DISCOVERING STATISTICS USING
IBM SPSS STATISTICS

CATISFIED CUSTOMERS

Diego
(Megan Chapman)

Tonks
(Erica Eckert)

Sarah Dahl's
Cat

Cody
(Andrea Luu)

Prof Fluffypants
(Sanj Choudhury)

Coltrane
(Krista Soria)

Nightshade
(Dave Verkuijl)

Sams
(Claudia Pama)

Kamaji & Choccy
(Emily Margaret-Gay)

DISCOVERING STATISTICS USING IBM SPSS STATISTICS

AND SEX AND DRUGS AND ROCK 'N' ROLL

4TH EDITION

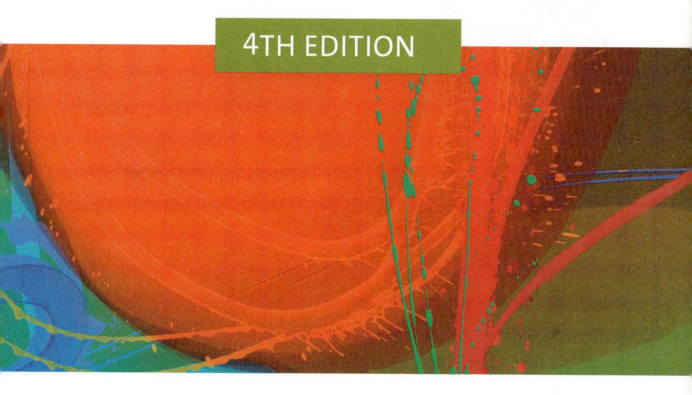

ANDY FIELD

Los Angeles | London | New Delhi
Singapore | Washington DC

Los Angeles | London | New Delhi
Singapore | Washington DC

SAGE Publications Ltd
1 Oliver's Yard
55 City Road
London EC1Y 1SP

SAGE Publications Inc.
2455 Teller Road
Thousand Oaks, California 91320

SAGE Publications India Pvt Ltd
B 1/I 1 Mohan Cooperative Industrial Area
Mathura Road
New Delhi 110 044

SAGE Publications Asia-Pacific Pte Ltd
3 Church Street
#10-04 Samsung Hub
Singapore 049483

Editor: Michael Carmichael
Development editor: Robin Lupton
Digital content assistant: Tanushri Shukla
Production editor: Ian Antcliff
Copyeditor: Richard Leigh
Proofreaders: Louise Harnby; Kate Harrison; Anna Gilding; Jennifer Hinchliffe
Indexer: David Rudeforth
Marketing manager: Ben Griffin-Sherwood
Cover design: Wendy Scott
Typeset by: C&M Digitals (P) Ltd, Chennai, India
Printed: in Canada by Transcontinental Printing Inc
Printed on paper from sustainable resources

Library of Congress Control Number: 2012944559

British Library Cataloguing in Publication data

A catalogue record for this book is available from the British Library

ISBN 978-1-4462-4917-8
ISBN 978-1-4462-4918-5 (pbk)

CONTENTS

PREFACE

Karma Police, arrest this man, he talks in maths, he buzzes like a fridge, he's like a detuned radio

Radiohead, 'Karma Police', *OK Computer* (1997)

Introduction

Many behavioural and social science students (and researchers for that matter) despise statistics. Most of us have a non-mathematical background, which makes understanding complex statistical equations very difficult. Nevertheless, the evil goat-warriors of Satan force our non-mathematical brains to apply themselves to what is the very complex task of becoming a statistics expert. The end result, as you might expect, can be quite messy. The one weapon that we have is the computer, which allows us to neatly circumvent the considerable disability of not understanding mathematics. Computer programs such as IBM SPSS Statistics, SAS, R and the like provide an opportunity to teach statistics at a conceptual level without getting too bogged down in equations. The computer to a goat-warrior of Satan is like catnip to a cat: it makes them rub their heads along the ground and purr and dribble ceaselessly. The only downside of the computer is that it makes it really easy to make a complete idiot of yourself if you don't really understand what you're doing. Using a computer without any statistical knowledge at all can be a dangerous thing. Hence this book.

My first aim is to strike a good balance between theory and practice: I want to use the computer as a tool for teaching statistical concepts in the hope that you will gain a better understanding of both theory and practice. If you want theory and you like equations then there are certainly better books: Howell (2012), Stevens (2002) and Tabachnick and Fidell (2012) have taught (and continue to teach) me more about statistics than you could possibly imagine. (I have an ambition to be cited in one of these books, but I don't think that will ever happen.) However, if you want a stats book that also discusses digital rectal stimulation then you have just spent your money wisely.

Too many books create the impression that there is a 'right' and 'wrong' way to do statistics. Data analysis is more subjective than is often made out. Therefore, although I make recommendations, within the limits imposed by the senseless destruction of rainforests, I hope to give you enough background in theory to enable you to make your own decisions about how best to conduct your analysis.

A second (ridiculously ambitious) aim is to make this the only statistics book that you'll ever need to buy. It's a book that I hope will become your friend from first year at university right through to your professorship. The start of the book is aimed at first-year undergraduates (Chapters 1–9), and then we move onto second-year undergraduate level material (Chapters 5, 8 and 10–15) before a dramatic climax that should keep postgraduates tickled

(Chapters 16–20). There should be something for everyone in each chapter also, and to help you gauge the difficulty of material, I flag the level of each section within each chapter (more on that in a moment).

My final and most important aim is to make the learning process fun. I have a sticky history with maths. This extract is from my school report at the age of 11:

| MATHEMATICS ADDL. MATHS. | 43 | 59 | 27 | D | C | *His work shows lack of discipline in thought and presentation. I hope it will mature next year.* | *LM* |

CHEMISTRY

The '27' in the report is to say that I came equal 27th with another student out of a class of 29. That's pretty much bottom of the class. The 43 is my exam mark as a percentage. Oh dear. Four years later (at 15) this was my school report:

NAME ...Andrew...Field............... FORM .4(1)   SUBJECT ...Mathematics..

EXAM	
ATTAINMENT	
EFFORT	

Andrew's progress in Mathematics has been remarkable. From being a weaker candidate who lacked confidence he has developed into a budding Mathematician. He should achieve a good grade.

Date...27/6/88   *B.A. Greate* ....Subject Teacher

The catalyst of this remarkable change was having a good teacher: my brother, Paul. I owe my life as an academic to Paul's ability to teach me stuff in an engaging way – something my maths teachers failed to do. Paul's a great teacher because he cares about bringing out the best in people, and he was able to make things interesting and relevant to me. He got the 'good teaching' genes in the family, but wasted them by not becoming a teacher; however, they're a little less wasted because his approach inspires mine. I strongly believe that people appreciate the human touch, and so I try to inject a lot of my own personality and sense of humour (or lack of) into *Discovering Statistics Using …* books. Many of the examples in this book, although inspired by some of the craziness that you find in the real world, are designed to reflect topics that play on the minds of the average student (i.e., sex, drugs, rock and roll, celebrity, people doing crazy stuff). There are also some examples that are there simply because they made me laugh. So, the examples are light-hearted (some have said 'smutty', but I prefer 'light-hearted') and by the end, for better or worse, I think you will have some idea of what goes on in my head on a daily basis. I apologize to those who think it's crass, hate it, or think that I'm undermining the seriousness of science, but, come on, what's not funny about a man putting an eel up his anus?

I never believe that I meet my aims, but previous editions have certainly been popular. I enjoy the rare luxury of having complete strangers emailing me to tell me how wonderful I am. (Admittedly, there are also emails calling me a pile of gibbon excrement, but you have to take the rough with the smooth.) The second edition of this book also won the British Psychological Society book award in 2007. However, with every new edition, I fear that the changes I make will ruin all of my previous hard work. Let's see what those changes are.

What do you get for your money?

This book takes you on a journey (and I try my best to make it a pleasant one) not just of statistics but also of the weird and wonderful contents of the world and my brain. It's full of daft, bad jokes, and smut. Aside from the smut, I have been forced reluctantly to include some academic content. In essence it contains everything I know about statistics (actually, more than I know …). It also has these features:

- **Everything you'll ever need to know**: I want this book to be good value for money, so it guides you from complete ignorance (Chapter 1 tells you the basics of doing research) to being an expert on multilevel modelling (Chapter 20). Of course no book that it's physically possible to lift will contain everything, but I think this one has a fair crack. It's pretty good for developing your biceps also.

- **Stupid faces**: You'll notice that the book is riddled with stupid faces, some of them my own. You can find out more about the pedagogic function of these 'characters' in the next section, but even without any useful function they're nice to look at.

- **Data sets**: There are about 132 data files associated with this book on the companion website. Not unusual in itself for a statistics book, but my data sets contain more sperm (not literally) than other books. I'll let you judge for yourself whether this is a good thing.

- **My life story**: Each chapter is book-ended by a chronological story from my life. Does this help you to learn about statistics? Probably not, but hopefully it provides some light relief between chapters.

- **SPSS tips**: SPSS does weird things sometimes. In each chapter, there are boxes containing tips, hints and pitfalls related to SPSS.

- **Self-test questions**: Given how much students hate tests, I thought the best way to commit commercial suicide was to liberally scatter tests throughout each chapter. These range from simple questions to test what you have just learned to going back to a technique that you read about several chapters before and applying it in a new context. All of these questions have answers to them on the companion website so that you can check on your progress.

- **Companion website**: The companion website contains an absolutely insane amount of additional material, all of which is described in the section about the companion website.

- **Digital stimulation**: No, not the aforementioned type of digital stimulation, but brain stimulation. Many of the features on the companion website will be accessible from tablets and smartphones, so that when you're bored in the cinema you can read about the fascinating world of heteroscedasticity instead.

- **Reporting your analysis**: Every chapter has a guide to writing up your analysis. How you write up an analysis varies a bit from one discipline to another, but my guides should get you heading in the right direction.

- **Glossary**: Writing the glossary was so horribly painful that it made me stick a vacuum cleaner into my ear to suck out my own brain. You can find my brain in the bottom of the vacuum cleaner in my house.

- **Real-world data**: Students like to have 'real data' to play with. The trouble is that real research can be quite boring. However, just for you, I trawled the world for examples of research on really fascinating topics (in my opinion). I then stalked the authors of the research until they gave me their data. Every chapter has a real research example.

What do you get that you didn't get last time?

I suppose if you have spent your hard-earned money on the previous edition it's reasonable that you want a good reason to spend more money on this edition. In some respects it's hard to quantify all of the changes in a list: I'm a better writer than I was 4 year ago, so there is a lot of me rewriting things because I think I can do it better than before. I spent 6 months solidly on the updates, so suffice it to say that a lot has changed; but anything you might have liked about the previous edition probably hasn't changed:

- **IBM SPSS compliance**: This edition was written using versions 20 and 21 of IBM SPSS Statistics. IBM bring out a new SPSS each year and this book gets rewritten about every 4 years, so, depending on when you buy the book, it may not reflect the latest version. This shouldn't bother you because one edition of SPSS is usually much the same as another (see Section 3.2).

- **New! Mediation and Moderation**: Even since the first edition I have been meaning to do a chapter on mediation and moderation, because they are two very widely used techniques. With each new edition I have run out of energy. Not this time though: I wrote it in the middle of the update before I managed to completely burn myself out. Chapter 10 is brand spanking new and all about mediation and moderation.

- **New! Structure**: My publishers soiled their underwear at the thought of me changing the structure because they think lecturers who use the book don't like this sort of change. They might have a point, but I changed it anyway. So, logistic regression (a complex topic) has moved towards the end of the book, and non-parametric tests (a relatively straightforward topic) have moved towards the beginning. In my opinion this change enables the book's story to flow better.

- **New! Focus**: Statistical times are a-changing, and people are starting to appreciate the limitations of significance testing, so I have discussed this more in Chapter 2, and the points made there permeate the rest of the book. The theme of 'everything being the same model' has run through all editions of the book, but I have made this theme even more explicit this time.

- **New! Tasks**: There are 111 more Smart Alex tasks, and 8 more Labcoat Leni tasks. This, of course, means there are quite a lot more pages of answers to these tasks on the companion website.

- **New! Bootstrapping**: The SPSS bootstrapping procedure is covered in every chapter where it is relevant.

- **New! Process diagrams**: Every chapter has a diagrammatic summary of the key steps that you go through for a particular analysis.

- **New! Love story**: Every chapter has a diagrammatic summary at the end (*Brian's attempt to woo Jane*). More interesting, though, Brian Haemorrhage has fallen in love with Jane Superbrain (see next section) and these diagrams follow Brian's attempts to convince Jane to go on a date with him.

- **New! Characters**: I enjoy coming up with new characters, and this edition has a crazy hippy called Oditi, and a deranged philosopher called Confusius (see the next section).

- **New-ish! Assumptions**: I've never really liked the way I dealt with assumptions, so I completely rewrote Chapter 5 to try to give more of a sense of when assumptions actually matter.

Every chapter had a serious edit/rewrite, but here is a chapter-by-chapter run-down of the more substantial changes:

- **Chapter 1 (Doing research)**: I added some more material on reporting data. I added stuff about variance and standard deviations, and expanded the discussion of p-values.

- **Chapter 2 (Statistical theory)**: I added material on estimating parameters, significance testing and its limitations, problems with one-tailed tests, running multiple tests (i.e., familywise error), confidence intervals and significance, sample size and significance, effect sizes (including Cohen's d and meta-analysis), and reporting basic statistics. It's changed a lot.

- **Chapter 3 (IBM SPSS)**: No dramatic changes.

- **Chapter 4 (Graphs)**: I moved the discussion of outliers into Chapter 5, which meant I had to rewrite one of the examples. I now include population pyramids also.

- **Chapter 5 (Assumptions)**: I completely rewrote this chapter. It's still about assumptions, but I try to explain when they matter and what they bias. Rather than dealing with assumptions separately in every chapter, because everything in the book is a linear model, I deal with the assumptions of linear models here. Therefore, this chapter acts as a single reference point for all subsequent chapters. I also cover other sources of bias such as outliers (which used to be scattered about in different chapters).

- **Chapter 6 (Non-parametric models)**: This is a fully updated and rewritten chapter on non-parametric statistics. It used to be later in the book, but now flows gracefully on from the discussion of assumptions.

- **Chapter 7 (Correlation)**: No dramatic changes.

- **Chapter 8 (Regression)**: I restructured this chapter so that most of the theory is now at the beginning and most of the SPSS is at the end. I did a fair bit of editing, too, moved categorical predictors into Chapter 10, and integrated simple and multiple regression more.

- **Chapter 9 (t-tests)**: The old version of this chapter used spider examples, but someone emailed me to say that this freaked them out, so I changed the example to be about cloaks of invisibility. Hopefully that won't freak anyone out. I restructured a bit, too, so that the theory is in one place and the SPSS in another.

- **Chapter 10 (Mediation and moderation)**: This chapter is completely new.

- **Chapter 11 (GLM 1)**: I gave more prominence to ANOVA as a general linear model because this makes it easier to think about assumptions and bias. I moved some of the more technical bits of the SPSS interpretation into boxes so that you can ignore them if you wish.

- **Chapter 12 (GLM 2)**: Again some restructuring and a bit more discussion on whether the covariate and predictor need to be independent.

- **Chapters 13–15 (GLM 3–5)**: These haven't changed much. I restructured each one a bit, edited down/rewrote a lot and gave more prominence to the GLM way of thinking.

- **Chapter 16 (MANOVA)**: I gave the writing a bit of a polish, but no real content changes.

- **Chapter 17 (Factor analysis)**: I added some stuff to the theory to make the distinction between principal component analysis (PCA) and factor analysis (FA) clearer. The chapter used to focus on PCA, but I changed it so that the focus is on FA. I edited out 3000 words of my tedious, repetitive, superfluous drivel.

- **Chapters 18 and 19 (Categorical data and logistic regression):** Because these chapters both deal with categorical outcomes, I rewrote them and put them together. The basic content is the same as before.

- **Chapter 20 (Multilevel models):** I polished the writing a bit and updated, but there are no changes that will upset anyone.

Goodbye

The first edition of this book was the result of two years (give or take a few weeks to write up my Ph.D.) of trying to write a statistics book that I would enjoy reading. With each new edition I try not just to make superficial changes but also to rewrite and improve everything (one of the problems with getting older is you look back at your past work and think you can do things better). This fourth edition is the culmination of about 6 years of full-time work (on top of my actual job). This book has literally consumed the last 15 years or so of my life, and each time I get a nice email from someone who found it useful I am reminded that it is the most useful thing I'll ever do with my life. It began and continues to be a labour of love. It still isn't perfect, and I still love to have feedback (good or bad) from the people who matter most: you.

Andy

 www.facebook.com/profandyfield

 @ProfAndyField

 www.youtube.com/user/ProfAndyField

 discoveringstatistics.blogspot.co.uk

HOW TO USE THIS BOOK

When the publishers asked me to write a section on 'How to use this book' it was tempting to write 'Buy a large bottle of Olay anti-wrinkle cream (which you'll need to fend off the effects of ageing while you read), find a comfy chair, sit down, fold back the front cover, begin reading and stop when you reach the back cover.' However, I think they wanted something more useful.☺

What background knowledge do I need?

In essence, I assume that you know nothing about statistics, but that you have a very basic grasp of computers (I won't be telling you how to switch them on, for example) and maths (although I have included a quick revision of some very basic concepts, so I really don't assume much).

Do the chapters get more difficult as I go through the book?

Yes, more or less: Chapters 1–9 are first-year degree level, Chapters 8–15 move into second-year degree level, and Chapters 16–20 discuss more technical topics. However, my main aim is to tell a statistical story rather than worrying about what level a topic is at. Many books teach different tests in isolation and never really give you a grasp of the similarities between them; this, I think, creates an unnecessary mystery. Most of the tests in this book are the same thing expressed in slightly different ways. I want the book to tell this story, and I see it as consisting of seven parts:

- Part 1 (Doing research and introducing linear models): Chapters 1–3.
- Part 2 (Exploring data): Chapters 4–6.
- Part 3 (Linear models with continuous predictors): Chapters 7 and 8.
- Part 4 (Linear models with continuous or categorical predictors): Chapters 9–15.
- Part 5 (Linear models with multiple outcomes): Chapter 16 and 17.
- Part 6 (Linear models with categorical outcomes): Chapters 18–19.
- Part 7 (Linear models with hierarchical data structures): Chapter 20.

This structure might help you to see the method in my madness. If not, to help you on your journey I've coded each section with an icon. These icons are designed to give you an idea of the difficulty of the section. It doesn't mean you can skip the sections (but see Smart Alex in the next section), but it will let you know whether a section is at about your level, or whether it's going to push you. It's based on a wonderful categorization system using the letter 'I':

① *Introductory*, which I hope means that everyone should be able to understand these sections. These are for people just starting their undergraduate courses.

② *Intermediate*. Anyone with a bit of background in statistics should be able to get to grips with these sections. They are aimed at people who are perhaps in the second year of their degree, but they can still be quite challenging in places.

③ *In at the deep end*. These topics are difficult. I'd expect final-year undergraduates and recent postgraduate students to be able to tackle these sections.

④ *Incinerate your brain*. These are difficult topics. I would expect these sections to be challenging for undergraduates, but postgraduates with a reasonable background in research methods shouldn't find them too much of a problem.

Why do I keep seeing silly faces everywhere?

Brian Haemorrhage: Brian is a really nice guy, and he has a massive crush on Jane Superbrain. He's seen her around the university campus carrying her jars of brains (see below). Whenever he sees her, he gets a knot in his stomach and he imagines slipping a ring onto her finger on a beach in Hawaii, as their friends and family watch through their gooey eyes. Jane never even notices him; this makes him very sad. His friends have told him that the only way she'll marry him is if he becomes a statistics genius (and changes his surname). Therefore, he's on a mission to learn statistics. It's his last hope of impressing Jane, settling down and living happily ever after. At the moment he knows nothing, but he's about to embark on a journey that will take him from statistically challenged to a genius, in 900 pages. Along his journey he pops up and asks questions, and at the end of each chapter he flaunts his newly found knowledge to Jane in the hope she'll go on a date with him.

New! Confusius: The great philosopher Confucius had a lesser-known brother called Confusius. Jealous of his brother's great wisdom and modesty, Confusius vowed to bring confusion to the world. To this end, he built the confusion machine. He puts statistical terms into it, and out of it come different names for the same concept. When you see Confusius he will be alerting you to statistical terms that mean the same thing.

Cramming Sam: Samantha thinks statistics is a boring waste of time and she just wants to pass her exam and forget that she ever had to know anything about normal distributions. She appears and gives you a summary of the key points that you need to know. If, like Samantha, you're cramming for an exam, she will tell you the essential information to save you having to trawl through hundreds of pages of my drivel.

Curious Cat: He also pops up and asks questions (because he's curious). The only reason he's here is because I wanted a cat in the book … and preferably one that looks like mine. Of course the educational specialists think he needs a specific role, and so his role is to look cute and make bad cat-related jokes.

Jane Superbrain: Jane is the cleverest person in the whole universe. A mistress of osmosis, she acquired vast statistical knowledge by stealing the brains of statisticians and eating them. Apparently they taste of sweaty tank tops. Having devoured some top statistics brains and absorbed their knowledge, she knows all of the really hard stuff. She appears in boxes to tell you advanced things that are a bit tangential to the main text. Her friends tell her that a half-whit called Brian is in love with her, but she doesn't know who he is.

Labcoat Leni: Leni is a budding young scientist and he's fascinated by real research. He says, 'Andy, man, I like an example about using an eel as a cure for constipation as much as the next guy, but all of your data are made up. We need some real examples, dude!' So off Leni went: he walked the globe, a lone data warrior in a thankless quest for real data. He turned up at universities, cornered academics, kidnapped their families and threatened to put them in a bath of crayfish unless he was given real data. The generous ones relented, but others? Well, let's just say their families are sore. So, when you see Leni you know that you will get some real data, from a real research study to analyse. Keep it real.

New! Oditi's Lantern: Oditi believes that the secret to life is hidden in numbers and that only by large-scale analysis of those numbers shall the secrets be found. He didn't have time to enter, analyse and interpret all of the data in the world, so he established the cult of undiscovered numerical truths. Working on the principle that if you gave a million monkeys typewriters, one of them would re-create Shakespeare, members of the cult sit at their computers crunching numbers in the hope that one of them will unearth the hidden meaning of life. To help his cult Oditi has set up a visual vortex called 'Oditi's Lantern'. When Oditi appears it is to implore you to stare into the lantern, which basically means there is a video tutorial to guide you.

Oliver Twisted: With apologies to Charles Dickens, Oliver, like the more famous fictional London urchin, is always asking 'Please, Sir, can I have some more?' Unlike Master Twist though, our young Master Twisted wants more statistics information. Of course he does, who wouldn't? Let us not be the ones to disappoint a young, dirty, slightly smelly boy who dines on gruel. When Oliver appears he's telling you that there is additional information to be found on the companion website. (It took a long time to write, so someone please actually read it.)

Satan's Personal Statistics Slave: Satan is a busy boy – he has all of the lost souls to torture in hell; then there are the fires to keep fuelled, not to mention organizing enough carnage on the planet's surface to keep Norwegian black metal bands inspired. Like many of us, this leaves little time for him to analyse data, and this makes him very sad. So, he has his own personal slave, who, also like some of us, spends all day dressed in a gimp mask and tight leather pants in front of IBM SPSS analysing Satan's data. Consequently, he knows a thing or two about SPSS, and when Satan's busy spanking a goat, he pops up in a box with SPSS tips.

Smart Alex: Alex is a very important character because he appears when things get particularly difficult. He's basically a bit of a smart alec, and so whenever you see his face you know that something scary is about to be explained. When the hard stuff is over he reappears to let you know that it's safe to continue. You'll also find that Alex gives you tasks to do at the end of each chapter to see whether you're as smart as he is.

Why do I keep seeing QR codes?

MobileStudy: QR stands for 'quantum reality', and if you download a QR scanner and scan one of these funny little barcode things into your mobile device (smartphone, tablet, etc...) it will transport you and your device into a quantum reality in which left is right, time runs backwards, drinks pour themselves out of your mouth into bottles, and statistics is interesting. Scanning these codes will be your gateway to revision resources such as Chapter Introductions, Cramming Sam's Tips, Interactive Multiple Choice Questions, and more. Don't forget to add MobileStudy to your favourites on your device so you can revise any time you like – even on the toilet!

What is on the companion website?

In this age of downloading, CD-ROMs are for losers (at least that's what the 'kids' tell me), so I've put my cornucopia of additional funk on that worldwide interweb thing. To enter my world of delights, go to www.sagepub.co.uk/field4e. The website contains resources for students and lecturers alike, with additional content from some of the characters from the book.

- **Testbank:** There is a comprehensive testbank of multiple choice and numeracy questions for instructors. This comes in two flavours: (1) Testbank files supporting a range of disciplines are available for lecturers to upload into their online teaching system; (2) A powerful, online, instructional tool for students and lecturers called WebAssign®. WebAssign® allows instructors to assign questions for exams and assignments which can be automatically graded for formative and summative assessment. WebAssign® also supports student revision by allowing them to learn at their own pace and practise statistical principles again and again until they master them. To further assist learning WebAssign® also gives feedback on right and wrong answers and provides students with access to an electronic version of the textbook to further their study.

- **Data files:** You need data files to work through the examples in the book and they are all on the companion website. We did this so that you're forced to go there and once you're there Sage will flash up subliminal messages to make you buy more of their books.

- **Resources for different subject areas:** I am a psychologist and although I tend to base my examples around the weird and wonderful, I do have a nasty habit of resorting to psychology when I don't have any better ideas. I realize that not everyone is as psychologically oriented as me, so my publishers have recruited some non-psychologists to provide data files and an instructor's testbank of multiple-choice questions for those studying or teaching in **business and management**, **education**, **sport sciences** and **health sciences**. You have no idea how happy I am that I didn't have to write those.

- **Webcasts:** Whenever you see Oditi in the book it means that there is a webcast to accompany the chapter. These are hosted on my YouTube channel (www.youtube.com/user/ProfAndyField), which I have amusingly called μ-Tube (see what I did there?). You can also get to them via the companion website.

- **Self-assessment multiple-choice questions:** Organized by chapter, these will allow you to test whether wasting your life reading this book has paid off so that you can annoy your friends by walking with an air of confidence into the examination. If you fail said exam, please don't sue me.

- **Flashcard glossary**: As if a printed glossary wasn't enough, my publishers insisted that you'd like an electronic one too. Have fun here flipping through terms and definitions covered in the textbook; it's better than actually learning something.

- **Oliver Twisted's pot of gruel**: Oliver Twisted will draw your attention to the 300 pages or so of more technical information that we have put online so that (1) the planet suffers a little less, and (2) you won't die when the book falls off of your bookshelf onto your head.

- **Labcoat Leni solutions**: For all of the Labcoat Leni tasks in the book there are full and detailed answers on the companion website.

- **Smart Alex answers**: Each chapter ends with a set of tasks for you to test your newly acquired expertise. The chapters are also littered with self-test questions. The companion website contains around 300 pages (that's a different 300 pages to the 300 above) of detailed answers. Will I ever stop writing?

- **PowerPoint slides**: I can't come and teach you all in person (although you can watch my lectures on YouTube). Instead I rely on a crack team of highly skilled and super-intelligent pan-dimensional beings called 'lecturers'. I have personally grown each and every one of them in a greenhouse in my garden. To assist in their mission to spread the joy of statistics I have provided them with PowerPoint slides for each chapter. If you see something weird on their slides that upsets you, then remember that's probably my fault.

- **Links**: Every website has to have links to other useful websites, and the companion website is no exception.

- **Cyberworms of knowledge**: I have used nanotechnology to create cyberworms that crawl down your broadband connection, pop out of the USB port of your computer and fly through space into your brain. They rearrange your neurons so that you understand statistics. You don't believe me? Well, you'll never know for sure unless you visit the companion website ….

Happy reading, and don't get distracted by Facebook and Twitter.

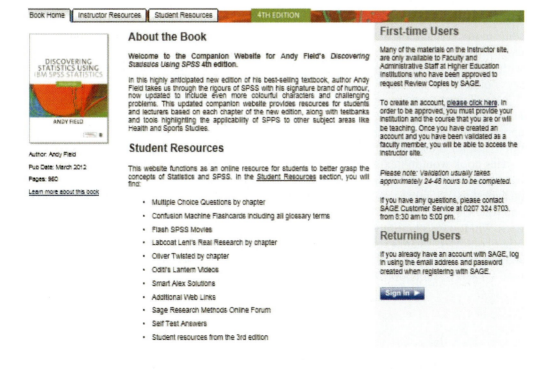

ACKNOWLEDGEMENTS

This book (in all its SPSS, SAS and R versions) wouldn't have happened if not for Dan Wright's unwarranted faith in the ability of a then postgraduate to write the first SPSS edition. Numerous other people have contributed to previous editions of this book. I don't have room to list them all, but particular thanks are due to to Dan (again), David Hitchin, Laura Murray, Gareth Williams, Lynne Slocombe and Kate Lester, who gave me significant amounts of feedback on various incarnations of this text. For this edition, lots of people sent me very helpful emails, but in particular Maria de Ridder (for a very helpful document of suggestions) and Thom Baguley (for feedback on Chapter 5 at very short notice).

Special thanks to Jeremy Miles for his help with various versions of this book over the years. Part of his 'help' involves ranting on at me about things I've written being, and I quote, 'bollocks'. Nevertheless, working on the SAS and R versions of this book with him has influenced me enormously. He's also been a very nice person to know over the past few years (apart from when he's ranting on at me about …).

Thanks to the following for sending me their raw data – it's an honour for me to include their fascinating research in my book: Rebecca Ang, Philippe Bernard, Hakan Çetinkaya, Tomas Chamorro-Premuzic, Graham Davey, Mike Domjan, Gordon Gallup, Nicolas Guéguen, Sarah Johns, Eric Lacourse, Nate Lambert, Sarah Marzillier, Karlijn Massar, Geoffrey Miller, Peter Muris, Laura Nichols, Nick Perham, Achim Schüetzwohl, Mirjam Tuk, and Lara Zibarras.

I appreciate everyone who has taken time to write nice reviews of this book on the various Amazon (and other) websites around the world; the success of this book has been in no small part due to these people being so positive and constructive in their feedback. Thanks also to everyone who contributes so enthusiastically to my Facebook page: I hit some motivational dark times during this edition, but feeling the positive vibes from readers always got me back on track (especially the photos of cats, dogs, parrots and lizards with this book☺). I continue to be amazed and bowled over by the nice things that people say about the book.

Not all contributions are as tangible as those above. Very early in my career Graham Hole made me realize that teaching research methods didn't have to be dull. My whole approach to teaching has been to steal all of his good ideas, and he has had the good grace not to ask for them back! He is a rarity in being brilliant, funny *and* nice.

This book wouldn't exist without the generous support of IBM who allow me to beta-test SPSS Statistics and keep me up to date with the software (www-01.ibm.com/software/analytics/spss). I wrote this edition on a Mac but used Windows for the screen shots. Mac and Mac OS are trademarks of Apple Inc., registered in the United States and other countries; Windows is a registered trademark of Microsoft Corporation in the United States and other countries. Thanks to Jess Knott at TechSmith (www.techsmith.com) who provided support for Camtasia (which I use to record and edit my webcasts) and Snagit (which I used for screen shots) for Mac; she also breathed new life into some of my old webcasts. I created most diagrams and flowcharts in this book using OmniGraffle (www.omnigroup.com). Although it is unhealthy to love a piece of software, I love OmniGraffle and if I ever meet the authors I will buy them beer, and plenty of it.

My publishers, Sage, are rare in being a large, successful company that manages to maintain a family feel. Like any family, I don't always see eye-to-eye with them, and sometimes we drive each other mad, but we wouldn't want to be without each other. They generously co-funded my wife to help update the web materials for this book. My editor Mike takes his fair share of crap from me (what does he expect, he supports Tottenham?), but I always appreciate his unfaltering enthusiasm, support and willingness to make things happen. Thanks to everyone at Sage, but especially Ian, Karen (who supports a proper football team) and Ziyad (who doesn't know what football is) for their help and support over many years.

You'll notice the book is riddled with nicely drawn characters. I didn't draw them. The ones that survived from the previous edition are thanks to Alex Lee. Special thanks to Laura-Jane at Anelina Illustrations (www.anelinaillustrations.com) for my caricature, Oditi and Confusius. It was great working with you.

I always write listening to music. For this edition I predominantly enjoyed (my neighbours less so): Absu, Anathema, Anthrax, Animals as Leaders, Audrey Horne, The Beyond, Black Breath, Black Tusk, Black Sabbath, Blue Öyster Cult, Blut Aus Nord, Deathspell Omega, Deep Purple, Foo Fighters, Genesis, Graveyard, Ihsahn, Iron Maiden, Jethro Tull, Kiss, Manowar, Marillion, Meshuggah (a lot), Metallica, Mastodon, Motörhead, Opeth (a lot), Primal Rock Rebellion, Rainbow, Rush, Secrets of the Moon, Status Quo, Steve Wilson, Storm Corrosion, Sylosis, Torche, Uriah Heep, Watain, and Wolves in the Throne Room.

All this book-writing nonsense requires many lonely hours of typing. Without some wonderful friends to drag me out of my dimly lit room from time to time I'd be even more of a gibbering cabbage than I already am. Peter Muris, Birgit Mayer, and especially Leonora Wilkinson gave me a lot of support while writing previous editions of this book. For this edition, and in most cases all of the previous ones, my eternal gratitude goes to Graham Davey, Ben Dyson, Martin Watts, Sam Cartwright-Hatton, Mark Franklin and their lovely families for reminding me that there is more to life than work. You'd also be hard pushed to find more supportive, loving and proud parents than mine. I also throw out a robust set of horns to my brothers of metal Doug Martin and Rob Mepham for letting me deafen them with my drumming (www.myspace.com/fracturepattern). I also became an uncle while writing this update, so thanks to Melody for being small and cute.

For someone who spends his life writing, I'm constantly surprised at how incapable I am of finding words to express how wonderful my wife Zoë is. She has a never-ending supply of patience, love, support and optimism (even when her husband is a grumpy, sleep-deprived, withered, self-doubting husk). As if that wasn't enough, she also did the lion's share of the updating of the accompanying web materials and SPSS screen shots for this edition. I never forget, not even for a nanosecond, how lucky I am.

With thanks to the following people for their feedback on the fourth edition

Mahmood Ali, University of Greenwich
Rory Allen, Goldsmiths, University of London
Rob Angell, University of Cardiff
Derek Ashford, Manchester Metropolitan University
Chris Askew, Kingston University
Mirjam Baars, University of Amsterdam
Theodoros Bampouras, University of Cumbria
Kirsten Bartlett, Sheffield Hallam University
Roger Bennett, London Metropolitan University
Kanishka Bhattacharya, Oxford University
Kate Black, University of Chester
Ian Boardley, University of Birmingham
Nicola Brown, St Mary's University College
Douglas Bryson, ESC Rennes School of Business
Hannah Buchanan-Smith, University of Stirling
Louise Bunce, London Metropolitan University
Scott Burnet, Southampton Solent University
Robert Busching, University of Potsdam
Katherine Cagney, Waterford Institute of Technology
Ian Charity, Newcastle Business School
Sam Chenery-Morris, University Campus Suffolk
I-Chant Chiang, Quest University Canada
Nikki Coghill, University of Bristol
Graham Cookson, King's College London
Julie Davies, Bangor University
Matthew Davis, University of Leeds
Rutger de Graaf, University of Amsterdam
Peter de Waal, Utrecht University
Pedro Dias, Catholic University of Portugal
Gerlof Donga, Hogeschool van Amsterdam
Michelle Ellefson, University of Cambridge
Chris Fife-Schaw, University of Surrey
Liam Foster, University of Sheffield
Pauline Fox, University of West London
Robert Francis, King's College London
Benjamin Gardner, University College London
Lise Georgeson, St Mary's University College
Elisabeth Götze, Vienna University of Economics and Business
Martijn Goudbeek, Tilburg University
Hannah Greatwood, Leeds Metropolitan University
Suzanne Hacking, University of Central Lancashire
Sebastian Hagen, University of Leipzig
Carol Haigh, Manchester Metropolitan University
Julie Hall, Birmingham City University
Karen Hambly, University of Kent
Karolina Hansen, Friedrich Schiller University Jena
Azmi Hassali, Universiti Sains Malaysia
Erica Hepper, University of Southampton
Beryl Hilberink-Schulpen, Radboud University Nijmegen
Henriette Hogh, University of Surrey
Lee Hulbert-Williams, University of Wolverhampton
Gerry Humphris, University of St Andrews
Martyn Jarvis, University of Glamorgan
Domhnall Jennings, Newcastle University
Paul Jepson, University of Birmingham

Stephen Johnston, Swansea University
Marie Juanchich, Kingston University
Serdar Karabati, Bilgi University
Roshni Khatri, University of Northampton
Paul Kiff, University of East London
Thomas Koch, LMU Munich
Wolfgang Kotowski, University of Zurich
Wander Lowie, University of Groningen
Ruth Lowry, University of Chichester
John Mallett, University of Ulster
Chris Mamo, Cork Institute of Technology
Irene Manaras, University of Hertfordshire
Anne Manyande, University of West London
Jesse Martin, Bangor University
Carla Martins, University of Minho
Paul McCarthy, Glasgow Caledonian University
Philip McDonald, Leeds Trinity University College
Margaret McGrath, National University of Ireland, Galway
Gary Mckenna, University of the West of Scotland
Alistair McMillan, University of Sheffield
Juanjo Medina, University of Manchester
Remo Mombarg, Hanze University of Applied Sciences, Groningen
Maria Mos, Tilburg University
Eyob Mulat-Weldemeskel, London Metropolitan University
Drew Munn, University of Northampton
Tony Myers, Newman University College
Rich Neil, Cardiff Metropolitan University
Dennis Nigbur, Canterbury Christ Church University
Louis Passfield, University of Kent
Monique Pollmann, Tilburg University
Michelle Pyer, University of Northampton
Shahid Qureshi, Institute of Business Administration, Karachi
Eric Rietzschel, University of Groningen
Claire-Marie Roberts, University of Worcester
Janet Robertson, Lancaster University
Petros Roussos, University of Athens
Tom Scherndl, University of Salzburg
Kim Schildkamp, University of Twente
Shivani Sharma, University of Hertfordshire
Luke Sloan, Cardiff University
Sandrino Smeets, Radboud University Nijmegen
Andy Smith, Leeds Metropolitan University
Martin Southam, Canterbury Christ Church University
Adrian Thompson, University of Birmingham
Jayne Tidd, Teesside University
Alastair Tomlinson, Cardiff Metropolitan University
Alison Tresidder, University of Bedfordshire
Ivo van der Lans, Wageningen University
Frans Van der Slik, Radboud University Nijmegen
Marcel van Egmond, University of Amsterdam
Nel Verhoeven, University College Roosevelt Academy
Paresh Wankhade, Liverpool Hope University
Maggie Whittaker, University of Essex
Bob Williams, Durham University

Dedication

Like the previous editions, this book is dedicated to my brother Paul and my cat Fuzzy, because one of them is a constant source of intellectual inspiration and the other wakes me up in the morning by sitting on me and purring in my face until I give him cat food: mornings will be considerably more pleasant when my brother gets over his love of cat food for breakfast.☺

SYMBOLS USED IN THIS BOOK

Mathematical operators

Σ	This symbol (called sigma) means 'add everything up'. So, if you see something like Σx_i it just means 'add up all of the scores you've collected'.
Π	This symbol means 'multiply everything'. So, if you see something like Πx_i it just means 'multiply all of the scores you've collected'.
$\sqrt{x}$	This means 'take the square root of x'.

Greek symbols

α	The probability of making a Type I error
β	The probability of making a Type II error
β_i	Standardized regression coefficient
ε	Usually stands for 'error'
η^2	Eta squared
μ	The mean of a population of scores
ρ	The correlation in the population
σ	The standard deviation in a population of data
σ^2	The variance in a population of data
$\sigma_{\bar{x}}$	The standard error of the mean
τ	Kendall's tau (non-parametric correlation coefficient)
χ^2	Chi-square test statistic
χ^2_F	Friedman's ANOVA test statistic
ω^2	Omega squared (an effect size measure). This symbol also means 'expel the contents of your intestine immediately into your trousers'; you will understand why in due course.

English symbols

b_i	The regression coefficient (unstandardized), I tend to use it for any coefficient in a linear model.
df	Degrees of freedom
e_i	The error associated with the ith person
F	F-ratio (test statistic used in ANOVA)
H	Kruskal–Wallis test statistic
k	The number of levels of a variable (i.e., the number of treatment conditions), or the number of predictors in a regression model
ln	Natural logarithm
MS	The mean squared error: the average variability in the data.
N, n, n_i	The sample size. N usually denotes the total sample size, whereas n usually denotes the size of a particular group
P	Probability (the probability value, p-value or significance of a test are usually denoted by p)
r	Pearson's correlation coefficient
r_s	Spearman's rank correlation coefficient
r_b, r_{pb}	Biserial correlation coefficient and point-biserial correlation coefficient, respectively
R	The multiple correlation coefficient
R^2	The coefficient of determination (i.e., the proportion of data explained by the model)
s	The standard deviation of a sample of data
s^2	The variance of a sample of data
SS	The sum of squares, or sum of squared errors, to give it its full title
SS_A	The sum of squares for variable A
SS_M	The model sum of squares (i.e., the variability explained by the model fitted to the data)
SS_R	The residual sum of squares (i.e., the variability that the model can't explain – the error in the model)
SS_T	The total sum of squares (i.e., the total variability within the data)
t	Test statistic for Student's t-test
T	Test statistic for Wilcoxon's matched-pairs signed-rank test
U	Test statistic for the Mann–Whitney test
W_s	Test statistic for Wilcoxon's rank-sum test
$\bar{X}$	The mean of a sample of scores
z	A data point expressed in standard deviation units

SOME MATHS REVISION

Two negatives make a positive: Although in life two wrongs don't make a right, in mathematics they do! When we multiply a negative number by another negative number, the result is a positive number. For example, $-2 \times -4 = 8$.

A negative number multiplied by a positive one makes a negative number: If you multiply a positive number by a negative number then the result is another negative number. For example, $2 \times -4 = -8$, or $-2 \times 6 = -12$.

BODMAS: This is an acronym for the order in which mathematical operations are performed: Brackets, Order, Division, Multiplication, Addition, and Subtraction. Mostly these operations are self-explanatory (e.g., always calculate things within brackets first) except for 'order', which refers to power terms such as squares. Four squared, or 4^2, used to be called four raised to the order of 2, hence the word 'order' in BODMAS (also, if we used 'power', we'd end up with BPDMAS, which doesn't roll off the tongue quite so nicely). Let's look at an example of BODMAS: what would be the result of $1 + 3 \times 5^2$? The answer is 76 (not 100 as some of you might have thought). There are no brackets so the first thing is to deal with the order term: 5^2 is 25, so the equation becomes $1 + 3 \times 25$. There is no division, so we can move on to multiplication: 3×25, which gives us 75. BODMAS tells us to deal with addition next: $1 + 75$, which gives us 76 and the equation is solved. If I'd written the original equation as $(1 + 3) \times 5^2$, then the answer would have been 100 because we deal with the brackets first: $(1 + 3) = 4$, so the equation becomes 4×5^2. We then deal with the order term, so the equation becomes $4 \times 25 = 100$.

http://www.bbc.co.uk/schools/gcsebitesize/maths/ is a good site for revising basic maths.

Why is my evil lecturer forcing me to learn statistics?

1

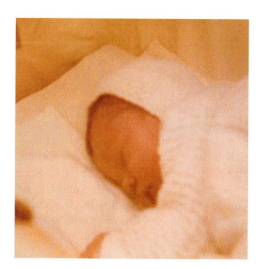

1.1. What will this chapter tell me? ①

I was born on 21 June 1973. Like most people, I don't remember anything about the first few years of life, and like most children I went through a phase of driving my dad mad by asking 'Why?' every five seconds. With every question, the word 'dad' got longer and whinier: 'Dad, why is the sky blue?', 'Daaad, why don't worms have legs?', 'Daaaaaaaaad, where do babies come from?' Eventually, my dad could take no more and whacked me around the face with a golf club.[1]

My torrent of questions reflected the natural curiosity that children have: we all begin our voyage through life as inquisitive little scientists. At the age of 3, I was at my friend

[1] He was practising in the garden when I unexpectedly wandered behind him at the exact moment he took a back swing. It's rare that a parent enjoys the sound of their child crying, but on this day it filled my dad with joy because my wailing was tangible evidence he hadn't killed me, which he thought he might have done. Had he hit me with the club end rather than the shaft he probably would have. Fortunately (for me) I survived, although some might argue that this incident goes some way to explaining the way my brain functions.

Obe's party (just before he left England to return to Nigeria, much to my distress). It was a hot day, and there was an electric fan blowing cold air around the room. My 'curious little scientist' brain was working through what seemed like a particularly pressing question: 'What happens when you stick your finger in a fan?' The answer, as it turned out, was that it hurts – a lot.[2] At the age of 3, we intuitively know that to answer questions you need to collect data, even if it causes us pain.

My curiosity to explain the world never went away, which is why I'm a scientist. The fact you're reading this book means that the inquisitive 3-year-old in you is alive and well and wants to answer new and exciting questions too. To answer these questions you need 'science' and science has a **pilot fish** called 'statistics' that hides under its belly eating ectoparasites. That's why your evil lecturer is forcing you to learn statistics. Statistics is a bit like sticking your finger into a revolving fan blade: sometimes it's very painful, but it does give you answers to interesting questions. I'm going to try to convince you in this chapter that statistics are an important part of doing research. We will overview the whole research process, from why we conduct research in the first place, through how theories are generated, to why we need data to test these theories. If that doesn't convince you to read on then maybe the fact that we discover whether Coca-Cola kills sperm will. Or perhaps not.

1.2. What the hell am I doing here? I don't belong here ①

You're probably wondering why you have bought this book. Maybe you liked the pictures, maybe you fancied doing some weight training (it *is* heavy), or perhaps you needed to reach something in a high place (it *is* thick). The chances are, though, that given the choice of spending your hard-earned cash on a statistics book or something more entertaining (a nice novel, a trip to the cinema, etc.) you'd choose the latter. So, why have you bought the book (or downloaded an illegal PDF of it from someone who has way too much time on their hands if they can scan a 900-page textbook)? It's likely that you obtained it because you're doing a course on statistics, or you're doing some research, and you need to know how to analyse data. It's possible that you didn't realize when you started your course or research that you'd have to know about statistics but now find yourself inexplicably wading, neck high, through the Victorian sewer that is data analysis. The reason why you're in the mess that you find yourself in is that you have a curious mind. You might have asked yourself questions like why people behave the way they do (psychology), why behaviours differ across cultures (anthropology), how businesses maximize their profit (business), how the dinosaurs died (palaeontology), whether eating tomatoes protects you against cancer (medicine, biology), whether it is possible to build a quantum computer (physics, chemistry), whether the planet is hotter than it used to be and where (geography, environmental studies). Whatever it is you're studying or researching, the reason why you're studying it is probably that you're interested in answering questions. Scientists are curious people, and you probably are too. However, it might not have occurred to you that to answer interesting questions, you need two things: data and an explanation for those data.

The answer to 'what the hell are you doing here?' is, therefore, simple: to answer interesting questions you need data. One of the reasons why your evil statistics lecturer is forcing you to learn about numbers is that they are a form of data and are vital to the research process. Of course there are forms of data other than numbers that can be used to test

---

[2] In the 1970s fans didn't have helpful protective cages around them to prevent idiotic 3-year-olds sticking their fingers into the blades.

and generate theories. When numbers are involved the research involves **quantitative methods**, but you can also generate and test theories by analysing language (such as conversations, magazine articles, media broadcasts, etc.). This involves **qualitative methods** and it is a topic for another book not written by me. People can get quite passionate about which of these methods is *best*, which is a bit silly because they are complementary, not competing, approaches and there are much more important issues in the world to get upset about. Having said that, all qualitative research is rubbish.[3]

1.2.1. The research process ①

How do you go about answering an interesting question? The research process is broadly summarized in Figure 1.2. You begin with an observation that you want to understand, and this observation could be anecdotal (you've noticed that your cat watches birds when they're on TV but not when jellyfish are on)[4] or could be based on some data (you asked several cat owners to keep diaries of their cat's TV habits and have noticed that lots of them watch birds on TV). From your initial observation you generate explanations, or theories, for those observations, from which you can make predictions (hypotheses). Here's where the data come into the process because to test your predictions you need data. First you collect some relevant data (and to do that you need to identify things that can be measured) and then you analyse those data. The analysis of the data may support your theory or give you cause to modify the theory. As such, the processes of data collection

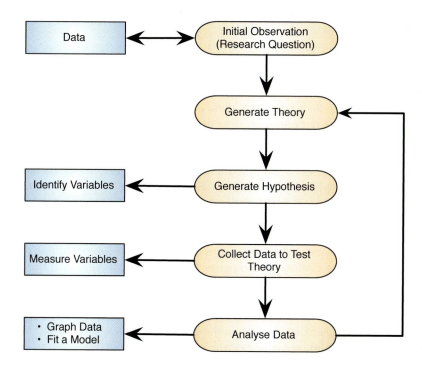

FIGURE 1.2
The research process

[3] This is a joke. Like many of my jokes, there are people who won't find it remotely funny. Passions run high between qualitative and quantitative researchers, so its inclusion will likely result in me being hunted down, locked in a room and forced to do discourse analysis by a hoard of rabid qualitative researchers.

[4] My cat does actually climb up and stare at the TV when it's showing birds flying about.

and analysis and generating theories are intrinsically linked: theories lead to data collection/analysis and data collection/analysis informs theories. This chapter explains this research process in more detail.

1.3. Initial observation: finding something that needs explaining ①

The first step in Figure 1.2 was to come up with a question that needs an answer. I spend rather more time than I should watching reality TV. Over many years I used to swear that I wouldn't get hooked on *Big Brother*, and yet year upon year I would find myself glued to the TV screen waiting for the next contestant's meltdown (I am a psychologist, so really this is just research). I used to wonder why there are so many contestants with really unpleasant personalities on the show (my money is on narcissistic personality disorder).[5] A lot of scientific endeavour starts this way: not by watching *Big Brother*, but by observing something in the world and wondering why it happens.

Having made a casual observation about the world (*Big Brother* contestants on the whole have profound personality defects), I need to collect some data to see whether this observation is true (and not a biased observation). To do this, I need to define one or more **variables** that I would like to measure. There's one variable in this example: the personality of the contestant. I could measure this variable by giving them one of the many well-established questionnaires that measure personality characteristics. Let's say that I did this and I found that 75% of contestants did have narcissistic personality disorder. These data support my observation: a lot of *Big Brother* contestants have extreme personalities.

1.4. Generating theories and testing them ①

The next logical thing to do is to explain these data (Figure 1.2). One explanation could be that people with narcissistic personality disorder are more likely to audition for *Big Brother* than those without. This is a **theory**. Another possibility is that the producers of *Big Brother* are more likely to select people who have narcissistic personality disorder to be contestants than those with less extreme personalities. This is another theory. We verified our original observation by collecting data, and we can collect more data to test these theories. We can make two predictions from these two theories. The first is that the number of people turning up for an audition who have narcissistic personality disorder will be higher than the general level in the population (which is about 1%). A prediction from a theory, like this one, is known as a **hypothesis** (see Jane Superbrain Box 1.1). We could test this hypothesis by getting a team of clinical psychologists to interview each person at the *Big Brother* audition and diagnose them as having narcissistic personality disorder or not. A prediction from our second theory is that if the *Big Brother* selection panel are more likely to choose people with narcissistic personality disorder then the rate of this disorder in the final contestants will be even higher than the rate in the group of people going for auditions. This is another hypothesis. Imagine we collected these data; they are in Table 1.1.

In total, 7662 people turned up for the audition. Our first hypothesis is that the percentage of people with narcissistic personality disorder will be higher at the audition than the

---

[5] This disorder is characterized by (among other things) a grandiose sense of self-importance, arrogance, lack of empathy for others, envy of others and belief that others envy them, excessive fantasies of brilliance or beauty, the need for excessive admiration and exploitation of others.

JANE SUPERBRAIN 1.1

When is a hypothesis not a hypothesis? ①

A good theory should allow us to make statements about the state of the world. Statements about the world are good things: they allow us to make sense of our world, and to make decisions that affect our future. One current example is global warming. Being able to make a definitive statement that global warming is happening, and that it is caused by certain practices in society, allows us to change these practices and, hopefully, avert catastrophe. However, not all statements can be tested using science. Scientific statements are ones that can be verified with reference to empirical evidence, whereas non-scientific statements are ones that cannot be empirically tested. So,

statements such as 'The Led Zeppelin reunion concert in London in 2007 was the best gig ever',[6] 'Lindt chocolate is the best food' and 'This is the worst statistics book in the world' are all non-scientific; they cannot be proved or disproved. Scientific statements can be confirmed or disconfirmed empirically. 'Watching *Curb Your Enthusiasm* makes you happy', 'Having sex increases levels of the neurotransmitter dopamine' and 'Velociraptors ate meat' are all things that can be tested empirically (provided you can quantify and measure the variables concerned). Non-scientific statements can sometimes be altered to become scientific statements, so 'The Beatles were the most influential band ever' is non-scientific (because it is probably impossible to quantify 'influence' in any meaningful way) but by changing the statement to 'The Beatles were the best-selling band ever' it becomes testable (we can collect data about worldwide album sales and establish whether the Beatles have, in fact, sold more records than any other music artist). Karl Popper, the famous philosopher of science, believed that non-scientific statements were nonsense and had no place in science. Good theories should, therefore, produce hypotheses that are scientific statements.

TABLE 1.1 A table of the number of people at the Big Brother audition split by whether they had narcissistic personality disorder and whether they were selected as contestants by the producers

	No Disorder	Disorder	Total
Selected	3	9	12
Rejected	6805	845	7650
Total	6808	854	7662

general level in the population. We can see in the table that of the 7662 people at the audition, 854 were diagnosed with the disorder, this is about 11% (854/7662 × 100) which is much higher than the 1% we'd expect. Therefore, this hypothesis is supported by the data. The second hypothesis was that the *Big Brother* election panel have a bias to chose people with narcissistic personality disorder. If we look at the 12 contestants that they selected, 9 of them had the disorder (a massive 75%). If the producers did not have a bias we would have expected only 11% of the contestants to have the disorder (the same rate as was found when we considered everyone who turned up for the audition). The data again support our hypothesis. Therefore, my initial observation that contestants have personality disorders was verified by data, then my theory was tested using specific hypotheses that were also verified using data. Data are *very* important!

I would now be smugly sitting in my office with a contented grin on my face because my theories and observations were well supported by the data. Perhaps I would quit while I was

---

[6] It was pretty awesome actually.

ahead and retire. It's more likely, though, that having solved one great mystery, my excited mind would turn to another. I would lock myself in a room to watch *Big Brother*. Days later, the door would open, and a stale odour would waft out like steam rising from the New York subway. Through this green cloud, my bearded face would emerge, my eyes squinting at the shards of light that cut into my pupils. Stumbling forwards, I would open my mouth to lay waste to my scientific rivals with my latest profound observation: 'personality-disordered contestants, despite their obvious character flaws, enter the house convinced that the public will love them and that they will win'.[7] I would croak before collapsing on the floor. The hypothesis we could take from this observation is that if I asked the contestants if they thought that they would win, the people with a personality disorder would say 'yes'.

Let's imagine I tested my hypothesis by measuring contestants' expectations of success in the show, by asking them 'Do you think you will win *Big Brother*?'. Let's suppose that 7 of 9 contestants with personality disorders said that they thought they would win, which confirms my observation. Next, I would come up with another theory (I'll spare you a repeat of the 'locked in a room' scenario): these contestants think that they will win because they don't realize that they have a personality disorder. The related hypothesis is that if I asked these people whether their personalities were different from other people they would say 'no'. As before, I would collect some more data and perhaps ask those who thought that they would win whether they thought that their personalities were different from the norm. All 7 contestants said that they thought their personalities were different from the norm. These data seem to contradict my theory. This is known as **falsification**, which is the act of disproving a hypothesis or theory.

It's unlikely that we would be the only people interested in why individuals who go on *Big Brother* have extreme personalities and think that they will win. Imagine these researchers discovered that people with narcissistic personality disorder think that: (1) they are more interesting than others; (2) they deserve success more than others; and (3) others like them because they have 'special' personalities.

This additional research is even worse news for my theory: if contestants didn't realize that they had a personality different from the norm then you wouldn't expect them to think that they were more interesting than others, and you certainly wouldn't expect them to think that others would like their unusual personalities. In general, this means that my theory sucks: it cannot explain all of the data, predictions from the theory are not supported by subsequent data, and it cannot explain other research findings. At this point I would start to feel intellectually inadequate and people would find me curled up on my desk in floods of tears wailing and moaning about my failing career (no change there then).

At this point, a rival scientist, Fester Ingpant-Stain, appears on the scene with a rival theory to mine. In his new theory, he suggests that the problem is not that personality-disordered contestants don't realize that they have a personality disorder (or at least a personality that is unusual), but that they falsely believe that this special personality is perceived positively by other people (to put it another way, they believe that their personality makes them likeable, not dislikeable). One hypothesis from this model is that if personality-disordered contestants are asked to evaluate what other people think of them, then they will overestimate other people's positive perceptions. To test this hypothesis, Fester Ingpant-Stain collected yet more data. When each contestant came to the diary room[8] they had to fill out a questionnaire evaluating all of the other contestants' personalities, and also answer each question about themselves but from the perspective of each of their housemates. (So,

---

[7] One of the things I like about *Big Brother* in the UK is that year upon year the winner tends to be a nice person, which does give me faith that humanity favours the nice.

[8] For those of you who don't watch *Big Brother*, this is a special room where 'Big Brother' (i.e., a disembodied voice) can talk to contestants in private (away from other contestants; obviously these conversations are broadcast to a few hundred thousand viewers).

for every contestant there is a measure of what they thought of every other contestant, and also a measure of what they believed every other contestant thought of them.) He found out that the contestants with personality disorders did overestimate their housemates' opinions of them; conversely, the contestants without personality disorders had relatively accurate impressions of what others thought of them. These data, irritating as they would be for me, support the rival theory that the contestants with personality disorders know they have unusual personalities but believe that these characteristics are ones that others would feel positive about. Fester Ingpant-Stain's theory is quite good: it explains the initial observations and brings together a range of research findings. The end result of this whole process (and my career) is that we should be able to make a general statement about the state of the world. In this case we could state that '*Big Brother* contestants who have personality disorders overestimate how much other people like their personality characteristics'.

SELF-TEST   Based on what you have read in this section, what qualities do you think a scientific theory should have?

1.5. Collect data to test your theory ①

In looking at the process of generating theories and hypotheses, we have already seen the importance of data in testing those hypotheses or deciding between competing theories. This section looks at the process of data collection in more detail: in essence, we need to decide on two things: (1) what to measure, and (2) how to measure it.

1.5.1. Variables ①

The question of what to measure is easy enough to answer: to test hypotheses we need to measure variables. Variables are just things that can change (or vary); they might vary between people (e.g., IQ, behaviour) or locations (e.g., unemployment) or even time (e.g., mood, profit, number of cancerous cells). Most hypotheses can be expressed in terms of two variables: a proposed cause and a proposed outcome. For example, if we take the scientific statement 'Coca-Cola is an effective spermicide'[9] then the proposed cause is Coca-Cola and the proposed effect is dead sperm. Both the cause and the outcome are variables: for the cause we could vary the type of drink, and for the outcome these drinks will kill different amounts of sperm. The key to testing scientific statements is to measure these two variables.

1.5.1.1. Independent and dependent variables ①

A variable that we think is a cause is known as an **independent variable** (because its value does not depend on any other variables). A variable that we think is an effect is called a **dependent variable** because the value of this variable depends on the cause (independent

---

[9] Actually, there is a long-standing urban myth that a post-coital douche with the contents of a bottle of Coke is an effective contraceptive. Unbelievably, this hypothesis has been tested and Coke does affect sperm motility, and different types of Coke are more or less effective – Diet Coke is best apparently (Umpierre, Hill, & Anderson, 1985). In case you decide to try this out, I feel it worth mentioning that a Coke douche is ineffective at preventing pregnancy.

variable). These terms are very closely tied to experimental methods in which the cause is manipulated by the experimenter (as we will see in Section 1.5.5). However, researchers can't always manipulate variables (for example, if you wanted see whether smoking causes lung cancer you wouldn't lock a bunch of people in a room for 30 years and force them to smoke) and so sometimes they use correlational methods instead (Section 1.5.4). In this context it doesn't make sense to talk of dependent and independent variables because all variables are essentially dependent variables. I prefer to use the terms **predictor variable** and **outcome variable** in place of dependent and independent variable. This is not a personal whimsy: in experimental work the cause (independent variable) is a predictor, and the effect (dependent variable) is an outcome, and in correlational work we can talk of one or more (predictor) variables predicting (statistically at least) one or more outcome variables.

CRAMMING SAM'S TIPS   Some important terms

When doing research there are some important generic terms for variables that you will encounter:

- *Independent variable*: A variable thought to be the cause of some effect. This term is usually used in experimental research to denote a variable that the experimenter has manipulated.
- *Dependent variable*: A variable thought to be affected by changes in an independent variable. You can think of this variable as an outcome.
- *Predictor variable*: A variable thought to predict an outcome variable. This is basically another term for independent variable (although some people won't like me saying that; I think life would be easier if we talked only about predictors and outcomes).
- *Outcome variable*: A variable thought to change as a function of changes in a predictor variable. This term could be synonymous with 'dependent variable' for the sake of an easy life.

1.5.1.2. Levels of measurement ①

Variables can take on many different forms and levels of sophistication. The relationship between what is being measured and the numbers that represent what is being measured is known as the **level of measurement**. Broadly speaking, variables can be categorical or continuous, and can have different levels of measurement.

A **categorical variable** is made up of categories. A categorical variable that you should be familiar with already is your species (e.g., human, domestic cat, fruit bat, etc.). You are a human or a cat or a fruit bat: you cannot be a bit of a cat and a bit of a bat, and neither a batman nor (despite many fantasies to the contrary) a catwoman exist (not even one in a nice PVC suit). A categorical variable is one that names distinct entities. In its simplest form it names just two distinct types of things, for example male or female. This is known as a **binary variable**. Other examples of binary variables are being alive or dead, pregnant or not, and responding 'yes' or 'no' to a question. In all cases there are just two categories and an entity can be placed into only one of the two categories.

When two things that are equivalent in some sense are given the same name (or number), but there are more than two possibilities, the variable is said to be a **nominal variable**. It should be obvious that if the variable is made up of names it is pointless to do arithmetic on them (if you multiply a human by a cat, you do not get a hat). However, sometimes numbers are used to denote categories. For example, the numbers worn by players in a sports team. In rugby, the numbers on shirts denote specific field positions, so the number 10 is always worn by the fly-half,[10] and the number 2 is always the hooker (the ugly-looking player at the front of the scrum). These numbers do not tell us anything other than what position the player plays. We could equally have shirts with FH and H instead of 10 and 2. A number 10 player is not necessarily better than a number 2 (most managers would not want their fly-half stuck in the front of the scrum!). It is equally daft to try to do arithmetic with nominal scales where the categories are denoted by numbers: the number 10 takes penalty kicks, and if the coach found that his number 10 was injured he would not get his number 4 to give number 6 a piggy-back and then take the kick. The only way that nominal data can be used is to consider frequencies. For example, we could look at how frequently number 10s score tries compared to number 4s.

JANE SUPERBRAIN 1.2

Self-report data ①

A lot of self-report data are ordinal. Imagine two judges on *The X Factor* were asked to rate Billie's singing on a 10-point scale. We might be confident that a judge who gives a rating of 10 found Billie more talented than one who gave a rating of 2, but can we be certain that the first judge found her five times more talented than the second? What if both judges gave a rating of 8: could we be sure they found her equally talented? Probably not: their ratings will depend on their subjective feelings about what constitutes talent (the quality of singing? showmanship? dancing?). For these reasons, in any situation in which we ask people to rate something subjective (e.g., their preference for a product, their confidence about an answer, how much they have understood some medical instructions) we should probably regard these data as ordinal, although many scientists do not.

So far the categorical variables we have considered have been unordered (e.g., different brands of Coke with which you're trying to kill sperm), but they can be ordered too (e.g., increasing concentrations of Coke with which you're trying to skill sperm). When categories are ordered, the variable is known as an **ordinal variable**. Ordinal data tell us not only that things have occurred, but also the order in which they occurred. However, these data tell us nothing about the differences between values. *The X Factor* is a TV show broadcast across the globe in which hopeful singers compete to win a recording contract. It is a hugely popular show, which could (if you take a depressing view) reflect the fact that Western society values 'luck' more than hard work. (This comment in no way reflects my bitterness at spending years learning musical instruments and trying to create original music, only to be beaten to musical fame and fortune by a 15-year-old who can sing, sort of.) Anyway, imagine the three winners of a particular *X Factor* series were Billie, Freema and Elizabeth. The names of the winners don't provide any information about where they came in the contest; however, labelling them according to their performance does – first, second and third. These categories are ordered. In using ordered categories we now know that the woman who won was better than the women who came second and third. We still know nothing about the differences between categories, though. We don't, for example, know how much better the winner was than the runners-up: Billie might have been an easy victor, getting many more votes than Freema and Elizabeth, or it might have been a very close contest that she won by only a single vote. Ordinal data, therefore, tell us more

---

[10] Unlike, for example, NFL American football where a quarterback could wear any number from 1 to 19.

than nominal data (they tell us the order in which things happened) but they still do not tell us about the differences between points on a scale.

The next level of measurement moves us away from categorical variables and into continuous variables. A **continuous variable** is one that gives us a score for each person and can take on any value on the measurement scale that we are using. The first type of continuous variable that you might encounter is an **interval variable**. Interval data are considerably more useful than ordinal data, and most of the statistical tests in this book rely on having data measured at this level. To say that data are interval, we must be certain that equal intervals on the scale represent equal differences in the property being measured. For example, on *www.ratemyprofessors.com* students are encouraged to rate their lecturers on several dimensions (some of the lecturers' rebuttals of their negative evaluations are worth a look). Each dimension (helpfulness, clarity, etc.) is evaluated using a 5-point scale. For this scale to be interval it must be the case that the difference between helpfulness ratings of 1 and 2 is the same as the difference between say 3 and 4, or 4 and 5. Similarly, the difference in helpfulness between ratings of 1 and 3 should be identical to the difference between ratings of 3 and 5. Variables like this that look interval (and are treated as interval) are often ordinal – see Jane Superbrain Box 1.2.

JANE SUPERBRAIN 1.3

Continuous and discrete variables ①

The distinction between discrete and continuous variables can be blurred. For one thing, continuous variables can be measured in discrete terms; for example,

when we measure age we rarely use nanoseconds but use years (or possibly years and months). In doing so we turn a continuous variable into a discrete one (the only acceptable values are years). Also, we often treat discrete variables as if they were continuous. For example, the number of boyfriends/girlfriends that you have had is a discrete variable (it will be, in all but the very weirdest cases, a whole number). However, you might read a magazine that says 'the average number of boyfriends that women in their 20s have has increased from 4.6 to 8.9'. This assumes that the variable is continuous, and of course these averages are meaningless: no one in their sample actually had 8.9 boyfriends.

Ratio variables go a step further than interval data by requiring that in addition to the measurement scale meeting the requirements of an interval variable, the ratios of values along the scale should be meaningful. For this to be true, the scale must have a true and meaningful zero point. In our lecturer ratings this would mean that a lecturer rated as 4 would be twice as helpful as a lecturer rated with a 2 (who would in turn be twice as helpful as a lecturer rated as 1). The time to respond to something is a good example of a ratio variable. When we measure a reaction time, not only is it true that, say, the difference between 300 and 350 ms (a difference of 50 ms) is the same as the difference between 210 and 260 ms or between 422 and 472 ms, but it is also true that distances along the scale are divisible: a reaction time of 200 ms is twice as long as a reaction time of 100 ms and half as long as a reaction time of 400 ms.

Continuous variables can be, well, continuous (obviously) but also discrete. This is quite a tricky distinction (Jane Superbrain Box 1.3). A truly continuous variable can be measured to any level of precision, whereas a **discrete variable** can take on only certain values (usually whole numbers) on the scale. What does this actually mean? Well, our example of rating lecturers on a 5-point scale is an example of a discrete variable. The range of the scale is 1–5, but you can enter only values of 1, 2, 3, 4 or 5; you cannot enter a value of 4.32 or 2.18. Although a continuum exists underneath the scale (i.e., a rating of 3.24 makes sense), the actual values that the variable takes on are limited. A continuous variable would be something like age, which can be measured at an infinite level of precision (you could be 34 years, 7 months, 21 days, 10 hours, 55 minutes, 10 seconds, 100 milliseconds, 63 microseconds, 1 nanosecond old).

CRAMMING SAM'S TIPS   Levels of measurement

Variables can be split into categorical and continuous, and within these types there are different levels of measurement:

- Categorical (entities are divided into distinct categories):
  - Binary variable: There are only two categories (e.g., dead or alive).
  - Nominal variable: There are more than two categories (e.g., whether someone is an omnivore, vegetarian, vegan, or fruitarian).
  - Ordinal variable: The same as a nominal variable but the categories have a logical order (e.g., whether people got a fail, a pass, a merit or a distinction in their exam).
- Continuous (entities get a distinct score):
  - Interval variable: Equal intervals on the variable represent equal differences in the property being measured (e.g., the difference between 6 and 8 is equivalent to the difference between 13 and 15).
  - Ratio variable: The same as an interval variable, but the ratios of scores on the scale must also make sense (e.g., a score of 16 on an anxiety scale means that the person is, in reality, twice as anxious as someone scoring 8).

1.5.2. Measurement error ①

It's one thing to measure variables, but it's another thing to measure them accurately. Ideally we want our measure to be calibrated such that values have the same meaning over time and across situations. Weight is one example: we would expect to weigh the same amount regardless of who weighs us, or where we take the measurement (assuming it's on Earth and not in an anti-gravity chamber). Sometimes variables can be measured directly (profit, weight, height) but in other cases we are forced to use indirect measures such as self-report, questionnaires and computerized tasks (to name a few).

It's been a while since I mentioned sperm, so let's go back to our Coke as a spermicide example. Imagine we took some Coke and some water and added them to two test tubes of sperm. After several minutes, we measured the motility (movement) of the sperm in the two samples and discovered no difference. A few years passed, as you might expect given that Coke and sperm rarely top scientists' research lists, before another scientist, Dr Jack Q. Late, replicated the study. Dr Late found that sperm motility was worse in the Coke sample. There are two measurement-related issues that could explain his success and our failure: (1) Dr Late might have used more Coke in the test tubes (sperm might need a critical mass of Coke before they are affected); (2) Dr Late measured the outcome (motility) differently than us.

The former point explains why chemists and physicists have devoted many hours to developing standard units of measurement. If you had reported that you'd used 100 ml of Coke and 5 ml of sperm, then Dr Late could have ensured that he had used the same amount – because millilitres are a standard unit of measurement we would know that Dr Late used exactly the same amount of Coke that we used. Direct measurements such as the millilitre provide an objective standard: 100 ml of a liquid is known to be twice as much as only 50 ml.

The second reason for the difference in results between the studies could have been to do with how sperm motility was measured. Perhaps in our original study we measured motility using absorption spectrophotometry, whereas Dr Late used laser light-scattering techniques.[11] Perhaps his measure is more sensitive than ours.

There will often be a discrepancy between the numbers we use to represent the thing we're measuring and the actual value of the thing we're measuring (i.e., the value we would get if we could measure it directly). This discrepancy is known as **measurement error**. For example, imagine that you know as an absolute truth that you weigh 83 kg. One day you step on the bathroom scales and they say 80 kg. There is a difference of 3 kg between your actual weight and the weight given by your measurement tool (the scales): this is a measurement error of 3 kg. Although properly calibrated bathroom scales should produce only very small measurement errors (despite what we might want to believe when it says we have gained 3 kg), self-report measures will produce larger measurement error because factors other than the one you're trying to measure will influence how people respond to our measures. For example, if you were completing a questionnaire that asked you whether you had stolen from a shop, would you admit it, or might you be tempted to conceal this fact?

1.5.3. Validity and reliability ①

One way to try to ensure that measurement error is kept to a minimum is to determine properties of the measure that give us confidence that it is doing its job properly. The first property is **validity**, which is whether an instrument actually measures what it sets out to measure. The second is **reliability**, which is whether an instrument can be interpreted consistently across different situations.

Validity refers to whether an instrument measures what it was designed to measure (e.g., does your lecturer helpfulness rating scale actually measure lecturers' helpfulness?); a device for measuring sperm *motility* that actually measures sperm *count* is not valid. Things like reaction times and physiological measures are valid in the sense that a reaction time does in fact measure the time taken to react and skin conductance does measure the conductivity of your skin. However, if we're using these things to infer other things (e.g., using skin conductance to measure anxiety) then they will be valid only if there are no other factors other than the one we're interested in that can influence them.

Criterion validity is whether you can establish that an instrument measures what it claims to measure through comparison to objective criteria. In an ideal world, you assess this by relating scores on your measure to real-world observations. For example, we could take an objective measure of how helpful lecturers were and compare these observations to student's ratings of helpfulness on *ratemyprofessors.com*. When data are recorded simultaneously using the new instrument and existing criteria, then this is said to assess **concurrent validity**; when data from the new instrument are used to predict observations at a later point in time, this is said to assess **predictive validity**.

Assessing criterion validity (whether concurrently or predictively) is often impractical because objective criteria that can be measured easily may not exist. Also, with attitudes it might be the person's perception of reality rather than reality itself that you're interested

---

[11] In the course of writing this chapter I have discovered more than I think is healthy about the measurement of sperm motility.

in (you might not care whether a person *is* a psychopath but whether they *think* they are a psychopath). With self-report measures/questionnaires we can also assess the degree to which individual items represent the construct being measured, and cover the full range of the construct (content validity).

Validity is a necessary but not sufficient condition of a measure. A second consideration is reliability, which is the ability of the measure to produce the same results under the same conditions. To be valid the instrument must first be reliable. The easiest way to assess reliability is to test the same group of people twice: a reliable instrument will produce similar scores at both points in time (test–retest reliability). Sometimes, however, you will want to measure something that does vary over time (e.g., moods, blood-sugar levels, productivity). Statistical methods can also be used to determine reliability (we will discover these in Chapter 17).

SELF-TEST   What is the difference between reliability and validity?

1.5.4. Correlational research methods ①

So far we've looked at the question of *what* to measure and discovered that to answer scientific questions we measure variables (which can be collections of numbers or words). We also saw that to get accurate answers we need accurate measures. We move on now to look at the question of *how* data are collected. If we simplify things quite a lot then there are two ways to test a hypothesis: either by observing what naturally happens, or by manipulating some aspect of the environment and observing the effect it has on the variable that interests us.

In correlational or cross-sectional research we observe what naturally goes on in the world without directly interfering with it, whereas in experimental research we manipulate one variable to see its effect on another. In correlational research we observe natural events; we can do this by either taking a snapshot of many variables at a single point in time, or by measuring variables repeatedly at different time points (known as longitudinal research). For example, we might measure pollution levels in a stream and the numbers of certain types of fish living there; lifestyle variables (smoking, exercise, food intake) and disease (cancer, diabetes); workers' job satisfaction under different managers; or children's school performance across regions with different demographics. Correlational research provides a very natural view of the question we're researching because we are not influencing what happens and the measures of the variables should not be biased by the researcher being there (this is an important aspect of ecological validity).

At the risk of sounding like I'm absolutely obsessed with using Coke as a contraceptive (I'm not, but my discovery that people in the 1950s and 1960s actually tried this has, I admit, intrigued me), let's return to that example. If we wanted to answer the question 'Is Coke an effective contraceptive?' we could administer questionnaires about sexual practices (quantity of sexual activity, use of contraceptives, use of fizzy drinks as contraceptives, pregnancy, etc.). By looking at these variables we could see which variables correlate with pregnancy, and in particular whether people reliant on Coca-Cola as a form of contraceptive were more likely to end up pregnant than those using other contraceptives, and less likely than those using no contraceptives at all. This is the only way to answer a question like this because we cannot manipulate any of these variables particularly easily. Even if we could, it would be totally unethical to insist on some people using Coke as a contraceptive (or indeed to do anything that would make a person likely to produce a child that they didn't intend to produce). However, there is a price to pay, which relates to causality: correlational research tells us nothing about the causal influence of variables.

1.5.5. Experimental research methods ①

Most scientific questions imply a causal link between variables; we have seen already that dependent and independent variables are named such that a causal connection is implied (the dependent variable *depends* on the independent variable). Sometimes the causal link is very obvious, as in the research question 'Does low self-esteem cause dating anxiety?' Sometimes the implication might be subtler; for example, in 'Is dating anxiety all in the mind?' the implication is that a person's mental outlook causes them to be anxious when dating. Even when the cause–effect relationship is not explicitly stated, most research questions can be broken down into a proposed cause (in this case mental outlook) and a proposed outcome (dating anxiety). Both the cause and the outcome are variables: for the cause, some people will perceive themselves in a negative way (so it is something that varies); and for the outcome, some people will get more anxious on dates than others (again, this is something that varies). The key to answering the research question is to uncover how the proposed cause and the proposed outcome relate to each other; are the people who have a low opinion of themselves the same people that are more anxious on dates?

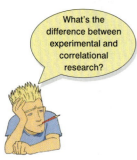

What's the difference between experimental and correlational research?

David Hume (see Hume, 1739–40, 1748, for more detail),[12] an influential philosopher, said that to infer cause and effect: (1) cause and effect must occur close together in time (contiguity); (2) the cause must occur before an effect does; and (3) the effect should never occur without the presence of the cause. These conditions imply that causality can be inferred through corroborating evidence: cause is equated to high degrees of correlation between contiguous events. In our dating example, to infer that low self-esteem caused dating anxiety, it would be sufficient to find that whenever someone had low self-esteem they would feel anxious when on a date, that the low self-esteem emerged before the dating anxiety did, and the person should never have dating anxiety if they haven't been suffering from low self-esteem.

In the previous section on correlational research, we saw that variables are often measured simultaneously. The first problem with doing this is that it provides no information about the contiguity between different variables: we might find from a questionnaire study that people with low self-esteem also have dating anxiety but we wouldn't know whether the low self-esteem or the dating anxiety came first. Longitudinal research addresses this issue to some extent, but there is a still a problem with Hume's idea that causality can be inferred from corroborating evidence.

Let's imagine that we find that there are people who have low self-esteem but do not get dating anxiety. This finding doesn't violate Hume's rules: he doesn't say anything about the cause happening without the effect. It could be that both low self-esteem and dating anxiety are caused by a third variable (e.g., poor social skills which might make you feel generally worthless but also put pressure on you in dating situations). This illustrates a second problem with correlational evidence: the *tertium quid* ('a third person or thing of indeterminate character'). For example, a correlation has been found between having breast implants and suicide (Koot, Peeters, Granath, Grobbee, & Nyren, 2003). However, it is

---

[12] Both of these can be read online at http://www.utilitarian.net/hume/ or by doing a Google search for David Hume.

unlikely that having breast implants causes you to commit suicide – presumably, there is an external factor (or factors) that causes both; for example, low self-esteem might lead you to have breast implants and also attempt suicide. These extraneous factors are sometimes called **confounding variables** or confounds for short.

The shortcomings of Hume's criteria led John Stuart Mill (1865) to add a further criterion: that all other explanations of the cause–effect relationship be ruled out. Put simply, Mill proposed that, to rule out confounding variables, an effect should be present when the cause is present and that when the cause is absent the effect should be absent also. Mill's ideas can be summed up by saying that the only way to infer causality is through comparison of two controlled situations: one in which the cause is present and one in which the cause is absent. This is what *experimental methods* strive to do: to provide a comparison of situations (usually called *treatments* or *conditions*) in which the proposed cause is present or absent.

As a simple case, we might want to look at the effect of motivators on learning about statistics. I might, therefore, randomly split[13] some students into three different groups in which I change my style of teaching in the seminars on the course:

- **Group 1 (positive reinforcement)**: During seminars I congratulate all students in this group on their hard work and success. Even when they get things wrong, I am supportive and say things like 'that was very nearly the right answer; you're coming along really well' and then give them a nice piece of chocolate.

- **Group 2 (punishment)**: This group receives seminars in which I give relentless verbal abuse to all of the students even when they give the correct answer. I demean their contributions and am patronizing and dismissive of everything they say. I tell students that they are stupid, worthless and shouldn't be doing the course at all. In other words, this group receives normal university-style seminars.☺

- **Group 3 (no motivator)**: Students are not praised or punished but instead I give them no feedback at all.

The thing that I have manipulated is the motivator (positive reinforcement, punishment or no motivator). As we have seen, this variable is known as the independent variable and in this situation it is said to have three levels, because it has been manipulated in three ways (i.e., the motivator has been split into three types: positive reinforcement, punishment and none). The outcome in which I am interested is statistical ability, and I could measure this variable using a statistics exam after the last seminar. As we have seen, this outcome variable is the dependent variable because we assume that these scores will depend upon the type of teaching method used (the independent variable). The critical thing here is the inclusion of the 'no motivator' group because this is a group in which our proposed cause (motivator) is absent, and we can compare the outcome in this group against the two situations in which the proposed cause is present. If the statistics scores are different in each of the motivation groups (cause is present) compared to the group for which no motivator was given (cause is absent) then this difference can be attributed to the type of motivator used. In other words, the motivator used caused a difference in statistics scores (Jane Superbrain Box 1.4).

1.5.5.1. Two methods of data collection ①

When we collect data in an experiment, we can choose between two methods of data collection. The first is to manipulate the independent variable using different entities. This method is the one described above, in which different groups of entities take part in each

---

[13] This random assignment of students is important, but we'll get to it later.

JANE SUPERBRAIN 1.4

Causality and statistics ①

People sometimes get confused and think that certain statistical procedures allow causal inferences and others don't. This isn't true; it's the fact that in experiments we manipulate the causal variable systematically to see

its effect on an outcome (the effect). In correlational research we observe the co-occurrence of variables; we do not manipulate the causal variable first and then measure the effect, therefore we cannot compare the effect when the causal variable is present against when it is absent. In short, we cannot say which variable causes a change in the other; we can merely say that the variables co-occur in a certain way. The reason why some people think that certain statistical tests allow causal inferences is that historically certain tests (e.g., ANOVA, *t*-tests, etc.) have been used to analyse experimental research, whereas others (e.g., regression, correlation) have been used to analyse correlational research (Cronbach, 1957). As you'll discover, these statistical procedures are, in fact, mathematically identical.

experimental condition (a **between-groups**, **between-subjects**, or **independent design**). The second method is to manipulate the independent variable using the same entities. In our motivation example, this means that we give a group of students positive reinforcement for a few weeks and test their statistical abilities and then begin to give this same group punishment for a few weeks before testing them again, and then finally give them no motivator and test them for a third time (a **within-subject** or **repeated-measures design**). As you will discover, the way in which the data are collected determines the type of test that is used to analyse the data.

1.5.5.2. Two types of variation ①

Imagine we were trying to see whether you could train chimpanzees to run the economy. In one training phase they are sat in front of a chimp-friendly computer and press buttons that change various parameters of the economy; once these parameters have been changed a figure appears on the screen indicating the economic growth resulting from those parameters. Now, chimps can't read (I don't think) so this feedback is meaningless. A second training phase is the same except that if the economic growth is good, they get a banana (if growth is bad they do not) – this feedback is valuable to the average chimp. This is a repeated-measures design with two conditions: the same chimps participate in condition 1 *and* in condition 2.

Let's take a step back and think what would happen if we did *not* introduce an experimental manipulation (i.e., there were no bananas in the second training phase so condition 1 and condition 2 were identical). If there is no experimental manipulation then we expect a chimp's behaviour to be similar in both conditions. We expect this because external factors such as age, gender, IQ, motivation and arousal will be the same for both conditions (a chimp's gender etc. will not change from when they are tested in condition 1 to when they are tested in condition 2). If the performance measure is reliable (i.e., our test of how well they run the economy), and the variable or characteristic that we are measuring (in this case ability to run an economy) remains stable over time, then a participant's performance in condition 1 should be very highly related to their performance in condition 2. So, chimps who score highly in condition 1 will also score highly in condition 2, and those who have low scores for condition 1 will have low scores in condition 2. However, performance won't be *identical*; there will be small differences in performance created by unknown factors. This variation in performance is known as **unsystematic variation**.

If we introduce an experimental manipulation (i.e., provide bananas as feedback in one of the training sessions), then we do something different to participants in condition 1 than what we do to them in condition 2. So, the *only* difference between conditions 1 and 2 is the manipulation that the experimenter has made (in this case that the chimps get bananas as a positive reward in one condition but not in the other).[14] Therefore, any differences between the means of the two conditions are probably due to the experimental manipulation. So, if the chimps perform better in one training phase than the other then this *has* to be due to the fact that bananas were used to provide feedback in one training phase but not the other. Differences in performance created by a specific experimental manipulation are known as **systematic variation**.

Now let's think about what happens when we use different participants – an independent design. In this design we still have two conditions, but this time different participants participate in each condition. Going back to our example, one group of chimps receives training without feedback, whereas a second group of different chimps does receive feedback on their performance via bananas.[15] Imagine again that we didn't have an experimental manipulation. If we did nothing to the groups, then we would still find some variation in behaviour between the groups because they contain different chimps who will vary in their ability, motivation, propensity to get distracted from running the economy by throwing their own faeces, and other factors. In short, the type of factors that were held constant in the repeated-measures design are free to vary in the independent design. So, the unsystematic variation will be bigger than for a repeated-measures design. As before, if we introduce a manipulation (i.e., bananas) then we will see additional variation created by this manipulation. As such, in both the repeated-measures design and the independent design there are always two sources of variation:

- **Systematic variation**: This variation is due to the experimenter doing something in one condition but not in the other condition.

- **Unsystematic variation**: This variation results from random factors that exist between the experimental conditions (such as natural differences in ability, the time of day, etc.).

Statistical tests are usually based on the idea of estimating how much variation there is in performance, and comparing how much of this is systematic to how much is unsystematic.

In a repeated-measures design, differences between two conditions can be caused by only two things: (1) the manipulation that was carried out on the participants, or (2) any other factor that might affect the way in which an entity performs from one time to the next. The latter factor is likely to be fairly minor compared to the influence of the experimental manipulation. In an independent design, differences between the two conditions can also be caused by one of two things: (1) the manipulation that was carried out on the participants, or (2) differences between the characteristics of the entities allocated to each of the groups. The latter factor in this instance is likely to create considerable random variation both within each condition and between them. When we look at the effect of our experimental manipulation, it is always against a background of 'noise' caused by random, uncontrollable differences between our conditions. In a repeated-measures design this 'noise' is kept to a minimum and so the effect of the experiment is

---

[14] Actually, this isn't the only difference because by condition 2 they have had some practice (in condition 1) at running the economy; however, we will see shortly that these practice effects are easily eradicated.

[15] Obviously I mean they receive a banana as a reward for their correct response and not that the bananas develop little banana mouths that sing them a little congratulatory song.

more likely to show up. This means that, other things being equal, repeated-measures designs have more power to detect effects than independent designs.

1.5.6. Randomization ①

In both repeated-measures and independent designs it is important to try to keep the unsystematic variation to a minimum. By keeping the unsystematic variation as small as possible we get a more sensitive measure of the experimental manipulation. Generally, scientists use the randomization of entities to treatment conditions to achieve this goal. Many statistical tests work by identifying the systematic and unsystematic sources of variation and then comparing them. This comparison allows us to see whether the experiment has generated considerably more variation than we would have got had we just tested participants without the experimental manipulation. Randomization is important because it eliminates most other sources of systematic variation, which allows us to be sure that any systematic variation between experimental conditions is due to the manipulation of the independent variable. We can use randomization in two different ways depending on whether we have an independent or repeated-measures design.

Let's look at a repeated-measures design first. I mentioned earlier (in a footnote) that when the same entities participate in more than one experimental condition they are naive during the first experimental condition but they come to the second experimental condition with prior experience of what is expected of them. At the very least they will be familiar with the dependent measure (e.g., the task they're performing). The two most important sources of systematic variation in this type of design are:

- **Practice effects**: Participants may perform differently in the second condition because of familiarity with the experimental situation and/or the measures being used.

- **Boredom effects**: Participants may perform differently in the second condition because they are tired or bored from having completed the first condition.

Although these effects are impossible to eliminate completely, we can ensure that they produce no systematic variation between our conditions by counterbalancing the order in which a person participates in a condition.

We can use randomization to determine in which order the conditions are completed. That is, we randomly determine whether a participant completes condition 1 before condition 2, or condition 2 before condition 1. Let's look at the teaching method example and imagine that there were just two conditions: no motivator and punishment. If the same participants were used in all conditions, then we might find that statistical ability was higher after the punishment condition. However, if every student experienced the punishment after the no motivator seminars then they would enter the punishment condition already having a better knowledge of statistics than when they began the no motivator condition. So, the apparent improvement after punishment would not be due to the experimental manipulation (i.e., it's not because punishment works), but because participants had attended more statistics seminars by the end of the punishment condition compared to the no motivator one. We can use randomization to ensure that the number of statistics seminars does not introduce a systematic bias by randomly assigning students to have the punishment seminars first or the no motivator seminars first.

If we turn our attention to independent designs, a similar argument can be applied. We know that participants in different experimental conditions will differ in many respects (their IQ, attention span, etc.). Although we know that these confounding variables contribute to the variation between conditions, we need to make sure that these variables contribute to the unsystematic variation and *not* the systematic variation. A good example is the effects of alcohol on behaviour. You might give one group of people 5 pints of beer, and keep a second group sober, and then count how many times you can persuade them to do a fish impersonation. The effect that alcohol has varies because people differ in their tolerance: teetotal people can become drunk on a small amount, while alcoholics need to consume vast quantities before the alcohol affects them. If you allocated a bunch of hardened drinkers to the condition that consumed alcohol, and teetotal people to the no alcohol condition then you might find that alcohol doesn't increase the number of fish impersonations you get. However, this finding could be because (1) alcohol does not make people engage in frivolous activities, or (2) the hardened drinkers were unaffected by the dose of alcohol. You have no way to dissociate these explanations because the groups varied not just on dose of alcohol but also their tolerance of alcohol (the systematic variation created by their past experience with alcohol cannot be separated from the effect of the experimental manipulation). The best way to reduce this eventuality is to randomly allocate participants to conditions: by doing so you minimize the risk that groups differ on variables other than the one you want to manipulate.

SELF-TEST   Why is randomization important?

1.6. Analysing data ①

The final stage of the research process is to analyse the data you have collected. When the data are quantitative this involves both looking at your data graphically (Chapter 4) to see what the general trends in the data are, and fitting statistical models to the data (all other chapters). Given that the rest of book is dedicated to this process, we'll begin here by looking at a few fairly basic ways to look at and summarize the data you have collected.

1.6.1.   Frequency distributions ①

Once you've collected some data a very useful thing to do is to plot a graph of how many times each score occurs. This is known as a **frequency distribution**, or **histogram**, which is a graph plotting values of observations on the horizontal axis, with a bar showing how many times each value occurred in the data set. Frequency distributions can be very useful for assessing properties of the distribution of scores. We will find out how to create these types of charts in Chapter 4.

Frequency distributions come in many different shapes and sizes. It is quite important, therefore, to have some general descriptions for common types of distributions. In an ideal world our data would be distributed symmetrically around the centre of all scores. As such, if we drew a vertical line through the centre of the distribution then it should look the same on both sides. This is known as a **normal distribution** and is characterized by the bell-shaped curve with which you might already be familiar. This shape basically implies that the majority of scores

What is a frequency distribution and when is it normal?

FIGURE 1.3
A 'normal' distribution (the curve shows the idealized shape)

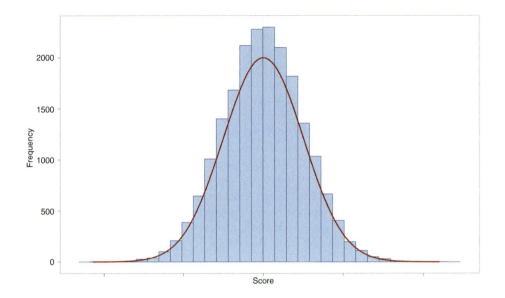

lie around the centre of the distribution (so the largest bars on the histogram are all around the central value). Also, as we get further away from the centre the bars get smaller, implying that as scores start to deviate from the centre their frequency is decreasing. As we move still further away from the centre our scores become very infrequent (the bars are very short). Many naturally occurring things have this shape of distribution. For example, most men in the UK are around 175 cm tall,[16] some are a bit taller or shorter but most cluster around this value. There will be very few men who are really tall (i.e., above 205 cm) or really short (i.e., under 145 cm). An example of a normal distribution is shown in Figure 1.3.

There are two main ways in which a distribution can deviate from normal: (1) lack of symmetry (called **skew**) and (1) pointyness (called **kurtosis**). Skewed distributions are not symmetrical and instead the most frequent scores (the tall bars on the graph) are clustered at one end of the scale. So, the typical pattern is a cluster of frequent scores at one end of the scale and the frequency of scores tailing off towards the other end of the scale. A skewed distribution can be either *positively skewed* (the frequent scores are clustered at the lower end and the tail points towards the higher or more positive scores) or *negatively skewed* (the frequent scores are clustered at the higher end and the tail points towards the lower or more negative scores). Figure 1.4 shows examples of these distributions.

Distributions also vary in their kurtosis. Despite sounding like some kind of exotic disease, kurtosis refers to the degree to which scores cluster at the ends of the distribution (known as the *tails*) and this tends to express itself in how pointy a distribution is (but there are other factors that can affect how pointy the distribution looks – see Jane Superbrain Box 1.5). A distribution with *positive kurtosis* has many scores in the tails (a so-called heavy-tailed distribution) and is pointy. This is known as a **leptokurtic** distribution. In contrast, a distribution with *negative kurtosis* is relatively thin in the tails (has light tails) and tends to be flatter than normal. This distribution is called **platykurtic**. Ideally, we want our data to be normally distributed (i.e., not too skewed, and not too many or too few scores at the extremes!). For everything there is to know about kurtosis read DeCarlo (1997).

In a normal distribution the values of skew and kurtosis are 0 (i.e., the tails of the distribution are as they should be).[17] If a distribution has values of skew or kurtosis above or

---

[16] I am exactly 180 cm tall. In my home country this makes me smugly above average. However, I often visit the Netherlands where the average male height is 185 cm (a massive 10 cm higher than the UK), and where I feel like a bit of a dwarf.

[17] Sometimes no kurtosis is expressed as 3 rather than 0, but SPSS uses 0 to denote no excess kurtosis.

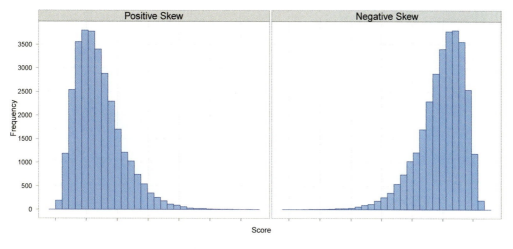

FIGURE 1.4
A positively (left) and negatively (right) skewed distribution

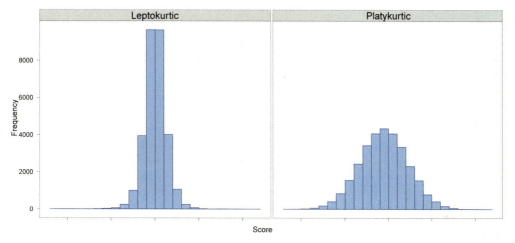

FIGURE 1.5
Distributions with positive kurtosis (leptokurtic, left) and negative kurtosis (platykurtic, right)

below 0 then this indicates a deviation from normal: Figure 1.5 shows distributions with kurtosis values of +2.6 (left panel) and −0.09 (right panel).

1.6.2. The centre of a distribution ①

We can also calculate where the centre of a frequency distribution lies (known as the **central tendency**). There are three measures commonly used: the mode, the median and the mean.

1.6.2.1. The mode ①

The **mode** is simply the score that occurs most frequently in the data set. This is easy to spot in a frequency distribution because it will be the tallest bar. To calculate the mode, simply place the data in ascending order (to make life easier), count how many times each score occurs, and the score that occurs the most is the mode. One problem with the mode is that it can often take on several values. For example, Figure 1.6 shows an example of a distribution with two modes (there are two bars that are the highest), which is said to be **bimodal**, and

FIGURE 1.6

Examples of bimodal (left) and multimodal (right) distributions

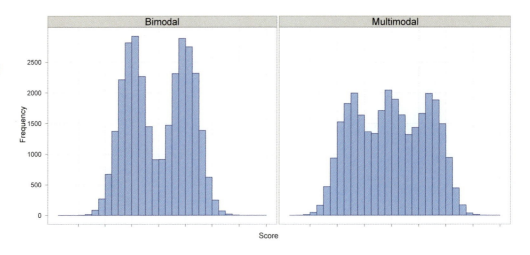

three modes (data sets with more than two modes are **multimodal**). Also, if the frequencies of certain scores are very similar, then the mode can be influenced by only a small number of cases.

1.6.2.2. The median ①

Another way to quantify the centre of a distribution is to look for the middle score when scores are ranked in order of magnitude. This is called the **median**. Facebook is a popular social networking website in which users can sign up to be 'friends' of other users. Imagine we looked at the number of friends that a selection of 11 Facebook users had. Figure 1.7

What are the mode, median and mean?

shows the number of friends that each of the 11 Facebook users had: 57, 40, 103, 234, 93, 53, 116, 98, 108, 121, 22.

To calculate the median, we first arrange these scores into ascending order: 22, 40, 53, 57, 93, 98, 103, 108, 116, 121, 234.

Next, we find the position of the middle score by counting the number of scores we have collected (n), adding 1 to this value, and then dividing by 2. With 11 scores, this gives us $(n + 1)/2 = (11 + 1)/2 = 12/2 = 6$. Then, we find the score that is positioned at the location we have just calculated. So, in this example we find the sixth score (see Figure 1.7).

This process works very nicely when we have an odd number of scores (as in this example) but when we have an even number of scores there won't be a middle value. Let's imagine that we decided that because the highest score was so big (almost twice as large as the next biggest number), we would ignore it. (For one thing, this person is far too popular and we hate them.) We have only 10 scores now. Figure 1.8 shows this situation. As before, we rank-order these scores: 22, 40, 53, 57, 93, 98, 103, 108, 116, 121. We then calculate the position of the middle score, but this time it is $(n + 1)/2 = 11/2 = 5.5$, which means that the median is halfway between the fifth and sixth scores. To get the median we add these two scores and divide by 2. In this example, the fifth score in the ordered list was 93 and the sixth score was 98. We add these together ($93 + 98 = 191$) and then divide this value by 2 ($191/2 = 95.5$). The median number of friends was, therefore, 95.5.

The median is relatively unaffected by extreme scores at either end of the distribution: the median changed only from 98 to 95.5 when we removed the extreme score of 234. The median is also relatively unaffected by skewed distributions and can be used with ordinal, interval and ratio data (it cannot, however, be used with nominal data because these data have no numerical order).

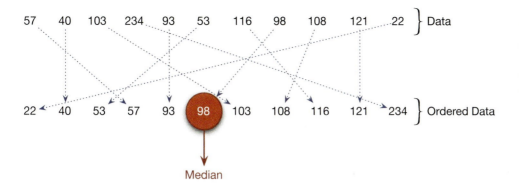

FIGURE 1.7
The median is simply the middle score when you order the data

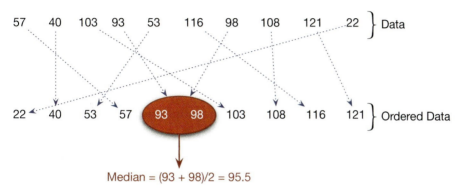

FIGURE 1.8
When the data contains an even number of scores, the median is the average of the middle two values

1.6.2.3. The mean ①

The **mean** is the measure of central tendency that you are most likely to have heard of because it is simply the average score and the media are full of average scores.[18] To calculate the mean we simply add up all of the scores and then divide by the total number of scores we have. We can write this in equation form as:

$$\bar{X} = \frac{\sum_{i=1}^{n} x_i}{n} \tag{1.1}$$

This may look complicated, but the top half of the equation simply means 'add up all of the scores' (the x_i just means 'the score of a particular person'; we could replace the letter i with each person's name instead), and the bottom bit means divide this total by the number of scores you have got (n). Let's calculate the mean for the Facebook data. First, we first add up all of the scores:

$$\sum_{i=1}^{n} x_i = 22 + 40 + 53 + 57 + 93 + 98 + 103 + 108 + 116 + 121 + 234$$

$$= 1045$$

We then divide by the number of scores (in this case 11):

$$\bar{X} = \frac{\sum_{i=1}^{n} x_i}{n} = \frac{1045}{11} = 95$$

---

[18] I wrote this on 15 February, and to prove my point the BBC website ran a headline about how PayPal estimates that Britons will spend an average of £71.25 each on Valentine's Day gifts, but uSwitch.com said that the average spend would be only £22.69. The media is full of lies and contradictions.

The mean is 95 friends, which is not a value we observed in our actual data. In this sense the mean is a statistical model – more on this in the next chapter.

SELF-TEST   Compute the mean but excluding the score of 234.

If you calculate the mean without our most popular person (i.e., excluding the value 234), the mean drops to 81.1 friends. One disadvantage of the mean is that it can be influenced by extreme scores. In this case, the person with 234 friends on Facebook increased the mean by about 14 friends; compare this difference with that of the median. Remember that the median hardly changed if we included or excluded 234, which illustrates how the median is less affected by extreme scores than the mean. While we're being negative about the mean, it is also affected by skewed distributions and can be used only with interval or ratio data.

If the mean is so lousy then why do we use it all of the time? One very important reason is that it uses every score (the mode and median ignore most of the scores in a data set). Also, the mean tends to be stable in different samples.

1.6.3.   The dispersion in a distribution ①

It can also be interesting to try to quantify the spread, or dispersion, of scores in the data. The easiest way to look at dispersion is to take the largest score and subtract from it the smallest score. This is known as the **range** of scores. For our Facebook friends data, if we order these scores we get 22, 40, 53, 57, 93, 98, 103, 108, 116, 121, 234. The highest score is 234 and the lowest is 22; therefore, the range is 234 − 22 = 212. One problem with the range is that because it uses only the highest and lowest score it is affected dramatically by extreme scores.

SELF-TEST   Compute the range but excluding the score of 234.

If you have done the self-test task you'll see that without the extreme score the range drops dramatically from 212 to 99: less than half the size.

One way around this problem is to calculate the range when we exclude values at the extremes of the distribution. One convention is to cut off the top and bottom 25% of scores and calculate the range of the middle 50% of scores – known as the **interquartile range**. Let's do this with the Facebook data. First we need to calculate what are called **quartiles**. Quartiles are the three values that split the sorted data into four equal parts. First we calculate the median, which is also called the *second quartile*, which splits our data into two equal parts. We already know that the median for these data is 98. The **lower quartile** is the median of the lower half of the data and the **upper quartile** is the median of the upper half of the data. As a rule of thumb the median is not included in the two halves when they are split (this is convenient if you have an odd number of values), but you can include it (although which half you put it in is another question). Figure 1.9 shows how we would

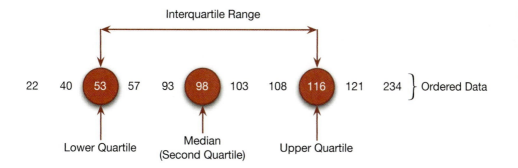

FIGURE 1.9
Calculating
quartiles and
the interquartile
range

calculate these values for the Facebook data. Like the median, if each half of the data had an even number of values in it then the upper and lower quartiles would be the average of two values in the data set (therefore, the upper and lower quartile need not be values that actually appear in the data). Once we have worked out the values of the quartiles, we can calculate the interquartile range, which is the difference between the upper and lower quartile. For the Facebook data this value would be $116-53 = 63$. The advantage of the interquartile range is that it isn't affected by extreme scores at either end of the distribution. However, the problem with it is that you lose a lot of data (half of it in fact).

It's worth noting here that quartiles are special cases of things called **quantiles**. Quantiles are values that split a data set into equal portions, and in the case of quartiles they are quantiles that split the data into four equal parts. However, you can have other quantiles such as **percentiles** (points that split the data into 100 equal parts), **noniles** (points that split the data into nine equal parts) and so on.

SELF-TEST   Twenty-one heavy smokers were put on a treadmill at the fastest setting. The time in seconds was measured until they fell off from exhaustion:

18, 16, 18, 24, 23, 22, 22, 23, 26, 29, 32, 34, 34, 36, 36, 43, 42, 49, 46, 46, 57

Compute the mode, median, mean, upper and lower quartiles, range and interquartile range.

If we want to use all of the data rather than half of it, we can calculate the spread of scores by looking at how different each score is from the centre of the distribution. If we use the mean as a measure of the centre of a distribution then we can calculate the difference between each score and the mean, which is known as the **deviance**:

$$\text{deviance} = x_i - \bar{x} \tag{1.2}$$

If we want to know the total deviance then we could add up the deviances for each data point. In equation form, this would be:

$$\text{total deviance} = \sum_{i=1}^{n}(x_i - \bar{x}) \tag{1.3}$$

The sigma symbol (Σ) simply means 'add up all of what comes after', and the 'what comes after' in this case is the deviances. So, this equation simply means 'add up all of the deviances'.

TABLE 1.2   Table showing the deviations of each score from the mean

Number of Friends (x_i)	Mean ($\bar{x}$)	Deviance ($x_i - \bar{x}$)	Deviance squared ($x_i - \bar{x})^2$
22	95	−73	5329
40	95	−55	3025
53	95	−42	1764
57	95	−38	1444
93	95	−2	4
98	95	3	9
103	95	8	64
108	95	13	169
116	95	21	441
121	95	26	676
234	95	139	19321

$$\sum_{i=1}^{n} x_i - \bar{x} = 0 \qquad \sum_{i=1}^{n}(x_i - \bar{x})^2 = 32246$$

Let's try this with the Facebook data. Table 1.2 shows the number of friends for each person in the Facebook data, the mean, and the difference between the two. Note that because the mean is at the centre of the distribution, some of the deviations are positive (scores greater than the mean) and some are negative (scores smaller than the mean). Consequently, when we add the scores up, the total is zero. Therefore, the 'total spread' is nothing. This conclusion is as silly as a tapeworm thinking it can get to have tea with the Queen of England simply by donning a bowler hat and pretending to be a human.

To overcome this problem, we could ignore the minus signs when we add the deviations up. There's nothing wrong with doing this, but people tend to square the deviations which has a similar effect (because a negative number multiplied by another negative number becomes positive). The final column of Table 1.2 shows these squared deviances. We can add these squared deviances up to get the **sum of squared errors, SS** (often just called the *sum of squares*); unless your scores are all exactly the same, the resulting value will be bigger than zero, indicating that there is some deviance from the mean. As an equation we would write:

$$\text{sum of squared errors (SS)} = \sum_{i=1}^{n}(x_i - \bar{x})^2 \tag{1.4}$$

Again, the sigma symbol means 'add up all of the things that follow' and what follows is the squared deviances (or squared errors as it's more commonly known). We can use the sum of squares as an indicator of the total dispersion, or total deviance of scores from the mean. The problem with using the total is that its size will depend on how many scores we have in the data. The sum of squares for the Facebook data is 32,246, but if we added another 11 scores that value would increase (other things being equal, it will more or less double in size). The total dispersion is a bit of a nuisance then because we can't compare it across samples that differ in size. Therefore, it can be useful to work not with the total dispersion, but the average dispersion, which is also know as the **variance**. We have seen that an average is simply the total of scores divided by the number of scores, therefore, the variance is simply the sum of squares divided by the number of observations (N). Actually, we normally divide the SS by the number of observations minus 1 (the reason why is explained in the next chapter and Jane Superbrain Box 2.2):

$$\text{variance}\left(s^2\right) = \frac{\text{SS}}{N-1} = \frac{\sum_{i=1}^{n}(x_i - \bar{x})^2}{N-1} = \frac{32{,}246}{10} = 3224.6 \tag{1.5}$$

As we have seen, the variance is the average error between the mean and the observations made. There is one problem with the variance as a measure: it gives us a measure in units squared (because we squared each error in the calculation). In our example we would have to say that the average error in our data was 3224.6 friends squared. It makes very little sense to talk about friends squared, so we often take the square root of the variance (which ensures that the measure of average error is in the same units as the original measure). This measure is known as the **standard deviation** and is simply the square root of the variance:

$$s = \sqrt{\frac{\sum_{i=1}^{n}(x_i - \bar{x})^2}{N-1}}$$
$$= \sqrt{3224.6}$$
$$= 56.79 \tag{1.6}$$

The sum of squares, variance and standard deviation are all measures of the dispersion or spread of data around the mean. A small standard deviation (relative to the value of the mean itself) indicates that the data points are close to the mean. A large standard deviation (relative to the mean) indicates that the data points are distant from the mean. A standard deviation of 0 would mean that all of the scores were the same. Figure 1.10 shows the overall ratings (on a 5-point scale) of two lecturers after each of five different lectures. Both lecturers had an average rating of 2.6 out of 5 across the lectures. However, the first lecturer had a standard deviation of 0.55 (relatively small compared to the mean). It should be clear from the graph that ratings for this lecturer were consistently close to the mean rating. There was a small fluctuation, but generally his lectures did not vary in popularity. Put another way, the scores are not spread too widely around the mean. The second lecturer, however, had a standard deviation of 1.82 (relatively high compared to the mean). The ratings for this second lecturer are more spread from the mean than the first: for some lectures he received very high ratings, and for others his ratings were appalling.

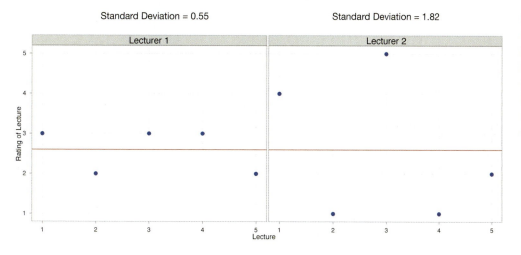

FIGURE 1.10
Graphs illustrating data that have the same mean but different standard deviations

1.6.4. Using a frequency distribution to go beyond the data ①

Another way to think about frequency distributions is not in terms of how often scores actually occurred, but how likely it is that a score would occur (i.e., probability). The word 'probability' induces suicidal ideation in most people (myself included) so it seems fitting that we use an example about throwing ourselves off a cliff. Beachy Head is a large, windy cliff on the Sussex coast (not far from where I live) that has something of a reputation for attracting suicidal people, who seem to like throwing themselves off it (and after several months of rewriting this book I find my thoughts drawn towards that peaceful chalky cliff top more and more often). Figure 1.12 shows a frequency distribution of some completely made-up data of the number of suicides at Beachy Head in a year by people of different ages (although I made these data up, they are roughly based on general suicide statistics such as those in Williams, 2001). There were 172 suicides in total and you can see that the suicides were most frequently aged between about 30 and 35 (the highest

JANE SUPERBRAIN 1.5

The standard deviation and the shape of the distribution ①

The variance and standard deviation tell us about the shape of the distribution of scores. If the mean represents the data well then most of the scores will cluster close to

the mean and the resulting standard deviation is small relative to the mean. When the mean is a worse representation of the data, the scores cluster more widely around the mean and the standard deviation is larger. Figure 1.11 shows two distributions that have the same mean (50) but different standard deviations. One has a large standard deviation relative to the mean ($SD = 25$) and this results in a flatter distribution that is more spread out, whereas the other has a small standard deviation relative to the mean ($SD = 15$) resulting in a more pointy distribution in which scores close to the mean are very frequent but scores further from the mean become increasingly infrequent. The main message is that as the standard deviation gets larger, the distribution gets fatter. This can make distributions look platykurtic or leptokurtic when, in fact, they are not.

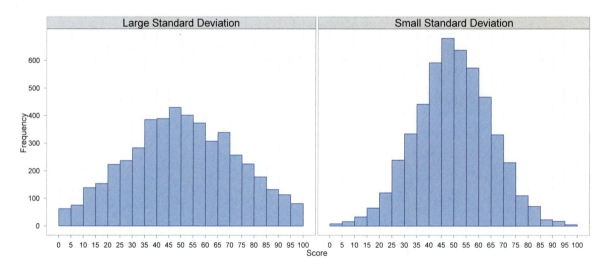

FIGURE 1.11   Two distributions with the same mean, but large and small standard deviations

CHAPTER 1   WHY IS MY EVIL LECTURER FORCING ME TO LEARN STATISTICS?

29

SCANLON, T. J., ET AL. (1993). *BRITISH MEDICAL JOURNAL, 307,* 1584–1586.

LABCOAT LENI'S REAL RESEARCH 1.1

Is Friday the 13th unlucky? ①

Many of us are superstitious, and a common superstition is that Friday the 13th is unlucky. Most of us don't literally think that someone in a hockey mask is going to kill us, but many people are wary. Scanlon and colleagues, in a tongue-in-cheek study (Scanlon, Luben, Scanlon, & Singleton, 1993), looked at accident statistics at hospitals in the South West Thames region of the UK. They took statistics both for Friday the 13th and Friday the 6th (the week before) in different months in 1989, 1990, 1991 and 1992. They looked at both emergency admissions of accidents and poisoning, and transport accidents.

Calculate the mean, median, standard deviation and interquartile range for each type of accident and on each date. Answers are in the additional material on the companion website.

Date	Accidents and Poisoning		Traffic Accidents	
	Friday 6th	Friday 13th	Friday 6th	Friday 13th
October 1989	4	7	9	13
July 1990	6	6	6	12
September 1991	1	5	11	14
December 1991	9	5	11	10
March 1992	9	7	3	4
November 1992	1	6	5	12

bar). The graph also tells us that, for example, very few people aged above 70 committed suicide at Beachy Head.

We can think of frequency distributions in terms of probability. To explain this, imagine that someone asked you, 'How likely is it that a person who committed suicide at Beach Head is older than 70?' What would your answer be? The chances are that if you looked at the frequency distribution you might respond 'not very likely' because you can see that only 3 people out of the 172 suicides were aged over 70. What about if someone asked you, 'How likely is it that a 34-year-old committed suicide?' Again, by looking at the graph, you might say 'it's relatively likely' because that is the highest bar so it is the age at which people were most likely to commit suicide. What about if someone asked, 'How likely is it that someone who committed suicide was aged 30–35?' The bars representing these ages are shaded a darker blue in Figure 1.12. The question about the likelihood of a suicide being aged 30–35 is really asking, 'How big is the dark blue area of Figure 1.12 compared to the total size of all bars?' We can find out the size of the dark blue region by adding the values of the bars (8 + 4 + 6 + 4 + 11 + 3 = 36); therefore, the dark blue area represents 36 people. The total size of all bars is simply the total number of suicides recorded (i.e., 172). If the dark blue area represents 36 people, and the total area represents 172 people, then if we compare the dark blue to the total area we get 36/172 = .21. This proportion can be converted to a percentage by multiplying by 100, which gives us 21%. Therefore, our answer might be, 'It's quite likely that someone who committed suicide was aged 30–35 because 21% of the sample, or around 1 in every 5 people that committed suicide, were in that age range.' A very important point here is that the size of the bars relate directly to the probability of an event occurring.

Hopefully these illustrations show that we can use the frequencies of different scores, and the area of a frequency distribution, to estimate the probability that a particular score will occur. A probability value can range from 0 (there's no chance whatsoever of the event happening) to 1 (the event will definitely happen). So, for example, when I talk to

FIGURE 1.12
Frequency
distribution
showing the
number of
suicides at
Beachy Head in
a year, by age

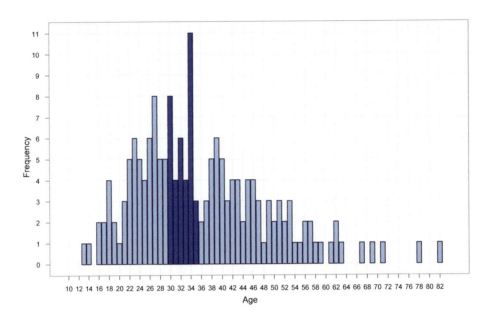

my publishers I tell them there's a probability of 1 that I will have completed the revisions to this book by May. However, when I talk to anyone else, I might, more realistically, tell them that there's a .10 probability of me finishing the revisions on time (or put another way, a 10% chance, or 1 in 10 chance that I'll complete the book in time). In reality, the probability of my meeting the deadline is 0 (not a chance in hell) because I never manage to meet publishers' deadlines. If probabilities don't make sense to you then just ignore the decimal point and think of them as percentages instead (i.e., a .10 probability that something will happen is a 10% chance that something will happen).

I've talked in vague terms about how frequency distributions can be used to get a rough idea of the probability of a score occurring. However, we can be precise. For any distribution of scores we could, in theory, calculate the probability of obtaining a score of a certain size – it would be incredibly tedious and complex to do it, but we could. To spare our sanity, statisticians have identified several common distributions. For each one they have worked out mathematical formulae (known as **probability density functions**) that specify idealized versions of these distributions. We could draw such a function by plotting the value of the variable (x) against the probability of it occurring (y).[19] The resulting curve is known as a **probability distribution**; for a normal distribution (Section 1.6.1) it would look like Figure 1.13, which has the characteristic bell shape that we saw in Figure 1.3.

A probability distribution is just like a histogram except that the lumps and bumps have been smoothed out so that we see a nice smooth curve. However, like a frequency distribution, the area under this curve tells us something about the probability of a value occurring. Just like we did in our Beachy Head example, we could use the area under the curve between

two values to tell us how likely it is that a score fell within a particular range. For example, the blue shaded region in Figure 1.13 corresponds to the probability of a score being z or greater. The normal distribution is not the only distribution that has been precisely specified by people with enormous brains. There are many distributions that have characteristic shapes and have been specified with a probability density function. We'll encounter some of these other distributions throughout the book, for example, the t-distribution, chi-square (χ^2) distribution and F-distribution. For now, the important thing to remember is that all of these distributions have something in common: they are all defined by an equation that enables us to calculate precisely the probability of obtaining a given score.

[19] Actually we usually plot something called the density, which is closely related to the probability.

CHAPTER 1 WHY IS MY EVIL LECTURER FORCING ME TO LEARN STATISTICS?

31

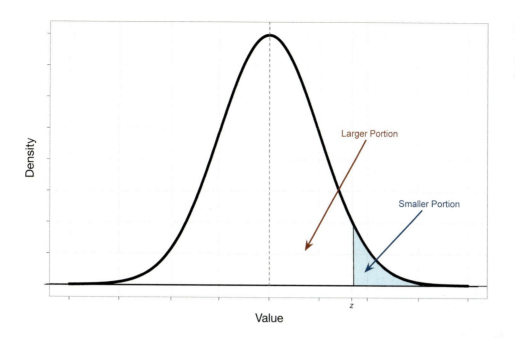

FIGURE 1.13
The normal
probability
distribution

As we have seen, distributions can have different means and standard deviations. This isn't a problem for the probability density function – it will still give us the probability of a given value occurring – but it is a problem for us because probability density functions are difficult enough to spell, let alone to use to compute probabilities. Therefore, to avoid a brain meltdown we often use a normal distribution with a mean of 0 and a standard deviation of 1 as a standard. This has the advantage that we can pretend that the probability density function doesn't exist and use tabulated probabilities (as in the Appendix) instead. The obvious problem is that not all of the data we collect will have a mean of 0 and standard deviation of 1. For example, for the Beachy Head data the mean is 36.16 and the standard deviation is 13.03. However, any data set can be converted into a data set that has a mean of 0 and a standard deviation of 1. First, to centre the data around zero, we take each score (X) and subtract from it the mean of all scores ($\bar{X}$). To ensure the data have a standard deviation of 1, we divide the resulting score by the standard deviation (s), which we recently encountered. The resulting scores are denoted by the letter z and are known as *z-scores*. In equation form, the conversion I've just described is:

$$z = \frac{X - \bar{X}}{s} \tag{1.7}$$

The table of probability values that have been calculated for the standard normal distribution is shown in the Appendix. Why is this table important? Well, if we look at our suicide data, we can answer the question 'What's the probability that someone who threw themselves off of Beachy Head was 70 or older?' First we convert 70 into a z-score. We saw that the mean was 36.16 and the standard deviation was 13.03, so our score of 70 expressed as a z-score is:

$$z = \frac{70 - 36.16}{13.03} = 2.60$$

We can now use this value, rather than the original value of 70, to compute an answer to our question.

Figure 1.14 shows (an edited version of) the tabulated values of the standard normal distribution from the Appendix of this book. This table gives us a list of values of z, and the density (y) for each value of z, but, most important, it splits the distribution at the value of z and tells us the size of the two areas under the curve that this division creates. For example, when z is 0, we are at the mean or centre of the distribution so it splits the area under the curve exactly in half. Consequently both areas have a size of .5 (or 50%). However, any value of z that is not zero will create different sized areas, and the table tells us the size of the larger and smaller portion. For example, if we look up our z-score of 2.6, we find that the smaller portion (i.e., the area above this value, or the blue area in Figure 1.14) is .0044, or put another way, only 0.44%. I explained before that these areas relate to probabilities, so in this case we could say that there is only a 0.44% chance that a suicide victim would be 70 years old or more. By looking at the larger portion (the area below 2.60) we get .9956, or put another way, there's a 99.56% chance that a suicide victim was younger than 70 years old. Note that these two proportions add up to 1 (or 100%), so the total area under the curve is 1.

Another useful thing we can do (you'll find out just how useful in due course) is to work out limits within which a certain percentage of scores fall. With our Beachy Head example, we looked at how likely it was that a suicide victim was aged between 30 and 35; we could ask a similar question such as 'what is the range of ages between which the middle 95% of suicides fall?'. To answer this we need to use the table the opposite way around. We know that the total area under the curve is 1 (or 100%), so to discover the limits within which 95% of scores fall we're asking, 'What is the value of z that cuts off 5% of the scores?' It's not quite as simple as that because if we want the *middle* 95%, then we want to cut off scores from both ends. Given the distribution is symmetrical, if we want to cut off 5% of scores overall but we want to take some from both extremes of scores, then the percentage of scores we want to cut off of each end will be 5%/2 = 2.5% (or .025 as a proportion). If we cut off 2.5% of scores from each end then in total we'll have cut off 5% scores, leaving us with the middle 95% (or 0.95 as a proportion) – see Figure 1.15. To find out what value of z cuts off the top area of .025, we look down the column 'smaller portion' until we reach .025; we then read off the corresponding value of z. This value is 1.96 (see Figure 1.14) and because the distribution is symmetrical around zero, the value that cuts off the bottom .025 will be the same but a minus value (–1.96). Therefore, the middle 95% of z-scores fall between –1.96 and 1.96. If we wanted to know the limits between which the middle 99% of scores would fall, we could do the same: now we would want to cut off 1% of scores, or 0.5% from each end. This equates to a proportion of .005. We look up .005 in the *smaller portion* part of the table and the nearest value we find is .00494, which equates to a z-score of 2.58 (see Figure 1.14). This tells us that 99% of z-scores lie between –2.58 and 2.58. Similarly (have a go) you can show that 99.9% of them lie between –3.29 and 3.29. Remember these values (1.96, 2.58 and 3.29) because they'll crop up time and time again.

SELF-TEST   Assuming the same mean and standard deviation for the Beachy Head example above, what's the probability that someone who threw themselves off Beachy Head was 30 or younger?

1.6.5. Fitting statistical models to the data ①

Having looked at your data (and there is a lot more information on different ways to do this in Chapter 4), the next step of the research process is to fit a statistical model to the

A.1. Table of the standard normal distribution

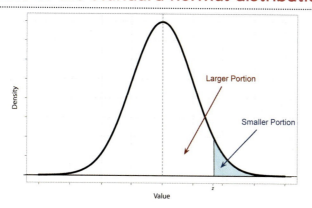

FIGURE 1.14
Using tabulated
values of
the standard
normal
distribution

z	Larger Portion	Smaller Portion	y	z	Larger Portion	Smaller Portion	y
.00	.50000	.50000	.3989	.12	.54776	.45224	.3961
.01	.50399	.49601	.3989	.13	.55172	.44828	.3956
.02	.50798	.49202	.3989	.14	.55567	.44433	.3951
.03	.51197	.48803	.3988	.15	.55962	.44038	.3945
.04	.51595	.48405	.3986	.16	.56356	.43644	.3939
1.56	.94062	.05938	.1182	1.86	.96856	.03144	.0707
1.57	.94179	.05821	.1163	1.87	.96926	.03074	.0694
1.58	.94295	.05705	.1145	1.88	.96995	.03005	.0681
1.59	.94408	.05592	.1127	1.89	.97062	.02938	.0669
1.60	.94520	.05480	.1109	1.90	.97128	.02872	.0656
1.61	.94630	.05370	.1092	1.91	.97193	.02807	.0644
1.62	.94738	.05262	.1074	1.92	.97257	.02743	.0632
1.63	.94845	.05155	.1057	1.93	.97320	.02680	.0620
1.64	.94950	.05050	.1040	1.94	.97381	.02619	.0608
1.65	.95053	.04947	.1023	1.95	.97441	.02559	.0596
1.66	.95154	.04846	.1006	1.96	.97500	.02500	.0584
1.67	.95254	.04746	.0989	1.97	.97558	.02442	.0573
1.68	.95352	.04648	.0973	1.98	.97615	.02385	.0562
2.26	.98809	.01191	.0310	2.56	.99477	.00523	.0151
2.27	.98840	.01160	.0303	2.57	.99492	.00508	.0147
2.28	.98870	.01130	.0297	2.58	.99506	.00494	.0143
2.29	.98899	.01101	.0290	2.59	.99520	.00480	.0139
2.30	.98928	.01072	.0283	2.60	.99534	.00466	.0136
2.31	.98956	.01044	.0277	2.61	.99547	.00453	.0132

FIGURE 1.15
The probability
density function
of a normal
distribution

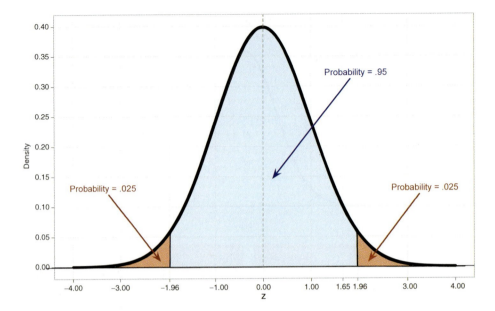

data. That is to go where eagles dare, and no one should fly where eagles dare; but to become scientists we have to, so the rest of this book attempts to guide you through the various models that you can fit to the data.

1.7. Reporting data ①

1.7.1. Dissemination of research ①

Having established a theory and collected and started to summarize data, you might want to tell other people what you have found. This sharing of information is a fundamental part of being a scientist. As discoverers of knowledge, we have a duty of care to the world to present what we find in a clear and unambiguous way, and with enough information that others can challenge our conclusions. Tempting as it may be to cover up the more unsavoury aspects of our results, science should be about 'the truth'. We tell the world about our findings by presenting them at conferences and in articles published in scientific **journals**. A scientific journal is a collection of articles written by scientists on a vaguely similar topic. A bit like a magazine, but more tedious. These articles can describe new research, review existing research, or might put forward a new theory. Just like you have magazines such as *Modern Drummer*, which is about drumming, or *Vogue*, which is about fashion (or Madonna, I can never remember which), you get journals such as *Journal of Anxiety Disorders*, which publishes articles about anxiety disorders, and *British Medical Journal*, which publishes articles about medicine (not specifically British medicine, I hasten to add). As a scientist, you submit your work to one of these journals and they will consider publishing it. Not everything a scientist writes will be published. Typically, your manuscript will be given to an 'editor' who will be a fairly eminent scientist working in that research area who has agreed, in return for their soul, to make decisions about whether or not to publish articles. This editor will send your manuscript out to review, which means they send it to other experts in your research area and ask those experts to assess the quality of the work. The reviewers' role is to provide a constructive and even-handed overview of the strengths and weaknesses of your article and the research contained within it. Once these reviews are complete the editor reads them all, and assimilates the comments with his or her own views on the manuscript and decides whether or not to publish it (in reality, you'll be asked to make revisions at least once before a final acceptance).

The review process is an excellent way to get some really useful feedback on what you have done, and very often throws up things that you hadn't considered. The flip side is that when people scrutinize your work they don't always say nice things. Early on in my career I found this process quite difficult: often you have put months of work into the article and it's only natural that you want your peers to receive it well. When you do get negative feedback, and even the most respected scientists do, it can be easy to feel like you're not good enough. At those times, it's worth remembering that if you're not affected by criticism then you're probably not human; every scientist I know has moments when they doubt themselves.

1.7.2. Knowing how to report data ①

An important part of publishing your research is how you present and report your data. You will typically do this through a combination of graphs (see Chapter 4) and written descriptions of the data. Throughout this book I will give you guidance about how to present data and write up results. The difficulty is that different disciplines have different conventions. In my area of science (psychology) we typically follow the publication guidelines of the American Psychological Association, APA (American Psychological Association, 2010), but even within psychology different journals have their own idiosyncratic rules about how to report data. Therefore, my advice will be based on the APA guidelines (because on the whole they are sensible) with a bit of my own personal opinion thrown in when there isn't a specific APA 'rule'. However, when reporting data for assignments or for publication it is always advisable to check the specific guidelines of your tutor or the journal.

Despite the 'rules' that you'll find floating around, and the fact that some people would have you believe that if you deviate from any of these rules in even the most subtle of ways then you will unleash the four horsemen of the apocalypse onto the world to obliterate humankind, rules are no substitute for common sense. Although some people treat the APA style guide like a holy sacrament, its job is not to lay down intractable laws, but to offer a guide so that everyone is consistent in what they do. It does not tell you what to do in every situation but does offer sensible guiding principles that you can extrapolate to most situations you'll encounter.

1.7.3. Some initial guiding principles ①

When reporting data your first decision is whether to use text, a graph or a table. You want to be succinct so you shouldn't present the same values in multiple ways: if you have a graph showing some results then don't also produce a table of the same results: it's a waste of space. The APA gives the following guidelines:

✓ Choose a mode of presentation that optimizes the understanding of the data.

✓ If you present three or fewer numbers then try using a sentence.

✓ If you need to present between 4 and 20 numbers consider a table.

✓ If you need to present more than 20 numbers then a graph is often more useful than a table.

Of these, I think the first is most important: I can think of countless situations where I would want to use a graph rather than a table to present 4–20 values because a graph will show up the pattern of data most clearly. Similarly, I can imagine some graphs presenting more than 20 numbers being an absolute mess. This takes me back to my point about rules being no substitute for common sense, and the most important thing is to present the data in a way that makes it easy for the reader to digest. We'll look at how to present graphs in Chapter 4 and we'll look at tabulating data in various chapters when we discuss how best to report the results of particular analyses.

A second general issue is how many decimal places to use when reporting numbers. The guiding principal from the APA (which I think is sensible) is that the fewer decimal places the better, which means that you should round as much as possible but bear in mind the precision of the measure you're reporting. This principle again reflects making it easy for the reader to understand the data. Let's look at an example. Sometimes when a person doesn't respond to someone, they will ask, 'What's wrong? Has the cat got your tongue?' Actually, my cat has a large collection of carefully preserved human tongues that he keeps in a box under the stairs. Periodically he'll get one out, pop it in his mouth and wander around the neighbourhood scaring people with his big tongue. If I measured the difference in length between his actual tongue and his fake human tongue, I might report this difference as 0.0425 metres, 4.25 centimetres, or 42.5 millimetres. This example illustrates three points: (1) I needed a different number of decimal places (4, 2 and 1, respectively) to convey the same information in each case; (2) 4.25 cm is probably easier for someone to digest than 0.0425 metres because it uses fewer decimal places, and (3) my cat is odd. The first point demonstrates that it's not the case that you should always use, say, two decimal places; you should use however many you need in a particular situation. The second point implies that if you have a very small measure it's worth considering whether you can use a different scale to make the numbers more palatable.

Finally, every set of guidelines will include advice on how to report specific analyses and statistics. For example, when describing data with a measure of central tendency, the APA suggests you use M (capital M in italics) to represent the mean but is fine with you using the mathematical notation ($\bar{X}$) too. However, you should be consistent: if you use M to represent the mean you should do so throughout your article. There is also a sensible principle that if you report a summary of the data such as the mean, you should also report the appropriate measure of the spread of scores. Then people know not just the central location of the data, but also how spread out it was. Therefore, whenever we report the mean, we typically report the standard deviation also. The standard deviation is usually denoted by SD, but it is also common to simply place it in parentheses as long as you indicate that you're doing so in the text. Here are some examples from this chapter:

- ✓ Andy has 2 friends on Facebook. On average, a sample of other users ($N = 11$) had considerably more, $M = 95$, $SD = 56.79$.

- ✓ The number of suicides at Beachy Head per year, $\bar{X} = 36$, $SD = 13$, was higher than the national average.

- ✓ By reading this chapter we discovered that (SD in parentheses), on average, people have 95 (56.79) friends on Facebook and there are 36 (13) suicides per year at Beachy Head.

Note that in the first example, I used N to denote the size of the sample. This is a common abbreviation: a capital N represents the entire sample and a lower case n represents a subsample (e.g., the number of cases within a particular group). Similarly, when we report medians, there is a specific notation (the APA suggests Mdn) and we should report the range or interquartile range as well (the APA do not have an abbreviation for either of these terms but IQR is commonly used for the interquartile range). Therefore, we could report:

- ✓ Andy has 2 friends on Facebook. A sample of other users ($N = 11$) typically had more, $Mdn = 98$, $IQR = 63$.

- ✓ Andy has 2 friends on Facebook. A sample of other users ($N = 11$) typically had more, $Mdn = 98$, $range = 212$.

1.8. Brian's attempt to woo Jane ①

Brian Haemorrhage is in love with Jane Superbrain. Jane never even acknowledges his existence because she thinks he's an idiot. She likes people who know about statistics. At the end of each chapter Brian will appear and show off his newly acquired knowledge to see whether Jane is impressed enough to go on a date with him. We'll also see how she reacts to his attempt to woo her (Figure 1.16).

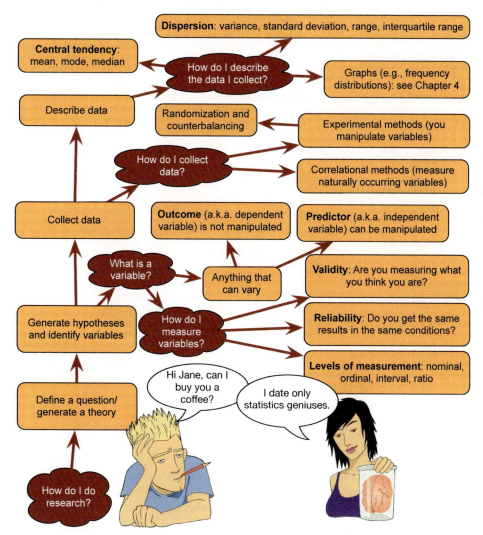

FIGURE 1.16   What Brian learnt from this chapter

1.9. What next? ①

It is all very well discovering that if you stick your finger into a fan or get hit around the face with a golf club it hurts, but what if these are isolated incidents? It's better if we can somehow extrapolate from our data and draw more general conclusions. Even better, perhaps we can start to make predictions about the world: if we can predict when a golf club is going to appear out of nowhere then we can better move our faces. The next chapter looks at fitting models to the data and using these models to draw conclusions that go beyond the data we collected.

My early childhood wasn't all full of pain. On the contrary it was filled with a lot of fun: the nightly 'from how far away can I jump into bed' competition (which sometimes involved a bit of pain) and being carried by my brother and dad to bed as they hummed Chopin's *Marche Funèbre* before lowering me between two beds as though being buried in a grave. It was more fun than it sounds.

1.10. Key terms that I've discovered

Between-groups design
Between-subjects design
Bimodal
Binary variable
Boredom effect
Categorical variable
Central tendency
Concurrent validity
Confounding variable
Content validity
Continuous variable
Correlational research
Counterbalancing
Criterion validity
Cross-sectional research
Dependent variable
Deviance
Discrete variable
Ecological validity
Experimental research
Falsification
Frequency distribution
Histogram
Hypothesis
Independent design
Independent variable

Interquartile range
Interval variable
Journal
Kurtosis
Leptokurtic
Level of measurement
Longitudinal research
Lower quartile
Mean
Measurement error
Median
Mode
Multimodal
Negative skew
Nominal variable
Nonile
Normal distribution
Ordinal variable
Outcome variable
Percentile
Platykurtic
Positive skew
Practice effect
Predictive validity
Predictor variable
Probability density function (PDF)

Probability distribution
Qualitative methods
Quantitative methods
Quantile
Quartile
Randomization
Range
Ratio variable
Reliability
Repeated-measures design
Second quartile
Skew
Standard deviation
Systematic variation
Sum of squared errors
Tertium quid
Test–retest reliability
Theory
Unsystematic variance
Upper quartile
Validity
Variables
Variance
Within-subject design
z-scores

1.11. Smart Alex's tasks

Smart Alex knows everything there is to know about statistics and SPSS. He also likes nothing more than to ask people stats questions just so that he can be smug about how much he knows. So, why not really annoy him and get all of the answers right!

- **Task 1**: What are (broadly speaking) the five stages of the research process? ①
- **Task 2**: What is the fundamental difference between experimental and correlational research? ①
- **Task 3**: What is the level of measurement of the following variables? ①

The number of downloads of different bands' songs on iTunes
The names of the bands that were downloaded
Their positions in the iTunes download chart
The money earned by the bands from the downloads
The weight of drugs bought by the bands with their royalties
The type of drugs bought by the bands with their royalties
The phone numbers that the bands obtained because of their fame

The gender of the people giving the bands their phone numbers
The instruments played by the band members
The time they had spent learning to play their instruments

- **Task 4**: Say I own 857 CDs. My friend has written a computer program that uses a webcam to scan the shelves in my house where I keep my CDs and measure how many I have. His program says that I have 863 CDs. Define measurement error. What is the measurement error in my friend's CD-counting device? ①

- **Task 5**: Sketch the shape of a normal distribution, a positively skewed distribution and a negatively skewed distribution. ①

- **Task 6:** In 2011 I got married and we went to Disney World in Florida for our honeymoon. We bought some bride and groom Micky Mouse hats and wore them around the parks. The staff at Disney are really nice and upon seeing our hats would say 'congratulations' to us. We counted how many times people said congratulations over 7 days of the honeymoon: 5, 13, 7, 14, 11, 9, 17. Calculate the mean, median, sum of squares, variance and standard deviation of these data. ①

- **Task 7:** In this chapter we used an example of the time taken for 21 heavy smokers to fall off a treadmill at the fastest setting (18, 16, 18, 24, 23, 22, 22, 23, 26, 29, 32, 34, 34, 36, 36, 43, 42, 49, 46, 46, 57). Calculate the sum of squares, variance and standard deviation of these data. ①

- **Task 8:** Sports scientists sometimes talk of a 'red zone', which is a period during which players in a team are more likely to pick up injuries because they are fatigued. When a player hits the red zone it is a good idea to rest them for a game or two. At a prominent London football club that I support, they measured how many consecutive games the 11 first team players could manage before hitting the red zone: 10, 16, 8, 9, 6, 8, 9, 11, 12, 19, 5. Calculate the mean, standard deviation, median, range and interquartile range. ①

- **Task 9:** Celebrities always seem to be getting divorced. The (approximate) lengths of some celebrity marriages in days are: 240 (J-Lo and Cris Judd), 144 (Charlie Sheen and Donna Peele), 143 (Pamela Anderson and Kid Rock), 72 (Kim Kardashian, if you can call her a celebrity), 30 (Drew Barrymore and Jeremy Thomas), 26 (Axl Rose and Erin Everly), 2 (Britney Spears and Jason Alexander), 150 (Drew Barrymore again, but this time with Tom Green), 14 (Eddie Murphy and Tracy Edmonds), 150 (Renee Zellweger and Kenny Chesney), 1657 (Jennifer Aniston and Brad Pitt). Compute the mean, median, standard deviation, range and interquartile range for these lengths of celebrity marriages. ①

- **Task 10:** Repeat Task 9 but excluding Jennifer Anniston and Brad Pitt's marriage. How does this affect the mean, median, range, interquartile range, and standard deviation. What do the differences in values between Tasks 9 and 10 tell us about the influence of unusual scores on these measures? ①

Answers can be found on the companion website.

1.12. Further reading

Field, A. P., & Hole, G. J. (2003). *How to design and report experiments*. London: Sage. (I am rather biased, but I think this is a good overview of basic statistical theory and research methods.)

Miles, J. N. V., & Banyard, P. (2007). *Understanding and using statistics in psychology: A practical introduction*. London: Sage. (A fantastic and amusing introduction to statistical theory.)

Wright, D. B., & London, K. (2009). *First steps in statistics* (2nd ed.). London: Sage. (This book is a very gentle introduction to statistical theory.)

Everything you never wanted to know about statistics

2.1. What will this chapter tell me? ①

Although I had learnt a lot about golf clubs randomly appearing out of nowhere and hitting you around the face, I still felt that there was much about the world that I didn't understand. For one thing, could I learn to predict the presence of these golf clubs that seemed inexplicably drawn towards my apparently magnetic head? A child's survival depends upon being able to predict reliably what will happen in certain situations; consequently they develop a model of the world based on the data they have (previous experience) and they then test this model by collecting new data/experiences. Based on how well the new experiences fit with their original model, a child might revise their model of the world.

According to my parents (conveniently I have no memory of this at all), while at nursery school the model of the world that I was most enthusiastic to try out was 'If I get my penis out, it will be really funny'. To my considerable disappointment, this model turned out to be a poor predictor of positive outcomes. Thankfully for all concerned, I soon revised this model of the world to be 'If I get my penis out at nursery school the teachers and mummy and daddy will be quite annoyed'. This revised model was a better 'fit' of the observed data. Fitting models that accurately reflect the observed data is important to establish whether a theory is true.

You'll be relieved to know that this chapter is not about my penis but is about fitting statistical models. We edge sneakily away from the frying pan of research methods and trip accidentally into the fires of statistics hell. We will start to see how we can use the properties of data to go beyond our observations and to draw inferences about the world at large. This chapter lays the foundation for the whole of the rest of the book.

2.2. Building statistical models ①

We saw in the previous chapter that scientists are interested in discovering something about a phenomenon that we assume actually exists (a 'real-world' phenomenon). These real-world phenomena can be anything from the behaviour of interest rates in the economic market to the behaviour of undergraduates at the end-of-exam party. Whatever the phenomenon we desire to explain, we collect data from the real world to test our hypotheses about that phenomenon. Testing these hypotheses involves building statistical models of the phenomenon of interest.

Let's begin with an analogy. Imagine an engineer wishes to build a bridge across a river. That engineer would be pretty daft if she just built any old bridge, because it might fall down. Instead, the engineer collects data from the real world: she looks at existing bridges and sees from what materials they are made, their structure, size and so on (she might even collect data about whether these bridges are still standing). She uses this information to construct an idea of what her new bridge will be (this is a 'model'). It's expensive and impractical for her to build a full size version of her bridge, so she builds a scaled-down version. The model may differ from reality in several ways – it will be smaller for a start – but the engineer will try to build a model that best fits the situation of interest based on the data available.

Why do we build statistical models?

Once the model has been built, it can be used to predict things about the real world: for example, the engineer might test whether the bridge can withstand strong winds by placing the model in a wind tunnel. It is important that the model is an accurate representation of the real world or her conclusions based on the model can't be extrapolated to the real-world bridge.

Scientists do much the same: they build (statistical) models of real-world processes in an attempt to predict how these processes operate under certain conditions (see Jane Superbrain Box 2.1). Unlike engineers, we don't have access to the real-world situation and so we can only ever *infer* things about psychological, societal, biological or economic processes based upon the models we build. However, just like the engineer, we want our model to be as accurate as possible so that we can be confident that the predictions we make about the real world are also accurate; the statistical model we build must represent the data collected (the *observed data*) as closely as possible. The degree to which a statistical model represents the data collected is known as the **fit** of the model.

Figure 2.2 illustrates three models that an engineer might build to represent the real-world bridge that she wants to create. The first model is an excellent representation of the real-world situation and is said to be a *good fit*. If the engineer uses this model to make predictions about the real world then, because it so closely resembles reality, she can be confident that these predictions will be accurate. So, if the model collapses in a strong wind, then there is a good chance that the real bridge would collapse also. The second model has some similarities to the real world: the model includes some of the basic structural features, but there are some big differences too (e.g., the absence of one of the supporting towers).

FIGURE 2.2
Fitting models
to real-world
data (see text for
details)

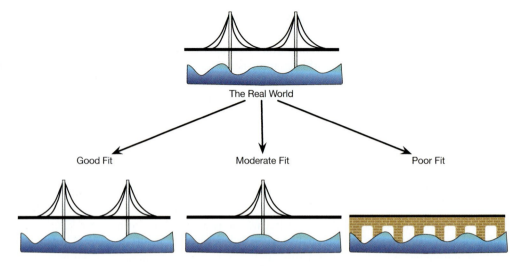

We might consider this model to have a *moderate fit* (i.e., there are some similarities to reality but also some important differences). If the engineer uses this model to make predictions about the real world then these predictions may be inaccurate or even catastrophic (e.g., the model predicts that the bridge will collapse in a strong wind, causing the real bridge to be closed down, creating 100-mile tailbacks with everyone stranded in the snow, all of which was unnecessary because the real bridge was perfectly safe – the model was a bad representation of reality). We can have some confidence, but not complete confidence, in predictions from this model. The final model is completely different to the real-world situation; it bears no structural similarities to the real bridge and is a *poor fit*. Any predictions based on this model are likely to be completely inaccurate. Extending this analogy to science, if our model is a poor fit of the observed data then the predictions we make from it will be equally poor.

2.3. Populations and samples ①

As scientists, we are interested in finding results that apply to an entire **population** of entities. For example, psychologists want to discover processes that occur in all humans, biologists might be interested in processes that occur in all cells, economists want to build models that apply to all salaries, and so on. A population can be very general (all human beings) or very narrow (all male ginger cats called Bob). Usually, scientists strive to infer things about general populations rather than narrow ones. For example, it's not very interesting to conclude that psychology students with brown hair who own a pet hamster named George recover more quickly from sports injuries if the injury is massaged (unless you happen to be a psychology student with brown hair who has a pet hamster named George, like René Koning[1]). It will have a much wider impact if we can conclude that *everyone's* sports injuries are aided by massage.

Remember that our bridge-building engineer could not make a full-size model of the bridge she wanted to build and instead built a small-scale model and tested it under various conditions. From the results obtained from the small-scale model the engineer could infer things about how the full-sized bridge will respond. The small-scale model may respond differently to a full-sized version of the bridge, but the larger the model, the more likely it is to behave in the same way as the full-size bridge. This metaphor can be extended to

---

[1] A brown-haired psychology student with a hamster called Sjors (Dutch for George, apparently) who emailed me to weaken my foolish belief that I'd generated an obscure combination of possibilities.

JANE SUPERBRAIN 2.1

Types of statistical models ①

Scientists (especially behavioural and social ones) tend to describe data with **linear models**, which are models based upon a straight line The scientific literature is riddled with research that uses analysis of variance (ANOVA) and regression to analyse the data; these methods are identical systems based on linear models (Cohen, 1968), yet they have different names and, in psychology at least, are used largely in different contexts due to historical divisions in methodology (Cronbach, 1957).

Let's look at an example. The Honesty Lab (www.honestylab.com) looked at how people evaluated dishonest acts. Participants evaluated the dishonesty of acts based on watching videos of people confessing to those acts. I haven't seen the results in an academic journal, but the media would have us believe that the more likeable the perpetrator was, the more positively their dishonest acts were viewed. Imagine we took 100 people and gave them a random dishonest act, described by the perpetrator. We asked them to evaluate the honesty of the act (from 0 = appalling behaviour to 10 = it's OK really) and how much they liked the person (0 = not at all, 10 = a lot).

We could represent these hypothetical data on a scatterplot in which each dot represents an individual's rating on both variables (see Section 4.8). Figure 2.3 shows two versions of the same data, but the left has a linear (straight) and the right a non-linear (curved) model fit. These graphs illustrate how we can fit different types of models to the same data. Both graphs show that the more you like the perpetrator the more positively you rate their dishonest act. However, the curved line shows a more subtle pattern: the trend to be more forgiving of likeable people really kicks in when the likeableness rating rises above 4. Below 4 (when people are really not likeable) all deeds are rated fairly low (the red line is quite flat), but as people become likeable (above about 4) the line slopes up more strongly, suggesting that as likeableness rises above this value, people become increasingly more forgiving of dishonest acts. Neither of the two models is necessarily correct, but one model will fit the data better than another; this is why when we use statistical models it is important for us to assess how well a given model fits the data.

Linear models tend to get fitted to data because they are less complex (despite 900 pages of statistics hell, I don't really discuss non-linear models in this book). This may have created two types of bias: (1) many 'models' in the scientific literature might not be the ones that fit best (because the authors didn't try out a non-linear model); and (2) many data sets might not have been published because a linear model was a poor fit, but the scientists gave up and didn't try out a non-linear one (which perhaps would have been a good fit). It is useful to plot your data first: if your plot seems to suggest a non-linear model then investigate this possibility (and email me complaining about how I don't cover non-linear models in this book).

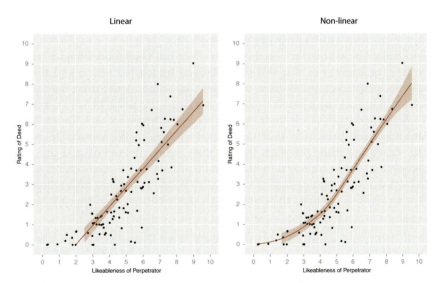

FIGURE 2.3   A scatterplot of the same data with a linear model fitted (left), and with a non-linear model fitted (right)

scientists: we rarely, if ever, have access to every member of a population (the real-size bridge). Psychologists cannot collect data from every human being and ecologists cannot observe every male ginger cat called Bob. Therefore, we collect data from a small subset of the population known as a **sample** (the scaled-down bridge) and use these data to infer things about the population as a whole. The bigger the sample, the more likely it is to reflect the whole population. If we take several random samples from the population, each of these samples will give us slightly different results. However, on average, large samples should be fairly similar.

2.4. Statistical models ①

Many centuries ago there existed a cult of elite mathematicians. They spent 200 years trying to solve an equation that they believed would give them eternal life. However, one of them forgot that when you multiply two minus numbers you get a plus, and instead of gaining immortality they accidentally released Cthulu from his underwater city. It's amazing how small computational mistakes in maths can have these sorts of consequences. Anyway, the only way they could agree to get Cthulu to go back to his entrapment was if they promised to infect the minds of humanity with confusion. They set about this task by taking the simple and elegant idea of a statistical model and reinventing that idea in hundreds of seemingly different ways (Figure 2.4). They described each model as though it were completely different from the rest. Confusion indeed infected the minds of students. They kept their secret that all statistical models could be described in one simple, easy-to-understand equation locked away in a wooden box with Cthulu's head burned unto the lid. 'No one will open a box with a big squid head burnt into it', they thought. They were right, until a Greek fisherman stumbled upon the box and, thinking it contained some vintage calamari, opened it. Disappointed with the contents, he sold the script inside on eBay. I bought it for €3. I can now reveal to you the key that will unlock the mystery of statistics for ever: everything in this book (and statistics generally) boils down to the following equation:

$$\text{outcome}_i = (\text{model}) + \text{error}_i \tag{2.1}$$

This equation just means that the data we observe can be predicted from the model we choose to fit to the data plus some amount of error.[2] The 'model' in the equation will vary depending on the design of your study, the type of data you have and what it is you're trying to achieve with your model. Consequently, the model can also vary in its complexity. No matter how long the equation that describes your model might be, you can just close your eyes, reimagine it as the word 'model' (much less scary) and think of the equation above: we predict an outcome variable from some model (that may or may not be hideously complex) but it won't predict perfectly so there will be some error in there too.

Statistical models are made up of variables and **parameters**. As we have seen, variables are measured constructs that vary across entities in the sample. In contrast, parameters are estimated from the data (rather than being measured) and are (usually) constants believed to represent some fundamental truth about the relations between variables in the model. Some examples of parameters with which you might be familiar are: the mean and median (which estimate the centre of the distribution) and the correlation and regression

---

[2] The little *i* (e.g., outcome*ᵢ*) simply refers to the *i*th score. Imagine we had three scores collected from Andy, Jeremy and Zoë, we could replace the *i* with a name, so if we wanted to predict Zoë's score we could change the equation to: outcome$_{\text{Zoë}}$ = model + error$_{\text{Zoë}}$. The *i* just reflects the fact that the value of the outcome and the error will be different for each person.

FIGURE 2.4
Thanks to the
Confusion
machine a
simple equation
is made to
seem like lots
of completely
separate tests

coefficients (which estimate the relationship between two variables). Statisticians try to confuse you by giving different parameters different symbols and letters (X for the mean, r for the correlation, b for regression coefficients) but it's much less confusing if we just use the letter b. If we're interested only in summarizing the outcome, as we are when we compute a mean, then we won't have any variables in the model, only a parameter, so we could write our equation as:

$$\text{outcome}_i = (b) + \text{error}_i \tag{2.2}$$

However, often we want to predict an outcome from a variable. We usually denote predictor variables with the letter X, therefore our model will be:

$$\text{outcome}_i = (bX_i) + \text{error}_i \tag{2.3}$$

Now we're predicting the value of the outcome for a particular entity (i) from its score on the predictor variable (X_i). The predictor variable has a parameter (b) attached to it, which tells us something about the relationship between the predictor (X_i) and outcome.

If we want to predict an outcome from two predictors then we can add another predictor to the model too:

$$\text{outcome}_i = (b_1 X_{1i} + b_2 X_{2i}) + \text{error}_i \tag{2.4}$$

Now we're predicting the value of the outcome for a particular entity (i) from its score on two predictor variables (X_{1i} and X_{2i}). Each predictor variable has a parameter (b) attached to it, which tells us something about the relationship between that predictor and the outcome. We could carry on expanding the model with more variables, but that will make our brains hurt so let's not. In each of these equations I have kept brackets around the model, which aren't necessary, but I think it helps you to see what the model is in each case.

Hopefully what you can take from this section is that all of this book boils down to a very simple idea: we can predict values of an outcome variable based on some kind of model. The form of the model changes but there will always be some error, and there will always be parameters that tell us about the shape or form of the model.

To work out what the model looks like we have to estimate the parameters (i.e., the value(s) of b). You'll hear the phrases 'estimate the parameter' or 'parameter estimates' a lot in statistics, and you might wonder why we use the word 'estimate'. Surely statistics has evolved enough that we can compute exact values of things and not merely estimate them. As I mentioned before, we're interested in drawing conclusions about a population (to which we didn't have access). In other words, we want to know what our model might look like in the whole population. Given that our model is defined by parameters, this amounts to saying that we don't care about the parameters in our sample; we care about the parameters in the population. The problem is that we don't know what the parameters in the population are because we didn't measure the population; we measured only a sample. However, we can use the sample data to *estimate* what the population parameters are likely to be. That's why we use the word 'estimate', because when we calculate parameters based on sample data they are only estimates (i.e., a 'best guess') of what the true parameter is in the population. Let's make these ideas a bit more concrete with a very simple model indeed: the mean.

2.4.1. The mean as a statistical model ①

We encountered the mean in Section 1.6.2.3, where I briefly mentioned that it was a statistical model of the data because it is a hypothetical value and not necessarily one that is observed in the data. For example, if we took five statistics lecturers and measured the number of friends that they had, we might find the following data: 1, 2, 3, 3 and 4. If we want to know the mean number of friends, this can be calculated by adding the values we obtained, and dividing by the number of values measured: $(1 + 2 + 3 + 3 + 4)/5 = 2.6$. It is impossible to have 2.6 friends (unless you chop someone up with a chainsaw and befriend their arm, which frankly is probably not beyond your average statistics lecturer) so the mean value is a *hypothetical* value: it is a model created to summarize the data. The mean is simply a summary of the outcome variable (we aren't trying to predict it from other variables) so our model is:

$$\text{outcome}_i = (b) + \text{error}_i$$

in which the parameter, b, is the mean. The important thing is that we can use the value of the mean (or any parameter) computed in our sample to estimate the value in the population (which is the value in which we're actually interested). We basically just assume that the value of the mean in the sample (2.6) is the same as the value in the population.

2.4.2. Assessing the fit of a model: sums of squares and variance revisited ①

With any statistical model we have to assess the fit (to return to our bridge analogy, we need to know how closely our model bridge resembles the real bridge that we want to build). With most statistical models we can determine whether the model is accurate by looking at how different our real data are from the model that we have created. As I explained in the previous section, the easiest way to do this is to look at the difference between the data we observed and the model fitted. Let's look what happens when we make a prediction for lecturer 1; we observed that they had one friend and the model (i.e., the mean of all lecturers) predicts 2.6. Therefore, equation (2.1) becomes:

$$\text{outcome}_{\text{lecturer1}} = \bar{X} + \varepsilon_{\text{lecturer 1}}$$
$$1 = 2.6 + \varepsilon_{\text{lecturer 1}}$$
$$\varepsilon_{\text{lecturer 1}} = 1 - 2.6$$

From this we can work out that the error is $1 - 2.6$, or -1.6. You might notice that all we have done here is calculate the deviance, which we encountered in Section 1.6.3. The

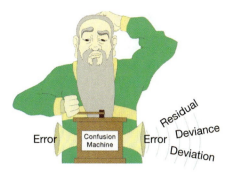

FIGURE 2.5
Thanks to the Confusion machine there are lots of terms that basically refer to error

deviance is just another word for *error* (Figure 2.5). A more general way to think of the deviance or error is by rearranging equation (2.1):

$$\text{deviance} = \text{outcome}_i - \text{model}_i \tag{2.5}$$

In other words, the error or deviance for a particular entity is the score predicted by the model for that person subtracted from the observed score for that entity. Figure 2.6 shows the number of friends that each statistics lecturer had, and also the mean number that we calculated earlier on. The line representing the mean can be thought of as our model, and the circles are the observed data. The diagram also has a series of vertical lines that connect each observed value to the mean value. These lines represent the error or deviance of the model for each lecturer. The first lecturer had only 1 friend (a glove puppet of an ostrich called Kevin) and we have already seen that the error for this lecturer is −1.6. This error is a negative number, and represents the fact that our model *overestimates* this lecturer's popularity: it predicts that he will have 2.6 friends but actually he has only 1 (bless him!).

We know the accuracy or 'fit' of the model for lecturer 1, but we want to know the fit of the model overall. We saw in Section 1.6.3 that we can't just add deviances because some errors are positive and others negative and so we'd get a total of zero:

$$\text{total error} = \text{sum of errors}$$

$$= \sum_{i=1}^{n} \left(\text{outcome}_i - \text{model}_i\right)$$

$$= (-1.6) + (-0.6) + (0.4) + (0.4) + (1.4) = 0$$

We also saw in Section 1.6.3 that one way around this problem is to square the errors. This would give us:

$$\text{sum of squared errors} \, (\text{SS}) = \sum_{i=1}^{n} \left(\text{outcome}_i - \text{model}_i\right)^2$$

$$= (-1.6)^2 + (-0.6)^2 + (0.4)^2 + (0.4)^2 + (1.4)^2$$

$$= 2.56 + 0.36 + 0.16 + 0.16 + 1.96$$

$$= 5.20$$

Does this equation look familiar? It ought to, because it's the same as equation (1.4) for the sum of squares in Section 1.6.3 – the only difference is that equation (1.4) was specific to when our model is the mean, so the 'model' was replaced with the symbol for the mean

FIGURE 2.6
Graph showing
the difference
between the
observed
number of
friends that
each statistics
lecturer had,
and the mean
number of
friends

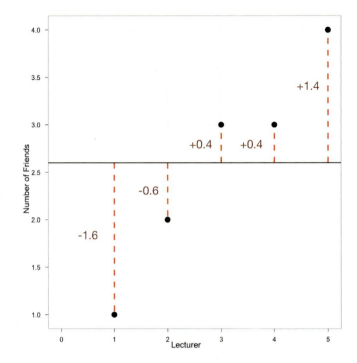

$(\bar{x})$, and the outcome was replaced by the letter x (which is a commonly used to represent a score on a variable):

$$\sum_{i=1}^{n}\left(\text{outcome}_i - \text{model}_i\right)^2 = \sum_{i=1}^{n}(x_i - \bar{x})^2$$

However, when we're thinking about models more generally, this illustrates that we can think of the total error in terms of this general equation:

$$\text{Total error} = \sum_{i=1}^{n}\left(\text{observed}_i - \text{model}_i\right)^2 \tag{2.6}$$

This equation shows how something we have used before (the sum of squares) can be used to assess the total error in any model (not just the mean).

We saw in Section 1.6.3 that although the sum of squared errors (SS) is a good measure of the accuracy of our model, it depends upon the amount of data that has been collected – the more data points, the higher the SS. We also saw that we can overcome this problem by using the average error, rather than the total. To compute the average error we simply divide the sum of squares (i.e., the total error) by the number of values (N) that we used to compute that total. We again come back to the problem that we're usually interested in the error in the model in the population (not the sample). To estimate the mean error in the population we need to divide not by the number of scores contributing to the total, but by the degrees of freedom (df), which is the number of scores used to compute the total adjusted for the fact that we're trying to estimate the population value (Jane Superbrain Box 2.2):

$$\text{mean squared error} = \frac{SS}{df} = \frac{\sum_{i=1}^{n}\left(\text{outcome}_i - \text{model}_i\right)^2}{N-1} \tag{2.7}$$

JANE SUPERBRAIN 2.2

Degrees of freedom ②

The concept of degrees of freedom (*df*) is a very difficult one to explain. I'll begin with an analogy. Imagine you're the manager of a sports team (I'll try to keep it general so you can think of whatever sport you follow, but in my mind I'm thinking about soccer). On the morning of the game you have a team sheet with (in the case of soccer) 11 empty slots relating to the positions on the playing field. Different players have different positions on the field that determine their role (defence, attack etc.) and to some extent their physical location (left, right, forward, back). When the first player arrives, you have the choice of 11 positions in which to place this player. You place their name in one of the slots and allocate them to a position (e.g., striker) and, therefore, one position on the pitch is now occupied. When the next player arrives, you have the choice of 10 positions but you still have the freedom to choose which position this player is allocated (they could be put in defence, midfield, etc.). However, as more players arrive, you become more limited in your choices: perhaps you have enough defenders so you need to start allocating some people to attack, where

you have positions unfilled. Eventually you'll reach the point at which 10 positions have been filled and the final player arrives. With this player you have no freedom to choose where they play – there is only one position left. Therefore there are 10 degrees of freedom; that is, for 10 players you have some degree of choice over where they play, but for one player you have no choice. The degrees of freedom are one less than the number of players.

In statistical terms the degrees of freedom relate to the number of observations that are free to vary. If we take a sample of four observations from a population, then these four scores are free to vary in any way (they can be any value). However, if we then use this sample of four observations to calculate the mean squared error in the population, we have to use the mean of the sample as an estimate of the population's mean. Thus we hold one parameter constant. Say that the mean of the sample was 10; then we assume that the population mean is 10 also and we keep this value constant. With this parameter fixed, can all four scores from our sample vary? The answer is no, because to ensure that the population mean is 10 only three values are free to vary. For example, if the values in the sample were 8, 9, 11, 12 (mean = 10) and we changed three of these values to 7, 15 and 8, then the final value *must* be 10 so that the mean is 10 also. Therefore, if we hold one parameter constant then the degrees of freedom must be one less than the number of scores used to calculate that parameter. This fact explains why when we use a sample to estimate the mean squared error (or indeed the standard deviation) of a population, we divide the sums of squares by $N - 1$ rather than N alone.

Does this equation look familiar? Again, it ought to, because it's a more general form of the equation for the variance (equation (1.5)). Our model is the mean, so let's replace the 'model' with the mean ($\bar{x}$), and the 'outcome' with the letter x (to represent a score on the outcome). Lo and behold, the equation transforms into that of the variance:

$$\text{mean squared error} = \frac{SS}{df} = \frac{\sum_{i=1}^{n}(x_i - \bar{x})^2}{N-1} = \frac{5.20}{4} = 1.30$$

To sum up, we can use the sum of squared error and the mean squared error to assess the fit of a model. When our model is the mean, the mean squared error has a special name: the variance. As such, the variance is a special case of a more general principle that we can apply to more complex models, which is that the fit of the model can be assessed with either the sum of squared errors or the mean squared error. Both of these measures give us an idea of how well a model fits the data: large values relative to the model indicate a lack of fit. Think back to Figure 1.10, which showed students' ratings of five lectures given by two lecturers. These lecturers differed in their mean squared error:[3] lecturer 1 had a smaller mean squared error than lecturer 2. Compare their graphs: the ratings for lecturer 1 were consistently close to the mean rating, indicating that the mean is a good representation of the observed data – it is a good fit. The ratings for lecturer 2, however, were more spread from the mean: for some lectures he received very high ratings, and for others his ratings were terrible. Therefore, the mean is not such an good representation of the observed scores – it is a poor fit.

2.4.3. Estimating parameters ①

We have seen that models are defined by parameters, and these parameters need to be estimated from the data that we collect. We used an example of the mean because it was familiar, but it will also illustrate a general principle about how parameters are estimated. Let's imagine that one day we walked down the road and fell into a hole. Not just any old hole, though, but a hole created by a rupture in the space–time continuum. We slid down the hole, which turned out to be a sort of U-shaped tunnel under the road, and we emerged out of the other end to find that not only were we on the other side of the road, but we'd gone back in time a few hundred years. Consequently, statistics had not been invented and neither had the equation to compute the mean. Happier times than now, you might think, until a slightly odorous and beardy tramp accosts you, demanding to know the average number of friends that a lecturer has. If we didn't know the equation for computing the mean, how might we do it? We could just guess, and then see how well our guess fits the data. Remember, we're trying to estimate the parameter b in equation (2.2):

$$\text{outcome}_i = b + \text{error}_i$$

We know already that we can rearrange this equation to give us the error for each person:

$$\text{error}_i = \text{outcome}_i - b$$

If we add the error for each person then we'll get the sum of squared errors, which we can use as a measure of 'fit'. Imagine we begin by guessing that the mean number of friends that a lecturer has is 2. We can compute the error for each lecturer by subtracting this value from the number of friends they actually had. We then square this value to get rid of any minus signs, and we add up these squared errors. Table 2.1 shows this process, and we find that by guessing a value of 2, we end up with a total squared error of 7. Now let's take another guess; this time we'll guess that b is 3. Again we can compute the sum of squared error as a measure of 'fit'. This model (i.e., this guess) is better than the last because the total squared error is smaller than before: it is only 6. We could then take a third guess and do the same, and then carry on guessing and calculating the error for each guess. We could do this, if we led tragic lives and had nothing better to do, but we don't so we won't; except, actually I have plotted the results on a graph. Figure 2.7 shows the sum of squared error that you would get for various values of the parameter b. Note that, as we just calculated, when b is 2 we get an error of 7, and when it is 3 we get an error of 6. The shape of the graph is interesting, though, because the error is least when $b = 2.6$. The error you get for this value of b is 5.2. Do these values seem familiar? They should, because they are the mean and sum of squared error we calculated earlier for these data. This example illustrates that the equation for the mean is designed to estimate that parameter so as to minimize the error. In other words, it is the value of b that has the least error. This doesn't necessarily mean that this value of b is a good fit for the data, but it is a better fit than any other value you might have chosen.

---

[3] I reported the standard deviation but this value is the square root of the variance (a.k.a. the mean square error).

TABLE 2.1 Guessing the mean

Number of friends (x_i)	b_1	Squared error $(x_i - b_1)^2$	b_2	Squared error $(x_i - b_2)^2$
1	2	1	3	4
2	2	0	3	1
3	2	1	3	0
3	2	1	3	0
4	2	4	3	1
		$\displaystyle\sum_{i=1}^{n}\left(x_i - b_1\right)^2 = 7$		$\displaystyle\sum_{i=1}^{n}\left(x_i - b_2\right)^2 = 6$

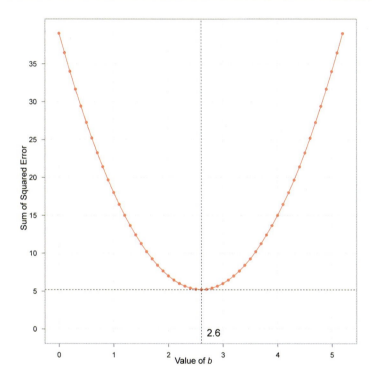

FIGURE 2.7
Graph showing the sum of squared error for different 'guesses' of the mean (b)

   Throughout the book we will fit lots of different models to data sets, not just means, and they will all have parameters that need to be estimated. Although the equations for estimating these parameters will differ, they are based on this principle of minimizing error: they will give you the parameter that has the least error given the data you have. Again, it's worth reiterating that this is not the same thing as the parameter being accurate or representative of the population: it could just be the best of a bad bunch. This section has focused on the principle of minimizing the sum of squared error and this is known as the **method of least squares**. However, we'll also encounter other methods later in the book.

2.5. Going beyond the data ①

We have looked at how we can fit a statistical model to a set of observations to summarize those data. It's one thing to summarize the data that you have actually collected, but in Chapter 1 we saw that good theories should say something about the wider world. It's one thing to be able to say that a sample of high-street stores in Brighton improved profits by placing cats in their store windows, but it's more useful to be able to say, based on our sample, that all high-street stores can increase profits by placing cats in their window displays.

2.5.1.   The standard error ①

In Chapter 1 we saw that the standard deviation tells us about how well the mean represents the sample data. However, if we're using the sample mean to estimate this parameter in the population, then we need to know well it represents the values in the population. This is particularly important because if you take several samples from a population, they will differ slightly. Imagine that we were interested in the student ratings of all lecturers (so lecturers in general are the population). We could take a sample from this population, and when we do we are taking one of many possible samples. If we were to take several samples from the same population, then each sample would have its own mean, and some of these sample means will be different. Figure 2.8 illustrates the process of taking samples from a population. Imagine for a fleeting second that we eat some magic beans that transport us to an astral plane where we can see for a few short, but beautiful, seconds the ratings of all lectures in the world. We're in this astral plane just long enough to compute the mean of these ratings (which given the size of the population implies we're there a few days). Thanks to our astral adventure we know as an absolute fact that the mean of all ratings is 3 (this is the *population mean*, μ, the parameter that we're trying to estimate).

Back in the real world, we don't have access to the population – and we've run out of magic beans – so we use a sample. For each sample we calculate the average, or *sample mean*. Let's imagine we took nine different samples (as in Figure 2.8); you can see that some of the samples have the same mean as the population but some have different means: the first sample of lecturers were, on average, rated as 3, but the second sample were, on average, rated as only 2. This illustrates sampling variation: that is, samples will vary because they contain different members of the population; a sample that by chance includes some very good lecturers will have a higher average than a sample that, by chance, includes some awful lecturers. If we were to plot the sample means as a frequency distribution, or histogram,[4] we would see that three samples had a mean of 3, means of 2 and 4 occurred in two samples each, and means of 1 and 5 occurred in only one sample each. The end result is a nice symmetrical distribution known as a sampling distribution. A sampling distribution is the frequency distribution of sample means (or whatever parameter you're trying to estimate) from the same population. You need to imagine that we're taking hundreds or thousands of samples to construct a sampling distribution – I'm using nine to keep the diagram simple. The sampling distribution is a bit like a unicorn: we can imagine what one looks like, we can appreciate its beauty, and we can wonder at its magical feats, but the sad truth is that you'll never see a real one. They both exist as ideas rather than real things. You would never go out and actually collect thousands of samples and draw a frequency distribution of their means; instead very clever statisticians have worked out what these distributions look like and how they behave.

The sampling distribution tells us about the behaviour of samples from the population, and you'll notice that it is centred at the same value as the mean of the population (i.e., 3). Therefore, if we took the average of all sample means we'd get the value of the population mean. We can use the sampling distribution to tell us how representative a sample is of the population. Think back to the standard deviation. We used the standard

---

[4] This is just a graph of possible values of the sample mean plotted against the number of samples that have a mean of that value – see Section 1.6.1 for more details.

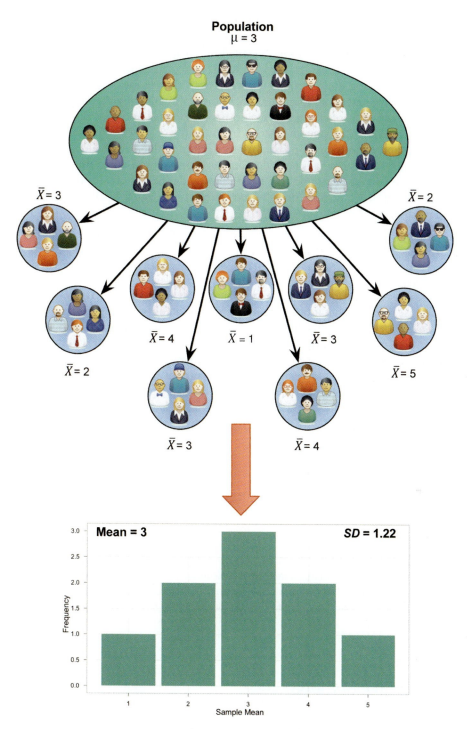

FIGURE 2.8
Illustration of
the standard
error (see text
for details)

deviation as a measure of how representative the mean was of the observed data. A small standard deviation represented a scenario in which most data points were close to the mean, while a large standard deviation represented a situation in which data points were widely spread from the mean. If our 'observed data' are sample means then the standard deviation of these sample means would similarly tell us how widely spread (i.e., how representative) sample means are around their average. Bearing in mind that the average of the sample means is the same as the population mean, the standard deviation of the sample means would therefore tell us how widely sample means are spread around the population mean: put another way, it tells us whether sample means are typically representative of the population mean.

The standard deviation of sample means is known as the **standard error of the mean (SE)** or **standard error** for short. In the land where unicorns exist, the standard error could be calculated by taking the difference between each sample mean and the overall mean, squaring these differences, adding them up, and then dividing by the number of samples. Finally, the square root of this value would need to be taken to get the standard deviation of sample means: the standard error. In the real world, we cannot collect hundreds of samples and so we rely on approximations of the standard error. Luckily for us, some exceptionally clever statisticians have demonstrated something called the **central limit theorem**, which tells us that as samples get large (usually defined as greater than 30), the sampling distribution has a normal distribution with a mean equal to the population mean, and a standard deviation of

$$\sigma_{\bar{X}} = \frac{s}{\sqrt{N}} \tag{2.8}$$

We will return to the central limit theorem in more detail in Chapter 5, but I've mentioned it here because it tells us that if our sample is large we can use equation (2.8) to approximate the standard error (because it is the standard deviation of the sampling distribution).[5] When the sample is relatively small (fewer than 30) the sampling distribution is not normal: it has a different shape, known as a *t*-distribution, which we'll come back to later. A final point is that our discussion here has been about the mean, but everything we have learnt about sampling distributions applies to other parameters too: any parameter that can be calculated in a sample has a hypothetical sampling distribution and standard error.

CRAMMING SAM'S TIPS   **The standard error**

The standard error is the standard deviation of sample means. As such, it is a measure of how representative a sample is likely to be of the population. A large standard error (relative to the sample mean) means that there is a lot of variability between the means of different samples and so the sample we have might not be representative of the population. A small standard error indicates that most sample means are similar to the population mean and so our sample is likely to be an accurate reflection of the population.

2.5.2. Confidence intervals ②

2.5.2.1. Calculating confidence intervals ②

As a brief recap, we usually use a sample value as an estimate of a parameter (e.g., the mean) in the population. We've just seen that the estimate of a parameter (e.g., the mean) will differ across samples, and we can use the standard error to get some idea of the extent

---

[5] In fact it should be the *population* standard deviation (*s*) that is divided by the square root of the sample size; however, for large samples this is a reasonable approximation.

to which these estimates differ. We can also use this information to calculate boundaries within which we believe the population will fall. Such boundaries are called confidence intervals. Although what I'm about to describe applies to any parameter, we'll stick with the mean again to keep things consistent with what you have already learnt.

Domjan, Blesbois, and Williams (1998) examined the learnt release of sperm in Japanese quail. The basic idea is that if a quail is allowed to copulate with a female quail in a certain context (an experimental chamber) then this context will serve as a cue to copulation and this in turn will affect semen release (although during the test phase the poor quail were tricked into copulating with a terry cloth with an embalmed female quail head stuck on top).[6] Anyway, if we look at the mean amount of sperm released in the experimental chamber, there is a true mean (the mean in the population); let's imagine it's 15 million sperm. Now, in our actual sample, we might find the mean amount of sperm released was 17 million. Because we don't know the true mean, we don't really know whether our sample value of 17 million is a good or bad estimate of this value. So rather than fixating on the single value in the sample, we could use an interval estimate instead: we use our sample value as the mid-point, but set a lower and upper limit as well. So, we might say, we think the true value of the mean sperm release is somewhere between 12 million and 22 million sperm (note that 17 million falls exactly between these values). Of course, in this case the true value (15 million) does falls within these limits. However, what if we'd set smaller limits? What if we'd said we think the true value falls between 16 and 18 million (again, note that 17 million is in the middle)? In this case the interval does not contain the true value of the mean. Let's now imagine that you were particularly fixated with Japanese quail sperm, and you repeated the experiment 50 times using different samples. Each time you did the experiment you constructed an interval around the sample mean as I've just described. Figure 2.9 shows this scenario: the dots represent the mean for each sample, with the lines sticking out of them representing the intervals for these means. The true value of the mean (the mean in the population) is 15 million and is shown by a vertical line. The first thing to note is that the sample means are different from the true mean (this is because of sampling variation as described in the previous section). Second, although most of the intervals do contain the true mean (they cross the vertical line, meaning that the value of 15 million sperm falls somewhere between the lower and upper boundaries), a few do not.

What is a confidence interval?

The crucial thing is to construct them in such a way that they tell us something useful. Therefore, we calculate them so that they have certain properties: in particular they tell us the likelihood that they contain the true value of the parameter we're trying to estimate (in this case, the mean). Typically we look at 95% confidence intervals, and sometimes 99% confidence intervals, but they all have a similar interpretation: they are limits constructed such that for a certain percentage of samples (be that 95% or 99%) the true value of the population parameter will fall within these limits. So, when you see a 95% confidence interval for a mean, think of it like this: if we'd collected 100 samples, calculated the mean and then calculated a confidence interval for that mean (a bit like in Figure 2.9) then for 95 of these samples, the confidence intervals we constructed would contain the true value of the mean in the population.

To calculate the confidence interval, we need to know the limits within which 95% of means will fall. We know (in large samples) that the sampling distribution of means will be normal, and the normal distribution has been precisely defined such that it has a mean of 0 and a standard deviation of 1. We can use this information to compute the probability of a score occurring, or the limits between which a certain percentage of scores fall (see Section 1.6.4). It is no coincidence that when I explained all of this in Section 1.6.4, I used

---

[6] This may seem a bit sick, but the male quails didn't appear to mind too much, which probably tells us all we need to know about male mating behaviour.

The confidence intervals of the sperm counts of Japanese quail (horizontal axis) for 50 different samples (vertical axis)

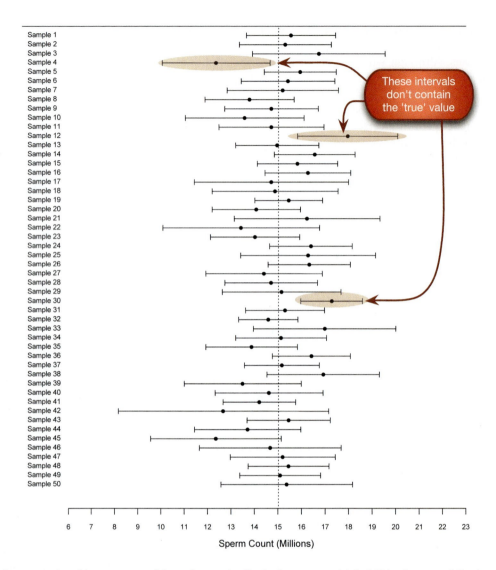

the example of how we would work out the limits between which 95% of scores fall; that is precisely what we need to know if we want to construct a 95% confidence interval. We discovered in Section 1.6.4 that 95% of z-scores fall between -1.96 and 1.96. This means that if our sample means were normally distributed with a mean of 0 and a standard error of 1, then the limits of our confidence interval would be -1.96 and $+1.96$. Luckily we know from the central limit theorem that in large samples (above about 30) the sampling distribution will be normally distributed (see Section 2.5.1). It's a pity then that our mean and standard deviation are unlikely to be 0 and 1 – but only because we need to convert scores so that they do have a mean of 0 and standard deviation of 1 (z-scores) using equation (1.7):

$$z = \frac{X - \bar{X}}{s}$$

If we know that our limits are -1.96 and 1.96 as z-scores, then to find out the corresponding scores in our raw data we can replace z in the equation (because there are two values, we get two equations):

$$1.96 = \frac{X - \bar{X}}{s} \qquad -1.96 = \frac{X - \bar{X}}{s}$$

We rearrange these equations to discover the value of X:

$$1.96 \times s = X - \bar{X} \qquad\qquad -1.96 \times s = X - \bar{X}$$

$$(1.96 \times s) + \bar{X} = X \qquad\qquad (-1.96 \times s) + \bar{X} = X$$

Therefore, the confidence interval can easily be calculated once the standard deviation (s in the equation) and mean ($\bar{X}$ in the equation) are known. However, we use the standard error and not the standard deviation because we're interested in the variability of *sample* means, not the variability in observations within the sample. The lower boundary of the confidence interval is, therefore, the mean minus 1.96 times the standard error, and the upper boundary is the mean plus 1.96 standard errors:

$$\text{lower boundary of confidence interval} = \bar{X} - (1.96 \times SE)$$

$$\text{upper boundary of confidence interval} = \bar{X} + (1.96 \times SE)$$

(2.9)

As such, the mean is always in the centre of the confidence interval. We know that 95% of confidence intervals contain the population mean, so we can assume this confidence interval contains the true mean; therefore, if the interval is small, the sample mean must be very close to the true mean. Conversely, if the confidence interval is very wide then the sample mean could be very different from the true mean, indicating that it is a bad representation of the population. You'll find that confidence intervals will come up time and time again throughout this book.

2.5.2.2. Calculating other confidence intervals ②

The example above shows how to compute a 95% confidence interval (the most common type). However, we sometimes want to calculate other types of confidence interval such as a 99% or 90% interval. The 1.96 and -1.96 in equation (2.9) are the limits within which 95% of z-scores occur. If we want to compute confidence intervals for a value other than 95% then we need to look up the value of z for the percentage that we want. For example, we saw in Section 1.6.4 that z-scores of -2.58 and 2.58 are the boundaries that cut off 99% of scores, so we could use these values to compute 99% confidence intervals. In general then, we could say that confidence intervals are calculated as:

$$\text{lower boundary of confidence interval} = \bar{X} - \left(z_{\frac{1-p}{2}} \times SE \right)$$

$$\text{upper boundary of confidence interval} = \bar{X} + \left(z_{\frac{1-p}{2}} \times SE \right)$$

(2.10)

in which p is the probability value for the confidence interval. So, if you want a 95% confidence interval, then you want the value of z for $(1-0.95)/2 = .025$. Look this up in the 'smaller portion' column of the table of the standard normal distribution (look back at Figure 1.14) and you'll find that z is 1.96. For a 99% confidence interval we want z for $(1-0.99)/2 = .005$, which from the table is 2.58 (Figure 1.14). For a 90% confidence interval we want z for $(1-0.90)/2 = .05$, which from the table is 1.64 (Figure 1.14). These values of z are multiplied by the standard error (as above) to calculate the confidence interval. Using these general principles, we could work out a confidence interval for any level of probability that takes our fancy.

2.5.2.3. Calculating confidence intervals in small samples ②

The procedure that I have just described is fine when samples are large, because the central limit theorem tells us that the sampling distribution will be normal. However, for small samples, as I have mentioned before, the sampling distribution is not normal; it has a t-distribution. The t-distribution is a family of probability distributions that change shape as the sample size gets bigger (when the sample is very big, it has the shape of a normal distribution). To construct a confidence interval in a small sample we use the same principle as before but instead of using the value for z we use the value for t:

$$\text{lower boundary of confidence interval} = \bar{X} - \left(t_{n-1} \times SE\right)$$

$$\text{upper boundary of confidence interval} = \bar{X} - \left(t_{n-1} \times SE\right)$$

(2.11)

The $n - 1$ in the equations is the degrees of freedom (see Jane Superbrain Box 2.2) and tells us which of the t-distributions to use. For a 95% confidence interval we find the value of t for a two-tailed test with probability of .05, for the appropriate degrees of freedom.

SELF-TEST   In Section 1.6.2.2 we came across some data about the number of friends that 11 people had on Facebook. We calculated the mean for these data as 95 and standard deviation as 56.79.

- Calculate a 95% confidence interval for this mean.
- Recalculate the confidence interval assuming that the sample size was 56.

2.5.2.4. Showing confidence intervals visually ②

Confidence intervals provide us with very important information about a parameter, and, therefore, you often see them displayed on graphs. (We will discover more about how to create these graphs in Chapter 4.) The confidence interval is usually displayed using something called an error bar, which just looks like the letter 'I'. An error bar can represent the standard deviation, or the standard error, but more often than not it shows the 95%

What's an error bar?

confidence interval of the mean. So, often when you see a graph showing the mean, perhaps displayed as a bar or a symbol (Section 4.6), it is accompanied by this funny I-shaped bar.

We have seen that any two samples can have slightly different means (and the standard error tells us a little about how different we can expect sample means to be). We have seen that the 95% confidence interval is an interval constructed such that in 95% of samples the true value of the population mean will fall within its limits. Therefore, the confidence interval tells us the limits within which the population mean is likely to fall. By comparing the confidence intervals of different means (or other parameters) we can get some idea about whether the means came from the same or different populations.

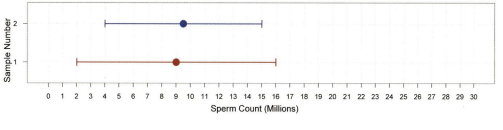

FIGURE 2.10
Two overlapping 95% confidence intervals

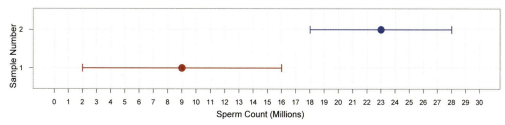

FIGURE 2.11
Two 95% confidence intervals that don't overlap

Taking our previous example of quail sperm, imagine we had a sample of quail and the mean sperm release had been 9 million sperm with a confidence interval of 2 to 16. Therefore, we know that the population mean is probably between 2 and 16 million sperm. What if we now took a second sample of quail and found the confidence interval ranged from 4 to 15? This interval overlaps a lot with our first sample (Figure 2.10). The fact that the confidence intervals overlap in this way tells us that these means could plausibly come from the same population: in both cases the intervals are likely to contain the true value of the mean (because they are constructed such that in 95% of studies they will), and both intervals overlap considerably, so they contain many similar values.

What if the confidence interval for our second sample ranged from 18 to 28? If we compared this to our first sample we'd get Figure 2.11. These confidence intervals don't overlap at all, so one confidence interval, which is likely to contain the population mean, tells us that the population mean is somewhere between 2 and 16 million, whereas the other confidence interval, which is also likely to contain the population mean, tells us that the population mean is somewhere between 18 and 28 million. This contradiction suggests two possibilities: (1) our confidence intervals both contain the population mean, but they come from different populations (and, therefore, so do our samples); or (2) both samples come from the same population but one of the confidence intervals doesn't contain the population mean. If we've used 95% confidence intervals then we know that the second possibility is unlikely (this happens only 5 times in 100 or 5% of the time), so the first explanation is more plausible.

OK, I can hear you all thinking, 'So what if the samples come from a different population?' Well, this has a very important implication in experimental research. When we do an experiment, we introduce some form of manipulation between two or more conditions (see

CRAMMING SAM'S TIPS   **Confidence intervals**

- A confidence interval for the mean is a range of scores constructed such that the population mean will fall within this range in 95% of samples.
- The confidence interval is not an interval within which we are 95% confident that the population mean will fall.

Section 1.5.5). If we have taken two random samples of people, and we have tested them on some measure, then we expect these people to belong to the same population. If their sample means are so different as to suggest that they come from different populations, then this is likely to be because our experimental manipulation has induced a difference between the samples. Therefore, error bars showing 95% confidence intervals are useful, because if the bars of any two means do not overlap then we can infer that these means are from different populations – they are significantly different. We will return to this point in Section 2.6.1.9.

2.6. Using statistical models to test research questions ①

In Chapter 1 we saw that research was a five-stage process (Figure 1.2). This chapter has looked at the final stage, in which we analyse the data and fit a statistical model to them to see whether or not it supports our initial predictions. I have shown that we can use a sample of data to estimate what's happening in a larger population to which we don't have access. We have also seen (using the mean as an example) that we can fit a statistical model to a sample of data and assess how well it fits. However, we have yet to see how fitting models like these can help us to test our research predictions. How do statistical models help us to test complex hypotheses such as 'Is there a relationship between the amount of gibberish that people speak and the amount of vodka jelly they've eaten?' or 'Does reading this chapter improve your knowledge of research methods?'.

2.6.1. Null hypothesis significance testing ①

The first approach we'll discuss is called null hypothesis significance testing (NHST), which is a cumbersome name for an equally cumbersome process. NHST is the most commonly taught approach to testing research questions with statistical models. It arose out of two different approaches to the problem of how to use data to test theories: (1) Ronald Fisher's idea of computing probabilities to evaluate evidence, and (2) Jerzy Neyman and Egon Pearson's idea of competing hypotheses.

2.6.1.1. Fisher's *p*-value ①

Fisher (1925/1991) (Figure 2.12) described an experiment designed to test a claim by a woman that she could determine, by tasting a cup of tea, whether the milk or the tea was added first to the cup. Fisher thought that he should give the woman some cups of tea, some of which had the milk added first and some of which had the milk added last, and see whether she could correctly identify them. The woman would know that there are an equal number of cups in which milk was added first or last but wouldn't know in which order the cups were placed. If we take the simplest situation in which there are only two cups, then the woman has 50% chance of guessing correctly. If she did guess correctly we wouldn't be that confident in concluding that she can tell the difference between cups in which the milk was added and cups in which it was added last, because even by guessing she would be correct half of the time. However, what about if we complicated things by having six cups? There are 20 orders in which these cups can be arranged and the woman would guess the correct order only 1 time in 20 (or 5% of the time). If she got the correct order we would be much more confident that she could genuinely tell the difference (and bow down in awe

FIGURE 2.12
Sir Ronald
A. Fisher,
the cleverest
person ever
($p < .0001$)

of her finely tuned palette). If you'd like to know more about Fisher and his tea-tasting antics, see David Salsburg's excellent book *The lady tasting tea* (Salsburg, 2002). For our purposes the take-home point is that only when there was a very small probability that the woman could complete the tea task by luck alone would we conclude that she had genuine skill in detecting whether milk was poured into a cup before or after the tea.

It's no coincidence that I chose the example of six cups above (where the tea-taster had a 5% chance of getting the task right by guessing), because scientists tend to believe that 5% is a useful threshold for confidence: only when there is a 5% chance (or .05 probability) of getting the data we have if no effect exists are we confident enough to accept that the effect is genuine.[7] Fisher's basic point was that you should calculate the probability of an event and evaluate this probability within the research context. Although Fisher felt a $p = .01$ would be strong evidence to back up a hypothesis, and perhaps a $p = .20$ would be weak evidence, he never said $p = .05$ was in any way a special number.

2.6.1.2. Types of hypothesis ①

In contrast to Fisher, Neyman and Pearson believed that scientific statements should be split into testable hypotheses. The hypothesis or prediction from your theory would normally be that an effect will be present. This hypothesis is called the **alternative hypothesis** and is denoted by H_1. (It is sometimes also called the **experimental hypothesis**, but because this term relates to a specific type of methodology it's probably best to use 'alternative hypothesis'.) There is another type of hypothesis called the **null hypothesis**, which is denoted by H_0. This hypothesis is the opposite of the alternative hypothesis and so usually states that an effect is absent.

Often when I write, my thoughts are drawn towards chocolate. I believe that I would eat less of it if I could stop thinking about it. However, according to Morewedge, Huh, and Vosgerau (2010), that's not true. In fact, they found that people ate less of a food if they had previously imagined eating it. Imagine we did a similar study; we might generate the following hypotheses:

- Alternative hypothesis: if you imagine eating chocolate you will eat less of it.

- Null hypothesis: if you imagine eating chocolate you will eat the same amount as normal.

---

[7] Of course, in reality, it might not be true – we're just prepared to believe that it is.

The reason why we need the null hypothesis is that we cannot prove the experimental hypothesis using statistics, but we can collect evidence to reject the null hypothesis. If our data give us confidence to reject the null hypothesis then this provides support for our experimental hypothesis. However, be aware that even if we can reject the null hypothesis, this doesn't prove the experimental hypothesis – it merely supports it. So, rather than talking about accepting or rejecting a hypothesis (which some textbooks tell you to do) we should talk about 'the chances of obtaining the data we've collected assuming that the null hypothesis is true'.

Imagine in our study that we took 100 people and measured how many pieces of chocolate they usually eat (day 1). On day 2, we got them to imagine eating chocolate and again measured how much chocolate they ate that day. Imagine that we found that 75% of people ate less chocolate on the second day than the first. When we analyse our data, we are really asking, 'Assuming that imagining eating chocolate has no effect whatsoever, is it likely that 75% of people would eat less chocolate on the second day?' Intuitively the answer is that the chances are very low: if the null hypothesis is true, then everyone should eat the same amount of chocolate on both days. Therefore, we are very unlikely to have got the data that we did if the null hypothesis were true.

What if we found that only 1 person (1%) at less chocolate on the second day? If the null hypothesis is true and imaging eating chocolate has no effect whatsoever on consumption, then no people should eat less on the second day. The chances of getting these data if the null hypothesis is true are, therefore, higher than before.

When we collect data to test theories we have to work in these terms: we cannot talk about the null hypothesis being true or the experimental hypothesis being true, we can only talk in terms of the probability of obtaining a particular set of data if, hypothetically speaking, the null hypothesis was true. We will elaborate on this idea in the next section.

Hypotheses can be directional or non-directional. A directional hypothesis states that an effect will occur, but it also states the direction of the effect. For example, 'if you imagine eating chocolate you will eat less of it' is a one-tailed hypothesis because it states the direction of the effect (people will eat less). A non-directional hypothesis states that an effect will occur, but it doesn't state the direction of the effect. For example, 'imagining eating chocolate affects the amount of chocolate you eat' does not tell us whether they will eat more or less.

SELF-TEST   What are the null and alternative hypotheses for the following questions?

- 'Is there a relationship between the amount of gibberish that people speak and the amount of vodka jelly they've eaten?'
- 'Does reading this chapter improve your knowledge of research methods?'

2.6.1.3. The basic principles of NHST ①

NHST is a blend of Fisher's idea of using the probability value p as an index of the weight of evidence against a null hypothesis, and Jerzy Neyman and Egon Pearson's idea of testing a null hypothesis *against* an alternative hypothesis (Neyman & Pearson, 1933). There was no love lost between these competing statisticians (Jane Superbrain Box 2.3). NHST is a system designed to tell us whether the alternative hypothesis is likely to be true – it helps us to confirm or reject our predictions. Crudely put, this is the logic:

- We assume that the null hypothesis is true (i.e., there is no effect).

- We fit a statistical model to our data that represents the alternative hypothesis and see how well it fits (in terms of the variance it explains).

JANE SUPERBRAIN 2.3

Who said statistics was dull? Part 1 ①

Students often think that statistics is dull, but back in the early 1900s it was anything but dull, with various prominent figures entering into feuds on a soap opera scale. One particularly impressive feud was between Ronald Fisher and Jerzy Neyman. On 28 March 1935 Neyman delivered a talk to the Royal Statistical Society, at which Fisher was present, in which he criticized some of Fisher's most important work. Fisher's directly attacked Neyman in his discussion of the paper at the same meeting: he more or less said that Neyman didn't know what he was talking about and didn't understand the background material on which his work was based. He may as well have said, 'I put it to you, sir, that you are a fool, an imbecile, a man so incapacitated by stupidity that in a battle of wits with a single-cell amoeba, the amoeba would fancy its chances.' He didn't say that, but I like to imagine that he did.

Relations soured so much that while they both worked at University College London, Neyman openly attacked many of Fisher's ideas in lectures to his students. The two feuding groups even took afternoon tea (a common practice in the British academic community of the time) in the same room but at different times! The truth behind who fuelled these feuds is, perhaps, lost in the mists of time, but Zabell (1992) makes a sterling effort to unearth it. Basically, the founders of modern statistical methods were a bunch of squabbling children. Nevertheless, these men were astonishingly gifted individuals. Fisher, in particular, was a world leader in genetics, biology and medicine as well as possibly the most original mathematical thinker ever (Barnard, 1963; Field, 2005c; Savage, 1976).

- To determine how well the model fits the data, we calculate the probability (called the *p*-value) of getting that 'model' if the null hypothesis were true.

- If that probability is very small (the usual criterion is .05 or less) then we conclude that the model fits the data well (i.e., explains a lot of the variation in scores) and we assume our initial prediction is true: we gain confidence in the alternative hypothesis.

The thing to remember is that we can never be completely sure that either hypothesis is correct; all we can do is to calculate the probability that our model would fit if there were no effect in the population (i.e., the null hypothesis is true). As this probability decreases, we gain greater confidence that the alternative hypothesis is correct and that the null hypothesis can be rejected. This process works only if we make our predictions before we collect the data (see Jane Superbrain Box 2.4).

2.6.1.4. Test statistics ①

NHST relies on fitting a 'model' to the data and then evaluating the probability of this 'model' given the assumption that no effect exists. I have been deliberately vague about what the 'model' is, but the time has come to lift the veil of secrecy. To do this we need to return to the concepts of systematic and unsystematic variation that we encountered in Section 1.5.5.2. Systematic variation is variation that can be explained by the model that we've fitted to the data (and, therefore, due to the hypothesis that we're testing). Unsystematic variation is variation that cannot be explained by the model that we've fitted. In other words, it is error, or variation not attributable to the effect we're investigating. The simplest way, therefore, to test whether the model fits the data, or whether our hypothesis is a good explanation of the data we have observed, is to compare the systematic variation

JANE SUPERBRAIN 2.4

Cheating in research ①

NHST works only if you generate your hypotheses and decide on your criteria for whether an effect is significant before collecting the data. Imagine I wanted to place a bet on who would win the soccer World Cup. Being English, I might bet on England to win the tournament. To do this I'd: (1) place my bet, choosing my team (England) and odds available at the betting shop (e.g., 6/4); (2) see which team wins the tournament; (3) collect my winnings (or more likely not).

To keep everyone happy, this process needs to be equitable: the betting shops set their odds such that they're not paying out too much money (which keeps them happy), but so that they do pay out sometimes (to keep the customers happy). The betting shop can offer any odds before the tournament has ended, but it can't change them once the tournament is over (or the last game has started). Similarly, I can choose any team

before the tournament, but I can't then change my mind half way through, or after the final game.

The research process is similar: we can choose any hypothesis (soccer team) before the data are collected, but we can't change our minds halfway through data collection (or after data collection). Likewise we have to decide on our probability level (or betting odds) before we collect data. If we do this, the process works. However, researchers sometimes cheat. They don't formulate hypotheses before they conduct their experiments; they change them when the data are collected (like me changing my team after the World Cup is over), or worse still they decide on them after the data are collected. With the exception of some procedures called *post hoc* tests, this is cheating. Similarly, researchers can be guilty of choosing which significance level to use after the data are collected and analysed, like a betting shop changing the odds after the tournament.

If you change your hypothesis or the details of your analysis you increase the chance of finding a significant result, but you also make it more likely that you will publish results that other researchers can't reproduce (which is embarrassing). If, however, you follow the rules carefully and do your significance testing at the 5% level you at least know that in the long run at most only 1 result out of every 20 will risk this public humiliation. (Thanks to David Hitchin for this box, and apologies to him for introducing soccer into it.)

against the unsystematic variation. In doing so we look at a simple signal-to-noise ratio: we compare how good the model/hypothesis is against how bad it is (the error):

$$\text{Test statistic} = \frac{\text{signal}}{\text{noise}} = \frac{\text{variance explained by the model}}{\text{variance not explained by the model}} = \frac{\text{effect}}{\text{error}} \qquad (2.12)$$

This ratio of systematic to unsystematic variance or effect to error is a **test statistic**, and you'll discover later in the book that there are lots of them: t, F and χ^2, to name only three. The exact form of this equation changes depending on which test statistic you're calculating, but the important thing to remember is that they all, crudely speaking, represent the same thing: signal-to-noise or the amount of variance explained by the model we've fitted to the data compared to the variance that can't be explained by the model (see Chapters 8 and 9 in particular for a more detailed explanation). The reason why this ratio is so useful is intuitive really: if our model is good then we'd expect it to be able to explain more variance than it can't explain. In this case, the test statistic will be greater than 1 (but not necessarily significant).

A test statistic is a statistic for which we know how frequently different values occur. I mentioned the t-distribution, chi-square (χ^2) distribution and F-distribution in Section 1.6.4 and said that they are all defined by an equation that enables us to calculate precisely the probability of obtaining a given score. Therefore, if a test statistic comes from one of these distributions we can calculate the probability of obtaining a certain value (just as we could estimate the probability of getting a score of a certain size from a frequency distribution in Section 1.6.4). This probability is the p-value that Fisher described and in NHST it is used to estimate how likely it would be that we would get a test statistic at least as big as the one we have *if there were no effect* (i.e., the null hypothesis were true).

Test statistics can be a bit scary, so let's imagine that they're cute kittens. Kittens are typically very small (about 100 g at birth on average), but every so often a cat will give birth to a big one (say, 150 g). A 150 g kitten is rare, so the probability of finding one is very small. Conversely, 100 g kittens are very common so the probability of finding one is quite high. Test statistics are the same as kittens in this respect: small ones are quite common and large ones are rare. So, if we do some research (i.e., give birth to a kitten) and calculate a test statistic (weigh the kitten) we can calculate the probability of obtaining a value (weight) at least that large. The more variation our model explains compared to the variance it can't explain, the bigger the test statistic will be (i.e., the more the kitten weighs), and the more unlikely it is to occur by chance (like our 150 g kitten). Like kittens, as test statistics get bigger the probability of them occurring becomes smaller. If we use conventional NHST then when this probability falls below a certain value (usually $p < .05$), we accept this as giving us enough confidence to assume that the test statistic is as large as it is because our model explains a sufficient amount of variation to reflect what's genuinely happening in the real world (the population). The test statistic is said to be *significant*. Given that the statistical model that we fit to the data reflects the hypothesis that we set out to test, then a significant test statistic tells us that the model would be unlikely to fit this well if the there was no effect in the population (i.e., the null hypothesis was true). Therefore, we reject our null hypothesis and gain confidence that the alternative hypothesis is true. If, however, the probability of obtaining a test statistic at least as big as the one we have (if the null hypothesis were true) is too large (typically $p > .05$) then the test statistic is said to be non-significant and we reject the alternative hypothesis (see Section 2.6.2.1 for a discussion of what 'statistically significant' actually means).

2.6.1.5. One- and two-tailed tests ②

We saw in Section 2.6.1.2 that hypotheses can be directional (e.g., 'the more someone reads this book, the more they want to kill its author') or non-directional (i.e., 'reading more of this book could increase or decrease the reader's desire to kill its author'). A statistical model that tests a directional hypothesis is called a **one-tailed test**, whereas one testing a non-directional hypothesis is known as a **two-tailed test**.

Imagine we wanted to discover whether reading this book increased or decreased the desire to kill me. If we have no directional hypothesis then there are three possibilities. (1) People who read this book want to kill me more than those who don't so the difference (the mean for those reading the book minus the mean for non-readers) is positive. Correlationally, the more of the book you read, the more you want to kill me – a positive relationship. (2) People who read this book want to kill me less than those who don't so the difference (the mean for those reading the book minus the mean for non-readers) is negative. Correlationally, the more of the book you read, the less you want to kill me – a negative relationship. (3) There is no difference between readers and non-readers in their desire to kill me – the mean for readers minus the mean for non-readers is exactly zero. Correlationally, there is no relationship between reading this book and wanting to kill me. This final option is the null hypothesis. The direction of the test statistic (i.e., whether it is positive or negative) depends on whether the difference is positive or negative. Assuming there is a positive difference or relationship (reading this book makes you want to kill me), then to detect this difference we have to take account of the fact that the mean for readers is bigger than for non-readers (and so derive a positive test statistic). However, if we've predicted incorrectly and actually reading this book makes readers want to kill me less then the test statistic will actually be negative.

Why do you need two tails?

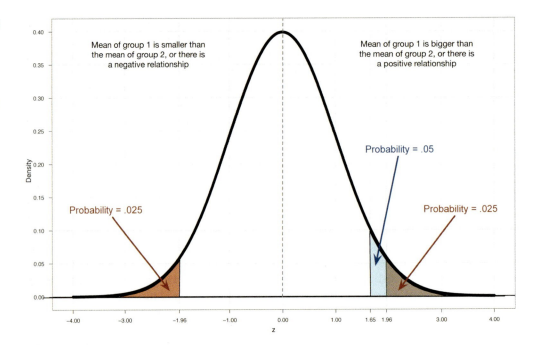

What are the consequences of this? Well, if at the .05 level we needed to get a test statistic bigger than, say, 10 and the one we get is actually −12, then we would reject the hypothesis even though a difference does exist. To avoid this we can look at both ends (or tails) of the distribution of possible test statistics. This means we will catch both positive and negative test statistics. However, doing this has a price because to keep our criterion probability of .05 we have to split this probability across the two tails: so we have .025 at the positive end of the distribution and .025 at the negative end. Figure 2.13 shows this situation – the red tinted areas are the areas above the test statistic needed at a .025 level of significance. Combine the probabilities (i.e., add the two tinted areas together) at both ends and we get .05, our criterion value.

If we have made a prediction, then we put all our eggs in one basket and look only at one end of the distribution (either the positive or the negative end, depending on the direction of the prediction we make). So, in Figure 2.13, rather than having two small red tinted areas at either end of the distribution that show the significant values, we have a bigger area (the blue tinted area) at only one end of the distribution that shows significant values. Note that this blue area contains within it the red area as well as an extra bit of blue area. Consequently, we can just look for the value of the test statistic that would occur by chance with a probability of .05. In Figure 2.13, the blue tinted area is the area above the positive test statistic needed at a .05 level of significance (1.64); this value is smaller than the value that begins the area for the .025 level of significance (1.96). This means that if we make a specific prediction then we need a smaller test statistic to find a significant result (because we are looking in only one tail of the distribution), but if our prediction happens to be in the wrong direction then we'll miss out on detecting the effect that does exist. This final point is very important, so let me rephrase it: if you do a one-tailed test and the results turn out to be in the opposite direction to what you predicted you must ignore them, resist all temptation to interpret them, and accept (no matter how much it pains you) the null hypothesis. If you don't do this, then you have done a two-tailed test using a different level of significance from the one you set out to use (and Jane Superbrain Box 2.4 explains why that is a bad idea).

I have explained one- and two-tailed tests because people expect to find them explained in statistics textbooks. However, there are a few reasons why you should think long and hard about whether one-tailed tests are a good idea. Wainer (1972) quotes John Tukey (one of the great modern statisticians) as responding to the question 'Do you mean to say that one should *never* do a one-tailed test?' by saying, 'Not at all. It depends upon to whom you are speaking. *Some people will believe anything*' (italics added). Why might Tukey have been so sceptical?

As I have said already, if the result of a one-tailed test is in the opposite direction to what you expected, *you cannot and must not reject the null hypothesis*. In other words, you must completely ignore that result even though it is poking you in the arm and saying, 'Look at me; I'm intriguing and unexpected.' The reality is that when scientists see interesting and unexpected findings their natural instinct is to want to explain them. Therefore, one-tailed tests are dangerous because, just as a mermaid lures a lonely sailor to his death by being beguiling and interesting, one-tailed tests lure lonely scientists to their academic death by throwing up beguiling and unpredicted results.

A related point is that one-tailed tests are appropriate only if a result in the opposite direction to that expected would result in the same action as a non-significant result (Lombardi & Hurlbert, 2009; Ruxton & Neuhaeuser, 2010). There are some limited circumstances in which this might be the case. First, if a result in the opposite direction would be theoretically meaningless or impossible to explain even if you wanted to (Kimmel, 1957). Second, imagine you're testing a new drug to treat depression. You predict it will be better than existing drugs. If it is not better than existing drugs (non-significant p) you would not approve the drug; however, it was significantly worse than existing drugs (significant p but in the opposite direction) you would also not approve the drug. In both situations, the drug is not approved.

Finally, one-tailed tests encourage cheating. If you do a two-tailed test and find that your p is .06, then you would conclude that your results were not significant (because .06 is bigger than the critical value of .05). Had you done this test one-tailed, however, the p you would get would be half of the two-tailed value (.03). This one-tailed value would be significant at the conventional level (because .03 is less than .05). Therefore, if we find a two-tailed p that is just non-significant, we might be tempted to pretend that we'd always intended to do a one-tailed test because our 'one-tailed' p-value is significant. But we can't change our rules after we have collected data (Jane Superbrain Box 2.4) so we must conclude that the effect is not significant. Although scientists hopefully don't do this sort of thing deliberately, people do get confused about what is and isn't permissible. Two recent surveys of practice in ecology journals concluded that 'all uses of one-tailed tests in the journals surveyed seemed invalid'. (Lombardi & Hurlbert, 2009) and that only one in 17 papers using one-tailed tests were justified in doing so (Ruxton & Neuhaeuser, 2010). The bottom line is that you should use one-tailed tests only if you have a very good reason to do so.

2.6.1.6. Type I and Type II errors ①

Neyman and Pearson identified two types of errors that we can make when we test hypotheses. When we use test statistics to tell us about the true state of the world, we're trying to see whether there is an effect in our population. There are two possibilities: there is, in reality, an effect in the population, or there is, in reality, no effect in the population. We have no way of knowing which of these possibilities is true; however, we can look at test statistics and their associated probability to tell us which of the two is more likely. Obviously, it is important that we're as accurate as possible. There are two mistakes we can make: a Type I and a Type II error. A **Type I error** occurs when we believe that there is a genuine effect in our population, when in fact there isn't. If we use the conventional criterion then the probability of this error is .05 (or 5%) when there is no effect in the population – this value is known as the **α-level**. Assuming there is no effect in our population, if we replicated our data collection 100 times we could expect that on five occasions we would obtain a test statistic large enough to make us think that there was a genuine effect in the population even though there isn't. The opposite is a **Type II error**, which occurs when we believe that there is no effect in the population when, in reality, there is. This would occur when we obtain a small test statistic (perhaps because there is a lot of natural variation between our samples). In an ideal world, we want the probability of this error to be very small (if there is an effect in the population then it's important that we can detect it). Cohen (1992) suggests that the maximum acceptable probability of a Type II error would be .2 (or 20%) – this is called the β-level. That would mean that if we took 100 samples of data from a population in which an effect exists, we would fail to detect that effect in 20 of those samples (so we'd miss 1 in 5 genuine effects).

There is obviously a trade-off between these two errors: if we lower the probability of accepting an effect as genuine (i.e., make α smaller) then we increase the probability that we'll reject an effect that does genuinely exist (because we've been so strict about the level at which we'll accept that an effect is genuine). The exact relationship between the Type I and Type II error is not straightforward because they are based on different assumptions: to make a Type I error there has to be no effect in the population, whereas to make a Type II error the opposite is true (there has to be an effect that we've missed). So, although we know that as the probability of making a Type I error decreases, the probability of making a Type II error increases, the exact nature of the relationship is usually left for the researcher to make an educated guess (Howell, 2012, gives a great explanation of the trade-off between errors).

2.6.1.7. Inflated error rates ①

As we have seen, if a test uses a .05 level of significance then the chance of making a Type I error is only 5%. Logically then, the probability of no Type I errors is .95 (95%) for each test. However, in science it's rarely the case that we can get a definitive answer to our research question using a single test on our data: we often need to conduct several tests. For example, imagine we wanted to look at factors that affect how viral a video becomes on YouTube. You might predict that the amount of humour and innovation in the video will be important factors. To test this, you might look at the relationship between the number of hits and measures of both the humour content and the innovation. However, you probably ought to also look at whether innovation and humour content are related too. Therefore, you would need to do three tests. If we assume that each test is independent (which in this case they won't be, but it enables us to multiply the probabilities) then the overall probability of no Type I errors will be $(.95)^3 = .95 \times .95 \times .95 = .857$, because the probability of no Type I errors is .95 for each test and there are three tests. Given that the probability of no Type I errors is .857, then the probability of making at least one Type I error is this number subtracted from 1 (remember that the maximum probability of any event occurring is 1). So, the probability of at least one Type I error is $1 - .857 = .143$, or 14.3%. Therefore, across this group of tests, the probability of making a Type I error has increased from 5% to 14.3%, a value greater than the conventional criterion. This error rate across statistical tests conducted on the same data is known as the familywise or experimentwise error rate. Our scenario with three tests is relatively simple, and the effect of carrying out several tests is not severe, but imagine that we increased the number of tests from three to ten. The familywise error rate can be calculated using the following equation (assuming you use a .05 level of significance).

$$\text{familywise error} = 1 - (0.95)^n \tag{2.13}$$

In this equation n is the number of tests carried out on the data. With 10 tests carried out, the familywise error rate is $1 - .95^{10} = .40$, which means that there is a 40% chance of having made at least one Type I error.

FIGURE 2.14
Carlo
Bonferroni
before the
celebrity of his
correction led
to drink, drugs
and statistics
groupies

To combat this build-up of errors we can adjust the level of significance for individual tests such that the overall Type I error rate (α) across all comparisons remains at .05. There are several ways in which the familywise error rate can be controlled. The most popular (and easiest) way is to divide α by the number of comparisons, k:

$$P_{\text{Crit}} = \frac{\alpha}{k}$$

Therefore, if we conduct 10 tests, we use .005 as our criterion for significance. In doing so, we ensure that the cumulative Type I error remains below .05. This method is known as the **Bonferroni correction** (Figure 2.14). There is a trade-off for controlling the familywise error rate, and that is a loss of statistical power, which is the next topic on our agenda.

2.6.1.8. Statistical power ②

We have seen that the it is important to control the Type I error rate so that we don't too often mistakenly think that an effect is significant when it is not. The opposite problem relates to the Type II error, which is how often we will miss an effect in the population that genuinely exists. If we set the Type II error rate high then we will be likely to miss a lot of genuine effects, but if we set it low we will be less likely to miss effects. The ability of a test to find an effect is known as its statistical **power** (not to be confused with statistical *powder*, which is an illegal substance that makes you understand statistics better). The power of a test is the probability that a given test will find an effect assuming that one exists in the population. This is the opposite of the probability that a given test will *not* find an effect assuming that one exists in the population, which as we have seen is the β-level (i.e., Type II error rate). Therefore, the power of a test can be expressed as $1 - \beta$. Given that Cohen (1988, 1992) recommends a .2 probability of failing to detect a genuine effect (see above) the corresponding level of power would be $1 - .2$, or .8. Therefore, we usually aim to achieve a power of .8, or put another way, an 80% chance of detecting an effect if one genuinely exists. The power of a statistical test depends on the following:[8]

[8] It will also depend on whether the test is a one- or two-tailed test (see Section 2.6.1.5), but, as we have seen, you'd normally do a two-tailed test.

1   How big the effect actually is, because bigger effects will be easier to spot. This is known as the effect size and we'll discuss it in Section 2.7.1).

2   How strict we are about deciding that an effect is significant. The more strict we are, the harder it will be to 'find' an effect. This strictness is reflected in the α-level. This brings us back to our point in the previous section about correcting for multiple tests. If we use a more conservative Type I error rate for each test (such as a Bonferroni correction) then the probability of rejecting an effect that does actually exist is increased (we're more likely to make a Type II error). In other words, when we apply a Bonferroni correction the tests will have less power to detect effects.

3   The sample size: we saw earlier in this chapter that larger samples are better approximations of the population; therefore, they have less sampling error. Remember that test statistics are basically a signal-to-noise ratio, so given that large samples have less 'noise' they make it easier to find the 'signal'.

Given that power $(1 - \beta)$, the α-level, sample size, and the size of the effect are all linked, if we know three of these things, then we can find out the remaining one. There are two things that scientists do with this knowledge:

1   **Calculate the power of a test**: Given that we've conducted our experiment, we will have already selected a value of α, we can estimate the effect size based on our sample data, and we will know how many participants we used. Therefore, we can use these values to calculate $1 - \beta$, the power of our test. If this value turns out to be .8 or more we can be confident that we achieved sufficient power to detect any effects that might have existed, but if the resulting value is less, then we might want to replicate the experiment using more participants to increase the power.

2   **Calculate the sample size necessary to achieve a given level of power**: We can set the value of α and $1 - \beta$ to be whatever we want (normally .05 and .8, respectively). We can also estimate the likely effect size in the population by using data from past research. Even if no one had previously done the exact experiment that we intend to do, we can still estimate the likely effect size based on similar experiments. Given this information, we can calculate how many participants we would need to detect that effect (based on the values of α and $1 - \beta$ that we've chosen).

The point of calculating the power of a test after the experiment has always been lost on me a bit: if you find a non-significant effect then you didn't have enough power, if you found a significant effect then you did. Using power to calculate the necessary sample size is the more common and, in my opinion, more useful thing to do. The actual computations are very cumbersome, but there are computer programs available that will do them for you. *G*Power* is a free and powerful (excuse the pun) tool, there is a package *pwr* that can be used in the open source statistics package R, and you can buy software such as *nQuery Adviser*, *Power and Precision* and *PASS* (Power Analysis and Sample Size) too. Also, Cohen (1988) provides extensive tables for calculating the number of participants for a given level of power (and vice versa).

OLIVER TWISTED

Please, Sir, can I have some more … power?

'I've got the power!' sings Oliver as he pops a huge key up his nose and starts to wind the clockwork mechanism of his brain. If, like Oliver, you like to wind up your brain, the companion website contains links to the various packages for doing power analysis and sample-size estimation. If that doesn't quench your thirst for knowledge then you're a grain of salt.

2.6.1.9. Confidence intervals and statistical significance ②

I mentioned earlier (Section 2.5.2.4) that if 95% confidence intervals didn't overlap then we could conclude that the means come from different populations, and, therefore, they are significantly different. I was getting ahead of myself a bit because this comment alluded to the fact that there is a relationship between statistical significance and confidence intervals. Cumming and Finch (2005) have three guidelines that are shown in Figure 2.15:

1 95% confidence intervals that just about touch end-to-end (as in the top left panel of Figure 2.15) represent a *p*-value for testing the null hypothesis of no differences of approximately .01.

2 If there is a gap between the upper end of one 95% confidence interval and the lower end of another (as in the top right panel of Figure 2.15) then $p < .01$.

3 A *p*-value of .05 is represented by *moderate* overlap between the bars (the bottom panels of Figure 2.15).

Theses guidelines are poorly understood by many researchers. In one study (Belia, Fidler, Williams, & Cumming, 2005), 473 researchers from medicine, psychology and behavioural neuroscience were shown a graph of means and confidence intervals for two independent groups and asked to move one of the error bars up or down on the graph until they showed a 'just significant difference' (at $p < .05$). The sample ranged from new researchers to very experienced ones, but surprisingly this experience did not predict their responses. In fact, only a small percentage of researchers could position the confidence intervals correctly to show a just significant difference (15% of psychologists, 20% of behavioural neuroscientists and 16% of medics). The most frequent response was to position the confidence intervals more or less at the point where they stop overlapping (i.e., a *p*-value of approximately .01). Very few researchers (even experienced ones) realized that moderate overlap between confidence intervals equates to the standard *p*-value of .05 for accepting significance.

What do we mean by moderate overlap? Cumming (2012) defines it as half the length of the average margin of error (MOE). The MOE is half the length of the confidence interval (assuming it is symmetric), so it's the length of the bar sticking out in one direction from the mean. In the bottom left of Figure 2.15 the confidence interval for sample 1 ranges from 4 to 14 so has a length of 10 and an MOE of half this value (i.e., 5). For sample 2, it ranges from 11.5 to 21.5 so again a distance of 10 and an MOE of 5. The average MOE is therefore $(5 + 5)/2 = 5$. Moderate overlap would be half of this value (i.e., 2.5). This is the amount of overlap between the two confidence intervals in the bottom left of Figure 2.15. Basically, then, if the confidence intervals are the same length, then $p = .05$ is represented by an overlap of about a quarter of the confidence interval. In the more likely scenario of confidence intervals with different lengths, the interpretation of overlap is more difficult. In the bottom right of Figure 2.15 the confidence interval for sample 1 again ranges from 4 to 14 so has a length of 10 and an MOE of 5. For sample 2, it ranges from 12 to 18 so a distance of 6 and an MOE of half this value, 3. The average MOE is therefore $(5 + 3)/2 = 4$. Moderate overlap would be half of this value (i.e., 2). The two confidence intervals in the bottom left of Figure 2.15 overlap by 2 points on the scale, so this again equates to a *p* of around .05.

2.6.1.10. Sample size and statistical significance ②

When we discussed power, we saw that it is intrinsically linked with the sample size. Given that power is the ability of a test to find an effect that genuinely exists, and we 'find' an

FIGURE 2.15

The relationship
between
confidence
intervals and
statistical
significance

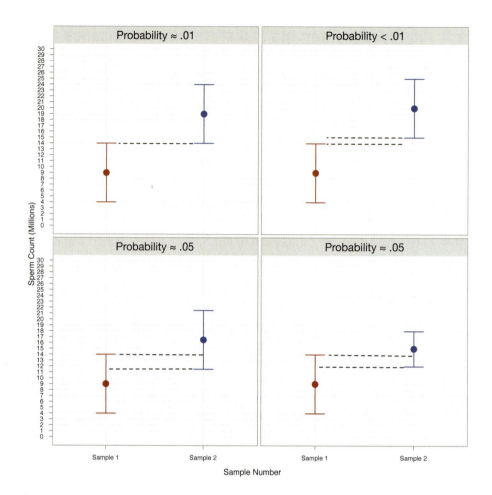

FIGURE 2.15

The relationship between confidence intervals and statistical significance

effect by having a statistically significant result (i.e., $p < .05$), there is also a connection between the sample size and the p-value associated with a test statistic. We can demonstrate this connection with two examples. Apparently male mice 'sing' to female mice to try to attract them as mates (Hoffmann, Musolf, & Penn, 2012); I'm not sure what they sing, but I like to think it might be 'This mouse is on fire' by AC/DC, or perhaps 'Mouses of the Holy' by Led Zeppelin, or even 'The mouse Jack built' by Metallica. It's probably not 'Terror and hubris in the mouse of Frank Pollard' by Lamb of God. That would just be weird. Anyway, many a young man has spent time wondering how best to attract female mates, so to help them out, imagine we did a study in which we got two groups of 10 heterosexual young men to go up to a woman that they found attractive and either engage them in conversation (group 1) or sing them a song (group 2). We measured how long it was before the woman ran away. Imagine we repeated this experiment but using 100 men in each group.

Figure 2.16 shows the results of these two experiments. The data are identical data: in both cases the singing group had a mean of 10 and a standard deviation of 3, and the conversation group had a mean of 12 and a standard deviation of 3. Remember that the only difference between the two experiments is that one collected 10 scores per sample, and the other 100 scores per sample.

SELF-TEST   Compare the graphs in Figure 2.16. What effect does the difference in sample size have? Why do you think it has this effect?

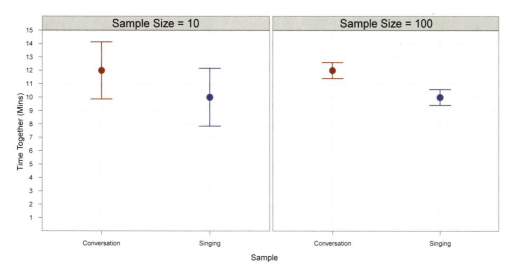

FIGURE 2.16
Graph showing two data sets with the same means and standard deviations but based on different sized samples

Notice in Figure 2.16 that the means for each sample are the same in both graphs, but the confidence intervals are much narrower when the samples contain 100 scores compared to when they contain only 10 scores. You might think that this is odd given that I said that all of the standard deviations were the same (i.e., 3). If you think back to how the confidence interval is computed, it is the mean plus or minus 1.96 times the standard error. The standard error is the standard deviation divided by the square root of the sample size (see equation (2.8)); therefore, as the sample size gets larger, the standard error (and, therefore, confidence interval) will get smaller.

We saw in the previous section that if the confidence intervals of two samples are the same length then a p of around .05 is represented by an overlap of about a quarter of the confidence interval. Therefore, we can see that even though the means and standard deviations are identical in both graphs, the study that has only 10 scores per sample is not significant (the bars overlap quite a lot; in actual fact $p = .15$) but the study that has 100 scores per sample shows a highly significant difference (the bars don't overlap at all, $p < .001$). Remember, the means and standard deviations are *identical* in the two graphs, but the sample size affects the standard error and hence the significance.

Taking this relationship to the extreme, we can illustrate that with a big enough sample even a completely meaningless difference between two means can be deemed significant with $p < .05$. Figure 2.17 shows such a situation. This time, the singing group has a mean of 10.00 ($SD = 3$) and the conversation group has a mean of 10.01 ($SD = 3$): a difference of 0.01 – a very small difference indeed. The main graph looks very odd: the means look identical and there are no confidence intervals. In fact, the confidence intervals are so narrow that they merge into a single line. The figure also shows a zoomed image of the confidence intervals (note that the values on the vertical axis now range from 9.98 to 10.02 so the entire range of values we're showing is only 0.04). As you can see, the sample means are 10 and 10.01 as mentioned before,[9] but now we have zoomed in on the image we can see the confidence intervals. Note that the confidence intervals show an overlap of about a quarter, which equates to a significance value of about $p = .05$ (for these data the actual value of p is .044). How is it possible that we have two sample means that are almost identical (10 and 10.01), and have the same standard deviations, but are significantly different? The answer is again the sample size: there are 1 million cases in each sample, so the standard errors are minuscule.

This section has made two important points. First, the sample size affects whether a difference between samples is deemed significant or not. In large samples small differences

---

[9] The mean of the singing group looks bigger than 10, but this is only because we have zoomed in so much that it's actual value of 10.00147 is noticeable.

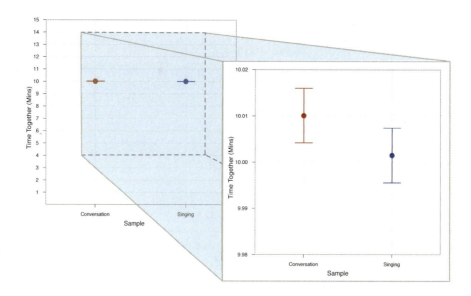

FIGURE 2.17
A very small difference between means based on an enormous sample size (n = 1,000,000 per group)

can be significant, and in small samples large differences can be non-significant. This point relates to power: large samples have more power to detect effects. Second, even a difference of practically zero can be deemed 'significant' if the sample size is big enough. Remember that test statistics are effectively the ratio of signal to noise, and the standard error is our measure of 'sampling noise'. The standard error is estimated from the sample size, and the bigger the sample size, the smaller the standard error. Therefore, bigger samples have less 'noise', so even a small signal can be detected.

2.6.2. Problems with NHST ②

NHST is the dominant method for testing theories using statistics. It is compelling because it offers a rule-based framework for deciding whether to believe in a particular hypothesis.

CRAMMING SAM'S TIPS   Null hypothesis significance testing

- NHST is a widespread method for assessing scientific theories. The basic idea is that we have two competing hypotheses: one says that an effect exists (the *alternative hypothesis*) and the other says that an effect doesn't exist (the *null hypothesis*). We compute a test statistic that represents the alternative hypothesis and calculate the probability that we would get a value as big as the one we have if the null hypothesis were true. If this probability is less than .05 we reject the idea that there is no effect, say that we have a *statistically significant* finding and throw a little party. If the probability is greater than .05 we do not reject the idea that there is no effect, we say that we have a *non-significant* finding and we look sad.
- We can make two types of error: we can believe that there is an effect when, in reality, there isn't (*a Type I error*); and we can believe that there is not an effect when, in reality, there is (*a Type II error*).
- The power of a statistical test is the probability that it will find an effect when one actually exists.
- The significance of a test statistic is directly linked to the sample size: the same effect will have different *p*-values in different sized samples: small differences can be deemed 'significant' in large samples, and large effects might be deemed 'non-significant' in small samples.

It is also appealing to teach because even if your students don't understand the logic behind NHST, most of them can get to grips with the idea that a $p < .05$ is 'significant' and a $p > .05$ is not. Like baking a cake, it offers a recipe which, if followed correctly, seems to provide 'the right answer'. No one likes to get things wrong and, at face value, NHST gives a pretty clear steer about what is the 'right' conclusion and what is the 'wrong' one. However, here are two of my favourite quotes about NHST:

The almost universal reliance on merely refuting the null hypothesis is a terrible mistake, is basically unsound, poor scientific strategy, and one of the worst things that ever happened in the history of psychology. (Meehl, 1978, p. 817)

NHST; I resisted the temptation to call it Statistical Hypothesis Inference Testing. (Cohen, 1994, p. 997)

This section explains these two highly respected people's cynicism by describing why, despite its widespread use, NHST is a fundamentally flawed process (see Ziliak & McCloskey, 2008, for a more in-depth discussion).

2.6.2.1. What can we conclude from statistical significance testing? ②

That the effect is important? Statistical significance is not the same thing as actual importance because the p-value from which we determine significance is affected by sample size (Section 2.6.1.10). Therefore, we should not be fooled by that phrase 'statistically significant', because even if the p-value is less than .05 it doesn't necessarily follow that the effect is important: very small and unimportant effects can turn out to be statistically significant just because huge numbers of people have been used in the study (Figure 2.17), and very large and important effects can be missed simply because the sample size was too small.

A non-significant result means that the null hypothesis is true? Actually, no. If the p-value is greater than .05 then we can decide to reject the alternative hypothesis, but this is not the same thing as the null hypothesis being true: a non-significant result tells us is that the effect is not big enough to be found but it doesn't tell us that the effect is zero. In fact, the null hypothesis is *never* true because we know from sampling distributions (see Section 2.5.1) that two random samples will have slightly different means, and even though these differences can be very small (e.g., one mean might be 10 and another might be 10.00001) they are nevertheless different (Cohen, 1990). As we have seen before, even such a small difference would be deemed as statistically significant if a big enough sample were used (think back to Figure 2.17). Therefore, a non-significant result should never be interpreted (despite the fact that it often is) as 'no difference between means' or 'no relationship between variables'.

A significant result means that the null hypothesis is false? Wrong again. A significant test statistic is based on probabilistic reasoning, which severely limits what we can conclude. Cohen (1994), who was an incredibly lucid writer on statistics, points out that formal reasoning relies on an initial statement of fact followed by a statement about the current state of affairs, and an inferred conclusion. This syllogism illustrates what I mean:

- If a man has no arms then he can't play guitar.
  - This man plays guitar.
  - Therefore, this man has arms.

The syllogism starts with a statement of fact that allows the end conclusion to be reached because you can deny the man has no arms (the antecedent) by denying that he can't play guitar (the consequent). A comparable version of the null hypothesis is:

- If the null hypothesis is correct, then this test statistic cannot occur.
  - This test statistic has occurred.
  - Therefore, the null hypothesis is false.

This is all very nice except that the null hypothesis is not represented in this way because it is based on probabilities. Instead it should be stated as follows:

- If the null hypothesis is correct, then this test statistic is highly unlikely.
  - This test statistic has occurred.
  - Therefore, the null hypothesis is highly unlikely.

If we go back to the guitar example we could get a similar statement:

- If a man plays guitar then he probably doesn't play for Fugazi (this is true because there are thousands of people who play guitar but only two who play guitar in the band Fugazi!).
  - Guy Picciotto plays for Fugazi.
  - Therefore, Guy Picciotto probably doesn't play guitar.

This should hopefully seem completely ridiculous – the conclusion is wrong because Guy Picciotto does play guitar. This illustrates a common fallacy in hypothesis testing.

To sum up then, although NHST is set up to test which of two competing hypotheses (the null or the alternate) is likely to be correct, the process is flawed because the significance of the test tells us nothing about the null hypothesis: it is never true.

2.6.2.2. All-or-nothing thinking ②

Another major problem with NHST is that it encourages all or nothing thinking: if $p < .05$ then an effect is significant, but if $p > .05$ it is not. One ridiculous scenario that is easy to imagine is that you have two effects, based on the same sample sizes, and one has $p = .0499$, and the other $p = .0501$. If you apply the NHST recipe book then the first effect is significant and the second is not. Is that really the case, when the ps differ by only .0002? Of course it's not the case; these effects are very similar. There is nothing magic about the criterion of $p < .05$; it is merely a convenient rule of thumb that has become popular for fairly arbitrary reasons (see Jane Superbrain Box 2.5). Nevertheless, the recipe-book nature of NHST encourages us to think in these very black and white terms. The dogmatic application of the .05 rule can mislead us.

Students are often very scared of statistics. One day a man called Dr Richard Weeping claimed to have found a cure for statistics anxiety: a potion containing badger sweat, a tear from a new-born child, a teaspoon of Guinness, some cat saliva and sherbet. Imagine that 10 researchers all did a study in which they compared anxiety levels in students who had taken the potion to those who had taken a placebo potion (water). If the potion didn't work, then there should be a difference of zero between these group means (the null hypothesis) but if it does work then those that took the potion should be less anxious than those taking the placebo (which will show up in a positive difference between the groups). The results of the 10 studies are shown in Figure 2.18 along with the p-value within each study.

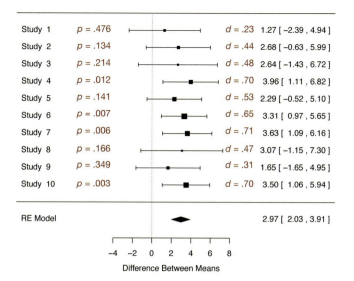

FIGURE 2.18
Results of 10
different studies
looking at the
difference
between two
interventions. The
squares show the
mean difference
between
groups (a
positive number
shows that the
intervention group
were less anxious
than the control)

SELF-TEST   Based on what you have learnt so far, which of the following statements best reflects your view of Dr Weeping's potion?

A   The evidence is equivocal, we need more research.

B   All of the mean differences show a positive effect of the intervention, therefore, we have consistent evidence that the treatment works.

C   Four of the studies show a significant result ($p < .05$), but the other six do not. Therefore, the studies are inconclusive: some suggest that the intervention is better than placebo, but others suggest there's no difference. The fact that more than half of the studies showed no significant effect means that the treatment is not (on balance) more successful in reducing anxiety than the control.

D   I want to go for C, but I have a feeling it's a trick question.

Based on what I have told you about NHST you should have answered C: only 4 of the 10 studies have a 'significant' result, which isn't very compelling evidence for Dr Weeping's magic potion. Now pretend you know nothing about NHST, look at the confidence intervals, and think about what we know about overlapping confidence intervals.

SELF-TEST   Now you've looked at the confidence intervals, which of the earlier statements best reflects your view of Dr Weeping's potion?

I would hope that some of you have changed your mind to option B. If you're still sticking with option C then let me try to convince you otherwise. First, 10 out of 10 studies show a positive effect of the potion (none of the means are below zero), and even though sometimes this positive effect is not always 'significant', it is consistently positive. The confidence intervals overlap with each other substantially in all studies, suggesting

JANE SUPERBRAIN 2.5

Why do we use .05? ①

This criterion of 95% confidence, or a .05 probability, forms the basis of NHST and yet there is very little justification for it. How it arose is a complicated mystery to unravel. Fisher believed that you calculate the probability of an event and evaluate this probability within the research context. Although Fisher felt that $p = .01$ would be strong evidence to back up a hypothesis, and perhaps $p = .20$ would be weak evidence, he objected to Neyman's use of an alternative hypothesis (among other things). Conversely, Neyman objected to Fisher's exact probability approach (Berger, 2003; Lehmann, 1993). The confusion arising from both parties' hostility to each other's ideas led scientists, over time, to create a sort of bastard child of both approaches. That bastard child is NHST. I use the word 'bastard' advisedly.

During the decades of confusion in which Fisher and Neyman's ideas have been fused into a sort of moronic Frankenstein, the probability of .05 rose to prominence. The reason why is probably because back in the days before computers, scientists had to compare their test statistics against published tables of 'critical values' (they did not have SPSS to calculate exact probabilities for them). These critical values had to be calculated by exceptionally clever people like Fisher. In his incredibly influential textbook *Statistical methods for research workers* (Fisher, 1925),[10] Fisher produced tables of these critical values, but to save space produced tables for particular probability values (.05, .02 and .01). The impact of this book should not be underestimated (to get some idea of its influence 25 years after publication, see Mather, 1951; Yates, 1951) and these tables were very frequently used – even Neyman and Pearson admitted the influence that these tables had on them (Lehmann, 1993). This disastrous combination of researchers confused about the Fisher and Neyman–Pearson approaches and the availability of critical values for only certain levels of probability led to a trend to report test statistics as being significant at the now infamous $p < .05$ and $p < .01$ (because critical values were readily available at these probabilities). However, Fisher believed that the dogmatic use of a fixed level of significance was silly: 'no scientific worker has a fixed level of significance at which from year to year, and in all circumstances, he rejects hypotheses; he rather gives his mind to each particular case in the light of his evidence and his ideas' (Fisher, 1956).

that all studies have sampled the same population. Again, this implies great consistency in the studies: they all throw up population effects of a similar size. Remember that the confidence interval will contain the actual population value in 95% of samples. Look at how much of the confidence intervals are above zero across the 10 studies: even in studies for which the confidence interval includes zero (implying that the population effect might be zero) the majority of the bar is greater than zero. Again, this suggests very consistent evidence that the population value is greater than zero (i.e., the potion works). Therefore, looking at the confidence intervals rather than just focusing on significance allows us to see the consistency in the data: rather than having conflicting results (which the NHST approach implied), we actually have very consistent results: in all studies the effect of the potion was positive and, taking all 10 studies into account, there's good reason to think that the population effect is likely to be greater than zero.

2.7. Modern approaches to theory testing ②

The pitfalls of NHST have led to a shift in pervasive view of how to evaluate evidence for a hypothesis or theory. We are some way off of discarding the shackles of NHST completely,

[10] You can read this online at http://psychclassics.yorku.ca/Fisher/Methods/

and this is, in part, because generations of scientists have been taught this approach and it continues to be the default option taught to budding scientists like yourself. Nevertheless, the shift in conventional wisdom is tangible. In my discipline (psychology), the American Psychological Association (APA) set up a task force not too long ago to produce guidelines for the reporting of data in their journals. This report acknowledged the limitations of NHST but also appreciated that a sea change in practice would not happen; therefore, they didn't recommend against NHST but suggested (sensibly in my opinion) that scientists report useful things like confidence intervals and effect sizes to help them (and readers) evaluate the research findings without dogmatic reliance on *p*-values (Wilkinson, 1999). We have looked at confidence intervals, but not effect sizes, and it is to these that we now turn.

2.7.1. Effect sizes ②

One of the problems we identified with NHST was that significance does not tell us about the importance of an effect. The solution to this criticism is to measure the size of the effect that we're testing in a standardized way. When we measure the size of an effect (be that an experimental manipulation or the strength of a relationship between variables) it is known as an **effect size**. An effect size is simply an objective and (usually) standardized measure of the magnitude of the observed effect. The fact that the measure is standardized just means that we can compare effect sizes across different studies that have measured different variables, or have used different scales of measurement (so an effect size based on speed in milliseconds could be compared to an effect size based on heart rates). As I mentioned before, the APA recommends reporting these effect sizes, so it's a habit well worth getting into.

2.7.1.1. Cohen's *d* ②

Many measures of effect size have been proposed, the most common of which are Cohen's *d*, Pearson's correlation coefficient *r* (Chapter 6) and the odds ratio (Chapters 18 and 19). As we shall see throughout the book, there are others, but these three are the simplest to understand. Let's think back to our study of whether singing gets you a date in Section 2.6.1.10. If we wanted to quantify the effect between the singing and conversation groups, how might we do it? A fairly simple thing to do would be to take the differences between means. The conversation group had a mean of 12 minutes (before the woman ran away), and the singing group a mean of 10 minutes. So, the effect of singing compared to conversation is 10–12 = –2 minutes. This is an effect size. Singing had a detrimental effect on how long the woman stayed, by –2 minutes. That's fairly easy to compute and understand, but it has two small inconveniences. First, the difference in means will be expressed in the units of measurement for the particular study. In this particular example, this inconvenience isn't really an inconvenience at all because minutes mean something to us: we can all imagine what an extra 2 minutes of time with someone would be like. We can also have an idea of what 2 minutes with someone is like relative to the amount of time we usually spend talking to random people. However, if we'd measured what the women thought of the men rather than how much time they spent with them, then interpretation is more tricky: 2 units of 'thought' or 'positivity' or whatever is less tangible to us than 2 minutes of time. The second inconvenience is that although the difference between means gives us an indication of the 'signal', it does not tell us about the

Can we measure the importance of an effect?

'noise' in the measure. Is 2 minutes of time a lot or a little relative to the 'normal' amount of time spent talking to strangers?

We can remedy both of these problems in the same way. We saw earlier in this chapter that the standard deviation is a measure of 'error' or 'noise' in the data, and we saw in Section 1.6.4 that if we divide by the standard deviation then the result is a score expressed in standard deviation units (i.e., a *z*-score). Therefore, if we divide the difference between means by the standard deviation we get a signal-to-noise ratio, but we also get a value that is expressed in standard deviation units (and can, therefore, be compared in different studies that used different measures). What I have just described is **Cohen's *d*** and we can express it formally as:

$$\hat{d} = \frac{\bar{X}_1 - \bar{X}_2}{s} \tag{2.15}$$

I have put a hat on the *d* to remind us that we're really interested in the effect size in the population, but because we can't measure that directly, we estimate it from the sample.[11] The hat means 'estimate of'. Therefore, *d* is simply the difference between means divided by the standard deviation. However, we had two standard deviations, so which one should we use? Sometimes we assume that group variances (and therefore standard deviations) are equal (see Chapter 5) and if they are we can just pick a standard deviation from one of the groups because it won't matter. In our singing for a date example, the standard deviations were identical in the two groups (*SD* = 3) so it doesn't matter which one we pick; we would get:

$$\frac{\bar{X}_{\text{Singing}} - \bar{X}_{\text{Conversation}}}{\sigma} = \frac{10 - 12}{3} = -0.667$$

This effect size means that if a man sang rather than having a normal conversation, the time the woman spent with him was reduced by 0.667 standard deviations. That's quite a bit.

Cohen (1988, 1992) has made some widely used suggestions about what constitutes a large or small effect: *d* = 0.2 (small), 0.5 (medium) and 0.8 (large). For our singing data this would mean we have a medium to large effect size. However, as Cohen acknowledged, these benchmarks encourage the kind of lazy thinking that we were trying to avoid and ignore the context of the effect such as the measurement instruments and general norms in a particular research area. Lenth put it nicely when he said that when we interpret effect sizes we're not trying to sell T-shirts: 'I'll have the Metallica tour effect size in a medium, please' (Baguley, 2004; Lenth, 2001).

Sometimes groups do not have equal standard deviations, and in those cases there are two main options. First, the standard deviation of the control group or baseline is often used. This makes sense because any intervention or experimental manipulation might be expected to change not just the mean but also the spread of scores. Therefore, the control group/baseline standard deviation will be a more accurate estimate of the standard deviation for the measure you're using. In our singing study, we would use the conversation group standard deviation because you wouldn't normally go up to someone and start singing. Therefore, *d* would represent the amount of time less that women spent with singing men than talking men relative to the normal variation in time that women spend with strange men who talk to them.

---

[11] The value for the population is expressed as:

$$d = \frac{\bar{\mu}_1 - \bar{\mu}_2}{\sigma}$$

It's the same equation, but because we're dealing with population values rather than ones from the sample, the hat over the *d* is gone, the means are expressed with μ and the standard deviation with σ.

The second option is to pool the standard deviations of the two groups using (if your groups are independent) this equation:

$$s_p = \sqrt{\frac{(N_1-1)s_1^2 + (N_2-1)s_2^2}{N_1 + N_2 - 2}} \tag{2.16}$$

in which N is the sample size of each group and s is the standard deviation. For the singing data, because the standard deviations and sample sizes are the same in the two groups this pooled estimate will be the same as the standard deviation (i.e., 3):

$$s_p = \sqrt{\frac{(10-1)3^2 + (10-1)3^2}{10+10-2}} = \sqrt{\frac{81+81}{18}} = \sqrt{9} = 3$$

When the group standard deviations are different, this pooled estimate can be useful; however, it changes the meaning of d because we're now comparing the difference between means against all of the background 'noise' in the measure, not just the noise that you would expect to find in normal circumstances.

SELF-TEST Compute Cohen's d for the effect of singing when a sample size of 100 was used (right-hand graph in Figure 2.16).

If you did the self-test you should have got the same result as before: −0.667. That's because the difference in sample size did not affect the means or standard deviations and, therefore, will not affect the effect size. Other things being equal, effect sizes are not affected by sample size, unlike p-values. Therefore, by using effect sizes we overcome one of the major problems with NHST. In reality, the situation is not quite this simple because, like any parameter, you will get better estimates of the population value in large samples than small ones. So, although the sample size doesn't affect the computation of your effect size in the sample, it does affect how closely the sample effect size matches that of the population (known as the *precision*).

SELF-TEST Compute Cohen's d for the effect in Figure 2.17. The exact mean of the singing group was 10, and for the conversation group was 10.01. In both groups the standard deviation was 3.

If you did the self-test then you will have found that the effect size for our larger study was $d = -0.003$. In other words, very small indeed. Remember that when we looked at p-values, this very small effect indeed was deemed statistically significant.

SELF-TEST Look at Figures 2.16 and 2.17. Compare what we concluded about these three data sets based on p-values, with what we conclude using effect sizes.

When we looked at the data sets in Figures 2.16 and 2.17 and their corresponding *p*-values, we concluded the following:

- Figure 2.16: Two experiments with identical means and standard deviations yield completely opposite conclusions when using a *p*-value to interpret them (the study based on 10 scores per group was not significant but the study based on 100 scores per group was).

- Figure 2.17: Two virtually identical means are deemed to be significantly different based on a *p*-value.

If we use effect sizes to guide our interpretations we would conclude the following:

- Figure 2.16: Two experiments with identical means and standard deviations yield identical conclusions when using an effect size to interpret them (both studies had $d = 0.667$).

- Figure 2.17: Two virtually identical means are deemed to be not very different at all based on an effect size ($d = 0.003$, which is tiny).

With these examples I hope to have convinced you that effect sizes offer us something that is less misleading than NHST.

2.7.1.2. The correlation coefficient ②

Many of you will be familiar with Pearson's correlation coefficient, *r*, as a measure of the strength of relationship between two variables (and we'll cover it in Chapter 6 if you're not). As such, it is an effect size. It might surprise you though that it can also be used to quantify the strength of an experimental effect. The reason why you might be surprised by this revelation is that students are usually taught about the correlation coefficient within the context of non-experimental research. If you think about it, though, it's not really surprising: *r* quantifies the relationship between two variables, so if one of those variables represents an experimental manipulation and the other represents an outcome variable then *r* would quantify the relationship between the experimental manipulation and the outcome. In other words, it would quantify the experimental effect. Of course, it's a bit more complex than that but I don't want to get ahead of myself, and we'll discover more about *r* as an effect size measure in Chapters 6, 9 and 11.

Like with *d*, Cohen (1988, 1992) suggested some 'T-shirt sizes' for *r*:

- $r = .10$ (small effect): In this case the effect explains 1% of the total variance.

- $r = .30$ (medium effect): The effect accounts for 9% of the total variance.

- $r = .50$ (large effect): The effect accounts for 25% of the variance.

It's worth bearing in mind that *r* is not measured on a linear scale, so an effect with $r = .6$ isn't twice as big as one with $r = .3$. It is worth remembering my earlier caveat that these 'canned' effect sizes are no substitute for evaluating an effect size within the context of the research domain that it is being used.

There are many reasons to like *r* as an effect size measure, one of them being that it is constrained to lie between 0 (no effect) and 1 (a perfect effect).[12] However, there are situ-

---

[12] The correlation coefficient can also be negative (but not below −1), which is useful when we're measuring a relationship between two variables because the sign of *r* tells us about the direction of the relationship, but in experimental research the sign of *r* merely reflects the way in which the experimenter coded their groups (see Chapter 6).

ations in which d may be favoured; for example, when group sizes are very discrepant, r can be quite biased compared to d (McGrath & Meyer, 2006).

2.7.2. Meta-analysis ②

Throughout the first two chapters I have alluded to how scientists often test similar theories and hypotheses. An important part of science is replicating results, and it is rare that a single study gives a definitive answer to a scientific question. In Section 2.6.2.2 we looked at an example of 10 experiments that had all explored whether a potion reduces statistics anxiety compared to a placebo (water). The summary of these studies was shown in Figure 2.18. Earlier, we concluded that, based on p-values, we would conclude that there were inconsistent results: 4 studies show a significant effect of the potion and 6 do not. However, based on the confidence intervals, we would conclude the opposite: that the findings across the studies were quite consistent and that it was likely that the effect in the population was positive. Also in this figure, although you wouldn't have known what they were at the time, are the values of Cohen's d for each study.

 SELF-TEST Look back at Figure 2.18. Based on the effect sizes, is your view of the efficacy of the potion more in keeping with what we concluded based on p-values or based on confidence intervals?

The 10 studies summarized in Figure 2.18 have ds ranging from .23 (other things being equal, smallish) to .71 (other things being equal, fairly large). All of the effect sizes are positive: no studies showed worse anxiety after taking the potion. Therefore, the effect sizes are very consistent: all studies show positive effects and the potion, at worst, had an effect of about a quarter of a standard deviation, and, at best, an effect of almost three-quarters of a standard deviation. Our conclusions are remarkably similar to what we concluded when we looked at the confidence intervals, that is, there is consistent evidence of a positive effect in the population. Wouldn't it be nice if we could use these studies to get a definitive estimate of the effect in the population? Well, we can, and this process is known as **meta-analysis**. It sounds hard, doesn't it?

What wouldn't be hard would be to summarize these 10 studies by taking an average of the effect sizes:

$$\overline{d} = \frac{\sum_{i=1}^{k} d_i}{n} = \frac{0.23 + 0.44 + 0.48 + 0.70 + 0.53 + 0.65 + 0.71 + 0.47 + 0.31 + 0.70}{10} = 0.52$$

Congratulations you have done your first meta-analysis – well, sort of. It wasn't that hard was it? Obviously there's more to it than that, but at a very basic level a meta-analysis involves computing effect sizes for a series of studies that investigated the same research question, and taking an average of those effect sizes. At a less simple level we don't use a normal average; we use what's known as a weighted average: in a meta-analysis each effect size is weighted by its precision (i.e., how good an estimate of the population it is) before the average is computed. By doing this, large studies, which will yield effect sizes that are more likely to closely approximate the population, are given more 'weight' than smaller studies, which should have yielded imprecise effect size estimates.

CRAMMING SAM'S TIPS   **Effect sizes**

- An effect size is a way of measuring the size of an observed effect, usually relative to the background error.
- Cohen's *d* is the difference between two means divided by the standard deviation of the mean of the control group, or a pooled estimated based on the standard deviations of both groups.
- Pearson's correlation coefficient, *r*, is also a versatile effect size measure.

Meta-analysis is not easily done in SPSS so there isn't a lot of point in me discussing it in more detail in a book about SPSS. However, I think it is worth knowing what it does and being aware of it because, in many ways, it is the natural endpoint of alternative approaches to the NHST. If you're interested then I have written some fairly accessible tutorials on doing a meta-analysis using SPSS (Field & Gillett, 2010) and also using a free software package called R (Field, 2012). There are also numerous good books and articles on meta-analysis that will get you started (e.g., Cooper, 2010; Field, 2001, 2003, 2005a, 2005b; Hedges, 1992; Hunter & Schmidt, 2004).

2.8. Reporting statistical models ②

In Section 1.7 we looked at some general principles for reporting data. Now that we have learnt a bit about fitting statistical models, we can add to these guiding principles. We learnt in this chapter that we can construct confidence intervals around a parameter such as the mean. Such an interval tells us something about the limits within which the population value will fall and, therefore, it is very important to report this. It is important to tell readers the type of confidence interval used (e.g., 95%) and in general we use the format [lower boundary, upper boundary] to present the actual values. So, if we had a mean of 30 and the confidence interval ranged from 20 to 40, we might write $M = 30$, 95% CI [20, 40]. If we were reporting lots of 95% confidence intervals it might be easier to state the level at the start of our results and just use the square brackets:

✓ 95% confidence intervals are reported in square brackets. Fear reactions were higher, $M = 9.86$ [7.41, 12.31] when Andy's cat Fuzzy wore a fake human tongue compared to when he didn't, $M = 6.58$ [3.47, 9.69].

We also saw that when we fit a statistical model we calculate a test statistic and a *p*-value associated with it. We conclude that an effect (our model) is significant if this *p*-value is less than .05. Historically, people would report *p*-values as being either less than or greater than .05. They would write things like:

✗ Fear reactions were significantly higher when Andy's cat Fuzzy wore a fake human tongue compared to when he didn't, $p < .05$.

If an effect was very significant – for example, if the p-value was less than .01 or even .001 – they would also use these two criteria to indicate a 'very significant' finding:

    × The number of cats intruding into the garden was significantly less when Fuzzy wore a fake human tongue compared to when he didn't, $p < .01$.

Similarly, non-significant effects would be reported in much the same way (note this time that p is reported as greater than .05):

    × Fear reactions were not significantly different when Fuzzy wore a David Beckham mask compared to when he didn't, $p > .05$.

In the days before computers it made sense to use these standard benchmarks for reporting significance because it was a bit of a pain to compute exact significance values (Jane Superbrain Box 2.5). However, computers make computing p-values a piece of ps, so we have no excuse for using these conventions. The APA now recommends reporting exact p-values for both significant and non-significant results. The reason is that reporting effects as $p > .05$ tells us very little about the size of the effect: perhaps the p was .06, or perhaps it was .92. These would be dramatically different effects, but based on knowing only that $p > .05$ we would consider them as exactly the same. Therefore, we should report exact p-values because it gives the reader more information than simply knowing that the p-value was less or more than a random threshold like .05. A possible exception is the threshold of .001. If we find a p-value of .0000234 then for the sake of space and everyone's sanity it would be reasonable to report $p < .001$.

The other thing is that because p-values depend on things like the sample size (see Section 2.6.1.10) it is highly advisable to report effect sizes as well as p-values (actually I'd argue instead of, but that's a bit radical and won't get your paper accepted in an academic journal). Effect sizes allow the reader to see very clearly the magnitude of the effects you have observed without being blinded by the all-or-nothing thinking that has attached itself to hypothesis testing and p-values (Section 2.6.2.2). So, we should report significance tests like this (note the presence of exact p-values and effect sizes):

    ✓ Fear reactions were significantly higher when Andy's cat Fuzzy wore a fake human tongue compared to when he didn't, $p = .023$, $d = 0.54$.

    ✓ The number of cats intruding into the garden was significantly less when Fuzzy wore a fake human tongue compared to when he didn't, $p = .007$, $d = 0.76$.

    ✓ Fear reactions were not significantly different when Fuzzy wore a David Beckham mask compared to when he didn't, $p = .18$, $d = 0.22$.

2.9. Brian's attempt to woo Jane ①

This chapter has taken us through a huge amount of statistical theory. Surely this will be enough for Brian to impress Jane (Figure 2.19)?

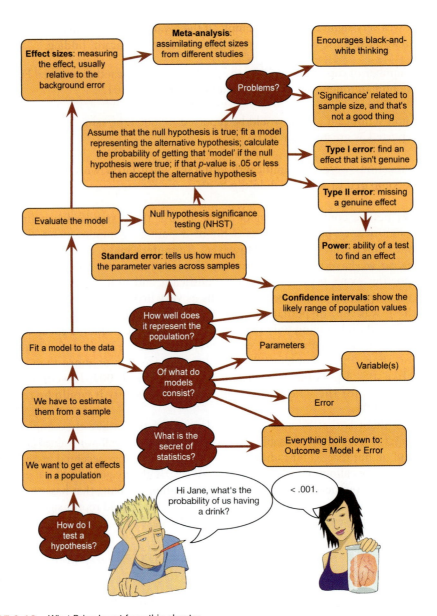

FIGURE 2.19 What Brian learnt from this chapter

2.10. What next? ①

Although I managed to get myself into trouble at nursery school, it was nevertheless a safe and nurturing place to be. However, at some point in our lives we all have to leave the safety of a familiar place and try out new things. I can't remember anything about how I felt about leaving nursery because it was a very long time ago, but given how massively neurotic I am, it's hard to believe that I was anything other than anxious. Still, you can't stay in nursery school for ever. Soon you have to find new pastures in which to wave your penis, and the new pasture into which I headed was primary school (or 'elementary school', as I believe it's called in the US). This was a scary new environment, a bit like SPSS might be for you. The question is, how do we cope with new and scary environments? It is this conundrum to which we now turn.

2.11. Key terms that I've discovered

α-level	Experimentwise error rate	Sample
Alternative hypothesis	Familywise error rate	Sampling distribution
β-level	Fit	Sampling variation
Bonferroni correction	Linear model	Standard error
Central limit theorem	Meta-analysis	Standard error of the
Cohen's *d*	Method of least squares	mean (SE)
Confidence interval	Null hypothesis	Test statistic
Degrees of freedom	One-tailed test	Two-tailed test
Deviance	Parameter	Type I error
Effect size	Population	Type II error
Experimental hypothesis	Power	

2.12. Smart Alex's tasks

- **Task 1**: Why do we use samples? ①

- **Task 2**: What is the mean and how do we tell if it's representative of our data? ①

- **Task 3**: What's the difference between the standard deviation and the standard error? ①

- **Task 4**: In Chapter 1 we used an example of the time in seconds taken for 21 heavy smokers to fall off a treadmill at the fastest setting (18, 16, 18, 24, 23, 22, 22, 23, 26, 29, 32, 34, 34, 36, 36, 43, 42, 49, 46, 46, 57). Calculate the standard error and 95% confidence interval for these data. ②

- **Task 5**: What do the sum of squares, variance and standard deviation represent? How do they differ? ①

- **Task 6**: What is a test statistic and what does it tell us? ①

- **Task 7**: What are Type I and Type II errors? ①

- **Task 8**: What is an effect size and how is it measured? ②

- **Task 9**: What is statistical power? ②

- **Task 10**: Figure 2.16 shows two experiments that looked at the effect of singing versus conversation on how much time a woman would spend with a man. In both experiments the means were 10 (singing) and 12 (conversation), the standard deviations in all groups were 3, but the group sizes were 10 per group in the first experiment and 100 per group in the second. Compute the values of the confidence intervals displayed in the figure. ②

- **Task 11**: Figure 2.17 shows a similar study to that in Task 10, but the means were 10 (singing) and 10.01 (conversation), the standard deviations in both groups were 3, and each group contained 1 million people. Compute the values of the confidence intervals displayed in the figure. ②

- **Task 12**: In Chapter 1 (Task 8) we looked at an example of how many games it took a sportsperson before they hit the 'red zone'. Calculate the standard error and confidence interval for those data. ②

- **Task 13**: At a rival club to the one I support, they similarly measured the number of consecutive games it took their players before they reached the red zone. The data are: 6, 17, 7, 3, 8, 9, 4, 13, 11, 14, 7. Calculate the mean, standard deviation, and confidence interval for these data. ②

- **Task 14**: Compute and interpret Cohen's *d* for the difference in the mean number of games it took players to become fatigued in the two teams mentioned in the previous two tasks. ②

- **Task 15**: In Chapter 1 (Task 9) we looked at the length in days of nine celebrity marriages. Here are the length in days of eight marriages, one being mine and the other seven being those of some of my friends and family (in all but one case up to the day I'm writing this, which is 8 March 2012, but in the 91-day case it was the entire duration – this isn't my marriage, in case you're wondering): 210, 91, 3901, 1339, 662, 453, 16672, 21963, 222. Calculate the mean, standard deviation and confidence interval for these data. ②

- **Task 16**: Calculate and interpret Cohen's *d* for the difference in the mean duration of the celebrity marriages in Chapter 1 and those in Task 15. ②

- **Task 17**: What are the problems with null hypothesis significance testing? ②

Answers can be found on the companion website.

2.13. Further reading

Cohen, J. (1990). Things I have learned (so far). *American Psychologist*, *45*, 1304–1312.

Cumming, G. (2012). *Understanding the new statistics: Effect sizes, confidence intervals, and meta-analysis*. New York: Routledge. (A really great book that elaborates on much of material that I cover in this chapter. Cumming takes a really refreshing and modern perspective on the material, and I recommend this book very highly.)

The IBM SPSS Statistics environment

3

FIGURE 3.1
All I want for Christmas is … some tasteful wallpaper

3.1. What will this chapter tell me? ①

At about 5 years old I moved from nursery (note that I moved; I was not 'kicked out' for showing my …) to primary school. Even though my older brother was already there, I remember being really scared about going. None of my nursery school friends were going to the same school and I was terrified about meeting all of these new children. I arrived in my classroom and, as I'd feared, it was full of scary children. In a fairly transparent ploy to make me think that I'd be spending the next 6 years building sand castles, the teacher told me to play in the sand pit. While I was nervously trying to discover whether I could build a pile of sand high enough to bury my head in it, a boy came and joined me. He was Jonathan Land, and he was really nice. Within an hour he was my new best friend (5-year-olds are fickle …) and I loved school. Sometimes new environments seem more scary than they really are. This chapter introduces you to what might seem like a scary new environment: IBM SPSS Statistics. The SPSS environment is a generally more unpleasant environment in which to spend time than your normal environment; nevertheless, we have to spend time there if we are to analyse our data. The purpose of this chapter is, therefore, to put you in a sand pit with a 5-year-old called Jonathan. I will orient you in your new home and everything will be fine. We will explore the key windows in SPSS (the *data editor*, *viewer* and the *syntax editor*) and also look at how to create variables, enter data and adjust the properties of your variables. We finish off by looking at how to load files and save them.

3.2. Versions of IBM SPSS Statistics ①

This book is based primarily on version 21 of *IBM SPSS Statistics* (I'm just going to call it SPSS from now on); however, don't be fooled too much by version numbers because SPSS release 'new' versions each year, and as you might imagine, not much changes in a year. Occasionally IBM have a major overhaul, but most of the time you can get by with a book that doesn't explicitly cover the latest version (or indeed the version you're using): a bit of common sense will see you through. So, this edition, although dealing with version 21, will happily cater for earlier versions (certainly back to version 18). I also suspect it'll be useful with versions 22 onwards when they appear (although it's always a possibility that IBM may decide to change everything just to annoy me).

3.3. Windows versus MacOS ①

Recent versions of SPSS use a program called Java. The cool thing about Java is that it is platform independent, which means it works on Windows, MacOS, and even Linux. The Windows and MacOS versions of SPSS differ very little (if at all) because it is built using Java. They look a bit different because MacOS looks different than Windows (you can get the Mac version of SPSS to display itself like the Windows version, although why on earth you'd want to do that I have no idea), but they are not. Therefore, although I have taken the screenshots from Windows because the vast majority of readers will use Windows, you can use this book if you have a Mac. In fact, I wrote it on a Mac.

3.4. Getting started ①

SPSS mainly uses two windows: the **data editor** (this is where you input your data and carry out statistical functions) and the **viewer** (this is where the results of any analysis appear). There are several additional windows that can be activated such as the **syntax editor** (see Section 3.9), which allows you to enter SPSS commands manually (rather than using the window-based menus). For beginners, the syntax window is redundant because you can carry out most analyses by clicking merrily with your mouse. However, there are additional functions that can be accessed using syntax and this can often save you time. Consequently, strange people who enjoy statistics can find numerous uses for syntax and dribble excitedly when discussing it. There are sections of the book where I'll force you to use syntax, but mainly because I wish to drown in a pool of my own excited dribble.

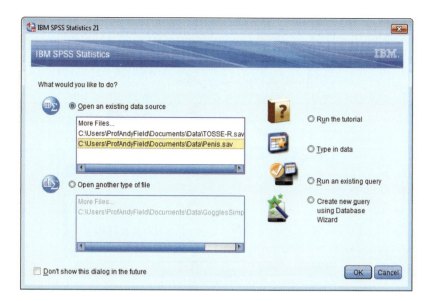

FIGURE 3.2
The start-up
window of IBM
SPSS

Once SPSS has been activated, a start-up window will appear (see Figure 3.2), which allows you to select various options. If you already have a data file on disk that you would like to open then select *Open an existing data source* by clicking on the ○ so that it looks like ◉: this is the default option. In the space underneath this option there will be a list of recently used data files that you can select with the mouse. To open a selected file click on ⌐OK⌐. If you want to open a data file that isn't in the list then simply select *More Files…* and click on ⌐OK⌐. This action will open a standard Explorer window that allows you to browse your computer and find the file you want (see Section 3.11). It might be the case that you want to open something other than a data file, for example a *viewer* document containing the results of your last analysis. You can do this by selecting *Open another type of file* by clicking on the ○ (so that it looks like ◉) and either selecting a file from the list or selecting *More Files…* and browsing your computer. If you're starting a new analysis (as we are here) then you'll want to type your data into a new data editor. Therefore, you select *Type in data* (by again clicking on the appropriate ○) and then click on ⌐OK⌐. This action will load a blank *data editor* window.

3.5. The data editor ①

The main SPSS window includes a data editor for entering data. This window is where most of the action happens. At the top of this screen is a menu bar similar to the ones you might have seen in other programs. Figure 3.3 shows this menu bar and the data editor. There are several menus at the top of the screen (e.g., File Edit View) that can be activated by using the computer mouse to move the on-screen arrow onto the desired menu and then pressing the left mouse button once (I'll call pressing this button as *clicking*). When you have clicked on a menu, a menu box will appear that displays a list of options that can be activated by moving the on-screen arrow so that it is pointing at the desired option and then clicking with the mouse. Often, selecting an option from a menu makes a window appear; these windows are referred to as *dialog boxes*. When referring to selecting options in a menu I will use images to notate the menu paths; for example, if I were to say that you should select the *Save As …* option in the *File* menu, you will see File Save As… .

The data editor has two views: the **data view** and the **variable view**. The data view is for entering data, and the variable view is for defining characteristics of the variables within the

FIGURE 3.3
The SPSS data editor

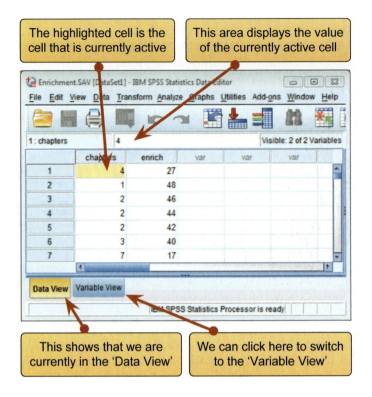

The highlighted cell is the cell that is currently active

This area displays the value of the currently active cell

This shows that we are currently in the 'Data View'

We can click here to switch to the 'Variable View'

data editor. Notice at the bottom of the data editor that there are two tabs labelled 'Data View' and 'Variable View' (Data View Variable View); all we do to switch between these two views is click on these tabs (the highlighted tab tells you which view you're in, although it will be obvious). Let's look at some general features of the data editor, features that don't change when we switch between the data view and the variable view. First off, let's look at the menus.

You'll find that within the menus in Windows some letters are underlined: these underlined letters represent the *keyboard shortcut* for accessing that function. It is possible to select many functions without using the mouse, and with a bit of practice these shortcuts are faster than manoeuvring the mouse arrow to the appropriate place on the screen. In Windows, the letters underlined in the menus indicate that the option can be obtained by simultaneously pressing *Alt* on the keyboard and the underlined letter. So, to access the *Save As…* option, using only the keyboard, you should press *Alt* and F on the keyboard simultaneously (which activates the *File* menu), then, keeping your finger on the *Alt* key, press A (which is the underlined letter).[1] In MacOS, keyboard shortcuts are listed in the menus; for example, you can save a file by simultaneously pressing ⌘ and S (I will denote these shortcuts as ⌘ + S). Below is a brief reference guide to each of the menus and some of the options that they contain. We will discover the wonders of each menu as we progress through the book:

- **File** This menu contains all of the options that are customarily found in *File* menus: you can save data, graphs or output, open previously saved files and print graphs, data or output.

- **Edit** This menu contains edit functions for the data editor. In SPSS it is possible to *cut* and *paste* blocks of numbers from one part of the data editor to another (which can be very handy when you realize that you've entered lots of numbers in the wrong

[1] In Windows XP these underlined letters seemed to disappear, but they reappear if you press *Alt*.

place). You can also use ⊞ Options… to select various preferences such as the font that is used for the output. The default preferences are fine for most purposes.

- View This menu deals with system specifications such as whether you have grid lines on the data editor, or whether you display value labels (exactly what value labels are will become clear later).

- Data This menu allows you to make changes to the data editor. The important features are ⊞ Insert Variable, which is used to insert a new variable into the data editor (i.e., add a column); ⊞ Insert Cases, which is used to add a new row of data between two existing rows of data; ⊞ Split File…, which is used to split the file by a grouping variable (see Section 5.3.2.4); and ⊞ Select Cases…, which is used to run analyses on only a selected sample of cases.

- Transform You should use this menu if you want to manipulate one of your variables in some way. For example, you can use *recode* to change the values of certain variables (e.g., if you wanted to adopt a slightly different coding scheme for some reason) – see SPSS Tip 10.2. The *compute* function is also useful for transforming data (e.g., you can create a new variable that is the average of two existing variables). This function allows you to carry out any number of calculations on your variables (see Section 5.4.4.2).

- Analyze The fun begins here, because the statistical procedures lurk in this menu. Below is a brief guide to the options in the statistics menu that will be used during the course of this book (this is only a small portion of what is available):

  ○ Descriptive Statistics ▸ This menu is for conducting descriptive statistics (mean, mode, median, etc.), frequencies and general data exploration. There is also a command called *crosstabs* that is useful for exploring frequency data and performing tests such as chi-square, Fisher's exact test and Cohen's kappa.

  ○ Compare Means ▸ This is where you can find *t*-tests (related and unrelated – Chapter 9) and one-way independent ANOVA (Chapter 11).

  ○ General Linear Model ▸ This menu is for more complex ANOVA such as two-way (unrelated, related or mixed), one-way ANOVA with repeated measures and multivariate analysis of variance (MANOVA) – see Chapters 12 to 16.

  ○ Mixed Models ▸ This menu can be used for running multilevel linear models (MLMs). At the time of writing I know absolutely nothing about these, but seeing as I've promised to write a chapter on them I'd better go and do some reading. With luck you'll find a chapter on it later in the book, or 30 blank sheets of paper. It could go either way.

  ○ Correlate ▸ It doesn't take a genius to work out that this is where the correlation techniques are kept. You can do bivariate correlations such as Pearson's *R*, Spearman's rho (ρ) and Kendall's tau (τ) as well as partial correlations (see Chapter 6).

  ○ Regression ▸ There are a variety of regression techniques available in SPSS. You can do simple linear regression, multiple linear regression (Chapter 8) and more advanced analyses such as logistic regression (Chapter 19).

  ○ Loglinear ▸ Loglinear analysis is hiding in this menu, waiting for you, and ready to pounce like a tarantula from its burrow (Chapter 18).

  ○ Dimension Reduction ▸ You'll find factor analysis here (Chapter 17).

  ○ Scale ▸ Here you'll find reliability analysis (Chapter 17).

- ○ <u>N</u>onparametric Tests ▸ There are a variety of non-parametric statistics available such the chi-square goodness-of-fit statistic, the binomial test, the Mann–Whitney test, the Kruskal–Wallis test, Wilcoxon's test and Friedman's ANOVA (Chapter 6).

- <u>G</u>raphs SPSS has some graphing facilities and this menu is used to access the Chart Builder (see Chapter 4). The types of graphs you can do include bar charts, histograms, scatterplots, box–whisker plots, pie charts and error bar graphs.

- <u>U</u>tilities In this menu there is an option, Data File <u>C</u>omments... , that allows you to comment on your data set. This can be quite useful because you can write yourself notes about from where the data come, or the date they were collected and so on.

- Add-<u>o</u>ns SPSS sell several add-ons that can be accessed through this menu. For example, they have a program called *Sample Power* that computes the sample size required for studies, and power statistics (see Section 2.6.1.7). However, because most people won't have these add-ons (including me) I'm not going to discuss them in the book.

- <u>W</u>indow This menu allows you to switch from window to window. So, if you're looking at the output and you wish to switch back to your data sheet, you can do so using this menu. There are icons to shortcut most of the options in this menu, so it isn't particularly useful.

- <u>H</u>elp This is an invaluable menu because it offers you online help on both the system itself and the statistical tests. The statistics help files are fairly incomprehensible at times (the program is not designed to teach you statistics) and are certainly no substitute for acquiring a good book like this, erm, I mean acquiring a good knowledge of your own. However, they can get you out of a sticky situation.

At the top of the data editor window are a set of *icons* (see Figure 3.3) that are shortcuts to frequently used facilities in the menus. Using the icons saves you time. Below is a brief list of these icons and their functions.

This icon gives you the option to open a previously saved file (if you are in the data editor, SPSS assumes you want to open a data file; if you are in the output viewer, it will offer to open a viewer file).

This icon allows you to save files. It will save the file you are currently working on (be it data or output). If the file hasn't already been saved it will produce the *Save Data As* dialog box.

SPSS TIP 3.1   Save time and avoid RSI ①

By default, when you try to open a file from SPSS it will go to the directory in which the program is stored on your computer. This is fine if you happen to store all of your data and output in that folder, but if not then you will find yourself spending time navigating around your computer trying to find your data. If you use SPSS as much as I do then this has two consequences: (1) all those seconds have added up to weeks navigating my computer when I could have been doing something useful like playing my drum kit; (2) I have increased my chances of getting RSI in my wrists, and if I'm going to get RSI in my wrists I can think of more enjoyable ways to achieve it than navigating my computer (drumming again, obviously). Luckily, we can avoid wrist death by telling SPSS where we'd like it to start looking for files. Select Edit Options... to open the Options dialog box below and select the File Locations tab.

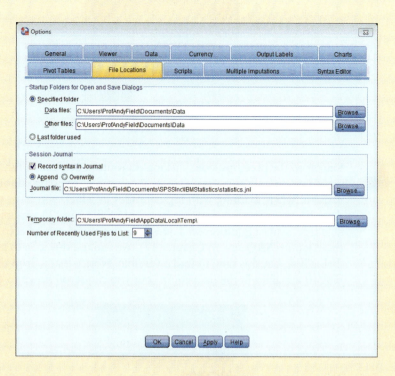

This dialog box allows you to select a folder in which SPSS will initially look for data files and other files. For example, I keep all of my data files in a single folder called, rather unimaginatively, 'Data'. In the dialog box here I have clicked on Browse... and then navigated to my data folder. SPSS will use this as the default location when I try to open files and my wrists are spared the indignity of RSI. You can also select the option for SPSS to use the Last folder used, in which case SPSS remembers where you were last time it was loaded and uses that folder when you open files.

 This icon activates a dialog box for printing whatever you are currently working on (either the data editor or the output). The exact print options will depend on the printer you use. By default SPSS will print everything in the output window, so a useful way to save trees is to print only a selection of the output (see SPSS Tip 3.5).

 Clicking on this icon will activate a list of the last 12 dialog boxes that you used. You can select any box from the list and it will appear on the screen. This icon makes it easy for you to repeat parts of an analysis.

 This icon implies to me (what with the big arrow and everything) that if you click on it SPSS will send a miniaturizing ray our of your monitor that shrinks you and then sucks you into a red cell in the data editor, where you will spend the rest of your days fighting decimal points with your bare hands. Fortunately, this icon does not do this, but instead enables you to go directly to a case (a row in the data editor). This button is useful if you are working on large data files: if you were analysing a survey with 3000 respondents it would get pretty tedious scrolling down the data sheet to find the responses of participant 2407. By clicking on this icon you can skip straight to the case by typing the case number required (in our example 2407) into this dialog box:

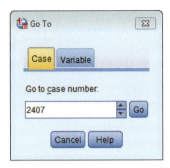

 Similar to the previous icon, clicking this button activates a function that enables you to go directly to a variable (i.e., a column in the data editor). As before, this is useful when working with big data files in which you have many columns of data. In the example below, we have a data file with 23 variables and each variable represents a question on a questionnaire and is named accordingly (we'll use this data file, **SAQ.sav**, in Chapter 17). We can use this icon to activate the *Go To* dialog box, but this time to find a variable. Notice that a drop-down box lists the first 10 variables in the data editor, but you can scroll down to go to others.

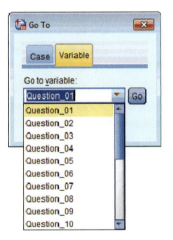

 Clicking on this icon opens a dialog box that shows you the variables in the data editor and summary information about each one. The dialog box below shows the information for the file that we used for the previous icon. We have selected the first variable in this file, and we can see the variable name (question_01), the label (Statistics makes me cry), the measurement level (ordinal), and the value labels (e.g., the number 1 represents the response of 'strongly agree').

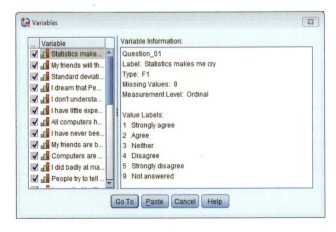

I initially thought that this icon would allow me to spy on my neighbours, but this shining diamond of excitement was snatched cruelly from me by the cloaked thief that is SPSS. Instead, click this button to search for words or numbers in your data file and output window. In the data editor it will search within the variable (column) that is currently active. This option is useful if, for example, you realize from a graph of your data that you have typed 20.02 instead of 2.02 (see Section 4.4): you can simply search for 20.02 within that variable and replace that value with 2.02:

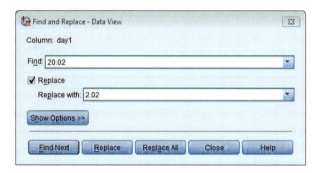

Clicking on this icon inserts a new case in the data editor (so it creates a blank row at the point that is currently highlighted in the data editor). This function is very useful if you need to add new data at a particular point in the data editor.

Clicking on this icon creates a new variable to the left of the variable that is currently active (to activate a variable simply click once on the name at the top of the column).

Clicking on this icon is a shortcut to the Data ⊞ Split File... function (see Section 5.3.2.4). There are often situations in which you might want to analyse groups of cases separately. In SPSS we differentiate groups of cases by using a coding variable (see Section 3.5.2.3), and this function lets us divide our output by such a variable. For example, we might test males and females on their statistical ability. We can code each participant with a number that represents their gender (e.g., 1 = female, 0 = male). If we then want to know the mean statistical ability of each gender we simply ask the computer to split the file by the variable **Gender**. Any subsequent analyses will be performed on the men and women separately. There are situations across many disciplines where this might be useful: sociologists and economists might want to look at data from different geographic locations separately, biologists might wish to analyse different groups of mutated mice, and so on.

This icon shortcuts to the Data ⚖ Weight Cases... function. This function is necessary when we come to input frequency data (see Section 18.5.2.2) and is useful for some advanced issues in survey sampling.

This icon is a shortcut to the Data ⊞ Select Cases... function. If you want to analyse only a portion of your data, this is the option for you. This function allows you to specify what cases you want to include in the analysis.

Clicking on this icon will either display or hide the value labels of any coding variables. We often group people together and use a coding variable to let the computer know that a certain participant belongs to a certain group. For example, if we coded gender as 1 = female, 0 = male then the computer knows that every time it comes across the value 1 in the **Gender** column, that person is a female. If you press this icon, the coding will appear on the data editor rather than the numerical values; so, you will see the words *male* and *female* in the **Gender** column rather than a series of numbers. This idea will become clear in Section 3.5.2.3.

3.5.1. Entering data into the data editor ①

When you first load SPSS it will provide a blank data editor with the title *Untitled1* (this of course is daft because once it has been given the title 'untitled' it ceases to be untitled). When inputting a new set of data, you must input your data in a logical way. The SPSS data editor is arranged such that *each row represents data from one entity while each column represents a variable*. There is no discrimination between independent and dependent variables: both types should be placed in a separate column. The key point is that each row represents one entity's data (be that entity a human, mouse, tulip, business, or water sample). Therefore, any information about that case should be entered across the data editor. For example, imagine you were interested in sex differences in perceptions of pain created by hot and cold stimuli. You could place some people's hands in a bucket of very cold water for a minute and ask them to rate how painful they thought the experience was on a scale of 1 to 10. You could then ask them to hold a hot potato and again measure their perception of pain. Imagine I was a participant. You would have a single row representing my data, so there would be a different column for my name, my gender, my pain perception for cold water and my pain perception for a hot potato: Andy, male, 7, 10.

The column with the information about my gender is a grouping variable: I can belong to either the group of males or the group of females, but not both. As such, this variable is a between-group variable (different people belong to different groups). Rather than representing groups with words, in SPSS we use numbers. This involves assigning each group a number, and then telling SPSS which number represents which group. Therefore, between-group variables are represented by a single column in which the group to which the person belonged is defined using a number (see Section 3.5.2.3). For example, we might decide that if a person is male then we give them the number 0, and if they're female we give them the number 1. We then tell SPSS that every time it sees a 1 in a particular column the person is a female, and every time it sees a 0 the person is a male. Variables that specify to which of several groups a person belongs can be used to split data files (so in the pain example you could run an analysis on the male and female participants separately – see Section 5.3.2.4).

Finally, the two measures of pain are a repeated measure (all participants were subjected to hot and cold stimuli). Therefore, levels of this variable (see SPSS Tip 3.2) can be entered in separate columns (one for pain to a hot stimulus and one for pain to a cold stimulus).

SPSS TIP 3.2   Entering data ①

There is a simple rule for how variables should be placed in the SPSS data editor: data from different things go in different rows of the data editor, whereas data from the same things go in different columns of the data editor. As such, each person (or mollusc, goat, organization, or whatever you have measured) is represented in a different row. Data within each person (or mollusc, etc.) go in different columns. So, if you've prodded your mollusc, or human, several times with a pencil and measured how much it twitches as an outcome, then each prod will be represented by a column.

In experimental research this means that any variable measured with the same participants (a repeated measure) should be represented by several columns (each column representing one level of the repeated-measures variable). However, any variable that defines different groups of things (such as when a between-groups design is used and different participants are assigned to different levels of the independent variable) is defined using a single column. This idea will become clearer as you learn about how to carry out specific procedures. (This golden rule is broken in mixed models, but until Chapter 19 we can overlook this annoying anomaly.)

The data editor is made up of lots of *cells*, which are boxes in which data values can be placed. When a cell is active it becomes highlighted in orange (as in Figure 3.3). You can move around the data editor, from cell to cell, using the arrow keys ← ↑ ↓ → (found on the right of the keyboard) or by clicking the mouse on the cell that you wish to activate. To enter a number into the data editor simply move to the cell in which you want to place the data value, type the value, then press the appropriate arrow button for the direction in which you wish to move. So, to enter a row of data, move to the far left of the row, type the value and then press → (this process inputs the value and then moves you into the next cell on the right).

The first step in entering your data is to create some variables using the variable view of the data editor, and then to input your data using the data view of the data editor. We'll go through these two steps by working through an example.

3.5.2. The variable view ①

Before we input any data into the data editor, we need to create the variables. To create variables we use the variable view of the data editor. To access this view click on the 'Variable View' tab at the bottom of the data editor (Data View | Variable View); the contents of the window will change (see Figure 3.4).

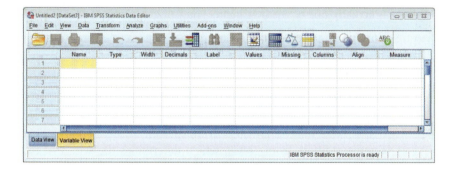

FIGURE 3.4
The 'Variable View' of the SPSS Data Editor

Every row of the variable view represents a variable, and you set characteristics of a particular variable by entering information into the following labelled columns (play around and you'll get the hang of it):

Name — You can enter a name in this column for each variable. This name will appear at the top of the corresponding column in the data view, and helps you to identify variables in the data view. You can more or less write what you like, but there are certain symbols you can't use (mainly symbols that have other uses in SPSS such as +, −, &), and you can't use spaces. (It can be useful to use a 'hard space', which replaces the space with an underscore; for example, Andy_Field instead of Andy Field.) If you use a character that SPSS doesn't like you'll get an error message saying that the variable name is invalid when you click on a different cell, or try to move off the cell using the arrow keys.

Type — You can have different types of data. Mostly you will use **numeric variables** (which means that the variable contains numbers and is the default). You will come across **string variables**, which consist of strings of letters. If you wanted to type in people's names, for example, you would need to change the variable type to be string rather than numeric. You can also have **currency variables** (i.e., £s, $s, €s) and **date variables** (e.g., 21-06-1973)

Width

By default, when a new variable is created, SPSS sets it up to be *numeric* and to store 8 digits/characters, but you can change this value by typing a new number in this column in the dialog box. For numeric variables 8 digits is fine (unless you have very large numbers), but for string variables you will often make this value bigger (you can't write a lot in only 8 characters). This characteristic differs from Columns in that it affects what is stored in the variable rather than what is displayed in the data editor.

Decimals

Another default setting is to have 2 decimal places displayed. (You'll notice that if you don't change this option then when you type in whole numbers to the data editor SPSS adds a decimal place with two zeros after it, which can be disconcerting.) If you want to change the number of decimal places for a given variable then replace the 2 with a new value or increase or decrease the value using ▲.

Label

The name of the variable (see above) has some restrictions on characters, and you also wouldn't want to use huge long names at the top of your columns (they become hard to read). Therefore, you can write a longer variable description in this column. This may seem pointless, but is actually one of the best habits you can get into (see SPSS Tip 3.3).

Values

This column is for assigning numbers to represent groups of people (see Section 3.5.2.3 below).

Missing

This column is for assigning numbers to missing data (see Section 3.5.3 below).

Columns

Enter a number into this column to determine the width of the column, that is, how many characters are displayed in the column. (This characteristic differs from Width, which determines the width of the variable itself – you could have a variable of 10 characters but by setting the column width to 8 you would see only 8 of the 10 characters of the variable in the data editor.) It can be useful to increase the column width if you have a string variable (Section 3.5.2.1) that exceeds 8 characters, or a coding variable (Section 3.5.2.3) with value labels that exceed 8 characters.

Align

You can use this column to select the alignment of the data in the corresponding column of the data editor. You can choose to align the data to the ≣ Left, ≣ Right or ≣ Center.

Measure

This is where you define the level at which a variable was measured (*Nominal*, *Ordinal* or *Scale* – Section 1.5.1.2).

Role

There are some procedures in SPSS that attempt to run analyses automatically without you needing to think about what you're doing (one example is the *Automatic Linear Modeling* option in the *Regression* part of the *Analyze* menu). To think on your behalf, SPSS needs to know whether a variable is a predictor (↘ Input), an outcome (◉ Target), both (◉ Both, although I'm not sure how that works out in practice), a variable that splits the analysis by different groups (▦ Split), a variable that selects out part of the data (▦ Partition), or a variable that has no pre-defined role (None). These roles can be useful if you're chugging out huge numbers of analyses and want to automate them, but most readers of this book won't be. It's also rarely a good idea to let a computer do your thinking for you, so I'm also not a fan of the procedures in SPSS that attempt to select variables on your behalf (they have their place, but that place is not in this book). Therefore, I'm not going to talk about roles any more than I already have.

Let's use the variable view to create some variables. Imagine we were interested in looking at the differences between lecturers and students. We took a random sample of five psychology lecturers from the University of Sussex and five psychology students and then measured how many friends they had, their weekly alcohol consumption (in units), their yearly income and how neurotic they were (higher score is more neurotic). These data are in Table 3.1.

SPSS TIP 3.3   Naming variables ①

Surely it's a waste of my time to type in long names for my variables when I've already given them a short name. I can understand why it would seem to be so, but as you go through your course accumulating data files, you will be grateful that you did. Imagine you had a variable called 'number of times I wanted to shoot myself during Andy Field's statistics lecture'; then you might have called the column in SPSS 'shoot'. If you don't add a more detailed label, SPSS will use this variable name in all of the output from an analysis. That's all well and good, but what happens in three weeks' time when you look at your data and output again? The chances are that you'll probably think 'What did shoot stand for? Number of shots at goal? Number of shots I drank?' Imagine the chaos you could get into if you had used an acronym for the variable 'wait at news kiosk'. I have many data sets with variables called things like 'sftg45c', and if I didn't give them proper labels I would be in all sorts of trouble. Get into a good habit and label all of your variables.

TABLE 3.1   Some data with which to play

Name	Birth Date	Job	No. of Friends	Alcohol (Units)	Income (p.a.)	Neuroticism
Ben	03-Jul-1977	Lecturer	5	10	20,000	10
Martin	24-May-1969	Lecturer	2	15	40,000	17
Andy	21-Jun-1973	Lecturer	0	20	35,000	14
Paul	16-Jul-1970	Lecturer	4	5	22,000	13
Graham	10-Oct-1949	Lecturer	1	30	50,000	21
Carina	05-Nov-1983	Student	10	25	5,000	7
Karina	08-Oct-1987	Student	12	20	100	13
Doug	16-Sep-1989	Student	15	16	3000	9
Mark	20-May-1973	Student	12	17	10,000	14
Zoë	12-Nov-1984	Student	17	18	10	13

3.5.2.1. Creating a string variable ①

The first variable in our data set is the name of the lecturer/student. This variable is a *string variable* because it consists of names. To create this variable follow these steps:

1 Click in the first white cell in the column labelled *Name*.

2 Type the word 'Name'.

3 Move off this cell using the arrow keys on the keyboard (you can also just click on a different cell, but this is a very slow way of doing it).

You've just created your first variable! Notice that once you've typed a name, SPSS creates default settings for the variable (such as assuming it's numeric and assigning 2 decimal places). The problem is that SPSS has assumed that we want a numeric variable (i.e., numbers) but we don't; we want to enter people's names, so we need a *string* variable. Therefore, we have to change the variable type. Move into the column labelled ⬚ Type ⬚ using the arrow keys on the keyboard. The cell will now look like this Numeric ⬚ . Click on ⬚ to activate the dialog box in Figure 3.5. By default, SPSS selects the numeric variable type (◉ Numeric) — see the left panel of Figure 3.5. To change the variable to a string variable, click on ◉ String and the dialog box will change to look like the right panel of Figure 3.5. You can choose how many characters you want in your string variable (i.e., the maximum number of characters you will type for a given case of data). The default is 8, which is fine for us because our longest name is only six letters; however, if we were entering surnames as well, we would need to increase this value. When you have finished, click on ⬚OK⬚ to return to the variable view.

Now, because I want you to get into good habits, move to the cell in the ⬚ Label ⬚ column and type a description of the variable, such as 'Participant's First Name'. Finally, we can specify the level at which a variable was measured (see Section 1.5.1.2) by going to the column labelled *Measure* and selecting either *Nominal*, *Ordinal* or *Scale* from the drop-down list. In this case, we have a string variable, so they represent only names of cases and provide no information about the order of cases, or the magnitude of one case compared to another. Therefore, we need to select ⬚ Nominal ⬚ .

Once the variable has been created, you can return to the data view by clicking on the 'Data View' tab at the bottom of the data editor (Data View Variable View). The contents of the window will change, and you'll notice that the first column now has the label *Name*. To enter the data, click on the white cell at the top of the column labelled *Name* and type the first name, 'Ben'. To register this value in this cell, simply move to a different cell; because we are entering data down a column, the most sensible way to do this is to press the ↓ key on the keyboard. This action moves you down to the next cell, and the word 'Ben' should appear in the cell above. Enter the next name, 'Martin', and then press ↓ to move down to the next cell, and so on.

FIGURE 3.5
Defining a string variable

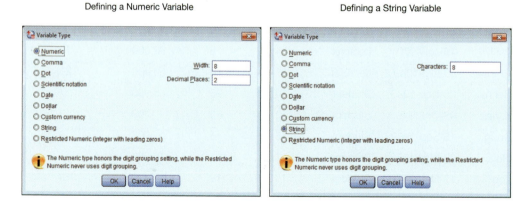

3.5.2.2. Creating a date variable ①

Notice that the second column in our table contains dates (birth dates, to be exact). To enter date variables into SPSS we use the same procedure as with the previous variable, except that we need to change the variable type. First, move back to the 'Variable View' using the tab at the bottom of the data editor (Data View Variable View). As with the previous variable, move to the cell in row 2 of the column labelled *Name* (under the previous variable you created). Type the word 'Birth_Date' (note that we have used a hard space to separate the words). Move into the column labelled Type using the → key on the keyboard (SPSS will create default settings in the other columns). The cell will look like this Numeric . Click on ⋯ to activate the dialog box in Figure 3.6. By default, SPSS selects the numeric variable type (⦿ Numeric), and we can change this setting by clicking on ⦿ Date. The dialog box will change to look like the right panel of Figure 3.6. You can then choose your preferred date format; being British, I am used to the days coming before the month and I have stuck with the default option of dd-mmm-yyyy (i.e., 21-Jun-1973), but Americans, for example, will be used to the month and date being the other way around and could select mm/dd/yyyy (06/21/1973). When you have selected a format for your dates, click on OK to return to the variable view. Finally, move to the cell in the column labelled *Label* and type 'Date of Birth'.

Now that the variable has been created, you can return to the data view by clicking on the 'Data View' tab (Data View Variable View) and input the dates of birth. The second column now has the label *Birth_Date*; click on the white cell at the top of this column and type the first value, 03-Jul-1977. To register this value in this cell, move down to the next cell by pressing the ↓ key on the keyboard. Now enter the next date, and so on.

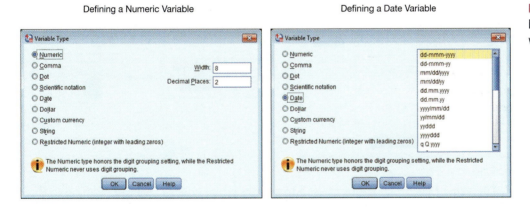

Defining a Numeric Variable   Defining a Date Variable

FIGURE 3.6
Defining a date variable

3.5.2.3. Creating coding variables ①

A coding variable (also known as a grouping variable) uses numbers to represent different groups of data. As such, it is a *numeric variable*, but these numbers represent names (i.e., it is a nominal variable). These groups of data could be levels of a treatment variable in an experiment, different groups of people (men or women, an experimental group or a control group, ethnic groups, etc.), different geographic locations, different organizations, etc. In experiments, coding variables represent independent variables that have been measured between groups (i.e., different entities were assigned to different groups). If you were to run an experiment with one group of entities in an experimental condition and a different group of entities in a control group, you might assign the experimental group a code of 1 and the control group a code of 0. When you come to put the data into the data editor you would create a variable (which you might call **group**) and type in the value 1 for any participants in the experimental group, and 0 for any participants in the control group. These codes tell SPSS that all of the cases that have been assigned the value 1 should be treated as belonging to the same group, and likewise for the cases assigned the value 0. In situations other than experiments, you might use codes to distinguish naturally occurring groups (e.g., you might give students a code of 1 and lecturers a code of 0).

We have a coding variable in our data: the one describing whether a person was a lecturer or student. To create this coding variable, we follow the steps for creating a normal variable, but we also have to tell SPSS which numeric codes have been assigned to which groups. So, first of all, return to the variable view (Data View | Variable View) if you're not already in it and then move to the cell in the third row of the data editor and in the column labelled *Name* type a name (let's call it **Group**). I'm still trying to instil good habits, so move along the third row to the column called *Label* and give the variable a full description such as 'Is the person a lecturer or a student?' Then to define the group codes, move along the row to the column labelled Values and into this cell: None .... Click on ... to access the *Value Labels* dialog box (see Figure 3.7).

FIGURE 3.7
Defining coding
variables and
their values

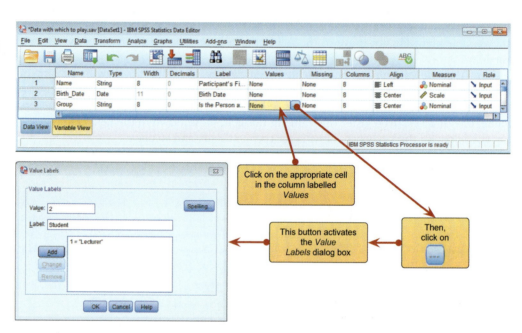

The *Value Labels* dialog box is used to specify group codes. This can be done in three easy steps. First, click in the white space next to where it says *Value* (or press *Alt* and *U* at the same time) and type in a code (e.g., 1). These codes are completely arbitrary; for the sake of convention people typically use 0, 1, 2, 3, etc., but in practice you could have a code of 495 if you were feeling particularly arbitrary. The second step is to click in the white space below, next to where it says *Value Label* (or press *Tab*, or *Alt* and *E* at the same time) and type in an appropriate label for that group. In Figure 3.7 I have already defined a code of 1 for the lecturer group, and then I have typed in 2 as my code and given this a label of *Student*. The third step is to add this coding to the list by clicking on Add . When you have defined all of your coding values you can click on Spelling... and SPSS will check your variable labels for spelling errors (which can be very handy if you are as bad at spelling as I am). To finish, click on OK ; if you click on OK and have forgotten to add your final coding to the list, SPSS will display a message warning you that any 'pending changes will be lost'. In plain English this message tells you to go back and click on Add before continuing. Finally, coding variables always represent categories and so the level at which they are measured is nominal (or ordinal if the categories have a meaningful order). Therefore, you should specify the level at which the variable was measured by going to the column labelled *Measure* and selecting  Nominal (or Ordinal if the groups have a meaningful order) from the drop-down list.

Having defined your codes, switch to the data view and type these numerical values into the appropriate column; so if a person was a lecturer, type 1, but if they were a student then type 2 (see SPSS Tip 3.4). You can get SPSS to display the numeric codes, or the value labels that you assigned to them by clicking on (see Figure 3.9), which is pretty groovy. Figure 3.9 shows how the data should be arranged: remember that each row of the data editor represents data from one entity and in this example our entities were people (arguably in the case of the lecturers). The first five participants were lecturers whereas participants 6–10 were students.

When using a coding variable it is impossible for a participant to belong to more than one category; therefore, in experimental research we use this kind of variable to enter independent variables that have been measured using a between-groups design (i.e.,

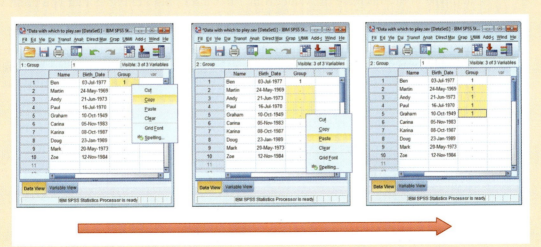

FIGURE 3.8 Copying and pasting into empty cells

FIGURE 3.9
Coding values
in the data
editor with the
value labels
switched off
and on

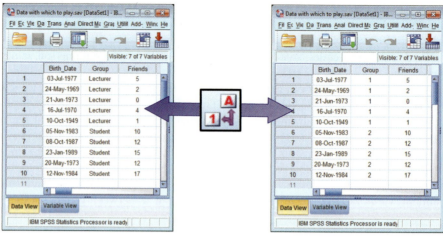

Value Labels On   Value Labels Off

when different entities have been tested in both the experimental and the control group). However, in repeated-measures designs (within subjects) each participant is tested in every condition and so we would not use this sort of coding variable.

3.5.2.4. Creating a numeric variable ①

Numeric variables are the easiest ones to create because SPSS assumes this format for data. Our next variable is **No. of friends**; to create this variable we move back to the variable view using the tab at the bottom of the data editor (Data View Variable View). As with the previous variables, move to the cell in row 4 of the column labelled *Name* (under the previous variable you created). Type the word 'Friends'. Move into the column labelled Type using the → key on the keyboard. As with the previous variables we have created, SPSS has assumed that this is a numeric variable, so the cell will look like this Numeric . We can leave this as it is, because we want to enter a numeric variable.

Notice that our data for the number of friends has no decimal places (unless you are a very strange person indeed, you can't have 0.23 of a friend). Move to the Decimals column and type '0' (or decrease the value from 2 to 0 using ⬍) to tell SPSS that you don't want any decimal places.

Next, let's continue our good habit of naming variables and move to the cell in the column labelled *Label* and type 'Number of Friends'. Finally, we can specify the level at which a variable was measured (see Section 1.5.1.2) by going to the column labelled *Measure* and selecting ⚖ Scale from the drop-down list (this will have been done automatically actually, but it's worth checking).

SELF-TEST   Why is the 'Number of Friends' variable a scale variable?

Once the variable has been created, you can return to the data view by clicking on the 'Data View' tab at the bottom of the data editor (Data View Variable View). The contents of the window will change, and you'll notice that the fourth column now has the label *Friends*. To enter the data, click on the white cell at the top of the column labelled *Friends* and type the first value, 5. To register this value in this cell, we have to move to a different cell; and because we are entering data down a column, the most sensible way to do this is to press the ↓ key on the keyboard. This action moves you down to the next cell, and the number 5 should appear in the cell above. Enter the next number, 2, and then press ↓ to move down to the next cell, and so on.

SELF-TEST Having created the first four variables with a bit of guidance, try to enter the rest of the variables in Table 3.1 yourself.

3.5.3. Missing values ①

Although as researchers we strive to collect complete sets of data, it is often the case that we have missing data. Missing data can occur for a variety of reasons: in long

LABCOAT LENI'S REAL RESEARCH 3.1

Gonna be a rock 'n' roll singer ①

AC/DC are one one of the best-selling hard rock bands in history with around 100 million certified sales, and an estimated 200 million actual sales. In 1980 their original singer Bon Scott died of alcohol poisoning and choking on his own vomit. He was replaced by Brian Johnson, who has been their singer ever since. Debate rages with unerring frequency within the rock music press over who is the better frontman. The conventional wisdom seems to be that Bon Scott was better, although personally, and I seem to be somewhat in the minority here, I prefer Brian Johnson. Anyway, Robert Oxoby, in a playful paper, decided to put this argument to bed once and for all (Oxoby, 2008).

Using a task from experimental economics called the ultimatum game, individuals are assigned the role of either proposer or responder and paired randomly. Proposers were allocated $10 from which they had to make a financial offer to the responder (i.e., $2). The responder can accept or reject this offer. If the offer is rejected neither party gets any money, but if the offer is accepted the

responder keeps the offered amount (e.g., $2), and the proposer keeps the original amount minus what they offered (e.g., $8). For half of the participants the song 'It's a long way to the top' sung by Bon Scott was playing in the background; for the remainder 'Shoot to thrill' sung by Brian Johnson was playing. Oxoby measured the offers made by proposers, and the minimum offers accepted by responders (called the minimum acceptable offer). He reasoned that people would accept lower offers and propose higher offers when listening to something they like (because of the 'feel-good factor' the music creates). Therefore, by comparing the value of offers made and the minimum acceptable offers in the two groups he could see whether people have more of a feel-good factor when listening to Bon or Brian. The offers made (in dollars) are[2] as follows (there were 18 people per group):

- Bon Scott group: 1, 2, 2, 2, 2, 3, 3, 3, 3, 3, 4, 4, 4, 4, 4, 5, 5, 5
- Brian Johnson group: 2, 3, 3, 3, 3, 3, 4, 4, 4, 4, 4, 5, 5, 5, 5, 5, 5, 5

Enter these data into the SPSS data editor, remembering to include value labels, to set the measure property, to give each variable a proper label, and to set the appropriate number of decimal places. Answers are on the companion website, and my version of how this file should look can be found in **Oxoby (2008) Offers.sav.**

---

[2] These data are estimated from Figures 1 and 2 in the paper because I couldn't get hold of the author to get the original data files.

questionnaires participants accidentally (or, depending on how paranoid you're feeling, deliberately just to piss you off) miss out questions; in experimental procedures mechanical faults can lead to a datum not being recorded; and in research on delicate topics (e.g., sexual behaviour) participants may exert their right not to answer a question. However, just because we have missed out on some data for a participant, that doesn't mean that we have to ignore the data we do have (although it sometimes creates statistical difficulties). Nevertheless, we do need to tell SPSS that a value is missing for a particular case. The principle behind missing values is quite similar to that of coding variables in that we choose a number to represent the missing data point. This value tells SPSS that there is no recorded value for a participant for a certain variable. The computer then ignores that cell of the data editor (it does not use the value you select in the analysis). You need to be careful that the chosen code doesn't correspond to any naturally occurring data value. For example, if we tell the computer to regard the value 9 as a missing value and several participants genuinely scored 9, then the computer will treat their data as missing when, in reality, they are not.

To specify missing values click in the column labelled Missing in the variable view (Data View Variable View) and then click on ⋯ to activate the *Missing Values* dialog box in Figure 3.10. By default SPSS assumes that no missing values exist, but if you do have data with missing values you can choose to define them in one of three ways. The first is to select discrete values (by clicking on the circle next to where it says *Discrete missing values*) which are single values that represent missing data. SPSS allows you to specify up to three discrete values to represent missing data. The reason why you might choose to have several numbers to represent missing values is that you can assign a different meaning to each discrete value. For example, you could have the number 8 representing a response of 'not applicable', a code of 9 representing a 'don't know' response, and a code of 99 meaning that the participant failed to give any response. As far as the computer is concerned it will ignore any data cell containing these values; however, using different codes may be a useful way to remind you of why a particular score is missing. Usually, one discrete value is enough and in an experiment in which attitudes are measured on a 100-point scale (so scores vary from 1 to 100) you might choose 666 to represent missing values because (1) this value cannot occur in the data that have been collected and (2) missing data create statistical problems, and you will regard the people who haven't given you responses as children of Satan. The second option is to select a range of values to represent missing data and this is useful in situations in which it is necessary to exclude data falling between two points. So, we could exclude all scores between 5 and 10. The final option is to have a range of values and one discrete value.

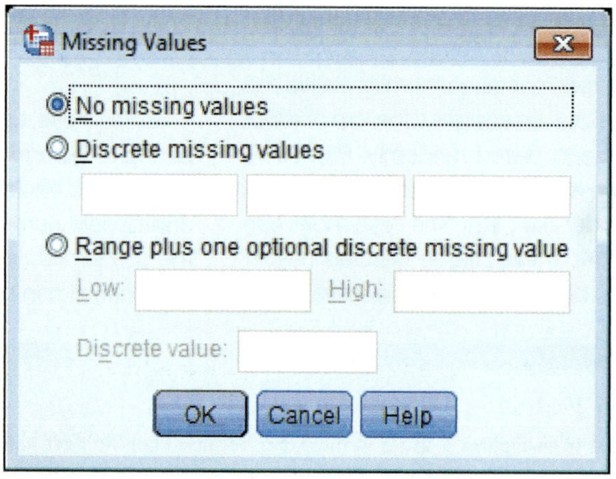

FIGURE 3.10
Defining missing values

ODITI'S LANTERN

Entering data

'I, Oditi, believe that the secrets of life have been hidden in a complex numeric code. Only by "analysing" these sacred numbers can we reach true enlightenment. To crack the code I must assemble thousands of followers to analyse and interpret these numbers (it's a bit like the chimps and typewriters theory). I need you to follow me. To spread the numbers to other followers you must store them in an easily distributable format called a "data file". You, my follower, are loyal and loved, and to assist you my lantern displays a tutorial on how to use it.'

3.6. Importing data ①

We can also import data into SPSS from other software packages such as Microsoft Excel, R, SAS, and Systat. The easiest way is probably to export the data from these packages as a tab-delimited or comma-separated text file (*.txt*, *.dat* or *.csv*) and then use the `File` `Read Text Data...` menu to activate the wizard for importing text data. This process will also read Excel format files (*.xls*) into SPSS.

ODITI'S LANTERN

Editing tables

'I, Oditi, have become aware that some of the sacred numbers that hide the secrets of life are contained within files other than those of my own design. We cannot afford to miss vital clues that lurk among these rogue files. Like all good cults, we must convert all to our cause, even data files. Should you encounter one of these files, you must convert it to the SPSS format. My lantern shows you how.'

3.7. The SPSS viewer ①

Alongside the SPSS data editor window, there is a second window known as the *SPSS viewer*. The SPSS viewer displays all of the output from SPSS: analysis results, graphs, error messages – pretty much everything you could want, except for photos of your cat. Although it is all-singing and all-dancing, sadly my prediction in previous editions of this book that the *SPSS viewer* will one day include a tea-making facility have not come to fruition (IBM take note☺). Figure 3.11 shows the basic layout of the viewer window. On the right-hand side there is a large space in which the output is displayed. SPSS displays both graphs and the results of statistical analyses in this part of the viewer. It is also possible to edit a graph (Section 4.9) or table by double-clicking on it. There is a tree diagram on the left-hand side of the viewer that displays the structure of the output. This tree diagram provides an easy way of accessing specific parts of the output, which is useful when you have conducted several analyses. The tree structure is fairly self-explanatory: every time you do something in SPSS (such as drawing a graph or running a statistical procedure), it lists this procedure as a main heading.

In Figure 3.11 I ran a graphing procedure followed by a univariate analysis of variance (ANOVA) and these names appear as main headings in the tree diagram. For each

FIGURE 3.11
The SPSS
viewer

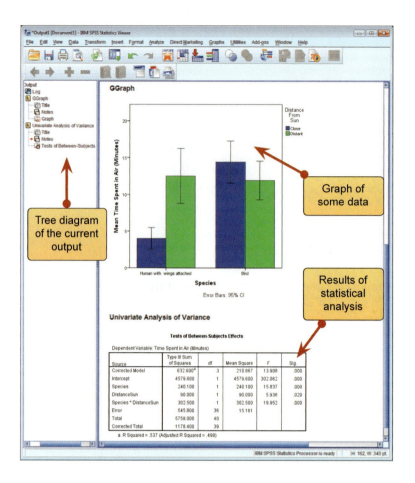

ODITI'S LANTERN

Importing data into SPSS

'I, Oditi, impart to you, my loyal posse, the knowledge that SPSS will conceal the secrets of life within tables of output. Like the author of this book, these tables appear flat and lifeless; however, if you give them a poke they have hidden depths. Often you will need to seek out the hidden codes within the tables. To do this double-click on them. This will reveal the "layers" of the table. Stare into my lantern and find out how.'

procedure there are a series of sub-headings that represent different parts of the analysis. For example, in the ANOVA procedure, which you'll learn more about later in the book, there are several sections to the output such as *Tests of Between-Subjects Effects* (as you will discover, this is the table containing the main results). You can skip to any one of these sub-components of the ANOVA output by clicking on the appropriate branch of the tree diagram. So, if you wanted to skip straight to the between-groups effects you should move the on-screen arrow to the left-hand portion of the window and click where it says *Tests of Between-Subjects Effects*. This action will highlight this part of the output in the main part of the viewer (see SPSS Tip 3.5).

There are several icons in the output viewer window that help you to do things quickly without using the drop-down menus. Some of these icons are the same as those described

SPSS TIP 3.5   **Printing and saving the planet** ①

Rather than printing all of your output on reams of paper, you can help the planet by printing only a selection of the output. You can do this by using the tree diagram in the SPSS viewer to select parts of the output for printing. For example, if you decided that you wanted to print out a graph but you didn't want to print the whole output, you can click on the word *Graph* in the tree structure and that graph will become highlighted in the output. It is then possible through the *Print* dialog box to select to print only the selected part of the output.

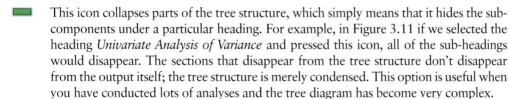

It is worth noting that if you click on a main heading (such as *Univariate Analysis of Variance*) then SPSS will highlight not only that main heading but all of the sub-components as well. This is useful for printing the results of a single statistical procedure.

for the data editor window, so I will concentrate mainly on the icons that are unique to the viewer window:

 When this icon is pressed in the viewer window it activates a dialog box for printing the output (see SPSS Tip 3.5).

 This icon returns you to the data editor. I'm not sure what the big red star is all about.

 This icon takes you to the last output in the viewer (so it returns you to the last procedure you conducted).

 This icon *promotes* the currently active part of the tree structure to a higher branch of the tree. For example, in Figure 3.11 the *Tests of Between-Subjects Effects* are a sub-component under the heading of *Univariate Analysis of Variance*. If we wanted to promote this part of the output to a higher level (i.e., to make it a main heading) then this is done using this icon.

 This icon is the opposite of the above in that it *demotes* parts of the tree structure. For example, in Figure 3.11 if we didn't want the *Univariate Analysis of Variance* to be a unique section we could select this heading and demote it so that it becomes part of the previous heading (the *Graph* heading). This button is useful for combining parts of the output relating to a specific research question.

 This icon collapses parts of the tree structure, which simply means that it hides the sub-components under a particular heading. For example, in Figure 3.11 if we selected the heading *Univariate Analysis of Variance* and pressed this icon, all of the sub-headings would disappear. The sections that disappear from the tree structure don't disappear from the output itself; the tree structure is merely condensed. This option is useful when you have conducted lots of analyses and the tree diagram has become very complex.

This icon expands any collapsed sections. By default all of the main headings are displayed in the tree diagram in their expanded form. If, however, you have opted to collapse part of the tree diagram (using the icon above) then you can use this icon to undo your dirty work.

This icon and the following one allow you to show and hide parts of the output itself. So you can select part of the output in the tree diagram and click on this icon and that part of the output will disappear. It isn't erased, but it is hidden from view. This icon is similar to the collapse icon listed above except that it affects the output rather than the tree structure. This is useful for hiding less relevant parts of the output.

 This icon undoes the previous one, so if you have hidden a selected part of the output from view and you click on this icon, that part of the output will reappear. By default, all parts of the output are shown, so this icon is not active; it will become active only once you have hidden part of the output.

 Although this icon looks like it has a slot in which to insert a CD, unfortunately it does not play music for you; it inserts a new heading into the tree diagram. For example, if you had several statistical tests that related to one of many research questions you could insert a main heading and then demote the headings of the relevant analyses so that they all fall under this new heading.

 Assuming you had done the above, you can use this icon to provide your new heading with a title. The title you type in will actually appear in your output. So, you might have a heading like 'Research question number 1' which tells you that the analyses under this heading relate to your first research question.

 This final icon is used to place a text box in the output window. You can type anything into this box. In the context of the previous two icons, you might use a text box to explain what your first research question is (e.g., 'My first research question is whether or not boredom has set in by the end of the first chapter of my book. The following analyses test the hypothesis that boredom levels will be significantly higher at the end of the first chapter than at the beginning.').

ODITI'S LANTERN

The SPSS viewer window

'I, Oditi, believe that by "analysing" the sacred numbers we can find the answers to life. I have given you the tools to spread these numbers far and wide, but to interpret these numbers we need "the Viewer". This is like an X-ray that reveals what is beneath the raw numbers. Use the Viewer wisely, my loyal friends, because if you stare long enough you will see into your very soul. Stare into my lantern and see a tutorial on the Viewer.'

SPSS TIP 3.6   Funny numbers ①

You might notice that SPSS sometimes reports numbers with the letter 'E' placed in the mix just to confuse you. For example, you might see a value such as 9.612 E−02 and many students find this notation confusing. Well, this notation means 9.61×10^{-2}, which might be a more familiar notation or could be even more confusing. Think of E−02 as meaning 'move the decimal place 2 places to the left', so 9.612 E−02 becomes 0.09612. If the notation reads 9.612 E−01, then that would be 0.9612, and if it reads 9.612 E−03, that would be 0.009612. Likewise, think of E+02 (notice the minus sign has changed) as meaning 'move the decimal place 2 places to the right'. So 9.612 E+02 becomes 961.2.

3.8. Exporting SPSS output ①

If you want to share your SPSS output with other people who don't have SPSS Statistics installed you have two choices: (1) export the output into a software package that they do have (such as Microsoft Word) or in the Portable Document Format (PDF) that can be read by free software such as Adobe's Acrobat Reader; (2) get them to install the IBM SPSS **Smartreader**, which is free from the IBM SPSS website. The SPSS Smartreader is basically a free version of the viewer window that enables people to look at SPSS output.

ODITI'S LANTERN

Exporting SPSS output

'In order that I, the almighty Oditi, can discover the secrets within the numbers, my followers must spread these numbers around the world. But some of the non-believers do not have SPSS, therefore we must send them a link to the Smartreader. I have also given to you, my loyal brethren, a tutorial on how to export SPSS output into word. These are the tools you will need to spread the word. Go forth and stare into my lantern.'

3.9. The syntax editor ③

I mentioned earlier that sometimes it's useful to use SPSS syntax. Syntax is a language of commands for carrying out statistical analyses and data manipulations. Most of the time you'll do the things you need to use using SPSS dialog boxes, but SPSS syntax can be useful. For one thing, there are certain things you can do with syntax that you can't do through dialog boxes (admittedly most of these things are fairly advanced, but there will be a few places in this book where I show you some nice tricks using syntax). The second reason for using syntax is if you often carry out very similar analyses on data sets. In these situations it is often quicker to do the analysis and save the syntax as you go along. Fortunately this is easily done because many dialog boxes in SPSS have a Paste button. When you've specified your analysis using the dialog box, if you click on this button it will paste the syntax into a syntax editor window for you. To open a syntax editor window simply use the menus File New ▶ Syntax and a blank syntax editor will appear as in Figure 3.12. In this window you can type your syntax commands into the command area. Like grammatical rules when we write, there are a set of rules that need to be followed so that SPSS 'understands' the syntax. For example, one rule is that each line has to end with a full stop. If you make a syntax error (i.e., break one of the rules), SPSS produces an error message in the viewer window. The messages themselves are often indecipherable until you get some experience of translating them, but they do helpfully identify the line in the syntax window in which the error occurred. Notice that in the syntax window each line is numbered so that you can easily find the line in which the error occurred. As we go through the book I'll show you a few things that will give you a flavour of how syntax can be used. Most of you won't have to use it, but for those that do this flavour will hopefully be enough to start you on your way.

The syntax window has a navigation area (rather like the viewer window). When you have a large file of syntax commands this navigation area can be helpful for negotiating your way to the bit of syntax that you actually need. Once you've typed in your syntax you have to run it using the Run menu. Run All will run all of the syntax in the window, or you can highlight a selection of your syntax using the mouse and use Run ▶ Selection to process the selected syntax (clicking on ▶ will also do this). You can also run the syntax a command

FIGURE 3.12
A new syntax window (top) and a syntax window with some syntax in it (bottom)

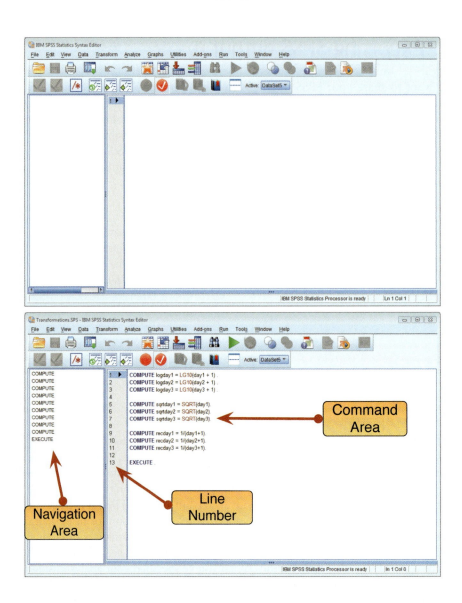

at a time from either the current command (Run Step Through ▸ From Current), or the beginning (Run Step Through ▸ From Start). You can also run all the syntax from the cursor to the end of the syntax window (Run ➞I To End). Another thing to note is that in SPSS you can have several data files open at once. Rather than have a syntax window for each data file, which could get confusing, you can use the same syntax window, but select the data set that you want to run the syntax commands on before you run them using the drop-down list DataSet1 ▾.

ODITI'S LANTERN
Sin-tax

'I, Oditi, leader of the cult of undiscovered numerical truths, require my brethren to focus only on the discovery of those truths. To focus their minds I shall impose a tax on sinful acts. Sinful acts (such as dichotomizing a continuous variable) can distract from the pursuit of truth. To implement this tax, followers will need to use the sin-tax window. Stare into my lantern to see a tutorial on how to use it.'

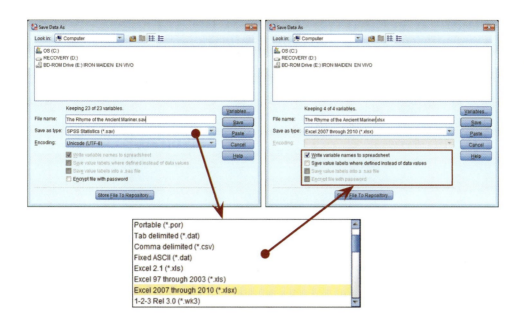

FIGURE 3.13
The *Save Data As* dialog box

3.10. Saving files ①

Most of you should be familiar with how to save files. Like most software, you can use the 💾 icon (or use the menus File 💾 Save or File Save As...). If the file is a new file, then clicking on this icon will activate the *Save As...* dialog box (see Figure 3.13). If you are in the data editor when you select *Save As* ... then SPSS will save the data file you are currently working on, but if you are in the viewer window then it will save the current output. As with any file, you need to select a location at which to store the file: your hard drive (💾), a CD, DVD, or Blu-ray disk (💿), a USB stick (▬) or other external drive (🖥). Once you have chosen a main location, the dialog box will display all of the available folders on that particular device. Once you have selected a folder in which to save your file, type a name in the space next to where it says *File name*. If you have sensitive data then you can password encrypt it by selecting ☑ Encrypt file with password. By default, the file will be saved in an SPSS format, so if it is a data file the file extension will be *.sav*, if it is a viewer document it will be *.spv*, and if it is a syntax files it will be *.sps*. Once a file has previously been saved, it can be saved again (updated) by clicking on 💾. This icon appears in both the data editor and the viewer, and the file saved depends on the window that is currently active. The file will be saved in the location at which it is currently stored.

You can save data in formats other than SPSS. Three of the most useful are Microsoft Excel files (*.xls*, *.xlsx*), comma-separated values (*.csv*) and tab-delimited text (*.dat*). The latter two file types are basically just text files, which means that they can be opened by virtually any spreadsheet software you can think of (including Excel, OpenOffice, Numbers, R, SAS, and Systat). To save your data file in a different format, click on SPSS Statistics (*.sav) ▼ and select one from the drop down list (Figure 3.13). You'll notice that if you select a format other than SPSS, the ☐ Save value labels where defined instead of data values option becomes active. If you leave this option unselected then any coding variables (Section 3.5.2.3) will be exported as the number entered for each group, but if you select it then the value labels will be exported as text strings.

3.11. Retrieving a file ①

Throughout this book you will work with data files that you need to download from the companion website. To load files into SPSS use the 📂 icon or select File Open ▶

FIGURE 3.14
Dialog box to
open a file

and then 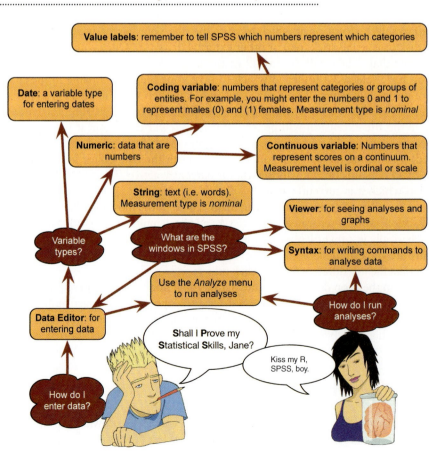 Data... to open a data file, Output... to open a viewer file, or Syntax to open a syntax file. This process opens the standard dialog box in Figure 3.14. I'm sure you have used this kind of dialog box many times before: navigate to wherever you saved the files and open it either by selecting it with the mouse and then clicking on Open, or by double-clicking on the icon next to the file you want (e.g., double-clicking on 🔴). The data/output/syntax will then appear in the appropriate window. If you are in the data editor and you want to open a viewer file, then click on SPSS Statistics (*.sav) ▼ and a list of alternative file formats will be displayed. Click on the appropriate file type (viewer document (*.*spv*), syntax file (*.*sps*), Microsoft Excel file (*.*xls*), text file (*.*dat*, *.*txt*)) and any files of that type will be displayed for you to open.

3.12. Brian's attempt to woo Jane ①

FIGURE 3.15
What Brian learnt
from this chapter

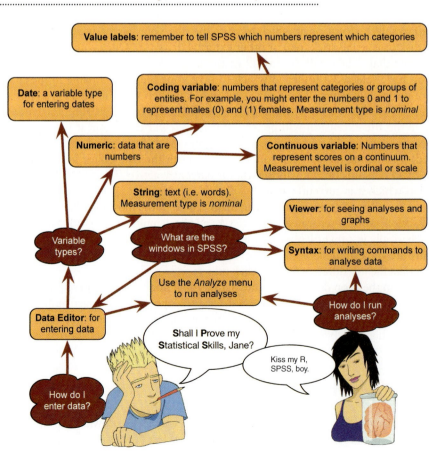

3.13. What next? ①

We discovered that I was scared of my new school. This fear was quite rationale because at the time I grew up in England some idiot politician had decided that all school children had to drink a small bottle of milk at the start of the day. To be fair the government supplied the milk, I think, for free. However, most free things come at a price. The milk was usually delivered early in the morning and then left in the hottest place someone could find until we children arrived hopping and skipping into the playground. Upon arriving at school we were given one of these bottles and very small straw and were forced to drink. The straw was a blessing really because it filtered out the lumps that had inevitably formed in the gently curdling milk. Politicians take note: if you want children to enjoy school, don't force-feed them warm, lumpy milk. Despite gagging on warm milk every morning, primary school was a very happy time indeed. With the help of Jonathan Land my confidence grew. With this new confidence I began to feel comfortable not just at school but in the world at large. It was time to explore.

3.14. Key terms that I've discovered

Currency variable	Numeric variable	Syntax editor
Data editor	Smartreader	Variable view
Data view	String variable	Viewer
Date variable		

3.15. Smart Alex's tasks

- **Task 1**: Smart Alex's first task for this chapter is to save the data that you've entered in this chapter. Save it somewhere on the hard drive of your computer (or a USB stick if you're not working on your own computer). Give it a sensible title and save it somewhere easy to find (perhaps create a folder called 'My Data Files' where you can save all of your files when working through this book). ①

- **Task 2**: The data below show the score (out of 20) for 20 different students, some of whom are male and some female, and some of whom were taught using positive reinforcement (being nice) and others who were taught using punishment (electric shock). Enter these data into SPSS and save the file as **Method Of Teaching.sav**. (Clue: the data should not be entered in the same way that they are laid out below.) ①

Male		Female	
Electric Shock	Being Nice	Electric Shock	Being Nice
15	10	6	12
14	9	7	10
20	8	5	7
13	8	4	8
13	7	8	13

- **Task 3**: Thinking back to Labcoat Leni's Real Research 3.1, Oxoby also measured the minimum acceptable offer; these MAOs (in dollars) are below (again, these are approximations based on the graphs in the paper). Enter these data into the SPSS data editor and save this file as **Oxoby (2008) MAO.sav**. ①

  - Bon Scott group: 2, 3, 3, 3, 3, 4, 4, 4, 4, 4, 4, 4, 4, 5, 5, 5, 5, 5

  - Brian Johnson group: 0, 1, 2, 2, 3, 3, 3, 3, 3, 4, 4, 4, 4, 4, 4, 4, 4, 1

- **Task 4**: According to some highly unscientific research done by a UK department store chain and reported in *Marie Claire* magazine (http://ow.ly/9Dxvy) shopping is good for you: they found that the average woman spends 150 minutes and walks 2.6 miles when she shops, burning off around 385 calories. In contrast, men spend only about 50 minutes shopping, covering 1.5 miles. This was based on strapping a pedometer on a mere 10 participants. Although I don't have the actual data, some simulated data based on these means are below. Enter these data into SPSS and save them as **Shopping Exercise.sav**. ①

Male		Female	
Distance	**Time**	**Distance**	**Time**
15	0.16	1.40	22
30	0.40	1.81	140
37	1.36	1.96	160
65	1.99	3.02	183
103	3.61	4.82	245

- **Task 5**: I was taken by two new stories. The first was about a Sudanese man who was forced to marry a goat after being caught having sex with it (http://ow.ly/9DyyP). I'm not sure he treated the goat to a nice dinner in a posh restaurant before taking advantage of her, but either way you have to feel sorry for the goat. I'd barely had time to recover from that story when another appeared about an Indian man forced

Goat		Dog	
Animal Liking	**Life Satisfaction**	**Animal Liking**	**Life Satisfaction**
69	47	16	52
25	6	65	66
31	47	39	65
29	33	35	61
12	13	19	60
49	56	53	68
25	42	27	37
35	51	44	72
51	42		
40	46		
23	27		
37	48		

to marry a dog to atone for stoning two dogs and stringing them up in a tree 15 years earlier (http://ow.ly/9DyFn). Why anyone would think it's a good idea to enter a dog into matrimony with a man with a history of violent behaviour towards dogs is beyond me. Still, I wondered whether a goat or dog made a better spouse. I found some other people who had been forced to marry goats and dogs and measured their life satisfaction and how much they like animals. Enter these data into SPSS and save as **Goat or Dog.sav**. ①

- **Task 6**: One of my favourite activities, especially when trying to do brain-melting things like writing statistics books, is drinking tea. I am English, after all. Fortunately, tea improves your cognitive function, well, in old Chinese people at any rate (Feng, Gwee, Kua, & Ng, 2010). I may not be Chinese and I'm not *that* old, but I nevertheless enjoy the idea that tea might help me think. Here's some data based on Feng et al.'s study that measured the number of cups of tea drunk and cognitive functioning in 15 people. Enter these data into SPSS and save the file as **Tea Makes You Brainy 15.sav**. ①

Cups of Tea	Cognitive Functioning
2	60
4	47
3	31
4	62
2	44
3	41
5	49
5	56
2	45
5	56
1	57
3	40
3	54
4	34
1	46

- **Task 7**: Men get homicidal and suicidal in response to infidelity, whereas women feel undesirable and insecure (Shackelford, LeBlanc, & Drass, 2000). Let's imagine we did some similar research: we took some men and women and got their partners to tell them they had slept with someone else. We then took each person to two shooting galleries and each time gave them a gun and 100 bullets. In one gallery was a human-shaped target with a picture of their own face on it, and in the other was a target with their partner's face on it. They were left alone with each target for 5 minutes and the number of bullets used was measured. The data are below; enter them into SPSS and save them as **Infidelity.sav** (clue: they are not entered in the format in the table). ①

Male		Female	
Partner's Face	Own Face	Partner's Face	Own Face
69	33	70	97
76	26	74	80
70	10	64	88
76	51	43	100
72	34	51	100
65	28	93	58
82	27	48	95
71	9	51	83
71	33	74	97
75	11	73	89
52	14	41	69
34	46	84	82

Answers can be found on the companion website.

3.16. Further reading

There are many good introductory SPSS books on the market that go through similar material to this chapter. Pallant's *SPSS survival manual* and Kinnear and Gray's *SPSS XX made simple* (insert a version number where I've typed XX, because they update it regularly) are both excellent guides for people new to SPSS. There are many others on the market as well, so have a hunt around.

Exploring data with graphs

4

4.1. What will this chapter tell me? ①

As I got a bit older I used to love exploring. At school they would teach you about maps and how important it was to know where you were going and what you were doing. I used to have a more relaxed view of exploration and there is a little bit of a theme of me wandering off to whatever looked most exciting at the time. I got lost at a holiday camp once when I was about 3 or 4. I remember nothing about this, but apparently my parents were frantically running around trying to find me while I was happily entertaining myself (probably by throwing myself head first out of a tree or something). My older brother, who was supposed to be watching me, got a bit of flak for that, but he was probably working out equations to bend time and space at the time. He did that a lot when he was 7. The careless explorer in me hasn't really gone away: in new cities I tend to just wander off and hope for the best, usually get lost and so far haven't managed to die (although I tested my luck once by wandering through part of New Orleans where apparently tourists get mugged a lot – it seemed fine to me). When exploring data you can't afford not to have a map; to explore data in the way that the 6-year-old me used to explore the world is to spin around 8000 times while drunk and then run along the edge of a cliff. Wright (2003) quotes Rosenthal, who said that researchers should 'make friends with their data'. This wasn't meant to imply that people who use statistics may as well befriend their data because the data are the only friend they'll have; instead Rosenthal meant that researchers often rush their analysis. Wright makes the analogy of a fine wine: you should savour the bouquet and delicate flavours to truly enjoy the experience. That's perhaps overstating the joys of data analysis, but rushing your analysis is, I suppose, a bit like gulping down a bottle of wine: the outcome is messy and incoherent. To negotiate your way around your data you need a map. Maps of data are called graphs, and it is into this tranquil and tropical ocean that we now dive (with a compass and ample supply of oxygen, obviously).

4.2. The art of presenting data ①

4.2.1. What makes a good graph? ①

I want to begin by talking about some general issues when presenting data. SPSS and other packages make it very easy to produce snazzy-looking graphs (see Section 4.9), and you may find yourself losing consciousness at the excitement of colouring your graph bright pink (really, it's amazing how excited my psychology students get at the prospect of bright pink graphs – personally I'm not a fan of pink). Much as pink graphs might send a twinge of delight down your spine, I want to urge you to remember why you're drawing the graph – it's not to make yourself (or others) purr with delight at the pinkness of your graph; it's to present information (dull, perhaps, but true).

Tufte (2001) wrote an excellent book about how data should be presented. He points out that graphs should do the following, among other things:

- ✓ Show the data.

- ✓ Induce the reader to think about the data being presented (rather than some other aspect of the graph, like how pink it is).

- ✓ Avoid distorting the data.

- ✓ Present many numbers with minimum ink.

- ✓ Make large data sets (assuming you have one) coherent.

- ✓ Encourage the reader to compare different pieces of data.

- ✓ Reveal the underlying message of the data.

However, graphs often don't do these things (see Wainer, 1984, for some examples). Let's look at an example of a bad graph. When searching around for the worst example of a graph that I have ever seen, it turned out that I didn't need to look any further than myself – it's in the first edition of this book (Field, 2000). Overexcited by SPSS's ability to add pointless fluff to graphs (like 3-D effects, fill effects and so on – Tufte calls these **chartjunk**), I literally went into some weird orgasmic state and produced an absolute abomination (I'm surprised Tufte didn't kill himself just so he could turn in his grave at the sight of it). The only

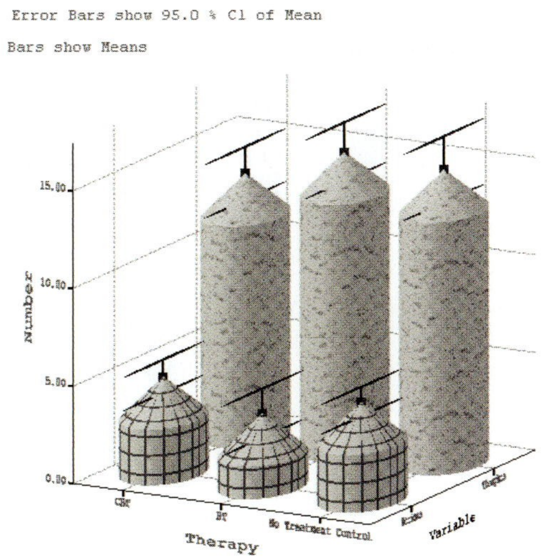

FIGURE 4.2
A cringingly
bad example of
a graph from
the first edition
of this book

consolation was that because the book was published in black and white, it's not bloody pink! The graph is reproduced in Figure 4.2. What's wrong with this graph?

- ✖ The bars have a 3-D effect: Never use 3-D plots for a graph plotting two variables because it obscures the data.[1] In particular, 3-D effects make it hard to see the values of the bars: in Figure 4.2, for example, the 3-D effect makes the error bars almost impossible to read.

- ✖ Patterns: The bars also have patterns, which, although very pretty, distract the eye from what matters (namely the data). These are completely unnecessary.

- ✖ Cylindrical bars: Were my data so sewage-like that I wanted to put them in silos? The cylinder effect muddies the data and distracts the eye from what is important.

- ✖ Badly labelled y-axis: 'Number' of what? Delusions? Fish? Cabbage-eating sea lizards from the eighth dimension? Idiots who don't know how to draw graphs?

Now, take a look at the alternative version of this graph (Figure 4.3). Can you see what improvements have been made?

- ✓ A 2-D plot: The completely unnecessary third dimension is gone, making it much easier to compare the values across therapies and thoughts/behaviours.

- ✓ The y-axis has a more informative label: We now know that it was the number of obsessive thoughts or actions per day that was being measured.

- ✓ Distractions: There are fewer distractions like patterns, cylindrical bars and the like.

- ✓ Minimum ink: I've got rid of superfluous ink by getting rid of the axis lines and by using lines on the bars rather than grid lines to indicate values on the y-axis. Tufte would be pleased.

4.2.2. Lies, damned lies, and … erm … graphs ①

Governments lie with statistics, but scientists shouldn't. How you present your data makes a huge difference to the message conveyed to the audience. As a big fan of cheese, I'm often

---

[1] If you do 3-D plots when you're plotting only two variables then a bearded statistician will come to your house, lock you in a room and make you write I μυστ νοτ δο 3–Δ γραπησ 75,172 times on the blackboard. Really, they will.

FIGURE 4.3
Figure 4.2
drawn properly

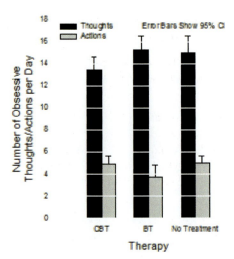

curious about whether the urban myth that it gives you nightmares is true. Shee (1964) reported the case of a man who had nightmares about his workmates: 'He dreamt of one, terribly mutilated, hanging from a meat-hook.[2] Another he dreamt of falling into a bottomless abyss. When cheese was withdrawn from his diet the nightmares ceased.' This would not be good news if you were the minister for cheese in your country.

Figure 4.4 shows two graphs that, believe it or not, display exactly the same data: the number of nightmares had after eating cheese. The first panel shows how the graph should probably be scaled. The y-axis reflects the maximum of the scale, and this creates the correct impression: that people have more nightmares about colleagues hanging from meat-hooks if they eat cheese before bed. However, as minister for cheese, you want people to think the opposite; all you have to do is rescale the graph (by extending the y-axis way beyond the average number of nightmares) and there suddenly seems to be a little difference. Tempting as it is, don't do this (unless, of course, you plan to be a politician at some point in your life).

FIGURE 4.4
Two graphs
about cheese

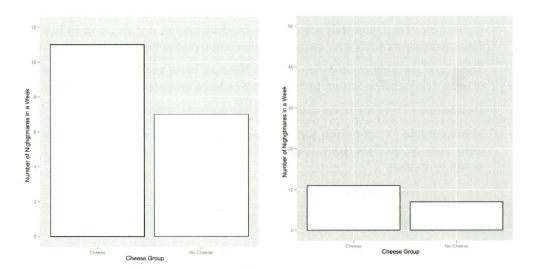

[2] I have similar dreams, but that has more to do with some of my workmates than with cheese.

CRAMMING SAM'S TIPS   Graphs

- The vertical axis of a graph is known as the *y*-axis (or ordinate) of the graph.
- The horizontal axis of a graph is known as the *x*-axis (or abscissa) of the graph.

If you want to draw a good graph follow the cult of Tufte:

✓ Don't create false impressions of what the data actually show (likewise, don't hide effects) by scaling the *y*-axis in some weird way.

✓ Abolish chartjunk: Don't use patterns, 3-D effects, shadows, pictures of spleens, photos of your Uncle Fred or anything else.

✓ Avoid excess ink: This is a bit radical, but if you don't need the axes, then get rid of them.

4.3. The SPSS chart builder ①

You are probably drooling like a rabid dog to get into the statistics and to discover the answer to your really interesting research question, so aren't graphs just a waste of your precious time? Data analysis is a bit like Internet dating (actually it's not, but bear with me). You can scan through the vital statistics and find a perfect match (good IQ, tall, physically fit, likes arty French films, etc.) and you'll think you have found the perfect answer to your question. However, if you haven't seen a picture, then you don't really know how to interpret this information – your perfect match might turn out to be Rimibald the Poisonous, King of the Colorado River Toads, who has genetically combined himself with a human to further his plan to start up a lucrative rodent farm (they like to eat small rodents).[3] Data analysis is much the same: inspect your data with a picture, see how it looks and only then can you interpret the more vital statistics.

Although SPSS's graphing facilities are quite versatile (you can edit most things – see Section 4.9), they are still quite limited for repeated-measures data (for this reason some of the graphs in this book are done using a package called ggplot2 for the software R – in case you're wondering why you can't replicate them in SPSS). To draw graphs in SPSS we use the all-singing and all-dancing **Chart Builder**.[4]

Figure 4.5 shows the basic *Chart Builder* dialog box, which is accessed through the Graphs 🔳 Chart Builder... menu. There are some important parts of this dialog box:

- *Gallery*: For each type of graph, a gallery of possible variants is shown. Double-click on an icon to select a particular type of graph.

- *Variable list*: The variables in the data editor are listed here. These can be dragged into *drop zones* to specify what is shown in a given graph.

---

[3] On the plus side, he would have a long sticky tongue and if you smoke his venom (which, incidentally, can kill a dog) you'll hallucinate (if you're lucky, you'd hallucinate that he wasn't a Colorado river toad–human hybrid).

[4] Unfortunately it's dancing like an academic at a conference disco and singing 'I will always love you' in the wrong key after 34 pints of beer.

FIGURE 4.5
The SPSS
Chart Builder

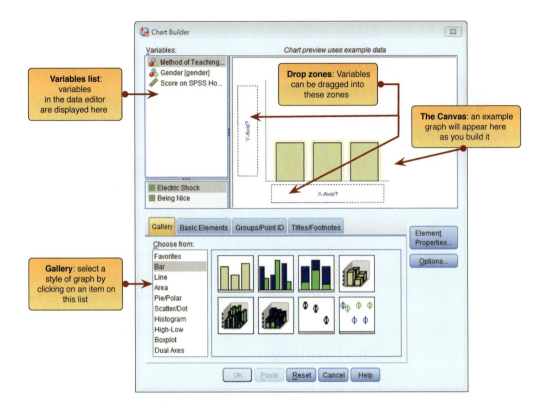

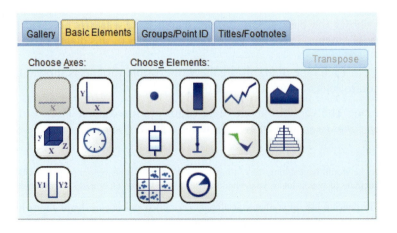

- *The canvas*: This is the main area in the dialog box and is where a preview of the graph is displayed as you build it.

- *Drop zones*: These zones are designated with blue dotted lines. You can drag variables from the variable list into these zones.

There are two ways to build a graph: the first is by using the gallery of predefined graphs, and the second is by building a graph on an element-by-element basis. The gallery is the default option and this tab (Gallery Basic Elements Groups/Point ID Titles/Footnotes) is automatically selected; however, if you want to build your graph from basic elements then click on the *Basic Elements* tab (Gallery Basic Elements Groups/Point ID Titles/Footnotes). This changes the bottom of the dialog box in Figure 4.5 to look like Figure 4.6.

FIGURE 4.6
Building a
graph from
basic elements

SPSS TIP 4.1   Strange dialog boxes ①

When you first use the chart builder to draw a graph you will see a dialog box that seems to signal an impending apocalypse. In fact, SPSS is just helpfully(?!) reminding you that for the Chart Builder to work, you need to have set the level of measurement correctly for each variable. That is, when you defined each variable you must have set them correctly to be scale, ordinal or nominal (see Section 3.5.2). This is because SPSS needs to know whether variables are categorical (nominal) or continuous (scale) when it creates the graphs. If you 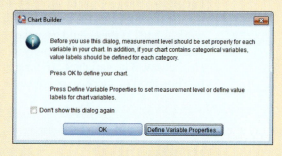 have been diligent and set these properties when you entered the data then click on OK to make the dialog disappear. If you forgot to set the level of measurement for any variables then click on Define Variable Properties to go to a new dialog box in which you can change the properties of the variables in the data editor.

We will have a look at building various graphs throughout this chapter rather than trying to explain everything in this introductory section (see also SPSS Tip 4.1). Most graphs that you are likely to need can be obtained using the gallery view, so I will tend to stick with this method.

4.4. Histograms ①

We encountered histograms (frequency distributions) in Chapter 1; they're a useful way to look at the shape of your data and also for spotting problems (more on that in the next chapter). We will now learn how to create one in SPSS. My wife and I spent our honeymoon at Disney World in Orlando, Florida.[5] It was two of the best weeks of my life and, although some people find the Disney experience a bit nauseating, we loved it. There is absolutely nothing wrong with spending two weeks around people who constantly congratulate you on your marriage, and are nice to you. The world could do with more 'nice' in it. The one exception to my tolerance of Disney was their obsession with dreams coming true and wishing on stars. Don't misunderstand me, I love the idea of having dreams (I haven't yet given up the idea that one day Steve Harris from Iron Maiden might call requiring my drumming services for their next world tour; nor have I stopped thinking, despite all of the physical evidence to the contrary, that I could step in and help out my favourite soccer team at their time of need). Dreams are good, but a completely blinkered view that they'll come true without any work on your part is less healthy. My chances of playing drums for Iron Maiden will be greatly enhanced by me practising, forging some kind of name for myself as a professional drummer, and incapacitating their current drummer (sorry, Nicko). I think it highly unlikely that merely 'wishing on a star' will make my dream come true. I wonder if the seismic increase in youth internalizing disorders is (Twenge, 2000), in part, caused

---

[5] Although not necessarily representative of our Disney experience, I have put a video of a bat fellating itself at the Animal Kingdom on my YouTube channel. It won't help you to learn statistics.

by millions of Disney children reaching the rather depressing realization that wishing on a star didn't work.

Sorry, I started that paragraph in the happy glow of honeymoon memories but somewhere in the middle turned into a misery guts. Anyway, I collected some data from 250 people on their level of success using a composite measure involving their salary, quality of life and how closely their life matches their aspirations. This gave me a score from 0 (complete failure) to 100 (complete success). I then implemented an intervention: I told people that for the next 5 years they should either wish upon a star for their dreams to come true or work as hard as they could to make their dreams come true. I measured their success again 5 years later. People were randomly allocated to these two instructions. The data are in **Jiminy Cricket.sav**. The variables are **Strategy** (hard work or wishing on a star), **Success_Pre** (their baseline level of success) and **Success_Post** (their level of success after 5 years).

SELF-TEST   What does a histogram show?

First, access the chart builder as in Figure 4.5 and then select *Histogram* in the list labelled *Choose from* to bring up the gallery shown in Figure 4.7. This gallery has four icons representing different types of histogram, and you should select the appropriate one either by double-clicking on it, or by dragging it onto the canvas in the chart builder:

⇒ *Simple histogram*: Use this option when you just want to see the frequencies of scores for a single variable.

⇒ *Stacked histogram*: If you had a grouping variable (e.g., whether people worked hard or wished upon a star) you could produce a histogram in which each bar is split by group. In this example, each bar would have two colours, one representing people who worked hard and the other people who wished upon a star. This is a good way to compare the relative frequency of scores across groups (e.g., were those who worked hard more successful than those who wished upon a star?).

⇒ *Frequency polygon*: This option displays the same data as the simple histogram, except that it uses a line instead of bars to show the frequency, and the area below the line is shaded.

⇒ *Population pyramid*: Like a stacked histogram, this shows the relative frequency of scores in two populations. It plots the variable (e.g., success after 5 years) on the vertical axis and the frequencies for each population on the horizontal: the populations appear back to back on the graph. If the bars either side of the dividing line are equally long then the distributions have equal frequencies.

We are going to do a simple histogram first, so double-click on the icon for a simple histogram (Figure 4.7). The *Chart Builder* dialog box will show a preview of the graph in the canvas area. At the moment it's not very exciting (top of Figure 4.8) because we haven't told SPSS which variables we want to plot. Note that the variables in the data editor are listed on the left-hand side of the chart builder, and any of these variables can be dragged into any of the spaces surrounded by blue dotted lines (called *drop zones*).

A histogram plots a single variable (*x*-axis) against the frequency of scores (*y*-axis), so all we need to do is select a variable from the list and drag it into ⌞ X-Axis? ⌟. Let's do this for the post-intervention success scores. Click on this variable (**Success_Post**) in the list and

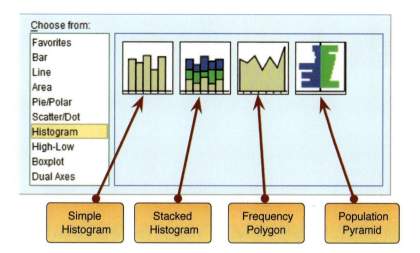

FIGURE 4.7
The histogram gallery

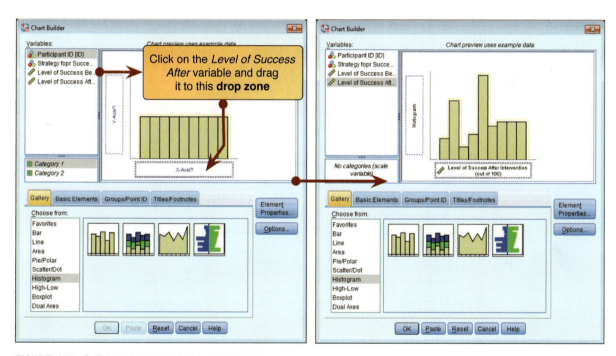

FIGURE 4.8   Defining a histogram in the chart builder

drag it to [X-Axis?] as shown in Figure 4.8; you will now find the histogram previewed on the canvas. (Although SPSS calls the resulting graph a preview, it's not really because it does not use your data to generate this image – it is a preview only of the general form of the graph, and not what your specific graph will actually look like.) To draw the histogram click on [OK] (see also SPSS Tip 4.2).

The resulting histogram is shown in Figure 4.10. You can see that the distribution is quite lumpy: although there is a peak of scores around 50 (the mid-point of the scale), there are quite a few scores at the high end, and fewer at the low end. This creates the impression of negative skew, but it's not quite as simple as that. To help us to dig a bit deeper it might be helpful to plot the histogram separately for those who wished upon a star and those who worked hard: after all, if the intervention was a success then their distributions should be from different populations.

SPSS TIP 4.2   Further histogram options ①

You might notice another dialog box floating about making a nuisance of itself (if not, then consider yourself lucky, or click on Element Properties). This dialog box allows you to edit various features of a histogram (Figure 4.9). For example, you can change the statistic displayed: the default is *Histogram*, but if you wanted to express values as a percentage rather than a frequency, you could select *Histogram Percent*. You can also decide manually how you want to divide up your data to compute frequencies.

If you click on Set Parameters... then another dialog box appears (Figure 4.9), in which you can determine properties of the 'bins' used to make the histogram. You can think of a bin as, well, a rubbish bin (this is a pleasing analogy, as you will see): on each rubbish bin you write a score (e.g., 3), or a range of scores (e.g., 1–3), then you go through each score in your data set and throw it into the rubbish bin with the appropriate label on it (so a score of 2 gets thrown into the bin labelled 1–3). When you have finished throwing your data into these rubbish bins, you count how many scores are in each bin. A histogram is created in much the same way; either SPSS can decide how the bins are labelled (the default) or you can decide. Our success scores range from 0 to 100, therefore we might decide that our bins should begin with 0 and we could set the ⦿ Custom value for anchor: property to 0. We might also decide that we want each bin to contain scores between whole numbers (i.e., 0–1, 1–2, 2–3, etc.), in which case we could set the ⦿ Interval width: to be 1. This what I've done in Figure 4.9, but for the time being leave the default settings (i.e., everything set to ⦿ Automatic).

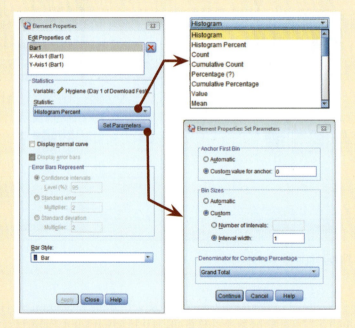

FIGURE 4.9   Element properties of a histogram

To compare frequency distributions of several groups simultaneously, we can use a population pyramid. Click on the population pyramid icon (Figure 4.7) to display the template for this graph on the canvas. Then from the variable list select the variable representing the success scores after the intervention and drag it into Distribution Variable? to set it as the variable that you want to plot. Then select the variable **Strategy** and drag it to Split Variable? to set it as the variable for which you want to plot different distributions. The dialog should now look

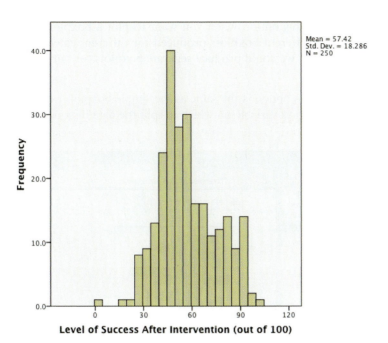

FIGURE 4.10
Histogram of
the post-
intervention
success scores

like Figure 4.11 – the variable names are displayed in the drop zones, and the canvas now displays a preview of our graph (e.g., there are two histograms representing each strategy for success). Click on OK to produce the graph.

The resulting population pyramid (Figure 4.12) shows that for those who wished upon a star there is a fairly normal distribution centred at about the mid-point of the success scale (50%). A small minority manage to become successful just by wishing, but most just end up sort of averagely successful. Those who work hard show a skewed distribution, where a large proportion of people (relative to those wishing) become very successful, and fewer people are around or below the mid-point of the success scale. Hopefully, this example shows how a population pyramid can be a very good way to visualize differences in distributions in different groups (or populations).

SELF-TEST Produce a histogram and population pyramid for the success scores *before* the intervention.

4.5. Boxplots (box–whisker diagrams) ①

A **boxplot** or box–whisker diagram is a really useful way to display your data. At the centre of the plot is the *median*, in a box the top and bottom of which are the limits within which the middle 50% of observations fall (the inter-quartile range, IQR). Sticking out of the top and bottom of the box are two whiskers which show the top and bottom 25% of scores (approximately). First, we will make some boxplots using the chart builder and then we'll look at what they tell us in more detail.

In the chart builder (Figure 4.5) select *Boxplot* in the list labelled *Choose from* to bring up the gallery shown in Figure 4.13. There are three types of boxplot you can choose:

Did someone say a box of whiskas?

⇒ *Simple boxplot*: Use this option when you want to plot a boxplot of a single variable, but you want different boxplots produced for different categories in the data (for these success data we could produce separate boxplots for our two intervention groups).

⇒ *Clustered boxplot*: This option is the same as the simple boxplot, except that you can select a second categorical variable on which to split the data. Boxplots for this second

FIGURE 4.11
Defining a population pyramid in the chart builder

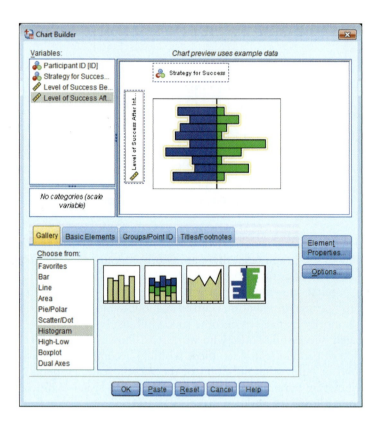

FIGURE 4.12
Population pyramid of success scores (5 years after different strategies were implemented)

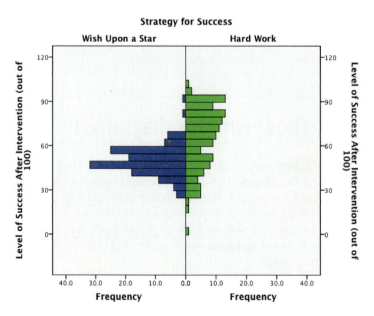

Oxoby, R. J. (2008). *Economic Enquiry*, 47(3), 598–602.

LABCOAT LENI'S REAL RESEARCH 4.1

Gonna be a rock 'n' roll singer (again) ①

In Labcoat Leni's Real Research 3.1 we came across a study that compared economic behaviour while different music by AC/DC played in the background. Specifically, they manipulated whether the background song was sung by their original singer (Bon Scott) or his replacement (Brian Johnson). They measured how many offers participants accepted (**Oxoby (2008) Offers.sav**) and what the minimum offer was that they would accept (**Oxoby (2008) MOA.sav**). See Labcoat Leni's Real Research 3.1 for more detail on the study. We entered the data for this study in the previous chapter; now let's graph it. Produce separate population pyramids for the number of offers and the minimum acceptable offer and in both cases split the data by which singer was singing in the background music. Compare these plots with Figures 1 and 2 in the original article.

variable are produced in different colours. For example, we might have measured whether our people believed in the power of wishing or not. We could produce boxplots not just for the wishers and workers, but within these groups we could have different-coloured boxplots for those who believe in the power of wishing and those who do not.

⇒ *1-D Boxplot*: Use this option when you want to see a boxplot for a single variable. (This differs from the simple boxplot in that no categorical variable is selected for the *x*-axis.)

In the data file of success scores we have information about whether people worked hard or wished upon a star. Let's plot this information. To make a boxplot of the post-intervention success scores for our two groups, double-click on the *simple boxplot* icon (Figure 4.13), then from the variable list select the **Success_Post** variable and drag it into Y-Axis? and select the variable **Strategy** and drag it to X-Axis? . The dialog should now look like Figure 4.14 – note that the variable names are displayed in the drop zones, and the canvas now displays a preview of our graph (i.e., there are two boxplots, one for wishers and one for hard workers). Click on OK to produce the graph.

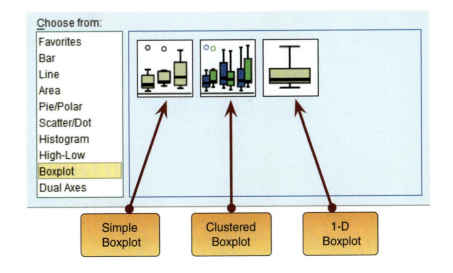

FIGURE 4.13
The boxplot gallery

FIGURE 4.14
Completed
dialog box for a
simple boxplot

FIGURE 4.14
Completed
dialog box for a
simple boxplot

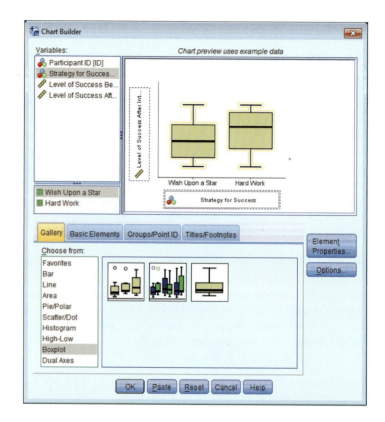

Figure 4.15 shows the boxplots for the success data. Notice that there is a tinted box, which represents the IQR (i.e., the middle 50% of scores). It's clear that the middle 50% of scores are more spread out for the hard-work group than for those who wished on a star because the box is much longer. Within the box, there is a thick horizontal line, which shows the median. The workers had a higher median than the wishers, indicating greater success

FIGURE 4.15
Boxplot of
success scores
5 years after
implementing
a strategy of
working hard or
wishing upon
a star

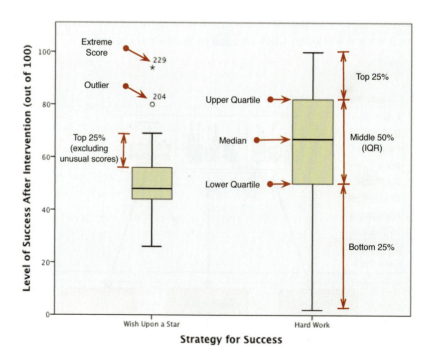

overall. The top and bottom of the tinted box represent the upper and lower quartile, respectively (see Section 1.6.3). The distance between the top of the box and the top of the whisker shows the range of the top 25% of scores (approximately); similarly, the distance between the bottom of the box and the end of the bottom whisker shows the range of the lowest 25% of scores (approximately). I say 'approximately' because SPSS looks for unusual cases before creating the whiskers: any score greater than the upper quartile plus 1.5 times the IQR is deemed to be an 'outlier' (more on those in Chapter 5), and any case greater than the upper quartile plus 3 times the IQR is labelled an 'extreme case'. The same rules are applied to cases below the lower quartile. Therefore, when there are no unusual cases, the whiskers show the top and bottom 25% of scores exactly, but when there are unusual cases they will show the top and bottom 25% of scores only approximately because the unusual cases are excluded. The whiskers also tell us about the range of scores because the top and bottom of the whiskers show the lowest and highest scores *excluding unusual cases*.

In terms of the success scores, we can see that the range of scores was much wider for the workers than the wishers, but the wishers contained an outlier (which SPSS shows as a circle) and an extreme score (which SPSS shows as an asterisk). SPSS labels these cases with the row number from the data editor (in this case 204 and 229), which can help you to identify these scores in the data, check that they were entered correctly, or look for reasons why this score might have been unusual. Like histograms, boxplots also tell us whether the distribution is symmetrical or skewed. If the whiskers are the same length then the distribution is symmetrical (the range of the top and bottom 25% of scores is the same); however, if the top or bottom whisker is much longer than the opposite whisker then the distribution is asymmetrical (the range of the top and bottom 25% of scores is different). The scores from those wishing on a star look symmetrical because the two whiskers are similar lengths, but the hard-work group shows signs of skew because the lower whisker is longer than the upper one.

SELF-TEST Produce boxplots for the success scores before the intervention.

4.6. Graphing means: bar charts and error bars ①

Bar charts are the usual way to display means. How you create these graphs in SPSS depends largely on how you collected your data (whether the means come from independent cases and so are independent, or came from the same cases and so are related). For this reason we will look at a variety of situations. Our starting point is always the chart builder (Figure 4.5). In this dialog box select *Bar* in the list labelled *Choose from* to bring up the gallery shown in Figure 4.16. This gallery has eight icons representing different types of bar chart, and you should select the appropriate one either by double-clicking on it, or by dragging it onto the canvas.

⇒ *Simple bar*: Use this option when you just want to see the means of scores across different groups of cases. For example, you might want to plot the mean ratings of two films.

⇒ *Clustered bar*: If you had a second grouping variable you could produce a simple bar chart (as above) but with bars produced in different colours for levels of a second grouping variable. For example, you could have ratings of the two films, but for each film have a bar representing ratings of 'excitement' and another bar showing ratings of 'enjoyment'.

FIGURE 4.16
The bar chart gallery

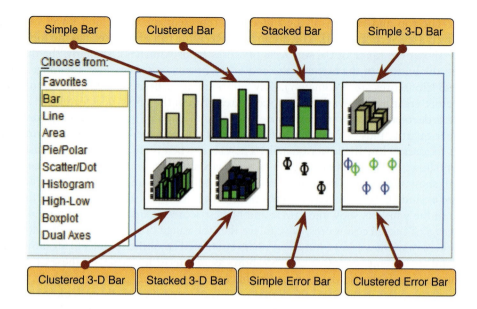

⇒ *Stacked bar*: This is really the same as the clustered bar, except that the different-coloured bars are stacked on top of each other rather than placed side by side.

⇒ *Simple 3-D bar*: This is also the same as the clustered bar, except that the second grouping variable is displayed not by different-coloured bars but by an additional axis. Given what I said in Section 4.2 about 3-D effects obscuring the data, my advice is not to use this type of graph, but to stick to a clustered bar chart.

⇒ *Clustered 3-D bar*: This is like the clustered bar chart, except that you can add a third categorical variable on an extra axis. The means will almost certainly be impossible for anyone to read on this type of graph so don't use it.

⇒ *Stacked 3-D bar*: This graph is the same as the clustered 3-D graph, except the different-coloured bars are stacked on top of each other instead of standing side by side. Again, this is not a good type of graph for presenting data clearly.

⇒ *Simple error bar*: This is the same as the simple bar chart, except that, instead of bars, the mean is represented by a dot, and a line represents the precision of the estimate of the mean (usually the 95% confidence interval is plotted, but you can plot the standard deviation or standard error of the mean instead). You can add these error bars to a bar chart anyway, so really the choice between this type of graph and a bar chart with error bars is largely down to personal preference.

⇒ *Clustered error bar*: This is the same as the clustered bar chart, except that the mean is displayed as a dot with an error bar around it. These error bars can also be added to a clustered bar chart.

4.6.1. Simple bar charts for independent means ①

To begin with, imagine that a film company director was interested in whether there was really such a thing as a 'chick flick' (a film that typically appeals to women more than men). He took 20 men and 20 women and showed half of each sample a film that was supposed to be a 'chick flick' (*Bridget Jones's Diary*), and the other half of each sample a film that didn't fall into the category of 'chick flick' (*Memento*, a brilliant film by the way). In all cases he measured their arousal[6] as an indicator of how much they enjoyed the film. The data are in a file called **ChickFlick.sav** on the companion website. Load this file now.

Let's plot the mean rating of the two films. We have just one grouping variable (the film) and one outcome (the arousal); therefore, we want a simple bar chart. In the chart builder double-click on the icon for a simple bar chart (Figure 4.16). On the canvas you will see a graph and two drop zones: one for the *y*-axis and one for the *x*-axis. The *y*-axis needs to be the dependent variable, or the thing you've measured, or more simply the thing for which you want to display the mean. In this case it would be **arousal**, so select arousal from the variable list and drag it into the *y*-axis drop zone (Y-Axis?). The *x*-axis should be the variable by which we want to split the arousal data. To plot the means for the two films, select the variable **film** from the variable list and drag it into the drop zone for the *x*-axis (X-Axis?).

Figure 4.17 also shows some other options: the *Element Properties* dialog box should appear when you select the type of graph you want, but if it doesn't, then click on . There are three important features of this dialog box. The first is that, by default, the bars will display the mean value. This is fine, but just note that you can plot other summary statistics such as the median or mode. Second, just because you've selected a simple bar chart doesn't mean that you have to have a bar chart. You can select to show an I-bar (the bar is reduced to a line with bars showing the top and bottom), or just a whisker (the bar is reduced to a vertical line). The I-bar and whisker options might be useful when you're not planning on showing error bars, but because we are going to show error bars we should stick with a bar. Finally, you can ask SPSS to add error bars to your bar chart to create an **error bar chart** by selecting ☑ Display error bars . You have a choice of what your error bars represent. Normally, error bars show the 95% confidence interval (see Section 2.5.2), and I have selected this option (◉ Confidence intervals).[7] Note, though, that you can change the width of the confidence interval displayed by changing the '95' to a different value. You can also display the standard error (the default is to show 2 standard errors, but you can change this to 1) or standard deviation (again, the default is 2, but this could be changed to 1 or another value). It's important that when you change these properties you click on Apply : if you don't then the changes will not be applied to chart builder. The completed dialog box is in Figure 4.17. Click on OK to produce the graph.

How do I plot an error bar graph?

Figure 4.18 shows the resulting bar chart. This graph displays the means (and the confidence interval of those means) and shows us that on average, people were more aroused by *Memento* than they were by *Bridget Jones's Diary*. However, we originally wanted to look for gender effects, so this graph isn't really telling us what we need to know. The graph we need is a *clustered graph*.[8]

4.6.2. Clustered bar charts for independent means ①

To do a clustered bar chart for means that are independent (i.e., have come from different groups) we need to double-click on the clustered bar chart icon in the chart builder (Figure

---

[6] I had an email from someone expressing her 'disgust' at measuring arousal while watching a film. This reaction surprised me because to a psychologist (like me) 'arousal' means a heightened emotional response, the sort of heightened emotional response you might get from watching a film you like. Apparently if you're the sort of person who complains about the contents of textbooks then 'arousal' means something different. I can't think what.

[7] It's also worth mentioning at this point that because confidence intervals are constructed assuming a normal distribution, you should plot them only when this is a reasonable assumption (see Section 2.5.2).

[8] You can also use a drop-line graph, which is described in Section 4.8.6.

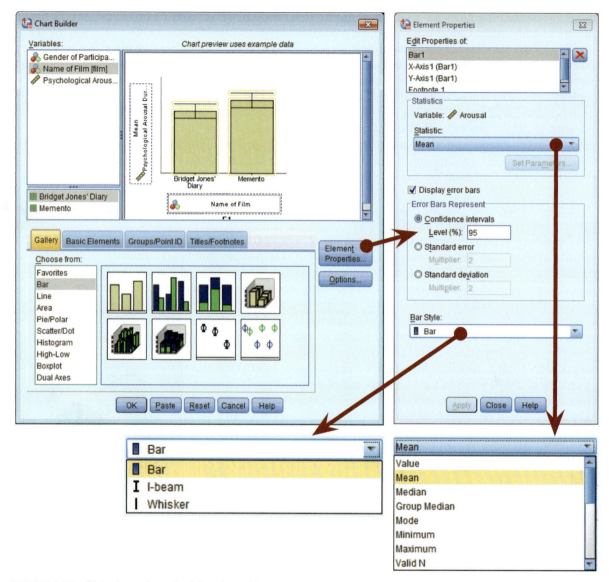

FIGURE 4.17   Dialog boxes for a simple bar chart with error bar

4.16). On the canvas you will see a graph as with the simple bar chart but there is now an extra drop zone: `Cluster on X: set color`. All we need to do is to drag our second grouping variable into this drop zone. As with the previous example, select **arousal** from the variable list and drag it into `Y-Axis?`, then select **film** from the variable list and drag it into `X-Axis?`. In addition, select the **Gender** variable and drag it into `Cluster on X: set color`. This will mean that bars representing males and females will be displayed in different colours (but see SPSS Tip 4.3). As in the previous section, select error bars in the properties dialog box and click on `Apply` to apply them to the chart builder. Figure 4.19 shows the completed chart builder. Click on `OK` to produce the graph.

Figure 4.20 shows the resulting bar chart. Like the simple bar chart, this graph tells us that arousal was overall higher for *Memento* than for *Bridget Jones's Diary*, but it also splits this information by gender. The mean arousal for *Bridget Jones's Diary* shows that males were actually more aroused during this film than females. This indicates they enjoyed the film more than the women did. Contrast this with *Memento*, for which arousal levels are

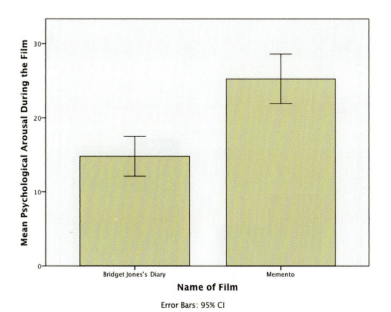

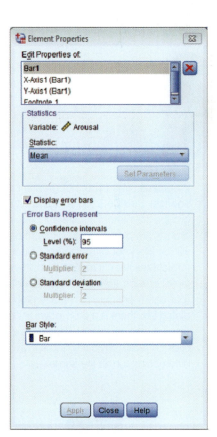

FIGURE 4.18
Bar chart of the
mean arousal
for each of the
two films

FIGURE 4.19 Dialog boxes for a clustered bar chart with error bar

comparable in males and females. On the face of it, this contradicts the idea of a 'chick flick': it actually seems that men enjoy chick flicks more than chicks do (probably because it's the only help we get to understand the workings of the female mind).

FIGURE 4.20
Bar chart of the mean arousal for each of the two films

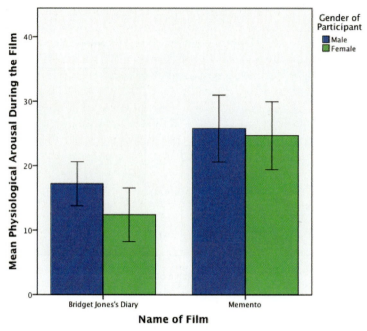

Error Bars: 95% CI

SPSS TIP 4.3   Colours and Patterns? ①

By default, when you plot graphs on which you group the data by some categorical variable (e.g., a clustered bar chart or a grouped scatterplot) these groups are plotted in different colours. You can change this default so that the groups are plotted using different patterns. In a bar chart this means that bars will be filled not with different colours, but with different patterns. With a scatterplot (see later) it means that different symbols are used to plot data from different groups. To make this change, double-click in the [Cluster on X: set color] drop zone (bar chart) or [Set color] (scatterplot) to bring up a new dialog box. Within this dialog box there is a drop-down list labelled *Distinguish Groups by* within which you can select *Color* or *Pattern*. To change the default, select *Pattern* and then click on [OK]. Obviously you can switch back to displaying different groups in different colours in the same way.

4.6.3. Simple bar charts for related means ①

Graphing means from the same entities is slightly more tricky, but as they say, if you're going to die, die with your boots on. So, let's put our boots on and hopefully not die. Hiccups can be a serious problem: Charles Osborne apparently got a case of hiccups while slaughtering a hog (well, who wouldn't?) that lasted 67 years. People have many methods for stopping hiccups (a surprise, holding your breath), and medical science has put its collective mind to the task too. The official treatment methods include tongue-pulling manoeuvres, massage of the carotid artery, and, believe it or not, digital rectal massage (Fesmire, 1988). I don't know the details of what the digital rectal massage involved, but I can probably imagine. Let's say we wanted to put digital rectal massage to the test (erm, as a cure for hiccups I mean). We took 15 hiccup sufferers, and during about of hiccups administered each of the three procedures (in random order and at intervals of 5 minutes) after taking a baseline of how many hiccups they had per minute. We counted the number of hiccups in the minute after each procedure. Load the file **Hiccups.sav**. Note that these data are laid out in different columns; there is no grouping variable that specifies the interventions, because each patient experienced all interventions. In the previous two examples we have used grouping variables to specify aspects of the graph (e.g., we used the grouping variable **film** to specify the *x*-axis). For repeated-measures data we will not have these grouping variables and so the process of building a graph is a little more complicated (but only a little).

How do I plot a bar graph of repeated-measures data?

To plot the mean number of hiccups, go to the chart builder and double-click on the icon for a simple bar chart (Figure 4.16). As before, you will see a graph on the canvas with drop zones for the *x*- and *y*-axes. Previously we specified the column in our data that contained data from our outcome measure on the *y*-axis, but for these data we have four columns containing data on the number of hiccups (the outcome variable). What we have to do then is to drag all four of these variables from the variable list into the *y-axis* drop zone. We have to do this simultaneously. First, we need to select multiple items in the variable list: to do this select the first variable by clicking on it with the mouse. The variable will be highlighted in blue. Now, hold down the *Ctrl* key (or *Cmd* if you're on a Mac) on the keyboard and click on a second variable. Both variables are now highlighted. Again, hold down the *Ctrl* key and click on a third variable in the variable list and so on for the fourth. In cases in which you want to select a list of consecutive variables, you can do this very quickly by simply clicking on the first variable that you want to select (in this case **Baseline**), hold down the *Shift* key (also on a Mac) on the keyboard and then click on the last variable that you want to select (in this case **Digital Rectal Massage**); notice that all of the variables in between have been selected too. Once the four variables are selected you can drag them by clicking on any one of the variables and then dragging them into [Y-Axis?] as shown in Figure 4.21.

Once you have dragged the four variables onto the *y*-axis drop zone a new dialog box appears (Figure 4.22). This box tells us that SPSS is creating two temporary variables. One is called **Summary**, which is going to be the outcome variable (i.e., what we measured – in this case the number of hiccups per minute). The other is called **Index**, which will represent our independent variable (i.e., what we manipulated – in this case the type of intervention). SPSS uses these temporary names because it doesn't know what our particular variables represent, but we should change them to something more helpful. Just click on [OK] to get rid of this dialog box.

We need to edit some of the properties of the graph. Figure 4.23 shows the options that need to be set: if you can't see this dialog box then click on [Element Properties] in the chart builder. In the left panel of Figure 4.23 just note that I have selected to display error bars (see the previous two sections for more information). The middle panel is accessed by clicking on *X-Axis1 (Bar1)* in the list labelled *E*d*it Properties of* which allows us to edit properties of the horizontal axis. The first thing we need to do is give the axis a title and I have typed *Intervention* in the space labelled *Axis Label*. This label will appear on the graph. Also, we can change the order of our variables if we want to by selecting a variable in the list labelled *O*r*der* and moving it up or down using [↑] and [↓]. If we change our mind about displaying one of our variables then we can also remove it from the list by selecting it and clicking on [×]. Click on [Apply] for these changes to take effect. The right panel of Figure 4.23 is accessed by clicking on *Y-Axis1 (Bar1)* in the list labelled *E*d*it Properties of* which allows us to edit properties of the vertical axis. The main change that I have made here is to give

FIGURE 4.21
Specifying
a simple bar
chart for
repeated-
measures data

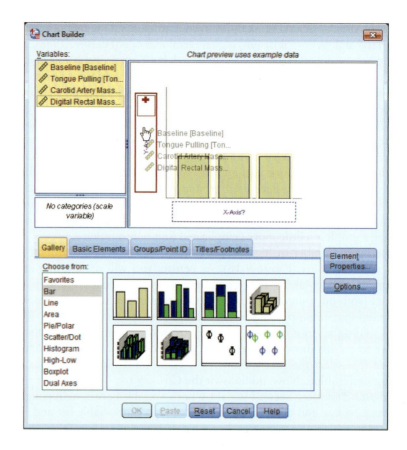

FIGURE 4.22
The *Create
Summary
Group* dialog
box

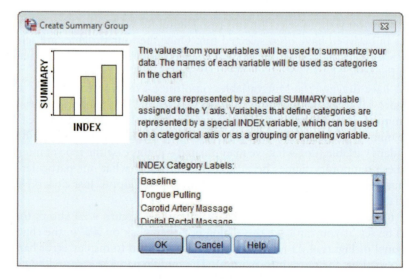

the axis a label so that the final graph has a useful description on the axis (by default it will just display 'Mean', which isn't very helpful). I have typed 'Mean Number of Hiccups Per Minute' in the box labelled *Axis Label*. Also note that you can use this dialog box to set the scale of the vertical axis (the minimum value, maximum value and the major increment, which is how often a mark is made on the axis). Mostly you can let SPSS construct the scale automatically and it will be fairly sensible – and even if it's not you can edit it later. Click on Apply to apply the changes.

FIGURE 4.23 Setting *Element Properties* for a repeated-measures graph

Figure 4.24 shows the completed chart builder. Click on [OK] to produce the graph. The resulting bar chart in Figure 4.25 displays the mean (and the confidence interval for the mean)[9] number of hiccups at baseline and after the three interventions. Note that the axis labels that I typed in have appeared on the graph. We can conclude that the amount of hiccups after tongue pulling was about the same as at baseline; however, carotid artery massage reduced hiccups, but not by as much as a good old fashioned digital-rectal massage. The moral here is: if you have hiccups, find something digital and go amuse yourself for a few minutes.

4.6.4. Clustered bar charts for related means ①

Now we have seen how to plot means that are related (i.e., show different conditions applied to the same group of cases), you might well wonder what you do if you have a second independent variable that had been measured in the same sample. You'd do a clustered bar chart, right? Wrong? Actually, the SPSS chart builder doesn't appear to be able to cope with this situation at all – at least not that I can work out from playing about with it. (Cue a deluge of emails along the general theme of 'Dear Professor Field, I was recently looking through my FEI Titan 80-300 monochromated scanning transmission electron microscope

---

[9] The error bars on graphs of repeated-measures designs aren't actually correct, as we will see in Chapter 9; I don't want to go into the reasons why here, but if you're doing a graph of your own data then you should read Section 9.6.2 first.

FIGURE 4.24
Completed
chart builder
for a repeated-
measures
graph

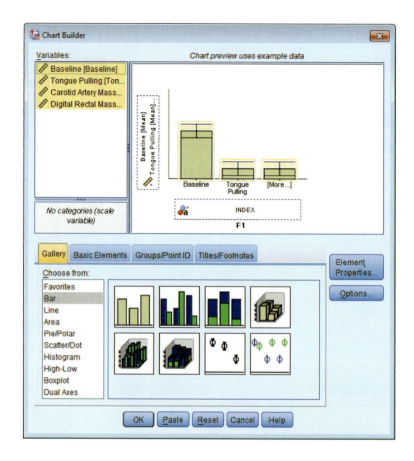

LABCOAT LENI'S REAL RESEARCH 4.2

Seeing red ①

JOHNS, S. E., ET AL. (2012). *PLOS ONE*, 7(4), E34669.

It is believed that males have a biological predis-position towards the colour red because it is sexu-ally salient. The theory suggests that women use the colour red as a proxy signal for genital colour to indi-cate ovulation and sexual proceptivity. If this hypoth-esis is true then using the colour red in this way would have to attract men (otherwise it's a pointless strat-egy). In a novel study, Sarah Johns tested this idea by manipulating the colour of four pictures of female genitalia to make them increasing shades of red (pale pink, light pink, dark pink, red). Heterosexual males rated the resulting 16 pictures from 0 (unattractive) to 100 (attractive). The data are in the file **Johns et al. (2012).sav**. Draw and error bar graph of the mean rat-ings for the four different colours. Do you think men preferred red genitals? (Remember, if the theory is cor-rect then red should be rated highest.) Answers are on the companion website. (We analyse these data at the end of Chapter 15.)

and I think I may have found your brain. I have enclosed it for you – good luck finding it in the envelope. May I suggest that you take better care next time there is a slight gust of wind or else, I fear, it might blow out of your head again. Yours, Professor Enormobrain. PS Doing clustered charts for related means in SPSS is simple for anyone whose mental acumen can raise itself above that of a louse.')

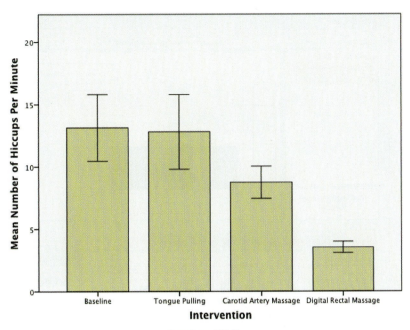

FIGURE 4.25
Bar chart of the mean number of hiccups at baseline and after various interventions

4.6.5. Clustered bar charts for 'mixed' designs ①

The chart builder might not be able to do charts for multiple repeated-measures variables, but it can graph what is known as a mixed design (see Chapter 15). This is a design in which you have one or more independent variables measured using different groups, and one or more independent variables measured using the same sample. Basically, the chart builder can produce a graph provided you have only one repeated-measure variable.

My students like to text-message during my lectures (I assume they text the person next to them to say, 'Bloody hell, this guy is so boring I need to poke out my own eyes'). What will happen to future generations, though? Not only will they develop miniature thumbs; they might not learn correct written English. Imagine we conducted an experiment in which a group of 25 children were encouraged to send text messages on their mobile phones over a 6-month period. A second group of 25 children were discouraged from sending text messages for the same period by being given armbands that administered painful shocks in the presence of microwaves (like those emitted from phones).[10] The outcome was a percentage score on a grammatical test that was measured both before and after the intervention. The first independent variable was, therefore, text message use (text messagers versus controls) and the second was the time at which grammatical ability was assessed (baseline or after 6 months). The data are in the file **Text Messages.sav**.

To graph these data we need to follow the procedure for graphing related means in Section 4.6.3. Our repeated-measures variable is time (whether grammatical ability was measured at baseline or 6 months) and is represented in the data file by two columns, one for the baseline data and the other for the follow-up data. In the chart builder select these two variables simultaneously by clicking on one and then holding down the *Ctrl* key (*Cmd* on a Mac) on

---

[10] Although this punished them for any attempts to use a mobile phone, because other people's phones also emit microwaves, an unfortunate side effect was that these children acquired a pathological fear of anyone talking on a mobile phone.

FIGURE 4.26
Selecting the
repeated-
measures
variable in the
chart builder

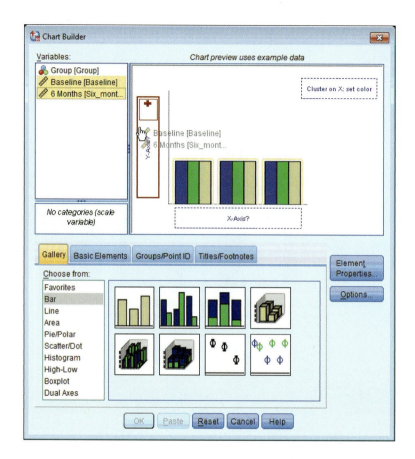

the keyboard and clicking on the other. When they are both highlighted click on either one and drag it into [Y-Axis?] as shown in Figure 4.26. The second variable (whether children text messaged or not) was measured using different children and so is represented in the data file by a grouping variable (**group**). This variable can be selected in the variable list and dragged into [Cluster on X: set color]. The two groups will be displayed as different-coloured bars. The finished chart builder is in Figure 4.27. Click on [OK] to produce the graph.

SELF-TEST   Use what you learnt in Section 4.6.3 to add error bars to this graph and to label both the *x*- (I suggest 'Time') and *y*-axis (I suggest 'Mean Grammar Score (%)')

Figure 4.28 shows the resulting bar chart. It shows that at baseline (before the intervention) the grammar scores were comparable in our two groups; however, after the intervention, the grammar scores were lower in the text messagers than in the controls. Also, if you compare the two blue bars you can see that text messagers' grammar scores have fallen over the 6 months; compare this to the controls (green bars) whose grammar scores are fairly similar over time. We could, therefore, conclude that text messaging has a detrimental effect on children's understanding of English grammar and civilization will crumble, with Abaddon rising cackling from his bottomless pit to claim our wretched souls. Maybe.

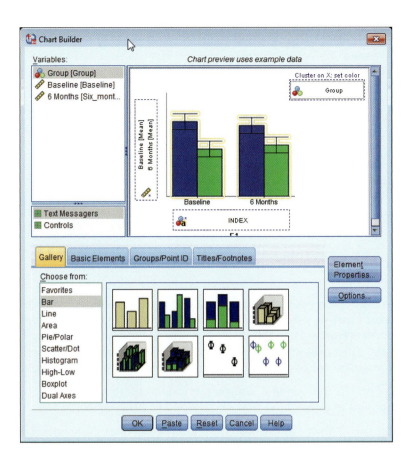

FIGURE 4.27
Completed dialog box for an error bar graph of a mixed design

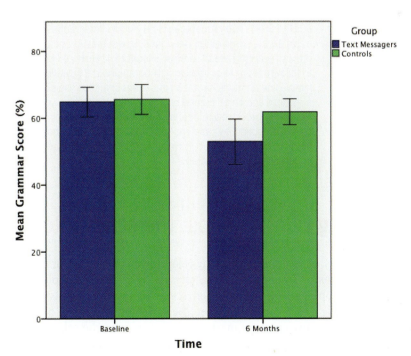

Error Bars: 95% CI

FIGURE 4.28
Error bar graph of the mean grammar score over 6 months in children who were allowed to text-message versus those who were forbidden

FIGURE 4.29

The line chart gallery

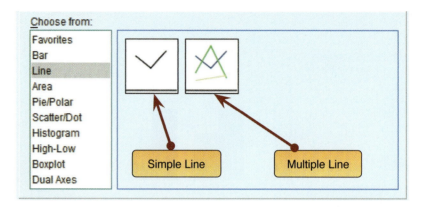

4.7. Line charts ①

Line charts are bar charts but with lines instead of bars. Therefore, everything we have just done with a bar chart we can display as a line chart instead. As ever, our starting point is the chart builder (Figure 4.5). In this dialog box select *Line* in the list labelled *Choose from* to bring up the gallery shown in Figure 4.29. This gallery has two icons and you should select the appropriate one by either double-clicking on it or dragging it onto the canvas.

⇒ *Simple line*: Use this option when you just want to see the means of scores across different groups of cases.

⇒ *Multiple line*: This is equivalent to the clustered bar chart in the previous section, in that you can plot means of a particular variable but produce different-coloured lines for each level of a second variable.

SELF-TEST   The procedure for producing line graphs is basically the same as for bar charts except that you get lines on your graphs instead of bars. Therefore, you should be able to follow the previous sections for bar charts but selecting a simple line chart instead of a simple bar chart, and selecting a multiple line chart instead of a clustered bar chart. I would like you to produce line charts of each of the bar charts in the previous section. In case you get stuck, the self-test answers that can be downloaded from the companion website will take you through it step by step.

4.8. Graphing relationships: the scatterplot ①

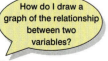

How do I draw a graph of the relationship between two variables?

Sometimes we need to look at the relationships between variables (rather than their means or frequencies). A **scatterplot** is a graph that plots each person's score on one variable against their score on another. It tells us whether there seems to be a relationship between the variables, what kind of relationship it is and whether any cases are markedly different from the others. Drawing a scatterplot using SPSS is dead easy. As usual, our starting point is the chart builder (Figure 4.5). In this dialog box select *Scatter/Dot* in the list labelled *Choose from* to bring up the gallery shown in Figure 4.30. This gallery has eight icons representing different types of scatterplot, and you should select the appropriate one by either double-clicking on it or dragging it onto the canvas.

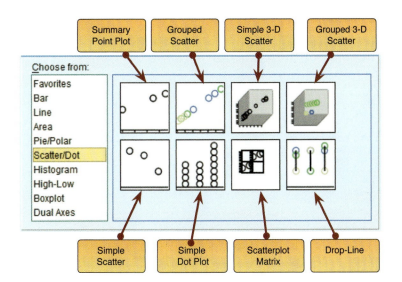

FIGURE 4.30
The scatter/dot gallery

⇒ *Simple scatter*: Use this option when you want to plot values of one continuous variable against another.

⇒ *Grouped scatter*: This is like a simple scatterplot, except that you can display points belonging to different groups in different colours (or symbols).

⇒ *Simple 3-D scatter*: Use this option to plot values of one continuous variable against values of two others.

⇒ *Grouped 3-D scatter*: Use this option if you want a to plot values of one continuous variable against two others, but differentiating groups of cases with different-coloured dots.

⇒ *Summary point plot*: This graph is the same as a bar chart (see Section 4.6), except that a dot is used instead of a bar.

⇒ *Simple dot plot*: Otherwise known as a **density plot**, this graph is similar to a histogram (see Section 4.4), except that rather than having a summary bar representing the frequency of scores, a density plot shows each individual score as a dot. This can be useful, like a histogram, for looking at the shape of a distribution.

⇒ *Scatterplot matrix*: This option produces a grid of scatterplots showing the relationships between multiple pairs of variables.

⇒ *Drop-line:* This option produces a graph that is similar to a clustered bar chart (see, for example, Section 4.6.2) but with a dot representing a summary statistic (e.g., the mean) instead of a bar, and with a line connecting means of different groups. This can be useful for comparing statistics, such as the mean, across different groups.

4.8.1. Simple scatterplot ①

This type of scatterplot is for looking at just two variables. For example, a psychologist was interested in the effects of exam stress on exam performance. So, she devised and validated a

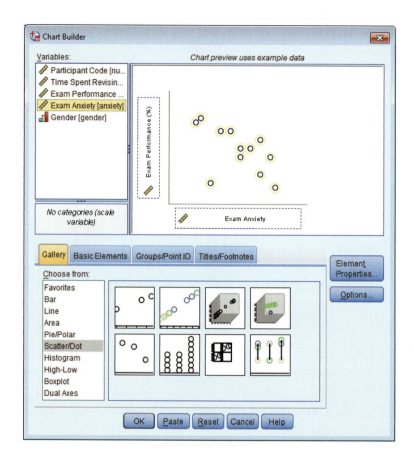

questionnaire to assess state anxiety relating to exams (called the Exam Anxiety Questionnaire, or EAQ). This scale produced a measure of anxiety scored out of 100. Anxiety was measured before an exam, and the percentage mark of each student on the exam was used to assess the exam performance. The first thing that the psychologist should do is draw a scatterplot of the two variables (her data are in the file **ExamAnxiety.sav** and you should load this file into SPSS).

In the chart builder double-click on the icon for a simple scatterplot (Figure 4.31). On the canvas you will see a graph and two drop zones: one for the *y*-axis and one for the *x*-axis. The *y*-axis needs to be the dependent variable (the outcome that was measured).[11] In this case the outcome is Exam Performance (%), so select it from the variable list and drag it into the *y*-axis drop zone (Y-Axis?). The horizontal axis should display the independent variable (the variable that predicts the outcome variable). In this case is it is **ExamAnxiety**, so click on this variable in the variable list and drag it into the drop zone for the *x*-axis (X-Axis?). Figure 4.31 shows the completed chart builder. Click on OK to produce the graph.

Figure 4.32 shows the resulting scatterplot; yours won't have a funky line on it yet, but don't get too depressed about it because I'm going to show you how to add this line very soon. The scatterplot tells us that the majority of students suffered from high levels of anxiety (there are very few cases that had anxiety levels below 60). Also, there are no obvious outliers in that most points seem to fall within the vicinity of other points. There also seems to be some general trend in the data, shown by the line, such that higher levels of anxiety are associated with lower exam scores and low levels of anxiety are almost always associated

---

[11] In experimental research the independent variable is usually plotted on the horizontal axis and the dependent variable on the vertical axis because changes in the independent variable (the variable that the experimenter has manipulated) cause changes in the dependent variable. In correlational research, variables are measured simultaneously and so no cause-and-effect relationship can be established. As such, these terms are used loosely.

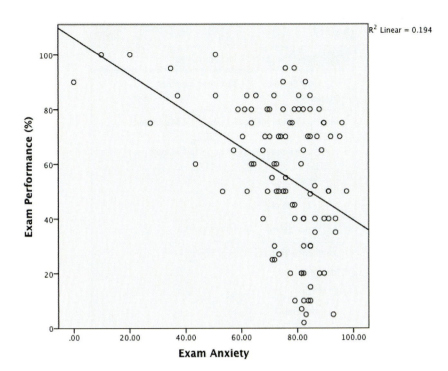

FIGURE 4.32
Scatterplot of
exam anxiety
and exam
performance

with high examination marks. Another noticeable trend in these data is that there were no
cases having low anxiety and low exam performance – in fact, most of the data are clustered
in the upper region of the anxiety scale.

Often when you plot a scatterplot it is useful to plot a line that summarizes the relationship
between variables (this is called a **regression line** and we will discover more about
it in Chapter 8). All graphs in SPSS can be edited by double-clicking on them in
the SPSS viewer to open them in the SPSS chart editor (see Figure 4.39). For more
detail on editing graphs, see Section 4.9; for now, just click on ⬚ in the chart editor
to open the *Properties* dialog box (Figure 4.33). Using this dialog box, we can add a
line to the graph that represents the overall mean of all data, a linear (straight line)
model, a quadratic model, a cubic model and so on (these trends are described in
Section 11.4.5). Let's look at the linear regression line; select this option and then
click on Apply to apply the changes to the graph. It should now look like Figure
4.32. A variation on the scatterplot is the catterplot, which is useful for plotting unpredictable
data (Jane Superbrain Box 4.1).

> How do I fit
> a regression line
> to a scatterplot?

4.8.2. Grouped scatterplot ①

What if we want to see whether male and female students had different reactions to exam
anxiety? To do this, we need a grouped scatterplot. This type of scatterplot is for looking
at two continuous variables, but when you want to colour data points by a third categorical
variable. Sticking with our previous example, we could look at the relationship between
exam anxiety and exam performance in males and females (our grouping variable). To do
this we double-click on the grouped scatter icon in the chart builder (Figure 4.30). As in
the previous example, we select **Exam Performance (%)** from the variable list and drag it
into the [Y-Axis?] drop zone, and select **Exam Anxiety** and drag it into [X-Axis?] drop
zone. There is an additional drop zone ([Set color]) into which we can drop any categorical
variable. In this case, **Gender** is the only categorical variable in our variable list, so select it

FIGURE 4.33
Properties
dialog box
for a simple
scatterplot

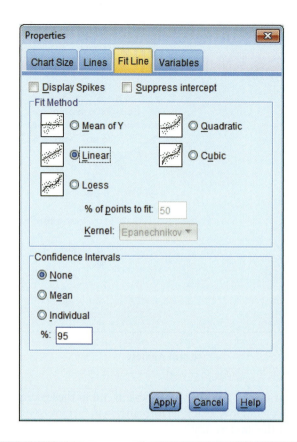

JANE SUPERBRAIN 4.1

Catterplots ①

The catterplot is a variation on the scatterplot that was designed by Herman Garfield to overcome the difficulty that sometimes emerges when plotting very unpredictable data. He named it the catterplot because, of all the things he could think of that were unpredictable, cat behaviour topped his list. To illustrate the catterplot, open the data in the file **Catterplot.sav.** These data measure two variables: the time since last feeding a cat **(DinnerTime)**, and how loud their purr is **(Meow)**. In SPSS, to create a catterplot you follow the same procedure as a simple scatterplot: select **DinnerTime** and drag it into the drop zone for the *x*-axis (X-Axis?),

then select **Meow** and drag it to the *y*-axis drop zone (Y-Axis?). Click on OK to produce the graph.

The catterplot is shown in Figure 4.34. You might expect that there is a positive relationship between the variables: the longer time since being fed, the more vocal the cat becomes. However, the graph shows something quite different: there doesn't seem to be a consistent relationship.[12]

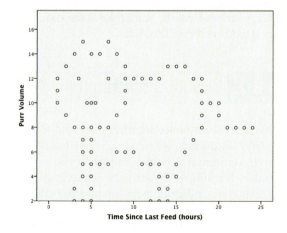

FIGURE 4.34   A catterplot

[12] I'm hugely grateful to Lea Raemaekers for sending me these data.

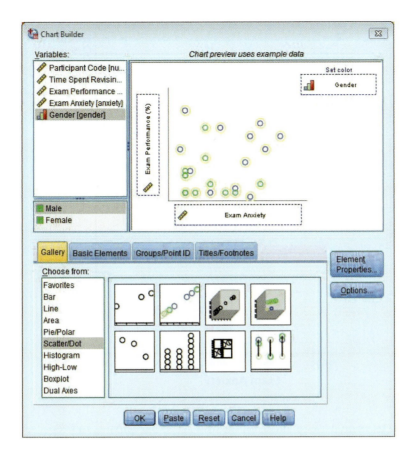

FIGURE 4.35
Completed
Chart Builder
dialog box
for a grouped
scatterplot

and drag it into this drop zone. (If you want to display the different genders using different-shaped symbols rather than different-coloured symbols then read SPSS Tip 4.3). Figure 4.35 shows the completed chart builder. Click on [OK] to produce the graph.

Figure 4.36 shows the resulting scatterplot; as before, I have added regression lines, but this time I have added different lines for each group. We saw in the previous section that graphs can be edited by double-clicking on them in the SPSS viewer to open them in the SPSS chart editor (Figure 4.39). We also saw that we could fit a regression line that summarized the whole data set by clicking on ⬈. We could do this again, if we wished. However, having split the data by gender, it might be more interesting to fit separate lines for our two groups. This is easily achieved by clicking on ⬈ in the chart editor. As before, this action opens the *Properties* dialog box (Figure 4.33) and we can ask for a linear model to be fitted to the data (see the previous section); however, when we click on [Apply] SPSS will fit a separate line for the men and women. These lines (Figure 4.36) tell us that the relationship between exam anxiety and exam performance was slightly stronger in males (the line is steeper) indicating that men's exam performance was more adversely affected by anxiety than women's exam anxiety. (Whether this difference is significant is another issue – see Section 7.6.1.)

4.8.3. Simple and grouped 3-D scatterplots ①

One of the few times you can use a 3-D graph without a statistician locking you in a room and whipping you with his beard is a scatterplot. A 3-D scatterplot displays the relationship between three variables, and the reason why it's all right to use a 3-D graph in this context is that the third dimension tells us something useful (it isn't there to look pretty). As an example, imagine our researcher decided that exam anxiety might not be the only factor

FIGURE 4.36
Scatterplot of exam anxiety and exam performance split by gender

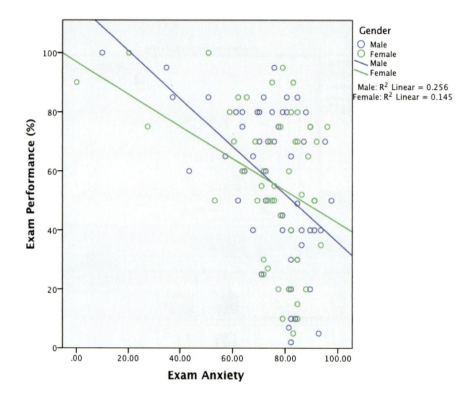

contributing to exam performance. So, she also asked participants to keep a revision diary from which she calculated the number of hours spent revising for the exam. She might want to look at the relationships between these variables simultaneously, and she could do this using a 3-D scatterplot. Personally, I don't think a 3-D scatterplot is a clear way to present data – a matrix scatterplot (Section 4.8.4) is better – but if you want to do one, see Oliver Twisted.

4.8.4. Matrix scatterplot ①

Instead of plotting several variables on the same axes on a 3-D scatterplot (which can be difficult to interpret), I think it's better to plot a matrix of 2-D scatterplots. This type of plot allows you to see the relationship between all combinations of many different pairs of variables. Let's use the same example that we have just used: the relationships between

OLIVER TWISTED

Please, Sir, can I have some more … dimensions?

'I need to discover how to bend space and time so that I can escape from Dickensian London and enter the twenty-first century, where when you pick a pocket or two you get an iPhone rather than a snotty hanky. To do this I need extra dimensions – preferably fourth ones', says Oliver. At present SPSS won't let you manipulate the space–time continuum, but it will let you add an extra dimension to a scatterplot. To find out how, look at the additional material.

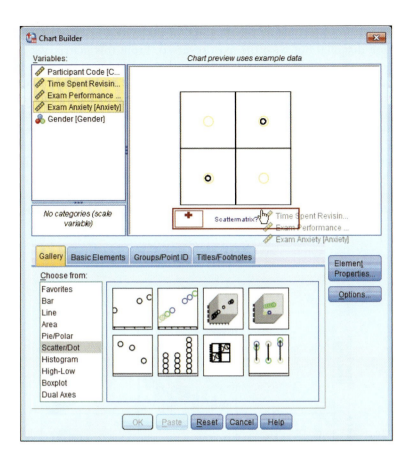

FIGURE 4.37
Chart Builder
dialog box
for a matrix
scatterplot

exam performance, exam anxiety and time spent revising. First, access the chart builder and double-click on the icon for a scatterplot matrix (Figure 4.30). A different type of graph than what you've seen before will appear on the canvas, and it has only one drop zone (Scattermatrix?). We need to drag all of the variables that we would like to see plotted against each other into this single drop zone. We have dragged multiple variables into a drop zone in previous sections, but, to recap, we first need to select multiple items in the variable list: to do this select the first variable (**Time Spent Revising**) by clicking on it with the mouse. The variable will be highlighted. Now, hold down the *Ctrl* key (*Cmd* on a Mac) and click on a second variable (**Exam Performance %**). Both variables are now highlighted. Again, hold down the *Ctrl* key and click on a third variable (**Exam Anxiety**). (We could also have simply clicked on **Time Spent Revising**, then held down the *Shift* key and then clicked on **Exam Anxiety**.) Once the three variables are selected, drag them into Scattermatrix? as shown in Figure 4.37. Click on OK to produce the graph.

The six scatterplots in Figure 4.38 represent the various combinations of each variable plotted against each other variable. So, the grid references represent the following plots:

- **B1**: revision time (*Y*) against exam performance (*X*)

- **C1**: revision time (*Y*) against anxiety (*X*)

- **C2**: exam performance (*Y*) against anxiety (*X*)

- **A2**: exam performance (*Y*) against revision time (*X*)

- **A3**: anxiety (*Y*) against revision time (*X*)

- **B3**: anxiety (*Y*) against exam performance (*X*)

Thus, the three scatterplots below the diagonal of the matrix are the same plots as the ones above the diagonal but with the axes reversed. From this matrix we can see that revision time and anxiety are inversely related (the more time spent revising, the less anxiety the participant had about the exam). Also, in the scatterplot of revision time against anxiety (grids C1 and A3) it looks like there is one possible unusual case – a single participant who spent very little time revising yet suffered very little anxiety about the exam. As all participants who had low anxiety scored highly on the exam, we can deduce that this person also did well on the exam (don't you just hate a smart alec?). We could choose to examine this case more closely if we believed that their behaviour was caused by some external factor (such as taking brain-pills!). Matrix scatterplots are very convenient for examining pairs of relationships between variables (see SPSS Tip 4.4). However, they can become very confusing indeed if you plot them for more than three or four variables.

FIGURE 4.38
Matrix scatterplot of exam performance, exam anxiety and revision time. Grid references have been added for clarity

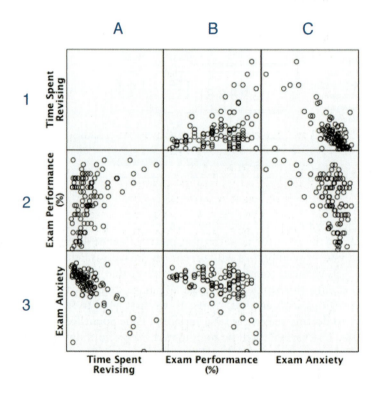

SPSS TIP 4.4   **Regression lines on a scatterplot matrix ①**

You can add regression lines to each scatterplot in the matrix in exactly the same way as for a simple scatterplot. First, double-click on the scatterplot matrix in the SPSS viewer to open it in the SPSS chart editor, then click on ⬚ to open the *Properties* dialog box. Using this dialog box add a line to the graph that represents the linear model (this should be set by default). Click on ⬚Apply to apply the changes. Each panel of the matrix should now show a regression line.

4.8.5. Simple dot plot or density plot ①

I mentioned earlier that the simple dot plot, or density plot as it is also known, is a histogram except that each data point is plotted (rather than using a single summary bar to show each frequency). Like a histogram, the data are still placed into bins (SPSS Tip 4.2) but a dot is used to represent each data point. As such, you should be able to follow the instructions for a histogram to draw one.

SELF-TEST Doing a simple dot plot in the chart builder is quite similar to drawing a histogram. Reload the **Jiminy Cricket.sav** data and see if you can produce a simple dot plot of the success scores after the intervention. Compare the resulting graph to the earlier histogram of the same data (Figure 4.10). Remember that your starting point is to double-click on the icon for a simple dot plot in the chart builder (Figure 4.30). The instructions for drawing a histogram (Section 4.4) might then help – if not, there is full guidance in the additional material on the companion website.

4.8.6. Drop-line graph ①

I also mentioned earlier that the drop-line plot is fairly similar to a clustered bar chart (or line chart) except that each mean is represented by a dot (rather than a bar), and within groups these dots are linked by a line (contrast this with a line graph where dots are joined across groups, rather than within groups). The best way to see the difference is to plot one and to do this you can apply what you were told about clustered line graphs (Section 4.6.2) to this new situation.

SELF-TEST Doing a drop-line plot in the chart builder is quite similar to drawing a clustered bar chart. Reload the **ChickFlick.sav** data and see if you can produce a drop-line plot of the arousal scores. Compare the resulting graph to the earlier clustered bar chart of the same data (Figure 4.20). The instructions in Section 4.6.2 might help.

SELF-TEST Now see if you can produce a drop-line plot of the **Text Messages.sav** data from earlier in this chapter. Compare the resulting graph to the earlier clustered bar chart of the same data (Figure 4.28). The instructions in Section 4.6.5 might help.

Remember that your starting point for both tasks is to double-click on the icon for a drop-line plot in the chart builder (Figure 4.30). There is full guidance for both examples in the additional material on the companion website.

FIGURE 4.39
Opening a
graph for
editing in the
SPSS chart
editor

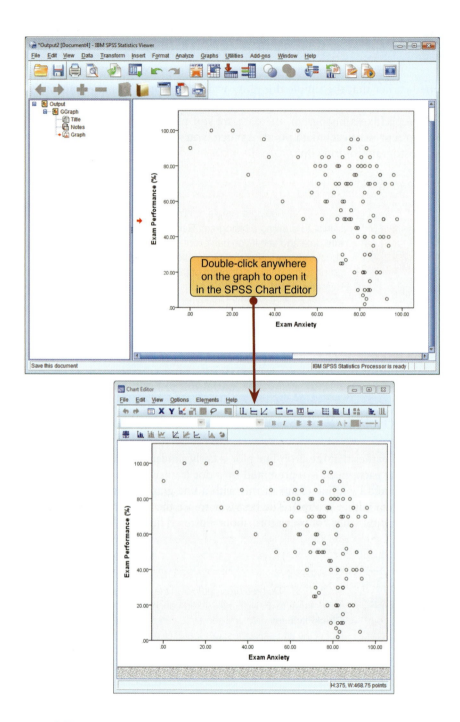

4.9. Editing graphs ①

We have already seen how to add regression lines to scatterplots (Section 4.8.1). You can edit almost every aspect of the graph by double-clicking on the graph in the SPSS viewer to open it in a new window called the **Chart Editor** (Figure 4.39). Once in the chart editor you can click on virtually anything that you want to change and change it. There are also many buttons that you can click on to add elements to the graph (such as grid lines, regression lines and data labels). You can change the bar colours, the axes titles, the scale of each axis and so on. You can also do things like make the bars three-dimensional. However, tempting

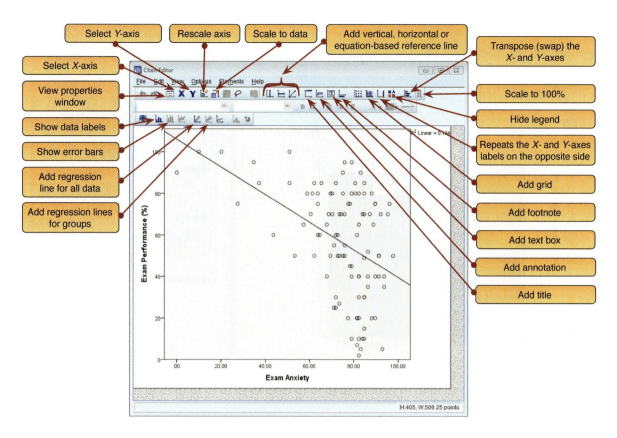

FIGURE 4.40   The chart editor

as these tools may be (it can look quite pretty) try to remember the advice I gave at the start of this chapter when editing your graphs.

Once in the chart editor (Figure 4.40) there are several icons that you can click on to change aspects of the graph. Whether a particular icon is active depends on the type of chart that you are editing (e.g., the icon to fit a regression line will not work on a bar chart). The figure tells you what most of the icons do, and to be honest most of them are fairly self-explanatory (you don't need me to explain what the icon for adding a title does). I would suggest playing around with these features.

OLIVER TWISTED

Please, Sir, can I have some more … graphs?

'Blue and green should never be seen!', shrieks Oliver with so much force that his throat starts to hurt. 'This graph offends my delicate artistic sensibilities. It *must* be changed immediately!' Never fear, Oliver. Using the editing functions in SPSS, it's possible to create some very tasteful graphs. These facilities are so extensive that I could probably write a whole book on them. In the interests of saving trees, I have prepared a tutorial that can be downloaded from the companion website. We look at an example of how to edit an error bar chart to make it conform to some of the guidelines that I talked about at the beginning of this chapter. In doing so we will look at how to edit the axes, add grid lines, change the bar colours, change the background and borders. It's a very extensive tutorial.

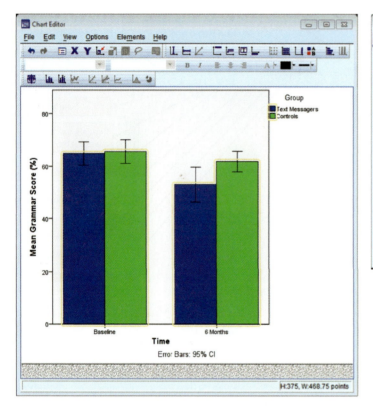

FIGURE 4.41   To select an element in the graph simply click on it and its *Properties* dialog box will appear

ODITI'S LANTERN

Editing graphs

'I, Oditi, have been dazzled and confused by the pinkness of many a graph. Those who seek to prevent our worthy mission do bedazzle us with their pink and lime green monstrosities. These colours burn our retinas until we can no longer see the data within the sacred drawings of truth. To complete our mission to find the secret of life we must make the sacred drawings palatable to the human eye. Stare into my lantern to find out how.'

You can also edit parts of the graph by selecting them and then changing their properties. To select part of the graph simply click on it; it will become highlighted in orange and a new dialog box will appear (Figure 4.41). This *Properties* dialog box enables you to change virtually anything about the item that you have selected. Rather than spend a lot of time here showing you the various properties (there are lots) there is a tutorial in the additional website material (see Oliver Twisted).

4.10. Brian's attempt to woo Jane ①

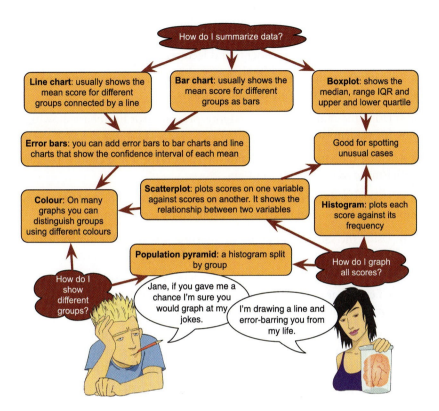

FIGURE 4.42
What Brian learnt from this chapter

4.11. What next? ①

We have discovered that when it comes to graphs, minimal is best: no pink, no 3-D effects, no pictures of Errol your pet ferret superimposed on the graph – oh, and did I mention no pink? Graphs are a useful way to visualize life. Around the age of 5 I was trying to visualize my future and, like many boys, my favoured career choices were going into the army (goodness only know why, but a possibly explanation is that I was too young to comprehend mortality and death) and becoming a famous sports person. On balance, I seemed to favour the latter, and like many a UK-born child my sport of choice was football (or soccer, as people outside of the UK sometimes like to call it to avoid confusion with a game in which a ball is predominantly passed through the hands, and not the feet, but is bizarrely also called football). It is to this chapter of my life that we now turn.

4.12. Key terms that I've discovered

Bar chart	Chartjunk	Line chart
Boxplot (box–whisker plot)	Density plot	Regression line
Chart Builder	Error bar chart	Scatterplot
Chart Editor		

4.13. Smart Alex's tasks

- **Task 1**: Using the data from Chapter 2 (which you should have saved, but if you didn't, re-enter it from Table 3.1), plot and interpret an error bar chart showing the mean number of friends for students and lecturers. ①

- **Task 2**: Using the same data, plot and interpret an error bar chart showing the mean alcohol consumption for students and lecturers. ①

- **Task 3**: Using the same data, plot and interpret an error line chart showing the mean income for students and lecturers. ①

- **Task 4**: Using the same data, plot and interpret error a line chart showing the mean neuroticism for students and lecturers. ①

- **Task 5**: Using the same data, plot and interpret a scatterplot with regression lines of alcohol consumption and neuroticism grouped by lecturer/student. ①

- **Task 6**: Using the same data, plot and interpret a scatterplot matrix with regression lines of alcohol consumption, neuroticism and number of friends. ①

- **Task 7**: Using the **Infidelity.sav** data from Chapter 3 (see Task 7 in that chapter), plot a clustered error bar chart of the mean number of bullets used against the self and the partner for males and females. ①

- **Task 8**: Using the **Method Of Teaching.sav** data from Chapter 3 (see Task 2 in that chapter), plot a clustered error line chart of the mean score when electric shocks were used compared to being nice, and plot males and females as different coloured lines. ①

- **Task 9**: Using the **Shopping Exercise.sav** data from Chapter 3 (see Task 4 in that chapter), plot two error bar graphs comparing men and women (*x*-axis): one for the distance walked, and the other of the time spent shopping. ①

- **Task 10**: Using the **Goat or Dog.sav** data from Chapter 3 (see Task 5 in that chapter), plot two error bar graphs comparing scores when married to a goat or a dog (*x*-axis): one for the animal liking variable, and the other of the life satisfaction. ①

- **Task 11**: Using the same data as above, plot a scatterplot of animal liking scores against life satisfaction (plot scores for those married to dogs or goats in different colours). ①

- **Task 12**: Using the **Tea Makes You Brainy 15.sav** data from Chapter 3 (see Task 6 in that chapter), plot a scatterplot showing the number of cups of tea drunk (*x*-axis) against cognitive functioning (*y*-axis). ①

Answers can be found on the companion website.

4.14. Further reading

Tufte, E. R. (2001). *The visual display of quantitative information* (2nd ed.). Cheshire, CT: Graphics Press.

Wainer, H. (1984). How to display data badly. *American Statistician, 38*, 137–147.

Wickham, H. (2009). *ggplot2: Elegant graphics for data analysis*. New York: Springer-Verlag.

Wilkinson, L. (2005). *The grammar of graphics*. New York: Springer-Verlag.

Wright, D. B., & Williams, S. (2003). Producing bad results sections. *The Psychologist, 16*, 646–648.

http://junkcharts.typepad.com/ is an amusing look at bad graphs.

The beast of bias

FIGURE 5.1
My first failed
career choice
was a soccer
star

5.1. What will this chapter tell me? ①

Like many young boys in the UK my first career choice was to become a soccer star. My grand-dad (Harry) had been something of a local soccer hero in his day, and I wanted nothing more than to be like him. Harry had a huge influence on me: he had been a goalkeeper, and conse-quently I became a goalkeeper too. This decision, as it turned out, wasn't a great one because I was a bit short for my age, which meant that I never got picked to play in goal for my school. Instead, a taller boy was always chosen. I was technically a better goalkeeper than the other boy, but the trouble was that the opposition could just lob the ball over my head (so, technique aside, I was a worse goalkeeper). Instead, I typically got played at left back ('left back in the changing room' as the joke used to go) because, despite being right footed, I could kick with my left one too. The trouble was, having spent years trying to emulate my granddad's goal-keeping skills, I didn't really have a clue what a left back was supposed to do.[1] Consequently,

[1] In the 1970s at primary school, no one actually bothered to teach you anything about how to play soccer; they just shoved 11 boys onto a pitch and hoped for the best.

I didn't exactly shine in the role, and for many years that put an end to my believing that I could play soccer. This example shows that a highly influential thing (like your granddad) can bias the conclusions you come to and that this can lead to quite dramatic consequences. The same thing happens in data analysis: sources of influence and bias lurk within the data, and unless we identify and correct for them we'll end up becoming goalkeepers despite being a short arse. Or something like that.

5.2. What is bias? ①

You will all be familiar with the term 'bias'. For example, if you've ever watched a sports game you'll probably have accused a referee of being 'biased' at some point, or perhaps you've watched a TV show like *The X Factor* and felt that one of the judges was 'biased' towards the acts that they mentored. In these contexts, bias means that someone isn't evaluating the evidence (e.g., someone's singing) in an objective way: there are other things affecting their conclusions. Similarly, when we analyse data there can be things that lead us to the wrong conclusions.

A bit of revision. We saw in Chapter 2 that, having collected data, we usually fit a model that represents the hypothesis that we want to test. This model is usually a linear model, which takes the form of equation (2.4). To remind you, it looks like this:

$$\text{outcome}_i = \left(b_1 X_{1i} + b_2 X_{2i} + \cdots + b_n X_{ni}\right) + \text{error}_i$$

Therefore, we predict an outcome variable from some kind of model. That model is described by one or more predictor variables (the Xs in the equation) and parameters (the bs in the equation) that tell us something about the relationship between the predictor and the outcome variable. Finally, the model will not predict the outcome perfectly, so for each observation there will be some error.

When we fit a model to the data, we estimate the parameters and we usually use the method of least squares (Section 2.4.3). We're not interested in our sample so much as a more general population to which we don't have access, so we use the sample data to estimate the value of the parameters in the population (that's why we call them estimates rather than values). When we estimate a parameter we also compute an estimate of how well it represents the population such as a standard error (Section 2.5.1) or confidence interval (Section 2.5.2). We also can test hypotheses about these parameters by computing test statistics and their associated probabilities (p-values, Section 2.6.1). Therefore, when we think about bias, we need to think about it within three contexts:

1 things that bias the parameter estimates (including effect sizes);

2 things that bias standard errors and confidence intervals;

3 things that bias test statistics and p-values.

These situations are related: first, if the standard error is biased then the confidence interval will be too because it is based on the standard error; second, test statistics are usually based on the standard error (or something related to it), so if the standard error is biased test statistics will be too; and third, if the test statistic is biased then so too will its p-value. It is important that we identify and eliminate anything that might affect the information that we use to draw conclusions about the world: if our test statistic is inaccurate (or biased) then our conclusions will be too.

Sources of bias come in the form of a two-headed, fire-breathing, green-scaled beast that jumps out from behind a mound of blood-soaked moss to try to eat us alive. One of its heads goes by the name of unusual scores, or 'outliers', whereas the other is called 'violations of assumptions'. These are probably names that led to it being teased at school, but, what the hell, it could breath fire from both heads so it could handle it. Onward into battle …

5.2.1.   Assumptions ①

What are assumptions?

Most of our potential sources of bias come in the form of violations of assumptions, and you will often hear or read about 'assumptions' of statistical tests. An assumption is a condition that ensures that what you're attempting to do works. For example, when we assess a model using a test statistic, we have usually made some assumptions, and if these assumptions are true then we know that we can take the test statistic (and, therefore, p-value) associated with a model at face value and interpret it accordingly. Conversely, if any of the assumptions are not true (usually referred to as a violation) then the test statistic and p-value will be inaccurate and could lead us to the wrong conclusion if we interpret them at face value.

Assumptions are often presented so that it seems like different statistical procedures have their own unique set of assumptions. However, because we're usually fitting variations of the linear model to our data (see Section 2.4), all of the tests in this book basically have the same assumptions. These assumptions relate to the quality of the model itself, and the test statistics used to assess it (which are usually **parametric tests** based on the normal distribution). The main assumptions that we'll look at are:

- additivity and linearity;
- normality of something or other;
- homoscedasticity/homogeneity of variance;
- independence.

5.2.2.   Outliers ①

I mentioned that the first head of the beast of bias is called 'outliers'. An **outlier** is a score very different from the rest of the data. Let's look at an example. When I published my first book (the first edition of this book), I was very excited and I wanted everyone in the world to love my new creation and me. Consequently, I obsessively checked the book's ratings on amazon.co.uk. Customer ratings can range from 1 to 5 stars, where 5 is the best. Back in 2002, my first book had seven ratings (in the order given) of 2, 5, 4, 5, 5, 5, and 5. All but one of these ratings are fairly similar (mainly 5 and 4) but the first rating was quite different from the rest – it was a rating of 2 (a mean and horrible rating). Figure 5.2 plots seven reviewers on the horizontal axis and their ratings on the vertical axis. There is also a dotted horizontal line that represents the mean rating (4.43, as it happens). It should be clear that all of the scores except one lie close to this line. The score of 2 is very different and lies some way below the mean. This score is an example of an outlier – a weird and unusual person (I mean, score) that deviates from the rest of humanity (I mean, data set). The solid horizontal line represents the mean of the scores when the outlier is not included (4.83). This line is higher than the original mean, indicating that by ignoring this score the mean increases (by 0.4). This example shows how a single score, from some

FIGURE 5.2

The first seven customer ratings of this book on www.amazon.co.uk (in about 2002). The first score biases the mean

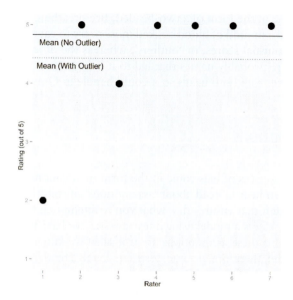

mean-spirited badger turd, can bias a parameter such as the mean: the first rating of 2 drags the average down. Based on this biased estimate, new customers might erroneously conclude that my book is worse than the population actually thinks it is. Although I am consumed with bitterness about this whole affair, it has at least given me a great example of an outlier.

The example illustrates that outliers can bias a parameter estimate, but it has an even greater influence on the error associated with that estimate. Back in Section 2.4.1 we looked at example of the number of friends that 5 statistics lecturers had. The data were 1, 3, 4, 3, 2, the mean was 2.6 and the sum of squared error was 5.2. Let's replace one of the scores with an outlier by changing the 4 to a 10. The data are now: 1, 3, 10, 3, and 2.

SELF-TEST   Compute the mean and sum of squared error for the new data set.

If you did the self-test, you should find that the mean of the data set with the outlier is 3.8 and the sum of squared error is 50.8. Figure 5.3 shows these values; like Figure 2.7 it shows the sum of squared error (y-axis) associated with different potential values of the mean (the parameter we're estimating, b). For both the original data set and the one with the outlier the estimate for the mean is the optimal estimate: it is the one with the least error, which you can tell by the fact the curve converges on the values of the mean (2.6 and 3.8). The presence of the outlier, however, pushes the curve to the right (i.e., it makes the mean higher) and pushes it upwards too (i.e., it makes the sum of squared error larger). By comparing how far the curves shift horizontally compared to vertically you should (I hope) get a clear sense that the outlier affects the sum of squared error more dramatically than it affects the parameter estimate itself. This is because we use squared errors, so any bias created by the outlier is magnified by the fact that deviations are squared.[2]

---

[2] In this example, the difference between the outlier and the mean (the deviance) is $10 - 3.8 = 6.2$. The deviance squared is $6.2^2 = 38.44$. Therefore, of the 50.8 units of error that we have, a whopping 38.44 are attributable to the outlier.

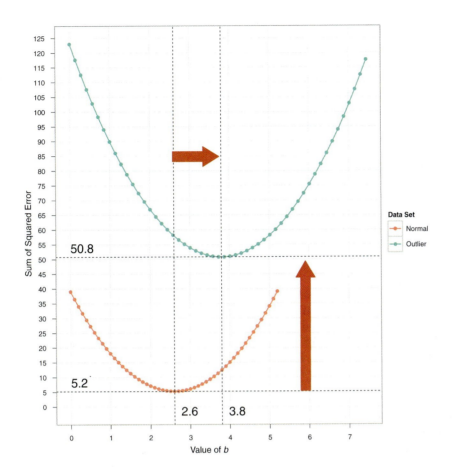

FIGURE 5.3
The effect of
an outlier on
a parameter
estimate (the
mean) and its
associated
estimate of error
(the sum of
squared errors)

We have seen that outliers can bias estimates of parameters (such as the mean), and also dramatically affect the sum of squared errors. This latter point is important because the sum of squared errors is used compute the standard deviation, which in turn is used to estimate the standard error, which itself is used to calculate confidence intervals around the parameter estimate. Therefore, if the sum of squared errors is biased, so are the standard error and the confidence intervals associated with the parameter estimate. In addition, most test statistics are based on sums of squares so these will be biased too by outliers.

5.2.3. Additivity and linearity ①

The second head of the beast of bias is called 'violation of assumptions'. The first assumption we'll look at is additivity and linearity. The vast majority of statistical models in this book are based on the linear model, which takes this form:

$$\text{outcome}_i = \left(b_1 X_{1i} + b_2 X_{2i} + \cdots + b_n X_{ni}\right) + \text{error}_i$$

The assumption of additivity and linearity means that the outcome variable is, in reality, linearly related to any predictors (i.e., their relationship can be summed up by a straight line – think back to Jane Superbrain Box 2.1), and that if you have several predictors then their combined effect is best described by adding their effects together. In other words, it means that the process we're trying to model can be accurately described as:

$$b_1 X_{1i} + b_2 X_{2i} + \cdots + b_n X_{ni}$$

This assumption is the most important because if it is not true then even if all other assumptions are met, your model is invalid because you have described it incorrectly. It's a bit like calling your pet cat a dog: you can try to get it to go in a kennel, or to fetch sticks, or to sit when you tell it to, but don't be surprised when its behaviour isn't what you expect because even though you've a called it a dog, it is in fact a cat. Similarly, if you have described your statistical model inaccurately it won't behave itself and there's no point in interpreting its parameter estimates or worrying about significance tests of confidence intervals: the model is wrong.

5.2.4. Normally distributed something or other ①

The second assumption relates to the normal distribution, which we encountered in Chapter 1 and so we know what it looks like and we (hopefully) understand it. The normal distribution is relevant to many of the things we want to do when we fit models to data and assess them:

- **Parameter estimates**: The mean is a parameter, and we saw in the previous section (the Amazon ratings) that extreme scores can bias it. This illustrates that estimates of parameters are affected by non-normal distributions (such as those with outliers). Parameter estimates differ in how much they are biased in a non-normal distribution: the median, for example, is less biased by skewed distributions than the mean.

- **Confidence intervals**: We use values of the standard normal distribution to compute the confidence interval (Section 2.5.2.1) around a parameter estimate (e.g., the mean, or a b in equation (2.4)). Using values of the standard normal distribution makes sense only if the parameter estimates actually come from one.

- **Null hypothesis significance testing**: If we want to test a hypothesis about a model (and, therefore, the parameter estimates within it) using the framework described in Section 2.6.1 then we assume that the parameter estimates have a normal distribution. We assume this because the test statistics that we use (which we will learn about in due course) have distributions related to the normal distribution (such as the t, F and chi-square distributions), so if our parameter estimate is normally distributed then these test statistics and p-values will be accurate.

- **Errors**: We've seen that any model we fit will include some error (it won't predict the outcome variable perfectly). We also saw that we could calculate the error for each case of data (called the deviance or residual). If these residuals are normally distributed in the population then using the method of least squares to estimate the parameters (the bs in equation (2.4)) will produce better estimates than other methods.

5.2.4.1. The assumption of normality ②

Many people take the 'assumption of normality' to mean that your data need to be normally distributed. However, that isn't what it means. In fact, there is an awful lot of confusion about what it does mean. We have just looked at ways in which normality might introduce bias, and this list hints that the 'assumption of normality' might mean different things in different contexts:

1 For confidence intervals around a parameter estimate (e.g., the mean, or a b in equation (2.4)) to be accurate, that estimate must come from a normal distribution.

2 For significance tests of models (and the parameter estimates that define them) to be accurate the *sampling distribution* of what's being tested must be normal.

For example, if testing whether two means are different, the data do not need to be normally distributed, but the sampling distribution of means (or differences between means) does. Similarly, if looking at relationships between variables, the significance tests of the parameter estimates that define those relationships (the bs in equation (2.4)) will be accurate only when the sampling distribution of the estimate is normal.

3 For the estimates of the parameters that define a model (the bs in equation (2.4)) to be optimal (have the least possible error given the data) the residuals (the error$_i$ in equation 2.4) in the population must be normally distributed. This is true mainly if we use the method of least squares (Section 2.4.3), which we often do.

The misconception that people often have about the data themselves needing to be normally distributed probably stems from the fact that if the data are normally distributed then it's reasonable to assume that the errors in the model and the sampling distribution are too (and remember, we don't have direct access to the sampling distribution, so we have to make educated guesses about its shape). Therefore, the assumption of normality tends to get translated as 'your data need to be normally distributed', even though that's not really what it means (see Jane Superbrain Box 5.1 for some more information).

5.2.4.2. The central limit theorem revisited ③

To understand when and if we need to worry about the assumption of normality we need to revisit the central limit theorem,[3] which we encountered in Section 2.5.1. Imagine

JANE SUPERBRAIN 5.1

The assumption of normality with categorical predictors ②

Although it is often the shape of the sampling distribution that matters, researchers tend to look at the scores on the outcome variable (or the residuals) when assessing normality. An important thing to remember is that when you have a categorical predictor variable (such as people falling into different groups) you wouldn't expect the overall distribution of the outcome (or residuals) to be normal. For example, if you have seen the movie *The* *Muppets*, you will know that muppets live among us. Imagine you predicted that muppets are happier than humans (on TV they seem to be). You collect happiness scores in some muppets and some humans and plot the frequency distribution. You get the graph on the left of Figure 5.4 and decide that your data are not normal: you think that you have violated the assumption of normality. However, you haven't because you predicted that humans and muppets will differ in happiness; in other words, you predict that they come from different populations. If we plot separate frequency distributions for humans and muppets (right of Figure 5.4) you'll notice that within each group the distribution of scores is very normal. The data are as you predicted: muppets are happier than humans and so the centre of their distribution is higher than that of humans. When you combine all of the scores this gives you a bimodal distribution (i.e., two humps). This example illustrates that it is not the normality of the outcome (or residuals) overall that matters, but normality at each unique level of the predictor variable.

[3] The 'central' in the name refers to the theorem being important and far-reaching and has nothing to do with centres of distributions.

FIGURE 5.4   A distribution that looks non-normal (left) could be made up of different groups of normally distributed scores

we have a population of scores that is not normally distributed. Figure 5.5 shows such a population containing scores of how many friends statistics lecturers have: it is very skewed, with most lecturers having only one friend, and the frequencies declining as the number of friends increases to the maximum score of 7 friends. I'm not tricking you; this population is as far removed from the bell-shaped normal curve as it looks. Imagine that I took samples of 5 scores from this population and in each sample I estimated a parameter (let's say I computed the mean) and then replaced the scores. In fact, I took 5000 samples, and consequently I have 5000 values of the parameter estimate (each one from a different sample). Let's look what happens when we plot these 5000 values in a frequency distribution. The frequency distribution of the 5000 parameter estimates from the 5000 samples is on the far left of Figure 5.5. This is the sampling distribution of the parameter estimate. Note that it is quite skewed, but not as skewed as the population. Imagine now that I repeated the sampling process, but this time my samples each contained 30 scores instead of only 5. The resulting distribution of the 5000 parameter estimates is in the centre of Figure 5.5. There is still skew in this sampling distribution but it is a lot more normal than when the samples were based on only 5 scores. Finally, I repeated the whole process but this time took samples of 100 scores rather than 30. The resulting distribution of the 5000 parameter estimates is basically normal (right of Figure 5.5). As our sample sizes got bigger the sampling distributions became more normal, up to point at which the sample is big enough that the sampling distribution is normal – despite the fact that the population of scores was very non-normal indeed. This is the central limit theorem: regardless of the shape of the population, parameter estimates of that population will have a normal distribution provided the samples are 'big enough' (see Jane Superbrain Box 5.2).

5.2.4.3. When does the assumption of normality matter? ②

The central limit theorem means that *there are a variety of situations in which we can assume normality regardless of the shape of our sample data* (Lumley, Diehr, Emerson, & Chen, 2002). Let's think back to the things affected by normality:

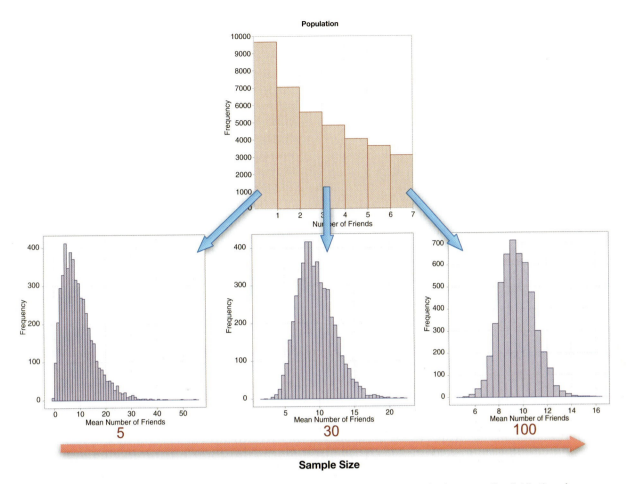

FIGURE 5.5 Parameter estimates sampled from a non-normal population. As the sample size increases, the distribution of those parameters becomes increasingly normal

ODITI'S LANTERN

The central limit theorem

'I, Oditi, believe that the central limit theorem is key to unlocking the hidden truths that the cult strives to find. The true wonder of the CLT cannot be understood by a static diagram and the ramblings of a damaged mind. Only by staring into my lantern can you see the CLT at work in all its glory. Go forth and look into the abyss.'

1 For confidence intervals around a parameter estimate (e.g., the mean, or a *b* in equation (2.4)) to be accurate, that estimate must come from a normal distribution. The central limit theorem tells us that in large samples the estimate will have come from a normal distribution regardless of what the sample or population data look like. Therefore, if we are interested in computing confidence intervals then we don't need to worry about the assumption of normality if our sample is large enough.

2 For significance tests of models to be accurate the sampling distribution of what's being tested must be normal. Again, the central limit theorem

Does normality matter?

JANE SUPERBRAIN 5.2

Size really does matter ②

How big is 'big enough' for the central limit theorem to kick in? The widely accepted value is a sample size of 30, and we saw in Figure 5.4 that with samples of this size we started to get a sampling distribution that approximated normal. However, we also saw that with samples of 100 we got a better approximation of normal. As with most things in statistics, there isn't a simple answer: how big is 'big enough' depends on the distribution of the population. In light-tailed distributions (where outliers are rare) an *N* as small as 20 can be 'large enough', but in heavy-tailed distributions (where outliers are common) then up to 100 or even 160 might be necessary. If the distribution has a lot of skew and kurtosis you might need a very large sample indeed for the central limit theorem to work. It also depends on the parameter that you're trying to estimate (Wilcox, 2010, discusses this issue in detail).

tells us that in large samples this will be true no matter what the shape of the population. Therefore, the shape of our data shouldn't affect significance tests *provided our sample is large enough*. However, the extent to which test statistics perform as they should do in large samples varies across different test statistics, and we will deal with these idiosyncratic issues in the appropriate chapter.

3   For the estimates of model parameters (the *b*s in equation (2.4)) to be optimal (using the method of least squares) the residuals in the population must be normally distributed. The method of least squares will always give you an estimate of the model parameters that minimizes error, so in that sense you don't need to assume normality of anything to fit a linear model and estimate the parameters that define it (Gelman & Hill, 2007). However, there are other methods for estimating model parameters, and if you happen to have normally distributed errors then the estimates that you obtained using the method of least squares will have less error than the estimates you would have got using any of these other methods.

To sum up then, if all you want to do is estimate the parameters of your model then normality doesn't really matter. If you want to construct confidence intervals around those parameters, or compute significance tests relating to those parameters, then the assumption of normality matters in small samples, but because of the central limit theorem we don't really need to worry about this assumption in larger samples (but see Jane Superbrain Box 5.2). In practical terms, as long as your sample is fairly large, outliers are a more pressing concern than normality. Although we tend to think of outliers as isolated very extreme cases, you can have outliers that are less extreme but are not isolated cases. These outliers can dramatically reduce the power of significance tests (Jane Superbrain Box 5.3).

5.2.5.   Homoscedasticity/homogeneity of variance ②

The second assumption we'll explore relates to variance (Section 1.6.3), which can affect the two main things that we might do when we fit models to data:

JANE SUPERBRAIN 5.3

Stealth outliers ③

Although we often think of outliers as one or two very extreme scores, sometimes they soak themselves in radar-absorbent paint and contort themselves into strange shapes so as to avoid detection. These 'stealth outliers' (that's my name for them; no one else calls them that) hide undetected in data sets, radically affecting analyses. Imagine you collected happiness scores, and when you plotted the frequency distribution it looked like Figure 5.6 (left). You might decide that this distribution is normal, because it has the characteristic beli-shaped curve. However, it is not: it is a **mixed normal distribution** or **contaminated normal distribution** (Tukey, 1960). The happiness scores on the left of Figure 5.6 are made up of two distinct populations: 90% of scores are from

humans, but 10% are from muppets (we saw in Jane Superbrain Box 5.1 that they live among us). Figure 5.6 (right) reproduces this overall distribution (the blue one), but also shows the unique distributions for the humans (red) and muppets (Kermit-coloured green) that contribute to it.

The human distribution is a perfect normal distribution, but the curve for the muppets is flatter and heavier in the tails, showing that muppets are more likely than humans to be extremely happy (like Kermit) or extremely miserable (like Statler and Waldorf). When these populations combine, the muppets contaminate the perfectly normal distribution of humans: the combined distribution (blue) has slightly more scores in the extremes than a perfect normal distribution (red). The muppet scores have affected the overall distribution even though (1) they make up only 10% of the scores; and (2) their scores are more frequent at the extremes of 'normal' and not radically different like you might expect an outlier to be. These extreme scores inflate estimates of the population variance (think back to Jane Superbrain Box 1.5). Mixed normal distributions are very common and they reduce the power of significance tests – see Wilcox (2010) for a thorough account of the problems associated with these distributions.

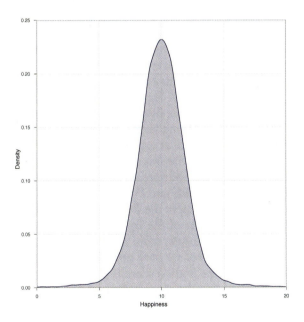

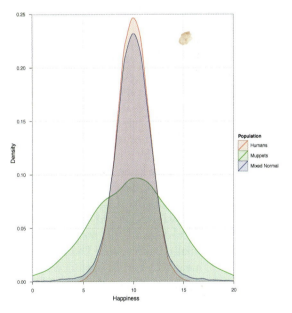

FIGURE 5.6 An apparently normal distribution (left), which is actually a 'mixed normal' distribution made up of two populations (right)

- **Parameters**: If we use the method of least squares (Section 2.4.3) to estimate the parameters in the model, then this will give us optimal estimates if the variance of the outcome variable is equal across different values of the predictor variable.

- **Null hypothesis significance testing**: Test statistics often assume that the variance of the outcome variable is equal across different values of the predictor variable. If this is not the case then these test statistics will be inaccurate.

Therefore, to make sure our estimates of the parameters that define our model and significance tests are accurate we have to assume homoscedasticity (also known as homogeneity of variance).

5.2.5.1. What is homoscedasticity/homogeneity of variance? ②

In designs in which you test several groups of participants this assumption means that each of these samples comes from populations with the same variance. In correlational designs, this assumption means that the variance of the outcome variable should be stable at all levels of the predictor variable. In other words, as you go through levels of the predictor variable, the variance of the outcome variable should not change. Let's illustrate this idea with an example. An audiologist was interested in the effects of loud concerts on people's hearing. She sent 10 people on tour with the loudest band she could find, Motörhead. These people went to concerts in Brixton (London), Brighton, Bristol, Edinburgh, Newcastle, Cardiff and Dublin, and the audiologist measured for how many hours after the concert these people had ringing in their ears.

The top of Figure 5.7 shows the number of hours that each person (represented by a circle) had ringing in his or her ears after each concert. The squares show the average number of hours of ringing in the ears after each concert. A line connects these means so that we can see the general trend. For each concert, the circles are the scores from which the mean is calculated. We can see in both graphs that the means increase as the people go to more concerts: there is a cumulative effect of the concerts on ringing in the ears. The graphs don't differ with respect to the means (which are roughly the same), but do differ in the *spread* of scores around the mean. The bottom of Figure 5.7 removes the data and replaces it with a bar that shows the range of the scores displayed in the top figure. In the left-hand graphs, the green bars are roughly the same length, which tells us that the spread of scores around the mean was roughly the same at each concert. This is what we mean by **homogeneity of variance** or **homoscedasticity**:[4] the spread of scores for hearing loss is the same at each level of the concert variable (i.e., the spread of scores is the same at Brixton, Brighton, Bristol, Edinburgh, Newcastle, Cardiff and Dublin). The right-hand side of Figure 5.7 shows a different scenario: the scores after the Brixton concert (which are again displayed by the green lines in the bottom part of the figure) are quite tightly packed around the mean (the vertical distance from the lowest score to the highest score is small), but after the Dublin show (for example) the scores are very spread out around the mean (the vertical distance from the lowest score to the highest score is large). In general, the green bars on the right differ in length, showing that the spread of scores was different at each concert. This scenario is an example of **heterogeneity of variance** or **heteroscedasticity**: at some levels of the concert variable the variance of scores is different than at other levels (graphically, the vertical distance from the lowest to highest score is different after different concerts).

---

[4] My explanation is a bit simplified because usually we're making the assumption about the errors in the model and not the data themselves, but the two things are related.

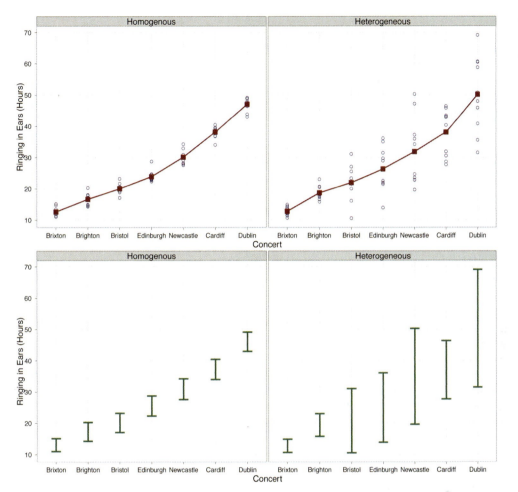

FIGURE 5.7
Graphs
illustrating
data with
homogeneous
(left) and
heterogeneous
(right) variances

5.2.5.2. When does homoscedasticity/homogeneity of variance matter? ②

In terms of estimating the parameters within a linear model, if we assume equality of variance then the estimates we get using the method of least squares will be optimal. If variances for the outcome variable differ along the predictor variable then the estimates of the parameters within the model will not be optimal. The method of least squares will produce 'unbiased' estimates of parameters even when homogeneity of variance can't be assumed, but better estimates can be achieved using different methods, for example, by using weighted least squares in which each case is weighted by a function of its variance. Therefore, if all you care about is estimating the parameters of the model in your sample then you don't need to worry about homogeneity of variance in most cases: the method of least squares will produce unbiased estimates (Hayes & Cai, 2007).

However, unequal variances/heteroscedasticity creates a bias and inconsistency in the estimate of the standard error associated with the parameter estimates in your model (Hayes & Cai, 2007). As such, your confidence intervals and significance tests for the parameter estimates will be biased, because they are computed using the standard error. Confidence intervals can be 'extremely inaccurate' when homogeneity of variance/homoscedasticity cannot be assumed (Wilcox, 2010). Therefore, if you want to look at the confidence intervals around your model parameter estimates or to test the significance of the

Does homowhateveritis matter?

model or its parameter estimates then homogeneity of variance matters. Some test statistics are designed to be accurate even when this assumption is violated, and we'll discuss these in the appropriate chapters.

5.2.6. Independence ②

This assumption means that the errors in your model (the error$_i$ in equation (2.4)) are not related to each other. Imagine Paul and Julie were participants in an experiment where they had to indicate whether they remembered having seen particular photos. If Paul and Julie were to confer about whether they'd seen certain photos then their answers would *not* be independent: Julie's response to a given question would depend on Paul's answer. We know already that if we estimate a model to predict their responses, there will be error in those predictions and because Paul and Julie's scores are not independent the errors associated with these predicted values will also not be independent. If Paul and Julie were unable to confer (if they were locked in different rooms) then the error terms should be independent (unless they're telepathic): the error in predicting Paul's response should not be influenced by the error in predicting Julie's response.

The equation that we use to estimate the standard error (equation (2.8)) is valid only if observations are independent. Remember that we use the standard error to compute confidence intervals and significance tests, so if we violate the assumption of independence then our confidence intervals and significance tests will be invalid. If we use the method of least squares, then model parameter estimates will still be valid but not optimal (we could get better estimates using a different method). In general, if this assumption is violated, we should apply the techniques covered in Chapter 20, so it is important to identify whether the assumption is violated.

5.3. Spotting bias ②

5.3.1. Spotting outliers ②

When they are isolated, extreme cases and outliers are fairly easy to spot using graphs such as histograms and boxplots; it is considerably trickier when outliers are more subtle (using z-scores may be useful – Jane Superbrain Box 5.4). Let's look at an example. A biologist was worried about the potential health effects of music festivals. She went to the Download Music Festival[5] (those of you outside the UK can pretend it is Roskilde Festival, Ozzfest, Lollopalooza, Wacken or something) and measured the hygiene of 810 concert-goers over the three days of the festival. She tried to measure every person on every day but, because it was difficult to track people down, there were missing data on days 2 and 3. Hygiene was measured using a standardized technique (don't worry, it *wasn't* licking the person's armpit) that results in a score ranging between 0 (you smell like a corpse that's been left to rot up a skunk's arse) and 4 (you smell of sweet roses on a fresh spring day). I know from bitter experience that sanitation is not always great at these places (the Reading Festival seems particularly bad) and so the biologist predicted that personal hygiene would go down dramatically over the three days of the festival. The data can be found in **DownloadFestival.sav**.

---

[5] http://www.downloadfestival.co.uk

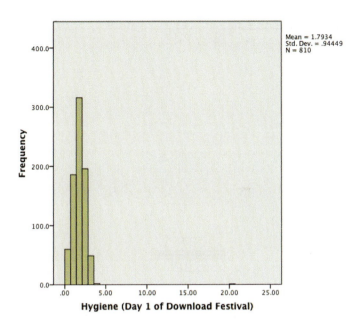

FIGURE 5.8

Histogram of the
day 1 Download
Festival hygiene
scores

SELF-TEST   Using what you learnt in Section 4.4, plot
a histogram of the hygiene scores on day 1 of
the festival.

The resulting histogram is shown in Figure 5.8. The first thing that should leap out at you is that there is one case that is very different from the others. All of the scores appear to be squashed up at one end of the distribution because they are all less than 5 (yielding a very pointy distribution) except for one, which has a value of 20. This score is an obvious outlier because it is above the top of our scale (remember our hygiene scale ranged only from 0 to 4). It must be a mistake. However, with 810 cases, how on earth do we find out which case it was? You could just look through the data, but that would certainly give you a headache, and so instead we can use a boxplot (see Section 4.5), which is another very useful way to spot outliers.

SELF-TEST   Using what you learnt in Section 4.5, plot a
boxplot of the hygiene scores on day 1 of the festival.

The resulting boxplot is shown in Figure 5.9. The outlier that we detected in the histogram has shown up as an extreme score (*) on the boxplot. SPSS helpfully tells us the number of the case (611) that's producing this outlier. If we go to the data editor (data view), we can locate this case quickly by clicking on 🔲 and typing 611 in the dialog box that appears. That takes us straight to case 611. Looking at this case reveals a score of 20.02, which is probably a mistyping of 2.02. We'd have to go back to the raw data and check. We'll assume we've checked the raw data and this score should be 2.02, so replace the value 20.02 with the value 2.02 before we continue this example.

FIGURE 5.9
Boxplot of
hygiene scores
on day 1 of
the Download
Festival

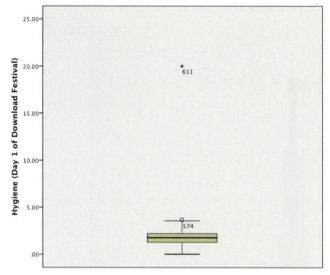

FIGURE 5.10
Histogram (left)
and boxplot
(right) of
hygiene scores
on day 1 of
the Download
Festival after
removing the
extreme score

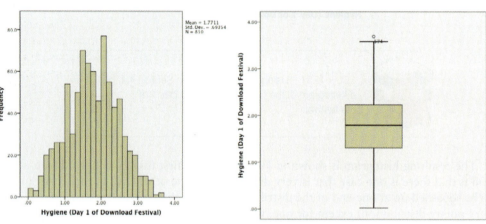

SELF-TEST   Now we have removed the outlier in the data,
re-plot the histogram and boxplot.

Figure 5.10 shows the histogram and boxplot for the data after the extreme case has
been corrected. The distribution looks amazingly normal: it is nicely symmetrical and
doesn't seem too pointy or flat. Neither plot indicates any particularly extreme scores: the
boxplot suggests that case 574 is a mild outlier, but the histogram doesn't seem to show any
cases as being particularly out of the ordinary.

SELF-TEST   Produce boxplots for the day 2 and day 3
hygiene scores and interpret them.

SELF-TEST   Re-plot theses scores but splitting by **Gender**
along the x-axis. Are there differences between men and women?

5.3.2. Spotting normality ①

5.3.2.1. Using graphs to spot normality ①

Frequency distributions are not only good for spotting outliers; they are the natural choice for looking at the shape of the distribution as a whole. We have already plotted a histogram of the day 1 scores (Figure 5.10). The **P-P plot** (probability–probability plot) is another useful graph for checking normality; it plots the cumulative probability of a variable against the cumulative probability of a particular distribution (in this case we would specify a

JANE SUPERBRAIN 5.4

Using z-scores to find outliers ③

We saw in Section 1.6.4 that *z*-scores express scores in terms of a distribution with a mean of 0 and a standard deviation of 1. By converting our data to *z*-scores we can use benchmarks that we can apply to any data set (regardless of what its original mean and standard deviation were) to search for outliers. We can get SPSS to do this conversion using the `Analyze Descriptive Statistics ▶` `Descriptives...` dialog box. Select the variable(s) to convert (such as day 2 of the hygiene data as in the diagram) and tick the *Save standardized values as variables* option (Figure 5.11). SPSS will create a new variable in the data editor (with the same name prefixed with the letter *z*).

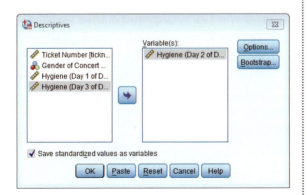

FIGURE 5.11   Saving *z*-scores

To look for outliers we can count how many *z*-scores fall within certain important limits. If we ignore whether

the *z*-score is positive or negative (called the 'absolute value'), then in a normal distribution we'd expect about 5% to be greater than 1.96 (we often use 2 for convenience), 1% to have absolute values greater than 2.58, and none to be greater than about 3.29. To get SPSS to do the counting for you, use the syntax file **Outliers (Percentage of Z-scores).sps** (on the companion website), which will produce a table for day 2 of the Download Festival hygiene data. Load this file and run the syntax (see Section 3.9). It uses the following commands:

```
DESCRIPTIVES
VARIABLES= day2/SAVE.
COMPUTE zday2= abs(zday2).
EXECUTE.
```

These commands use the *descriptives* function on the variable **day2** to save the *z*-scores in the data editor (as a variable called **zday2**). We then use the *compute* command to change **zday2** so that it contains the absolute values.

```
RECODE
  zday2 (3.29 thru highest = 1)(2.58 thru highest = 2)
(1.96 thru highest = 3)(Lowest thru 1.95 = 4).
  EXECUTE.
```

These commands recode the variable **zday2** so that if a value is greater than 3.29 it's assigned a code of 1, if it's greater than 2.58 it's assigned a code of 2, if it's greater than 1.96 it's assigned a code of 3, and if it's less than 1.95 it gets a code of 4.

```
VALUE LABELS zday2
  4 'Normal range' 3 'Potential Outliers (z > 1.96)' 2
'Probable Outliers (z > 2.58)' 1 'Extreme (z-score > 3.29)'.
```

This syntax assigns appropriate labels to the codes we defined above.

```
FREQUENCIES
VARIABLES= zday2
/ORDER=ANALYSIS.
```

Finally, this syntax uses the *frequencies* command to produce a table (Output 5.1) telling us the percentage of 1s, 2s, 3s and 4s found in the variable **zday2**. Thinking about what we know about the absolute values of z-scores, we would expect to see only 5% (or less) with an values greater than 1.96, 1% (or less) with values greater than 2.58, and very few cases above 3.29. The column labelled *Cumulative Percent* tells us the corresponding percentages for the hygiene

scores on day 2: 0.8% of cases were above 3.29 (extreme cases), 2.3% (compared to the 1% we'd expect) had values greater than 2.58, and 6.8% (compared to the 5% we would expect) had values greater than 1.96. The remaining cases (which, if you look at the *Valid Percent*, constitute 93.2%) were in the normal range. All in all these percentages are broadly consistent with what we'd expect in a normal distribution (around 95% were in the normal range).

Zscore: Hygiene (Day 2 of Download Festival)

		Frequency	Percent	Valid Percent	Cumulative Percent
Valid	Extreme (z-score > 3.29)	2	.2	.8	.8
	Probable Outliers (z > 2.58)	4	.5	1.5	2.3
	Potential Outliers (z > 1.96)	12	1.5	4.5	6.8
	Normal range	246	30.4	93.2	100.0
	Total	264	32.6	100.0	
Missing	System	546	67.4		
Total		810	100.0		

OUTPUT 5.1

normal distribution). The data are ranked and sorted, then for each rank the corresponding z-score is calculated to create an 'expected value' that the score should have in a normal distribution. Next, the score itself is converted to a z-score (see Section 1.6.4). The actual z-score is plotted against the expected z-score. If the data are normally distributed then the actual z-score will be the same as the expected z-score and you'll get a lovely straight diagonal line. This ideal scenario is helpfully plotted on the graph and your job is to compare the data points to this line. If values fall on the diagonal of the plot then the variable is normally distributed; however, when the data sag consistently above or below the diagonal then this shows that the kurtosis differs from a normal distribution, and when the data points are S-shaped, the problem is skewness.

To get a P-P plot use Analyze Descriptive Statistics ▸ 🗔 P-P Plots... to access the dialog box in Figure 5.12.[6] There's not a lot to say about this dialog box because the default options will compare any variables selected to a normal distribution, which is what we want (although note that there is a drop-down list of different distributions against which you could compare your data). Select the three hygiene score variables in the variable list (click on the day 1 variable, then hold down *Shift* and select the day 3 variable and the day 2 scores will be selected as well). Transfer the selected variables to the box labelled *Variables* by clicking on ◄. Click on OK to draw the graphs.

SELF-TEST   Using what you learnt in Section 4.4, plot histograms for the hygiene scores for days 2 and 3 of the Download Festival.

Figure 5.13 shows the histograms (from the self-test tasks) and the corresponding P-P plots. We've looked at the day 1 scores in the previous section and concluded that they

[6] You'll notice in the same menu something called a Q-Q plot, which is very similar and which we'll discuss later.

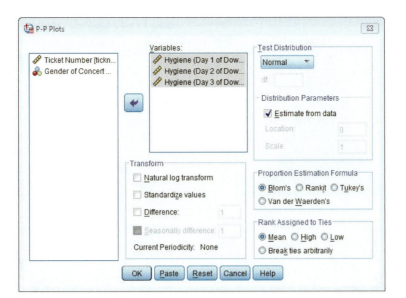

FIGURE 5.12
Dialog box for
obtaining P-P
plots

looked quite normal. The P-P plot echoes this view because the data points all fall very
close to the 'ideal' diagonal line. However, the distributions for days 2 and 3 are not nearly
as symmetrical as day 1: they both look positively skewed. Again, this can be seen in the
P-P plots by the data points deviating away from the diagonal. In general, this seems to suggest that by days 2 and 3, hygiene scores were much more clustered around the low end of
the scale. Remember that the lower the score, the less hygienic the person is, so generally
people became smellier as the festival progressed. The skew occurs because a substantial
minority insisted on upholding their levels of hygiene (against all odds) over the course of
the festival (baby wet-wipes are indispensable, I find).

5.3.2.2. Using numbers to spot normality ①

Graphs are particularly useful for looking at normality in big samples; however, in smaller
samples it can be useful to explore the distribution of the variables using the *frequencies*
command (Analyze Descriptive Statistics ▸ 📊 Frequencies…). The main dialog box is shown in Figure
5.14. The variables in the data editor are listed on the left-hand side, and they can be transferred to the box labelled *Variable(s)* by clicking on a variable (or highlighting several with
the mouse) and then clicking on 🔹. If a variable listed in the *Variable(s)* box is selected, it
can be transferred back to the variable list by clicking on the arrow button (which should
now be pointing in the opposite direction). By default, SPSS produces a frequency distribution of all scores in table form. However, there are two other dialog boxes that can be
selected that provide other options. The *Statistics* dialog box is accessed by clicking on
Statistics…, and the *Charts* dialog box is accessed by clicking on Charts… .

The *Statistics* dialog box allows you to select ways to describe a distribution, such as
measures of central tendency (mean, mode, median), measures of variability (range, standard deviation, variance, quartile splits), measures of shape (kurtosis and skewness). Select
the mean, mode, median, standard deviation, variance and range. To check that a distribution of scores is normal, we can look at the values of kurtosis and skewness (see Section
1.6.1). The *Charts* option provides a simple way to plot the frequency distribution of
scores (as a bar chart, a pie chart or a histogram). We've already plotted histograms of our
data so we don't need to select these options, but you could use these options in future
analyses. When you have selected the appropriate options, return to the main dialog box
by clicking on Continue. Once in the main dialog box, click on OK to run the analysis.

FIGURE 5.13
Histograms
(left) and P-P
plots (right)
of the hygiene
scores over the
three days of
the Download
Festival

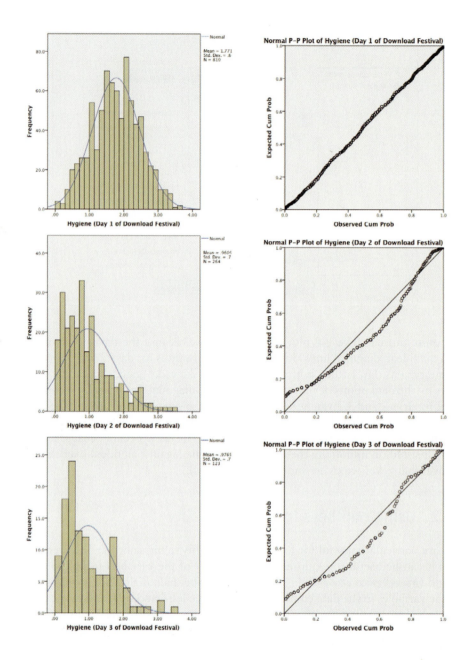

Output 5.2 shows the table of descriptive statistics for the three variables in this example. On average, hygiene scores were 1.77 (out of 5) on day 1 of the festival, but went down to 0.96 and 0.98 on days 2 and 3, respectively. The other important measures for our purposes are the skewness and the kurtosis (see Section 1.6.1), both of which have an associated standard error.

There are different ways to calculate skewness and kurtosis, but SPSS uses methods that give values of zero in a normal distribution. Positive values of skewness indicate a pile-up of scores on the left of the distribution, whereas negative values indicate a pile-up on the right. Positive values of kurtosis indicate a pointy and heavy-tailed distribution, whereas negative values indicate a flat and light-tailed distribution. The further the value is from zero, the more likely it is that the data are not normally distributed. For day 1 the skew value is very close to zero (which is good) and kurtosis is a little negative. For days 2 and 3, though, there is a skewness of around 1 (positive skew).

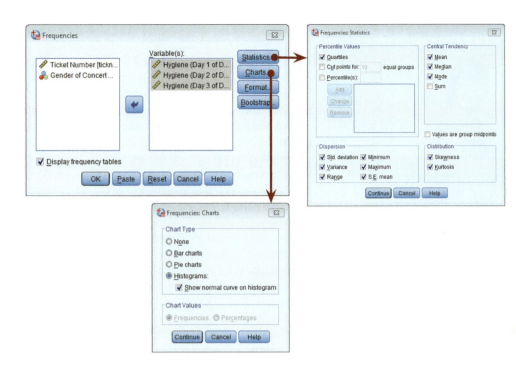

FIGURE 5.14
Dialog boxes for the *frequencies* command

OUTPUT 5.2

Statistics

		Hygiene (Day 1 of Download Festival)	Hygiene (Day 2 of Download Festival)	Hygiene (Day 3 of Download Festival)
N	Valid	810	264	123
	Missing	0	546	687
Mean		1.7711	.9609	.9765
Std. Error of Mean		.02437	.04436	.06404
Median		1.7900	.7900	.7600
Mode		2.00	.23	.44ª
Std. Deviation		.69354	.72078	.71028
Variance		.481	.520	.504
Skewness		-.004	1.095	1.033
Std. Error of Skewness		.086	.150	.218
Kurtosis		-.410	.822	.732
Std. Error of Kurtosis		.172	.299	.433
Range		3.67	3.44	3.39
Minimum		.02	.00	.02
Maximum		3.69	3.44	3.41
Percentiles	25	1.3050	.4100	.4400
	50	1.7900	.7900	.7600
	75	2.2300	1.3500	1.5500

a. Multiple modes exist. The smallest value is shown

OLIVER TWISTED

Please, Sir, can I have some more … frequencies?

In your output you will also see tabulated frequency distributions of each variable. This table is reproduced in the additional online material along with a description.

We can convert these values to z-scores (Section 1.6.4), which enables us to (1) compare skew and kurtosis values in different samples that used different measures, and (2) calculate a p-value that tells us if the values are significantly different from 0 (i.e., normal). Although

JANE SUPERBRAIN 5.5

Significance tests and assumptions ②

Throughout this section we will look at various significance tests that have been devised to look at whether assumptions are violated. These include tests of whether a distribution is normal (the Kolmogorov–Smirnoff and Shapiro–Wilk tests), tests of homogeneity of variances (Levene's test), and tests of significance of skew and kurtosis. Although I cover these tests because people expect to see these sorts of things in introductory statistics books, there is a fundamental problem with using them. They are all based on null hypothesis significance testing, and this means that (1) in large samples they can be significant even for small and unimportant effects, and (2) in small samples they will lack power to detect violations of assumptions (Section 2.6.1.10).

We have also seen in this chapter that the central limit theorem means that as sample sizes get larger, the assumption of normality matters less because the sampling distribution will be normal regardless of what our population (or indeed sample) data look like. So, the problem is that in large samples, where we don't need to worry about normality, a test of normality is more likely to be significant, and therefore likely to make us worry about and correct for something that doesn't need to be corrected or worried about. Conversely, in small samples, where we might want to worry about normality, a significance test won't have the power to detect non-normality and so is likely to encourage us not to worry about something that we probably ought to. Therefore, the best advice is that if your sample is large then don't use significance tests of normality; in fact, don't worry too much about normality at all. In small samples pay attention if your significance tests are significant but resist being lulled into a false sense of security if they are not.

there are good reasons not to do this (see Jane Superbrain Box 5.5), if you want to you can do it by subtracting the mean of the distribution (in this case zero) from the score and then dividing by the standard error of the distribution.

$$z_{\text{skewness}} = \frac{S - 0}{SE_{\text{skewness}}} \qquad z_{\text{kurtosis}} = \frac{K - 0}{SE_{\text{kurtosis}}}$$

In the above equations, the values of S (skewness) and K (kurtosis) and their respective standard errors are produced by SPSS. These z-scores can be compared against values that you would expect to get if skew and kurtosis were not different from 0 (see Section 1.6.4). So, an absolute value greater than 1.96 is significant at $p < .05$, above 2.58 is significant at $p < .01$ and above 3.29 is significant at $p < .001$. However, you really should use these criteria only in small samples: in larger samples examine the shape of the distribution visually, interpret the value of the skewness and kurtosis statistics, and possibly don't even worry about normality at all (Jane Superbrain Box 5.5).

Did someone say Smirnov? Great, I need a drink after all this data analysis!

For the hygiene scores, the z-score of skewness is $-0.004/0.086 = 0.047$ on day 1, $1.095/0.150 = 7.300$ on day 2 and $1.033/0.218 = 4.739$ on day 3. It is pretty clear then that although on day 1 scores are not at all skewed, on days 2 and 3 there is a very significant positive skew (as was evident from the histogram). The kurtosis z-scores are: $-0.410/0.172 = -2.38$ on day 1, $0.822/0.299 = 2.75$ on day 2 and $0.732/0.433 = 1.69$ on day 3. These values indicate significant problems with skew, kurtosis or both (at $p < .05$) for all three days; however, because of the large sample, this isn't surprising and so we can take comfort from the central limit theorem.

Another way of looking at the problem is to see whether the distribution of scores deviates from a comparable normal distribution. The **Kolmogorov–Smirnov**

CRAMMING SAM'S TIPS   Skewness and kurtosis

- To check that the distribution of scores is approximately normal, we need to look at the values of skewness and kurtosis in the output.
- Positive values of skewness indicate too many low scores in the distribution, whereas negative values indicate a build-up of high scores.
- Positive values of kurtosis indicate a pointy and heavy-tailed distribution, whereas negative values indicate a flat and light-tailed distribution.
- The further the value is from zero, the more likely it is that the data are not normally distributed.
- You can convert these scores to z-scores by dividing by their standard error. If the resulting score (when you ignore the minus sign) is greater than 1.96 then it is significant ($p < .05$).
- Significance tests of skew and kurtosis should not be used in large samples (because they are likely to be significant even when skew and kurtosis are not too different from normal).

test and Shapiro–Wilk test do this: they compare the scores in the sample to a normally distributed set of scores with the same mean and standard deviation. If the test is non-significant ($p > .05$) it tells us that the distribution of the sample is not significantly different from a normal distribution (i.e., it is probably normal). If, however, the test is significant ($p < .05$) then the distribution in question is significantly different from a normal distribution (i.e., it is non-normal). These tests seem great: in one easy procedure they tell us whether our scores are normally distributed (nice!). However, Jane Superbrain Box 5.5 explains some really good reasons not to use them. If you insist on using them, bear Jane's advice in mind and always plot your data as well and try to make an informed decision about the extent of non-normality based on converging evidence.

The Kolmogorov–Smirnov (K-S; Figure 5.15) test is accessed through the *explore* command (Analyze Descriptive Statistics ▸ 🔍 Explore…). Figure 5.16 shows the dialog boxes for this command. First, enter any variables of interest in the box labelled *Dependent List* by highlighting them on the left-hand side and transferring them by clicking on ▸. For this example, select the hygiene scores for the three days. If you click on Statistics… a dialog box appears, but the default option is fine (it will produce means, standard deviations and so on). The more interesting option for our current purposes is accessed by clicking on Plots…. In this dialog box select the option ☑ Normality plots with tests, and this will produce both

Is it possible to test whether I am normal?

the K-S test and some *normal quantile–quantile (Q-Q) plots*. A Q-Q plot is very similar to the P-P plot that we encountered in Section 5.3.2 except that it plots the quantiles (Section 1.6.3) of the data instead of every individual score in the data. The expected quantiles are a straight diagonal line, whereas the observed quantiles are plotted as individual points. The Q-Q plot can be interpreted in the same way as a P-P plot: any deviation of the dots from the diagonal line represents a deviation from normality. Kurtosis is shown up by the dots sagging above or below the line, whereas skew is shown up by the dots snaking around the line in an 'S' shape. If you have a lot of scores, Q-Q plots can be easier to interpret than P-P plots because they will display fewer values.

By default, SPSS will produce boxplots (split according to group if a factor has been specified) and stem-and-leaf diagrams as well. We also need to click on Options… to tell SPSS how to deal with missing values. This is important because although we start off with 810 scores on

FIGURE 5.15
Andrei
Kolmogorov,
wishing he had a
Smirnov

FIGURE 5.16
Dialog boxes
for the *explore*
command

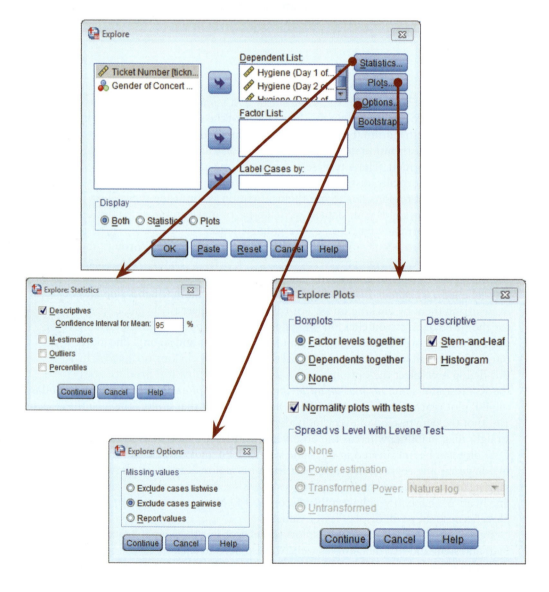

day 1, by day 2 we have only 264 and by day 3 only 123. By default, SPSS will use only cases for which there are valid scores on all of the selected variables. This would mean that for day 1, even though we have 810 scores, it will use only the 123 cases for which there are scores on all three days. This is known as excluding cases *listwise*. However, we want it to use all of the scores it has on a given day, which is known as *pairwise*. There's more information on these two methods in SPSS Tip 5.1. Once you have clicked on [Options...], select *Exclude cases pairwise*, then click on [Continue] to return to the main dialog box and click on [OK] to run the analysis.

SPSS will produce a table of descriptive statistics (mean, etc.) that should have the same values as the tables obtained using the frequencies procedure. The important table is that of the K-S test (Output 5.3). This table includes the test statistic itself, the degrees of freedom (which should equal the sample size) and the significance value of this test. Remember that a significant value (*Sig.* less than .05) indicates a deviation from normality. For day 1 the K-S test is just about non-significant ($p = .097$), which is surprisingly close to significant given how normal the day 1 scores looked in the histogram (Figure 5.13). However, the sample size on day 1 is very large ($N = 810$) and the significance of the K-S test for these data shows how in large samples even small and unimportant deviations from normality might be deemed significant by this test (Jane Superbrain Box 5.5). For days 2 and 3 the test is highly significant, indicating that these distributions are not normal, which is likely to reflect the skew seen in the histograms for these data (Figure 5.13).

SPSS TIP 5.1   Pairwise or listwise? ①

Many of the analyses in this book have additional options that can be accessed by clicking on [Options...]. Often the resulting *Options* dialog box will ask you if you want to exclude cases 'pairwise', 'analysis by analysis' or 'listwise'. Let's imagine we wanted to use our hygiene scores to compare mean scores on days 1 and 2, days 1 and 3, and days 2 and 3. First, we can exclude cases listwise, which means that if a case has a missing value for any variable, then they are excluded from the whole analysis. So, for example, if we had the hygiene score for a person (let's call her Melody) at the festival on days 1 and 2, but not day 3, then Melody's data will be excluded for all of the comparisons mentioned above. Even though we have her data for days 1 and 2, we won't use them for that comparison – *they would be completely excluded from the analysis*. Another option is to excluded cases on a *pairwise* (a.k.a. *analysis-by-analysis* or *test-by-test*) basis, which means that Melody's data will be excluded only for analyses for which she has missing data: so her data would be used to compare days 1 and 2, but would be excluded for the other comparisons (because we don't have her score on day 3).

Tests of Normality

OUTPUT 5.3

	Kolmogorov-Smirnov[a]			Shapiro-Wilk		
	Statistic	df	Sig.	Statistic	df	Sig.
Hygiene (Day 1 of Download Festival)	.029	810	.097	.996	810	.032
Hygiene (Day 2 of Download Festival)	.121	264	.000	.908	264	.000
Hygiene (Day 3 of Download Festival)	.140	123	.000	.908	123	.000

a. Lilliefors Significance Correction

OLIVER TWISTED

Please, Sir, can I have some more … normality tests?

'There is another test reported in the table (the Shapiro–Wilk test)', whispers Oliver as he creeps up behind you, knife in hand, 'and a footnote saying that the '"Lilliefors significance correction" has been applied. What the hell is going on?' (If you do the K-S test through the Nonparametric Tests menu rather than the Explore menu this correction is not applied.) Well, Oliver, all will be revealed in the additional material for this chapter on the companion website: you can find out more about the K-S test, and information about the Lilliefors correction and Shapiro–Wilk test. What are you waiting for?

5.3.2.3. Reporting the K-S test ①

The test statistic for the K-S test is denoted by *D*, and we should report the degrees of freedom (*df*) from the table in brackets after the *D*. We can report the results in Output 5.3 in the following way:

✓ The hygiene scores on day 1, $D(810) = 0.029$, $p = .097$, did not deviate significantly from normal; however, day 2, $D(264) = 0.121$, $p < .001$, and day 3, $D(123) = 0.140$, $p < .001$, scores were both significantly non-normal.

CRAMMING SAM'S TIPS   **Normality tests**

- The K-S test can be used to see if a distribution of scores significantly differs from a normal distribution.
- If the K-S test is significant (*Sig.* in the SPSS table is less than .05) then the scores are significantly different from a normal distribution.
- Otherwise, scores are approximately normally distributed.
- The Shapiro–Wilk test does much the same thing, but it has more power to detect differences from normality (so this test might be significant when the K-S test is not).
- **Warning**: In large samples these tests can be significant even when the scores are only slightly different from a normal distribution. Therefore, I don't particularly recommend them and they should always be interpreted in conjunction with histograms, P-P or Q-Q plots, and the values of skew and kurtosis.

5.3.2.4. Normality within groups and the split file command ①

We saw earlier that when predictor variables are formed of categories, if you decide that you need to check the assumption of normality then you need to do it within each group separately (Jane Superbrain Box 5.1). For example, for the hygiene scores we have data for males and females (in the variable **Gender**). If we made some prediction about there being differences in hygiene between males and females at a music festival then we should look at normality within males and females separately. There are several ways to produce basic descriptive statistics for separate groups. First, I will introduce you to the *split file* function. This function allows you to specify a grouping variable (remember, these variables are used to specify categories of cases). Any subsequent procedure in SPSS is then carried out on *each category of cases separately*.

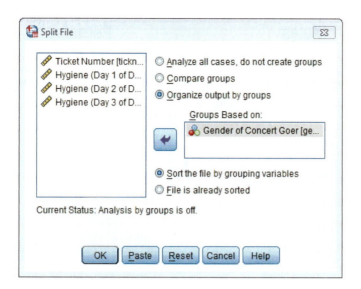

FIGURE 5.17
Split File dialog box

If we want to obtain separate descriptive statistics for males and females in our festival hygiene scores, we can split the file, and then proceed using the *frequencies* command described in the previous section. To split the file, select Data ⬛ Split File... or click on ⬛. In the resulting dialog box (Figure 5.17) select the option *Organize output by groups*. Once this option is selected, the *Groups Based on* box will activate. Select the variable containing the group codes by which you wish to repeat the analysis (in this example select **Gender**), and drag it to the box or click on ⬛. By default, SPSS will sort the file by these groups (i.e., it will list one category followed by the other in the data editor). Once you have split the file, use the *frequencies* command (see the previous section). Let's request statistics for all three days as in Figure 5.14.

Can I analyse groups of data?

Output 5.4 shows the results, which have been split into two tables: the results for males and the results for females. Males scored lower then females on all three days of the festival (i.e., they were smellier). The values of skew and kurtosis are similar for males and females on days 2 and 3, but differ a little on day 1: as already indicated, males show a very slight positive skew (0.200) but for females the skew is slightly negative (−0.176). In both cases the skew on day 1 is very small. Figure 5.18 shows the histograms of hygiene scores split according to the gender of the

Male

Female

OUTPUT 5.4

Statistics[a]

		Hygiene (Day 1 of Download Festival)	Hygiene (Day 2 of Download Festival)	Hygiene (Day 3 of Download Festival)
N	Valid	315	104	56
	Missing	0	211	259
Mean		1.6021	.7733	.8291
Std. Error of Mean		.03620	.05847	.07210
Median		1.5800	.6700	.7300
Mode		2.00	.23	.44
Std. Deviation		.64241	.59630	.53954
Variance		.413	.356	.291
Skewness		.200	1.476	.719
Std. Error of Skewness		.137	.237	.319
Kurtosis		−.101	3.134	−.268
Std. Error of Kurtosis		.274	.469	.628
Range		3.47	3.35	2.09
Minimum		.11	.00	.02
Maximum		3.58	3.35	2.11

a. Gender of Concert Goer = Male

Statistics[a]

		Hygiene (Day 1 of Download Festival)	Hygiene (Day 2 of Download Festival)	Hygiene (Day 3 of Download Festival)
N	Valid	495	160	67
	Missing	0	335	428
Mean		1.8787	1.0829	1.0997
Std. Error of Mean		.03164	.06078	.09896
Median		1.9400	.8900	.8500
Mode		2.02	.85	.38
Std. Deviation		.70396	.76876	.81001
Variance		.496	.591	.656
Skewness		−.176	.870	.869
Std. Error of Skewness		.110	.192	.293
Kurtosis		−.397	.089	.069
Std. Error of Kurtosis		.219	.381	.578
Range		3.67	3.38	3.39
Minimum		.02	.06	.02
Maximum		3.69	3.44	3.41

a. Gender of Concert Goer = Female

Distributions of hygiene scores for males (left) and females (right) over three days (top to bottom) of a music festival

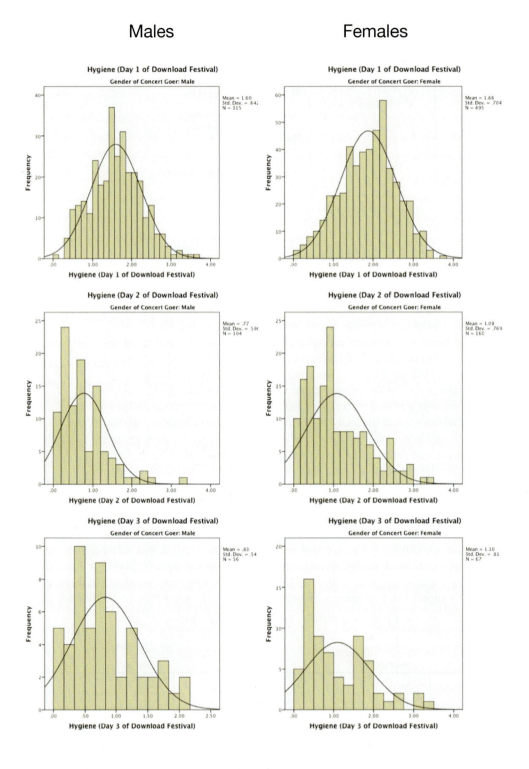

festival-goer. Male and female scores have similar distributions. On day 1 they are fairly normal (although females perhaps show a very slight negative skew, which indicates a higher proportion of them were at the higher end of hygiene scores than males). On days 2 and 3 both males and females show the characteristic positive skew that we saw in the sample as a whole. It looks as though proportionally more females are in the skewed end of the distribution (i.e., at the hygienic end).

We can also do K-S tests within the different groups by repeating the analysis we did earlier (Figure 5.16); because the *split file* command is switched on, we'd get the K-S test performed on males and females separately. An alterative method is to split the analysis by group from within the *explore* command itself. First, switch *split file* off by clicking on Data ▦ Split File... (or click on ▦) to activate the dialog box in Figure 5.17. Select *Analyze all cases, do not create groups* and click on ⬭ OK ⬭. The *split file* function is now off and analyses will be conducted on the data as whole. Next, activate the *explore* command just as we did before: Analyze Descriptive Statistics ▸ ⬭ Explore.... We can ask for separate tests for males and females by placing **Gender** in the box labelled *Factor List* as in Figure 5.21 and selecting the same options as described earlier. Let's do this for the day 1 hygiene scores. You should see the table in Output 5.5, which shows that the distribution of hygiene scores was normal for males (the value of *Sig.* is greater than .05) but not for females (the value of *Sig.* is smaller than .05).

OUTPUT 5.5

Tests of Normality

	Gender of Concert Goer	Kolmogorov-Smirnov[a]			Shapiro-Wilk		
		Statistic	df	Sig.	Statistic	df	Sig.
Hygiene (Day 1 of Download Festival)	Male	.035	315	.200[*]	.993	315	.119
	Female	.053	495	.002	.993	495	.029

[*]. This is a lower bound of the true significance.

a. Lilliefors Significance Correction

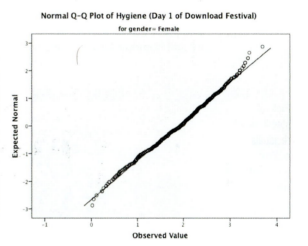

Male   Female

FIGURE 5.19 Normal Q-Q plots of hygiene scores for day 1 of the music festival

SPSS also produces a normal Q-Q plot (see Figure 5.19). Despite the K-S having completely different outcomes for males and females, the Q-Q plots are remarkably similar: there is no sign of a major problem with kurtosis (the dots do not particularly sag above or below the line) and there is some slight skew (the female graph in particular has a slight S-shape). However, both graphs show that the quantiles fall very close to the diagonal line, which, let's not forget, represents a perfect normal distribution. For the females the graph is at odds with the significant K-S test, and this illustrates my earlier point that if you have a large sample then tests like K-S will lead you to conclude that even very minor deviations from normality are 'significant'.

SELF-TEST Compute and interpret a K-S test and Q-Q plots for males and females for days 2 and 3 of the music festival.

5.3.3.　Spotting linearity and heteroscedasticity/heterogeneity of variance ②

5.3.3.1.　Using graphs to spot problems with linearity or homoscedasticity ②

It might seem odd that I have chosen to look at the assumption of linearity and homosce-dasticity together. However, there is a graph that shows up problems with both of these assumptions. These assumptions both relate to the errors (a.k.a. residuals) in the model we fit to the data. We can create a scatterplot of the values of the residuals against the values of the outcome predicted by our model. In doing so we're looking at whether there is a systematic relationship between what comes out of the model (the predicted values) and the errors in the model. Normally we convert the predicted values and errors to z-scores,[7] so this plot is sometimes referred to as *zpred vs. zresid*. If linearity and homoscedasticity hold true then there should be no systematic relationship between the errors in the model and what the model predicts. Looking at this graph can, therefore, kill two birds with one stone. If this graph funnels out, then the chances are that there is heteroscedasticity in the data. If there is any sort of curve in this graph then the chances are that the data have broken the assumption of linearity.

Figure 5.20 shows several examples of the plot of standardized residuals against standard-ized predicted values. The top left panel shows a situation in which the assumptions of linear-ity and homoscedasticity have been met. The top right panel shows a similar plot for a data

FIGURE 5.20
Plots of standardized residuals against predicted (fitted) values

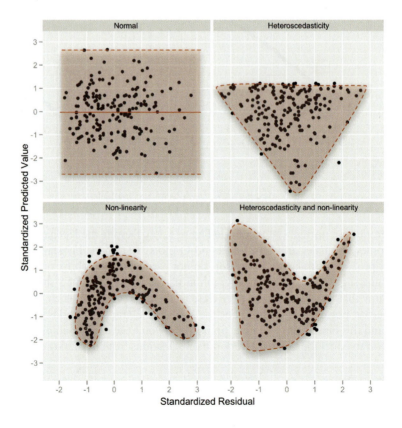

[7] Theses standardized errors are called standardized residuals, which we'll discuss in Chapter 8.

set that violates the assumption of homoscedasticity. Note that the points form a funnel: they become more spread out across the graph. This funnel shape is typical of heteroscedasticity and indicates increasing variance across the residuals. The bottom left panel shows a plot of some data in which there is a non-linear relationship between the outcome and the predictor: there is a clear curve in the residuals. Finally, the bottom right panel illustrates data that not only have a non-linear relationship, but also show heteroscedasticity. Note first the curved trend in the residuals, and then also note that at one end of the plot the points are very close together whereas at the other end they are widely dispersed. When these assumptions have been violated you will not see these exact patterns, but hopefully these plots will help you to understand the general anomalies you should look out for. We'll look at an example of how this graph is used in Chapter 8, but for the time being just be aware of the patterns to look out for.

5.3.3.2. Spotting heteroscedasticity/heterogeneity of variance using numbers ②

Remember that homoscedasticity/homogeneity of variance means that as you go through levels of one variable, the variance of the other should not change. If you've collected groups of data then this means that the variance of your outcome variable or variables should be the same in each of these groups. You'll sometimes come across **Levene's test** (Levene, 1960), which tests the null hypothesis that the variances in different groups are equal. It's a very simple and elegant test that works by doing a one-way ANOVA (see Chapter 11) on the deviation scores; that is, the absolute difference between each score and the mean of the group from which it came (see Glass, 1966, for a very readable explanation).[8] For now, all you need to know is that if Levene's test is significant at $p \neq .05$ then you conclude that the null hypothesis is incorrect and that the variances are significantly different – therefore, the assumption of homogeneity of variances has been violated. If, however, Levene's test is non-significant (i.e., $p > .05$) then the variances are roughly equal and the assumption is tenable. Although Levene's test can be selected as an option in many of the statistical tests that require it, it's best to look at it when you're exploring data because it informs the model you fit. As with the K-S test (and other tests of normality), when the sample size is large, small differences in group variances can produce a Levene's test that is significant (Jane Superbrain Box 5.5). There are also other very strong arguments for not using it (Jane Superbrain Box 5.6).

Some people also look at **Hartley's F**$_{max}$, also known as the **variance ratio** (Pearson & Hartley, 1954). This is the ratio of the variances between the group with the biggest variance and the group with the smallest variance. This ratio was compared to critical values in a table published by Hartley. Although this ratio isn't used very often, if you want the critical values (for a .05 level of significance) see Oliver Twisted. The critical values depend on the number of cases per group, and the number of variances being compared. For example, with sample sizes (n) of 10 per group, an F_{max} of less than 10 is more or less always going to be non-significant, with 15–20 per group the ratio needs to be less than about 5, and with samples of 30–60 the ratio should be below about 2 or 3.

5.3.3.3. If you still decide to do Levene's test ②

We can get Levene's test using the *Explore* menu that we used in the previous section. Sticking with the hygiene scores, we'll compare the variances of males and females on day 1

---

[8] We haven't covered ANOVA yet, so this explanation won't make much sense to you now, but in Chapter 11 we will look in more detail at how Levene's test works.

JANE SUPERBRAIN 5.6

Is Levene's test worth the effort? ②

Statisticians used to recommend testing for homogeneity of variance using Levene's test and, if the assumption was violated, using an adjustment to correct for it. However, people have stopped using this approach for two reasons. First, when you have violated this assumption it only matters if you have unequal group sizes: if you don't have unequal group sizes, this assumption is pretty much irrelevant, and can be ignored. Second, the tests of homogeneity of variance like Levene's tend to work very well when you have equal group sizes and large samples (when it doesn't matter as much if you have violated the assumption) and don't work as well with unequal group sizes and smaller samples (which is exactly when it does matter). Plus, there are adjustments to correct for violations of this assumption that can often be applied (as we shall see) which would be a right nuisance if you had to do them by hand, but are very easy to do if you have a computer. In most cases, if you have violated the assumption then a correction is made – and if you haven't violated the assumption, a correction is not made. So, you might as well always do the adjustment and forget about the assumption. If you're really interested in this issue, I like the article by Zimmerman (2004).

OLIVER TWISTED

Please, Sir, can I have some more … Hartley's F_{max}?

Oliver thinks that it's stupid to talk about the variance ratio without the critical values. 'No critical values?' he laughed. 'That's the most stupid thing I've seen since I was at Sussex Uni and I saw my statistics lecturer, Andy Fie…'. Well, go choke on your gruel, you Dickensian bubo, because the full table of critical values is in the additional material for this chapter on the companion website.

of the festival. Use `Analyze Descriptive Statistics` ▶ `Explore…` to open the dialog box in Figure 5.21. Transfer the **day1** variable from the list on the left-hand side to the box labelled *Dependent List* by clicking on the ⬆ next to this box; because we want to split the output by the grouping variable to compare the variances, select the variable **Gender** and transfer it to the box labelled *Factor List* by clicking on the appropriate ⬆. Then click on `Plots…` to open the other dialog box in Figure 5.21. To get Levene's test we need to select one of the options where it says *Spread vs. level with Levene test*. If you select ◉ `Untransformed`, Levene's test is carried out on the raw data (a good place to start). When you've finished with this dialog box click on `Continue` to return to the main *Explore* dialog box and then click on `OK` to run the analysis.

Output 5.6 shows the table for Levene's test. The test can be based on differences between scores and the mean, and between scores and the median. The median is slightly preferable (because it is less biased by outliers). When using both the mean ($p = .030$) and the median ($p = .037$) the significance values are less than .05, indicating a significant difference between the male and female variances. To calculate the variance ratio, we need to divide the largest variance by the smallest. You should find the variances in your output, but if not, we obtained these values in Output 5.4. The male variance was 0.413 and the female one 0.496; the variance ratio is, therefore, $0.496/0.413 = 1.2$. In essence the variances are practically equal. So, why does Levene's test tell us they are significantly different? The answer is because the sample sizes are so large: we had 315 males and 495 females, so

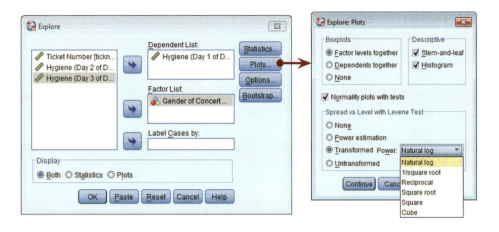

FIGURE 5.21
Exploring groups of data and obtaining Levene's test

Test of Homogeneity of Variance

OUTPUT 5.6

		Levene Statistic	df1	df2	Sig.
Hygiene (Day 1 of Download Festival)	Based on Mean	4.736	1	808	.030
	Based on Median	4.354	1	808	.037
	Based on Median and with adjusted df	4.354	1	805.066	.037
	Based on trimmed mean	4.700	1	808	.030

even this very small difference in variances is shown up as significant by Levene's test (Jane Superbrain Box 5.5). Hopefully this example convinces you to treat these tests cautiously.

5.3.3.4. Reporting Levene's test ①

Levene's test can be denoted by the letter F and there are two different degrees of freedom. As such you can report it, in general form, as $F(df_1, df_2)$ = value, p = p-value. So, for the results in Output 5.6 we could say:

✓ For the hygiene scores on day 1 of the festival, the variances were unequal for for males and females, $F(1, 808) = 4.74$, $p = .03$.

CRAMMING SAM'S TIPS **Homogeneity of variance**

- Homogeneity of variance/homoscedasticity is the assumption that the spread of outcome scores is roughly equal at different points on the predictor variable.
- This can be tested by looking at a plot of the standardized predicted values from your model against the standardized residuals *(zpred vs. zresid)*.
- When comparing groups, this assumption can be tested with Levene's test and the variance ratio (Hartley's F_{max}).
  - If Levene's test is significant *(Sig.* in the SPSS table is less than .05) then the variances are significantly different in different groups.
  - Otherwise, homogeneity of variance can be assumed.
  - The variance ratio is the largest group variance divided by the smallest. This value needs to be smaller than the critical values in the additional material.
- **Warning**: There are good reasons not to use tests like Levene's test. In large samples Levene's test can be significant even when group variances are not very different. Therefore, it should be interpreted in conjunction with the variance ratio.

5.4. Reducing bias ②

Having looked at potential sources of bias, the next issue is how to reduce the impact of bias. Essentially there are four methods for correcting problems with the data, which can be remembered with the handy acronym of TWAT (or WATT, if you prefer):

- **Trim the data**: Delete a certain amount of scores from the extremes.

- **Winsorizing**: Substitute outliers with the highest value that isn't an outlier.

- **Analyse with robust methods**: This typically involves a technique known as bootstrapping.

- **Transform the data**: This involves applying a mathematical function to scores to try to correct any problems with them.

Probably the best of these choices is to use **robust tests**, which is a term applied to a family of procedures to estimate statistics that are reliable even when the normal assumptions of the statistic are not met (Section 5.4.3). Let's look at each technique in more detail.

5.4.1. Trimming the data ②

Trimming the data means deleting some scores from the extremes, and it takes many forms. In its simplest form it could be deleting the data from the person who contributed the outlier. However, this should be done only if you have good reason to believe that this case is not from the population that you intended to sample. For example, if you were investigating factors that affected how much cats purr and one cat didn't purr at all, this would likely be an outlier (all cats purr). Upon inspection, if you discovered that this cat was actually a dog wearing a cat costume (hence why it didn't purr), then you'd have grounds to exclude this case because it comes from a different population (dogs who like to dress as cats) than your target population (cats).

More often, trimming involves removing extreme scores using one of two rules: (1) a percentage based rule; and (2) a standard deviation based rule. A percentage based rule would be, for example, deleting the 10% of highest and lowest scores. Let's look at an example. Meston and Frohlich (2003) report a study showing that heterosexual people rate a picture of someone of the opposite sex as more attractive after riding a roller coaster compared to before. Imagine we took 20 people as they came off of the Rockit roller-coaster at Universal Studios in Orlando[9] and asked them to rate the attractiveness of someone in a photograph on a scale of 0 (looks like Jabba the Hutt) to 10 (my eyes have just exploded because they weren't designed to gaze upon such beauty). Figure 5.22 shows these scores. As you can see, most people gave ratings above the mid-point of the scale: they were pretty positive in their ratings. However, there were two people who gave zeros. If we were to trim 5% of the data from either end, this would mean deleting one score at each extreme (there are 20 scores and 5% of 20 is 1). Figure 5.22 shows that this involves deleting a 0 and an 8. We could compute a 5% trimmed mean by working out the mean for this trimmed data set. Similarly, Figure 5.22 shows that with 20 scores, a 10% trim would mean deleting two scores from each extreme, and a 20% trim would entail deleting four scores from each extreme. If you take trimming to its extreme then you get the median, which is the value left when you have trimmed all but the middle score. If we calculate the

---

[9] I have a video of my wife and me on this rollercoaster during our honeymoon. I swear quite a lot on it, but I might stick it on my YouTube channel so you can laugh at what a cissy I am.

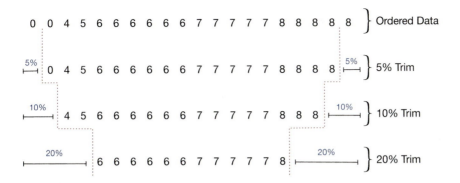

FIGURE 5.22
Illustration of
trimming data

mean in a sample that has been trimmed in this way, it is called (unsurprisingly) a **trimmed mean**. A similar robust measure of location is the **M-estimator**, which differs from a trimmed mean in that the amount of trimming is determined empirically. In other words, rather than the researcher deciding before the analysis how much of the data to trim, an M-estimator determines the optimal amount of trimming necessary to give a robust estimate of, say, the mean. This has the obvious advantage that you never over- or under-trim your data. However, the disadvantage is that it is not always possible to reach a solution.

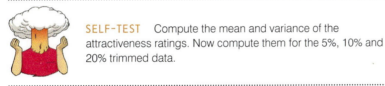

SELF-TEST   Compute the mean and variance of the attractiveness ratings. Now compute them for the 5%, 10% and 20% trimmed data.

If you do the self-test you should find that the mean rating was 6 with a variance of 5.37. The 5% trimmed mean is 6.22, the 10% trimmed mean is 6.50, and the 20% trimmed mean is 6.58. The means get higher in this case because the trimming is reducing the impact of the few scores that were very small (the couple of miserable gits who gave ratings of 0). What happens to the variances? For the overall sample it is 5.37, but for the 5%, 10%, and 20% trimmed data you get 3.59, 1.20 and 0.45, respectively. The variances get smaller (and more stable) because, again, the outliers have less impact. We saw earlier that the accuracy of the mean and variance depends on a symmetrical distribution, but a trimmed mean (and variance) will be relatively accurate even when the distribution is not symmetrical, because by trimming the ends of the distribution we remove outliers and skew that bias the mean. Some robust methods work by taking advantage of the properties of the trimmed mean.

Standard deviation based rules involve calculating the mean and standard deviation of a set of scores, and then removing values that are a certain number of standard deviations greater than the mean. For example, when analysing reaction time data (which is notoriously messy) it is very common to remove any reaction times greater than (or below) 2.5 standard deviations above the mean (Ratcliff, 1993). For the roller coaster data the standard deviation is 2.32, so 2.5 times the standard deviation is 5.8. The mean was 6, therefore, we would delete scores greater than $6 + 5.8 = 11.8$, of which there were none (it was only a 10-point scale); we would also delete scores less than $6 - 5.8 = 0.2$, which means deleting the two scores of zero because they are the only scores less than 0.2. If we recalculate the mean excluding these two zeros we get 6.67 and a variance of 1.29. Again, you can see that this method reduces the impact of extreme scores. However, there is one fundamental problem with standard deviation based trimming, which is that the mean and standard deviation are both highly influenced by outliers (see Section 5.2.2); therefore, if you have outliers in the data the criterion you use to reduce their impact has already been biased by them.

When it comes to implementing these methods in SPSS, there isn't a simple way to do it. Although SPSS will calculate a 5% trimmed mean for you if you use the *explore* command (Figure 5.16), it won't remove the actual cases from the data set, so to do tests based on a trimmed sample you would need to manually trim the data (or do it using syntax commands) or use the *select cases* command (see Oditi's Lantern).

5.4.2.   Winsorizing ①

Winsorizing the data involves replacing outliers with the next highest score that is *not* an outlier. It's perfectly natural to feel uncomfortable at the idea of changing the scores you collected to different values. It feels a bit like cheating. However, you need to bear in mind that if the score you're changing is very unrepresentative of the sample as a whole and biases your statistical model then it's not cheating at all; it's improving your accuracy.[10] What *is* cheating is not dealing with extreme cases that bias the results in favour of your hypothesis, or changing scores in a systematic way other than to reduce bias (again, perhaps to support your hypothesis).

There are some subtle variations on winsorizing, such as replacing extreme scores with a score 3 standard deviations from the mean. A *z*-score of 3.29 constitutes an outlier (see 5.3.1) so we can calculate what score would give rise to a *z*-score of 3.29 (or perhaps 3) by rearranging the *z*-score equation, which gives us $X = (z \times s) + \bar{X}$. All we're doing is calculating the mean ($\bar{X}$) and standard deviation (*s*) of the data and, knowing that *z* is 3 (or 3.29 if you want to be exact), adding three times the standard deviation to the mean and replacing our outliers with that score. As with trimming, this is something you would need to do manually in SPSS or use the *select cases* command (see Oditi's Lantern).

ODITI'S LANTERN

Select Cases

'I, Oditi, believe that those who would try to prevent our cult from discovering the truths behind the numbers have placed dead herrings within the data. These rotting numerical fish permeate our models and infect the nostrils of understanding with their putrid stench. We must banish them; we mush select only the good data, the pure data, the data uncontaminated by piscene putrefaction. You, the trooper of truth, must stare into my lantern to discover how to select cases using SPSS.'

5.4.3.   Robust methods ③

By far the best option if you have irksome data (other than sticking a big samurai sword through your head) is to use a test that is robust to violations of assumptions and outliers. In other words, tests that are relatively unaffected by irksome data. The first set of tests are ones that do not rely on the assumption of normally distributed data (see

---

[10] It is worth making the point that having outliers is interesting in itself, and if you don't think they represent the population then you need to ask yourself why they are different. The answer to the question might be a fruitful topic of more research.

Chapter 6).[11] One thing that you will quickly discover about non-parametric tests is that they have been developed for only a fairly limited range of situations. So, happy days if you want to compare two means, but sad and lonely days listening to Joy Division if you have a complex experimental design.

What are robust methods?

A much more promising approach is to use robust methods, which I mentioned earlier. These tests have developed as computers have got more sophisticated (doing these tests without computers would be only marginally less painful than ripping off your skin and diving into a bath of salt). How these tests work is beyond the scope of this book (and my brain), but two simple concepts will give you the general idea. The first we have already looked at: robust measures of the centre of the distribution such as the trimmed mean and M-estimators. The second is the bootstrap (Efron & Tibshirani, 1993), which is a very simple and elegant idea. The problem that we have is that we don't know the shape of the sampling distribution, but normality in our data allows us to infer that the sampling distribution is normal (and hence we can know the probability of a particular test statistic occurring). Lack of normality prevents us from knowing the shape of the sampling distribution unless we have big samples. Bootstrapping gets around this problem by estimating the properties of the sampling distribution from the sample data. Figure 5.23 illustrates the process: in effect, the sample data are treated as a population from which smaller samples (called bootstrap samples) are taken (putting each score back before a new one is drawn from the sample). The parameter of interest (e.g., the mean) is calculated in each bootstrap sample. This process is repeated perhaps 2000 times. The end result is that we have 2000 parameter estimates, one from each bootstrap sample. There are two things we can do with these estimates: the first is to order them and work out the limits within which 95% of them fall. For example, in Figure 5.23, 95% of bootstrap sample means fall between 2 and 9. We can use these values as an estimate of the limits of the 95% confidence interval of the parameter. The result is known as a percentile bootstrap confidence interval (because it is based on the values between which 95% of bootstrap sample estimates fall). The second thing we can do is to calculate the standard deviation of the parameter estimates from the bootstrap samples and use it as the standard error of parameter estimates. Therefore, when we use bootstrapping, we're effectively getting the computer to use our sample data to mimic the sampling process described in Section 2.5. An important point to remember is that because bootstrapping is based on taking random samples from the data you've collected, the estimates you get will be slightly different every time. This is nothing to worry about. For a fairly gentle introduction to the concept of bootstrapping, see Wright, London, and Field (2011).

SPSS implements bootstrapping in some contexts, which we'll encounter as we go through various chapters. Some procedures have a bootstrap option, which can be accessed by clicking on `Bootstrap...` to activate the dialog box in Figure 5.24 (see Oditi's Lantern). Select ☑ Perform bootstrapping to activate bootstrapping for the procedure you're currently doing. In terms of the options, SPSS will compute a 95% percentile confidence interval (◉ Percentile), but you can change the method to a slightly more accurate one (Efron & Tibshirani, 1993) called a bias corrected and accelerated confidence interval (◉ Bias corrected accelerated (BCa)). You can also change the confidence level by typing a number other than 95 in the box labelled *Level(%)*. By default, SPSS uses 1000 bootstrap samples, which is a reasonable number, and you certainly wouldn't need to use more than 2000.

There are versions of common procedures such as ANOVA, ANCOVA, correlation and multiple regression based on trimmed means and bootstrapping that enable you to ignore

---

[11] For convenience a lot of textbooks refer to these tests as *non-parametric tests* or *assumption-free* tests and stick them in a separate chapter. Actually neither of these terms is particularly accurate (none of these tests is assumption-free), but in keeping with tradition I've put them in Chapter 6, on their own, feeling lonely and ostracized from their 'parametric' counterparts.

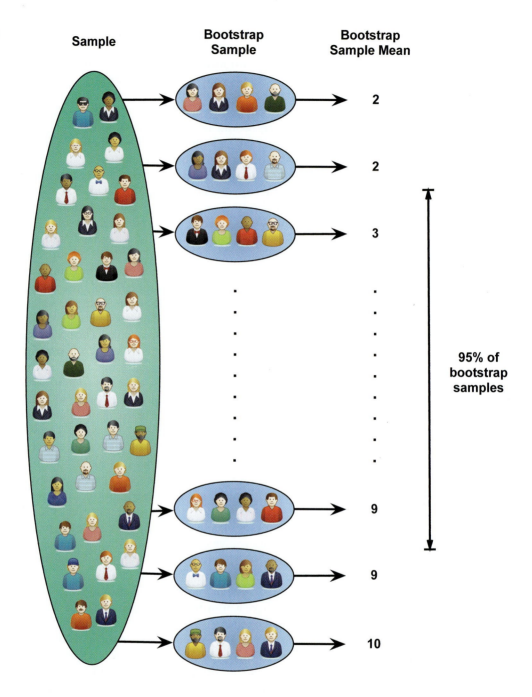

FIGURE 5.23
Illustration of
the percentile
bootstrap

everything we have discussed about bias in this chapter. That's a happy story, but one with a tragic ending because you can't implement them directly in SPSS. The definitive guide to these tests is Wilcox's (2012) outstanding book. Thanks to Wilcox, these tests can be implemented using a free statistics program called R (www.r-project.org). There is a plug-in for SPSS that enables you to use R via the SPSS interface, but it's fiddly to get working and once it is working all it really does is allow you to type the commands that you would type into R. Therefore, I find it much easier just to use R. If you want to go down that route, then I have written a version of this textbook for R that covers these robust tests in some detail (Field, Miles, & Field, 2012). (Sorry, that was a shameless plug.)

FIGURE 5.24
Dialog box for the standard bootstrap

ODITI'S LANTERN

Bootstrapping

'I, Oditi, believe that R is so-called because it makes you shout "Arrghhh!!?" You, my followers, are precious to me and I would not want you to place your sensitive body parts into that guillotine. Instead, stare into my lantern to see how we can use bootstrapping within SPSS.'

5.4.4. Transforming data ②

The final thing that you can do to combat problems with normality and linearity is to transform your data. The idea behind transformations is that you do something to every score to correct for distributional problems, outliers, lack of linearity or unequal variances. Although some students often (understandably) think that transforming data sounds dodgy (the phrase 'fudging your results' springs to some people's minds!), in fact it isn't because you do the same thing to all of your scores. As such, transforming the data changes the form of the relationships between variables but the relative differences between people for a given variable stay the same, so we can still quantify those relationships. However, it does change the differences between different variables (because it changes the units of measurement). Therefore, if you are looking at relationships between variables (e.g., regression) just transform the problematic variable, but if you are looking at differences between variables (e.g., change in a variable over time) then you need to transform all of those variables.

What is a data transformation?

For example, our festival hygiene data were not normal on days 2 and 3 of the festival. Now, we might want to look at how hygiene levels changed across the three days (i.e.,

JANE SUPERBRAIN 5.7

*To transform or not to transform,
that is the question* ③

Not everyone thinks that transforming data is a good idea: Glass, Peckham, and Sanders (1972) commented in a review that 'the payoff of normalizing transformations in terms of more valid probability statements is low, and they are seldom considered to be worth the effort' (p. 241). The issue is quite complicated (especially for this early in the book), but essentially we need to know whether the statistical models we apply perform better on transformed data than they do when applied to data that violate the assumption that the transformation corrects. The question of whether to transform is linked to what test you are performing on your data and whether it is robust (see Section 5.4).

A good case in point is the *F*-test in ANOVA (see Chapter 11), which is often claimed to be robust (Glass et al., 1972). Early findings suggested that *F* performed as it should in skewed distributions and that transforming the data helped as often as it hindered the accuracy of *F* (Games & Lucas, 1966). However, in a lively but informative exchange, Levine and Dunlap (1982) showed that transformations of skew did improve the performance of *F*. In response, Games (1983) argued

that their conclusion was incorrect, which Levine and Dunlap (1983) contested in a response to the response. Finally, in a response to the response to the response, Games (1984) pointed out several important issues:

1. As we've seen, the central limit theorem (Section 5.2.4.2) tells us that in large samples the sampling distribution will be normal regardless. Lots of early research did show that with samples of 40 the sampling distribution was, as predicted, normal. However, this research focused on distributions with light tails, and with heavy-tailed distributions larger samples would be necessary to invoke the central limit theorem (Wilcox, 2012). Transformations might be useful for such distributions.

2. By transforming the data you change the hypothesis being tested (when using a log transformation and comparing means you change from comparing arithmetic means to comparing geometric means). Transformation also means that you're now addressing a different construct to the one originally measured, and this has obvious implications for interpreting that data (Grayson, 2004).

3. In small samples it is tricky to determine normality one way or another (see Jane Superbrain Box 5.5).

4. The consequences for the statistical model of applying the 'wrong' transformation could be worse than the consequences of analysing the untransformed scores.

Given these issues, unless you're correcting for a lack of linearity I would use robust procedures, where possible, in preference to transforming the data.

compare the mean on day 1 to the means on days 2 and 3 to see if people got smellier). The data for days 2 and 3 were skewed and need to be transformed, but because we might later compare the data to scores on day 1, we would also have to transform the day 1 data (even though scores were not skewed). If we don't change the day 1 data as well, then any differences in hygiene scores we find from day 1 to day 2 or 3 will be due to us transforming one variable and not the others. However, if we were going to look at the relationship between day 1 and day 2 scores (not the difference between them) we could transform only the day 2 scores and leave the day 1 scores alone.

5.4.4.1. Choosing a transformation ②

There are various transformations that you can do to the data that are helpful in correcting various problems. However, whether these transformations are necessary or useful is quite a complex issue (see Jane Superbrain Box 5.7).[12] Nevertheless, because they *are* used,

---

[12] Although there aren't statistical consequences of transforming data, there may be empirical or scientific implications that outweigh the statistical benefits (see Jane Superbrain Box 5.7).

TABLE 5.1   Data transformations and their uses

Data Transformation	Can Correct For
Log transformation (log(X_i)): Taking the logarithm of a set of numbers squashes the right tail of the distribution. As such it's a good way to reduce positive skew. This transformation is also very useful if you have problems with linearity (it can sometimes make a curvilinear relationship linear). However, you can't get a log value of zero or negative numbers, so if your data tend to zero or produce negative numbers you need to add a constant to all of the data before you do the transformation. For example, if you have zeros in the data then do log(X_i + 1), or if you have negative numbers add whatever value makes the smallest number in the data set positive.	Positive skew, positive kurtosis, unequal variances, lack of linearity
Square root transformation ($\sqrt{X_i}$): Taking the square root of large values has more of an effect than taking the square root of small values. Consequently, taking the square root of each of your scores will bring any large scores closer to the centre – rather like the log transformation. As such, this can be a useful way to reduce positive skew; however, you still have the same problem with negative numbers (negative numbers don't have a square root).	Positive skew, positive kurtosis, unequal variances, lack of linearity
Reciprocal transformation ($1/X_i$): Dividing 1 by each score also reduces the impact of large scores. The transformed variable will have a lower limit of 0 (very large numbers will become close to 0). One thing to bear in mind with this transformation is that it reverses the scores: scores that were originally large in the data set become small (close to zero) after the transformation, but scores that were originally small become large after the transformation. For example, imagine two scores of 1 and 10; after the transformation they become 1/1 = 1, and 1/10 = 0.1: the small score becomes larger than the large score after the transformation. However, you can avoid this by reversing the scores before the transformation, by finding the highest score and changing each score to the highest score minus the score you're looking at. So, you do a transformation $1/(X_{Highest} - X_i)$. Like the log transformation, you can't take the reciprocal of 0 (because 1/0 = infinity) so if you have zeros in the data you need to add a constant to all scores before doing the transformation.	Positive skew, positive kurtosis, unequal variances
Reverse score transformations: Any one of the above transformations can be used to correct negatively skewed data, but first you have to reverse the scores. To do this, subtract each score from the highest score obtained, or the highest score + 1 (depending on whether you want your lowest score to be 0 or 1). If you do this, don't forget to reverse the scores back afterwards, or to remember that the interpretation of the variable is reversed: large scores have become small and small scores have become large.	Negative skew

Table 5.1 shows some common transformations and their uses.[13] The way to decide which transformation to use is by good old fashioned trial and error: try one out, see if it helps and if it doesn't then try a different one.

Trying out different transformations can be quite time-consuming. However, if heterogeneity of variance is your issue then we can see the effect of a transformation quite quickly. In Section 5.3.3.3 we saw how to use the *explore* function to get Levene's test. In

[13] You'll notice in this section that I keep writing X_i. We saw in Chapter 1 that this refers to the observed score for the ith person (so the i could be replaced with the name of a particular person, thus for Graham, $X_i = X_{Graham}$ is Graham's score, and for Carol, $X_i = X_{Carol}$ is Carol's score).

that section we ran the analysis selecting the raw scores (◉ U̲ntransformed). However, if the variances turn out to be unequal, as they did in our example, you can use the same dialog box (Figure 5.21) but select ◉ T̲ransformed. When you do this you should notice a drop-down list that becomes active and if you click on this you'll notice that it lists several transformations including the ones that I have just described. If you select a transformation from this list (*Natural log* perhaps or *Square root*) then SPSS will calculate what Levene's test would be if you were to transform the data using this method. This can save you a lot of time trying out different transformations.

5.4.4.2. The *compute* function ②

To do transformations on SPSS we use the *compute* command, which enables us to carry out functions (such as adding or multiplying) on columns of data in the data editor. To access the *Compute Variable* dialog box, select Transform ▦ Compute Variable… . Figure 5.25 shows the main dialog box; it has a list of functions on the right-hand side, a calculator-like keyboard in the centre and a blank space that I've labelled the command area. You type a name for a new variable in the area labelled *Target Variable* and then you write some kind of

FIGURE 5.25
*Compute
Variable* dialog
box command

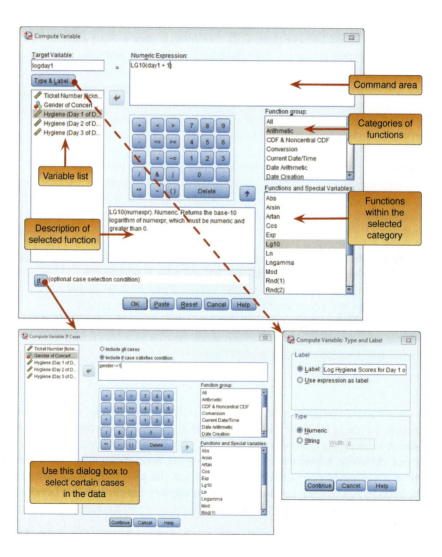

command in the command area to tell SPSS how to create this new variable. You use a combination of existing variables selected from the list on the left, and numeric expressions. So, for example, you could use it like a calculator to add variables (i.e., add two columns in the data editor to make a third). However, you can also use it to generate data without using existing variables too. There are hundreds of built-in functions that SPSS has grouped together. In the dialog box these groups are listed in the area labelled *Function group*; upon selecting a function group, a list of available functions within that group will appear in the box labelled *Functions and Special Variables*. If you select a function, then a description of that function appears in the white box indicated in Figure 5.25. You can enter variable names into the command area by selecting the variable required from the variables list and then clicking on ▸. Likewise, you can select a certain function from the list of available functions and enter it into the command area by clicking on ▴.

First type a variable name in the box labelled *Target Variable*, then click on `Type & Label...` and another dialog box appears, where you can give the variable a descriptive label and specify whether it is a numeric or string variable (see Section 3.5.2). When you have written your command for SPSS to execute, click on `OK` to run the command and create the new variable. If you type in a variable name that already exists in the data editor then SPSS will tell you and ask you whether you want to replace this existing variable. If you respond with *Yes* then SPSS will replace the data in the existing column with the result of the *compute* command; if you respond with *No* then nothing will happen and you will need to rename the target variable. If you're computing a lot of new variables it can be quicker to use syntax (see SPSS Tip 5.2).

Let's first look at some of the simple functions:

Addition: This button places a plus sign in the command area. For example, with our hygiene data, 'day1 + day2' creates a column in which each row contains the hygiene score from the column labelled day1 added to the score from the column labelled day2 (e.g., for participant 1: $2.65 + 1.35 = 4$).

Subtraction: This button places a minus sign in the command area. For example, if we wanted to calculate the change in hygiene from day 1 to day 2 we could type 'day2 − day1'. This creates a column in which each row contains the score from the column labelled day1 subtracted from the score from the column labelled day2 (e.g., for participant 1: $2.65 − 1.35 = 1.30$).

Multiply: This button places a multiplication sign in the command area. For example, 'day1*day2' creates a column that contains the score from the column labelled day1 multiplied by the score from the column labelled day2 (e.g., for participant 1: $2.65 \times 1.35 = 3.58$).

Divide: This button places a division sign in the command area. For example, 'day1/day2' creates a column that contains the score from the column labelled day1 divided by the score from the column labelled day2 (e.g., for participant 1: $2.65/1.35 = 1.96$).

Exponentiation: This button raises the preceding term to the power of the succeeding term. So, 'day1**2' creates a column that contains the scores in the day1 column raised to the power of 2 (i.e., the square of each number in the day1 column: for participant 1, $2.65^2 = 7.02$). Likewise, 'day1**3' creates a column with values of day1 cubed.

Less than: This operation is usually used for 'include case' functions. If you click on the `If...` button, a dialog box appears that allows you to select certain cases on which to carry out the operation. So, if you typed 'day1 < 1', then SPSS would carry out the compute function only for those participants whose hygiene score on day 1 of the festival was less than 1 (i.e., if day1 was 0.99 or less). So, we might use this if we wanted to look only at the people who were already smelly on the first day of the festival.

Less than or equal to: This operation is the same as above except that in the example above, cases that are exactly 1 would be included as well.

 More than: This operation is used to include cases above a certain value. So, if you clicked on and then typed 'day1 > 1' then SPSS will carry out any analysis only on cases for which hygiene scores on day 1 of the festival were greater than 1 (i.e., 1.01 and above). This could be used to exclude people who were already smelly at the start of the festival. We might want to exclude them because these people will contaminate the data (not to mention our nostrils) because they reek of putrefaction to begin with so the festival cannot further affect their hygiene.

 More than or equal to: This operation is the same as above but will include cases that are exactly 1 as well.

 Equal to: You can use this operation to include cases for which participants have a specific value. So, if you clicked on and typed 'day1 = 1' then only cases that have a value of exactly 1 for the day1 variable are included. This is most useful when you have a coding variable and you want to look at only one of the groups. For example, if we wanted to look only at females at the festival we could type 'gender = 1', and then the analysis would be carried out on only females (who are coded as 1 in the data).

Not equal to: This operation will include all cases except those with a specific value. So, 'gender¬ = 1' (as in Figure 5.25) will carry out the compute command only on the males and exclude females (because they have a 1 in the gender column).

Some of the most useful functions are listed in Table 5.2, which shows the standard form of the function, the name of the function, an example of how the function can be used and what SPSS would output if that example were used. There are several basic functions for calculating means, standard deviations and sums of columns. There are also functions such as the square root and logarithm that are useful for transforming data that are skewed, and we will use these functions now. For the interested reader, the SPSS help files have details of all of the functions available through the *Compute Variable* dialog box (click on [Help] when you're in the dialog box).

5.4.4.3. The log transformation in SPSS ②

Let's use *compute* to transform our data. Open the main *compute* dialog box by selecting [Transform] [Compute Variable...]. Enter the name **logday1** into the box labelled *Target Variable*, click on [Type & Label...] and give the variable a more descriptive name such as *Log transformed hygiene scores for day 1 of Download festival*. In the list box labelled *Function group* click on *Arithmetic* and then in the box labelled *Functions and Special Variables* click on *Lg10* (this is the log transformation to base 10; *Ln* is the natural log) and transfer it to the command area by clicking on [↑]. When the command is transferred, it appears in the command area as 'LG10(?)' and the question mark should be replaced with a variable name (which can be typed manually or transferred from the variables list). So replace the question mark with the variable **day1** by either selecting the variable in the list and dragging it across, clicking on [→], or just typing 'day1' where the question mark is.

For the day 2 hygiene scores there is a value of 0 in the original data, and there is no logarithm of the value 0. To overcome the problem we add a constant to our original scores before we take the log of those scores. Any constant will do (although sometimes it can matter), provided that it makes all of the scores greater than 0. In this case our lowest score

TABLE 5.2 Some useful compute functions

Function	Name	Example Input	Output
MEAN(?,?,..)	Mean	Mean(day1, day2, day3)	For each row, SPSS calculates the average hygiene score across the three days of the festival
SD(?,?,..)	Standard deviation	SD(day1, day2, day3)	Across each row, SPSS calculates the standard deviation of the values in the columns labelled *day1*, *day2* and *day3*
SUM(?,?,..)	Sum	SUM(day1, day2)	For each row, SPSS adds the values in the columns labelled *day1* and *day2*
SQRT(?)	Square root	SQRT(day2)	Produces a column containing the square root of each value in the column labelled *day2*
ABS(?)	Absolute value	ABS(day1)	Produces a variable that contains the absolute value of the values in the column labelled *day1* (i.e., the signs are ignored, so −5 becomes +5 and +5 stays as +5)
LG10(?)	Base 10 logarithm	LG10(day1)	Produces a variable that contains the logarithmic values (to base 10) of the variable *day1*.
RV.NORMAL (mean, stddev)	Normal random numbers	Normal(20, 5)	Produces a variable of pseudo-random numbers from a normal distribution with a mean of 20 and a standard deviation of 5.

is 0 in the data so we could add 1 to all of the scores to ensure that all scores are greater than zero. Even though this problem affects the day 2 scores, we need to be consistent and do the same to the day 1 scores as we will do with the day 2 scores. Therefore, make sure the cursor is still inside the brackets and click on ⬚ and then ⬚. The final dialog box should look like Figure 5.25. Note that the expression reads LG10(day1 + 1); that is, SPSS will add one to each of the day 1 scores and then take the log of the resulting values. Click on ⬚ to create a new variable **logday1** containing the transformed values.

SELF-TEST Have a go at creating similar variables **logday2** and **logday3** for the day 2 and day 3 data. Plot histograms of the transformed scores for all three days.

5.4.4.4. The square root transformation on SPSS ②

To do a square root transformation, we run through the same process, by using a name such as **sqrtday1** in the box labelled *Target Variable* (and click on ⬚ to give the variable a more descriptive name). In the list box labelled *Function group* click on *Arithmetic* and then in the box labelled *Functions and Special Variables* click on *Sqrt* and drag it to the command area or click on ⬚. When the command is transferred, it appears in the command area as SQRT(?). Replace the question mark with the variable **day1** by selecting the variable in the list and dragging it, clicking on ⬚, or just typing 'day1' where the question mark is. The final expression will read *SQRT(day1)*. Click on ⬚ to create the variable.

SELF-TEST   Repeat this process for **day2** and **day3** to create variables called **sqrtday2** and **sqrtday3**. Plot histograms of the transformed scores for all three days.

5.4.4.5. The reciprocal transformation on SPSS ②

To do a reciprocal transformation on the data from day 1, we could use a name such as **recday1** in the box labelled *Target Variable*. Then we can simply click on [1] and then [/]. Ordinarily you would select the variable name that you want to transform from the list and drag it across, click on [→] or just type the name of the variable. However, the day 2 data contain a zero value and if we try to divide 1 by 0 then we'll get an error message (you can't divide by 0). We need to add a constant to our variable just as we did for the log transformation. Any constant will do, but 1 is a convenient number for these data. So, instead of selecting the variable we want to transform, click on [()]; this places a pair of brackets into the box labelled *Numeric Expression*. Then make sure the cursor is between these two brackets and select the variable you want to transform from the list and transfer it across by clicking on [→] (or type the name of the variable manually). Now click on [+] and then [1] (or type '+ 1'

SPSS TIP 5.2   **Using syntax to compute new variables ③**

If you're computing a lot of new variables it can be quicker to use syntax. I've written the file **Transformations.sps** to do all nine of the transformations that we've discussed. Open this file and you'll see these commands in the syntax window (see Section 3.9):

COMPUTE logday1 = LG10(day1 + 1).

COMPUTE logday2 = LG10(day2 + 1).

COMPUTE logday3 = LG10(day3 + 1).

COMPUTE sqrtday1 = SQRT(day1).

COMPUTE sqrtday2 = SQRT(day2).

COMPUTE sqrtday3 = SQRT(day3).

COMPUTE recday1 = 1/(day1+1).

COMPUTE recday2 = 1/(day2+1).

COMPUTE recday3 = 1/(day3+1).

EXECUTE.

Each *compute* command above does the equivalent of what you'd do using the *Compute Variable* dialog box in Figure 5.25. So, the first three lines ask SPSS to create three new variables (**logday1**, **logday2** and **logday3**), which are the log transformations of the variables **day1**, **day2** and **day3** plus 1. The next three lines create new variables called **sqrtday1**, **sqrtday2** and **sqrtday3** by using the *SQRT* function to take the square root of **day1**, **day2** and **day3**, respectively. The next three lines do the reciprocal transformation in much the same way. The final line has the command *execute* without which none of the *compute* commands beforehand will be executed. Note also that every line ends with a full stop.

using your keyboard). The box labelled *Numeric Expression* should now contain the text *1/ (day1 + 1)*. Click on OK to create a new variable containing the transformed values.

SELF-TEST   Repeat this process for **day2** and **day3**. Plot histograms of the transformed scores for all three days.

5.4.4.6. The effect of transformations ②

Figure 5.26 shows the distributions for days 1 and 2 of the festival after the three different transformations. Compare these to the untransformed distributions in Figure 5.13. Now, you can see that all three transformations have cleaned up the hygiene scores for day 2: the positive skew is reduced (the square root transformation in particular has been useful). However, because our hygiene scores on day 1 were more or less symmetrical to begin

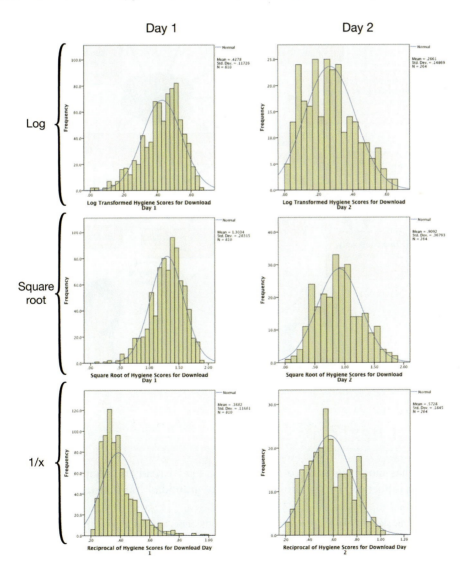

FIGURE 5.26

Distributions of the hygiene data on day 1 and day 2 after various transformations with, they have now become slightly negatively skewed for the log and square root transformation, and positively skewed for the reciprocal transformation.[14] If we're using scores from day 2 alone or looking at the relationship between day 1 and day 2, then we could use the transformed scores; however, if we wanted to look at the *change* in scores then we'd have to weigh up whether the benefits of the transformation for the day 2 scores outweigh the problems it creates in the day 1 scores – data analysis can be frustrating sometimes.☺

5.5. Brian's attempt to woo Jane ①

FIGURE 5.27
What Brian learnt from this chapter

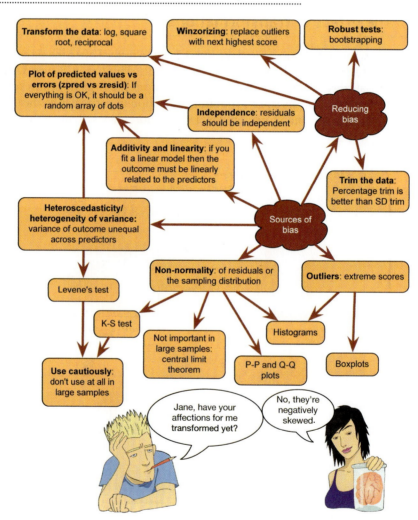

5.6. What next? ①

This chapter has taught us how to identify bias. Had I read this chapter I might have avoided being influenced by my idolization of my granddad[15] and instead realized that I

---

[14] The reversal of the skew for the reciprocal transformation is because, as I mentioned earlier, the reciprocal has the effect of reversing the scores.

[15] Oddly enough, despite absolutely worshipping the ground my granddad walked on, I ended up supporting a different team than him: he supported a certain north London team close to where we grew up and I support their local rivals.

could be a useful midfield player. From there a successful career in soccer would undoubtedly have unfolded in front of me. Or, as anyone who has seen me play will realize, perhaps not. Still, I sort of had the last laugh on the goalkeeping front. At the end of my time at primary school we had a five-a-side tournament between local schools so that kids from different schools could get to know each other before going to secondary school together. My goalkeeping nemesis was, of course, chosen to play and I was the substitute. In the first game he had a shocker, and I was called up to play in the second game during which I made a series of dramatic and acrobatic saves (at least they are in my memory). I did likewise in the next game, and my nemesis had to sit out the whole of the rest of the tournament. Perhaps this should have encouraged me to pursue being goalkeeper at my new school. However, five-a-side goals are shorter than normal goals, so my height wasn't an issue and that was my last time trying to get into the school football team – I just gave up. Years later when I started playing again, I regretted this decision: not because I could have been a professional soccer player, but just because I missed many years of enjoying playing. Instead, I read books and immersed myself in music. Unlike my cleverer older brother who was reading Albert Einstein's papers (well, Isaac Asimov) as an embryo, my literary preferences were more in keeping with my intellect …

5.7. Key terms that I've discovered

Bootstrap	Independence	Parametric test
Contaminated normal distribution	Kolmogorov–Smirnov test	Q-Q plot
Hartley's F_{max}	Levene's test	Robust test
Heterogeneity of variance	M-estimator	Shapiro–Wilk test
Heteroscedasticity	Mixed normal distribution	Transformation
Homogeneity of variance	Normally distributed data	Trimmed mean
Homoscedasticity	Outlier	Variance ratio
	P-P plot	Weighted least squares

5.8. Smart Alex's tasks

- **Task 1**: Using the **ChickFlick.sav** data from Chapter 4, check the assumptions of normality and homogeneity of variance for the two films (ignore **Gender**): are the assumptions met? ①

- **Task 2**: The file **SPSSExam.sav** contains data regarding students' performance on an SPSS exam. Four variables were measured: **exam** (first-year SPSS exam scores as a percentage), **computer** (measure of computer literacy in percent), **lecture** (percentage of SPSS lectures attended) and **numeracy** (a measure of numerical ability out of 15). There is a variable called **uni** indicating whether the student attended Sussex University (where I work) or Duncetown University. Compute and interpret descriptive statistics for **exam, computer, lecture**, and **numeracy** for the sample as a whole. ①

- **Task 3**: Calculate and interpret the z-scores for skewness for all variables. ①

- **Task 4**: Calculate and interpret the z-scores for kurtosis for all variables. ①

- **Task 5**: Use the *split file* command to look at and interpret the descriptive statistics for **numeracy** and **exam**. ①

- **Task 6**: Repeat Task 5 but for the computer literacy and percentage of lectures attended. ①

- **Task 7**: Conduct and interpret a K-S test for **numeracy** and **exam**. ①

- **Task 8**: Conduct and interpret a Levene's test for **numeracy** and **exam**. ①

- **Task 9**: Transform the **numeracy** scores (which are positively skewed) using one of the transformations described in this chapter. Do the data become normal? ②

- **Task 10**: Use the *explore* command to see what effect a natural log transformation would have on the four variables measured in **SPSSExam.sav**.

Answers can be found on the companion website.

5.9. Further reading

Tabachnick, B. G., & Fidell, L. S. (2012). *Using multivariate statistics* (6th ed.). Boston: Allyn & Bacon. (They have the definitive guide to screening data.)

Wilcox, R. R. (2005). *Introduction to robust estimation and hypothesis testing* (2nd ed.). Burlington, MA: Elsevier. (Quite technical, but this is the definitive book on robust methods.)

Wilcox, R. R. (2010). *Fundamentals of modern statistical methods: Substantially improving power and accuracy*. New York: Springer-Verlag. (A fantastic book on bias in statistical methods that expands upon many of the points in this chapter and is written by someone who actually knows what he's talking about.)

Non-parametric models

FIGURE 6.1
I came first in the competition for who has the smallest brain

6.1. What will this chapter tell me? ①

When we were learning to read at primary school, we used to read versions of stories by the famous storyteller Hans Christian Andersen. One of my favourites was the story of the ugly duckling. This duckling was a big ugly grey bird, so ugly that even a dog would not bite him. The poor duckling was ridiculed, ostracized and pecked by the other ducks. Eventually, it became too much for him and he flew to the swans, the royal birds, hoping that they would end his misery by killing him because he was so ugly. Still, life sometimes throws up surprises and as he stared into the water, he saw not an ugly grey bird but a beautiful swan. Data are much the same. Sometimes they're just big, grey and ugly and don't do any of the things that they're supposed to do. When we get data like these, we swear at them, curse them, peck them and hope that they'll fly away and be killed by the swans. Alternatively, we can try to force our data into becoming beautiful swans. That's what this chapter is all about: trying to make an ugly duckling of a data set turn into a swan. Be careful what you wish your data to be, though: a swan can break your arm.[1]

---

[1] Although it is theoretically possible, apparently you'd have to be weak boned, and swans are nice and wouldn't do that sort of thing.

6.2. When to use non-parametric tests ①

We discovered in the last chapter that there are many things that can bias the conclusions from a statistical model. We also looked at several ways to reduce this bias. Sometimes, however, no matter how hard you try, you will find that you can't correct the problems in your data. This is a particular problem if you have small samples and can't, therefore, rely on the central limit theorem

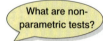

to get you out of trouble. However, there is a small family of tests that can be used to test hypotheses that don't make many of the assumptions that we looked at in the last chapter. They are called **non-parametric tests** or 'assumption-free tests' because they make fewer assumptions than the other tests that we'll look at in this book.[2] In general, you are better off trying to use a robust test than a non-parametric test, but we'll look at non-parametric tests because (1) the range of robust tests is limited in SPSS; and (2) non-parametric tests are a nice gentle way for us to look at the idea of using a statistical test to evaluate a hypothesis.

All of the tests in this chapter overcome the problem of the shape of the distribution of scores by **ranking** the data: that is, finding the lowest score and giving it a rank of 1, then finding the next highest score and giving it a rank of 2, and so on. This process results in high scores being represented by large ranks, and low scores being represented by small ranks. The analysis is then carried out on the ranks rather than the actual data. By using the ranks we eliminate the effect of outliers: imagine you have 20 data points and the two highest scores are 30 and 60 (a difference of 30); these scores will have ranks of 19 and 20 (a difference of 1). In much the same way, ranking irons out problems with skew. Some people believe that non-parametric tests have less power than their parametric counterparts, but this is not always true (Jane Superbrain Box 6.1). In this chapter, we'll look at carrying out

JANE SUPERBRAIN 6.1

Non-parametric tests and statistical power ②

Ranking the data is a useful way to reduce the impact of outliers or weird distributions, but there is a price to pay: by ranking the data we lose some information about the magnitude of differences between scores. Consequently, non-parametric tests can be less powerful than their parametric counterparts. Remember that statistical power (Section 2.6.1.7) is the ability of a test to find an effect that genuinely exists, so we're saying that if there is a genuine effect in our data then a parametric test is more likely to detect it than a non-parametric one. However, this statement is true only *if the assumptions*

described in Chapter 5 are met. So, if we use a parametric test and a non-parametric test on the same data, and those data meet the appropriate assumptions, then the parametric test will have greater power to detect the effect than the non-parametric test.

The problem is that to define the power of a test we need to be sure that it controls the Type I error rate (the number of times a test will find a significant effect when in reality there is no effect to find – see Section 2.6.1.5). We saw in Chapter 2 that this error rate is normally set at 5%. We know that when the sampling distribution is normally distributed, the Type I error rate of tests based on this distribution is indeed 5%, and so we can work out the power. However, when the sampling distribution is not normal, the Type I error rate of tests based on this distribution won't be 5% (in fact we don't know what it is for sure, as it will depend on the shape of the distribution) and so we have no way of calculating power (because power is linked to the Type I error rate – see Section 2.6.1.7). So, although you often hear of non-parametric tests having less power (i.e., an increased chance of a Type II error), this is true only if the sampling distribution is normal.

---

[2] Some people might tell you that non-parametric tests are 'distribution-free tests' because they make *no* assumptions about the distribution of the data. However, they *do* make distributional assumptions but just not normality: the ones in this chapter, for example, all assume a continuous distribution.

and interpreting four of the most common non-parametric procedures: the Mann–Whitney test, the Wilcoxon signed-rank test, Friedman's test and the Kruskal–Wallis test.

6.3. General procedure of non-parametric tests in SPSS ①

All of the non-parametric tests in this chapter have a similar window structure through which you specify the analysis. To begin with, then, we'll have a look at the general procedure for all of the tests we use in this chapter before looking at each specific test in turn. If you want to compare groups containing different entities then select `Analyze Nonparametric Tests ▶ ⚠ Independent Samples...`. But if you're comparing scores that were taken from the same entities but under different conditions then select `Analyze Nonparametric Tests ▶ ⚠ Related Samples...`. Both menus take you to a similar dialog box that has three tabs:

`Objective Fields Settings` This dialog box is very similar regardless of whether you have scores from the same entities or different ones: as Figure 6.2 shows, in both cases you are given the choice to compare scores automatically (which basically means that SPSS selects a test for you, and I don't recommend this option because it's not a good idea to let a computer think on your behalf), or to select the analysis yourself (`◉ Customize analysis`).

`Objective Fields Settings` Selecting this tab will take you to a screen in which you select the variables that you want to analyse. Within this screen, if you have set roles for your variables in the data editor (Section 3.5.2) then SPSS will take an educated guess, based on these roles, as to what analysis you want to do (`◉ Use predefined roles`). However, if you have not set roles, or if you don't think it's wise to let SPSS guess what you might want to do, then you can specify the variables within the analysis yourself (`◉ Use custom field assignments`). Although the exact look of this tab changes depending on whether you have independent or related samples, in both cases you will find a list of variables on the left-hand side labelled *Fields*. By default, it will show all variables (All) but you can filter this list to show only nominal/categorical variables (🔵) or only scale variables (📏). In general your outcome variable will be scale (📏) and your predictor nominal (🔵), so these filters can help you to find the appropriate variable. You can also toggle between showing the variable name and the variable label in the list by clicking 🔖. On the right-hand side will be a box labelled *Test Fields*, which is where you place outcome variables within an analysis, and sometimes there will be a box labelled *Groups* where you can place categorical predictors. We'll look at the exact configuration of this box within each analysis. For now, I just want you to get the idea that it's pretty similar regardless of which non-parametric test we're doing.

`Objective Fields Settings` Selecting this tab takes you to a screen where you can select the test that you wish to perform. You can let SPSS pick a test for you (`◉ Automatically choose the tests based on the data`), but I'd recommend making the decisions yourself (`◉ Customize tests`). Regardless of the type of test you're doing you can set the significance level (the default is .05), the confidence interval level (the default is 95%) and whether to exclude cases listwise or test-by-test (see SPSS Tip 5.1) by clicking on *Test Options* (see Figure 6.3). Similarly, if you have categorical variables and missing values you can choose to exclude or include these missing values by selecting *User-Missing Values* and checking the appropriate option (see Figure 6.3). The default option is to exclude them, which makes sense a lot of the time.

The exact windows will change depending on whether you're comparing scores from the same entities or different entities, but this summary hopefully gives you a sense of the similarities in the process. The general process for any non-parametric analysis, then, is:

1 Because I don't like the automated functions in SPSS, choose ⊙ Customize analysis in the Objective Fields Settings tab (Figure 6.2).

2 Specify your predictor and outcome variables using the Objective Fields Settings tab.

3 Choose the test you want to do using the Objective Fields Settings tab and, although the default settings are fine, you can change any options for the test if necessary (Figure 6.3).

ODITI'S LANTERN

Non-parametric tests

'I, Oditi, am impressed with your progress. You are now ready to take your first steps towards understanding the hidden meanings behind the data. However, I love and value your precious brains, and and do not want them to end up like a fly on a windshield. Stare into my lantern to discover how to test hypotheses with all of the non-parametric tests covered in this chapter.'

FIGURE 6.2

Dialog boxes for the *Objective* tab of the Non-parametric Tests menu

Scores from different entities   Scores from the same entities

FIGURE 6.3

Dialog box for the *Settings* tab when choosing *Test Options* and *User-Missing Values*

Test options   User-missing values

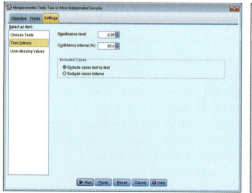
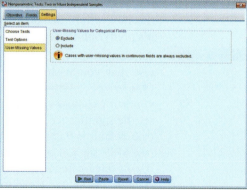

6.4. Comparing two independent conditions: the Wilcoxon rank-sum test and Mann–Whitney test ①

Imagine that you have a hypothesis that two groups of different entities will differ from each other on some variable. For example, a neurologist might collect data to investigate the depressant effects of certain recreational drugs. She tested 20 clubbers in all: 10 were given an ecstasy tablet to take on a Saturday night and 10 were allowed to drink only alcohol. Levels of depression were measured using the Beck Depression Inventory (BDI) the day after (Sunday) and midweek (Wednesday). The data are in Table 6.1. You might have two hypotheses: between those who took alcohol and those that took ecstasy, depression levels will be different the day after (hypothesis 1) and mid-week (hypothesis 2). To test these hypotheses, we need to fit a model that compares the distribution in the alcohol group to that in the ecstasy group.

SELF-TEST What are the null hypotheses for these hypotheses?

TABLE 6.1 Data for drug experiment

Participant	Drug	BDI (Sunday)	BDI (Wednesday)
1	Ecstasy	15	28
2	Ecstasy	35	35
3	Ecstasy	16	35
4	Ecstasy	18	24
5	Ecstasy	19	39
6	Ecstasy	17	32
7	Ecstasy	27	27
8	Ecstasy	16	29
9	Ecstasy	13	36
10	Ecstasy	20	35
11	Alcohol	16	5
12	Alcohol	15	6
13	Alcohol	20	30
14	Alcohol	15	8
15	Alcohol	16	9
16	Alcohol	13	7
17	Alcohol	14	6
18	Alcohol	19	17
19	Alcohol	18	3
20	Alcohol	18	10

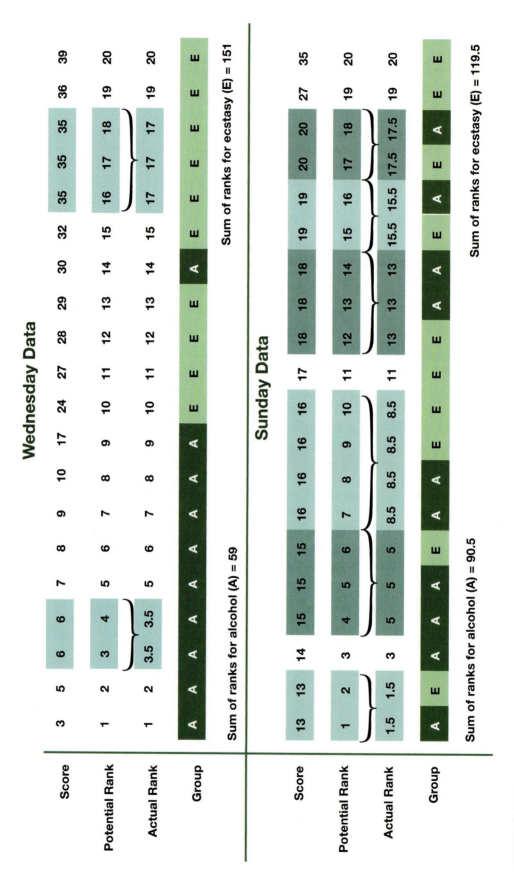

FIGURE 6.4   Ranking the depression scores

When you want to compare the distributions in two conditions and these conditions contain different entities, then you have two choices: the **Mann–Whitney test** (Mann & Whitney, 1947) and **Wilcoxon's rank-sum test** (Wilcoxon, 1945). Both tests are equivalent, and there's another Wilcoxon test, which gets extremely confusing. These tests are the non-parametric equivalent of the independent *t*-test, which we'll discover in Chapter 9.

6.4.1. Theory ②

The logic behind the Wilcoxon rank-sum and Mann–Whitney tests is incredibly elegant. First, let's imagine a scenario in which there is no difference in depression levels between ecstasy and alcohol users. If you were to rank the data *ignoring the group to which a person belonged* from lowest to highest (i.e., give the lowest score a rank of 1 and the next lowest a rank of 2, etc.), if there's no difference between the groups then you should find a similar number of high and low ranks in each group; specifically, if you added up the ranks, then you'd expect the summed total of ranks in each group to be about the same. Now think about what would happen if there was a difference between the groups. Let's

imagine that the ecstasy group is more depressed than the alcohol group. If you rank the scores as before, then you would expect the higher ranks to be in the ecstasy group and the lower ranks to be in the alcohol group. Again, if we summed the ranks in each group, we'd expect the sum of ranks to be higher in the ecstasy group than in the alcohol group. The Mann–Whitney and Wilcoxon rank-sum tests both work on this principle. In fact, when the groups have unequal numbers of participants in them, the test statistic (W_s) for the Wilcoxon rank-sum test is simply the sum of ranks in the group that contains the fewer people; when the group sizes are equal, it's the value of the smaller summed rank.

SMART
ALEX
ONLY

How do I rank data?

Let's have a look at how ranking works in practice. Figure 6.4 shows the ranking process for both the Wednesday and Sunday data. To begin with, let's use our data for Wednesday, because it's more straightforward. First, just arrange the scores in ascending order, and attach a label to remind you which group they came from (I've used A for alcohol and E for ecstasy). Then, starting at the lowest score, assign potential ranks starting with 1 and going up to the number of scores you have. The reason why I've called these potential ranks is that sometimes the same score occurs more than

FIGURE 6.5
Frank Wilcoxon

once in a data set (e.g., in these data a score of 6 occurs twice, and a score of 35 occurs three times). These are called *tied ranks* and these values need to be given the same rank, so all we do is assign a rank that is the average of the potential ranks for those scores. So, with our two scores of 6, because they would've been ranked as 3 and 4, we take an average of these values (3.5) and use this value as the rank for both occurrences of the score. Likewise, with the three scores of 35, we have potential ranks of 16, 17 and 18; we again use the average of these three ranks, $(16 + 17 + 18)/3 = 17$. When we've ranked the data, we add up all of the ranks for the two groups. So, add the ranks for the scores that came from the alcohol group (you should find the sum is 59) and then add the ranks for the scores that came from the ecstasy group (this value should be 151). We take the lowest of these sums to be our test statistic, so the test statistic for the Wednesday data is $W_s = 59$.

SELF-TEST   Based on what you have just learnt, try ranking the Sunday data. (The answers are in Figure 6.4 – there are lots of tied ranks and the data are generally horrible.)

You should find that when you've ranked the Sunday data, and added the ranks for the two groups, the sum of ranks for the alcohol group is 90.5 and for the ecstasy group is 119.5. The lowest of these sums is our test statistic, so the test statistic for the Sunday data is $W_s = 90.5$. The next issue is: how do we determine whether this test statistic is significant? It turns out that the mean ($\bar{W}_s$) and standard error of this test statistic ($SE_{\bar{W}_s}$) can be easily calculated from the sample sizes of each group (n_1 is the sample size of group 1 and n_2 is the sample size of group 2):

$$\bar{W}_s = \frac{n_1(n_1 + n_2 + 1)}{2}$$

$$SE_{\bar{W}_s} = \sqrt{\frac{n_1 n_2(n_1 + n_2 + 1)}{12}}$$

For our data, we actually have equal-sized groups and there are 10 people in each, so n_1 and n_2 are both 10. Therefore, the mean and standard deviation are:

$$\bar{W}_s = \frac{10(10 + 10 + 1)}{2} = 105$$

$$SE_{\bar{W}_s} = \sqrt{\frac{(10 \times 10)(10 + 10 + 1)}{12}} = 13.23$$

If we know the test statistic, the mean of test statistics and the standard error, then we can easily convert the test statistic to a z-score using the equation that we came across back in Chapter 1:

$$z = \frac{X - \bar{X}}{s} = \frac{W_s - \bar{W}_s}{SE_{\bar{W}_s}}$$

If we calculate this value for the Sunday and Wednesday depression scores we get:

$$z_{\text{Sunday}} = \frac{W_s - \bar{W}_s}{SE_{\bar{W}_s}} = \frac{90.5 - 105}{13.23} = -1.10$$

$$z_{\text{Wednesday}} = \frac{W_s - \bar{W}_s}{SE_{\bar{W}_s}} = \frac{59 - 105}{13.23} = -3.48$$

If these values are bigger than 1.96 (ignoring the minus sign) then the test is significant at $p < .05$. Thus, there is a significant difference between the groups on Wednesday, but not on Sunday.

The procedure I've actually described is the Wilcoxon rank-sum test. The Mann–Whitney test, with which many of you may be more familiar, is basically the same. It is based on a test statistic U, which is derived in a fairly similar way to the Wilcoxon procedure (in fact there's a direct relationship between the two). If you're interested, U is calculated using an equation in which n_1 and n_2 are the sample sizes of groups 1 and 2 respectively, and R_1 is the sum of ranks for group 1:

$$U = n_1 n_2 + \frac{n_1(n_1 + 1)}{2} - R_1$$

So, for our data we'd get the following (remember we have 10 people in each group and the sum of ranks for group 1, the ecstasy group, was 119.5 for the Sunday data and 151 for the Wednesday data):

$$U_{\text{Sunday}} = (10 \times 10) + \frac{10(11)}{2} - 119.50 = 35.50$$

$$U_{\text{Wednesday}} = (10 \times 10) + \frac{10(11)}{2} - 151.00 = 4.00$$

SPSS produces both statistics and there is a direct relationship between the two, so it doesn't really matter which one you choose.

EVERYBODY

6.4.2. Inputting data and provisional analysis ①

SELF-TEST See whether you can use what you have learnt about data entry to enter the data in Table 6.1 into SPSS.

When the data are collected using different participants in each group, we need to input the data using a coding variable. So, the data editor will have three columns of data. The first column is a coding variable (called something like **Drug**), which, in this case, will have only two codes (for convenience I suggest 1 = ecstasy group and 2 = alcohol group). The second column will have values for the dependent variable (BDI) measured the day after (call this variable **Sunday_BDI**) and the third will have the midweek scores on the same questionnaire (call this variable **Wednesday_BDI**). When you enter the data into SPSS remember to tell the computer that a code of 1 represents the group that was given ecstasy and a code of 2 represents the group that was restricted to alcohol (see Section 3.5.2.3). Save the file as **Drug.sav**.

First, we could run some exploratory analyses on the data. Given we have a small sample (10 per group) it's probably worth using tests of normality and homogeneity of variance (but see Jane Superbrain Box 5.5). For normality, because we're going to be looking for group differences, we need to run the analyses for each group separately.

SELF-TEST Carry out some analyses to test for normality and homogeneity of variance in these data (see Sections 5.3.2 and 5.3.3).

FIGURE 6.6

Normal Q-Q plots of depression scores after ecstasy and alcohol on Sunday and Wednesday

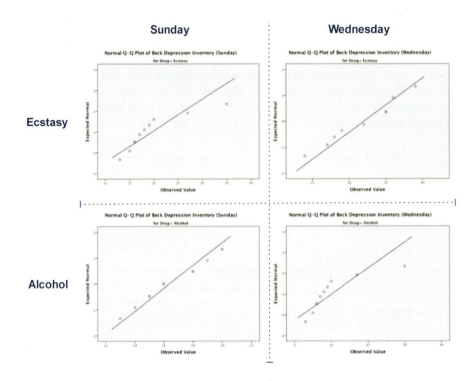

OUTPUT 6.1

Tests of Normality

		Kolmogorov–Smirnov[a]			Shapiro–Wilk		
	Type of Drug	Statistic	df	Sig.	Statistic	df	Sig.
Beck Depression Inventory (Sunday)	Ecstasy	.276	10	.030	.811	10	.020
	Alcohol	.170	10	.200[*]	.959	10	.780
Beck Depression Inventory (Wednesday)	Ecstasy	.235	10	.126	.941	10	.566
	Alcohol	.305	10	.009	.753	10	.004

*. This is a lower bound of the true significance.

a. Lilliefors Significance Correction

Test of Homogeneity of Variance

		Levene Statistic	df1	df2	Sig.
Beck Depression Inventory (Sunday)	Based on Mean	3.644	1	18	.072
	Based on Median	1.880	1	18	.187
	Based on Median and with adjusted df	1.880	1	10.076	.200
	Based on trimmed mean	2.845	1	18	.109
Beck Depression Inventory (Wednesday)	Based on Mean	.508	1	18	.485
	Based on Median	.091	1	18	.766
	Based on Median and with adjusted df	.091	1	11.888	.768
	Based on trimmed mean	.275	1	18	.606

The results of our exploratory analysis are shown in Output 6.1 and Figure 6.6. The normal Q-Q plots show quite clear deviations from normality for ecstasy on Sunday and alcohol on Wednesday because the dots deviate from the diagonal line. The tables in Output 6.1 confirm these observations: for the Sunday data the distribution for ecstasy, $D(10) = 0.28$, $p = .02$, appears to be non-normal whereas the alcohol data, $D(10) = 0.17$, $p = .78$, were normal; conversely, for the Wednesday data, although the data for ecstasy were normal, $D(10) = 0.24$, $p = .566$, the data for alcohol were significantly non-normal, $D(10) = 0.31$, $p = .004$. Remember that we can tell this by whether the significance of the K-S and Shapiro–Wilk tests are less than .05 (and, therefore, significant) or greater than .05 (and, therefore, non-significant, *ns*). These findings alert us to the fact that the sampling distribution might also be non-normal for the Sunday and Wednesday data and that a non-parametric test might be appropriate given that our sample is small. The second table in Output 6.1 shows the results of Levene's test. For the Sunday data, $F(1, 18) = 3.64$, $p = .072$, and for Wednesday, $F(1, 18) = 0.51$, $p = .485$, the variances are not significantly different, indicating that the assumption of homogeneity has been met.

6.4.3. The Mann–Whitney test using SPSS ①

To run a Mann–Whitney test you need to follow the general procedure outlined in Section 6.3, first of all selecting `Analyze Nonparametric Tests ▸ ▲ Independent Samples…`. When you reach the `Objective Fields Settings` tab you should see all of the variables in the data editor listed in the box labelled *Fields*. If you have assigned roles for the variables in the data editor `◉ Use predefined roles` will be selected and SPSS will have automatically assigned your variables. If you haven't assigned roles then `◉ Use custom field assignments` will be selected and you'll need to assign variables yourself. Select both dependent variables from the list (click on **Beck Depression Inventory (Sunday)** then, holding down *Ctrl* (*Cmd* on a Mac), click on **Beck Depression Inventory (Wednesday)** and drag them to the box labelled *Test Fields* (or click on `➡`). Next, select the independent variable, in this case **Type of Drug**, and transfer it to the box labelled *Groups*. The completed dialog box is shown in Figure 6.7.

Next, select the `Objective Fields Settings` tab to activate the test options. You can let SPSS pick a test for you (`◉ Automatically choose the tests based on the data`), but you have more options available if you select `◉ Customize tests`. To do a Mann–Whitney test simply check `☑ Mann-Whitney U (2 samples)` (Figure 6.7). The dialog box also provides the facility to do tests other than the Mann–Whitney test, and these alternatives are explained in SPSS Tip 6.1. To run the analysis click on `▶ Run`.

SPSS TIP 6.1   **Other options for the Mann–Whitney test ②**

In the main dialog box there are some other tests that can be selected:

- **Kolmogorov–Smirnov Z**: In Chapter 5 we met a Kolmogorov–Smirnov test that tested whether a sample was from a normally distributed population. This is a different test. In fact, it tests whether two groups have been drawn from the same population (regardless of what that population may be). In effect, this means it does much the same as the Mann–Whitney test. However, this test tends to have better power than the Mann–Whitney test when sample sizes are less than about 25 per group, and so is worth selecting if that's the case.
- **Moses extreme reactions**: Great name – makes me think of a bearded man standing on Mount Sinai reading a stone tablet and then suddenly bursting into a wild rage, smashing the tablet and screaming 'What do you mean, do not worship any other God?' Sadly, this test isn't as exciting as my mental image. It's a bit like a non-parametric Levene's test (Section 5.3.3.2); it basically compares the variability of scores in the two groups.
- **Wald–Wolfowitz runs**: Despite sounding like a particularly bad case of diarrhoea, this test is another variant on the Mann–Whitney test. In this test the scores are rank-ordered as in the Mann–Whitney test, but rather than analysing the ranks, this test looks for 'runs' of scores from the same group within the ranked order. Now, if there's no difference between groups then obviously ranks from the two groups should be randomly interspersed. However, if the groups are different then you should see more ranks from one group at the lower end and more ranks from the other group at the higher end. By looking for clusters of scores in this way the test can determine if the groups differ.

FIGURE 6.7
Dialog boxes
for the Mann–
Whitney test

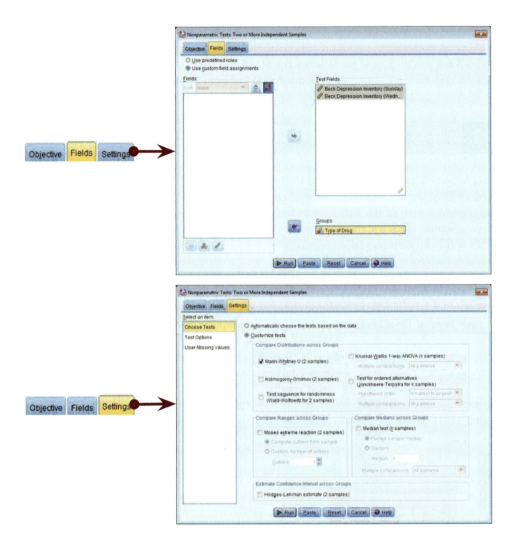

6.4.4. Output from the Mann–Whitney test ①

With all non-parametric tests, SPSS displays a summary table of the analysis in the viewer, but to see the details of the analysis, you need to double-click on this table to open the *model viewer* window (see Figure 6.8). This window is divided into two panels: the left panel shows the summary table of any analyses that you have done, and the right panel shows the details of the analysis. In this example, we analysed group differences for both Sunday and Wednesday, hence the summary table has two rows: one for Sunday and one for Wednesday. To see the results of the Sunday analysis appear in the right-hand panel you need to select that analysis in the left-hand panel. Once selected, the row becomes shaded in the left-hand panel (as shown in Figure 6.8). If we wanted to see the results of the analysis on the Wednesday data we would need to click somewhere on the second row of the table in the left-hand panel. This row would then become shaded within the table and the output in the right-hand panel would change to show the corresponding output.

I explained earlier that the Mann–Whitney test works by looking at differences in the ranked positions of scores in different groups. Therefore, the first part of the output is a graph summarizing the data after they have been ranked. SPSS shows us the distribution of ranks in the two groups (alcohol and ecstasy) and the mean rank in each condition (see

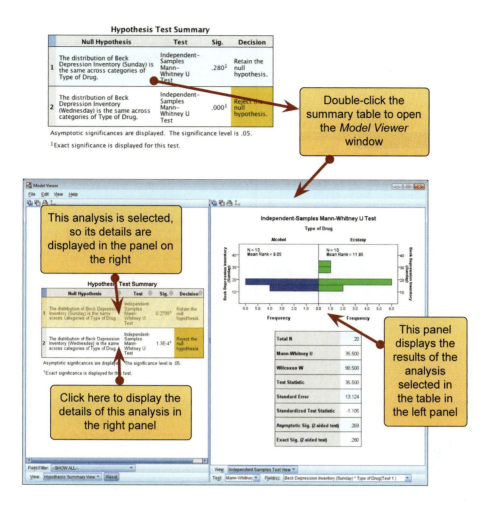

FIGURE 6.8
With non-parametric tests you must double-click the summary table within the viewer window to open up the model viewer window

Output 6.2). Remember that the Mann–Whitney test relies on scores being ranked from lowest to highest; therefore, the group with the lowest mean rank is the group with the greatest number of lower scores in it. Similarly, the group that has the highest mean rank should have a greater number of high scores within it. Therefore, this graph can be used to ascertain which group had the highest scores, which is useful in case we need to interpret a significant result. For example, we can see for the Sunday data that the distributions in the two groups are almost identical (the ecstasy has a couple of higher ranks but otherwise the bars look the same) and the mean ranks are similar (9.05 and 11.95); conversely, in the Wednesday group the distribution of ranks is shifted upwards in the ecstasy group compared to the alcohol group and this is reflected in a much bigger mean rank (15.10 compared to 5.90).

There is a table underneath the graph showing the test statistics for the Mann–Whitney test, the Wilcoxon procedure and the corresponding z-score. Note that the values of U, W_s and the z-score are the same as we calculated in Section 6.4.1 (phew!). The rows labelled *Asymptotic Sig.* and *Exact Sig.* tell us the probability that a test statistic of at least that magnitude would occur if there were no difference between groups. The fact there are two p-values simply reflects two different ways to compute them; our sample is fairly small, so we'll use the exact method (see Jane Superbrain Box 6.2). For these data, the Mann–Whitney test is non-significant for the depression scores taken on the Sunday because the p-value of .280 is greater than the critical value of .05. This finding indicates that ecstasy is no more of a depressant, the day after taking it, than alcohol: both groups report comparable levels of depression. This confirms what we concluded from the mean ranks and distribution of ranks. For the midweek measures the results are highly significant because the exact p-value, given as .000, is less than the critical value of .05. In this case we can say that $p < .001$ because the

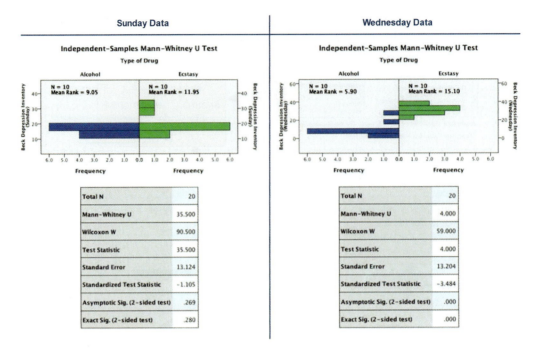

Total N	20
Mann–Whitney U	35.500
Wilcoxon W	90.500
Test Statistic	35.500
Standard Error	13.124
Standardized Test Statistic	–1.105
Asymptotic Sig. (2–sided test)	.269
Exact Sig. (2–sided test)	.280

Total N	20
Mann–Whitney U	4.000
Wilcoxon W	59.000
Test Statistic	4.000
Standard Error	13.204
Standardized Test Statistic	–3.484
Asymptotic Sig. (2–sided test)	.000
Exact Sig. (2–sided test)	.000

JANE SUPERBRAIN 6.2

Exact tests ②

You'll notice in the output that SPSS calculates the *p*-value for non-parametric tests in two ways. The first method, called the *asymptotic* method, gives you a sort of approximation that in large samples will be a perfectly serviceable answer. However, when samples are small, or the data are particularly poorly distributed, it doesn't give you a good answer. The *exact* method is more computationally difficult (but we don't care, because our computer is doing the computations for us) and gives us an exact significance value. You should use this exact significance in small samples (by which I mean anything under 50 really). There is a third method, which isn't available through the non-parametric menus that we're using, but is available for some other tests so we might as well learn about it now. The **Monte Carlo method**[3] is slightly less labour-intensive than computing an exact *p*-value. This method is like bootstrapping (Section 5.4.3) and involves creating a distribution similar to that found in the sample and then taking several samples (the default is 10,000) from this distribution. From those samples the mean significance value and the confidence interval around it can be created.

---

[3] If you're wondering why it's called the Monte Carlo method, it's because back in the late 1800s when Karl Pearson was trying to simulate data, he didn't have a computer to do it for him, so he used to toss coins. A lot. That is, until a friend suggested that roulette wheels, if unbiased, were excellent random number generators. Rather than trying to persuade the Royal Society to fund trips to Monte Carlo casinos to collect data from their roulette wheels, he purchased copies of *Le Monaco*, a weekly Paris periodical that published exactly the data that he required, at the cost of 1 franc (Pearson, 1894; Plackett, 1983). When simulated data are used to test a statistical method, or to estimate a statistic, it is known as the Monte Carlo method even though we use computers now and not roulette wheels.

observed p is very small indeed. This finding also confirms what we suspected based on the distribution of ranks and mean ranks: the ecstasy group (mean rank = 15.10) had significantly higher levels of depression midweek than the alcohol group (mean rank = 5.90).

6.4.5. Calculating an effect size ②

It's important to report effect sizes so that people have a standardized measure of the size of the effect you observed, which they can compare to other studies. SPSS doesn't calculate an effect size for us, but we can calculate approximate effect sizes really easily thanks to the fact that SPSS converts the test statistics into a z-score. The equation to convert a z-score into the effect size estimate, r, is as follows (from Rosenthal, 1991, p. 19):

$$r = \frac{z}{\sqrt{N}}$$

in which z is the z-score that SPSS produces and N is the size of the study (i.e., the number of total observations) on which z is based. In this case Output 6.2 tells us that z is -1.11 for the Sunday data and -3.48 for the Wednesday data. We had 10 ecstasy users and 10 alcohol users, and so the total number of observations was 20. The effect sizes are therefore:

$$r_{Sunday} = \frac{-1.11}{\sqrt{20}} = -.25$$

$$r_{Wednesday} = \frac{-3.48}{\sqrt{20}} = -.78$$

This represents a small to medium effect for the Sunday data (it is below the .3 criterion for a medium effect size) and a huge effect for the Wednesday data (the effect size is well above the .5 threshold for a large effect). The Sunday data show how a fairly large effect size can still be non-significant in a small sample (see Section 2.6.1.10).

6.4.6. Writing the results ①

For the Mann–Whitney test, we need to report only the test statistic (which is denoted by U) and its significance. Also, in keeping with good practice (Section 2.8) we ought to include the effect size and report exact values of p (rather than summary values such as $p < .05$). So, we could report something like:

✓ Depression levels in ecstasy users ($Mdn = 17.50$) did not differ significantly from alcohol users ($Mdn = 16.00$) the day after the drugs were taken, $U = 35.50$, $z = -1.11$, $p = .280$, $r = -.25$. However, by Wednesday, ecstasy users ($Mdn = 33.50$) were significantly more depressed than alcohol users ($Mdn = 7.50$), $U = 4.00$, $z = -3.48$, $p < .001$, $r = -.78$.

I've reported the median for each condition because this statistic is more appropriate than the mean for non-parametric tests. You can get these values by running descriptive statistics (Section 5.3.2.2), or you could report the mean ranks instead of the median. We could also choose to report Wilcoxon's test rather than Mann–Whitney's U statistic and this would be as follows:

✓ Depression levels in ecstasy users (*Mdn* = 17.50) did not significantly differ from alcohol users (*Mdn* = 16.00) the day after the drugs were taken, $W_s = 90.50$, $z = -1.11$, $p = .280$, $r = -.25$. However, by Wednesday, ecstasy users (*Mdn* = 33.50) were significantly more depressed than alcohol users (*Mdn* = 7.50), $W_s = 59.00$, $z = -3.48$, $p < .001$, $r = -.78$.

CRAMMING SAM'S TIPS   **Mann–Whitney test**

- The Mann–Whitney test and Wilcoxon rank-sum test compare two conditions when different participants take part in each condition and the resulting data have unusual cases or violate any assumption in Chapter 5.
- Look at the row labelled *Asymptotic Sig.* or *Exact Sig.* (if your sample is small). If the value is less than .05 then the two groups are significantly different.
- The values of the mean ranks tell you how the groups differ (the group with the highest scores will have the highest mean rank).
- Report the *U* statistic (or W_s if you prefer), the corresponding *z* and the significance value. Also report the medians and their corresponding ranges (or draw a boxplot).
- Calculate the effect size and report this too.

6.5. Comparing two related conditions: the Wilcoxon signed-rank test ①

The **Wilcoxon signed-rank test** (Wilcoxon, 1945), not to be confused with the rank-sum test in the previous section, is used in situations in which there are two sets of scores to compare, but these scores come from the same participants. It is the non-parametric equivalent of the paired-samples *t*-test, which we'll encounter in Chapter 9. Imagine the experimenter in the previous section was now interested in the *change* in depression levels, within people, for each of the two drugs. We now want to compare the BDI scores on Sunday to those on Wednesday. We still have to use a non-parametric test because the distributions of scores for both drugs were non-normal on one of the two days, implying (because the sample is small) that the sampling distribution will be non-normal too (see Output 6.1).

6.5.1. Theory of the Wilcoxon signed-rank test ②

SMART
ALEX
ONLY

The Wilcoxon signed-rank test is based on the differences between scores in the two conditions you're comparing. Once these differences have been calculated they are ranked (just like in Section 6.4.1) but the sign of the difference (positive or negative) is assigned to the rank. If we use the same data as before we can compare depression scores on Sunday to those on Wednesday for the two drugs separately.

Table 6.2 shows the ranking for these data. Remember that we're ranking the two drugs separately. First, we calculate the difference between Sunday and Wednesday (that's just Sunday's score subtracted from Wednesday's). If the difference is zero (i.e., the scores are the same on Sunday and Wednesday) then we exclude these data from the ranking. We make a note of the sign of the difference (positive or negative) and then rank the differences (starting with the smallest) ignoring whether they are positive or negative. The ranking is the same as in Section 6.4.1, and

TABLE 6.2   Ranking data in the Wilcoxon signed-rank test

BDI Sunday	BDI Wednesday	Difference	Sign	Rank	Positive Ranks	Negative Ranks
			Ecstasy			
15	28	13	+	2.5	2.5	
35	35	0	Exclude			
16	35	19	+	6	6	
18	24	6	+	1	1	
19	39	20	+	7	7	
17	32	15	+	4.5	4.5	
27	27	0	Exclude			
16	29	13	+	2.5	2.5	
13	36	23	+	8	8	
20	35	15	+	4.5	4.5	
					Total = 36	0
			Alcohol			
16	5	−11	−	9		9
15	6	−9	−	7		7
20	30	10	+	8	+8	
15	8	−7	−	3.5		3.5
16	9	−7	−	3.5		3.5
13	7	−6	−	2		2
14	6	−8	−	5.5		5.5
19	17	−2	−	1		1
18	3	−15	−	10		10
18	10	−8	−	5.5		5.5
					Total = 8	47

we deal with tied scores in exactly the same way. Finally, we collect together the ranks that came from a positive difference between the conditions, and add them up to get the sum of positive ranks (T_+). We also add up the ranks that came from negative differences between the conditions to get the sum of negative ranks (T_-). So, for ecstasy, $T_+ = 36$ and $T_- = 0$ (in fact there were no negative ranks), and for alcohol, $T_+ = 8$ and $T_- = 47$. The test statistic is T_+, and so it is 36 for ecstasy and 8 for alcohol.

To calculate the significance of the test statistic (T), we again look at the mean ($\bar{T}$) and standard error ($SE_{\bar{T}}$), which, like the Mann–Whitney and rank-sum test in the previous section, are functions of the sample size, n (because we used the same participants, there is only one sample size):

$$\bar{T} = \frac{n(n+1)}{4}$$

$$SE_{\bar{T}} = \sqrt{\frac{n(n+1)(2n+1)}{24}}$$

In both groups, n is simply 10 (because that's how many participants were used). However, remember that for our ecstasy group we excluded two people because they had differences of zero, therefore the sample size we use is 8, not 10. This gives us:

$$\bar{T}_{Ecstasy} = \frac{8(8+1)}{4} = 18$$

$$SE_{\bar{T}_{Ecstasy}} = \sqrt{\frac{8(8+1)(16+1)}{24}} = 7.14$$

For the alcohol group there were no exclusions so we get:

$$\bar{T}_{Alcohol} = \frac{10(10+1)}{4} = 27.50$$

$$SE_{\bar{T}_{Alcohol}} = \sqrt{\frac{10(10+1)(20+1)}{24}} = 9.81$$

As before, if we know the test statistic, the mean of test statistics and the standard error, then we can easily convert the test statistic to a z-score using the equation that we came across way back in Chapter 1 and the previous section:

$$z = \frac{X - \bar{X}}{s} = \frac{T - \bar{T}}{SE_{\bar{T}}}$$

If we calculate this value for the ecstasy and alcohol depression scores we get:

$$z_{Ecstasy} = \frac{T - \bar{T}}{SE_{\bar{T}}} = \frac{36 - 18}{7.14} = 2.52$$

$$z_{Alcohol} = \frac{T - \bar{T}}{SE_{\bar{T}}} = \frac{8 - 27.5}{9.81} = -1.99$$

If these values are bigger than 1.96 (ignoring the minus sign) then the test is significant at $p < .05$. So, it looks as though there is a significant difference between depression scores on Wednesday and Sunday for both ecstasy and alcohol.

EVERYBODY

6.5.2.   Running the analysis ①

To do the same analysis on SPSS we can use the same data as before, but because we want to look at the change for each drug *separately*, we need to use the *split file* command and ask SPSS to split the file by the variable **Type of Drug**. This process ensures that any subsequent analysis is done for the ecstasy group and the alcohol group separately.

SELF-TEST   Split the file by **Drug** (see Section 5.3.2.4).

To run a Wilcoxon test you need to follow the general procedure outlined in Section 6.3, first of all selecting Analyze Nonparametric Tests ▸ Related Samples.... When you reach the Objective Fields Settings tab you will see all of the variables in the data editor listed in the box labelled *Fields*. If you have assigned roles for the variables in the data editor ◉ Use predefined roles will be selected and SPSS will have automatically assigned your variables. If you haven't assigned roles then ◉ Use custom field assignments will be selected and you'll need to assign variables yourself. Select both dependent variables from the list (click on **Beck Depression Inventory (Sunday)** then, holding down *Ctrl* (*Cmd* on a Mac), click on **Beck Depression Inventory (Wednesday)** and drag them to the box labelled *Test Fields* (or click on ➡). The completed dialog box is shown in Figure 6.9. Next, select the Objective Fields Settings tab to activate the test options. You can let SPSS pick a test for you (◉ Automatically choose the tests based on the data), but you have more options available if you select ◉ Customize tests (see SPSS Tip 6.2). To do a Wilcoxon test check ☑ Wilcoxon matched-pair signed-rank (2 samples) (Figure 6.9). To run the analysis click on ▶ Run.

6.5.3. Output for the ecstasy group ①

If you have split the file, then the first set of results obtained will be for the ecstasy group (Output 6.3). The summary table tells you that the significance of the test was .012 and helpfully suggests that you reject the null hypothesis. Let's not be ordered around by SPSS,

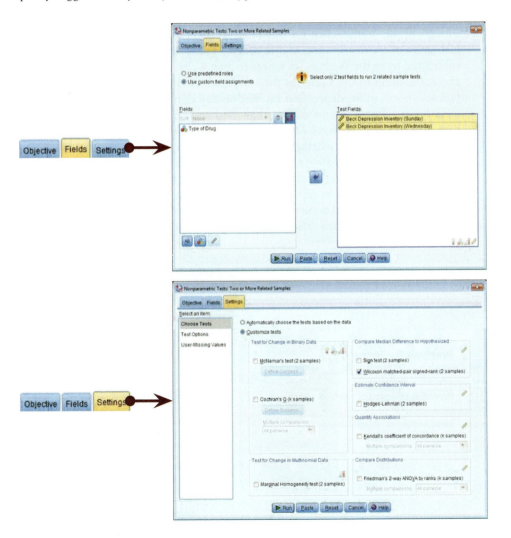

FIGURE 6.9
Dialog boxes for the Wilcoxon signed-rank test

SPSS TIP 6.2   Other options for the Wilcoxon signed-rank test ②

In the main dialog box there are some other tests that can be selected:

- **Sign**: The sign test does the same thing as the Wilcoxon signed-rank test, except that it is based only on the direction of difference (positive or negative). The magnitude of change is completely ignored (unlike in the Wilcoxon test, where the rank tells us something about the relative magnitude of change). For these reasons the sign test lacks power (it's not very good at detecting effects) unless sample sizes are very small (six or less). So, frankly, I don't see the point.
- **McNemar**: This test is useful when you have nominal rather than ordinal data. It's typically used when you're looking for changes in people's scores and it compares the number of people who changed their response in one direction (i.e., scores increased) to those who changed in the opposite direction (scores decreased). So, this test needs to be used when you've got two related dichotomous variables.
- **Marginal Homogeneity**: This produces an extension of McNemar's test but for ordinal variables. It does much the same as the Wilcoxon test, as far as I can tell.

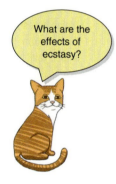

What are the effects of ecstasy?

though. If we double-click on this table to enter the model viewer we will see a histogram of the distribution of differences. These differences are the Sunday scores subtracted from the Wednesday scores (which we're told underneath the histogram) and correspond to the values in the *Difference* column in Table 6.2. A positive difference means more depression on Wednesday than Sunday, a negative difference means more depression on Sunday than Wednesday, and a difference of zero means that depression levels were identical on Sunday and Wednesday. The histogram is colour-coded based on whether ranks are positive or negative: positive ranks appear as brown bars, and negative ranks as blue bars. You might notice that there are no blue bars, which tells us that there were no negative ranks. Therefore, the histogram is a very quick indication of the ratio of positive to negative ranks: in this case all ranks are positive (or tied) and none are negative. We are told the same in the legend to the histogram: there were 8 positive differences, 0 negative differences and 2 ties.

OUTPUT 6.3

Hypothesis Test Summary

	Null Hypothesis	Test	Sig.	Decision
1	The median of differences between Beck Depression Inventory (Sunday) and Beck Depression Inventory (Wednesday) equals 0.	Related-Samples Wilcoxon Signed Rank Test	.012	Reject the null hypothesis.

Asymptotic significances are displayed. The significance level is .05.

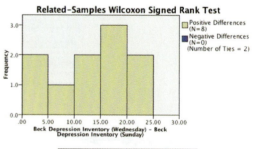

Related–Samples Wilcoxon Signed Rank Test

Positive Differences (N=8)
Negative Differences (N=0)
(Number of Ties = 2)

Total N	10
Test Statistic	36.000
Standard Error	7.124
Standardized Test Statistic	2.527
Asymptotic Sig. (2–sided test)	.012

In Section 6.5.1 I explained that the test statistic, T, is the sum of positive ranks, so our test value here is 36. I also showed how this value can be converted to a z-score, and in doing so we can compute exact significance values based on the normal distribution. Underneath the histogram in Output 6.3 is a table that tells us the test statistic (36), its standard error (7.12) and the z-score (2.53), which all correspond (more or less) to the values we computed by hand in Section 6.5.1. This z-score has a significance value of $p = .012$. This value is less than the standard critical value of .05, so we conclude that there is a significant change in depression scores from Sunday to Wednesday (i.e., we reject the null hypothesis). From the histogram we know that this test statistic is based on there being many more positive differences (i.e., scores being higher on Wednesday than Sunday), therefore, we can conclude that when taking ecstasy there was a significant increase in depression (as measured by the BDI) from the morning after to midweek.

6.5.4. Output for the alcohol group ①

The second set of results obtained will be for the alcohol group (Output 6.4). The summary table tells you that the significance of the test was .047 and again suggests that we reject the null hypothesis. As before, double-click on this table to enter the model viewer. Notice that for the alcohol group (unlike the ecstasy group) we have different coloured bars: the brown bars represent positive differences and the blue bars negative differences. For the ecstasy group we see only brown bars, but for the alcohol group we see the complete opposite: the bars are predominantly blue. This indicates that, on the whole, differences between Wednesday and Sunday were negative. In other words, scores were generally higher on Sunday than they were on Wednesday. Again, these differences are the same as those in the *Difference* column in Table 6.2. The legend of the graph confirms that there was only 1 positive difference, 9 negative differences and 0 ties.

As before, there is a table below the histogram that tells us the test statistic (8), its standard error (9.80), and the corresponding z-score (–1.99). (These are the values we calculated in Section 6.5.1; I point this out merely because I'm so amazed that my hand calculations actually worked.) The p-value associated with the z-score is .047, which means that there's a probability of .047 that we would get a value of z as large as the

OUTPUT 6.4

Related–Samples Wilcoxon Signed Rank Test

Hypothesis Test Summary

	Null Hypothesis	Test	Sig.	Decision
1	The median of differences between Beck Depression Inventory (Sunday) and Beck Depression Inventory (Wednesday) equals 0.	Related–Samples Wilcoxon Signed Rank Test	.047	Reject the null hypothesis.

Asymptotic significances are displayed. The significance level is .05.

Total N	10
Test Statistic	8.000
Standard Error	9.798
Standardized Test Statistic	–1.990
Asymptotic Sig. (2–sided test)	.047

one we have if there were no effect in the population; because this value is less than the critical value of .05 we conclude that there is a significant difference in depression scores. Based on the fact that the histogram showed predominantly negative differences (i.e., scores higher on Sunday than on Wednesday) we know that there was a significant *decline* in depression (as measured by the BDI) from the morning after to midweek in the alcohol group.

The results of the ecstasy and alcohol groups show that there is an opposite effect when alcohol is taken to when ecstasy is taken. After taking alcohol depression is higher the morning after than midweek, whereas after taking ecstasy, depression increases from the morning after to midweek. A different effect across different groups or conditions is known as an interaction (i.e., you get one effect under certain circumstances and a different effect under other circumstances). You can't look at these effects directly using non-parametric tests, but as we explore more common statistical models we will look at these interaction effects in detail (see Chapters 10 and 13).

6.5.5. Calculating an effect size ②

The effect size can be calculated in the same way as for the Mann–Whitney test (see the equation in Section 6.4.5). In this case Outputs 6.3 and 6.4 tell us that for the ecstasy group z is 2.53, and for the alcohol group it is -1.99. In both cases we had 20 observations (although we only used 10 people and tested them twice, it is the number of observations, not the number of people, that is important here). The effect size is therefore:

$$r_{\text{Ecstasy}} = \frac{2.53}{\sqrt{20}} = .57$$

$$r_{\text{Alcohol}} = \frac{-1.99}{\sqrt{20}} = -.44$$

This represents a large change in levels of depression when ecstasy is taken (it is above Cohen's benchmark of .5) and a medium to large change in depression when alcohol is taken (it is between Cohen's criteria of .3 and .5 for a medium and large effect, respectively).

6.5.6. Writing the results ①

For the Wilcoxon test, we need to report only the test statistic (which is denoted by the letter *T*), its exact significance and an effect size (see Section 2.8). So, we could report something like:

✓ For ecstasy users, depression levels were significantly higher on Wednesday (*Mdn* = 33.50) than on Sunday (*Mdn* = 17.50), *T* = 36, *p* = .012, *r* = .57. However, for alcohol users the opposite was true: depression levels were significantly lower on Wednesday (*Mdn* = 7.50) than on Sunday (*Mdn* = 16.0), *T* = 8, *p* = .047, *r* = −.44.

You can get the median values by running descriptive statistics (Section 5.3.2.2). Alternatively, we could report the values of *z*:

✓ For ecstasy users, depression levels were significantly higher on Wednesday (*Mdn* = 33.50) than on Sunday (*Mdn* = 17.50), *z* = 2.53, *p* = .012, *r* = .57. However, for alcohol users the opposite was true: depression levels were significantly lower on Wednesday (*Mdn* = 7.50) than on Sunday (*Mdn* = 16.0), *z* = −1.99, *p* = .047, *r* = −.44.

CRAMMING SAM'S TIPS   Wilcoxon signed-rank test

- The Wilcoxon signed-rank test compares two conditions when the same participants take part in each condition and the resulting data have unusual cases or violate any assumption in Chapter 5.
- Look at the row labelled *Asymptotic Sig. (2-sided test)*. If the value is less than .05 then the two conditions are significantly different.
- Look at the histogram and numbers of positive or negative differences to tell you how the groups differ (the greater number of differences in a particular direction tells you the direction of the result).
- Report the *T*-statistic, the corresponding *z*, the exact significance value and an effect size. Also report the medians and their corresponding ranges (or draw a boxplot).

LABCOAT LENI'S REAL RESEARCH 6.1

Having a quail of a time? ①

MATTHEWS, R. C., ET AL. (2007). *PSYCHOLOGICAL SCIENCE*. 18(9), 758–762.

We encountered some research in Chapter 2 in which we discovered that you can influence aspects of male quail's sperm production through 'conditioning'. The basic idea is that the male is granted access to a female for copulation in a certain chamber (e.g., one that is coloured green) but gains no access to a female in a different context (e.g., a chamber with a tilted floor). The male, therefore, learns that when he is in the green chamber his luck is in, but if the floor is tilted then frustration awaits. For other males the chambers will be reversed (i.e., they get sex only when in the chamber with the tilted floor). The human equivalent (well, sort of) would be if you always managed to pull in the Funky Buddha Lounge but never in the Honey Club.[4] During the test phase, males get to mate in both chambers. The question is: after the males have learnt that they will get a mating opportunity in a certain context, do they produce more sperm or better-quality sperm when mating in that context compared to the control context? (That is, are

you more of a stud in the Honey Club? OK, I'm going to stop this analogy now.)

Mike Domjan and his colleagues predicted that if conditioning evolved because it increases reproductive fitness then males who mated in the context that had previously signalled a mating opportunity would fertilize a significantly greater number of eggs than males that mated in their control context (Matthews, Domjan, Ramsey, & Crews, 2007). They put this hypothesis to the test in an experiment that is utter genius. After training, they allowed 14 females to copulate with two males (counterbalanced): one male copulated with the female in the chamber that had previously signalled a reproductive opportunity (**Signalled**), whereas the second male copulated with the same female but in the chamber that had not previously signalled a mating opportunity (**Control**). Eggs were collected from the females for 10 days after the mating and a genetic analysis was used to determine the father of any fertilized eggs.

The data from this study are in the file **Matthews et al. (2007).sav**. Labcoat Leni wants you to carry out a Wilcoxon signed-rank test to see whether more eggs were fertilized by males mating in their signalled context compared to males in their control context.

Answers are in the additional material on the companion website (or look at page 760 in the original article).

---

[4] These are both clubs in Brighton that I don't go to because I'm too old for that sort of thing, but actually I didn't go even when I was younger because my social skills aren't really at that level of sophistication.

6.6. Differences between several independent groups: the Kruskal–Wallis test ①

We have looked a how to fit a model that represents differences between two groups or conditions, but what happens when there are more than two groups? In these situations we can use two other tests: the Kruskal–Wallis test, which is used when the groups or conditions contain independent scores; and the Friedman test, which we use when the scores are related. Let's look at the Kruskal–Wallis test first (Kruskal & Wallis, 1952). This test assesses the hypothesis that multiple independent groups come from different populations, so we use it to look for differences between groups of scores when those scores have come from different entities, and if we want to counteract the presence of unusual cases or we have violated one of the assumptions from Chapter 5. If you'd like to know a bit more about William Kruskal (Figure 6.10) then there is a lovely biography by Fienberg, Stigler, and Tanur (2007).

I read a story in a newspaper claiming that scientists had discovered that the chemical genistein, which is naturally occurring in soya, was linked to lowered sperm counts

FIGURE 6.10
William Kruskal

in Western males. It turns out that the study was actually conducted on rats and found no link to lowered sperm counts, but there was evidence of abnormal sexual development in male rats (probably because this chemical acts like oestrogen). The journalist naturally interpreted this as a clear link to apparently declining sperm counts in Western males (never trust what you read in the newspapers). Anyway, as a vegetarian who eats lots of soya products and probably would like to have kids one day, I might want to test this idea in humans rather than rats. Suppose I took 80 males and split them into four groups that varied in the number of soya meals they ate per week over a year-long period. The first group was a control group and had no soya meals at all per week (i.e., none in the whole year); the second group had one soya meal per week (that's 52 over the year); the third group had four soya meals per week (that's 208 over the year); and the final group had seven soya meals a week (that's 364 over the year). At the end of the year, all of the participants were sent away to produce some sperm that I could count (when I say 'I', I mean someone else in a laboratory as far away from me as humanly possible).[5]

6.6.1. Theory of the Kruskal–Wallis test ②

SMART
ALEX
ONLY

The theory for the Kruskal–Wallis test is very similar to that for the Mann–Whitney (and Wilcoxon rank-sum) test, so before reading on, look back at Section 6.4.1. Like the Mann–Whitney test, the Kruskal–Wallis test is based on ranked data. So, to begin with, you order the scores from lowest to highest, ignoring the group to which the score belongs, and then assign the lowest score a rank of 1, the next highest a rank of 2 and so on (see Section 6.4.1 for more detail). When you've ranked the data you collect the scores back into their

---

[5] In case any medics are reading this chapter, these data are made up and, because I have absolutely no idea what a typical sperm count is, they're probably ridiculous. I apologize, and you can laugh at my ignorance.

TABLE 6.3 Data for the soya example with ranks

No Soya		1 Soya Meal		4 Soya Meals		7 Soya Meals	
Sperm (millions)	Rank	Sperm (millions)	Rank	Sperm (millions)	Rank	Sperm (millions)	Rank
0.35	4	0.33	3	0.40	6	0.31	1
0.58	9	0.36	5	0.60	10	0.32	2
0.88	17	0.63	11	0.96	19	0.56	7
0.92	18	0.64	12	1.20	21	0.57	8
1.22	22	0.77	14	1.31	24	0.71	13
1.51	30	1.53	32	1.35	27	0.81	15
1.52	31	1.62	34	1.68	35	0.87	16
1.57	33	1.71	36	1.83	37	1.18	20
2.43	41	1.94	38	2.10	40	1.25	23
2.79	46	2.48	42	2.93	48	1.33	25
3.40	55	2.71	44	2.96	49	1.34	26
4.52	59	4.12	57	3.00	50	1.49	28
4.72	60	5.65	61	3.09	52	1.50	29
6.90	65	6.76	64	3.36	54	2.09	39
7.58	68	7.08	66	4.34	58	2.70	43
7.78	69	7.26	67	5.81	62	2.75	45
9.62	72	7.92	70	5.94	63	2.83	47
10.05	73	8.04	71	10.16	74	3.07	51
10.32	75	12.10	77	10.98	76	3.28	53
21.08	80	18.47	79	18.21	78	4.11	56
Total (R_i)	927		883		883		547
Average ($\bar{R}_i$)	46.35		44.15		44.15		27.35

groups and add up the ranks for each group. The sum of ranks for each group is denoted by R_i (where i is used to denote the particular group). Table 6.3 shows the raw data for this example along with the ranks.

SELF-TEST Have a go at ranking the data and see if you get the same results as me.

Once the sum of ranks has been calculated for each group, the test statistic, H, is calculated as follows:

$$H = \frac{12}{N(N+1)} \sum_{i=1}^{k} \frac{R_i^2}{n_i} - 3(N+1) \tag{6.1}$$

In this equation, R_i is the sum of ranks for each group, N is the total sample size (in this case 80) and n_i is the sample size of a particular group (in this case we have equal sample sizes and they are all 20). Therefore, all we really need to do for each group is square the sum of ranks and divide this value by the sample size for that group. We then add up these values. That deals with the middle part of the equation; the rest of it involves calculating various values based on the total sample size. For these data we get:

$$H = \frac{12}{80(81)}\left(\frac{927^2}{20} + \frac{883^2}{20} + \frac{883^2}{20} + \frac{547^2}{20}\right) - 3(81)$$

$$= \frac{12}{6480}(42966.45 + 38984.45 + 38984.45 + 14960.45) - 243$$

$$= 0.0019(135895.8) - 243$$

$$= 251.66 - 243$$

$$= 8.659$$

EVERYBODY

This test statistic has a distribution from the family of chi-square distributions (see Chapter 18). Whereas the standard normal distribution is defined by a mean of 0 and a standard deviation of 1, the chi-square distribution is defined by a single value, the degrees of freedom, which is one less than the number of groups ($k - 1$), in this case 3.

6.6.2. Follow-up analysis ②

The Kruskal–Wallis test tells us that, overall, groups come from different populations. However, if we have four groups like we have in this example, we don't know specifically which groups differ. Are all of the groups different, or are just two of them different? We need some way to tease apart the overall effect. The simplest thing we can do is to compare all pairs of groups (known as **pairwise comparisons**). In our current example, this would entail six tests: none vs. 1 meal; none vs. 4 meals; none vs. 7 meals; 1 vs. 4 meals; 1 vs. 7 meals; and 4 vs. 7 meals. At a very basic level we could simply perform six Mann–Whitney tests making each of these comparisons. However, we saw in Section 2.6.1.7 that when we do lots of tests on the same data we inflate the familywise error rate: in other words, there is more than a 5% chance that we'll make at least one Type I error. Ideally, we want to know that, over all of the tests we do, we still have only a 5% chance of making a Type I error. We also saw that one way to achieve this is to use a lower probability as our threshold for significance. Therefore, one way of teasing apart the effects after a Kruskal–Wallis test is to compare every pair of groups, but to adjust the p-value so that overall, across all of the tests, the Type I error rate remains at 5%.

We saw in Section 2.6.1.8 that by being stricter about what p-value you deem to be significant you reduce the power of the tests (you throw out the baby with the bathwater). An alternative is to use a stepped procedure. The one SPSS uses begins by ordering the groups based on the sum of ranks from smallest to largest (if there are ties, the median is used to decide the order). For our data the rank sums were: 7 meals (rank sum = 547, median = 1.33), 4 meals (rank sum = 883, median = 2.90), 1 meal (rank sum = 883, median = 2.60), no meals (rank sum = 927, median = 3.1). Therefore, the group order would be: 7 meals, 1 meal, 4 meals, and no meals. Figure 6.11 shows how the step-down process works. Step 1 is to see whether the first ordered group is the same as the second (i.e., is there a significant difference?). If they are the same, you then put in the third group and see if all three are the same. If they are, you put in the fourth group and see if all four are the same. If at any point you find a significant difference (i.e., the groups are not the same) then you stop,

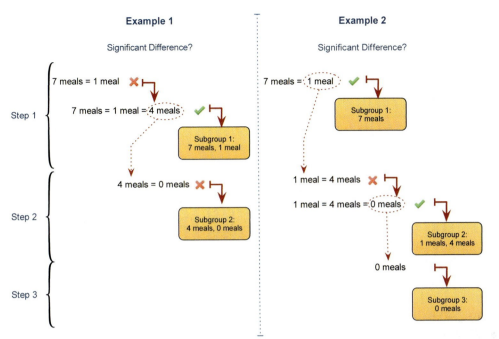

FIGURE 6.11

The non-parametric step-down procedure

carry the group that you included last into the next step, and consider the groups you don't carry forward as a subset (i.e., they are the same). In step 2 you repeat the same process. So (Figure 6.11, Example 1), we start with the first two groups in our ordered list (7 meals and 1 meal). They are not significantly different so we add in group 3 (4 meals). This makes the groups significantly different, so we carry 4 meals into the second step, and conclude that 7 meals and 1 meal are homogeneous groups (i.e., the same). In step 2, we compare 4 meals to the one remaining group (no meals). These groups are not different so we put them in a different subgroup and stop the process. In Example 2, we start with the first two groups in our ordered list (7 meals and 1 meal). They are significantly different so we carry the 1 meal group into the second step, and conclude that 7 meals is a group on its own. In step 2, we compare 1 meal to 4 meals. They are not significantly different so we add in no meals. This makes the groups significantly different, so we carry no meals into the third step, and conclude that 4 meals and 1 meal are homogenous groups. In step 3 we have only one group so there's nothing left to compare it with, and we conclude that it is a group on its own.

These follow-up procedures might seem quite complicated, so don't worry if you don't fully understand them – we will discuss these issues in more detail later on in the book. The main take-home message is that if we have more than two groups to compare we need to follow up the main analysis to find out exactly where the differences between groups lie.

6.6.3. Inputting data and provisional analysis ①

SELF-TEST   See whether you can enter the data in Table 6.3 into SPSS (you don't need to enter the ranks). Then conduct some exploratory analyses on the data (see Sections 5.3.2 and 5.3.3).

When the data are collected using different participants in each group, we input the data using a coding variable. So, the data editor will have two columns of data. The first column

FIGURE 6.12
Normal Q-Q
plots of sperm
counts after
different doses
of soya meals
per week

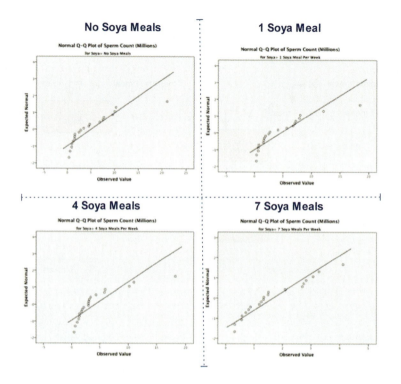

is a coding variable (called something like **Soya**), which, in this case, will have four codes
(for convenience I suggest 1 = no soya, 2 = one soya meal per week, 3 = four soya meals
per week and 4 = seven soya meals per week). The second column will have values for
the dependent variable (sperm count) measured at the end of the year (call this variable
Sperm). When you enter the data into SPSS, remember to tell the computer which group is
represented by which code (see Section 3.5.2.3). The data can be found in the file **Soya.sav**.

   The results of your exploratory analysis are shown in Figure 6.12 and Output 6.5. The
normal Q-Q plots show quite clear deviations from normality for all four groups because
the dots deviate from the diagonal line. We don't really need to do anything more than
look at these graphs – the evidence of non-normality is plain to see and formal tests can be

OUTPUT 6.5

Tests of Normality

	Number of Soya Meals Per Week	Kolmogorov–Smirnov[a]			Shapiro–Wilk		
		Statistic	df	Sig.	Statistic	df	Sig.
Sperm Count (Millions)	No Soya Meals	.181	20	.085	.805	20	.001
	1 Soya Meal Per Week	.207	20	.024	.826	20	.002
	4 Soya Meals Per Week	.267	20	.001	.743	20	.000
	7 Soya Meals Per Week	.204	20	.028	.912	20	.071

a. Lilliefors Significance Correction

Test of Homogeneity of Variance

		Levene Statistic	df1	df2	Sig.
Sperm Count (Millions)	Based on Mean	5.117	3	76	.003
	Based on Median	2.860	3	76	.042
	Based on Median and with adjusted df	2.860	3	58.107	.045
	Based on trimmed mean	4.070	3	76	.010

problematic (see Jane Superbrain Box 5.5). However, given that we would assess normality separately for each group, and within each group the sample is quite small ($n = 20$), if tests of normality are significant then we can take this as evidence of non-normality (because if the test has found a deviation in such a small sample, then it's probably a fairly substantial deviation). If you do these tests (Output 6.5) you'll find that the Kolmogorov–Smirnov test was not significant for the control group, $D(20) = .181$, $p = .085$, but the more accurate Shapiro–Wilk test is ($p = .001$). Data for the group that ate one soya meal per week were significantly different from normal, $D(20) = .207$, $p = .002$, as were the data for those who ate 4, $D(20) = .267$, $p < .001$, and 7, $D(20) = .204$, $p = .028$. Levene's test also shows that the assumption of homogeneity of variance has been violated, $F(3, 76) = 5.12$, $p = .003$, because the p-value in the table is less than .05. As such, these data are not normally distributed, and the groups have heterogeneous variances: a sad story.

6.6.4. Doing the Kruskal–Wallis test in SPSS ①

To run a Kruskal–Wallis test, follow the general procedure outlined in Section 6.3, first of all selecting **Analyze Nonparametric Tests ▸ ▲ Independent Samples…**. When you reach the **Objective Fields Settings** tab you should see all of the variables in the data editor listed in the box labelled *Fields*. If you have assigned roles for the variables in the data editor ◉ **Use predefined roles** will be selected and SPSS will have automatically assigned your variables. If you haven't assigned roles then ◉ **Use custom field assignments** will be selected and you'll need to assign variables yourself. Select the dependent variable from the list (click on **Sperm Count (Millions)**) and drag it to the box labelled *Test Fields* (or click on ◆). Next, select the independent variable (the grouping variable), in this case **Soya**, and drag it to the box labelled *Groups*. The completed dialog box is shown in Figure 6.13.

Next, select the **Objective Fields Settings** tab to activate the test options. You can let SPSS pick a test for you (◉ **Automatically choose the tests based on the data**), but you have more options available if you select ◉ **Customize tests** (see SPSS Tip 6.3). To do a Kruskal–Wallis test check ☑ **Kruskal-Wallis 1-way ANOVA (k samples)** (Figure 6.13). Next to this option there is a drop-down list labelled *Multiple comparisons*. This option allows us to look at differences between individual groups. Within this list there are two options, which we discussed earlier: to compare every group against every other group (*All pairwise*) or to use a step-down method (*Stepwise step-down*). You can also ask for the Jonckheere–Terpstra trend test. This is useful if you want to see whether the medians of the groups increase or decrease in a linear way. For the time being don't select this option, but we will look at this test in due course. To run the analysis click on **▶ Run**.

FIGURE 6.13
Dialog boxes
for the Kruskal–
Wallis test

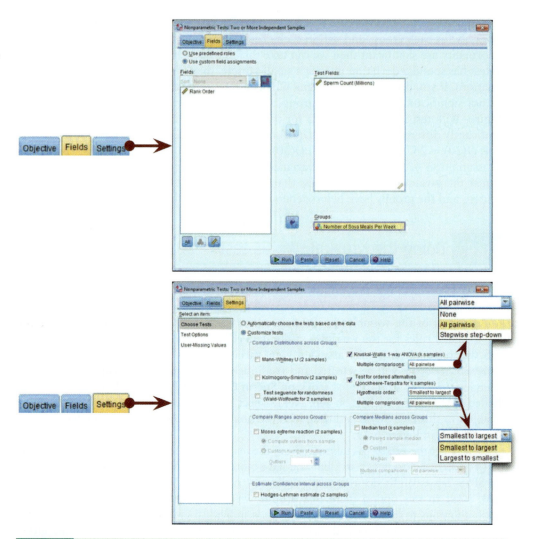

6.6.5. Output from the Kruskal–Wallis test ①

6.6.5.1. The main analysis ①

Output 6.6 shows the summary table, which tells us the *p*-value of the test (.034) and gives us a little message of advice telling us to reject the null hypothesis. Double-click this summary table to open up the model viewer window, which shows the same summary table, but also a more detailed output containing the test statistic, *H*, for the Kruskal–Wallis (8.659, the same value that we calculated earlier), its associated degrees of freedom (in this case we had four groups so the degrees of freedom are 4 − 1, or 3) and the significance. The crucial thing to look at is the significance value, which is .034; because this value is less than .05 we could conclude that the amount of soya meals eaten per week does significantly affect sperm counts.

As we discussed earlier, this overall effect tells us that sperm counts were different in some of the groups, but we don't know specifically which groups differed. One way to see which groups differ is to look at a boxplot (see Section 5.3.2.2) of the groups. SPSS produces a boxplot for us in Output 6.6. The first thing to note is that there are some outliers (note the circles and asterisks that lie above the top whiskers) – these are men who produced a particularly rampant quantity of sperm. Using the control as our baseline, the medians of the first three groups seem quite similar; however, the median of the group, which ate seven soya meals per week, does seem a little lower, so perhaps this is where the

Independent-Samples Kruskal-Wallis Test   OUTPUT 6.6

Hypothesis Test Summary

	Null Hypothesis	Test	Sig.	Decision
1	The distribution of Sperm Count (Millions) is the same across categories of Number of Soya Meals Per Week.	Independent-Samples Kruskal-Wallis Test	.034	Reject the null hypothesis.

Asymptotic significances are displayed. The significance level is .05.

Total N	80
Test Statistic	8.659
Degrees of Freedom	3
Asymptotic Sig. (2–sided test)	.034

1. The test statistic is adjusted for ties.

difference lies. However, these conclusions are subjective. What we really need are some follow-up analyses like those we discussed in Section 6.6.2.

6.6.5.2. Follow-up analysis ②

There are two ways to follow up a Kruskal–Wallis test in SPSS, as we saw in Section 6.6.2, and the output you see depends on whether you selected *All pairwise* or *Stepwise step-down* in the drop-down list labelled *Multiple comparisons* when you ran the analysis (Figure 6.13). In both cases, the output of these tests won't be immediately visible in the model viewer window. The right-hand side of the model viewer window shows the main output by default (labelled the *Independent Samples Test View*), but we can change what is visible in the right-hand panel by using the drop-down list at the bottom of the window labelled *View*. By clicking on this drop-down list you'll see several options, including *Pairwise Comparisons* (if you selected *All pairwise* when you ran the analysis) or *Homogeneous Subsets* (if you selected *Stepwise step-down*). Selecting this option displays the output for the follow-up analysis in the right-hand panel of the model viewer, and to switch back to the main output you would use the same drop-down list but select *Independent Samples Test View* (Figure 6.14).

Let's look at the pairwise comparisons first. The output from this type of follow-up analysis is shown in Output 6.7. The diagram at the top shows the average rank within each group: so, for example, the average rank in the 7 meal group was 27.35, and for the no soya meals group was 46.35. This diagram will also highlight differences between groups by using a different coloured line to connect them (in the current example, there are no significant differences between groups, which is why all of the connecting lines are black). The table underneath shows all of the possible comparisons: 7 vs. 1 soya meals, 7 vs. 4 soya meals, 7 vs. no soya meals, 1 vs. 4 soya meals, 1 vs. no soya meals, and 4 vs. no soya meals. In each case the test statistic is the difference between the mean ranks of those groups. For 7 vs. 1 soya meal, this will be $44.15 - 27.35 = 16.80$, for no soya meals vs. 4 soya meals this value is $46.35 - 44.15 = 2.20$, and so on. These test statistics are converted into z-scores by dividing by their standard errors, and these z-scores have exact p-values associated with them. For example, the 7 vs. 1 soya meal comparison has a z-score of 2.286 and the exact p-value for this z is .022. However, as I mentioned in Section 6.6.2, we have to make sure that we adjust the p-value for the number of tests we have done. The column labelled *Adj.*

Sig. contains these adjusted *p*-values, and it is this column that we need to interpret (no matter how tempted we are to interpret the one labelled *Sig.*). Looking at this column, none of the values fall below our criterion of .05 (although the comparison between 7 soya meals and no soya meals comes fairly close with a *p* = .058, and this reminds us that significance testing encourages black and white thinking and effect sizes might be useful).

To sum up, despite the significant overall effect, none of the specific comparisons between groups indicates a significant difference in sperm counts due to differing amounts of soya consumption. The effect we got seems to mainly reflect the fact that eating soya seven times per week lowers (I know this from the mean ranks) sperm counts compared to eating no soya, although even this comparison was just non-significant.

If you chose the *Stepwise step-down* procedure for following up the Kruskal–Wallis test then the output is rather different. This method does not compare every group with every other group, which means that we don't have to be so strict in adjusting the *p*-values because we're not doing so many significance tests on the same data. Output 6.8 shows the output of this procedure, which is labelled *Homogeneous Subsets* in the *View* drop-down list. (Remember that you can only conduct one type of follow-up analysis, so you

FIGURE 6.14
Changing the main output view to the pairwise comparisons view

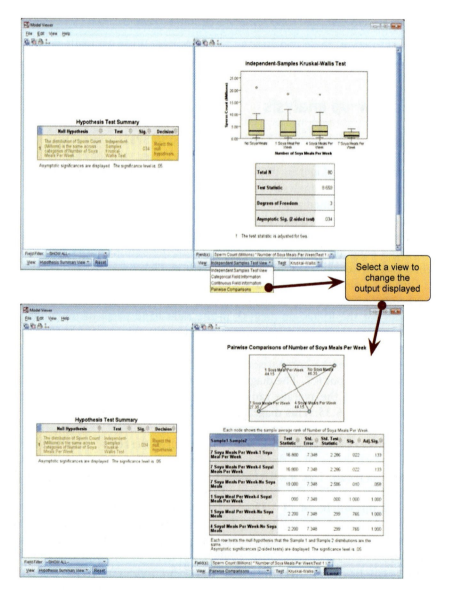

OUTPUT 6.7

Pairwise Comparisons of Number of Soya Meals Per Week

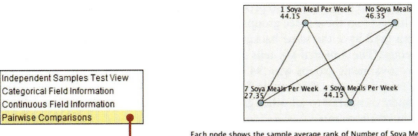

Each node shows the sample average rank of Number of Soya Meals Per Week.

Sample1-Sample2	Test Statistic	Std. Error	Std. Test Statistic	Sig.	Adj.Sig.
7 Soya Meals Per Week-1 Soya Meal Per Week	16.800	7.348	2.286	.022	.133
7 Soya Meals Per Week-4 Soya Meals Per Week	16.800	7.348	2.286	.022	.133
7 Soya Meals Per Week-No Soya Meals	19.000	7.348	2.586	.010	.058
1 Soya Meal Per Week-4 Soya Meals Per Week	.000	7.348	.000	1.000	1.000
1 Soya Meal Per Week-No Soya Meals	2.200	7.348	.299	.765	1.000
4 Soya Meals Per Week-No Soya Meals	2.200	7.348	.299	.765	1.000

Each row tests the null hypothesis that the Sample 1 and Sample 2 distributions are the same.
Asymptotic significances (2-sided tests) are displayed. The significance level is .05.

OUTPUT 6.8

Homogeneous Subsets based on Sperm Count (Millions)

		Subset	
		1	2
Sample[1]	7 Soya Meals Per Week	27.350	
	1 Soya Meal Per Week		44.150
	4 Soya Meals Per Week		44.150
	No Soya Meals		46.350
Test Statistic		.[2]	.118
Sig. (2-sided test)		.	.943
Adjusted Sig. (2-sided test)		.	.943

Homogeneous subsets are based on asymptotic significances. The significance level is .05.

[1] Each cell shows the sample average rank of Sperm Count (Millions).

[2] Unable to compute because the subset contains only one sample.

will have either *Pairwise Comparisons* in the drop-down list or *Homogeneous Subsets*, not both.) This output clusters similar (homogeneous) groups together in the same columns of the resulting table (and colour-codes them to make the differences clear). From column 1, we can see that the group that ate 7 soya meals a week clusters on its own. In other words, comparing it with the next highest ranking group (the 1 soya meal group) produced a significant difference. Consequently, the 1 soya meal group is moved into a different subset in column 2 and is compared to the next highest ranking group (4 soya meals), and this did not lead to a significant difference, so then they were compared to the no soya meals group too, which also produced no significant difference (think back to Figure 6.11). The fact that these three groups (1, 4 and no soya meals) are clustered within the same column (and have the same background colour) tells us that they are the same (i.e., homogeneous). The *Adjusted Sig.* tells us that the *p*-value associated with comparing the 1, 4 and no soya meals groups was .943, which means not at all significant. We can sum these results up by saying that having 7 soya meals per week seemed to lower sperm counts significantly compared to all other groups, but all other doses of soya had no significant effect on sperm counts.

6.6.6. Testing for trends: the Jonckheere–Terpstra test ②

Back in Section 6.6.4 I mentioned that you could select an option for the Jonckheere–Terpstra test, ☑ Test for ordered alternatives (Jonckheere-Terpstra for k samples) (Jonckheere, 1954; Terpstra, 1952). This statistic tests for an ordered pattern to the medians of the groups you're comparing. Essentially it does the same thing as the Kruskal–Wallis test (i.e., it tests for a difference between the medians of the groups) but it incorporates information about whether the order of the groups is meaningful. As such, you should use this test when you expect the groups you're comparing to produce a meaningful order of medians. So, in the current example we expect that the more soya a person eats, the more their sperm count will go down. Therefore, the control group should have the highest sperm count, those having one soya meal per week should have a lower sperm count, the sperm count in the four meals per week group should be smaller still, and the seven meals per week group should have the lowest sperm count. Therefore, there is an order to our medians: they should decrease across the groups. Conversely there might be situations where you expect your medians to increase. For example, there's a phenomenon in psychology known as the 'mere exposure effect', which basically means that the more you're exposed to something, the more you'll like it. Record companies put this to good use by making sure songs are played on radio for about 2 months prior to their release, so on the day of release everyone loves the song and is dying to have it and rushes out to buy it, sending it to number one.[6] Anyway, if you took three groups and exposed them to a song 10 times, 20 times and 30 times respectively and then measured how much people liked the song, you'd expect the medians to increase. Those who heard it 10 times would like it a bit, but those who heard it 20 times would like it more, and those who heard it 30 times would like it the most.

The Jonckheere–Terpstra test was designed for these situations. In SPSS, we can select between two options (Figure 6.13):

- *Smallest to largest*, which tests whether the first group differs from the second group, which in turn differs from the third group, which in turn differs from the fourth and so on until the last group.

- *Largest to smallest*, which tests whether the last group differs from the group before, which in turn differs from the group before and so on until the first group.

In both cases the test just looks at differences across ordered groups; it does not distinguish between whether there is an increase or decrease over the groups. As such, the test determines whether the medians of the groups *ascend or descend* in the *order*

---

[6] In most cases the mere exposure effect seems to have the reverse effect on me: the more I hear the manufactured rubbish that gets into the charts, the more I want to rid my brain of the mental anguish it creates by ramming hot irons into my ears and making myself deaf.

specified by the coding variable. The coding variable is important, therefore, because it must code groups in the order that you expect the medians to change (to repeat, it doesn't matter whether you expect them to increase or decrease). For our soya example, we coded our groups as 1 = no soya, 2 = one soya meal per week, 3 = four soya meals per week and 4 = seven soya meals per week, so in this context we would test whether the median sperm count increases or decreases across the groups when they're ordered in that way. Obviously we could change the coding scheme and test whether the medians were ordered in a different way. Figure 6.13 shows how to specify the test, so rerun the analysis (as in Section 6.6.4) but selecting the Jonckheere–Terpstra (*Smallest to largest*) instead of the Kruskal–Wallis test.

Output 6.9 shows the output from the Jonckheere–Terpstra test for the soya data. Like the Kruskal–Wallis test, the viewer window will display only a summary table, which tells us the *p*-value of the test (.013) and advises us to reject the null hypothesis. Double-clicking on this table opens up a more detailed results table in the model viewer window. The output tells us the value of test-statistic, *J*, which is 912. In large samples (more than about eight per group) this test statistic has a sampling distribution that is normal, and a mean and standard deviation that are easily defined and calculated. Knowing these things, we can convert to a *z*-score, which we are told is −2.476. As with any *z*-score, we can ascertain the *p*-value associated with it, in this case .013. This value indicates a significant trend in the medians because it is lower than the critical value of .05. The sign of the *z*-score tells us something useful, though: if it is positive then it indicates a trend of ascending medians (i.e., the medians get bigger as the values of the coding variable get bigger), but if it is negative (as it is here) it indicates a trend of descending medians (the medians get smaller as the value of the coding variable gets bigger). In this example, because we set the test option to be *Smallest to largest* (Figure 6.13) and we coded the variables as 1 = no soya, 2 = one soya meal per week, 3 = four soya meals per week and 4 = seven soya meals per week, the negative value of *z* means that the medians get smaller as we go from no soya to one soya meal, to four soya meals and on to seven soya meals.[7]

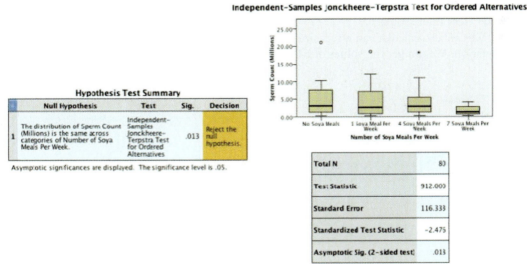

OUTPUT 6.9

---

[7] If you're bored, rerun the test but specify *Largest to smallest*. The results will be identical except that the *z* will be 2.476 rather than −2.476. This positive value shows an ascending trend, rather than a descending one. This will happen because by selecting *Largest to smallest* we would be looking at the medians in the opposite direction (i.e., from 7 to 4 to 1 to no meals) to selecting *Smallest to largest* (i.e., from no to 1 to 4 to 7 meals).

OLIVER TWISTED

Please Sir, can I have some more … Jonck?

'I want to know how the Jonckheere–Terpstra Test actually works', complains Oliver. Of course you do, Oliver, sleep is hard to come by these days. I am only too happy to oblige, my little syphilitic friend. The additional material for this chapter on the companion website has a complete explanation of the test and how it works. I bet you're glad you asked.

6.6.7. Calculating an effect size ②

Unfortunately there isn't an easy way to convert a Kruskal–Wallis test statistic that has more than 1 degree of freedom to an effect size r. You could use the significance value of the Kruskal–Wallis test statistic to find an associated value of z from a table of probability values for the normal distribution (like that in the Appendix). From this you could use the conversion to r that we used in Section 6.4.5. However, this kind of effect size is rarely that useful (because it's summarizing a general effect). In most cases it's more interesting to know the effect size for a focused comparison (such as when comparing two things). For this reason, I'd suggest just calculating effect sizes for the pairwise tests we used to follow up the main analysis. Table 6.4 shows how you would do this for these data. For each comparison we get the z-score from the column labelled *Std. Test Statistic* in Output 6.7. Each comparison compared two groups of 20 people, so the total N for a given comparison is 40. We use the square root of this value ($\sqrt{40} = 6.32$) to compute r, which is $z/\sqrt{N}$). We can see from the table that the effect sizes were medium to large for 7 meals compared to all other groups. Despite the fact that the significance tests for these comparisons were non-significant, there seems to be something meaningful going on. All other comparisons yielded very small effect sizes (less than $r = .1$).

We can also calculate an effect size for Jonckheere's test if we want to by using the same equation. We can get the values of z (−2.476) and N (80) from Output 6.9:

$$r_{\text{Jonckheere}} = \frac{-2.476}{\sqrt{80}}$$

$$= -.28$$

TABLE 6.4 Calculating effect sizes for pairwise comparisons

Comparison	z	$\sqrt{N}$	r
7 vs. 1 meal	2.286	6.32	.362
7 vs. 4 meals	2.286	6.32	.362
7 vs. no meals	2.586	6.32	.409
1 vs. 4 meals	0.000	6.32	.000
1 vs. no meals	0.299	6.32	.047
4 vs. no meals	0.299	6.32	.047

6.6.8. Writing and interpreting the results ①

For the Kruskal–Wallis test, we need only report the test statistic (which we saw earlier is denoted by H), its degrees of freedom and its significance. So, we could report something like:

✓ Sperm counts were significantly affected by eating soya meals, $H(3) = 8.66$, $p = .034$.

However, we need to report the follow-up tests as well (including their effect sizes):

✓ Sperm counts were significantly affected by eating soya meals, $H(3) = 8.66$, $p = .034$. Pairwise comparisons with adjusted p-values showed that there were no significant differences between sperm counts when people ate 7 soya meals per week compared to 4 meals ($p = .133$, $r = .36$), 1 meal ($p = .133$, $r = .36$), or no meals ($p = .058$, $r = .41$). There were also no significant differences in sperm counts between those eating 4 soya meals per week and those eating 1 meal ($p = 1.00$, $r = .00$) and no meals ($p = 1.00$, $r = .05$). Finally, there were no significant differences in sperm counts between those eating 1 soya meal per week and those eating none ($p = 1.00$, $r = .05$).

✓ Sperm counts were significantly affected by eating soya meals, $H(3) = 8.66$, $p = .034$. Step-down follow-up analysis showed that if soya is eaten every day it significantly reduces sperm counts compared to eating none; however, eating soya less than every day has no significant effect on sperm counts, $p = .943$ ('phew!' says the vegetarian book author).

Or, we might want to report our trend:

✓ Sperm counts were significantly affected by eating soya meals, $H(3) = 8.66$, $p = .034$. Jonckheere's test revealed a significant trend in the data: as more soya was eaten, the median sperm count decreased, $J = 912$, $z = -2.48$, $p = .013$, $r = -.28$.

CRAMMING SAM'S TIPS   **The Kruskal–Wallis test**

- The Kruskal–Wallis test compares several conditions when different participants take part in each condition and the resulting data have unusual cases or violate any assumption in Chapter 5.
- Look at the row labelled *Asymptotic Sig*. If the value is less than .05 then the groups are significantly different.
- You can follow up the main analysis with pairwise comparisons, comparing each group against each other group in pairs, but correcting the resulting p-value of each test so that the overall error rate remains at 5%.
- If you predict that the means will increase or decrease across your groups in a certain order then do Jonckheere's trend test.
- Report the H-statistic, the degrees of freedom and the significance value for the main analysis. For any follow-up tests, report an effect size (you can also report the corresponding z-score and significance value). Also report the medians and their corresponding ranges (or draw a boxplot).

6.7. Differences between several related groups: Friedman's ANOVA ①

The Kruskal–Wallis test enables us to compare groups of scores that are independent (come from different entities), but what happens if we want to compare several groups but the scores

ÇETINKAYA, H., & DOMJAN, M. (2006) *JOURNAL OF COMPARATIVE PSYCHOLOGY*, 120(4), 427–432.

LABCOAT LENI'S REAL RESEARCH 6.2

Eggs-traordinary ①

There seems to be a lot of sperm in this book (not literally I hope) – it's possible that I have a mild obsession. We saw in Labcoat Leni's Real Research 6.1 that male quail fertilized more eggs if they had been trained to be able to predict when a mating opportunity would arise. However, some quail develop fetishes. Really. In the previous example the type of compartment acted as a predictor of an opportunity to mate, but in studies where a terrycloth object acts as a sign that a mate will shortly become available, some quail start to direct their sexual behaviour towards the terrycloth object. (I may regret this analogy, but in human terms if you imagine that everytime you were going to have sex with your boyfriend you gave him a green towel a few moments before seducing him, then after enough seductions he would start rubbing his crotch against any green towel he saw. If you've ever wondered why your boyfriend rubs his crotch on green towels, then I hope this explanation has been enlightening.) In evolutionary terms, this fetishistic behaviour seems counterproductive because sexual behaviour becomes directed towards something that cannot provide reproductive success.

However, perhaps this behaviour serves to prepare the organism for the 'real' mating behaviour.

Hakan Çetinkaya and Mike Domjan conducted a brilliant study in which they sexually conditioned male quail (Çetinkaya & Domjan, 2006). All quail experienced the terrycloth stimulus and an opportunity to mate, but for some the terrycloth stimulus immediately preceded the mating opportunity (paired group) whereas for others they experienced it 2 hours after the mating opportunity (this was the control group because the terrycloth stimulus did not predict a mating opportunity). In the paired group, quail were classified as fetishistic or not depending on whether they engaged in sexual behaviour with the terrycloth object.

During a test trial the quail mated with a female and the researchers measured the percentage of eggs fertilized, the time spent near the terrycloth object, the latency to initiate copulation, and copulatory efficiency. If this fetishistic behaviour provides an evolutionary advantage then we would expect the fetishistic quail to fertilize more eggs, initiate copulation faster and be more efficient in their copulations.

The data from this study are in the file **Çetinkaya & Domjan (2006).sav.** Labcoat Leni wants you to carry out a Kruskal–Wallis test to see whether fetishist quail produced a higher percentage of fertilized eggs and initiated sex more quickly.

Answers are in the additional material on the companion website (or look at pages 429–430 in the original article).

are dependent (i.e., they come from the same entities)? In this situation we can use **Friedman's ANOVA** (Friedman, 1937). Friedman's test is used for testing differences between conditions when there are more than two conditions and the same entities have provided scores in all conditions (so, each case contributes several scores to the data), and when we want to counteract the presence of unusual cases or we have violated one of the assumptions from Chapter 5.

Young people can become obsessed with body weight and diets, and because the media insist on ramming ridiculous images of stick-thin celebrities down our throats (should that be 'into our eyes'?) and brainwashing us into believing that these emaciated corpses are actually attractive, we all end up terribly depressed that we're not perfect (because we don't have a couple of slugs stuck to our faces instead of lips). Then corporate parasites jump on our vulnerability by making loads of money on diets that will help us attain the body beautiful. Not wishing to miss out on this great opportunity to exploit people's insecurities, I came up with the Andikins diet.[8] The principle is that you follow my lifestyle: you eat no meat, drink lots of Darjeeling tea, eat shedloads of lovely European cheese, lots of fresh crusty bread, pasta, chocolate at every available opportunity (especially when writing books), then enjoy a few beers at the weekend, play soccer twice a week and play your drum kit for an hour a day or until your neighbour threatens to saw your arms off and beat you around the head with them for making so much noise. To test the efficacy of my wonderful new diet, I took 10 women who thought that they needed to lose weight and

---

[8] Not to be confused with the Atkins diet, obviously.☺

put them on this diet for two months. Their weight was measured in kilograms at the start of the diet and then after one month and two months.

6.7.1. Theory of Friedman's ANOVA ②

The theory for Friedman's ANOVA is much the same as for the other tests we've seen in this chapter: it is based on ranked data. To begin with, you place your data for different conditions into different columns (in this case there were three conditions so we have three columns). The data for the diet example are in Table 6.5; note that the data are in different columns and so each row represents the weight of a different person. The next thing we have to do is rank the data *for each person*. So, we start with person 1, we look at their scores (in this case person 1 weighed 63.75 kg at the start, 65.38 kg after one month on the diet, and 81.34 kg after two months on the diet), and then we give the lowest one a rank of 1, the next highest a rank of 2 and so on (see Section 6.4.1 for more detail). When you've ranked the data for the first person, you move onto the next person, and starting at 1 again, rank their lowest score, then rank the next highest as 2 and so on. You do this for all people from whom you've collected data. You then simply add up the ranks for each condition (R_i, where i is used to denote the particular group).

SELF-TEST Have a go at ranking the data and see if you get the same results as in Table 6.5.

TABLE 6.5 Data for the diet example with ranks

	Weight			Weight		
	Start	**Month 1**	**Month 2**	**Start (Ranks)**	**Month 1 (Ranks)**	**Month 2 (Ranks)**
Person 1	63.75	65.38	81.34	1	2	3
Person 2	62.98	66.24	69.31	1	2	3
Person 3	65.98	67.70	77.89	1	2	3
Person 4	107.27	102.72	91.33	3	2	1
Person 5	66.58	69.45	72.87	1	2	3
Person 6	120.46	119.96	114.26	3	2	1
Person 7	62.01	66.09	68.01	1	2	3
Person 8	71.87	73.62	55.43	2	3	1
Person 9	83.01	75.81	71.63	3	2	1
Person 10	76.62	67.66	68.60	3	1	2
			R_i	19	20	21

Once the sum of ranks has been calculated for each group, the test statistic, F_r, is calculated as:

$$F_r = \left[\frac{12}{Nk(k+1)} \sum_{i=1}^{k} R_i^2 \right] - 3N(k+1) \tag{6.2}$$

In this equation, R_i is the sum of ranks for each group, N is the total sample size (in this case 10) and k is the number of conditions (in this case 3). This equation is very similar to that for the Kruskal–Wallis test (compare equations (6.1) and (6.2)). All we need to do for each condition is square the sum of ranks and then add up these values. That deals with the middle part of the equation; the rest of it involves calculating various values based on the total sample size and the number of conditions. For these data we get:

$$F_r = \left[\frac{12}{(10 \times 3)(3+1)} \left(19^2 + 20^2 + 21^2 \right) \right] - (3 \times 10)(3+1)$$

$$= \frac{12}{120}(361 + 400 + 441) - 120$$

$$= 0.1(1202) - 120$$

$$= 120.2 - 120$$

$$= 0.2$$

EVERYBODY

When the number of people tested is large (bigger than about 10) this test statistic, like the Kruskal–Wallis test in the previous section, has a chi-square distribution (see Chapter 18) and this distribution is defined by one value, the degrees of freedom, which is one less than the number of groups ($k - 1$), in this case 2.

6.7.2. Inputting data and provisional analysis ①

SELF-TEST   Using what you know about inputting data, try to enter these data into SPSS and run some exploratory analyses (see Chapter 5).

When the data are collected using the same participants in each condition, the data are entered using different columns. So, the data editor will have three columns of data. The first column is for the data from the start of the diet (called something like **Start**), the second column will have values for the weights after one month (called **Month1**) and the final column will have the weights at the end of the diet (called **Month2**). The data can be found in the file **Diet.sav**.

The results of the exploratory analysis are shown in Figure 6.15 and Output 6.10. The normal Q-Q plots show quite clear deviations from normality for all three time points because the dots deviate from the diagonal line. These graphs are evidence enough that our data are not normal, and because our sample size is small we can't rely on the central limit theorem to get us out of trouble. If you're keen on normality tests, we can certainly use significance in these tests to demonstrate a lack of normality because the sample size is small and so a significant result will have to be because of a fairly substantial problem. (It's worth noting that non-significance in this context tells us nothing useful because our sample size is so small.) If you do these tests (Output 6.10), you'll find that the Kolmogorov–Smirnov test is not significant for the initial weights at the start of the diet, $D(10) = .23$, $p = .15$, but the more accurate Shapiro–Wilk test is significant, $p = .009$. The data one month into the diet were significantly different from normal, $D(10) = .34$, $p = .002$. The data at the end of the diet were not significantly non-normal, $D(10) = .20$, $p = .200$, but this finding

Baseline

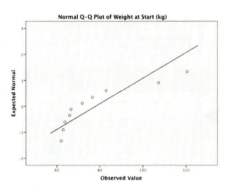

FIGURE 6.15
Q-Q plots of the diet data

1 Month

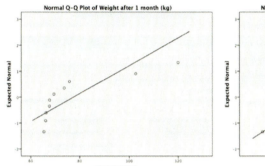

2 Months

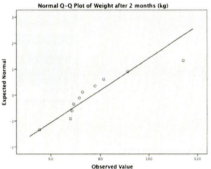

Tests of Normality

OUTPUT 6.10

	Kolmogorov–Smirnov[a]			Shapiro-Wilk		
	Statistic	df	Sig.	Statistic	df	Sig.
Weight at Start (kg)	.228	10	.149	.784	10	.009
Weight after 1 month (kg)	.335	10	.002	.685	10	.001
Weight after 2 months (kg)	.203	10	.200[*]	.877	10	.121

*. This is a lower bound of the true significance.

a. Lilliefors Significance Correction

isn't helpful because the lack of significance could simply be due to the small sample size (Section 2.6.1.10). In combination, the tests and Q-Q plots suggest non-normal data or unusual cases at all time points.

6.7.3. Doing Friedman's ANOVA in SPSS ①

Again you need to follow the general procedure outlined in Section 6.3, first of all selecting Analyze Nonparametric Tests ▸ ▲ Related Samples... When you reach the Objective Fields Settings tab you will see all of the variables in the data editor listed in the box labelled *Fields*. If you have assigned roles for the variables in the data editor ⦿ Use predefined roles will be selected and SPSS will have automatically assigned your variables. If you haven't assigned roles then ⦿ Use custom field assignments will be selected and you'll need to assign variables yourself. Select the three variables that represent the dependent variable at the different levels of the independent variable from the list:

FIGURE 6.16
Dialog boxes
for Friedman's
ANOVA

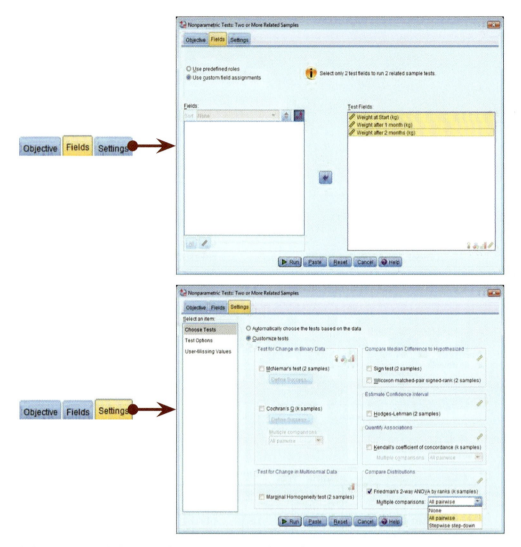

click on **Start** and then, holding down the *Ctrl* (*Cmd* on a Mac) key, click on **Month1** and **Month2**. Drag them to the box labelled *Test Fields* (or click on). The completed dialog box is shown in Figure 6.16.

Next, select the tab to activate the test options. You can let SPSS pick a test for you (Automatically choose the tests based on the data), but you have more options available if you select Customize tests (see SPSS Tip 6.4). To do a Friedman test check ☑ Friedman's 2-way ANOVA by ranks (k samples); next to this option there is a drop-down list labelled *Multiple comparisons* (Figure 6.16) just as there was for the Kruskal–Wallis test. This option allows us to look at differences between individual groups. Within this list there are two options, which we discussed earlier: to compare every group against every other group (*All pairwise*) or to use a step-down method (*Stepwise step-down*). To run the analysis click on ▶ Run.

6.7.4. Output from Friedman's ANOVA ①

Output 6.11 shows the summary table, which tells us the *p*-value of the test (.905) and advises us to retain the null hypothesis. Double-click this summary table to open up the model viewer window, which shows the same summary table, but also a more detailed output containing the test statistic, F_r, for the Friedman test (0.2, which we calculated earlier),

SPSS TIP 6.4 Other options for Friedman's ANOVA ②

In the main dialog box there are some other tests that can be selected:

- **Kendall's W** (coefficient of concordance): This is similar to Friedman's ANOVA but is used specifically for looking at the agreement between raters. If, for example, we asked 10 different women to rate the attractiveness of Justin Timberlake, David Beckham and Barack Obama, we could use this test to look at the extent to which they agree. This test is particularly useful because, like the correlation coefficient, Kendall's *W* has a limited range: it ranges from 0 (no agreement between judges) to 1 (complete agreement between judges).
- **Cochran's Q**: This test is an extension of McNemar's test (see SPSS Tip 6.2) and is basically a Friedman test for when you have dichotomous data. So imagine you asked 10 people whether they'd like to snog Justin Timberlake, David Beckham and Barack Obama and they could answer only yes or no. If we coded responses as 0 (no) and 1 (yes) we could do the Cochran test on these data.

OUTPUT 6.11

Hypothesis Test Summary

	Null Hypothesis	Test	Sig.	Decision
1	The distributions of Weight at Start (kg), Weight after 1 month (kg) and Weight after 2 months (kg) are the same.	Related-Samples Friedman's Two-Way Analysis of Variance by Ranks	.905	Retain the null hypothesis.

Asymptotic significances are displayed. The significance level is .05.

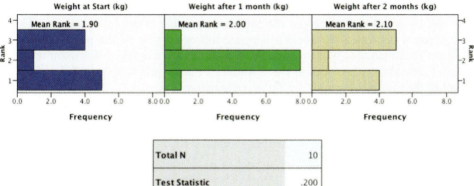

Related-Samples Friedman's Two-Way Analysis of Variance by Ranks

Total N	10
Test Statistic	.200
Degrees of Freedom	2
Asymptotic Sig. (2–sided test)	.905

1. Multiple comparisons are not performed because the overall test retained the null hypothesis of no differences.

its associated degrees of freedom (in this case we had 3 groups so the they are 3 − 1, or 2) and the significance. The significance value is .905, which is well above .05, therefore we could conclude that the Andikins diet does not have any effect: the weights didn't significantly change over the course of the diet.

The output also shows us the distribution of ranks across the three groups. It's clear that the mean rank is very similar across the three time points: it is 1.90 (baseline), 2.00 (1 month) and 2.10 (2 months), which shows that the mean rank changes very little over time. This explains the lack of significance of the test statistic.

6.7.5. Following-up Friedman's ANOVA ②

As with the Kruskal–Wallis test, there are two ways to follow-up a Friedman test: we can compare all groups, or we can use a step-down procedure (Section 6.6.2). The output you see depends on whether you selected *All pairwise* or *Stepwise step-down* in the drop-down list labelled *Multiple comparisons* when you ran the analysis (Figure 6.16). As with the Kruskal–Wallis test, the output of these tests won't be immediately visible in the model viewer window. To see them we need to use the drop-down list at the bottom of the window labelled *View*. By clicking on this drop-down list you'll see several options including *Pairwise Comparisons* (if you selected *All pairwise* when you ran the analysis) or *Homogeneous Subsets* (if you selected *Stepwise step-down*). However, for these data you won't see anything in the drop-down list. That's because SPSS produces these tests only if the overall analysis is significant; because our overall analysis wasn't significant, we have no follow-up tests. This decision is sensible: why would you want to unpick an effect that isn't significant in the first place? However, if you get a significant overall effect you could examine follow-up analyses in exactly the same way as we did for the Kruskal–Wallis test.

6.7.6. Calculating an effect size ②

It's most sensible (in my opinion at least) to calculate effect sizes for any comparisons you've done after the ANOVA. In this example we didn't have any follow-up analyses because the overall effect was non-significant. However, effect sizes for these comparisons might still be useful so that people can see the magnitude of group differences. This is a slight dilemma because SPSS doesn't compute follow-up tests in the presence of a non-significant Friedman test. What we'd have to do instead is a series of Wilcoxon tests (from which we can extract a z-score). In this example, we have only three groups, so if we compare all of the groups we simply get three comparisons:

- Test 1: Weight at the start of the diet compared to at one month.

- Test 2: Weight at the start of the diet compared to at two months.

- Test 3: Weight at one month compared to at two months.

 SELF-TEST   Carry out the three Wilcoxon tests suggested above (see Figure 6.9).

Output 6.12 shows the Wilcoxon signed-rank test statistics from doing the three comparisons. As we saw in Section 6.5.5, it's straightforward to get an effect size *r* from the Wilcoxon signed-rank test. For the first comparison (start weight versus 1 month) Output 6.12 shows us that *z* is −0.051, and because this is based on comparing two conditions

Baseline - 1 Month			Baseline - 2 Months			1 Month - 2 Months	
Total N	10		Total N	10		Total N	10
Test Statistic	27.000		Test Statistic	25.000		Test Statistic	26.000
Standard Error	9.811		Standard Error	9.811		Standard Error	9.811
Standardized Test Statistic	-.051		Standardized Test Statistic	-.255		Standardized Test Statistic	-.153
Asymptotic Sig. (2-sided test)	.959		Asymptotic Sig. (2-sided test)	.799		Asymptotic Sig. (2-sided test)	.878

OUTPUT 6.12

each containing 10 observations, we had 20 observations in total (remember it isn't important that the observations come from the same people). The effect size is therefore:

$$r_{\text{Start−1 Month}} = \frac{-0.051}{\sqrt{20}} = -.01$$

For the second comparison (start weight vs. 2 months) Output 6.12 shows us that z is −0.255, and this was again based on 20 observations. The effect size is therefore:

$$r_{\text{Start−2 Months}} = \frac{-0.255}{\sqrt{20}} = -.06$$

For the final comparison (1 month vs. 2 months) Output 6.12 shows us that z is −0.153 and this was again based on 20 observations. The effect size is therefore:

$$r_{\text{Start−1 Month}} = \frac{-0.153}{\sqrt{20}} = -.03$$

Unsurprisingly, given the lack of significance of the Friedman test, these all represent virtually non-existent effects: they are all very close to zero.

6.7.7. Writing and interpreting the results ①

For Friedman's ANOVA we need only report the test statistic, which is denoted by χ^2_F, its degrees of freedom and significance.[9] So, we could report something like:

✓ The weight of participants did not significantly change over the two months of the diet, $\chi^2(2) = 0.20$, $p = .91$.

Although with no significant initial analysis we wouldn't report follow-up tests for these data, in case you need to, you should say something like this:

✓ The weight of participants did not significantly change over the two months of the diet, $\chi^2(2) = 0.20$, $p = .91$. Wilcoxon tests were used to follow up this finding. It appeared that weight didn't significantly change from the start of the diet to one month, $T = 27$, $r = −.01$, from the start of the diet to two months, $T = 25$, $r = −.06$, or from one month to two months, $T = 26$, $r = −.03$. We can conclude that the Andikins diet, like its creator, is a complete failure.

[9] The test statistic is sometimes denoted without the F as χ^2.

CRAMMING SAM'S TIPS   Friedman's ANOVA

- Friedman's ANOVA compares several conditions when the same participants take part in each condition and the resulting data have unusual cases or violate any assumption in Chapter 5.
- Look at the row labelled *Asymptotic Sig.* If the value is less than .05 then the conditions are significantly different.
- You can follow up the main analysis with pairwise comparisons. Which compare each group against each other group in pairs, but correcting the resulting *p*-value of each test so that the overall error rate remains at 5%.
- Report the χ^2 statistic, the degrees of freedom and the significance value for the main analysis. For any follow-up tests, report an effect size (you can also report the corresponding *z* and the significance value).
- Report the medians and their ranges (or draw a boxplot).

6.8. Brian's attempt to woo Jane ①

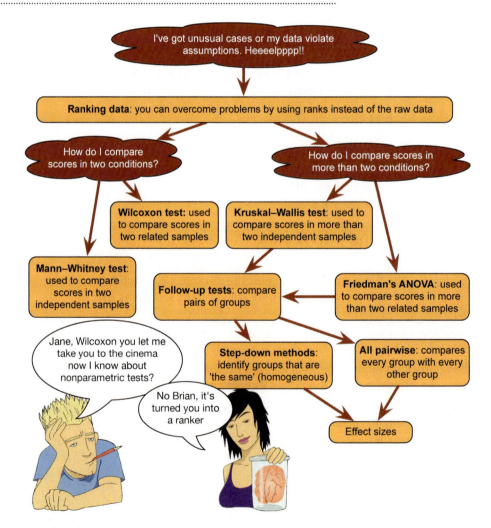

FIGURE 6.17   What Brian learnt from this chapter

6.9. What next? ①

'You promised us swans', I hear you cry, 'and all we got was Kruskal this, and Wilcoxon that – where were the bloody swans?!' Well, the Queen owns them all so I wasn't allowed to have them. Nevertheless, this chapter did negotiate Dante's eighth circle of hell (Malebolge), where data of deliberate and knowing evil dwell. That is, data don't always behave themselves. Unlike the data in this chapter, my formative years at school were spent being very well-behaved and uninteresting. However, a mischievous and rebellious streak was growing inside. Perhaps the earliest signs were my taste in music. Even from about the age of 3 music was my real passion: one of my earliest memories is of listening to my dad's rock and soul records (back in the days of vinyl) while waiting for my older brother to come home from school. I still have a nostalgic obsession with vinyl. The first record I asked my parents to buy me was 'Take on the world' by Judas Priest, which I'd heard on *Top of the Pops* (a now defunct UK TV show) and liked. Watching the Priest on *Top of the Pops* is a very vivid memory – it had a huge impact. This record came out in 1978 when I was 5. Some people think that this sort of music corrupts young minds. Let's see if it did …

6.10. Key terms that I've discovered

Cochran's *Q*	Mann–Whitney test	Pairwise comparisons
Friedman's ANOVA	McNemar's test	Ranking
Jonckheere–Terpstra test	Median test	Sign test
Kendall's *W*	Monte Carlo method	Wald–Wolfowitz runs
Kolmogorov-Smirnov *Z*	Moses extreme reactions	Wilcoxon rank-sum test
Kruskal–Wallis test	Non-parametric tests	Wilcoxon signed-rank test

6.11. Smart Alex's tasks

- **Task 1:** A psychologist was interested in the cross-species differences between men and dogs. She observed a group of dogs and a group of men in a naturalistic setting (20 of each). She classified several behaviours as being dog-like (urinating against trees and lamp posts, attempts to copulate with anything that moved, and attempts to lick their own genitals). For each man and dog she counted the number of dog-like behaviours displayed in a 24-hour period. It was hypothesized that dogs would display more dog-like behaviours than men. The data are in the file **MenLikeDogs. sav**. Analyse them with a Mann–Whitney test. ①

- **Task 2:** There's been speculation over the years about the influence of subliminal messages on records. Both Ozzy Osbourne and Judas Priest have been accused of putting backward masked messages on their albums that subliminally influence poor unsuspecting teenagers into doing things like blowing their heads off with shotguns. A psychologist was interested in whether backward masked messages really did have an effect. He took the master tapes of Britney Spears's 'Baby one more time' and created a second version that had the masked message 'deliver your soul to the dark lord' repeated in the chorus. He took this version, and the original, and played one version (randomly) to a group of 32 people. He took the same group six months later and played them whatever version they hadn't heard the time before. So each person heard both the original, and the version with the masked message, but at different points in time. The psychologist measured the number of goats that were sacrificed in the week after listening to each version. It was hypothesized that the backward message would lead to more goats being sacrificed. The data are in the file **DarkLord.sav**. Analyse them with a Wilcoxon signed-rank test. ①

- **Task 3**: A psychologist was interested in the effects of television programmes on domestic life. She hypothesized that through 'learning by watching', certain programmes might actually encourage people to behave like the characters within them. This in turn could affect the viewer's own relationships (depending on whether the programme depicted harmonious or dysfunctional relationships). She took episodes of three popular TV shows and showed them to 54 couples, after which the couple were left alone in the room for an hour. The experimenter measured the number of times the couple argued. Each couple viewed all three of the TV programmes at different points in time (a week apart) and the order in which the programmes were viewed was counterbalanced over couples. The TV programmes selected were *EastEnders* (which typically portrays the lives of extremely miserable, argumentative, London folk who like nothing more than to beat each other up, lie to each other, sleep with each other's wives and generally show no evidence of any consideration to their fellow humans), *Friends* (which portrays a group of unrealistically considerate and nice people who love each other oh so very much – but I love it anyway), and a National Geographic programme about whales (this was a control). The data are in the file **Eastenders.sav**. Access them and conduct Friedman's ANOVA on the data. ①

- **Task 4**: A researcher was interested in trying to prevent coulrophobia (fear of clowns) in children. She decided to do an experiment in which different groups of children (15 in each) were exposed to different forms of positive information about clowns. The first group watched some adverts for McDonald's in which their mascot Ronald McDonald is seen cavorting about with children and going on about how they should love their mums. A second group was told a story about a clown who helped some children when they got lost in a forest (although what on earth a clown was doing in a forest remains a mystery). A third group was entertained by a real clown, who came into the classroom and made balloon animals for the children.[10] A final group acted as a control and had nothing done to them at all. The researcher took self-report ratings of how much the children liked clowns, resulting in a score for each child that could range from 0 (not scared of clowns at all) to 5 (very scared of clowns). The data are in the file **coulrophobia.sav**. Access them and conduct a Kruskal–Wallis test. ①

- **Task 5**: Thinking back to Labcoat Leni's Real Research 3.1, test whether the number of offers was significantly different in people listening to Bon Scott compared to those listening to Brian Johnson. Remember the data are in **Oxoby (2008) Offers.sav**. Compare your results to those reported by Oxoby (2008). ①

- **Task 6**: Repeat the analysis above but for the minimum acceptable offer (remember these data are in the file **Oxoby (2008) MAO.sav**). See Chapter 3, Task 3. ①

- **Task 7**: Using the data in **Shopping Exercise.sav** (Chapter 3, Task 4), test whether men and women spent significantly different amounts of time shopping. ①

- **Task 8**: Using the same data, test whether men and women walked significantly different distances while shopping. ①

---

[10] Unfortunately, the first time they attempted the study the clown accidentally burst one of the balloons. The noise frightened the children and they associated that fear response with the clown. All 15 children are currently in therapy for coulrophobia.

- **Task 9**: Using the data in **Goat or Dog.sav** (Chapter 3, Task 5), test whether people married to goats and dogs differed significantly in their life satisfaction. ①

- **Task 10**: Use the **SPSSExam.sav** (Chapter 5, Task 2) data to test whether students at Sussex and Duncetown universities differed significantly in their SPSS exam scores, their numeracy, their computer literacy, and the number of lectures attended. ①

- **Task 11**: Use the **DownloadFestival.sav** data from Chapter 5 to test whether hygiene levels changed significantly over the three days of the festival. ①

Answers can be found on the companion website.

6.12. Further reading

Siegel, S., & Castellan, N. J. (1988). *Nonparametric statistics for the behavioral sciences* (2nd ed.). New York: McGraw-Hill. (This is a seminal text on non-parametric statistics, and is the only book seriously worth recommending as 'further' reading. It is probably not a good book for stats-phobes, but if you've coped with my chapter then this book will be an excellent next step.)

Wilcox, R. R. (2010). *Fundamentals of modern statistical methods: Substantially improving power and accuracy*. New York: Springer. (A fantastic book that looks at lots of other approaches to dealing with problem data beyond the ones I have covered in this chapter.)

7 Correlation

7.1. What will this chapter tell me? ①

When I was 8 years old, my parents bought me a guitar for Christmas. Even then, I'd desperately wanted to play the guitar for years. I could not contain my excitement at getting this gift (had it been an *electric* guitar I think I would actually have exploded with excitement). The guitar came with a 'learn to play' book, and after a little while of trying to play what was on page 1 of this book, I readied myself to unleash a riff of universe-crushing power onto the world (well, 'Skip to my Lou' actually). But I couldn't do it. I burst into tears and ran upstairs to hide.[1] My dad sat with me and said 'Don't worry, Andy, everything is hard to begin with, but the more you practise the easier it gets.' In his comforting words, my dad was inadvertently teaching me about the relationship, or correlation, between two variables. These two variables could be related in three ways: (1) *positively related*,

[1] This is not a dissimilar reaction to the one I have when publishers ask me for new editions of statistics textbooks.

meaning that the more I practised my guitar, the better a guitar player I would become (i.e., my dad was telling me the truth); (2) *not related* at all, meaning that as I practised the guitar my playing ability would remain completely constant (i.e., my dad had fathered a cretin); or (3) *negatively related*, which would mean that the more I practised the guitar the worse a guitar player I would become (i.e., my dad had fathered an indescribably strange child). This chapter looks first at how we can express the relationships between variables statistically by looking at two measures: *covariance* and the *correlation coefficient*. We then discover how to carry out and interpret correlations in SPSS. The chapter ends by looking at more complex measures of relationships; in doing so it acts as a precursor to the chapter on multiple regression.

7.2. Modelling relationships ①

In Chapter 4 I stressed the importance of looking at your data graphically before running any other analysis on them. I want to begin by reminding you that our starting point with a correlation analysis should be to look at some scatterplots of the variables we have measured. I am not going to repeat how to get SPSS to produce these graphs, but I am going to urge you (if you haven't done so already) to read Section 4.8 before embarking on the rest of this chapter.

Way back in Chapter 2 we started talking about fitting models to your data, and that these models represented the hypothesis you're trying to test. In the previous chapter we started to look at this process using a very specific set of models that are applied to ranked data and are useful when the data contain unusual cases or fail to meet the assumptions we discussed in Chapter 5. However, when these assumptions are met we can start to use a model known as the general linear model, which is an incredibly versatile and simple model. In fact, we've already encountered it. In Section 2.4 we discussed fitting models to the data and I mentioned that everything in statistics boils down to one simple idea (expressed in equation (2.1)):

$$\text{outcome}_i = (\text{model}) + \text{error}_i$$

To recap, this equation means that the data we observe can be predicted from the model we choose to fit to the data plus some amount of error. The 'model' in the equation will vary depending on the design of your study, the type of data you have and what it is you're trying to achieve with your model. If we want to model a relationship between variables then we're trying to predict an outcome variable from a predictor variable. Therefore, we need to factor the predictor variable into the model. As we saw in equation (2.3), we usually denote predictor variables with the letter *X*, so our model will be:

$$\text{outcome}_i = (bX_i) + \text{error}_i$$

This just means 'the outcome for an entity is predicted from the predictor variable plus some error'. As we have seen before, the model is described by a parameter, *b*, which in this context represents the relationship between the predictor variable (*X*) and the outcome. We use the sample data to estimate this parameter. Therefore, when we look at linear relationships between variables, this is the model we fit. We're interested in estimating the value of *b* because this will tell us how strong the relationship between the predictor and outcome is. When there is only one predictor variable in the model, *b* is known as the Pearson product-moment correlation coefficient (and, just to confuse us, is denoted by the *letter r*). How might we estimate this parameter? Like a quest for fire, we could search across the land … or, we could use maths.

7.2.1. A detour into the murky world of covariance ①

The simplest way to look at whether two variables are associated is to look at whether they *covary*. To understand what covariance is, we first need to think back to the concept of variance that we met in Chapter 2. Remember that the variance of a single variable represents the average amount that the data vary from the mean. Numerically, it is described by:

$$\text{variance} \left(s^2 \right) = \frac{\sum_{i=1}^{n} \left(x_i - \bar{x} \right)^2}{N-1} = \frac{\sum_{i=1}^{n} \left(x_i - \bar{x} \right) \left(x_i - \bar{x} \right)}{N-1} \tag{7.1}$$

The mean of the sample is represented by $\bar{x}$, x_i is the data point in question and N is the number of observations (see Section 2.4.1). If two variables are related, then changes in one variable should be met with similar changes in the other variable. Therefore, when one variable deviates from its mean we would expect the other variable to deviate from its mean in a similar way. To illustrate what I mean, imagine we took five people and subjected them to a certain number of advertisements promoting toffee sweets, and then measured how many packets of those sweets each person bought during the next week. The data are in Table 7.1, as well as the mean and standard deviation (*s*) of each variable.

TABLE 7.1

Participant:	1	2	3	4	5	Mean	s
Adverts Watched	5	4	4	6	8	5.4	1.67
Packets Bought	8	9	10	13	15	11.0	2.92

   If there were a relationship between these two variables, then as one variable deviates from its mean, the other variable should deviate from its mean in the same or the directly opposite way. Figure 7.2 shows the data for each participant (green circles represent the number of packets bought and blue circles represent the number of adverts watched); the green line is the average number of packets bought and the blue line is the average number of adverts watched. The vertical lines represent the differences (remember that these differences are called *deviations* or *residuals*) between the observed values and the mean of the relevant variable. The first thing to notice about Figure 7.2 is that there is a very similar pattern of deviations for both variables. For the first three participants the observed values are below the mean for both variables, for the last two people the observed values are above the mean for both variables. This pattern is indicative of a potential relationship between the two variables (because it seems that if a person's score is below the mean for one variable then their score for the other will also be below the mean).
   So, how do we calculate the exact similarity between the patterns of differences of the two variables displayed in Figure 7.2? One possibility is to calculate the total amount of deviation, but we would have the same problem as in the single-variable case: the positive and negative deviations would cancel out (see Section 1.6.3). Also, by adding the deviations, we would gain little insight into the *relationship* between the variables. In the single-variable case, we squared the deviations to eliminate the problem of positive and negative deviations cancelling each other out. When there are two variables, rather than squaring each deviation, we can multiply the deviation for one variable by the corresponding deviation for the

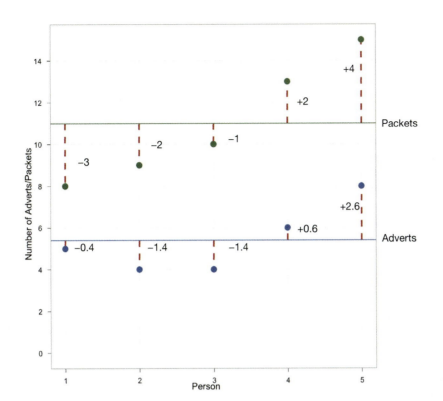

FIGURE 7.2
Graphical display of the differences between the observed data and the means of two variables

second variable. If both deviations are positive or negative then this will give us a positive value (indicative of the deviations being in the same direction), but if one deviation is positive and one negative then the resulting product will be negative (indicative of the deviations being opposite in direction). When we multiply the deviations of one variable by the corresponding deviations of a second variable, we get what is known as the **cross-product deviations**. As with the variance, if we want an average value of the combined deviations for the two variables, we must divide by the number of observations (we actually divide by $N-1$ for reasons explained in Jane Superbrain Box 2.2). This averaged sum of combined deviations is known as the **covariance**. We can write the covariance in equation form:

$$\text{covariance}(x, y) = \frac{\sum_{i=1}^{n}(x_i - \bar{x})(y_i - \bar{y})}{N - 1} \tag{7.2}$$

You will notice that the equation is the same as the equation for variance (equation (1.5)), except that instead of squaring the differences, we multiply them by the corresponding difference of the second variable. For the data in Table 7.1 and Figure 7.2 we reach the following value:

$$
\begin{aligned}
\text{covariance}(x, y) &= \frac{\sum_{i=1}^{n}(x_i - \bar{x})(y_i - \bar{y})}{N - 1} \\
&= \frac{(-0.4)(-3) + (-1.4)(-2) + (-0.4)(-1) + (0.6)(2) + (2.6)(4)}{N - 1} \\
&= \frac{1.2 + 2.8 + 1.4 + 1.2 + 10.4}{4} \\
&= \frac{17}{4} \\
&= 4.25
\end{aligned}
$$

Calculating the covariance is a good way to assess whether two variables are related to each other. A positive covariance indicates that as one variable deviates from the mean, the other variable deviates in the same direction. On the other hand, a negative covariance indicates that as one variable deviates from the mean (e.g., increases), the other deviates from the mean in the opposite direction (e.g., decreases). However, the covariance depends upon the scales of measurement used: it is not a standardized measure. For example, if we use the data above and assume that they represented two variables measured in miles then the covariance is 4.25 square miles (as calculated above). If we then convert these data into kilometres (by multiplying all values by 1.609) and calculate the covariance again then we should find that it increases to 11 square kilometres. This dependence on the scale of measurement is a problem because it means that we cannot compare covariances in an objective way – so, we cannot say whether a covariance is particularly large or small relative to another data set unless both data sets were measured in the same units.

7.2.2. Standardization and the correlation coefficient ①

To overcome the problem of dependence on the measurement scale, we need to convert the covariance into a standard set of units. This process is known as **standardization**. We need a unit of measurement into which any scale of measurement can be converted, and typically we use the *standard deviation*. We came across this measure in Section 1.6.3 and saw that, like the variance, it is a measure of the average deviation from the mean. If we divide any distance from the mean by the standard deviation, it gives us that distance in standard

FIGURE 7.3
Karl Pearson

deviation units. For example, for the data in Table 7.1, the standard deviation for the number of packets bought is approximately 3.0 (the exact value is 2.91). In Figure 7.2 we can see that the observed value for participant 1 was 3 packets less than the mean (so there was an error of −3 packets of sweets). If we divide this deviation, −3, by the standard deviation, which is approximately 3, then we get a value of −1. This tells us that the difference between participant 1's score and the mean was −1 standard deviation. So, we can express the deviation from the mean for a participant in standard units by dividing the observed deviation by the standard deviation.

It follows from this logic that if we want to express the covariance in a standard unit of measurement we can simply divide by the standard deviation. However, there are two variables and, hence, two standard deviations. Now, when we calculate the covariance we actually calculate two deviations (one for each variable) and then multiply them. Therefore, we do the same for the standard deviations: we multiply them and divide by the product of this multiplication. The standardized covariance is known as a *correlation coefficient* and is defined as follows:

$$r = \frac{\text{cov}_{xy}}{s_x s_y} = \frac{\sum_{i=1}^{n}(x_i - \bar{x})(y_i - \bar{y})}{(N-1)s_x s_y} \tag{7.3}$$

in which s_x is the standard deviation of the first variable and s_y is the standard deviation of the second variable (all other letters are the same as in the equation defining covariance). This coefficient, r, is known as the **Pearson product-moment correlation coefficient**

JANE SUPERBRAIN 7.1

Who said statistics was dull? Part 2 ①

We saw in Jane Superbrain Box 2.3 that Fisher and Neyman had a feud over their different views of hypothesis testing. Fisher seemed to believe that if you're going to feud with one of your prominent peers, you may as well feud with them all, and he famously didn't see eye-to-eye

with Karl Pearson either. This wasn't a great career move on Fisher's part, given that Pearson was senior to him and wielded an awful lot of influence through his journal *Biometrika*. The feud began when Pearson published a paper of Fisher's in his journal but made comments in his editorial that, to the casual reader, belittled Fisher's work. Two years later, Pearson's group published work following on from Fisher's paper without consulting him. The antagonism persisted with Fisher turning down a job to work in Pearson's group and publishing 'improvements' on Pearson's ideas. Fisher's 'improvements' were greeted by Pearson in much the same way as a cat would be welcomed into a fish tank. Pearson for his part wrote in his own journal about apparent errors made by Fisher (Barnard, 1963; Field, 2005c; Savage, 1976). Yes, statistics was never dull back then.

or **Pearson's correlation coefficient** (for a really nice explanation of why it was originally called the 'product-moment' correlation, see Miles & Banyard, 2007) and was invented by Karl Pearson (see Figure 7.3 and Jane Superbrain Box 7.1).[2] If we look back at Table 7.1 we see that the standard deviation for the number of adverts watched (s_x) was 1.67, and for the number of packets of crisps bought (s_y) was 2.92. If we multiply these together we get $1.67 \times 2.92 = 4.88$. Now, all we need to do is take the covariance, which we calculated a few pages ago as being 4.25, and divide by these multiplied standard deviations. This gives us $r = 4.25/4.88 = .87$.

By standardizing the covariance we end up with a value that has to lie between -1 and $+1$ (if you find a correlation coefficient less than -1 or more than $+1$ you can be sure that something has gone hideously wrong). A coefficient of $+1$ indicates that the two variables are perfectly positively correlated, so as one variable increases, the other increases by a proportionate amount. Conversely, a coefficient of -1 indicates a perfect negative relationship: if one variable increases, the other decreases by a proportionate amount. A coefficient of zero indicates no linear relationship at all and so if one variable changes, the other stays the same. We also saw in Section 2.7.1 that because the correlation coefficient is a standardized measure of an observed effect, it is a commonly used measure of the size of an effect and that values of $\pm.1$ represent a small effect, $\pm.3$ is a medium effect and $\pm.5$ is a large effect (although I re-emphasize my caveat that these canned effect sizes are no substitute for interpreting the effect size within the context of the research literature).

There are two types of correlation. What we have just described is a **bivariate correlation**, which is a correlation between two variables. You can also compute a **partial correlation**, which quantifies the relationship between two variables while 'controlling' the effect of one or more additional variables. We will look at partial correlations in due course.

---

[2] You will find Pearson's product-moment correlation coefficient denoted by both r and R. Typically, the upper-case form is used in the context of regression because it represents the multiple correlation coefficient; however, for some reason, when we square r (as in Section 7.4.2.2) an upper case R is used. Don't ask me why – it's just to confuse us.

7.2.3. The significance of the correlation coefficient ③

Although we can interpret the size of a correlation coefficient directly (Section 2.7.1), we have seen in Chapter 2 that scientists like to test hypotheses using probabilities. In the case of a correlation coefficient we can test the hypothesis that the correlation is different from zero (i.e., different from 'no relationship'). If we find that our observed coefficient was very unlikely to be as big as it is if there was no effect in the population then we can gain confidence that the relationship that we have observed is statistically meaningful.

There are two ways that we can go about testing this hypothesis. The first is to use our trusty z-scores that keep cropping up in this book. As we have seen, z-scores are useful because we know the probability of a given value of z occurring, if the distribution from which it comes is normal. There is one problem with Pearson's r, which is that it is known to have a sampling distribution that is not normally distributed. This is a bit of a nuisance, but luckily thanks to our friend Fisher we can adjust r so that its sampling distribution *is* normal, as follows (Fisher, 1921):

$$z_r = \frac{1}{2} \log_e \left(\frac{1+r}{1-r} \right)$$

(7.4)

The resulting z_r has a standard error of:

$$SE_{z_r} = \frac{1}{\sqrt{N-3}}$$

(7.5)

For our advert example, our $r = .87$ becomes 1.33 with a standard error of .71.

We can then transform this adjusted r into a z-score just as we have done for raw scores, and for skewness and kurtosis values in previous chapters. If we want a z-score that represents the size of the correlation relative to a particular value, then we simply compute a z-score using the value that we want to test against and the standard error. Normally we want to see whether the correlation is different from 0, in which case we can subtract 0 from the observed value of r and divide by the standard error (in other words, we just divide z_r by its standard error):

$$z = \frac{z_r}{SE_{z_r}}$$

(7.6)

For our advert data this gives us 1.33/.71 = 1.87. We can look up this value of z (1.87) in the table for the normal distribution in the Appendix and get the one-tailed probability from the column labelled 'Smaller Portion' (think back to Section 1.6.4). In this case the value is .0307. To get the two-tailed probability we simply multiply this value by 2, which gives us .0614. As such the correlation is not significant, because $p > .05$.

In fact, the hypothesis that the correlation coefficient is different from 0 is usually (SPSS, for example, does this) tested not using a z-score, but using a different test statistic called a t-statistic with $N - 2$ degrees of freedom. This statistic can be obtained directly from r:

$$t_r = \frac{r\sqrt{N-2}}{\sqrt{1-r^2}}$$

(7.7)

So you might wonder then why I told you about z-scores. Partly it was to keep the discussion framed in concepts with which you are already familiar (we don't encounter the t-statistic properly for a few chapters), but also it is useful background information for the next section.

7.2.4. Confidence intervals for r ③

We saw in Chapter 2 that confidence intervals tell us something about the likely value (in this case of the correlation) in the population. To compute them for r, we can take advantage of what we learnt in the previous section about converting r to z_r (to make the sampling distribution normal), and use the associated standard errors. We can then construct a confidence interval in the usual way, for example, a 95% confidence interval is calculated as (see equation (2.9)):

$$\text{lower boundary of confidence interval} = \overline{X} - (1.96 \times SE)$$

$$\text{upper boundary of confidence interval} = \overline{X} + (1.96 \times SE)$$

In the case of our transformed correlation coefficients these equations become:

$$\text{lower boundary of confidence interval} = z_r - \left(1.96 \times SE_{z_r}\right)$$

$$\text{upper boundary of confidence interval} = z_r + \left(1.96 \times SE_{z_r}\right)$$

For our advert data this gives us $1.33 - (1.96 \times .71) = -0.062$ and $1.33 + (1.96 \times .71) = 2.72$. Remember that these values are in the z_r metric, but we can convert back to a correlation coefficient using:

$$r = \frac{e^{2z_r} - 1}{e^{2z_r} + 1} \tag{7.8}$$

This gives us an upper bound of $r = .991$ and a lower bound of -0.062 (because this value is so close to zero the transformation to z has no impact).

I was moaning earlier on about how SPSS doesn't make tea for you. Another thing that it doesn't do is compute these confidence intervals for you. However, it does something even better (than computing confidence intervals, not than making tea): it computes a bootstrap confidence interval. We learnt about the percentile bootstrap confidence interval in Section 5.4.3: it is a confidence interval that is derived from the actual data and, therefore, we know it will be accurate even when the sampling distribution of r is not normal. This is very good news indeed.

OLIVER TWISTED

*Please Sir, can I have some more …
confidence intervals?*

'These confidence intervals are rubbish', says Oliver. 'they're too confusing and I hate equations, and the values we get will only be approximate. Can't we get SPSS to do it for us while we check Facebook?' Well, no you can't. Except you sort of can with some syntax. I've written some SPSS syntax, which will compute confidence intervals for r for you. To find out more, read the additional material for this chapter on the companion website. Or check Facebook, the choice is yours.

CRAMMING SAM'S TIPS   **Correlation**

- A crude measure of the relationship between variables is the covariance.
- If we standardize this value we get Pearson's correlation coefficient, r.
- The correlation coefficient has to lie between -1 and $+1$.
- A coefficient of $+1$ indicates a perfect positive relationship, a coefficient of -1 indicates a perfect negative relationship, and a coefficient of 0 indicates no linear relationship at all.
- The correlation coefficient is a commonly used measure of the size of an effect: values of $\pm.1$ represent a small effect, $\pm.3$ is a medium effect and $\pm.5$ is a large effect. However, if you can, try to interpret the size of correlation within the context of the research you've done rather than blindly following these benchmarks.

7.2.5. A word of warning about interpretation: causality ①

It's important to remember that correlation coefficients give no indication of the direction of *causality*. So, in our example, although we can conclude that as the number of adverts watched increases, the number of packets of toffees bought increases also, we cannot say that watching adverts *causes* you to buy packets of toffees. There are two problems:

- **The third-variable problem or *tertium quid***: We came across this problem in Section 1.5.5. To recap, in any correlation, causality between two variables cannot be assumed because there may be other measured or unmeasured variables affecting the results.

- **Direction of causality**: Correlation coefficients say nothing about which variable causes the other to change (see also Jane Superbrain Box 1.4). Even if we could ignore the third-variable problem, and we could assume that the two correlated variables were the only important ones, the correlation coefficient doesn't indicate in which direction causality operates. So, although it is intuitively appealing to conclude that watching adverts causes us to buy packets of toffees, there is no *statistical* reason why buying packets of toffees cannot cause us to watch more adverts. Although the latter conclusion makes less intuitive sense, statistically it is no less true than the other conclusion.

7.3. Data entry for correlation analysis using SPSS ①

Data entry when looking at relationships between variables is straightforward because each variable is entered in a separate column. So, for each variable you have measured, create a variable in the data editor with an appropriate name, and enter a participant's scores across one row of the data editor. There may be occasions on which you have one or more categorical variables (such as gender) and these variables can also be entered in a column (but remember to define appropriate value labels). As an example, if we wanted to calculate the correlation between the two variables in Table 7.1 we would enter these data as in Figure 7.4. You can see that each variable is entered in a separate column, and each row represents a single individual's data (so the first consumer saw 5 adverts and bought 8 packets).

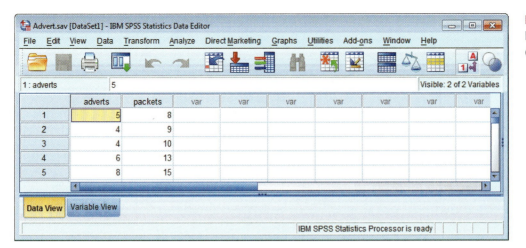

FIGURE 7.4
Data entry for correlation

SELF-TEST Enter the advert data and use the chart editor to produce a scatterplot of the data (number of packets bought on the *y*-axis, and adverts watched on the *x*-axis).

7.4. Bivariate correlation ①

Figure 7.5 shows a general procedure when considering computing a bivariate correlation coefficient. First, you must check for sources of bias as outlined in Chapter 5. The two most important ones in this context are probably linearity and normality. Remember that we're fitting a linear model to the data, so if the relationship between variables is not linear then this model is invalid, and you might need to transform the data. To meet this requirement, the outcome variable needs to be measured at the interval level (see Section 1.5.1.2) and the predictor variable must be interval also (although, as we shall see, one exception is that it can be a categorical variable provided there are only two categories – we'll get onto this in Section 7.4.5). As far as normality is concerned, we care about this only if we want confidence intervals or significance tests and if the sample size is small (Section 5.2.4.2).

If the data have outliers or are not normal (and the sample is small) you can use versions of the correlation coefficient that work on ranked data (just like the tests in the previous chapter). Two examples are Spearman's rho (Section 7.4.3) and Kendall's tau (Section 7.4.4). By ranking the data, the impact of outliers will be reduced. However, given that normality matters only for inferring significance and computing confidence intervals, we could also use a bootstrap method to compute the confidence interval, then we don't need to worry at all about the distribution.

In Chapter 4 we looked at an example relating to exam anxiety: a psychologist was interested in the effects of exam stress and revision on exam performance. She had devised and validated a questionnaire to assess state anxiety relating to exams (called the Exam Anxiety Questionnaire, or EAQ). This scale produced a measure of anxiety scored out of 100. Anxiety was measured before an exam, and the percentage mark of each student on the exam was used to assess the exam performance. She also measured the number of hours spent revising. These data are in **Exam Anxiety.sav**. We already created scatterplots for these data (Section 4.8) so we don't need to do that again; however, we could look at the distributions of the three main variables.

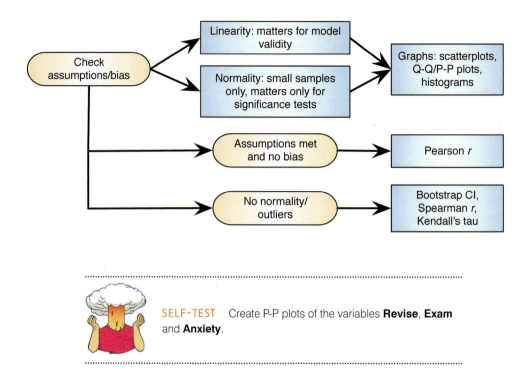

FIGURE 7.5
The general process for conducting correlation analysis

SELF-TEST   Create P-P plots of the variables **Revise**, **Exam** and **Anxiety**.

The P-P plots are shown in Figure 7.6. From these plots it's very clear that exam performance is fairly normally distributed (the dots hover close to the line) but for exam revision and exam anxiety there is evidence of skew (the dots snake around the diagonal line). This could be a problem if we want to do significance tests or look at confidence intervals; the sample contains 103 observations, which is reasonably large, and possibly large enough for the central limit theorem to relieve us of concerns about normality. However, it would be advisable to use the bootstrap function to get robust confidence intervals. We might also consider using a rank-based method to compute the correlation coefficient itself.

FIGURE 7.6
P-P plots for the exam anxiety variables

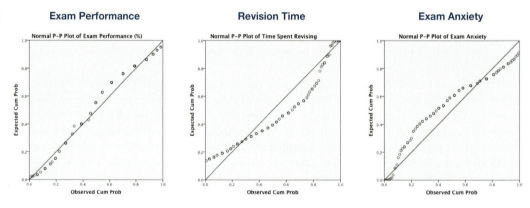

7.4.1. General procedure for running correlations in SPSS ①

To conduct a bivariate correlation you need to find the *Correlate* option of the *Analyze* menu. The main dialog box is accessed by selecting Analyze Correlate ▸ Bivariate... and is shown in Figure 7.7. Using the dialog box, it is possible to select which of three

ODITI'S LANTERN
Correlations

'I, Oditi, understand the importance of relationships. Being leader of the cult of undiscovered numerical truths, no one wants a relationship with me. This truth makes me sad. I need my cult to help me better understand relationships so that I might have one and leave my empty and soulless existence behind. To this end, we must look within the data and quantify all relationships we find. Stare into my lantern and discover how ... stare too long and possibly you'll never have another relationship.'

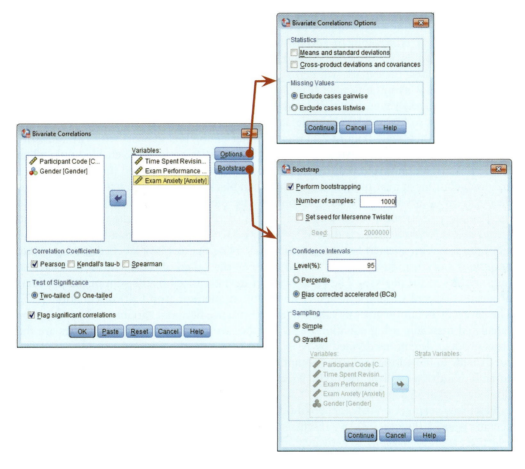

FIGURE 7.7
Dialog box for conducting a bivariate correlation

correlation statistics you wish to perform. The default setting is Pearson's product-moment correlation, but you can also calculate Spearman's correlation and Kendall's correlation – we will see the differences between these correlation coefficients in due course.

Having accessed the main dialog box, you should find that the variables in the data editor are listed on the left-hand side of the dialog box (Figure 7.7). There is an empty box labelled *Variables* on the right-hand side. You can select any variables from the list using the mouse and transfer them to the *Variables* box by dragging them there or clicking on . SPSS will create a table of correlation coefficients for all of the combinations of variables. This table is called a correlation matrix. For our current example, select the variables **Exam performance**, **Exam anxiety** and **Time spent revising** and transfer them to the *Variables* box by clicking on . Having selected the variables of interest, you can choose

OLIVER TWISTED

Please Sir, can I have some more … options?

Oliver is so excited to get onto analysing his data that he doesn't want me to spend pages waffling on about options that you will probably never use. 'Stop writing, you waffling fool', he says. 'I want to analyse my data.' Well, he's got a point. If you want to find out more about what the Options... do in correlation, then the additional material for this chapter on the companion website will tell you.

between three correlation coefficients: Pearson's product-moment correlation coefficient (☑ Pearson), Spearman's rho (☑ Spearman) and Kendall's tau (☑ Kendall's tau-b). Any of these can be selected by clicking on the appropriate tick-box with a mouse.

In addition, it is possible to specify whether or not the test is one- or two-tailed. Therefore, if you have a directional hypothesis (e.g., 'the more anxious someone is about an exam, the worse their mark will be') you could click on ⊙ One-tailed, whereas if you have a non-directional hypothesis (i.e., 'I'm not sure whether exam anxiety will improve or reduce exam marks') you could click on ⊙ Two-tailed. In Section 2.6.1.5 I advised against one-tailed tests, so I would leave the default of ⊙ Two-tailed.

If you click on Options... (Figure 7.7) then another dialog box appears with two *Statistics* options and two options for *Missing Values*. The *Statistics* options are enabled only when Pearson's correlation is selected; if Pearson's correlation is not selected then these options are disabled (they appear in light grey rather than black and you can't activate them). This deactivation occurs because these two options are meaningful only for interval data and the Pearson correlation is used with that kind of data. If you select the tick-box labelled *Means and standard deviations* then SPSS will produce the mean and standard deviation of all of the variables selected for analysis. If you activate the tick-box labelled *Cross-product deviations and covariances* then SPSS will give you the values of these statistics for each of the variables in the analysis. The cross-product deviations tell us the sum of the products of mean corrected variables, which is simply the numerator (top half) of equation (7.2). The covariances option gives us values of the covariance between variables, which could be calculated manually using equation (7.2). In other words, these covariance values are the cross-product deviations divided by $N − 1$ and represent the unstandardized correlation coefficient. In most instances you will not need to use these options, but they occasionally come in handy (see Oliver Twisted). We can also decide how to deal with missing values (look back to SPSS Tip 5.1).

Finally, we can get bootstrapped confidence intervals for the correlation coefficient by clicking Bootstrap... (Figure 7.7). We discussed this dialog box in Section 5.4.3; to recap, you select ☑ Perform bootstrapping to activate bootstrapping for the correlation coefficient, and to get a 95% confidence interval click ⊙ Percentile or ⊙ Bias corrected accelerated (BCa). For this analysis, let's ask for a bias corrected (BCa) confidence interval.

7.4.2. Pearson's correlation coefficient ①

7.4.2.1. Running Pearson's *r* in SPSS ①

We have already seen how to access the main dialog box and select the variables for analysis earlier in this section (Figure 7.7). To obtain Pearson's correlation coefficient simply select the appropriate box (☑ Pearson) – SPSS selects this option by default – and click on OK to run the analysis.

Correlation
coefficients

OUTPUT 7.1
Output for
a Pearson's
correlation

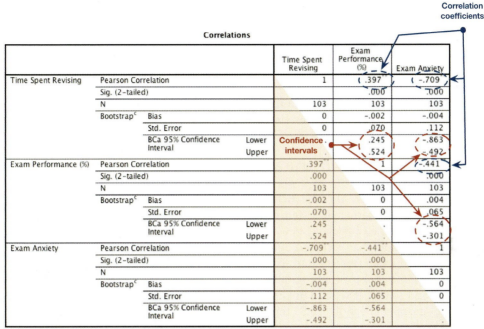

Correlations

			Time Spent Revising	Exam Performance (%)	Exam Anxiety
Time Spent Revising	Pearson Correlation		1	.397**	−.709**
	Sig. (2–tailed)			.000	.000
	N		103	103	103
	Bootstrap[c]	Bias	0	−.002	−.004
		Std. Error	0	.070	.112
	BCa 95% Confidence Interval	Lower	Confidence intervals	.245	−.863
		Upper		.524	−.492
Exam Performance (%)	Pearson Correlation		.397**	1	−.441**
	Sig. (2–tailed)		.000		.000
	N		103	103	103
	Bootstrap[c]	Bias	−.002	0	.004
		Std. Error	.070	0	.065
	BCa 95% Confidence Interval	Lower	.245	.	−.564
		Upper	.524		−.301
Exam Anxiety	Pearson Correlation		−.709**	−.441**	1
	Sig. (2–tailed)		.000	.000	
	N		103	103	103
	Bootstrap[c]	Bias	−.004	.004	0
		Std. Error	.112	.065	0
	BCa 95% Confidence Interval	Lower	−.863	−.564	.
		Upper	−.492	−.301	

**. Correlation is significant at the 0.01 level (2–tailed).

*. Correlation is significant at the 0.05 level (2–tailed).

c. Unless otherwise noted, bootstrap results are based on 1000 bootstrap samples

Output 7.1 provides a matrix of results, which looks bewildering, but it's not as bad as it looks. For one thing, the information in the top part of the table (not shaded) is the same as in the bottom half (which I have shaded), so we can effectively ignore half of the table. The first row tells us about time spent revising. This row is subdivided so first we are told the correlation coefficients with the other variables: $r = .397$ with exam performance and $r = −.709$ with exam anxiety. The second major row in the table tells us about exam performance, and from this part of the table we can get the correlation coefficient for its relationship with exam anxiety, $r = −.441$. Directly underneath each correlation coefficient we're told the significance value of the correlation and the sample size (N) on which it is based. The significance values are all less than .001 (as indicated by the double asterisk after the coefficient). This significance value tells us that the probability of getting a correlation coefficient this big in a sample of 103 people if the null hypothesis were true (there was no relationship between these variables) is very low (close to zero in fact). All of the significance values are below the standard criterion of .05, indicating a 'statistically significant' relationship.

Given the lack of normality in some of the variables, we should be more concerned with the bootstrapped confidence intervals than the significance *per se*: this is because the bootstrap confidence intervals will be unaffected by the distribution of scores, but the significance value might be. These confidence intervals are labelled *BCa 95% Confidence Interval* and you're given two values: the upper boundary and the lower boundary. For the relationship between revision time and exam performance the interval is .245 to .524, for revision time and exam anxiety it is −.863 to −.492, and for exam anxiety and exam performance it is −.564 to −.301. There are two important points here. First, because the confidence intervals are derived empirically using a random sampling procedure (i.e., bootstrapping) the results will be slightly different each time you run the analysis. Therefore, the confidence intervals you get won't be the same as the ones in Output 7.1, and that's normal and nothing to worry about. Second, think about what a correlation of zero represents: it is no effect whatsoever. A confidence interval is the boundary between which the population value falls (in 95% of samples), therefore, if this interval crosses zero it means that the population value could be zero (i.e., no effect at all). If it crosses zero it also means that the population value could be a negative number (i.e., a negative relationship) or a positive one (i.e., a positive relationship); in other words, we can't be sure if the true relationship goes in one direction or the complete opposite. For our three correlation coefficients none of the intervals cross zero, therefore we can be confident that there is a genuine effect in the population. In psychological terms, this all means that as anxiety about an exam increases, the percentage mark obtained in that exam decreases. Conversely, as the amount of time revising increases, the percentage obtained in the exam increases. Finally, as revision time increases, the student's anxiety about the exam decreases. So there is a complex interrelationship between the three variables.

7.4.2.2. Using R^2 for interpretation ①

Although we cannot make direct conclusions about causality from a correlation, we can take the correlation coefficient a step further by squaring it. The correlation coefficient squared (known as the **coefficient of determination**, R^2) is a measure of the amount of variability in one variable that is shared by the other. For example, we may look at the relationship between exam anxiety and exam performance. Exam performances vary from person to person because of any number of factors (different ability, different levels of preparation and so on). If we add up all of this variability (rather like when we calculated the sum of squares in Section 1.6.3) then we would have an estimate of how much variability exists in exam performances. R^2 tells us how much of this variability is shared by exam anxiety. These two variables had a correlation of -0.4410 and so the value of R^2 will be $(-0.4410)^2 = 0.194$, which means that 0.194 of the variability in exam performance is shared by exam anxiety. It's a bit easier to think of this value as a percentage rather than a proportion, which we can do by multiplying by 100. In this example, then, exam anxiety shares 19.4% of the variability in exam performance. To put this value into perspective, this leaves 80.6% of the variability still to be accounted for by other variables.

You'll often see people write things about R^2 that imply causality: they might write 'the variance in *y accounted for* by *x*', or 'the variation in one variable *explained* by the other'. However, although R^2 is an extremely useful measure of the substantive importance of an effect, it cannot be used to infer causal relationships. Exam anxiety might well share 19.4% of the variation in exam scores, but it does not necessarily cause this variation.

7.4.3. Spearman's correlation coefficient ①

Spearman's correlation coefficient, denoted by r_s (Figure 7.8), is a non-parametric statistic based on ranked data (see Chapter 6) and so can be useful to minimize the effects of extreme scores or the effects of violations of the assumptions discussed in Chapter 5. You'll sometimes hear the test referred to as Spearman's rho (pronounced 'row', as in 'row your boat gently down the stream'). Spearman's test works by first ranking the data (see Section 6.4.1), and then applying Pearson's equation (equation (7.3)) to those ranks (Spearman, 1910).

I was born in England, which has some bizarre traditions. One such oddity is the World's Biggest Liar Competition held annually at the Santon Bridge Inn in Wasdale (in the Lake District). The contest honours a local publican, 'Auld Will Ritson', who in the nineteenth century was famous in the area for his far-fetched stories (one such tale being that Wasdale turnips were big enough to be hollowed out and used as garden sheds). Each year locals are encouraged to attempt to tell the biggest lie in the world (lawyers and politicians are apparently banned from the competition). Over the years there have been tales of mermaid farms, giant moles, and farting sheep blowing holes in the ozone layer. (I am thinking of entering next year and reading out some sections of this book.)

What if my data are not parametric?

Imagine I wanted to test a theory that more creative people will be able to create taller tales. I gathered
together 68 past contestants from this competition and
noted where they were placed in the competition (first,
second, third, etc.) and also gave them a creativity
questionnaire (maximum score 60). The position in the
competition is an ordinal variable (see Section 1.5.1.2)
because the places are categories but have a meaningful
order (first place is better than second place and so on).
Therefore, Spearman's correlation coefficient should
be used (Pearson's *r* requires interval or ratio data). The
data for this study are in the file **The Biggest Liar.sav**.
The data are in two columns: one labelled **Creativity**
and one labelled **Position** (there's actually a third vari-
able in there but we will ignore it for the time being). For the **Position** variable, each of the
categories described above has been coded with a numerical value. First place has been coded
with the value 1, with positions being labelled 2, 3 and so on. Note that for each numeric code
I have provided a value label (just like we did for coding variables). I have also set the *Measure*
property of this variable to  Ordinal .

FIGURE 7.8
Charles
Spearman,
ranking
furiously

The procedure for doing a Spearman correlation is the same as for a Pearson correlation except that in the *Bivariate Correlations* dialog box (Figure 7.7), we need to select
☑ Spearman and deselect the option for a Pearson correlation. As with the Pearson correlation, we should use the Bootstrap... option to get some robust confidence intervals.

Output 7.2 shows the output for a Spearman correlation on the variables **Creativity** and
Position. The output is very similar to that of the Pearson correlation: a matrix is displayed
giving the correlation coefficient between the two variables (−.373), underneath is the
significance value of this coefficient (.002) and finally the sample size (68).[3] We also have
a BCa 95% confidence interval that ranges from −.604 to −.114.[4] The fact that the confidence interval does not cross zero (and the significance is less than .05) tells us that there is
a significant negative relationship between creativity scores and how well someone did in
the World's Biggest Liar Competition: as creativity increased, position decreased.

OUTPUT 7.2

Correlations

				Creativity	Position in Best Liar Competition
Spearman's rho	Creativity	Correlation Coefficient		1.000	−.373*
		Sig. (2−tailed)		.	.002
		N		68	68
		Bootstrap[c]	Bias	.000	.007
			Std. Error	.000	.125
		BCa 95% Confidence Interval	Lower	.	−.604
			Upper	.	−.114
	Position in Best Liar Competition	Correlation Coefficient		−.373**	1.000
		Sig. (2−tailed)		.002	.
		N		68	68
		Bootstrap[c]	Bias	.007	.000
			Std. Error	.125	.000
		BCa 95% Confidence Interval	Lower	−.604	.
			Upper	−.114	.

**. Correlation is significant at the 0.01 level (2−tailed).

*. Correlation is significant at the 0.05 level (2−tailed).

c. Unless otherwise noted, bootstrap results are based on 1000 bootstrap samples

[3] It is good to check that the value of N corresponds to the number of observations that were made. If it doesn't
then data may have been excluded for some reason.

[4] Remember that these confidence intervals are based on a random sampling procedure so the values you get will
differ slightly from mine, and will change if you rerun the analysis.

This might seem contrary to what we predicted until you remember that a low number means that you did well in the competition (a low number such as 1 means you came first, and a high number like 4 means you came fourth). Therefore, our hypothesis is supported: as creativity increased, so did success in the competition.

SELF-TEST   Did creativity cause success in the World's Biggest Liar Competition?

7.4.4. Kendall's tau (non-parametric) ①

Kendall's tau, τ, is another non-parametric correlation and it should be used rather than Spearman's coefficient when you have a small data set with a large number of tied ranks. This means that if you rank all of the scores and many scores have the same rank, then Kendall's tau should be used. Although Spearman's statistic is the more popular of the two coefficients, there is much to suggest that Kendall's statistic is actually a better estimate of the correlation in the population (see Howell, 1997, p. 293). As such, we can draw more accurate generalizations from Kendall's statistic than from Spearman's. To carry out Kendall's correlation on the world's biggest liar data, simply follow the same steps as for Pearson and Spearman correlations but select ☑ Kendall's tau-b and deselect the Pearson and Spearman options. The output is much the same as for Spearman's correlation.

You'll notice from Output 7.3 that the actual value of the correlation coefficient is closer to zero than the Spearman correlation (it has increased from −.373 to −.300). Despite the difference in the correlation coefficients, we can still interpret this result as being a highly significant relationship because the significance value of .001 is less than .05 and the robust confidence interval does not cross zero (−.491 to −.100). However, Kendall's value is a more accurate gauge of what the correlation in the population would be. As with the Pearson correlation, we cannot assume that creativity caused success in the World's Best Liar Competition.

OUTPUT 7.3

Correlations

					Creativity	Position in Best Liar Competition
Kendall's tau_b	Creativity	Correlation Coefficient			1.000	−.300**
		Sig. (2–tailed)			.	.001
		N			68	68
		Bootstrap[c]	Bias		.000	.001
			Std. Error		.000	.098
			BCa 95% Confidence Interval	Lower	.	−.491
				Upper	.	−.100
	Position in Best Liar Competition	Correlation Coefficient			−.300**	1.000
		Sig. (2–tailed)			.001	.
		N			68	68
		Bootstrap[c]	Bias		.001	.000
			Std. Error		.098	.000
			BCa 95% Confidence Interval	Lower	−.491	.
				Upper	−.100	.

**. Correlation is significant at the 0.01 level (2–tailed).

*. Correlation is significant at the 0.05 level (2–tailed).

c. Unless otherwise noted, bootstrap results are based on 1000 bootstrap samples

7.4.5.   Biserial and point-biserial correlations ③

The biserial and point-biserial correlation coefficients are distinguished by only a conceptual difference yet their statistical calculation is quite different. These correlation coefficients are used when one of the two variables is dichotomous (i.e., it is categorical with only two categories). An example of a dichotomous variable is being pregnant, because a woman can be either pregnant or not (she cannot be 'a bit pregnant'). Often it is necessary to investigate relationships between two variables when one of the variables is dichotomous. The difference between the use of biserial and point-biserial correlations depends on whether the dichotomous variable is discrete or continuous. This difference is very subtle. A discrete, or true, dichotomy is one for which there is no underlying continuum between the categories. An example of this is whether someone is dead or alive: a person can be only dead or alive, they can't be 'a bit dead'. Although you might describe a person as being 'half-dead' – especially after a heavy drinking session – they are clearly still alive if they are still breathing! Therefore, there is no continuum between the two categories. However, it is possible to have a dichotomy for which a continuum does exist. An example is passing or failing a statistics test: some people will only just fail, while others will fail by a large margin; likewise some people will scrape a pass, while others will excel. So although participants fall into only two categories there is an underlying continuum along which they lie. Hopefully, it is clear that in this case there is some kind of continuum underlying the dichotomy, because some people passed or failed more dramatically than others. The **point-biserial correlation** coefficient (r_{pb}) is used when one variable is a discrete dichotomy (e.g., pregnancy), whereas the **biserial correlation** coefficient (r_b) is used when one variable is a continuous dichotomy (e.g., passing or failing an exam). The biserial correlation coefficient cannot be calculated directly in SPSS: first you must calculate the point-biserial correlation coefficient and then use an equation to adjust it.

SMART ALEX ONLY

Imagine that I was interested in the relationship between the gender of a cat and how much time it spent away from home (what can I say? I love cats, so these things interest me). I had heard that male cats disappeared for substantial amounts of time on long-distance roams around the neighbourhood (something about hormones driving them to find mates) whereas female cats tended to be more homebound. So, I used this as a purr-fect (sorry!) excuse to go and visit lots of my friends and their cats. I took a note of the gender of the cat and then asked the owners to note down the number of hours that their cat was absent from home over a week. Clearly the time spent away from home is measured at an interval level – and let's assume it meets the other assumptions of parametric data – while the gender of the cat is discrete dichotomy. A point-biserial correlation has to be calculated and this is simply a Pearson correlation when the dichotomous variable is coded with 0 for one category and 1 for the other (actually you can use any values and SPSS will change the lower one to 0 and the higher one to 1 when it does the calculations). So, to conduct these correlations in SPSS assign the **Gender** variable a coding scheme as described in Section 3.5.2.3 (in the saved data the coding is 1 for a male and 0 for a female). The **Time** variable simply has time in hours recorded as normal. These data are in the file **pbcorr.sav**.

SELF-TEST   Carry out a Pearson correlation on these data (as in Section 7.4.2.1).

EVERYBODY

Congratulations: if you did the self-test task then you have just conducted your first point-biserial correlation. See, despite the horrible name, it's really quite easy to do. You should find that you have the same output as Output 7.4, which shows the correlation matrix of **Time** and **Gender**. The point-biserial correlation coefficient is $r_{pb} = .378$, which has a significance value of .003. The significance test for this correlation is actually the same as performing an independent-samples *t*-test on the data (see Chapter 9). The sign of the correlation (i.e., whether the relationship was positive or negative) will depend entirely on which way round the coding of the dichotomous variable was done. To prove that this is the case, the data file **pbcorr.sav** has an extra variable called **Recode** which is the same as the variable **Gender** except that the coding is reversed (1 = female, 0 = male). If you repeat the Pearson correlation using **Recode** instead of **Gender** you will find that the correlation coefficient becomes -0.378. The sign of the coefficient is completely dependent on which category you assign to which code and so we must ignore all information about the direction of the relationship. However, we can still interpret R^2 as before. In this example, $R^2 = 0.378^2 = .143$. Hence, we can conclude that gender accounts for 14.3% of the variability in time spent away from home.

OUTPUT 7.4

Correlations

			Time away from home (hours)	Gender of cat
Time away from home (hours)	Pearson Correlation		1	.378**
	Sig. (2–tailed)			.003
	N		60	60
	Bootstrap[c]	Bias	0	-.004
		Std. Error	0	.114
		BCa 95% Confidence Interval	Lower	.	.160
			Upper	.	.584
Gender of cat	Pearson Correlation		.378**	1
	Sig. (2–tailed)		.003	
	N		60	60
	Bootstrap[c]	Bias	-.004	0
		Std. Error	.114	0
		BCa 95% Confidence Interval	Lower	.160	.
			Upper	.584	.

**. Correlation is significant at the 0.01 level (2–tailed).

*. Correlation is significant at the 0.05 level (2–tailed).

c. Unless otherwise noted, bootstrap results are based on 1000 bootstrap samples

OLIVER TWISTED

Please Sir, can I have some more … biserial correlation?

'Some of the male cats were neutered and so there might be a continuum of maleness that underlies the gender variable, you nugget brain', Oliver hurls at me. 'We need to convert the point-biserial correlation into the biserial correlation coefficient (r_b). I think you're Fagin your knowledge of how to do this.' Oliver, if you go to the companion website you'll find that I am not artfully dodging how to do the conversion.

CRAMMING SAM'S TIPS **Correlations**

- We can measure the relationship between two variables using correlation coefficients.
- These coefficients lie between −1 and +1.
- Pearson's correlation coefficient, r, is a parametric statistic and requires interval data for both variables. To test its significance we assume normality too.
- Spearman's correlation coefficient, r_s, is a non-parametric statistic and requires only ordinal data for both variables.
- Kendall's correlation coefficient, τ, is like Spearman's r_s but probably better for small samples.
- The point-biserial correlation coefficient, r_{pb}, quantifies the relationship between a continuous variable and a variable that is a discrete dichotomy (e.g., there is no continuum underlying the two categories, such as dead or alive).
- The biserial correlation coefficient, r_b, quantifies the relationship between a continuous variable and a variable that is a continuous dichotomy (e.g., there is a continuum underlying the two categories, such as passing or failing an exam).

7.5. Partial correlation ②

7.5.1. The theory behind part and partial correlation ③

SMART
ALEX
ONLY

I mentioned earlier that there is a type of correlation that can be done that allows you to look at the relationship between two variables when the effects of a third variable are held constant. For example, analyses of the exam anxiety data (in the file **Exam Anxiety. sav**) showed that exam performance was negatively related to exam anxiety, but positively related to revision time, and revision time itself was negatively related to exam anxiety. This scenario is complex, but given that we know that revision time is related to both exam anxiety and exam performance, then if we want a pure measure of the relationship between exam anxiety and exam performance, we need to take account of the influence of revision time. Using the values of R^2 for these relationships, we know that exam anxiety accounts for 19.4% of the variance in exam performance, that revision time accounts for 15.7% of the variance in exam performance and that revision time accounts for 50.2% of the variance in exam anxiety. If revision time accounts for half of the variance in exam anxiety, then it seems feasible that at least some of the 19.4% of variance in exam performance that is accounted for by anxiety is the same variance that is accounted for by revision time. As such, some of the variance in exam performance explained by exam anxiety is not *unique* and can be accounted for by revision time. A correlation between two variables in which the effects of other variables are held constant is known as a **partial correlation**.

Let's return to our example of exam scores, revision time and exam anxiety to illustrate the principle behind partial correlation (Figure 7.9). In part 1 of the diagram there is a box for exam performance that represents the total variation in exam scores (this value would be the variance of exam performance). There is also a box that represents the variation in exam anxiety (again, this is the variance of that variable). We know already that exam

FIGURE 7.9
Diagram
showing the
principle
of partial
correlation

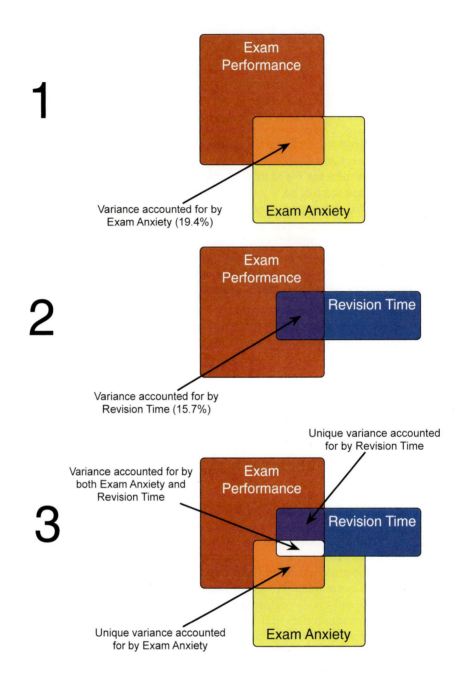

anxiety and exam performance share 19.4% of their variation (this value is the correlation coefficient squared). Therefore, the variations of these two variables overlap (because they share variance) creating a third box (the orange box). The overlap of the boxes representing exam performance and exam anxiety is the common variance. Likewise, in part 2 of the diagram the shared variation between exam performance and revision time is illustrated. Revision time shares 15.7% of the variation in exam scores. This shared variation is represented by the area of overlap (the purple box). We know that revision time and exam anxiety also share 50% of their variation; therefore, it is very probable that some of the variation in exam performance shared by exam anxiety is the same as the variance shared by revision time.

Part 3 of the diagram shows the complete picture. The first thing to note is that the boxes representing exam anxiety and revision time have a large overlap (this is because they share 50% of their variation). More important, when we look at how revision time and anxiety contribute to exam performance we see that there is a portion of exam performance that is shared by both anxiety and revision time (the white area). However, there are still small chunks of the variance in exam performance that are unique to the other two variables. So, although in part 1 exam anxiety shared a large chunk of variation in exam performance, some of this overlap is also shared by revision time. If we remove the portion of variation that is also shared by revision time, we get a measure of the unique relationship between exam performance and exam anxiety. We use partial correlations to find out the size of the unique portion of variance. Therefore, we could conduct a partial correlation between exam anxiety and exam performance while 'controlling' for the effect of revision time. Likewise, we could carry out a partial correlation between revision time and exam performance while 'controlling' for the effects of exam anxiety.

7.5.2. Partial correlation in SPSS ③

Reload the **Exam Anxiety.sav** file so that, as I suggested above, we can conduct a partial correlation between exam anxiety and exam performance while 'controlling' for the effect of revision time. To access the *Partial Correlations* dialog box (Figure 7.10) select Analyze Correlate ▸ ⯌ Partial…. This dialog box lists all of the variables in the data editor on the left-hand side and there are two empty spaces on the right-hand side. The space labelled *Variables* is for listing the variables that you want to correlate and the space labelled *Controlling for* is for declaring any variables the effects of which you want to control. In the example I have described, we want to look at the unique effect of exam anxiety on exam performance and so we want to correlate the variables **exam** and **anxiety** while controlling for **revise**. Figure 7.10 shows the completed dialog box.

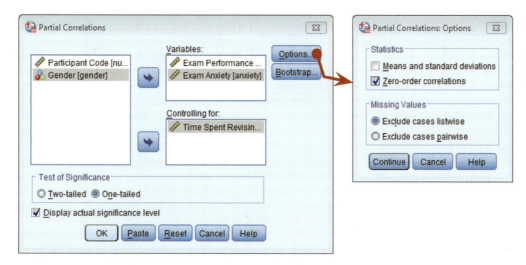

FIGURE 7.10
Main dialog box for conducting a partial correlation

Clicking on Options… accesses options similar to those in bivariate correlation, and within this dialog box you can select *Zero-order correlations*, which are the Pearson correlation coefficients without controlling for any other variables. In this example, if we select the tick-box for zero-order correlations SPSS will produce a correlation matrix of **anxiety**, **exam** and **revise**. If you haven't conducted bivariate correlations before the partial correlation then this is a useful way to compare the correlations that haven't been controlled against those that have. This comparison gives you some insight into the contribution of different variables. We already have the zero-order correlations in Output 7.1 so don't tick this box, just be aware that you can. Finally, as with all of the other correlations we can use the Bootstrap option to get some robust confidence intervals. In this instance we have controlled for one variable and this is known as a *first-order partial correlation*. It is possible to control for the effects of two variables (a *second-order partial correlation*), three variables (a *third-order partial correlation*) and so on.

Output 7.5 shows the output for the partial correlation of exam anxiety and exam performance controlling for revision time. This table is a matrix of correlations for the variables **anxiety** and **exam** but controlling for the effect of revision. Note that the top and bottom of the table contain identical values, so we can ignore one half of the table. First, notice that the partial correlation between exam performance and exam anxiety is $-.247$, which is considerably less than the correlation when the effect of revision time is not controlled for ($r = -.441$). In fact, the correlation coefficient is nearly half what it was before. Although this correlation is still statistically significant (its p-value is still below .05) and the confidence interval [$-.434$, $-.005$] still doesn't contain zero, the relationship is diminished. In terms of variance, the value of R^2 for the partial correlation is .06, which means that exam anxiety now shares only 6% of the variance in exam performance (compared to 19.4% when revision time was not controlled). Running this analysis has shown us that exam anxiety alone does explain some of the variation in exam scores, but there is a complex relationship between anxiety, revision and exam performance that might otherwise have been ignored. Although causality is still not certain, because relevant variables are being included, the third variable problem is, at least, being addressed to some degree.

OUTPUT 7.5
Output from a partial correlation

Correlations

Control Variables				Exam Performance (%)	Exam Anxiety
Time Spent Revising	Exam Performance (%)	Correlation		1.000	−.247
		Significance (2–tailed)		.	.012
		df		0	100
		Bootstrap[a]	Bias	.000	.010
			Std. Error	.000	.102
			BCa 95% Confidence Interval Lower	.	−.434
			Upper	.	−.005
	Exam Anxiety	Correlation		−.247	1.000
		Significance (2–tailed)		.012	.
		df		100	0
		Bootstrap[a]	Bias	.010	.000
			Std. Error	.102	.000
			BCa 95% Confidence Interval Lower	−.434	.
			Upper	−.005	.

a. Unless otherwise noted, bootstrap results are based on 1000 bootstrap samples

Partial correlations can be done when variables are dichotomous (including the 'third' variable). So, for example, we could look at the relationship between bladder relaxation (did the person wet themselves or not?) and the number of large tarantulas crawling up the person's leg, controlling for fear of spiders (the first variable is dichotomous, but the second variable and 'controlled for' variable are continuous). Similarly, to use an earlier example, we could examine the relationship between creativity and success in the world's greater liar contest controlling for whether someone had previous experience in the competition (and therefore had some idea of the type of tale that would win) or not. In this latter case the 'controlled for' variable is dichotomous.[5]

---

[5] Both these examples are, in fact, simple cases of hierarchical regression (see the next chapter) and the first example is also an example of analysis of covariance. This may be confusing now, but illustrates what I have repeatedly said about all statistical models being variations of the same linear model.

7.5.3. Semi-partial (or part) correlations ②

In the next chapter, we will come across another form of correlation known as a **semi-partial correlation** (also referred to as a **part correlation**). While I'm babbling on about partial correlations it is worth explaining the difference between this type of correlation and a semi-partial correlation. When we do a partial correlation between two variables, we control for the effects of a third variable. Specifically, the effect that the third variable has on *both* variables in the correlation is controlled. In a semi-partial correlation we control for the effect that the third variable has on only one of the variables in the correlation. Figure 7.11 illustrates this principle for the exam performance data. The partial correlation that we calculated took account not only of the effect of revision on exam performance, but also of the effect of revision on anxiety. If we were to calculate the semi-partial correlation for the same data, this would control for only the effect of revision on exam performance (the effect of revision on exam anxiety is ignored). Partial correlations are most useful for looking at the unique relationship between two variables when other variables are ruled out. Semi-partial correlations are, therefore, useful when trying to explain the variance in one particular variable (an outcome) from a set of predictor variables. (Bear this in mind when you read Chapter 8.)

Partial Correlation   Semi-partial Correlation

FIGURE 7.11
The difference between a partial and a semi-partial correlation

CRAMMING SAM'S TIPS   **Partial and semi-partial correlations**

- A partial correlation quantifies the relationship between two variables while accounting for the effects of a third variable on both variables in the original correlation.
- A semi-partial correlation quantifies the relationship between two variables while accounting for the effects of a third variable on only one of the variables in the original correlation.

7.6. Comparing correlations ③

7.6.1. Comparing independent *rs* ③

Sometimes we want to know whether one correlation coefficient is bigger than another. For example, when we looked at the effect of exam anxiety on exam performance, we might have been interested to know whether this correlation was different in men and women. We could compute the correlation in these two samples, but then how would we assess whether the difference was meaningful?

 SELF-TEST   Use the *split file* command to compute the correlation coefficient between exam anxiety and exam performance in men and women.

If we did this, we would find that the correlations were $r_{Male} = -.506$ and $r_{Female} = -.381$. These two samples are independent; that is, they contain different entities. To compare these correlations we can again use what we discovered in Section 7.2.3 to convert these coefficients to z_r (just to remind you, we do this because it makes the sampling distribution normal and, therefore, we know the standard error). If we do the conversion, then we get z_r (males) $= -.557$ and z_r (females) $= -.401$. We can calculate a z-score of the differences between these correlations as:

$$z_{Difference} = \frac{z_{r_1} - z_{r_2}}{\sqrt{\dfrac{1}{N_1 - 3} + \dfrac{1}{N_2 - 3}}}$$

(7.9)

We had 52 men and 51 women so we would get:

$$z_{Difference} = \frac{-0.557 - (-0.401)}{\sqrt{\dfrac{1}{49} + \dfrac{1}{48}}} = \frac{-0.156}{0.203} = -0.768$$

We can look up this value of z (0.768, we can ignore the minus sign) in the table for the normal distribution in the Appendix and get the one-tailed probability from the column labelled 'Smaller Portion'. In this case the value is .221. To get the two-tailed probability we simply multiply the one-tailed probability value by 2, which gives us .442. As such the correlation between exam anxiety and exam performance is not significantly different in men and women (see Oliver Twisted for how to do this in SPSS).

7.6.2.   Comparing dependent *rs* ③

If you want to compare correlation coefficients that come from the same entities then things are a little more complicated. You can use a *t*-statistic to test whether a difference between two dependent correlations from the same sample is significant. For example, in our exam anxiety data we might want to see whether the relationship between exam anxiety (*x*) and exam performance (*y*) is stronger than the relationship between revision (*z*) and exam performance. To calculate this, all we need are the three *rs* that quantify the relationships between these variables: r_{xy}, the relationship between exam anxiety and exam performance (–.441); r_{zy}, the relationship between revision and exam performance (.397); and r_{xz}, the relationship between exam anxiety and revision (–.709). The *t*-statistic is computed as (Chen & Popovich, 2002):

$$t_{\text{Difference}} = \left(r_{xy} - r_{zy}\right)\sqrt{\frac{(n-3)(1+r_{xz})}{2\left(1 - r_{xy}^2 - r_{xz}^2 - r_{zy}^2 + 2r_{xy}r_{xz}r_{zy}\right)}}$$ (7.10)

Admittedly that equation looks hideous, but really it's not too bad: it just uses the three correlation coefficients and the sample size N. Place the numbers from the exam anxiety example in (N was 103) and you should end up with:

$$t_{\text{Difference}} = (-.838)\sqrt{\frac{29.1}{2(1 - .194 - .503 - .158 + 0.248)}} = -5.09$$

This value can be checked against the appropriate critical value in the Appendix with $N - 3$ degrees of freedom (in this case 100). The critical values in the table are 1.98 ($p < .05$) and 2.63 ($p < .01$), two-tailed. As such we can say that the correlation between exam anxiety and exam performance was significantly higher than the correlation between revision time and exam performance (this isn't a massive surprise, given that these relationships went in opposite directions to each other).

EVERYBODY

OLIVER TWISTED

Please Sir, can I have some more … comparing of correlations?

'Are you having a bloody laugh with that equation?' yelps Oliver. 'I'd rather smother myself with cheese sauce and lock myself in a room full of hungry mice.' Yes, yes, Oliver, enough of your sexual habits. To spare the poor mice I have written some SPSS syntax to run the comparisons mentioned in this section. For a guide on how to use them read the additional material for this chapter. Go on, be nice to the mice!

7.7. Calculating the effect size ①

Calculating effect sizes for correlation coefficients couldn't be easier because, as we saw earlier in the book, correlation coefficients *are* effect sizes. So, no calculations (other than those you have already done) are necessary. However, although the Spearman and Kendall correlations are comparable to Pearson's r in many respects (their power, for example, is similar under parametric conditions), there are two important differences (Strahan, 1982).

First, we can square the value of Pearson's r to get the proportion of shared variance, R^2. For Spearman's r_s we can do this too because it uses the same equation as Pearson's r. However, the resulting R_s^2 needs to be interpreted slightly differently: it is the proportion of variance in the *ranks* that two variables share. Having said this, R_s^2 is usually a good approximation of R^2 (especially in conditions of near-normal distributions). Kendall's τ, however, is not numerically similar to either r or r_s and so τ^2 does not tell us about the proportion of variance shared by two variables (or the ranks of those two variables). Second, Kendall's τ is 66–75% smaller than both Spearman's r_s and Pearson's r, but r and r_s are generally similar sizes (Strahan, 1982).

As such, if τ is used as an effect size it should be borne in mind that it is not comparable to r and r_s and should not be squared. A related issue is that

Can I use r^2 for non-parametric correlations?

the point-biserial and biserial correlations differ in size too (as we saw in this chapter, the biserial correlation was bigger than the point-biserial). In this instance you should be careful to decide whether your dichotomous variable has an underlying continuum, or whether it is a truly discrete variable. More generally, when using correlations as effect sizes you should remember (both when reporting your own analysis and when interpreting others) that the choice of correlation coefficient can make a substantial difference to the apparent size of the effect.

7.8. How to report correlation coefficients ①

Reporting correlation coefficients is pretty easy: you just have to say how big they are, report their confidence intervals, and report their significance value (although the significance value isn't *that* important because the correlation coefficient is an effect size in its own right). Some general points (see Sections 1.7.3 and 2.8) are as are follows: (1) if you follow the conventions of the American Psychological Association, there should be no zero before the decimal point for the correlation coefficient or the probability value (because neither can exceed 1); (2) coefficients are usually reported to 2 or 3 decimal places because this is a reasonable level of precision; (3) report 95% confidence intervals; (4) each correlation coefficient is represented by a different letter (and some of them are Greek); and (5) report exact p-values. Let's take a few examples from this chapter:

- ✓ There was no significant relationship between the number of adverts watched and the number of packets of sweets purchased, $r = .87$, $p = .054$.

- ✓ Bias corrected and accelerated bootstrap 95% CIs are reported in square brackets. Exam performance was significantly correlated with exam anxiety, $r = -.44$ [−.564, −.301], and time spent revising, $r = .40$ [.245, .524]; the time spent revising was also correlated with exam anxiety, $r = -.71$ [−.863, −.492] (all $ps < .001$).

- ✓ Creativity was significantly related to how well people did in the World's Biggest Liar competition, $r_s = -.37$, 95% BCa CI [−.604, −.114], $p = .002$.

- ✓ Creativity was significantly related to a person's placing in the World's Biggest Liar competition, $\tau = -.30$, 95% BCa CI [−.491, −.100], $p = .001$. (Note that I've quoted Kendall's τ.)

- ✓ The gender of the cat was significantly related to the time the cat spent away from home, $r_{pb} = .38$, 95% BCa CI [.160, .584], $p = .003$.

- ✓ The gender of the cat was significantly related to the time the cat spent away from home, $r_b = .48$, $p = .003$.

When we have lots of correlations a table can be useful. Our exam anxiety correlations could be reported as in Table 7.2. Note that above the diagonal I have reported the correlation coefficients and used symbols to represent different levels of significance. The confidence intervals are reported underneath. Under the table there is a legend to tell readers what the symbols represent. (Actually, none of the correlations were non-significant or had p bigger than .001 so most of these are here simply to give you a reference point – you would normally include only symbols that you had actually used in the table.) Finally, in the lower part of the table I have reported the sample sizes. These are all the same (103), but when you have missing data it is useful to report the sample sizes in this way because different values of the correlation will be based on different sample sizes. You could alternatively use the bottom part of the table to report exact *p*-values.

TABLE 7.2   An example of reporting a table of correlations

	Exam Performance	Exam Anxiety	Revision Time
Exam Performance	1	−.44*** [−.564, −.301]	.40*** [.245, .524]
Exam Anxiety	103	1	−.71*** [−.863, −.492]
Revision Time	103	103	1

ns = not significant (*p* > .05), * *p* < .05, ** *p* < .01, *** *p* < .001. BCa bootstrap 95% CIs reported in brackets.

LABCOAT LENI'S REAL RESEARCH 7.1

Why do you like your lecturers? ①

Chamorro-Premuzic, T., et al. (2008). *Personality and Individual Differences, 44*, 965–976.

As students you probably have to rate your lecturers at the end of the course. There will be some lecturers you like and others you hate. As a lecturer I find this process horribly depressing (although this has a lot to do with the fact that I tend to focus on negative feedback and ignore the good stuff). There is some evidence that students tend to pick courses of lecturers they perceive to be enthusiastic and good communicators. In a fascinating study, Tomas Chamorro-Premuzic and his colleagues (Chamorro-Premuzic, Furnham, Christopher, Garwood, & Martin, 2008) tested the hypothesis that students tend to like lecturers who are like themselves. (This hypothesis will have the students on my course who like my lectures screaming in horror.)

The authors measured students' own personalities using a very well-established measure (the NEO-FFI) which measures five fundamental personality traits: neuroticism, extroversion, openness to experience, agreeableness and conscientiousness. Students also completed a questionnaire in which they were given descriptions (e.g., 'warm: friendly, warm, sociable, cheerful, affectionate, outgoing') and asked to rate how much they wanted to see this in a lecturer from −5 (I don't want this characteristic at all) through 0 (the characteristic is not important) to +5 (I really want this characteristic in my lecturer). The characteristics were the same as those measured by the NEO-FFI.

As such, the authors had a measure of how much a student had each of the five core personality characteristics, but also a measure of how much they wanted to see those same characteristics in their lecturer. Tomas and his colleagues could then test whether, for instance, extroverted students want extroverted lecturers. The data from this study are in the file **Chamorro-Premuzic.sav**. Run Pearson correlations on these variables to see if students with certain personality characteristics want to see those characteristics in their lecturers. What conclusions can you draw? Answers are on the companion website (or look at Table 3 in the original article, which shows you how to report a large number of correlations).

7.9. Brian's attempt to woo Jane ①

FIGURE 7.12
What Brian
learnt from this
chapter

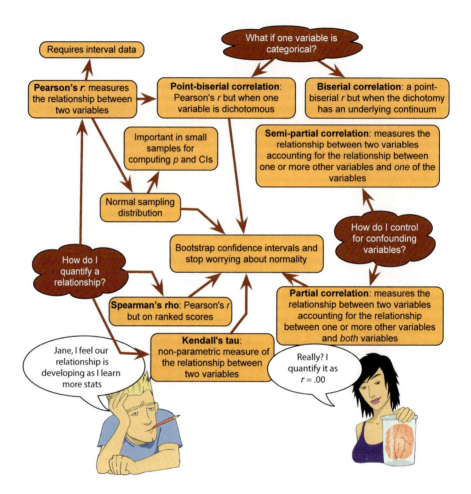

7.10. What next? ①

At the age of 8 my dad taught me a valuable lesson, which is that if you really want something then you need to work at it, and the harder you work at it the more likely you are to get what you want. I did practise my guitar and before long the tears had been replaced with a competent version of 'Skip to my Lou'. My dad had also had aspirations to be a musician when he was young and encouraged my new passion.[6] He found me a guitar teacher and found the money for lessons. These lessons illustrate how being a good student often depends on finding the right teacher. Ken Steers, despite his best efforts, was on a completely different wavelength to me. I wanted to learn some crushing metal riffs, and he wanted me to play through Bert Weedon's 'Play in a day' and learn trad jazz classics. As an adult, I wish I had paid more attention to Ken because I'd have been a better guitar player than I am; however, I was a terrible student and I adopted a strategy of selective practice: I'd practise if I wanted to do something but not if I thought it was 'boring'. Perhaps this is why I am still so obsessed with trying not to be a boring teacher. Nevertheless, my dad and

---

[6] My dad, like me, never made it in his band, but, unlike me, did sing on the UK TV show *Stars in Their Eyes*, which made us all pretty proud.

Ken did get me going and soon enough, like my favourite record of the time, I was ready to 'Take on the world'. Well, Wales at any rate …

7.11. Key terms that I've discovered

Biserial correlation	Kendall's tau	Semi-partial correlation
Bivariate correlation	Partial correlation	Spearman's correlation
Coefficient of determination	Pearson correlation	coefficient
Covariance	coefficient	Standardization
Cross-product deviations	Point-biserial correlation	

7.12. Smart Alex's tasks

- **Task 1**: A student was interested in whether there was a positive relationship between the time spent doing an essay and the mark received. He got 45 of his friends and timed how long they spent writing an essay (**hours**) and the percentage they got in the essay (**essay**). He also translated these grades into their degree classifications (**grade**): in the UK, a student can get a first-class mark (the best), an upper-second-class mark, a lower second, a third, a pass or a fail (the worst). Using the data in the file **EssayMarks. sav**, find out what the relationship was between the time spent doing an essay and the eventual mark in terms of percentage and degree class (draw a scatterplot too). ①

- **Task 2**: Using the **ChickFlick.sav** data from Chapter 3, find out if there is a relationship between gender and arousal. ①

- **Task 3**: Using the same data, what is the relationship between the film watched and arousal? ①

- **Task 4**: As a statistics lecturer, I am always interested in the factors that determine whether a student will do well on a statistics course. Imagine I took 25 students and looked at their degree grades for my statistics course at the end of their first year at university: first, upper second, lower second or third class (see Task 1). I also asked these students what grade they got in their high school maths exams. In the UK, GCSEs are school exams taken at age 16 that are graded A, B, C, D, E or F (an A grade is better than all of the lower grades). The data for this study are in the file **grades.sav**. Carry out the appropriate analysis to see if GCSE maths grades correlate with first-year statistics grades. ①

- **Task 5**: In Figure 2.3 we saw some data relating to people's ratings of dishonest acts and the likeableness of the perpetrator (for a full description see Jane Superbrain Box 2.1). Compute the Spearman correlation between ratings of dishonesty and likeableness of the perpetrator. The data are in **HonestyLab.sav**.

- **Task 6:** In Chapter 3 (Task 5) we looked at data from people who had been forced to marry goats and dogs and measured their life satisfaction and how much they like animals (**Goat or Dog.sav**). Is there a significant correlation between life satisfaction and the type of animal to which a person was married? ②

- **Task 7:** Repeat the analysis above, taking account of animal-liking when computing the correlation between life satisfaction and the animal to which a person was married. ②

- **Task 8:** In Chapter 3 (Task 6) we looked at data based on findings that the number of cups of tea drunk was related to cognitive functioning (Feng et al., 2010). The data are in the file **Tea Makes You Brainy 15.sav**. What is the correlation between tea drinking and cognitive functioning? Is there a significant effect? ①

- **Task 9**: The research in the previous example was replicated but in a larger sample (*N* = 716), which is the same as the sample size in Feng et al.'s research (**Tea Makes You Brainy 716.sav**). Conduct a correlation between tea drinking and cognitive functioning. Compare the correlation coefficient and significance in this large sample with the previous task. What statistical point do the results illustrate? ②

- **Task 10**: In Chapter 5 we looked at hygiene scores over three days of a rock music festival (**Download Festival.sav**). Using Spearman's correlation, were hygiene scores on day 1 of the festival significantly correlated with those on day 3? ①

- **Task 11**: Using the data in **Shopping Exercise.sav** (Chapter 3, Task 4) is there a significant relationship between the time spent shopping and the distance covered? ①

- **Task 12**: What effect does accounting for the effect of gender have on the relationship between the time spent shopping and the distance covered? ②

Answers can be found on the companion website.

7.13. Further reading

Chen, P. Y., & Popovich, P. M. (2002). *Correlation: Parametric and nonparametric measures.* Thousand Oaks, CA: Sage.

Howell, D. C. (2012). *Statistical methods for psychology* (8th ed.). Belmont, CA: Duxbury. (An excellent text that is a bit more technical than this book, so is a useful next step.)

Miles, J. N. V., & Banyard, P. (2007). *Understanding and using statistics in psychology: A practical introduction.* London: Sage. (A fantastic and amusing introduction to statistical theory.)

Wright, D. B., & London, K. (2009). *First steps in statistics* (2nd ed.). London: Sage. (This book is a very gentle introduction to statistical theory.)

Regression

8

8.1. What will this chapter tell me? ①

Although none of us can know the future, predicting it is so important that organisms are hard wired to learn about predictable events in their environment. We saw in the previous chapter that I received a guitar for Christmas when I was 8. My first foray into public performance was a weekly talent show at a holiday camp called 'Holimarine' in Wales (it doesn't exist any more because I am old and this was 1981). I sang a Chuck Berry song called 'My ding-a-ling'[1] and to my absolute amazement I won the competition.[2] Suddenly other 8-year-olds across the land (well, a ballroom in Wales) worshipped me (I made lots of friends after the competition). I had tasted success, it tasted like praline chocolate, and so I wanted to enter the competition in the second week of our holiday. To ensure success, I needed to know why I had won in the first week. One way to do this would have been to collect data and to use these data to predict people's evaluations of

---

[1] It appears that even then I had a passion for lowering the tone of things that should be taken seriously.

[2] I have a very grainy video of this performance recorded by my dad's friend on a video camera the size of a medium-sized dog that had to be accompanied at all times by a 'battery pack' the size and weight of a tank (see Oditi's Lantern).

children's performances in the contest from certain variables: the age of the performer, what type of performance they gave (singing, telling a joke, magic tricks), and perhaps how cute they looked. A regression analysis on these data would enable us to predict the future (success in next week's competition) based on values of the predictor variables. If, for example, singing was an important factor in getting a good audience evaluation, then I could sing again the following week; however, if jokers tended to do better then I could switch to a comedy routine. When I was 8 I wasn't the sad geek that I am today, so I didn't know about regression analysis (nor did I wish to know); however, my dad thought that success was due to the winning combination of a cherub-looking 8-year-old singing songs that can be interpreted in a filthy way. He wrote a song for me to sing about the keyboard player in the Holimarine Band 'messing about with his organ'. He said 'take this song, son, and steal the show' … and that's what I did: I came first again. There's no accounting for taste.

ODITI'S LANTERN

Words that go unspoken, deeds that go undone

'I, Oditi, do not want my followers to get distracted by playing with their ding-a-lings. To warn you all of the dangers of such frivolity, I have uncovered a song, sung by an innocent child, that explains the risks. Stare into my lantern and shake your booty to the funky tune.'

8.2. An introduction to regression ①

8.2.1. The simple linear model ①

In the previous chapter we started getting down to the nitty-gritty of the linear model that we've been discussing since way back in Chapter 2. We saw that if we wanted to look at the relationship between two variables we could use the model in equation (2.3):

$$\text{outcome}_i = (bX_i) + \text{error}_i$$

In this model, b is the correlation coefficient (more often denoted as r) and it is a standardized measure. However, we can also work with an unstandardized version of b, but in doing so we need to add something to the model:

$$\text{outcome}_i = (b_0 + b_1 X_i) + \text{error}_i$$

$$y_i = (b_0 + b_1 X_i) + \varepsilon_i$$

$$(8.1)$$

The important thing to note is that this equation keeps the fundamental idea that an outcome for a person can be predicted from a model (the stuff in brackets) and some error associated with that prediction (ε_i). We are still predicting an outcome variable (y_i) from a predictor variable (X_i) and a parameter, b_1, associated with the predictor variable that quantifies the relationship it has with the outcome variable. This model differs from that of a correlation only in that it uses an *unstandardized* measure of the relationship (b) and consequently we need to include a parameter that tells us the value of the outcome when the predictor is zero.[3] This parameter is b_0.

Focus on the model itself for a minute. Does it seem familiar? Let's imagine that instead of b_0 we use the letter c, and instead of b_1 we use the letter m. Let's also ignore the error term for the moment. We could predict our outcome as follows:

$$\text{outcome}_i = mx + c$$

Or if you're American, Canadian or Australian let's use the letter b instead of c:

$$\text{outcome}_i = mx + b$$

Perhaps you're French, Dutch or Brazilian, in which case let's use a instead of m:

$$\text{outcome}_i = ax + b$$

Do any of these look familiar to you? If not, there are two explanations: (1) you didn't pay enough attention at school, or (2) you're Latvian, Greek, Italian, Swedish, Romanian, Finnish or Russian – to avoid this section being even more tedious, I used only the three main international differences in the equation above. The different forms of the equation make an important point: the symbols or letters we use in an equation don't necessarily change it.[4] Whether we write $mx + c$ or $b_1X + b_0$ doesn't really matter, what matters is what the symbols represent. So, what do the symbols represent?

Hopefully, some of you recognized this model as 'the equation of a straight line'. I have talked throughout this book about fitting 'linear models', and linear simply means 'straight line'. So, it should come as no surprise that the equation we use is the one that describes a straight line. Any straight line can be defined by two things: (1) the slope (or gradient) of the line (usually denoted by b_1); and (2) the point at which the line crosses the vertical axis of the graph (known as the *intercept* of the line, b_0). These parameters b_1 and b_0 are known as the regression coefficients and will crop up time and time again in this book, where you may see them referred to generally as b (without any subscript) or ***bn*** (meaning the b associated with variable n). A particular line (i.e., model) will have a specific intercept and gradient.

Figure 8.2 shows a set of lines that have the same intercept but different gradients. For these three models, b_0 will be the same in each but the values of b_1 will differ in each model.

Figure 8.2 also shows models that have the same gradients (b_1 is the same in each model) but different intercepts (the b_0 is different in each model). I've mentioned already that b_1 quantifies the relationship between the predictor variable and the outcome, and Figure 8.2 illustrates this point. In Chapter 6 we saw how relationships can be either positive or negative (and I don't mean whether or not you and your partner argue all the time). A model with a positive b_1 describes a positive relationship, whereas a line with a negative b_1 describes a negative relationship. Looking at Figure 8.2 (left), the red line describes a positive relationship whereas the green line describes a negative relationship. As such, we can use a linear

---

[3] In case you're interested, by standardizing b, as we do when we compute a correlation coefficient, we're estimating b for standardized versions of the predictor and outcome variables (i.e., versions of these variables that have a mean of 0 and standard deviation of 1). In this situation b_0 drops out of the equation because it is the value of the outcome when the predictor is 0, and when the predictor and outcome are standardized then when the predictor is 0, the outcome (and hence b_0) will be 0 also.

[4] For example, you'll sometimes see equation (8.1) written as $Y_i = (\beta_0 + \beta_1X_i) + \varepsilon_i$. The only difference is that this equation has βs in it instead of bs. Both versions are the same thing, they just use different letters to represent the coefficients.

FIGURE 8.2
Lines that
share the same
intercept but
have different
gradients, and
lines with the
same gradients
but different
intercepts

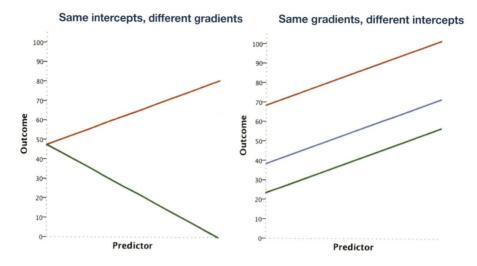

model (i.e., a straight line) to summarize the relationship between two variables: the gradient (b_1) tells us what the model looks like (its shape) and the intercept (b_0) tells us where the model is (its location in geometric space).

This is all quite abstract, so let's look at an example. Imagine that I was interested in predicting physical and downloaded album sales (outcome) from the amount of money spent advertising that album (predictor). We could summarize this relationship using a linear model by replacing the names of our variables into equation (8.1):

$$y_i = b_0 + b_1 X_i + \varepsilon_i$$

$$\text{album sales}_i = b_0 + b_1 \text{advertising budget}_i + \varepsilon_i \tag{8.2}$$

Once we have estimated the values of the bs we would be able to make a prediction about album sales by replacing 'advertising' with a number representing how much we wanted to spend advertising an album. For example, imagine that b_0 turned out to be 50 and b_1 turned out to be 100. Our model would be:

$$\text{album sales}_i = 50 + \left(100 \times \text{advertising budget}_i\right) + \varepsilon_i \tag{8.3}$$

Note that I have replaced the betas with their numeric values. Now, we can make a prediction. Imagine we wanted to spend £5 on advertising, we can replace the variable 'advertising budget' with this value and solve the equation to discover how many album sales we will get:

$$\text{album sales}_i = 50 + \left(100 \times 5\right) + \varepsilon_i$$

$$= 550 + \varepsilon_i$$

So, based on our model we can predict that if we spend £5 on advertising, we'll sell 550 albums. I've left the error term in there to remind you that this prediction will probably not be perfectly accurate. This value of 550 album sales is known as a **predicted value**.

8.2.2. The linear model with several predictors ②

We have seen that we can use a straight line to 'model' the relationship between two variables. However, life is usually more complicated than that: there are often numerous variables that might be related to the outcome of interest. To take our album sales example, we might expect variables other than simply advertising to have an effect. For example, how much someone hears songs from the album on the radio, or the 'look' of the band might have an influence. One of the beautiful things about the linear model is that it can be expanded to include as many predictors as you like. We hinted at this back in Chapter 2 (equation (2.4)). To add a predictor all we need to do is place it into the model and give it a b that estimates the relationship between that predictor and the outcome. For example, if we wanted to add the number of plays of the band on the radio per week (airplay), we could add this second predictor in general as:

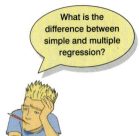

$$Y_i = \left(b_0 + b_1 X_{1i} + b_2 X_{2i}\right) + \varepsilon_i \tag{8.4}$$

Note that all that has changed is the addition of a second predictor (X_2) and an associated parameter (b_2). To make things more concrete, let's use the variable names instead:

$$\text{album sales}_i = b_0 + b_1 \text{advertising budget}_i + b_2 \text{airplay}_i + \varepsilon_i \tag{8.5}$$

The new model includes a b-value for both predictors (and, of course, the constant, b_0). If we estimate the b-values, we could make predictions about album sales based not only on the amount spent on advertising but also in terms of radio play. There are only two predictors in this model and so we could display this model graphically in three dimensions (Figure 8.3).

The tinted trapezium in the diagram (known as the regression *plane*) is described by equation (8.5) and the dots represent the observed data points. Like a regression line, a regression plane aims to give the best prediction for the observed data. However, there are invariably some differences between the model and the real-life data (this fact is evident because some of the dots do not lie exactly on the tinted area of the graph). The vertical distances between the regression plane and each data point are the errors or *residuals* in the model. The b-value for advertising describes the slope of the left and right sides of the

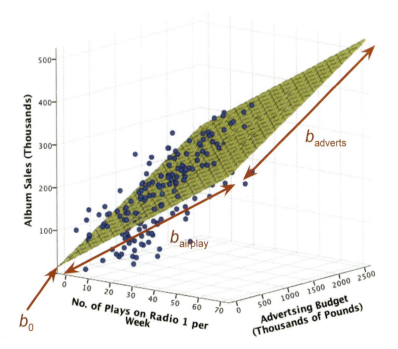

FIGURE 8.3

Scatterplot of the relationship between album sales, advertising budget and radio play regression plane, whereas the *b*-value for airplay describes the slope of the top and bottom of the regression plane. Just like simple regression, knowledge of these two slopes tells us about the shape of the model (what it looks like) and the intercept locates the regression plane in space.

It is fairly easy to visualize a regression model with two predictors, because it is possible to plot the regression plane using a 3-D scatterplot. However, multiple regression can be used with three, four or even ten or more predictors. Although you can't immediately visualize what such complex models look like, or visualize what the *b*-values represent, you should be able to apply the principles of these basic models to more complex scenarios. In fact, in general we can add as many predictors as we like, and the linear model will expand accordingly:

$$Y_i = \left(b_0 + b_1 X_{1i} + b_2 X_{2i} + \ldots + b_n X_{ni}\right) + \varepsilon_i \tag{8.6}$$

in which Y is the outcome variable, b_1 is the coefficient of the first predictor (X_1), b_2 is the coefficient of the second predictor (X_2), b_n is the coefficient of the *n*th predictor (X_{ni}), and ε_i is the error for the *i*th participant. (The parentheses aren't necessary, they're just there to make the connection to equation (8.1)). This equation illustrates that we can add in as many predictors as we like until we reach the final one (X_n), but each time we do, we assign it a regression coefficient (b).

To sum up, regression analysis is when we fit a linear model to our data and use it to predict values of an **outcome variable** (a.k.a. dependent variable) from one or more **predictor variables** (a.k.a. independent variables). With one predictor variable, the technique is sometimes referred to as **simple regression**, but when there are several predictors in the model we call it **multiple regression**. This tool is incredibly useful because it enables us to go a step beyond the data that we collected.

8.2.3. Estimating the model ②

We have seen that the linear model is a versatile model for summarizing the relationship between one or more predictor variables and an outcome variable. No matter how many predictors we have, the model can be described entirely by a constant (b_0) and by parameters associated with each predictor (bs). You might wonder how we estimate these parameters, and the quick answer is that we typically use the method of least squares that was described in Section 2.4.3. We saw then that we could assess the fit of a model (the example we used was the mean) by looking at the deviations between the model and the actual data collected. These deviations were the vertical distances between what the model predicted and each data point that was actually observed. We can do exactly the same to assess the fit of a regression line (which, like the mean, is a statistical model).

Figure 8.4 shows some data about advertising budget and album sales. A model has been fitted to these data (the straight line). The blue circles are the observed data. The line is the model. The green dots on the line are the predicted values. We saw earlier that predicted values are the values of the outcome variable calculated from the model. In other words, if we estimated the values of *b* that define the model and put these values into the linear model (as we did in equation (8.3)), then we insert different values for advertising budget, the predicted values are the resulting estimates of album sales. The question is what values of advertising budget to use to get these predicted values. One very useful thing to do is to use the values of the predictor that actually occurred in the data from which the model was estimated. If you think about it, this makes sense because if the model is a perfect fit of the data then for a given value of the predictor(s) the model should predict the same value of the outcome as was actually observed. In terms of Figure 8.4 this would mean that the green dots fall in exactly the same locations as the blue dots. As you can see, they don't, which shows that the model is not perfect (and it never will be): there is error in the predicted values – sometimes they overestimate the observed value of the outcome and sometimes they underestimate it. In regression, the differences between what the model predicts and the observed data are usually called **residuals** (they are the same as *deviations* when we looked at the mean) and they are the vertical dashed lines in Figure 8.4.

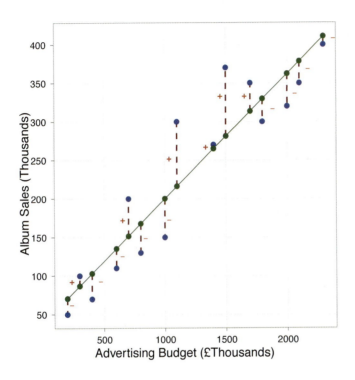

FIGURE 8.4
A scatterplot of some data with a line representing the general trend. The vertical lines (dotted) represent the differences (or residuals) between the line and the actual data

We saw in Chapter 2, equation (2.6), that if we want to calculate the total error in a model we do so by looking at the squared differences between the observed values of the outcome, and the predicted values that come from the model:

$$\text{Total error} = \sum_{i=1}^{n} \left(\text{observed}_i - \text{model}_i\right)^2 \tag{8.7}$$

Sometimes the predicted value of the outcome is less than the actual value and sometimes it is greater, meaning that sometimes the residuals are positive and sometimes they are negative. If we add the residuals, the positive ones will cancel out the negative ones, so we square them before we add them up (this idea should be familiar from Section 2.4.2). Therefore, to assess the error in a regression model, just like when we assessed the fit of the mean using the variance, we use a sum of squared errors, and because in regression we call these errors residuals, we refer to this total as the *sum of squared residuals* or **residual sum of squares** (SS_R). The residual sum of squares is a gauge of how well a particular line fits the data: if the squared differences are large, the line is not representative of the data; if the squared differences are small, the line is representative.

How do we find the optimal model to summarize our data? You could, if you were particularly bored, calculate the residual sum of squares for every possible line that could be fitted to your data and then compare these 'goodness-of-fit' measures. The one with the lowest SS_R would be the best fitting model. However, we have better things to do, so just like when we estimate the mean, we can use the method of least squares to estimate the parameters (*b*) that define the model for which the sum of squared errors is the minimum it can be (given the data). This method is known as **ordinary least squares (OLS)** regression. How exactly the method of least squares does this is beyond me: it uses a mathematical technique for finding maxima and minima to find the *b*-values that describe the model that minimizes the sum of squared differences.

I don't really know much more about it than that, to be honest, so with one predictor I tend to think of the process as a little bearded wizard called Nephwick the Line Finder who just magically finds lines of best fit. Yes, he lives inside your computer. For more complex models, Nephwick invites his brother Clungglewad the Beta Seeker for tea and cake inside your computer and together they stare into the tea leaves in their cups until the optimal beta-values are revealed to them. Then they compare beard growth since their last meeting. In short, they use the method of least squares to estimate the values of *b* that describe the **regression model** that best fits the data.

8.2.4. Assessing the goodness of fit, sums of squares, *R* and R^2 ①

Once Nephwick and Clungglewad have found the model of best fit, it is important that we assess how well this model fits the actual data (we assess the goodness of fit of the model). We do this because even though the model is the best one available, it can still be a lousy fit to the data. We saw above that the residual sum of squares, SS_R, is a measure of how much error there is in the model: it gives us an idea of how much error there is in prediction, but it doesn't tell us whether using the model is better than nothing. It is not enough to simply assess the error within the model, we need to compare it against a baseline to see whether it 'improves' how well we can predict the outcome. So, we fit the most basic model we can, we use equation (8.7) to calculate the fit of this baseline model. Then we fit the best model, and also calculate the error, SS_R, within it using equation (8.7). Basically if the best model is any good then it should have significantly less error within it than our basic model.

How do I tell if my model is good?

This is all quite abstract, so let's go back to our example of predicting album sales (*Y*) from the amount of money spent advertising that album (*X*). One day my boss came in to my office and said: 'Andy, I know you wanted to be a rock star and you've ended up working as my stats-monkey, but how many albums will we sell if we spend £100,000 on advertising?' If I didn't have an accurate model of the relationship between album sales and advertising, what would my best guess be? Probably the best answer I could give would be the mean number of album sales (say, 200,000) because on average that's how many albums we expect to sell. This response might well satisfy a brainless record company executive (who didn't offer my band a recording contract). However, what if he had asked: 'How many albums will we sell if we spend £1 on advertising?' Again, in the absence of any accurate information, my best guess would be to give the average number of sales (200,000). There is a problem: whatever amount of money is spent on advertising I always predict the same levels of sales. As such, the mean is a model of 'no relationship' at all between the variables. It should be pretty clear, then, that the mean is fairly useless as a model of a relationship between two variables – but it is the simplest model available.

So, as a basic strategy for predicting the outcome, we might choose to use the mean, because on average it will be a fairly good guess of an outcome. Using the mean as a model, we can calculate the difference between the observed values, and the values predicted by the mean (equation (8.7)). We saw in Section 2.4.1 that we square all of these differences to give us the sum of squared differences. This sum of squared differences is known as the **total sum of squares** (denoted SS_T) because it is the total amount of differences present when the most basic model is applied to the data. This value represents how good the mean is as a model of the observed data. Now, if we fit a more sophisticated model to the data, such as a regression model, we can again work out the differences between this new model and the observed data (again using equation (8.7)). This value is the residual sum of squares (SS_R) discussed in the previous section. This value represents the degree of inaccuracy when the best model is fitted to the data. We can use these two values to calculate how much better the regression model is than using a baseline model such as the mean (i.e., how much better the best possible model is than the worst model). The improvement in prediction resulting from using the regression model rather than the mean is calculated by calculating the difference between SS_T and SS_R. This difference shows us the reduction in the inaccuracy of the model resulting from fitting the regression model to the data. This improvement is the **model sum of squares** (SS_M). Figure 8.5 shows each sum of squares graphically for the example where the regression model is a line (i.e., one predictor) but the same principles apply with more than one predictor.

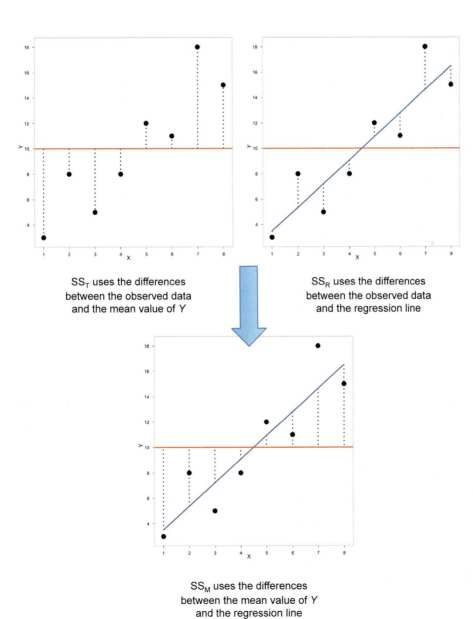

SS$_T$ uses the differences between the observed data and the mean value of Y

SS$_R$ uses the differences between the observed data and the regression line

SS$_M$ uses the differences between the mean value of Y and the regression line

FIGURE 8.5
Diagram showing from where the regression sums of squares derive

If the value of SS_M is large, then the regression model is very different from using the mean to predict the outcome variable. This implies that the regression model has made a big improvement to how well the outcome variable can be predicted. However, if SS_M is small then using the regression model is little better than using the mean (i.e., the regression model is no better than taking our 'best guess'). A useful measure arising from these sums of squares is the proportion of improvement due to the model. This is easily calculated by dividing the sum of squares for the model by the total sum of squares to give a quantity called R^2:

$$R^2 = \frac{SS_M}{SS_T} \qquad\qquad (8.8)$$

To express this value as a percentage you should multiply it by 100. This R^2 represents the amount of variance in the outcome explained by the model (SS_M) relative to how much variation there was to explain in the first place (SS_T); it is the same as the R^2 we met in Chapter 7 (Section 7.4.2.2) and it is interpreted in the same way: as a percentage, it represents the percentage of the variation in the outcome that can be explained by the model. We can take the square root of this value to obtain Pearson's correlation coefficient for the relationship between the values of the outcome predicted by the model and the values of the outcome we actually observed.[5] As such, the correlation coefficient provides us with a good estimate of the overall fit of the regression model (i.e., the correspondence between predicted values of the outcome and the actual values), and R^2 provides us with a gauge of the substantive size of the model fit.[6]

A second use of the sums of squares in assessing the model is through the F-test. I mentioned way back in Chapter 2 that test statistics (like F) are usually the amount of systematic variance divided by the amount of unsystematic variance, or, put another way, the model compared to the error in the model. This is true here: F is based upon the ratio of the improvement due to the model (SS_M) and the difference between the model and the observed data (SS_R). Actually, because the sums of squares depend on the number of differences that we have added up, we use the average sums of squares (referred to as the **mean squares** or MS). To work out the mean sums of squares we divide by the degrees of freedom (this is comparable to calculating the variance from the sums of squares – see Section 2.4.2). For SS_M the degrees of freedom are the number of variables in the model, and for SS_R they are the number of observations minus the number of parameters being estimated (i.e., the number of beta coefficients including the constant). The result is the mean squares for the model (MS_M) and the residual mean squares (MS_R). At this stage it isn't essential that you understand how the mean squares are derived (it is explained in Chapter 11). However, it is important that you understand that the **F-ratio**,

$$F = \frac{MS_M}{MS_R} \qquad\qquad (8.9)$$

is a measure of how much the model has improved the prediction of the outcome compared to the level of inaccuracy of the model. If a model is good, then we expect the improvement in prediction due to the model to be large (so MS_M will be large) and the difference between the model and the observed data to be small (so MS_R will be small). In

---

[5] This is the correlation between the green dots and the blue dots in Figure 8.4. With only one predictor in the model this value will be the same as the Pearson correlation coefficient between the predictor and outcome variable.

[6] When the model contains more than one predictor, people sometimes refer to R^2 as multiple R^2. This is another example of how people attempt to make statistics more confusing than it needs to be by referring to the same thing in different ways. The meaning and interpretation of R^2 are the same regardless of how many predictors you have in the model or whether you choose to call it multiple R^2: it is the squared correlation between values of the outcome predicted by the model and the values observed in the data.

short, a good model should have a large *F*-ratio (greater than 1 at least) because the top of equation (8.9) will be bigger than the bottom.

The exact magnitude of this *F*-ratio can be assessed using critical values for the corresponding degrees of freedom (as in the Appendix). The *F*-statistic can also be used to calculate the significance of R^2 using the following equation:

$$F = \frac{(N - k - 1)R^2}{k(1 - R^2)}$$ (8.10)

in which *N* is the number of cases or participants, and *k* is the number of predictors in the model. This *F* tests the null hypothesis that R^2 is zero (i.e., there is no improvement in the sum of squared error due to fitting the model).

8.2.5. Assessing individual predictors ①

We've seen that any predictor in a regression model has a coefficient (b_1), which in simple regression represents the gradient of the regression line. The value of *b* represents the change in the outcome resulting from a unit change in the predictor. If the model was useless at predicting the outcome, then if the value of the predictor changed, what might we expect the change in the outcome to be? Well, if the model was very bad then we would expect the change in the outcome to be zero. Think back to Figure 8.5 (see the panel representing SS_T) in which we saw that using the mean was a very bad way of predicting the outcome. In fact, the line representing the mean is flat, which means that as the predictor variable changes, the value of the outcome does *not* change (because for each level of the predictor variable, we predict that the outcome will equal the mean value). The important point here is that a bad model (such as the mean) will have regression coefficients of 0 for the predictors. A regression coefficient of 0 means: (1) a unit change in the predictor variable results in no change in the predicted value of the outcome (the predicted value of the outcome does not change at all); and with only one predictor in the model (2) the gradient of the regression line is 0, meaning that the regression line is flat. Hopefully, you'll see that logically if a variable significantly predicts an outcome, then it should have a *b*-value that is different from zero. This hypothesis is tested using a *t*-test (see Chapter 9). The **t-statistic** tests the null hypothesis that the value of *b* is 0: therefore, if it is significant we gain confidence in the hypothesis that the *b*-value is significantly different from 0 and that the predictor variable contributes significantly to our ability to estimate values of the outcome.

Like *F*, the *t*-statistic is also based on the ratio of explained variance to unexplained variance or error. Well, actually, what we're interested in here is not so much variance but whether the *b* we have is big compared to the amount of error in that estimate. To estimate how much error we could expect to find in *b* we use the standard error. The standard error tells us something about how different *b*-values would be across different samples (think back to Section 2.5.1). If the standard error is very small, then it means that most samples are likely to have a *b*-value similar to the one in our sample (because there is little variation across samples). The *t*-test tells us whether the *b*-value is different from 0 relative to the variation in *b*-values across samples. When the standard error is small even a small deviation from zero can reflect a meaningful difference because *b* is representative of the majority of possible samples.

Equation (8.11) shows how the *t*-test is calculated and you'll find a general version of this equation in Chapter 9 (equation (9.2)). The $b_{expected}$ is simply the value of *b* that we would expect to obtain if the null hypothesis were true. I mentioned earlier that the null hypothesis is that b is 0 and so this value can be replaced by 0. The equation simplifies to become the observed value of b divided by the standard error with which it is associated:

$$t = \frac{b_{\text{observed}} - b_{\text{expected}}}{SE_b}$$

$$= \frac{b_{\text{observed}}}{SE_b} \tag{8.11}$$

The values of t have a special distribution that differs according to the degrees of freedom for the test. In this context, the degrees of freedom are $N - p - 1$, where N is the total sample size and p is the number of predictors. In simple regression when we have only one predictor, this reduces down to $N - 2$. Having established which t-distribution needs to be used, the observed value of t can then be compared to the values that we would expect to find if there was no effect (i.e., $b = 0$): if t is very large then it is unlikely to have occurred when there is no effect (these values can be found in the Appendix). SPSS provides the exact probability that the observed value (or a larger one) of t would occur if the value of b was, in fact, 0. As a general rule, if this observed significance is less than .05, then scientists assume that b is significantly different from 0; put another way, the predictor makes a significant contribution to predicting the outcome.

8.3. Bias in regression models? ②

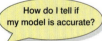

How do I tell if my model is accurate?

In Chapter 5 we saw that statistical models can be biased by unusual cases or by failing to meet certain assumptions. Therefore, when we have produced a model based on a sample of data, and assessed the fit, there are two important questions to ask: (1) is the model influenced by a small number of cases; and (2) can the model generalize to other samples? These questions are, in some sense, hierarchical because we wouldn't want to generalize a bad model. However, it is a mistake to think that because a model fits the observed data well we can draw conclusions beyond our sample. **Generalization** is a critical additional step, and if we find that our model is not generalizable, then we must restrict any conclusions based on the model to the sample used. In Section 8.3.1 we will look at how we establish whether a model has been biased by unusual cases, and in Section 8.3.2 we move on to look at how we assess whether a model can be used to make inferences beyond the sample of data that has been collected.

8.3.1. Is the model biased by unusual cases? ②

To answer the question of whether the model is influenced by a small number of cases, we can look for outliers and influential cases (the difference is explained in Jane Superbrain Box 8.1). We will look at these in turn.

8.3.1.1. Outliers and residuals ②

An outlier is a case that differs substantially from the main trend of the data (see Section 5.2.2). Outliers can affect the estimates of the regression coefficients. For example, Figure 8.6 uses the

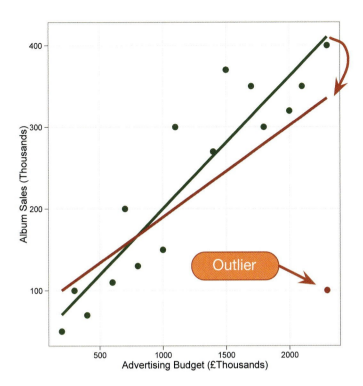

FIGURE 8.6
Graph demonstrating the effect of an outlier. The green line represents the original regression line for these data, whereas the red line represents the regression line when an outlier is present

same data as Figure 8.4 except that the score of one album has been changed to be an outlier (in this case an album that sold relatively few despite a very large advertising budget). The green line shows the original model, and the red line shows the model with the outlier included. The outlier has a dramatic effect on the regression model: the line becomes flatter (i.e., b_1 is smaller) and the intercept increases (i.e., b_0 is larger). If outliers affect the estimates of the bs that define the model then it is important to detect these cases.

How do you think that you might detect an outlier? Well, we know that an outlier, by its nature, is very different from all of the other scores. This being true, do you think that the model will predict that person's score very accurately? The answer is *no*: looking at Figure 8.6, it is evident that even though the outlier has biased the model, the model still predicts that one value very badly (the regression line is a long way from the outlier). Therefore, if we were to work out the differences between the data values that were collected, and the values predicted by the model, we could detect an outlier by looking for large differences. This process is the same as looking for cases that the model predicts inaccurately. We saw earlier that the differences between the values of the outcome predicted by the model and the values of the outcome observed in the sample are called *residuals*. These residuals represent the error present in the model. If a model fits the sample data well then all residuals will be small (if the model was a perfect fit of the sample data – all data points fall on the regression line – then all residuals would be zero). If a model is a poor fit of the sample data then the residuals will be large. Also, if any cases stand out as having a large residual, then they could be outliers.

SELF-TEST   Residuals are used to compute which of the three sums of squares?

The *normal* or **unstandardized residuals** described above are measured in the same units as the outcome variable and so are difficult to interpret across different models. All we can do is to look for residuals that stand out as being particularly large: we cannot define a universal cut-off point for what constitutes a large residual. To overcome this problem, we use standardized residuals, which are the residuals converted to *z*-scores (see Section 1.6.4), which means they are converted into standard deviation units (i.e., they are distributed around a mean of 0 with a standard deviation of 1). By converting residuals into *z*-scores (standardized residuals) we can compare residuals from different models and use what we know about the properties of *z*-scores to devise universal guidelines for what constitutes an acceptable (or unacceptable) value. For example, we know from Chapter 1 that in a normally distributed sample, 95% of *z*-scores should lie between −1.96 and +1.96, 99% should lie between −2.58 and +2.58, and 99.9% (i.e., nearly all of them) should lie between −3.29 and +3.29. Some general rules for standardized residuals are derived from these facts: (1) standardized residuals with an absolute value greater than 3.29 (we can use 3 as an approximation) are cause for concern because in an average sample a value this high is unlikely to occur; (2) if more than 1% of our sample cases have standardized residuals with an absolute value greater than 2.58 (we usually just say 2.5) there is evidence that the level of error within our model is unacceptable (the model is a fairly poor fit of the sample data); and (3) if more than 5% of cases have standardized residuals with an absolute value greater than 1.96 (we can use 2 for convenience) then there is also evidence that the model is a poor representation of the actual data.

A third form of residual is the Studentized residual, which is the unstandardized residual divided by an estimate of its standard deviation that varies point by point. These residuals have the same properties as the standardized residuals but usually provide a more precise estimate of the error variance of a specific case.

8.3.1.2. Influential cases ③

As well as testing for outliers by looking at the error in the model, it is also possible to look at whether certain cases exert undue influence over the parameters of the model. So, if we were to delete a certain case, would we obtain different regression coefficients? This type of analysis can help to determine whether the regression model is stable across the sample, or whether it is biased by a few influential cases. Again, this process will unveil outliers.

There are several residual statistics that can be used to assess the influence of a particular case. One statistic is the adjusted predicted value for a case when that case is excluded from the analysis. In effect, the computer calculates a new model without a particular case and then uses this new model to predict the value of the outcome variable for the case that was excluded. If a case does not exert a large influence over the model then we would expect the adjusted predicted value to be very similar to the predicted value when the case is included. Put simply, if the model is stable then the predicted value of a case should be the same regardless of whether or not that case was used to estimate the model. We can also look at the residual based on the adjusted predicted value: that is, the difference between the adjusted predicted value and the original observed value. This is the deleted residual. The deleted residual can be divided by the standard error to give a standardized value known as the Studentized deleted residual. This residual can be compared across different regression analyses because it is measured in standard units.

The deleted residuals are very useful to assess the influence of a case on the ability of the model to predict that case. However, they do not provide any information about how a case influences the model as a whole (i.e., the impact that a case has on the model's ability to predict *all* cases). One statistic that does consider the effect of a single case on the model as a whole is Cook's distance. Cook's distance is a measure of the overall influence of a case on the model, and Cook and Weisberg (1982) have suggested that values greater than 1 may be cause for concern.

A second measure of influence is **leverage** (sometimes called **hat values**), which gauges the influence of the observed value of the outcome variable over the predicted values. The average leverage value is defined as $(k + 1)/n$, in which k is the number of predictors in the model and n is the number of participants.[7] The maximum value for leverage is $(N - 1)/N$; however, SPSS calculates a version of the leverage that takes a maximum value of 1 (indicating that the case has complete influence over prediction).

- If no cases exert undue influence over the model then we would expect all of the leverage values to be close to the average value $((k + 1)/n)$.

- Hoaglin and Welsch (1978) recommend investigating cases with values greater than twice the average $(2(k + 1)/n)$.

- Stevens (2002) recommends using three times the average $(3(k + 1)/n)$ as a cut-off point for identifying cases having undue influence.

We will see how to use these cut-off points later. However, cases with large leverage values will not necessarily have a large influence on the regression coefficients because they are measured on the outcome variables rather than the predictors.

Related to the leverage values are the **Mahalanobis distances**, which measure the distance of cases from the mean(s) of the predictor variable(s). Look for the cases with the highest values. These distances have a chi-square distribution, with degrees of freedom equal to the number of predictors (Tabachnick & Fidell, 2012). One way to establish a cut-off point is to find the critical value of chi-square for the desired alpha level (values for $p = .05$ and .01 are in the Appendix). For example, with three predictors, a distance greater than 7.81 ($p = .05$) or 11.34 ($p = .01$) would be cause for concern. Barnett and Lewis (1978) have also produced a table of critical values dependent on the number of predictors and the sample size. From their work it is clear that even with large samples ($N = 500$) and five predictors, values above 25 are cause for concern. In smaller samples ($N = 100$) and with fewer predictors (namely, three), values greater than 15 are problematic, and in very small samples ($N = 30$) with only two predictors, values, greater than 11 should be examined.

It is possible to run the regression analysis with a case included and then rerun the analysis with that same case excluded. If we did this, undoubtedly there would be some difference between the b coefficients in the two regression equations. This difference would tell us how much influence a particular case has on the parameters of the regression model. To take a hypothetical example, imagine two variables that had a perfect negative relationship except for a single case (case 30). If a regression analysis was done on the 29 cases that were perfectly linearly related then we would get a model in which the predictor variable X perfectly predicts the outcome variable Y, and there are no errors. If we then ran the

FIGURE 8.7
Prasanta Chandra Mahalanobis staring into his distances

analysis but this time include the case that didn't conform (case 30), then the resulting model would have different parameters. Some data are stored in the file **DFBeta.sav** which illustrate such a situation.

---

[7] You may come across the average leverage denoted as p/n in which p is the number of parameters being estimated. In regression, we estimate parameters for each predictor and also for a constant and so p is equivalent to the number of predictors plus one $(k + 1)$.

SELF-TEST   Once you have read Section 8.4, run a regression first with all the cases included and then with case 30 deleted.

The results are summarized in Table 8.1, which shows: (1) the parameters for the regression model when the extreme case is included or excluded; (2) the resulting regression equations; and (3) the value of Y predicted from participant 30's score on the X variable (which is obtained by replacing the X in the regression equation with participant 30's score for X, which was 1).

When case 30 is excluded, these data have a perfect negative relationship; hence the coefficient for the predictor (b_1) is -1 (remember that in simple regression this term is the same as Pearson's correlation coefficient), and the coefficient for the constant (the intercept, b_0) is 31. However, when case 30 is included, both parameters are reduced[8] and the difference between the parameters is also displayed. The difference between a parameter estimated using all cases and estimated when one case is excluded is known as the **DFBeta**. DFBeta is calculated for every case and for each of the parameters in the model. So, in our hypothetical example, the DFBeta for the constant is -2, and the DFBeta for the predictor variable is 0.1. By looking at the values of DFBeta, it is possible to identify cases that have a large influence on the parameters of the regression model. Again, the units of measurement used will affect these values and so SPSS produces a **standardized DFBeta**. These standardized values are easier to use because universal cut-off points can be applied. In this case absolute values above 1 indicate cases that substantially influence the model parameters (although Stevens (2002) suggests looking at cases with absolute values greater than 2).

TABLE 8.1   The difference in the parameters of the regression model when one case is excluded

Parameter (b)	Case 30 Included	Case 30 Excluded	Difference
Constant (intercept)	29.00	31.00	−2.00
Predictor (gradient)	−0.90	−1.00	0.10
Model (regression line)	$y = -0.9x + 29$	$y = -1x + 31$	
Predicted Y	28.10	30.00	−1.90

A related statistic is the **DFFit**, which is the difference between the predicted value for a case when the model is calculated including that case and when the model is calculated excluding that case: in this example the value is -1.90 (see Table 8.1). If a case is not influential then its DFFit should be zero – hence, we expect non-influential cases to have small DFFit values. However, we have the problem that this statistic depends on the units of measurement of the outcome and so a DFFit of 0.5 will be very small if the outcome

---

[8] The value of b_1 is reduced because the data no longer have a perfect linear relationship and so there is now variance that the model cannot explain.

ranges from 1 to 100, but very large if the outcome varies from 0 to 1. Therefore, SPSS also produces standardized versions of the DFFit values (Standardized DFFit).

A final measure is the covariance ratio (CVR), which is a measure of whether a case influences the variance of the regression parameters. A description of the computation of this statistic leaves me dazed and confused, so suffice to say that when this ratio is close to 1 the case has very little influence on the variances of the model parameters. Belsey, Kuh, and Welsch (1980) recommend the following:

- If $CVR_i > 1 + [3(k + 1)/n]$ then deleting the ith case will damage the precision of some of the model's parameters.

- If $CVR_i < 1 − [3(k + 1)/n]$ then deleting the ith case will improve the precision of some of the model's parameters.

In both equations, k is the number of predictors, CVR_i is the covariance ratio for the ith participant, and n is the sample size.

8.3.1.3. A final comment on diagnostic statistics ②

EVERYBODY

There are a lot of diagnostic statistics that should be examined after a regression analysis, and it is difficult to summarize this wealth of material into a concise conclusion. However, one thing I would like to stress is a point made by Belsey et al. (1980) who noted the dangers inherent in these procedures. The point is that diagnostics are tools that enable you to see how good or bad your model is in terms of fitting the sampled data. They are a way of assessing your model. They are *not*, however, a way of justifying the removal of data points to effect some desirable change in the regression parameters (e.g., deleting a case that changes a non-significant b-value into a significant one). Stevens (2002), as ever, offers excellent advice:

> If a point is a significant outlier on Y, but its Cook's distance is < 1, there is no real need to delete that point since it does not have a large effect on the regression analysis. However, one should still be interested in studying such points further to understand why they did not fit the model. (p. 135)

8.3.2. Generalizing the model ②

When a regression analysis is done, an equation can be produced that is correct for the sample of observed values. However, we are usually interested in generalizing our findings outside of the sample. For a regression model to generalize we must be sure that underlying assumptions have been met, and to test whether the model does generalize we can look at cross-validating it.

8.3.2.1. Assumptions of the linear model ②

We have already looked at the main assumptions of the linear model and how to assess them in Chapter 5. I will recap the main ones in order of importance (Gelman & Hill, 2007):

- *Additivity and linearity*: The outcome variable should, in reality, be linearly related to any predictors and, with several predictors, their combined effect is best described

JANE SUPERBRAIN 8.1

The difference between residuals and influence statistics ③

To illustrate how residuals and influence statistics differ, imagine that the Mayor of London at the turn of the last century was interested in how drinking affected mortality. London is divided up into different regions called boroughs, and so he might measure the number of pubs and the number of deaths over a period of time in eight of his boroughs. The data are in a file called **pubs.sav**.

The scatterplot of these data (Figure 8.8) reveals that without the last case there is a perfect linear relationship (the dashed straight line). However, the presence of the last case (case 8) changes the line of best fit dramatically (although this line is still a significant fit to the data – do the regression analysis and see for yourself).

What's interesting about these data is when we look at the residuals and influence statistics. The standardized residual for case 8 is the second *smallest:* this outlier produces a very small residual (most of the non-outliers have larger residuals) because it sits very close to the line that has been fitted to the data. How can this be? Look at the influence statistics below and you'll see that

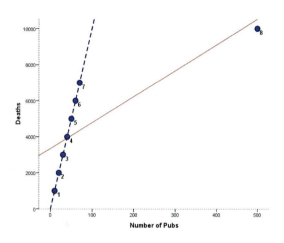

FIGURE 8.8   With non-parametric tests you must double-click the summary table within the viewer window to open up the model viewer window

they're massive for case 8: it exerts a huge influence over the model.

As always, when you see a statistical oddity you should ask what was happening in the real world. The last data point represents the City of London, a tiny area of only 1 square mile in the centre of London where very few people lived but where thousands of commuters (even then) came to work and had lunch in the pubs. Hence the pubs didn't rely on the resident population for their business and the residents didn't consume all of their beer. Therefore, there was a massive number of pubs. This illustrates that a case exerting a massive influence can produce a small residual – so look at both (I'm very grateful to David Hitchin for this example, and he in turn got it from Dr Richard Roberts.)

Case Summaries[a]

	Standardized Residual	Mahalanobis Distance	Cook's Distance	Centered Leverage Value	DFFIT	DFBETA Intercept	DFBETA pubs
1	-1.33839	.28515	.21328	.04074	-495.72692	-509.65184	1.39249
2	-.87895	.22370	.08530	.03196	-305.09716	-321.12768	.80153
3	-.41950	.16969	.01814	.02424	-137.20167	-147.10661	.33016
4	.03995	.12314	.00015	.01759	12.38769	13.45081	-.02658
5	.49940	.08403	.02294	.01200	147.81622	161.44976	-.27267
6	.95885	.05237	.08092	.00748	273.00807	297.67748	-.41116
7	1.41830	.02817	.17107	.00402	391.72124	422.81664	-.44422
8	-.27966	6.03375	227.14286	.86196	-39478.58473	3351.95531	-85.66108
Total N	8	8	8	8	8	8	8

a. Limited to first 100 cases.

by adding their effects together. In other words, the process we're trying to model can be described by the linear model. If this assumption isn't met then the model is invalid. You can sometimes transform variables to make their relationships linear (see Chapter 5).

- **Independent errors**: For any two observations the residual terms should be uncorrelated (i.e., independent). This eventuality is sometimes described as a lack of **autocorrelation**. If we violate the assumption of independence then our confidence intervals and significance tests will be invalid. However, in terms of the model parameters themselves, the estimates using the method of least squares will still be valid but not optimal (see Section 5.2.6). This assumption can be tested with the **Durbin–Watson test**, which tests for serial correlations between errors. Specifically, it tests whether adjacent residuals are correlated. The test statistic can vary between 0 and 4, with a value of 2 meaning that the residuals are uncorrelated. A value greater than 2 indicates a negative correlation between adjacent residuals, whereas a value below 2 indicates a positive correlation. The size of the Durbin–Watson statistic depends upon the number of predictors in the model and the number of observations. For accuracy, you should look up the exact acceptable values in Durbin and Watson's (1951) original paper. As a very conservative rule of thumb, values less than 1 or greater than 3 are definitely cause for concern; however, values closer to 2 may still be problematic, depending on your sample and model.

- *Homoscedasticity* (see Section 5.2.5): At each level of the predictor variable(s), the variance of the residual terms should be constant. This just means that the residuals at each level of the predictor(s) should have the same variance (homoscedasticity); when the variances are very unequal there is said to be heteroscedasticity. Violating this assumption invalidates our confidence intervals and significance tests. However, estimates of the model parameters (*b*) using the method of least squares are still valid but not optimal. This problem can be overcome using weighted least squares regression in which each case is weighted by a function of its variance.

- *Normally distributed errors* (see Section 5.2.4): It is assumed that the residuals in the model are random, normally distributed variables with a mean of 0. This assumption simply means that the differences between the model and the observed data are most frequently zero or very close to zero, and that differences much greater than zero happen only occasionally. Some people confuse this assumption with the idea that predictors have to be normally distributed. In fact, predictors do not need to be normally distributed. In small samples a lack of normality will invalidate confidence intervals and significance tests; in large samples it will not, because of the central limit theorem. If you are concerned only with estimating the model parameters (and not significance tests and confidence intervals) then this assumption barely matters. If you bootstrap confidence intervals then you really can ignore this assumption.

There are some other considerations that we have not yet discussed (see Berry, 1993):

- *Predictors are uncorrelated with 'external variables'*: *External variables* are variables that haven't been included in the regression model and that influence the outcome variable.[9] These variables can be thought of as similar to the 'third variable' that was discussed with reference to correlation. This assumption means that there should be no external variables that correlate with any of the variables included in the regression model. Obviously, if external variables do correlate with the predictors, then the conclusions we draw from the model become unreliable (because other variables exist that can predict the outcome just as well).

---

[9] Some authors refer to these external variables as part of an error term that includes any random factor in the way in which the outcome varies. However, to avoid confusion with the residual terms in the regression equations I have chosen the label 'external variables'. Although this term implicitly washes over any random factors, I acknowledge their presence here.

- *Variable types*: All predictor variables must be quantitative or categorical (with two categories), and the outcome variable must be quantitative, continuous and unbounded. By 'quantitative' I mean that they should be measured at the interval level and by 'unbounded' I mean that there should be no constraints on the variability of the outcome. If the outcome is a measure ranging from 1 to 10 yet the data collected vary between 3 and 7, then these data are constrained.

- *No perfect* **multicollinearity**: If your model has more than one predictor then there should be no perfect linear relationship between two or more of the predictors. So, the predictor variables should not correlate too highly (see Section 8.5.3).

- *Non-zero variance*: The predictors should have some variation in value (i.e., they do not have variances of 0). This is self-evident really.

As we saw in Chapter 5, violating these assumptions has implications mainly for significance tests and confidence intervals; the estimates of *b*s are not dependent on these assumptions (although least squares methods will be optimal when the assumptions are met). However, the confidence interval for a *b* tells us the boundaries within which the population values of that *b* are likely to fall. Therefore, if confidence intervals are inaccurate (as they are when these assumptions are broken) then we cannot accurately estimate the likely population value. This means we can't generalize our model to the population. When the assumptions are met, then, *on average* the regression model from the sample is the same as the population model. However, you should be clear that even when the assumptions are met, it is possible that a model obtained from a sample may not be the same as the population model – but the likelihood of them being the same is increased.

8.3.2.2. Cross-validation of the model ③

Even if we can't be confident that the model derived from our sample accurately represents the entire population, we can assess how well our model can predict the outcome in a different sample. Assessing the accuracy of a model across different samples is known as **cross-validation**. If a model can be generalized, then it must be capable of accurately predicting the same outcome variable from the same set of predictors in a different group of people. If the model is applied to a different sample and there is a severe drop in its predictive power, then the model clearly does *not* generalize. As a first rule of thumb, we should aim to collect enough data to obtain a reliable regression model (see the next section). Once we have a regression model there are two main methods of cross-validation:

- *Adjusted R^2*: SPSS computes an **adjusted R^2**. Whereas R^2 tells us how much of the variance in *Y* is accounted for by the regression model from our sample, the adjusted value tells us how much variance in *Y* would be accounted for if the model had been derived from the population from which the sample was taken. Therefore, the adjusted value indicates the loss of predictive power or **shrinkage**. SPSS derives the adjusted R^2 using Wherry's equation. This equation has been criticized because it tells us nothing about how well the regression model would predict scores of a different sample of data from the same population. One version of R^2 that does tell us how well the model cross-validates uses Stein's formula (see Stevens, 2002).

$$\text{adjusted } R^2 = 1 - \left[\left(\frac{n-1}{n-k-1} \right) \left(\frac{n-2}{n-k-2} \right) \left(\frac{n+1}{n} \right) \right] \left(1 - R^2 \right) \qquad (8.12)$$

In Stein's equation, R^2 is the unadjusted value, *n* is the number of participants and *k* is the number of predictors in the model. For the more mathematically minded of you, it is worth using this equation to cross-validate a regression model.

● *Data splitting*: This approach involves randomly splitting your sample data, computing a regression equation on both halves of the data and then comparing the resulting
models. When using stepwise methods (see Section 8.5.1.3), cross-validation is particularly important; you should run the stepwise regression on a random selection of
about 80% of your cases. Then force this model on the remaining 20% of the data.
By comparing values of the R^2 and b-values in the two samples you can tell how well
the original model generalizes (see Tabachnick & Fidell, 2012, for more detail).

8.3.3. Sample size in regression ③

In the previous section I said that it's important to collect enough data to obtain a reliable
regression model. Also, larger samples enable us to assume that our bs are from a normally
distributed sampling distribution because of the central limit theorem (Section 5.2.4.2).
Well, how much is enough?

You'll find a lot of rules of thumb floating about, the two most common being
that you should have 10 cases of data for each predictor in the model, or 15
cases of data per predictor. So, with five predictors, you'd need 50 or 75 cases
respectively (depending on the rule you use). These rules are very pervasive
but they oversimplify the issue. In fact, the sample size required will depend on
the size of effect that we're trying to detect (i.e., how strong the relationship
is that we're trying to measure) and how much power we want to detect these
effects. The simplest rule of thumb is that the bigger the sample size, the better:
the estimate of R that we get from regression is dependent on the number of
predictors, k, and the sample size, N. In fact, the expected R for random data is
$k/(N - 1)$ and so with small sample sizes random data can appear to show a strong effect:
for example, with six predictors and 21 cases of data, $R = 6/(21 - 1) = .3$ (a medium effect
size by Cohen's criteria described in Section 7.2.2). Obviously for random data we'd want
the expected R to be 0 (no effect) and for this to be true we need large samples (to take the
previous example, if we had 100 cases rather than 21, then the expected R would be a more
acceptable .06).

It's all very well knowing that larger is better, but researchers usually need some more concrete guidelines (much as we'd all love to collect 1000 cases of data, it isn't always practical).
As I've mentioned before, the sample size required depends on the size of the effect (i.e., how
well our predictors predict the outcome), how much statistical power we want to detect these
effects, and what we're testing (the significance of the b-values, or the significance of the
model overall). Figure 8.9 shows the sample size required[10] to achieve a high level of power
(I've taken Cohen's (1988) benchmark of .8) to test that the model is significant overall (i.e.,
R^2 is not equal to zero). I've varied the number of predictors and the size of expected effect:
I used $R^2 = .02$ (small), .13 (medium) and .26 (large), which correspond to benchmarks in
Cohen (1988). Broadly speaking, if your aim is to test the overall fit of the model: (1) if you
expect to find a large effect then a sample size of 77 will always suffice (with up to 20 predictors) and if there are fewer predictors then you can afford to have a smaller sample; (2) if
you're expecting a medium effect, then a sample size of 160 will always suffice (with up to
20 predictors), you should always have a sample size above 55, and with six or fewer predictors you'll be fine with a sample of 100; and (3) if you're expecting a small effect size then
just don't bother unless you have the time and resources to collect hundreds of cases of data.
Miles and Shevlin (2001) produce some more detailed graphs that are worth a look, but the
take-home message is that if you're looking for medium to large effects, sample sizes don't
need to be massive, regardless of how many predictors you have.

---

[10] I used the program G*Power, mentioned in Section 2.6.1.7, to compute these values.

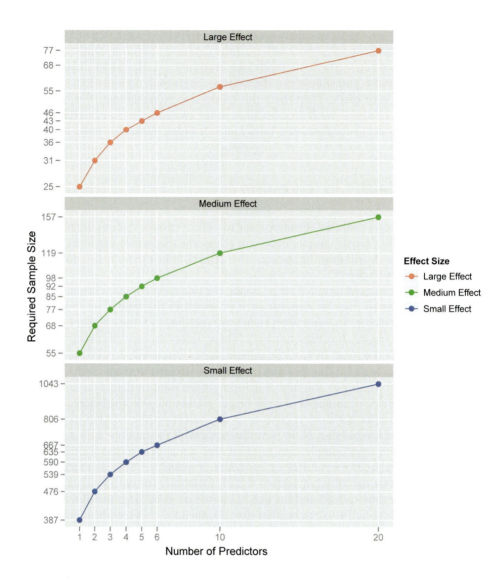

8.4. Regression using SPSS: One Predictor ①

To help clarify what we have learnt so far, we will go through an example of a regression with one predictor before looking in a bit more detail at models with several predictors. Earlier on I asked you to imagine that I worked for a record company and that my boss was interested in predicting album sales from advertising. There are some data for this example in the file **Album Sales.sav**. This data file has 200 rows, each one representing a different album. There are also several columns, one of which contains the sales (in thousands) of each album in the week after release (**Sales**) and one containing the amount (in thousands of pounds) spent promoting the album before release (**Adverts**). The other columns represent how many times songs from the album were played on radio in the week before release (**Airplay**), and how attractive people found the band out of 10 (**Attract**). Ignore these last two variables for now; we'll use them later. Note how the data are laid out (Figure 8.10): each variable is in a column and each row represents a different album. So, the first album had £10,260 spent advertising it, sold 330,000 copies, received 43 plays on Radio 1 the week before release, and was made by a band that the majority of people rated as gorgeous sex objects.

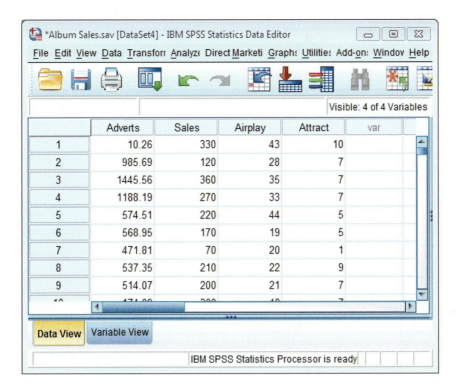

FIGURE 8.10
Data layout for
regression

8.4.1. Regression: the general procedure ①

Figure 8.11 shows the general process of conducting regression analysis. First, we should produce scatterplots to get some idea of whether the assumption of linearity is met, and also to look for any outliers or obvious unusual cases. At this stage we might transform the data to correct problems. Having done this initial screen for problems, we fit a model and save the various diagnostic statistics that we discussed in Section 8.3. If we want to generalize our model beyond the sample, or we are interested in interpreting significance tests and confidence intervals, then we examine these residuals to check for homoscedasticity, normality, independence and linearity (although this will likely be fine given our earlier screening). If we find problems then we take corrective action and re-estimate the model. This process might seem complex, but it's not as bad as it seems. Also, it's probably wise to use bootstrapped confidence intervals when we first estimate the model because then we can basically forget about things like normality.

SELF-TEST   Produce a scatterplot of sales (y-axis) against advertising budget (x-axis). Include the regression line.

The pattern of the data is shown in Figure 8.12, and it should be clear that a positive relationship exists: so, the more money spent advertising the album, the more it is likely

FIGURE 8.11
The process of fitting a regression model
.

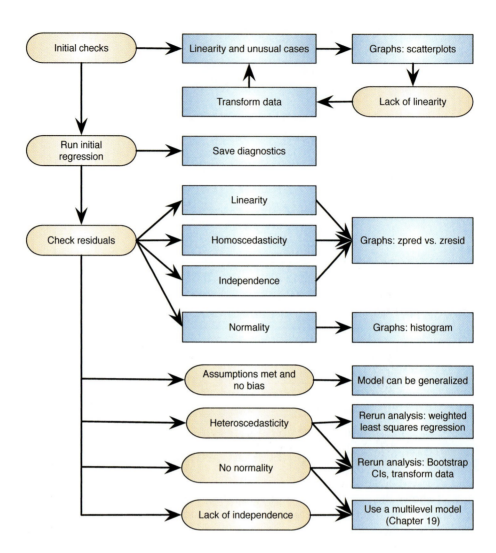

to sell. Of course there are some albums that sell well regardless of advertising (top left of scatterplot), but there are none that sell badly when advertising levels are high (bottom right of scatterplot). The scatterplot also shows the line of best fit for these data: bearing in mind that the mean would be represented by a flat line at around the 200,000 sales mark, the regression line is noticeably different.

8.4.2. Running a simple regression using SPSS ①

To do the analysis you need to access the main dialog box by selecting Analyze Regression ▸ Linear… . Figure 8.13 shows the resulting dialog box. There is a space labelled *Dependent* in which you should place the outcome variable (in this example **Sales**). So, select **Sales** from the list on the left-hand side, and transfer it by dragging it or clicking on . There is another space labelled *Independent(s)* in which any predictor variable should be placed. In simple regression we use only one predictor (in this example, **Adverts**) and so you should select **Adverts** from the list and click on to transfer it to the list of predictors. There are a variety of options available, but these will be explored within the context of multiple regression. However, we can get bootstrapped confidence intervals for the regression

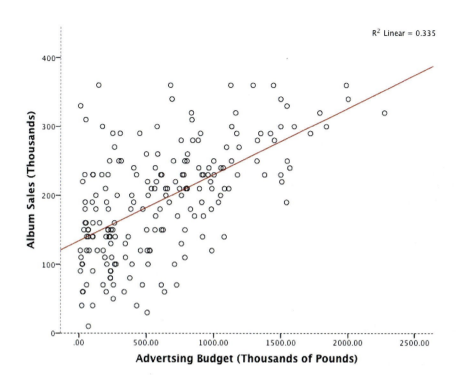

FIGURE 8.12
Scatterplot showing the relationship between album sales and the amount spent promoting the album

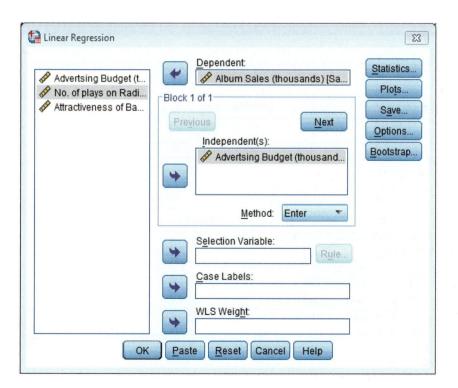

FIGURE 8.13
Main dialog box for regression

coefficients by clicking on `Bootstrap...` (see Section 5.4.3). Select ☑ Perform bootstrapping to activate bootstrapping, and to get a 95% confidence interval click ⦿ Bias corrected accelerated (BCa). Click on `OK` in the main dialog box to run the basic analysis.

8.4.3. | Interpreting a simple regression ①

8.4.3.1. Overall fit of the model ①

The first table provided by SPSS is a summary of the model (Output 8.1). This summary table provides the value of R and R^2 for the model that has been derived. For these data, R has a value of .578 and because there is only one predictor, this value represents the simple correlation between advertising and album sales (you can confirm this by running a correlation using what you were taught in Chapter 6). The value of R^2 is .335, which tells us that advertising expenditure can account for 33.5% of the variation in album sales. In other words, if we are trying to explain why some albums sell more than others, we can look at the variation in sales of different albums. There might be many factors that can explain this variation, but our model, which includes only advertising expenditure, can explain approximately 33% of it. This means that 66% of the variation in album sales cannot be explained by advertising alone. Therefore, there must be other variables that have an influence also.

The next part of the output (Output 8.2) reports an analysis of variance (ANOVA – see Chapter 11). The summary table shows the various sums of squares described in Figure 8.5 and the degrees of freedom associated with each. From these two values, the average sums of squares (the mean squares) can be calculated by dividing the sums of squares by the associated degrees of freedom. The most important part of the table is the F-ratio, which is calculated using equation (8.9), and the associated significance value of that F-ratio. For these data, F is 99.59, which is significant at $p < .001$ (because the value in the column labelled *Sig.* is less than .001). This result tells us that there is less than a 0.1% chance that an F-ratio this large would happen if the null hypothesis were true. Therefore, we can conclude that our regression model results in significantly better prediction of album sales than if we used the mean value of album sales. In short, the regression model overall predicts album sales significantly well.

OUTPUT 8.1

Model Summary

Model	R	R Square	Adjusted R Square	Std. Error of the Estimate
1	.578[a]	.335	.331	65.991

a. Predictors: (Constant), Advertsing Budget (thousands of pounds)

OUTPUT 8.2

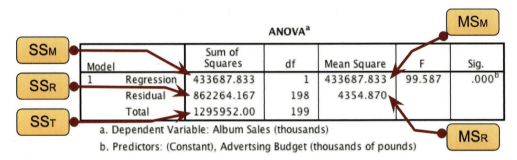

ANOVA[a]

Model		Sum of Squares	df	Mean Square	F	Sig.
1	Regression	433687.833	1	433687.833	99.587	.000[b]
	Residual	862264.167	198	4354.870		
	Total	1295952.00	199			

a. Dependent Variable: Album Sales (thousands)
b. Predictors: (Constant), Advertsing Budget (thousands of pounds)

8.4.3.2. Model parameters ①

The ANOVA tells us whether the model, overall, results in a significantly good degree of prediction of the outcome variable. However, the ANOVA doesn't tell us about the individual contribution of variables in the model (although in this simple case there is only one variable in the model and so we can infer that this variable is a good predictor). The table in Output 8.3 provides estimates of the model parameter (the beta values) and the significance of these values. We saw in equation (8.1) that b_0 was the Y intercept, and this value is the value B (in the SPSS output) for the constant. So, from the table, we can say that b_0 is 134.14, and this can be interpreted as meaning that when no money is spent on advertising (when $X = 0$), the model predicts that 134,140 albums will be sold (remember that our unit of measurement was thousands of albums). We can also read off the value of b_1 from the table, and this value represents the gradient of the regression line. It is 0.096. Although this value is the slope of the regression line, it is more useful to think of it as representing *the change in the outcome associated with a unit change in the predictor*. Therefore, if our predictor variable is increased by one unit (if the advertising budget is increased by 1), then our model predicts that 0.096 extra albums will be sold. Our units of measurement were thousands of pounds and thousands of albums sold, so we can say that for an increase in advertising of £1000 the model predicts 96 ($0.096 \times 1000 = 96$) extra album sales. As you might imagine, this investment is pretty bad for the album company: it invests £1000 and gets only 96 extra sales! Fortunately, as we already know, advertising accounts for only one-third of album sales.

How do I interpret b-values?

We saw earlier that, in general, values of the regression coefficient b represent the change in the outcome resulting from a unit change in the predictor and that if a predictor has a significant impact on our ability to predict the outcome then this b should be different from 0 (and big relative to its standard error). We also saw that the t-test tells us whether the b-value is different from 0. SPSS provides the exact probability that the observed value of t would occur if the value of b in the population were zero. If this observed significance is less than .05, then the result reflects a genuine effect (see Chapter 2). For both ts, the probabilities are given as .000 (zero to 3 decimal places) and so we can say that the probability of these t values (or larger) occurring if the values of b in the population were zero is less than .001. Therefore, the bs are significantly different from 0. In the case of the b for advertising budget this result means that the advertising budget makes a significant contribution ($p < .001$) to predicting album sales.

The bootstrap confidence interval tells us that the population value of b for advertising budget is likely to fall between .08 and .11, and because this interval doesn't include zero we would conclude that there is a genuine positive relationship between advertising budget and album sales in the population. Also, the significance associated with this confidence interval is $p = .001$, which is highly significant. Also, note that the bootstrap process involves re-estimating the standard error (it changes from .01 in the original table

OUTPUT 8.3

Coefficients[a]

Model		Unstandardized Coefficients		Standardized Coefficients	t	Sig.
		B	Std. Error	Beta		
1	(Constant)	134.140	7.537		17.799	.000
	Advertsing Budget (thousands of pounds)	.096	.010	.578	9.979	.000

a. Dependent Variable: Album Sales (thousands)

Bootstrap for Coefficients

Model		B	Bootstrap[a]				
			Bias	Std. Error	Sig. (2-tailed)	BCa 95% Confidence Interval	
						Lower	Upper
1	(Constant)	134.140	.356	8.214	.001	117.993	151.258
	Advertsing Budget (thousands of pounds)	.096	.000	.009	.001	.080	.113

a. Unless otherwise noted, bootstrap results are based on 1000 bootstrap samples

to a bootstrap estimate of .009). This is a very small change. For the constant, the standard error is 7.537 compared to the bootstrap estimate of 8.214, which is a difference of 0.677. The bootstrap confidence intervals and significance values are useful to report and interpret because they do not rely on assumptions of normality or homoscedasticity.

SELF-TEST How is the t in Output 8.3 calculated? Use the values in the table to see if you can get the same value as SPSS.

8.4.4. Using the model ①

So far, we have discovered that we have a useful model, one that significantly improves our ability to predict album sales. However, the next stage is often to use that model to make some predictions. The first stage is to define the model by replacing the b-values in equation (8.1) with the values from the output. In addition, we can replace the X and Y with the variable names so that the model becomes:

$$\text{album sales}_i = b_0 + b_1\text{advertising budget}_i$$

$$= 134.14 + \left(0.096 \times \text{ advertising budget}_i\right) \tag{8.13}$$

It is now possible to make a prediction about album sales, by replacing the advertising budget with a value of interest. For example, imagine a recording company executive wanted to spend £100,000 on advertising a new album. Remembering that our units are already in thousands of pounds, we can simply replace the advertising budget with 100. He would discover that album sales should be around 144,000 for the first week of sales:

$$\text{album sales}_i = 134.14 + \left(0.096 \times \text{ advertising budget}_i\right)$$

$$= 134.14 + \left(0.096 \times 100\right)$$

$$= 143.74 \tag{8.14}$$

CRAMMING SAM'S TIPS   **Simple regression**

- Simple regression is a way of predicting values of one variable from another.
- We do this by fitting a statistical model to the data in the form of a straight line.
- This line is the line that best summarizes the pattern of the data.
- We have to assess how well the line fits the data using:
  ○ R^2, which tells us how much variance is explained by the model compared to how much variance there is to explain in the first place. It is the proportion of variance in the outcome variable that is shared by the predictor variable.
  ○ F, which tells us how much variability the model can explain relative to how much it can't explain (i.e., it's the ratio of how good the model is compared to how bad it is).
  ○ the b-value, which tells us the gradient of the regression line and the strength of the relationship between a predictor and the outcome variable. If it is significant (*Sig.* < .05 in the SPSS table) then the predictor variable significantly predicts the outcome variable.

SELF-TEST How many albums would be sold if we spent £666,000 on advertising the latest CD by black metal band Abgott?

8.5. Multiple regression ②

Imagine that the record company executive was now interested in extending the model of albums sales to incorporate other variables. Before an album is released, the executive notes the amount spent on advertising, the number of times songs from the album are played on radio the week before release (**Airplay**), and the attractiveness of the band (**Attract**). He does this for 200 different albums (each made by a different band). Attractiveness was measured by asking a random sample of the target audience to rate the attractiveness of each band on a scale from 0 (hideous potato-heads) to 10 (gorgeous sex objects). The mode attractiveness given by the sample was used in the regression (because he was interested in what the majority of people thought, rather than the average of people's opinions).

When we want to build a model with several predictors, everything we have discussed so far still applies. It is important to remember that SPSS may appear to be very clever, but it is not. SPSS will happily generate output based on any garbage you decide to feed into it, it will not judge you or give any indication of whether the model is valid or generalizable. SPSS will provide the information necessary to assess these things, but we need to rely on our brains to evaluate the model – which is slightly worrying (especially if your brain is as small as mine).

The first thing to think about is what predictor variables to enter into the model. A great deal of care should be taken in selecting predictors for a model because the estimates of the regression coefficients depend upon the variables in the model. The predictors included and the way in which they are entered into the model can have a great impact. *Do not select hundreds of random predictors, bung them all into a regression analysis and hope for the best.* You should select predictors based on a sound theoretical rationale or well-conducted past research that has demonstrated their importance.[11] In our example, it seems logical that the band's image and radio play ought to affect sales, so these are sensible predictors. It would not be sensible to measure how much the album cost to make, because this won't affect sales directly: you would just be adding noise to the model. If predictors are being added that have never been looked at before (in your particular context) then select these new variables based on their substantive *theoretical* importance.

8.5.1. Methods of regression ②

In addition to the problem of selecting predictors, there are several ways in which variables can be entered into a model. When predictors are all completely uncorrelated, the order of variable entry has very little effect on the parameters calculated; however, we rarely have uncorrelated predictors and so the method of predictor selection is crucial.

---

[11] I might cynically qualify this suggestion by proposing that predictors be chosen based on past research that has utilized good methodology. If basing such decisions on regression analyses, select predictors based only on past research that has used regression appropriately and yielded reliable, generalizable models.

8.5.1.1. Hierarchical (blockwise entry) ②

In **hierarchical regression** predictors are selected based on past work and the researcher decides in which order to enter the predictors into the model. As a general rule, known predictors (from other research) should be entered into the model first in order of their importance in predicting the outcome. After known predictors have been entered, the experimenter can add any new predictors into the model. New predictors can be entered either all in one go, in a stepwise manner, or hierarchically (such that the new predictor suspected to be the most important is entered first).

8.5.1.2. Forced entry ②

Forced entry (or *Enter* as it is known in SPSS) is a method in which all predictors are forced into the model simultaneously. Like hierarchical, this method relies on good theoretical reasons for including the chosen predictors, but unlike hierarchical the experimenter makes no decision about the order in which variables are entered. Some researchers believe that this method is the only appropriate method for theory testing (Studenmund & Cassidy, 1987) because stepwise techniques are influenced by random variation in the data and so seldom give replicable results if the model is retested.

8.5.1.3. Stepwise methods ②

Stepwise regressions are generally frowned upon by statisticians. Nevertheless, SPSS makes it very easy to do and actively encourages it in the *Automatic Linear Modelling* process (probably because this function is aimed at people who don't know better) – see Oditi's Lantern. I'm assuming that you wouldn't wade through 1000 pages of my drivel unless you wanted to know better, so we'll give stepwise a wide birth. However, you probably ought to know what it does so you can understand why to avoid it.

In **stepwise regressions** decisions about the order in which predictors are entered into the model are based on a purely mathematical criterion. In the *forward* method, an initial model is defined that contains only the constant (b_0). The computer then searches for the predictor (out of the ones available) that best predicts the outcome variable – it does this by selecting the predictor that has the highest simple correlation with the outcome. If this predictor significantly improves the ability of the model to predict the outcome, then this predictor is retained in the model and the computer searches for a second predictor. The criterion used for selecting this second predictor is that it is the variable that has the largest semi-partial correlation with the outcome. In plain English, imagine that the first predictor can explain 40% of the variation in the outcome variable; then there is still 60% left unexplained. The computer searches for the predictor that can explain the biggest part of the remaining 60% (it is not interested in the 40% that is already explained). As such, this semi-partial correlation gives a measure of how much 'new variance' in the outcome can be explained by each remaining predictor (see Section 7.5). The predictor that accounts for the most new variance is added to the model and, if it makes a significant contribution to the predictive power of the model, it is retained and another predictor is considered.

The *stepwise* method in SPSS is the same as the forward method, except that each time a predictor is added to the equation, a removal test is made of the least useful predictor. As such, the regression equation is being reassessed constantly to see whether any redundant predictors can be removed. The *backward* method is the opposite of the forward method in that the computer begins by placing all predictors in the model and then calculating the contribution of each one by looking at the significance value of the *t*-test for each predictor. This significance value is compared against a removal criterion (which can be either an

ODITI'S LANTERN

Automatic linear modelling

'I, Oditi, come with a warning. Your desparation to bring me answers to numerical truths so as to gain a privileged place within my heart may lead you into the temptation that is SPSS's 'automatic linear modelling'. Automatic linear modelling promises answers without thought, and like a cat who is promised a fresh salmon, you will drool and purr in anticipation. If you want to find out more then stare into my lantern, but be warned, sometimes what looks like a juicy salmon is a rotting pilchard in disguise.'

absolute value of the test statistic or a probability value for that test statistic). If a predictor meets the removal criterion (i.e., if it is not making a statistically significant contribution to how well the model predicts the outcome variable) it is removed from the model and the model is re-estimated for the remaining predictors. The contribution of the remaining predictors is then reassessed.

8.5.1.4. Choosing a method ②

SPSS allows you to opt for any one of the methods described, and it is important to select an appropriate one. The short answer to which method to select is 'not stepwise', because stepwise methods rely on the computer selecting variables based upon mathematical criteria. Many writers argue that this takes many important methodological decisions out of the hands of the researcher. What's more, the models derived by computer often take advantage of random sampling variation and so decisions about which variables should be included will be based upon slight differences in their semi-partial correlation. However, these slight statistical differences may contrast dramatically with the theoretical importance of a predictor to the model.

Which method of regression should I use?

There is also the danger of overfitting the model (having too many variables in the model that essentially make little contribution to predicting the outcome) and underfitting it (leaving out important predictors).

The main problem with stepwise methods is that they assess the fit of a variable based on the other variables in the model. Jeremy Miles (who has worked with me on other books) uses the analogy of getting dressed to describe this problem. You wake up in the morning and you need to get dressed: on your dressing table (or floor, if you're me) you have underwear, some jeans, a T-shirt and jacket. Imagine these items are predictor variables. It's a cold day and you're trying to be warm. A stepwise method will put your trousers on first because they fit your goal best. It then looks around and tries the other clothes (variables). It tries to get you to put on your underwear but they won't fit over your jeans, so it decides they are 'a poor fit' and discards them. You end up leaving the house without your underwear. Later on during a university seminar you stand up and your trousers fall down revealing your genitals to the room. It's a mess. The problem is that the underwear was a poor fit only because when you tried to put them on you were already wearing jeans. In stepwise methods, variables might be considered bad predictors only because of what has already been put in the model.

For these reasons, stepwise methods are best avoided except for exploratory model building. If you do decide to use a stepwise method, then let the statistical blood be on your hands, not mine. Use the backward method rather than the forward method to minimize **suppressor effects**, which occur when a predictor has a significant effect but only when another variable is held constant. Forward selection is more likely than backward elimination to exclude predictors involved in suppressor effects. As such, the forward method runs a higher risk of making a Type II error (i.e., missing a predictor that does in fact predict the outcome). It is also advisable to cross-validate your model by splitting the data (see Section 8.3.2.2).

8.5.2. Comparing models ②

Hierarchical and (although obviously you'd never use them) stepwise methods involve adding predictors to the model in stages and it is, of course, useful to know whether these additions improve the model. Given that larger values of R^2 indicate better fit, a simple way to see whether a model has improved as a result of adding predictors to it would be to see whether R^2 for the new model is bigger than for the old model. In fact, it will always get bigger if we add predictors, so the issue is more whether it gets significantly bigger. We can assess the significance of the change in R^2 using equation (8.10), but because we're looking at the change in models we use the change in R^2 (R^2_{change}) and the R^2 of the newer model (R^2_{new}). We also use the change in the number of predictors (k_{change}) as well as the number of predictors in the new model (k_{new}). The equation is thus:

$$F_{change} = \frac{(N - k_{new} - 1)R^2_{change}}{k_{change}(1 - R^2_{new})}$$

(8.15)

We can compare models using this F-ratio. The problem with R^2 is that when you add more variables to the model, it will always go up. So, if you are deciding which of two models fits the data better, the model with more predictor variables in will always fit better. The **Akaike information criterion (AIC)**[12] is a measure of fit which penalizes the model for having more variables. If the AIC is bigger, the fit is worse; if the AIC is smaller, the fit is better. If you use the *Automated Linear Model* function in SPSS, then you can use the AIC to select models rather than the change in R^2. The AIC doesn't mean anything on its own: you cannot say that a value of the AIC of 10 is small, or that a value for the AIC of 1000 is large. The only thing you do with the AIC is compare it to other models with the same outcome variable: if it's getting smaller then the fit of your model is improving.

8.5.3. Multicollinearity ②

A final additional concern when we want to include more than one predictor in our model is multicollinearity, which exists when there is a strong correlation between two or more predictors. **Perfect collinearity** exists when at least one predictor is a perfect linear combination of the others (the simplest example being two predictors that are perfectly correlated – they have a correlation coefficient of 1). If there is perfect collinearity between predictors it becomes impossible to obtain unique estimates of the regression coefficients because there are an infinite number of combinations of coefficients that would work equally well. Put simply, if we have two predictors that are perfectly correlated, then the values of b for each variable are interchangeable. The good news is that perfect collinearity is rare in real-life data. The bad news is that less than perfect collinearity is virtually unavoidable. Low levels of collinearity pose little threat to the model estimates, but as collinearity increases there are three problems that arise:

---

[12] Hirotsugu Akaike (pronounced 'A-ka-ee-kay') was a Japanese statistician who gave his name to the AIC, which is used in a huge range of different places.

- **Untrustworthy *b*s**: As collinearity increases so do the standard errors of the *b* coefficients. If you think back to what the standard error represents, then big standard errors for *b* coefficients means that these *b*s are more variable across samples. Therefore, the *b* coefficient in our sample is less likely to represent the population. Crudely put, multicollinearity means that the *b*-values are less trustworthy. Don't lend them money and don't let them go out to dinner with your boy- or girlfriend. Of course, if the *b*s are variable from sample to sample then the resulting predictor equations will be unstable across samples too.

- **It limits the size of *R***: Remember that *R* is a measure of the correlation between the predicted values of the outcome and the observed values and that R^2 indicates the variance in the outcome for which the model accounts. Imagine a situation in which a single variable predicts the outcome variable fairly successfully (e.g., $R = .80$) and a second predictor variable is then added to the model. This second variable might account for a lot of the variance in the outcome (which is why it is included in the model), but the variance it accounts for is the same variance accounted for by the first variable. In other words, once the variance accounted for by the first predictor has been removed, the second predictor accounts for very little of the remaining variance (the second variable accounts for very little *unique variance*). Hence, the overall variance in the outcome accounted for by the two predictors is little more than when only one predictor is used (so *R* might increase from .80 to .82). This idea is connected to the notion of partial correlation that was explained in Chapter 7. If, however, the two predictors are completely uncorrelated, then the second predictor is likely to account for different variance in the outcome than that accounted for by the first predictor. So, although in itself the second predictor might account for only a little of the variance in the outcome, the variance it does account for is different to that of the other predictor (and so when both predictors are included, *R* is substantially larger, say .95). Therefore, having uncorrelated predictors is beneficial.

- **Importance of predictors**: Multicollinearity between predictors makes it difficult to assess the individual importance of a predictor. If the predictors are highly correlated, and each accounts for similar variance in the outcome, then how can we know which of the two variables is important? Quite simply, we can't – the model could include either one, interchangeably.

One way of identifying multicollinearity is to scan a correlation matrix of the predictor variables and see if any correlate very highly (by 'very highly' I mean correlations of above .80 or .90). This is a good 'ball park' method, but misses more subtle forms of multicollinearity. Luckily, SPSS produces various collinearity diagnostics, one of which is the **variance inflation factor (VIF)**. The VIF indicates whether a predictor has a strong linear relationship with the other predictor(s). Related to the VIF is the **tolerance** statistic, which is its reciprocal (1/VIF). Although there are no hard and fast rules about what value of the VIF should cause concern, there are some general guidelines:

- If the largest VIF is greater than 10 then there is cause for concern (Bowerman & O'Connell, 1990; Myers, 1990).

- If the average VIF is substantially greater than 1 then the regression may be biased (Bowerman & O'Connell, 1990).

- Tolerance below 0.1 indicates a serious problem.

- Tolerance below 0.2 indicates a potential problem (Menard, 1995).

Other measures that are useful in discovering whether predictors are dependent are the *eigenvalues of the scaled, uncentred cross-products matrix*, the *condition indexes* and the *variance proportions.* These statistics are extremely complex and will be covered as part of the interpretation of SPSS output (see Section 8.7.5). If none of this has made any sense then have a look at Hutcheson and Sofroniou (1999, pp. 78–85) who give a really clear explanation of multicollinearity.

8.6. Regression with several predictors using SPSS ②

Remember that for any regression we need to follow the general procedure outlined in Figure 8.11. So, first we might look at some scatterplots of the relationships between the outcome variable and the predictors. The resulting scatterplots for our album sales data are shown in Figure 8.14. We need to focus on the relationship between predictors and the outcome (album sales), and in Figure 8.14 I have shaded out the other scatterplots so we can focus on the three related to album sales.[13] We can see that although the data are messy in places, the three predictors have reasonably linear relationships with the outcome (album sales) and there are no obvious outliers.

FIGURE 8.14

Matrix scatterplot of the relationships between advertising budget, airplay, and attractiveness of the band and album sales

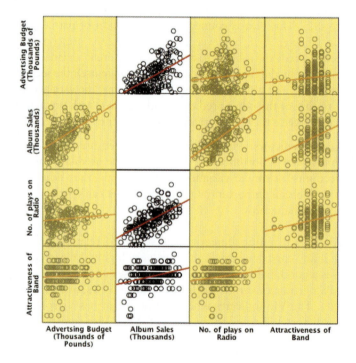

SELF-TEST   Produce a matrix scatterplot of **Sales**, **Adverts**, **Airplay** and **Attract** including the regression line.

[13] I had to edit the font size of the *x*- and *y*-axes to make it smaller (I used size 8); we looked at how to edit graphs in Oditi's Lantern in Chapter 4.

8.6.1. Main options ②

The executive has past research indicating that advertising budget is a significant predictor of album sales, and so he should include this variable in the model first. His new variables (**Airplay** and **Attract**) should, therefore, be entered into the model *after* advertising budget. This method is hierarchical (the researcher decides in which order to enter variables into the model based on past research). To do a hierarchical regression in SPSS we have to enter the variables in blocks (each block representing one step in the hierarchy). To get to the main *Regression* dialog box select Analyze Regression ▸ Linear…. We encountered this dialog box in Figure 8.13 when we looked at a model with only one predictor. Essentially, to set up the first block we do exactly what we did before. Select the outcome variable (album sales) and drag it to the box labelled *Dependent* (or click on). We also need to specify the predictor variable for the first block. We've decided that advertising budget should be entered into the model first, so select this variable in the list and drag it to the box labelled *Independent(s)* (or click on). Underneath the *Independent(s)* box, there is a drop-down menu for specifying the *Method* of regression (see Section 8.5.1). You can select a different method of variable entry for each block by clicking on Enter ▾, next to where it says *Method*. The default option is forced entry, and this is the option we want, but if you were carrying out more exploratory work, you might decide to use one of the stepwise methods (forward, backward, stepwise or remove).

Having specified the first block in the hierarchy, we need to move onto the second. To tell the computer that you want to specify a new block of predictors you must click on Next. This process clears the *Independent(s)* box so that you can enter the new predictors (you should also note that above this box it now reads *Block 2 of 2* indicating that you are in the second block of the two that you have so far specified). We decided that the second block would contain both of the new predictors and so you should click on **Airplay** and **Attract** (while holding down *Ctrl*, or *Cmd* if you use a Mac) in the variables list and drag them to the *Independent(s)* box or click on . The dialog box should now look like Figure 8.15. To move

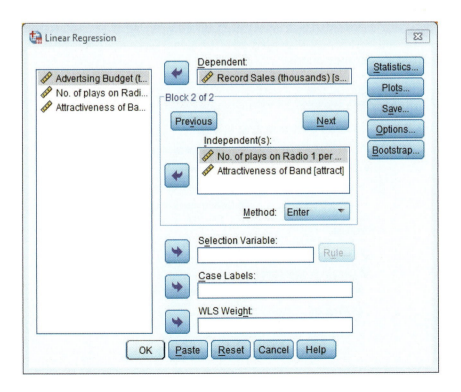

FIGURE 8.15
Main dialog box for block 2 of the multiple regression

between blocks use the Previous and Next buttons (so for example, to move back to block 1, click on Previous).

It is possible to select different methods of variable entry for different blocks in a hierarchy. So although we specified forced entry for the first block, we could now specify a stepwise method for the second. Given that we have no previous research regarding the effects of attractiveness and airplay on album sales, we might be justified in requesting a stepwise method for this block. However, because of the problems with stepwise methods, I am going to stick with forced entry for both blocks in this example.

8.6.2. Statistics ②

In the main *Regression* dialog box click on Statistics... to open a dialog box for selecting various important options relating to the model (see list below and Figure 8.16). Most of these options relate to the parameters of the model; however, there are procedures available for checking the assumptions of no multicollinearity (collinearity diagnostics) and independence of errors (Durbin–Watson). When you have selected the statistics you require (I recommend all but the covariance matrix as a general rule), click on Continue to return to the main dialog box.

- *Estimates*: This option is selected by default because it gives us the estimated coefficients of the regression model (i.e., the estimated *b*-values). Test statistics and their significance are produced for each regression coefficient: a *t*-test is used to see whether each *b* differs significantly from zero (see Section 8.2.5).

- *Confidence intervals*: This option produces confidence intervals for each of the unstandardized regression coefficients. Remember that if the assumptions of regression are not met these confidence intervals will be inaccurate and we should use bootstrap confidence intervals instead.

- *Covariance matrix*: This option produces a matrix of the covariances, correlation coefficients and variances between the regression coefficients of each variable in the model. A variance–covariance matrix is produced with variances displayed along the diagonal and covariances displayed as off-diagonal elements. The correlations are produced in a separate matrix.

FIGURE 8.16
Statistics dialog box for regression analysis

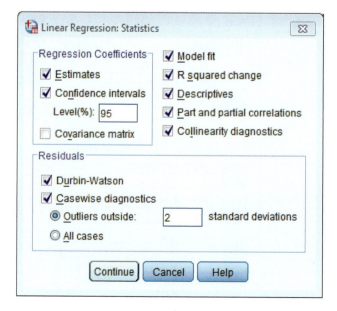

- *Model fit*: This option is vital and so is selected by default. It provides not only a statistical test of the model's ability to predict the outcome variable (the *F*-test described in Section 8.2.4), but also the value of *R*, the corresponding R^2 and the adjusted R^2.

- *R squared change*: This option displays the change in R^2 resulting from the inclusion of a new predictor (or block of predictors). This measure is a useful way to assess the contribution of new predictors (or blocks) to explaining variance in the outcome.

- *Descriptives*: If selected, this option displays a table of the mean, standard deviation and number of observations of all of the variables included in the analysis. A correlation matrix is also displayed showing the correlation between all of the variables and the one-tailed probability for each correlation coefficient. This option is extremely useful because the correlation matrix can be used to assess whether there is multicollinearity.

- *Part and partial correlations*: This option produces the zero-order correlation (the Pearson correlation) between each predictor and the outcome variable. It also produces the partial correlation between each predictor and the outcome, controlling for all other predictors in the model. Finally, it produces the part correlation (or semi-partial correlation) between each predictor and the outcome. This correlation represents the relationship between each predictor and the part of the outcome that is not explained by the other predictors in the model. As such, it measures the unique relationship between a predictor and the outcome (see Section 7.5).

- *Collinearity diagnostics*: This option is for obtaining collinearity statistics such as the VIF, tolerance, eigenvalues of the scaled, uncentred cross-products matrix, condition indexes and variance proportions (see Section 8.5.3).

- *Durbin-Watson*: This option produces the Durbin–Watson test statistic, which tests the assumption of independent errors. Unfortunately, SPSS does not provide the significance value of this test, so you must decide for yourself whether the value is different enough from 2 to be cause for concern (see Section 8.3.2.1).

- *Casewise diagnostics*: This option, if selected, lists the observed value of the outcome, the predicted value of the outcome, the difference between these values (the residual) and this difference standardized. Furthermore, it will list these values either for all cases, or just for cases for which the standardized residual is greater than 3 (when the ± sign is ignored). This criterion value of 3 can be changed, and I recommend changing it to 2 for reasons that will become apparent. A summary table of residual statistics indicating the minimum, maximum, mean and standard deviation of both the values predicted by the model and the residuals (see Section 8.6.4) is also produced.

8.6.3. Regression plots ②

Once you are back in the main dialog box, click on [Plots...] to activate the regression *Plots* dialog box shown in Figure 8.17. This dialog box provides the means to specify several graphs, which can help to establish the validity of some regression assumptions. Most of these plots involve various *residual* values, which will be described in more detail in Section 8.6.4.

On the left-hand side of the dialog box is a list of several variables.

- **DEPENDNT** (the outcome variable).

- ***ZPRED** (the standardized predicted values of the dependent variable based on the model). These values are standardized forms of the values predicted by the model.

- *ZRESID (the standardized residuals, or errors). These values are the standardized differences between the observed data and the values that the model predicts).

- *DRESID (the deleted residuals). See Section 8.3.1.1 for details.

- *ADJPRED (the adjusted predicted values). See Section 8.3.1.1 for details.

- *SRESID (the Studentized residual). See Section 8.3.1.1 for details.

- *SDRESID (the Studentized deleted residual). This value is the deleted residual divided by its standard error.

The variables listed in this dialog box all come under the general heading of residuals. In Section 5.3.3.1 we saw that a plot of *ZRESID (*y*-axis) against *ZPRED (*x*-axis) is useful for testing the assumptions of independent errors, homoscedasticity and linearity. A plot of *SRESID (*y*-axis) against *ZPRED (*x*-axis) will show up any heteroscedasticity also. Although often these two plots are virtually identical, the latter is more sensitive on a case-by-case basis. To create these plots simply select a variable from the list, and transfer it to the space labelled either *X* or *Y* (which refer to the axes) by clicking on . When you have selected two variables for the first plot (as is the case in Figure 8.17) you can specify a new plot by clicking on Next . This process clears the spaces in which variables are specified. If you click on Next and would like to return to the plot that you last specified, then simply click on Previous . You can specify up to nine plots.

You can also tick the box labelled *Produce all partial plots* which will produce scatterplots of the residuals of the outcome variable and each of the predictors when both variables are regressed separately on the remaining predictors. Regardless of whether the previous sentence made any sense to you, these plots have several important characteristics that make them worth inspecting. First, the gradient of the regression line between the two residual variables is equivalent to the coefficient of the predictor in the regression equation. As such, any obvious outliers on a partial plot represent cases that might have undue influence on a predictor's regression coefficient. Second, non-linear relationships between a predictor and the outcome variable are much more detectable using these plots. Finally, they are a useful way of detecting collinearity. For these reasons, I recommend requesting them.

There are several options for plots of the standardized residuals. First, you can select a *Histogram* of the standardized residuals (this is useful for checking the assumption of normality of errors). Second, you can ask for a *Normal probability plot*, which also provides

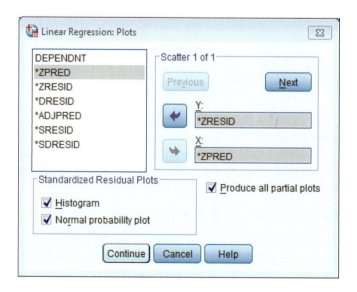

FIGURE 8.17
The *Plots*
dialog box

information about whether the residuals in the model are normally distributed. When you have selected the options you require, click on [Continue] to take you back to the main *Regression* dialog box.

8.6.4. Saving regression diagnostics ②

In Section 8.3 we met two types of regression diagnostics: those that help us assess how well our model fits our sample and those that help us detect cases that have a large influence on the model generated. In SPSS we can choose to save these diagnostic variables in the data editor (so SPSS will calculate them and then create new columns in the data editor in which the values are placed).

To save regression diagnostics you need to click on [Save] in the main *Regression* dialog box. This process activates the *Save* new variables dialog box (see Figure 8.18). Once this dialog box is active, it is a simple matter to tick the boxes next to the required statistics. Most of the available options were explained in Section 8.3, and Figure 8.18 shows what I consider to be a fairly basic set of diagnostic statistics. Standardized (and Studentized) versions of these diagnostics are generally easier to interpret, so I suggest selecting them in preference to the unstandardized versions. Once the regression has been run, SPSS creates a column in your data editor for each statistic requested and it has a standard set of variable names to describe each one. After the name, there will be a number that refers to the analysis that has been run. So, for the first regression run on a data set the variable names will be followed by a 1, if you carry out a second regression it will create a new set of variables with names followed by a 2, and so on. The names of the variables that will be created are below. When you have selected the diagnostics you require (by clicking in the appropriate boxes), click on [Continue] to return to the main *Regression* dialog box.

- **pre_1**: unstandardized predicted value;
- **zpr_1**: standardized predicted value;
- **adj_1**: adjusted predicted value;
- **sep_1**: standard error of predicted value;
- **res_1**: unstandardized residual;
- **zre_1**: standardized residual;
- **sre_1**: Studentized residual;
- **dre_1**: deleted residual;
- **sdr_1**: Studentized deleted residual;
- **mah_1**: Mahalanobis distance;
- **coo_1**: Cook's distance;
- **lev_1**: centred leverage value;
- **sdb0_1**: standardized DFBETA (intercept);
- **sdb1_1**: standardized DFBETA (predictor 1);
- **sdb2_1**: standardized DFBETA (predictor 2);
- **sdf_1**: standardized DFFIT;
- **cov_1**: covariance ratio.

FIGURE 8.18
Dialog box
for regression
diagnostics

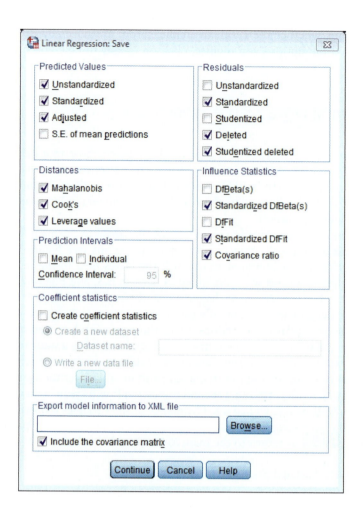

8.6.5. Further options ②

You can click on Options... to take you to the *Options* dialog box (Figure 8.19). The first set of options allows you to change the criteria used for entering variables in a stepwise regression. If you insist on doing stepwise regression, then it's probably best that you leave the default criterion of .05 probability for entry alone. However, you can make this criterion more stringent (.01). There is also the option to build a model that doesn't include a constant (i.e., has no Y intercept). This option should also be left alone. Finally, you can select a method for dealing with missing data points (see SPSS Tip 5.1). By default, SPSS excludes cases listwise, which in regression means that if a person has a missing value for any variable, then they are excluded from the whole analysis. So, for example, if our record company executive didn't have an attractiveness score for one of his bands, their data would not be used in the regression model. Another option is to exclude cases on a pairwise basis, which means that if a participant has a score missing for a particular variable, then their data are excluded only from calculations involving the variable for which they have no score. So, data for the band for which there was no attractiveness rating would still be used to calculate the relationships between advertising budget, airplay and album sales. However, if you do this, many of your variables may not make sense, and you can end up with absurdities such as R^2 either negative or greater than 1.0. So it's not a good option.

Another possibility is to replace the missing score with the average score for this variable and then include that case in the analysis (so our example band would be given an attractiveness

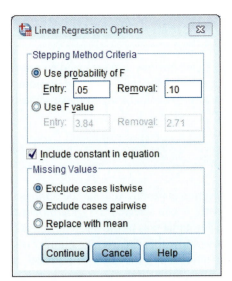

FIGURE 8.19
Options for linear regression

rating equal to the average attractiveness of all bands). The problem with this final choice is that it is likely to suppress the true value of the standard deviation (and, more importantly, the standard error). The standard deviation will be suppressed because for any replaced case there will be no difference between the mean and the score, whereas if data had been collected for that case there would, almost certainly, have been some difference between the score and the mean. Obviously, if the sample is large and the number of missing values small then this is not a serious consideration. However, if there are many missing values this choice is potentially dangerous because smaller standard errors are more likely to lead to significant results that are a product of the data replacement rather than a genuine effect. The final option is to use the *Missing Value Analysis* routine in SPSS. This is for experts. It makes use of the fact that if two or more variables are present and correlated for most cases in the file, and an occasional value is missing, you can replace the missing values with estimates far better than the mean (some of these features are described in Tabachnick & Fidell, 2012, Chapter 4).

8.6.6. Robust regression ②

We can get bootstrapped confidence intervals for the regression coefficients by clicking on Bootstrap... (see Section 5.4.3). However, this function doesn't work when we have used the Save... option to save residuals, so we can't use it now. We will return to robust regression in Section 8.8.

ODITI'S LANTERN

Regression

'I, Oditi, wish to predict when I can take over the world, and rule you pathetic mortals with will of pure iron … erm.. ahem, I mean, I wish to predict how to save cute kittens from the jaws of rabid dogs, because I'm nice like that, and have no aspirations to take over the world. This chapter is so long that some of you will die before you reach the end, so ignore the author's bumbling drivel and stare instead into my lantern of wonderment.'

8.7. Interpreting multiple regression ②

Having selected all of the relevant options and returned to the main dialog box, we need to click on OK to run the analysis. SPSS will spew out copious amounts of output in the viewer window, and we now turn to look at how to make sense of this information.

8.7.1. Descriptives ②

The output described in this section is produced using the options in the *Statistics* dialog box (see Figure 8.16). To begin with, if you selected the *Descriptives* option, SPSS will produce the table seen in Output 8.4. This table tells us the mean and standard deviation of each variable in our data set, so we now know that the average number of album sales was 193,200. This table isn't necessary for interpreting the regression model, but it is a useful summary of the data. In addition to the descriptive statistics, selecting this option produces a correlation matrix. This table shows three things. First, it shows the value of Pearson's correlation coefficient between every pair of variables (e.g., we can see that the advertising budget had a large positive correlation with album sales, $r = .578$). Second, the one-tailed significance of each correlation is displayed (e.g., the correlation above is significant, $p < .001$). Finally, the number of cases contributing to each correlation ($N = 200$) is shown.

You might notice that along the diagonal of the matrix the values for the correlation coefficients are all 1.00 (i.e., a perfect positive correlation). The reason for this is that

OUTPUT 8.4
Descriptive statistics for regression analysis

Descriptive Statistics

	Mean	Std. Deviation	N
Album Sales (Thousands)	193.20	80.699	200
Advertsing Budget (Thousands of Pounds)	614.4123	485.65521	200
No. of plays on Radio	27.50	12.270	200
Attractiveness of Band	6.77	1.395	200

Correlations

		Album Sales (Thousands)	Advertsing Budget (Thousands of Pounds)	No. of plays on Radio	Attractivenes s of Band
Pearson Correlation	Album Sales (Thousands)	1.000	.578	.599	.326
	Advertsing Budget (Thousands of Pounds)	.578	1.000	.102	.081
	No. of plays on Radio	.599	.102	1.000	.182
	Attractiveness of Band	.326	.081	.182	1.000
Sig. (1-tailed)	Album Sales (Thousands)	.	.000	.000	.000
	Advertsing Budget (Thousands of Pounds)	.000	.	.076	.128
	No. of plays on Radio	.000	.076	.	.005
	Attractiveness of Band	.000	.128	.005	.
N	Album Sales (Thousands)	200	200	200	200
	Advertsing Budget (Thousands of Pounds)	200	200	200	200
	No. of plays on Radio	200	200	200	200
	Attractiveness of Band	200	200	200	200

these values represent the correlation of each variable with itself, so obviously the resulting values are 1. The correlation matrix is extremely useful for getting a rough idea of the relationships between predictors and the outcome, and for a preliminary look for multicollinearity. If there is no multicollinearity in the data then there should be no substantial correlations ($r > .9$) between predictors.

If we look only at the predictors (ignore album sales) then the highest correlation is between the attractiveness of the band and the amount of airplay, which is significant at a .01 level ($r = .182$, $p = .005$). Despite the significance of this correlation, the coefficient is small and so it looks as though our predictors are measuring different things (there is no collinearity). We can see also that of all of the predictors the number of plays on radio correlates best with the outcome ($r = .599$, $p < .001$) and so it is likely that this variable will best predict album sales.

CRAMMING SAM'S TIPS   Descriptive statistics

- Use the descriptive statistics to check the correlation matrix for multicollinearity – that is, predictors that correlate too highly with each other, r > .9.

8.7.2. Summary of model ②

The next section of output describes the overall model (so it tells us whether the model is successful in predicting album sales). Remember that we chose a hierarchical method and so each set of summary statistics is repeated for each stage in the hierarchy. In Output 8.5 you should note that there are two models. Model 1 refers to the first stage in the hierarchy when only advertising budget is used as a predictor. Model 2 refers to when all three predictors are used. Output 8.5 is the *model summary* and this table was produced using the *Model fit* option. This option is selected by default in SPSS because it provides us with some very important information about the model: the values of R, R^2 and the adjusted R^2. If the *R squared change* and *Durbin-Watson* options were selected, then these values are included also (if they weren't selected you'll find that you have a smaller table).

Under the model summary table shown in Output 8.5 you should notice that SPSS tells us what the dependent variable (outcome) was and what the predictors were in each of the two models. In the column labelled R are the values of the multiple correlation coefficient

Model Summary^c

Model	R	R Square	Adjusted R Square	Std. Error of the Estimate	Change Statistics R Square Change	F Change	df1	df2	Sig. F Change	Durbin-Watson
1	.578^a	.335	.331	65.991	.335	99.587	1	198	.000	
2	.815^b	.665	.660	47.087	.330	96.447	2	196	.000	1.950

a. Predictors: (Constant), Advertsing Budget (Thousands of Pounds)

b. Predictors: (Constant), Advertsing Budget (Thousands of Pounds), Attractiveness of Band, No. of plays on Radio

c. Dependent Variable: Album Sales (Thousands)

OUTPUT 8.5 Regression model summary

between the predictors and the outcome. When only advertising budget is used as a predictor, this is the simple correlation between advertising and album sales (.578). In fact all of the statistics for model 1 are the same as the simple regression model earlier (see Section 8.4.3). The next column gives us a value of R^2, which we already know is a measure of how much of the variability in the outcome is accounted for by the predictors. For the first model its value is .335, which means that advertising budget accounts for 33.5% of the variation in album sales. However, when the other two predictors are included as well (model 2), this value increases to .665 or 66.5% of the variance in album sales. Therefore, if advertising accounts for 33.5%, we can tell that attractiveness and radio play account for an additional 33%.[14] So, the inclusion of the two new predictors has explained quite a large amount of the variation in album sales.

The adjusted R^2 gives us some idea of how well our model generalizes and ideally we would like its value to be the same as, or very close to, the value of R^2. In this example the difference for the final model is small (in fact the difference between the values is $.665 - .660 = .005$ or 0.5%). This shrinkage means that if the model were derived from the population rather than a sample it would account for approximately 0.5% less variance in the outcome. If you apply Stein's formula you'll get an adjusted value of .653 (Jane Superbrain Box 8.2), which is very close to the observed value of R^2 (.665) indicating that the cross-validity of this model is very good.

JANE SUPERBRAIN 8.2

Maths frenzy ③

We can have a look at how some of the values in the output are computed by thinking back to the theory part of the chapter. For example, looking at the change in R^2 for the first model, we have only one predictor (so $k = 1$) and 200 cases ($N = 200$), so the F comes from equation (8.10):[15]

$$F_{Model1} = \frac{(200 - 1 - 1)0.334648}{1(1 - 0.334648)} = 99.59$$

In model 2 in Output 8.5 two predictors have been added (attractiveness and radio play), so the new model has 3 predictors (k_{new}) and the previous model had only 1, which is a change of 2 (k_{change}). The addition of these two predictors increases R^2 by .330 (R^2_{change}), making the R^2 of the new model .665 (R^2_{new}).[16] The F-ratio for this change comes from equation (8.15):

$$F_{change} = \frac{(N - 3 - 1)0.33}{2(1 - 0.664668)} = 96.44$$

We can also apply Stein's formula (equation (8.12)) to R^2 to get some idea of its likely value in different samples. We replace n with the sample size (200) and k with the number of predictors (3):

$$adjusted\ R^2 = 1 - \left[\left(\frac{n-1}{n-k-1}\right)\left(\frac{n-2}{n-k-2}\right)\left(\frac{n+1}{n}\right)\right](1 - R^2)$$

$$= 1 - \left[(1.015)(1.015)(1.005)\right](0.335)$$

$$= 1 - 0.347$$

$$= .653$$

---

[14] That is, 33% = 66.5% – 33.5% (this value is the *R Square Change* in the table).

[15] To get the same values as SPSS we have to use the exact value of R^2, which is 0.3346480676231 (if you don't believe me double-click on the table in the SPSS output that reports this value, then double-click on the cell of the table containing the value of R^2 and you'll see that .335 becomes the value just mentioned).

[16] The more precise value is 0.664668.

The change statistics are provided only if requested, and these tell us whether the change in R^2 is significant. In Output 8.5, the change is reported for each block of the hierarchy. So, model 1 causes R^2 to change from 0 to .335, and this change in the amount of variance explained gives rise to an F-ratio of 99.59, which is significant with a probability less than .001. In model 2, in which attractiveness and radio play have been added as predictors, R^2 increases by .330, making the R^2 of the new model .665. This increase yields an F-ratio of 96.44 (Jane Superbrain Box 8.2), which is significant ($p < .001$). The change statistics therefore tell us about the difference made by adding new predictors to the model.

Finally, if you requested the Durbin–Watson statistic it will be found in the last column of the table in Output 8.5. This statistic informs us about whether the assumption of independent errors is tenable (see Section 8.3.2.1). As a conservative rule I suggested that values less than 1 or greater than 3 should definitely raise alarm bells (although I urge you to look up precise values for the situation of interest). The closer to 2 that the value is, the better, and for these data the value is 1.950, which is so close to 2 that the assumption has almost certainly been met.

Output 8.6 shows the next part of the output, which contains an ANOVA that tests whether the model is significantly better at predicting the outcome than using the mean as a 'best guess'. Specifically, the F-ratio represents the ratio of the improvement in prediction that results from fitting the model, relative to the inaccuracy that still exists in the model (see Section 8.2.4). This table is again split into two sections, one for each model. We are told the value of the sum of squares for the model (this value is SS_M in Section 8.2.4 and represents the improvement in prediction resulting from fitting a regression line to the data rather than using the mean as an estimate of the outcome). We are also told the residual sum of squares (this value is SS_R in Section 8.2.4 and represents the total difference between the model and the observed data). We are also told the degrees of freedom (df) for each term. In the case of the improvement due to the model, this value is equal to the number of predictors (1 for the first model and 3 for the second), and for SS_R it is the number of observations (200) minus the number of coefficients in the regression model. The first model has two coefficients (one for the predictor and one for the constant) whereas the second has four (one for each of the three predictors and one for the constant). Therefore, model 1 has 198 degrees of freedom whereas model 2 has 196. The average sum of squares (MS) is then calculated for each term by dividing the SS by the df. The F-ratio is calculated by dividing the average improvement in prediction by the model (MS_M) by the average difference between the model and the observed data (MS_R). If the improvement due to fitting the regression model is much greater than the inaccuracy within the model then the value of F will be greater than 1, and SPSS calculates the exact probability of obtaining the value of F by chance. For the initial model the F-ratio is 99.59, $p < .001$. For the second the F-ratio is 129.498 – also highly significant

OUTPUT 8.6

ANOVA[a]

Model		Sum of Squares	df	Mean Square	F	Sig.
1	Regression	433687.833	1	433687.833	99.587	.000[b]
	Residual	862264.167	198	4354.870		
	Total	1295952.00	199			
2	Regression	861377.418	3	287125.806	129.498	.000[c]
	Residual	434574.582	196	2217.217		
	Total	1295952.00	199			

a. Dependent Variable: Album Sales (Thousands)

b. Predictors: (Constant), Advertising Budget (Thousands of Pounds)

c. Predictors: (Constant), Advertising Budget (Thousands of Pounds), Attractiveness of Band, No. of plays on Radio

($p < .001$). We can interpret these results as meaning that both models significantly improved our ability to predict the outcome variable compared to not fitting the model.

8.7.3. Model parameters ②

So far we have looked at whether or not the model has improved our ability to predict the outcome variable. The next part of the output is concerned with the parameters of the model. Output 8.7 shows the model parameters for both steps in the hierarchy. Now, the first step in our hierarchy was to include advertising budget (as we did for the simple regression earlier in this chapter) and so the parameters for the first model are identical to the parameters obtained in Output 8.3. Therefore, we will discuss only the parameters for the final model (in which all predictors were included). The format of the table of coefficients will depend on the options selected. The confidence interval for the *b*-values, collinearity diagnostics and the part and partial correlations will be present only if selected in the dialog box in Figure 8.16.

Remember that in multiple regression the model takes the form of equation (8.6), and in that equation there are several unknown parameters (the *b*-values). The first part of the table gives us estimates for these *b*-values, and these values indicate the individual contribution of each predictor to the model. By replacing the *b*-values in equation (8.6) we can define our specific model as:

$$\text{sales}_i = b_0 + b_1\text{advertising}_i + b_2\text{airplay}_i + b_3\text{attractiveness}_i$$
$$= -26.61 + \left(0.08\ \text{advertising}_i\right) + \left(3.37\ \text{airplay}_i\right) + \left(11.09\ \text{attractiveness}_i\right) \quad (8.16)$$

The *b*-values tell us about the relationship between album sales and each predictor. If the value is positive we can tell that there is a positive relationship between the predictor and the outcome, whereas a negative coefficient represents a negative relationship. For these data all three predictors have positive *b*-values indicating positive relationships. So, as advertising budget increases, album sales increase; as plays on the radio increase, so do album sales; and finally, more attractive bands will sell more albums. The *b*-values tell us more than this, though. They tell us to what degree each predictor affects the outcome *if the effects of all other predictors are held constant*.

Coefficients^a

Model		Unstandardized Coefficients		Standardized Coefficients	t	Sig.	95.0% Confidence Interval for B	
		B	Std. Error	Beta			Lower Bound	Upper Bound
1	(Constant)	134.140	7.537		17.799	.000	119.278	149.002
	Advertising Budget (Thousands of Pounds)	.096	.010	.578	9.979	.000	.077	.115
2	(Constant)	−26.613	17.350		−1.534	.127	−60.830	7.604
	Advertising Budget (Thousands of Pounds)	.085	.007	.511	12.261	.000	.071	.099
	No. of plays on Radio	3.367	.278	.512	12.123	.000	2.820	3.915
	Attractiveness of Band	11.086	2.438	.192	4.548	.000	6.279	15.894

a. Dependent Variable: Album Sales (Thousands)

Coefficients^a

Model		Correlations			Collinearity Statistics	
		Zero-order	Partial	Part	Tolerance	VIF
1	Advertising Budget (Thousands of Pounds)	.578	.578	.578	1.000	1.000
2	Advertising Budget (Thousands of Pounds)	.578	.659	.507	.986	1.015
	No. of plays on Radio	.599	.655	.501	.959	1.043
	Attractiveness of Band	.326	.309	.188	.963	1.038

a. Dependent Variable: Album Sales (Thousands)

OUTPUT 8.7
Coefficients of the regression model[17]

- **Advertising budget** ($b = 0.085$): This value indicates that as advertising budget increases by one unit, album sales increase by 0.085 units. Both variables were measured in thousands; therefore, for every £1000 more spent on advertising, an extra 0.085 thousand albums (85 albums) are sold. This interpretation is true only if the effects of attractiveness of the band and airplay are held constant.

- **Airplay** ($b = 3.367$): This value indicates that as the number of plays on radio in the week before release increases by one, album sales increase by 3.367 units. Therefore, every additional play of a song on radio (in the week before release) is associated with an extra 3.367 thousand albums (3367 albums) being sold. This interpretation is true only if the effects of attractiveness of the band and advertising are held constant.

- **Attractiveness** ($b = 11.086$): This value indicates that a band rated one unit higher on the attractiveness scale can expect additional album sales of 11.086 units. Therefore, every unit increase in the attractiveness of the band is associated with an extra 11.086 thousand albums (11,086 albums) being sold. This interpretation is true only if the effects of radio airplay and advertising are held constant.

Each of the beta values has an associated standard error indicating to what extent these values would vary across different samples, and these standard errors are used to determine whether or not the b-value differs significantly from zero. As we saw in Section 8.4.3.2, a t-statistic can be derived that tests whether a b-value is significantly different from 0. With only one predictor a significant value of t indicates that the slope of the regression line is significantly different from horizontal, but with many predictors it is not so easy to visualize what the value tells us. Instead, it is easiest to conceptualize the t-tests as measures of whether the predictor is making a significant contribution to the model. Therefore, if the t-test associated with a b-value is significant (if the value in the column labelled *Sig.* is less than .05) then the predictor is making a significant contribution to the model. The smaller the value of *Sig.* (and the larger the value of t), the greater the contribution

---

[17] To spare your eyesight I have split this part of the output into two tables; however, it should appear as one long table in the SPSS viewer.

of that predictor. For this model, the advertising budget, $t(196) = 12.26$, $p < .001$, the amount of radio play prior to release, $t(196) = 12.12$, $p < .001$ and attractiveness of the band, $t(196) = 4.55$, $p < .001$, are all significant predictors of album sales.[18] Remember that these significance tests are accurate only if the assumptions discussed in Chapter 5 are met. From the magnitude of the t-statistics we can see that the advertising budget and radio play had a similar impact, whereas the attractiveness of the band had less impact.

The b-values and their significance are important statistics to look at; however, the standardized versions of the b-values are probably easier to interpret (because they are not dependent on the units of measurement of the variables). The standardized beta values (labelled as Beta, β_i) tell us the number of standard deviations that the outcome will change as a result of one standard deviation change in the predictor. The standardized beta values are all measured in standard deviation units and so are directly comparable: therefore, they provide a better insight into the 'importance' of a predictor in the model. The standardized beta values for airplay and advertising budget are virtually identical (.512 and .511 respectively) indicating that both variables have a comparable degree of importance in the model (this concurs with what the magnitude of the t-statistics told us). To interpret these values literally, we need to know the standard deviations of all of the variables, and these values can be found in Output 8.4.

- **Advertising budget** (*standardized β = .511*): This value indicates that as advertising budget increases by one standard deviation (£485,655), album sales increase by 0.511 standard deviations. The standard deviation for album sales is 80,699 and so this constitutes a change of 41,240 sales (0.511 × 80,699). Therefore, for every £485,655 more spent on advertising, an extra 41,240 albums are sold. This interpretation is true only if the effects of attractiveness of the band and airplay are held constant.

- **Airplay** (*standardized β = .512*): This value indicates that as the number of plays on radio in the week before release increases by one standard deviation (12.27), album sales increase by 0.512 standard deviations. The standard deviation for album sales is 80,699 and so this constitutes a change of 41,320 sales (0.512 × 80,699). Therefore, if Radio 1 plays the song an extra 12.27 times in the week before release, 41,320 extra album sales can be expected. This interpretation is true only if the effects of attractiveness of the band and advertising are held constant.

- **Attractiveness** (*standardized β = .192*): This value indicates that a band rated one standard deviation (1.40 units) higher on the attractiveness scale can expect additional album sales of 0.192 standard deviations units. This constitutes a change of 15,490 sales (0.192 × 80,699). Therefore, a band with an attractiveness rating 1.40 higher than another band can expect 15,490 additional sales. This interpretation is true only if the effects of radio airplay and advertising are held constant.

 SELF-TEST   Think back to what the confidence interval of the mean represented (Section 2.5.2). Can you work out what the confidence interval for b represents?

---

[18] For all of these predictors I wrote $t(196)$. The number in brackets is the degrees of freedom. We saw in Section 8.2.5 that in regression the degrees of freedom are $N - p - 1$, where N is the total sample size (in this case 200) and p is the number of predictors (in this case 3). For these data we get $200 - 3 - 1 = 196$.

We are also given the confidence intervals for the betas (again these are accurate only if the assumptions discussed in Chapter 5 are met). Imagine that we collected 100 samples of data measuring the same variables as our current model. For each sample we could create a regression model to represent the data. If the model is reliable then we hope to find very similar parameters (bs) in all samples. The confidence intervals of the unstandardized beta values are boundaries constructed such that in 95% of samples these boundaries contain the population value of b (see Section 2.5.2). Therefore, if we'd collected 100 samples, and calculated the confidence intervals for b, we are saying that 95% of these confidence intervals would contain the true value of b. Therefore, we can be fairly confident that the confidence interval we have constructed for this sample will contain the true value of b in the population. This being so, a good model will have a small confidence interval, indicating that the value of b in this sample is close to the true value of b in the population. The sign (positive or negative) of the b-values tells us about the direction of the relationship between the predictor and the outcome. Therefore, we would expect a very bad model to have confidence intervals that cross zero, indicating that in the population the predictor could have a negative relationship to the outcome but could also have a positive relationship. In this model the two best predictors (advertising and airplay) have very tight confidence intervals, indicating that the estimates for the current model are likely to be representative of the true population values. The interval for attractiveness is wider (but still does not cross zero), indicating that the parameter for this variable is less representative, but nevertheless significant.

If you asked for part and partial correlations, then they will appear in the output in separate columns of the table. The zero-order correlations are the simple Pearson's correlation coefficients (and so correspond to the values in Output 8.4). The partial correlations represent the relationships between each predictor and the outcome variable, controlling for the effects of the other two predictors. The part correlations represent the relationship between each predictor and the outcome, controlling for the effect that the other two variables have on the outcome. In effect, these part correlations represent the unique relationship that each predictor has with the outcome. If you opt to do a stepwise regression, you would find that variable entry is based initially on the variable with the largest zero-order correlation and then on the part correlations of the remaining variables. Therefore, airplay would be entered first (because it has the largest zero-order correlation), then advertising budget (because its part correlation is bigger than attractiveness) and then finally attractiveness – try running a forward stepwise regression on these data to see if I'm right. Finally, we are given details of the collinearity statistics, but these will be discussed in Section 8.7.5.

CRAMMING SAM'S TIPS   Model parameters

- The individual contribution of variables to the regression model can be found in the *Coefficients* table from SPSS. If you have done a hierarchical regression then look at the values for the final model.
- For each predictor variable, you can see if it has made a significant contribution to predicting the outcome by looking at the column labelled *Sig.* (values less than .05 are significant).
- The standardized beta values tell you the importance of each predictor (bigger absolute value = more important).
- The tolerance and VIF values will also come in handy later on, so make a note of them.

8.7.4. Excluded variables ②

At each stage of a regression analysis SPSS provides a summary of any variables that have not yet been entered into the model. In a hierarchical model, this summary has details of the variables that have been specified to be entered in subsequent steps, and in stepwise regression this table contains summaries of the variables that SPSS is considering entering into the model. For this example, there is a summary of the excluded variables (Output 8.8) for the first stage of the hierarchy (there is no summary for the second stage because all predictors are in the model). The summary gives an estimate of each predictor's beta value if it was entered into the equation at this point and calculates a *t*-test for this value. In a stepwise regression, SPSS should enter the predictor with the highest *t*-statistic and will continue entering predictors until there are none left with *t*-statistics that have significance values less than .05. The partial correlation also provides some indication as to what contribution (if any) an excluded predictor would make if it were entered into the model.

OUTPUT 8.8

Excluded Variables[a]

Model		Beta In	t	Sig.	Partial Correlation	Collinearity Statistics		
						Tolerance	VIF	Minimum Tolerance
1	No. of plays on Radio	.546[b]	12.513	.000	.665	.990	1.010	.990
	Attractiveness of Band	.281[b]	5.136	.000	.344	.993	1.007	.993

a. Dependent Variable: Album Sales (Thousands)

b. Predictors in the Model: (Constant), Advertsing Budget (Thousands of Pounds)

8.7.5. Assessing multicollinearity ②

Output 8.7 provided some measures of whether there is collinearity in the data. Specifically, it provided the VIF and tolerance statistics (with tolerance being 1 divided by the VIF). We can apply the guidelines from Section 8.5.3 to our model. The VIF values are all well below 10 and the tolerance statistics all well above 0.2; therefore, we can safely conclude that there is no collinearity within our data. To calculate the average VIF we simply add the VIF values for each predictor and divide by the number of predictors (*k*):

$$\overline{\text{VIF}} = \frac{\sum_{i=1}^{k} \text{VIF}_i}{k} = \frac{1.015 + 1.043 + 1.038}{3} = 1.032$$

The average VIF is very close to 1 and this confirms that collinearity is not a problem for this model.

SPSS also produces a table of eigenvalues of the scaled, uncentred cross-products matrix, condition indexes and variance proportions. There is a lengthy discussion, and example, of collinearity in Section 19.8.2 and how to detect it using variance proportions, so I will limit myself now to saying that we are looking for large variance proportions on the same *small* eigenvalues (Jane Superbrain Box 8.3). Therefore, in Output 8.9 we look at the bottom few rows of the table (these are the small eigenvalues) and look for any variables that both have high variance proportions for that eigenvalue. The variance proportions vary between 0 and 1, and for each predictor should be distributed across different dimensions (or eigenvalues). For this model, you can see that each predictor has most of its variance loading onto a different dimension (advertising has 96% of variance on dimension 2, airplay has 93% of variance on dimension 3 and attractiveness has 92% of variance on dimension 4).

These data represent a classic example of no multicollinearity. For an example of when collinearity exists in the data and some suggestions about what can be done, see Chapters 19 (Section 19.8.2) and 17 (Section 17.3.3.3).

Collinearity Diagnostics[a]

OUTPUT 8.9

Model	Dimension	Eigenvalue	Condition Index	Variance Proportions			
				(Constant)	Advertsing Budget (Thousands of Pounds)	No. of plays on Radio	Attractivenes s of Band
1	1	1.785	1.000	.11	.11		
	2	.215	2.883	.89	.89		
2	1	3.562	1.000	.00	.02	.01	.00
	2	.308	3.401	.01	.96	.05	.01
	3	.109	5.704	.05	.02	.93	.07
	4	.020	13.219	.94	.00	.00	.92

a. Dependent Variable: Album Sales (Thousands)

CRAMMING SAM'S TIPS Multicollinearity

- To check for multicollinearity, use the VIF values from the table labelled *Coefficients* in the SPSS output.
- If these values are less than 10, then there probably isn't cause for concern.
- If you take the average of VIF values, and it is not substantially greater than 1, then there's also no cause for concern.

JANE SUPERBRAIN Box 8.3

What are eigenvectors and eigenvalues? ④

The definitions and mathematics of eigenvalues and eigenvectors are very complicated and most of us need not worry about them (although they do crop up again in Chapters 16 and 17). However, although the mathematics is hard, they are quite easy to visualize. Imagine we have two variables: the salary a supermodel earns in a year, and how attractive she is. Also imagine these two

variables are normally distributed and so can be considered together as a bivariate normal distribution. If these variables are correlated, then their scatterplot forms an ellipse: if we draw a dashed line around the outer values of the scatterplot we get something oval shaped (Figure 8.20). We can draw two lines to measure the length and height of this ellipse. These lines are the *eigenvectors* of the original correlation matrix for these two variables (a vector is just a set of numbers that tells us the location of a line in geometric space). Note that the two lines we've drawn (one for height and one for width of the oval) are perpendicular; that is, they are at 90 degrees to each other, which means that they are independent of one another. So, with two variables, eigenvectors are just lines measuring the length and height of the ellipse that surrounds the scatterplot of data for those variables.

If we add a third variable (e.g., the length of experience of the supermodel) then all that happens is our scatterplot

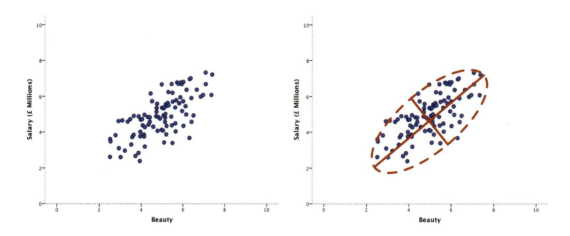

FIGURE 8.20   A scatterplot of two variables forms an ellipse

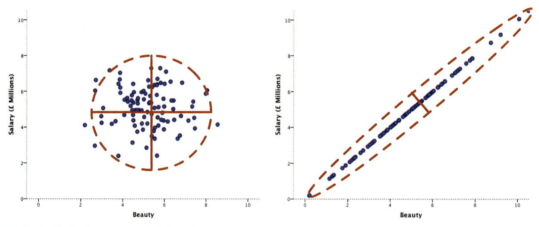

FIGURE 8.21   Perfectly uncorrelated (left) and correlated (right) variables

gets a third dimension, the ellipse turns into something shaped like a rugby ball (or American football), and because we now have a third dimension (height, width and depth) we get an extra eigenvector to measure this extra dimension. If we add a fourth variable, a similar logic applies (although it's harder to visualize): we get an extra dimension, and an eigenvector to measure that dimension. Each eigenvector has an *eigenvalue* that tells us its length (i.e., the distance from one end of the eigenvector to the other). So, by looking at all of the eigenvalues for a data set, we know the dimensions of the ellipse or rugby ball: put more generally, we know the dimensions of the data. Therefore, the eigenvalues show how evenly (or otherwise) the variances of the matrix are distributed.

In the case of two variables, the *condition* of the data is related to the ratio of the larger eigenvalue to the smaller. Figure 8.21 shows the two extremes: when there is no relationship at all between variables (left), and

when there is a perfect relationship (right). When there is no relationship, the scatterplot will be contained roughly within a circle (or a sphere if we had three variables). If we draw lines that measure the height and width of this circle we'll find that these lines are the same length. The eigenvalues measure the length, therefore the eigenvalues will also be the same. So, when we divide the largest eigenvalue by the smallest we'll get a value of 1 (because the eigenvalues are the same). When the variables are perfectly correlated (i.e., there is perfect collinearity) then the scatterplot forms a straight line and the ellipse surrounding it will also collapse to a straight line. Therefore, the height of the ellipse will be very small indeed (it will approach zero). Therefore, when we divide the largest eigenvalue by the smallest we'll get a value that tends to infinity (because the smallest eigenvalue is close to zero). Therefore, an infinite condition index is a sign of deep trouble.

8.7.6. Bias in the model: casewise diagnostics ②

The final stage of the general procedure outlined in Figure 8.11 is to check the residuals for evidence of bias. We do this in two stages. The first is to examine the casewise diagnostics, and the second is to check the assumptions discussed in Chapter 5. SPSS produces a summary table of the residual statistics, and these should be examined for extreme cases. Output 8.10 shows any cases that have a standardized residual less than −2 or greater than 2 (remember that we changed the default criterion from 3 to 2 in Figure 8.16). I mentioned in Section 8.3.1.1 that in an ordinary sample we would expect 95% of cases to have standardized residuals within about ±2. We have a sample of 200, therefore it is reasonable to expect about 10 cases (5%) to have standardized residuals outside of these limits. From Output 8.10 we can see that we have 12 cases (6%) that are outside the limits: therefore, our sample is within 1% of what we would expect. In addition, 99% of cases should lie within ±2.5 and so we would expect only 1% of cases to lie outside these limits. From the cases listed here, it is clear that two cases (1%) lie outside of the limits (cases 164 and 169). Therefore, our sample appears to conform to what we would expect for a fairly accurate model. These diagnostics give us no real cause for concern except that case 169 has a standardized residual greater than 3, which is probably large enough for us to investigate further.

Casewise Diagnostics[a]

OUTPUT 8.10

Case Number	Std. Residual	Album Sales (Thousands)	Predicted Value	Residual
1	2.125	330	229.92	100.080
2	−2.314	120	228.95	−108.949
10	2.114	300	200.47	99.534
47	−2.442	40	154.97	−114.970
52	2.069	190	92.60	97.403
55	−2.424	190	304.12	−114.123
61	2.098	300	201.19	98.810
68	−2.345	70	180.42	−110.416
100	2.066	250	152.71	97.287
164	−2.577	120	241.32	−121.324
169	3.061	360	215.87	144.132
200	−2.064	110	207.21	−97.206

a. Dependent Variable: Album Sales (Thousands)

You may remember that in Section 8.6.4 we asked SPSS to save various diagnostic statistics. You should find that the data editor now contains columns for these variables. It is perfectly acceptable to check these values in the data editor, but you can also get SPSS to list the values in your viewer window too. To list variables you need to use the *Case Summaries* command, which can be found by selecting Analyze Reports ▸ Case Summaries… . Figure 8.22 shows the dialog box for this function. Simply select the variables that you want to list and transfer them to the box labelled *Variables* by clicking on ▸. By default, SPSS will limit the output to the first 100 cases, but if you want to list all of your cases then deselect this option (see also SPSS Tip 8.1). It is also very important to select the *Show case numbers* option to enable you to tell the case number of any problematic cases.

To save space, Output 8.11 shows the influence statistics for 12 cases that I selected. None of them have a Cook's distance greater than 1 (even case 169 is well below this criterion) and so none of the cases has an undue influence on the model. The average leverage can be calculated as $(k + 1)/n = 4/200 = 0.02$, and so we are looking for values either twice as large as this (0.04) or three times as large (0.06) depending on which statistician

FIGURE 8.22
The *Summarize Cases* dialog box

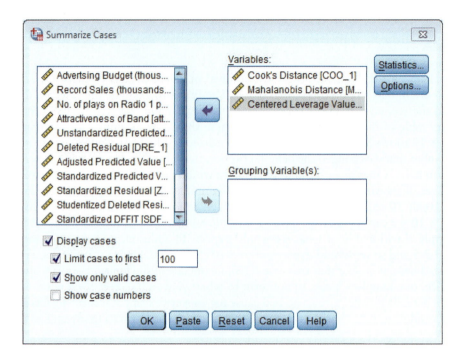

SPSS TIP 8.1   Selecting cases ③

In large data sets, a useful strategy when summarizing cases is to use SPSS's *Select Cases* function (see Section 5.4.2) and to set conditions that will select problematic cases. For example, you could create a variable that selects cases with a Cook's distance greater than 1 by running this syntax:

```
USE ALL.
COMPUTE cook_problem=(COO_1 > 1).
VARIABLE LABELS cook_problem 'Cooks distance greater than 1'.
VALUE LABELS cook_problem 0 'Not Selected' 1 'Selected'.
FILTER BY cook_problem.
EXECUTE.
```

This syntax creates a variable called **cook_problem**, based on whether Cook's distance is greater than 1 (the *compute* command), it labels this variable as 'Cooks distance greater than 1' (the *variable labels* command), sets value labels to be 1 = include, 0 = exclude (the *value labels* command), and finally filters the data set by this new variable (the *filter by* command). Having selected cases, you can use case summaries to see which cases meet the condition you set (in this case having Cook's distance greater than 1).

you trust most (see Section 8.3.1.2). All cases are within the boundary of three times the average and only case 1 is close to two times the average.

Finally, from our guidelines for the Mahalanobis distance we saw that with a sample of 100 and three predictors, values greater than 15 were problematic. Also, with three predictors, values greater than 7.81 are significant ($p < .05$). None of our cases come close to

Case Summaries[a]

	Case Number	Standardized DFBETA Intercept	Standardized DFBETA Adverts	Standardized DFBETA Airplay	Standardized DFBETA Attract	Standardized DFFIT	COVRATIO
1	1	-.31554	-.24235	.15774	.35329	.48929	.97127
2	2	.01259	-.12637	.00942	-.01868	-.21110	.92018
3	10	-.01256	-.15612	.16772	.00672	.26896	.94392
4	47	.06645	.19602	.04829	-.17857	-.31469	.91458
5	52	.35291	-.02881	-.13667	-.26965	.36742	.95995
6	55	.17427	-.32649	-.02307	-.12435	-.40736	.92486
7	61	.00082	-.01539	.02793	.02054	.15562	.93654
8	68	-.00281	.21146	-.14766	-.01760	-.30216	.92370
9	100	.06113	.14523	-.29984	.06766	.35732	.95888
10	164	.17983	.28988	-.40088	-.11706	-.54029	.92037
11	169	-.16819	-.25765	.25739	.16968	.46132	.85325
12	200	.16633	-.04639	.14213	-.25907	-.31985	.95435
Total N	12	12	12	12	12	12	12

a. Limited to first 100 cases.

Case Summaries[a]

	Case Number	Cook's Distance	Mahalanobis Distance	Centered Leverage Value
1	1	.05870	8.39591	.04219
2	2	.01089	.59830	.00301
3	10	.01776	2.07154	.01041
4	47	.02412	2.12475	.01068
5	52	.03316	4.81841	.02421
6	55	.04042	4.19960	.02110
7	61	.00595	.06880	.00035
8	68	.02229	2.13106	.01071
9	100	.03136	4.53310	.02278
10	164	.07077	6.83538	.03435
11	169	.05087	3.14841	.01582
12	200	.02513	3.49043	.01754
Total N	12	12	12	12

a. Limited to first 100 cases.

exceeding the criterion of 15, although a few would be deemed 'significant' (e.g., case 1). The evidence does not suggest major problems with no influential cases within our data (although all cases would need to be examined to confirm this fact).

We can look also at the DFBeta statistics to see whether any case would have a large influence on the regression parameters. An absolute value greater than 1 is a problem and in all cases the values lie within ±1, which shows that these cases have no undue influence over the regression parameters.

There is also a column for the covariance ratio. We saw in Section 8.3.1.2 that we need to use the following criteria:

- $\text{CVR}_i > 1 + [3(k + 1)/n] = 1 + [3(3 + 1)/200] = 1.06,$
- $\text{CVR}_i < 1 - [3(k + 1)/n] = 1 - [3(3 + 1)/200] = 0.94.$

Therefore, we are looking for any cases that deviate substantially from these boundaries. Most of our 12 potential outliers have CVR values within or just outside these boundaries. The only case that causes concern is case 169 (again) whose CVR is some way below the bottom limit. However, given the Cook's distance for this case, there is probably little cause for alarm.

You would have requested other diagnostic statistics, and from what you know from the earlier discussion of them you would be well advised to glance over them in case of any unusual cases in the data. However, from this minimal set of diagnostics we appear to have a fairly reliable model that has not been unduly influenced by any subset of cases.

CRAMMING SAM'S TIPS   **Residuals**

You need to look for cases that might be influencing the regression model:

- Look at standardized residuals and check that no more than 5% of cases have absolute values above 2, and that no more than about 1% have absolute values above 2.5. Any case with a value above about 3 could be an outlier.
- Look in the data editor for the values of Cook's distance: any value above 1 indicates a case that might be influencing the model.
- Calculate the average leverage (the number of predictors plus 1, divided by the sample size) and then look for values greater than twice or three times this average value.
- For Mahalanobis distance, a crude check is to look for values above 25 in large samples (500) and values above 15 in smaller samples (100). However, Barnett and Lewis (1978) should be consulted for more detailed analysis.
- Look for absolute values of DFBeta greater than 1.
- Calculate the upper and lower limit of acceptable values for the covariance ratio, CVR. The upper limit is 1 plus three times the average leverage, while the lower limit is 1 minus three times the average leverage. Cases that have a CVR that falls outside these limits may be problematic.

8.7.7. Bias in the model: assumptions ②

The general procedure outlined in Figure 8.11 suggests that, having fitted a model, we need to look for evidence of bias, and the second stage of this process is to check some assumptions. I urge you to review Chapter 5 to remind yourself of the main assumptions and the implications of violating them. We have already looked for collinearity within the data and used Durbin–Watson to check whether the residuals in the model are independent. We saw in Section 5.3.3.1 that we can look for heteroscedasticity and non-linearity using a plot of standardized residuals against standardized predicted values. We asked for this plot in Section 8.6.3. If everything is OK then this graph should look like a random array of dots, if the graph funnels out then that is a sign of heteroscedasticity and any curve suggests non-linearity (see Figure 5.20). Figure 8.23 (top left) shows the graph for our model. Note how the points are randomly and evenly dispersed throughout the plot. This pattern is indicative of a situation in which the assumptions of linearity and homoscedasticity have been met. Compare this with the examples in Figure 5.20.

Figure 8.23 also shows the partial plots, which are scatterplots of the residuals of the outcome variable and each of the predictors when both variables are regressed separately on the remaining predictors. Obvious outliers on a partial plot represent cases that might have undue influence on a predictor's regression coefficient, and non-linear relationships and heteroscedasticity can be detected using these plots as well. For advertising budget (Figure 8.23, top right) the partial plot shows the strong positive relationship to album sales. There are no obvious outliers on this plot, and the cloud of dots is evenly spaced out around the line, indicating homoscedasticity. For airplay (Figure 8.23, bottom left) the partial plot shows a strong positive relationship to album sales. The pattern of the residuals is similar to advertising (which would be expected, given the similarity of the standardized betas of these predictors). There are no obvious outliers on this plot, and the cloud of dots is evenly spaced around the line, indicating homoscedasticity. For attractiveness (Figure 8.23, bottom right) the plot again shows a positive relationship to album sales. The relationship looks less linear than for the other predictors, and the dots show some funnelling, indicating greater spread

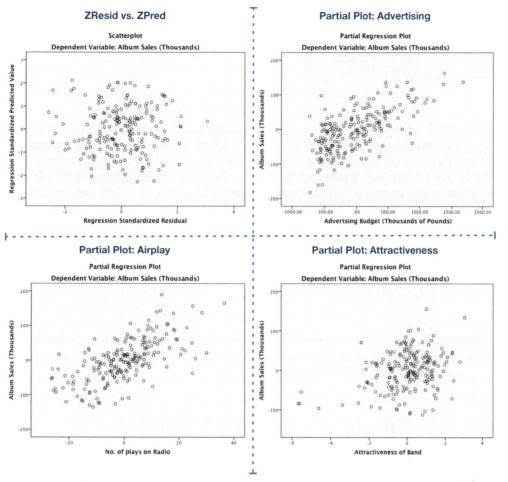

FIGURE 8.23
Plot of
standardized
predicted
values against
standardized
residuals (top
left), and partial
plots of album
sales against
advertising
(top right),
airplay (bottom
left) and
attractiveness
of the band
(bottom right)

at high levels of attractiveness. There are no obvious outliers on this plot, but the funnel-shaped cloud of dots might indicate a violation of the assumption of homoscedasticity.

To test the normality of residuals, we look at the histogram and normal probability plot selected in Figure 8.17. Figure 8.24 shows the histogram and normal probability plot of the data for the current example. Compare these to examples of non-normality in Section 5.3.2.1. For the album sales data, the distribution is very normal: the histogram is symmetrical and approximately bell-shaped. The P-P plot shows up deviations from normality as deviations

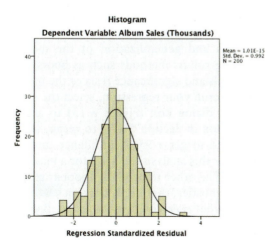

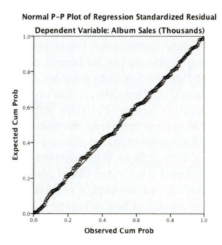

FIGURE 8.24
Histograms
and normal
P-P plots
of normally
distributed
residuals (left-
hand side) and
non-normally
distributed
residuals (right-
hand side)

CRAMMING SAM'S TIPS   **Model assumptions**

- Look at the graph of ZRESID* plotted against ZPRED*. If it looks like a random array of dots then this is good. If the dots seem to get more or less spread out over the graph (look like a funnel) then this is probably a violation of the assumption of homogeneity of variance. If the dots have a pattern to them (i.e., a curved shape) then this is probably a violation of the assumption of linearity. If the dots seem to have a pattern and are more spread out at some points on the plot than others then this probably reflects violations of both homogeneity of variance *and* linearity. Any of these scenarios puts the validity of your model into question. Repeat the above for all partial plots too.
- Look at histograms and P-P plots. If the histograms look like normal distributions (and the P-P plot looks like a diagonal line), then all is well. If the histogram looks non-normal and the P-P plot looks like a wiggly snake curving around a diagonal line then things are less good. Be warned, though: distributions can look very non-normal in small samples even when they are normal.

from the diagonal line (see Section 5.3.2.1). For our model, the dots lie almost exactly along the diagonal, which as we know indicates a normal distribution: hence this plot also suggests that the residuals are normally distributed.

8.8. What if I violate an assumption? Robust regression ②

We could summarize by saying that our model appears, in most senses, to be both accurate for the sample and generalizable to the population. The only slight glitch is some concern over whether attractiveness ratings had violated the assumption of homoscedasticity. Therefore, we could conclude that in our sample, advertising budget and airplay are fairly equally important in predicting album sales. Attractiveness of the band is a significant predictor of album sales but is less important than the other two predictors (and probably needs verification because of possible heteroscedasticity). The assumptions seem to have been met and so we can probably assume that this model would generalize to any album being released. However, this won't always be the case: there will be times when you uncover problems. It's worth looking carefully at Chapter 5 to see exactly what the implications are of violating assumptions, but in brief it will invalidate significance tests, confidence intervals and generalization of the model. These problems can be largely overcome by using robust methods such as bootstrapping (Section 5.4.3) to generate confidence intervals and significance tests of the model parameters. Therefore, if you uncover problems, rerun your regression, select the same options as before, but click ⬚Bootstrap⬚ in the main dialog box (Figure 8.13) to access the bootstrap function. We discussed this dialog box in Section 5.4.3; to recap, select ☑ Perform bootstrapping to activate bootstrapping, and to get a 95% confidence interval click ◉ Per̲centile or ◉ B̲ias corrected accelerated (BCa). For this analysis, let's ask for a bias corrected and accelerated (BCa) confidence interval. The other thing is that bootstrapping doesn't appear to work if you ask SPSS to save diagnostics; therefore, click on ⬚Save...⬚ to open the dialog box in Figure 8.18 and *make sure that everything is deselected*. Back in the main dialog box, click on ⬚OK⬚ to run the analysis.

ONG, E. Y. L., ET AL. (2011). *PERSONALITY AND INDIVIDUAL DIFFERENCES.* 50(2), 180–185.

LABCOAT LENI'S REAL RESEARCH 8.1

I want to be loved (on Facebook) ①

Social media websites such as Facebook seem to have taken over the world. These websites offer an unusual opportunity to carefully manage your self-presentation to others (i.e., you can try to appear to be cool when in fact you write statistics books, appear attractive when you have huge pustules all over your face, fashionable when you wear 1980s heavy metal band T-shirts, and so on). Ong et al. (2011) conducted an interesting study that examined the relationship between narcissism and behaviour on Facebook in 275 adolescents. They measured the **Age**, **Gender** and **Grade** (at school), as well as extroversion and narcissism. They also measured how

often (per week) these people updated their Facebook status (**FB_Status**), and also how they rated their own profile picture on each of four dimensions: coolness, glamour, fashionableness and attractiveness. These ratings were summed as an indicator of how positively they perceived the profile picture they had selected for their page (**FB_Profile_TOT**). They hypothesized that narcissism would predict, above and beyond the other variables, the frequency of status updates, and how positive a profile picture the person chose. To test this, they conducted two hierarchical regressions: one with **FB_Status** as the outcome and one with **FB_Profile_TOT** as the outcome. In both models they entered **Age, Gender** and **Grade** in the first block, then added extroversion (**NEO_FFI**) in a second block, and finally narcissism (**NPQC_R**) in a third block. The data from this study are in the file **Ong et al. (2011).sav**. Labcoat Leni wants you to replicate their two hierarchical regressions and create a table of the results for each. Answers are on the companion website (or look at Table 2 in the original article).

The main difference will be a table of bootstrap confidence intervals for each predictor and their significance value.[19] These tell us that advertising, $b = 0.09$ [0.07, 0.10], $p = .001$, airplay, $b = 3.37$ [2.74, 4.02], $p = .001$, and attractiveness of the band, $b = 11.09$ [6.46, 15.01], $p = .001$, all significantly predict album sales. Note that as before, the bootstrapping

OUTPUT 8.12

Coefficients[a]

Model		Unstandardized Coefficients B	Std. Error	Standardized Coefficients Beta	t	Sig.	95.0% Confidence Interval for B Lower Bound	Upper Bound
1	(Constant)	134.140	7.537		17.799	.000	119.278	149.002
	Advertsing Budget (Thousands of Pounds)	.096	.010	.578	9.979	.000	.077	.115
2	(Constant)	-26.613	17.350		-1.534	.127	-60.830	7.604
	Advertsing Budget (Thousands of Pounds)	.085	.007	.511	12.261	.000	.071	.099
	No. of plays on Radio	3.367	.278	.512	12.123	.000	2.820	3.915
	Attractiveness of Band	11.086	2.438	.192	4.548	.000	6.279	15.894

a. Dependent Variable: Album Sales (Thousands)

Bootstrap for Coefficients

Model		B	Bias	Std. Error	Sig. (2-tailed)	BCa 95% Confidence Interval Lower	Upper
1	(Constant)	134.140	-.116	7.952	.001	120.108	148.793
	Advertsing Budget (Thousands of Pounds)	.096	.000	.008	.001	.079	.112
2	(Constant)	-26.613	.489	16.295	.097	-55.403	8.595
	Advertsing Budget (Thousands of Pounds)	.085	.000	.007	.001	.072	.098
	No. of plays on Radio	3.367	.010	.321	.001	2.735	4.022
	Attractiveness of Band	11.086	-.119	2.221	.001	6.458	15.013

a. Unless otherwise noted, bootstrap results are based on 1000 bootstrap samples

[19] Remember that because of how bootstrapping works the values in your output will be slightly different than mine, and different again if you rerun the analysis.

process involves re-estimating the standard errors, so these have changed for each predictor (although not dramatically). The main benefit of the bootstrap confidence intervals and significance values is that they do not rely on assumptions of normality or homoscedasticity, so they give us an accurate estimate of the true population value of b for each predictor.

8.9. How to report multiple regression ②

If your model has several predictors then you can't really beat a summary table as a concise way to report your model. As a bare minimum, report the betas, their confidence interval, significance value and some general statistics about the model (such as the R^2). The standardized beta values and the standard errors are also very useful. Personally I like to see the constant as well because then readers of your work can construct the full regression model if they need to. For hierarchical regression you should report these values at each stage of the hierarchy. So, basically, you want to reproduce the table labelled *Coefficients* from the SPSS output and omit some of the non-essential information. For the example in this chapter we might produce a table like that in Table 8.2.

Look back through the SPSS output in this chapter and see if you can work out from where the values came. Things to note are: (1) I've rounded off to 2 decimal places throughout because this is a reasonable level of precision given the variables measured; (2) for the standardized betas there is no zero before the decimal point (because these values shouldn't exceed 1) but for all other values less than 1 the zero is present; (3) often you'll see that the significance of the variable is denoted by an asterisk with a footnote to indicate the significance level being used, but it's better practice to report exact p-values; (4) the R^2 for the initial model and the change in R^2 (denoted as ΔR^2) for each subsequent step of the model are reported below the table; and (5) in the title I have mentioned that confidence intervals and standard errors in the table are based on bootstrapping – this information is important for readers to know.

TABLE 8.2   Linear model of predictors of album sales, with 95% bias corrected and accelerated confidence intervals reported in parentheses. Confidence intervals and standard errors based on 1000 bootstrap samples

	b	$SE\ B$	β	p
Step 1				
Constant	134.14 (120.11, 148.79)	7.95		$p = .001$
Advertising Budget	0.10 (0.08, 0.11)	0.01	.58	$p = .001$
Step 2				
Constant	−26.61 (−55.40, 8.60)	16.30		$p = .097$
Advertising Budget	0.09 (0.07, 0.10)	0.01	.51	$p = .001$
Plays on BBC Radio 1	3.37 (2.74, 4.02)	0.32	.51	$p = .001$
Attractiveness	11.09 (6.46, 15.01)	2.22	.19	$p = .001$

Note. $R^2 = .34$ for Step 1; $\Delta R^2 = .33$ for Step 2 (ps < .001).

CHAMORRO-PREMUZIC, T., et al. (2008), *PERSONALITY AND INDIVIDUAL DIFFERENCES*, 44, 965–976.

LABCOAT LENI'S REAL RESEARCH 8.2

Why do you like your lecturers? ①

In the previous chapter we encountered a study by Chamorro-Premuzic et al. in which they measured students' personality characteristics and asked them to rate how much they wanted these same characteristics in their lecturers (see Labcoat Leni's Real Research 7.1 for a full description). In that chapter we correlated these scores; however, we could go a step further and see whether students' personality characteristics predict the characteristics that they would like to see in their lecturers.

The data from this study are in the file **Chamorro-Premuzic.sav.** Labcoat Leni wants you to carry out five multiple regression analyses: the outcome variable in each of the five analyses is the ratings of how much students want to see neuroticism, extroversion, openness to experience, agreeableness and conscientiousness. For each of these outcomes, force age and gender into the analysis in the first step of the hierarchy, then in the second block force in the five student personality traits (neuroticism, extroversion, openness to experience, agreeableness and conscientiousness). For each analysis create a table of the results. Answers are on the companion website (or look at Table 4 in the original article).

8.10. Brian's attempt to woo Jane ①

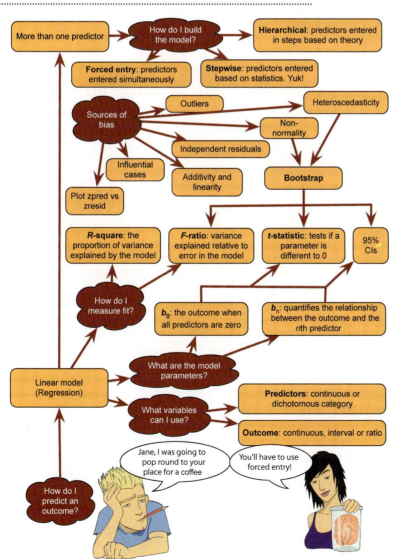

FIGURE 8.25
What Brian learnt from this chapter

8.11.   What next? ①

This chapter is possibly the longest book chapter ever written, and if you feel like you aged several years while reading it then, well, you probably have (look around, there are cobwebs in the room, you have a long beard, and when you go outside you'll discover a second ice age has been and gone, leaving only you and a few woolly mammoths to populate the planet). However, on the plus side, you now know more or less everything you ever need to know about statistics. Really, it's true; you'll discover in the coming chapters that everything else we discuss is basically a variation of this chapter. So, although you may be near death having spent your life reading this chapter (and I'm certainly near death having written it) you are officially a stats genius – well done!

We started the chapter by discovering that at 8 years old I could have really done with regression analysis to tell me which variables are important in predicting talent competition success. Unfortunately I didn't have regression, but fortunately I had my dad instead (and he's better than regression). He correctly predicted the recipe for superstardom, but in doing so he made me hungry for more. I was starting to get a taste for the rock-idol lifestyle: I had friends, a fortune (well, two gold-plated winner's medals), fast cars (a bike) and dodgy-looking 8-year-olds were giving me suitcases full of lemon sherbet to lick off of mirrors. The only things needed to complete the job were a platinum selling album and a heroin addiction. However, before that my parents and teachers were about to impress reality upon my young mind …

8.12.   Key terms that I've discovered

Adjusted predicted value	Heteroscedasticity	Residual sum of squares
Adjusted R^2	Hierarchical regression	Shrinkage
Autocorrelation	Homoscedasticity	Simple regression
b_i	Independent errors	Standardized DFBeta
β_i	Leverage	Standardized DFFit
Cook's distance	Mahalanobis distances	Standardized residuals
Covariance ratio (CVR)	Mean squares	Stepwise regression
Cross-validation	Model sum of squares	Studentized deleted residuals
Deleted residual	Multicollinearity	Studentized residuals
DFBeta	Multiple r	Suppressor effects
DFFit	Multiple regression	t-statistic
Dummy variables	Ordinary least squares (OLS)	Tolerance
Durbin–Watson test	Outcome variable	Total sum of squares
F-ratio	Perfect collinearity	Unstandardized residuals
Generalization	Predicted value	Variance inflation factor (VIF)
Goodness of fit	Predictor variable	
Hat values	Residual	

8.13.   Smart Alex's tasks

- **Task 1:** In Chapter 3 (Task 6) we looked at data based on findings that the number of cups of tea drunk was related to cognitive functioning (Feng et al., 2010). The data are in the file **Tea Makes You Brainy 716.sav**. Using the model that predicts cognitive functioning from tea drinking, what would cognitive functioning be if someone drank 10 cups of tea? Is there a significant effect? ①

- **Task 2**: Run a regression analysis for the **pubs.sav** data in Jane Superbrain Box 8.1 predicting **mortality** from the number of **pubs**. Try repeating the analysis but bootstrapping the confidence intervals. ②

- **Task 3**: In Jane Superbrain Box 2.1 we saw some data (**HonestyLab.sav**) relating to people's ratings of dishonest acts and the likeableness of the perpetrator. Run a regression using bootstrapping to predict ratings of dishonesty from the likeableness of the perpetrator. ②

- **Task 4**: A fashion student was interested in factors that predicted the salaries of cat-walk models. She collected data from 231 models. For each model she asked them their salary per day on days when they were working (**Salary**), their age (**Age**), how many years they had worked as a model (**Years**), and then got a panel of experts from modelling agencies to rate the attractiveness of each model as a percentage, with 100% being perfectly attractive (**Beauty**). The data are in the file **Supermodel. sav**. Unfortunately, this fashion student bought a substandard statistics textbook and so doesn't know how to analyse her data.☺ Can you help her out by conducting a multiple regression to see which variables predict a model's salary? How valid is the regression model? ②

- **Task 5**: A study was carried out to explore the relationship between **Aggression** and several potential predicting factors in 666 children who had an older sibling. Variables measured were **Parenting_Style** (high score = bad parenting practices), **Computer_ Games** (high score = more time spent playing computer games), **Television** (high score = more time spent watching television), **Diet** (high score = the child has a good diet low in harmful additives), and **Sibling_Aggression** (high score = more aggression seen in their older sibling). Past research indicated that parenting style and sibling aggression were good predictors of the level of aggression in the younger child. All other variables were treated in an exploratory fashion. The data are in the file **Child Aggression.sav**. Analyse them with multiple regression. ②

- **Task 6**: Repeat the analysis in Labcoat Leni's Real Research 8.1 using bootstrapping for the confidence intervals. What are the confidence intervals for the regression parameters? ①

- **Task 7**: Coldwell, Pike, and Dunn (2006) investigated whether household chaos predicted children's problem behaviour over and above parenting. From 118 families they recorded the age and gender of the youngest child (**Child_age** and **Child_ gender**). They then interviewed the child about their relationship with their mum using the Berkeley Puppet Interview (BPI), which measures (1) warmth/enjoyment (**Child_warmth**), and (2) anger/hostility (**Child_anger**). Higher scores indicate more anger/hostility and warmth/enjoyment, respectively. Each mum was interviewed about their relationship with the child resulting in scores for relationship positivity (**Mum_pos**) and relationship negativity (**Mum_neg**). Household chaos (**Chaos**) was assessed using the Confusion, Hubbub, and Order Scale. The outcome variable was the child's adjustment (**sdq**): the higher the score, the more problem behaviour the child is reported to be displaying. The data are in the file **Coldwell et al. (2006).sav**. Conduct a hierarchical regression in three steps: (1) enter child age and gender; (2) add the variables measuring parent–child positivity, parent–child negativity, parent–child warmth and parent–child anger; (3) add chaos. Is household chaos predictive of children's problem behaviour over and above parenting? ③

Answers can be found on the companion website.

8.14. Further reading

Baguley, T. (2012). *Serious stats: A guide to advanced statistics for the behavioural sciences*. Basingstoke: Palgrave Macmillan.

Bowerman, B. L., & O'Connell, R. T. (1990). *Linear statistical models: An applied approach* (2nd ed.). Belmont, CA: Duxbury. (This text is only for the mathematically minded or postgraduate students, but provides an extremely thorough exposition of regression analysis.)

Miles, J. N. V., & Shevlin, M. (2001). *Applying regression and correlation: A guide for students and researchers*. London: Sage. (This is an extremely readable text that covers regression in loads of detail but with minimum pain – highly recommended.)

Comparing two means

9

FIGURE 9.1
Practising for my career as a rock star by slaying the baying throng of Grove Primary School at the age of 10 (note the girl with her hands covering her ears)

9.1. What will this chapter tell me? ①

We saw in the previous chapter that I had successfully conquered the holiday camps of Wales with my singing and guitar playing (and the Welsh know a thing or two about good singing). I had jumped on a snowboard called oblivion and thrown myself down the black run known as world domination. About 10 metres after starting this slippery descent I hit the lumpy patch of ice called 'adults'. I was 9, life was fun, and yet every adult I encountered seemed obsessed with my future. 'What do you want to be when you grow up?' they would ask. Would I be a surgeon, a lawyer, a teacher? I was 9 and 'grown up' was a lifetime away. All I knew was that I was going to marry Clair Sparks (more on her in the next chapter) and be a rock legend who didn't need to worry about such adult matters as having a job. It was a difficult question, but adults require answers and I wasn't going to let them know that I didn't care about 'grown-up' matters. Like all good scientists I drew upon past data: I hadn't tried conducting brain surgery, neither did I have experience of sentencing psychopaths to prison sentences for eating their husbands, nor had I taught anyone. I had, however, had a go at singing and playing guitar; therefore, I predicted I would be a rock star. However, even at this early age I realized that not all adults would appreciate the raw talent that would surely see me parading across the lighted stage in front of tens of thousands of people. Some of them might not think that rock stardom was a good career prospect. I needed to convince them. Adults tend to think money is important, so I decided I should demonstrate that rock stars earn more money than, say, a 'respectable' profession such as being a teacher. I could gather some teachers and rock stars, find out what their salaries were and compare them. Effectively I'd be 'predicting' salary from two categories: rock star or teacher. This would require a *t*-test. I didn't know about *t*-tests when I was 9. Happy days.

9.2. Looking at differences ①

So far we have tended to focus on relationships between variables; however, sometimes researchers are interested in looking at differences between groups of people. In particular, in experimental research we often want to manipulate what happens to people so that we can make causal inferences. The simplest form of experiment that can be done is one with only one independent variable that is manipulated in only two ways and only one outcome is measured. More often than not the manipulation of the independent variable involves having an experimental condition and a control group (see Field & Hole, 2003). Some examples of this kind of design are:

- Is the movie *Scream 2* scarier than the original *Scream*? We could measure heart rates (which indicate anxiety) during both films and compare them.

- Does listening to Andy's favourite music while you work improve your work? You could get some people to write an essay (or book) listening to my favourite music (as listed in the Acknowledgements), and then write a different essay when working in silence (this is a control group). You could then compare the essay grades.

- Do diet pills work? Suppose we take two groups of people and randomly assign one group a programme of diet pills and the other group a programme of sugar pills (which they believe will help them lose weight). If the people who take the dieting pills lose more weight than those on the sugar pills we can infer that the diet pills caused the weight loss.

Manipulating the independent variable systematically is a powerful research tool because it goes one step beyond merely observing variables.[1] This chapter is the first of many that look at this kind of research scenario, and we start with the simplest scenario: when we have two groups, or, to be more specific, when we want to compare two means. As we have seen (Chapter 1), there are two different ways of collecting data: we can either expose different people to different experimental manipulations (*between-group* or *independent* design), or take a single group of people and expose them to different experimental manipulations at different points in time (a *repeated-measures* or *within-subjects* design). Sometimes people are tempted to compare artificially created groups by, for example, dividing people into groups based on a median score; however, this is generally a bad idea (see Jane Superbrain Box 9.1).

---

[1] People sometimes get confused and think that certain statistical procedures allow causal inferences and others don't (see Jane Superbrain Box 1.4).

JANE SUPERBRAIN 9.1

Are median splits the devil's work? ②

In research papers you sometimes see that people have analysed their data using a 'median split'. For example, there is a stereotype that science fiction fans are recluses with no social skills. If you wanted to test this you might measure knowledge of the film *Star Wars* and social skills. You might then take the median score on *Star Wars* knowledge and classify anyone with a score above the median as a '*Star Wars* fan', and those below the median as a 'non-fan'. In doing this you 'dichotomize' a continuous variable. This practice is quite common, but is it sensible?

MacCallum, Zhang, Preacher, and Rucker (2002) wrote a splendid paper pointing out various problems in turning a perfectly decent continuous variable into a categorical variable:

1 Imagine there are four people: Peter, Birgit, Jip and Kiki. We measure how much they know about *Star Wars* as a percentage and get Jip (100%), Kiki (60%), Peter (40%) and Birgit (0%). If we split these four people at the median (50%) then we're saying that Jip and Kiki are the same (they get a score of 1 = fanatic) and Peter and Birgit are the same (they both get a score of 0 = not a fanatic). In reality, Kiki and Peter are the most similar of the four people, but they have been put in different groups. So, median splits change the original information quite dramatically (Peter and Kiki are originally very similar but become very different after the split, Jip and Kiki are relatively dissimilar originally but become identical after the split).

2 Effect sizes get smaller: If you correlate two continuous variables then the effect size will be larger than if you correlate the same variables after one of them has been dichotomized. Effect sizes also get smaller in ANOVA and regression.

3 There is an increased chance of finding spurious effects.

So, if your supervisor has just told you to do a median split, have a good think about whether it is the right thing to do and read up on the topic (I recommend DeCoster, Gallucci, & Iselin, 2011; DeCoster, Iselin, & Gallucci, 2009; MacCallum, et al., 2002). One of the rare situations in which dichotomizing a continuous variable is justified, according to MacCallum et al., is when there is a clear theoretical rationale for distinct categories of people based on a meaningful break point (i.e., not the median); for example, phobic versus not phobic based on diagnosis by a trained clinician would be a legitimate dichotomization of anxiety.

9.2.1. An example: are invisible people mischievous? ①

Two news stories caught my eye that related to some physics research (Di Falco, Ploschner, & Krauss, 2010). In the first headline (November 2010) the *Daily Mirror* (a UK newspaper) reported 'Scientists make Harry Potter's invisible cloak'. I'm not really a *Harry Potter* aficionado,[2] so it wasn't his mention that caught my attention, but the idea of being able to don a cloak that would render me invisible and able to get up to mischief was very exciting indeed. Where could I buy one? By February 2011 the same newspaper was reporting on a different piece of research (Chen, et al., 2011), but it came with a slightly more sedate headline: 'Harry Potter-style "invisibility cloak" built by scientists'.

Needless to say, scientists hadn't actually made Harry Potter's cloak of invisibility. Di Falco et al. had created a flexible material (Metaflex) that had optical properties that

---

[2] Perhaps I should be, given that a UK newspaper once tagged me 'the Harry Potter of the social sciences' (http://www.discoveringstatistics.com/docs/thes_170909.pdf). I wasn't sure whether this made me a heroic wizard battling against the evil forces of statistics, or an adult with a mental age of 11.

meant that if you layered it up you might be able to create something around which light would bend. Not exactly a cloak in the clothing sense of the word, but easier to wear than, say, a slab of granite. Chen et al. also hadn't made a 'cloak of invisibility' in the clothing sense, but had created a calcite lump of invisibility. This could hide small objects (centimetres and millimetres in scale): you could conceal my brain but little else. Nevertheless, with a suitably large piece of calcite in tow, I could theoretically hide my whole body (although people might get suspicious of the apparently autonomous block of calcite manoeuvring itself around the room on a trolley).

Although the newspapers probably overstated the case a little, these are two very exciting pieces of research that bring the possibility of a cloak of invisibility closer to a reality. So, I imagine a future in which we have some cloaks of invisibility to test out. As a psychologist (with his own slightly mischievous streak) I might be interested in the effect that wearing a cloak of invisibility has on people's tendency for mischief. I took 24 participants and placed them in an enclosed community. The community was riddled with hidden cameras so that we could record mischievous acts. Half of the paricipants were given cloaks of invisibility: they were told not to tell anyone else about their cloak and they could wear it whenever they liked. We measured how many mischievous acts they performed in a week. These data are in Table 9.1.

TABLE 9.1   Data from **Invisibility.sav**

Participant	Cloak	Mischief
1	0	3
2	0	1
3	0	5
4	0	4
5	0	6
6	0	4
7	0	6
8	0	2
9	0	0
10	0	5
11	0	4
12	0	5
13	1	4
14	1	3
15	1	6
16	1	6
17	1	8
18	1	5
19	1	5
20	1	4
21	1	2
22	1	5
23	1	7
24	1	5

SELF-TEST   Enter these data into SPSS.

The file **Invisibility.sav** shows how you should have entered the data: the variable **Cloak** records whether or not a person was given a cloak (**cloak** = 1) or not (**cloak** = 0), and **Mischief** is how many mischievous acts were performed.

SELF-TEST   Produce some descriptive statistics for these data (using *Explore*).

Output 9.1 (your table will have more stuff in it – I edited mine down to save space) shows some descriptive statistics for these data: notice that more mischievous acts were performed by people who had an invisibility cloak, $M = 5$, 95% CI [3.95, 6.05], $SD = 1.65$, than those that did not, $M = 3.75$, 95% CI [2.53, 4.97], $SD = 1.91$. Not that we should trust these tests (see Jane Superbrain Box 5.5), but both groups' scores are normally distributed because the K-S tests have significance values greater than .05.

Descriptives

OUTPUT 9.1

Cloak of invisibility			Statistic	Std. Error
Mischievous Acts	No Cloak	Mean	3.75	.552
		95% Confidence Interval for Mean	Lower Bound	2.53	
			Upper Bound	4.97	
		5% Trimmed Mean	3.83	
		Median	4.00	
		Variance	3.659	
		Std. Deviation	1.913	
		Skewness	-.789	.637
		Kurtosis	-.229	1.232
	Cloak	Mean	5.00	.477
		95% Confidence Interval for Mean	Lower Bound	3.95	
			Upper Bound	6.05	
		5% Trimmed Mean	5.00	
		Median	5.00	
		Variance	2.727	
		Std. Deviation	1.651	
		Skewness	.000	.637
		Kurtosis	.161	1.232

Tests of Normality

	Cloak of invisibility	Kolmogorov–Smirnov[a]			Shapiro-Wilk		
		Statistic	df	Sig.	Statistic	df	Sig.
Mischievous Acts	No Cloak	.219	12	.118	.913	12	.231
	Cloak	.167	12	.200*	.973	12	.936

*. This is a lower bound of the true significance.

a. Lilliefors Significance Correction

9.2.2. Categorical predictors in the linear model ①

If we want to compare differences between the means of two groups, all we are really doing is predicting an outcome based on membership of two groups. For our invisibility example, we're predicting the number of mischievous acts from whether or not someone had a cloak of invisibility. This is a regression with one dichotomous predictor. The b for the model will reflect the differences between the mean levels of mischief between the two groups, and the resulting t-test will, therefore, tell us whether the difference between means is different from zero (because, remember, the t-test tests whether $b = 0$).

The astute among you might be thinking 'bs show relationships, not differences between means – what is this fool going on about?'. You might be starting to mistrust me, or are stuffing the book back in a box to post it back for a refund. I wouldn't blame you, because I used to think this too. To tame a land like the complex, thorny, weed-infested, Andy-eating and tarantula-inhabited world of statistics you need an epiphany, and mine came in the form of a paper by Cohen (1968). This paper showed me how when we compare means we are also using a linear model, which turned my statistical world into a beautiful meadow filled with bleating little lambs all jumping for joy at the wonder of life.

Recall from Chapter 2 that all statistical models are more or less elaborate versions of this model:

$$\text{outcome}_i = (\text{model}) + \text{error}_i$$

If we want to use a linear model, then we saw that this general equation becomes equation (8.1) in which the model is defined by parameters: b_0 tells us the value of the outcome when the predictor is zero, and b_1 quantifies the relationship between the predictor (X_i) and outcome (Y_i). We've seen this equation lots of times, but let's make it a bit more concrete for our example. We can use this equation to predict the variable **Mischief** from the group to which a person belongs (the variable **Cloak**):

$$Y_i = (b_0 + b_1 X_{1i}) + \varepsilon_i$$

$$\text{Mischief}_i = (b_0 + b_1 \text{Cloak}_i) + \varepsilon_i \tag{9.1}$$

The problem we have is that **Cloak** is a nominal variable: people had a 'cloak' or 'no cloak'. We can't put words into a statistical model because it will burn a hole in the ozone layer. Instead, we have to convert this variable into numbers – in exactly the same way as we do when we enter nominal variables into SPSS (see Section 3.5.2.3). When we enter nominal variables into SPSS it doesn't really matter what numbers we choose, but if we're going to stick numbers into a mathematical model then it does matter which number we choose to represent the categories of a nominal variable. There are different ways to code variables (which we won't get into here); one of them is to use **dummy variables**. We'll look at these in more detail in Section 10.5.1, but in essence it means we code a baseline category with a 0, and other categories with a 1. In this example there are two categories, our baseline category is no cloak (this is the control condition) and so we assign these participants a 0 for the variable cloak, and the 'experimental' group is those who were given a cloak and so we assign these a 1. In fact, this is the same coding we used in the SPSS file. Let's plug these numbers into the model and see what happens.

First, let's imagine someone is in the no cloak condition. What would be the best prediction we could make of the number of mischievous acts for someone in that group? Our best guess would be the group mean (which is 3.75 in Output 9.1). So, the value of Y in the equation will be the group mean $\bar{X}_{\text{No Cloak}}$, and the value of the **Cloak** variable will be 0. As such, equation (9.1) becomes (if we ignore the residual term):

$$\text{Mischief}_i = b_0 + b_1 \text{Cloak}_i$$

$$\bar{X}_{\text{No Cloak}} = b_0 + (b_1 \times 0)$$

$$b_0 = \bar{X}_{\text{No Cloak}}$$

$$b_0 = 3.75$$

Therefore, b_0 (the intercept) is equal to the mean of the no cloak group (i.e., it is the mean of the group coded as 0). Now let's look at what happens when we use the model to predict mischief in people who had an invisibility cloak. Again, the outcome we'd predict for such a person would be the mean of the cloak group $\bar{X}_{\text{Cloak}}$, which was 5 in Output 9.1, and the value of the **Cloak** variable will be 1. Remembering that we have just found out that b_0 is equal to the mean of the no cloak group ($\bar{X}_{\text{No Cloak}}$), equation (9.1) becomes:

$$\text{Mischief}_i = b_0 + b_1 \text{Cloak}_i$$

$$\bar{X}_{\text{Cloak}} = b_0 + (b_1 \times 1)$$

$$\bar{X}_{\text{Cloak}} = b_0 + b_1$$

$$\bar{X}_{\text{Cloak}} = \bar{X}_{\text{No Cloak}} + b_1$$

$$b_1 = \bar{X}_{\text{Cloak}} - \bar{X}_{\text{No Cloak}}$$

b_1, therefore, represents the difference between the group means (in this case $5 - 3.75 = 1.25$). As such, we can compare two group means using the same linear model that we have used throughout the book. In this model, b_1 represents the difference between group means, and b_0 is equal to the mean of the group coded as 0. We have seen that a *t*-test is used to ascertain whether the regression coefficient (b_1) is equal to 0; and in this context it will be testing whether the difference between group means is equal to 0.

SELF-TEST To prove that I'm not making it up as I go along, run a regression on the data in **Invisibility.sav** with **Cloak** as the predictor and **Mischief** as the outcome. **Cloak** is coded using zeros and ones as for the dummy variable described above.

The resulting SPSS output should contain the regression summary table shown in Output 9.2. The first thing to notice is the value of the constant (b_0): its value is 3.75, the same as the mean of the base category (the no cloak group). The second thing to notice is that the value of the regression coefficient b_1 is 1.25, which is the difference between the two group means ($5 - 3.75 = 1.25$). Finally, the *t*-statistic, which tests whether b_1 is significantly different from zero, is not significant because the significance value is greater than .05, which means that the difference between means (1.25) is not significantly different from 0. This section has demonstrated that differences between means can be represented in terms of linear models, and this concept is essential in understanding the following chapters on the general linear model.

OUTPUT 9.2

Coefficients[a]

Model		Unstandardized Coefficients		Standardized Coefficients	t	Sig.
		B	Std. Error	Beta		
1	(Constant)	3.750	.516		7.270	.000
	Cloak of invisibility	1.250	.730	.343	1.713	.101

a. Dependent Variable: Mischievous Acts

9.3. The *t*-test ①

What's the difference between the independent- and paired-samples *t*-test?

So far we have looked at how we can include a categorical predictor in our linear model to test for differences between two means. This approach is useful in showing you the simplistic joy that is the linear model, and to keep the thread of linear models running through the book. However, what I have just described is not normally how people think about comparing means, and is not how SPSS likes us to compare means. This is because people do not want you to realize that most statistical models are the same because it will make them look less clever. The other reason is that what I've just explained gets complicated when we want to look at repeated-measures designs. Therefore, when testing difference between two means, people tend to think of the *t*-test as a separate entity.

In this section we'll look at the theoretical underpinnings of the test. There are, in fact, two different *t*-tests and the one you use depends on whether the independent variable was manipulated using the same participants or different:

- **Independent-samples *t*-test**: This test is used when there are two experimental conditions and different participants were assigned to each condition (this is sometimes called the *independent-measures* or *independent-means t*-test).

- **Paired-samples *t*-test**: This test is used when there are two experimental conditions and the same participants took part in both conditions of the experiment (Figure 2.5).

FIGURE 9.2
Thanks to the Confusion Machine there are lots of terms for the paired samples *t*-test

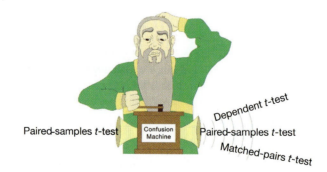

9.3.1. Rationale for the *t*-test ①

Both *t*-tests have a similar rationale, which is based on what we learnt in Chapter 2 about hypothesis testing:

- Two samples of data are collected and the sample means calculated. These means might differ by either a little or a lot.

- If the samples come from the same population, then we expect their means to be roughly equal (see Section 2.5.1). Although it is possible for their means to differ by chance, we would expect large differences between sample means to occur very infrequently. Under the null hypothesis we assume that the experimental manipulation has no effect on the participants: therefore, we expect the sample means to be very similar.

- We compare the difference between the sample means that we collected to the difference between the sample means that we would expect to obtain if there were no effect (i.e., if the null hypothesis were true). We use the standard error (see Section 2.5.1) as a gauge of the variability between sample means. If the standard error is small, then we expect most samples to have very similar means. When the standard error is large, large differences in sample means are more likely. If the difference between the samples we have collected is larger than we would expect based on the standard error then we can assume one of two things:

  ○ There is no effect and sample means in our population fluctuate a lot and we have, by chance, collected two samples that are atypical of the population from which they came.

  ○ The two samples come from different populations but are typical of their respective parent population. In this scenario, the difference between samples represents a genuine difference between the samples (and so the null hypothesis is unlikely).

- The larger the observed difference between the sample means, the more confident we become that the second explanation is correct. If the null hypothesis is incorrect, then we gain confidence that the two sample means differ because of the different experimental manipulation imposed on each sample.

I mentioned in Section 2.6.1.4 that most test statistics are a signal-to-noise ratio: the 'variance explained by the model' divided by the 'variance that the model can't explain'. In other words, effect/error. When comparing two means, the 'model' that we fit to the data (the effect) is the difference between the two group means. We saw also in Chapter 2 that means vary from sample to sample (sampling variation) and that we can use the standard error as a measure of how much means fluctuate (in other words, the error in the estimate of the mean). Therefore, we can also use the standard error of the differences between the two means as an estimate of the error in our model (or the error in the difference between means). Therefore, we calculate the *t*-test as follows:

$$t = \frac{\begin{array}{c}\text{observed difference} \\ \text{between sample means}\end{array} - \begin{array}{c}\text{expected difference} \\ \text{between population means} \\ \text{(if null hypothesis is true)}\end{array}}{\begin{array}{c}\text{estimate of the standard error of the} \\ \text{difference between two sample means}\end{array}} \tag{9.2}$$

The top half of the equation is the 'model' (our model being that the difference between means is bigger than the expected difference, which in most cases will be 0 – we expect the difference between means to be different than zero). The bottom half is the 'error'. So, just as I said in Chapter 2, we're basically getting the test statistic by dividing the model (or effect) by the error in the model. The exact form that this equation takes depends on whether the same or different participants were used in each experimental condition.

9.3.2. The independent *t*-test equation explained ①

Let's first look at the situation in which different entities have been tested in the different conditions of your experiment. This is a situation in which the independent *t*-test is used. If you choose not to think about the *t*-test as a form of regression, then you can think of it in terms of two different equations that differ depending on whether the samples contain an equal number of people. We can calculate the *t*-statistic by using a numerical version of equation (9.2); in other words, we are comparing the model or effect against the error. When different participants participate in different conditions, pairs of scores will differ not just because of the experimental manipulation, but also because of other sources of variance (such as individual differences between participants' motivation, IQ, etc.). Therefore, we make comparisons on a *per-condition* basis (by looking at the overall effect in a condition):

$$t = \frac{(\bar{X}_1 - \bar{X}_2) - (\mu_1 - \mu_2)}{\text{estimate of the standard error}} \tag{9.3}$$

We look at differences between the overall means of the two samples and compare them to the differences we would expect to get between the means of the two populations from which the samples come. If the null hypothesis is true then the samples have been drawn from the same population. Therefore, under the null hypothesis $\mu_1 = \mu_2$ and therefore $\mu_1 - \mu_2 = 0$. Therefore, under the null hypothesis the equation becomes:

$$t = \frac{\bar{X}_1 - \bar{X}_2}{\text{estimate of the standard error}} \tag{9.4}$$

For the independent *t*-test we are looking at differences between groups and so we divide by the standard deviation of differences between groups. We can apply the logic of sampling distributions to this situation. Now, imagine we took several pairs of samples – each pair containing one sample from the two different populations – and compared the means of these samples. From what we have learnt about sampling distributions, we know that the majority of samples from a population will have fairly similar means. Therefore, if we took several pairs of samples (from different populations), the differences between the sample means will be similar across pairs. However, often the difference between a pair of sample means will deviate by a small amount and very occasionally it will deviate by a large amount. If we could plot a sampling distribution of the differences between every pair of sample means that could be taken from two populations, then we would find that it had a normal distribution with a mean equal to the difference between population means $(\mu_1 - \mu_2)$. The sampling distribution would tell us by how much we can expect the means of two (or more) samples to differ. As before, the standard deviation of the sampling distribution (the standard error) tells us how variable the differences between sample means are by chance alone. If the standard deviation is high then large differences between sample means can occur by chance; if it is small then only small differences between sample means are expected. It, therefore, makes sense that we use the standard error of the sampling distribution to assess whether the difference between two sample means is statistically meaningful or simply a chance result. Specifically, we divide the difference between sample means by the standard deviation of the sampling distribution.

So, how do we obtain the standard deviation of the sampling distribution of differences between sample means? Well, we use the **variance sum law**, which states that the variance of a difference between two independent variables is equal to the sum of their variances (see, for example, Howell, 2012). This statement means that the variance of the sampling distribution is equal to the sum of the variances of the two populations from which the samples were taken. We saw earlier that the standard error is the standard deviation of the sampling distribution of a population. We can use the sample standard deviations to calculate the standard error of each population's sampling distribution:

$$SE \text{ of sampling distribution of population } 1 = \frac{s_1}{\sqrt{N_1}}$$

$$SE \text{ of sampling distribution of population } 2 = \frac{s_2}{\sqrt{N_2}}$$

Therefore, remembering that the variance is simply the standard deviation squared, we can calculate the variance of each sampling distribution:

$$\text{variance of sampling distribution of population } 1 = \left(\frac{s_1}{\sqrt{N_1}}\right)^2 = \frac{s_1^2}{N_1}$$

$$\text{variance of sampling distribution of population } 2 = \left(\frac{s_2}{\sqrt{N_2}}\right)^2 = \frac{s_2^2}{N_2}$$

The variance sum law means that to find the variance of the sampling distribution of differences we merely add together the variances of the sampling distributions of the two populations:

$$\text{variance of sampling distribution of differences} = \frac{s_1^2}{N_1} + \frac{s_2^2}{N_2}$$

To find out the standard error of the sampling distribution of differences we merely take the square root of the variance (because variance is the standard deviation squared):

$$SE \text{ of sampling distribution of differences} = \sqrt{\frac{s_1^2}{N_1} + \frac{s_2^2}{N_2}}$$

Therefore, equation (9.4) becomes:

$$t = \frac{\bar{X}_1 - \bar{X}_2}{\sqrt{\dfrac{s_1^2}{N_1} + \dfrac{s_2^2}{N_2}}} \tag{9.5}$$

Equation (9.5) is true only when the sample sizes are equal. Often in science it is not possible to collect samples of equal size (because, for example, people may not complete an experiment). When we want to compare two groups that contain different numbers of participants, equation (9.5) is not appropriate. Instead the pooled variance estimate *t*-test is used which takes account of the difference in sample size by *weighting* the variance of each sample. We saw in Chapter 1 that large samples are better than small ones because they more closely approximate the population; therefore, we weight the variance by the size of sample on which it's based (we actually weight by the number of degrees of freedom, which is the sample size minus 1). Therefore, the pooled variance estimate is:

$$s_p^2 = \frac{(n_1 - 1)s_1^2 + (n_2 - 1)s_2^2}{n_1 + n_2 - 2} \tag{9.6}$$

This is simply a weighted average in which each variance is multiplied (weighted) by its degrees of freedom, and then we divide by the sum of weights (or sum of the two degrees of freedom). The resulting weighted average variance is then just replaced in the t-test equation:

$$t = \frac{\bar{X}_1 - \bar{X}_2}{\sqrt{\dfrac{s_p^2}{n_1} + \dfrac{s_p^2}{n_2}}} \qquad\qquad (9.7)$$

We can compare the value of t obtained against the maximum value we would expect to get if the null hypothesis were true in a t-distribution with the same degrees of freedom (these values can be found in the Appendix); if the value we obtain exceeds this critical value we can be confident that this reflects an effect of our independent variable. One thing that should be apparent from the equation for t is that to compute it you don't actually need any raw data. All you need are the means, standard deviations and sample sizes (see SPSS Tip 9.1).

The derivation of the t-statistic is merely to provide a conceptual grasp of what we are doing when we carry out a t-test on SPSS. Therefore, if you don't know what on earth I'm babbling on about then don't worry about it (just spare a thought for my cat: he has to listen to this rubbish all the time), because SPSS knows how to do it and that's all that matters.

9.3.3. The paired-samples t-test equation explained ①

As with the independent t-test, the paired-samples t-test is a numeric version of equation (9.2). It compares the mean difference between our samples ($\bar{D}$) and the difference that we would expect to find between population means (μ_D), and then takes into account the standard error of the differences ($s_D/\sqrt{N}$):

$$t = \frac{\bar{D} - \mu_D}{s_D / \sqrt{N}} \qquad\qquad (9.8)$$

If the null hypothesis is true, then we expect there to be no difference between the population means (hence $\mu_D = 0$).

I said that the lower half of equation (9.8) is the standard error of differences. The standard error was introduced in Section 2.5.1 and is the standard deviation of the sampling distribution. Have a look back at this section now to refresh your memory about sampling distributions and the standard error. Sampling distributions have several properties that are important. For one thing, if the population is normally distributed then so is the sampling distribution; in fact, if the samples contain more than about 50 scores the sampling distribution should be normally distributed. The mean of the sampling distribution is equal to the mean of the population, so the average of all possible sample means should be the same as the population mean. Therefore, on average, a sample mean will be very close to the population mean and only rarely will it be substantially different from that of the population. A final property of a sampling distribution is that its standard deviation is equal to the standard deviation of the population divided by the square root of the number of observations in the sample. As I mentioned before, this standard deviation is known as the standard error.

All of this is true also if we look at *differences* between sample means. If you were to take several pairs of samples from a population and calculate their means, then you

SPSS TIP 9.1   **Computing *t* from means, *SD*s and *N*s** ③

Using syntax, you can compute an independent *t*-test in SPSS from only the two group means, the two group standard deviations and the two group sizes. Open a data editor window and set up six new variables: ***x1*** (mean of group 1), ***x2*** (mean of group 2), ***sd1*** (standard deviation of group 1), ***sd2*** (standard deviation of group 2), ***n1*** (sample size of group 1) and ***n2*** (sample size of group 2). Type the values of each of these in the first row of the data editor. Open a syntax window and type the following:

COMPUTE df = n1+n2−2.

COMPUTE poolvar = (((n1−1)*(sd1 ** 2))+((n2−1)*(sd2 ** 2)))/df.

COMPUTE t = (x1−x2)/sqrt(poolvar*((1/n1)+(1/n2))).

COMPUTE sig = 2*(1−(CDF.T(abs(t),df))).

Variable labels sig 'Significance (2-tailed)'.

EXECUTE.

The first line computes the degrees of freedom, the second computes the pooled variance, s_p^2, the third computes *t* and the fourth its two-tailed significance. All of these values will be created in a new column in the data editor. The line beginning 'Variable labels' simply labels the significance variable so that we know that it is two-tailed. If you want to display the results in the SPSS viewer you could type:

SUMMARIZE

  /TABLES= x1 x2 df t sig

  /FORMAT=VALIDLIST NOCASENUM TOTAL LIMIT=100

  /TITLE='T-test'

  /MISSING=VARIABLE

  /CELLS=NONE.

These commands will produce a table of the variables **x1**, **x2**, **df**, **t** and **sig** so you'll see the means of the two groups, the degrees of freedom, the value of *t* and its two-tailed significance.

You can run lots of *t*-tests at the same time by putting different values for the means, SDs and sample sizes in different rows. If you do this, though, I suggest having a string variable called **Outcome** in the file in which you type what was being measured (or some other information so that you can identify to what the *t*-test relates).

I have put these commands in a syntax file called **Independent t from means.sps**. My file is actually a bit more complicated because it calculates an effect size measure (Cohen's *d*). For an example of how to use this file, see Labcoat Leni's Real Research 9.1.

could calculate the difference between their means. On average sample means will be very similar to the population mean, therefore, on average, most samples will have very similar means. Therefore, most of the time, the difference between sample means from the same population will be zero, or close to zero. However, sometimes one or both of the samples could have a mean very deviant from the population mean, and so it is possible to obtain large differences between sample means by chance alone. However, this would happen less frequently.

BOARD, B. J., & FRITZON, K. (2005). *PSYCHOLOGY, CRIME & LAW*, *11(1)*, 17–32.

LABCOAT LENI'S REAL RESEARCH 9.1

You don't have to be mad here, but it helps ③

In the UK you often see the 'humorous' slogan 'You don't have to be mad to work here, but it helps' stuck up in work places. Well, Board and Fritzon (2005) took this a step further by measuring whether 39 senior business managers and chief executives from leading UK companies were mad (well, had personality disorders, PDs). They gave them the Minnesota Multiphasic Personality Inventory Scales for DSM III Personality Disorders (MMPI-PD), which is a well-validated measure of 11 personality

disorders: histrionic, narcissistic, antisocial, borderline, dependent, compulsive, passive-aggressive, paranoid, schizotypal, schizoid and avoidant. They needed a comparison group, and what better one to choose than 317 legally classified psychopaths at Broadmoor Hospital (a famous high-security psychiatric hospital in the UK).

The authors report the means and SDs for these two groups in Table 2 of their paper. Using these values and the syntax file **Independent t from means.sps**, we can run *t*-tests on these means. Use the file **Board and Fritzon 2005.sav** and the syntax file to run *t*-tests to see whether managers score higher on personality disorder questionnaires than legally classified psychopaths. Report these results. What do you conclude? Answers are on the companion website (or Table 2 in the original article).

In fact, if you plotted these differences between sample means as a histogram, you would again have a sampling distribution with all of the properties previously described. The standard deviation of this sampling distribution is called the standard error of differences. A small standard error tells us that most pairs of samples from a population will have very similar means (i.e., the difference between sample means should normally be very small). A large standard error tells us that sample means can deviate quite a lot from the population mean and so differences between pairs of samples can be quite large by chance alone.

In an experiment, a person's score in condition 1 will be different to their score in condition 2, and this difference could be very large or very small. If we calculate the differences between each person's score in each condition and add up these differences we would get the total amount of difference. If we then divide this total by the number of participants we get the average difference (thus how much, on average, a person's score differed between condition 1 and condition 2). This average difference is $\bar{D}$ in equation (9.8), and it is an indicator of the systematic variation in the data (i.e., it represents the experimental effect). We need to compare this systematic variation against some kind of measure of the 'systematic variation that we could naturally expect to find'.

In Chapter 2 we saw that the standard error was a measure of how representative a mean is of the population. In this context, we know that if we had taken two random samples from a population (and not done anything to these samples) then the means could be different just by chance. The standard error tells us by how much these samples could differ. A small standard error means that sample means should be quite similar, so a big difference between two sample means is unlikely. In contrast, a large standard error tells us that big differences between the means of two random samples are more likely. Therefore it makes sense to compare the average difference between means against the standard error of these differences. This gives us a test statistic that, as I've said numerous times in previous chapters, represents model/error. Our model is the average difference between condition means, and we divide by the standard error, which represents the error associated with this model (i.e., how similar two random samples are likely to be from this population).

Therefore, by dividing by the standard error we are doing two things: (1) standardizing the average difference between conditions (this just means that we can compare values of *t* without having to worry about the scale of measurement used to measure the outcome variable); and (2) contrasting the difference between means that we have against the difference that we could *expect* to get based on how well the samples represent the populations from which they came. If the standard error is large, then large differences between samples are more common (because the distribution of differences is more spread out). Conversely, if the standard error is small, then large differences between sample means are uncommon (because the distribution is very narrow and centred around zero). Therefore, if the average difference between our samples is large, and the standard error of differences is small, then we can be confident that the difference we observed in our sample is not a chance result. If this is the case then it must have been caused by the experimental manipulation.

As we've seen before, we can't measure standard errors directly – we have to estimate them based on the data we have. We can do this with an equation or using bootstrapping. We saw in Section 2.5.1 that the standard error is simply the standard deviation divided by the square root of the sample size; likewise the standard error of differences ($\sigma_{\bar{D}}$) is simply the standard deviation of differences obtained within the sample (s_D) divided by the square root of the sample size (N):

$$\sigma_{\bar{D}} = \frac{s_D}{\sqrt{N}} \qquad (9.9)$$

If the standard error of differences is a measure of the unsystematic variation within the data, and the sum of difference scores represents the systematic variation, then it should be clear that the t-statistic is simply the ratio of the systematic variation in the experiment to the unsystematic variation. If the experimental manipulation creates any kind of effect, then we would expect the systematic variation to be much greater than the unsystematic variation (so at the very least, t should be greater than 1). If the experimental manipulation is unsuccessful then we might expect the variation caused by individual differences to be much greater than that caused by the experiment (so t will be less than 1). We can compare the obtained value of t against the maximum value we would expect to get, if there was no effect in the population, in a t-distribution with the same degrees of freedom (these values can be found in the Appendix); if the value we obtain exceeds this critical value we conclude that our experimental manipulation has had an effect.

9.4. Assumptions of the *t*-test ①

Both the independent t-test and the paired-samples t-test are *parametric tests* based on the normal distribution and, therefore, the sources of bias identified in Chapter 5 apply. These assumptions and how to identify them were explained in Chapter 5, so I won't go into them again here. However, it is worth saying that for the paired-samples t-test the assumption of normality means that the sampling distribution of the *differences* between scores should be normal, not the scores themselves (see Section 9.6.2). Let's look at how to do these tests using SPSS.

9.5. The independent *t*-test using SPSS ①

9.5.1. The general procedure ①

I have probably bored most of you to the point of wanting to eat your own legs by now. Equations are boring, and SPSS was invented to help us minimize our contact with them. Using

FIGURE 9.3
The general
process for
performing a
t-test

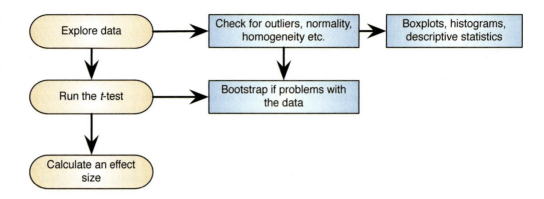

our invisibility data again (**Invisibility.sav**), we have 12 people who were given an invisibility cloak and 12 who were not (the groups are coded using the variable **Cloak**). Remember that the number of mischievous acts they performed was measured (**Mischief**). I have already described how the data are arranged (see Section 9.2.1), so we can move straight on to doing the test itself. Figure 9.3 shows the general process for performing a *t*-test: as with fitting any model, we start by looking for the sources of bias identified in Chapter 5. Having satisfied ourselves that assumptions are met and outliers dealt with, we run the test. We can also consider using bootstrapping if any of the test assumptions were not met. Finally, we compute an effect size.

9.5.2. Exploring data and testing assumptions ①

We have already got some descriptive statistics and looked at distributional assumptions in Section 9.2.1. In the interests of space we won't go over this analysis again in detail, but we found evidence of normality in each group, and we saw that the mean number of mischievous acts was higher for those with a cloak ($M = 5$) than those without ($M = 3.75$). To look at homogeneity of variance (Section 5.3.3) SPSS produces Levene's test when you run the *t*-test.

SELF-TEST   Produce an error bar chart of the **Invisibility.sav** data (**Cloak** will be on the *x*-axis and **Mischief** on the *y*-axis).

9.5.3. Compute the independent *t*-test ①

To run an independent *t*-test, we need to access the main dialog box by selecting Analyze Compare Means ▸ Independent-Samples T Test… (see Figure 9.4). Once the dialog box is activated, select the dependent variable from the list (click on **Mischief**) and transfer it to the box labelled *Test Variable(s)* by dragging it or clicking on →. If you want to carry out *t*-tests on several dependent variables then you can select other dependent variables and transfer them to the variables list. However, there are good reasons why it is not a good idea to carry out lots of tests (see Section 2.6.1.7).

Next, we need to select an independent variable (the grouping variable). In this case, we need to select **Cloak** and then transfer it to the box labelled *Grouping Variable*. When your grouping variable has been selected, the Define Groups… button will become active and you should click on it

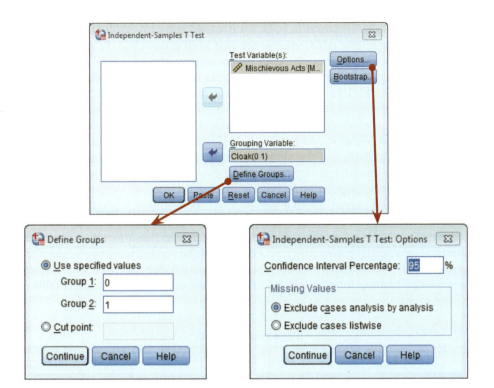

FIGURE 9.4
Dialog boxes
for the
independent-
samples *t*-test

to activate the *Define Groups* dialog box. SPSS needs to know what numeric codes you assigned to your two groups, and there is a space for you to type the codes. In this example, we coded our no cloak group as 0 and our cloak group as 1, and so these are the codes that we type. Alternatively you can specify a *Cut point*, in which case SPSS will assign all cases greater than or equal to that value to one group and all the values below the cut point to the second group. This facility is useful if you are testing different groups of participants based on something like a median split (see Jane Superbrain Box 9.1) – you would simply type the median value in the box labelled *Cut point*. When you have defined the groups, click on Continue to return to the main dialog box. If you click on Options... then another dialog box appears that gives you the chance to change the width of the confidence interval that is calculated. The default setting is for a 95% confidence interval and this is fine; however, if you want to be stricter about your analysis you could choose a 99% confidence interval but you run a higher risk of failing to detect a genuine effect (a Type II error). You can also select how to deal with missing values (see SPSS Tip 5.1). To run the analysis click on OK in the main dialog box.

If we have potential bias in the data we can reduce its impact by using bootstrapping (Section 5.4.3) to generate confidence intervals for the difference between means. We can select this option by clicking Bootstrap... in the main dialog box to access the bootstrap function. We discussed this dialog box in Section 5.4.3; to recap, select ☑ Perform bootstrapping to activate bootstrapping, and to get a 95% confidence interval click ◉ Percentile or ◉ Bias corrected accelerated (BCa). For this analysis, let's ask for a bias corrected and accelerated (BCa) confidence interval. Back in the main dialog box, click on OK to run the analysis.

9.5.4. Output from the independent *t*-test ①

The output from the independent *t*-test contains only three tables (two if you don't opt for bootstrapping). The first table (Output 9.3) provides summary statistics for the two experimental conditions (if you don't ask for bootstrapping this table will be a bit more straightforward). From this table, we can see that both groups had 12 participants (row labelled *N*). The group who had no cloak, on average, performed 3.75 mischievous acts with a standard deviation of 1.913. What's more, the standard error of that group is 0.552 ($SE = 1.913/\sqrt{12} = 1.913/3.464 = 0.552$). The bootstrap SE estimate is 0.53, and the boot-strapped confidence interval for the mean ranges from 2.92 to 4.58. Those who were given an invisibility cloak performed, on average, 5 acts, with a standard deviation of 1.651, a standard error of 0.477 ($SE = 1.651/\sqrt{12} = 1.651/3.464 = 0.477$). The bootstrap standard error is a bit lower at 0.46, and the confidence interval for the mean ranges from 4.33 to 5.67. Note that the confidence intervals for the two groups overlap, implying that they might be from the same population.

The second table of output (Output 9.4) contains the main test statistics. The first thing to notice is that there are two rows containing values for the test statistics: one row is labelled *Equal variances assumed*, while the other is labelled *Equal variances not assumed*. In Chapter 5, we saw that parametric tests assume that the variances in experimental groups are roughly equal. We also saw in Jane Superbrain Box 5.6 that there are adjustments that can be made in situations in which the variances are not equal. The rows of the table relate to whether or not this assumption has been broken.

OUTPUT 9.3

Paired Samples Statistics

				Bootstrap[a]			
						BCa 95% Confidence Interval	
			Statistic	Bias	Std. Error	Lower	Upper
Pair 1	Mischief (No Invisibility Cloak)	Mean	3.75	.01	.53	2.92	4.58
		N	12				
		Std. Deviation	1.913	-.127	.354	1.311	2.229
		Std. Error Mean	.552				
	Mischief (Invisibility Cloak)	Mean	5.00	.00	.46	4.33	5.67
		N	12				
		Std. Deviation	1.651	-.117	.307	1.168	1.881
		Std. Error Mean	.477				

a. Unless otherwise noted, bootstrap results are based on 1000 bootstrap samples

OUTPUT 9.4

Independent Samples Test

		Levene's Test for Equality of Variances		t-test for Equality of Means						
									95% Confidence Interval of the Difference	
		F	Sig.	t	df	Sig. (2-tailed)	Mean Difference	Std. Error Difference	Lower	Upper
Mischievous Acts	Equal variances assumed	.545	.468	-1.713	22	.101	-1.250	.730	-2.763	.263
	Equal variances not assumed			-1.713	21.541	.101	-1.250	.730	-2.765	.265

We saw in Section 5.3.3 that we can use Levene's test to see whether variances are different in different groups, and SPSS produces this test for us (but see Jane Superbrain Box 5.6). Remember that Levene's test is similar to a *t*-test in that it tests the hypothesis that the variances in the two groups are equal (i.e., the difference between the variances is zero). Therefore, if Levene's test is significant at $p \leq .05$, it suggests that the assumption of homogeneity of variances has been violated. If, however, Levene's test is non-significant (i.e., $p > .05$) then we can assume that the variances are roughly equal and the assumption is tenable. For these data, Levene's test is non-significant (because $p = .468$, which is greater than .05) and so we should read the test statistics in the row labelled *Equal variances assumed*. Had Levene's test been significant, then we would have read the test statistics from the row labelled *Equal variances not assumed*.

Having established that the assumption of homogeneity of variances is met, we can look at the *t*-test itself. We are told the mean difference ($\bar{X}_{\text{No Cloak}} - \bar{X}_{\text{Cloak}} = 3.75 - 5 = -1.25$) and the standard error of the sampling distribution of differences, which is calculated using the lower half of equation (9.5):

$$\sqrt{\frac{s_1^2}{N_1} + \frac{s_2^2}{N_2}} = \sqrt{\frac{1.913^2}{12} + \frac{1.651^2}{12}}$$

$$= \sqrt{0.305 + 0.227}$$

$$= \sqrt{0.532}$$

$$= 0.730$$

The t-statistic is calculated by dividing the mean difference by the standard error of the sampling distribution of differences ($t = -1.25/0.730 = -1.71$). The value of t is then assessed against the value of t you might expect to get if there was no effect in the population when you have certain degrees of freedom. For the independent t-test, degrees of freedom are calculated by adding the two sample sizes and then subtracting the number of samples ($df = N_1 + N_2 - 2 = 12 + 12 - 2 = 22$). SPSS produces the exact significance value of t, and we are interested in whether this value is less than or greater than .05. In this case the two-tailed value of p is .101, which is greater than .05, and so we would have to conclude that there was no significant difference between the means of these two samples. In terms of the experiment, we can infer that having a cloak of invisibility did not significantly affect the amount of mischief a person got up to. Note that the value of t and the significance value are the same as when we ran the same test as a regression (see Output 9.2).[3]

Some people use a one-tailed probability when they have made a specific prediction (e.g., if they predicted that having an invisibility cloak would lead to more mischief). We can get this probability by diving the two-tailed probability by 2, which in this case is .101/2 =.0505 (which is still not significant). However, I don't recommend you do this for reasons outlined in Section 2.6.1.5.

Bootstrap for Independent Samples Test   OUTPUT 9.5

		Mean Difference	Bootstrap[a]			
			Bias	Std. Error	BCa 95% Confidence Interval	
					Lower	Upper
Mischievous Acts	Equal variances assumed	-1.250	.003	.726	-2.606	.043
	Equal variances not assumed	-1.250	.003	.726	-2.606	.043

a. Unless otherwise noted, bootstrap results are based on 1000 bootstrap samples

Output 9.5 shows the results of the bootstrapping (if you selected it). You can see that the bootstrapping procedure has been applied to re-estimate the standard error of the mean difference (which is estimated as .726 rather than .730, the value in Output 9.4).[4] SPSS also computes a bootstrapped confidence interval for the difference between means are computed. The difference between means is −1.25, and the confidence interval ranges from −2.606 to 0.043. The confidence interval implies that the difference between means in the

---

[3] In fact, the value of the t-statistic is the same but has a positive sign rather than negative. You'll remember from the discussion of the point biserial correlation in Section 7.4.5 that when you correlate a dichotomous variable the direction of the correlation coefficient depends entirely upon which cases are assigned to which groups. Therefore, the direction of the t-statistic here is similarly influenced by which group we select to be the base category (the category coded as 0).

[4] Remember that the values for the standard error and confidence interval you get will differ from mine because of the way bootstrapping works.

TUK, M. A., ET AL. (2011). *PSYCHOLOGICAL SCIENCE*, 22(5), 627–633.

LABCOAT LENI'S REAL RESEARCH 9.2

Bladder control ①

Visceral factors that require us to engage in self-control (such as a filling bladder) can affect our inhibitory abilities in unrelated domains. In a fascinating study by Tuk, Trampe, and Warlop (2011) participants were given five cups of water: one group were asked to drink them all, whereas another was asked to take a sip from each. This manipulation led one group to have full bladders and the other group relatively empty bladders (**Drink_Group**). Later on, these participants were given eight trials on which they had to choose between a small financial reward that they would receive soon (SS) or a large financial reward for which they would wait longer (LL). They counted how many trials participants choose the LL reward as an indicator of inhibitory control (**LL_Sum**). Do a *t*-test to see whether people with full bladders inhibited more than those without (**Tuk et al. (2011).sav**). Answers are on the companion website, or see p. 6.29 of the original article.

population could be negative, positive or even zero (because the interval ranges from a negative value to a positive one). In other words, it's possible that the true difference between means is zero – no difference at all. Therefore, this bootstrap confidence interval confirms our conclusion that having a cloak of invisibility seems not to affect acts of mischief.

9.5.5. Calculating the effect size ②

Even though our *t*-statistic is not statistically significant, this doesn't necessarily mean that our effect is unimportant in practical terms. To discover whether the effect is substantive we can compute effect sizes (see Section 2.7.1). Converting a *t*-value into an *r*-value is fairly easy; we can use the following equation (e.g., Rosenthal, 1991; Rosnow & Rosenthal, 2005):

$$r = \sqrt{\frac{t^2}{t^2 + df}}$$ (9.10)

We know the value of *t* and the *df* from the SPSS output and so we can compute *r* as follows:

$$r = \sqrt{\frac{-1.713^2}{-1.713^2 + 22}} = \sqrt{\frac{2.93}{24.93}} = 0.34$$

If you think back to our benchmarks for effect sizes this represents a medium effect (it is around .3, the threshold for a medium effect). Therefore, even though the effect was non-significant, it still represented a fairly substantial effect.

We could instead compute Cohen's *d* (Section 2.7.1.1), using the two means (5 and 3.75) and the standard deviation of the control group (no cloak):

$$\hat{d} = \frac{\overline{X}_{\text{Cloak}} - \overline{X}_{\text{No Cloak}}}{s_{\text{No Cloak}}} = \frac{5 - 3.75}{1.91} = 0.65$$

This means that there is 0.65 of a standard deviation difference between the two groups in terms of their mischief making, which again is a fairly substantial effect.

ODITI'S LANTERN

t-tests

'I, Oditi, leader of the cult of undiscovered numerical truths, do not like differences. Everyone must conform to my cultish ideas, my view is the only view, and we must wage war on those who dare to have different views. Only by locating differences can we eliminate them and turn the world into mindless clones. Stare into my lantern to discover how to detect these differences. The more you stare, the more you will find yourself agreeing with everything I say …'

9.5.6. Reporting the independent *t*-test ①

As we have seen before, there is a fairly standard way to report any test statistic: you usually state the finding to which the test relates and then report the test statistic, its degrees of freedom and the probability value of that test statistic. An estimate of the effect size should be reported too. The SPSS output tells us that the value of t was -1.71; that the number of degrees of freedom on which this was based was 22; and that it was not significant, $p = .101$. We can also see the means for each group. We could write this as:

✓ On average, participants given a cloak of invisibility engaged in more acts of mischief ($M = 5$, $SE = 0.48$), than those not given a cloak ($M = 3.75$, $SE = 0.55$). This difference, -1.25, BCa 95% CI [-2.606, 0.043], was not significant $t(22) = -1.71$, $p = .101$; however, it did represent a medium-sized effect, $d = 0.65$.

CRAMMING SAM'S TIPS   The independent *t*-test

- The independent *t*-test compares two means, when those means have come from different groups of entities.
- Look at the column labelled *Levene's Test for Equality of Variance*. If the *Sig.* value is less than .05 then the assumption of homogeneity of variance has been broken and you should look at the row in the table labelled *Equal variances not assumed*. If the *Sig.* value of Levene's test is bigger than .05 then you should look at the row in the table labelled *Equal variances assumed*.
- Look at the column labelled *Sig.* If the value is less than .05 then the means of the two groups are significantly different.
- Look at the table labelled *Bootstrap for Independent Samples Test* to get a robust confidence interval for the difference between means.
- Look at the values of the means to tell you how the groups differ.
- Report the mean difference and its confidence interval, the *t*-statistic, the degrees of freedom and the significance value. Also report the means and their corresponding standard errors (or draw an error bar chart).
- Calculate and report the effect size. Go on, you can do it.☺

Note how we've reported the means in each group (and standard errors), the mean difference and its bootstrapped confidence interval, and the test statistic, its degrees of freedom and *p*-value. Try to avoid writing vague, unsubstantiated things like this:

   ✗ People weren't more mischievous ($t = -1.71$).

More mischievous than what? Where are the *df*? Was the result statistically significant? Was the effect important (what was the effect size)?

9.6. Paired-samples *t*-test using SPSS ①

9.6.1. Entering data ①

Let's imagine that we had collected the cloak of invisibility data using a repeated measures design; this is not because I am too lazy to think up a different data set, but because it allows me to illustrate various things. So, the data will be identical. In this scenario we might have recorded everyone's natural level of mischievous acts in a week, then given them an invisibility cloak and counted the number of mischievous acts in the next week.[5]

SELF-TEST   Enter the data in Table 9.1 into SPSS, but assuming that a repeated-measures design was used.

   The data would now be arranged differently in SPSS. Instead of having a coding variable, and a single column with mischief scores in, we would arrange the data in two columns (one representing the **Cloak** condition and one representing the **No_Cloak** condition). The data are in **Invisibility RM.sav** if you had difficulty entering them into SPSS yourself.

9.6.2. Exploring data and testing assumptions ①

We talked about the assumption of normality in Chapter 5 and discovered that parametric tests (like the paired-samples *t*-test) assume that the sampling distribution is normal. This should be true in large samples, but in small samples people often check the normality of their data because if the data themselves are normal then the sampling distribution is likely to be also. With the paired-samples *t*-test we analyse the *differences* between scores because we're interested in the sampling distribution of these differences (not the raw data). Therefore, if you want to test for normality before a paired-samples *t*-test then what you should do is compute the differences between scores, and then check if this new variable is normally distributed (or use a big sample and not worry about normality☺). It is

---

[5] In theory we'd counterbalance the weeks so that some people had the cloak and then it was taken away, while others had no cloak but were then given one. However, given the research scenario relied on participants not knowing about the cloaks of invisibility it might be best just to have a baseline phase and then give everyone their cloak at the same time (unaware that others were getting cloaks too).

possible to have two measures that are highly non-normal and produce beautifully distributed differences.

 SELF-TEST   Using the **Invisibility RM.sav** data, compute the differences between the cloak and no cloak conditions and check the assumption of normality for these differences.

9.6.2.1. A problem with error bar graphs of repeated-measures designs ①

We saw in Chapter 4 that it is important to visualize group differences using error bars. We're now going to look at a problem that occurs when we graph repeated-measures error bars.

 SELF-TEST   Produce an error bar chart of the **Invisibility RM.sav** data (**Cloak** on the x-axis and **Mischief** on the y-axis).

In one of the earlier self-tests I asked you to produce an error bar graph for the data when we treated it as an independent design, and now we have produced one from a repeated-measures design. Figure 9.5 shows these graphs; remember that the data are exactly the same, all that has changed is whether we pretended the design used the same participants (repeated-measures) or different (independent). Now, we discovered in Chapter 1 that repeated-measures designs eliminate some extraneous variables (such as age, IQ and so on) and so can give us more sensitivity in the data. Therefore, we would expect our graphs to be different: the repeated-measures graph should reflect the increased sensitivity in the design. Looking at the two error bar graphs, can you spot this difference between the graphs?

Hopefully your answer was 'no' because, of course, the graphs are identical. This similarity reflects the fact that when you create an error bar graph of repeated-measures data, SPSS treats the data as though different groups of participants were used. In other words,

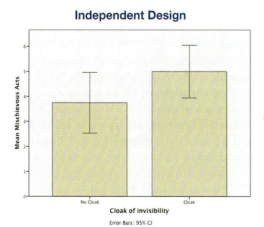

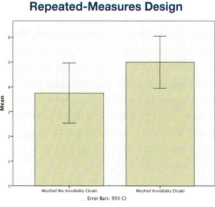

FIGURE 9.5
Two error bar graphs of the invisibility data. The data on the left are treated as though they are different participants, whereas those on the right are treated as though they are from the same participants

the error bars do not reflect the 'true' error around the means for repeated-measures designs. We can correct this problem manually. It's a bit of a faff, but that's what we will discover now.

9.6.2.2 Step 1: Calculate the mean for each participant ②

To correct the repeated-measures error bars, we need to use the *compute* command that we encountered in Chapter 5. To begin with, we need to calculate the average mischief for each participant and so we use the *Mean* function. Access the main *Compute* dialog box by selecting Transform ▦ Compute Variable… . Enter the name **Mean** into the box labelled *Target Variable* and then in the list labelled *Function group* select *Statistical* and then in the list labelled *Functions and Special Variables* select *Mean*. Transfer this command to the command area by clicking on ⬆. When the command is transferred, it appears in the command area as *MEAN(?,?)*; the question marks should be replaced with variable names (which can be typed manually or transferred from the variables list). So replace the first question mark with the variable **No_Cloak** and the second one with the variable **Cloak**. The completed dialog box should look like Figure 9.6. Click on ⬚OK⬚ to create this new variable, which will appear as a new column in the data editor.

FIGURE 9.6
Using the
compute
function to
calculate the
mean of two
columns

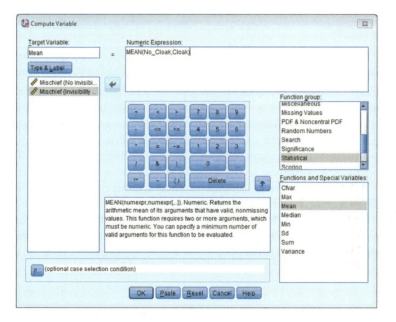

9.6.2.3. Step 2: Calculate the grand mean ②

The **grand mean** is the mean of all scores (regardless of which condition the score comes from) and so for the current data this value will be the mean of all 24 scores. One way to calculate this is by hand (i.e., add up all of the scores and divide by 24); however, an easier way is to use the means that we have just calculated. The means we have just calculated are the average score for each participant and so if we take the average of those mean scores, we will have the mean of all scores (i.e., the grand mean) – phew, there were a lot of means in that sentence. OK, to do this we can use a useful little gadget called the *descriptives* command (you could also use the *explore* or *frequencies* functions that we came across in Chapter 5, but as I've already covered those we'll try something different). Access the *descriptives* command by selecting Analyze Descriptive Statistics ▸ ▦ Descriptives… . The dialog box in

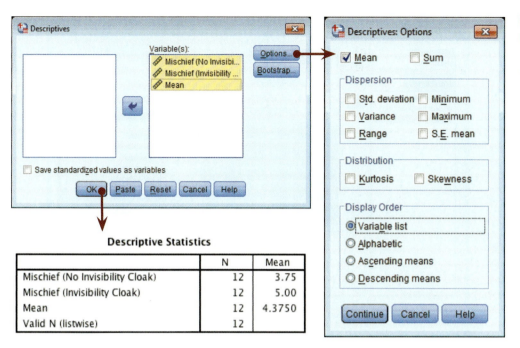

FIGURE 9.7
Dialog boxes and output for descriptive statistics

Figure 9.7 should appear. The *descriptives* command is used to get basic descriptive statistics for variables and clicking on Options... activates a second dialog box. Select the variable **Mean** from the list and transfer it to the box labelled *Variable(s)* by clicking on →. Then use the *Options* dialog box to specify only the mean (you can leave the default settings as they are, but we are interested only in the mean). If you run this analysis the output should provide you with some self-explanatory descriptive statistics for each of the three variables (assuming you selected all three). You should see that we get the mean of the no cloak condition, and the mean of the cloak condition, but it's the final variable in which we're interested: the mean of the cloak and no cloak conditions (**Mean**). The average of this variable is the grand mean, and you can see from the summary table that its value is 4.375. We will use this grand mean in the following calculations.

9.6.2.4. Step 3: Calculate the adjustment factor ②

If you look at the variable labelled **Mean**, you should notice that the values for each participant are different, which tells us that some people were more mischievous than others across the conditions. The fact that participants' mean mischief scores differ represents individual differences between different people (so it represents the fact that some of the participants are generally more mischievous than others). These differences in natural mischievousness contaminate the error bar graphs, which is why if we don't adjust the values that we plot, we will get the same graph as if an independent design had been used. Loftus and Masson (1994) argue that to eliminate this contamination we should equalize the means between participants (i.e., adjust the scores in each condition such that when we take the mean score across conditions, it is the same for all participants). To do this, we need to calculate an adjustment factor by subtracting each participant's mean score from the grand mean. We can use the *compute* function to do this calculation. Activate the *Compute* dialog box, give the target variable a name (I suggest **Adjustment**) and then use the command '4.375-mean'. This command will take the grand mean (4.375) and subtract from it each participant's average mischief level (see Figure 9.8).

FIGURE 9.8
Calculating the
adjustment
factor

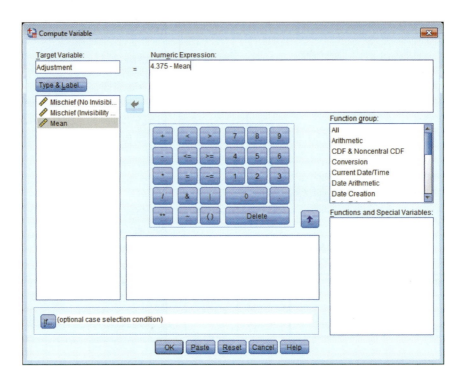

This process creates a new variable in the data editor called **Adjustment**. The scores in the **Adjustment** column represent the difference between each participant's mean mischief levels and the mean mischief level across all participants. You'll notice that some of the values are positive, and these are participants who were less mischievous than average. Other participants were more mischievous than average and they have negative adjustment scores. We can now use these adjustment values to eliminate the between-subjects differences in mischief.

9.6.2.5. Step 4: Create adjusted values for each variable ②

So far, we have calculated the difference between each participant's mean score and the mean score of all participants (the grand mean). This difference can be used to adjust the existing scores for each participant. First we'll adjust the scores in the **No_Cloak** condition. Once again, we can use the *compute* command to make the adjustment. Activate the *Compute* dialog box in the same way as before, and then title our new variable **No_Cloak_Adjusted** (you can then click on Type & Label… and give this variable a label such as 'No Cloak Condition: Adjusted Values'). All we are going to do is to add each participant's score in the **No_Cloak** condition to their adjustment value. Select the variable **No_Cloak** and transfer it to the command area by clicking on ⇥, then click on ⊞ and select the variable **Adjustment** and transfer it to the command area by clicking on ⇥. The completed dialog box is shown in Figure 9.9. Now do the same thing for the variable **Cloak**: create a variable called **Cloak_Adjusted** that contains the values of **Cloak** added to the value in the **Adjustment** column.

Now, the variables **Cloak_Adjusted** and **No_Cloak_Adjusted** represent the mischief experienced in each condition, adjusted so as to eliminate any between-subjects differences. If you don't believe me, then use the *compute* command to create a variable **Mean2** that is the average of **Cloak_Adjusted** and **No_Cloak_Adjusted** (just like we did in Section 9.6.2.2). You should find that the value in this column is the same for every participant,

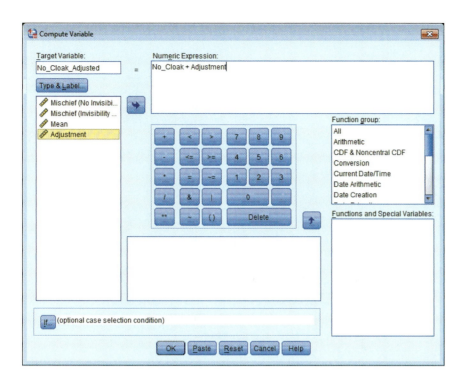

FIGURE 9.9
Adjusting
the values of
No_Cloak

thus proving that the between-subjects variability in means is gone: the value will be 4.375 (i.e., the grand mean).

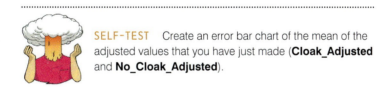

SELF-TEST Create an error bar chart of the mean of the adjusted values that you have just made (**Cloak_Adjusted** and **No_Cloak_Adjusted**).

The resulting error bar graph is shown in Figure 9.10. Compare this graph to the graphs in Figure 9.5 – what differences do you see? The first thing to notice is that the means in the two conditions have not changed. However, the error bars have changed: they have got smaller. Also, whereas in Figure 9.5 the error bars overlap, in this new graph they do not. In Chapter 2 we discovered that when error bars do not overlap we can be fairly confident that our samples have not come from the same population (and so our experimental manipulation has been successful). Therefore, when we plot the proper error bars for the repeated-measures data it shows the extra sensitivity that this design has: the differences between conditions appear to be significant, whereas when different participants are used, there does not appear to be a significant difference. (Remember that the means in both situations are identical, but the sampling error is smaller in the repeated-measures design.) I expand upon this point in Section 9.7.

9.6.3. Computing the paired-samples *t*-test ①

To conduct a paired-samples *t*-test, we need to access the main dialog box by selecting Analyze Compare Means ▶ Paired-Samples T Test... (Figure 9.11). Once the dialog box is

FIGURE 9.10
Error bar
graph of the
adjusted values
of the data in
**Invisibility
RM.sav**

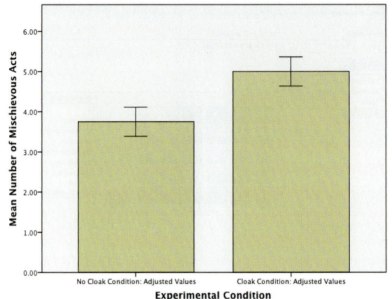

FIGURE 9.10
Error bar
graph of the
adjusted values
of the data in
**Invisibility
RM.sav**

FIGURE 9.11
Main dialog box
for paired-
samples *t*-test

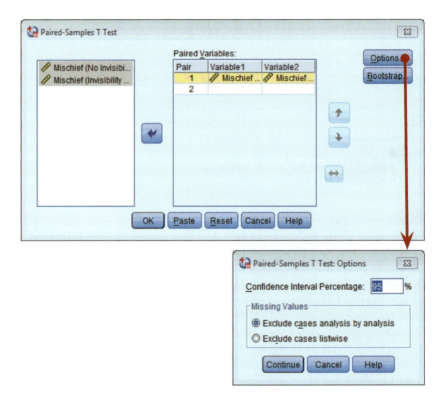

activated, you need to select pairs of variables to be analysed. In this case we have only one
pair (**Cloak** vs. **No_Cloak**). To select a pair you should click on the first variable that you
want to select (in this case **No_Cloak**), then hold down the *Ctrl* key (*Cmd* on a Mac) and
select the second (in this case **Cloak**). To transfer these two variables to the box labelled
Paired Variables, click on . (You can also select each variable individually and transfer
it by clicking on , but selecting both variables as just described is quicker.) If you want
to carry out several *t*-tests then you can select another pair of variables, transfer them to

the variables list, then select another pair and so on. If you click on [Options...] then another dialog box appears that gives you the same options as for the independent *t*-test. Similarly, you can click on [Bootstrap...] to access the bootstrap function (Section 5.4.3). As with the independent *t*-test, select ☑ Perform bootstrapping and ◉ Bias corrected accelerated (BCa). Back in the main dialog box, click on [OK] to run the analysis.

9.6.3.1. Output from the paired-samples *t*-test ①

The resulting output produces four tables (three if you don't select bootstrapping). Output 9.6 shows a table of summary statistics for the two experimental conditions (if you don't ask for bootstrapping this table will be a bit more straightforward). For each condition we are told the mean, the number of participants (*N*), the standard deviation and standard error. These values are the same as when we treated the data as an independent design and were described in Section 9.5.4.

Output 9.6 also shows the Pearson correlation between the two conditions. When repeated measures are used it is possible that the experimental conditions will correlate (because the data in each condition come from the same people and so there could be some constancy in their responses). SPSS provides the value of Pearson's *r* and the two-tailed significance value (see Chapter 7). For these data the experimental conditions yield a very large correlation coefficient, $r = .806$, which is highly significant, $p = .002$, and has a bootstrap confidence interval that doesn't include zero, BCa 95% CI [.185, .965].

Output 9.7 shows us whether the difference between the means of the two conditions was large enough *not* to be a chance result. First, the table tells us the mean difference between the mean scores of each condition: $3.75 - 5 = -1.25$ (this value is $\bar{D}$ in equation (9.8)). The table also reports the standard deviation of the differences between the means and, more importantly, the standard error of the differences between participants' scores in each condition. The test statistic, *t*, is calculated by dividing the mean of differences by the standard error of differences (see equation (9.8): $t = -1.25/0.329 = -3.804$). The size of *t* is compared against known values based on the degrees of freedom. When the same participants have been used, the degrees of freedom are the sample size minus 1 ($df = N - 1 = 11$). SPSS uses the degrees of freedom to calculate the exact probability that a value of *t* as big as the one obtained could occur if there was no difference between population means. This probability value is in the column labelled *Sig*. SPSS provides the two-tailed probability, which is the probability when no prediction was made about the direction of group differences and the one I recommend using (see Section 2.6.1.5). The two-tailed probability for the invisibility data is very low ($p = .003$); it tells us that there is only a 0.3% chance that a value of *t* at least this big could occur if the null hypothesis were true. We are interested in whether this value is less than or greater than .05, and because the value of *p* is less than .05 we can conclude that there was a significant difference between the means of these two samples. In terms of the experiment, we can infer that having a cloak of invisibility significantly affected the amount of mischief a person got up to, $t(11) = -3.80$, $p = .003$. This result was predicted by the error bar chart in Figure 9.10.

Finally, this output provides a 95% confidence interval for the mean difference.[6] However, a more robust confidence interval, estimated using bootstrapping, is produced in Output 9.8. remember that confidence intervals are constructed such that in 95% of samples the intervals

---

[6] These intervals represent the value of two (well, 1.96 to be precise) standard errors either side of the mean of the sampling distribution (Section 2.5.2). For these data, in which the mean difference was –1.25 and the standard error was 0.329, these limits will be $-1.25 \pm (1.96 \times 0.329)$. However, because we're using the *t*-distribution, not the normal distribution, we use the critical value of *t* to compute the confidence intervals. This value is (with df = 11 in this example) 2.201 (two-tailed), which gives us $-1.25 \pm (2.201 \times 0.329)$.

OUTPUT 9.6

Paired Samples Statistics

			Statistic	Bootstrap[a]			
				Bias	Std. Error	BCa 95% Confidence Interval	
						Lower	Upper
Pair 1	Mischief (No Invisibility Cloak)	Mean	3.75	−.02	.52	2.83	4.50
		N	12				
		Std. Deviation	1.913	−.110	.341	1.311	2.234
		Std. Error Mean	.552				
	Mischief (Invisibility Cloak)	Mean	5.00	.00	.46	4.17	5.75
		N	12				
		Std. Deviation	1.651	−.087	.309	1.114	1.992
		Std. Error Mean	.477				

a. Unless otherwise noted, bootstrap results are based on 1000 bootstrap samples

Paired Samples Correlations

		N	Correlation	Sig.	Bootstrap for Correlation[a]			
					Bias	Std. Error	BCa 95% Confidence Interval	
							Lower	Upper
Pair 1	Mischief (No Invisibility Cloak) & Mischief (Invisibility Cloak)	12	.806	.002	−.019	.160	.185	.965

a. Unless otherwise noted, bootstrap results are based on 1000 bootstrap samples

OUTPUT 9.7

Paired Samples Test

		Paired Differences							
		Mean	Std. Deviation	Std. Error Mean	95% Confidence Interval of the Difference		t	df	Sig. (2-tailed)
					Lower	Upper			
Pair 1	Mischief (No Invisibility Cloak) − Mischief (Invisibility Cloak)	−1.250	1.138	.329	−1.973	−.527	−3.804	11	.003

OUTPUT 9.8

Bootstrap for Paired Samples Test

		Mean	Bootstrap[a]				
			Bias	Std. Error	Sig. (2-tailed)	BCa 95% Confidence Interval	
						Lower	Upper
Pair 1	Mischief (No Invisibility Cloak) − Mischief (Invisibility Cloak)	−1.250	−.019	.323	.004	−1.667	−.833

a. Unless otherwise noted, bootstrap results are based on 1000 bootstrap samples

contain the true value of the mean difference. So, assuming that this sample's confidence interval is one of the 95 out of 100 that contains the population value, we can say that the true mean difference lies between −1.67 and −0.83. The importance of this interval is that it does not contain zero (both limits are negative), which tells us that the true value of the mean difference is unlikely to be zero. In other words, there is an effect in the population reflecting more mischievous acts performed when someone is given an invisibility cloak.

9.6.4. Calculating the effect size ①

According to Rosenthal (1991), we can compute the effect size direct from the value of t, just as we did for the independent t-test. In this case, we take the value of t and the df from the SPSS output and compute r as:

$$r = \sqrt{\frac{(-3.804)^2}{(-3.804)^2 + 11}} = \sqrt{\frac{14.47}{25.47}} = .75$$

GELMAN, A., & WEAKLIEM, D. (2009). *AMERICAN SCIENTIST*, 97, 310–316.

LABCOAT LENI'S REAL RESEARCH 9.3

The beautiful people ①

Apparently there are more beautiful women in the world than there are handsome men. Satoshi Kanazawa explains this finding in terms of good-looking parents being more likely to have a baby daughter as their first child than a baby son. Perhaps more controversially, he suggests that, from an evolutionary point of view, beauty is a more valuable trait for women than for men (Kanazawa, 2007). In a playful and very informative paper, Andrew Gelman and David Weakliem discuss various statistical errors and misunderstandings, some of which have implications for Kanazawa's claims. The 'playful' part of the paper is that to illustrate their point they collected data on the 50 most beautiful celebrities (as listed by *People* magazine) of 1995-2000. They counted how many male and female children they had as of 2007. If Kanazawa is correct, these beautiful people would have produced more girls than boys. Do a *t*-test to find out whether they did. The data are in **Gelman & Weakliem (2009).sav**. Answers are on the companion website.

This value represents a very large effect (it is above .5, the threshold for a large effect). Therefore, as well as being statistically significant, this effect is a substantive finding. You may notice that the effect has grown: it was .34 when we treated the data as though it was from an independent design. This growth in the effect size might seem slightly odd given that we used exactly the same data (but see Section 9.7). Dunlap, Cortina, Vaslow, and Burke (1996) would agree, and have shown that using a *t* from a paired-samples *t*-test leads to an overestimation of the population effect size (although they discussed *d* rather than *r*). You could instead compute Cohen's *d* (Section 2.7.1.1) as we did in Section 9.5.5:

$$\hat{d} = \frac{\bar{X}_{\text{Cloak}} - \bar{X}_{\text{No Cloak}}}{s_{\text{No Cloak}}} = \frac{5 - 3.75}{1.91} = 0.65$$

Note that the change in design does not affect the calculation at all; therefore, the effect size doesn't change as a result of the type of design used and we can interpret it as before. In this respect it might be preferable to *r*.

9.6.5. Reporting the paired-samples *t*-test ①

We can basically report the same information for paired-samples *t*-test as for the independent *t*-test, but obviously the confidence intervals, degrees of freedom and values of *t* and *p* have changed:

✓ On average, participants given a cloak of invisibility engaged in more acts of mischief (*M* = 5, *SE* = 0.48), than those not given a cloak (*M* = 3.75, *SE* = 0.55). This difference, −1.25, BCa 95% CI [−1.67, −0.83], was significant *t*(11) = −3.80, *p* = .003, and represented a medium-sized effect, *d* = 0.65.

CRAMMING SAM'S TIPS   **Paired-samples *t*-test**

- The paired-samples *t*-test compares two means, when those means have come from the same entities.
- Look at the column labelled *Sig*. If the value is less than .05 then the means of the two conditions are significantly different.
- Look at the values of the means to tell you how the conditions differ.
- Look at the table labelled *Bootstrap for Paired Samples Test* to get a robust confidence interval for the difference between means.
- Report the mean difference and its confidence interval, the *t*-statistic, the degrees of freedom and the significance value. Also report the means and their corresponding standard errors (or draw an error bar chart).
- Calculate and report the effect size too.

9.7. Between groups or repeated measures? ①

The two examples in this chapter are interesting (honestly!) because they illustrate the difference between data collected using the same participants and data collected using different participants. The two examples in this chapter use the same scores in each condition. When analysed as though the data came from the same participants the result was a significant difference between means, but when analysed as though the data came from different participants there was no significant difference between group means. This may seem like a puzzling finding – after all, the numbers were identical in both examples. The effect size (*d*) did not change, reflecting the fact that the data were the same and the effect was the same, all that changed was the significance of that effect. This example illustrates the relative *power* of repeated-measures designs. When the same participants are used across conditions the unsystematic variance (often called the error variance) is reduced dramatically, making it easier to detect any systematic variance. It is often assumed that the way in which you collect data is irrelevant, and in terms of the size of effect it sort of is, but if you're interested in significance then it matters a fair bit. Researchers have carried out studies using the same participants in experimental conditions, then replicated the study using different participants, and used the method of data collection as an independent variable in the analysis. Typically, they have found that the method of data collection interacts significantly with the results found (see Erlebacher, 1977).

9.8. What if I violate the test assumptions? ②

In Chapter 5 we looked at various sources of bias and how to correct for them. In the case of comparing two means, there are adjustments that can be made to the *t*-test when the assumption of homogeneity of variance is broken, and if other assumptions are broken we've encountered other tests that compare two groups and make fewer assumptions: the *Wilcoxon signed-rank test* (Section 6.5), *Wilcoxon rank-sum test* and *Mann–Whitney test* (Section 6.4). However, I wouldn't use these tests: I would take the usual steps to reduce the impact of obvious outliers, and use the bootstrapped confidence interval for the mean difference. This confidence interval should be robust to the sources of bias that we have discussed in the book.

9.9. Brian's attempt to woo Jane ①

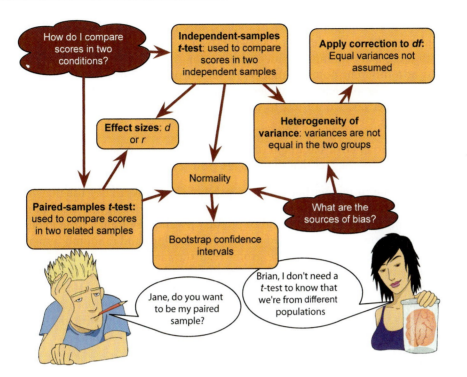

FIGURE 9.12
What Brian learnt
from this chapter

9.10. What next? ①

I'd announced to my parents that my career of choice was that of rock star. Obviously I hadn't presented them with a *t*-test showing how much more money I would earn compared to a university professor, but even if I had, I'm not sure it would have mattered. My parents were quite happy for me to live this fantasy provided that I entertained the possibility that it might not work out and had a plan B. Preferably a plan B that was a little bit more sensible than being a rock star. At the age of 10, I think my plan B was probably to be a soccer star. One way or another I wanted my career to involve being a star, so if it wasn't rock, then soccer would do. However, we've seen already that I was at a genetic disadvantage when it came to soccer, but not so much when it came to rock stardom: my dad, after all, was quite musical. All I had to do was make it happen. The first step, I reasoned, was to build a fan base and the best place to start a fan base is among your friends. With that in mind, I put on my little denim jacket with Iron Maiden patches sewn onto it, threw my guitar over my back and headed off down the rocky road of stardom. The first stop was my school.

9.11. Key terms that I've discovered

Dependent *t*-test	Independent *t*-test	Standard error of differences
Dummy variables	Paired-samples *t*-test	Variance sum law
Grand mean		

9.12. Smart Alex's tasks

- **Task 1**: Is arachnophobia (fear of spiders) specific to real spiders or will pictures of spiders evoke similar levels of anxiety? Twelve arachnophobes were asked to play with a big hairy tarantula spider with big fangs and an evil look in its eight eyes, and at a different point in time were shown only pictures of the same big hairy tarantula. The participants' anxiety was measured in each case. The data are in **Big Hairy Spider.sav**. Do a *t*-test to see whether anxiety is higher for real spiders than for pictures. ①

- **Task 2**: Plot an error bar graph of the above data (remember to make the necessary adjustments for the fact that the data are from a repeated-measures design.) ②

- **Task 3**: One of my pet hates is 'pop psychology' books. They usually spout non-sense that is unsubstantiated by science and give psychology a very bad name. As part of my plan to rid the world of popular psychology I did a little experiment. I took two groups of people who were in relationships and randomly assigned them to one of two conditions. One group read the famous popular psychology book *Women are from Bras and men are from Penis*, whereas another group read *Marie Claire*. I tested only 10 people in each of these groups, and the dependent variable was an objective measure of their happiness with their relationship after reading the book. The data are in the file **Penis.sav**. Analyse them with the appropriate *t*-test. ①

- **Task 4**: Imagine Twaddle and Sons, the publishers of *Women are from Bras and men are from Penis*, were upset about my claims that their book was as useful as a paper umbrella. They designed their own experiment in which participants read their book and one of my books (Field & Hole, 2003) at different times. Relationship happiness was measured after reading each book. They used a sample of 500 participants, but got each participant to take part in both conditions (in counterbalanced order and with a six-month delay). Does reading their wonderful contribution to popular psychology lead to greater relationship happiness compared to my tedious book about experiments? The data are in **Field&Hole.sav**. ①

- **Task 5**: In Chapter 3 (Task 5) we looked at data from people who had been forced to marry goats and dogs and measured their life satisfaction as well as how much they like animals (**Goat or Dog.sav**). Conduct a *t*-test to see whether life satisfaction depends upon the type of animal to which a person was married. ①

- **Task 6**: What do you notice about the *t*-value and significance above compared to when you ran the analysis as a regression in Chapter 8, Task 2? ①

- **Task 7**: In Chapter 5 we looked at hygiene scores over three days of a rock music festival (**Download Festival.sav**). Do a paired-samples *t*-test to see whether hygiene scores on day 1 differed from those on day 3. ①

- **Task 8**: Analyse the data in Chapter 6, Task 1 (whether men and dogs differ in their dog-like behaviours – **MenLikeDogs.sav**) using an independent *t*-test with bootstrapping. Do you reach the same conclusions? ②

- **Task 9**: Analyse the data in Chapter 6, Task 2 (whether the type of music you hear influences goat sacrificing – **DarkLord.sav**) using an matched-samples *t*-test with bootstrapping. Do you reach the same conclusions? ②

- **Task 10**: Thinking back to Labcoat Leni's Real Research 3.1, test whether the number of offers was significantly different in people listening to Bon Scott compared to those listening to Brian Johnson, using an independent *t*-test and bootstrapping. Do your results differ from Oxoby (2008)? (The data are in **Oxoby (2008) Offers.sav.**) ②

Answers can be found on the companion website.

9.13. Further reading

Field, A. P., & Hole, G. (2003). *How to design and report experiments*. London: Sage. (In my completely unbiased opinion this is a useful book to get some more background on experimental methods.)

Miles, J. N. V., & Banyard, P. (2007). *Understanding and using statistics in psychology: A practical introduction*. London: Sage. (A fantastic and amusing introduction to statistical theory.)

Wilcox, R. R. (2010). *Fundamentals of modern statistical methods: Substantially improving power and accuracy*. New York: Springer. (Looks at robust approaches to analysing differences between means.)

Wright, D. B., & London, K. (2009). *First steps in statistics* (2nd ed.). London: Sage. (This book has very clear introductions to the *t*-test.)

Moderation, mediation and more regression

FIGURE 10.1
My 10th birthday. (From left to right) My brother Paul (who still hides behind cakes rather than have his photo taken), Paul Spreckley, Alan Palsey, Clair Sparks and me

10.1. What will this chapter tell me? ①

Having successfully slayed audiences at holiday camps around the country, my next step towards global domination was my primary school. I had learnt another Chuck Berry song ('Johnny B. Goode'), but also broadened my repertoire to include songs by other artists (I have a feeling 'Over the edge' by Status Quo was one of them).[1] Needless to say, when the opportunity came to play at a school assembly I jumped at it. The headmaster tried to have me banned,[2] but the show went on. It was a huge success (I want to reiterate my earlier

---

[1] This would have been about 1982, so just before they became the most laughably bad band on the planet. Some would argue that they were *always* the most laughably bad band on the planet, but they were the first band that I called my favourite band.

[2] Seriously! Can you imagine a headmaster banning a 10-year-old from assembly? By this time I had an electric guitar and he used to play hymns on an acoustic guitar; I can assume only that he somehow lost all perspective on the situation and decided that a 10-year-old blasting out some Quo in a squeaky little voice was subversive or something.

point that 10-year-olds are very easily impressed). My classmates carried me around the playground on their shoulders. I was a hero. Around this time I had a childhood sweetheart called Clair Sparks. Actually, we had been sweethearts since before my newfound rock legend status. I don't think the guitar playing and singing impressed her much, but she rode a motorbike (really, a little child's one) which impressed *me* quite a lot; I was utterly convinced that we would one day get married and live happily ever after. I was utterly convinced, that is, until she ran off with Simon Hudson. Being 10, she probably literally did run off with him – across the playground. I remember telling my parents and them asking me how I felt about it. I told them I was being philosophical about it. I probably didn't know what philosophical meant at the age of 10, but I knew that it was the sort of thing you said if you were pretending not to be bothered about being dumped.

If I hadn't been philosophical, I might have wanted to look at what had lowered Clair's relationship satisfaction. We've seen in previous chapters that we could predict things like relationship satisfaction using regression. Perhaps it's predicted from your partner's love of rock bands like Status Quo (I don't recall Clair liking that sort of thing). However, life is usually more complicated than this; for example, your partner's love of rock music probably depends on your own love of rock music. For example, if you both like rock music then your love of the same music might have an additive effect, giving you huge relationship satisfaction (*moderation*), or perhaps the relationship between your partner's love of rock and your own relationship satisfaction can be explained by your own music tastes (*mediation*). In the previous chapter we also saw that regression could be done with a dichotomous predictor (e.g., rock fan or not) but what if you wanted to categorize musical taste into several categories (rock, hip-hop, R & B etc.)? Surely you can't use multiple categories as a predictor in regression? This chapter extends what we know about regression to these more complicated scenarios. First we look at two common regression-based models – moderation and mediation – before expanding what we already know about categorical predictors.

10.2. Installing custom dialog boxes in SPSS ②

Although you can do both moderation and mediation analysis in SPSS manually, it's a bit of a faff. It will require you to create new variables using the *compute* command, and in the case of mediation analysis it will limit what you can do considerably. By far the best way to tackle moderation and mediation is to use the *PROCESS* command. This is not part of SPSS; it exists only because Andrew Hayes and his colleague Kristopher Preacher have spent an enormous amount of time writing a range of tools for doing moderation and mediation analyses (e.g., Hayes & Matthes, 2009; Preacher & Hayes, 2004, 2008a). These tools were previously available only through syntax, and for inexperienced users were a bit scary and fiddly. Andrew Hayes wrote the *PROCESS* custom dialog box (Hayes, 2012) to wrap the Preacher and Hayes mediation and moderation tools in a convenient menu and dialog box interface. It's pretty much the best thing to happen to moderation and mediation analysis in a long time. While using these tools, I strongly suggest you spare a thought of gratitude that there are people like Hayes and Preacher in the world who invest their spare time doing cool stuff like this that makes it possible for you to analyse your data without having a nervous breakdown. Even if you think you are having a nervous breakdown, trust me it's not as big as the one you'd be having if *PROCESS* didn't exist.

The *PROCESS* tool is what's known as a custom dialog box. SPSS includes the ability to add your own menus and dialog boxes, which means that you can write your own functions using syntax, but then create a custom menu and dialog box for yourself so that you can access the syntax through a nice point and click menu. Of course, most of us will never use this feature, but Andrew Hayes has. Essentially, he provides a file (**process.spd**) that you download, which installs a new menu into the Analyze Regression ▶ menu.

From this menu you access a dialog box that can be used to do moderation and mediation analysis.

You install *PROCESS* in three easy steps, which are illustrated in Figure 10.2 (MacOS users can ignore step 2):

1 *Download the install file*: Download the file **process.spd** from Andrew Hayes' website: http://www.afhayes.com/spss-sas-and-mplus-macros-and-code.html. Save this file onto your computer.

2 *Start SPSS as an administrator*: To install the tool in Windows, you need to start IBM SPSS as an administrator. To do this, make sure that SPSS isn't already running, and then click on the start menu ( ). Select ▸ All Programs , which will display a list of programs installed on your machine. Within that list, there should be a folder called *IBM SPSS Statistics*. Select that folder to display its contents. You should see this icon within that folder: Σ IBM SPSS Statistics 20 (don't be worried if the number is different from 20, it just refers to the version of SPSS that you have installed). Click on this icon with the *right mouse button* to activate the menu in Figure 10.2. Within this menu select (you're back to using the left mouse button now) Run as administrator . This action opens SPSS but allows it to make changes to your computer. A dialog box will appear that asks you whether you want to let SPSS make changes to your computer and you should select Yes .

3 Once SPSS has loaded select Utilities Custom Dialogs ▸ Install Custom Dialog..., which will open a standard dialog box for opening files (Figure 10.2). Locate the file **process.spd**, select it, and click on Open . This will install the *PROCESS* menu and dialog boxes into SPSS. If you get an error message, the most likely explanation is that you haven't opened SPSS as an administrator (see step 2). Once the installation is complete you'll find that the *PROCESS* menu has been added to the existing Analyze Regression ▸ menu (Figure 10.3).

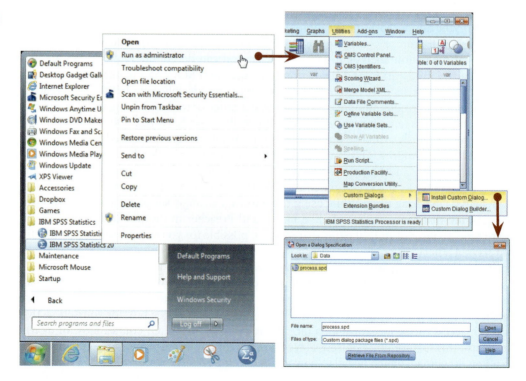

FIGURE 10.2
Installing the *PROCESS* menu

10.3. Moderation: interactions in regression ③

10.3.1. The conceptual model ③

So far we have looked at individual predictors in the linear model. However, it is possible for a statistical model to include the combined effect of two or more predictor variables on an outcome. The combined effect of two variables on another is known conceptually as **moderation**, and in statistical terms as an **interaction effect**. We'll start with the conceptual and we'll use an example of whether violent video games make people antisocial. Video games are among the favourite online activities for young people: two-thirds of 5–16-year-olds have their own video games console, and 88% of boys aged 8–15 own at least one games console (Ofcom (Office of Communications), 2008). Although playing violent video games can enhance visuospatial acuity, visual memory, probabilistic inference, and mental rotation (Feng, Spence, & Pratt, 2007; Green & Bavelier, 2007; Green, Pouget, & Bavelier, 2010; Mishra, Zinni, Bavelier, & Hillyard, 2011), compared to games such as Tetris, these games have also been linked to increased aggression in youths (Anderson & Bushman, 2001). Another predictor of aggression and conduct problems is callous-unemotional traits such as lack of guilt, lack of empathy, and callous use of others for personal gain (Rowe, Costello, Angold, Copeland, & Maughan, 2010). Imagine a scientist wanted to look at the relationship between playing violent video games such as Grand Theft Auto, MadWorld and Manhunt and aggression. She gathered data from 442 youths (**Video Games.sav**). She measured their aggressive behaviour (**Aggression**), callous unemotional traits (**CaUnTs**), and the number of hours per week they play video games (**Vid_Games**).

What is moderation?

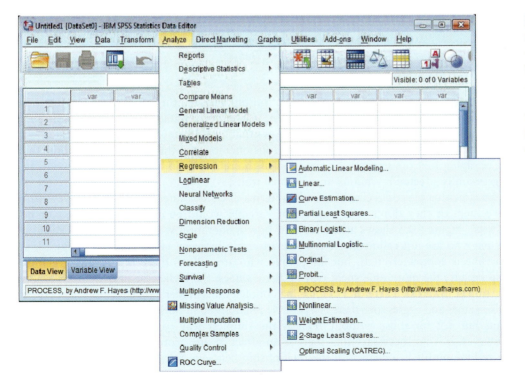

FIGURE 10.3
After installation, the *PROCESS* menu appears as part of the existing *Regression* menu

FIGURE 10.4
Diagram of the *conceptual* moderation model

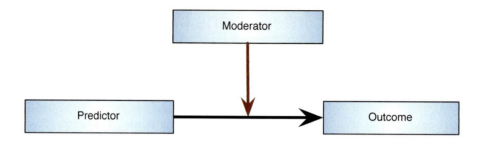

FIGURE 10.5
A categorical moderator (callous traits)

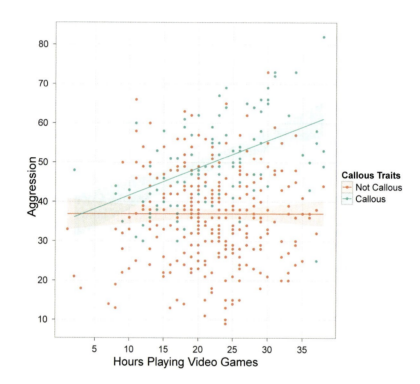

Let's assume we're interested in the relationship between the hours spent playing these games (predictor) and aggression (outcome). The conceptual model of moderation is shown in Figure 10.4, and this diagram shows that a **moderator** variable is one that affects the relationship between two others. If callous-unemotional traits were a moderator then we're saying that the strength or direction of the relationship between game playing and aggression is affected by callous-unemotional traits.

Imagine that we could classify people in terms of callous-unemotional traits: they either have them or they don't. Our moderator variable would be categorical (callous or not callous). Figure 10.5 shows an example of how moderation would work in this case: for people who are not callous there is no relationship between video games and aggression (the line is completely flat), but for people who are callous there is a positive relationship because the more time spent playing these games, the higher the aggression levels (the line slopes upwards). Therefore, callous-unemotional traits moderate the relationship between video games and aggression: there is a positive relationship in those with callous-unemotional traits but not for those without. This is the simplest way to think about moderation. However, it is not necessary that there is an effect in one group but not in the other, all we're looking for is a change in the relationship between video games and aggression in the two callousness groups. It could be that the effect is weakened or changes direction.

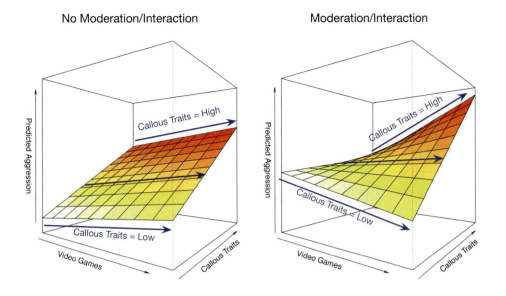

No Moderation/Interaction   Moderation/Interaction

FIGURE 10.6
A continuous moderator (callous traits)

If we measure the moderator variable along a continuum it becomes a bit trickier to visualize, but the basic interpretation stays the same. Figure 10.6 shows two graphs that display the relationships between the time spent playing video games, aggression and callous-unemotional traits (measured along a continuum rather than as two groups). We're still interested in how the relationship between video games and aggression changes as a function of callous-unemotional traits. We can do this by comparing the slope of the regression plane for time spent gaming at low and high values of callous traits. To help you I have added blue arrows that show the relationship between video games and aggression. In the left of the diagram you can see that at the low end of the callous-unemotional traits scale, there is a slight positive relationship between playing video games and aggression (as time playing games increases so does aggression). At the high end of the callous-unemotional traits scale, we see a very similar relationship between video games and aggression (the ends of the regression planes slope at the same angle). The same is also true at the middle of the callous-unemotional traits scale. This is a case of no interaction or no moderation. The right of Figure 10.6 shows an example of moderation: at low values of callous-unemotional traits the plane slopes downwards, indicating a slightly negative relationship between playing video games and aggression, but at the high end of callous-unemotional traits the plane slopes upwards, indicating a strong positive relationship between gaming and aggression. At the midpoint of the callous-unemotional traits scale, the relationship between video games and aggression is relatively flat. So, as we move along the callous-unemotional traits variable, the relationship between gaming and aggression changes from slightly negative to neutral to strongly positive. We can say that the relationship between violent video games and aggression is moderated by callous-unemotional traits.

10.3.2. The statistical model ②

Now we know what moderation is conceptually, let's look at how we explore these effects within a statistical model. Figure 10.7 shows how we conceptualize moderation statistically: we predict the outcome from the predictor variable, the proposed moderator, and the interaction of the two. It is the interaction effect that tells us whether moderation has occurred, but *we must include the predictor and moderator as well for the interaction term to be valid*. This point is very important. In our example, then, we'd be looking at doing a

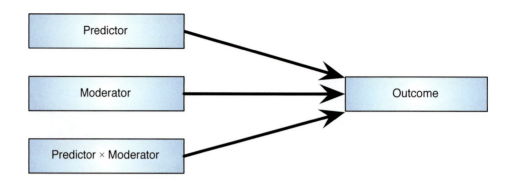

regression in which aggression was the outcome, and we would predict it from video game playing, callous-unemotional traits and their interaction.

All of the general linear models we've considered in this book take the general form of:

$$\text{outcome}_i = (\text{model}) + \text{error}_i$$

When we encountered multiple regression in Chapter 8 we saw that this model was written as (see equation (8.6)):

$$Y_i = (b_0 + b_1 X_{1i} + b_2 X_{2i} + \cdots + b_n X_{ni}) + \varepsilon_i$$

Therefore, our basic regression model for this example would be:

$$\text{Aggression}_i = (b_0 + b_1 \text{Gaming}_i + b_2 \text{Callous}_i) + \varepsilon_i$$

However, to test for moderation we need to consider the interaction between gaming and callous-unemotional traits. If we want to include this term too, then we have seen before that we can extend the linear model to include extra terms, and each time we do we assign them a parameter (*b*). A model that tests for moderation, therefore, is as follows (first expressed generally and then in terms of this specific example):

$$Y_i = (b_0 + b_1 A_i + b_2 B_i + b_3 A B_i) + \varepsilon_i$$

$$\text{Aggression}_i = (b_0 + b_1 \text{Gaming}_i + b_2 \text{Callous}_i + b_3 \text{Interaction}_i) + \varepsilon_i \qquad (10.1)$$

10.3.3. Centring variables ②

When an interaction term is included in the model the *b* parameters have a specific meaning: for the individual predictors they represent the regression of the outcome on that predictor when the other predictor is zero. So, in equation (10.1), b_1 represents the relationship between aggression and gaming when callous traits are zero, and b_2 represents the relationship between aggression and callous traits when someone spends zero hours gaming per week. In our particular example this interpretation isn't problematic because zero is a meaningful score for both predictors: it's plausible that a child spends no hours playing video games, and it is plausible that a child gets a score of 0 on the continuum of callous-unemotional traits. However, there are often situations where it makes no sense for a predictor to have a score of zero. Imagine that rather than measuring how much a child played violent video games we'd measured their heart rate while playing the games as an indicator of their physiological reactivity to them:

$$\text{Aggression}_i = \left(b_0 + b_1 \text{Heart Rate}_i + b_2 \text{Callous}_i + b_3 \text{Interaction}_i\right) + \varepsilon_i$$

In this model b_2 is the regression of aggression on callous traits when someone has a heart rate of zero while playing the games. This b makes no sense unless we're interested in knowing something about the relationship between callous traits and aggression in youths who die (and therefore have a heart rate of zero) while playing these games. It's fair to say that in the unlikely event that playing a video game actually killed someone, we wouldn't really have to worry one way or another about them subsequently developing aggression. Hopefully this example illustrates that the presence of the interaction term makes the bs for the main predictors uninterpretable in many situations.

For this reason, it is common to transform the predictors using grand mean centring. Centring refers to the process of transforming a variable into deviations around a fixed point. This fixed point can be any value that you choose, but typically it's the grand mean. When we calculated z-scores in Chapter 1 we used grand mean centring because the first step was to take each score and subtract from it the mean of all scores. This is grand mean centring. Like z-scores, the subsequent scores are centred on zero, but unlike z-scores we don't care about expressing the centred scores as standard deviations.[3] Therefore, grand mean centring for a given variable is achieved by taking each score and subtracting from it the mean of all scores (for that variable).

What is centring and do I need to do it?

Centring the predictors has no effect on the b for highest-order predictor, but will affect the bs for the lower-order predictors. 'Highest-order' and 'lower-order' refer to how many variables are involved: so the gaming × callous traits interaction is a higher-order effect than the effect of gaming alone because it involves two variables rather than one. So, in our model (equation (10.1)), whether or not we centre the predictors will have no effect on b_3 (the parameter for the interaction) but it will change the values of b_1 and b_2 (the parameters for gaming and callous traits). As we have seen, if we don't centre the gaming and callous variables, then the bs represent the effect of the predictor when the other predictor is zero. However, if we centre the gaming and callous variables then the bs represent the effect of the predictor when the other predictor is its mean value. For example, b_2 represents the relationship between aggression and callous traits for someone who spends the average number of hours gaming per week.

Therefore, centring is particularly important when your model contains an interaction term because it makes the bs for lower-order effects interpretable. There are good reasons for not caring about the lower-order effects when the higher-order interaction involving those effects is significant, but when it is not, centring will make interpreting the main effects easier. For example, if the gaming × callous traits interaction is significant, then it's not clear why we would be interested in the individual effects of gaming and callous traits. In any case, with centred variables the bs for individual predictors have two interpretations: (1) they are the effect of that predictor at the mean value of the sample; and (2) they are the average effect of the predictor across the range of scores for the other predictors. To explain the second interpretation, imagine we took everyone who spent no hours gaming and computed the regression between aggression and callous traits and noted the b, then we took everyone who played games for 1 hour and did the same, then we took everyone who gamed for 2 hours per week and did the same. We continued doing this until we had computed regressions for every different value of the hours spent gaming. We'd have a lot of bs: each one representing the relationship between callous traits and aggression but for

[3] Remember that with z-scores we go a step further and divide the centred scores by the standard deviation of the original data, which changes the units of measurements to standard deviations.

different amounts of gaming. If we took an average of these *b*s then we'd get the same value as the *b* for callous traits (centred) when we use it as a predictor with gaming (centred) and their interaction.

The *PROCESS* tool will do the centring for us so we don't really need to worry too much about how it's done, but because centring is useful in other analyses Oliver Twisted has some additional material that shows you how to do it manually for this example.

OLIVER TWISTED

*Please, Sir, can I have
some more … centring?*

'Recentgin', babbles Oliver as he stumbles drunk out of Mrs Moonshine's alcohol emporium. 'I've had some recent gin.' I think you mean *centring* Oliver, not *recentgin*. If you want to know how to centre your variables using SPSS, then the additional material for this chapter on the companion website will tell you.

10.3.4. Creating interaction variables ②

Equation (10.1) contains a variable called 'Interaction', but the data file does not. The question you might well ask is how we enter a variable into the model that doesn't exist in the data set. We can create it, and it's easier than you might think. Mathematically speaking, when we look at the combined effect of two variables (an interaction) we are literally looking at the effect of the two variables multiplied together. So the interaction variable in this case would literally be the scores on the time spent gaming multiplied by the scores for callous-unemotional traits. That's why interactions are denoted as *variable 1 × variable 2*. The way we'll do moderation analysis in SPSS creates the interaction variable for you, but the self-help task gives you some practice at doing it manually (which might be handy for future reference).

SELF-TEST   Follow Oliver Twisted's instructions to create the centred variables **CUT_Centred** and **Vid_Centred**. Then use the *compute* command to create a new variable called **Interaction** in the **Video Games.sav** file, which is **CUT_Centred** multiplied by **Vid_Centred**.

10.3.5. Following up an interaction effect ②

As we have already seen, moderation is shown by a significant interaction between variables. However, if the moderation effect is significant, then we need to delve a bit deeper to find out the nature of the moderation. In our example, we're predicting that the moderator (callous traits) will influence the relationship between playing violent video games and aggression. If the interaction of callous traits and time spent gaming is a significant predictor of aggression then we know that we have a moderation effect, but we don't know the nature of the effect. It could be that the time spent gaming always has a positive relationship with aggression, but that relationship gets stronger the more a person has callous traits. Alternatively, perhaps in people low on callous traits the time spent gaming *reduces* aggression but it *increases* aggression in those high on callous traits (i.e., the relationship reverses). To find out what is going on we need to do something known as **simple slopes analysis** (Aiken & West, 1991; Rogosa, 1981).

The idea behind simple slopes analysis is fairly straightforward and it's really no different than what was illustrated in Figure 10.6. When describing that figure I talked about comparing the relationship between the predictor (time spent gaming) and outcome (aggression) at low and high levels of the moderator (callous traits). For example, in the right panel of Figure 10.6, we saw that time spent gaming and aggression had a slightly negative relationship at low levels of callous traits, but a fairly strong positive relationship at high levels of callous traits. This is the essence of simple slopes analysis: we work out the regression equations for the predictor and outcome and low, high and average levels of the moderator. The 'high' and 'low' levels can be anything you like, but *PROCESS* uses 1 standard deviation above and below the mean value of the moderator. Therefore, in our example, we would get the regression model for aggression predicted from hours spent gaming for the average value of callous traits, for 1 standard deviation above the mean value of callous traits and for one standard deviation below the mean value of callous traits. We compare these slopes both in terms of their significance, and the value and direction of the b to see whether the relationship between hours spent gaming and aggression changes at different levels of callous traits.

A slightly different approach is to look at how the relationship between the predictor and outcome changes at lots of different values of the moderator (not just at high, low and mean values). One such approach implemented by *PROCESS* is based on Johnson and Neyman (1936). Essentially, it computes the regression model for the predictor and outcome at lots of different values of the moderator. For each model it computes the significance of the regression slope so you can see for which values of the moderator the relationship between the predictor and outcome is significant. It returns a 'zone of significance',[4] which consists of two values of the moderator. Typically, for values in between these two values of the moderator the predictor does not significantly predict the outcome. Values below the lower value and above the upper value are values of the moderator for which the predictor significantly predicts the outcome.

10.3.6. Running the analysis ②

Given that moderation is demonstrated through a significant interaction between the predictor and moderator in a regression, we could follow the general procedure for fitting linear models in Chapter 8 (Figure 8.11). We would first centre the predictor and moderator, then create the interaction term as discussed already, then run a forced entry regression with the centred predictor, centred moderator and the interaction of the two centred variables as predictors. The advantage of this approach is that we can inspect sources of bias in the model.

SELF-TEST Assuming you have done the other self-test, run a regression predicting **Aggression** from **CUT_Centred**, **Vid_Centred** and **Interaction**.

Using the *PROCESS* tool (if you haven't installed it yet, see Section 10.2) has several advantages over using the normal regression tools: (1) it will centre predictors for us; (2) it computes the interaction term automatically; and (3) it will do simple slopes analysis. To access the dialog boxes in Figure 10.8 select Analyze Regression ▶

---

[4] I have to be careful not to confuse this with my wife, who is the Zoë of significance.

PROCESS, by Andrew F. Hayes (http://www.afhayes.com). The variables in your data file will be listed in the box labelled *Data File Variables*. Select the outcome variable (in this case **Aggression**) and drag it to the box labelled *Outcome Variable (Y)*, or click on ⏩. Similarly, select the predictor variable (in this case **Vid_Games**) and drag it to the box labelled *Independent Variable (X)*. Finally, select the moderator variable (in this case **CaUnTs**) and drag it to the box labelled *M Variable(s)*, or click on ⏩. This box is where you specify any moderators (you can have more than one).

PROCESS can test 74 different types of model, and these models are listed in the drop-down box labelled *Model Number*. If you want to investigate all 74 different models then have a look at the PROCESS documentation (http://www.afhayes.com/public/process.pdf). Simple moderation analysis is represented by model 1, but the default model is 4 (mediation, which we'll look at next). Therefore, activate this drop-down list and select 1 ⏷. The rest of the options in this dialog box are for models other than simple moderation, so we'll ignore them.

If you click on Options another dialog box will appear containing four useful options for moderation. Selecting (1) *Mean center for products* centres the predictor and moderator for you; (2) *Heteroscedasticity-consistent SEs* means we need not worry about having heteroscedasticity in the model; (3) *OLS/ML confidence intervals* produces confidence intervals for the model, and I've tried to emphasize the importance of these throughout the book; and (4) *Generate data for plotting* is helpful for interpreting and visualizing the simple slopes analysis. Talking of simple slopes analysis, if you click on Conditioning, you can change whether you want simple slopes at ±1 standard deviation of the mean of the moderator (the default, which is fine) or at percentile points (it uses the 10th, 25th, 50th, 75th and 90th percentiles). It is useful to select the *Johnson-Neyman* method to get a zone of significance for the moderator. Back in the main dialog box, click on OK to run the analysis.

FIGURE 10.8
The dialog boxes for running moderation analysis

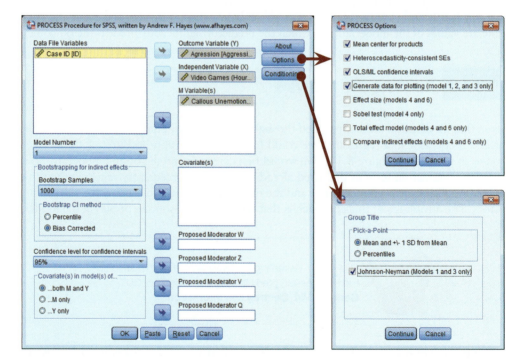

10.3.7. Output from moderation analysis ②

The first thing to notice about the output is it appears as text rather than being nicely formatted in tables. Try not to let this formatting disturb you. If your output looks odd

SPSS TIP 10.1   Troubleshooting *PROCESS* ②

There are a few things worth knowing about *PROCESS* that might help to prevent weird stuff happening.

- If the variable names entered into *PROCESS* are longer than 8 characters, it shortens them to 8 characters. Therefore, if you enter variables with similar long names *PROCESS* will get confused. For example, if you had two variables in the data editor called **NumberOfNephariousActs** and **NumberOfBlackSabbathAlbumsOwned** they would both be shortened to **numberof** (or possibly **number~1** and **number~2**) and *PROCESS* will get confused about which variable is which. If your output looks weird, then check your variable names.
- Don't call any of your variables **xxx** (I'm not sure why you would) because that is a reserved variable name in *PROCESS*, so naming a variable **xxx** will confuse it.
- *PROCESS* is also confused by string variables, so only enter numeric variables.

or contains warnings, or has a lot of zeros in it, it might be worth checking the variables that you input into *PROCESS* (SPSS Tip 10.1). However, assuming everything has gone smoothly, you should see Output 10.1, which is the main moderation analysis. This output is pretty much the same as the table of regression coefficients that we saw in Chapter 8. We're told the *b*-value for each predictor, and the associated standard errors (which have been adjusted for heteroscedasticity because we asked for them to be). Each *b* is compared to zero using a *t*-test, which is computed from the beta divided by its standard error. The confidence interval for the *b* is also produced (because we asked for it). Moderation is shown up by a significant interaction effect, and in this case the interaction is highly significant, $b = 0.027$, 95% CI [0.013, 0.041], $t = 3.71$, $p < .001$, indicating that the relationship between the time spent gaming and aggression is moderated by callous traits.

SELF-TEST   Assuming you did the previous self-test, compare the table of coefficients that you got with those in Output 10.1.

To interpret the moderation effect we can examine the simple slopes, which are shown in Output 10.2. Essentially, the table shows us the results of three different regressions: the regression for time spent gaming as a predictor of aggression (1) when callous traits are low (to be precise when the value of callous traits is –9.6177); (2) at the mean value of callous traits (because we centred callous traits its mean value is zero as indicated in the output); and (3) when the value of callous traits is 9.6177 (i.e., high). We can interpret these three regressions as we would any other: we're interested in the value of *b* (called *Effect* in the output), and its significance. From what we have already learnt about regression we can interpret the three models as follows:

1 When callous traits are low, there is a non-significant negative relationship between time spent gaming and aggression, $b = -0.091$, 95% CI [–0.299, 0.117], $t = -0.86$, $p = .392$.

2 At the mean value of callous traits, there is a significant positive relationship between time spent gaming and aggression, $b = 0.170$, 95% CI [0.020, 0.319], $t = 2.23$, $p = .026$.

3 When callous traits are high, there is a significant positive relationship between time spent gaming and aggression, $b = 0.430$, 95% CI [0.231, 0.628], $t = 4.26$, $p < .001$.

These results tell us that the relationship between time spent playing violent video games and aggression only really emerges in people with average or greater levels of callous-unemotional traits.

OUTPUT 10.1

```
************************************************************************
Model = 1
    Y = Aggressi
    X = Vid_Game
    M = CaUnTs


Sample size
      442
************************************************************************
Outcome: Aggressi
Model Summary
          R         R-sq         F        df1        df2          p
       .6142       .3773     90.5311     3.0000   438.0000      .0000
Model
             coeff         se          t          p       LLCI       ULCI
constant    39.9671      .4750    84.1365      .0000    39.0335    40.9007
CaUnTs        .7601      .0466    16.3042      .0000      .6685      .8517
Vid_Game      .1696      .0759     2.2343      .0260      .0204      .3188
int_1         .0271      .0073     3.7051      .0002      .0127      .0414

Interactions:

 int_1    Vid_Game    X     CaUnTs
```

OUTPUT 10.2

```
************************************************************************
Conditional effect of X on Y at values of the moderator(s)
     CaUnTs     Effect        se          t          p       LLCI       ULCI
    -9.6177     -.0907      .1058      -.8568      .3920     -.2986      .1173
      .0000      .1696      .0759      2.2343      .0260      .0204      .3188
     9.6177      .4299      .1010      4.2562      .0000      .2314      .6284
Values for quantitative moderators are the mean and plus/minus one SD from mean
```

Output 10.3 shows the output of the Johnson–Neyman method, and this gives a different approach to simple slopes. First we're told the boundaries of the zone of significance: it is between −17.1002 and −0.7232. Remember that these are the values of the centred version of the callous-unemotional traits variable, and define regions within which the relationship between the time spent gaming and aggression is significant. The table underneath gives a detailed breakdown of these regions. Essentially it's doing something quite similar to the simple slopes analysis: it takes different values of callous and unemotional traits and for each one computes the b (*Effect*) and its significance for the relationship between the time spent gaming and aggression. I have annotated the output to show the boundaries of the zone of significance. If you look at the column labelled p you can see that we start off with a significant negative relationship between time spent gaming and aggression, $b = -0.334$, 95% CI [−0.645, −0.022], $t = -2.10$, $p = .036$. As we move up to the next value of callous traits (−17.1002), the relationship between time spent gaming and aggression is still significant ($p = .0500$), but at the next value it becomes non-significant ($p = .058$). Therefore, the

```
*********************** JOHNSON-NEYMAN TECHNIQUE **************************

Moderator value(s) defining Johnson-Neyman significance region(s)
    -17.1002
      -.7232

Conditional effect of X on Y at values of the moderator (M)
    CaUnTs       Effect        se          t           p         LLCI        ULCI
   -18.5950      -.3336      .1587     -2.1027       .0361      -.6454      -.0218      ] Significant
   -17.1002      -.2931      .1492     -1.9654       .0500      -.5863       .0000
   -16.4450      -.2754      .1451     -1.8987       .0583      -.5605       .0097
   -14.2950      -.2172      .1319     -1.6467       .1003      -.4765       .0420
   -12.1450      -.1590      .1194     -1.3319       .1836      -.3937       .0756
    -9.9950      -.1009      .1077      -.9361       .3497      -.3126       .1109      Not
    -7.8450      -.0427      .0972      -.4390       .6609      -.2338       .1484      significant
    -5.6950       .0155      .0882       .1757       .8606      -.1579       .1889
    -3.5450       .0737      .0813       .9059       .3655      -.0862       .2336
    -1.3950       .1319      .0771      1.7111       .0878      -.0196       .2833
     -.7232       .1501      .0763      1.9654       .0500       .0000       .3001
      .7550       .1901      .0759      2.5053       .0126       .0410       .3392
     2.9050       .2482      .0779      3.1878       .0015       .0952       .4013
     5.0550       .3064      .0829      3.6980       .0002       .1436       .4693
     7.2050       .3646      .0903      4.0360       .0001       .1871       .5422
     9.3550       .4228      .0997      4.2386       .0000       .2267       .6188
    11.5050       .4810      .1106      4.3490       .0000       .2636       .6983      Significant
    13.6550       .5392      .1225      4.4013       .0000       .2984       .7799
    15.8050       .5973      .1352      4.4188       .0000       .3317       .8630
    17.9550       .6555      .1484      4.4160       .0000       .3638       .9473
    20.1050       .7137      .1621      4.4017       .0000       .3950      1.0324
    22.2550       .7719      .1762      4.3814       .0000       .4256      1.1181
    24.4050       .8301      .1905      4.3580       .0000       .4557      1.2044

******************************************************************************
```

threshold for significance ends at −17.1002 (which we were told at the top of the output). As we increase the value of callous-unemotional traits the relationship between time spent gaming and aggression remains non-significant until the value of callous-unemotional traits is −0.723, at which point it just crosses the threshold for significance again. For all subsequent values of callous-unemotional traits the relationship between time spent gaming and aggression is significant. Looking at the *b*-values themselves (in the column labelled *Effect*) we can also see that with increases in callous-unemotional traits the strength of relationship between time spent gaming and aggression goes from a small negative effect ($b = -0.334$) to a fairly strong positive one ($b = 0.830$).

The final way we can look at these effects is by graphing them. In Figure 10.8 we asked *PROCESS* to generate data for plotting and these data are at the bottom of the output (see Figure 10.9). We're given values of the variable **Vid_Games** (-6.9622, 0, 6.9622) and of **CaUnTs** (-9.6177, 0, 9.6177). These values are not important in themselves, but they correspond to low, mean and high values of the variable. The **yhat** tells us the predicted values of the outcome (aggression) for these combinations of the predictors. For example, when **Vid_Games** and **CaUnTs** are both low (−6.9622 and −9.6177, respectively) the predicted value of aggression is 33.2879, when both variables are at their mean (0 and 0), the predicted value of aggression is 39.9671, and so on. To create a simple slopes graph we need to put these values in a data file. The simplest way to create the new data file is to create coding variables that represent low, mean and high (use any codes you like). Then enter all combinations of these codes. For example, in Figure 10.9 I've created variables called **Games** and **CaUnTs** both of which are coding variables (1 = low, 2 = mean, 3 = high) and then entered the combinations of these codes that correspond to the *PROCESS* output (e.g., low–low, mean–low, high–low), then I have typed in the corresponding predicted values from the *PROCESS* output. Hopefully you can see from Figure 10.9 how the output from *PROCESS* corresponds to the new data file. You can access this file as **Video Game Graph.sav** if you can't work out how to create it yourself. Having transferred the output to a data file, we can draw line graphs using what we learnt in Chapter 4.

FIGURE 10.9
Entering data
for graphing
simple slopes

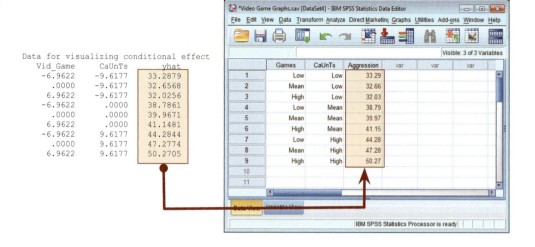

```
Data for visualizing conditional effect
  Vid_Game    CaUnTs         yhat
  -6.9622    -9.6177      33.2879
    .0000    -9.6177      32.6568
   6.9622    -9.6177      32.0256
  -6.9622      .0000      38.7861
    .0000      .0000      39.9671
   6.9622      .0000      41.1481
  -6.9622     9.6177      44.2844
    .0000     9.6177      47.2774
   6.9622     9.6177      50.2705
```

SELF-TEST Draw a multiple line graph of **Aggression** (*y*-axis)
against **Games** (*x*-axis) with different-coloured lines for different
values of **CaUnTs**.

The resulting graph from the self-test is shown in Figure 10.10. The graph shows what
we found from the simple slopes analysis: when callous traits are low (blue line) there is
a non-significant negative relationship between time spent gaming and aggression; at the
mean value of callous traits (green line) there is small positive relationship between time
spent gaming and aggression; and this relationship gets even stronger at high levels of callous traits (beige line).

FIGURE 10.10
Simple slopes
equations of
the regression
of aggression
on video games
at three levels
of callous traits

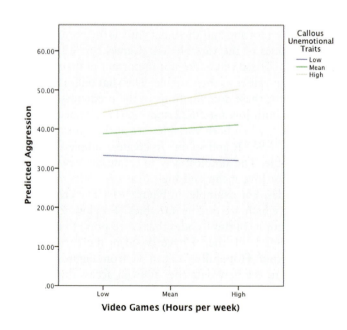

SELF-TEST Now draw a multiple line graph of **Aggression** (y-axis) against **CaUnTs** (x-axis) with different-coloured lines for different values of **Games**.

10.3.8. Reporting moderation analysis ②

Moderation analysis is just regression, so we can report it in the same way as described in Section 8.9. My personal preference would be to produce a table such as Table 10.1.

TABLE 10.1 Linear model of predictors of aggression

	b	SE B	t	p
Constant	39.97 [39.03, 40.90]	0.475	84.13	*p* < .001
Callous Traits (centred)	0.76 [0.67, 0.85]	0.047	16.30	*p* < .001
Gaming (centred)	0.17 [0.02, 0.32]	0.076	2.23	*p* = .026
Callous Traits x Gaming	0.027 [0.01, 0.04]	0.007	3.71	*p* < .001

Note. R^2 = .38.

CRAMMING SAM'S TIPS   Moderation

- Moderation occurs when the relationship between two variables changes as a function of a third variable. For example, the relationship between watching horror films and feeling scared at bedtime might increase as a function of how vivid an imagination a person has.
- Moderation is tested using a regression in which the outcome (fear at bedtime) is predicted from a predictor (how many horror films are watched), the moderator (imagination) and the interaction of these variables.
- Predictors should be centred before the analysis.
- The interaction of two variables is simply the scores on the two variables multiplied together.
- If the interaction is significant then moderation is present.
- If moderation is found, follow up the analysis with simple slopes analysis. This analysis looks at the relationship between the predictor and outcome at low, mean and high levels of the moderator.

10.4. Mediation ②

10.4.1. The conceptual model ②

What is mediation?

Whereas moderation alludes to the combined effect of two variables on an outcome, **mediation** refers to a situation when the relationship between a predictor variable and an outcome variable can be explained by their relationship to a third variable (the **mediator**). The top of Figure 10.11 shows a basic relationship between a predictor and an outcome (denoted as *c*). However, the bottom of the figure shows that these variables are also related to a third variable in specific ways: (1) the predictor also predicts the mediator through the path denoted by *a*; (2) the mediator predicts the outcome through the path denoted by *b*. The relationship between the predictor and outcome will probably be different when the mediator is also included in the model and so is denoted *c'*. The letters denoting each path (*a*, *b*, *c* and *c'*) represent the unstandardized regression coefficient between the variables connected by the arrow; therefore, they symbolize the strength of relationship between variables. Mediation is said to have occurred if the strength of the relationship between the predictor and outcome is reduced by including the mediator (i.e., the regression parameter for *c'* is smaller than for *c*). Perfect mediation occurs when *c'* is zero: in other words, the relationship between the predictor and outcome is completely wiped out by including the mediator in the model.

This description is all a bit abstract, so let's use an example. My wife and I often wonder what the important factors are in making a relationship last. For my part, I don't really understand why she'd want to be with a balding heavy rock fan with an oversized collection of vinyl and musical instruments and an unhealthy love of *Doctor Who* and numbers. It is important I gather as much information as possible about keeping her happy because the odds are stacked against me. For her part I have no idea why she wonders: her very existence makes me happy. Perhaps if you are in a relationship you have wondered how to make it last too.

FIGURE 10.11
Diagram of a basic mediation model

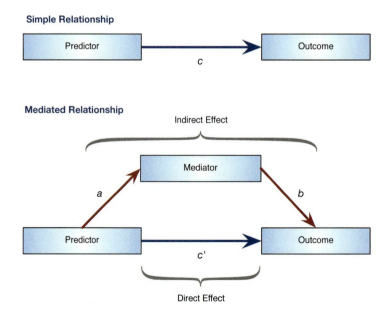

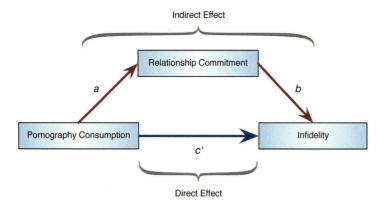

FIGURE 10.12
Diagram of
a mediation
model from
Lambert et al.
(2012)

During our cyber-travels, Mrs Field and I have discovered that physical attractiveness (McNulty, Neff, & Karney, 2008), conscientiousness and neuroticism (good for us) predict marital satisfaction (Claxton, O'Rourke, Smith, & DeLongis, 2012). Pornography use probably doesn't: it is related to infidelity (Lambert, Negash, Stillman, Olmstead, & Fincham, 2012). Mediation is really all about the variables that explain relationships like these: it's unlikely that everyone who catches a glimpse of some porn suddenly rushes out of their house to have an affair – presumably it leads to some kind of emotional or cognitive change that undermines the love glue that holds us and our partners together. Lambert et al. tested this hypothesis. Figure 10.12 shows their mediator model: the initial relationship is that between pornography consumption (the predictor) and infidelity (the outcome), and they hypothesized that this relationship is mediated by commitment (the mediator). This model suggests that the relationship between pornography consumption and infidelity isn't a direct effect but operates through a reduction in relationship commitment. For this hypothesis to be true: (1) pornography consumption must predict infidelity in the first place (path c); (2) pornography consumption must predict relationship commitment (path a); (3) relationship commitment must predict infidelity (path b); and (4) the relationship between pornography consumption and infidelity should be smaller when relationship commitment is included in the model than when it isn't. We can distinguish between the **direct effect** of pornography consumption on infidelity, which is the relationship between them controlling for relationship commitment, and the **indirect effect**, which is the effect of pornography consumption on infidelity through relationship commitment (Figure 10.12).

10.4.2.   The statistical model ②

Unlike moderation, the statistical model for mediation is basically the same as the conceptual model: it is characterized in Figure 10.11. Historically, this model was tested through a series of regression analyses, which reflect the four conditions necessary to demonstrate mediation (Baron & Kenny, 1986). I have mentioned already that the letters denoting the paths in Figure 10.11 represent the unstandardized regression coefficients for the relationships between variables denoted by the path. Therefore, to estimate any one of these paths, we want to know the unstandardized regression coefficient for the two variables involved. For example, Baron and Kenny suggested in their seminal paper that mediation is tested through three regression models (see also Judd & Kenny, 1981):

1   A regression predicting the outcome from the predictor variable. The regression coefficient for the predictor gives us the value of c in Figure 10.11.

2 A regression predicting the mediator from the predictor variable. The regression coefficient for the predictor gives us the value of *a* in Figure 10.11.

3 A regression predicting the outcome from both the predictor variable and the mediator. The regression coefficient for the predictor gives us the value of *c'* in Figure 10.11, and the regression coefficient for the mediator gives us the value of *b*.

These models test the four conditions of mediation: (1) the predictor variable must significantly predict the outcome variable in model 1; (2) the predictor variable must significantly predict the mediator in model 2; (3) the mediator must significantly predict the outcome variable in model 3; and (4) the predictor variable must predict the outcome variable less strongly in model 3 than in model 1.

In Lambert et al.'s (2012) study, all participants had been in a relationship for at least a year. The researchers measured pornography consumption on a scale from 0 (low) to 8 (high), but this variable, as you might expect, was skewed (most people had low scores) so they analysed log-transformed values (**LnConsumption**). They also measured commitment to their current relationship (**Commitment**) on a scale from 1 (low) to 5 (high). Infidelity was measured in terms of questions asking whether the person had committed a physical act (**Infidelity**) that they or their partner would consider to be unfaithful (0 = no, 1 = one of them would consider it unfaithful, 2 = both of them would consider the act unfaithful),[5] and also in terms of the number of people they had 'hooked up' with in the previous year (**Hook_Ups**), which would mean during a time period in which they were in their current relationship.[6] The actual data from Lambert et al.'s study are in the file **Lambert et al. (2012).sav**.

SELF-TEST   Run the three regressions necessary to test mediation for Lambert et al.'s data: (1) a regression predicting **Infidelity** from **LnConsumption**; (2) a regression predicting **Commitment** from **LnConsumption**; and (3) a regression predicting **Infidelity** from both **LnConsumption** and **Commitment**. Is there evidence of mediation?

Many people still use this approach to test mediation: Baron and Kenny's article has been cited over 35,000 times in scientific papers, which gives you some idea of how influential this method has been. I think it is very useful for illustrating the principles of mediation and for understanding what mediation means. However, the method of regressions has some limitations. The main one is the fourth criterion by which mediation is assessed: *the predictor variable must predict the outcome variable less strongly in model 3 than in model 1*. Although we know that perfect mediation is shown when the relationship between the predictor and outcome is reduced to zero in model 3, usually this doesn't happen. Instead, you see a reduction in the relationship between the predictor and outcome, rather than the relationship being reduced to zero. This raises the question of how much of a reduction is necessary to infer mediation.

Although Baron and Kenny advocated looking at the sizes of the regression parameters, in practice people tend to look for a change in significance; so, mediation would occur if the relationship between the predictor and outcome was significant ($p < .05$) when looked at in isolation (model 1) but not significant ($p > .05$) when the mediator is included too (model 3). This approach can lead to all sorts of silliness because of the all-or-nothing

---

[5] I've coded this variable differently from the original data to make interpretation of it more intuitive, but it doesn't affect the results.

[6] A 'hook-up' was defined to participants as 'when two people get together for a physical encounter and don't necessarily expect anything further (e.g., no plan or intention to do it again)'.

thinking that p-values encourage. You could have a situation in which the b-value for the relationship between the predictor and outcome changes very little in models with and without the mediator, but the p-value shifts from one side of the threshold to another (e.g., from $p =.049$ when the mediator isn't included to $p =.051$ when it is). Even though the p-values have changed from significant to not significant, the change is very small, and the size of the relationship between the predictor and outcome will not have changed very much at all. Similarly, you could have a situation where the b for the relationship between the predictor and the outcome reduces a lot when the mediator is included, but remains significant in both cases. For example, perhaps when looked at in isolation the relationship between the predictor and outcome is $b = 0.46$, $p < .001$, but when the mediator is included as a predictor as well it reduces to $b = 0.18$, $p = .042$. You'd conclude (based on significance) that no mediation had occurred despite the fact that relationship between the predictor and outcome is less than half its original value.

An alternative is to estimate the indirect effect and its significance. The indirect effect is illustrated in Figures 10.11 and 10.12: it is the combined effects of paths a and b. The significance of this effect can be assessed using the **Sobel test** (Sobel, 1982). If the Sobel test is significant it means that the predictor significantly affects the outcome variable via the mediator. In other words, there is significant mediation. This test works well in large samples, but you're better off computing confidence intervals for the indirect effect using bootstrap methods (Section 5.4.3). Now that computers make it easy for us to estimate the indirect effect (i.e., the effect of mediation) and its confidence interval, this practice is becoming increasingly common and is preferable to Baron and Kenny's regressions and the Sobel test because it's harder to get sucked into the black-and-white thinking of significance testing (Section 2.6.2.2). People tend to apply Baron and Kenny's method in a way that is intrinsically bound to looking for 'significant' relationships, whereas estimating the indirect effect and its confidence interval allows us to simply report the degree of mediation observed in the data.

10.4.3. Effect sizes of mediation ③

If we're going to look at the size of the indirect effect to judge whether mediation has occurred, then it's useful to have effect size measures to help us (see Section 2.7.1). Many effect size measures have been proposed and are discussed in detail elsewhere (MacKinnon, 2008; Preacher & Kelley, 2011). The simplest is to look at the regression coefficient for the indirect effect and its confidence interval. Figure 10.11 shows us that the indirect effect is the combined effect of paths a and b. We have also seen that a and b are unstandardized regression coefficients for the relationships between variables denoted by the path. To find the combined effect of these paths, we simply multiply these regression coefficients:

$$\text{indirect effect} = ab \tag{10.2}$$

The resulting value is an unstandardized regression coefficient like any other, and consequently is expressed in the original units of measurement. As we have seen, it is sometimes useful to look at standardized regression parameters, because these can be compared across different studies using different outcome measures (see Chapter 8). MacKinnon (2008) suggested standardizing this measure by dividing by the standard deviation of the outcome variable:

$$\text{indirect effect (partially standardized)} = \frac{ab}{s_{\text{Outcome}}} \tag{10.3}$$

This standardizes the indirect effect with respect to the outcome variable, but not the predictor or mediator. As such, it is sometimes referred to as the partially standardized indirect effect. To fully standardize the indirect effect we would need to multiply the partially standardized measures by the standard deviation of the predictor variable (Preacher & Hayes, 2008b):

$$\text{indirect effect (standardized)} = \frac{ab}{s_{\text{Outcome}}} \times s_{\text{Predictor}} \tag{10.4}$$

This measure is sometimes called the **index of mediation**. This measure is useful in that it can be compared across different mediation models that use different measures of the predictor, outcome and mediator. Reporting this measure would be particularly helpful if anyone decides to include your research in a meta-analysis.

A different approach to estimating the size of the indirect effect is to look at the size of the indirect effect relative to either the total effect of the predictor or the direct effect of the predictor. For example, if we wanted the ratio of the indirect effect (ab) to the total effect (c) we could use the regression parameters from the various regressions displayed in Figure 10.11:

$$P_M = \frac{ab}{c} \tag{10.5}$$

Similarly, if we want to express the indirect effect as a ratio of the direct effect (c'), the regressions give us everything we need:

$$R_M = \frac{ab}{c'} \tag{10.6}$$

These ratio-based measures only really re-describe the original indirect effect. Both are very unstable in small samples, and MacKinnon (2008) advises against using P_M and R_M in samples smaller than 500 and 5000, respectively. Also, although it is tempting to think of P_M as a proportion (because it is the ratio of the indirect effect compared to the *total* effect) it is not: it can exceed 1 and even take on negative values (Preacher & Kelley, 2011). For these reasons, these ratio measures are probably best avoided.

In regression we used R^2 as a measure of the proportion of variance explained by a predictor (or several predictors). We can compute a form of R^2 for the indirect effect, which tells us the proportion of variance explained by the indirect effect. MacKinnon (2008) proposes several versions, but *PROCESS* computes this one:

$$R_M^2 = R_{Y,M}^2 - \left(R_{Y,MX}^2 - R_{Y,X}^2 \right) \tag{10.7}$$

This uses the proportion of variance in the outcome variables explained by the predictor ($R_{Y,X}^2$), the mediator ($R_{Y,M}^2$), and both ($R_{Y,MX}^2$). It can be interpreted as the variance in the outcome that is shared by the mediator and the predictor, but that cannot be attributed to either in isolation. Again, this measure is not bound to fall between 0 and 1, and it's possible to get negative values (which usually indicate suppression effects rather than mediation).

The final measure that I'll consider was proposed by Preacher and Kelley (2011) and is called kappa-squared (κ^2). If you read the original article, it is full of scary equations that make this measure very difficult to explain. However, at a conceptual level it is a very simple and elegant idea: kappa-squared expresses the indirect effect as a ratio to the maximum possible indirect effect that you could have found given the design of your study:

$$\kappa^2 = \frac{ab}{\max(ab)} \tag{10.8}$$

The scary maths comes into play in how the maximum possible value of the indirect effect is computed. However, we have computers to do that for us, so let's just imagine that a frog called Hugglefrall sticks his big slimy tongue out and numbers attach themselves to it. He then swirls the numbers around in his mouth, does that funny expanding throat thing that frogs sometimes do, and then belches out the value for us. Beyond that, all we need to know is that kappa is a proportion and we can interpret it as such: values of 0 mean the indirect effect is very small relative to the maximum possible value, and values close to 1 mean that it is as large as it could possibly be given the design that we have. Not that I should really encourage this sort of thing, but in terms of what constitutes a large effect, κ^2 can be equated to the values used for R^2: a small effect is .01, a medium effect would be around .09, and a large effect in the region of .25 (Preacher & Kelley, 2011).

PROCESS computes all of the effect size measures that I have discussed, but of them all probably the most useful are the unstandardized and standardized indirect effect and κ^2. All of the measures discussed have accompanying confidence intervals and are unaffected by sample sizes (although note my earlier comments about the variability of P_M and R_M in small samples). However, P_M, R_M and R_M^2 cannot be interpreted easily because they allude to being proportions but are not, and all of the measures apart from κ^2 are unbounded, which again makes interpretation tricky (Preacher & Kelley, 2011).

10.4.4. Running the analysis ②

Assuming we're going to test Lambert's mediation model (Figure 10.12) by estimating the indirect effect rather than through a Baron and Kenny style mediation analysis, then we can again use Hayes's *PROCESS* tool (see Section 10.2 if you haven't installed it yet). To access the dialog boxes in Figure 10.13 select Analyze Regression ▸ PROCESS, by Andrew F. Hayes (http://www.afhayes.com). The variables in your data file will be listed in the box labelled *Data File Variables*. Select the outcome variable (in this case **Infidelity**) and drag it to the box labelled *Outcome Variable (Y)*, or click on ➡. Similarly, select the predictor variable (in this case **LnConsumption**) and drag it to the box labelled *Independent Variable (X)*. Finally, select the mediator variable (in this case **Commitment**) and drag it to the box labelled *M Variable(s)*, or click on ➡. This box is where you specify any mediators (you can have more than one).

As I mentioned before, *PROCESS* can test many different types of model, and simple mediation analysis is represented by model 4 (this model is selected by default). Therefore, make sure that 4 ▾ is selected in the drop-down list under *Model Number*. Unlike moderation, there are other options in this dialog box that are useful: for example, to test the indirect effects we will use bootstrapping to generate a confidence interval around the indirect effect. By default *PROCESS* uses 1000 bootstrap samples, and will compute bias corrected and accelerated confidence intervals. These default options are fine, but just be aware that you can ask for percentile bootstrap confidence intervals instead (see Section 5.4.3).

If you click on Options another dialog box will appear containing four useful options for mediation. Selecting (1) *Effect size* produces the estimates of the size of the indirect effect

FIGURE 10.13
The dialog boxes for running mediation analysis

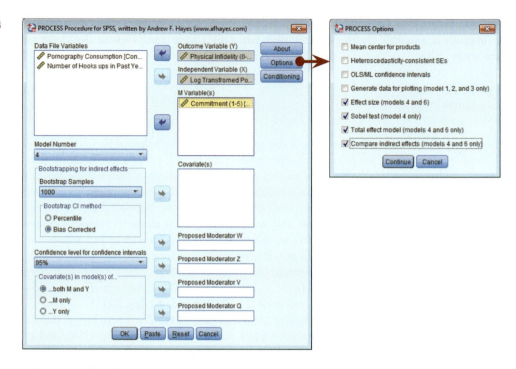

ODITI'S LANTERN

moderation and mediation

'I, Oditi, want you to join my cult of undiscovered numerical truths. I also want you to stare into my lantern to gain statistical enlightenment. It's possible that statistical knowledge mediates the relationship between staring into my lantern and joining my cult … or it could be mediated by neurological changes to your brain created by the subliminal messages in the videos. Stare into my lantern to find out about mediation and moderation.'

discussed in Section 10.4.3;[7] (2) *Sobel test* produces a significance test of the indirect effect devised by Sobel; (3) *Total effect model* produces the direct effect of the predictor on the outcome (in this case the regression of infidelity predicted from pornography consumption); and (4) *Compare indirect effects* will, when you have more than one mediator in the model, estimate the effect and confidence interval for the difference between the indirect effects resulting from these mediators. This final option is useful when you have more than one mediator to compare their relative importance in explaining the relationship between the predictor and outcome. However, we have only a single mediator so we don't need to select this option (you can select it if you like, but it won't change the output produced). None of the options activated by clicking on [Conditioning] apply to simple mediation models, so we can ignore this button and click [OK] to run the analysis.

10.4.5. Output from mediation analysis ②

As with moderation, the output appears as text. Output 10.4 shows the first part of the output, which initially tells us the name of the outcome (*Y*), the predictor (*X*) and the mediator (*M*)

---

[7] R_M^2 and κ^2 are produced only for models with a single mediator. Although I don't look at more complex models, bear this in mind if you run models including more than one mediator, or covariates.

variables, which have been shortened to 8 letters (SPSS Tip 10.1). This is useful for double-checking we have entered the variables in the correct place: the outcome is infidelity, the predictor consumption, and the mediator is commitment. The next part of the output shows us the results of the simple regression of commitment predicted from pornography consumption (i.e., path a in Figure 10.12). This output is interpreted just as we would interpret any regression: we can see that pornography consumption significantly predicts relationship commitment, $b = -0.47$, $t = -2.21$, $p = .028$. The R^2 value tells us that pornography consumption explains 2% of the variance in relationship commitment, and the fact that the b is negative tells us that the relationship is negative also: as consumption increases, commitment declines (and vice versa).

OUTPUT 10.4

```
*************************************************************************
Model = 4

    Y = Infideli

    X = LnConsum

    M = Commitme

Sample size

       239

*************************************************************************

Outcome: Commitme


Model Summary

          R         R-sq           F          df1          df2            p
      .1418        .0201      4.8633       1.0000     237.0000        .0284

Model

               coeff          se           t            p
constant      4.2027       .0545     77.1777        .0000

LnConsum      -.4697       .2130     -2.2053        .0284
```

Output 10.5 shows the results of the regression of infidelity predicted from both pornography consumption (i.e., path c' in Figure 10.12) and commitment (i.e., path b in Figure 10.12). We can see that pornography consumption significantly predicts infidelity even with relationship commitment in the model, $b = 0.46$, $t = 2.35$, $p = .02$; relationship commitment also significantly predicts infidelity, $b = -0.27$, $t = -4.61$, $p <.001$. The R^2 value tells us that the model explains 11.4% of the variance in infidelity. The negative b for commitment tells us that as commitment increases, infidelity declines (and vice versa), but the positive b for consumption indicates that as pornography consumption increases, infidelity increases also. These relationships are in the predicted direction.

OUTPUT 10.5

```
*************************************************************************
Outcome: Infideli

Model Summary

          R         R-sq           F          df1          df2            p
      .3383        .1144     15.2453       2.0000     236.0000        .0000

Model

               coeff          se           t            p
constant      1.3704       .2518      5.4433        .0000

Commitme      -.2710       .0587     -4.6128        .0000

LnConsum       .4573       .1946      2.3505        .0196
```

Output 10.6 shows the total effect of pornography consumption on infidelity (outcome). You will get this bit of the output only if you selected *Total effect model* in Figure 10.13. The total effect is the effect of the predictor on the outcome when the mediator is not present in the model – in other words, path *c* in Figure 10.11. When relationship commitment is not in the model, pornography consumption significantly predicts infidelity, $b = 0.58$, $t = 2.91$, $p = .004$. The R^2 value tells us that the model explains 3.46% of the variance in infidelity. As is the case when we include relationship commitment in the model, pornography consumption has a positive relationship with infidelity (as shown by the positive *b*-value).

OUTPUT 10.6

```
************************* TOTAL EFFECT MODEL ***************************

Outcome: Infideli

 Model Summary
          R         R-sq          F          df1         df2           p
      .1859        .0346     8.4866       1.0000    237.0000       .0039

 Model
              coeff         se           t           p
constant      .2315       .0513      4.5123       .0000

LnConsum      .5846       .2007      2.9132       .0039
```

Output 10.7 is the most important part of the output because it displays the results for the indirect effect of pornography consumption on infidelity (i.e., the effect via relationship commitment). First, we're told the effect of pornography consumption on infidelity in isolation (the total effect), and these values replicate the model in Output 10.6. Next, we're told the effect of pornography consumption on infidelity when relationship commitment is included as a predictor as well (the direct effect). These values replicate those in Output 10.5. The first bit of new information is the *Indirect effect of X on Y*, which in this case is the indirect effect of pornography consumption on infidelity. We're given an estimate of this effect ($b = 0.127$) as well as a bootstrapped standard error and confidence interval. As we have seen many times before, 95% confidence intervals contain the true value of a parameter in 95% of samples. Therefore, we tend to assume that our sample isn't one of the 5% that does not contain the true value and use them to infer the population value of an effect. In this case, assuming our sample is one of the 95% that 'hits' the true value, we know that the true *b*-value for the indirect effect falls between 0.023 and 0.335.[8] This range does not include zero, and remember that $b = 0$ would mean 'no effect whatsoever'; therefore, the fact that the confidence interval does not contain zero means that there is likely to be a genuine indirect effect. Put another way, relationship commitment is a mediator of the relationship between pornography consumption and infidelity.

The rest of Output 10.7 you will see only if you selected *Effect size* in Figure 10.13; it contains various standardized forms of the indirect effect. In each case they are accompanied by a bootstrapped confidence interval. We discussed these measures of effect size in Section 10.4.3, and rather than interpret them all I'll merely note that for each one you get an estimate along with a confidence interval based on a bootstrapped standard error. As with the unstandardized indirect effect, if the confidence intervals don't contain zero then we can be confident that the true effect size is different from 'no effect'. In other words, there is mediation. All of the effect size measures have confidence intervals that don't include zero, so whatever one we look at we can be fairly confident that the indirect effect is greater than 'no effect'. Focusing on the most useful of these

---

[8] Remember that because of the nature of bootstrapping you will get slightly different values in your output.

effect sizes, the standardized b for the indirect effect, its value is $b =.041$, 95% BCa CI [.007, .103], and similarly, $\kappa^2 =.041$, 95% BCa CI [.008,.104]. κ^2 is bounded between 0 and 1, so we can interpret this as the indirect effect being about 4.1% of the maximum value that it could have been, which is a fairly small effect. We might, therefore, want to look for other potential mediators to include in the model in addition to relationship commitment.

```
***************** TOTAL, DIRECT, AND INDIRECT EFFECTS ********************
Total effect of X on Y
    Effect        SE         t          p
    .5846       .2007     2.9132      .0039

Direct effect of X on Y
    Effect        SE         t          p
    .4573       .1946     2.3505      .0196

Indirect effect of X on Y
            Effect     Boot SE    BootLLCI    BootULCI
Commitme    .1273      .0716       .0232       .3350

Partially standardized indirect effect of X on Y
            Effect     Boot SE    BootLLCI    BootULCI
Commitme    .1818      .1002       .0325       .4684

Completely standardized indirect effect of X on Y
            Effect     Boot SE    BootLLCI    BootULCI
Commitme    .0405      .0220       .0073       .1032

Ratio of indirect to total effect of X on Y
            Effect     Boot SE    BootLLCI    BootULCI
Commitme    .2177     1.9048       .0348      1.4074

Ratio of indirect to direct effect of X on Y
            Effect     Boot SE    BootLLCI    BootULCI
Commitme    .2783     6.4664       .0222      6.7410

R-squared mediation effect size (R-sq_med)
            Effect     Boot SE    BootLLCI    BootULCI
Commitme    .0138      .0101       .0017       .0480

Preacher and Kelley (2011) Kappa-squared
            Effect     Boot SE    BootLLCI    BootULCI
Commitme    .0411      .0218       .0080       .1044
```

OUTPUT 10.7

The final part of the output (Output 10.8) shows the results of the Sobel test. As I have mentioned before, it is better to interpret the bootstrap confidence intervals than formal tests of significance; however, if you selected *Sobel test* in Figure 10.13 this is what you will see. Again, we're given the size of the indirect effect ($b = 0.127$), the standard error, associated z-score ($z = 1.95$) and p-value ($p = .051$).[9] The p-value isn't quite under the not-at-all magic .05 threshold so technically we'd conclude that there isn't a significant indirect effect, but this just shows you how misleading these kind of tests can be: every single effect size had a confidence interval not containing zero, so there is compelling evidence that there is a small but meaningful mediation effect.

---

[9] You might remember in regression, we calculate a test statistic (t) by dividing the regression coefficient by its standard error (as in equation (8.11)). We do the same here except we get a z instead of a t: $z = 0.1273/0.0652 = 1.9526$.

MASSAR, K., ET AL. (2012). PERSONALITY AND INDIVIDUAL DIFFERENCES, 52, 106–109.

OUTPUT 10.8

```
Normal theory tests for indirect effect
    Effect        se          Z          p
    .1273       .0652      1.9526      .0509
```

LABCOAT LENI'S REAL RESEARCH 10.1

I heard that Jane has a boil and kissed a tramp ②

Everyone likes a good gossip from time to time, but apparently it has an evolutionary function. One school of thought is that gossip is used as a way to derogate sexual competitors – especially by questioning their appearance and sexual behaviour. For example, if you've got your eyes on a guy, but he has his eyes on Jane, then a good strategy is to spread gossip that Jane has a massive pus-oozing boil on her stomach and that she kissed a smelly vagrant called Aqualung. Apparently men rate gossiped-about women as less attractive, and they were more influenced by the gossip if it came from a woman with a high mate value (i.e., attractive and sexually desirable). Karlijn Massar and her colleagues hypothesized that if this theory is true then (1) younger women will gossip more because there is more mate competition at younger ages; and (2) this relationship will be mediated by the mate value of the person (because for those with high mate value gossiping for the purpose of sexual competition will be more effective). Eighty-three women aged from 20 to 50 (**Age**) completed questionnaire measures of their tendency to gossip (**Gossip**) and their sexual desirability (**Mate_Value**). Test Massar et al.'s mediation model using Baron and Kenny's method (as they did) but also using *PROCESS* to estimate the indirect effect (**Massar et al. (2011).sav**). Answers are on the companion website (or look at Figure 1 in the original article, which shows the parameters for the various regressions).

10.4.6. Reporting mediation analysis ②

Some people report only the indirect effect in mediation analysis, and possibly the Sobel test. However, I have repeatedly favoured using bootstrap confidence intervals, so you should report these, and preferably the effect size κ^2 and its confidence interval:

✓ There was a significant indirect effect of pornography consumption on infidelity through relationship commitment, $b = 0.127$, BCa CI [0.023, 0.335]. This represents a relatively small effect, $\kappa^2 = .041$, 95% BCa CI [.008, .104]

This is fine, but it can be quite useful to present a diagram of the mediation model, and indicate on it the regression coefficients, the indirect effect and its bootstrapped confidence intervals. For the current example, we might produce something like Figure 10.14.

FIGURE 10.14
Model of pornography consumption as a predictor of infidelity, mediated by relationship commitment. The confidence interval for the indirect effect is a BCa bootstrapped CI based on 1000 samples

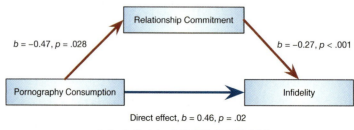

CRAMMING SAM'S TIPS Mediation

- Mediation is when the strength of the relationship between a predictor variable and outcome variable is reduced by including another variable as a predictor. Essentially, mediation equates to the relationship between two variables being 'explained' by a third. For example, the relationship between watching horror films and feeling scared at bedtime might be explained by scary images appearing in your head.
- Mediation is tested by assessing the size of the *indirect effect* and its confidence interval. If the confidence interval contains zero then we cannot be confident that a genuine mediation effect exists. If the confidence interval doesn't contain zero, then we can conclude that mediation has occurred.
- The size of the indirect effect can be expressed using kappa-squared (κ^2). Values of 0 mean that the indirect effect is very small relative to its maximum possible value, and values close to 1 mean that it is as large as it could possibly be given the research design. A small effect is .01, a medium effect would be around .09, and a large effect in the region of .25.

10.5. Categorical predictors in regression ③

We saw in the previous chapter that it is possible to include a categorical predictor in a regression model when there are only two categories: we simply code these categories with 0 and 1.[10] However, often you'll collect data about groups of people in which there are more than two categories (e.g., ethnic group, gender, socio-economic status, diagnostic category). You might want to include these groups as predictors in the regression model. Given that we have seen how to include categorical predictors with two categories into a regression model (Section 9.2.2), it shouldn't be too inconceivable that we could then extend this model to incorporate several predictors that had two categories; therefore, if we want to include a predictor with more than two categories, all we need to do is convert it to several variables each of which has two categories. This is the essence of dummy coding.

10.5.1. Dummy coding ③

10.5.1.1. What is dummy coding? ③

The obvious problem with wanting to use categorical variables as predictors is that often you'll have more than two categories. For example, if you'd collected data on religion you might have categories of Muslim, Jewish, Hindu, Catholic, Buddhist, Protestant, Jedi.[11] Clearly these groups cannot be distinguished using a single variable coded with zeros and ones. Therefore, we use what are called **dummy variables**, which is a way of representing groups of people using only zeros and ones. To do it, we have to create several variables; in fact, the number of variables we need is one less than the number of groups we're recoding.

---

[10] We saw in Section 9.2.2 why we use 0 and 1, and I elaborate on this issue in Section 11.2.1.

[11] For those of you not in the UK, we had a census here a few years back in which a significant portion of people put down Jedi as their religion.

There are eight basic steps:

1 Count the number of groups you want to recode and subtract 1.

2 Create as many new variables as the value you calculated in step 1. These are your dummy variables.

3 Choose one of your groups as a baseline against which all other groups will be compared. Normally you'd pick the control group, or, if you don't have a specific hypothesis, the group that represents the majority of people (because it might be interesting to compare other groups against the majority).

4 Having chosen a baseline group, assign that group values of 0 for all of your dummy variables.

5 For your first dummy variable, assign the value 1 to the first group that you want to compare against the baseline group. Assign all other groups 0 for this variable.

6 For the second dummy variable assign the value 1 to the second group that you want to compare against the baseline group. Assign all other groups 0 for this variable.

7 Repeat this process until you run out of dummy variables.

8 Place all of your dummy variables into the regression analysis in the same block.

Let's try this out using an example. In Chapter 5 we encountered a biologist who was worried about the potential health effects of music festivals. She collected some data at the Download Festival, which is a music festival specializing in heavy metal. The biologist was worried that the findings that she had were a function of the fact that she had tested only one type of person: metal fans. Perhaps it's only metal fans who get smellier at festivals (as a metal fan, I would at this point sacrifice the biologist to Odin for being so prejudiced). To find out whether the type of music a person likes predicts whether hygiene decreases over the festival, the biologist went to the Glastonbury Music Festival, which has an eclectic clientele. Again, she measured the hygiene of concertgoers over the three days of the festival using a technique that results in a score ranging between 0 (you smell like you've bathed in sewage) and 4 (you smell of freshly baked bread). The data are in the file called **GlastonburyFestivalRegression.sav**. This file contains the hygiene scores for each of three days of the festival as well as a variable called **change**, which is the change in hygiene over the three days of the festival (so it's the change from day 1 to day 3).[12] The biologist categorized people according to their musical affiliation: she used the label 'indie kid' for people who mainly like alternative music, 'metaller' for people who like heavy metal, and 'crusty' for people who like hippy/folky/ambient type of stuff. Anyone not falling into these categories was labelled 'no musical affiliation'. In the data file she coded these groups 1, 2, 3 and 4, respectively.

We have four groups, so there will be three dummy variables (one less than the number of groups). The first step is to choose a baseline group. We're interested in comparing those that have different musical affiliations against those that don't, so our baseline category will be 'no musical affiliation'. We give this group a code of 0 for all of our dummy variables. For our first dummy variable, we could look at the 'crusty' group, and to do this we give anyone who was a crusty a code of 1, and everyone else a code of 0. For our second dummy variable, we

TABLE 10.2   Dummy coding for the Glastonbury Festival data

	Dummy Variable 1	Dummy Variable 2	Dummy Variable 3
No Affiliation	0	0	0
Indie Kid	0	0	1
Metaller	0	1	0
Crusty	1	0	0

---

[12] Not everyone could be measured on day 3, so there is a change score only for a subset of the original sample.

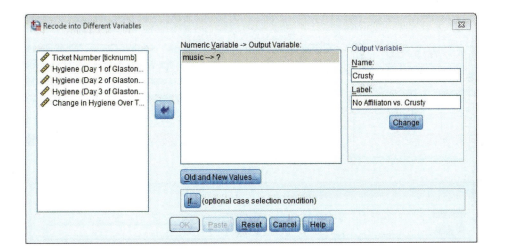

FIGURE 10.15
Recode dialog box

could look at the 'metaller' group, and to do this we give anyone who was a metaller a code of 1, and everyone else a code of 0. Our final dummy variable will code the 'indie kid' category. To do this, we give anyone who was an indie kid a code of 1, and everyone else a code of 0. The resulting coding scheme is shown in Table 10.2. Note that each group has a code of 1 on only one of the dummy variables (except the base category, which is always coded as 0).

10.5.1.2. The *recode* function ③

We looked at why dummy coding works in Section 9.2.2, so let's look at how to recode our grouping variable into these dummy variables using SPSS. To recode variables you need to use the *recode* function. Select Transform ▸ Recode into Different Variables… to access the dialog box in Figure 10.15. The *Recode* dialog box lists all of the variables in the data editor, and you need to select the one you want to recode (in this case **music**) and transfer it to the box labelled *Numeric Variable* → *Output Variable* by clicking on ▸. You then need to name the new variable (the *Output Variable* as SPSS calls it) by going to the part labelled *Output Variable* and typing a name for your first dummy variable in the box labelled *Name* (let's call it **Crusty**). You can give this variable a more descriptive name by typing something in the box labelled *Label* (for this first dummy variable I've labelled it 'No Affiliation vs. Crusty'). Click on Change to transfer this new variable to the box labelled *Numeric Variable* → *Output Variable* (this box should now say *music* → *Crusty*).

Having defined the first dummy variable, we need to tell SPSS how to recode the values of the variable **music** into the values that we want for the new variable, **Crusty**. To do this, click on Old and New Values… to access the dialog box in Figure 10.16. This dialog box is used to change values of the original variable into different values for the new variable. For our first dummy variable, we want anyone who was a crusty to get a code of 1 and everyone else to get a code of 0. Now, crusty was coded with the value 3 in the original variable, so you need to type the value 3 in the section labelled *Old Value* in the box labelled *Value*. The new value we want is 1, so we need to type the value 1 in the section labelled *New Value* in the box labelled *Value*. When you've done this, click on Add to add this change to the list of changes (the list is displayed in the box labelled *Old* → *New*, which should now say *3 → 1* as in the diagram). The next thing we need to do is to change the remaining groups to have a value of 0 for the first dummy variable. To do this just select ⦿ All other values and type the value 0 in the section labelled *New Value* in the box labelled *Value*.[13] When you've

---

[13] Using this ⦿ All other values option is fine when you don't have missing values in the data, but just note that when you do (as is the case here) cases with both system-defined and user-defined missing values will be included in the recode. One way around this is to recode only cases for which there is a value (see Oliver Twisted). The alternative is to recode missing values specifically using the ⦿ Range: option. It is also a good idea to use the *frequencies* or *crosstabs* commands after a recode and check that you have caught all of these missing values.

OLIVER TWISTED

Please, Sir, can I have some more … recoding?

'Our data set has missing values', worries Oliver. 'What do we do if we only want to recode cases for which we have data?' Well, we can set some other options. If you want to know more, the additional material for this chapter on the companion website will tell you. Stop worrying, Oliver, everything will be OK.

FIGURE 10.16
Recode
dialog box for changing old values to new (see also SPSS Tip 10.2)

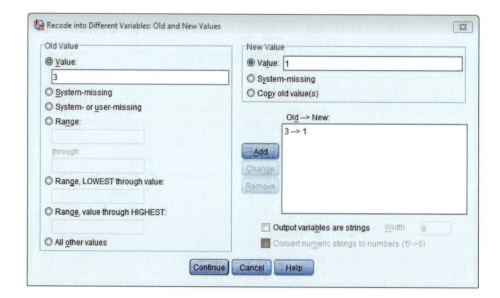

done this, click on [Add] to add this change to the list of changes (this list will now also say *ELSE → 0*). When you've done this, click on [Continue] to return to the main dialog box, and then click on [OK] to create the first dummy variable. This variable will appear as a new column in the data editor, and you should notice that it will have a value of 1 for anyone originally classified as a crusty and a value of 0 for everyone else.

SELF-TEST Try creating the remaining two dummy variables (call them **Metaller** and **Indie_Kid**) using the same principles.

10.5.2.   SPSS output for dummy variables ③

Let's assume you've created the three dummy coding variables (if you're stuck there is a data file called **GlastonburyDummy.sav** (the 'Dummy' refers to the fact it has dummy variables in it – I'm not implying that if you need to use this file you're a dummy☺). With dummy variables, you have to enter all related dummy variables in the same block (so use the *Enter* method).

SPSS TIP 10.2   Using syntax to recode ③

If you're doing a lot of recoding it soon becomes pretty tedious using the dialog boxes all of the time. I've written the syntax file, **RecodeGlastonburyData.sps**, to create all of the dummy variables we've discussed. Load this file and run the syntax, or type the following into a new syntax window (see Section 3.9):

```
DO IF(1-MISSING(change)).
RECODE music (3=1)(ELSE = 0) INTO Crusty.
RECODE music (2=1)(ELSE = 0) INTO Metaller.
RECODE music (1=1)(ELSE = 0) INTO Indie_Kid.
END IF.
VARIABLE LABELS Crusty 'No Affiliation vs. Crusty'.
VARIABLE LABELS Metaller 'No Affiliation vs. Metaller'.
VARIABLE LABELS Indie_Kid 'No Affiliation vs. Indie Kid'.
VARIABLE LEVEL Crusty Metaller Indie_Kid (Nominal).
FORMATS Crusty Metaller Indie_Kid (F1.0).
EXECUTE.
```

Each *recode* command does the equivalent of the dialog box in Figure 10.16. So, the three lines beginning *recode* ask SPSS to create three new variables (**Crusty, Metaller** and **Indie_Kid**), which are based on the original variable **music**. For the first variable, if **music** is 3 then it becomes 1, and every other value becomes 0. For the second, if **music** is 2 then it becomes 1, and every other value becomes 0, and so on for the third dummy variable. Note that all of these *recode* commands are within an *if* statement (beginning *do if* and ending with *end if*). This tells SPSS to carry out the *recode* commands only if a certain condition is met. The condition we have set is (*1- MISSING(change)*). *MISSING* is a built-in command that returns 'true' (i.e., the value 1) for a case that has a system- or user-defined missing value for the specified variable; it returns 'false' (i.e., the value 0) if a case has a value. Hence, *MISSING(change)* returns a value of 1 for cases that have a missing value for the variable **change** and 0 for cases that do have values. We want to recode the cases that *do* have a value for the variable change, therefore we use '*1−MISSING(change)*'. This command reverses *MISSING(change)* so that it returns 1 (true) for cases that have a value for the variable **change** and 0 (false) for system- or user-defined missing values. To sum up, the statement *DO IF (1−MISSING(change))* tells SPSS 'Do the following *recode* commands if the case has a value for the variable **change**.'

The *variable labels* command tells SPSS to assign the text in the quotations as labels for the variables **Crusty, Metaller**, and **Indie_Kid**, respectively. It then sets these three variables to be 'nominal', and the *formats* command changes the variables to have a width of 1 and 0 decimal places (hence the 1.0). The *execute* is essential: without it none of the commands beforehand will be executed. Note also that every line ends with a full stop.

SELF-TEST Use what you learnt in Chapter 8 to run a multiple regression using the change scores as the outcome, and the three dummy variables (entered in the same block) as predictors.

Let's have a look at the output. Output 10.9 shows the model statistics. We see that by entering the three dummy variables we can explain 7.6% of the variance in the change in hygiene scores (the R^2 value × 100%). In other words, 7.6% of the variance in the change in hygiene can be explained by the musical affiliation of the person. The ANOVA (which shows the same thing as the R^2 change statistic because there is only one step in this regression) tells us that the model is significantly better at predicting the change in hygiene scores

Model Summary

Model	R	R Square	Adjusted R Square	Std. Error of the Estimate	R Square Change	F Change	df1	df2	Sig. F Change
					Change Statistics				
1	.276[a]	.076	.053	.68818	.076	3.270	3	119	.024

a. Predictors: (Constant), No Affiliation vs. Indie Kid, No Affiliation vs. Crusty, No Affiliation vs. Metaller

b. Predictors: (Constant), No Affiliation vs. Indie Kid, No Affiliation vs. Metaller, No Affiliation vs. Crusty

ANOVA[a]

Model		Sum of Squares	df	Mean Square	F	Sig.
1	Regression	4.646	3	1.549	3.270	.024[b]
	Residual	56.358	119	.474		
	Total	61.004	122			

a. Dependent Variable: Change in Hygiene Over The Festival

b. Predictors: (Constant), No Affiliation vs. Indie Kid, No Affiliation vs. Crusty, No Affiliation vs. Metaller

c. Predictors: (Constant), No Affiliation vs. Indie Kid, No Affiliation vs. Metaller, No Affiliation vs. Crusty

than having no model (put another way, the 7.6% of variance that can be explained is a significant amount).

Output 10.10 shows a basic *Coefficients* table for the dummy variables, which is the more interesting part of the output. The first thing to notice is that each dummy variable appears in the table with a useful label (such as No Affiliation vs. Crusty) because when we recoded our variables we gave each variable a useful label; if we hadn't done this then the table would contain the less helpful variable names of Crusty, Metaller and Indie_Kid. The labels that I have used remind me of what each dummy variable represents. The first dummy variable (No Affiliation vs. Crusty) shows the difference between the change in hygiene scores for the no affiliation group and the crusty group. Remember that the beta value tells us the change in the outcome due to a unit change in the predictor. In this case, a unit change in the predictor is the change from 0 to 1. By including all three dummy variables at the same time, zero will represent our baseline category (no affiliation). For this variable 1 represents 'Crusty'. Therefore, the change from 0 to 1 represents the change from no affiliation to Crusty. Therefore, this variable represents the difference in the change in hygiene scores for a crusty, relative to someone with no musical affiliation. This difference is the difference between the two group means (see Section 9.2.2).

To illustrate this fact, I've produced a table (Output 10.11) of the group means for each of the four groups and also the difference between the means for each group and the *no affiliation* group. These means represent the average change in hygiene scores for the three groups (i.e., the mean of each group on our outcome variable). If we calculate the difference in these means for the no affiliation group and the crusty group we get, crusty − no affiliation = $(-0.966) - (-0.554) = -0.412$. In other words, the change in hygiene scores is greater for the crusty group than it is for the no affiliation group (crusties' hygiene decreases more over the festival than those with no musical affiliation). This value is the same as the *unstandardized* beta value in Output 10.10. So, the beta values tell us the relative difference between each group and the group that we chose as a baseline category. This beta value is converted to a *t*-statistic and the significance of this *t* reported. As we've seen before this *t*-statistic tests whether the beta value is 0; therefore, when we have two categories coded with 0 and 1, it tests whether the difference between group means is 0. If it is significant then the group coded with 1 is significantly different from the baseline category – so, it's testing the difference between two means, which is the context in which students are most familiar with the *t*-statistic (see Chapter 9). For our first dummy variable, the *t*-test is significant, and the beta value has a negative value so we could say that the change in hygiene scores goes down as a person changes from having no affiliation to being a crusty. Bear in mind that a decrease in hygiene scores represents greater change (you're becoming smellier) so what this actually means is that hygiene decreased significantly more in crusties compared to those with no musical affiliation.

OUTPUT 10.10

Coefficients[a]

Model		Unstandardized Coefficients		Standardized Coefficients	t	Sig.	95.0% Confidence Interval for B	
		B	Std. Error	Beta			Lower Bound	Upper Bound
1	(Constant)	-.554	.090		-6.134	.000	-.733	-.375
	No Affiliation vs. Crusty	-.412	.167	-.232	-2.464	.015	-.742	-.081
	No Affiliation vs. Metaller	.028	.160	.017	.177	.860	-.289	.346
	No Affiliation vs. Indie Kid	-.410	.205	-.185	-2.001	.048	-.816	-.004

a. Dependent Variable: Change in Hygiene Over The Festival

Bootstrap for Coefficients

Model		B	Bootstrap[a]				BCa 95% Confidence Interval	
			Bias	Std. Error	Sig. (2-tailed)		Lower	Upper
1	(Constant)	-.554	.005	.097	.001		-.736	-.349
	No Affiliation vs. Crusty	-.412	-.011	.179	.030		-.733	-.101
	No Affiliation vs. Metaller	.028	-.006	.149	.847		-.262	.293
	No Affiliation vs. Indie Kid	-.410	-.010	.201	.049		-.813	-.043

a. Unless otherwise noted, bootstrap results are based on 1000 bootstrap samples

OLAP Cubes

OUTPUT 10.11

Variables=Change in Hygiene Over The Festival

Musical Affiliation	Mean	Std. Deviation	N
Indie Kid	-0.964	0.670	14
Metaller	-0.526	0.576	27
Crusty	-0.966	0.760	24
No Musical Affiliation	-0.554	0.708	58
Crusty - No Musical Affiliation	-0.412	0.052	-34
Metaller - No Musical Affiliation	0.028	-0.133	-31
Indie Kid - No Musical Affiliation	-0.410	-0.038	-44
Total	-0.675	0.707	123

Our next dummy variable compares metallers to those that have no musical affiliation. The beta value again represents the difference in the change in hygiene scores for a person with no musical affiliation compared to a metaller. The difference in the group means for the no affiliation group and the metaller group is metaller − no affiliation = $(-0.526) - (-0.554) = 0.028$. This value is again the same as the unstandardized beta value in Output 10.10. For this second dummy variable, the t-test is not significant. We could conclude that the change in hygiene scores is similar if a person changes from having no affiliation to being a metaller: the change in hygiene scores is not predicted by whether someone is a metaller compared to if they have no musical affiliation.

For the final dummy variable, we're comparing indie kids to those that have no musical affiliation. The beta value again represents the shift in the change in hygiene scores if a person has no musical affiliation, compared to someone who is an indie kid. The difference in the group means for the no affiliation group and the indie kid group is indie kid − no affiliation = $(-0.964) - (-0.554) = -0.410$. It should be no surprise to you by now that this is the unstandardized beta value in Output 10.10. The t-test is significant, and the beta value has a negative value so, as with the first dummy variable, we could say that the change in hygiene scores goes down as a person changes from having no affiliation to being an indie kid. Bear in mind that a decrease in hygiene scores represents more change (you're becoming smellier) so this actually means that hygiene decreased significantly more in indie kids compared to those with no musical affiliation. We could report the results as in Table 10.3 (note I've included the bootstrap confidence intervals).

So, overall this analysis has shown that compared to having no musical affiliation, crusties and indie kids get significantly smellier across the three days of the festival, but

TABLE 10.3 Linear model of predictors of the change in hygiene scores (95% bias corrected and accelerated confidence intervals reported in parentheses). Confidence intervals and standard errors based on 1000 bootstrap samples

	b	SE B	β	p
Constant	−0.55 (−0.74, −0.35)	0.10		p = .001
No Affiliation vs. Crusty	−0.41 (−0.73, −0.10)	0.18	−.23	p = .030
No Affiliation vs. Metaller	0.03 (−0.26, 0.29)	0.15	.02	p = .847
No Affiliation vs. Indie Kid	−0.41 (−0.81, −0.04)	0.20	−.19	p = .049

Note. $R^2 = .08$ ($p = .024$).

metallers don't. This section has introduced some really complex ideas that I expand upon in Chapter 11. It might all be a bit much to take in, and so if you're confused or want to know more about why dummy coding works in this way I suggest reading Section 11.2.1 and then coming back here. Alternatively, read Hardy's (1993) excellent monograph.

10.6. Brian's attempt to woo Jane ①

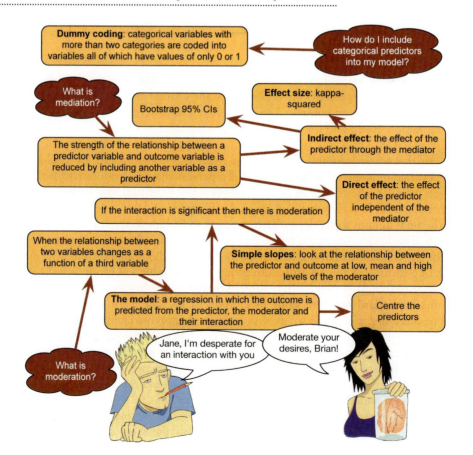

10.7. What next? ①

We started this chapter by looking at my relative failures as a human being compared to Simon Hudson. I then bleated on excitedly about moderation and mediation, which could explain why Clair Sparks chose Simon Hudson all those years ago. Perhaps she could see the writing on the wall! I was true to my word to my parents, though, and I was philosophical about it. I set my sights elsewhere during the obligatory lunchtime game of kiss chase. However, my life was about to change beyond all recognition. Not that I believe in fate, but if I did I would have believed that the wrinkly and hairy hand of fate (I don't know why but I always imagine it wrinkly, hairy and in need of a manicure) had decided that I was far too young to be getting distracted by such things as girls. Waggling its finger at me, it plucked me out of primary school and cast me down into what can only be described as hell, also known as an all-boys' school. It's fair to say that my lunchtime primary school game of kiss chase was the last I would see of girls for quite some time …

10.8. Key terms that I've discovered

Grand mean centring	Interaction effect	Moderator
Direct effect	Mediation	Simple slopes analysis
Index of mediation	Mediator	Sobel test
Indirect effect	Moderation	

10.9. Smart Alex's tasks

- **Task 1**: McNulty et al. (2008) found a relationship between a person's **Attractiveness** and how much **Support** they give their partner as newlyweds. Is this relationship moderated by gender (i.e., whether the data were from the husband or wife)? The data are in **McNulty et al. (2008).sav**.[14] ②

- **Task 2**: Produce the simple slopes graphs for the above example. ②

- **Task 3**: McNulty et al. (2008) also found a relationship between a person's **Attractiveness** and their relationship **Satisfaction** as newlyweds. Using the same data as the previous examples, is this relationship moderated by gender? ②

- **Task 4**: In the chapter we tested a mediation model of infidelity for Lambert et al.'s data using Baron and Kenny's regressions. Repeat this analysis, but using **Hook_Ups** as the measure of infidelity. ②

- **Task 5**: Repeat the above analysis but using the *PROCESS* tool to estimate the indirect effect and its confidence interval. ②

- **Task 6**: In Chapter 3 (Task 5) we looked at data from people who had been forced to marry goats and dogs and measured their life satisfaction as well as how much they like animals (**Goat or Dog.sav**). Run a regression predicting life satisfaction from the type of animal to which a person was married. Write out the final model. ②

---

[14] These are not the actual data from the study, but are simulated to mimic the findings in Table 1 of the original paper.

- **Task 7:** Repeat the analysis above but include animal liking in the first block, and type of animal in the second block. Do your conclusions about the relationship between type of animal and life satisfaction change? ②

- **Task 8:** Using the **GlastonburyDummy.sav** data, which you should've already analysed, comment on whether you think the model is reliable and generalizable. ③

- **Task 9:** Tablets like the iPad are very popular. A company owner was interested in how to make his brand of tablets more desirable. He collected data on how cool people perceived a product's advertising to be (**Advert_Cool**), how cool they thought the product was (**Product_Cool**), and how desirable they found the product (**Desirability**). Test his theory that the relationship between cool advertising and product desirability is mediated by how cool people think the product is (**Tablets.sav**). Am I showing my age by using the word 'cool'? ③

Answers can be found on the companion website.

10.10. Further reading

Cohen, J., Cohen, P., Aiken, L., & West, S. (2003). *Applied multiple regression/correlation analysis for the behavioral sciences*. Mahwah, NJ: Erlbaum.

Hardy, M. A. (1993). *Regression with dummy variables*. Sage University Paper Series on Quantitative Applications in the Social Sciences, 07-093. Newbury Park, CA: Sage.

Hayes, A. F. (2013). *An introduction to mediation, moderation, and conditional process analysis*. New York: Guilford Press.

Comparing several means: ANOVA (GLM 1)

11.1. What will this chapter tell me? ①

There are pivotal moments in everyone's life, and one of mine was at the age of 11. Where I grew up in England there were three choices when leaving primary school and moving on to secondary school: (1) state school (where most people go); (2) grammar school (where clever people who pass an exam called the Eleven Plus go); and (3) private school (where rich people go). My parents were not rich and I am not clever and consequently I failed my Eleven Plus, so private school and grammar school (where my clever older brother had gone) were out. This left me to join all of my friends at the local state school. I could not have been happier. Imagine everyone's shock when my parents received a letter saying that some extra spaces had become available at the grammar school; although the local authority could scarcely believe it and had checked the Eleven Plus papers several million times to confirm their findings, I was next on their list. I could not have been unhappier. So, I waved goodbye to all of my friends and trundled off to join my brother at Ilford County High School for Boys (a school that still hit students with a cane if they were particularly bad and that, for some considerable time and with good reason, had 'H.M. Prison' painted in huge white letters on its roof). It was goodbye to normality, and hello to six years of learning how not to function in society. I often wonder how my life would have turned out had I not gone to this school; in the parallel universes where the letter didn't arrive and the parallel Andy went to state school, or where his parents were rich and he went to private school, what became of him? If we wanted to compare these three situations we couldn't use a *t*-test because there are more than two conditions.[1] However, this chapter tells us all about the statistical models that we use to analyse situations in which we want to compare more than two conditions: analysis of variance (or ANOVA to its friends). This chapter will begin by explaining the theory of ANOVA when different participants are used (*independent ANOVA*). We'll then look at how to carry out the analysis in SPSS and interpret the results.

11.2. The theory behind ANOVA ②

11.2.1. Using a linear model to compare means ②

We saw in Chapter 9 that if we include a predictor variable containing two categories into the linear model then the resulting *b* for that predictor compares the difference between the mean score for the two categories. We also saw in Chapter 10 that if we want to include a categorical predictor that contains more than two categories, this can be achieved by recoding that variable into several categorical predictors each of which has only two categories (dummy coding). We can flip this idea on its head to ask how we can use a linear model to compare differences between the means of more than two groups. The answer is the same: we use dummy coding to represent the groups and stick them in a linear model. Many people are taught that to compare differences between several means we use 'ANOVA' and to look at relationships between variables we use 'regression' (Jane Superbrain Box 11.1). ANOVA and regression are often taught as though they are completely unrelated tests. However, as we have already seen in Chapter 8, we test the fit of a regression model with an ANOVA (the *F*-test). In fact, ANOVA is just a special case of the linear model (i.e., regression) we have used throughout the book.

There are several good reasons why I think ANOVA is best understood as a linear model. First, it provides a familiar context: I wasted many trees trying to explain regression, so why not use this base of knowledge to explain a new concept (it should make it easier to understand)? Second, the traditional method of teaching ANOVA (known as the variance ratio method) is fine for simple designs, but becomes impossibly cumbersome in more complex situations (such as analysis of covariance). The regression model extends very logically to these more complex designs without anyone needing to get bogged down in mathematics. Finally, the variance ratio method becomes extremely unmanageable in unusual circumstances such as when you have unequal sample sizes.[2] The regression method makes these situations considerably simpler. Although these reasons are good enough, SPSS very much deals with ANOVA in a regression-y sort of way (known as the general linear model, or GLM).

I have mentioned that ANOVA is a way of comparing the ratio of systematic variance to unsystematic variance in an experimental study. The ratio of these variances is known

---

[1] Really, this is the least of our problems: there's the small issue of needing access to parallel universes.

[2] Having said this, it is well worth the effort in trying to obtain equal sample sizes in your different conditions because unbalanced designs do cause statistical complications (see Section 11.3).

JANE SUPERBRAIN 11.1

Why do people think ANOVA and regression are different things? ②

There is a historical reason why people sometimes think of ANOVA and regression as being separate tests, which is that two distinct branches of methodology developed in the social sciences: correlational research and experimental research. Researchers interested in controlled experiments adopted ANOVA

as their statistic of choice whereas those looking for real-world relationships adopted multiple regression. As we all know, scientists are intelligent, mature and rational people and so neither group was tempted to slag off the other and claim that their own choice of methodology was far superior to the other (yeah, right!). With the divide in methodologies came a chasm between the statistical methods adopted by the two opposing camps (Cronbach, 1957, documents this divide in a lovely article). This divide has lasted many decades, to the extent that now students are generally taught regression and ANOVA in very different contexts and many textbooks teach ANOVA in an entirely different way from regression. Although many considerably more intelligent people than me have attempted to redress the balance (notably the great Jacob Cohen, 1968), I am passionate about making my own small, feeble-minded attempt to enlighten you.

as the *F*-ratio. However, any of you who have read Chapter 8 should recognize the *F*-ratio (see Section 8.2.4) as a way to assess how well a regression model can predict an outcome compared to the error within that model. If you haven't read Chapter 8 (surely not!), have a look before you carry on (it should only take you a couple of weeks to read). How can the *F*-ratio be used to test differences between means *and* whether a regression model fits the data? The answer is that when we test differences between means we *are* fitting a regression model and using *F* to see how well it fits the data, but the regression model contains only categorical predictors (i.e., grouping variables). So, just as the *t*-test could be represented by the linear regression equation (see Section 9.2.2), ANOVA can be represented by the multiple regression equation in which the number of predictors is one less than the number of categories of the independent variable.

Let's take an example. There was a lot of excitement, when I wrote the first edition of this book, surrounding the drug Viagra. Admittedly there's less excitement now, but it has been replaced by an alarming number of spam emails on the subject (for which I'll no doubt be grateful in 15 years' time), so I'm going to stick with the example. Viagra is a sexual stimulant (used to treat impotence) that broke into the black market under the belief that it will make someone a better lover (oddly enough, there was a glut of journalists taking the stuff at the time in the name of 'investigative journalism'... hmmm!). In the psychology literature sexual performance issues have been linked to a loss of libido (Hawton, 1989). Suppose we tested this belief by taking three groups of participants and administering one group with a placebo (such as a sugar pill), one group with a low dose of Viagra and one with a high dose. The dependent variable was an objective measure of libido (I will tell you only that it was measured over the course of a week – the rest I will leave to your own imagination). The data are in Table 11.1 and can be found in the file **Viagra.sav** (which is described in detail later in this chapter).

If we want to predict levels of libido from the different levels of Viagra then we can use the general equation that keeps popping up:

$$\text{outcome}_i = (\text{model}) + \text{error}_i$$

TABLE 11.1 Data in **Viagra.sav**

	Placebo	Low Dose	High Dose
	3	5	7
	2	2	4
	1	4	5
	1	2	3
	4	3	6
$\bar{X}$	2.20	3.20	5.00
s	1.30	1.30	1.58
s^2	1.70	1.70	2.50
Grand mean = **3.467** Grand SD = **1.767** Grand variance = **3.124**			

If we want to use a linear model, then we saw in Section 9.2.2 that when there are only two groups we could replace the 'model' in this equation with a linear regression equation with one dummy variable to describe two groups. This dummy variable was a categorical variable with two numeric codes (0 for one group and 1 for the other). With three groups, however, we can extend this idea and use a multiple regression model with two dummy variables. We also saw in Section 10.5 that we can extend the model to any number of groups and the number of dummy variables needed will be one less than the number of categories of the independent variable. In the two-group case, we assigned one category as a base category (remember that in Section 9.2.2 we chose the no cloak condition to act as a base) and this category was coded with 0. When there are three categories we also need a base category and you should choose the condition to which you intend to compare the other groups. Usually this category will be the control group. In most well-designed experiments there will be a group of participants who act as a baseline for other categories. This baseline group should act as the reference or base category, although the group you choose will depend upon the particular hypotheses that you want to test. In unbalanced designs (in which the group sizes are unequal) it is important that the base category contains a fairly large number of cases to ensure that the estimates of the regression coefficients are reliable. In the Viagra example, we can take the placebo control group as the base category. We are interested in comparing both the high- and low-dose groups to the group that received no Viagra at all. If the placebo group is the base category then the two dummy variables that we have to create represent the other two conditions: so, we should have one dummy variable called High and the other one called Low. The resulting equation is:

$$\text{Libido}_i = b_0 + b_2 \text{High}_i + b_1 \text{Low}_i + \varepsilon_i \tag{11.1}$$

In equation (11.1), a person's libido can be predicted from knowing their group code (i.e., the code for the High and Low dummy variables) and the intercept (b_0) of the model. The dummy variables in equation (11.1) can be coded in several ways, but the simplest way is as we did in Section 10.5. The base category is always coded as 0. If a participant was given a high dose of Viagra then they are coded with a 1 for the High dummy variable and 0 for all other variables. If a participant was given a low dose of Viagra then they are coded with the value 1 for the Low dummy variable and coded with 0 for all other variables. Using this coding scheme, we can express each group by combining the codes of the two dummy variables (see Table 11.2).

TABLE 11.2   Dummy coding for the three-group experimental design

Group	Dummy Variable 1 (High)	Dummy Variable 2 (Low)
Placebo	0	0
Low Dose Viagra	0	1
High Dose Viagra	1	0

When the predictor is made up of groups, the predicted values (the value of libido in equation (11.1)) will be the group mean because for a given individual the best guess of their score will be the mean of the group to which they belong. Knowing this we can look at the model for each group.

Let's examine the model for the *placebo group*. In this group both the High and Low dummy variables are coded as 0. The predicted value for the model will be the mean of the placebo group. Therefore, if we ignore the error term (ε_i), the regression equation becomes:

$$\text{Libido}_i = b_0 + (b_2 \times 0) + (b_1 \times 0)$$
$$\text{Libido}_i = b_0$$
$$\overline{X}_{\text{Placebo}} = b_0$$

This is a situation in which the high- and low-dose groups have both been excluded (because they are coded with 0). We are looking at predicting the level of libido when both doses of Viagra are ignored, and so the predicted value will be the mean of the placebo group (because this group is the only one included in the model). Hence, the intercept of the regression model, b_0, is always the mean of the base category (in this case the mean of the placebo group).

If we examine the *high-dose group*, the dummy variable High will be coded as 1 and the dummy variable Low will be coded as 0. If we replace the values of these codes in equation (11.1) the model becomes:

$$\text{Libido}_i = b_0 + (b_2 \times 1) + (b_1 \times 0)$$
$$\text{Libido}_i = b_0 + b_2$$

We know already that b_0 is the mean of the placebo group. If we are interested in only the high-dose group then the model should predict that the value of Libido for a given participant equals the mean of the high-dose group. Given this information, the equation becomes:

$$\text{Libido}_i = b_0 + b_2$$
$$\overline{X}_{\text{High}} = \overline{X}_{\text{Placebo}} + b_2$$
$$b_2 = \overline{X}_{\text{High}} - \overline{X}_{\text{Placebo}}$$

Hence, b_2 represents the difference between the means of the high-dose and placebo groups.

Finally, let's look at the model for the *low-dose group*. Now the dummy variable Low is coded as 1 (and hence High is coded as 0). Therefore, the regression equation becomes:

$$\text{Libido}_i = b_0 + (b_2 \times 0) + (b_1 \times 1)$$
$$\text{Libido}_i = b_0 + b_1$$

We know that the intercept is equal to the mean of the base category and that for the low-dose group the predicted value should be the mean libido for a low dose. Therefore the model reduces to:

$$\text{Libido}_i = b_0 + b_1$$
$$\bar{X}_{\text{Low}} = \bar{X}_{\text{Placebo}} + b_1$$
$$b_1 = \bar{X}_{\text{Low}} - \bar{X}_{\text{Placebo}}$$

Hence, b_1 represents the difference between the means of the low-dose group and the placebo group. This form of dummy variable coding is the simplest, but, as we will see later, there are other ways in which variables can be coded to test specific hypotheses. These alternative coding schemes are known as *contrasts* (see Section 11.4.2). The idea behind contrasts is that you code the dummy variables in such a way that the b-values represent differences between groups that you are interested in testing.

SELF-TEST   To illustrate exactly what is going on I have created a file called **dummy.sav.** This file contains the Viagra data but with two additional variables **(dummy1** and **dummy2)** that specify to which group a data point belongs (as in Table 10.2). Access this file and run multiple regression analysis using **libido** as the outcome and **dummy1** and **dummy2** as the predictors. If you're stuck on how to run the regression then read Chapter 8 again.

The resulting analysis is shown in Output 11.1. It might be a good idea to remind yourself of the group means from Table 11.1. The first thing to notice is that, just as in the regression chapter, an ANOVA has been used to test the overall fit of the model. This test is significant, $F(2, 12) = 5.12$, $p = .025$. Given that our model represents the group differences, this ANOVA tells us that using group means to predict scores is significantly better than using the overall mean: in other words, the group means are significantly different.

In terms of the regression coefficients, the constant (b_0) is equal to the mean of the base category (the placebo group). The regression coefficient for the first dummy variable (b_2) is equal to the difference between the means of the high-dose group and the placebo group $(5.0 - 2.2 = 2.8)$. Finally, the regression coefficient for the second dummy variable (b_1) is equal to the difference between the means of the low-dose group and the placebo group $(3.2 - 2.2 = 1)$. This analysis demonstrates how the regression model represents the three-group situation. We can see from the significance values of the t-tests that the difference between the high-dose group and the placebo group (b_2) is significant because $p = .008$, which is less than .05. The difference between the low-dose and the placebo group is not, however, significant $(p = .282)$.

A four-group experiment can be described by extending the three-group scenario. We looked at a four-group situation in Section 10.5 (so look back there to refresh your memory). As before, we specify one category as a base category (a control group), and assign this category a code of 0 for all dummy variables. The remaining three conditions will have a code of 1 for the dummy variable that described that condition and a code of 0 for the other dummy variables. Table 11.3 illustrates how the coding scheme would work.

11.2.2.   Logic of the *F*-ratio ②

If differences between group means can be expressed as a linear model, then it shouldn't surprise you that we can test these differences with an *F*-ratio. We learnt in Chapter 8

OUTPUT 11.1

ANOVA[b]

Model		Sum of Squares	df	Mean Square	F	Sig.
1	Regression	20.133	2	10.067	5.119	.025[a]
	Residual	23.600	12	1.967		
	Total	43.733	14			

a. Predictors: (Constant), Dummy Variable 2, Dummy Variable 1

b. Dependent Variable: Libido

Coefficients[a]

Model		Unstandardized Coefficients B	Unstandardized Coefficients Std. Error	Standardized Coefficients Beta	t	Sig.
1	(Constant)	2.200	.627		3.508	.004
	Dummy Variable 1	2.800	.887	.773	3.157	.008
	Dummy Variable 2	1.000	.887	.276	1.127	.282

a. Dependent Variable: Libido

TABLE 11.3   Dummy coding for the four-group experimental design

	Dummy Variable 1	Dummy Variable 2	Dummy Variable 3
Group 1	1	0	0
Group 2	0	1	0
Group 3	0	0	1
Group 4 (base)	0	0	0

that the F-ratio tests the overall fit of a regression model to a set of observed data. It is the ratio of how good the model is compared to how bad it is (its error). When the model is based on group means, our predictions from the model are those means. If the group means are the same then our ability to predict the observed data will be poor (F will be small) but if the means differ we will be able to better discriminate between cases from different groups (F will be large). So, in this context F basically tells us whether the group means are different.

Figure 11.2 shows the Viagra data in graphical form (including the group means, the overall mean, and the difference between each case and the group mean). We want to test the hypothesis that the means of three groups are different (so the null hypothesis is that the group means are the same). If the group means were all the same, then we would not expect the placebo group to differ from the low-dose group or the high-dose group, and we would not expect the low-dose group to differ from the high-dose group. Therefore, in Figure 11.2 the three coloured lines would be in the same vertical position (the exact position would be the grand mean – the solid horizontal line in the figure). We can see from the diagram that the group means are different because the coloured lines (the group means) are in different vertical positions. We have just found out that in the regression model, b_2 represents the difference between the means of the placebo and the high-dose group, and b_1 represents the difference in means between the low-dose and placebo groups. These two distances are represented in Figure 11.2 by the vertical arrows. If the null hypothesis is true and all the groups have the same means, then these b coefficients should be zero (because if the group means are equal then the difference between them will be zero).

The logic of ANOVA follows from what we already know about linear models:

- The simplest model we can fit to a set of data is the grand mean (the mean of the outcome variable). This basic model represents 'no effect' or 'no relationship between the predictor variable and the outcome'.

- We can fit a different model to the data collected that represents our hypotheses. If this model fits the data well then it must be better than using the grand mean.

- The intercept and one or more parameters (*b*) describe the model.

- The parameters determine the shape of the model that we have fitted; therefore, the bigger the coefficients, the greater the deviation between the model and the grand mean.

- In experimental research the parameters (*b*) represent the differences between group means. The bigger the differences between group means, the greater the difference between the model and the grand mean.

- If the differences between group means are large enough, then the resulting model will be a better fit of the data than the grand mean.

- If this is the case we can infer that our model (i.e., predicting scores from the group means) is better than not using a model (i.e., predicting scores from the grand mean). Put another way, our group means are significantly different.

Just as we have done before, we use the *F*-ratio to compare the improvement in fit due to using the model (rather than the grand mean) to the error that still remains. In other words, the *F*-ratio is the ratio of the explained to the unexplained variation. We calculate this variation using sums of squares (look back at Section 8.2.4 to refresh your memory), which might sound complicated, but isn't as bad as you think (see Jane Superbrain Box 11.2).

JANE SUPERBRAIN 11.2

ANOVA boils down to one equation (well, sort of) ②

At every stage of the ANOVA we're assessing variation (or deviance) from a particular model (be that the most basic model or the most sophisticated model). We saw back in Section 2.4.1 that the extent to which a model deviates from the observed data can be expressed, in general, in the form of equation (2.6), repeated here as follows:

$$\text{Total error} = \sum_{i=1}^{n} \left(\text{observed}_i - \text{model}_i \right)^2 \tag{11.2}$$

So, in ANOVA, as in regression, we use this equation to calculate the fit of the most basic model, and then the fit of the best model (the line of best fit). If the best model is any good then it should fit the data significantly better than our basic model.

All of the sums of squares in ANOVA are variations on this one basic equation: all that changes is what we use as the model, and what the corresponding observed data are. As you read through the various sections on the sums of squares, hopefully you'll see that the equations for sums of squares are all basically variations on this equation.

11.2.3. Total sum of squares (SS_T) ②

To find the total amount of variation within our data we calculate the difference between each observed data point and the grand mean. We then square these differences and add them together to give us the total sum of squares (SS_T):

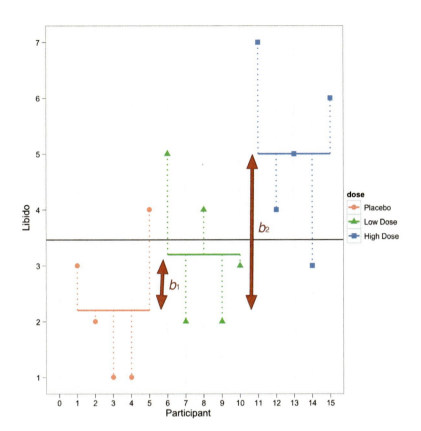

FIGURE 11.2
The Viagra data in graphical form. The coloured horizontal lines represent the mean libido of each group. The shapes represent the libido of individual participants (different shapes indicate different experimental groups). The dark horizontal line is the average libido of all participants

$$SS_T = \sum_{i=1}^{N}(x_i - \overline{x}_{grand})^2$$ (11.3)

We also saw in Section 2.4.1 that the variance and the sums of squares are related such that variance, $s^2 = SS/(N-1)$, where N is the number of observations. Therefore, we can calculate the total sums of squares from the variance of all observations (the **grand variance**) by rearranging the relationship ($SS = s^2(N-1)$). The grand variance is the variation between all scores, regardless of the experimental condition from which the scores come. Figure 11.3 shows the different sums of squares graphically (note the similarity to Figure 8.5 which we looked at when we learnt about regression). The top left panel shows the total sum of squares: it is the sum of the squared distances between each point and the solid horizontal line (which represents the mean of all scores).

The grand variance for the Viagra data is given in Table 11.1, and if we count the number of observations we find that there were 15 in all. Therefore, SS_T is calculated as follows:

$$\begin{aligned}
SS_T &= s^2_{grand}(N-1)\\
&= 3.124(15-1)\\
&= 3.124 \times 14\\
&= 43.74
\end{aligned}$$

Before we move on, it is important to understand degrees of freedom, so have a look back at Jane Superbrain Box 2.2 to refresh your memory. We saw before that when we estimate population values, the degrees of freedom are typically one less than the number of scores used to calculate the population value. This is because to get these estimates we have to hold something constant in the population (in this case the mean), which leaves

FIGURE 11.3
Graphical
representation
of the different
sums of
squares in
ANOVA designs

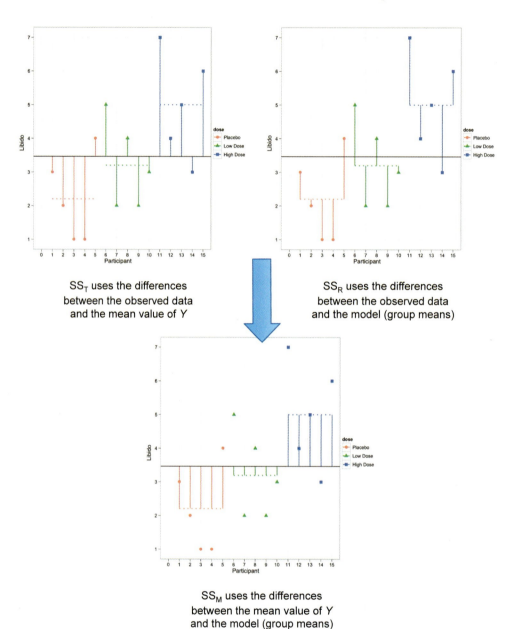

SS$_T$ uses the differences
between the observed data
and the mean value of Y

SS$_R$ uses the differences
between the observed data
and the model (group means)

SS$_M$ uses the differences
between the mean value of Y
and the model (group means)

all but one of the scores free to vary. For SS$_T$, we used the entire sample (i.e., 15 scores) to calculate the sums of squares and so the total degrees of freedom (df_T) are one less than the total sample size (N - 1). For the Viagra data, this value is 14.

11.2.4. Model sum of squares (SS$_M$) ②

So far we know that the total amount of variation within the data is 43.74 units. We now need to know how much of this variation the regression model can explain. In the ANOVA scenario the model is based upon differences between group means, and so the model sum of squares tells us how much of the total variation can be explained by the fact that different data points come from different groups.

In Section 8.2.4 we saw that the model sum of squares is calculated by taking the difference between the values predicted by the model and the grand mean (see Figure 8.5). In ANOVA, the values predicted by the model are the group means (the coloured dashed horizontal lines in Figure 11.3). The bottom panel in Figure 11.3 shows the model sum of squared error: it is the sum of the squared distances between what the model predicts for each data point (i.e., the dotted horizontal line for the group to which the data point belongs) and the overall mean of the data (the solid horizontal line).

For each participant the value predicted by the model is the mean for the group to which the participant belongs. In the Viagra example, the predicted value for the five participants in the placebo group will be 2.2, for the five participants in the low-dose condition it will be 3.2, and for the five participants in the high-dose condition it will be 5. The model sum of squares requires us to calculate the differences between each participant's predicted value and the grand mean. These differences are then squared and added together (for reasons that should be clear in your mind by now). We know that the predicted value for participants in a particular group is the mean of that group. Therefore, the easiest way to calculate SS_M is to do the following:

- Calculate the difference between the mean of each group and the grand mean.

- Square each of these differences.

- Multiply each result by the number of participants within that group (n_k).

- Add the values for each group together.

The mathematical expression for this process is:

$$SS_M = \sum_{k=1}^{k} n_k (\bar{x}_k - \bar{x}_{\text{grand}})^2 \tag{11.4}$$

Using the means from the Viagra data, we can calculate SS_M as follows:

$$SS_M = 5(2.200 - 3.467)^2 + 5(3.200 - 3.467)^2 + 5(5.000 - 3.467)^2$$

$$= 5(-1.267)^2 + 5(-0.267)^2 + 5(1.533)^2$$

$$= 8.025 + 0.355 + 11.755$$

$$= 20.135$$

The degrees of freedom (df_M) for SS_M will always be one less than the number of 'things' used to calculate the SS. We use the three group means so this value will be the number of groups minus one (which you'll see denoted as $k-1$). So, in the three-group case the degrees of freedom is 2 (because the calculation of the sums of squares is based on the group means, two of which will be free to vary in the population if the third is held constant).

11.2.5. Residual sum of squares (SS_R) ②

We now know that there are 43.74 units of variation to be explained in our data, and that our model can explain 20.14 of these units (nearly half). The final sum of squares is the residual sum of squares (SS_R), which tells us how much of the variation cannot be explained by the model. This value is the amount of variation caused by extraneous factors such as individual differences in weight, testosterone or whatever. Knowing SS_T and SS_M already, the simplest way to calculate SS_R is to subtract SS_M from SS_T ($SS_R = SS_T - SS_M$); however, telling you to do this provides little insight into what is being calculated and, of course, if you've messed up the calculations of either SS_M or SS_T (or both!) then SS_R will be incorrect also.

We saw in Section 8.2.4 that the residual sum of squares is the difference between what the model predicts and what was actually observed. In ANOVA, the values predicted by the model are the group means (the coloured dashed horizontal lines in Figure 11.3). The top left panel shows the residual sum of squared error: it is the sum of the squared distances between each point and the dotted horizontal line for the group to which the data point belongs.

We already know that, for a given participant, the model predicts the mean of the group to which that person belongs. Therefore, SS_R is calculated by looking at the difference between the score obtained by a person and the mean of the group to which the person belongs. In graphical terms, the vertical lines in Figure 11.2 represent this sum of squares. These distances between each data point and the group mean are squared and then added together to give the residual sum of squares, SS_R:

$$SS_R = \sum \left(x_{ik} - \bar{x}_k \right)^2 \tag{11.5}$$

Now, the sum of squares for each group represents the sum of squared differences between each participant's score in that group and the group mean. Therefore, we can express SS_R as $SS_R = SS_{\text{group 1}} + SS_{\text{group 2}} + SS_{\text{group 3}} + \dots$. Given that we know the relationship between the variance and the sums of squares, we can use the variances for each group of the Viagra data to create an equation like we did for the total sum of squares. As such, SS_R can be expressed as:

$$SS_R = \sum s_k^2 \left(n_k - 1 \right) \tag{11.6}$$

This just means take the variance from each group (s_k^2) and multiply it by one less than the number of people in that group ($n_k - 1$). When you've done this for each group, add them all up. For the Viagra data, this gives us:

$$\begin{aligned} SS_R &= s_{\text{group 1}}^2 \left(n_1 - 1 \right) + s_{\text{group 2}}^2 \left(n_2 - 1 \right) + s_{\text{group 3}}^2 \left(n_3 - 1 \right) \\ &= 1.70 \left(5 - 1 \right) + 1.70 \left(5 - 1 \right) + 2.50 \left(5 - 1 \right) \\ &= \left(1.70 \times 4 \right) + \left(1.70 \times 4 \right) + \left(2.50 \times 4 \right) \\ &= 6.8 + 6.8 + 10 \\ &= 23.60 \end{aligned}$$

The degrees of freedom for SS_R (df_R) are the total degrees of freedom minus the degrees of freedom for the model ($df_R = df_T - df_M = 14 - 2 = 12$). Put another way, it's $N - k$: the total sample size, N, minus the number of groups, k.

11.2.6. Mean squares ②

SS_M tells us the *total* variation that the regression model (e.g., the experimental manipulation) explains and SS_R tells us the *total* variation that is due to extraneous factors. However, because both of these values are summed values they will be influenced by the number of scores that were summed; for example, SS_M used the sum of only 3 different values (the group means) compared to SS_R and SS_T, which used the sum of 12 and 15 values, respectively. To eliminate this bias we can calculate the average sum of squares (known as the *mean squares*, MS), which is simply the sum of squares divided by the degrees of freedom. The reason why we divide by the degrees of freedom rather than the number of parameters used to calculate the SS is that we are trying to extrapolate to a population and so some parameters within that populations will be held constant (this is the same reason why we divide by $N - 1$ when calculating the variance; see Jane Superbrain Box 2.2). So, for the Viagra data we find the following mean squares:

$$MS_M = \frac{SS_M}{df_M} = \frac{20.135}{2} = 10.067$$

$$MS_R = \frac{SS_R}{df_R} = \frac{23.60}{12} = 1.967$$

MS_M represents the average amount of variation explained by the model (e.g., the systematic variation), whereas MS_R is a gauge of the average amount of variation explained by extraneous variables (the unsystematic variation).

11.2.7. The *F*-ratio ②

The *F*-ratio is a measure of the ratio of the variation explained by the model and the variation explained by unsystematic factors. In other words, it is the ratio of how good the model is against how bad it is (how much error there is). It can be calculated by dividing the model mean squares by the residual mean squares:

$$F = \frac{MS_M}{MS_R}$$

(11.7)

As with the independent *t*-test, the *F*-ratio is, therefore, a measure of the ratio of systematic variation to unsystematic variation. In experimental research, it is the ratio of the experimental effect to the individual differences in performance. An interesting point about the *F*-ratio is that because it is the ratio of systematic variance to unsystematic variance, if its value is less than 1 then it must, by definition, represent a non-significant effect. This is because if the *F*-ratio is less than 1 it means that MS_R is greater than MS_M, which in real terms means that there is more unsystematic than systematic variance. You can think of this in terms of the effect of natural differences being greater than differences brought about by the experiment. In this scenario, we can, therefore, be sure that our experimental manipulation has been unsuccessful (because it has brought about less change than if we left our participants alone). For the Viagra data, the *F*-ratio is:

$$F = \frac{MS_M}{MS_R} = \frac{10.067}{1.967} = 5.12$$

This value is greater than 1, which indicates that the experimental manipulation had some effect above and beyond the effect of individual differences in performance. However, it doesn't yet tell us whether the *F*-ratio is large enough to not be a chance result. To discover this we can compare the obtained value of *F* against the maximum value we would expect to get by chance if the group means were equal in an *F*-distribution with the same degrees of freedom (these values can be found in Appendix 3); if the value we obtain exceeds this critical value we can be confident that this reflects an effect of our independent variable (because this value would be very unlikely if there were no effect in the population). In this case, with 2 and 12 degrees of freedom the critical values are 3.89 ($p = .05$) and 6.93 ($p = .01$). The observed value, 5.12, is, therefore, significant at the .05 level but not significant at the .01 level. The exact significance produced by SPSS should, therefore, fall somewhere between .05 and .01 (which, incidentally, it does).

What does an
ANOVA tell me?

We saw in regression that the *F*-test assesses the overall fit of the model to the data. When the model is one that compares means, the *F*-test assesses whether 'overall' there are differences between means: it does not provide specific information about which groups were affected (the regression parameters do, but we'll come back to that later). For this reason, ANOVA is sometimes called an *omnibus* test. Therefore, assuming an experiment was conducted with three different groups, if we fit a model comparing the group means then a significant *F*-ratio tells us that the means of these three samples are not equal (i.e., that $\bar{X}_1 = \bar{X}_2 = \bar{X}_3$ is *not* true). However, there are several ways in which the means can differ. The first possibility is that all three sample means are significantly different ($\bar{X}_1 \neq \bar{X}_2 \neq \bar{X}_3$). A second possibility is that the means of groups 1 and 2 are the same but group 3 has a significantly different mean from both of the other groups ($\bar{X}_1 = \bar{X}_2 \neq \bar{X}_3$). Another possibility is that groups 2 and 3 have similar means but group 1 has a significantly different mean ($\bar{X}_1 \neq \bar{X}_2 = \bar{X}_3$). Finally, groups 1 and 3 could have similar means but group 2 has a significantly different mean from both ($\bar{X}_1 = \bar{X}_3 \neq \bar{X}_2$). So, in an experiment, the *F*-ratio tells us only that the experimental manipulation has had some effect, but it doesn't tell us specifically what the effect was.

It might seem a bit unhelpful that an ANOVA doesn't tell you which groups are different from which, given that having gone to the trouble of running an experiment, you probably need to know more than 'there's a difference somewhere or other'. You might wonder, therefore, why we don't just carry out a lot of *t*-tests, which would tell us very specifically whether pairs of group means differ. Actually, the reason has already been explained in Section 2.6.1.7: every time you run multiple tests on the same data you inflate the potential Type I errors that you make. However, we'll return to this point in Section 11.5 when we look at how we follow up an ANOVA to discover where the group differences lie.

11.3. Assumptions of ANOVA ③

If ANOVA is simply a linear model then all of the potential sources of bias discussed in Chapter 5 apply. In terms of normality, what matters is that scores *within groups* are normally distributed (see Jane Superbrain Box 5.1).

As with any linear model, there is an assumption that the variance of the outcome is steady as the predictor changes (in this context it means that variances in the groups are equal). This assumption can be tested using Levene's test, which tests the null hypothesis that the variances of the groups are the same (see Section 5.3.3.2). Basically, it is an ANOVA test conducted on the absolute differences between the observed scores and the mean or median of the group from which each score came (see Oliver Twisted). If Levene's test is significant (i.e., the *p*-value is less than .05) then we can say that the variances are significantly different. This would mean that we would have to take steps to rectify this matter. For example, we can adjust the *F*-test to correct the problem (just as we could with the *t*-test). SPSS offers us two corrected versions of the *F*-ratio: the **Brown–Forsythe *F*** (Brown & Forsythe, 1974), and **Welch's *F*** (Welch, 1951). If you're really bored, these two statistics are discussed in Jane Superbrain Box 11.3.

JANE SUPERBRAIN 11.3

What do I do in ANOVA when the homogeneity of variance assumption is broken? ③

In Section 11.3 I mentioned that when group sizes are unequal, violations of the assumption of homogeneity of variance can have quite serious consequences. SPSS incorporates options for two alternative *F*-ratios, which have been derived to be robust when homogeneity of variance has been violated. The first is the Brown and Forsythe (1974) *F*-ratio, which is fairly easy to explain. I mentioned earlier that when group sizes are unequal and the large groups have the biggest variance, then this biases the *F*-ratio to be conservative. If you think back to equation (11.6), this makes perfect sense because to calculate SS_R variances are multiplied by their sample size (minus one), so in this situation you get a large sample size cross-multiplied with a large variance, which will inflate the value of SS_R. What effect does this have on the *F*-ratio? Well, the *F*-ratio is proportionate to SS_M/SS_R, so if SS_R is big, then the *F*-ratio gets smaller (which is why it would be more conservative: its value is being overly reduced). Brown and Forsythe get around this problem by weighting the group variances not by their sample size, but by the inverse of their sample sizes (actually they use *n*/*N*, so it's the

sample size as a proportion of the total sample size). This means that the impact of large sample sizes with large variance is reduced:

$$F_{BF} = \frac{SS_M}{SS_{R_{BF}}} = \frac{SS_M}{\sum s_k^2 \left(1 - \frac{n_k}{N}\right)}$$

For the Viagra data, SS_M is the same as before (20.135), so the equation becomes:

$$F_{BF} = \frac{20.135}{s_{group1}^2 \left(1 - \frac{n_{group1}}{N}\right) + s_{group2}^2 \left(1 - \frac{n_{group2}}{N}\right) + s_{group3}^2 \left(1 - \frac{n_{group3}}{N}\right)}$$

$$= \frac{20.135}{1.7\left(1 - \frac{5}{15}\right) + 1.7\left(1 - \frac{5}{15}\right) + 2.5\left(1 - \frac{5}{15}\right)}$$

$$= \frac{20.135}{3.933}$$

$$= 5.119$$

This statistic is evaluated using degrees of freedom for the model and error terms. For the model, df_M is the same as before (i.e., $k - 1 = 2$), but an adjustment is made to the residual degrees of freedom, df_R.

The second correction is Welch's (1951) *F* – see Oliver Twisted.

The obvious question is which of the two procedures is best? Tomarken and Serlin (1986) review these and other techniques and seem to conclude that both techniques control the Type I error rate well (i.e., when there's no effect in the population you do indeed get a non-significant *F*). However, in terms of power (i.e., which test is best at detecting an effect when it exists), the Welch test seems to fare the best except when there is an extreme mean that has a large variance.

OLIVER TWISTED

Please Sir, can I have some more … Levene's test?

'Liar! Liar! Pants on fire', screams Oliver, his cheeks red and eyes about to explode. 'You promised in Chapter 5 to explain Levene's test properly and you haven't, you spatula head.' True enough, Oliver, I do have a spatula for a head. I also have a very nifty little demonstration of Levene's test in the additional material for this chapter on the companion website. It will tell you more than you could possibly want to know. Let's go fry an egg …

11.3.2. Is ANOVA robust? ③

You often hear people say 'ANOVA is a robust test', which means that it doesn't matter much if we break the assumptions of the test: the *F* will still be accurate. There is some truth to this statement, but it is also an oversimplification of the situation. For one thing, the term *ANOVA* covers many different situations and the performance of *F* has been investigated in only some of those situations. Remember from Chapter 5 that we mainly care about normality if we want to assess significance or construct confidence intervals. There are two issues to consider around the significance of *F*. First, does *F* control the Type I error rate or is it significant even when there are no differences between means? Second, does *F* have enough power (i.e., is it able to detect differences when they are there)? Let's have a look at the evidence.

Looking at normality first, Glass et al. (1972) reviewed a lot of evidence that suggests that *F* controls the Type I error rate well under conditions of skew, kurtosis and non-normality. Skewed distributions seem to have little effect on the error rate and power for two-tailed tests (but can have serious consequences for one-tailed tests). However, some of this evidence has been questioned (see Jane Superbrain Box 5.7). In terms of kurtosis, leptokurtic distributions make the Type I error rate too low (too many null effects are significant) and consequently the power is too high; platykurtic distributions have the opposite effect. The effects of kurtosis seem unaffected by whether sample sizes are equal or not. One study that is worth mentioning in a bit of detail is by Lunney (1970) who investigated the use of ANOVA in about the most non-normal situation you could imagine: when the dependent variable is binary (it could have values of only 0 or 1). The results showed that when the group sizes were equal, ANOVA was accurate when there were at least 20 degrees of freedom and the smallest response category contained at least 20% of all responses. If the smaller response category contained less than 20% of all responses then ANOVA performed accurately only when there were 40 or more degrees of freedom. The power of *F* also appears to be relatively unaffected by non-normality (Donaldson, 1968). This evidence suggests that *when group sizes are equal* the *F*-statistic can be quite robust to violations of normality. However, when group sizes are not equal the accuracy of *F* is affected by

OLIVER TWISTED

Please Sir, can I have some more … Welch's F?

'You're only telling us about the Brown–Forsythe *F* because you don't understand Welch's *F*', taunts Oliver. 'Andy, Andy, brains all sandy ….' Whatever, Oliver. Like the Brown–Forsythe *F*, Welch's *F* adjusts *F* and the residual degrees of freedom to combat problems arising from violations of the homogeneity of variance assumption. There is a lengthy explanation about Welch's *F* in the additional material available on the companion website. Oh, and Oliver, microchips are made of sand.

skew, and non-normality also affects the power of F in quite unpredictable ways (Wilcox, 2012). One situation that Wilcox describes shows that when means are equal the error rate (which should be 5%) can be as high as 18%. If you make the differences between means bigger you should find that power increases, but actually he found that initially power *decreased* (although it increased when he made the group differences bigger still). As such F can be biased when normality is violated.

In terms of violations of the assumption of homogeneity of variance, ANOVA is fairly robust in terms of the error rate when sample sizes are equal. However, when sample sizes are unequal, ANOVA is not robust to violations of homogeneity of variance (this is why earlier on I said it's worth trying to collect equal-sized samples of data across conditions). When groups with larger sample sizes have larger variances than the groups with smaller sample sizes, the resulting F-ratio tends to be conservative. That is, it's more likely to produce a non-significant result when a genuine difference does exist in the population. Conversely, when the groups with larger sample sizes have smaller variances than the groups with smaller samples sizes, the resulting F-ratio tends to be liberal. That is, it is more likely to produce a significant result when there is no difference between groups in the population (put another way, the Type I error rate is not controlled) – see Glass et al. (1972) for a review. When variances are proportional to the means then the power of F seems to be unaffected by the heterogeneity of variance and trying to stabilize variances does not substantially improve power (Budescu, 1982; Budescu & Appelbaum, 1981). Problems resulting from violations of homogeneity of variance assumption can be corrected (see Jane Superbrain Box 11.3).

Violations of the assumption of independence are very serious indeed. Scariano and Davenport (1987) showed that when this assumption is broken (i.e., observations across groups are correlated) then the Type I error rate is substantially inflated. For example, if scores are made to correlate moderately (say, with a Pearson coefficient of .5), then when comparing three groups of 10 observations per group the Type I error rate is .74 (remember that we'd expect it to be .05). Therefore, if observations are correlated you might think that you are working with the accepted .05 error rate (i.e., you'll incorrectly find a significant result only 5% of the time) when in fact your error rate is closer to .74 (i.e., you'll find a significant result on 74% of occasions when, in reality, there is no effect in the population).

11.3.3.   What to do when assumptions are violated ②

In Chapter 5 we discussed methods for correcting problems (e.g., the bias reduction methods in Section 5.4). We can correct for homogeneity of variance by adjusting F itself, but normality might require transforming the data. We can also use the Kruskal–Wallis test from Chapter 6, which does not assume normality. There are also robust methods available to compare independent means (and even medians) that involve, for example, using 20% trimmed means or a bootstrap, but SPSS doesn't do any of them directly. They can be done using a package called R, and once you've mastered SPSS you could consider mastering that software as well. These tests are explained in the sister textbook for R (Field et al., 2012).

11.4. Planned contrasts ②

The F-ratio tells us only whether the model fitted to the data accounts for more variation than extraneous factors, but it doesn't tell us where the differences between groups lie. So, if the F-ratio is large enough to be statistically significant, then we know only that one or more of the differences between means are statistically significant (e.g., either b_2 or b_1 is statistically significant). It is, therefore, necessary after conducting an ANOVA to carry out further analysis to find out which groups differ. In multiple regression, each *b* coefficient is tested individually using a *t*-test and we could do the same for ANOVA. However, we would need to carry out two *t*-tests, which would inflate the familywise error rate (see Section 2.6.1.7). Therefore, we need a way to contrast the different groups without inflating the Type I error rate. There are two ways in which to achieve this goal. The first is to break down the variance accounted for by the model into component parts; the second is to compare every group (as if conducting several *t*-tests) but to use a stricter acceptance criterion such that the familywise error rate does not rise above .05. The first option can be done using planned comparisons (also known as **planned contrasts**)[3] whereas the latter option is done using *post hoc* **tests** (see Section 11.5). The difference between planned comparisons and *post hoc* tests is that planned comparisons are done when you have specific hypotheses that you want to test, whereas *post hoc* tests are done when you have no specific hypotheses. Let's first look at planned contrasts.

11.4.1. Choosing which contrasts to do ②

In the Viagra example we could have had very specific hypotheses. For one thing, we would expect any dose of Viagra to change libido compared to the placebo group. As a second hypothesis, we might believe that a high dose should increase libido more than a low dose. To do planned comparisons, these hypotheses must be derived *before* the data are collected. It is fairly standard in science to want to compare experimental conditions to the control conditions as the first contrast, and then to see where the differences lie between the experimental groups. ANOVA is based upon splitting the total variation into two component parts: the variation due to the experimental manipulation (SS_M) and the variation due to unsystematic factors (SS_R) (see Figure 11.4).

Planned comparisons take this logic a step further by breaking down the variation due to the experiment into component parts (see Figure 11.5). The exact comparisons that are carried out depend upon the hypotheses you want to test. Figure 11.5 shows a situation in which the experimental variance is broken down to look at how much variation is created by the two drug conditions compared to the placebo condition (*contrast 1*). Then the variation explained by taking Viagra is broken down to see how much is explained by taking a high dose relative to a low dose (*contrast 2*).

Typically, students struggle with the notion of planned comparisons, but there are three rules that can help you to work out what to do:

1 If we have a control group this is usually because we want to compare it against the other groups.

2 Each contrast must compare only two 'chunks' of variation.

3 Once a group has been singled out in a contrast it can't be used in another contrast.

Let's look at these rules in reverse order. First, if a group is singled out in one comparison, then it should not reappear in another comparison. The important thing to remember is that we are breaking down one chunk of variation into smaller independent chunks. In Figure 11.5 contrast 1 involved comparing the placebo group to the experimental groups; because the placebo group is singled out, it should not be incorporated into any other contrasts. You can think of partitioning variance as being similar to slicing up a cake. You

---

[3] The terms *comparison* and *contrast* are used interchangeably.

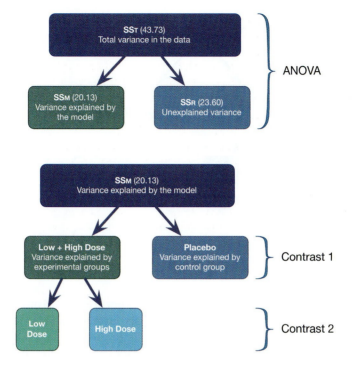

FIGURE 11.4
Partitioning variance for ANOVA

FIGURE 11.5
Partitioning of experimental variance into component comparisons

begin with a cake (the total sum of squares) and you then cut this cake into two pieces (SS_M and SS_R). You then take the piece of cake that represents SS_M and divide this up into smaller pieces. Once you have cut off a piece of cake you cannot stick that piece back onto the original slice, and you cannot stick it onto other pieces of cake, but you can divide it into smaller pieces of cake. Likewise, once a slice of variance has been split from a larger chunk, it cannot be attached to any other pieces of variance, it can only be subdivided into smaller chunks of variance. All of this talk of cake is making me hungry, but hopefully it illustrates the point.

If you follow the independence of contrasts rule that I've just explained (the cake slicing), and always compare only two pieces of variance, then you should always end up with one less contrast than the number of groups; that is, there will be $k - 1$ contrasts (where k is the number of conditions you're comparing).

Second, each contrast must compare only two chunks of variance. This rule is so that we can draw firm conclusions about what the contrast tells us. The *F*-ratio tells us that some of our means differ, but not which ones, and if we were to perform a contrast on more than two chunks of variance we would have the same problem. By comparing only two chunks of variance we can be sure that a significant result represents a difference between these two portions of variation.

Finally, in research we often use at least one control condition, and in the vast majority of experimental designs we predict that the experimental conditions will differ from the control condition(s). As such, the biggest hint that I can give you is that when planning comparisons the chances are that your first contrast should be one that compares all of the experimental groups with the control group(s). Once you have done this first comparison, any remaining comparisons will depend upon which of the experimental groups you predict will differ.

To illustrate these principles, Figures 11.6 and 11.7 show the contrasts that might be done in a four-group experiment. The first thing to notice is that in both scenarios there are three possible comparisons (one less than the number of groups). Also, every contrast compares only two chunks of variance. What's more, in both scenarios the first contrast is the same: the experimental groups are compared against the control group(s). In Figure

FIGURE 11.6

Partitioning variance for planned comparisons in a four-group experiment using one control group

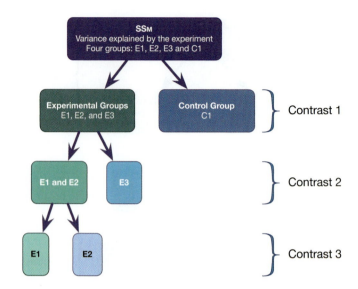

11.6 there is only one control condition and so this portion of variance is used only in the first contrast (because it cannot be broken down any further). In Figure 11.7 there are two control groups, and so the portion of variance due to the control conditions (contrast 1) can be broken down again so as to see whether or not the scores in the control groups differ from each other (contrast 3).

In Figure 11.6, the first contrast contains a chunk of variance that is due to the three experimental groups and this chunk of variance is broken down by first looking at whether groups E1 and E2 differ from E3 (contrast 2). It is equally valid to use contrast 2 to compare groups E1 and E3 to E2, or to compare groups E2 and E3 to E1. The exact comparison that you choose depends upon your hypotheses. For contrast 2 in Figure 11.6 to be valid we need to have a good reason to expect group E3 to be different from the other two groups. The third comparison in Figure 11.6 depends on the comparison chosen for contrast 2. Contrast 2 necessarily had to involve comparing two experimental groups against a third, and the experimental groups chosen to be combined must be separated in the final comparison. As a final point, you'll notice that in Figures 11.6 and 11.7, once a group has been singled out in a comparison, it is never used in any subsequent contrasts.

When we carry out a planned contrast, we compare 'chunks' of variance, and these chunks often consist of several groups. It is perhaps confusing to understand exactly what these contrasts tell us. Well, when you design a contrast that compares several groups to one other group, you are comparing the means of the groups in one chunk with the mean of the group in the other chunk. As an example, for the Viagra data I suggested that an appropriate first contrast would be to compare the two dose groups with the placebo group. The means of the groups are 2.20 (placebo), 3.20 (low dose) and 5.00 (high dose) and so the first comparison, which compared the two experimental groups to the placebo, is comparing 2.20 (the mean of the placebo group) to the average of the other two groups ((3.20 + 5.00)/2 = 4.10). If this first contrast turns out to be significant, then we can conclude that 4.10 is significantly greater than 2.20, which in terms of the experiment tells us that the average of the experimental groups is significantly different from the average of the controls. You can probably see that logically this means that, if the standard errors are the same, the experimental group with the highest mean (the high-dose group) will be significantly different from the mean of the placebo group. However, the experimental group with the lower mean (the low-dose group) might not necessarily differ from the placebo group; we have to use the final comparison to make sense of the experimental conditions. For the Viagra data the final comparison looked at

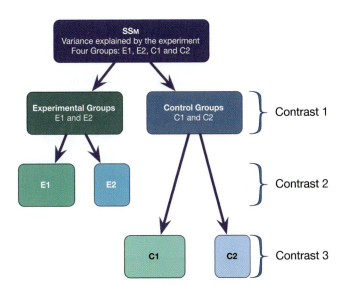

FIGURE 11.7
Partitioning
variance
for planned
comparisons
in a four-group
experiment
using two
control groups

whether the two experimental groups differ (i.e., is the mean of the high-dose group significantly different from the mean of the low-dose group?). If this comparison turns out to be significant then we can conclude that having a high dose of Viagra significantly affected libido compared to having a low dose. If the comparison is non-significant then we have to conclude that the dosage of Viagra made no significant difference to libido. In this latter scenario it is likely that both doses affect libido more than placebo, whereas the former case implies that having a low dose may be no different to having a placebo. However, the word *implies* is important here: it is possible that the low-dose group might not differ from the placebo. To be completely sure we must carry out *post hoc* tests.

11.4.2. Defining contrasts using weights ②

Hopefully by now you have got some idea of how to plan which comparisons to do (i.e., if your brain hasn't exploded yet). Much as I'd love to tell you that all of the hard work is now over and SPSS will magically carry out the comparisons that you've selected, I can't because it won't. To get SPSS to carry out planned comparisons we need to tell it which groups we would like to compare, and doing this can be quite complex. In fact, when we carry out contrasts we assign values to certain variables in the regression model (sorry, I'm afraid I have to start talking about regression again) – just as we did when we used dummy coding for the main ANOVA. To carry out contrasts we assign certain values to the dummy variables in the regression model. Whereas before we defined the experimental groups by assigning the dummy variables values of 1 or 0, when we perform contrasts we use different values to specify which groups we would like to compare. The resulting coefficients in the regression model (b_2 and b_1) represent the comparisons in which we are interested. The values assigned to the dummy variables are known as **weights**.

This procedure is horribly confusing, but there are a few basic rules for assigning values to the dummy variables to obtain the comparisons you want. I will explain these simple rules before showing how the process actually works. Remember the previous section when you read through these rules, and remind yourself of what I mean by a 'chunk' of variation.

- **Rule 1**: Choose sensible comparisons. Remember that you want to compare only two chunks of variation and that if a group is singled out in one comparison, that group should be excluded from any subsequent contrasts.

- **Rule 2**: Groups coded with positive weights will be compared against groups coded with negative weights. So, assign one chunk of variation positive weights and the opposite chunk negative weights.

- **Rule 3**: The sum of weights for a comparison should be zero. If you add up the weights for a given contrast the result should be zero.

- **Rule 4**: If a group is not involved in a comparison, automatically assign it a weight of zero. If we give a group a weight of zero then this eliminates that group from all calculations.

- **Rule 5**: For a given contrast, the weights assigned to the group(s) in one chunk of variation should be equal to the number of groups in the opposite chunk of variation.

OK, let's follow some of these rules to derive the weights for the Viagra data. The first contrast we chose was to compare the two experimental groups against the control:

Therefore, the first chunk of variation contains the two experimental groups, and the second chunk contains only the placebo group. Rule 2 states that we should assign one chunk positive weights, and the other negative. It doesn't matter which way round we do this, but for convenience let's assign chunk 1 positive weights, and chunk 2 negative weights:

Using rule 5, the weight we assign to the groups in chunk 1 should be equivalent to the number of groups in chunk 2. There is only one group in chunk 2 and so we assign each group in chunk 1 a weight of 1. Likewise, we assign a weight to the group in chunk 2 that is equal to the number of groups in chunk 1. There are two groups in chunk 1 so we give the placebo group a weight of 2. Then we combine the sign of the weights with the magnitude to give us weights of -2 (placebo), 1 (low dose) and 1 (high dose):

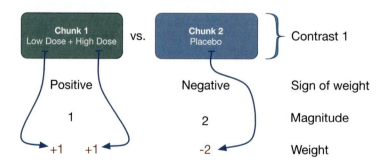

Rule 3 states that for a given contrast, the weights should add up to zero, and by following rules 2 and 5 this rule will always be followed (if you haven't followed these rules properly then this will become clear when you add the weights). So, let's check by adding the weights: sum of weights = $1 + 1 - 2 = 0$.

The second contrast was to compare the two experimental groups, and so we want to ignore the placebo group. Rule 4 tells us that we should automatically assign this group a weight of 0 (because this will eliminate this group from any calculations). We are left with two chunks of variation: chunk 1 contains the low-dose group and chunk 2 contains the high-dose group. By following rules 2 and 5 it should be obvious that one group is assigned a weight of +1 while the other is assigned a weight of −1. If we add the weights for contrast 2 we should find that they again add up to zero: sum of weights = 1 − 1 + 0 = 0.

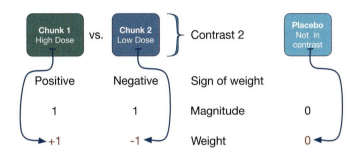

The weights for each contrast are codings for the two dummy variables in the following equation:

$$\text{Libido}_i = b_0 + b_1 \text{Contrast}_{1i} + b_2 \text{Contrast}_{2i} \tag{11.8}$$

Hence, these codings can be used in a multiple regression model in which b_2 represents contrast 1 (comparing the experimental groups to the control), b_1 represents contrast 2 (comparing the high-dose group to the low-dose group), and b_0 is the grand mean. Each group is specified now not by the 0 and 1 coding scheme that we initially used, but by the coding scheme for the two contrasts. A code of −2 for contrast 1 and a code of 0 for contrast 2 identify participants in the placebo group. Likewise, the high-dose group is identified by a code of 1 for both variables, and the low-dose group has a code of 1 for one contrast and a code of −1 for the other (see Table 11.4).

It is important that the weights for a comparison sum to zero because it ensures that you are comparing two unique chunks of variation. Therefore, SPSS can perform a *t*-test. A more important consideration is that when you multiply the weights for a particular group, these products should also add up to zero (see final column of Table 11.4). If the products add to zero then we can be sure that the contrasts are *independent* or **orthogonal**. It is important for interpretation that contrasts are orthogonal. When we used dummy variable coding and ran a regression on the Viagra data, I commented that we couldn't look at the individual *t*-tests done on the regression coefficients because the familywise error rate is inflated (see Section 2.6.1.7). However, if the contrasts are independent then the *t*-tests

TABLE 11.4   Orthogonal contrasts for the Viagra data

Group	Dummy Variable 1 (Contrast₁)	Dummy Variable 2 (Contrast₂)	Product Contrast₁ × Contrast₂
Placebo	−2	0	0
Low Dose	1	−1	−1
High Dose	1	1	1
Total	0	0	0

done on the b coefficients are independent also and so the resulting p-values are uncorrelated. You might think that it is very difficult to ensure that the weights you choose for your contrasts conform to the requirements for independence but, provided you follow the rules I have laid out, you should always derive a set of *orthogonal* comparisons. You should double-check by looking at the sum of the multiplied weights and if this total is not zero then go back to the rules and see where you have gone wrong.

Earlier on, I mentioned that when you used contrast codings in dummy variables in a regression model the b-values represented the differences between the means that the contrasts were designed to test. Although it is reasonable for you to trust me on this issue, for the more advanced students I'd like to take the trouble to show you how the regression model works (this next part is not for the faint-hearted …). When we do planned contrasts, the intercept b_0 is equal to the grand mean (i.e., the value predicted by the model when group membership is not known), which when group sizes are equal is:

$$b_0 = \text{grand mean} = \frac{\bar{X}_{\text{High}} + \bar{X}_{\text{Low}} + \bar{X}_{\text{Placebo}}}{3}$$

If we use the contrast codings for the *placebo group* (see Table 11.4), the predicted value of libido equals the mean of the placebo group. The regression equation can, therefore, be expressed as:

$$\text{Libido}_i = b_0 + b_1 \text{Contrast}_{i1} + b_2 \text{Contrast}_{2i}$$

$$\bar{X}_{\text{Placebo}} = \left(\frac{\bar{X}_{\text{High}} + \bar{X}_{\text{Low}} + \bar{X}_{\text{Placebo}}}{3} \right) + (-2b_1) + (b_2 \times 0)$$

Now, if we rearrange this equation and then multiply everything by 3 (to get rid of the fraction) we get:

$$2b_1 = \left(\frac{\bar{X}_{\text{High}} + \bar{X}_{\text{Low}} + \bar{X}_{\text{Placebo}}}{3} \right) - \bar{X}_{\text{Placebo}}$$

$$6b_1 = \bar{X}_{\text{High}} + \bar{X}_{\text{Low}} + \bar{X}_{\text{Placebo}} - 3\bar{X}_{\text{Placebo}}$$

$$6b_1 = \bar{X}_{\text{High}} + \bar{X}_{\text{Low}} - 2\bar{X}_{\text{Placebo}}$$

We can then divide everything by 2 to reduce the equation to its simplest form:

$$3b_1 = \left(\frac{\bar{X}_{\text{High}} + \bar{X}_{\text{Low}}}{2} \right) - \bar{X}_{\text{Placebo}}$$

$$b_1 = \frac{1}{3} \left[\left(\frac{\bar{X}_{\text{High}} + \bar{X}_{\text{Low}}}{2} \right) - \bar{X}_{\text{Placebo}} \right]$$

This equation shows that b_1 represents the difference between the average of the two experimental groups and the control group:

$$3b_1 = \left(\frac{\bar{X}_{High} + \bar{X}_{Low}}{2} \right) - \bar{X}_{Placebo}$$

$$= \frac{5 + 3.2}{2} - 2.2$$

$$= 1.9$$

We planned contrast 1 to look at the difference between the average of the experimental groups and the control and so it should now be clear how b_1 represents this difference. The observant among you will notice that rather than being the true value of the difference between experimental and control groups, b_1 is actually a third of this difference ($b_1 = 1.9/3 = 0.633$). This division controls the familywise error by making the regression coefficient equal to the actual difference divided by the number of groups in the contrast (in this case 3).

For the situation in which the codings for the *high-dose group* (see Table 11.4) are used, the predicted value of libido is the mean for the high-dose group, and so the regression equation becomes:

$$\text{Libido}_i = b_0 + b_1 \text{Contrast}_{1i} + b_2 \text{Contrast}_{2i}$$

$$\bar{X}_{High} = b_0 + (b_1 \times 1) + (b_2 \times 1)$$

$$b_2 = \bar{X}_{High} - b_1 - b_0$$

We know already what b_1 and b_0 represent, so we place these values into the equation and then multiply by 3 to get rid of some of the fractions:

$$b_2 = \bar{X}_{High} - b_1 - b_0$$

$$b_2 = \bar{X}_{High} - \frac{1}{3} \left[\left(\frac{\bar{X}_{High} + \bar{X}_{Low}}{2} \right) - \bar{X}_{Placebo} \right] - \frac{\bar{X}_{High} + \bar{X}_{Low} + \bar{X}_{Placebo}}{3}$$

$$3b_2 = 3\bar{X}_{High} - \left[\left(\frac{\bar{X}_{High} + \bar{X}_{Low}}{2} \right) - \bar{X}_{Placebo} \right] - \bar{X}_{High} + \bar{X}_{Low} + \bar{X}_{Placebo}$$

If we multiply everything by 2 to get rid of the other fraction, expand all of the brackets and then simplify the equation we get:

$$6b_2 = 6\bar{X}_{High} - \left(\bar{X}_{High} + \bar{X}_{Low} - 2\bar{X}_{Placebo} \right) - 2\left(\bar{X}_{High} + \bar{X}_{Low} + \bar{X}_{Placebo} \right)$$

$$6b_2 = 6\bar{X}_{High} - \bar{X}_{High} - \bar{X}_{Low} + 2\bar{X}_{Placebo} - 2\bar{X}_{High} - 2\bar{X}_{Low} - 2\bar{X}_{Placebo}$$

$$6b_2 = 3\bar{X}_{High} - 3\bar{X}_{Low}$$

Finally, we can divide the equation by 6 to find out what b_2 represents (remember that $3/6 = 1/2$):

$$b_2 = \frac{\overline{X}_{High} - \overline{X}_{Low}}{2}$$

We planned contrast 2 to look at the difference between the experimental groups:

$$\overline{X}_{High} - \overline{X}_{Low} = 5 - 3.2 = 1.8$$

It should now be clear how b_2 represents this difference. Again, rather than being the absolute value of the difference between the experimental groups, b_2 is actually half of this difference ($1.8/2 = 0.9$). The familywise error is again controlled, by making the regression coefficient equal to the actual difference divided by the number of groups in the contrast (in this case 2).

SELF-TEST   To illustrate these principles, I have created a file called **Contrast.sav** in which the Viagra data are coded using the contrast coding scheme used in this section. Run multiple regression analyses on these data using **libido** as the outcome and using **dummy1** and **dummy2** as the predictor variables (leave all default options).

EVERYBODY

Output 11.2 shows the result of this regression. The main ANOVA for the model is the same as when dummy coding was used (compare it to Output 11.1), showing that the model fit is the same (it should be because the model represents the group means and these have not changed); however, the regression coefficients have now changed. The first thing to notice is that the intercept is the grand mean, 3.467 (see, I wasn't telling lies). Second, the regression coefficient for contrast 1 is one-third of the difference between the average of the experimental conditions and the control condition (see above). Finally, the regression coefficient for contrast 2 is half of the difference between the experimental groups (see above). So, when a planned comparison is done in ANOVA a t-test is conducted comparing the mean of one chunk of variation with the mean of a different chunk. From the significance values of the t-tests we can see that our experimental groups were significantly different from the control ($p = .029$) but that the experimental groups were not significantly different ($p = .065$).

OUTPUT 11.2

Coefficients[a]

Model		Unstandardized Coefficients		Standardized Coefficients		
		B	Std. Error	Beta	t	Sig.
1	(Constant)	3.467	.362		9.574	.000
	Dummy Variable 1	.633	.256	.525	2.474	.029
	Dummy Variable 2	.900	.443	.430	2.029	.065

a. Dependent Variable: Libido

11.4.3. Non-orthogonal comparisons ②

Contrasts don't have to be orthogonal: non-orthogonal contrasts are comparisons that are in some way related, and the best way to get them is to disobey rule 1 in the previous section. Using my cake analogy again, non-orthogonal comparisons are where you slice

CRAMMING SAM'S TIPS   **Planned contrasts**

- After an ANOVA you need more analysis to find out which groups differ.
- When you have generated specific hypotheses before the experiment use *planned contrasts*.
- Each contrast compares two 'chunks' of variance. (A chunk can contain one or more groups.)
- The first contrast will usually be experimental groups against control groups.
- The next contrast will be to take one of the chunks that contained more than one group (if there were any) and divide it in to two chunks.
- You then repeat this process: if there are any chunks in previous contrasts that contained more than one group that haven't already been broken down into smaller chunks, then create a new contrast that breaks it down into smaller chunks.
- Carry on creating contrasts until each group has appeared in a chunk on its own in one of your contrasts.
- The number of contrasts you end up with should be one less than the number of experimental conditions. If not, you've done it wrong.
- In each contrast assign a 'weight' to each group that is the value of the number of groups in the opposite chunk in that contrast.
- For a given contrast, randomly select one chunk, and for the groups in that chunk change their weights to be negative numbers.
- Breathe a sigh of relief.

up your cake and then try to stick slices of cake together again. So, for the Viagra data a set of non-orthogonal contrasts might be to have the same initial contrast (comparing experimental groups against the placebo), but then to compare the high-dose group to the placebo. This disobeys rule 1 because the placebo group is singled out in the first contrast but used again in the second contrast. The coding for this set of contrasts is shown in Table 11.5; looking at the last column, it is clear that when you multiply and add the codings from the two contrasts the sum is not zero. This tells us that the contrasts are not orthogonal.

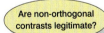
Are non-orthogonal contrasts legitimate?

There is nothing intrinsically wrong with performing non-orthogonal contrasts. However, if you choose to perform this type of contrast you must be very careful about how you interpret the results. With non-orthogonal contrasts, the comparisons you do are related and so the resulting test statistics and *p*-values will be correlated to some extent. For this reason you should use a more conservative probability level to accept that a given contrast is statistically meaningful (see Section 11.5).

TABLE 11.5   Non-orthogonal contrasts for the Viagra data

Group	Dummy Variable 1 (Contrast$_1$)	Dummy Variable 2 (Contrast$_2$)	Product Contrast$_1$ × Contrast$_2$
Placebo	−2	−1	2
Low Dose	1	0	0
High Dose	1	1	1
Total	0	0	3

11.4.4. Standard contrasts ②

Although under most circumstances you will design your own contrasts, there are special contrasts that have been designed to compare certain situations. Some of these contrasts are orthogonal, while others are non-orthogonal.

Table 11.6 shows the contrasts that are available in SPSS for procedures such as logistic regression (see Section 19.5.6), factorial ANOVA and repeated-measures ANOVA (see Chapters 13 and 14). Although the exact codings are not provided in Table 11.6, examples of the comparisons done in a three- and four-group situation are given (where the groups are respectively labelled 1, 2, 3 and 1, 2, 3, 4). When you code variables in the data editor, SPSS will treat the lowest-value code as group 1, the next highest code as group 2, and so on. Therefore, depending on which comparisons you want to make you should code your grouping variable appropriately (and then use Table 11.6 as a guide to which comparisons SPSS will carry out). One thing that clever readers might be able to work out about the contrasts in Table 11.6 is which are orthogonal (i.e., **Helmert** and **difference contrasts**) and which are non-orthogonal (**deviation**, **simple** and **repeated contrasts**). You might also notice

TABLE 11.6 Standard contrasts available in SPSS

Name	Definition	Contrast	Three Groups		Four Groups	
Deviation (first)	Compares the effect of each category (except first) to the overall experimental effect	1	2	vs. (1,2,3)	2	vs. (1,2,3,4)
		2	3	vs. (1,2,3)	3	vs. (1,2,3,4)
		3			4	vs. (1,2,3,4)
Deviation (last)	Compares the effect of each category (except last) to the overall experimental effect	1	1	vs. (1,2,3)	1	vs. (1,2,3,4)
		2	2	vs. (1,2,3)	2	vs. (1,2,3,4)
		3			3	vs. (1,2,3,4)
Simple (first)	Each category is compared to the first category	1	1	vs. 2	1	vs. 2
		2	1	vs. 3	1	vs. 3
		3			1	vs. 4
Simple (last)	Each category is compared to the last category	1	1	vs. 3	1	vs. 4
		2	2	vs. 3	2	vs. 4
		3			3	vs. 4
Repeated	Each category (except the first) is compared to the previous category	1	1	vs. 2	1	vs. 2
		2	2	vs. 3	2	vs. 3
		3			3	vs. 4
Helmert	Each category (except the last) is compared to the mean effect of all subsequent categories	1	1	vs. (2, 3)	1	vs. (2, 3, 4)
		2	2	vs. 3	2	vs. (3, 4)
		3			3	vs. 4
Difference (reverse Helmert)	Each category (except the first) is compared to the mean effect of all previous categories	1	3	vs. (2, 1)	4	vs. (3, 2, 1)
		2	2	vs. 1	3	vs. (2, 1)
		3			2	vs. 1

that the comparisons calculated using simple contrasts are the same as those given by using the dummy variable coding described in Table 11.2.

11.4.5. Polynomial contrasts: trend analysis ②

One type of contrast deliberately omitted from Table 11.6 is the polynomial contrast. This contrast tests for trends in the data and in its most basic form it looks for a linear trend (i.e., that the group means increase proportionately). However, there are other trends such as quadratic, cubic and quartic trends that can be examined. Figure 11.8 shows examples of the types of trend that can exist in data sets. The *linear* trend should be familiar to you all by now and represents a simply proportionate change in the value of the dependent variable across ordered categories (the diagram shows a positive linear trend but of course it could be negative). A quadratic trend is where there is a curve in the line (the curve can be more subtle than in the figure). An example of this is a situation in which a drug enhances performance on a task at first but then as the dose increases the performance tails off or drops. To find a quadratic trend you need at least three groups because with two groups the means of the dependent variable can't be connected by anything other than a straight line. A cubic trend is where there are two changes in the direction of the trend. So, for example, the mean of the dependent variable at first goes up across the first couple of categories of the independent variable, then goes down across the succeeding categories, but then goes up again across the last few categories. To have two changes in the direction of the mean

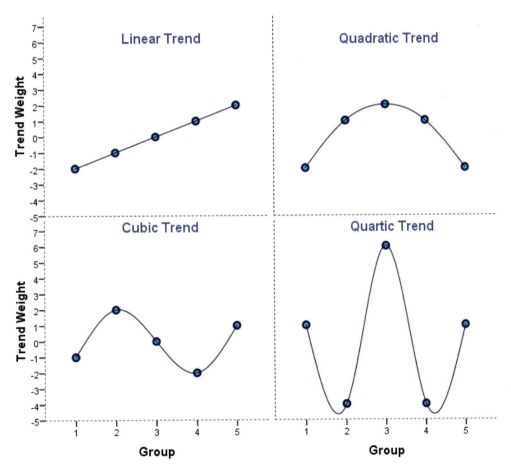

FIGURE 11.8

Examples of linear, quadratic, cubic and quartic trends across five groups

you must have at least four categories of the independent variable. The final trend that you are likely to come across is the **quartic trend**, and this trend has three changes of direction (so you need at least five categories of the independent variable).

Polynomial trends should be examined in data sets in which it makes sense to order the categories of the independent variable (so, for example, if you have administered five doses of a drug it makes sense to examine the five doses in order of magnitude). For the Viagra data there are only three groups and so we can expect to find only a linear or quadratic trend (and it would be pointless to test for any higher-order trends).

Each of these trends has a set of codes for the dummy variables in the regression model, so we are doing the same thing that we did for planned contrasts except that the codings have already been devised to represent the type of trend of interest. In fact, the graphs in Figure 11.8 have been constructed by plotting the coding values for the five groups. Also, if you add the codes for a given trend the sum will equal zero and if you multiply the codes you will find that the sum of the products also equals zero. Hence, these contrasts are orthogonal. The great thing about these contrasts is that you don't need to construct your own coding values to do them, because the codings already exist.

11.5. *Post hoc* procedures ②

Often people have no specific *a priori* predictions about the data they have collected and instead they rummage around the data looking for any differences between means that they can find. It's a bit like a statistical lucky dip. It sounds a bit dodgy, but I try to think of it as 'finding the differences that I should have predicted if only I'd been clever enough'.

Post hoc tests consist of **pairwise comparisons** that are designed to compare all different combinations of the treatment groups. So, it is rather like taking every pair of groups and performing a *t*-test on each pair. Now, this might seem like a particularly stupid thing to say (but then again, I am particularly stupid) in the light of what I have already told you about the problems of inflated familywise error rates in Section 2.6.1.7. However, pairwise comparisons control the familywise error by correcting the level of significance for each test such that the overall Type I error rate (α) across all comparisons remains at .05. There are several ways in which the familywise error rate can be controlled, and we have already discussed one of the most popular: the Bonferroni correction (Section 2.6.1.7).

There are other methods too (SPSS does about 18 different ones). Although I would love to go into tedious details about how all of the various *post hoc* tests work, there is really very little point. For one thing, there are some excellent texts already available for those who wish to know (Klockars & Sax, 1986; Toothaker, 1993). By far the best reason, though, is that to explain them I would have to learn about them first. I may be a nerd, but even I draw the line at reading up on 18 different *post hoc* tests. However, it *is* important that you know which *post hoc* tests perform best according to three important criteria: (1) does the test control the Type I error rate; (2) does the test control the Type II error rate (i.e., does the test have good statistical power); and (3) is the test robust?

SMART
ALEX
ONLY

11.5.1.   Type I and Type II error rates for *post hoc* tests ②

The Type I error rate and the statistical power of a test are linked. Therefore, there is always a trade-off: if a test is conservative (the probability of a Type I error is small) then it is likely to lack statistical power (the probability of a Type II error will be high). So it is important that multiple comparison procedures control the Type I error rate but without a substantial loss in power. If a test is too conservative then we are likely to reject differences between means that are, in reality, meaningful.

The *least significant difference* (LSD) pairwise comparison makes no attempt to control the Type I error and is equivalent to performing multiple *t*-tests on the data. The only difference is that the LSD requires the overall ANOVA to be significant. The *Studentized Newman–Keuls* procedure is also a very liberal test and lacks control over the familywise error rate. *Bonferroni's* and *Tukey's* tests both control the Type I error rate very well but are conservative tests (they lack statistical power). Of the two, Bonferroni has more power when the number of comparisons is small, whereas Tukey is more powerful when testing large numbers of means. Tukey generally has greater power than *Dunn* and *Scheffé*. The *Ryan, Einot, Gabriel and Welsch Q* procedure (REGWQ) has good power and tight control of the Type I error rate. In fact, when you want to test all pairs of means this procedure is probably the best. However, when group sizes are different this procedure should not be used.

11.5.2.   Are *post hoc* procedures robust? ②

Most research on *post hoc* tests has looked at whether the test performs well when the group sizes are different (an unbalanced design), when the population variances are very different, and when data are not normally distributed. The good news is that most multiple comparison procedures perform relatively well under small deviations from normality. The bad news is that they perform badly when group sizes are unequal and when population variances are different.

Hochberg's GT2 and *Gabriel's* pairwise test procedure were designed to cope with situations in which sample sizes are different. Gabriel's procedure is generally more powerful but can become too liberal when the sample sizes are very different. Also, Hochberg's GT2 is very unreliable when the population variances are different and so should be used only when you are sure that this is not the case. There are several multiple comparison procedures that have been specially designed for situations in which population variances differ. SPSS provides four options for this situation: *Tamhane's T2*, *Dunnett's T3*, *Games–Howell* and *Dunnett's C*. Tamhane's T2 is conservative and Dunnett's T3 and C keep very tight Type I error control. The Games–Howell procedure is the most powerful but can be liberal when sample sizes are small. However, Games–Howell is also accurate when sample sizes are unequal.

EVERYBODY

11.5.3.   Summary of *post hoc* procedures ②

The choice of comparison procedure will depend on the exact situation you have and whether it is more important for you to keep strict control over the familywise error rate or to have greater statistical power. However, some general guidelines can be drawn (Toothaker, 1993). When you have equal sample sizes and you are confident that your population variances are similar, use REGWQ or Tukey as both have good power and tight control over the Type I error rate. Bonferroni is generally conservative, but if you want guaranteed control over the Type I error rate then this is the test to use. If sample sizes are slightly different then use Gabriel's procedure because it has greater power, but if sample sizes are very different use Hochberg's GT2. If there is any doubt that the population variances are equal then use the Games–Howell procedure because this generally seems to offer the best performance. I recommend running the Games–Howell procedure in addition to any other tests you might select because of the uncertainty of knowing whether the population variances are equivalent.

CRAMMING SAM'S TIPS   *Post hoc* **tests**

- After an ANOVA you need a further analysis to find out which groups differ.
- When you have no specific hypotheses before the experiment, use *post hoc tests*.
- When you have equal sample sizes and group variances are similar use REGWQ or Tukey.
- If you want guaranteed control over the Type I error rate then use Bonferroni.
- If sample sizes are slightly different then use Gabriel's procedure, but if sample sizes are very different use Hochberg's GT2.
- If there is any doubt that group variances are equal then use the Games–Howell procedure.

Although these general guidelines provide a convention to follow, be aware of the other procedures available and when they might be useful (e.g., Dunnett's test is the only multiple comparison that allows you to test means against a control mean).

11.6. Running one-way ANOVA in SPSS ②

11.6.1. General procedure of one-way ANOVA ②

Hopefully you should all have some appreciation for the theory behind ANOVA, so let's put that theory into practice by conducting an ANOVA test on the Viagra data. As with the independent *t*-test we need to enter the data into the data editor using a coding variable to specify to which of the three groups the data belong. So, the data must be entered in two

FIGURE 11.9
Overview of the general procedure for one-way ANOVA

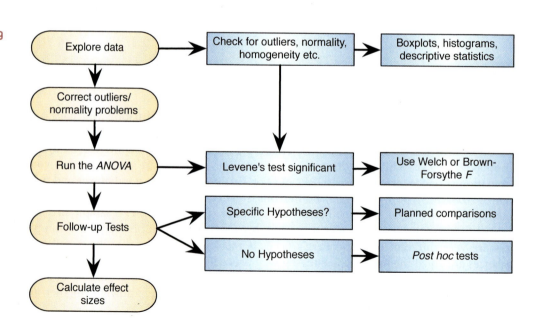

columns (one called **dose** which specifies how much Viagra the participant was given and one called **libido** which indicates the person's libido over the following week). The data are in the file **Viagra.sav,** but I recommend entering them by hand to gain practice in data entry. I have coded the grouping variable so that 1 = placebo, 2 = low dose and 3 = high dose (see Section 3.5.2.3).

ANOVA is a linear model, so we should look back at the general procedure for linear models in Chapter 8. Figure 11.9 highlights the steps that are specific to one-way ANOVA. As with any analyses, begin by graphing the data and looking for and correcting sources of bias.

SELF-TEST   Produce a line chart with error bars for the Viagra data.

As we'll see, we can test for homogeneity of variance with Levene's test (although note my reservations about this test from Chapter 5): if there's a problem, we simply look at a different part of the SPSS output, which gives us versions of *F* corrected for this problem (Section 11.3.1).

To conduct one-way ANOVA we have to access the main dialog box by selecting Analyze Compare Means ▸ 🔢 One-Way ANOVA... (Figure 11.10). This dialog box has a space in which you can list one or more dependent variables and a second space to specify a grouping variable, or *factor*. Factor is another term for independent variable and should not be confused with the factors that we will come across when we learn about factor analysis. For the Viagra data we need select only **libido** from the variables list and drag it to the box labelled *Dependent List* (or click on 🔽). Then select the grouping variable **dose** and drag it to the box labelled *Factor (or* click on 🔽).

One thing that I dislike about SPSS is that in various procedures, such as one-way ANOVA, the program encourages the user to carry out multiple tests, which as we have seen is not a good thing. For example, in this procedure you are allowed to specify several dependent variables on which to conduct several ANOVAs. In reality, if you had measured several dependent variables (say you had measured not just libido but physiological arousal and anxiety too) it would be preferable to analyse these data using MANOVA rather than treating each dependent measure separately (see Chapter 16).

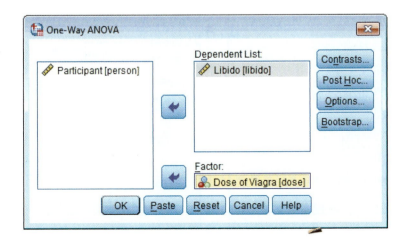

FIGURE 11.10
Main dialog box for one-way ANOVA

11.6.2.   Planned comparisons using SPSS ②

If you click on [Contrasts...] you access the dialog box that allows you to conduct the planned comparisons described in Section 11.4.

The dialog box is shown in Figure 11.11 and has two sections. The first section is for specifying trend analyses. If you want to test for trends in the data then tick the box labelled *Polynomial*. Once this box is ticked, you can select the degree of polynomial you would like. The Viagra data have only three groups and so the highest degree of trend there can be is a quadratic trend (see Section 11.4.3). Now, it is important from the point of view of trend analysis that we have coded the grouping variable in a meaningful order. Also, we expect libido to be smallest in the placebo group, to increase in the low-dose group and then to increase again in the high-dose group. To detect a meaningful trend, we need to have coded these groups in ascending order. We have done this by coding the placebo group with the lowest value 1, the low-dose group with the middle value 2 and the high-dose group with the highest coding value of 3. If we coded the groups differently, this would influence both whether a trend is detected and, if a trend is detected, whether it is statistically meaningful.

For the Viagra data there are only three groups and so we should select the polynomial option ☑ Polynomial then select a quadratic degree by clicking on [Linear ▼] and then select *Quadratic* (the drop-down list should now say [Quadratic ▼]). If a quadratic trend is selected SPSS will test for both linear and quadratic trends.

The lower part of the dialog box in Figure 11.11 is for specifying any planned comparisons. To conduct planned comparisons we need to tell SPSS what weights to assign to each group. The first step is to decide which comparisons you want to do and then what weights must be assigned to each group for each of the contrasts. We have already gone through this process in Section 11.4.2, so we know that the weights for contrast 1 were −2 (placebo group), +1 (low-dose group) and +1 (high-dose group). We will specify this contrast first. It is important to make sure that you enter the correct weight for each group, so you should remember that the first weight that you enter should be the weight for the *first* group (i.e., the group coded with the lowest value in the data editor). For the Viagra data, the group coded with the lowest value was the placebo group (which had a code of 1) so we should enter the weighting for this group first. Click in the box labelled *Coefficients* with the mouse and then type '−2' in this box and click on [Add]. Next, we need to input the weight for the second group, which for the Viagra data is the low-dose group (because this group was coded in the data editor with the second-highest value). Click in the box

FIGURE 11.11

Dialog box for conducting planned comparisons

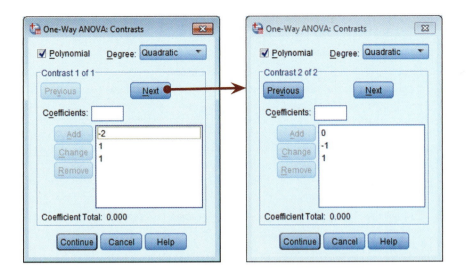

FIGURE 11.12
Contrasts
dialog box
completed
for the two
contrasts of the
Viagra data

labelled *Coefficients* with the mouse and then type '1' in this box and click on [Add]. Finally, we need to input the weight for the last group, which for the Viagra data is the high-dose group (because this group was coded with the highest value in the data editor). Click in the box labelled *Coefficients* with the mouse and then type '1' in this box and click on [Add]. The box should now look like Figure 11.12 (left).

Once you have inputted the weights you can change or remove any one of them by using the mouse to select the weight that you want to change. The weight will then appear in the box labelled *Coefficients* where you can type in a new weight and then click on [Change]. Alternatively, you can click on any of the weights and remove it completely by clicking [Remove]. Underneath the weights SPSS calculates the coefficient total, which, as we saw in Section 11.4.2, should equal zero. If the coefficient number is anything other than zero you should go back and check that the contrasts you have planned make sense and that you have followed the appropriate rules for assigning weights.

Once you have specified the first contrast, click on [Next]. The weights that you have just entered will disappear and the dialog box will now read *Contrast 2 of 2*. We know from Section 11.4.2 that the weights for contrast 2 were: 0 (placebo group), −1 (low-dose group) and +1 (high-dose group). We can specify this contrast as before. Remembering that the first weight we enter will be for the placebo group, we must enter the value 0 as the first weight. Click in the box labelled *Coefficients* with the mouse and then type '0' and click on [Add]. Next, we need to input the weight for the low-dose group by clicking in the box labelled *Coefficients* and then typing '−1' and clicking on [Add]. Finally, we need to input the weight for the high-dose group by clicking in the box labelled *Coefficients* and then typing '+1' and clicking on [Add]. The box should now look like Figure 11.12 (right). Notice that the weights add up to zero as they did for contrast 1. It is imperative that you remember to input zero weights for any groups that are not in the contrast. When all of the planned contrasts have been specified, click on [Continue] to return to the main dialog box.

11.6.3. *Post hoc* tests in SPSS ②

Having told SPSS which planned comparisons to do, we can choose to do *post hoc* tests. In theory, if we have done planned comparisons we shouldn't need to do *post hoc* tests (because we have already tested the hypotheses of interest). Likewise, if we choose to

FIGURE 11.13
Dialog box for
specifying *post
hoc* tests

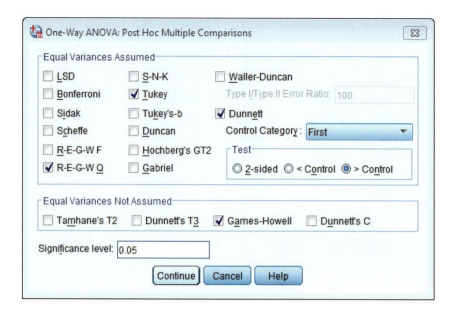

conduct *post hoc* tests then we should not need to do planned contrasts (because we have no hypotheses to test). However, for the sake of space we will conduct some *post hoc* tests on the Viagra data. Click on [Post Hoc...] in the main dialog box to access the *post hoc* tests dialog box (Figure 11.13).

In Section 11.5.3, I recommended various *post hoc* procedures for various situations. For the Viagra data there are equal sample sizes and so we need not use Gabriel's test. We should use Tukey's test and REGWQ and check the findings with the Games–Howell procedure. We have specific hypotheses that both the high- and low-dose groups should differ from the placebo group and so we could use Dunnett's test to examine these hypotheses. Once you have selected Dunnett's test, change the control category (the default is to use the [Last ▾] category) to specify that the [First ▾] category be used as the control category (because the placebo group was coded with the lowest value). You can also choose whether to conduct a two-tailed test (⦿ 2-sided) or a one-tailed test. If you choose a one-tailed test (which I advised against in Section 2.6.1.5) then you must predict whether you believe that the mean of the control group will be less than a particular experimental group (⦿ > Control) or greater than a particular experimental group (⦿ < Control). These are all of the *post hoc* tests that need to be specified and when the completed dialog box looks like Figure 11.13 click on [Continue] to return to the main dialog box.

11.6.4. Options ②

The options for one-way ANOVA are fairly straightforward (Figure 11.14). First you can ask for some descriptive statistics, which will produce a table of the means, standard deviations, standard errors, ranges and confidence intervals for the means of each group. This option is useful to select because it assists in interpreting the final results. If you select *Homogeneity of variance test* then the output will report Levene's test, which tests the hypothesis that the variances of each group are equal (see Section 5.3.3.2). It is definitely worth selecting either or both of *Brown-Forsythe* and *Welch* so that you can interpret these if you're concerned about having unequal variances (there is a decent case for just interpreting these tests all of the time). There is also an option to have a *Means plot*, and if this option is selected then a line graph of the group means will be produced in the output. The resulting graph is a leprotic tramp compared to what we can create using the chart

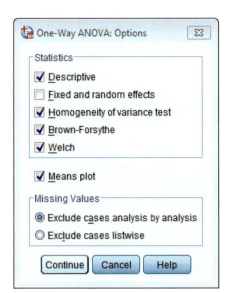

FIGURE 11.14
Options for
one-way
ANOVA

builder and, as I have said before, it's best to graph your data *before* the analysis, not during it. Finally, the options let us specify whether we want to exclude cases on a listwise basis or on a per-analysis basis (SPSS Tip 5.1). This option is useful only if you are conducting several ANOVAs on different dependent variables. The first option (*Exclude cases analysis by analysis*) excludes any case that has a missing value for either the independent or the dependent variable used in that particular analysis. *Exclude cases listwise* will exclude from *all analyses* any case that has a missing value for the independent variable or any of the dependent variables specified. If you stick to good practice and don't conduct hundreds of ANOVAs on different dependent variables the default settings are fine.

11.6.5. Bootstrapping ②

Also in the main dialog box is the alluring Bootstrap... button. We know that bootstrapping is a good way to overcome bias, and this button glistens and tempts us with the promise of untold riches, like a diamond in a bull's rectum. However, if you use bootstrapping it'll be as disappointing as if you reached for that diamond only to discover that it's a piece of glass. You might, not unreasonably, think that if you select bootstrapping it'd do a nice bootstrap of the *F*-statistic for you. It won't. It will bootstrap confidence intervals around the means (if you ask for descriptive statistics), contrasts and differences between means (i.e., the *post*

ODITI'S LANTERN

One-Way ANOVA

'I, Oditi, have made great progress in unearthing the hidden truth behind the numbers. This morning, one of my loyal followers reported to me that, based on an ANOVA he'd done, all dogs are controlled by cats who hide small remote controls up their rectums and manipulate them with their tongues. Everytime you see a cat 'cleaning' itself, there will be a dog nearby chasing its tail. Listen carefully and you can hear the cat laughing to itself. Be warned, cats are merely piloting the technology, and soon they will control us too, turning us into heated chairs and food vendors. We must find out more. Stare into my lantern so that you too can use ANOVA.'

FIGURE 11.15
Error bar (95%
CI) chart of the
Viagra data

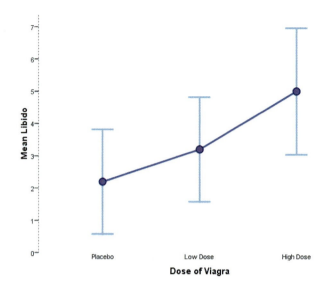

hoc tests). This, of course, can be useful, but the main test won't be bootstrapped. For this example, we have a very small data set so bootstrapping is going to go haywire anyway, so we won't select it. Click on [OK] in the main dialog box to run the analysis.

11.7. Output from one-way ANOVA ②

You should find that the output looks the same as what follows. If not, we should panic because one of us has done it wrong – hopefully not me or a lot of trees have died for nothing. Figure 11.15 shows a line chart with error bars from the self-test earlier in the chapter (I have edited my graph; see if you can use the SPSS chart editor to make yours look like mine). All of the error bars overlap a fair bit, indicating that, at face value, there might not be between-group differences (see Section 2.6.1.9). The line that joins the means seems to indicate a linear trend in that, as the dose of Viagra increases, so does the mean level of libido.

11.7.1. Output for the main analysis ②

Output 11.3 shows the table of descriptive statistics for the Viagra data. The first thing to notice is that the means and standard deviations correspond to those shown in Table 11.1. In addition, we are told the standard error. Remember that the standard error is the standard deviation of the sampling distribution of these data (so for the placebo group, if you took lots of samples from the population from which these data come, the means of these samples would have a standard deviation of 0.5831). We are also given confidence intervals for the mean. Assuming that this sample is one of the 95% that contain the true value, then the true value of the mean is between 0.5811 and 3.8189. Although these diagnostics are not immediately important, we will refer back to them throughout the analysis.

The next part of the output (Output 11.4) shows Levene's test (see Section 5.3.3.2). In this case, Levene's test is testing whether the variances of the three groups are significantly different. If Levene's test is significant (i.e., the value of *Sig.* is less than .05) then the variances are significantly different. This would mean we had violated the assumption

Descriptives

Libido

	N	Mean	Std. Deviation	Std. Error	95% Confidence Interval for Mean		Minimum	Maximum
					Lower Bound	Upper Bound		
Placebo	5	2.20	1.304	.583	.58	3.82	1	4
Low Dose	5	3.20	1.304	.583	1.58	4.82	2	5
High Dose	5	5.00	1.581	.707	3.04	6.96	3	7
Total	15	3.47	1.767	.456	2.49	4.45	1	7

of homogeneity of variance: we could rectify the problem by transforming the data and reanalysing these transformed values (see Chapter 5), but given the apparent utility of Welch's F and the Brown–Forsythe F, you might as well look at those (I'd probably suggest reporting Welch's F over the Brown–Forsythe F unless you have an extreme mean that is also causing the problem with the variances). For these data the variances are very similar (hence the high probability value); in fact, if you look at Output 11.3 you'll see that the variances of the placebo and low-dose groups are identical.

Test of Homogeneity of Variances

Libido

Levene Statistic	df1	df2	Sig.
.092	2	12	.913

Output 11.5 shows the main ANOVA summary table. The table is divided into between-groups effects (effects due to the model – the experimental effect) and within-group effects (this is the unsystematic variation in the data). The between-groups effect is further broken down into a linear and quadratic component, and these components are the trend analyses described in Section 11.4.5. The between-groups effect labelled *Combined* is the overall experimental effect. In this row we are told the sums of squares for the model (SS_M = 20.13), and this value corresponds to the value calculated in Section 11.2.4. The degrees of freedom are equal to 2 and the mean square for the model corresponds to the value calculated in Section 11.2.6 (10.067). The sum of squares and mean squares represent the experimental effect.

This overall effect is then broken down because we asked SPSS to conduct trend analyses of these data (we will return to these trends in due course). Had we not specified this in Section 11.6.2, then these two rows of the summary table would not have been produced. The row labelled *Within Groups* gives details of the unsystematic variation within the data (the variation due to natural individual differences in libido and different reactions to Viagra). The table tells us how much unsystematic variation exists (the residual sum of squares, SS_R) and this value (23.60) corresponds to the value calculated in Section 11.2.5. The table then gives the average amount of unsystematic variation, the mean square (MS_R), which corresponds to the value (1.967) calculated in Section 11.2.6.

The test of whether the group means are the same is represented by the F-ratio for the combined between-groups effect. The value of this ratio is 5.12, which is the same as was calculated in Section 11.2.7. The final column labelled *Sig.* tells us the probability of getting an F at least this big if there wasn't a difference between means in the population (see also SPSS Tip 11.1). In this case, there is a probability of .025 that an F-ratio of this size would occur if in reality there was no effect (that's only a 2.5% chance). We have seen in previous chapters that we use a cut-off point of .05 as a criterion for statistical significance.

Hence, because the observed significance value is less than .05 we can say that there was a significant effect of Viagra. However, at this stage we still do not know exactly what the effect of Viagra was (we don't know which groups differed). One thing that is interesting here is that we obtained a significant experimental effect yet our error bar plot suggested that no significant difference would be found. This contradiction illustrates how the error bar chart can act only as a rough guide to the data.

OUTPUT 11.5

ANOVA

Libido

			Sum of Squares	df	Mean Square	F	Sig.
Between Groups	(Combined)		20.133	2	10.067	5.119	.025
	Linear Term	Contrast	19.600	1	19.600	9.966	.008
		Deviation	.533	1	.533	.271	.612
	Quadratic Term	Contrast	.533	1	.533	.271	.612
Within Groups			23.600	12	1.967		
Total			43.733	14			

Knowing that the overall effect of Viagra was significant, we can now look at the trend analysis. The trend analysis breaks down the experimental effect to see whether it can be explained by either a linear or a quadratic relationship in the data. First, let's look at the linear component. This comparison tests whether the means increase across groups in a linear way. Again the sum of squares and mean squares are given, but the most important things to note are the value of the F-ratio and the corresponding significance value. For the linear trend the F-ratio is 9.97 and this value is significant at a .008 level. Therefore, we can say that as the dose of Viagra increased from nothing to a low dose to a high dose, libido increased proportionately. Moving onto the quadratic trend, this comparison is testing whether the pattern of means is curvilinear (i.e., is represented by a curve that has one bend). The error bar graph of the data suggests that the means cannot be represented by a curve and the results for the quadratic trend bear this out. The F-ratio for the quadratic trend is non-significant (in fact, the value of F is less than 1, which immediately indicates that this contrast will not be significant).

OUTPUT 11.6

Robust Tests of Equality of Means

Libido

	Statistic[a]	df1	df2	Sig.
Welch	4.320	2	7.943	.054
Brown–Forsythe	5.119	2	11.574	.026

a. Asymptotically F distributed.

Finally, Output 11.6 shows Welch's and the Brown–Forsythe F-ratios. As it turned out, we didn't need these because our Levene's test was not significant, indicating that our variances were similar. However, when homogeneity of variance has been violated you should look at these F-ratios *instead* of the ones in the main table. If you're interested in how these values are calculated then look at Jane Superbrain Box 11.3, but to be honest it's just confusing; you're much better off just looking at the values in Output 11.6 and trusting that they do what they're supposed to do (you should also note that the error degrees of freedom have been adjusted and you should remember this when you report the values).

SPSS TIP 11.1   **One and two-tailed tests in ANOVA** ②

A question I get asked a lot by students is: 'is the significance of the ANOVA one- or two-tailed, and if it's two-tailed can I divide by 2 to get the one-tailed value?' I told you earlier not to do that sort of thing anyway (see Section 2.6.1.5), but it's particularly daft in this context because to do a one-tailed test you have to be making a directional hypothesis (e.g., the mean for cats is greater than for dogs). When comparing more than two means (as you do with ANOVA) you can't make a directional hypothesis: you can predict only that the means will differ somehow. Therefore, it's invalid to halve the significance value of an *F*.

11.7.2.   Output for planned comparisons ②

In Section 11.6.2 we told SPSS to conduct two planned comparisons: one to test whether the control group was different from the two groups which received Viagra, and one to see whether the two doses of Viagra made a difference to libido. Output 11.7 shows the results of the planned comparisons that we requested for the Viagra data. The first table displays the contrast coefficients; these values are the ones that we entered in Section 11.6.2 and it is well worth looking at this table to double-check that the contrasts are comparing what they are supposed to. As a quick rule of thumb, remember that when we do planned comparisons we arrange the weights such that we compare any group with a positive weight against any group with a negative weight. Therefore, the table of weights shows that contrast 1 compares the placebo group against the two experimental groups, and contrast 2 compares the low-dose group to the high-dose group. It is useful to check this table to make sure that the weights that we entered into SPSS are the ones we intended.

The second table gives the statistics for each contrast. The first thing to notice is that statistics are produced for situations in which the group variances are equal, and when they are unequal. If Levene's test was significant then you should read the part of the table labelled *Does not assume equal variances*. However, for these data Levene's test was not significant and we can, therefore, use the part of the table labelled *Assume equal variances*. The table tells us the value of the contrast itself, which is the weighted sum of the group means. This value is obtained by taking each group mean, multiplying it by the weight for

Contrast Coefficients

OUTPUT 11.7

	Dose of Viagra		
Contrast	Placebo	Low Dose	High Dose
1	–2	1	1
2	0	–1	1

Contrast Tests

		Contrast	Value of Contrast	Std. Error	t	df	Sig. (2–tailed)
Libido	Assume equal variances	1	3.80	1.536	2.474	12	.029
		2	1.80	.887	2.029	12	.065
	Does not assume equal variances	1	3.80	1.483	2.562	8.740	.031
		2	1.80	.917	1.964	7.720	.086

the contrast of interest, and then adding these values together.[4] The table also gives the standard error of each contrast and a *t*-statistic. The *t*-statistic is derived by dividing the contrast value by the standard error ($t = 3.8/1.5362 = 2.47$) and is compared against critical values of the *t*-distribution. The significance value of the contrast is given in the final column and this value is two-tailed. Hence, for contrast 1, we can say that taking Viagra significantly increased libido compared to the control group ($p = .029$), but contrast 2 tells us that a high dose of Viagra did not significantly affect libido compared to a low dose ($p = .065$). Of course contrast 2 is almost significant, which demonstrates my earlier caution about how this process can lead to all-or-nothing thinking (Section 2.6.2.2).

11.7.3.   Output for *post hoc* tests ②

If we had no specific hypotheses about the effect that Viagra might have on libido then we could carry out *post hoc* tests to compare all groups of participants with each other. In fact, we asked SPSS to do this (see Section 11.6.3) and the results of this analysis are shown in Output 11.8. This table shows the results of Tukey's test (known as Tukey's HSD)[5], the Games–Howell procedure and Dunnett's test, which were all specified earlier on. If we look at Tukey's test first (because we have no reason to doubt that the population variances are unequal), it is clear from the table that each group of participants is compared to all of the remaining groups. For each pair of groups the difference between group means is displayed, the standard error of that difference, the significance level of that difference and a 95% confidence interval. First of all, the placebo group is compared to the low-dose group and reveals a non-significant difference (*Sig.* is greater than .05), but when compared to the high-dose group there is a significant difference (*Sig.* is less than .05).

SELF-TEST   Our planned comparison showed that any dose of Viagra produced a significant increase in libido, yet the *post hoc* tests indicate that a low dose does not. Why is there this contradiction?

In Section 11.4.2, I explained that the first planned comparison would compare the experimental groups to the placebo group. Specifically, it would compare the average of the two group means of the experimental groups ($(3.2 + 5.0)/2 = 4.1$) to the mean of the placebo group (2.2). So, it was assessing whether the difference between these values ($4.1 - 2.2 = 1.9$) was significant. In the *post hoc* tests, when the low dose is compared to the placebo, the contrast is testing whether the difference between the means of these two groups is significant. The difference in this case is only 1, compared to a difference of 1.9 for the planned comparison. This explanation illustrates how it is possible to have apparently contradictory results from planned contrasts and *post hoc* comparisons. More important, it illustrates how careful we must be in interpreting planned contrasts.

The low-dose group is then compared to both the placebo group and the high-dose group. The first thing to note is that the contrast involving the low-dose and placebo groups is identical to the one just described. The only new information is the comparison between the two experimental conditions. The group means differ by 1.8, which is not significant. This result is the same as our planned comparison (contrast 2).

---

[4] For the first contrast this value is: $\sum \bar{X} W = (2.2 \times (-2)) + (3.2 \times 1) + (5 \times 1) = 3.8$

[5] The HSD stands for 'honestly significant difference', which has a slightly dodgy ring to it if you ask me.

Multiple Comparisons

Dependent Variable: Libido

	(I) Dose of Viagra	(J) Dose of Viagra	Mean Difference (I–J)	Std. Error	Sig.	95% Confidence Interval Lower Bound	95% Confidence Interval Upper Bound
Tukey HSD	Placebo	Low Dose	−1.000	.887	.516	−3.37	1.37
		High Dose	−2.800*	.887	.021	−5.17	−.43
	Low Dose	Placebo	1.000	.887	.516	−1.37	3.37
		High Dose	−1.800	.887	.147	−4.17	.57
	High Dose	Placebo	2.800*	.887	.021	.43	5.17
		Low Dose	1.800	.887	.147	−.57	4.17
Games–Howell	Placebo	Low Dose	−1.000	.825	.479	−3.36	1.36
		High Dose	−2.800*	.917	.039	−5.44	−.16
	Low Dose	Placebo	1.000	.825	.479	−1.36	3.36
		High Dose	−1.800	.917	.185	−4.44	.84
	High Dose	Placebo	2.800*	.917	.039	.16	5.44
		Low Dose	1.800	.917	.185	−.84	4.44
Dunnett t (>control)[b]	Low Dose	Placebo	1.000	.887	.227	−.87	
	High Dose	Placebo	2.800*	.887	.008	.93	

*. The mean difference is significant at the 0.05 level.

b. Dunnett t-tests treat one group as a control, and compare all other groups against it.

Next, the table describes the Games–Howell test. A quick inspection reveals the same pattern of results: the only groups that differed significantly were the high-dose and placebo groups. These results give us confidence in our conclusions from Tukey's test because even if the population variances are not equal (which seems unlikely given that the sample variances are very similar), then the profile of results still holds true.

Finally, Dunnett's test is described, and you'll hopefully remember that we asked the computer to compare both experimental groups against the control using a one-tailed hypothesis that the mean of the control group would be smaller than both experimental groups. Even as a one-tailed hypothesis, levels of libido in the low-dose group are equivalent to the placebo group. However, the high-dose group has a significantly higher libido than the placebo group.

The table in Output 11.9 shows the results of Tukey's test and the REGWQ test. These tests display subsets of groups that have the same means. Therefore, Tukey's test creates two subsets of groups with statistically similar means. The first subset contains the placebo and low-dose groups (indicating that these two groups have the similar means) whereas the second subset contains the high- and low-dose groups. These results demonstrate that the placebo group has a similar mean to the low-dose group but not the high-dose group, and that the low-dose group has a similar mean to both the placebo and high-dose groups. In other words, the only groups that have significantly different means are the high-dose and placebo groups. The tests provide a significance value for each subset and it's clear from these significance values that the groups in subsets have non-significant means (as indicated by values of *Sig.* that are greater than .05).

Libido

	Dose of Viagra	N	Subset for alpha = 0.05 1	Subset for alpha = 0.05 2
Tukey HSD[a]	Placebo	5	2.20	
	Low Dose	5	3.20	3.20
	High Dose	5		5.00
	Sig.		.516	.147
Ryan–Einot–Gabriel–Welsch Range	Placebo	5	2.20	
	Low Dose	5	3.20	3.20
	High Dose	5		5.00
	Sig.		.282	.065

Means for groups in homogeneous subsets are displayed.

a. Uses Harmonic Mean Sample Size = 5.000.

CRAMMING SAM'S TIPS   **One-way ANOVA**

- The one-way independent ANOVA compares several means, when those means have come from different groups of people; for example, if you have several experimental conditions and have used different participants in each condition.
- When you have generated specific hypotheses before the experiment use *planned comparisons*, but if you don't have specific hypotheses use *post hoc* tests.
- There are lots of different *post hoc* tests: when you have equal sample sizes and homogeneity of variance is met, use REGWQ or Tukey's HSD. If sample sizes are slightly different then use Gabriel's procedure, but if sample sizes are very different use Hochberg's GT2. If there is any doubt about homogeneity of variance use the Games–Howell procedure.
- Test for homogeneity of variance using Levene's test. Find the table with this label: if the value in the column labelled *Sig.* is less than.05 then the assumption is violated. If this is the case go to the table labelled *Robust Tests of Equality of Means*. If homogeneity of variance has been met (the significance of Levene's test is greater than.05) go to the table labelled *ANOVA*.
- In the table labelled *ANOVA* (or *Robust Tests of Equality of Means* – see above), look at the column labelled *Sig.* If the value is less than.05 then the means of the groups are significantly different.
- For contrasts and *post hoc* tests, again look to the columns labelled *Sig.* to discover if your comparisons are significant (they will be if the significance value is less than.05).

These calculations use the harmonic mean sample size. The **harmonic mean** is a weighted version of the mean that takes account of the relationship between variance and sample size. Although you don't need to know the intricacies of the harmonic mean, it is useful that the harmonic sample size is used because it reduces bias that might be introduced through having unequal sample sizes. However, as we have seen, these tests are still biased when sample sizes are unequal.

11.8. Calculating the effect size ②

One thing you will notice is that SPSS doesn't routinely provide an effect size for one-way independent ANOVA. However, we saw in equation (9.10) that:

$$R^2 = \frac{SS_M}{SS_T}$$

Of course we know these values from the SPSS output. So we can calculate r^2 using the between-groups effect (SS_M), and the total amount of variance in the data (SS_T) – although for some bizarre reason it's usually called **eta squared,** η^2. It is then a simple matter to take the square root of this value to give us the effect size r:

$$r^2 = \eta^2 = \frac{SS_M}{SS_T} = \frac{20.13}{43.73} = .46$$
$$r = \sqrt{.46} = .68$$

Using the benchmarks for effect sizes, this represents a large effect (it is above the .5 threshold for a large effect). Therefore, the effect of Viagra on libido is a substantive finding.

Gallup, G. G. J., et al. (2003). *Evolution and Human Behavior, 24*, 277–289.

LABCOAT LENI'S REAL RESEARCH 11.1

Scraping the barrel? ①

Evolution has endowed us with many beautiful things (cats, dolphins, the Great Barrier Reef, etc.) all selected to fit their ecological niche. Given evolution's seemingly limitless capacity to produce beauty, it's something of a wonder how it managed to produce such a monstrosity as the human penis. One theory is that the penis evolved into the shape that it is because of sperm competition. Specifically, the human penis has an unusually large glans (the 'bell-end', as it's affectionately known) compared to other primates, and this may have evolved so that the penis can displace seminal fluid from other males by 'scooping it out' during intercourse. To put this idea to the test, Gordon Gallup and his colleagues came up with an ingenious study (Gallup et al., 2003). Armed with various female masturbatory devices from Hollywood Exotic Novelties, an artificial vagina from California Exotic Novelties, and some water and cornstarch to make fake sperm, they loaded the artificial vagina with 2.6 ml of fake sperm and inserted one of three female sex toys into it before withdrawing it. Over several trials, three different female sex toys were used:

a control phallus that had no coronal ridge (i.e., no bell-end), a phallus with a minimal coronal ridge (small bell-end) and a phallus with a coronal ridge.

They measured sperm displacement as a percentage using the following equation (included here because it is more interesting than all of the other equations in this book):

$$\frac{\text{Weight of vagina with semen} - \text{weight of vagina following insertion and removal of phallus}}{\text{Weight of vagina with semen} - \text{weight of empty vagina}} \times 100$$

As such, 100% means that all of the sperm was displaced by the phallus, and 0% means that none of the sperm was displaced. If the human penis evolved as a sperm displacement device then Gallup et al. predicted: (1) that having a bell-end would displace more sperm than not; and (2) the phallus with the larger coronal ridge would displace more sperm than the phallus with the minimal coronal ridge. The conditions are ordered (no ridge, minimal ridge, normal ridge) so we might also predict a linear trend. The data can be found in the file **Gallup et al.sav.** Draw an error bar graph of the means of the three conditions. Conduct a one-way ANOVA with planned comparisons to test the two hypotheses above. What did Gallup et al. find? Answers are on the companion website (or look at pages 280–281 in the original article).

However, this measure of effect size is slightly biased because it is based purely on sums of squares from the sample and no adjustment is made for the fact that we're trying to estimate the effect size in the population. Therefore, we often use a slightly more complex measure called omega squared (ω^2). This effect size estimate is still based on the sums of squares that we've met in this chapter, but like the *F*-ratio it uses the variance explained by the model, and the error variance (in both cases the average variance, or mean squared error, is used):

$$\omega^2 = \frac{SS_M - (df_M)MS_R}{SS_T + MS_R}$$

The df_M in the equation is the degrees of freedom for the effect, which you can get from the SPSS output (in the case of the main effect this is the number of experimental conditions minus one). So, in this example we'd get:

$$\omega^2 = \frac{20.13 - (2)1.97}{43.73 + 1.97}$$

$$= \frac{16.19}{45.70}$$

$$= .35$$

$$\omega = .60$$

As you can see, this has led to a slightly lower estimate to using r, and in general ω is a more accurate measure. Although in the sections on ANOVA I will use ω as my effect size measure, think of it as you would r (because it's basically an unbiased estimate of r anyway). People normally report ω^2 and it has been suggested that values of .01, .06 and .14 represent small, medium and large effects, respectively (Kirk, 1996). Remember, though, that these are rough guidelines and that effect sizes need to be interpreted within the context of the research literature.

Most of the time it isn't that interesting to have effect sizes for the overall ANOVA because it's testing a general hypothesis. Instead, we really want effect sizes for the contrasts (because these compare only two things, so the effect size is considerably easier to interpret). Planned comparisons are tested with the t-statistic and, therefore, we can use the same equation as in Section 9.6.4:

$$r_{\text{Contrast}} = \sqrt{\frac{t^2}{t^2 + df}}$$

We know the value of t and the df from SPSS Output 10.7 and so we can compute r as follows:

$$r_{\text{Contrast1}} = \sqrt{\frac{2.474^2}{2.474^2 + 12}} = \sqrt{\frac{6.12}{18.12}} = .58$$

If you think back to our benchmarks for effect sizes this represents a large effect (it is above .5, the threshold for a large effect). Therefore, as well as being statistically significant, this effect is large and so represents a substantive finding. For contrast 2 we get:

$$r_{\text{Contrast2}} = \sqrt{\frac{2.029^2}{2.029^2 + 12}} = \sqrt{\frac{4.12}{16.12}} = .51$$

This too is a substantive finding and represents a large effect size.

11.9. Reporting results from one-way independent ANOVA ②

When we report an ANOVA, we have to give details of the F-ratio and the degrees of freedom from which it was calculated. For the experimental effect in these data the F-ratio was derived by dividing the mean squares for the effect by the mean squares for the residual. Therefore, the degrees of freedom used to assess the F-ratio are the degrees of freedom for the effect of the model ($df_M = 2$) and the degrees of freedom for the residuals of the model ($df_R = 12$). Therefore, the correct way to report the main finding would be:

✓ There was a significant effect of Viagra on levels of libido, $F(2, 12) = 5.12$, $p = .025$, $\omega = .60$.

Notice that the value of the F-ratio is preceded by the values of the degrees of freedom for that effect. The linear contrast can be reported in much the same way:

✓ There was a significant linear trend, $F(1, 12) = 9.97$, $p = .008$, $\omega = .62$, indicating that as the dose of Viagra increased, libido increased proportionately.

Notice that the degrees of freedom have changed to reflect how the F-ratio was calculated. I've also included an effect size measure (have a go at calculating this as we did for the main

F-ratio and see if you get the same value). Also, we have reported the exact *p*-value. We can also report our planned contrasts:

✓ Planned contrasts revealed that having any dose of Viagra significantly increased libido compared to having a placebo, $t(12) = 2.47$, $p = .029$, $r = .58$, but having a high dose did not significantly increase libido compared to having a low dose, $t(12) = 2.03$, $p = .065$, $r = .51$.

11.10. Key terms that I've discovered

Analysis of variance (ANOVA)	Grand variance	Polynomial contrast
Brown–Forsythe *F*	Harmonic mean	*Post hoc* tests
Cubic trend	Helmert contrast	Quadratic trend
Deviation contrast	Independent ANOVA	Quartic trend
Difference contrast (reverse Helmert contrast)	Omega squared	Repeated contrast
	Orthogonal	Simple contrast
Eta squared, η^2	Pairwise comparisons	Weights
Experimentwise error rate	Planned contrasts	Welch's *F*
Familywise error rate		

11.11. Brian's attempt to woo Jane ①

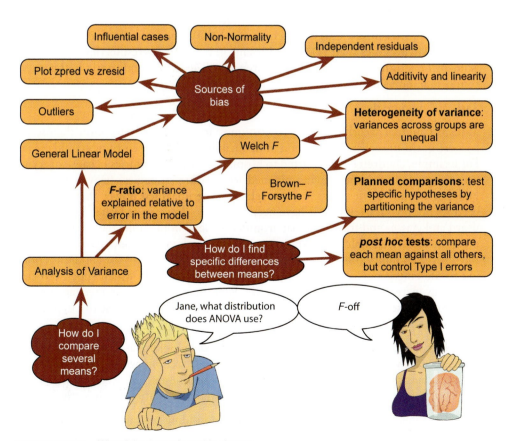

FIGURE 11.16 What Brian learnt from this chapter

11.12. What next? ①

My life was changed by a letter that popped through the letterbox one day saying only that I could go to the local grammar school if I wanted to. When my parents told me, rather than being in celebratory mood, they were very downbeat; they knew how much it meant to me to be with my friends and how I had got used to my apparent failure. Sure enough, my initial reaction was to say that I wanted to go to the local school. I was unwavering in this view. Unwavering, that is, until my brother convinced me that being at the same school as him would be really cool. It's hard to measure how much I looked up to him, and still do, but the fact that I willingly subjected myself to a lifetime of social dysfunction just to be with him is a measure of sorts. As it turned out, being at school with him was not always cool – he was bullied for being a boffin (in a school of boffins) and being the younger brother of a boffin made me a target. Luckily, unlike my brother, I was stupid and played football, which seemed to be good enough reasons for them to leave me alone. Most of the time.

11.13. Smart Alex's tasks

- **Task 1**: To test how different teaching methods affected students' knowledge I took three statistics courses where I taught the same material. For one course I wandered around with a large cane and beat anyone who asked daft questions or got questions wrong (*punish*). In the second I encouraged students to discuss things that they found difficult and gave anyone working hard a nice sweet (*reward*). For the final course I remained indifferent and neither punished nor rewarded students' efforts (*indifferent*). As the dependent measure I took the students' percentage exam marks. The data are in the file **Teach.sav.** Carry out a one-way ANOVA and use planned comparisons to test the hypotheses that: (1) reward results in better exam results than either punishment or indifference; and (2) indifference will lead to significantly better exam results than punishment. ②

- **Task 2***:* Compute the effect sizes for the previous task. ②

- **Task 3**: Children wearing superhero costumes are more likely to harm themselves because of the unrealistic impression of invincibility that these costumes could create. For example, children have reported to hospital with severe injuries because of trying 'to initiate flight without having planned for landing strategies' (Davies, Surridge, Hole, & Munro-Davies, 2007). I can relate to the imagined power that a costume bestows upon you; even now, I have been known to dress up as Fisher by donning a beard and glasses and trailing a goat around on a lead in the hope that it might make me more knowledgeable about statistics. Imagine we had data (**Superhero.sav**) about the severity of **injury** (on a scale from 0, no injury, to 100, death) for children reporting to the emergency centre at hospitals and information on which superhero costume they were wearing (**hero**): Spiderman, Superman, the Hulk or a teenage mutant ninja turtle. Use one-way ANOVA and multiple comparisons to test the hypotheses that different costumes give rise to more severe injuries. ②

- **Task 4**: In Chapter 6 (Section 6.6) there are some data looking at whether eating soya meals reduces your sperm count. Have a look at this section, access the data for that example, but analyse them with ANOVA. What's the difference between what you find and what is found in Section 6.6.5? Why do you think this difference has arisen? ②

- **Task 5**: Mobile phones emit microwaves, and so holding one next to your brain for large parts of the day is a bit like sticking your brain in a microwave oven and pushing the 'cook until well done' button. If we wanted to test this experimentally, we could get six groups of people and strap a mobile phone on their heads (so that they can't remove it). Then, by remote control, we turn the phones on for a certain amount of time each day. After six months, we measure the size of any tumour (in mm^3) close to the site of the phone antenna (just behind the ear). The six groups experienced 0, 1, 2, 3, 4 or 5 hours per day of phone microwaves for six months. Carry out an ANOVA to see if tumours increased with greater daily exposure. The data are in **Tumour.sav.** ②

- **Task 6:** Using the Glastonbury data from Chapter 8 (**GlastonburyFestival.sav**), carry out a one-way ANOVA on the data to see if the change in hygiene (**change**) is significant across people with different musical tastes (**music**). Do a simple contrast to compare each group against 'No Affiliation'. Compare the results to those described in Section 10.5. ②

- **Task 7:** Labcoat Leni's Real Research 6.2 describes an experiment (Çetinkaya & Domjan, 2006) on quails with fetishes for terrycloth objects. (Really, it does.) You were asked to analyse two of the variables that they measured with a Kruskal–Wallis test. However, there were two other outcome variables (time spent near the terrycloth object and copulatory efficiency). These data can be analysed with one-way ANOVA. Read Labcoat Leni's Real Research 6.2 to remind yourself of the full story then carry out a one-way ANOVA and Bonferroni *post hoc* tests on the time spent near the terrycloth object. ②

- **Task 8:** Repeat the analysis above but using copulatory efficiency as the outcome. ②

- **Task 9:** A sociologist wanted to compare murder rates (**Murder**) each month in a year at three high profile locations in London (**Street**). Run an ANOVA with bootstrapping on the *post hoc* tests to see in which streets the most murders happened (**Murder.sav**). ②

Answers can be found on the companion website.

11.14. Further reading

Howell, D. C. (2012). *Statistical methods for psychology* (8th ed.). Belmont, CA: Wadsworth. (Or you might prefer his *Fundamental statistics for the behavioral sciences*. Both are excellent texts.)

Klockars, A. J., & Sax, G. (1986). *Multiple comparisons.* Sage University Paper Series on Quantitative Applications in the Social Sciences, 07-061. Newbury Park, CA: Sage.

Rosenthal, R., Rosnow, R. L., & Rubin, D. B. (2000). *Contrasts and effect sizes in behavioural research: a correlational approach.* Cambridge: Cambridge University Press. (A fantastic book on planned comparisons by three of the great writers on statistics.)

Toothaker, L. E. (1993). *Multiple comparison procedures.* Sage University Paper Series on Quantitative Applications in the Social Sciences, 07-089. Newbury Park, CA: Sage.

12

Analysis of covariance, ANCOVA (GLM 2)

FIGURE 12.1
Davey Murray (guitarist from Iron Maiden) and me backstage in London in 1986; my grimace reflects the utter terror I was feeling at meeting my hero

12.1. What will this chapter tell me? ②

My road to rock stardom had taken a bit of a knock with my unexpected entry to an all-boys' grammar school (rock bands and grammar schools really didn't go together). I needed to be inspired and I turned to the masters: Iron Maiden. I first heard Iron Maiden at the age of 11 when a friend of mine lent me *Piece of Mind* and told me to listen to 'The Trooper'. It was, to put it mildly, an epiphany. I became their smallest (I was 11) biggest fan and started to obsess about them in the unhealthiest way possible. I started stalking the man who ran their fan club with letters, and, bless him, he replied. Eventually this stalking paid off and he arranged for me to go backstage when they played the Hammersmith Odeon in London (now the Hammersmith Apollo) on 5 November 1986 (*Somewhere on Tour* in case you're interested). Not only was it the first time that I had seen them live, but I got to meet them too. It's hard to put into words how bladder-splittingly exciting that night was. I was so utterly awe-struck that I managed to say precisely no words to them. Soon to become a theme in my life, a social situation had provoked me to make an utter fool of myself.[1]

When it was over I was in no doubt that this was the best day of my life. In fact, I thought, I should just kill myself there and then because nothing would ever be as good as that again.[2] This may be true, but I have subsequently had many other very nice experiences, so who is to say that they were not better? I could compare experiences to see which one is the best, but there is an important confound: my age. At the age of 13, meeting Iron Maiden was bowel-weakeningly exciting, but adulthood (sadly) dulls your capacity for this kind of unqualified joy of life. Therefore, to really see which experience was best, I would have to take account of the variance in enjoyment that is attributable to my age at the time. This will give me a purer measure of how much variance in my enjoyment is attributable to the event itself. This chapter describes analysis of covariance, which extends the basic idea of ANOVA from the previous chapter to situations when we want to factor in other variables that influence the outcome variable.

12.2. What is ANCOVA? ②

12.2.1.1. When to use ANCOVA ②

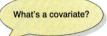

In the previous chapter we saw how one-way ANOVA could be characterized in terms of a multiple regression equation that used dummy variables to code group membership. In addition, in Chapter 8 we saw how multiple regression could incorporate several continuous predictor variables. It should, therefore, be no surprise that the regression equation for ANOVA can be extended to include one or more continuous variables that predict the outcome (or dependent variable). Continuous variables such as these, that are not part of the main experimental manipulation but have an influence on the dependent variable, are known as **covariates** and they can be included in an ANOVA analysis. When we measure covariates and include them in an analysis of variance we call it analysis of covariance (or **ANCOVA** for short). This chapter focuses on this technique.

In the previous chapter, we used an example about looking at the effects of Viagra on libido. Let's think about things other than Viagra that might influence libido: well, the obvious one is the libido of the participant's sexual partner (after all 'it takes two to tango'!), but there are other things too such as other medication that suppresses libido (such as antidepressants or the contraceptive pill) and fatigue. If these variables (the covariates) are measured, then it is possible to control for the influence they have on the dependent variable by including them in the regression model. From what we know of hierarchical regression (see Chapter 8) it should be clear that if we enter the covariate into the regression model first, and then enter the dummy variables representing the experimental manipulation, we can see what effect an independent variable has *after* the effect of the covariate. As such, we *partial out* the effect of the covariate. Here are two reasons for including covariates in ANOVA:

- **To reduce within-group error variance**: In the discussion of ANOVA and *t*-tests we got used to the idea that we assess the effect of an experiment by comparing the amount of variability in the data that the experiment can explain against the variability that it cannot explain. If we can explain some of this 'unexplained' variance (SS_R) in terms of other variables (covariates), then we reduce the error variance, allowing us to assess more accurately the effect of the independent variable (SS_M).

---

[1] In my teens I stalked many bands and Iron Maiden are by far the nicest of the bands I've met.

[2] Apart from my wedding day, as it turned out.

- **Elimination of confounds**: In any experiment, there may be unmeasured variables that confound the results (i.e., variables other than the experimental manipulation that affect the outcome variable). If any variables are known to influence the dependent variable being measured, then ANCOVA is ideally suited to remove the bias of these variables. Once a possible confounding variable has been identified, it can be measured and entered into the analysis as a covariate.

There are other reasons for including covariates in ANOVA, but because I do not intend to describe the computation of ANCOVA in any detail I recommend that the interested reader consult my favourite sources on the topic (Stevens, 2002; Wildt & Ahtola, 1978).

12.2.1.2. ANCOVA and the general linear model ②

Imagine that the researcher who conducted the Viagra study in the previous chapter suddenly realized that the libido of the participants' sexual partners would affect the participants' own libido (especially because the measure of libido was behavioural). Therefore, they repeated the study on a different set of participants, but this time took a measure of the partner's libido. The partner's libido was measured in terms of how often they tried to initiate sexual contact. The data for this example are in Table 12.1 and can be found in the file **ViagraCovariate.sav**. This file contains the variables **Dose** (1 = placebo, 2 = low dose, 3 = high dose), **Libido** (scores that correspond to the person's libido) and **Partner_Libido** (scores that correspond to the partner's libido).

SELF-TEST   Use SPSS to find the means and standard deviations of both the participant's libido and that of their partner in total, and within the three groups. (Answers are in Table 12.2.)

In the previous chapter, we saw that this experimental scenario could be characterized in terms of equation (11.1). Think back to what we know about multiple regression (Chapter 8) and you can hopefully see that this equation can be extended to include this covariate as follows:

$$\begin{aligned}
\text{Libido}_i &= b_0 + b_3 \text{Covariate}_i + b_2 \text{High}_i + b_1 \text{Low}_i + \varepsilon_i \\
&= b_0 + b_3 \text{Partner's libido}_i + b_2 \text{High}_i + b_1 \text{Low}_i + \varepsilon_i
\end{aligned} \tag{12.1}$$

As such, we can think about comparing the means of different groups in terms of a linear model (see Section 11.2.1) in which groups are coded as the dummy variables **High** and **Low**: **High** takes the value of 1 only for the high group, and **Low** takes a value of 1 only for the low group, in all other situations they have a value of 0.

We can think of ANCOVA as an extension of this model in which a covariate is added as a predictor to the model. This model will test the difference between group means *adjusted for the covariate*. Let's look at this idea with a practical example; although you would not normally do ANCOVA using the regression menu in SPSS, running the analysis this way will help us to understand what is going on conceptually.

SELF-TEST   Add two dummy variables to the file **ViagraCovariate.sav** that compare the low dose to the placebo (**Low_Placebo**) and the high dose to the placebo (**High_Placebo**) – see Section 11.2.1 for help. If you get stuck then download **ViagraCovariateDummy.sav**.

TABLE 12.1   Data from **ViagraCovariate.sav**

Dose	Participant's Libido	Partner's Libido
Placebo	3	4
	2	1
	5	5
	2	1
	2	2
	2	2
	7	7
	2	4
	4	5
Low Dose	7	5
	5	3
	3	1
	4	2
	4	2
	7	6
	5	4
	4	2
High Dose	9	1
	2	3
	6	5
	3	4
	4	3
	4	3
	4	2
	6	0
	4	1
	6	3
	2	0
	8	1
	5	0

TABLE 12.2   Means (and standard deviations) from **ViagraCovariate.sav**

Dose	Participant's Libido	Partner's Libido
Placebo	3.22 (1.79)	3.44 (2.07)
Low Dose	4.88 (1.46)	3.12 (1.73)
High Dose	4.85 (2.12)	2.00 (1.63)
Total	4.37 (1.96)	2.73 (1.86)

SELF-TEST Run a hierarchical regression analysis with **Libido** as the outcome. In the first block enter partner's libido (**Partner_Libido**) as a predictor, and then in a second block enter both dummy variables (Forced entry) – see Section 8.6 for help.

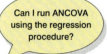

Can I run ANCOVA using the regression procedure?

The summary of the regression model resulting from the self-test (Output 12.1) shows us the goodness of fit of the model first when only the covariate is used in the model, and second when both the covariate and the dummy variables are used. Therefore, the difference between the values of R^2 (.288 −.061 =.227) represents the individual contribution of the dose of Viagra. We can say that the dose of Viagra accounted for 22.7% of the variation in libido, whereas partner's libido accounted for only 6.1%. This additional information provides some insight into the substantive importance of Viagra. The next table is the ANOVA table, which is again divided into two sections. The top half represents the effect of the covariate alone, while the bottom half represents the whole model (i.e., covariate and dose of Viagra included). Notice at the bottom of the ANOVA table (the bit for Model 2) that the entire model (partner's libido and the dummy variables) accounts for 31.92 units of variance (SS_M), there are 110.97 units in total (SS_T) and the unexplained variance (SS_R) is 79.05.

OUTPUT 12.1

Model Summary

Model	R	R Square	Adjusted R Square	Std. Error of the Estimate
1	.246[a]	.061	.027	1.929
2	.536[b]	.288	.205	1.744

a. Predictors: (Constant), Partner's Libido

b. Predictors: (Constant), Partner's Libido, Dummy Variable 1 (Placebo vs. Low), Dummy Variable 2 (Placebo vs. High)

ANOVA[a]

Model		Sum of Squares	df	Mean Square	F	Sig.
1	Regression	6.734	1	6.734	1.809	.189[b]
	Residual	104.232	28	3.723		
	Total	110.967	29			
2	Regression	31.920	3	10.640	3.500	.030[c]
	Residual	79.047	26	3.040		
	Total	110.967	29			

a. Dependent Variable: Libido

b. Predictors: (Constant), Partner's Libido

c. Predictors: (Constant), Partner's Libido, Dummy Variable 1 (Placebo vs. Low), Dummy Variable 2 (Placebo vs. High)

The table of regression coefficients (Output 12.2) is the interesting part of the output. Again, this table is split into two: the top half shows the effect when only the covariate is in the model and the bottom half contains the whole model. The *b*-values for the dummy variables represent the difference between the means of the low-dose group and the placebo group (**Low_Placebo**) and between the high-dose group and the placebo group (**High_Placebo**) – see Section 11.2.1 for an explanation. The means of the low- and high-dose groups were 4.88 and 4.85 respectively, and the mean of the placebo group was 3.22. Therefore, the *b*-values for the two dummy variables should be roughly the same (4.88 − 3.22 = 1.66 for **Low_Placebo** and 4.85 − 3.22 = 1.63 for **High_Placebo**). The astute among you might notice from the SPSS output that, in fact, the *b*-values are not only very different from each other (which shouldn't be the case because the high- and low-dose groups means are virtually the same), but also different from the values I've just calculated. Does this mean I've been lying to you for the past 50 pages about what the beta values represent? Well, even I'm not that horrible; the reason for this apparent anomaly is that the *b*-values in this regression represent the differences between the means of each group and the placebo when these means have been adjusted for the partner's libido.

These adjusted means come directly from the model. If we replace the *b* values in equation (12.1) with the values in Output 12.2, our model becomes:

$$\text{Libido}_i = 1.789 + 0.416 \text{ Partner's libido}_i + 2.225 \text{ High}_i + 1.786 \text{Low}_i \qquad (12.2)$$

Remember that **High** and **Low** are dummy variables such that **High** takes the value of 1 only for the high group, and **Low** takes a value of 1 only for the low group: in all other situations they have a value of 0. To get the adjusted means, we use this equation, but rather than replacing the covariate with an individual's score, we replace it with the mean value of the covariate from Table 12.2 (2.73) because we're interested in the predicted value for each group at the mean level of the covariate. For the placebo group, the dummy variables are both coded as 0, so we replace **High** and **Low** in the model with 0. The adjusted mean will, therefore, be:

$$\overline{\text{Libido}}_{\text{Placebo}} = 1.789 + \left(0.416 \times \overline{X}_{\text{Partner's libido}}\right) + \left(2.225 \times 0\right) + \left(1.786 \times 0\right)$$

$$\overline{\text{Libido}}_{\text{Placebo}} = 1.789 + \left(0.416 \times 2.73\right)$$

$$= 2.925$$

For the low-dose group, the dummy variable **Low** is 1 and **High** is 0, so the adjusted mean is:

$$\overline{\text{Libido}}_{\text{Low}} = 1.789 + \left(0.416 \times \overline{X}_{\text{Partner's libido}}\right) + \left(2.225 \times 0\right) + \left(1.786 \times 1\right)$$

$$\overline{\text{Libido}}_{\text{Low}} = 1.789 + \left(0.416 \times 2.73\right) + 1.786$$

$$= 4.71$$

For the high-dose group, the dummy variable **Low** is 0 and **High** is 1, so the adjusted mean is:

$$\overline{\text{Libido}}_{\text{High}} = 1.789 + \left(0.416 \times \overline{X}_{\text{Partner's libido}}\right) + \left(2.225 \times 1\right) + \left(1.786 \times 0\right)$$

$$\overline{\text{Libido}}_{\text{High}} = 1.789 + \left(0.416 \times 2.73\right) + 2.225$$

$$= 5.15$$

We can now see that the *b*-values for the two dummy variables represent the differences between these *adjusted* means (4.71 − 2.93 = 1.78 for **Low_Placebo** and 5.15 − 2.93 = 2.22 for **High_Placebo**). These adjusted means are the average amount of libido for each group at the mean level of partner's libido. This is why some people think of ANCOVA as 'controlling' for the covariate, because it compares the predicted group means at the average value of the covariate, so the groups are being compared at a level of the covariate that is the same for each group. However, as we shall see the 'controlling for the covariate' analogy is not a good one.

To reiterate, you don't usually run ANCOVA through the regression menus of SPSS (but see SPSS Tip 12.1); I have done so here to illustrate that ANCOVA is simply a regression model like all the others we have encountered in this book. It's not scary or complicated, it's the same model we've used countless times before.

Coefficients[a]

Model		Unstandardized Coefficients		Standardized Coefficients	t	Sig.
		B	Std. Error	Beta		
1	(Constant)	3.657	.634		5.764	.000
	Partner's Libido	.260	.193	.246	1.345	.189
2	(Constant)	1.789	.867		2.063	.049
	Partner's Libido	.416	.187	.395	2.227	.035
	Dummy Variable 1 (Placebo vs. Low)	1.786	.849	.411	2.102	.045
	Dummy Variable 2 (Placebo vs. High)	2.225	.803	.573	2.771	.010

a. Dependent Variable: Libido

12.3. Assumptions and issues in ANCOVA ③

ANCOVA is a linear model and, therefore, all of the sources of potential bias (and counteractive measures) discussed in Chapter 5 apply. However, there are two important additional considerations: (1) independence of the covariate and treatment effect; and (2) homogeneity of regression slopes.

12.3.1. Independence of the covariate and treatment effect ③

I said in the previous section that one use of ANCOVA is to reduce within-group error variance by allowing the covariate to explain some of this error variance. However, for this to be true the covariate must be independent of the experimental effect.

Figure 12.2 shows three different scenarios. Part A shows a basic ANOVA and is similar to Figure 11.4; it shows that the experimental effect (in our example libido) can be partitioned into two parts that represent the experimental or treatment effect (in this case the administration of Viagra) and the error or unexplained variance (i.e., factors that affect libido that we haven't measured). Part B shows the ideal scenario for ANCOVA in which the covariate shares its variance only with the bit of libido that is currently unexplained. In other words, it is completely independent of the treatment effect (it does not overlap with the effect of Viagra at all). This scenario is the only one in which ANCOVA is appropriate. Part C shows a situation in which people often use ANCOVA when they should not. In this situation the effect of the covariate overlaps with the experimental effect. In other words, the experimental effect is confounded with the effect of the covariate. In this situation, the covariate will reduce (statistically speaking) the experimental effect because it explains some of the variance that would otherwise be attributable to the experiment. When the covariate and the experimental effect (independent variable) are not independent, the treatment effect is obscured, spurious treatment effects can arise and at the very least the interpretation of the ANCOVA is seriously compromised (Wildt & Ahtola, 1978).

The problem of the covariate and treatment sharing variance is common and is ignored or misunderstood by many people (Miller & Chapman, 2001). Miller and Chapman are not the only people to point this out, but their paper is very readable and they cite many examples of people misapplying ANCOVA. Their main point is that when treatment groups differ on the covariate, putting the covariate into the analysis will not 'control for' or 'balance out' those differences (Lord, 1967, 1969). This situation arises mostly when participants are not randomly assigned to experimental treatment conditions. For example, anxiety and depression are closely correlated (anxious people tend to be depressed), so if you wanted to

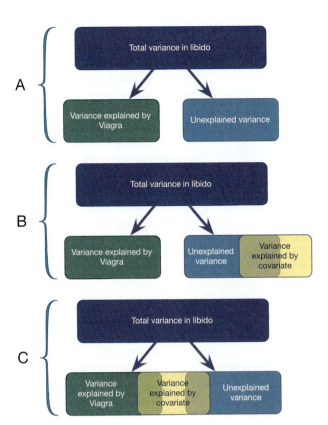

FIGURE 12.2
The role of the
covariate in
ANCOVA (see
text for details)

compare an anxious group of people against a non-anxious group on some task, the chances
are that the anxious group would also be more depressed than the non-anxious group. You
might think that by adding depression as a covariate into the analysis you can look at the
'pure' effect of anxiety, but you can't. This would be the situation in part C of Figure 12.2:
the effect of the covariate (depression) would contain some of the variance from the effect of
anxiety. Statistically speaking, all that we know is that anxiety and depression share variance;
we cannot separate this shared variance into 'anxiety variance' and 'depression variance',
it will always just be 'shared'. Another common example is if you happen to find that your
experimental groups differ in their ages. Placing age into the analysis as a covariate will not
solve this problem – it is still confounded with the experimental manipulation. ANCOVA is
not a magic solution to this problem (see Jane Superbrain Box 12.1).

   This problem can be avoided by randomizing participants to experimental groups, or by
matching experimental groups on the covariate (in our anxiety example, you could try to
find participants for the low anxious group who score high on depression). We can check
whether this problem is likely to be an issue by checking whether experimental groups differ
on the covariate before we run the ANCOVA. To use our anxiety example again, we could
test whether our high- and low-anxiety groups differ on levels of depression (with a t-test or
ANOVA). If the groups do not significantly differ then we can use depression as a covariate.

12.3.2. Homogeneity of regression slopes ③

When an ANCOVA is conducted we look at the overall relationship between the outcome
(dependent variable) and the covariate: we fit a regression line to the entire data set, ignoring to which group a person belongs. In fitting this overall model, we therefore assume that

JANE SUPERBRAIN 12.1

An interpretational or statistical requirement? ③

The treatment effect and covariate are simply predictor variables in a general linear model, yet despite several hundred pages discussing linear models, I haven't before mentioned that predictors should be completely independent. I've said that they shouldn't overlap too much (e.g., collinearity) but that's quite different than saying that they shouldn't overlap at all. If, in general, we don't care about predictors being independent in linear models, why should we care now? The short answer is we don't – there is no *statistical* requirement for the treatment variable and covariate to be independent.

However, there are situations in which ANCOVA can be biased when the covariate is not independent of the treatment variable. One situation, common in medical research, has been discussed a lot: an outcome (e.g.,

hypertension) is measured at baseline, and after a treatment intervention (with participants assigned to a treatment or control group). This design can be analysed using an ANCOVA in which treatment effects on post-intervention hypertension are analysed while covarying baseline levels of hypertension. In this scenario the independence of treatment and covariate variables means that baseline levels of hypertension are equal in the different treatment groups. According to Senn (2006), the idea that ANCOVA is biased unless treatment groups are equal on the covariate applies only when there is *temporal additivity*. To use our hypertension example, temporal additivity is the assumption that both treatment groups would experience the same change in hypertension over time if the treatment had no effect. In other words, had we left the two groups alone, their hypertension would change by exactly the same amount. Given that the groups have different overall levels of hypertension to begin with, this assumption might not be reasonable, which undermines the argument for requiring group equality in baseline measures.

To sum up, the independence of the covariate and treatment makes interpretation more straightforward but is not a statistical requirement. ANCOVA can be unbiased when groups differ on levels of the covariate, but, as Miller and Chapman point out, it creates an interpretational problem that ANCOVA cannot magic away.

this overall relationship is true for all groups of participants. This assumption is called the assumption of **homogeneity of regression slopes**. The best way to think of this assumption is to imagine plotting a scatterplot for each group of participants with the covariate on one axis and the outcome on the other. If the assumption is met then if you calculated and drew the regression line for each of these scatterplots, they should look more or less the same (i.e., the values of *b* in each group should be equal).

Let's try to make this concept a bit more concrete. Remember that the main example in this chapter looks at whether different doses of Viagra affect libido when including partner's libido as a covariate. The *homogeneity of regression slopes* assumption means that the relationship between the outcome (dependent variable) and the covariate is the same in each of our treatment groups. Figure 12.3 shows a scatterplot that displays this relationship (i.e., the relationship between partner's libido, the covariate, and the outcome, participant's libido) for each of the three experimental conditions. Each symbol represents the data from a particular participant, and the type of symbol tells us the group (circles = placebo, triangles = low dose, squares = high dose). The lines are the regression slopes for the particular group; they summarize the relationship between libido and partner's libido shown by the dots (blue = placebo group, green = low-dose group, red = high-dose group).

There is a positive relationship (the regression line slopes upwards from left to right) between partner's libido and participant's libido in both the placebo and low-dose conditions. In fact, the slopes of the lines for these two groups (blue and green) are very similar, showing that the relationship between libido and partner's libido is very similar in these

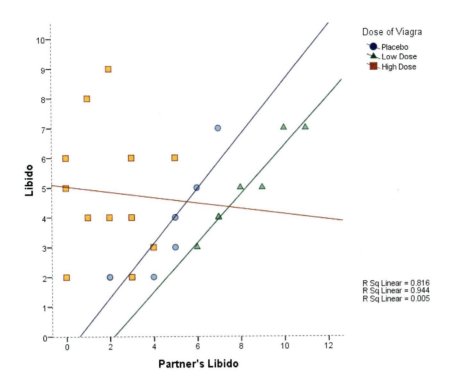

FIGURE 12.3
Scatterplot and regression lines of libido against partner's libido for each of the experimental conditions

two groups. This situation is an example of *homogeneity* of regression slopes. However, in the high-dose condition there appears to be a slightly negative relationship between libido and partner's libido. The slope of this line is very different than the slopes in the other two groups, suggesting *heterogeneity* of regression slopes (because the relationship between participant's libido and partner's libido is different in the high-dose group than the other two groups).

Although in a traditional ANCOVA, heterogeneity of regression slopes is a bad thing (Jane Superbrain Box 12.2), there are situations where you might actually expect regression slopes to differ across groups and this is, in itself, an interesting hypothesis. When research is conducted across different locations, you might reasonably expect the effects you get to differ slightly across those locations. For example, if you had a new treatment

JANE SUPERBRAIN 12.2

What are the consequences of violating the assumption of homogeneity of regression slopes? ②

When the assumption of homogeneity of regression slopes is met the resulting *F*-statistic can be assumed to have the corresponding *F*-distribution; however, when the assumption is not met the resulting *F*-statistic cannot be assumed to have the corresponding *F*-distribution, meaning that the resulting test statistic is being evaluated against a distribution different than the one that it actually has. Consequently, the Type I error rate of the test is inflated and the power to detect effects is not maximized (Hollingsworth, 1980). This is especially true when group sizes are unequal (Hamilton, 1977) and when the standardized regression slopes differ by more than .4 (Wu, 1984).

for backache, you might get several physiotherapists to try it out in different hospitals. You might expect the effect of the treatment to differ across these hospitals (because therapists will differ in expertise, the patients they see will have different problems and so on). As such, heterogeneity of regression slopes is not a bad thing *per se*. If you have violated the assumption of homogeneity of regression slopes, or if the variability in regression slopes is an interesting hypothesis in itself, then you can explicitly model this variation using multi-level linear models (see Chapter 20).

12.3.3. What to do when assumptions are violated ②

In Chapter 5 we discussed methods for correcting problems (e.g., bias reduction in Section 5.4). One practical solution is to use a bootstrap for the model parameters and *post hoc* tests so that these, at least, will be robust. This won't help for the main bits of the ANCOVA (the *F*-tests): there are robust versions of these tests but SPSS doesn't do them directly, and you'll have to delve into a package called R instead (Field et al., 2012).

12.4. Conducting ANCOVA in SPSS ②

12.4.1. General procedure ①

The general procedure for doing ANCOVA is much the same as it was for one-way ANOVA – they are, after all, both linear models. So, remind yourself of the general procedure for linear models in Chapter 8. Figure 12.4 shows a slightly simpler overview of the process that highlights some of the specific issues when conducting ANCOVA. As with any analysis, begin by graphing the data and looking for and correcting sources of bias.

12.4.2. Inputting data ①

We have already looked at the data (Table 12.1) and the data file (**ViagraCovariate.sav**). The file contains three columns: a coding variable called **Dose** (1 = placebo, 2 = low dose, 3 = high dose), a variable called **Libido** containing the scores for the person's libido, and a variable called **Partner_Libido** containing the scores for the partner's libido. The 30 rows correspond to each person's scores on these three variables.

12.4.3. Testing the independence of the treatment variable and covariate ②

In Section 12.3.1, I mentioned that if the covariate and treatment variable (independent variable) are independent then it makes interpretation of ANCOVA a lot more straightforward. In this case, the proposed covariate is partner's libido, and so we could check that this variable was roughly equal across levels of our independent variable. In other words, is the mean level of partner's libido roughly equal across our three Viagra groups? We can test this by running an ANOVA with **Partner_Libido** as the outcome and **Dose** as the predictor.

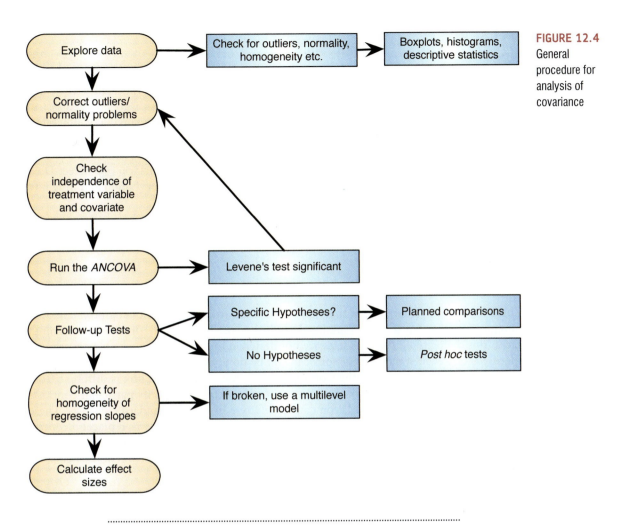

FIGURE 12.4
General procedure for analysis of covariance

SELF-TEST Conduct an ANOVA to test whether partner's libido (our covariate) is independent of the dose of Viagra (our independent variable).

Output 12.3 shows the results of such an ANOVA. The main effect of dose is not significant, $F(2, 27) = 1.98$, $p = .16$, which shows that the average level of partner's libido was roughly the same in the three Viagra groups. In other words, the means for partner's libido in Table 12.2 are not significantly different in the placebo, low- and high-dose groups. This result is good news for using partner's libido as a covariate in the analysis.

Tests of Between-Subjects Effects

OUTPUT 12.3

Dependent Variable:Partner's Libido

Source	Type III Sum of Squares	df	Mean Square	F	Sig.
Corrected Model	12.769ª	2	6.385	1.979	.158
Intercept	234.592	1	234.592	72.723	.000
Dose	12.769	2	6.385	1.979	.158
Error	87.097	27	3.226		
Total	324.000	30			
Corrected Total	99.867	29			

a. R Squared = .128 (Adjusted R Squared = .063)

12.4.4. The main analysis ②

Most of the *General Linear Model* (GLM) procedures in SPSS contain the facility to include one or more covariates. For designs that don't involve repeated measures it is easiest to conduct ANCOVA via the GLM *Univariate* procedure. To access the main dialog box select Analyze General Linear Model ▶ 🔢 Univariate... (see Figure 12.5). The main dialog box is similar to that for one-way ANOVA, except that there is a space to specify covariates. Select **Libido** and drag this variable to the box labelled *Dependent Variable* or click on 🔽. Select **Dose** and drag it to the box labelled *Fixed Factor(s)* and then select **Partner_Libido** and drag it to the box labelled *Covariate(s)*.

12.4.5. Contrasts

There are various dialog boxes that can be accessed from the main dialog box. The first thing to notice is that if a covariate is selected, the *post hoc* tests are disabled (you cannot access this dialog box). *Post hoc* tests are not designed for situations in which a covariate is specified; however, some comparisons can still be done using contrasts.

Click on ⬚ Contrasts... ⬚ to access the *Contrasts* dialog box. This dialog box is different from the one we met in Chapter 11 in that you cannot enter codes to specify particular contrasts (but see SPSS Tip 12.1). Instead, you can specify one of several standard contrasts. These standard contrasts were listed in Table 11.6. In this example, there was a placebo control condition (coded as the first group), so a sensible set of contrasts would be simple contrasts comparing each experimental group with the control. To select a type of contrast click on

FIGURE 12.5
Main dialog box for GLM univariate

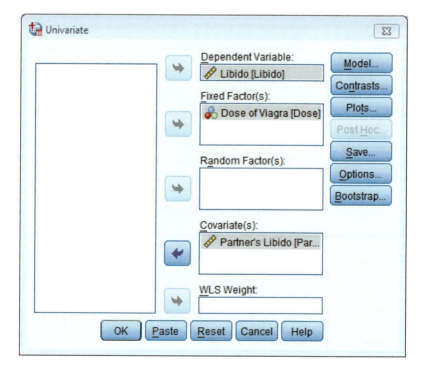

None ▾ to access a drop-down list of possible contrasts. Select a type of contrast (in this case *Simple*) from this list. For simple contrasts you have the option of specifying a reference category (which is the category against which all other groups are compared). By default the reference category is the last category but because for our data the control group was the first category (assuming that you coded placebo as 1) we need to change this option by selecting ◉ First. When you have selected a new contrast option, you must click on Change to register this change. The final dialog box should look like Figure 12.6. Click on Continue to return to the main dialog box.

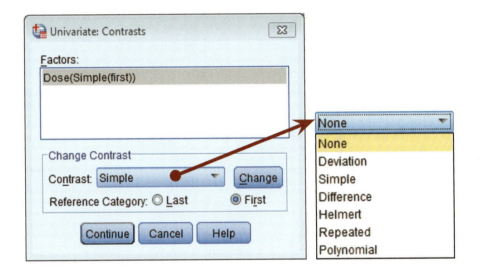

FIGURE 12.6
Options for standard contrasts in GLM univariate

12.4.6. Other options ②

You can get a limited range of *post hoc* tests by clicking on Options... to access the *Options* dialog box (see Figure 12.7). To specify *post hoc* tests, select the independent variable (in this case **Dose**) from the box labelled *Estimated Marginal Means: Factor(s) and Factor Interactions* and drag it to the box labelled *Display Means for* or click on ⬆. Once a variable has been transferred, the box labelled <u>C</u>ompare main effects becomes active and you should select this option (☑ Compare main effects). If this option is selected, the box labelled *Confidence interval adjustment* becomes active and you can click on LSD(none) ▾ to see a choice of three adjustment levels. The default is to have no adjustment and simply perform a Tukey LSD *post hoc* test (this option is not recommended); the second is to ask for a Bonferroni correction (recommended); the final option is to have a **Šidák correction**. The Šidák correction is similar to the Bonferroni correction but is less conservative and so should be selected if you are concerned about the loss of power associated with Bonferroni corrected values. For this example use the Šidák correction (we have used Bonferroni already in the book). As well as producing *post hoc* tests for the **Dose** variable, SPSS will create a table of estimated marginal means for this variable. These means provide an estimate of the *adjusted* group means (i.e., the means adjusted for the effect of the covariate). When you have selected the options required (see Jane Superbrain Box 12.3), click on Continue to return to the main dialog box.

SPSS TIP 12.1   Planned contrasts for ANCOVA ③

You may have noticed that there is no option for specifying planned contrasts like there was with one-way independent ANOVA (see Section 11.6.2). However, these contrasts can be done if we run the ANCOVA through the regression menu. Imagine you chose some planned contrasts as in Chapter 11, in which the first contrast compared the placebo group to all doses of Viagra, and the second contrast then compared the high and low doses (see Section 11.4). We saw in Sections 11.4 and 11.6.2 that to do this in SPSS we had to enter certain numbers to code these contrasts. For the first contrast we discovered an appropriate set of codes would be −2 for the placebo group and 1 for both the high- and low-dose groups. For the second contrast the codes would be 0 for the placebo group, −1 for the low-dose group and 1 for the high-dose group (see Table 11.4). If you want to do these contrasts for ANCOVA, then you enter these values as two dummy variables. So, for this example, we'd add a column called **Dummy1** and in that column we'd put the value −2 for every person who was in the placebo group, and the value 1 for all other participants. We'd then add a second column called **Dummy2**, in which we'd place the value 0 for everyone in the placebo group, −1 for everyone in the low-dose group and 1 for those in the high-dose group. The completed data would be as in the file **ViagraCovariateContrasts.sav**. Run the analysis as described in Section 12.2.1.2. The resulting output will begin with a model summary and ANOVA table that should be identical to those in Output 12.1 (because we've done the same thing as before, the only difference is how the model variance is subsequently broken down with the contrasts). The regression coefficients for the dummy variables will be different, though, because we've now specified different codes (Output 12.4).

Coefficients[a]

Model		Unstandardized Coefficients B	Unstandardized Coefficients Std. Error	Standardized Coefficients Beta	t	Sig.
1	(Constant)	3.657	.634		5.764	.000
	Partner's Libido	.260	.193	.246	1.345	.189
2	(Constant)	3.126	.625		5.002	.000
	Partner's Libido	.416	.187	.395	2.227	.035
	Dummy Variable 1 (Placebo vs. Low & High)	.668	.240	.478	2.785	.010
	Dummy Variable 2 (Low vs. High)	.220	.406	.094	.541	.593

a. Dependent Variable: Libido

OUTPUT 12.4

The first dummy variable compares the placebo group with the low- and high-dose groups. As such, it compares the adjusted mean of the placebo group (2.93) with the average of the adjusted means for the low- and high-dose groups ((4.71+5.15)/2 = 4.93). The b-value for the first dummy variable should therefore be the difference between these values: 4.93−2.93 = 2. However, we also discovered in a rather complex and boring bit of Section 11.4.2 that this value gets divided by the number of groups within the contrast (i.e., 3) and so will be 2/3 = 0.67 (as it is in the output). The associated t-statistic is significant, indicating that the placebo group was significantly different from the combined mean of the Viagra groups.

The second dummy variable compares the low- and high-dose groups, and so the b-value should be the difference between the adjusted means of these groups: 5.15−4.71 = 0.44. We again discovered in Section 11.4.2 that this value also gets divided by the number of groups within the contrast (i.e., 2) and so will be 0.44/2 = 0.22 (as in the output). The associated t-statistic is not significant (its significance is .59 which is greater than .05), indicating that the high-dose group did not produce a significantly higher libido than the low-dose group.

This illustrates how you can apply the principles from Section 11.4 to ANCOVA: although SPSS doesn't provide an easy interface to do planned contrasts, they can be done if you use the regression menus rather than the ANCOVA ones.

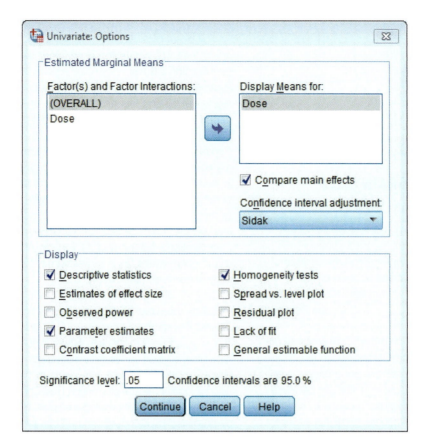

FIGURE 12.7
Options dialog box for GLM univariate

12.4.7. Bootstrapping and plots ②

There are other options available from the main dialog box. For example, if you have several independent variables you can plot them against each other (which is useful for interpreting interaction effects – see Section 13.6). Also, as with one-way ANOVA, the main dialog box has a Bootstrap button. Selecting this option will bootstrap confidence intervals around the estimated marginal means, parameter estimates and *post hoc* tests, but not the main *F*-test. This can be useful so select the options described in Section 5.4.3. Click on OK in the main dialog box to run the analysis.

12.5. Interpreting the output from ANCOVA ②

12.5.1. What happens when the covariate is excluded? ②

SELF-TEST   Run a one-way ANOVA to see whether the three groups differ in their levels of libido.

JANE SUPERBRAIN 12.3

Options for ANCOVA ②

The remaining options in this dialog box are as follows:

- *Descriptive statistics*: This option produces a table of means and standard deviations for each group.
- *Estimates of effect size*: This option produces the value of **partial eta squared (partial η^2)** – see Section 12.7 for a discussion.
- *Observed power*: This option provides an estimate of the probability that the statistical test could detect the difference between the observed group means (see Section 2.6.1.7). This measure is of little use because if the *F*-test is significant then the probability that the effect was detected will, of course, be high. Likewise, if group differences were small, the observed power would be low. I would advise that power calculations

are carried out before the experiment is conducted (see Section 2.6.1.8).

- *Parameter estimates*: This option produces a table of regression coefficients and their tests of significance for the variables in the regression model (see Section 12.5.2).
- *Contrast coefficient matrix*: This option produces matrices of the coding values used for any contrasts in the analysis. This option is useful only for checking which groups are being compared in which contrast.
- *Homogeneity tests*: This option produces Levene's test of the homogeneity of variance assumption (see Sections 5.3.3.2 and 11.7.1). In ANCOVA the assumption relates (as in regression) to the homogeneity of *residuals* (see Section 8.3).
- *Spread vs. level plot*: This option produces a chart that plots the mean of each group of a factor (*X*-axis) against the standard deviation of that group (*Y*-axis). This is a useful plot to check that there is no relationship between the mean and standard deviation. If a relationship exists then the data may need to be stabilized using a logarithmic transformation (see Chapter 5).
- *Residual plot*: This option produces plots of observed-by-predicted-by-standardized residual values. These plots can be used to assess the assumption of homoscedasticity.

ODITI'S LANTERN

ANCOVA

'I, Oditi, have discovered that covariates give us greater control. I like control, especially controlling people's minds and making them worship me, erm, I mean controlling their minds for the benevolent purpose of helping them to seek truth and personal enlightenment. As long as they are personally enlightened to worship me. In any case, stare into my lantern to discover more about using covariates and ANCOVA.'

Output 12.5 shows (for illustrative purposes) the ANOVA table for these data when the covariate is not included. It is clear from the significance value, which is greater than .05, that Viagra seems to have no significant effect on libido. It should also be noted that the total amount of variation to be explained (SS_T) is 110.97 (Corrected Total), of which the experimental manipulation accounted for 16.84 units (SS_M), with 94.12 unexplained (SS_R).

12.5.2. The main analysis ②

Output 12.6 shows the results of Levene's test (Section 5.3.3.2) and the ANOVA table when partner's libido is included in the model as a covariate. Levene's test is significant,

Tests of Between-Subjects Effects

Dependent Variable:Libido

Source	Type III Sum of Squares	df	Mean Square	F	Sig.
Corrected Model	16.844[a]	2	8.422	2.416	.108
Intercept	535.184	1	535.184	153.522	.000
Dose	16.844	2	8.422	2.416	.108
Error	94.123	27	3.486		
Total	683.000	30			
Corrected Total	110.967	29			

a. R Squared = .152 (Adjusted R Squared = .089)

indicating that the group variances are not equal (hence the assumption of homogeneity of variance has been violated). However, as I've mentioned in Section 5.3.3, Levene's test should be used with caution, and because ANCOVA is a linear model it is homogeneity of residuals that actually matters (and that's not what Levene's test looks at here). Ideally you'd inspect some plots of residuals as we did in Chapter 8, and if we bootstrap the parameter estimates and *post hoc* tests we can have confidence in these being robust.

The format of the ANOVA table is largely the same as without the covariate, except that there is an additional row of information about the covariate (**Partner_Libido**). Looking first at the significance values, it is clear that the covariate significantly predicts the dependent variable, because the significance value is less than .05. Therefore, the person's libido is influenced by their partner's libido. What's more interesting is that when the effect of partner's libido is removed, the effect of Viagra becomes significant ($p = .027$). The amount of variation accounted for by Viagra has increased to 25.19 units and the unexplained variance (SS_R) has been reduced to 79.05 units. Notice that SS_T has not changed; all that has changed is how that total variation is explained.[3]

How do I interpret ANCOVA?

Levene's Test of Equality of Error Variances[a]

Dependent Variable: Libido

F	df1	df2	Sig.
4.618	2	27	.019

Tests the null hypothesis that the error variance of the dependent variable is equal across groups.

a. Design: Intercept + Partner_Libido + Dose

Tests of Between-Subjects Effects

Dependent Variable: Libido

Source	Type III Sum of Squares	df	Mean Square	F	Sig.
Corrected Model	31.920[a]	3	10.640	3.500	.030
Intercept	76.069	1	76.069	25.020	.000
Partner_Libido	15.076	1	15.076	4.959	.035
Dose	25.185	2	12.593	4.142	.027
Error	79.047	26	3.040		
Total	683.000	30			
Corrected Total	110.967	29			

a. R Squared = .288 (Adjusted R Squared = .205)

[3] I often get asked what the *Corrected Model* represents in this table. It is the fit of the model overall (i.e., the model containing the intercept, **Partner_Libido** and **Dose**). Note that the SS of 31.92, *df* of 3, *F* of 3.5 and *p* of .03 are identical to the values in Output 12.1 (model 2), which tested the overall fit of this model when we ran the analysis as a regression.

OUTPUT 12.7

Estimates

Dependent Variable: Libido

Dose of Viagra	Mean	Std. Error	95% Confidence Interval		Bootstrap for Mean[gn]			
			Lower Bound	Upper Bound	Bias	Std. Error	BCa 95% Confidence Interval	
							Lower	Upper
Placebo	2.926[a]	.596	1.701	4.152	.030	.446	2.111	4.125
Low Dose	4.712[a]	.621	3.436	5.988	.033[go]	.392[go]	3.988[go]	5.620[go]
High Dose	5.151[a]	.503	4.118	6.184	.041	.651	3.923	6.771

a. Covariates appearing in the model are evaluated at the following values: Partner's Libido = 2.73.

gn. Unless otherwise noted, bootstrap results are based on 1000 bootstrap samples

go. Based on 999 samples

This example illustrates how ANCOVA can help us to exert stricter experimental control by taking account of confounding variables to give us a 'purer' measure of effect of the experimental manipulation. Without taking account of the libido of the participants' partners we would have concluded that Viagra had no effect on libido, yet it does. Looking back at the group means from Table 12.1 for the libido data, you might think that the significant ANOVA reflects a difference between the placebo group and the two experimental groups (because the low- and high-dose groups have very similar means, 4.88 and 4.85, whereas the placebo group mean is much lower at 3.22). However, we can't use these group means to interpret the effect because they have not been adjusted for the effect of the covariate. These original means tell us nothing about the group differences reflected by the significant ANCOVA. Output 12.7 gives the adjusted values of the group means (which we calculated in Section 12.2.1.2) and it is these values that should be used for interpretation (this is the main reason for selecting the *Display Means for* option). From these adjusted means you can see that libido increased across the three doses.

Output 12.8 shows the parameter estimates selected in the *Options* dialog box and their bootstrapped confidence intervals and *p*-values (bottom table). These estimates result from a regression analysis with **Dose** split into two dummy coding variables (see Section 12.2.1.2). The dummy variables are coded with the last category (the category coded with the highest value in the data editor – in this case the high-dose group) as the reference category. This reference category (labelled 'Dose=3' in the output) is coded with a 0 for both dummy variables (see Section 11.2.1 for a reminder of how dummy coding works). Dose=2, therefore, represents the difference between the group coded as 2 (low dose) and the reference category (high dose), and Dose=1 represents the difference between the group coded as 1 (placebo) and the reference category (high dose). The *b*-values represent the differences between the adjusted means in Output 12.7 and the significances of the *t*-tests tell us whether these adjusted group means differ significantly. The estimates of *b* in Output 12.8 correspond to the values that we computed in Section 12.2.1.2. So, the *b* for Dose = 1 is the difference between the adjusted means for the placebo group and the high-dose group, $2.926 - 5.151 = -2.225$, and the *b* for Dose = 2 is the difference between the adjusted means for the low-dose group and the high-dose group, $4.712 - 5.151 = -0.439$.

The degrees of freedom for the *t*-test of the *b* parameters are $N - p - 1$ (as is the case for multiple regression; see Section 8.2.5), in which N is the total sample size (in this case 30) and p is the number of predictors (in this case 3, the two dummy variables and the covariate). For these data, $df = 30 - 3 - 1 = 26$. Based on the bootstrapped significance and confidence intervals (remember you'll get different values than me because of how bootstrapping works), we could conclude that the high-dose differs significantly from the placebo group, $p = .016$ (Dose=1 in the table), but not from the low-dose group, $p = .556$, (Dose=2 in the table).

The final thing to notice is the value of *b* for the covariate (0.416), which is the same as in Output 12.2 (when we ran the analysis through the regression menu). This value tells us that if a partner's libido increases by one unit, then the person's libido should increase by just under half a unit (although there is nothing to suggest a causal link between the two); because

Parameter Estimates

Dependent Variable: Libido

Parameter	B	Std. Error	t	Sig.	95% Confidence Interval	
					Lower Bound	Upper Bound
Intercept	4.014	.611	6.568	.000	2.758	5.270
Partner_Libido	.416	.187	2.227	.035	.032	.800
[Dose=1]	-2.225	.803	-2.771	.010	-3.875	-.575
[Dose=2]	-.439	.811	-.541	.593	-2.107	1.228
[Dose=3]	0[a]	.	.	.	.	.

a. This parameter is set to zero because it is redundant.

Bootstrap for Parameter Estimates

Dependent Variable: Libido

Parameter	B	Bootstrap[a]				
		Bias	Std. Error	Sig. (2-tailed)	BCa 95% Confidence Interval	
					Lower	Upper
Intercept	4.014	.038	.815	.002	2.023	5.790
Partner_Libido	.416	-.024	.192	.046	.015	.686
[Dose=1]	-2.225	.007	.719	.016	-3.734	-.765
[Dose=2]	-.439	.029	.696	.556	-1.901	.904
[Dose=3]	0	0	0		.	.

a. Unless otherwise noted, bootstrap results are based on 1000 bootstrap samples

the coefficient is positive we know that as partner's libido increases so does their partner's. A negative coefficient would mean the opposite: as one increases, the other decreases.

12.5.3. Contrasts ②

Output 12.9 shows the result of the contrast analysis specified in Figure 12.6 and compares level 2 (low dose) against level 1 (placebo) as a first comparison, and level 3 (high dose) against level 1 (placebo) as a second comparison. These contrasts are consistent with what was specified: all groups are compared to the first group. The group differences are displayed: a difference value, standard error, significance value and 95% confidence interval. These results show that both the low-dose group (contrast 1, $p = .045$) and high-dose group (contrast 2, $p = .010$) had significantly different libidos than the placebo group (note that contrast 2 is identical to the regression parameters for Dose=1 in the previous section).

Output 12.10 shows the results of the Šidák corrected *post hoc* comparisons that were requested as part of the *Options* dialog box. The bottom table shows the bootstrapped significance and confidence intervals for these tests and because these will be robust we'll interpret this table (again, remember, your values will differ because of how bootstrapping works). There is a significant difference between the placebo group and both the low ($p = .003$) and high ($p = .021$) dose groups. The high and low-dose groups did not significantly differ ($p = .56$). It is interesting that the significant difference between the low-dose and placebo groups when bootstrapped ($p = .003$) is not present for the normal *post hoc* tests ($p = .130$). This could reflect properties of the data that have biased the non-robust version of the *post hoc* test.

12.5.4. Interpreting the covariate ②

I've already mentioned that the parameter estimates (Output 12.8) tell us how to interpret the covariate: the sign of the *b*-value tells us the direction of the relationship between the

OUTPUT 12.9

Contrast Results (K Matrix)

Dose of Viagra Simple Contrast[a]		Dependent Variable
		Libido
Level 2 vs. Level 1	Contrast Estimate	1.786
	Hypothesized Value	0
	Difference (Estimate – Hypothesized)	1.786
	Std. Error	.849
	Sig.	.045
	95% Confidence Interval for Difference Lower Bound	.040
	Upper Bound	3.532
Level 3 vs. Level 1	Contrast Estimate	2.225
	Hypothesized Value	0
	Difference (Estimate – Hypothesized)	2.225
	Std. Error	.803
	Sig.	.010
	95% Confidence Interval for Difference Lower Bound	.575
	Upper Bound	3.875

a. Reference category = 1

OUTPUT 12.10

Pairwise Comparisons

Dependent Variable: Libido

(I) Dose of Viagra	(J) Dose of Viagra	Mean Difference (I–J)	Std. Error	Sig.[b]	95% Confidence Interval for Difference[b]	
					Lower Bound	Upper Bound
Placebo	Low Dose	−1.786	.849	.130	−3.953	.381
	High Dose	−2.225[*]	.803	.030	−4.273	−.177
Low Dose	Placebo	1.786	.849	.130	−.381	3.953
	High Dose	−.439	.811	.932	−2.509	1.631
High Dose	Placebo	2.225[*]	.803	.030	.177	4.273
	Low Dose	.439	.811	.932	−1.631	2.509

Based on estimated marginal means

*. The mean difference is significant at the

b. Adjustment for multiple comparisons: Sidak.

Bootstrap for Pairwise Comparisons

Dependent Variable: Libido

(I) Dose of Viagra	(J) Dose of Viagra	Mean Difference (I–J)	Bootstrap[a]			BCa 95% Confidence Interval	
			Bias	Std. Error	Sig. (2–tailed)	Lower	Upper
Placebo	Low Dose	−1.786	−.003[b]	.535[b]	.003[b]	−2.778[b]	−.765[b]
	High Dose	−2.225	−.011	.760	.021	−3.752	−.832
Low Dose	Placebo	1.786	.003[b]	.535[b]	.003[b]	.663[b]	2.879[b]
	High Dose	−.439	−.008[b]	.745[b]	.558[b]	−1.937[b]	.935[b]
High Dose	Placebo	2.225	.011	.760	.021	.686	3.923
	Low Dose	.439	.008[b]	.745[b]	.558[b]	−.938[b]	1.945[b]

a. Unless otherwise noted, bootstrap results are based on 1000 bootstrap samples

b. Based on 999 samples

covariate and outcome variable. For these data the *b*-value was positive, indicating that as the partner's libido increases, so does the participant's libido. Another way to discover the same thing is to draw a scatterplot of the covariate against the outcome.

SELF-TEST   Produce a scatterplot of partner's libido (horizontal axis) against libido (vertical axis).

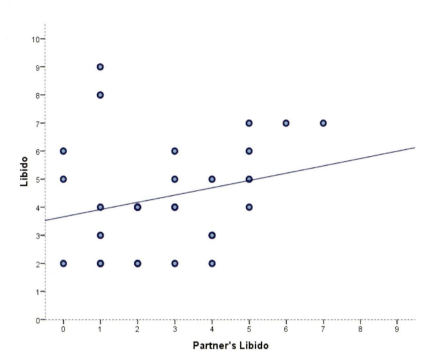

FIGURE 12.8
Scatterplot of libido against partner's libido

Figure 12.8 confirms that the effect of the covariate is that as partner's libido increases, so does the participant's libido (as shown by the slope of the regression line).

12.6. Testing the assumption of homogeneity of regression slopes ③

We saw earlier in the chapter that the assumption of homogeneity of regression slopes means that the relationship between the covariate and outcome variable (in this case **Partner_Libido** and **Libido**) should be similar at different levels of the predictor variable (in this case in the three **Dose** groups). Figure 12.3 showed scatterplots of the relationship between **Partner_Libido** and **Libido** in the three groups. This scatterplot showed that although this relationship was comparable in the low-dose and placebo groups, it appeared different in the high-dose group.

To test the assumption of homogeneity of regression slopes we need to rerun the ANCOVA, but this time use a customized model. Access the main dialog box as before and place the variables in the same boxes as before (so the finished box should look like Figure 12.5). To customize the model we need to access the *Model* dialog box (Figure 12.9) by clicking on [Model...]. To customize your model, select ◉ C̲ustom to activate the dialog box in Figure 12.9. The variables specified in the main dialog box are listed on the left-hand side. To test the assumption of homogeneity of regression slopes, we need to specify a model that includes the interaction between the covariate and independent variable. Ordinarily, the ANCOVA includes only the main effect of dose and partner's libido and does not include this interaction term. To test this interaction term it's important to still include the main effects of dose and partner so that the interaction term is tested controlling for these main effects. If we don't include the main effects then variance in libido may become attributed to the interaction term that would otherwise be attributed to main effects.

MURIS, P., ET AL. (2008). *CHILD PSYCHIATRY AND HUMAN DEVELOPMENT, 39*, 469–480.

LABCOAT LENI'S REAL RESEARCH 12.1

Space invaders ②

Anxious people tend to interpret ambiguous information in a negative way. For example, being highly anxious myself, if I overheard a student saying 'Andy Field's lectures are really *different*' I would assume that 'different' meant 'rubbish', but it could also mean 'refreshing' or 'innovative'. In an ingenious study Peter Muris and his colleagues addressed how these interpretational biases develop in children. Children imagined that they were astronauts who had discovered a new planet. Although the planet was similar to Earth, some things were different. They were given some scenarios about their time on the planet (e.g., 'On the street, you encounter a spaceman. He has a toy handgun and he fires at you …') and the child had to decide whether a positive ('You laugh: it is a water pistol and the weather is fine anyway') or negative ('Oops, this hurts! The pistol produces a red beam which burns your skin!') outcome occurred. After each response the child was told whether their choice

was correct. Half of the children were *always* told that the negative interpretation was correct, and the remainder were told that the positive interpretation was correct.

Over 30 scenarios children were trained to interpret their experiences on the planet as negative or positive. Muris et al. then measured interpretational biases in everyday life to see whether the training had created a bias to interpret things negatively. In doing so, they could ascertain whether children learn interpretational biases through feedback (e.g., from parents).

The data from this study are in the file **Muris et al (2008).sav**. The independent variable is **Training** (positive or negative) and the outcome was the child's interpretational bias score (**Interpretational_Bias**) – a high score reflects a tendency to interpret situations negatively. It is important to factor in the **Age** and **Gender** of the child and also their natural anxiety level (which they measured with a standard questionnaire of child anxiety called the **SCARED**) because these things affect interpretational biases also. Labcoat Leni wants you to carry out a one-way ANCOVA on these data to see whether **Training** significantly affected children's **Interpretational_Bias** using **Age**, **Gender** and **SCARED** as covariates. What can you conclude? Answers are on the companion website (or look at pages 475–476 in the original article).

Hence, to begin with you should select **Dose** and **Partner_Libido** (you can select both of them at the same time by holding down *Ctrl*, or *Cmd* on a Mac). Then, click on the drop-down menu and change it to [Main effects ▾]. Having selected this, click on [➡] to move the main effects of **Dose** and **Partner_Libido** to the box labelled *Model*. Next specify the interaction term by again selecting **Dose** and **Partner_Libido** simultaneously (as just described), then select [Interaction ▾] in the drop-down list and click on [➡]. This action moves the interaction of **Dose** and **Partner_Libido** to the box labelled *Model*. The finished dialog box should look like Figure 12.9. Click on [Continue] to return to the main dialog box and then click on [OK] to run the analysis.

Output 12.11 shows the main summary table for the ANCOVA, including the interaction term. The effects of the dose of Viagra and the partner's libido are still significant, but the main thing in which we're interested is the interaction term, so look at the significance value of the covariate by outcome interaction (**Dose×Partner_Libido**). If this effect is significant then the assumption of homogeneity of regression slopes has been broken. The effect here is significant ($p = .028$); therefore the assumption is not tenable. Although this finding is not surprising given the pattern of relationships shown in Figure 12.3, it does raise concern about the main analysis.

12.7. Calculating the effect size ②

We saw in the previous chapter that we can use eta squared, η^2, as an effect size measure in ANOVA. This effect size is just r^2 by another name and is calculated by dividing the effect

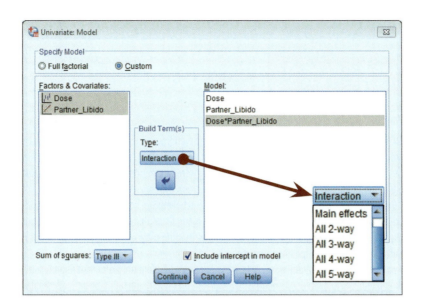

FIGURE 12.9
Model dialog box

Tests of Between-Subjects Effects

OUTPUT 12.11

Dependent Variable: Libido

Source	Type III Sum of Squares	df	Mean Square	F	Sig.
Corrected Model	52.346[a]	5	10.469	4.286	.006
Intercept	53.542	1	53.542	21.921	.000
Dose	36.558	2	18.279	7.484	.003
Partner_Libido	17.182	1	17.182	7.035	.014
Dose * Partner_Libido	20.427	2	10.213	4.181	.028
Error	58.621	24	2.443		
Total	683.000	30			
Corrected Total	110.967	29			

a. R Squared = .472 (Adjusted R Squared = .362)

of interest, SS_M, by the total amount of variance in the data, SS_T. As such, it is the proportion of total variance explained by an effect. In ANCOVA (and some of the more complex ANOVAs that we'll encounter in future chapters), we have more than one effect; therefore, we could calculate eta squared for each effect. However, we can also use an effect size measure called **partial eta squared (partial η^2)**. This differs from eta squared in that it looks not at the proportion of total variance that a variable explains, but at the proportion of variance that a variable explains that *is not explained by other variables in the analysis*. Let's look at this with our example; suppose we want to know the effect size of the dose of Viagra. Partial eta squared is the proportion of variance in libido that the dose of Viagra shares that is not attributed to partner's libido (the covariate). If you think about the variance that the covariate cannot explain, there are two sources: it cannot explain the variance attributable to the dose of Viagra, SS_{Viagra}, and it cannot explain the error variability, SS_R. Therefore, we use these two sources of variance instead of the total variability, SS_T, in the calculation. The difference between eta squared and partial eta squared is shown in the following equations:

$$\eta^2 = \frac{SS_{Effect}}{SS_{Total}} \tag{12.3}$$

$$Partial\,\eta^2 = \frac{SS_{Effect}}{SS_{Effect} + SS_{Residual}} \tag{12.4}$$

CRAMMING SAM'S TIPS   ANCOVA

- Analysis of covariance (ANCOVA) compares several means adjusted for the effect of one or more other variables (called *covariates*); for example, if you have several experimental conditions and want to adjust for the age of the participants.
- Before the analysis check that the independent variable(s) and covariate(s) are independent. You can do this using ANOVA or a *t*-test to check that levels of the covariate do not differ significantly across groups.
- In the table labelled *Tests of Between-Subjects Effects*, look at the column labelled *Sig.* for both the covariate and the independent variable. If the value is less than .05 then for the covariate it means that this variable has a significant relationship to the outcome variable; for the independent variable it means that the means are significantly different across the experimental conditions after adjusting them for the covariate.
- As with ANOVA, if you have generated specific hypotheses before the experiment use planned comparisons, but if you don't have specific hypotheses use *post hoc* tests. Although SPSS will let you specify certain standard contrasts, other planned comparisons will have to be done by analysing the data using the regression procedure in SPSS.
- For parameters and *post hoc* tests, look to the columns labelled *Sig.* to discover if your comparisons are significant (they will be if the significance value is less than .05). Use bootstrapping to get robust versions of these tests.
- In addition to the assumptions in Chapter 5, test for *homogeneity of regression slopes*. This has to be done by customizing the ANCOVA model in SPSS to look at the independent variable × covariate interaction.

We can get SPSS to produce partial eta squared for us (see Jane Superbrain Box 12.3). To illustrate its calculation let's look at our Viagra example. We need to use the sums of squares in Output 12.6 for the effect of dose (25.19), the covariate (15.08) and the error (79.05):

$$\text{Partial } \eta^2_{\text{Dose}} = \frac{\text{SS}_{\text{Dose}}}{\text{SS}_{\text{Dose}} + \text{SS}_{\text{Residual}}} = \frac{25.19}{25.19 + 79.05} = \frac{25.19}{104.24} = .24$$

$$\text{Partial } \eta^2_{\text{Partner's Libido}} = \frac{\text{SS}_{\text{Partner's Libido}}}{\text{SS}_{\text{Partner's Libido}} + \text{SS}_{\text{Residual}}} = \frac{15.08}{15.08 + 79.05} = \frac{15.08}{94.13} = .16$$

These values show that **Dose** explained a bigger proportion of the variance not attributable to other variables than **Partner_Libido**.

SELF-TEST   Rerun the ANCOVA but select ☑ Estimates of effect size in Figure 12.7. Do the values of partial eta squared match the ones we have just calculated?

As with ANOVA, you can also use omega squared (ω^2). However, as we saw in Section 11.8 this measure can be calculated only when we have equal numbers of participants in each group (which is not the case in this example). So, we're a bit stumped!

However, all is not lost because, as I've said many times already, the overall effect size is not nearly as interesting as the effect size for more focused comparisons. These are easy to calculate because we selected regression parameters (see Output 12.8) and so we have *t*-statistics for the covariate and comparisons between the low- and high-dose groups and the placebo and high-dose group. These t-statistics have 26 degrees of freedom (see Section 12.5.1). We can use the same equation as in Section 9.6.4:[4]

$$r_{Contrast} = \sqrt{\frac{t^2}{t^2 + df}}$$

Therefore we get (with t from Output 12.8):

$$r_{Covariate} = \sqrt{\frac{2.23^2}{2.23^2 + 26}} = \sqrt{\frac{4.97}{30.97}} = .40$$

$$r_{High\ Dose\ vs.\ Placebo} = \sqrt{\frac{-2.77^2}{-2.77^2 + 26}} = \sqrt{\frac{7.67}{33.67}} = .48$$

$$r_{High\ vs.\ Low\ Dose} = \sqrt{\frac{-0.54^2}{-0.54^2 + 26}} = \sqrt{\frac{0.29}{26.29}} = .11$$

If you think back to our benchmarks for effect sizes, the effect of the covariate and the difference between the high dose and the placebo both represent medium to large effect sizes (they're all between .4 and .5). Therefore, as well as being statistically significant, these effects are substantive findings. The difference between the high- and low-dose groups was a fairly small effect.

12.8. Reporting results ②

Reporting ANCOVA is much the same as reporting ANOVA, except we now have to report the effect of the covariate as well. For the covariate and the experimental effect we give details of the F-ratio and the degrees of freedom from which it was calculated. In both cases, the F-ratio was derived from dividing the mean squares for the effect by the mean squares for the residual. Therefore, the degrees of freedom used to assess the F-ratio are the degrees of freedom for the effect of the model ($df_M = 1$ for the covariate and 2 for the experimental effect) and the degrees of freedom for the residuals of the model ($df_R = 26$ for both the covariate and the experimental effect) – see Output 12.6. Therefore, the correct way to report the main findings would be:

- The covariate, partner's libido, was significantly related to the participant's libido, $F(1, 26) = 4.96$, $p = .035$, $r = .40$. There was also a significant effect of Viagra on levels of libido after controlling for the effect of partner's libido, $F(2, 26) = 4.14$, $p = .027$, partial $\eta^2 = .24$.

We can also report some contrasts (see Output 12.8):

- Planned contrasts revealed that having a high dose of Viagra significantly increased libido compared to having a placebo, $t(26) = -2.77$, $p = .01$, $r = .48$, but not compared to having a low dose, $t(26) = -0.54$, $p = .59$, $r = .11$.

---

[4] Strictly speaking, we have to use a slightly more elaborate procedure when groups are unequal. It's a bit beyond the scope of this book, but Rosnow, Rosenthal, and Rubin (2000) give a very clear account.

12.9. Brian's attempt to woo Jane ①

FIGURE 12.10
What Brian
learnt from this
chapter

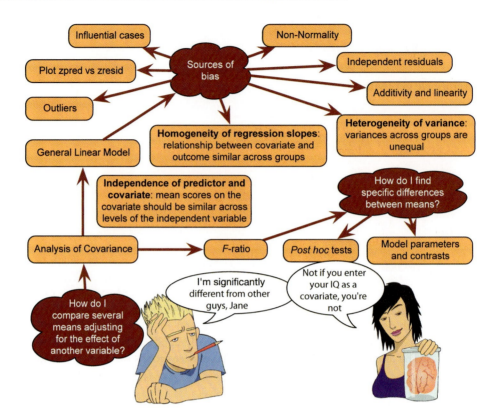

12.10. What next? ②

At the age of 13 I met my heroes, Iron Maiden, and very nice they were too. I've met them a couple of times since (not because they're my best buddies or anything exciting like that, but over the years the fan club has put on various events where you were actually allowed to stand next to them and gibber like a fool while they humoured you politely). You'll notice that the photo at the start of this chapter is signed by Dave Murray. This was possible not because I had my own darkroom installed backstage at Hammersmith Odeon in which I could quickly process photographs, or because I had access to time travel (sadly), but because I took the photo with me when I met him in 2000. I recounted the tale of how terrified I was about meeting him in 1986. If he thought I was some strange stalker he certainly didn't let on. Uncharacteristic of most people who've sold millions of albums, they're top blokes.

Anyway, having seen Iron Maiden in all of their glory, I was inspired. They still inspire me: I still rate them as the best live band I've ever seen (and I've seen them about 26 times so I ought to know). Although I had briefly been deflected from my destiny by the shock of grammar school, I was back on track. I *had* to form a band. There was just one issue: no one else played a musical instrument. The solution was easy: through several months of covert subliminal persuasion I convinced my two best friends (both called Mark, oddly enough) that they wanted nothing more than to start learning the drums and bass guitar. A power trio was in the making.

12.11. Key terms that I've discovered

Adjusted mean	Covariate	Partial eta squared (partial η^2)
Analysis of covariance (ANCOVA)	Homogeneity of regression slopes	Partial out
		Šidák correction

12.12. Smart Alex's tasks

- **Task 1**: A few years back I was stalked. You'd think they could have found someone a bit more interesting to stalk, but apparently times were hard. It could have been a lot worse than it was, but it wasn't particularly pleasant. I imagined a world in which a psychologist tried two different therapies on different groups of stalkers (25 stalkers in each group – this variable is called **Group**). To the first group of stalkers he gave what he termed cruel-to-be-kind therapy (every time the stalkers followed him around, or sent him a letter, the psychologist attacked them with a cattle prod). The second therapy was psychodyshamic therapy, in which stalkers were hypnotized and regressed into their childhood to discuss their penis (or lack of penis), their father's penis, their dog's penis and any other penis that sprang to mind (the seventh penis of a seventh penis and any other penis that sprang to mind). The psychologist measured the number of hours in the week that the stalker spent stalking their prey both before (**stalk1**) and after (**stalk2**) treatment. The data are in the file **Stalker.sav**. Analyse the effect of therapy on stalking behaviour after therapy, covarying for the amount of stalking behaviour before therapy. ②

- **Task 2**: Compute effect sizes and report the results from Task 1. ②

- **Task 3**: A marketing manager was interested in the therapeutic benefit of certain soft drinks for curing hangovers. He took 15 people out on the town one night and got them drunk. The next morning as they awoke, dehydrated and feeling as though they'd licked a camel's sandy feet clean with their tongue, he gave five of them water to drink, five of them Lucozade (a very nice glucose-based UK drink) and the remaining five a leading brand of cola (this variable is called **drink**). He measured how well they felt (on a scale from 0 = I feel like death to 10 = I feel really full of beans and healthy) two hours later (this variable is called **well**). He measured how **drunk** the person got the night before on a scale of 0 = as sober as a nun to 10 = flapping about like a haddock out of water on the floor in a puddle of their own vomit. The data are in the file **HangoverCure.sav**. Conduct an ANCOVA to see whether people felt better after different drinks when covarying for how drunk they were the night before. ②

- **Task 4**: Compute effect sizes and report the results from Task 3. ②

- **Task 5**: The highlight of the elephant calendar is the annual elephant soccer event in Nepal (http://news.bbc.co.uk/1/hi/8435112.stm). A heated argument burns between the African and Asian elephants. In 2010, the president of the Asian Elephant Football Association, an elephant named Boji, claimed that Asian elephants were more talented than their African counterparts. The head of the African Elephant Soccer Association, an elephant called Tunc, issued a press statement that read 'I make it a matter of personal pride never to take seriously any remark made by something that looks like an enormous scrotum'. I was called in to settle things. I collected data from the two types of elephants (**elephant**) over a season. For each elephant, I measured how many goals they scored in the season (**goals**) and how many years of experience the elephant had (**experience**). The data are in **Elephant Football.sav**. Analyse the effect of the type of elephant on goal scoring, covarying for the amount of football experience the elephant has. ②

- **Task 6**: In Chapter 3 (Task 5) we looked at data from people who had been forced to marry goats and dogs and measured their life satisfaction as well as how much they like animals (**Goat or Dog.sav**). Run an ANCOVA predicting life satisfaction from the type of animal to which a person was married and their animal liking score (covariate). ②

- **Task 7**: Compare your results for Task 6 to those for the corresponding task in Chapter 10. What differences do you notice, and why? ②

- **Task 8**: In Chapter 9 we compared the number of mischievous acts (**mischief2**) in people who had invisibility cloaks compared to those without (**cloak**). Imagine we also had information about the baseline number of mischievous acts in these participants (**mischief1**). Conduct an ANCOVA to see whether people with invisibility cloaks get up to more mischief than those without, when factoring in their baseline level of mischief (**Invisibility Baseline.sav**). ②

The answers are on the companion website.

12.13. Further reading

Howell, D. C. (2012). *Statistical methods for psychology* (8th ed.). Belmont, CA: Wadsworth. (Or you might prefer his *Fundamental statistics for the behavioral sciences*. Both are excellent texts.)

Miller, G. A., & Chapman, J. P. (2001). Misunderstanding analysis of covariance. *Journal of Abnormal Psychology*, 110, 40–48.

Rutherford, A. (2000). *Introducing ANOVA and ANCOVA: A GLM approach*. London: Sage.

Wildt, A. R., & Ahtola, O. (1978). *Analysis of covariance*. Sage University Paper Series on Quantitative Applications in the Social Sciences, 07-012. Newbury Park, CA: Sage. (This text is pretty high level but very comprehensive if you want to know the maths behind ANCOVA.)

Factorial ANOVA (GLM 3)

13

FIGURE 13.1
Andromeda coming to a living room near you in 1988 (L-R: Malcolm, me and the two Marks)

13.1. What will this chapter tell me? ②

After persuading my two friends (Mark and Mark) to learn the bass and drums, I took the rather odd decision to *stop* playing the guitar. I didn't stop, as such, but I focused on singing instead. In retrospect, I'm not sure why, because I am *not* a good singer. Mind you, I'm not a good guitarist either. The upshot was that a classmate, Malcolm, ended up as our guitarist. I really can't remember how or why we ended up in this configuration, but we called ourselves Andromeda, we learnt several Queen and Iron Maiden songs and we were truly awful. I have some recordings somewhere to prove just what a cacophony of tuneless drivel we produced, but the chances of them appearing on the companion website are slim at best. Suffice it to say, you'd be hard pushed to recognize *which* Iron Maiden and Queen songs we were trying to play. I try to comfort myself with the fact that we were only 14 or 15 at the time, but even youth does not excuse the depths of ineptitude to which we sank. Still, we garnered a reputation for being too loud in school assembly and we did a successful tour of our friends' houses (much to their parents' amusement, I'm sure). We even started to write a few songs (I wrote one called 'Escape From Inside' about the film *The Fly* that contained the wonderful rhyming couplet 'I am a fly, I want to die' – genius). The only thing that we did that resembled the activities of a 'proper' band was to split up due to 'musical differences'; these differences being that Malcolm wanted to write 15-part symphonies about a boy's journey to worship electricity pylons and discover a mythical beast called the cuteasaurus, whereas I wanted to write songs about flies and dying (preferably both). When we could not agree on a musical direction the split became inevitable. We could have tested empirically the best musical direction for the band if Malcolm and I had each written a 15-part symphony and a 3-minute song about a fly. If we'd played these songs to various people and measured their screams of agony then we could have ascertained the best musical direction to gain popularity. We have two variables that predict screams: whether Malcolm or I wrote the song (songwriter), and whether the song was a 15-part symphony or a song about a fly (song type). The one-way ANOVA that we encountered in Chapter 11 cannot deal with two predictor variables – this is a job for factorial ANOVA.

13.2. Theory of factorial ANOVA (independent designs) ②

In the previous two chapters we have looked at situations in which we've tried to test for differences between groups when there has been a single independent variable (i.e., one variable has been manipulated). However, at the beginning of Chapter 11 I said that one of the advantages of ANOVA was that we could look at the effects of more than one independent variable (and how these variables interact). This chapter extends what we already know about ANOVA to look at situations where there are two independent variables. We've already seen in the previous chapter that it's very easy to incorporate a second variable into the ANOVA framework when that variable is a continuous variable (i.e., not split into groups), but now we'll move onto to situations where there is a second independent variable that has been systematically manipulated by assigning people to different conditions.

13.2.1. Factorial designs ②

In the previous two chapters we have explored situations in which we have looked at the effects of a single independent variable on some outcome. However, independent variables often get lonely and want to have friends. Scientists are obliging individuals and often put a second (or third) independent variable into their designs to keep the others company. When an experiment has two or more independent variables it is known as a *factorial design* (this is because, as we have seen, variables are sometimes referred to as *factors*). There are several types of factorial design:

What is a factorial design?

- **Independent factorial design**: In this type of experiment there are several independent variables or predictors and each has been measured using different entities (between groups). We discuss this design in this chapter.

- **Repeated-measures (related) factorial design**: This is an experiment in which several independent variables or predictors have been measured, but the same entities have been used in all conditions. This design is discussed in Chapter 14.

- **Mixed design**: This is a design in which several independent variables or predictors have been measured; some have been measured with different entities whereas others used the same entities. This design is discussed in Chapter 15.

As you might imagine, analysing these types of experiments can get quite complicated. Fortunately, we can extend the ANOVA model that we encountered in the previous two chapters to deal with these more complicated situations. When we use ANOVA to analyse a situation in which there are two or more independent variables it is sometimes called **factorial ANOVA**; however, the specific names attached to different ANOVAs reflect the experimental design that they are being used to analyse (see Jane Superbrain Box 13.1). This section extends the one-way ANOVA model to the factorial case (specifically when there are two independent variables). In subsequent chapters we will look at repeated-measures designs, factorial repeated-measures designs and finally mixed designs.

JANE SUPERBRAIN 13.1

Naming ANOVAs ②

ANOVAs can be quite confusing because there appear to be lots of them. When you read research articles you'll quite often come across phrases like 'a two-way independent ANOVA was conducted', or 'a three-way repeated-measures ANOVA was conducted'. These names may look confusing but they are quite easy if you break them down. All ANOVAs have two things in common: they involve some quantity of independent variables, and these variables can be measured using either the same or different entities. If the same entities are used we typically use the term *repeated measures* and if different entities are used we use the term *independent*. When there are two or more independent variables, it's possible that some variables use the same entities whereas others use different entities. In this case

we use the term *mixed*. When we name an ANOVA, we are simply telling the reader how many independent variables we used and how they were measured. In general, we could call an ANOVA:

- a (number of independent variables)-way (how these variables were measured) ANOVA.

By remembering this you can understand the name of any ANOVA you come across. Look at these examples and try to work out how many variables were used and how they were measured:

- one-way independent ANOVA;
- two-way repeated-measures ANOVA;
- two-way mixed ANOVA;
- three-way independent ANOVA.

The answers you should get are:

- one independent variable measured using different entities;
- two independent variables both measured using the same entities;
- two independent variables, one measured using different entities and the other measured using the same entities;
- three independent variables all of which are measured using different entities.

13.2.2. Guess what? Factorial ANOVA is a linear model ③

Throughout this chapter we'll use an example that has two independent variables. This is known as a two-way ANOVA (see Jane Superbrain Box 13.1). I'll look at an example with two independent variables because this is the simplest extension of the ANOVAs that we have already encountered.

An anthropologist was interested in the effects of alcohol on mate selection in night-clubs. Her rationale was that after alcohol had been consumed, subjective perceptions of physical attractiveness would become more inaccurate (the well-known **beer-goggles effect**). She was also interested in whether this effect was different for men and women. She picked 48 students: 24 male and 24 female. She then took groups of eight participants to a nightclub and gave them no alcohol (participants received placebo drinks of alcohol-free lager), 2 pints of strong lager, or 4 pints of strong lager. At the end of the evening she took a photograph of the person that the participant was chatting up. She then got a pool of independent judges to assess the attractiveness of the person in each photograph (out of 100). The data are in Table 13.1 and **Goggles.sav**.

TABLE 13.1 Data for the beer-goggles effect

Alcohol	None		2 Pints		4 Pints	
Gender	Female	Male	Female	Male	Female	Male
	65	50	70	45	55	30
	70	55	65	60	65	30
	60	80	60	85	70	30
	60	65	70	65	55	55
	60	70	65	70	55	35
	55	75	60	70	60	20
	60	75	60	80	50	45
	55	65	50	60	50	40
Total	485	535	500	535	460	285
Mean	60.625	66.875	62.50	66.875	57.50	35.625
Variance	24.55	106.70	42.86	156.70	50.00	117.41

We saw in Section 11.2.1 that one-way ANOVA could be conceptualized as a regression equation (a general linear model). In this section we'll consider how we extend this linear model to incorporate two independent variables. To keep things as simple as possible I want you to imagine that we have only two levels of the alcohol variable in our example (none and 4 pints). As such, we have two predictor variables, each with two levels. All of the general linear models we've considered in this book take the general form of:

$$outcome_i = (model) + error_i$$

For example, when we encountered multiple regression in Chapter 8 we saw that this model was written as (see equation (8.6)):

$$Y_i = (b_0 + b_1X_{1i} + b_2X_{2i} + \cdots + b_nX_{ni}) + \varepsilon_i$$

Also, when we came across one-way ANOVA, we adapted this regression model to conceptualize our Viagra example, as (see equation (11.1)):

$$Libido_i = (b_0 + b_2High_i + b_1Low_i) + \varepsilon_i$$

In this model, the High and Low variables were dummy variables (i.e., variables that can take only values of 0 or 1). In our current example, we have two variables: **gender** (male or female) and **alcohol** (none and 4 pints). We can code each of these with zeros and ones (e.g., we could code gender as 0 = male, 1 = female, and we could code the alcohol variable as 0 = none, 1 = 4 pints). We could then directly copy the model we had in one-way ANOVA:

$$\text{Attractiveness}_i = \left(b_0 + b_1 \text{Gender}_i + b_2 \text{Alcohol}_i\right) + \varepsilon_i$$

However, this model does not consider the interaction between gender and alcohol. If we want to include this term too, then the model simply extends to become (first expressed generally and then in terms of this specific example):

$$\text{Attractiveness}_i = \left(b_0 + b_1 A_i + b_2 B_i + b_3 AB_i\right) + \varepsilon_i$$

$$\text{Attractiveness}_i = \left(b_0 + b_1 \text{Gender}_i + b_2 \text{Alcohol}_i + b_3 \text{Interaction}_i\right) + \varepsilon_i \qquad (13.1)$$

The question is: how do we code the interaction term? We saw how to do this in Section 10.3. The interaction term represents the combined effect of **alcohol** and **gender**; to get any interaction term in regression you simply multiply the variables involved. This is why you see interaction terms written as gender × alcohol, because in regression terms the interaction variable literally is the two variables multiplied by each other. Table 13.2 shows the resulting variables for the regression (note that the interaction variable is simply the value of the gender dummy variable multiplied by the value of the alcohol dummy variable). So, for example, a male receiving 4 pints of alcohol would have a value of 0 for the gender variable, 1 for the alcohol variable and 0 for the interaction variable. The group means for the various combinations of gender and alcohol are also included because they'll come in useful in due course.

TABLE 13.2 Coding scheme for factorial ANOVA

Gender	Alcohol	Dummy (Gender)	Dummy (Alcohol)	Interaction	Mean
Male	None	0	0	0	66.875
Male	4 Pints	0	1	0	35.625
Female	None	1	0	0	60.625
Female	4 Pints	1	1	1	57.500

To work out what the *b*-values represent in this model we can do the same as we did for the *t*-test and one-way ANOVA; that is, look at what happens when we insert values of our predictors (gender and alcohol). To begin with, let's see what happens when we look at men who had no alcohol. In this case, the value of gender is 0, the value of alcohol is 0 and the value of the interaction is also 0. The outcome we predict (as with one-way ANOVA) is the mean of this group (66.875), so our model becomes:

$$\text{Attractiveness}_i = \left(b_0 + b_1 \text{Gender}_i + b_2 \text{Alcohol}_i + b_3 \text{Interaction}_i\right) + \varepsilon_i$$
$$\bar{X}_{\text{Men, None}} = b_0 + \left(b_1 \times 0\right) + \left(b_2 \times 0\right) + \left(b_3 \times 0\right)$$
$$b_0 = \bar{X}_{\text{Men, None}}$$
$$= 66.875$$

So, the constant b_0 in the model represents the mean of the group for which all variables are coded as 0. As such it's the mean value of the base category (in this case men who had no alcohol).

Now let's see what happens when we look at females who had no alcohol. In this case, the gender variable is 1 and the alcohol and interaction variables are still 0. Also remember that b_0 is the mean of the men who had no alcohol. The outcome is the mean for women who had no alcohol. Therefore, the equation becomes:

$$\bar{X}_{\text{Women, None}} = b_0 + (b_1 \times 1) + (b_2 \times 0) + (b_3 \times 0)$$

$$\bar{X}_{\text{Women, None}} = b_0 + b_1$$

$$\bar{X}_{\text{Women, None}} = \bar{X}_{\text{Men, None}} + b_1$$

$$b_1 = \bar{X}_{\text{Women, None}} - \bar{X}_{\text{Men, None}}$$

$$= 60.625 - 66.875$$

$$= -6.25$$

So, b_1 in the model represents the difference between men and women who had no alcohol. More generally, we can say it's the effect of gender for the base category of alcohol (the base category being the one coded with 0, in this case no alcohol).

Now let's look at males who had 4 pints of alcohol. In this case, the gender variable is 0, the alcohol variable is 1 and the interaction variable is still 0. We can also replace b_0 with the mean of the men who had no alcohol. The outcome is the mean for men who had 4 pints. Therefore, the equation becomes:

$$\bar{X}_{\text{Men, 4 Pints}} = b_0 + (b_1 \times 0) + (b_2 \times 1) + (b_3 \times 0)$$

$$\bar{X}_{\text{Men, 4 Pints}} = b_0 + b_2$$

$$\bar{X}_{\text{Men, 4 Pints}} = \bar{X}_{\text{Men, None}} + b_2$$

$$b_2 = \bar{X}_{\text{Men, 4 Pints}} - \bar{X}_{\text{Men, None}}$$

$$= 35.625 - 66.875$$

$$= -31.25$$

So, b_2 in the model represents the difference between having no alcohol and 4 pints in men. Put more generally, it's the effect of alcohol in the base category of gender (i.e., the category of gender that was coded with a 0, in this case men).

Finally, we can look at females who had 4 pints of alcohol. In this case, the gender variable is 1, the alcohol variable is 1 and the interaction variable is also 1. We can also replace b_0, b_1 and b_2, with what we now know they represent. The outcome is the mean for women who had 4 pints. Therefore, the equation becomes:

$$\bar{X}_{\text{Women, 4 Pints}} = b_0 + (b_1 \times 1) + (b_2 \times 1) + (b_3 \times 1)$$

$$\bar{X}_{\text{Women, 4 Pints}} = b_0 + b_1 + b_2 + b_3$$

$$\bar{X}_{\text{Women, 4 Pints}} = \bar{X}_{\text{Men, None}} + \left(\bar{X}_{\text{Women, None}} - \bar{X}_{\text{Men, None}}\right) + \left(\bar{X}_{\text{Men, 4 Pints}} - \bar{X}_{\text{Men, None}}\right) + b_3$$

$$\bar{X}_{\text{Women, 4 Pints}} = \bar{X}_{\text{Women, None}} + \bar{X}_{\text{Men, 4 Pints}} - \bar{X}_{\text{Men, None}} + b_3$$

$$b_3 = \bar{X}_{\text{Men, None}} - \bar{X}_{\text{Women, None}} + \bar{X}_{\text{Women, 4 Pints}} - \bar{X}_{\text{Men, 4 Pints}}$$

$$b_3 = 66.875 - 60.625 + 57.500 - 35.625$$

$$b_3 = 28.125$$

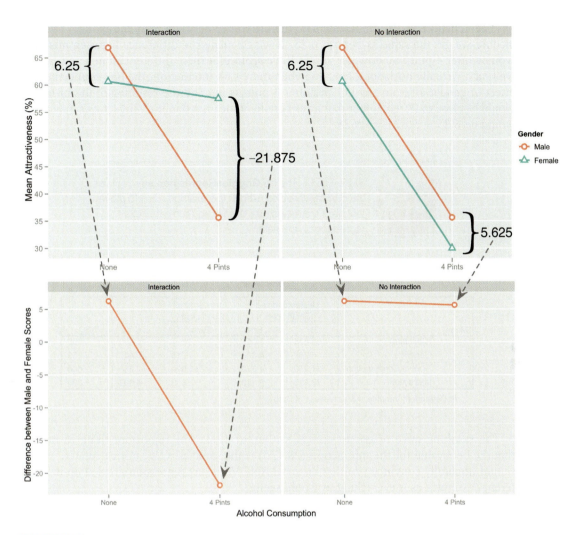

FIGURE 13.2 Breaking down what an interaction represents

So, b_3 in the model really compares the difference between men and women in the no alcohol condition to the difference between men and women in the 4-pint condition. Put another way, it compares the effect of gender after no alcohol to the effect of gender after 4 pints.[1] If you think about it in terms of an interaction graph, this makes perfect sense. For example, the top left-hand side of Figure 13.2 shows the interaction graph for these data. Now imagine we calculated the difference between men and women for the no alcohol groups. This would be the difference between the lines on the graph for the no alcohol group (the difference between group means, which is 6.25). If we then do the same for the 4-pints group, we find that the difference between men and women is −21.875. If we plotted these two values as a new graph we'd get a line connecting 6.25 to −21.875 (see the bottom left-hand side of Figure 13.2). This reflects the difference between the effect of gender after no alcohol compared to after 4 pints. We know that beta values represent gradients of lines, and in fact b_3 in our model is the gradient of this line (this is 6.25 − (−21.875) = 28.125).

Let's also see what happens if there isn't an interaction effect: the right-hand side of Figure 13.2 shows the same data except that the mean for the females who had 4 pints

---

[1] In fact, if you rearrange the terms in the equation you'll see that you can also phrase the interaction the opposite way around: it represents the effect of alcohol in men compared to women.

has been changed to 30. If we calculate the difference between men and women after no alcohol we get the same as before: 6.25. If we calculate the difference between men and women after 4 pints we now get 5.625. If we again plot these differences on a new graph, we find a virtually horizontal line. So, when there's no interaction, the line connecting the effect of gender after no alcohol and after 4 pints is flat and the resulting b_3 in our model would be close to 0 (remember that a zero gradient means a flat line). In fact its actual value would be $6.25 - 5.625 = 0.625$.

SELF-TEST   The file **GogglesRegression.sav** contains the dummy variables used in this example. Just to prove that all of this works, use this file and run a multiple regression on the data.

OUTPUT 13.1

Coefficients[a]

Model		Unstandardized Coefficients		Standardized Coefficients	t	Sig.
		B	Std. Error	Beta		
1	(Constant)	66.875	3.055		21.890	.000
	Gender	-6.250	4.320	-.219	-1.447	.159
	Alcohol Consumption	-31.250	4.320	-1.094	-7.233	.000
	Interaction	28.125	6.110	.853	4.603	.000

a. Dependent Variable: Attractiveness of Date

The resulting table of coefficients is in Output 13.1. The important thing to note is that the beta value for the interaction (28.125) is the same as we've just calculated, which should hopefully convince you that factorial ANOVA is just regression dressed up in a different costume – as is everything, it would seem.

What I hope to have shown you in this example is how even complex ANOVAs are just forms of regression (a general linear model). You'll be pleased to know (as I am, for that matter) that this is the last I'm going to say about ANOVA as a general linear model. I hope I've given you enough background so that you get a sense of the fact that we can just keep adding in independent variables into our model. All that happens is these new variables just get added into a multiple regression equation with an associated beta value (just like the regression chapter). Interaction terms can also be added simply by multiplying the variables that interact. These interaction terms will also have an associated beta value.

13.2.3.   Two-way ANOVA: behind the scenes ②

Now that we have a good conceptual understanding of factorial ANOVA as an extension of the basic idea of a linear model, we will turn our attention to some of the specific calculations that go on behind the scenes. The reason for doing this is that it should help you to understand what the output of the analysis means.

Two-way ANOVA is conceptually very similar to one-way ANOVA. Basically, we still find the total sum of squared errors (SS_T) and break this variance down into variance that can be explained by the experiment (SS_M) and variance that cannot be explained (SS_R). However, in two-way ANOVA, the variance explained by the experiment is made up of not one experimental manipulation but two. Therefore, we break the model sum of squares down into variance explained by the first independent variable (SS_A), variance explained

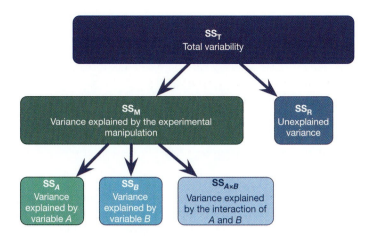

FIGURE 13.3
Breaking down
the variance
in two-way
ANOVA

by the second independent variable (SS_B) and variance explained by the interaction of these two variables ($SS_{A \times B}$) – see Figure 13.3.

13.2.4 Total sums of squares (SS_T) ②

We start off in the same way as we did for a one-way ANOVA. That is, we calculate how much variability there is between scores when we ignore the experimental condition from which they came. Remember from one-way ANOVA (equation (11.3)) that SS_T is calculated using the following equation:

$$SS_T = \sum_{i=1}^{N}\left(x_i - \overline{x}_{grand}\right)^2$$
$$= s_{grand}^2\left(N-1\right)$$

(13.2)

The grand variance is simply the variance of all scores when we ignore the group to which they belong. So if we treated the data as one big group it would look as follows:

65	50	70	45	55	30
70	55	65	60	65	30
60	80	60	85	70	30
60	65	70	65	55	55
60	70	65	70	55	35
55	75	60	70	60	20
60	75	60	80	50	45
55	65	50	60	50	40
Grand Mean = 58.33					

If we calculate the variance of all of these scores, we get 190.78 (try this on your calculator if you don't trust me). We used 48 scores to generate this value, and so N is 48. As such the equation becomes:

$$SS_T = s_{grand}^2 (N - 1)$$
$$= 190.78(48 - 1)$$
$$= 8966.66$$

The degrees of freedom for this SS will be $N - 1$, or 47.

13.2.5 Model sum of squares, SS_M ②

The next step is to work out the model sum of squares. As I suggested earlier, this sum of squares is then further broken into three components: variance explained by the first independent variable (SS_A), variance explained by the second independent variable (SS_B) and variance explained by the interaction of these two variables ($SS_{A \times B}$).

Before we break down the model sum of squares into its component parts, we must first calculate its value. We know we have 8966.66 units of variance to be explained, and our first step is to calculate how much of that variance is explained by our experimental manipulations overall (ignoring which of the two independent variables is responsible). When we did one-way ANOVA we worked out the model sum of squares by looking at the difference between each group mean and the overall mean (see Section 11.2.4). We can do the same here. We effectively have six experimental groups if we combine all levels of the two independent variables (three doses for the male participants and three doses for the females). So, given that we have six groups of different people we can then apply the equation for the model sum of squares that we used for one-way ANOVA (equation (11.4)):

$$SS_M = \sum_{k=1}^{k} n_k \left(\bar{x}_k - \bar{x}_{grand} \right)^2 \qquad (13.3)$$

The grand mean is the mean of all scores (we calculated this above as 58.33) and n is the number of scores in each group (i.e., the number of participants in each of the six experimental groups; eight in this case). Therefore, the equation becomes:

$$SS_M = 8(60.625 - 58.33)^2 + 8(66.875 - 58.33)^2 + 8(62.5 - 58.33)^2 + 8(66.875 - 58.33)^2$$
$$+ 8(57.5 - 58.33)^2 + 8(35.625 - 58.33)^2$$
$$= 8(2.295)^2 + 8(8.545)^2 + 8(4.17)^2 + 8(8.545)^2 + 8(-0.83)^2 + 8(-22.705)^2$$
$$= 42.1362 + 584.1362 + 139.1112 + 584.1362 + 5.5112 + 4124.1362$$
$$= 5479.167$$

The degrees of freedom for this SS will be the number of groups used, k, minus 1. We used six groups and so $df = 5$.

At this stage we know that the model (our experimental manipulations) can explain 5479.167 units of variance out of the total of 8966.66 units. The next stage is to further break down this model sum of squares to see how much variance is explained by our independent variables separately.

13.2.5.1. The main effect of gender, SS_A ②

To work out the variance accounted for by the first independent variable (in this case, gender) we need to group the scores according to which gender they belong. So, basically we ignore the amount of drink that has been drunk, and we just place all of the male scores into one group and all of the female scores into another. So, the data will look like Figure 13.4 (note that the first box contains the three female columns from our original table and the second box contains the male columns).

<table>
<tr><td colspan="3">A₁: Female</td><td colspan="3">A₂: Male</td></tr>
<tr><td>65</td><td>70</td><td>55</td><td>50</td><td>45</td><td>30</td></tr>
<tr><td>70</td><td>65</td><td>65</td><td>55</td><td>60</td><td>30</td></tr>
<tr><td>60</td><td>60</td><td>70</td><td>80</td><td>85</td><td>30</td></tr>
<tr><td>60</td><td>70</td><td>55</td><td>65</td><td>65</td><td>55</td></tr>
<tr><td>60</td><td>65</td><td>55</td><td>70</td><td>70</td><td>35</td></tr>
<tr><td>55</td><td>60</td><td>60</td><td>75</td><td>70</td><td>20</td></tr>
<tr><td>60</td><td>60</td><td>50</td><td>75</td><td>80</td><td>45</td></tr>
<tr><td>55</td><td>50</td><td>50</td><td>65</td><td>60</td><td>40</td></tr>
</table>

Mean Female = 60.21   Mean Male = 56.46

FIGURE 13.4
The main effect of gender

We can then apply the equation for the model sum of squares that we used to calculate the overall model sum of squares:

$$SS_A = \sum_{n=1}^{k} n_k \left(\bar{x}_k - \bar{x}_{grand} \right)^2 \tag{13.4}$$

The grand mean is the mean of all scores (above) and n is the number of scores in each group (i.e., the number of males and females; 24 in this case). Therefore, the equation becomes:

$$SS_{Gender} = 24(60.21 - 58.33)^2 + 24(56.46 - 58.33)^2$$

$$= 24(1.88)^2 + 24(-1.87)^2$$

$$= 84.8256 + 83.9256$$

$$= 168.75$$

The degrees of freedom for this SS will be the number of groups used, k, minus 1. We used two groups (males and females) and so $df = 1$. To sum up, the main effect of gender compares the mean of all males against the mean of all females (regardless of which alcohol group they were in).

13.2.5.2. The main effect of alcohol, SS_B ②

To work out the variance accounted for by the second independent variable (in this case, alcohol) we need to group the scores in the data set according to how much alcohol was consumed. So, basically we ignore the gender of the participant, and we just place all of the scores after no drinks in one group, the scores after 2 pints in another group and the scores after 4 pints in a third group. So, the data will look like Figure 13.5.

FIGURE 13.5

The main effect
of alcohol

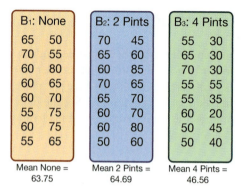

We can then apply the same equation for the model sum of squares that we used for the overall model sum of squares and for the main effect of gender:

$$SS_B = \sum_{n=1}^{k} n_k \left(\bar{x}_k - \bar{x}_{grand} \right)^2 \tag{13.5}$$

The grand mean is the mean of all scores (58.33 as before) and n is the number of scores in each group (i.e., the number of scores in each of the boxes above, in this case 16). Therefore, the equation becomes:

$$
\begin{aligned}
SS_{Alcohol} &= 16(63.75 - 58.33)^2 + 16(64.6875 - 58.33)^2 + 16(46.5625 - 58.33)^2 \\
&= 16(5.42)^2 + 16(6.3575)^2 + 16(-11.7675)^2 \\
&= 470.0224 + 646.6849 + 2215.5849 \\
&= 3332.292
\end{aligned}
$$

The degrees of freedom for this SS will be the number of groups used minus 1 (see Section 11.2.4). We used three groups and so $df = 2$. To sum up, the main effect of alcohol compares the means of the no alcohol, 2-pints and 4-pints groups (regardless of whether the scores come from men or women).

13.2.5.3. The interaction effect, $SS_{A \times B}$ ②

The final stage is to calculate how much variance is explained by the interaction of the two variables. The simplest way to do this is to remember that the SS_M is made up of three components (SS_A, SS_B and $SS_{A \times B}$). Therefore, given that we know SS_A and SS_B, we can calculate the interaction term using subtraction:

$$SS_{A \times B} = SS_M - SS_A - SS_B \tag{13.6}$$

Therefore, for these data, the value is:

$$
\begin{aligned}
SS_{A \times B} &= SS_M - SS_A - SS_B \\
&= 5479.167 - 168.75 - 3332.292 \\
&= 1978.125
\end{aligned}
$$

The degrees of freedom can be calculated in the same way, but are also the product of the degrees of freedom for the main effects (either method works):

$$df_{A \times B} = df_M - df_A - df_B \qquad df_{A \times B} = df_A \times df_B$$

$$= 5 - 1 - 2 \qquad\qquad\qquad = 1 \times 2$$

$$= 2 \qquad\qquad\qquad\qquad = 2$$

13.2.6. The residual sum of squares, SS_R ②

The residual sum of squares is calculated in the same way as for one-way ANOVA (see Section 11.2.5) and again represents individual differences in performance or the variance that can't be explained by factors that were systematically manipulated. We saw in one-way ANOVA that the value is calculated by taking the squared error between each data point and its corresponding group mean. An alternative way to express this is (see equation (11.6)):

$$SS_R = \sum s_k^2 (n_k - 1)$$

$$= s_{\text{group 1}}^2 (n_1 - 1) + s_{\text{group 2}}^2 (n_2 - 1) + \cdots + s_{\text{group } n}^2 (n_n - 1) \qquad (13.7)$$

So, we use the individual variances of each group and multiply them by one less than the number of people within the group (n). We have the individual group variances in our original table of data (Table 13.1) and there were eight people in each group (therefore, $n = 8$) and so the equation becomes:

$$SS_R = s_{\text{group 1}}^2 (n_1 - 1) + s_{\text{group 2}}^2 (n_2 - 1) + \cdots + s_{\text{group 6}}^2 (n_6 - 1)$$

$$= 24.55(8 - 1) + 106.7(8 - 1) + 42.86(8 - 1) + 156.7(8 - 1) + 50(8 - 1) + 117.41(8 - 1)$$

$$= (24.55 \times 7) + (106.7 \times 7) + (42.86 \times 7) + (156.7 \times 7) + (50 \times 7) + (117.41 \times 7)$$

$$= 171.85 + 746.9 + 300 + 1096.9 + 350 + 821.87$$

$$= 3487.52$$

The degrees of freedom for each group will be one less than the number of scores per group (i.e., 7). Therefore, if we add the degrees of freedom for each group, we get a total of $6 \times 7 = 42$.

13.2.7. The *F*-ratios ②

Each effect in a two-way ANOVA (the two main effects and the interaction) has its own *F*-ratio. To calculate these we have to first calculate the mean squares for each effect by taking the sum of squares and dividing by the respective degrees of freedom (think back to Section 11.2.6). We also need the mean squares for the residual term. So, for this example we'd have four mean squares calculated as follows:

$$MS_A = \frac{SS_A}{df_A} = \frac{168.75}{1} = 168.75$$

$$MS_B = \frac{SS_B}{df_B} = \frac{3332.292}{2} = 1666.146$$

$$MS_{A \times B} = \frac{SS_{A \times B}}{df_{A \times B}} = \frac{1978.125}{2} = 989.062$$

$$MS_R = \frac{SS_R}{df_R} = \frac{3487.52}{42} = 83.036.$$

The F-ratios for the two independent variables and their interactions are then calculated in the same way as for one-way ANOVA, by dividing their mean squares by the residual mean squares:

$$F_A = \frac{MS_A}{MS_R} = \frac{168.75}{83.036} = 2.032$$

$$F_B = \frac{MS_B}{MS_R} = \frac{1666.146}{83.036} = 20.065$$

$$F_{A \times B} = \frac{MS_{A \times B}}{MS_R} = \frac{989.062}{83.0362} = 11.911$$

SPSS computes an exact p-value for each of these F-ratios to tell us how likley these values are if there were no effect in the population. The main point is that two-way ANOVA is basically the same as one-way ANOVA except that the model sum of squares is partitioned into three parts: the effect of each of the independent variables and the effect of how these variables interact.

13.3. Assumptions of factorial ANOVA ③

Factorial ANOVA is again an extension of the linear model so all of the sources of potential bias (and counteractive measures) discussed in Chapter 5 apply (e.g., bias reduction in Section 5.4). If you have violated the assumption of homogeneity of variance then you can try to implement corrections based on the Welch procedure that was described in the previous chapter. However, this is quite technical, SPSS doesn't do it, and if you have anything more complicated than a 2 × 2 design then, really, it would be less painful to cover your body in paper cuts and bathe in chilli sauce (see Algina & Olejnik, 1984). One practical solution is to bootstrap the *post hoc* tests so that these will be robust. This won't help for main bits of the ANOVA (the F-tests): there are robust versions of factorial ANOVA but SPSS doesn't do them directly, and you'll have to delve into a package called R instead (Field et al., 2012).

13.4. Factorial ANOVA using SPSS ②

13.4.1. General procedure for factorial ANOVA ①

The steps in conducting a factorial ANOVA are the same as for one-way ANOVA, so refer back to Figure 11.9 as a guide.

13.4.2. Entering the data and accessing the main dialog box ②

We need to create two different coding variables in the data editor to represent gender and alcohol consumption. So, create a variable called **Gender** in the data editor. We have had a lot of experience with coding values, so you should be fairly happy about how to define value labels to represent the two genders: I recommend using the code male = 0 and female = 1. Once you have done this, you can enter a code of 0 or 1 in the gender column indicating to which group the person belonged. Create a second variable called **Alcohol** and assign group codes by using the *Labels* dialog box: I suggest placebo (no alcohol) = 1, 2 pints = 2 and 4 pints = 3. In the data editor, enter 1, 2 or 3 into the alcohol column to represent the amount of alcohol consumed by the participant. Remember that if you turn the *value labels* option on you will see text in the data editor rather than the numerical codes. The coding I have suggested is in Table 13.3.

TABLE 13.3 Coding two independent variables

Gender	Alcohol	Participant was
0	1	Male who consumed no alcohol
0	2	Male who consumed 2 pints
0	3	Male who consumed 4 pints
1	1	Female who consumed no alcohol
1	2	Female who consumed 2 pints
1	3	Female who consumed 4 pints

SELF-TEST Use the chart builder to plot a line graph (with error bars) of the attractiveness of the date with alcohol consumption on the *x*-axis and different coloured lines to represent males and females.

Once you have created the two coding variables, you can create a third variable in which to place the values of the dependent variable. Call this variable **Attractiveness** and use the *Labels* option to give it the fuller name of *Attractiveness of Date*.

In this example, there are two independent variables and different participants were used in each condition: the general factorial ANOVA procedure in SPSS is designed for analysing this design. To access the main dialog box select Analyze General Linear Model ▶ Univariate… .

OLIVER TWISTED

Please Sir, Can I … customize my model?

'My friend told me that there are different types of sums of squares', complains Oliver with an air of impressive authority. 'Why haven't you told us about them? Is it because you have a microbe for a brain?' No, Oliver, it's because everyone but you will find this very tedious. If you want to find out more about what the Model… button does, and the different types of sums of squares that can be used in ANOVA, then the additional material on the website will tell you.

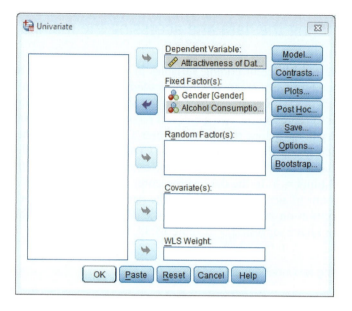

In the resulting dialog box (Figure 13.6) select the dependent variable **Attractiveness** from the variables list on the left-hand side and drag it to the space labelled *Dependent Variable* (or click on ➡). In the space labelled *Fixed Factor(s)* we need to place any independent variables relevant to the analysis. Select **Alcohol** and **Gender** in the variables list (to select these variables simultaneously hold down *Ctrl*, or *Cmd* on a Mac, while clicking on the variables) and drag them to the *Fixed Factor(s)* box (or click on ➡). There are various other spaces that are available for conducting more complex analyses such as random factors ANOVA (interested readers should consult Jackson & Brashers, 1994) and factorial ANCOVA, which extends the principles described at the beginning of this chapter to include a covariate (as in the previous chapter).

13.4.3. Graphing interactions ②

Once the relevant variables have been selected, you can click on `Plots...` to access the dialog box in Figure 13.7. This box allows you to select line graphs of your data, and these graphs are very useful for interpreting interaction effects (however, really we should plot graphs of the means before the data are analysed). We have only two independent variables, and the most useful plot is one that shows the interaction between these variables (the plot that displays levels of one independent variable against the other). In this case, the **interaction** graph will help us to interpret the combined effect of gender and alcohol consumption. Select **Alcohol** from the variables list on the left-hand side of the dialog box and drag it to the space labelled *Horizontal Axis* (or click on ➡). In the space labelled *Separate Lines* place the remaining independent variable, **Gender**. It doesn't matter which way round the variables are plotted; you should use your discretion as to which way produces the most sensible graph. When you have moved the two independent variables to the appropriate box, click on `Add` and this plot will be added to the list at the bottom of the box. You can plot a whole variety of graphs, and if you had a third independent variable, you would have the option of plotting different graphs for each level of that third variable by specifying a variable under the heading *Separate Plots*. When you have finished specifying graphs, click on `Continue` to return to the main dialog box.

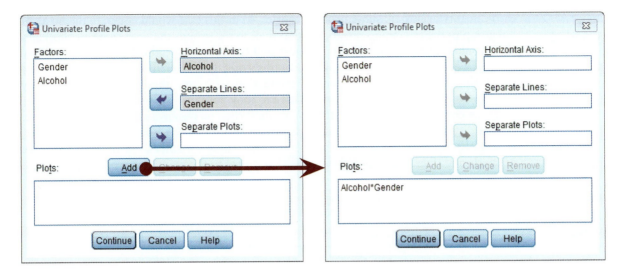

FIGURE 13.7   Defining plots of factorial ANOVA

13.4.4.   Contrasts ②

We saw in Chapter 11 that it's useful to follow up ANOVA with contrasts that break down the main effects and tell us where the differences between groups lie. For one-way ANOVA, SPSS has a procedure for entering codes that define the contrasts we want to do. However, for two-way ANOVA no such facility exists (although it can be done using syntax – see Oliver Twisted) and instead we are restricted to doing one of several standard contrasts. These standard contrasts are described in Table 11.6.

OLIVER TWISTED

Please Sir, can I have some more …contrasts?

'I don't want to use standard contrasts', sulks Oliver as he stamps his feet on the floor. 'They smell of rotting cabbage.' Actually, Oliver, I think the stench of rotting cabbage is because you stood your Dickensian self under Mr Mullycents' window when he emptied his toilet bucket into the street. Nevertheless, I do get asked a fair bit about how to do contrasts with syntax, and because I'm a complete masochist I've prepared a fairly detailed guide in the additional material for this chapter. These contrasts are useful to follow up a significant interaction effect.

We can use standard contrasts for this example. The effect of gender has only two levels, so we don't need contrasts for this main effect. The effect of alcohol has three levels: none, 2 pints and 4 pints. We could select a simple contrast for this variable, and use the first category as a reference category. This would compare the 2-pints group to the no alcohol group, and then compare the 4-pints category to the no alcohol group. As such, the alcohol groups would get compared to the no alcohol group. We could also select a *repeated* contrast. This would compare the 2-pints group to the no alcohol, and then the 4-pints group to the 2-pints group (so it moves through the groups comparing each group to the one before). Again, this might be useful. We could also do a *Helmert* contrast, which compares each category against all subsequent categories, so in this case would compare the no alcohol group to the remaining categories (that is all of the groups that had some alcohol) and then would move onto the 2-pints category and compare this to the 4-pints category. Any of these would be fine, but they give us contrasts only for the main effects. In reality, most of the time we want contrasts for our interaction term, and they can be obtained only through syntax (it looks like you might have to look at Oliver Twisted after all!).

To get contrasts for the main effect of alcohol, click on [Contrasts...] in the main dialog box. We have used the *Contrasts* dialog box before in Section 12.4.5, so refer back to that section to help you select a Helmert contrast for the alcohol variable. Once the contrasts have been selected (Figure 13.8), click on [Continue] to return to the main dialog box.

FIGURE 13.8
Defining
contrasts
in factorial
ANOVA

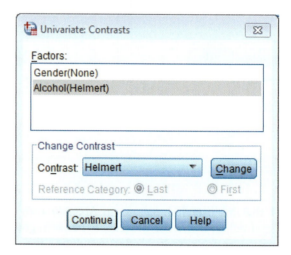

13.4.5. *Post hoc* tests ②

The dialog box for *post hoc* tests is obtained by clicking on [Post Hoc...] in the main dialog box (Figure 13.9). The variable **Gender** has only two levels and so we don't need to select *post hoc* tests for that variable (because any significant effects can reflect only the difference between males and females). However, there were three levels of the **Alcohol** variable (no alcohol, 2 pints and 4 pints); hence we can conduct *post hoc* tests (although remember that normally you would conduct contrasts *or post hoc* tests, not both). First, you should select the variable **Alcohol** from the box labelled *Factors* and transfer it to the box labelled *Post Hoc Tests for*: My recommendations for which *post hoc* procedures to use are in Section 11.5 (and I don't want to repeat myself). Suffice it to say that you should select the ones in Figure 13.9. Click on [Continue] to return to the main dialog box.

13.4.6. Bootstrapping and other options ②

Click on [Options...] to activate the same *Options* dialog box that we saw in the previous chapter (the options are explained in Jane Superbrain Box 12.3). The main thing is to get estimated marginal means by transferring all of the effects into the box labelled *Display Means for* (Figure 13.10). Some people will select *Homogeneity tests* to produce Levene's test (Section 5.3.3.2). You can also select ☑ Estimates of effect size if you want SPSS to calculate partial eta squared for you (see Section 12.7).

As with any ANOVA, the main dialog box contains the [Bootstrap...] button, which enables you to select bootstrapped confidence intervals for the estimated marginal means, descriptives

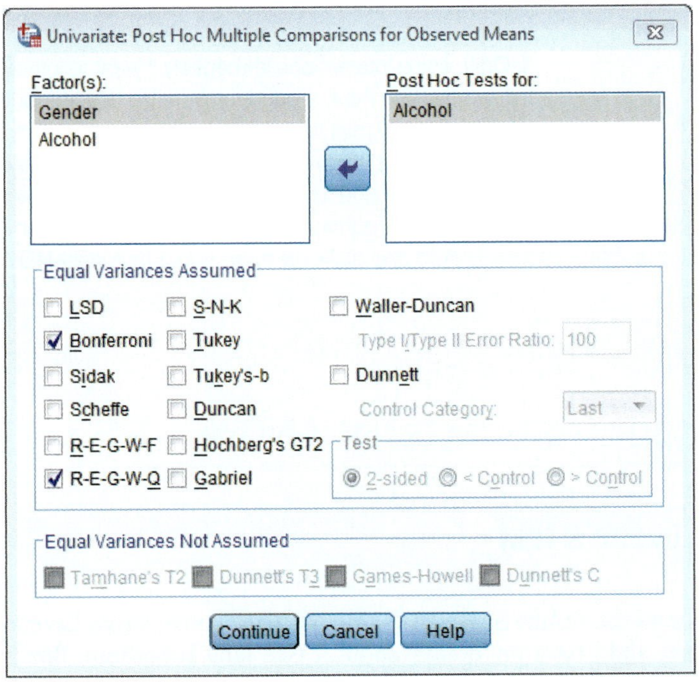

FIGURE 13.9
Dialog box for *post hoc* tests

and *post hoc* tests, but not the main *F*-test. The main use of these is if you plan to look at the *post hoc* tests, which we are, so select the options described in Section 5.4.3.

Once these options have been selected click on `Continue` to return to the main dialog box, then click on `OK` run the analysis.

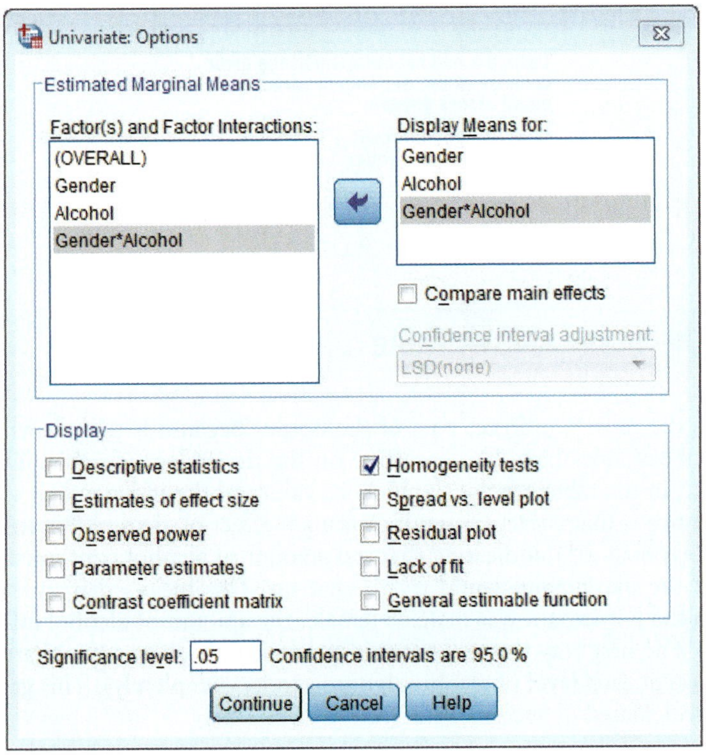

FIGURE 13.10
Dialog box for options

ODITI'S LANTERN

Factorial ANOVA

'I, Oditi, enjoy interactions immensely. I want to interact with all of my followers, invite them around to my large dessert ranch and let them sup on my tasty mint tea. I grow mint in my special mushroom patch, which gives it a unique flavour, and sometimes makes people obey my every command. I have learnt that interactions like these are powerful tools to understand the secrets of global domina … erm, I mean "life" and how to breed cute bunny rabbits of love. Stare into my lantern and discover more about factorial ANOVA.'

13.5. Output from factorial ANOVA ②

13.5.1. Levene's test ②

Output 13.2 shows the results of Levene's test. We have come across Levene's test numerous times before, and I have my doubts about it (see Jane Superbrain Box 5.6); however, in this case the non-significant result ($p = .202$) suggests the variance in attractiveness is roughly equal across the various combinations of gender and alcohol.

OUTPUT 13.2

Levene's Test of Equality of Error Variances[a]

Dependent Variable: Attractiveness of Date

F	df1	df2	Sig.
1.527	5	42	.202

Tests the null hypothesis that the error variance of the dependent variable is equal across groups.

a. Design: Intercept + Gender + Alcohol + Gender * Alcohol

13.5.2. The main ANOVA table ②

Output 13.3 is the most important part of the output because it tells us whether any of the independent variables have had an effect on the dependent variable. The important things to look at in the table are the significance values of the independent variables. The first thing to notice is that there is a significant main effect of alcohol (because the significance value is less than .05), indicating that the amount of alcohol consumed significantly affected whom the participant would try to chat up. This means that overall, when we ignore whether the participant was male or female, the amount of alcohol influenced their mate selection. The best way to see what this means is to look at a bar chart of the average attractiveness at each level of alcohol (ignore gender completely). This graph plots the means that we calculated in Section 13.2.5.2.

SELF-TEST Plot error bar graphs of the main effects of alcohol and gender.

OUTPUT 13.3

Tests of Between–Subjects Effects

Dependent Variable: Attractiveness of Date

Source	Type III Sum of Squares	df	Mean Square	F	Sig.
Corrected Model	5479.167[a]	5	1095.833	13.197	.000
Intercept	163333.333	1	163333.333	1967.025	.000
Gender	168.750	1	168.750	2.032	.161
Alcohol	3332.292	2	1666.146	20.065	.000
Gender * Alcohol	1978.125	2	989.062	11.911	.000
Error	3487.500	42	83.036		
Total	172300.000	48			
Corrected Total	8966.667	47			

a. R Squared = .611 (Adjusted R Squared = .565)

Figure 13.11 shows that when you ignore gender the overall attractiveness of the selected mate is very similar when no alcohol has been drunk and when 2 pints have been drunk (the means of these groups are approximately equal). Hence, this significant main effect is *likely* to reflect the drop in the attractiveness of the selected mates when 4 pints have been drunk. This finding seems to indicate that a person is willing to accept a less attractive mate after 4 pints.

The next part of Output 13.3 tells us about the main effect of gender. This time the F-ratio is not significant ($p = .161$). This effect means that overall, when we ignore

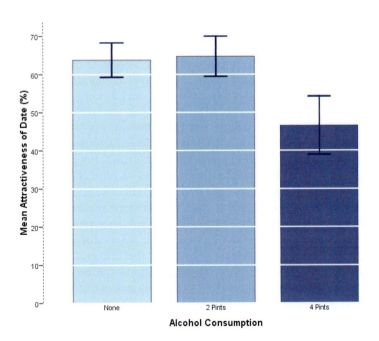

FIGURE 13.11
Graph showing the main effect of alcohol

FIGURE 13.12
Graph to show
the main effect
of gender on
mate selection

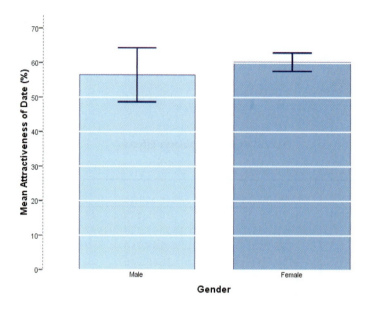

how much alcohol had been drunk, the gender of the participant did not influence the attractiveness of the partner that the participant selected. In other words, other things being equal, males and females selected equally attractive mates. The bar chart (which you hopefully produced for the self-test) of the average attractiveness of mates for men and women (ignoring how much alcohol had been consumed) reveals the meaning of this main effect. Figure 13.12 plots the means that we calculated in Section 13.2.5.1. This graph shows that the average attractiveness of the partners of male and female participants was fairly similar (the means are different by only 4%). Therefore, this non-significant effect reflects the fact that the mean attractiveness was similar. We can conclude from this that, *other things being equal*, men and women chose equally attractive partners.

Finally, Output 13.3 tells us about the interaction between the effect of gender and the effect of alcohol. The *F*-value is highly significant. What this actually means is that the effect of alcohol on mate selection was different for male participants than it was for females. The SPSS output includes a plot that we asked for (see Figure 13.7) which tells us something about the nature of this interaction effect (Figure 13.13 is a nicer version of the graph in your output). This graph plots the estimated marginal means, which you can find (along with their bootstrap confidence intervals) in Output 13.4. Figure 13.13 shows that for women, alcohol has very little effect: the attractiveness of their selected

partners is quite stable across the three conditions (as shown by the near-horizontal line). However, for the men, the attractiveness of their partners is stable when only a small amount has been drunk, but rapidly declines when more is drunk. The interaction tells us that alcohol has little effect on mate selection until 4 pints have been drunk and that the effect of alcohol is prevalent only in male participants. In short, women maintain high standards in their mate selection regardless of alcohol, whereas men have a few beers and then try to mate with anything on legs ☺. This example illustrates an important point because we concluded earlier that alcohol significantly affected how attractive a mate was selected (the **Alcohol** main effect); however, the interaction effect tells us that this is true only in males (females appear unaffected). In general, *you should not interpret main effects in the presence of a significant interaction effect involving that main effect.*

could do a simple effects analysis looking at the effect of gender at each level of alcohol. This would mean taking the average attractiveness of the date selected by men and comparing it to that for women after no drinks, then making the same comparison for 2 pints and then, finally, for 4 pints. Another way of looking at this is to say we would compare each triangle to the corresponding circle in Figure 13.13: based on the graph, we might expect to find no difference after no alcohol and after 2 pints (in both cases the triangle and circle are located in about the same position) but we would expect a difference after 4 pints (because the circle and triangle are quite far apart). The alternative way to do it would be to compare the mean attractiveness after no alcohol, 2 pints and 4 pints for men and then in a separate analysis do the same but for women. (This analysis would be like doing a one-way ANOVA on the effect of alcohol in men, and then doing a different one-way ANOVA for the effect of alcohol in women.) These analyses can't be run through the usual dialog boxes, but they can be run using syntax – see SPSS Tip 13.1.

SPSS TIP 13.1   Simple effects analysis in SPSS ③

Unfortunately, simple effects analyses can't be done through the dialog boxes and instead you have to use SPSS syntax (see Section 3.9 to remind you about the syntax window). The syntax you need to use in this example is:

```
GLM Attractiveness by gender alcohol
 /EMMEANS = TABLES(gender*alcohol) COMPARE(gender).
```

This syntax initiates the ANOVA by specifying the outcome or dependent variable (**Attractiveness**) and then the *by* command is followed by our independent variables (**Gender** and **Alcohol**). The line beginning /*EMMEANS* specifies the simple effects.

For example, *COMPARE(gender)* will look at the effect of gender at each level of alcohol. This syntax for looking at the effect of gender at different levels of alcohol is stored in a file called **GogglesSimpleEffects.sps** for you to look at should you not wish to go to the effort of typing the two lines above. Open this file (make sure you also have **Goggles.sav** loaded into the data editor) and run the syntax. The output you get will be the same as for the main analysis in the chapter but will contain an extra table at the end containing the simple effects (Output 13.6).

Univariate Tests

Dependent Variable: Attractiveness of Date

Alcohol Consumption		Sum of Squares	df	Mean Square	F	Sig.
None	Contrast	156.250	1	156.250	1.882	.177
	Error	3487.500	42	83.036		
2 Pints	Contrast	76.562	1	76.562	.922	.342
	Error	3487.500	42	83.036		
4 Pints	Contrast	1914.062	1	1914.062	23.051	.000
	Error	3487.500	42	83.036		

Each F tests the simple effects of Gender within each level combination of the other effects shown. These tests are based on the linearly independent pairwise comparisons among the estimated marginal means.

OUTPUT 13.6

Looking at the significance values for each simple effect, it appears that there was no significant difference between men and women at level 1 of alcohol (i.e., no alcohol), $p = .18$, or at level 2 of alcohol (2 pints), $p = .34$, but there was a very significant difference ($p < .001$) at level 3 of alcohol (4 pints, which judging from the graph reflects the fact that the mean for men is considerably lower than for women).

OLIVER TWISTED

Please Sir, can I have some more … simple effects?

'I want to impress my friends by doing a simple effects analysis by hand', boasts Oliver. You don't really need to know how simple effects analyses are calculated to run them, Oliver – but, since you asked, it is explained in the additional material available from the companion website.

13.5.5.   *Post hoc* analysis ②

The Bonferroni *post hoc* tests (Output 13.7) break down the main effect of alcohol and can be interpreted as if a one-way ANOVA had been conducted on the **Alcohol** variable (i.e., the reported effects for alcohol are collapsed with regard to gender). The tests show (both by the significance and whether the bootstrap confidence intervals cross zero) that when participants had drunk no alcohol or 2 pints of alcohol, they selected equally attractive mates, $p = 1.00$ (this is the maximum that p can be, which reflects the fact that the means are almost identical). However, after 4 pints had been consumed, participants selected significantly less attractive mates than after both 2 pints ($p < .001$) and no alcohol ($p < .001$).

The REGWQ test (Output 13.8) confirms that the means of the placebo and 2-pints conditions were equal, whereas the mean of the 4-pints group was different. It should again be noted that we wouldn't normally interpret these *post hoc* tests because main effects are not interesting when there is a significant interaction involving that main effect (as there is here).

In summary, we should conclude that alcohol has an effect on the attractiveness of selected mates. Overall, after a relatively small dose of alcohol (2 pints) humans are still in

OUTPUT 13.7

Multiple Comparisons

Dependent Variable: Attractiveness of Date

	(I) Alcohol Consumption	(J) Alcohol Consumption	Mean Difference (I–J)	Std. Error	Sig.	95% Confidence Interval Lower Bound	95% Confidence Interval Upper Bound
Bonferroni	None	2 Pints	−.94	3.222	1.000	−8.97	7.10
		4 Pints	17.19*	3.222	.000	9.15	25.22
	2 Pints	None	.94	3.222	1.000	−7.10	8.97
		4 Pints	18.13*	3.222	.000	10.09	26.16
	4 Pints	None	−17.19*	3.222	.000	−25.22	−9.15
		2 Pints	−18.13*	3.222	.000	−26.16	−10.09

Based on observed means.
The error term is Mean Square(Error) = 84.527.

*. The mean difference is significant at the

Bootstrap for Multiple Comparisons

Dependent Variable: Attractiveness of Date

	(I) Alcohol Consumption	(J) Alcohol Consumption	Mean Difference (I–J)	Bootstrap[a] Bias	Bootstrap[a] Std. Error	BCa 95% Confidence Interval Lower	BCa 95% Confidence Interval Upper
Bonferroni	None	2 Pints	−.94	.06	3.05	−6.72	5.23
		4 Pints	17.19	−.01	4.20	9.77	25.61
	2 Pints	None	.94	−.06	3.05	−5.07	6.56
		4 Pints	18.13	−.08	4.36	10.40	25.73
	4 Pints	None	−17.19	.01	4.20	−26.31	−8.52
		2 Pints	−18.13	.08	4.36	−27.33	−9.13

a. Unless otherwise noted, bootstrap results are based on 1000 bootstrap samples

Attractiveness of Date

	Alcohol Consumption	N	Subset 1	Subset 2
Ryan–Einot–Gabriel–Welsch Range[a]	4 Pints	16	46.56	
	None	16		63.75
	2 Pints	16		64.69
	Sig.		1.000	.772

Means for groups in homogeneous subsets are displayed.
Based on observed means.
The error term is Mean Square(Error) = 83.036.

a. Alpha =

control of their judgements and the attractiveness levels of chosen partners are consistent with a control group (no alcohol consumed). However, after a greater dose of alcohol, the attractiveness of chosen mates decreases significantly. This is the beer-goggles effect! More interestingly, the interaction shows a gender difference in the beer-goggles effect. Specifically, it looks as though men are significantly more likely to pick less attractive mates when drunk. Women, in comparison, manage to maintain their standards despite being drunk. What we still don't know is whether women will become susceptible to the beer-goggles effect at higher doses of alcohol.

CRAMMING SAM'S TIPS   Factorial ANOVA

- Two-way independent ANOVA compares several means when there are two independent variables and different entities have been used in all experimental conditions. For example, if you wanted to know whether different teaching methods worked better for different subjects, you could take students from four courses (Psychology, Geography, Management and Statistics) and assign them to either lecture-based or book-based teaching. The two variables are course and method of teaching. The outcome might be the end-of-year mark (as a percentage).
- You can test for homogeneity of variance using the table labelled *Levene's Test*: if the value in the column labelled *Sig.* is less than .05 then the assumption is violated.
- In the table labelled *Tests of Between-Subjects Effects*, look at the column labelled *Sig.* for all main effects and interactions; if the value is less than .05 then the effect is significant.
- To interpret a significant interaction look at an interaction graph or conduct simple effects analysis.
- You don't need to interpret main effects if an interaction effect involving that variable is significant.
- If you do interpret main effects then consult *post hoc* tests to see which groups differ: significance is shown by values in the columns labelled *Sig.* smaller than .05, and bootstrap confidence intervals that do not contain zero.
- Test the same assumptions as for any linear model (see Chapter 5).

13.6. Interpreting interaction graphs ②

We've already had a look at one interaction graph when we interpreted the analysis in this chapter. The key to understanding interactions is being able to interpret interaction graphs. In the example in this chapter we used Figure 13.13 to conclude that the interaction probably reflected the fact that men and women chose equally attractive dates after no alcohol

FIGURE 13.14

FIGURE 13.14

Another interaction graph

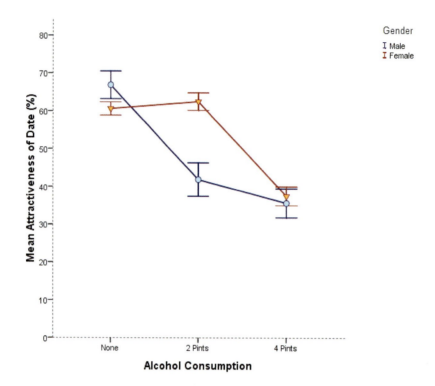

and 2 pints, but that at 4 pints men's standards dropped significantly more than women's. Imagine we'd got the profile of results shown in Figure 13.14; do you think we would've still got a significant interaction effect?

This profile of data probably would also give rise to a significant interaction term because, although the attractiveness of men and women's dates are similar after no alcohol and 4 pints of alcohol, there is a big difference after 2 pints. This reflects a scenario in which the beer-goggles effect is equally big in men and women after 4 pints (and doesn't exist after no alcohol) but kicks in quicker for men: the attractiveness of their dates plummets after 2 pints, whereas women maintain their standards until 4 pints (at which point they'd happily date an unwashed skunk). Let's try another example. Is there a significant interaction in Figure 13.15?

For the data in Figure 13.15 there is unlikely to be a significant interaction because the effect of alcohol is the same for men and women. So, for both men and women, the attractiveness of their dates after no alcohol is quite high, but after 2 pints all types drop by a similar amount (the slope of the male and female lines is about the same). After 4 pints there is a further drop and, again, this drop is about the same in men and women (the lines again slope at about the same angle). The fact that the line for males is lower than for females just reflects the fact that across all conditions, men have lower standards than their female counterparts: this reflects a main effect of gender (i.e., males generally chose less attractive dates than females at all levels of alcohol). There are two general points that we can make from these examples:

- Non-parallel lines on an interaction graph show up significant interactions. However, this doesn't mean that non-parallel lines *always* reflect significant interaction effects: it depends on how non-parallel the lines are.

- If the lines on an interaction graph cross then obviously they are not parallel and this can be a dead give-away that you have a possible significant interaction. However, if the lines of the interaction graph cross it isn't *always* the case that the interaction is significant.

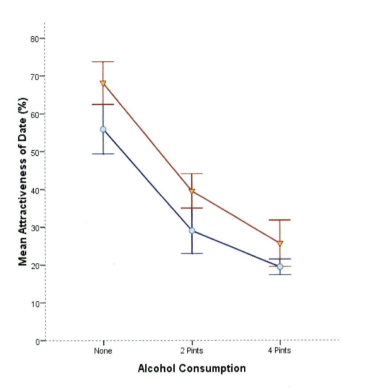

FIGURE 13.15
A graph
showing lack of
interaction

A further complication is that sometimes people draw bar charts rather than line charts. Figure 13.16 shows some bar charts of interactions between two independent variables. Panels (a) and (b) actually display the data from the example used in this chapter (why not have a go at plotting them?). As you can see, there are two ways to present the same data: panel (a) shows the data when levels of alcohol are placed along the *x*-axis and different-coloured bars are used to show means for males and females, and panel (b) shows the opposite scenario where gender is plotted on the *x*-axis and different colours distinguish the dose of alcohol. Both of these graphs show an interaction effect. What you're looking for is for the differences between coloured bars to be different at different points along the *x*-axis. So, for panel (a) you'd look at the difference between the light and dark blue bars for no alcohol, and then look to 2 pints and ask: 'Is the difference between the bars different than when I looked at no alcohol?' In this case the dark- and light-blue bars look the same at no alcohol as they do at 2 pints: hence, no interaction. However, you'd then move on to look at 4 pints, and you'd again ask: 'Is the difference between the light- and dark-blue bars different than it has been in any of the other conditions?' In this case the answer is yes: for no alcohol and 2 pints, the light- and dark-blue bars were about the same height, but at 4 pints the dark-blue bar is much higher than the light one. This shows an interaction: the pattern of responses changes at 4 pints. Panel (b) shows the same thing but plotted the other way around. Again we look at the pattern of responses. So, first we look at the men and see that the pattern is that the first two bars are the same height, but the last bar is much shorter. The interaction effect is shown up by the fact that for the women there is a different pattern: all three bars are about the same height.

SELF-TEST   What about panels (c) and (d): do you think there is an interaction?

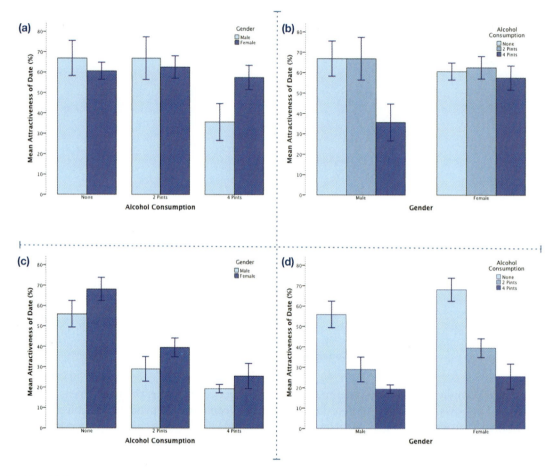

FIGURE 13.16   Bar charts showing interactions between two variables

LABCOAT LENI'S REAL RESEARCH 13.1

Going out on the pierce ②

GUÉGUEN, N. (2012), ALCOHOLISM: CLINICAL AND EXPERIMENTAL RESEARCH, 36(7), 1253–1256.

Tattoos and body piercings have become very popular since I was young. I have often contemplated having Ronald Fisher's face tattooed over my own so that people will think I'm a genius. But I digress. Research has shown that people who have tattoos and piercings are more likely to engage in risky behaviour. Nicolas Guéguen (2012) measured the level of intoxication (mass of alcohol per litre of breath exhaled, **Alcohol**) in 1965 French youths as they left bars. This measure was an indicator of risky behaviour. Each youth was also classified as having tattoos, piercings, both or neither (**Group**), and their gender was noted (**Gender**). The data are in the file **Gueguen (2012).sav**. Was the level of risk (i.e., alcohol) greater in groups who had tattoos and piercings? Did this effect interact with gender? Draw an error bar chart of the data too. Answers are on the companion website (or look at pages 1254–1255 in the original article).

Again, they display the same data in two different ways, but it's different data than what we've used in this chapter. First let's look at panel (c): for the no alcohol data, the dark bar is a little bit bigger than the light one; moving on to the 2-pints data, the dark bar is also a little bit taller than the light bar; and finally, for the 4-pints data, the dark bar is again higher than the light one. In all conditions the same pattern is shown – the dark-blue bar is a bit higher than the light-blue one (i.e., females pick more attractive dates than men regardless of alcohol consumption) – therefore, there is no interaction. Looking at panel (d), we see a similar result. For men, the pattern is that attractiveness ratings fall as more alcohol is drunk (the bars decrease in height) and then for the women we see the same pattern: ratings fall as more is drunk. This again is indicative of no interaction: the change in attractiveness due to alcohol is similar in men and women.

13.7. Calculating effect sizes ③

As we saw in previous chapters (e.g., Section 12.7), we can get SPSS to produce partial eta squared, η^2. However, you're well advised, for reasons explained in these other sections, to use omega squared (ω^2). The calculation of omega squared becomes somewhat more cumbersome in factorial designs ('somewhat' being one of my characteristic understatements). Howell (2012), as ever, does a wonderful job of explaining the complexities of it all (and has a nice table summarizing the various components for a variety of situations). Condensing all of this down, I'll just say that we need to first compute a variance component for each of the effects (the two main effects and the interaction term) and the error, and then use these to calculate effect sizes for each. If we call the first main effect A, the second main effect B and the interaction effect $A \times B$, then the variance components for each of these are based on the mean squares of each effect and the sample sizes on which they're based:

$$\hat{\sigma}_\alpha^2 = \frac{(a-1)(\mathrm{MS}_A - \mathrm{MS}_R)}{nab}$$

$$\hat{\sigma}_\beta^2 = \frac{(b-1)(\mathrm{MS}_B - \mathrm{MS}_R)}{nab}$$

$$\hat{\sigma}_{\alpha\beta}^2 = \frac{(a-1)(b-1)(\mathrm{MS}_{A\times B} - \mathrm{MS}_R)}{nab}$$

In these equations, a is the number of levels of the first independent variable, b is the number of levels of the second independent variable and n is the number of people per condition. Let's calculate these for our data. We need to look at Output 13.3 to find out the mean squares for each effect, and for the error term. Our first independent variable was alcohol. This had three levels (hence $a = 3$) and had a mean square of 1666.146. Our second independent variable was gender, which had two levels (hence $b = 2$) and a mean square of 168.75. The number of people in each group was 8 and the residual mean square was 83.036. Therefore, our equations become:

$$\hat{\sigma}_\alpha^2 = \frac{(3-1)(1666.146-83.036)}{8\times3\times2} = 65.96$$

$$\hat{\sigma}_\beta^2 = \frac{(2-1)(168.75-83.036)}{8\times3\times2} = 1.79$$

$$\hat{\sigma}_{\alpha\beta}^2 = \frac{(3-1)(2-1)(989.062-83.036)}{8\times3\times2} = 37.75$$

We also need to estimate the total variability and this is just the sum of these other variables and the residual mean square:

$$\hat{\sigma}^2_{total} = \hat{\sigma}^2_{\alpha} + \hat{\sigma}^2_{\beta} + \hat{\sigma}^2_{\alpha\beta} + MS_R$$

$$= 65.96 + 1.79 + 37.75 + 83.04$$

$$= 188.54$$

The effect size is then simply the variance estimate for the effect in which you're interested divided by the total variance estimate:

$$\omega^2_{effect} = \frac{\hat{\sigma}^2_{effect}}{\hat{\sigma}^2_{total}}$$

As such, for the main effect of alcohol we get:

$$\omega^2_{alcohol} = \frac{\hat{\sigma}^2_{alcohol}}{\hat{\sigma}^2_{total}} = \frac{65.96}{188.54} = .35$$

For the main effect of gender we get:

$$\omega^2_{gender} = \frac{\hat{\sigma}^2_{gender}}{\hat{\sigma}^2_{total}} = \frac{1.79}{188.54} = .009$$

For the interaction of gender and alcohol we get:

$$\omega^2_{alcohol \times gender} = \frac{\hat{\sigma}^2_{alcohol \times gender}}{\hat{\sigma}^2_{total}} = \frac{37.75}{188.54} = .20$$

To make these values comparable to r we can take the square root, which gives us effect sizes of .59 for alcohol, .09 for gender and .45 for the interaction term. As such, the effects of alcohol and the interaction are fairly large, but the effect of gender, which was non-significant in the main analysis, is very small indeed (close to zero in fact).

It's also possible to calculate effect sizes for our simple effects analysis (if you read Section 13.5.4). These effects have 1 degree of freedom for the model (which means they're comparing only two things) and in these situations F can be converted to r using the following equation (which just uses the F-ratio and the residual degrees of freedom):[2]

$$r = \sqrt{\frac{F(1, df_R)}{F(1, df_R) + df_R}}$$

[2] If your F compares more than two things then a different equation is needed (see Rosenthal et al., 2000, p. 44), but I think effect sizes for situations in which only two things are being compared are most useful because they have a clear interpretation.

Looking at SPSS Tip 13.1, we can see that we got *F*-ratios of 1.88, 0.92 and 23.05 for the effects of gender at no alcohol, 2 pints and 4 pints, respectively. For each of these, the degrees of freedom were 1 for the model and 42 for the residual. Therefore, we get the following effect sizes:

$$r_{\text{Gender (no alcohol)}} = \sqrt{\frac{1.88}{1.88 + 42}} = .21$$

$$r_{\text{Gender (2 pints)}} = \sqrt{\frac{0.92}{0.92 + 42}} = .15$$

$$r_{\text{Gender (4 pints)}} = \sqrt{\frac{23.05}{23.05 + 42}} = .60$$

Therefore, the effect of gender is very small at both no alcohol and 2 pints, but becomes large at 4 pints of alcohol.

EVERYBODY

13.8. Reporting the results of two-way ANOVA ②

As with the other ANOVAs we've encountered, we have to report the details of the *F*-ratio and the degrees of freedom from which it was calculated. For the effects of alcohol and the alcohol × gender interaction, the model degrees of freedom were $df_M = 2$, but for the effect of gender the degrees of freedom were only $df_M = 1$. For all effects, the degrees of freedom for the residuals were $df_R = 42$. We can, therefore, report the three effects from this analysis as follows:

✓ There was a significant main effect of the amount of alcohol consumed in the nightclub on the attractiveness of the mate selected, $F(2, 42) = 20.07$, $p < .001$, $\omega^2 = .35$. Bonferroni *post hoc* tests revealed that the attractiveness of selected dates was significantly lower after 4 pints than both after 2 pints and no alcohol (both $ps < .001$). There was no significant difference in the attractiveness of dates after 2 pints and no alcohol, $p = 1$.

✓ There was a non-significant main effect of gender on the attractiveness of selected mates, $F(1, 42) = 2.03$, $p = .161$, $\omega^2 = .009$.

✓ There was a significant interaction between the amount of alcohol consumed and the gender of the person selecting a mate, on the attractiveness of the partner selected, $F(2, 42) = 11.91$, $p < .001$, $\omega^2 = .20$. This effect indicates that males and females were affected differently by alcohol. Specifically, the attractiveness of partners was similar in males ($M = 66.88$, $SD = 10.33$) and females ($M = 60.63$, $SD = 4.96$) after no alcohol and 2 pints (males, $M = 66.88$, $SD = 12.52$; females, $M = 62.50$, $SD = 6.55$); however, attractiveness of partners selected by males ($M = 35.63$, $SD = 10.84$) was significantly lower than those selected by females ($M = 57.50$, $SD = 7.07$) after 4 pints.

DAVEY, G. C. L., ET AL. (2003). *JOURNAL OF BEHAVIOR THERAPY & EXPERIMENTAL PSYCHIATRY, 34,* 141–160.

LABCOAT LENI'S REAL RESEARCH 13.2

Don't forget your toothbrush? ②

We have all experienced that feeling after we have left the house of wondering whether we remembered to lock the door, close the window, or remove the bodies from the fridge in case the police turn up. This behaviour is common; however, people with obsessive compulsive disorder (OCD) tend to check things excessively. They might, for example, check whether they have locked the door so often that it takes them an hour to leave their house.

One theory suggests that this checking behaviour is caused by a combination of the mood you are in (positive or negative) interacting with the rules you use to decide when to stop a task (do you continue until you feel like stopping, or until you have done the task as best

as you can?). Davey, Startup, Zara, MacDonald, and Field (2003) tested this hypothesis by putting people into a negative, positive or no mood (**Mood**) and then asking them to generate as many things as they could that they should check before going on holiday (**Checks**). Within each mood group, half of the participants were instructed to generate as many items as they could, whereas the remainder were asked to generate items for as long as they felt like continuing the task (**Stop_Rule**). The data are in the file **Davey(2003).sav**.

Draw an error bar chart of the data and then conduct the appropriate analysis to test Davey et al.'s hypotheses that (1) people in negative moods who use an 'as many as can' stop rule would generate more items than those using a 'feel like continuing' stop rule; (2) people in a positive mood would generate more items when using a 'feel like continuing' stop rule compared to an 'as many as can' stop rule; (3) in neutral moods, the stop rule used won't have an effect.

Answers are on the companion website (or look at pages 148–149 in the original article).

13.9. Brian's attempt to woo Jane ①

FIGURE 13.17
What Brian learnt from this chapter

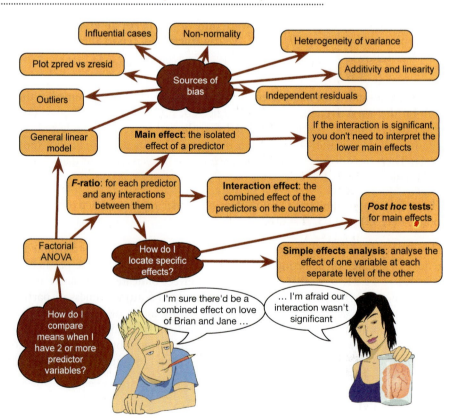

13.10. What next? ②

No sooner had I started my first band than it disintegrated. I went with drummer Mark to sing in a band called the Outlanders, who were much better musically but were not, if the truth be told, metal enough for me. They also sacked me after a very short period of time for not being able to sing like Bono (an insult at the time, but in retrospect …). So, that was two failed bands in very quick succession. You'd have thought that I might have been getting the message that perhaps singing wasn't the thing for me, but actually that message didn't sink in for quite some time (it still hasn't entirely). I needed a new master plan, and one was hatched one evening while walking along a cliff top in Cornwall. Fortunately, it wasn't a plan that involved throwing myself off into the sea …

13.11. Key terms that I've discovered

Beer-goggles effect	Interaction graph	Related factorial design
Factorial ANOVA	Mixed design	Simple effects analysis
Independent factorial design		

13.12. Smart Alex's tasks

- **Task 1**: People's musical tastes tend to change as they get older. My parents, for example, after years of listening to relatively cool music when I was a kid, subsequently hit their mid-forties and developed a worrying obsession with country and western music. This possibility worries me immensely because the future seems incredibly bleak if it is spent listening to Garth Brooks and thinking 'oh boy, did I underestimate Garth's immense talent when I was in my twenties'. So, I thought I'd do some research. I took two groups (**age**): young people (I arbitrarily decided that 'young' meant under 40 years of age) and older people (above 40 years of age). There were 45 people in each group, and I split each group into three smaller groups of 15 and assigned them to listen to Fugazi,[3] ABBA or Barf Grooks[4] (**music**). I got each person to rate it (**liking**) on a scale ranging from −100 (I hate this foul music) through 0 (I am completely indifferent) to +100 (I love this music so much I'm going to explode). The data are in the file **Fugazi.sav**. Conduct a two-way independent ANOVA on them. ②

- **Task 2**: Compute omega squared for the effects in Task 1 and report the results of the analysis. ③

- **Task 3**: In Chapter 3 we used some data that related to men and women's arousal levels when watching either *Bridget Jones's Diary* or *Memento* (**ChickFlick.sav**). Analyse these data to see whether men and women differ in their reactions to different types of films. ②

- **Task 4**: Compute omega squared for the effects in Task 3 and report the results of the analysis. ③

---

[3] See http://www.dischord.com

[4] A lesser-known country musician not to be confused with anyone who has a similar name and produces music that makes you want to barf.

- **Task 5**: In Chapter 3 we used some data that related to learning in men and women when either reinforcement or punishment was used in teaching (**Method Of Teaching. sav**). Analyse these data to see whether men's and women's learning differs according to the teaching method used. ②

- **Task 6**: At the start of this chapter I described a way of empirically researching whether I wrote better songs than my old band mate Malcolm, and whether this depended on the type of song (a symphony or song about flies). The outcome variable would be the number of screams elicited by audience members during the songs. These data are in the file **Escape From Inside.sav**. Draw an error bar graph (lines) and analyse these data. ②

- **Task 7**: Compute omega squared for the effects in Task 6 and report the results of the analysis. ③

- **Task 8**: Using SPSS Tip 13.1, change the syntax in **GogglesSimpleEffects.sps** to look at the effect of alcohol at different levels of gender. ③

- **Task 9**: There are reports of increases in injuries related to playing Nintendo Wii (http://ow.ly/ceWPj). These injuries were attributed mainly to muscle and tendon strains. A researcher hypothesized that a stretching warm-up before playing Wii would help lower injuries, and that athletes would be less susceptible to injuries because their regular activity makes them more flexible. She took 60 athletes and 60 non-athletes (**athlete**): half of them played Wii and half watched others playing as a control (**wii**), and within these groups half did a 5-minute stretch routine before playing/watching whereas the other half did not (**stretch**). The outcome was a pain score out of 10 (where 0 is no pain, and 10 is severe pain) after playing for 4 hours (**injury**). The data are in the file **Wii.sav**. Conduct a three-way ANOVA to test whether athletes are less prone to injury, and whether the prevention programme worked. ③

The answers are on the companion website.

13.13. Further reading

Howell, D. C. (2012). *Statistical methods for psychology* (8th ed.). Belmont, CA: Wadsworth. (Or you might prefer his *Fundamental statistics for the behavioral sciences*. Both are excellent texts.)

Rosenthal, R., Rosnow, R. L., & Rubin, D. B. (2000). *Contrasts and effect sizes in behavioural research: A correlational approach*. Cambridge: Cambridge University Press. (This is quite advanced but really cannot be bettered for contrasts and effect size estimation.)

Rosnow, R. L., & Rosenthal, R. (2005). *Beginning behavioral research: A conceptual primer* (5th ed.). Upper Saddle River, NJ: Pearson/Prentice Hall. (Has some wonderful chapters on ANOVA, with a particular focus on effect size estimation, and some very insightful comments on what interactions actually mean.)

Repeated-measures designs (GLM 4)

14

FIGURE 14.1
Scansion
in the early days;
I used to stare a
lot (L-R: me,
Mark and Mark)

14.1. What will this chapter tell me? ②

At the age of 15, I was on holiday with my friend Mark (the drummer) in Cornwall. I had a pretty decent mullet by this stage (nowadays I just wish I had enough hair to grow a mullet) and had acquired a respectable collection of heavy metal T-shirts from going to various gigs. We were walking along the cliff tops one evening at dusk reminiscing about our times in Andromeda. We came to the conclusion that the only thing we hadn't enjoyed about that band was Malcolm and that maybe we should reform it with a different guitarist.[1] As I was wondering who we could get to play guitar, Mark pointed out the blindingly

---

[1] I feel bad about saying this because Malcolm was a very nice guy and, to be honest, at that age (and some would argue beyond) I could be a bit of a cock.

obvious: I played guitar. So, when we got home Scansion was born.[2] As the singer, guitarist and songwriter I set about writing some songs. I moved away from writing about flies and set my sights on the pointlessness of existence, death, betrayal and so on. We had the dubious honour of being reviewed in the music magazine *Kerrang!* (in a live review they called us 'twee', which is really not what you want to be called if you're trying to make music so heavy that it ruptures the bowels of Satan). Our highlight, however, was playing a gig at the famous Marquee Club in London (this club has closed, not as a result of us playing there I hasten to add, but in its day it started the careers of people like Jimi Hendrix, the Who, Iron Maiden and Led Zeppelin).[3] This was the biggest gig of our career and it was essential that we played like we never had before. As it turned out, we did: I ran on stage, fell over and in the process de-tuned my guitar beyond recognition and broke the zip on my trousers. I spent the whole gig out of tune and spread-eagle to prevent my trousers falling down. Like I said, I'd never played like *that* before. We used to get quite obsessed with comparing how we played at different gigs. I didn't know about statistics then (happy days), but if I had I would have realized that we could rate ourselves and compare the mean ratings for different gigs; because we would always be the ones rating the gigs, this would be a repeated-measures design, so we would need a repeated-measures ANOVA to compare these means. That's what this chapter is about; hopefully it won't make our trousers fall down.

14.2. Introduction to repeated-measures designs ②

So far in this book, when looking at comparing means, we've concentrated on situations in which different entities contribute to different means; for example, different people take part in different experimental conditions. It doesn't have to be different people, it could be different plants, companies, plots of land, viral strains, goats or even different duck-billed platypuses (or whatever the plural is). I've completely ignored situations in which the same people (plants, goats, hamsters, seven-eyed green galactic leaders from space, or whatever) contribute to the different means. I've put it off long enough, and now I'm going to take you through what happens when we do ANOVA on repeated-measures data.

SELF-TEST   What is a repeated-measures design? (Clue: it is described in Chapter 1.)

'Repeated measures' is a term used when the same entities participate in all conditions of an experiment or provide data at multiple time points. For example, you might test the effects of alcohol on enjoyment of a party. Some people can drink a lot of alcohol without really feeling the consequences, whereas others, like myself, have only to sniff a pint of lager and they start flapping around on the floor waving their arms and legs around shouting 'Look at me, I'm Andy, King of the lost world of the Haddocks'. Therefore, it is important to control

---

[2] Scansion is a term for the rhythm of poetry. We got the name by searching through a dictionary until we found a word that we liked. Originally we didn't think it was 'metal' enough, and we decided that any self-respecting heavy metal band needed to have a big spiky 'X' in their name. So, for the first couple of years we spelt it 'Scanxion'. Like I said, I could be a bit of a cock back then.

[3] http://www.themarqueeclub.net

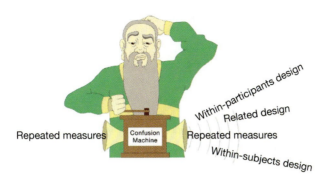

FIGURE 14.2
The confusion
machine has
created many
different ways to
refer to repeated-
measures
designs

for individual differences in tolerance to alcohol, and this can be achieved by testing the same people in all conditions of the experiment: participants could be given a questionnaire assessing their enjoyment of the party after they had consumed 1 pint, 2 pints, 3 pints and 4 pints of lager. There are lots of different ways to refer to this sort of design (Figure 14.2).

We saw in Chapter 1 that this type of design has several advantages; however, in Chapter 11 we saw that the accuracy of the *F*-test in ANOVA depends upon the assumption that scores in different conditions are independent (see Section 11.3). When repeated measures are used this assumption is violated: scores taken under different experimental conditions are likely to be related because they come from the same entities. As such, the conventional *F*-test will lack accuracy. The relationship between scores in different treatment conditions means that we have to make an additional assumption; put simplistically, we assume that the relationship between pairs of experimental conditions is similar (i.e., the level of dependence between experimental conditions is roughly equal). This assumption is called the assumption of **sphericity**, which, trust me, is a pain in the butt to pronounce when you're giving statistics lectures at 9 a.m. on a Monday.

14.2.1. The assumption of sphericity ②

The assumption of sphericity can be likened to the assumption of homogeneity of variance in between-groups ANOVA. Sphericity (denoted by ε and sometimes referred to as *circularity*) is a more general condition of **compound symmetry**. Compound symmetry holds true when both the variances across conditions are equal (this is the same as the homogeneity of variance assumption in between-groups designs) and the covariances between pairs of conditions are equal. So, we assume that the variation within experimental conditions is fairly similar and that no two conditions are any more dependent than any other two. Although compound symmetry has been shown to be a sufficient condition for ANOVA using repeated-measures data, it is not a necessary condition. Sphericity is a less restrictive form of compound symmetry and refers to the equality of variances of the *differences* between treatment levels. So, if you were to take each pair of treatment levels, and calculate the differences between each pair of scores, then it is necessary that these differences have approximately equal variances. As such, *you need at least three conditions for sphericity to be an issue.*

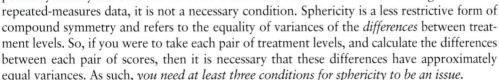

What is sphericity?

14.2.2. How is sphericity measured? ②

If we were going to check the assumption of sphericity by hand, which incidentally only a complete lunatic would do, then we could start by calculating the differences between pairs

TABLE 14.1 Hypothetical data to illustrate the calculation of the variance of the differences between conditions

Condition A	Condition B	Condition C	A−B	A−C	B−C
10	12	8	−2	2	4
15	15	12	0	3	3
25	30	20	−5	5	10
35	30	28	5	7	2
30	27	20	3	10	7
		Variance:	15.7	10.3	10.7

of scores in all combinations of the treatment levels. Once this has been done, we could calculate the variance of these differences. Table 14.1 shows data from an experiment with three conditions. The differences between pairs of scores are computed for each participant and the variance for each set of differences is calculated. Sphericity is met when these variances are roughly equal. For these data, sphericity will hold when:

$$\text{variance}_{A-B} \approx \text{variance}_{A-C} \approx \text{variance}_{B-C}$$

In these data there is some deviation from sphericity because the variance of the differences between conditions A and B (15.7) is greater than the variance of the differences between A and C (10.3) and between B and C (10.7). However, these data have *local circularity* (or local sphericity) because two of the variances of differences are very similar. Therefore, the sphericity assumption has been met for any multiple comparisons involving these conditions (for a discussion of local circularity see Rouanet & Lépine, 1970). The deviation from sphericity in the data in Table 14.1 does not seem too severe (all variances are *roughly* equal), but can we assess whether a deviation is severe enough to warrant action?

14.2.3. Assessing the severity of departures from sphericity ②

Sphericity can be assessed using **Mauchly's test**, which tests the hypothesis that the variances of the differences between conditions are equal. Therefore, if Mauchly's test statistic is significant (i.e., has a probability value less than .05) we conclude that there are significant differences between the variances of differences and, therefore, the condition of sphericity is not met. If, however, Mauchly's test statistic is non-significant (i.e., $p > .05$) then it is reasonable to conclude that the variances of differences are roughly equal. So, in short, if Mauchly's test is significant then we must be wary of the resulting F-ratios. However, like any significance test, Mauchly's test depends upon sample size: in big samples small deviations from sphericity can be significant, and in small samples large violations can be non-significant (see Jane Superbrain Box 5.5).

14.2.4. What is the effect of violating the assumption of sphericity? ③

Rouanet and Lépine (1970) provided a detailed account of the validity of the F-ratio under violations of the sphericity assumption (see also Mendoza, Toothaker, & Crain, 1976).

I summarized (Field, 1998) their findings in an article in a very obscure newsletter that no one can ever access (see Oliver Twisted). The take-home message is that for the F-ratio that we use in these situations, sphericity creates a loss of power and a test statistic that doesn't have the distribution that it's supposed to have (i.e., an F-distribution).

Sphericity also causes some amusing complications for *post hoc* tests (Jane Superbrain Box 14.1). If you don't want to worry about what these complications are then the take-home message is that when sphericity is violated, the Bonferroni method seems to be generally the most robust of the univariate techniques, especially in terms of power and control of the Type I error rate. When sphericity is definitely not violated, Tukey's test can be used.

OLIVER TWISTED

Please, Sir, can I have some more … sphericity?

'Balls …', says Oliver, '… are spherical, and I like balls. Maybe I'll like sphericity too if only you could explain it to me in more detail.' Be careful what you wish for, Oliver. In my youth I wrote an article called 'A bluffer's guide to sphericity', which I used to cite in this book, roughly on this page. Occasionally people ask me for it, so I thought I might as well reproduce it in the additional material for this chapter.

JANE SUPERBRAIN 14.1

Sphericity and post hoc *tests* ③

The violation of sphericity has implications for multiple comparisons. Again I summarize these in more detail online (see Oliver Twisted), but I have a few take-home messages here. Boik (1981) provided an estimable account of the effects of non-sphericity on *post hoc* tests in repeated-measures designs, and concluded that even very small departures from sphericity produce large biases in the F-test. He recommends against using these tests for repeated-measure contrasts. Maxwell (1980) systematically tested the power and alpha levels for five *post hoc* tests under repeated-measures conditions. The tests assessed were Tukey's wholly significant difference (WSD) test; Tukey's procedure but with a separate error term with either $(n - 1)$ df (labelled SEP1) or $(n - 1)(k - 1)$ df (labelled SEP2); Bonferroni's procedure (BON); and a multivariate approach, the Roy–Bose simultaneous confidence interval (SCI). He found that the multivariate approach was always 'too conservative for practical use' (p. 277) and this was most extreme when n (the number of participants) is small relative to k (the number of conditions). All variants of Tukey's test inflated the alpha rate unacceptably with increasing departures from sphericity. The Bonferroni method, however, was extremely robust (although *slightly* conservative) and controlled alpha levels regardless of the manipulation.

In terms of test power (the Type II error rate), Maxwell found WSD to be most powerful under conditions of non-sphericity in very small samples ($n = 8$) but this advantage was severely reduced in even slightly larger samples ($n = 15$). Keselman and Keselman (1988) extended Maxwell's work within unbalanced designs. They concluded that 'as the number of repeated treatment levels increases, BON is substantially more powerful than SCI' (p. 223). Therefore, although I've simplified the results somewhat, in terms of Type I error rates and power the Bonferroni method has much to recommend it.

14.2.5. What do you do if you violate sphericity? ②

You might think that if your data violate the sphericity assumption then you need to have a nervous breakdown, or book in to see a counsellor or something, but actually it just means that we need to adjust the degrees of freedom for any *F*-ratios affected by the violation. You can estimate sphericity in various ways (see below), resulting in a value that is 1 when your data are spherical and less than 1 when they are not. You multiply the degrees of freedom by this estimate, so when you have sphericity the degrees of freedom don't change (because you multiply them by 1) but when you don't the degrees of freedom decrease (because you multiply them by a value less than 1). Smaller degrees of freedom make the *p*-value associated with the *F*-ratio less significant. Therefore, by adjusting the degrees of freedom, we make the *F*-ratio more conservative when sphericity is violated. In doing so, we control the Type I error rate, which I was panicking about in the previous section.

The degrees of freedom are adjusted using estimates of sphericity advocated by Greenhouse and Geisser (1959) and Huynh and Feldt (1976). The calculation of these estimates is beyond the scope of this book (interested readers should consult Girden, 1992); we need know only that the three estimates differ. The **Greenhouse–Geisser estimate** (usually denoted as $\hat{\varepsilon}$) varies between $1/(k-1)$, where k is the number of repeated-measures conditions, and 1. For example, in a situation in which there are five conditions the lower limit of $\hat{\varepsilon}$ will be $1/(5-1)$, or .25 (known as the **lower-bound estimate** of sphericity).

Huynh and Feldt (1976) reported that when the Greenhouse–Geisser estimate is greater than .75 the correction is too conservative, and this can also be true when the sphericity estimate is as high as .90 (Collier, Baker, Mandeville, & Hayes, 1967). Huynh and Feldt, therefore, proposed their own less conservative correction (usually denoted as $\tilde{\varepsilon}$). However, $\tilde{\varepsilon}$ overestimates sphericity (Maxwell & Delaney, 1990). Many authors recommend that when estimates of sphericity are greater than .75 the **Huynh–Feldt estimate** should be used, but when the Greenhouse–Geisser estimate of sphericity is less than .75 or nothing is known about sphericity at all the Greenhouse–Geisser correction should be used (Barcikowski & Robey, 1984; Girden, 1992; Huynh & Feldt, 1976). Alternatively, Stevens (2002) suggests taking an average of the two estimates and adjusting the *df* by this average. We will see how these values are used in due course.

Given that violations of sphericity affect the accuracy of *F*, a second option when you have data that violate sphericity is to use a test other than *F*. The first possibility is to use multivariate test statistics (MANOVA), because they are not dependent upon the assumption of sphericity (see O'Brien & Kaiser, 1985). MANOVA is covered in Chapter 16, but SPSS produces multivariate test statistics in the context of repeated-measures ANOVA. However, there may be trade-offs in power between these univariate and multivariate tests (see Jane Superbrain Box 14.2). A more complex possibility is to analyse the data as a multilevel model (described in detail in Chapter 20).

14.3. Theory of one-way repeated-measures ANOVA ②

In a repeated-measures ANOVA the effect of our experiment is shown up in the within-participant variance (rather than in the between-groups variance). Remember that in independent ANOVA (Section 11.2) the within-participant variance is the residual variance (SS_R); it is the variance created by individual differences in performance. This variance is not contaminated by the experimental effect, because whatever manipulation we've

JANE SUPERBRAIN 14.2

Power in ANOVA and MANOVA ③

There is a trade-off in test power between univariate and multivariate approaches. Davidson (1972) compared the power of adjusted univariate techniques with those of Hotelling's T^2 (a MANOVA test statistic) and found that the univariate technique was relatively powerless to detect small reliable changes between highly correlated conditions when other less correlated conditions were also present. Mendoza, Toothaker, and Nicewander (1974) compared univariate and multivariate techniques under violations of compound symmetry (i.e., sphericity) and normality and found that as the degree of violation of compound symmetry increased the power of multivariate tests also increased whereas the power for univariate tests decreased. However, univariate tests tend to be more powerful than multivariate ones in small samples; Maxwell and Delaney (1990) noted that 'the multivariate approach should probably not be used if n is less than $a + 10$ (a is the number of levels for repeated measures)' (p. 602). To sum up, when you have a large violation of sphericity ($\varepsilon < .7$) and your sample size is greater than $a + 10$ then multivariate procedures are more powerful, but with small sample sizes or when sphericity holds ($\varepsilon > .7$) the univariate approach is preferred (Stevens, 2002). It is also worth noting that the power of MANOVA varies as a function of the correlations between dependent variables (see Jane Superbrain Box 16.1) and so the relationship between treatment conditions must be considered.

carried out has been done on different entities. However, when we carry out our experimental manipulation on the same entities the within-participant variance will be made up of two things: the effect of our manipulation and, as before, individual differences in performance. So, some of the within-participant variation comes from the effects of our experimental manipulation: we did different things in each experimental condition to the participants, and so variation in an individual's scores will partly be due to these manipulations. For example, if everyone scores higher in one condition than another, it's reasonable to assume that this happened because we did something different to the participants in that condition compared to the others. By doing the *same* thing to every participant within a particular condition, any variation that cannot be explained by the manipulation we've carried out must be due to random factors outside our control, unrelated to our experimental manipulations (we could call this 'error'). As in independent ANOVA, we use an F-ratio that compares the size of the variation due to our experimental manipulations to the size of the variation due to random factors; the only difference is in the way we calculate these variances. If the variance due to our manipulations is big relative to the variation due to random factors, we get a big value of F, and we can conclude that the observed results are unlikely to have occurred if there was no effect in the population.

Figure 14.3 shows how the variance is partitioned in a repeated-measures ANOVA. The important thing to note is that we have the same types of variances as in independent ANOVA: we have a total sum of squares (SS_T), a model sum of squares (SS_M) and a residual sum of squares (SS_R). The *only* difference between repeated-measures and independent ANOVA is from where those sums of squares come: in repeated-measures ANOVA the model and residual sums of squares are both part of the within-participant variance. Let's have a look at an example.

I'm a Celebrity, Get Me Out of Here! is a TV show in which celebrities (well, they're not really celebrities as such, more like ex-celebrities), in a pitiful attempt to salvage their careers (or just have careers in the first place), go and live in the jungle in Australia for a few weeks.

FIGURE 14.3
Partitioning
variance for
repeated-
measures
ANOVA

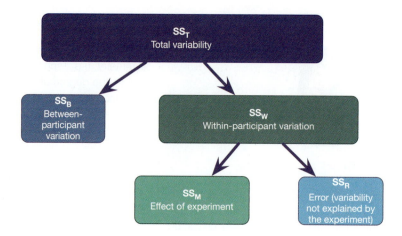

During the show these contestants have to do various humiliating and degrading tasks to win food for their camp mates. These tasks invariably involve creepy-crawlies in places where creepy-crawlies shouldn't go; for example, you might be locked in a coffin full of rats, forced to put your head in a bowl of large spiders, or have eels and cockroaches poured onto you. It's cruel, voyeuristic, gratuitous, car-crash TV, and I love it. As a vegetarian, a particular favourite task for me is the bushtucker trials in which the celebrities have to eat things like live stick insects, witchetty grubs, fish eyes and kangaroo testicles/penises. Honestly, seeing a fish eye exploding in someone's mouth scars your mental image of them for ever. I've often wondered (perhaps a little too much) which of the bushtucker foods is the most revolting. Imagine that I tested this idea by getting eight celebrities, and forcing them to eat four different animals (the aforementioned stick insect, kangaroo testicle, fish eye and witchetty grub) in counterbalanced order. On each occasion I measured the time it took the celebrity to retch, in seconds. This is a repeated-measures design because every celebrity eats every food. The independent variable was the type of food eaten and the dependent variable was the time taken to retch.

Table 14.2 shows the data for this example. There were four foods, each eaten by eight different celebrities. Their times taken to retch are shown in the table. In addition, the mean amount of time to retch for each celebrity is shown in the table (and the variance in the time taken to retch), and also the mean time to retch for each food. The total variance in retching time will, in part, be caused by the fact that different animals are more or less palatable (the manipulation), and will, in part, be caused by the fact that the celebrities themselves will differ in their constitution (individual differences).

TABLE 14.2   Data for the bushtucker example

Celebrity	Stick Insect	Kangaroo Testicle	Fish Eye	Witchetty Grub	Mean	s^2
1	8	7	1	6	5.50	9.67
2	9	5	2	5	5.25	8.25
3	6	2	3	8	4.75	7.58
4	5	3	1	9	4.50	11.67
5	8	4	5	8	6.25	4.25
6	7	5	6	7	6.25	0.92
7	10	2	7	2	5.25	15.58
8	12	6	8	1	6.75	20.92
Mean	8.13	4.25	4.13	5.75		

14.3.1. The total sum of squares, SS$_T$ ②

Remember from one-way independent ANOVA that SS$_T$ is calculated using the following equation:

$$SS_T = s_{grand}^2 (N - 1)$$

In repeated-measures designs the total sum of squares is calculated in exactly the same way. The grand variance in the equation is simply the variance of all scores when we ignore the group to which they belong. So if we treated the data as one big group it would look like Figure 14.4. The variance of these scores is 8.19 (try this on your calculator). We used 32 scores to generate this value, so N is 32. As such the equation becomes:

$$SS_T = s_{grand}^2 (N - 1)$$

$$= 8.19 (32 - 1)$$

$$= 253.89$$

The degrees of freedom for this sum of squares, as with the independent ANOVA, will be $N - 1$, or 31.

8	7	1	6
9	5	2	5
6	2	3	8
5	3	1	9
8	4	5	8
7	5	6	7
10	2	7	2
12	6	8	1

Grand Mean = 5.56
Grand Variance = 8.19

FIGURE 14.4
Treating the data as a single group

14.3.2. The within-participant sum of squares, SS$_W$ ②

The crucial difference in a repeated-measures design is the variance component called the within-participant variance, which represents individual differences within participants. When we looked at independent ANOVA we calculated individual differences as the residual sum of squares (SS$_R$) using equation (11.6):

$$SS_R = \sum_{i=1}^{n} (x_i - \bar{x}_i)^2$$

$$= s^2 (n - 1)$$

In an independent design we had different participants within each condition, so we needed to calculate this value within each condition and then add these values to give us a total:

$$SS_R = s_{group1}^2 (n_1 - 1) + s_{group\ 2}^2 (n_2 - 1) + s_{group\ 3}^2 (n_3 - 1) + \cdots + s_{group\ n}^2 (n_n - 1)$$

We do much the same thing in a repeated-measures design except that because we've subjected entities to more than one experimental condition, we're interested in the variation not within a group of entities (as in independent ANOVA) but within an entity. Therefore, we use the same equation but adapt it to look at participants rather than groups. So, if we call this sum of squares SS_W (for within-participant SS) we could write it as:

$$SS_W = s_{entity\ 1}^2 (n_1 - 1) + s_{entity\ 2}^2 (n_2 - 1) + s_{entity\ 3}^2 (n_3 - 1) + \cdots + s_{entity\ n}^2 (n_n - 1)$$

This equation means that we are looking at the variation in an individual's scores and then adding these variances for all the people in the study. The ns represent the number of scores on which the variances are based (i.e., the number of experimental conditions, or in this case the number of foods). All of the variances we need are in Table 14.2, so we can calculate SS_W as:

$$
\begin{aligned}
SS_W &= s_{Celebrity\ 1}^2 (n_1 - 1) + s_{Celebrity\ 2}^2 (n_2 - 1) + \ldots + s_{Celebrity\ n}^2 (n_n - 1) \\
&= 9.67(4-1) + 8.25(4-1) + 7.58(4-1) + 11.67(4-1) + 4.25(4-1) \\
&\quad + 0.92(4-1) + 15.58(4-1) + 20.92(4-1) \\
&= 29 + 24.75 + 22.75 + 35 + 12.75 + 2.75 + 46.75 + 62.75 \\
&= 236.50
\end{aligned}
$$

The degrees of freedom for each person are $n - 1$ (i.e., the number of conditions minus 1). To get the total degrees of freedom we add the dfs for all participants. So, with eight participants (celebrities) and four conditions (i.e., $n = 4$), there are 3 degrees of freedom for each celebrity and $8 \times 3 = 24$ degrees of freedom in total.

14.3.3. The model sum of squares, SS_M ②

So far, we know that the total amount of variation within the data is 253.58 units. We also know that 236.50 of those units are explained by the variance created by individuals' (celebrities') performances under different conditions. Some of this variation is the result of our experimental manipulation and some of this variation is random fluctuation. The next step is to work out how much variance is explained by our manipulation and how much is not.

In independent ANOVA, we worked out how much variation could be explained by our experiment (the model sum of squares) by looking at the means for each group and comparing these to the overall mean. So, we measured the variance resulting from the differences between group means and the overall mean (see equation (11.4)). We do exactly the same thing with a repeated-measures design:

$$SS_M = \sum_{k=1}^{k} n_k \left(\bar{x}_k - \bar{x}_{grand} \right)^2$$

Using the means from the bushtucker data (see Table 14.2), we can calculate SS_M as follows:

$$SS_M = 8(8.13 - 5.56)^2 + 8(4.25 - 5.56)^2 + 8(4.13 - 5.56)^2 + 8(5.75 - 5.56)^2$$

$$= 8(8.13 - 5.56)^2 + 8(4.25 - 5.56)^2 + 8(4.13 - 5.56)^2 + 8(5.75 - 5.56)^2$$

$$= 8(2.57)^2 + 8(-1.31)^2 + 8(-1.44)^2 + 8(0.196)^2$$

$$= 83.13$$

For SS_M, the degrees of freedom (df_M) are one less than the number of things used to calculate the sum of squares. We calculated the sum of squared errors using four means, therefore, the degrees of freedom will be 3. So, as with independent ANOVA the model degrees of freedom are always the number of conditions (k) minus 1:

$$df_M = k - 1 = 3$$

14.3.4. The residual sum of squares, SS_R ②

We now know that there are 253.58 units of variation to be explained in our data, and that the variation across our conditions accounts for 236.50 units. Of these 236.50 units, our experimental manipulation can explain 83.13 units. The final sum of squares is the residual sum of squares (SS_R), which tells us how much of the variation cannot be explained by the model. This value is the amount of variation caused by extraneous factors outside experimental control. Knowing SS_W and SS_M already, the simplest way to calculate SS_R is to subtract SS_M from SS_W:

$$SS_R = SS_W - SS_M$$

$$= 236.50 - 83.13$$

$$= 153.37$$

The degrees of freedom are calculated in a similar way:

$$df_R = df_W - df_M$$

$$= 24 - 3$$

$$= 21$$

14.3.5. The mean squares ②

SS_M tells us how much variation the model (e.g., the experimental manipulation) explains and SS_R tells us how much variation is due to extraneous factors. However, because both of these values are summed values, the number of scores that were summed influences them. As with independent ANOVA we eliminate this bias by calculating the average sum of squares (the *mean square*, MS), which is the sum of squares divided by the degrees of freedom:

$$MS_M = \frac{SS_M}{df_M} = \frac{83.13}{3} = 27.71$$

$$MS_R = \frac{SS_R}{df_R} = \frac{153.37}{21} = 7.30$$

MS_M represents the average amount of variation explained by the model (e.g., the systematic variation), whereas MS_R is a gauge of the average amount of variation explained by extraneous variables (the unsystematic variation).

14.3.6. The *F*-ratio ②

The *F*-ratio is a measure of the ratio of the variation explained by the model and the variation explained by unsystematic factors. It can be calculated by dividing the model mean square by the residual mean square. You should recall that this is exactly the same as for independent ANOVA:

$$F = \frac{MS_M}{MS_R}$$

So, as with the independent ANOVA, the *F*-ratio is still the ratio of systematic variation to unsystematic variation. As such, it is the ratio of the experimental effect to the effect on performance of unexplained factors. For the bushtucker data, the *F*-ratio is:

$$F = \frac{MS_M}{MS_R} = \frac{27.71}{7.30} = 3.79$$

This value is greater than 1, which indicates that the experimental manipulation had some effect above and beyond the effect of extraneous factors. As with independent ANOVA, this value can be compared against a critical value based on its degrees of freedom (which are df_M and df_R, which are 3 and 21 in this case).

14.3.7. The between-participants sum of squares ②

I mentioned that the total variation is broken down into a within-participant variation and a between-participants variation. We sort of forgot about the between-participants variation because we didn't need it to calculate the *F*-ratio. However, I will just briefly mention what it represents. The easiest way to calculate this term is by subtraction, because we know from Figure 14.3 that:

$$SS_T = SS_B + SS_W$$

We have already calculated SS_W and SS_T so by rearranging the equation and replacing the values of these terms, we get:

$$SS_B = SS_T - SS_W$$
$$= 253.89 - 236.50$$
$$= 17.39$$

This term represents individual differences between cases. So, in this example, different celebrities will have different tolerances for these sorts of food. This is shown by the means for the celebrities in Table 13.2. For example, celebrity 4 ($M = 4.50$) was, on average, more than 2 seconds quicker to retch than participant 8 ($M = 6.75$). Celebrity 8 had a better constitution than celebrity 4. The between-participants sum of squares reflects these differences between individuals. In this case only 17.39 units of variation in the times to retch can be explained by individual differences between our celebrities.

EVERYBODY

14.4. Assumptions in repeated-measures ANOVA ③

In addition to sphericity, because repeated-measures ANOVA is an extension of the linear model all of the sources of potential bias (and counteractive measures) discussed in Chapter 5 apply (see Section 5.4, for example). If these measures don't help then when you have only one independent variable you can use Friedman's ANOVA, which we discussed in Chapter 6. However, for factorial repeated-measures designs there is not a non-parametric counterpart. You will also discover that the Bootstrap... button is noticeable by its absence in the dialog box for repeated-measures ANOVA in SPSS. In fact, I haven't been able to find a robust version of the factorial repeated-measures design (not even in Wilcox's excellent book). So, in short, if the suggestions for overcoming bias in Chapter 5 don't help, then you're stuffed.

14.5. One-way repeated-measures ANOVA using SPSS ②

14.5.1. Repeated-measures ANOVA: the general procedure ②

The general procedure for repeated-measures ANOVA is much the same as for any other linear model, so remind yourself of the general procedure in Chapter 8. Figure 14.5 shows a simple overview that highlights some of the specific issues when using repeated measures.

14.5.2. The main analysis ②

Sticking with the bushtucker example, we know that *each row of the data editor should represent data from one entity, while each column represents a level of a variable* (SPSS Tip 3.2). Therefore, separate columns represent levels of a repeated-measure variable. As such, the data can be entered into the SPSS data editor in the same format as Table 14.2 (you don't need to include the columns labelled *Celebrity*, *Mean* or s^2 because they were included only to help me explain how this ANOVA is calculated). To begin with, create a

FIGURE 14.5
The process for conducting repeated-measures ANOVA

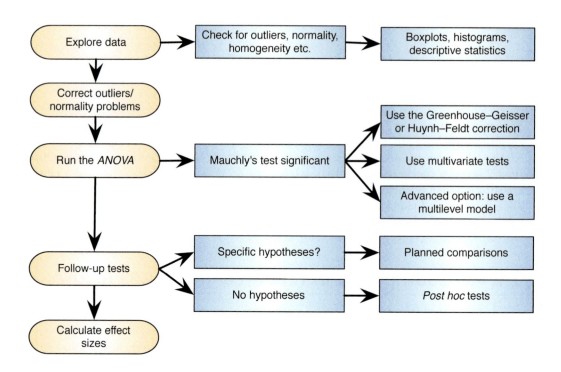

variable called **stick** and use the *Labels* dialog box to give this variable the full title 'Stick Insect'. In the next column, create a variable called **testicle**, and give this variable the full title 'Kangaroo Testicle'. The principle should now be clear: apply it to create the remaining variables called **eye** ('Fish Eye') and **witchetty** ('Witchetty Grub'). These data can also be found in the file **Bushtucker.sav**.

To conduct an ANOVA using a repeated-measures design, activate the *Define Factor(s)* dialog box by selecting Analyze General Linear Model ▸ GLM Repeated Measures… . In this dialog box (Figure 14.6), you are asked to supply a name for the within-subject (repeated-measures) variable. In this case the repeated-measures variable was the type of animal eaten in the bushtucker trial, so replace the word *factor1* with the word *Animal*. The name you give to the repeated-measures variable cannot have spaces in it. When you have given the repeated-measures factor a name, you have to tell SPSS how many levels there were to that variable (i.e., how many experimental conditions there were). In this case, there were four different animals eaten by each person, so enter the number 4 into the box labelled *Number of Levels*. Click on Add to add this variable to the list of repeated-measures variables. This variable will now appear in the white box at the bottom of the dialog box as *Animal (4)*. If your design has several repeated-measures variables then you can add more factors to the list (see the two-way ANOVA example below). When you have entered all of the repeated-measures factors that were measured click on Define to go to the main *Repeated Measures* dialog box.

The main dialog box (Figure 14.7) has a space labelled *Within-Subjects Variables* that contains a list of four question marks followed by a number. These question marks are for the variables representing the four levels of the independent variable. The variables corresponding to these levels should be selected and placed in the appropriate space. We have only four variables in the data editor, so it is possible to select all four variables at once (by clicking on the variable at the top, pressing the *Shift* key and then clicking on the last variable that you want to select). The selected variables can then be dragged to the box labelled *Within-Subjects Variables* (or click on ➡). When all four variables have been transferred, you can select various options for the analysis. There are several options that can be accessed with the buttons at the side of the main dialog box. These options are similar to the ones we have already encountered.

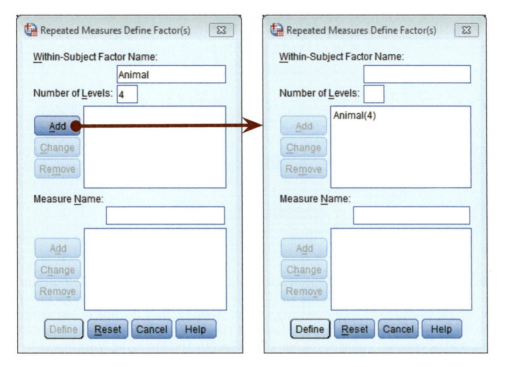

FIGURE 14.6
The *Define Factor(s)* dialog box for repeated-measures ANOVA

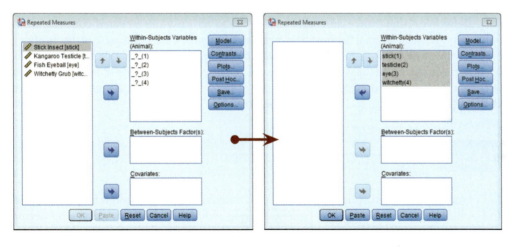

FIGURE 14.7
The main dialog box for repeated-measures ANOVA (before and after completion)

14.5.3. Defining contrasts for repeated measures ②

It is not possible to specify user-defined planned comparisons for repeated-measures designs in SPSS.[4] However, there is the option to conduct one of the many standard contrasts that we have come across previously (see Section 12.4.5 for details of changing contrasts). If you click on *Contrasts...* in the main dialog box you can access the *Contrasts* dialog box (Figure 14.8). The default contrast is a polynomial contrast, but to change this default

---

[4] Actually, as I mentioned in the previous chapter, you can, but only using SPSS syntax. Those who are not already feeling like sticking their head in an industrial-sized mincing machine can read the Oliver Twisted box in Chapter 13. Those who do feel like sticking their head in the aforementioned mincing machine can read it as well: it will have much the same effect (at least it did on me).

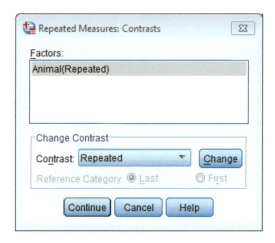

select a variable in the box labelled *Factors*, click on <kbd>Polynomial ▼</kbd>, select a contrast from the list and then click on <kbd>Change</kbd>. If you choose to conduct a simple contrast then you can specify whether you would like to compare groups against the first or last category. The first category would be the one entered as (1) in the main dialog box and, for these data, the last category would be the one entered as (4). Therefore, the order in which you enter variables in the main dialog box is important for the contrasts you choose.

There is no particularly good contrast for the data we have (the simple contrast is not very useful because we have no control category) so let's use the *repeated* contrast, which will compare each animal against the previous animal. This contrast can be useful in repeated-measures designs in which the levels of the independent variable have a meaning-ful order. An example is if you have measured the dependent variable at successive points in time, or administered increasing doses of a drug. When you have selected this contrast, click on <kbd>Continue</kbd> to return to the main dialog box.

14.5.4. *Post hoc* tests and additional options ③

As I've mentioned before, sphericity creates some entertaining complications for *post hoc* tests, and with respect to controlling the Type I error rate and having decent power the Bonferroni method fares pretty well (see Jane Superbrain Box 14.1).[5] When sphericity is definitely not violated, Tukey's test can be used, but if sphericity can't be assumed then the Games–Howell procedure, which uses a pooled error term, is preferable to Tukey's test. These sphericity-related complications mean that the standard *post hoc* tests that we have seen for independent designs are not available for repeated-measures analyses (you will find that if you access the dialog box for *post hoc* tests it will not list any repeated-measured factors).

The good news, though, is that you can do some basic *post hoc* procedures through the additional options. These options can be accessed by clicking on <kbd>Options...</kbd> in the main dialog box to open the *Options* dialog box (Figure 14.9). To specify *post hoc* tests, select the repeated-measures variable (in this case **Animal**) from the box labelled *Estimated Marginal Means: Factor(s) and Factor Interactions* and drag it to the box labelled *Display Means for* (or click on <kbd>➡</kbd>). Once a variable has been transferred, you will be able to select ☑ C̲ompare main effects. Once this option is selected, the box labelled *Confidence interval adjustment* becomes active and you can click on <kbd>LSD(none) ▼</kbd> to see a choice of three

---

[5] I also recommend David Howell's excellent discussion of *post hoc* tests in repeated-measures designs (http://www.uvm.edu/~dhowell/StatPages/More_Stuff/RepMeasMultComp/RepMeasMultComp.html).

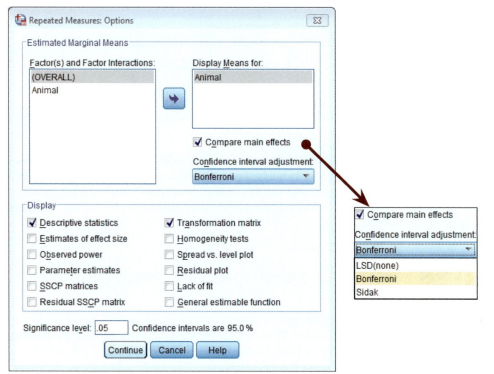

FIGURE 14.9
The *Options*
dialog box

adjustment levels. The default is to have no adjustment and simply perform a Tukey LSD *post hoc* test (this is not recommended). The second option is a Bonferroni correction (recommended for the reasons already mentioned), and the final option is a Šidák correction, which should be selected if you are concerned about the loss of power associated with Bonferroni corrected values.

The *Options* dialog box (Figure 14.9) has other useful options too. You can ask for descriptive statistics, which will provide the means, standard deviations and number of participants for each level of the independent variable. You can also ask for a transformation matrix, which provides the coding values for any contrast selected in the *Contrasts* dialog box (Figure 14.8) and is very useful for interpreting the contrasts in more complex designs. SPSS can also be asked to print out the hypothesis, error and residual sum of squares and cross-product matrices (SSCPs; see Chapter 16). You only need to bother with the option for homogeneity of variance tests when there is a between-groups factor as well (mixed designs – see the next chapter). You can also change the level of significance at which to test any *post hoc* tests; generally, the .05 level is acceptable. When you have selected the options of interest, click on Continue to return to the main dialog box, and then click on OK to run the analysis.

14.6. Output for one-way repeated-measures ANOVA ②

14.6.1. Descriptives and other diagnostics ①

Output 14.1 shows the initial diagnostics statistics. First, we are told the variables that represent each level of the independent variable. This box is useful to check that the variables

OUTPUT 14.1

Within–Subjects Factors

Measure: MEASURE_1

Animal	Dependent Variable
1	stick
2	testicle
3	eye
4	witchetty

Descriptive Statistics

	Mean	Std. Deviation	N
Stick Insect	8.13	2.232	8
Kangaroo Testicle	4.25	1.832	8
Fish Eyeball	4.13	2.748	8
Witchetty Grub	5.75	2.915	8

were entered in the correct order. The next table provides basic descriptive statistics for the four levels of the independent variable. From this table we can see that, on average, the time taken to retch was longest after eating the stick insect, and shortest after eating a testicle or eyeball. These mean values are useful for interpreting any effects that may emerge from the main analysis.

14.6.2 Assessing and correcting for sphericity: Mauchly's test ②

In Section 14.2.3 you were told that to assume sphericity Mauchly's test (see also SPSS Tip 14.1) should be non-significant. Output 14.2 shows Mauchly's test for the bushtucker data; sadly, the significance value (.047) is less than the critical value of .05, which means that the assumption of sphericity has been violated. The table also tells us the estimates of sphericity: the Greenhouse–Geisser estimate, $\hat{\varepsilon} = 0.533$, and the Huynh–Feldt estimate, $\tilde{\varepsilon} = .666$. To put these values into context, if the data are perfectly spherical then these estimates will be 1. For the Greenhouse–Geisser estimate, the lowest possible value is $1/(k-1)$, which with four conditions will be $1/(4-1) = 0.33$ (which is given as the lower-bound estimate in Output 14.2). The Greenhouse–Geisser estimate is closer to its lower limit of 0.33 than to the upper limit of 1, so we have a substantial deviation from sphericity. These estimates are used to correct the degrees of freedom for the F-ratio in the main part of the output (Jane Superbrain Box 14.3).

OUTPUT 14.2

Mauchly's Test of Sphericity[a]

Measure: MEASURE_1

Within Subjects Effect	Mauchly's W	Approx. Chi–Square	df	Sig.	Epsilon[b] Greenhouse–Geisser	Huynh–Feldt	Lower–bound
Animal	.136	11.406	5	.047	.533	.666	.333

Tests the null hypothesis that the error covariance matrix of the orthonormalized transformed dependent variables is proportional to an identity matrix.

a. Design: Intercept
   Within Subjects Design: Animal

b. May be used to adjust the degrees of freedom for the averaged tests of significance. Corrected tests are displayed in the Tests of Within–Subjects Effects table.

14.6.3. The main ANOVA ②

Output 14.4 shows the results of the ANOVA for the within-subject variable. This table can be read in much the same as for one-way between-group ANOVA (see Chapter 11). There is a sum of squares for the repeated-measures effect of **Animal**, which tells us how much of the total variability is explained by the experimental effect. Note the value of 83.13, which is the model sum of squares (SS_M) that we calculated in Section 14.3.3. There is also

SPSS TIP 14.1   My Mauchly's test looks weird ②

Sometimes the SPSS output for Mauchly's test looks strange: when you look at the significance, all you see is a dot. There is no significance value. This is the case in Output 14.3, which is from an ANOVA done comparing only the stick insect and kangaroo testicle conditions of our current example. Naturally, you fear that SPSS has gone crazy and is going to break into your bedroom at night and tattoo the equation for the Greenhouse–Geisser correction on your face. The reason why this happens is that (as I mentioned in Section 14.2.1) you need at least three conditions for sphericity to be an issue (read that section if you want to know why). Therefore, if you have a repeated-measures variable that has only two levels then sphericity is met. Hence, the estimates computed by SPSS are 1 (perfect sphericity) and the resulting significance test cannot be computed (hence the table has a value of 0 for the chi-square test and degrees of freedom and a blank space for the significance). It would be a lot easier if SPSS just didn't produce the table, but then I guess we'd all be confused about why the table hadn't appeared; maybe it should just print in big letters 'Hooray! Hooray! Sphericity has gone away!' We can dream.

Mauchly's Test of Sphericity[a]

Measure: MEASURE_1

Within Subjects Effect	Mauchly's W	Approx. Chi–Square	df	Sig.	Epsilon[b]		
					Greenhouse–Geisser	Huynh–Feldt	Lower-bound
Animal	1.000	.000	0	.	1.000	1.000	1.000

Tests the null hypothesis that the error covariance matrix of the orthonormalized transformed dependent variables is proportional to an identity matrix.

   a. Design: Intercept
       Within Subjects Design: Animal

   b. May be used to adjust the degrees of freedom for the averaged tests of significance. Corrected tests are displayed
      in the Tests of Within–Subjects Effects table.

OUTPUT 14.3

an error term, which is the amount of unexplained variation across the conditions of the repeated-measures variable. This value is 153.38, which is the residual sum of squares (SS_R) value that was calculated in Section 14.3.4. As I explained earlier, these sums of squares are converted into mean squares by dividing by the degrees of freedom. The F-ratio is obtained by dividing the mean squares for the experimental effect (27.71) by the error mean squares (7.30). As with between-group ANOVA, this test statistic represents the ratio of systematic variance to unsystematic variance. The value of $F = 3.79$ (the same as we calculated earlier) is then compared against a critical value for 3 and 21 degrees of freedom. SPSS displays the exact significance level for the F-ratio. The significance of F is .026, which is significant because it is less than the criterion value of .05. Based on this part of the table we would conclude that there was a significant difference between the four animals in their capacity to induce retching when eaten. However, this main test does not tell us which animals differed from each other.

Although this result seems plausible, we have learnt that violating the sphericity assumption makes the F-test inaccurate. We also know from Output 14.2 that we violated the assumption. As well as showing the F-ratio and associated degrees of freedom when sphericity is assumed, Output 14.4 also shows the results adjusted for the effect of sphericity. There are three possible adjustments based on the three estimates of sphericity in Output 14.2 (Greenhouse–Geisser, Huynh–Feldt, and the lower-bound value). These estimates

OUTPUT 14.4

Tests of Within-Subjects Effects

Measure: MEASURE_1

Source		Type III Sum of Squares	df	Mean Square	F	Sig.
Animal	Sphericity Assumed	83.125	3	27.708	3.794	.026
	Greenhouse–Geisser	83.125	1.599	52.001	3.794	.063
	Huynh–Feldt	83.125	1.997	41.619	3.794	.048
	Lower-bound	83.125	1.000	83.125	3.794	.092
Error(Animal)	Sphericity Assumed	153.375	21	7.304		
	Greenhouse–Geisser	153.375	11.190	13.707		
	Huynh–Feldt	153.375	13.981	10.970		
	Lower-bound	153.375	7.000	21.911		

JANE SUPERBRAIN 14.3

Adjusting for sphericity ②

The estimates of sphericity in Output 14.2 are used by SPSS to correct the degrees of freedom associated with the F statistic. This has the effect of changing the p-value for F (because by changing the degrees of

freedom, we change the shape of the F-distribution that is used to obtain p). Therefore, the F-ratio itself remains unchanged, but its degrees of freedom and p-value are adjusted.

The degrees of freedom are adjusted by multiplying them by the estimate of sphericity. For example, the Greenhouse–Geisser estimate of sphericity was 0.533 (Output 14.2). The original degrees of freedom for the model were 3; this value is corrected by multiplying by the estimate of sphericity (3 × 0.533 = 1.599). Likewise the error df was 21; this value is corrected in the same way (21 × 0.533 = 11.19). The F-ratio is then tested against a critical value with these new degrees of freedom (1.599, 11.19). The Huynh–Feldt correction is applied in the same way (see Oliver Twisted on sphericity).

are used to correct the degrees of freedom, which has the effect of increasing *p* (Jane Superbrain Box 14.3).

For these data the corrections result in the observed *F* being non-significant when using the Greenhouse–Geisser correction (because *p* > .05). However, using the Huynh–Feldt correction the *F*-value is still significant because the probability value of .048 is just below the criterion value of .05. I noted earlier that the Greenhouse–Geisser correction is probably too strict and that the Huynh–Feldt correction is probably not strict enough, and we see this here because one of them takes the significance value above our conventional .05 threshold while the other doesn't. This leaves us with the puzzling dilemma of whether or not to accept this *F*-statistic as significant (see Jane Superbrain Box 14.4).

Remember the earlier recommendation to use the Greenhouse–Geisser correction unless this estimate is greater than .75. Our Greenhouse–Geisser estimate is below this value (it is .533) so we ought to go with the Greenhouse–Geisser corrected *p* and conclude that there was no significant difference between means. We also saw earlier that Stevens (2002) recommends taking an average of the two estimates. In practical terms, rather than averaging the estimates, correcting the degrees of freedom manually and trying with an abacus or two to generate exact *p*-values, we could simply average the two *p*-values instead. In this case, the average of the two *p*-values is (.063 + .048)/2 = .056. Therefore, we would probably go with the Greenhouse–Geisser correction and conclude that the *F*-ratio is non-significant.

JANE SUPERBRAIN 14.4

Pointless p ②

In Section 2.6.2.2 I discussed the dangers of significance testing leading us to all-or-nothing thinking about our data. These data illustrate this point beautifully: the two sphericity corrections lead to significance values just above (.063) or just below (.048) the .05 criterion. These significance values differ by only .015 yet they lead to completely opposite conclusions. For these data, the decision about 'significance' has, in some ways, become rather arbitrary: if you choose one correction then the result is 'significant' but if you choose another it is not. The means themselves, and hence the size of effect, are unaffected by these sphericity corrections and so whether the *p*-value falls slightly above or slightly below .05 side-tracks us from the more important question of how big the effect was. We might be well advised to look at an effect size to see whether the effect is substantive regardless of its significance.

We also saw earlier that a final option, when you have data that violate sphericity, is to use multivariate test statistics (MANOVA), because they do not make this assumption (see O'Brien & Kaiser, 1985). MANOVA is covered in Chapter 16. Output 14.5 shows the multivariate test statistics for this example (details of these test statistics can be found in Section 16.4.4). The column displaying the significance values shows that the multivariate tests are significant (*p* = .002). This result supports a decision to conclude that there are significant differences between the times taken to retch after eating different animals.

Multivariate Tests[a]   OUTPUT 14.5

Effect		Value	F	Hypothesis df	Error df	Sig.
Animal	Pillai's Trace	.942	26.955[b]	3.000	5.000	.002
	Wilks' Lambda	.058	26.955[b]	3.000	5.000	.002
	Hotelling's Trace	16.173	26.955[b]	3.000	5.000	.002
	Roy's Largest Root	16.173	26.955[b]	3.000	5.000	.002

a. Design: Intercept
   Within Subjects Design: Animal

b. Exact statistic

14.6.4. Contrasts ②

The transformation matrix requested in the options is shown in Output 14.6. To interpret this table we can draw on our knowledge of contrast coding (see Chapter 11). The first thing to remember is that a code of 0 means that the group is not included in a contrast. Therefore, contrast 1 (labelled *Level 1 vs. Level 2*) ignores the fish eyeball and witchetty grub. The next thing to remember is that groups with a negative weight are compared to groups with a positive weight. For this first contrast, this means that the stick insect is compared against the kangaroo testicle. Using the same logic, contrast 2 (labelled *Level 2 vs. Level 3*) ignores the stick insect and witchetty grub and compares the kangaroo testicle with the fish eye.

SELF-TEST   What does contrast 3 (*Level 3 vs. Level 4*) compare?

Contrast 3 compares the fish eyeball with the witchetty grub. This pattern of contrasts is consistent with what we expect to get from a repeated contrast (i.e., all groups except the first are compared to the preceding category).

OUTPUT 14.6

Animal[a]

Measure: MEASURE_1

	Animal		
Dependent Variable	Level 1 vs. Level 2	Level 2 vs. Level 3	Level 3 vs. Level 4
Stick Insect	1	0	0
Kangaroo Testicle	-1	1	0
Fish Eyeball	0	-1	1
Witchetty Grub	0	0	-1

a. The contrasts for the within subjects factors are:
Animal: Repeated contrast

Above the transformation matrix, you'll find a summary table of the contrasts (Output 14.7). Each contrast is listed in turn, with an *F*-ratio that compares the two chunks of variation within the contrast. So, looking at the significance values from the table, we could say that celebrities took significantly longer to retch after eating the stick insect compared to the kangaroo testicle, $p = .002$ (*Level 1 vs. Level 2*), but that the time to retch was roughly the same after eating the kangaroo testicle and the fish eyeball, $p = .920$ (*Level 2 vs. Level 3*) and after eating a fish eyeball compared to eating a witchetty grub, $p = .402$ (*Level 3 vs. Level 4*).

OUTPUT 14.7

Tests of Within-Subjects Contrasts

Measure: MEASURE_1

Source	Animal	Type III Sum of Squares	df	Mean Square	F	Sig.
Animal	Level 1 vs. Level 2	120.125	1	120.125	22.803	.002
	Level 2 vs. Level 3	.125	1	.125	.011	.920
	Level 3 vs. Level 4	21.125	1	21.125	.796	.402
Error(Animal)	Level 1 vs. Level 2	36.875	7	5.268		
	Level 2 vs. Level 3	80.875	7	11.554		
	Level 3 vs. Level 4	185.875	7	26.554		

It's worth remembering that, by some criteria, our main effect of the type of animal eaten was not significant, and if this is the case then we really shouldn't look at these contrasts. Personally, given the multivariate tests, I would be inclined to conclude that the main effect of animal was significant, which is why I have interpreted these tests. The important point is that the sphericity in our data has illustrated that doing statistics is an art form more than a set of recipe-book rules that you follow to get the 'right' or 'wrong' answer. It's comforting to know that the computer does not have all of the answers – but it's alarming to realize that this means that we have to know some of the answers ourselves.

14.6.5.   *Post hoc* tests ②

If you selected *post hoc* tests for the repeated-measures variable in the *Options* dialog box (see Section 14.5.4), then the output viewer window will contain the table in Output 14.8.

Pairwise Comparisons   OUTPUT 14.8

Measure: MEASURE_1

(I) Animal	(J) Animal	Mean Difference (I–J)	Std. Error	Sig.[b]	95% Confidence Interval for Difference[b]	
					Lower Bound	Upper Bound
1	2	3.875*	.811	.012	.925	6.825
	3	4.000*	.732	.006	1.339	6.661
	4	2.375	1.792	1.000	−4.141	8.891
2	1	−3.875*	.811	.012	−6.825	−.925
	3	.125	1.202	1.000	−4.244	4.494
	4	−1.500	1.336	1.000	−6.359	3.359
3	1	−4.000*	.732	.006	−6.661	−1.339
	2	−.125	1.202	1.000	−4.494	4.244
	4	−1.625	1.822	1.000	−8.249	4.999
4	1	−2.375	1.792	1.000	−8.891	4.141
	2	1.500	1.336	1.000	−3.359	6.359
	3	1.625	1.822	1.000	−4.999	8.249

Based on estimated marginal means

*. The mean difference is significant at the

b. Adjustment for multiple comparisons: Bonferroni.

CRAMMING SAM'S TIPS   **One-way repeated-measures ANOVA**

- One-way repeated-measures ANOVA compares several means when those means have come from the same entities; for example, if you measured people's statistical ability each month over a year-long course.
- In repeated-measures ANOVA there is an additional assumption: *sphericity*. This assumption needs to be considered only when you have three or more repeated-measures conditions.
- Test for sphericity using *Mauchly's test*. Find the table with this label: if the value in the column labelled *Sig.* is less than .05 then the assumption is violated, if it is greater than .05 then sphericity can be assumed.
- The table labelled *Tests of Within-Subjects Effects* shows the main result of your ANOVA. If the assumption of sphericity has been met then look at the row labelled *Sphericity Assumed*. If the assumption was violated then read the row labelled *Greenhouse-Geisser* (you can also look at *Huynh-Feldt* but you'll have to read this chapter to find out the relative merits of the two procedures). Having selected the appropriate row, look at the column labelled *Sig.* If the value is less than .05 then the means of the groups are significantly different.
- For contrasts and *post hoc* tests, again look to the columns labelled *Sig.* to discover if your comparisons are significant (they will be if the significance value is less than .05).

This table is arranged similarly to that produced for between-groups *post hoc* tests: the difference between group means is displayed, along with the standard error, the significance value and a confidence interval for the difference between means. By looking at the significance values and the means (in Output 14.1) we can see that the time to retch was significantly longer after eating a stick insect compared to a kangaroo testicle ($p = .012$) and a fish eye ($p = .006$) but not compared to a witchetty grub ($p > .05$). The time to retch after eating a kangaroo testicle was not significantly different to after eating a fish eyeball or witchetty grub (both $ps > .05$). Finally, the time to retch was not significantly different after eating a fish eyeball compared to a witchetty grub ($p > .05$). Again, it's worth remembering that we wouldn't interpret these effects if we decide that the main effect of the type of animal eaten wasn't significant.

14.7. Effect sizes for repeated-measures ANOVA ③

SMART
ALEX
ONLY

As with independent ANOVA, the best measure of the overall effect size is omega squared (ω^2). However, just to make life even more complicated than it already is, the equations we've previously used for omega squared can't be used for repeated-measures data. If you do use the same equation on repeated-measures data it will slightly overestimate the effect size. For the sake of simplicity some people do use the same equation for one-way independent and repeated-measures ANOVAs (I'm guilty of this in another book), but I'm afraid that in this book we're going to hit simplicity in the face with Stingy the particularly poison-ridden jellyfish, and embrace complexity like a particularly hot date.

In repeated-measures ANOVA, the equation for omega squared is (hang onto your hat):

$$\omega^2 = \frac{\left[\dfrac{k-1}{nk}\left(MS_M - MS_R\right)\right]}{MS_R + \dfrac{MS_B - MS_R}{k} + \left[\dfrac{k-1}{nk}\left(MS_M - MS_R\right)\right]} \tag{14.1}$$

I know what you're thinking and it's something along the lines of 'are you having a laugh?' Well, no, I'm not, but really the equation isn't too bad if you break it down. First, there are some mean squares that we've come across before (and calculated before). There's the mean square for the model (MS_M) and the residual mean square (MS_R), both of which can be obtained from the ANOVA table that SPSS produces (Output 14.4). There's also k, the number of conditions in the experiment, which for these data would be 4 (there were four animals), and there's n, the number of people who took part (in this case, the number of celebrities, 8). The main problem is the term MS_B. Back at the beginning of Section 14.3 (Figure 14.3) I mentioned that the total variation is broken down into a within-participant variation and a between-participants variation. In Section 14.3.7 we saw that we could calculate this term from:

$$SS_T = SS_B + SS_W$$

The problem is that SPSS doesn't give us SS_W in the output, but we know that this is made up of SS_M and SS_R, which we are given. By substituting these terms and rearranging the equation we get:

$$SS_T = SS_B + SS_M + SS_R$$
$$SS_B = SS_T - SS_M - SS_R$$

The next problem is that SPSS, which is clearly trying to hinder us at every step, doesn't give us SS_T and I'm afraid (unless I've missed something in the output) you're just going to have to calculate it by hand (see Section 14.3.1). From the values we calculated earlier, you should get:

$$SS_B = 253.89 - 83.13 - 153.38$$
$$= 17.38$$

The next step is to convert this to a mean square by dividing by the degrees of freedom, which in this case are the number of people in the sample minus 1 ($N-1$):

$$MS_B = \frac{SS_B}{df_B} = \frac{SS_B}{N-1}$$
$$= \frac{17.38}{8-1}$$
$$= 2.48$$

Having done all this, and probably died of boredom in the process, we must now resurrect our corpses with renewed vigour for the effect size equation, which becomes:

$$\omega^2 = \frac{\left[\frac{4-1}{8\times4}(27.71-7.30)\right]}{7.30 + \frac{2.48-7.30}{4} + \left[\frac{4-1}{8\times4}(27.71-7.30)\right]}$$
$$= \frac{1.91}{8.01}$$
$$= .24$$

So, we get an omega squared of .24.

I've mentioned at various other points that it's more useful to have effect size measures for focused comparisons anyway (rather than the main ANOVA), and so a slightly easier approach to calculating effect sizes is to calculate them for the contrasts we did (see Output 14.7). For these we can use the equation that we've seen before to convert the F-values (because they all have 1 degree of freedom for the model) to r:

$$r = \sqrt{\frac{F(1, df_R)}{F(1, df_R)+df_R}}$$

For the three comparisons we did, we would get:

$$r_{\text{Stick insect vs. kangaroo testicle}} = \sqrt{\frac{22.80}{22.80+7}} = .87$$

$$r_{\text{Kangaroo testicle vs. fish eyeball}} = \sqrt{\frac{0.01}{0.01+7}} = .04$$

$$r_{\text{Fish eyeball vs. witchetty grub}} = \sqrt{\frac{0.80}{0.80+7}} = .32$$

The difference between the stick insect and the testicle was a large effect, between the fish eye and witchetty grub a medium effect, but between the testicle and eyeball a very small effect.

14.8. Reporting one-way repeated-measures ANOVA ②

When we report repeated-measures ANOVA, we give the same details as for an independent ANOVA. The only additional thing we should concern ourselves with is reporting the corrected degrees of freedom if sphericity was violated. Personally, I'm keen on reporting the results of sphericity tests as well. As with the independent ANOVA, the degrees of freedom used to assess the F-ratio are the degrees of freedom for the effect of the model (df_M = 1.60) and the degrees of freedom for the residuals of the model (df_R = 11.19). If you choose to report the sphericity test as well, you should report the chi-square approximation, its degrees of freedom and the significance value. It's also nice to report the degree of sphericity by reporting the epsilon value. Therefore, we could report the main finding as follows:

> ✓ Mauchly's test indicated that the assumption of sphericity had been violated, $\chi^2(5)$ = 11.41, p = .047, therefore Greenhouse–Geisser corrected tests are reported (ε = .53). The results show that the time to retch was not significantly affected by the type of animal eaten, $F(1.60, 11.19)$ = 3.79, p = .063, ω^2 = .24.

Alternatively, we could report the Huynh–Feldt corrected values:

> ✓ Mauchly's test indicated that the assumption of sphericity had been violated, $\chi^2(5)$ = 11.41, p = .047, therefore degrees of freedom were corrected using Huynh–Feldt estimates of sphericity (ε = .67). The results show that the time to retch was significantly affected by the type of animal eaten, $F(2, 13.98)$ = 3.79, p = .048, ω^2 = .24.

We could also report multivariate tests. There are four different test statistics, but in most situations you should probably report Pillai's trace, V (see Chapter 16). You should report the value of V as well as the associated F and its degrees of freedom (all from Output 14.6):

> ✓ Mauchly's test indicated that the assumption of sphericity had been violated, $\chi^2(5)$ = 11.41, p = .047, therefore multivariate tests are reported (ε = .53). The results show that the time to retch was significantly affected by the type of animal eaten, V = 0.94, $F(3, 5)$ = 26.96, p = .002, ω^2 = .24.

14.9. Factorial repeated-measures designs ②

We have seen already that simple between-groups designs can be extended to incorporate a second (or third) independent variable. It is equally easy to incorporate a second, third or even fourth independent variable into a repeated-measures analysis. There is evidence from advertising research that attitudes towards stimuli can be changed using positive imagery (e.g., Stuart, Shimp, & Engle, 1987). As part of an initiative to stop binge drinking in teenagers, the government funded some scientists to look at whether negative imagery could be used to make teenagers' attitudes towards alcohol more negative. The scientists designed

TABLE 14.3 Data from **Attitude.sav**

Drink	Beer			Wine			Water		
Image	+ve	−ve	Neut	+ve	−ve	Neut	+ve	−ve	Neut
Male	1	6	5	38	−5	4	10	−14	−2
	43	30	8	20	−12	4	9	−10	−13
	15	15	12	20	−15	6	6	−16	1
	40	30	19	28	−4	0	20	−10	2
	8	12	8	11	−2	6	27	5	−5
	17	17	15	17	−6	6	9	−6	−13
	30	21	21	15	−2	16	19	−20	3
	34	23	28	27	−7	7	12	−12	2
	34	20	26	24	−10	12	12	−9	4
	26	27	27	23	−15	14	21	−6	0
Female	1	−19	−10	28	−13	13	33	−2	9
	7	−18	6	26	−16	19	23	−17	5
	22	−8	4	34	−23	14	21	−19	0
	30	−6	3	32	−22	21	17	−11	4
	40	−6	0	24	−9	19	15	−10	2
	15	−9	4	29	−18	7	13	−17	8
	20	−17	9	30	−17	12	16	−4	10
	9	−12	−5	24	−15	18	17	−4	8
	14	−11	7	34	−14	20	19	−1	12
	15	−6	13	23	−15	15	29	−1	10

a study to address this issue by comparing the effects of negative imagery against positive and neutral imagery for different types of drinks. Table 14.3 illustrates the experimental design and contains the data for this example (each row represents a single participant).

Participants viewed a total of nine mock adverts over three sessions. In one session, they saw three adverts: (1) a brand of beer (Brain Death) presented with a negative image (a dead body with the slogan 'Drinking Brain Death makes your liver explode'); (2) a brand of wine (Dangleberry) presented in the context of a positive image (a sexy naked man or woman – depending on the participant's preference – and the slogan 'Drinking Dangleberry wine makes you irresistible'); and (3) a brand of water (Puritan) presented alongside a neutral image (a person watching television accompanied by the slogan 'Drinking Puritan water makes you behave completely normally'). In a second session (a week later), the participants saw the same three brands, but this time Brain Death was accompanied by the positive imagery, Dangleberry by the neutral image and Puritan by the negative. In a third session, the participants saw Brain Death accompanied by the neutral image, Dangleberry by the negative image and Puritan by the positive. After each advert participants were asked to rate the drinks on a scale ranging from −100 (dislike very much) through 0 (neutral) to 100 (like very much). The order of adverts was randomized, as was the order in which people participated in the three sessions. This design is quite complex. There are two independent variables: the type of drink (beer, wine or water) and the type of imagery used (positive, negative or neutral). These two variables completely cross over, producing nine experimental conditions.

14.9.1. The main analysis ②

To enter these data into SPSS remember that each row represents a single participant's data. If a person participates in all experimental conditions (in this case the person sees all types of stimuli presented with all types of imagery) then each experimental condition must be represented by a column in the data editor. In this experiment there are nine experimental conditions and so the data need to be entered in nine columns (so the format is identical to Table 14.3). Create the following nine variables in the data editor with the names as given. For each one, you should also enter a full variable name (see Section 3.5.2) for clarity in the output:

- beerpos = beer + sexy person
- beerneg = beer + corpse
- beerneut = beer + person watching TV
- winepos = wine + sexy person
- wineneg = wine + corpse
- wineneut = wine + person watching TV
- waterpos = water + sexy person
- waterneg = water + corpse
- waterneut = water + person watching TV

SELF-TEST   Once these variables have been created, enter the data as in Table 14.3. If you have problems entering the data then use the file **Attitude.sav.**

To access the define factors dialog box select **Analyze General Linear Model ▸ Repeated Measures...**. In the *Define Factor(s)* dialog box you are asked to supply a name for the within-subject (repeated-measures) variable. In this case there are two within-subject factors: **Drink** (beer, wine or water) and **Imagery** (positive, negative and neutral). Replace the word *factor1* with the word *Drink*. When you have given this repeated-measures factor a name, you have to tell the computer how many levels there were to that variable. In this case, there were three types of drink, so we have to enter the number 3 into the box labelled *Number of Levels*. Click on [Add] to add this variable to the list of repeated-measures variables. This variable will now appear in the white box at the bottom of the dialog box and appears as *Drink(3)*. We now have to repeat this process for the second independent variable. Enter the word *Imagery* into the space labelled *Within-Subject Factor Name* and then, because there were three levels of this variable, enter the number 3 into the space labelled *Number of Levels*. Click on [Add] to include this variable in the list of factors; it will appear as *Imagery(3)*. The finished dialog box is shown in Figure 14.10. When you have entered both of the within-subject factors click on [Define] to go to the main dialog box.

The main dialog box is essentially the same as when there is only one independent variable, except that there are now nine question marks (Figure 14.11). At the top of the

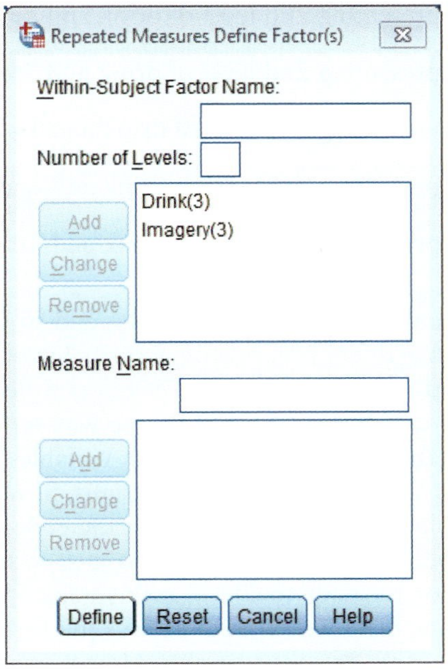

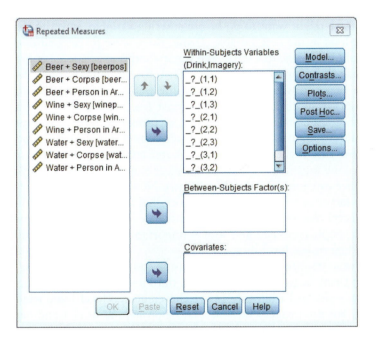

FIGURE 14.10
The *Define Factor(s)* dialog box for factorial repeated-measures ANOVA

FIGURE 14.11
The main dialog box for factorial repeated-measures ANOVA before completion

Within-Subjects Variables box, SPSS states that there are two factors: **Drink** and **Imagery**. In the box below there is a series of question marks followed by bracketed numbers. The numbers in brackets represent the levels of the factors (independent variables):

- _?_(1,1) $\Rightarrow$ variable representing 1st level of drink and 1st level of imagery
- _?_(1,2) $\Rightarrow$ variable representing 1st level of drink and 2nd level of imagery
- _?_(1,3) $\Rightarrow$ variable representing 1st level of drink and 3rd level of imagery
- _?_(2,1) $\Rightarrow$ variable representing 2nd level of drink and 1st level of imagery

- _?_(2,2) ⇒ variable representing 2nd level of drink and 2nd level of imagery

- _?_(2,3) ⇒ variable representing 2nd level of drink and 3rd level of imagery

- _?_(3,1) ⇒ variable representing 3rd level of drink and 1st level of imagery

- _?_(3,2) ⇒ variable representing 3rd level of drink and 2nd level of imagery

- _?_(3,3) ⇒ variable representing 3rd level of drink and 3rd level of imagery

In this example, there are two independent variables and so there are two numbers in the brackets. The first number refers to levels of the first factor listed above the box (in this case **Drink**). The second number in the bracket refers to levels of the second factor listed above the box (in this case **Imagery**). As with one-way repeated-measures ANOVA, you are required to replace these question marks with variables from the list on the left-hand side of the dialog box. With between-groups designs, in which coding variables are used, the levels of a particular factor are specified by the codes assigned to them in the data editor. However, in repeated-measures designs, no such coding scheme is used and so we determine which condition to assign to a level at this stage. For example, if we entered **beerpos** into the list first, then SPSS would treat beer as the first level of **Drink** and positive imagery as the first level of the **Imagery** variable. However, if we entered **wineneg** into the list first, SPSS would consider wine as the first level of **Drink**, and negative imagery as the first level of **Imagery**. For this reason, it is imperative that we think about the type of contrasts that we might want to do *before* entering variables into this dialog box. In this design, if we look at the first variable, **Drink**, there were three conditions, two of which involved alcoholic drinks. In a sense, the water condition acts as a control to whether the effects of imagery are specific to alcohol. Therefore, for this variable we might want to compare the beer and wine condition with the water condition. This comparison could be done by either specifying a simple contrast (see Table 11.6) in which the beer and wine conditions are compared to the water, or using a difference contrast in which both alcohol conditions are compared to the water condition before being compared to each other. In either case it is essential that the water condition be entered as either the first or last level of the independent variable **Drink** (because you can't specify the middle level as the reference category in a simple contrast). Now, let's think about the second factor. The imagery factor also has a control category that was not expected to change attitudes (neutral imagery). As before, we might be interested in using this category as a reference category in a simple contrast,[6] and so it is important that this neutral category is entered as either the first or last level.

Based on what has been discussed about using contrasts, it makes sense to have water as level 3 of the **Drink** factor and neutral as the third level of the imagery factor. The remaining levels can be decided arbitrarily. I have chosen beer as level 1 and wine as level 2 of the **Drink** factor. For the **Imagery** variable I chose positive as level 1 and negative as level 2. These decisions mean that the variables should be entered as in Figure 14.12.

Coincidentally, this order is the order in which variables are listed in the data editor. Actually it's not a coincidence: I thought ahead about what contrasts would be done, and then entered variables in the appropriate order! When these variables have been transferred, the dialog box should look like Figure 14.13. The buttons at the side of the screen have already been described for the one-independent-variable case and so I will describe only the buttons most relevant to this analysis.

---

[6] We expect positive imagery to improve attitudes, whereas negative imagery should make attitudes more negative. Therefore, it does not make sense to do a Helmert or difference contrast for this factor because the effects of the two experimental conditions will cancel each other out.

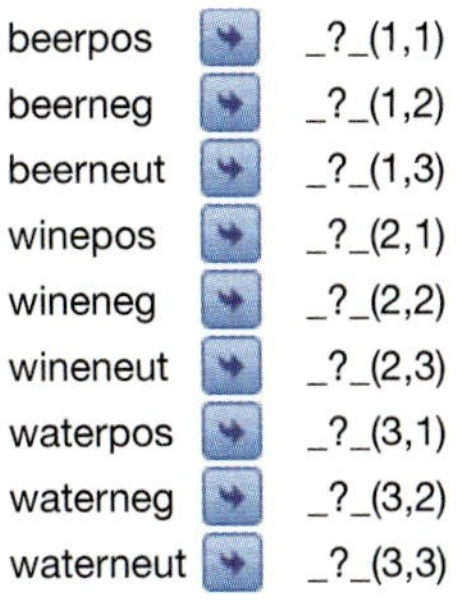

beerpos _?_(1,1)
beerneg _?_(1,2)
beerneut _?_(1,3)
winepos _?_(2,1)
wineneg _?_(2,2)
wineneut _?_(2,3)
waterpos _?_(3,1)
waterneg _?_(3,2)
waterneut _?_(3,3)

FIGURE 14.12 Variable allocations for the attitude data

Repeated Measures
Within-Subjects Variables
(Drink,Imagery):
beerneg(1,2)
beerneut(1,3)
winepos(2,1)
wineneg(2,2)
wineneut(2,3)
waterpos(3,1)
waterneg(3,2)
waterneu(3,3)
Model...
Contrasts...
Plots...
Post Hoc...
Save...
Options...
Between-Subjects Factor(s):
Covariates:
OK
Paste
Reset
Cancel
Help

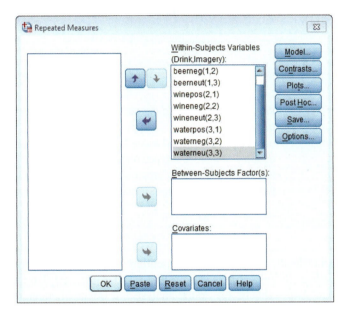

FIGURE 14.13 The main dialog box for factorial repeated-measures ANOVA after completion

14.9.2. Contrasts ②

As we've seen, there's no facility for entering contrast codes in repeated-measures designs (unless you use syntax) but we can use the standard contrasts (see Table 11.6). Figure 14.14 shows the dialog box for conducting contrasts and is obtained by clicking on Contrasts... in the main dialog box. In the previous section I described why it might be interesting to use the water and neutral conditions as base categories for the drink and imagery factors, respectively. We have used the *Contrasts* dialog box before in Sections 12.4.5 and 14.5.3, so all I will say is that you should select a simple contrast for each independent variable. For both independent variables, we entered the variables such that the control category was the last one; therefore, we need not change the reference category for the simple contrast. Once the contrasts have been selected, click on Continue to return to the main dialog box. An alternative to the contrasts available here is to do a simple effects analysis (see SPSS Tip 14.2).

14.9.3. Simple effects analysis ③

We saw in the previous chapter that we can use a technique called 'simple effects' analysis to break down an interaction term. This analysis looks at the effect of one independent

FIGURE 14.14
The *Contrasts* dialog box for factorial repeated-measures ANOVA

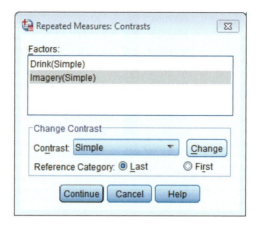

OLIVER TWISTED

Please, Sir, can I have some more … contrasts?

We can also follow up interaction effects with specially defined contrasts for the interaction term. Like simple effects, this can be done only using syntax and it's a fairly involved process. However, if this sounds like something you might want to do then the additional material for the previous chapter contains an example that I've prepared that walks you through specifying contrasts across an interaction.

variable at individual levels of the other independent variable. So, for this example, we could look at the effect of drink for positive imagery, then for negative imagery and then for neutral imagery. Alternatively, we could analyse the effect of imagery separately for beer, wine and water. With repeated-measures designs we can still do simple effects through SPSS syntax, but the syntax we use is slightly different – see SPSS Tip 14.2.

14.9.4. Graphing interactions ②

When we had only one independent variable, we ignored the possibility of specifying plots. However, if there are two or more factors, the *Profile Plots* dialog box is a convenient way to plot the means for each level of the factors (although really you should do some proper graphs before the analysis). To access this dialog box, click on ⟨ Plots... ⟩. Select **Drink** from the variables list on the left-hand side of the dialog box and drag it to the space labelled *Horizontal Axis* or click on ⟨➡⟩. In the space labelled *Separate Lines* we need to place the remaining independent variable, **Imagery**. As before, it is down to your discretion which way round the graph is plotted. When you have moved the two independent variables to the appropriate box, click on ⟨ Add ⟩ and this interaction graph will be added to the list at the bottom of the box (see Figure 14.15). When you have finished specifying graphs, click on ⟨Continue⟩ to return to the main dialog box.

14.9.5. Other options ②

As for the previous ANOVA, the *post hoc* tests are disabled because this design has only repeated-measures variables. However, as before we can access the *Options* dialog box by

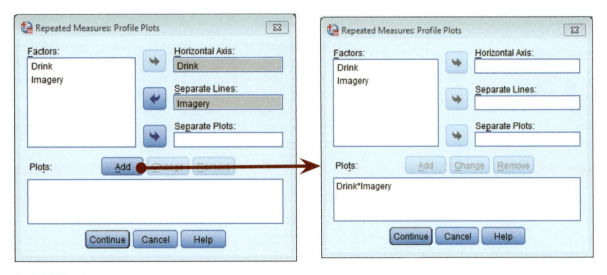

FIGURE 14.15 Defining profile plots in repeated-measures ANOVA

clicking on [Options...]. The options here are the same as for the one-way ANOVA. I recommend selecting some descriptive statistics. You might want to select some multiple comparisons by selecting all factors in the box labelled *Factor(s) and Factor Interactions* and dragging them to the box labelled *Display Means for,* or clicking on ➡ (see Figure 14.16). Having selected these variables, you should select ☑ Compare main effects and select an appropriate correction (I chose Bonferroni). These tests are interesting only if the interaction effect is not significant.

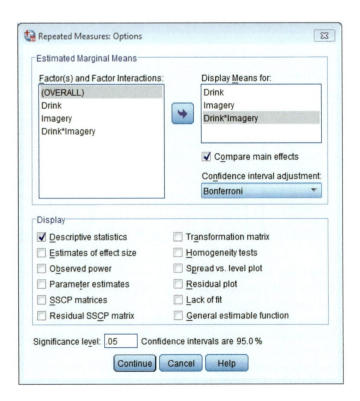

FIGURE 14.16
Options dialog box

ODITI'S LANTERN

Repeated-measures ANOVA

'I, Oditi, believe that we are closer to achieving our mission of understanding the secrets hidden within the numbers. The Earth is a sphere, and I believe that if I am to dominate, erm, I mean understand the Earth then I must educate you about sphere-icity. Knowledge of sphericity will unwire your neural connections and give you insight into analysing repeated-measures data. Come and stare into my lantern and feel your brain burn, but in a nice way.'

14.10. Output for factorial repeated-measures ANOVA ②

14.10.1. Descriptives and main analysis ②

Output 14.9 shows the initial output from this ANOVA. The first table lists the variables that have been included from the data editor and the level of each independent variable that they represent. This table is more important than it might seem, because it enables you to verify that you entered the variables in the correct order for the comparisons that you want to do. The second table is a table of descriptives and provides the mean and standard deviation for each of the nine conditions. The names in this table are the names I gave the variables in the data editor (therefore, if you didn't give these variables full names, this table will look slightly different).

The descriptives are interesting in that they tell us that the variability among scores was greatest when beer was used as a product (compare the standard deviations of the beer variables against the others). Also, when a corpse image was used, the ratings given to the products were negative (as expected) for wine and water but not for beer (so for some reason, negative imagery didn't seem to work when beer was used as a stimulus).

OUTPUT 14.9

Within-Subjects Factors

Measure: MEASURE_1

Drink	Imagery	Dependent Variable
1	1	beerpos
	2	beerneg
	3	beerneut
2	1	winepos
	2	wineneg
	3	wineneut
3	1	waterpos
	2	waterneg
	3	waterneu

Descriptive Statistics

	Mean	Std. Deviation	N
Beer + Sexy	21.05	13.008	20
Beer + Corpse	4.45	17.304	20
Beer + Person in Armchair	10.00	10.296	20
Wine + Sexy	25.35	6.738	20
Wine + Corpse	-12.00	6.181	20
Wine + Person in Armchair	11.65	6.243	20
Water + Sexy	17.40	7.074	20
Water + Corpse	-9.20	6.802	20
Water + Person in Armchair	2.35	6.839	20

Output 14.10 shows the results of Mauchly's sphericity test (see Section 14.2.3) for each of the three effects in the model (two main effects and one interaction). The significance values of these tests indicate that both the main effects of **Drink** and **Imagery** have violated this assumption and so the *F*-values should be corrected (see Section 14.6.2). For the interaction the assumption of sphericity is met (because $p > .05$) and so we need not correct the *F*-ratio for this effect.

Output 14.11 shows the results of the ANOVA (with corrected *F*-values). The output is split into sections that refer to each of the effects in the model and the error terms associated with

Mauchly's Test of Sphericity[a]

Measure: MEASURE_1

Within Subjects Effect	Mauchly's W	Approx. Chi-Square	df	Sig.	Epsilon[b]		
					Greenhouse-Geisser	Huynh-Feldt	Lower-bound
Drink	.267	23.753	2	.000	.577	.591	.500
Imagery	.662	7.422	2	.024	.747	.797	.500
Drink * Imagery	.595	9.041	9	.436	.798	.979	.250

Tests the null hypothesis that the error covariance matrix of the orthonormalized transformed dependent variables is proportional to an identity matrix.

a. Design: Intercept
   Within Subjects Design: Drink + Imagery + Drink * Imagery

b. May be used to adjust the degrees of freedom for the averaged tests of significance. Corrected tests are displayed in the Tests of Within-Subjects Effects table.

Tests of Within-Subjects Effects

Measure: MEASURE_1

Source		Type III Sum of Squares	df	Mean Square	F	Sig.
Drink	Sphericity Assumed	2092.344	2	1046.172	5.106	.011
	Greenhouse-Geisser	2092.344	1.154	1812.764	5.106	.030
	Huynh-Feldt	2092.344	1.181	1770.939	5.106	.029
	Lower-bound	2092.344	1.000	2092.344	5.106	.036
Error(Drink)	Sphericity Assumed	7785.878	38	204.892		
	Greenhouse-Geisser	7785.878	21.930	355.028		
	Huynh-Feldt	7785.878	22.448	346.836		
	Lower-bound	7785.878	19.000	409.783		
Imagery	Sphericity Assumed	21628.678	2	10814.339	122.565	.000
	Greenhouse-Geisser	21628.678	1.495	14468.490	122.565	.000
	Huynh-Feldt	21628.678	1.594	13571.496	122.565	.000
	Lower-bound	21628.678	1.000	21628.678	122.565	.000
Error(Imagery)	Sphericity Assumed	3352.878	38	88.234		
	Greenhouse-Geisser	3352.878	28.403	118.048		
	Huynh-Feldt	3352.878	30.280	110.729		
	Lower-bound	3352.878	19.000	176.467		
Drink * Imagery	Sphericity Assumed	2624.422	4	656.106	17.155	.000
	Greenhouse-Geisser	2624.422	3.194	821.778	17.155	.000
	Huynh-Feldt	2624.422	3.914	670.462	17.155	.000
	Lower-bound	2624.422	1.000	2624.422	17.155	.001
Error(Drink*Imagery)	Sphericity Assumed	2906.689	76	38.246		
	Greenhouse-Geisser	2906.689	60.678	47.903		
	Huynh-Feldt	2906.689	74.373	39.083		
	Lower-bound	2906.689	19.000	152.984		

these effects. Looking at the significance values, it is clear that there is a significant effect of the type of drink used as a stimulus, a significant main effect of the type of imagery used and a significant interaction between these two variables. I will examine each of these effects in turn.

14.10.1.1. The main effect of drink ②

The first part of Output 14.11 tells us the effect of the type of drink used in the advert. For this effect we must look at one of the corrected significance values because sphericity was violated (see above). All of the corrected values are significant and so we should report the conservative Greenhouse–Geisser corrected values of the degrees of freedom. This effect tells us that if we ignore the type of imagery that was used, participants rated some types of drink significantly differently.

FIGURE 14.17
Output and
graph of the
main effect of
drink

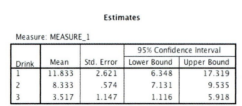

Estimates

Measure: MEASURE_1

Drink	Mean	Std. Error	95% Confidence Interval	
			Lower Bound	Upper Bound
1	11.833	2.621	6.348	17.319
2	8.333	.574	7.131	9.535
3	3.517	1.147	1.116	5.918

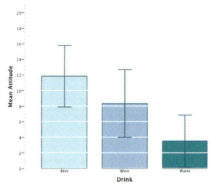

In Section 14.9.5 we requested that SPSS display means for all of the effects in the model (before conducting *post hoc* tests) and if you scan through your output you should find the table in Figure 14.17 in a section headed *Estimated Marginal Means*.[7] This table contains means for the main effect of drink with the associated standard errors. The levels of this variable are labelled 1, 2 and 3, and so we must think back to how we entered the variable to see which row of the table relates to which condition. We entered this variable with the beer condition first and the water condition last. Figure 14.17 also shows a graph of these means, which shows that beer and wine were rated higher than water (with beer being rated most highly). To see the nature of this effect we can look at the *post hoc* tests (see below) and the contrasts (see Section 14.10.2).

Output 14.12 shows the pairwise comparisons for the main effect of drink corrected using a Bonferroni adjustment. This table indicates that the significant main effect reflects a significant difference ($p = .001$) between levels 2 and 3 (wine and water). Curiously, the difference between the beer and water conditions is larger than that for wine and water, yet this effect is non-significant ($p = .066$). This inconsistency can be explained by looking at the standard error in the beer condition compared to the wine condition. The standard error for the wine condition is incredibly small and so the difference between means is relatively large (see Chapter 9).

SELF-TEST Try rerunning these *post hoc* tests but selecting the uncorrected values (LSD) in the *Options* dialog box (see Section 13.8.5). You should find that the difference between beer and water is now significant ($p = .02$).

This finding highlights the importance of controlling the error rate by using a Bonferroni correction. Had we not used this correction we could have concluded erroneously that beer was rated significantly more highly than water.

14.10.1.2. The main effect of imagery ②

Output 14.11 also indicates that the effect of the type of imagery used in the advert had a significant influence on participants' ratings of the stimuli. Again, we must look at one

---

[7] These means are obtained by taking the average of the means in Output 14.9 for a given condition. For example, the mean for the beer condition (ignoring imagery) is $\bar{X}_{Beer} = \dfrac{\bar{X}_{Beer+Sexy} + \bar{X}_{Beer+Corpse} + \bar{X}_{Beer+Neutral}}{3} = \dfrac{21.05 + 4.45 + 10.00}{3} = 11.83$.

Pairwise Comparisons

Measure: MEASURE_1

(I) Drink	(J) Drink	Mean Difference (I–J)	Std. Error	Sig.[b]	95% Confidence Interval for Difference[b]	
					Lower Bound	Upper Bound
1	2	3.500	2.849	.703	−3.980	10.980
	3	8.317	3.335	.066	−.438	17.072
2	1	−3.500	2.849	.703	−10.980	3.980
	3	4.817*	1.116	.001	1.886	7.747
3	1	−8.317	3.335	.066	−17.072	.438
	2	−4.817*	1.116	.001	−7.747	−1.886

Based on estimated marginal means

*. The mean difference is significant at the

b. Adjustment for multiple comparisons: Bonferroni.

Estimates

Measure: MEASURE_1

Imagery	Mean	Std. Error	95% Confidence Interval	
			Lower Bound	Upper Bound
1	21.267	.977	19.222	23.312
2	−5.583	1.653	−9.043	−2.124
3	8.000	.969	5.972	10.028

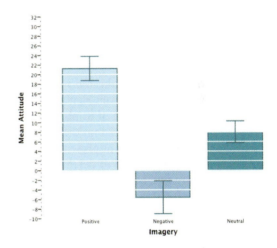

FIGURE 14.18 Output and graph of the main effect of imagery

of the corrected significance values because sphericity was violated (see above). All of the corrected values are highly significant, and so we can again report the Greenhouse–Geisser corrected values of the degrees of freedom. This effect tells us that if we ignore the type of drink that was used, participants' ratings of those drinks were different according to the type of imagery that was used.

In Section 14.9.5 we requested means for all of the effects in the model, and if you scan through your output you should find the table of means for the main effect of imagery with the associated standard errors (Figure 14.18). The levels of this variable are labelled 1, 2 and 3, and so we need to think back to how we entered the variable to see which row of the table relates to which condition. We entered this variable with the positive condition first and the neutral condition last. Figure 14.18 includes a graph of these means and shows that positive imagery resulted in very positive ratings (compared to the neutral imagery) and negative imagery resulted in negative ratings (especially compared to the effect of neutral imagery). Again, we can look at the *post hoc* tests (see below) and the contrasts (see Section 14.10.2).

Output 14.13 shows the pairwise comparisons for the main effect of imagery corrected using a Bonferroni adjustment. This table indicates that the significant main effect reflects significant differences ($p < .001$) between levels 1 and 2 (positive and negative), between levels 1 and 3 (positive and neutral) and between levels 2 and 3 (negative and neutral).

OUTPUT 14.13

Pairwise Comparisons

Measure:MEASURE_1

(I) Imagery	(J) Imagery	Mean Difference (I-J)	Std. Error	Sig.[a]	95% Confidence Interval for Difference[a]	
					Lower Bound	Upper Bound
1	2	26.850*	1.915	.000	21.824	31.876
	3	13.267*	1.113	.000	10.346	16.187
2	1	-26.850*	1.915	.000	-31.876	-21.824
	3	-13.583*	1.980	.000	-18.781	-8.386
3	1	-13.267*	1.113	.000	-16.187	-10.346
	2	13.583*	1.980	.000	8.386	18.781

Based on estimated marginal means

*. The mean difference is significant at the .05 level.

a. Adjustment for multiple comparisons: Bonferroni.

14.10.1.3. The interaction effect (drink × imagery) ②

Output 14.11 indicated that imagery interacted in some way with the type of drink used as a stimulus. From that table we should report that there was a significant interaction between the type of drink used and imagery associated with it, $F(4, 76) = 17.16$, $p < .001$. This effect tells us that the type of imagery used had a different effect depending on which type of drink it was presented alongside. As before, we can use the means that we requested in Section 14.9.5 to determine the nature of this interaction. This table is shown in Output 14.14 and is essentially the same as the initial descriptive statistics in Output 14.9, except that the standard errors are displayed rather than the standard deviations.

The means in Output 14.14 are used to create the plot that we requested in Section 14.9.4, and this graph is essential for interpreting the interaction. Figure 14.19 shows the interaction graph (modified to make it look nicer), and we are looking for non-parallel lines. The graph shows that the pattern of responding across drinks was similar when positive and neutral imagery were used. That is, ratings were positive for beer, they were slightly higher for wine and then they went down slightly for water. The fact that the line representing positive imagery is higher than the neutral line indicates that positive imagery gave rise to higher ratings than neutral imagery across all drinks. The bottom line (representing negative imagery) shows a different effect: ratings were lower for wine and water but not for beer.

OUTPUT 14.14

3. Drink * Imagery

Measure: MEASURE_1

Drink	Imagery	Mean	Std. Error	95% Confidence Interval	
				Lower Bound	Upper Bound
1	1	21.050	2.909	14.962	27.138
	2	4.450	3.869	-3.648	12.548
	3	10.000	2.302	5.181	14.819
2	1	25.350	1.507	22.197	28.503
	2	-12.000	1.382	-14.893	-9.107
	3	11.650	1.396	8.728	14.572
3	1	17.400	1.582	14.089	20.711
	2	-9.200	1.521	-12.384	-6.016
	3	2.350	1.529	-.851	5.551

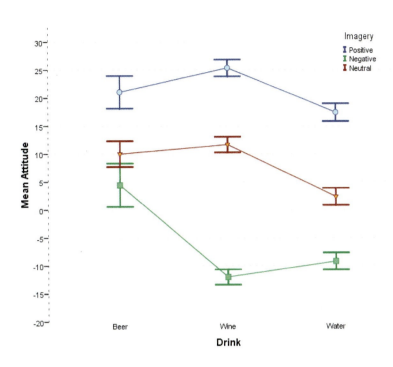

FIGURE 14.19

Interaction graph for **Attitude.sav.** The three lines represent the type of imagery: positive imagery (circles), negative imagery (squares) and neutral imagery (triangles)

Therefore, negative imagery had the desired effect on attitudes towards wine and water, but for some reason attitudes towards beer remained fairly neutral. Therefore, the interaction is likely to reflect the fact that negative imagery has a different effect than both positive and neutral imagery (because it decreases ratings rather than increasing them). This interaction is completely in line with the experimental predictions. To verify the interpretation of the interaction effect, we need to look at the contrasts that we requested in Section 14.9.2.

14.10.2. Contrasts for repeated-measures variables ②

In Section 14.9.2 we requested simple contrasts for the **Drink** variable (for which water was used as the control category) and for the **Imagery** category (for which neutral imagery was used as the control category). Output 14.16 shows the summary results for these contrasts. The table is split up into main effects and interactions, and each effect is split up into components of the contrast. So, for the main effect of drink, the first contrast compares level 1 (beer) against the base category (in this case, the last category, water). If you are confused as to which level is which, you are reminded that Output 14.9 lists them for you. This result is significant, $F(1, 19) = 6.22$, $p = .022$, which contradicts what was found using *post hoc* tests (see Output 14.12).

SELF-TEST   Why do you think that this contradiction has occurred?

The next contrast compares level 2 (wine) with the base category (water) and confirms the significant difference found with the *post hoc* tests, $F(1, 19) = 18.61$, $p < .001$. For the

SPSS TIP 14.2   Simple effects analysis in SPSS ③

With repeated-measures designs we can still do simple effects through SPSS syntax in much the same way as we did for between-groups designs. The syntax you need to use in this example is:

```
GLM beerpos beerneg beerneut winepos wineneg wineneut waterpos waterneg waterneut
  /WSFACTOR=Drink 3  Imagery 3
  /EMMEANS = TABLES(Drink*Imagery) COMPARE(Imagery).
```

This syntax initiates the ANOVA by specifying the variables in the data editor that relate to the levels of our repeated-measures variables. The /WSFACTORS command then defines the two repeated-measures variables that we have. The order that we list the variables from the data editor is important. So, because we've defined *Drink 3 Imagery 3*, SPSS starts at level 1 of drink, and then because we've specified three levels of imagery, it uses the first three variables listed as the levels of imagery at level 1 of drink. It then moves onto level 2 of drink and again looks to the next three variables in the list to be the relevant levels of imagery. Finally, it moves to level 3 of drink and uses the next three variables (the last three in this case) to be the levels of imagery. This is hard to explain, but look at the order of variables, and see that the first three relate to beer (and differ according to imagery), then the next three are wine and the three levels of imagery, and the final three are water ordered again according to imagery. (It would be equally valid to write /WSFACTORS Imagery 3 Drink 3, but only if initially we'd ordered the variables as beerpos winepos waterpos beerneg wineneg waterneg beerneut wineneut waterneut.)

The /EMMEANS command specifies the simple effects. *TABLES(Drink*Imagery)* requests a table of means for the interaction of drink and imagery and *COMPARE(Imagery)* will give us the simple effect of imagery at each level of drink separately. If we wanted to look at the effect of drink at each level of imagery, then we'd use *COMPARE(Drink)*. The syntax for looking at the effect of imagery at different levels of drink is stored in a file called **SimpleEffectsAttitude.sps**. Open this file (make sure you also have **Attitude.sav** loaded into the data editor) and run the syntax.

The resulting Output 14.15 gives us a multivariate test of the effect of imagery for each level of drink (because of the way we ordered the variables, 1 = beer, 2 = wine, 3 = water). Looking at the significance values for each simple effect, there were significant effects of imagery at all levels of drink.

Multivariate Tests

Drink		Value	F	Hypothesis df	Error df	Sig.
1	Pillai's trace	.593	13.122[a]	2.000	18.000	.000
	Wilks' lambda	.407	13.122[a]	2.000	18.000	.000
	Hotelling's trace	1.458	13.122[a]	2.000	18.000	.000
	Roy's largest root	1.458	13.122[a]	2.000	18.000	.000
2	Pillai's trace	.923	107.305[a]	2.000	18.000	.000
	Wilks' lambda	.077	107.305[a]	2.000	18.000	.000
	Hotelling's trace	11.923	107.305[a]	2.000	18.000	.000
	Roy's largest root	11.923	107.305[a]	2.000	18.000	.000
3	Pillai's trace	.939	138.795[a]	2.000	18.000	.000
	Wilks' lambda	.061	138.795[a]	2.000	18.000	.000
	Hotelling's trace	15.422	138.795[a]	2.000	18.000	.000
	Roy's largest root	15.422	138.795[a]	2.000	18.000	.000

Each F tests the multivariate simple effects of Imagery within each level combination of the other effects shown. These tests are based on the linearly independent pairwise comparisons among the estimated marginal means.

a. Exact statistic

OUTPUT 14.15

Tests of Within-Subjects Contrasts

Measure: MEASURE_1

Source	Drink	Imagery	Type III Sum of Squares	df	Mean Square	F	Sig.
Drink	Level 1 vs. Level 3		1383.339	1	1383.339	6.218	.022
	Level 2 vs. Level 3		464.006	1	464.006	18.613	.000
Error(Drink)	Level 1 vs. Level 3		4226.772	19	222.462		
	Level 2 vs. Level 3		473.661	19	24.930		
Imagery		Level 1 vs. Level 3	3520.089	1	3520.089	142.194	.000
		Level 2 vs. Level 3	3690.139	1	3690.139	47.070	.000
Error(Imagery)		Level 1 vs. Level 3	470.356	19	24.756		
		Level 2 vs. Level 3	1489.528	19	78.396		
Drink * Imagery	Level 1 vs. Level 3	Level 1 vs. Level 3	320.000	1	320.000	1.576	.225
		Level 2 vs. Level 3	720.000	1	720.000	6.752	.018
	Level 2 vs. Level 3	Level 1 vs. Level 3	36.450	1	36.450	.235	.633
		Level 2 vs. Level 3	2928.200	1	2928.200	26.906	.000
Error(Drink*Imagery)	Level 1 vs. Level 3	Level 1 vs. Level 3	3858.000	19	203.053		
		Level 2 vs. Level 3	2026.000	19	106.632		
	Level 2 vs. Level 3	Level 1 vs. Level 3	2946.550	19	155.082		
		Level 2 vs. Level 3	2067.800	19	108.832		

imagery main effect, the first contrast compares level 1 (positive) to the base category (the last category, neutral) and verifies the significant difference found with the *post hoc* tests, $F(1, 19) = 142.19$, $p < .001$. The second contrast confirms the significant difference in ratings found in the negative imagery condition compared to the neutral, $F(1, 19) = 47.07$, $p < .001$. These contrasts are all very well, but they tell us only what we already knew (although note the increased statistical power with these tests shown by the higher significance values). The contrasts become much more interesting when we look at the interaction term. To help us interpret these contrasts, Figure 14.20 reproduces the original interaction graph (Figure 14.19) but breaks it down to show only the means that each contrast compares.

14.10.2.1. Beer vs. water, positive vs. neutral imagery ②

The first interaction term looks at level 1 of drink (beer) compared to level 3 (water), when positive imagery (level 1) is used compared to neutral (level 3). This contrast is non-significant, $p = .225$. This result tells us that the increased liking found when positive imagery is used (compared to neutral imagery) is the same for both beer and water. In terms of the interaction graph (the top left of Figure 14.20) it means that the distance between the lines in the beer condition is the same as the distance between the lines in the water condition; the lines are approximately parallel, indicating no significant interaction effect. We could conclude that the improvement of ratings due to positive imagery compared to neutral is not affected by whether people are evaluating beer or water.

14.10.2.2. Beer vs. water, negative vs. neutral imagery ②

The second interaction term looks at level 1 of drink (beer) compared to level 3 (water), when negative imagery (level 2) is used compared to neutral (level 3). This contrast is significant, $F(1, 19) = 6.75$, $p = .018$. This result tells us that the decreased liking found when negative imagery is used (compared to neutral imagery) is different when beer is used compared to when water is used. In terms of the interaction graph (top right of Figure 14.20) it means that the distance between the red and green lines in the beer condition is significantly smaller than the distance between the red and green lines in the water condition. It seems that the decrease in ratings due to negative imagery (compared to neutral) found when water is used in the advert is smaller than when beer is used.

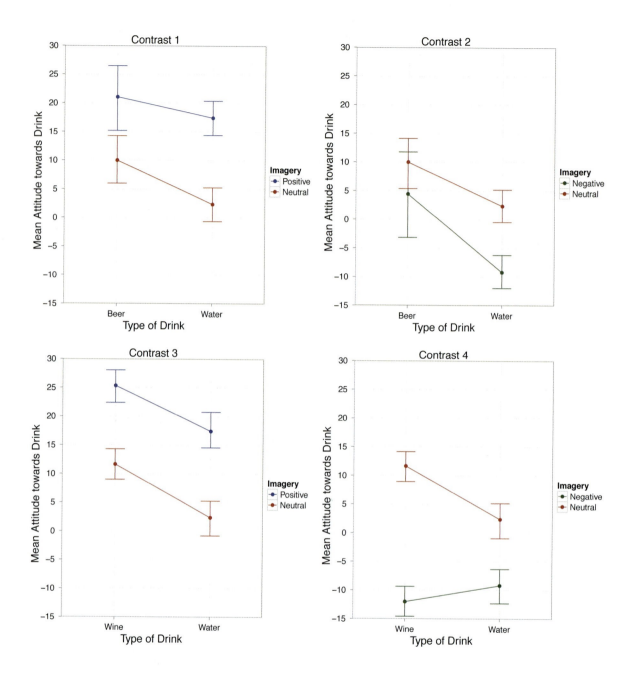

FIGURE 14.20 Graphs (not generated in SPSS, incidentally) illustrating the four contrasts in the attitude analysis

14.10.2.3. Wine vs. water, positive vs. neutral imagery ②

The third interaction term looks at level 2 of drink (wine) compared to level 3 (water), when positive imagery (level 1) is used compared to neutral (level 3). This contrast is non-significant, $p = .633$, indicating that the increased liking found when positive imagery is used (compared to neutral imagery) is similar for both wine and water. In terms of the interaction graph (the bottom left of Figure 14.20) it means that the distance between the red and blue lines in the wine condition is similar to the distance between the lines in the water condition.

The improvement of ratings due to positive imagery compared to neutral is not significantly affected by whether people are evaluating wine or water.

14.10.2.4. Wine vs. water, negative vs. neutral imagery ②

The final interaction term looks at level 2 of drink (wine) compared to level 3 (water), when negative imagery (level 2) is used compared to neutral (level 3). This contrast is significant, $F(1, 19) = 26.91$, $p < .001$. This result tells us that the decreased liking found when negative imagery is used (compared to neutral imagery) is different when wine is used compared to when water is used. In terms of the interaction graph (the bottom right of Figure 14.20) it means that the distance between the red and green lines in the wine condition is significantly larger than the distance between the lines in the water condition. We could conclude that the decrease in ratings due to negative imagery (compared to neutral) is significantly greater when wine is advertised than when water is advertised.

14.10.2.5. Limitations of these contrasts ②

These contrasts, by their nature, tell us nothing about the differences between the beer and wine conditions (or the positive and negative conditions), and different contrasts would have to be run to find out more. However, what is clear so far is that, relative to the neutral condition, positive images increased liking for the products more or less regardless of the product; however, negative imagery had a greater effect on wine and a lesser effect on beer. These differences were not predicted. Although it may seem tiresome to spend so long interpreting an analysis so thoroughly, you are well advised to take such a systematic approach if you want to truly understand the effects that you obtain. Interpreting interaction terms is complex, and I can think of a few well-respected researchers who still struggle with them, so don't feel disheartened if you find them hard. Try to be thorough, and break each effect down as much as possible using contrasts and graphs and hopefully you will find enlightenment.

CRAMMING SAM'S TIPS   Factorial repeated-measures ANOVA

- Two-way repeated-measures ANOVA compares several means when there are two independent variables, and the same entities have been used in all conditions.
- Test the assumption of *sphericity* when you have three or more repeated-measures conditions. Find the table labelled *Mauchly's test*: the assumption is violated if the value in the column labelled *Sig.* is less than .05. You should test this assumption for all effects (in a two-way ANOVA this means you test it for the effect of both variables and the interaction term).
- The table labelled *Tests of Within-Subjects Effects* shows the main result of your ANOVA. In a two-way ANOVA you will have three effects: a main effect of each variable and the interaction between the two. For *each* effect, if the assumption of sphericity has been met then look at the row labelled *Sphericity Assumed*. If the assumption was violated then read the row labelled *Greenhouse–Geisser* (you can also look at *Huynh–Feldt*, but you'll have to read this chapter to find out the relative merits of the two procedures). If the value in the column labelled *Sig.* is less than .05 then the effect is significant.
- Break down the main effects and interaction terms using contrasts. These contrasts appear in the table labelled *Tests of Within-Subjects Contrasts*; again look to the columns labelled *Sig.* to discover if your comparisons are significant (they will be if the significance value is less than .05).

14.11. Effect sizes for factorial repeated-measures ANOVA ③

SMART
ALEX
ONLY

Calculating omega squared for a one-way repeated-measures ANOVA was hair-raising enough, and, as I keep saying, effect sizes are really more useful when they describe a focused effect, so I'd advise calculating effect sizes for your contrasts when you've got a factorial design (and any main effects that compare only two groups). Output 14.16 shows the values for several contrasts, all of which have 1 degree of freedom for the model (i.e., they represent a focused and interpretable comparison) and 19 residual degrees of freedom. We can use these F-ratios and convert them to an effect size r, using a formula we've come across before:

$$r = \sqrt{\frac{F(1, df_R)}{F(1, df_R) + df_R}}$$

For the two comparisons we did for the drink variable (Output 14.16), we would get:

$$r_{\text{beer vs. water}} = \sqrt{\frac{6.22}{6.22 + 19}} = .50$$

$$r_{\text{wine vs. water}} = \sqrt{\frac{18.61}{18.61 + 19}} = .70$$

Therefore, both comparisons yielded very large effect sizes. For the two comparisons we did for the imagery variable (Output 14.16), we would get:

$$r_{\text{positive vs. neutral}} = \sqrt{\frac{142.19}{142.19 + 19}} = .94$$

$$r_{\text{negative vs. neutral}} = \sqrt{\frac{47.07}{47.07 + 19}} = .84$$

Again, both comparisons yield very large effect sizes. For the interaction term, we had four contrasts, but again we can convert them to r because they all have 1 degree of freedom for the model (Output 14.16):

$$r_{\text{beer vs. water, positive vs. neutral}} = \sqrt{\frac{1.58}{1.58 + 19}} = .28$$

$$r_{\text{beer vs. water, negative vs. neutral}} = \sqrt{\frac{6.75}{6.75 + 19}} = .51$$

$$r_{\text{wine vs. water, positive vs. neutral}} = \sqrt{\frac{0.24}{0.24 + 19}} = .11$$

$$r_{\text{wine vs. water, negative vs. neutral}} = \sqrt{\frac{26.91}{26.91 + 19}} = .77$$

PERHAM, N., & SYKORA, M. (2012). APPLIED COGNITIVE PSYCHOLOGY, 26(4), 550–555.

LABCOAT LENI'S
REAL RESEARCH 14.1

Are splattered cadavers distracting? ②

In Chapter 9, I used the example of whether listening to my favourite music would interfere with people's ability to write an essay. It turns out that Nick Perham has tested this hypothesis (sort of). He was interested in the effects of liked and disliked music (compared to quiet) on people's ability to remember things. Twenty-five participants were asked to remember lists of 8 letters. Perham and Sykora (2012) manipulated the background noise while each list was presented: it could be silence (the control), liked music or

disliked music. They used music that they believed most participants would like (a popular song called 'From Paris to Berlin' by Infernal) and dislike (Repulsion's 'Acid Bath', 'Eaten Alive' and 'Splattered Cadavers' – in other words, the sort of thing I listen to, although I don't actually have any stuff by Repulsion). Participants were asked to recall each list of 8 letters, which enabled the authors to calculate the probability of correctly recalling a letter in each position in the list. There are two variables: position in the list (which letter in the sequence is being recalled, 1 to 8) and sound playing when the list is presented (quiet, liked, disliked). Run a two-way repeated-measures ANOVA to see whether recall is affected by the type of sound played while learning the sequences (**Perham & Sykora (2012). sav**). Answers are on the companion website (or look at page 552 in the original article).

As such, the two effects that were significant (beer vs. water, negative vs. neutral and wine vs. water, negative vs. neutral) yield large effect sizes. The two effects that were not significant yielded a medium effect size (beer vs. water, positive vs. neutral) and a small effect size (wine vs. water, positive vs. neutral).

EVERYBODY

14.12. Reporting the results from factorial repeated-measures ANOVA ②

We can report a factorial repeated-measures ANOVA in much the same way as any other ANOVA. Remember that we've got three effects to report, and these effects might have different degrees of freedom. For the main effects of drink and imagery, the assumption of sphericity was violated so we'd have to report the Greenhouse–Geisser corrected degrees of freedom. We can, therefore, begin by reporting the violation of sphericity:

✓ Mauchly's test indicated that the assumption of sphericity had been violated for the main effects of drink, $\chi^2(2) = 23.75$, $p < .001$, and imagery, $\chi^2(2) = 7.42$, $p = .024$. Therefore degrees of freedom were corrected using Greenhouse–Geisser estimates of sphericity ($\varepsilon = .58$ for the main effect of drink and .75 for the main effect of imagery).

We can then report the three effects from this analysis as follows:

✓ Unless otherwise stated $p < .001$. There was a significant main effect of the type of drink on ratings of the drink, $F(1.15, 21.93) = 5.11$, $p = .011$. Contrasts revealed that ratings of beer, $F(1, 19) = 6.22$, $p = .022$, $r = .50$, and wine, $F(1, 19) = 18.61$, $r = .70$, were significantly higher than water.

✓ There was also a significant main effect of the type of imagery on ratings of the drinks, $F(1.50, 28.40) = 122.57$. Contrasts revealed that ratings after positive imagery were significantly higher than after neutral imagery, $F(1, 19) = 142.19$, $r = .94$. Conversely, ratings after negative imagery were significantly lower than after neutral imagery, $F(1, 19) = 47.07$, $r = .84$.

✓ There was a significant interaction effect between the type of drink and the type of imagery used, $F(4, 76) = 17.16$. This indicates that imagery had different effects on people's ratings depending on which type of drink was used. To break down this interaction, contrasts were performed comparing all drink types to their baseline (water) and all imagery types to their baseline (neutral imagery). These revealed significant interactions when comparing negative imagery to neutral imagery both for beer compared to water, $F(1, 19) = 6.75$, $p = .018$, $r = .51$, and wine compared to water, $F(1, 19) = 26.91$, $r = .77$. Looking at the interaction graph, these effects reflect that negative imagery (compared to neutral) lowered scores significantly more in water than it did for beer, and lowered scores significantly more for wine than it did for water. The remaining contrasts revealed no significant interaction term when comparing positive imagery to neutral imagery both for beer compared to water, $F(1, 19) = 1.58$, $p = .225$, $r = .28$, and wine compared to water, $F(1, 19) = 0.24$, $p = .633$, $r = .11$. However, these contrasts did yield small to medium effect sizes.

14.13. Brian's attempt to woo Jane ①

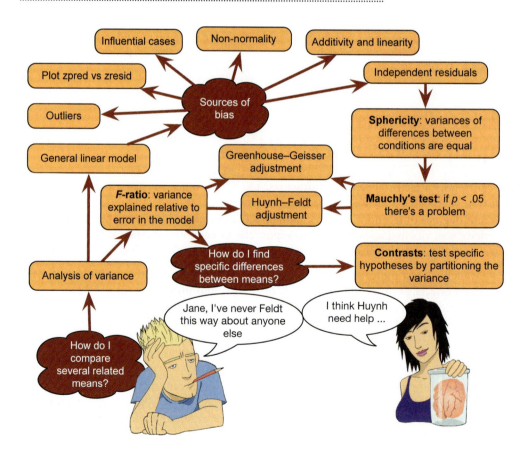

FIGURE 14.21   What Brian learnt from this chapter

14.14. What next? ②

By 16 I had started my first 'serious' band. We actually stayed together for about 7 years (with the same line-up, and we're still friends now) before Mark (drummer) moved to Oxford, I moved to Brighton to do my Ph.D., and rehearsing became a mammoth feat of organization. We had a track on a CD, some radio play and transformed from a thrash metal band to a blend of Fugazi, Nirvana and metal. I never split my trousers during a gig again (although I did once split my head open). Why didn't we make it? Well, Mark is an astonishingly good drummer so it wasn't his fault, the other Mark was an extremely good bassist too, and so all logic points towards the weak link being me. This fact was especially unfortunate given that I had three roles in the band (guitar, singing, songs) – my poor band mates never stood a chance.☺ I stopped playing music for quite a few years after we split. I still wrote songs (for personal consumption) but the three of us were such close friends that I couldn't bear the thought of playing with other people. At least not for a few years …

14.15. Key terms that I've discovered

Compound symmetry
Greenhouse–Geisser estimate
Huynh–Feldt estimate

Lower bound estimate
Mauchly's test

Repeated-measures ANOVA
Sphericity

14.16. Smart Alex's tasks

- **Task 1**: It is common that lecturers obtain reputations for being 'hard' or 'light' markers (or to use the students' terminology, 'evil manifestations from Beelzebub's bowels' and 'nice people') but there is often little to substantiate these reputations. A group of students investigated the consistency of marking by submitting the same essays to four different lecturers. The mark given by each lecturer was recorded for each of the eight essays. The independent variable was the lecturer who marked the essays and the dependent variable was the percentage mark given. The data are in the file **TutorMarks.sav**. Conduct a one-way ANOVA on these data by hand. ②

- **Task 2**: Repeat the analysis for Task 1 in SPSS and interpret the results. ②

- **Task 3**: Calculate the effect sizes for the analysis in Task 1. ③

- **Task 4**: The 'roving eye' effect is the propensity of people in relationships to 'eye up' members of the opposite sex. I took 20 men and fitted them with incredibly sophisticated glasses that could track their eye movements and record both the movement and the object being observed (this is the point at which it should be apparent that I'm making it up as I go along). Over four different nights I plied these poor souls with 1, 2, 3 or 4 pints of strong lager in a nightclub. Each night I measured how many different women they eyed up (a woman was categorized as having been eyed up if the man's eye moved from her head to her toe and back up again). The data are in the file **RovingEye.sav**. Analyse them with a one-way ANOVA. ②

- **Task 5**: In the previous chapter we came across the beer-goggles effect, a severe perceptual distortion occurring after imbibing several pints of alcohol that makes previously unattractive people suddenly become the hottest thing since Spicy Gonzalez's extra-hot Tabasco-marinated chillies. In short, one minute you're standing in a zoo admiring the orang-utans, and the next you're wondering why someone would put the adorable Zoë Field in a cage. Anyway, in that chapter, we demonstrated that the beer-goggles effect was stronger for men than for women, and took effect only after 2 pints. Imagine we followed this finding up. We took a sample of 26 men (because the effect is stronger in men) and gave them various doses of **Alcohol** over four different weeks (0 pints, 2 pints, 4 pints and 6 pints of lager). Each week (and, therefore, in each state of drunkenness) participants were asked to select a mate in a normal club (that had dim lighting) and then select a second mate in a specially designed club that had bright lighting. The second independent variable was whether the club had dim or bright lighting. The outcome measure was the attractiveness of each mate as assessed by a panel of independent judges. The data are in the file **BeerGogglesLighting.sav**. Analyse them with a two-way repeated-measures ANOVA. ②

- **Task 6**: Using SPSS Tip 14.2, change the syntax in **SimpleEffectsAttitude.sps** to look at the effect of drink at different levels of imagery. ③

- **Task 7**: A lot of my research looks at the effect of giving children information about animals. In one particular study (Field, 2006), I used three novel animals (the quoll, quokka and cuscus) and children were told negative things about one of the animals, positive things about another, and were given no information about the third (our control). I then asked the children to place their hands in three wooden boxes each of which they believed contained one of the aforementioned animals. The data are in the file **Field(2006).sav**. Draw an error bar graph of the means, then do some normality tests on the data. ①

- **Task 8**: Log-transform the scores in Task 7 and repeat the normality tests. ②

- **Task 9**: Conduct a one-way ANOVA on the log-transformed scores in Task 8. Do children take longer to put their hands in a box that they believe contains an animal about which they have been told nasty things? ②

Answers can be found on the companion website.

14.17. Further reading

Field, A. P. (1998). A bluffer's guide to sphericity. *Newsletter of the Mathematical, Statistical and Computing Section of the British Psychological Society*, 6(1), 13–22. (Available in the additional material for this chapter.)

Howell, D. C. (2012). *Statistical methods for psychology* (8th ed.). Belmont, CA: Wadsworth. (Or you might prefer his *Fundamental statistics for the behavioral sciences*. Both are excellent texts.)

Rosenthal, R., Rosnow, R. L., & Rubin, D. B. (2000). *Contrasts and effect sizes in behavioural research: A correlational approach*. Cambridge: Cambridge University Press. (This is quite advanced but really cannot be bettered for contrasts and effect size estimation.)

Mixed design ANOVA (GLM 5)

15

FIGURE 15.1
My 18th birthday
cake

15.1.1. What will this chapter tell me? ①

Most teenagers have anxiety and depression, but I probably had more than my fair share. The parasitic leech that was the all-boys' grammar school that I attended had feasted on my social skills, leaving in its wake a terrified husk. Although I had no real problem with playing my guitar and shouting in front of people, speaking to them was another matter entirely. In the band I felt at ease, in the real world I did not. Your 18th birthday is a time of great joy, where (in the UK at any rate) you cast aside the shackles of childhood and embrace the exciting new world of adult life. Your birthday cake might symbolize this happy transition by reflecting one of your great passions. Mine had a picture on it of a long-haired person who looked somewhat like me, slitting his wrists. That pretty much sums it up. Still, you can't lock yourself in your bedroom with your Iron Maiden albums for ever, and soon enough I tried to integrate with society. Between the ages of 16 and 18 this pretty much involved getting drunk. I quickly discovered that getting drunk made it much easier to speak to people, and getting *really* drunk made you unconscious and then the problem of speaking to people went away entirely. This situation was exacerbated by the sudden presence of girls in my social circle. I hadn't seen a girl since Clair Sparks; they were particularly problematic because not only did you have to talk to them, but what you said had to be really impressive because then they might become your girlfriend. Also, in 1990, girls didn't like to talk about Iron Maiden – they probably still don't. Speed dating[1] didn't exist back then, but if it had it would have been a sick and twisted manifestation of hell on earth for me. The idea of having a highly pressured social situation where you *have* to think of something witty and amusing to say or be thrown to the baying vultures of eternal loneliness would have had me injecting pure alcohol into my eyeballs; at least that way I could be in a coma and unable to see the disappointment on the faces of those forced to spend 3 minutes in my company. That's what this chapter is all about: speed dating, oh, and mixed ANOVA too, but if I mention that you'll move swiftly on to the next chapter when the bell rings.

15.2. Mixed designs ②

What is a mixed design?

If you thought that the previous chapter was bad, well, I'm about to throw an added complication into the mix. We can combine repeated-measures and independent designs, and this chapter looks at this situation. As if this wasn't bad enough, I'm also going to use this as an excuse to show you a design with three independent variables (at this point you should imagine me leaning back in my chair, cross-eyed, dribbling and laughing maniacally). A mixture of between-groups and repeated-measures variables is called a **mixed design**. It should be obvious that you need at least two independent variables for this type of design to be possible, but you can have more complex scenarios too (e.g., two between-groups and one repeated-measures, one between-groups and two repeated-measures, or even two of each).

SPSS allows you to test almost any design you might want to, and of virtually any degree of complexity. However, interaction terms are difficult enough to interpret with only two variables, so imagine how difficult they are if you include four. The best advice I can offer is to stick to three or fewer independent variables if you want to be able to interpret your interaction terms,[2] and certainly don't exceed four unless you want to give yourself a migraine.

This chapter will go through an example of a **mixed ANOVA**. There won't be any theory because you've probably had enough ANOVA theory by now to have a good idea of what's going on (you can read this as 'it's too complex for me and I'm going to cover up my own incompetence by pretending you don't need to know about it'). Essentially, though, as we have seen, any ANOVA is a linear model, so when we have three independent variables or predictors we simply add this third predictor into the linear model, give it a *b* and remember to also include any interactions involving the new predictor. We'll look at an example using SPSS and spend a bit of time developing your understanding of interactions and how to break them down using contrasts.

[1] In case speed dating goes out of fashion and no one knows what I'm going on about, the basic idea is that lots of men and women turn up to a venue (or just men or just women if it's a gay night), one-half of the group sit individually at small tables and the remainder choose a table, get 3 minutes to impress the other person at the table with their tales of heteroscedastic data, then a bell rings and they get up and move to the next table. Having worked around all of the tables, the end of the evening is spent either stalking the person whom you fancied or avoiding the hideous mutant who was going on about heterosomethingorother.

[2] Fans of irony will enjoy the four-way ANOVAs that I conducted in Field and Davey (1999) and Field and Moore (2005), to name but two examples.

15.3. Assumptions in mixed designs ②

If you have read any of the previous chapters on ANOVA you will be sick of me writing that ANOVA is an extension of the linear model and so all of the sources of potential bias (and counteractive measures) discussed in Chapter 5 apply (see Section 5.4, for example). But, there you go, I've just written it again. Of course, because mixed designs include both repeated measures and between-groups measures you have the double whammy of having to concern yourself with both homogeneity of variance *and* sphericity. It's enough to make you guzzle the ink from the octopus of inescapable despair. But don't: we know that a lack of sphericity is easily remedied by using the Greenhouse–Geisser correction.

The various other woes in Chapter 5 are more troublesome. As we saw in the previous chapter, the Bootstrap... button is absent in the dialog box for repeated-measures ANOVA. 'What about non-parametric tests?' you might ask. You wouldn't be alone: if I had £1 (or $1, €1 or whatever currency you fancy) for every time someone asked me what the non-parametric equivalent of mixed ANOVA was, I'd have a nice shiny new drum kit. The short answer is, there isn't one, but there *are* robust methods that can be used based on bootstrapping (Wilcox, 2012). They can't be done directly in SPSS but they can be implemented in R, and are explained in the sister textbook for that package (Field et al., 2012). Therefore, if the suggestions for overcoming bias in Chapter 5 don't help then stick an oxygen tank on your back and start swimming in the sea looking for that octopus …

15.4. What do men and women look for in a partner? ②

Lots of magazines go on and on about how men and women want different things from relationships (or perhaps it's just my wife's copies of *Marie Claire*, which I don't read – honestly). The big question seems to be: are looks or personality more important? Imagine you wanted to put this to the test. You devised a cunning plan whereby you'd set up a speed-dating night. Little did the people who came along know that you'd got some of your friends to act as the dates. Each date varied in their attractiveness (attractive, average or ugly) and their charisma (charismatic, average and dull), and by combining these characteristics you get nine different stooge dates. As such, your stooge dates were made up of nine different people. Three were extremely attractive people but differed in their personality: one had tonnes of charisma,[3] one had some charisma and the other was as dull as this book. Another three people were of average attractiveness, and again differed in their personality: one was highly charismatic, one had some charisma and the third was a dullard. The final three were, with no offense intended to pigs, pig-ugly, and again one was charismatic, one had some charisma and the final poor soul was mind-numbingly tedious. Obviously you had two sets of stooge dates: one set was male and the other female, so that your participants could match up with dates of their preferred gender.

The participants were not these nine stooges, but 10 men and 10 women who came to the speed-dating event that you had set up. Over the course of the evening they speed-dated all nine stooges of the gender that they'd normally date. After their 3-minute date, they rated how much they'd like to have a proper date with the person as a percentage (100% = 'I'd pay large sums of money for their phone number', 0% = 'I'd pay a large sum of money for a plane ticket to get me as far away from them as possible'). As such, each participant rated

---

[3] The highly attractive people with tonnes of charisma were, of course, taken to a remote cliff top and shot after the experiment because life is hard enough without having people like that floating around making you feel inadequate.

TABLE 15.1   Data from **LooksOrPersonality.sav** (Att = Attractive, Av = Average, Ug = Ugly)

Looks	High Charisma			Some Charisma			Dullard		
	Att	Av	Ugly	Att	Av	Ug	Att	Av	Ug
Male	86	84	67	88	69	50	97	48	47
	91	83	53	83	74	48	86	50	46
	89	88	48	99	70	48	90	45	48
	89	69	58	86	77	40	87	47	53
	80	81	57	88	71	50	82	50	45
	80	84	51	96	63	42	92	48	43
	89	85	61	87	79	44	86	50	45
	100	94	56	86	71	54	84	54	47
	90	74	54	92	71	58	78	38	45
	89	86	63	80	73	49	91	48	39
Female	89	91	93	88	65	54	55	48	52
	84	90	85	95	70	60	50	44	45
	99	100	89	80	79	53	51	48	44
	86	89	83	86	74	58	52	48	47
	89	87	80	83	74	43	58	50	48
	80	81	79	86	59	47	51	47	40
	82	92	85	81	66	47	50	45	47
	97	69	87	95	72	51	45	48	46
	95	92	90	98	64	53	54	53	45
	95	93	96	79	66	46	52	39	47

nine different people who varied in their attractiveness and personality. So, there are two repeated-measures variables: **Looks** (with three levels because the person could be attractive, average or ugly) and **Personality** (again with three levels because the person could have lots of charisma, have some charisma or be a dullard). The people giving the ratings could be male or female, so we should also include the gender of the person making the ratings (male or female), and this, of course, will be a between-groups variable. The data are in Table 15.1.

15.5. Mixed ANOVA in SPSS ②

15.5.1. Mixed ANOVA: the general procedure ②

The general procedure for mixed ANOVA is the same as any other linear model (see Chapter 8). Figure 15.2 shows a simpler overview that highlights some of the specific issues when using a mixed design.

15.5.2. Entering data ②

To enter these data into SPSS we use the same procedure as the two-way repeated-measures ANOVA. Remember that each row in the data editor represents a single participant's data.

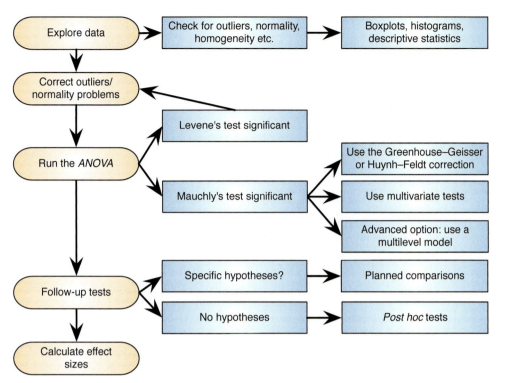

FIGURE 15.2
The process
for conducting
mixed ANOVA

If a person participates in all conditions (in this case they date all of the people who differ in attractiveness and all of the people who differ in their charisma) then each condition will be represented by a column in the data editor. In this experiment there are nine experimental conditions and so the data need to be entered in nine columns (the format is identical to Table 15.1). You will also need to create a coding variable to enter values for the gender of the participant (I used 1 = male, 2 = female).

SELF-TEST In the data editor create nine variables with the names and variable labels given in Figure 15.3. Create a variable Gender with value labels 1 = male, 2 = female.

Variable name	Variable label
att_high	Attractive and highly charismatic
av_high	Average and highly charismatic
ug_high	Ugly and highly charismatic
att_some	Attractive and some charisma
av_some	Average and some charisma
ug_some	Ugly and some charisma
att_none	Attractive and a dullard
av_none	Average and a dullard
ug_none	Ugly and a dullard

FIGURE 15.3
Variable names
and labels

SELF-TEST   Enter the data as in Table 15.1. If you have problems entering the data then use the file **Looks OrPersonality.sav.**

15.5.3.   The main analysis ②

First we have to define our repeated-measures variables, so access the *Define Factor(s)* dialog box by selecting Analyze General Linear Model ▸ Repeated Measures…. As with two-way repeated-measures ANOVA (see the previous chapter), we need to give names to our repeated-measures variables and specify how many levels they have. In this case there are two within-subject factors: **Looks** (attractive, average or ugly) and **Charisma** (high charisma, some charisma and dullard). In the *Define Factors(s)* dialog box replace the word *factor1* with the word *Looks*, then type 3 into the box labelled *Number of Levels*. Click on Add to add this variable to the list of repeated-measures variables. This variable will now appear in the white box at the bottom of the dialog box as *Looks(3)*. Now enter the word *Charisma* into the space labelled *Within-Subject Factor Name* and then, because there were three levels of this variable, enter the number 3 into the space labelled *Number of Levels*. Click on Add to include this variable in the list of factors; it will appear as *Charisma(3)*. The finished dialog box is shown in Figure 15.4. When you have entered both of the within-subject factors click on Define to go to the main dialog box.

The main dialog box in Figure 15.5 looks the same as in the previous chapter. At the top of the *Within-Subjects Variables* box, SPSS states that there are two factors: **Looks** and **Charisma**. In the box below there is a series of question marks followed by bracketed numbers. The numbers in brackets represent the levels of the independent variables – see the previous chapter for a more detailed explanation. There are two independent variables and so there are two numbers in the brackets. The first number refers to levels of the first factor listed above the box (in this case **Looks**), while the second refers to levels of the second factor listed above the box (in this case **Charisma**). As with the other repeated-measures ANOVAs we've come across, we have to replace the question marks with variables from the list on the left-hand side of the dialog box.

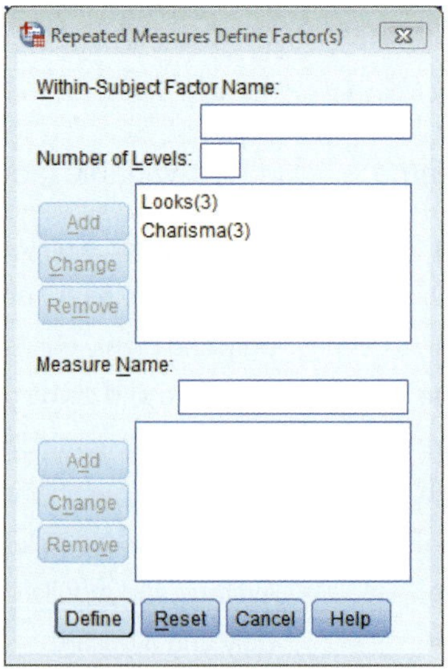

FIGURE 15.4

The *Define Factors(s)* dialog box for mixed design ANOVA with two repeated measures

Repeated Measures Define Factor(s)
Within-Subject Factor Name:
Number of Levels:
Add / Change / Remove — Looks(3), Charisma(3)
Measure Name:
Add / Change / Remove
Define   Reset   Cancel   Help

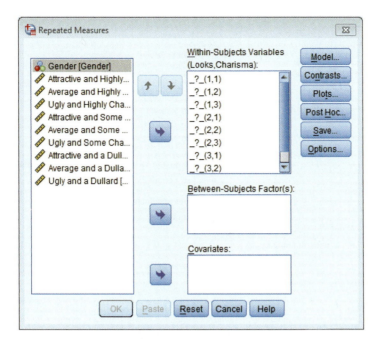

FIGURE 15.5
The main dialog
box for mixed
ANOVA before
completion

As in the previous chapter, we need to think about the type of contrasts that we might want to do *before* specifying variables in this dialog box. For the first variable, **Looks**, there were three conditions: attractive, average and ugly. In many ways it makes sense to compare the attractive and ugly conditions to the average because the average person represents the norm (although it wouldn't be wrong to, for example, compare attractive and average to ugly). This comparison could be done by specifying a simple contrast (see Table 11.6) provided that we make sure that average is coded as our first or last category. For the second factor, **Charisma**, there is also a category that represents the norm: some charisma. Again, we could use this as a control against which to compare our two extremes (high charisma and being a dullard). Therefore, we could again use a simple contrast to compare everything against 'some charisma' but we would need to enter this category as either the first or last level.

Based on this discussion about using contrasts, it makes sense to have average as level 3 of the **Looks** factor and some charisma as level 3 of the **Charisma** factor. The remaining levels can be decided arbitrarily. I have chosen attractive as level 1 and ugly as level 2 of the **Looks** factor. For the **Charisma** variable I chose high charisma as level 1 and none as level 2. These decisions mean that the variables should be entered as in Figure 15.6. I've deliberately made the order different from how the variables are listed in the data editor.

So far the procedure has been similar to other factorial repeated-measures designs. However, we have a mixed design here, so we also need to specify our between-groups factor as well. We do this by selecting **Gender** in the variables list and dragging it to the box

att_high	➡	_?_(1,1)
att_none	➡	_?_(1,2)
att_some	➡	_?_(1,3)
ug_high	➡	_?_(2,1)
ug_none	➡	_?_(2,2)
ug_some	➡	_?_(2,3)
av_high	➡	_?_(3,1)
av_none	➡	_?_(3,2)
av_some	➡	_?_(3,3)

FIGURE 15.6
Variable
allocations
for the speed
dating data

FIGURE 15.7
The main dialog box for mixed ANOVA after completion

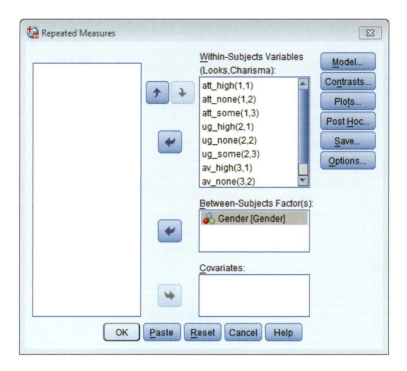

labelled *Between-Subjects Factors* (or click on ➡). The completed dialog box should look like Figure 15.7. I've already discussed the options for the buttons at the side of this dialog box, so I'll talk only about the ones of particular interest for this example.

15.5.4.   Other options ②

As we've seen before, there's no facility for entering contrast codes in repeated-measures designs (unless you use syntax) so we need to use the built-in contrasts (see Table 11.6). Figure 15.8 shows the dialog box for specifying contrasts, which is obtained by clicking on `Contrasts...` in the main dialog box. In the previous section I described why it might be interesting to use the average attractiveness and some charisma conditions as base categories for the **Looks** and **Charisma** factors, respectively. We have used the contrasts dialog box before in Sections 12.4.5 and 14.5.3, so all I will say is that you should select a simple contrast for both **Looks** and **Charisma**. In both cases, we specified the variables such that the control category was the last one; therefore, we need not change the reference category for the contrast. Once the contrasts have been selected, click on `Continue` to return to the main dialog box. **Gender** has only two levels (male or female) so we don't need to specify contrasts for this variable, nor do we need to select *post hoc* tests.[4]

We can plot a rough graph of the looks × charisma × gender interaction effect by clicking on `Plots...` to access the dialog box in Figure 15.9. Drag **Looks** to the slot labelled *Horizontal Axis*, **Charisma** to the slot labelled *Separate Lines*, and **Gender** to the slot

---

[4] If you want *post hoc* tests for your own data, then click on `Post Hoc...` to activate the *post hoc* test dialog box, which can be used as explained in Section 11.6.3.

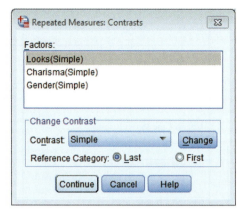

FIGURE 15.8

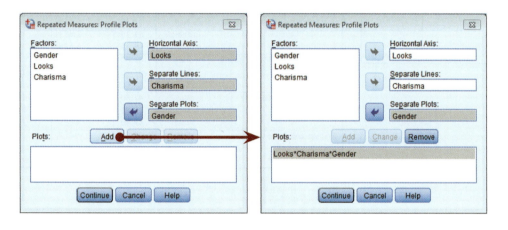

FIGURE 15.9
The *Profile Plots* dialog box for a three-way mixed ANOVA

labelled *Separate Plots*. When all three variables have been specified, don't forget to click on [Add] to add this combination to the list of plots. Specifying the graph in this way will plot the interaction graph for looks and charisma, but produce separate versions for male and female participants.

As far as other options are concerned, you should select the same ones that were chosen for the example in the previous chapter (see Section 14.9.5). It is worth selecting estimated marginal means for all effects (because these values will help you to understand any significant effects), but to save space I did not ask for confidence intervals for these effects because we have considered this part of the output in some detail already. When all of the appropriate options have been selected, run the analysis.

ODITI'S LANTERN

Mixed ANOVA

'I, Oditi, may be low on attractiveness but I am high on charisma. I'm high on a few other things too. Look deep into my charming eyes and you will find that you want to join the cult of undiscovered numerical truths. Our next lesson is mixed ANOVA, so stare into my lantern and immerse yourself ever deeper in the cult. You will awaken with a strange love of three-way interactions, and a desire to do only as I say.'

OUTPUT 15.1

Descriptive Statistics

	Gender	Mean	Std. Deviation	N
Attractive and Highly Charismatic	Male	88.30	5.697	10
	Female	89.60	6.637	10
	Total	88.95	6.057	20
Attractive and a Dullard	Male	87.30	5.438	10
	Female	51.80	3.458	10
	Total	69.55	18.743	20
Attractive and Some Charisma	Male	88.50	5.740	10
	Female	87.10	6.806	10
	Total	87.80	6.170	20
Ugly and Highly Charismatic	Male	56.80	5.731	10
	Female	86.70	5.438	10
	Total	71.75	16.274	20
Ugly and a Dullard	Male	45.80	3.584	10
	Female	46.10	3.071	10
	Total	45.95	3.252	20
Ugly and Some Charisma	Male	48.30	5.376	10
	Female	51.20	5.453	10
	Total	49.75	5.476	20
Average and Highly Charismatic	Male	82.80	7.005	10
	Female	88.40	8.329	10
	Total	85.60	8.022	20
Average and a Dullard	Male	47.80	4.185	10
	Female	47.00	3.742	10
	Total	47.40	3.885	20
Average and Some Charisma	Male	71.80	4.417	10
	Female	68.90	5.953	10
	Total	70.35	5.314	20

Within-Subjects Factors

Measure: MEASURE_1

Looks	Charisma	Dependent Variable
1	1	att_high
	2	att_none
	3	att_some
2	1	ug_high
	2	ug_none
	3	ug_some
3	1	av_high
	2	av_none
	3	av_some

15.6. Output for mixed factorial ANOVA ③

The initial output contains a table listing the repeated-measures variables from the data editor and the level of each independent variable that they represent. The second table contains descriptive statistics (mean and standard deviation) for each of the nine conditions, split according to whether participants were male or female (see Output 15.1). The names in this table are the names I gave the variables in the data editor (therefore, your output may differ slightly). These descriptive statistics show us the pattern of means across all conditions; we use these means to produce the graphs of the three-way interaction.

SELF-TEST   Output 15.2 shows the results of Mauchly's sphericity test. Based on what you have already learnt, was sphericity violated?

Output 15.2 shows the results of Mauchly's sphericity test for each of the three repeated-measures effects in the model. None of the effects violate the assumption of sphericity because all of the values in the column labelled *Sig.* are above .05; therefore, we can assume sphericity when we look at our *F*-statistics.

Output 15.3 shows the summary table of the repeated-measures effects in the ANOVA with corrected *F*-values. As with factorial repeated-measures ANOVA, the output is split into sections for each of the effects in the model and their associated error terms. The

Mauchly's Test of Sphericity[a]

Measure: MEASURE_1

Within Subjects Effect	Mauchly's W	Approx. Chi–Square	df	Sig.	Epsilon[b]		
					Greenhouse–Geisser	Huynh–Feldt	Lower-bound
Looks	.960	.690	2	.708	.962	1.000	.500
Charisma	.929	1.246	2	.536	.934	1.000	.500
Looks * Charisma	.613	8.025	9	.534	.799	1.000	.250

Tests the null hypothesis that the error covariance matrix of the orthonormalized transformed dependent variables is proportional to an identity matrix.

a. Design: Intercept + Gender
   Within Subjects Design: Looks + Charisma + Looks * Charisma

b. May be used to adjust the degrees of freedom for the averaged tests of significance. Corrected tests are displayed in the Tests of Within–Subjects Effects table.

OUTPUT 15.2

Tests of Within–Subjects Effects

OUTPUT 15.3

Measure: MEASURE_1

Source		Type III Sum of Squares	df	Mean Square	F	Sig.
Looks	Sphericity Assumed	20779.633	2	10389.817	423.733	.000
	Greenhouse–Geisser	20779.633	1.923	10803.275	423.733	.000
	Huynh–Feldt	20779.633	2.000	10389.817	423.733	.000
	Lower-bound	20779.633	1.000	20779.633	423.733	.000
Looks * Gender	Sphericity Assumed	3944.100	2	1972.050	80.427	.000
	Greenhouse–Geisser	3944.100	1.923	2050.527	80.427	.000
	Huynh–Feldt	3944.100	2.000	1972.050	80.427	.000
	Lower-bound	3944.100	1.000	3944.100	80.427	.000
Error(Looks)	Sphericity Assumed	882.711	36	24.520		
	Greenhouse–Geisser	882.711	34.622	25.496		
	Huynh–Feldt	882.711	36.000	24.520		
	Lower-bound	882.711	18.000	49.040		
Charisma	Sphericity Assumed	23233.600	2	11616.800	328.250	.000
	Greenhouse–Geisser	23233.600	1.868	12437.761	328.250	.000
	Huynh–Feldt	23233.600	2.000	11616.800	328.250	.000
	Lower-bound	23233.600	1.000	23233.600	328.250	.000
Charisma * Gender	Sphericity Assumed	4420.133	2	2210.067	62.449	.000
	Greenhouse–Geisser	4420.133	1.868	2366.252	62.449	.000
	Huynh–Feldt	4420.133	2.000	2210.067	62.449	.000
	Lower-bound	4420.133	1.000	4420.133	62.449	.000
Error(Charisma)	Sphericity Assumed	1274.044	36	35.390		
	Greenhouse–Geisser	1274.044	33.624	37.891		
	Huynh–Feldt	1274.044	36.000	35.390		
	Lower-bound	1274.044	18.000	70.780		
Looks * Charisma	Sphericity Assumed	4055.267	4	1013.817	36.633	.000
	Greenhouse–Geisser	4055.267	3.197	1268.295	36.633	.000
	Huynh–Feldt	4055.267	4.000	1013.817	36.633	.000
	Lower-bound	4055.267	1.000	4055.267	36.633	.000
Looks * Charisma * Gender	Sphericity Assumed	2669.667	4	667.417	24.116	.000
	Greenhouse–Geisser	2669.667	3.197	834.945	24.116	.000
	Huynh–Feldt	2669.667	4.000	667.417	24.116	.000
	Lower-bound	2669.667	1.000	2669.667	24.116	.000
Error(Looks*Charisma)	Sphericity Assumed	1992.622	72	27.675		
	Greenhouse–Geisser	1992.622	57.554	34.622		
	Huynh–Feldt	1992.622	72.000	27.675		
	Lower-bound	1992.622	18.000	110.701		

interactions between our between-groups variable of gender and the repeated-measures effects are included in this table also.

You should be aware by now that if the values in the column labelled *Sig.* are less than .05 for a particular effect then it is statistically significant. Working down from the top of the table we find a significant effects of **Looks**, the **Looks** × **Gender** interaction, **Charisma**, the **Charisma** × **Gender** interaction, the **Looks** × **Charisma** interaction and the **Looks** × **Charisma** × **Gender** interaction. Everything, basically. You wouldn't normally be interested in main effects when there are significant interactions, but for completeness we'll look at how to interpret each effect in turn, starting with the main effect of **Gender**.

SELF-TEST   What is the difference between a main effect and an interaction?

15.6.1.   The main effect of gender ②

Before looking at the main effect of gender we ought to check the assumption of homogeneity of variance using Levene's test (see Section 5.3.3.2).

SELF-TEST   Was the assumption of homogeneity of variance met (Output 15.4)?

SPSS produces a table listing Levene's test for all combinations of levels of any repeated-measures variables. Output 15.4 shows this table, and you can see that because all

LABCOAT LENI'S REAL RESEARCH 15.1

The objection of desire ③

There is a concern that images that portray women as sexually desirable objectify them. This idea was tested in an inventive study by Philippe Bernard (Bernard, Gervais, Allen, Campomizzi, & Klein, 2012). People find it harder to recognize upside-down (inverted) pictures than ones the right way up. This 'inversion effect' occurs for pictures of humans, but not for pictures of objects. Bernard et al. used this effect to test whether sexualized pictures of women are processed as objects. They presented people with pictures of sexualized (i.e., not wearing many clothes) males and females. Half of these pictures were inverted (**Inverted_Women** and **Inverted_Men**) and the

remainder were upright (**Upright_Women and Upright_Men**). They noted the **Gender** of the participant. After each trial participants were shown two pictures and asked to identify the one they had just seen. The outcome was the proportion of correctly identified pictures. An inversion effect is demonstrated by higher recognition scores for upright pictures than inverted ones. If sexualized females are processed as objects you would expect an inversion effect for the male pictures but not the female ones. The data are in **Bernard et al (2012). sav.** Conduct a three-way mixed ANOVA to see whether picture gender (male or female) and picture orientation (upright or inverted) interact. Include participant gender as the between-group factor. Follow up the analysis with *t*-tests looking at (1) the inversion effect for male pictures, (2) the inversion effect for female pictures, (3) the gender effect for upright pictures, and (4) the gender effect for inverted pictures. Answers are on the companion website (or look at page 470 in the original article).

BERNARD, P., ET AL. (2012). *PSYCHOLOGICAL SCIENCE*, 23(5), 469–471.

Levene's Test of Equality of Error Variances[a]

	F	df1	df2	Sig.
Attractive and Highly Charismatic	1.131	1	18	.302
Attractive and a Dullard	1.949	1	18	.180
Attractive and Some Charisma	.599	1	18	.449
Ugly and Highly Charismatic	.005	1	18	.945
Ugly and a Dullard	.082	1	18	.778
Ugly and Some Charisma	.124	1	18	.729
Average and Highly Charismatic	.102	1	18	.753
Average and a Dullard	.004	1	18	.950
Average and Some Charisma	1.763	1	18	.201

Tests the null hypothesis that the error variance of the dependent variable is equal across groups.

a. Design: Intercept + Gender
   Within Subjects Design: Looks + Charisma + Looks * Charisma

significance values are greater than .05 variances are homogeneous for all levels of the repeated-measures variables. If any values were significant, then we would have to try some of the corrective measures discussed in Chapter 5.

The main effect of gender is listed separately from the repeated-measures effects in a table labelled *Tests of Between-Subjects Effects*. This table (Output 15.5) reveals a non-significant effect because the significance of .946 is greater than the standard cut-off point of .05. This effect tells us that if we ignore all other variables, male participants' ratings were basically the same as females'. If you requested that SPSS display means for all of the effects in the analysis (I'll assume you did from now on) you should find tables of means in a section labelled *Estimated Marginal Means* in the output. Figure 15.10 shows this table for the main effect of gender alongside a plot of these means. It is clear from this graph that, overall, men and women's ratings were the same.

Tests of Between–Subjects Effects

Measure: MEASURE_1
Transformed Variable: Average

Source	Type III Sum of Squares	df	Mean Square	F	Sig.
Intercept	94027.756	1	94027.756	20036.900	.000
Gender	.022	1	.022	.005	.946
Error	84.469	18	4.693		

15.6.2. The main effect of looks ②

SELF-TEST Based on the previous section and what you have learned in previous chapters, can you interpret the main effect of looks? (Output 15.3)?

We came across the significant main effect of looks, $F(2, 36) = 423.73$, $p < .001$, in Output 15.3. This effect tells us that if we ignore all other variables, ratings were different for attractive, average and ugly dates. Figure 15.11 shows the *Estimated Marginal Means*

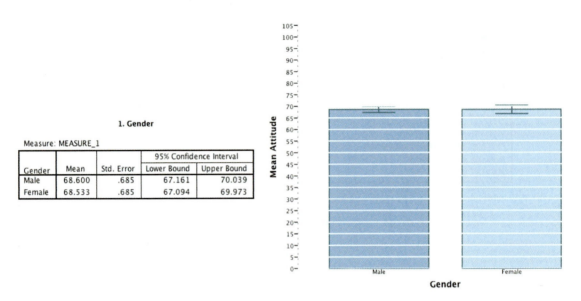

1. Gender

Measure: MEASURE_1

| Gender | Mean | Std. Error | 95% Confidence Interval | |
			Lower Bound	Upper Bound
Male	68.600	.685	67.161	70.039
Female	68.533	.685	67.094	69.973

FIGURE 15.10   Means and graph of the main effect of gender

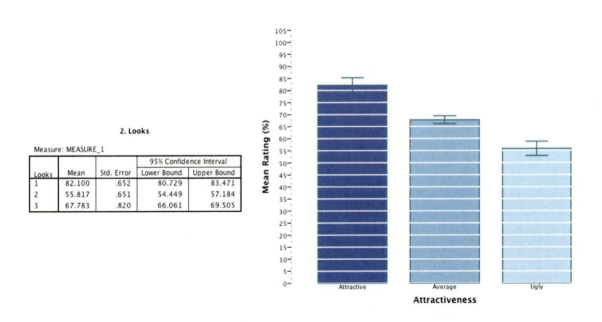

2. Looks

Measure: MEASURE_1

| Looks | Mean | Std. Error | 95% Confidence Interval | |
			Lower Bound	Upper Bound
1	82.100	.652	80.729	83.471
2	55.817	.651	54.449	57.184
3	67.783	.820	66.061	69.505

FIGURE 15.11   Means and graph of the main effect of looks

for the main effect of looks and a plot of these means. The levels of looks are labelled as 1, 2 and 3, and it's down to you to remember how you entered the variables (or you can look at the summary table that SPSS produces at the beginning of the output – see Output 15.1). If you did the same as I did then level 1 is attractive, level 2 is ugly and level 3 is average. From this table and plot you can see that as attractiveness falls, the mean rating falls too. So this main effect seems to reflect that the raters were more likely to express a greater interest in going out with attractive people than average or ugly people. However, we really need to look at some contrasts to find out exactly what's going on.

Output 15.6 shows the contrasts that we requested. For the time being, just look at the row labelled *Looks*. Remember that we did a simple contrast, and so we get a contrast comparing level 1 to level 3, and then comparing level 2 to level 3; because of the order in which we entered the variables, these contrasts represent attractive compared to average (level 1 vs. level 3) and ugly compared to average (level 2 vs. level 3). The values of F for each contrast, and their related significance values, tell us that the main effect of attractiveness represented the fact that attractive dates were rated significantly higher than average dates, $F(1, 18) = 226.99$, $p < .001$, and average dates were rated significantly higher than ugly ones, $F(1, 18) = 160.07$, $p < .001$.

15.6.3. The main effect of charisma ②

In Output 15.3 there was a significant main effect of charisma, $F(2, 36) = 328.25$, $p < .001$. This effect tells us that if we ignore all other variables, ratings were different for highly charismatic, averagely charismatic and dull people. The table labelled *Charisma* in the section headed *Estimated Marginal Means* tells us what this effect means (as shown in Figure 15.12 alongside a plot). Again, the levels of charisma are labelled as 1, 2 and 3. If you followed what I did then level 1 is high charisma, level 2 is dullard and level 3 is some charisma. This main effect seems to reflect that as charisma declines, the mean rating of the data falls too: raters expressed a greater interest in going out with charismatic people than average people or dullards.

We requested simple contrasts (the row labelled *Charisma* in Output 15.6), and because of the order in which we entered variables these contrasts represent high charisma compared

Tests of Within-Subjects Contrasts

Measure: MEASURE_1

Source	Looks	Charisma	Type III Sum of Squares	df	Mean Square	F	Sig.
Looks	Level 1 vs. Level 3		4099.339	1	4099.339	226.986	.000
	Level 2 vs. Level 3		2864.022	1	2864.022	160.067	.000
Looks * Gender	Level 1 vs. Level 3		781.250	1	781.250	43.259	.000
	Level 2 vs. Level 3		540.800	1	540.800	30.225	.000
Error(Looks)	Level 1 vs. Level 3		325.078	18	18.060		
	Level 2 vs. Level 3		322.067	18	17.893		
Charisma		Level 1 vs. Level 3	3276.800	1	3276.800	109.937	.000
		Level 2 vs. Level 3	4500.000	1	4500.000	227.941	.000
Charisma * Gender		Level 1 vs. Level 3	810.689	1	810.689	27.199	.000
		Level 2 vs. Level 3	665.089	1	665.089	33.689	.000
Error(Charisma)		Level 1 vs. Level 3	536.511	18	29.806		
		Level 2 vs. Level 3	355.356	18	19.742		
Looks * Charisma	Level 1 vs. Level 3	Level 1 vs. Level 3	3976.200	1	3976.200	21.944	.000
		Level 2 vs. Level 3	441.800	1	441.800	4.091	.058
	Level 2 vs. Level 3	Level 1 vs. Level 3	911.250	1	911.250	6.231	.022
		Level 2 vs. Level 3	7334.450	1	7334.450	88.598	.000
Looks * Charisma * Gender	Level 1 vs. Level 3	Level 1 vs. Level 3	168.200	1	168.200	.928	.348
		Level 2 vs. Level 3	6552.200	1	6552.200	60.669	.000
	Level 2 vs. Level 3	Level 1 vs. Level 3	1711.250	1	1711.250	11.701	.003
		Level 2 vs. Level 3	110.450	1	110.450	1.334	.263
Error(Looks*Charisma)	Level 1 vs. Level 3	Level 1 vs. Level 3	3261.600	18	181.200		
		Level 2 vs. Level 3	1944.000	18	108.000		
	Level 2 vs. Level 3	Level 1 vs. Level 3	2632.500	18	146.250		
		Level 2 vs. Level 3	1490.100	18	82.783		

OUTPUT 15.6

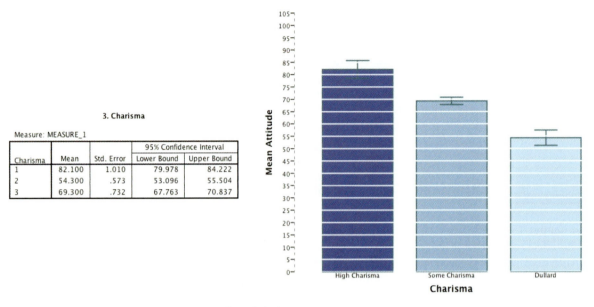

3. Charisma

Measure: MEASURE_1

Charisma	Mean	Std. Error	95% Confidence Interval	
			Lower Bound	Upper Bound
1	82.100	1.010	79.978	84.222
2	54.300	.573	53.096	55.504
3	69.300	.732	67.763	70.837

FIGURE 15.12   Means and graph of the main effect of charisma

to some charisma (level 1 vs. level 3) and no charisma compared to some charisma (level 2 vs. level 3). These contrasts tell us that the main effect of charisma is that highly charismatic dates were rated significantly higher than dates with some charisma, $F(1, 18) = 109.94$, $p <.001$, and dates with some charisma were rated significantly higher than dullards, $F(1, 18) = 227.94$, $p < .001$.

15.6.4.   The interaction between gender and looks ②

Gender significantly interacted with the attractiveness of the date, $F(2, 36) = 80.43$, $p < .001$ (Output 15.3). This effect tells us that the profile of ratings across dates of different attractiveness was different for men and women. We can again use the estimated marginal means to determine the nature of this interaction (you can get SPSS to plot this interaction using the dialog box in Figure 15.9). The means and interaction graph in Figure 15.13 show the meaning of this result. The graph shows that male (red line) and female (blue line) ratings are very similar for average-looking dates, but men give higher ratings (i.e., they're really keen to go out with these people) than women for attractive dates, but women express more interest in going out with ugly people than men. In general this interaction seems to suggest than men's interest in dating a person is more influenced by their looks than women's. Although both male's and female's interest decreases as attractiveness decreases, this decrease is more pronounced for men. This interaction can be clarified using the contrasts in Output 15.6.

15.6.4.1. Looks × gender interaction 1: attractive vs. average, male vs. female ②

The contrast for the first interaction term looks at level 1 of looks (attractive) compared to level 3 (average), comparing male and female scores. This contrast is highly significant, $F(1, 18) = 43.26$, $p <.001$, suggesting that the increased interest in attractive dates compared to average-looking dates found for men is significantly more than for women. So, in

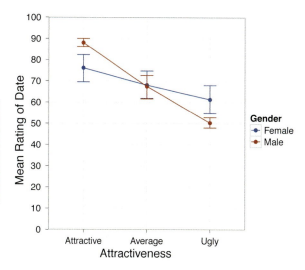

4. Gender * Looks

Measure: MEASURE_1

Gender	Looks	Mean	Std. Error	95% Confidence Interval	
				Lower Bound	Upper Bound
Male	1	88.033	.923	86.095	89.972
	2	50.300	.921	48.366	52.234
	3	67.467	1.159	65.031	69.902
Female	1	76.167	.923	74.228	78.105
	2	61.333	.921	59.399	63.267
	3	68.100	1.159	65.665	70.535

FIGURE 15.13 Means and graph of the gender × looks interaction

Figure 15.13 the slope of the red line (male) between attractive dates and average dates is steeper than the comparable blue line (women). The preferences for attractive dates, compared to average-looking dates, are greater for males than females.

15.6.4.2. Looks × gender interaction 2: ugly vs. average, male vs. female ②

The second contrast, which compares males and females at level 2 of looks (ugly) relative to level 3 (average) is highly significant, $F(1, 18) = 30.23$, $p < .001$. This tells us that the decreased interest in ugly dates compared to average-looking dates found for men is significantly more than for women. In Figure 15.13 the slope of the red line between the ugly and average dates is steeper than the corresponding blue line. The preferences for average-looking dates, compared to ugly dates, are greater for males than females.

15.6.5. The interaction between gender and charisma ②

Output 15.3 showed that gender significantly interacted with how charismatic the date was, $F(2, 36) = 62.45$, $p < .001$. This effect means that the profile of ratings across dates of different levels of charisma was different for men and women. The estimated marginal means and a plot of these means tell us the meaning of this interaction (see Figure 15.14). The graph shows the average male (red line) and female (blue line) ratings of dates of different levels of charisma, ignoring how attractive they were. The graph shows almost the reverse pattern to the gender × looks interaction: again male and female ratings are very similar for dates with normal amounts of charisma, but this time compared to women, men show more interest in dates low on charisma and less interest in very charismatic dates. In general, this interaction suggests that women's interest in dating a person is more influenced by their charisma than it is for men. Although both male's and female's interest decreases as charisma decreases, this decrease is more pronounced for females. We can break this interaction down using the contrasts in Output 15.6.

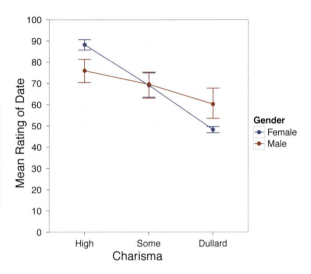

5. Gender * Charisma

Measure: MEASURE_1

Gender	Charisma	Mean	Std. Error	95% Confidence Interval	
				Lower Bound	Upper Bound
Male	1	75.967	1.428	72.966	78.967
	2	60.300	.810	58.598	62.002
	3	69.533	1.035	67.360	71.707
Female	1	88.233	1.428	85.233	91.234
	2	48.300	.810	46.598	50.002
	3	69.067	1.035	66.893	71.240

FIGURE 15.14   Means and graph of the gender × charisma interaction

15.6.5.1. Charisma × gender interaction 1: high vs. some charisma, male vs. female ②

The first contrast, which looks at level 1 of charisma (high charisma) compared to level 3 (some charisma), for males relative to females, is highly significant, $F(1, 18) = 27.20$, $p < .001$. This result tells us that the increased interest in highly charismatic dates compared to averagely charismatic dates found for women is significantly more than for men. In Figure 15.14 the slope of the blue line (female) between high charisma and some charisma is steeper than the corresponding red line (male). The preferences for very charismatic dates, compared to averagely charismatic dates, are greater for females than males.

15.6.5.2. Charisma × gender interaction 2: dullard vs. some charisma, male vs. female ②

The second contrast for the charisma × gender interaction looks at level 2 of charisma (dullard) compared to level 3 (some charisma), comparing male and female scores. This contrast is highly significant, $F(1, 18) = 33.69$, $p < .001$, and suggests that the decreased interest in dullard dates compared to averagely charismatic dates found for women is significantly more than for men. In Figure 15.14 the slope of the blue line (female) between some charisma and dullard is steeper than the corresponding red line (male): the preferences for dates with some charisma over dullards are greater for females than males.

15.6.6. The interaction between attractiveness and charisma ②

There was a significant attractiveness × charisma interaction in Output 15.3, $F(4, 72) = 36.63$, $p < .001$. This effect tells us that the profile of ratings across dates of different levels of charisma was different for attractive, average and ugly dates. We can unpick this interaction using the estimated marginal means, a plot (use the dialog box in Figure 15.9 to get a rough one), and contrasts. The graph (Figure 15.15) shows the mean ratings of dates of different levels of

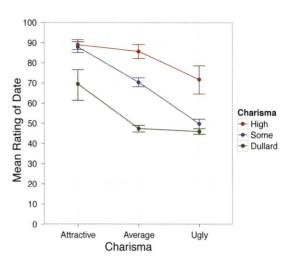

6. Looks * Charisma

Measure: MEASURE_1

Looks	Charisma	Mean	Std. Error	95% Confidence Interval	
				Lower Bound	Upper Bound
1	1	88.950	1.383	86.045	91.855
	2	69.550	1.019	67.409	71.691
	3	87.800	1.408	84.842	90.758
2	1	71.750	1.249	69.126	74.374
	2	45.950	.746	44.382	47.518
	3	49.750	1.211	47.206	52.294
3	1	85.600	1.721	81.985	89.215
	2	47.400	.888	45.535	49.265
	3	70.350	1.172	67.888	72.812

FIGURE 15.15   Means and graph of the looks × charisma interaction

attractiveness when the date also had high levels of charisma (red line), some charisma (blue line) and no charisma (green line). Look first at the difference between attractive and average-looking dates. The interest in highly charismatic dates doesn't change (the line is more or less flat between these two points), but for dates with some charisma or no charisma interest levels decline. So, if you have lots of charisma you can get away with being average-looking: people will still want to date you. Now look at the difference between average-looking and ugly dates. A different pattern is observed: for dates with no charisma there is little difference between ugly and average-looking people, but for those with charisma there is a decline in interest if you're ugly. It seems that if you're a dullard you need to be really attractive before people want to date you, but if you're ugly then having charisma won't help you much. The contrasts in Output 15.6 will pick apart these specific effects.

15.6.6.1. Looks × charisma interaction 1: attractive vs. average, high charisma vs. some charisma ②

The first contrast for the looks × charisma interaction investigates level 1 of looks (attractive) compared to level 3 of looks (average), for level 1 of charisma (high charisma) relative to level 3 of charisma (some charisma). This is like asking 'is the difference between high charisma and some charisma the same for attractive people and average-looking people?' The best way to understand this contrast is to focus on the relevant bit of the interaction graph in Figure 15.15, which I have reproduced in the top left of Figure 15.16. Interest (as indicated by high ratings) in attractive dates was the same regardless of whether they had high or average charisma; however, for average-looking dates, there was more interest when that person had high charisma rather than average. The contrast is highly significant, $F(1, 18) = 21.94$, $p < .001$, and tells us that as dates become less attractive there is a significantly greater decline in interest when charisma is average compared to when charisma is high.

15.6.6.2. Looks × charisma interaction 2: attractive vs. average, dullard vs. some charisma ②

The second contrast asked the question 'is the difference between no charisma and some charisma the same for attractive people and average-looking people?' It explores level 1 of

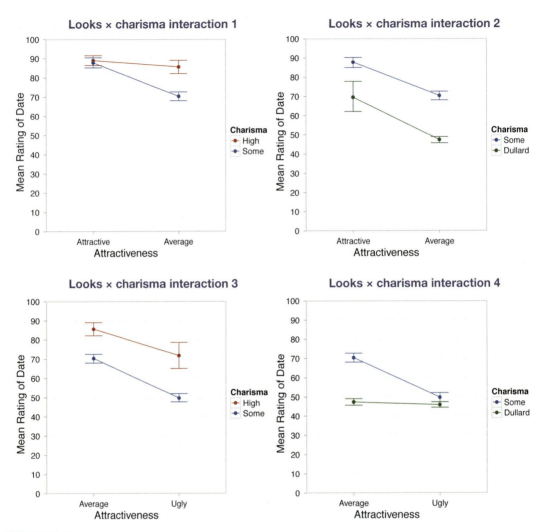

FIGURE 15.16   The looks × charisma interaction broken down into the four contrasts

looks (attractive) compared to level 3 of looks (average), in level 2 of charisma (dullard) relative to level 3 of charisma (some charisma). We can again focus on the relevant part of the interaction graph (Figure 15.15) which is reproduced in the top right of Figure 15.16. This graph shows that interest in attractive dates was higher when they had some charisma (blue) than when they were a dullard (green); the same is also true for average-looking dates. The two lines are fairly parallel, which is reflected in the non-significant contrast, $F(1, 18) = 4.09$, $p = .058$. It seems that as dates become less attractive there is a decline in interest both when charisma is low and when there is no charisma at all.

15.6.6.3. Looks × charisma interaction 3: ugly vs. average, high charisma vs. some charisma ②

The third contrast investigates level 2 of looks (ugly) relative to level 3 of looks (average), comparing level 1 of charisma (high charisma) to level 3 of charisma (some charisma). This contrast asks 'is the difference between high charisma and some charisma the same for ugly people and average-looking people?' The relevant part of the interaction graph is shown in the bottom left of Figure 15.16. Interest in dating decreases from average-looking dates to ugly ones in both high- and some-charisma dates; however, this fall is significantly greater in the low-charisma dates (the blue line is slightly steeper than the red), $F(1, 18) = 6.23$, $p = .022$. As dates become less attractive there is a significantly greater decline in interest when dates have some charisma compared to when they have a lot.

15.6.6.4. Looks × charisma interaction 4: ugly vs. average, dullard vs. some charisma ②

The final contrast addresses the question 'is the difference between no charisma and some charisma the same for ugly people and average-looking people?' It compares level 2 of looks (ugly) to level 3 of looks (average), in level 2 of charisma (dullard) relative to level 3 of charisma (some charisma). The relevant part of the interaction graph is shown in the bottom right of Figure 15.16. For average-looking dates, ratings were higher when they had some charisma than when they were a dullard, but for ugly dates the ratings were roughly the same regardless of the level of charisma. This contrast is highly significant, $F(1, 18) = 88.60$, $p < .001$.

15.6.7. The interaction between looks, charisma and gender ③

The significant looks × charisma × gender interaction in Output 15.3, $F(4, 72) = 24.12$, $p < .001$, tells us whether the looks × charisma interaction described above is the same for men and women (i.e., whether the combined effect of attractiveness of the date and their level of charisma is the same for male participants as for female subjects). The nature of this interaction is revealed in Figure 15.17, which shows the looks × charisma interaction for men and women separately (the means on which this graph is based appear in Output 15.7). The male graph shows that when dates are attractive, men will express a high interest regardless of charisma levels (the red, blue and green lines meet). At the opposite end of the attractiveness scale, when a date is ugly, regardless of charisma men will express very little interest (ratings are all low). The only time charisma makes any difference to a man is if the date is average-looking, in which case high charisma (red) boosts interest, being a dullard (green) reduces interest, and having a bit of charisma leaves things somewhere in between. The take-home message is that men are superficial cretins who are more interested in physical attributes.

How do I interpret a three way interaction?

 The picture for women is very different. If someone has high levels of charisma then it doesn't really matter what they look like, women will express an interest in them (the red line is relatively flat). At the other extreme, if the date is a dullard, then they will express no interest in them, regardless of how attractive they are (the green line is relatively flat). The only time attractiveness makes a difference is when someone has an average amount of charisma (the blue line), in which case being attractive boosts interest, and being ugly reduces it. Put another way, women prioritize charisma over physical appearance. Again, we can look at some contrasts to further break this interaction down (Output 15.6). These contrasts are similar to those for the looks × charisma interaction, but they now also take into account the effect of gender.

7. Gender * Looks * Charisma

Measure:MEASURE_1

Gender	Looks	Charisma	Mean	Std. Error	95% Confidence Interval	
					Lower Bound	Upper Bound
Male	1	1	88.300	1.956	84.191	92.409
		2	87.300	1.441	84.273	90.327
		3	88.500	1.991	84.317	92.683
	2	1	56.800	1.767	53.089	60.511
		2	45.800	1.055	43.583	48.017
		3	48.300	1.712	44.703	51.897
	3	1	82.800	2.434	77.687	87.913
		2	47.800	1.255	45.163	50.437
		3	71.800	1.657	68.318	75.282
Female	1	1	89.600	1.956	85.491	93.709
		2	51.800	1.441	48.773	54.827
		3	87.100	1.991	82.917	91.283
	2	1	86.700	1.767	82.989	90.411
		2	46.100	1.055	43.883	48.317
		3	51.200	1.712	47.603	54.797
	3	1	88.400	2.434	83.287	93.513
		2	47.000	1.255	44.363	49.637
		3	68.900	1.657	65.418	72.382

15.6.7.1. Looks × charisma × gender interaction 1: attractive vs. average, high charisma vs. some charisma, male vs. female ③

The first contrast for the looks × charisma × gender interaction compares level 1 of looks (attractive) to level 3 of looks (average), when level 1 of charisma (high charisma) is compared to level 3 of charisma (some charisma) in males relative to females, $F(1, 18) = 0.93, p = .348$. The relevant parts of Figure 15.17 are shown in the top left panel of Figure 15.18. It seems that interest in dating (as indicated by high ratings) attractive dates was the same regardless of whether they had high or average charisma (the blue and red dots are in the same place). However, for average-looking dates, there was more interest when that person had high charisma rather than some charisma (the blue dot is lower than the red dot). The non-significance of this contrast indicates that this pattern of results is very similar in males and females.

15.6.7.2. Looks × charisma × gender interaction 2: attractive vs. average, dullard vs. some charisma, male vs. female ③

The second contrast explores level 1 of looks (attractive) relative to level 3 of looks (average), when level 2 of charisma (dullard) is compared to level 3 of charisma (some charisma), in men compared to women. The relevant means are shown in the top right panel of Figure 15.18. The contrast is significant, $F(1, 18) = 60.67, p < .001$, which reflects the fact that the pattern of means is different for men and women. First, if we look at average-looking dates, more interest is expressed by both men and women when the date has some charisma than when they have none (and the distance between the blue and green lines is about the same). So the gender difference doesn't appear to be here. If we now look at attractive dates, we see that men are equally interested in their dates

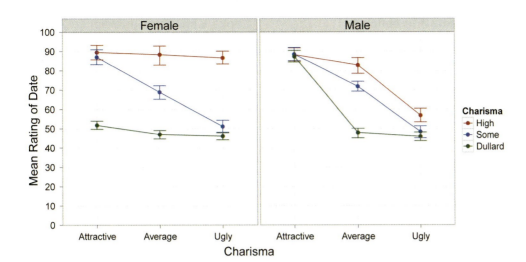

FIGURE 15.17
The looks × charisma interaction for men and women. Lines represent high charisma (red), some charisma (blue) and no charisma (green)

regardless of their charisma (the lines meet), but for women, they're much less interested in an attractive person if they are a dullard (the green dot is much lower than the blue).

Another way to look at this is that for dates with some charisma, the reduction in interest as attractiveness goes down is about the same in men and women (the blue lines have the same slope). However, for dates who are dullards, the decrease in interest if these dates are average-looking rather than attractive is much more dramatic in men than women (the green line is steeper for men than it is for women).

15.6.7.3. Looks × charisma × gender interaction 3: ugly vs. average, high charisma vs. some charisma, males vs. females ③

The third contrast was also significant, $F(1, 18) = 11.70$, $p = .003$. This contrast compares level 2 of looks (ugly) to level 3 of looks (average), in level 1 of charisma (high charisma) relative to level 3 of charisma (some charisma), in men compared to women. The bottom left panel of Figure 15.18 shows the relevant means. First, let's look at the men. For men, as attractiveness goes down, so does interest when the date has high charisma and when they have some charisma (the slopes of the red and blue lines are similar). So, regardless of charisma, there is a similar reduction in interest as attractiveness declines. Now let's look at the women. The picture is quite different: when charisma is high, there is no decline in interest as attractiveness falls (the red line is flat); however, when charisma is lower, the attractiveness of the date does matter and interest is lower in an ugly date than in an average-looking date (the blue line slopes down).

Another way to look at this is that for dates with some charisma, the reduction in interest as attractiveness goes down is about the same in men and women (the blue lines have similar slopes). However, for dates who have high charisma, the decrease in interest if these dates are ugly rather than average-looking is much more dramatic in men than women (the red line is steeper for men than it is for women).

15.6.7.4. Looks × charisma × gender interaction 4: ugly vs. average, dullard vs. some charisma, male vs. female ③

The final contrast was not significant, $F(1, 18) = 1.33$, $p = .263$. This contrast looks at the effect of gender when comparing level 2 of looks (ugly) to level 3 of looks (average),

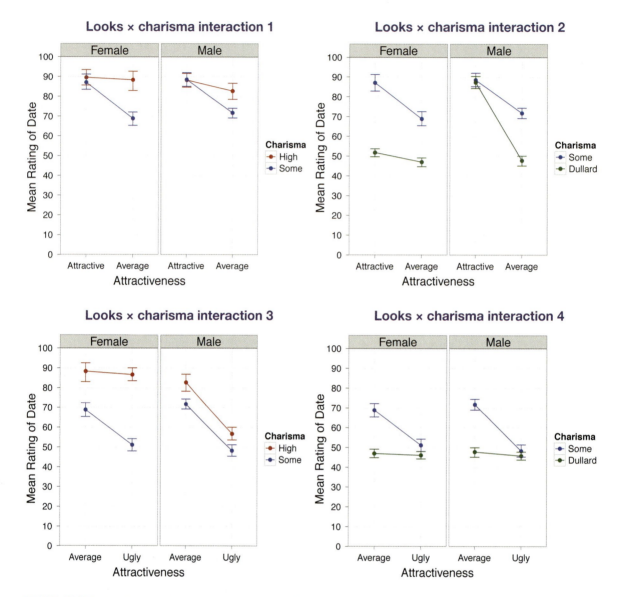

FIGURE 15.18   The looks × charisma × gender interaction broken down into the four contrasts

in level 2 of charisma (dullard) relative to level 3 of charisma (some charisma). The relevant means are displayed in the bottom right panel of Figure 15.18. Interest in ugly dates was the same regardless of whether they had some charisma or were a dullard (the blue and green dots are in the same place). For average-looking dates, there was more interest when that person had some charisma rather than if they were a dullard (the blue dot is higher than the green). Importantly, this pattern of results is very similar in males and females.

15.6.8. Conclusions ③

These contrasts tell us nothing about the differences between the attractive and ugly conditions, or the high-charisma and dullard conditions, because these were never compared. We could rerun the analysis and specify our contrasts differently to get these effects. However, what is clear from our data is that differences exist between men and women in terms of how they're affected by the looks and personality of potential dates. Men appear to be enthusiastic about dating anyone who is attractive regardless of how awful their personality. Women are almost completely the opposite: they are enthusiastic about dating anyone with a lot of charisma, regardless of how they look (and are unenthusiastic about dating people without charisma regardless of how attractive they look). The only consistency between men and women is that when there is some charisma (but not lots), the attractiveness influences how enthusiastic they are about dating the person.

What should be even clearer from this chapter is that when more than two independent variables are used in ANOVA, it yields complex interaction effects that require a great deal of concentration to interpret (imagine just how much your brain will throb when interpreting a four-way interaction). If faced with this particularly unpleasant scenario my best advice is to take a systematic approach to interpretation and plotting graphs is a useful way to proceed. It is also advisable to think carefully about the appropriate contrasts to use to answer the questions you have about your data. It is these contrasts that will help you to interpret interactions, so make sure you select sensible ones.

CRAMMING SAM'S TIPS   Mixed ANOVA

- Mixed ANOVA compares several means when there are two or more independent variables, and at least one of them has been measured using the same entities and at least one other has been measured using different entities.
- Test the assumption of sphericity for the repeated-measures variable(s) when they have three or more conditions using Mauchly's test. If the value in the column labelled *Sig.* is less than .05 then the assumption is violated. You should test this assumption for all effects (e.g., if there are two or more repeated-measures variables, test the assumption for all variables and the corresponding interaction terms).
- The table labelled *Tests of Within-Subjects Effects* shows the results of your ANOVA for the repeated-measures variables and all of the interaction effects. For *each* effect, if the assumption of sphericity has been met then look at the row labelled *Sphericity Assumed*. Otherwise, read the row labelled *Greenhouse-Geisser* or *Huynh-Feldt* (read the previous chapter to find out the relative merits of the two procedures). Having selected the appropriate row, look at the column labelled *Sig.* If the value is less than .05 then the means are significantly different.
- The table labelled *Tests of Between-Subjects Effects* shows the results of your ANOVA for the between-group variables. Look at the column labelled *Sig.* If the value is less than .05 then the means of the groups are significantly different.
- Break down the main effects and interaction terms using contrasts. These contrasts appear in the table labelled *Tests of Within-Subjects Contrasts*. Again look at the columns labelled *Sig.* to discover if your comparisons are significant (they are if the significance value is less than .05).
- Look at the means, or better still draw graphs, to help you interpret the contrasts.

15.7. Calculating effect sizes ③

I keep emphasizing the fact that effect sizes are really more useful when they summarize a focused effect. This also gives me a useful excuse to circumvent the complexities of omega squared in mixed designs (it's the road to madness, I assure you). Therefore, just calculate effect sizes for your contrasts when you've got a factorial design (and any main effects that compare only two groups). Output 15.6 shows the values for several contrasts, all of which

SMART
ALEX
ONLY

have 1 degree of freedom for the model (i.e., they represent a focused and interpretable comparison) and have 18 residual degrees of freedom. We can use these F-ratios and convert them to an effect size r, using a formula we've come across before:

$$r = \sqrt{\frac{F(1, df_R)}{F(1, df_R) + df_R}}$$

First, we can deal with the main effect of gender because this compares only two groups:

$$r_{gender} = \sqrt{\frac{0.005}{0.005 + 18}} = .02$$

For the two comparisons we did for the looks variable (Output 15.6), we would get:

$$r_{attractive\ vs.\ average} = \sqrt{\frac{226.99}{226.99 + 18}} = .96$$

$$r_{ugly\ vs.\ average} = \sqrt{\frac{160.07}{160.07 + 18}} = .95$$

Therefore, both comparisons yielded massive effect sizes. For the two comparisons we did for the charisma variable (Output 15.6), we would get:

$$r_{high\ vs.\ some} = \sqrt{\frac{109.94}{109.94 + 18}} = .93$$

$$r_{dullard\ vs.\ some} = \sqrt{\frac{227.94}{227.94 + 18}} = .96$$

Again, both comparisons yield massive effect sizes. For the looks × gender interaction, we again had two contrasts:

$$r_{attractive\ vs.\ average,\ male\ vs.\ female} = \sqrt{\frac{43.26}{43.26 + 18}} = .84$$

$$r_{ugly\ vs.\ average,\ male\ vs.\ female} = \sqrt{\frac{30.23}{30.23 + 18}} = .79$$

Again, these are massive effects. For the charisma × gender interaction, the two contrasts give us:

$$r_{high\ vs.\ some,\ male\ vs.\ female} = \sqrt{\frac{27.20}{27.20 + 18}} = .78$$

$$r_{dullard\ vs.\ some,\ male\ vs.\ female} = \sqrt{\frac{33.69}{33.69 + 18}} = .81$$

Yet again massive effects (yes, the data are fabricated). Moving onto the looks × charisma interaction, we get four contrasts:

$$r_{\text{attractive vs. average, high vs. some}} = \sqrt{\frac{21.94}{21.94+18}} = .74$$

$$r_{\text{attractive vs. average, dullard vs. some}} = \sqrt{\frac{4.09}{4.09+18}} = .43$$

$$r_{\text{ugly vs. average, high vs. some}} = \sqrt{\frac{6.23}{6.23+18}} = .51$$

$$r_{\text{ugly vs. average, dullard vs. some}} = \sqrt{\frac{88.60}{88.60+18}} = .91$$

All of these effects are in the medium to massive range. Finally, for the looks × charisma × gender interaction we had four contrasts:

$$r_{\text{attractive vs. average, high vs. some, male vs. female}} = \sqrt{\frac{0.93}{0.93+18}} = .22$$

$$r_{\text{attractive vs. average, dullard vs. some, male vs. female}} = \sqrt{\frac{60.67}{60.67+18}} = .88$$

$$r_{\text{ugly vs. average, high vs. some, male vs. female}} = \sqrt{\frac{11.70}{11.70+18}} = .63$$

$$r_{\text{ugly vs. average, dullard vs. some, male vs. female}} = \sqrt{\frac{1.33}{1.33+18}} = .26$$

As such, the two effects that were significant (attractive vs. average, dullard vs. some, male vs. female and ugly vs. average, high vs. some, male vs. female) yielded large effect sizes. The two effects that were not significant yielded close to medium effect sizes.

EVERYBODY

15.8. Reporting the results of mixed ANOVA ②

As you've probably gathered, when you have more than two independent variables there's a hell of a lot of information to report. I've mentioned a few times that when interaction effects are significant there's no point in interpreting main effects, so you can save space by not reporting them; however, some journals will expect you to report them anyway. In any case, certainly reserve the most detail for the effects that are central to your main hypothesis. Assuming we want to report all of our effects, we could do it something like this (although not as a list!):

✓ All effects are reported as significant at $p < .001$ unless otherwise stated. There was a significant main effect of the attractiveness of the date on interest expressed by participant, $F(2, 36) = 423.73$. Contrasts revealed that attractive dates were significantly more desirable than average-looking ones, $F(1, 18) = 226.99$, $r = .96$, and ugly dates were significantly less desirable than average-looking ones, $F(1, 18) = 160.07$, $r = .95$.

✓ There was also a significant main effect of the amount of charisma the date possessed on the interest expressed in dating them, $F(2, 36) = 328.25$. Contrasts revealed that dates with high charisma were significantly more desirable than dates with some charisma, $F(1, 18) = 109.94$, $r = .93$, and dullards were significantly less desirable than dates with some charisma, $F(1, 18) = 227.94$, $r = .96$.

✓ There was no significant effect of gender, indicating that ratings from male and female participants were similar, $F(1, 18) = 0.005$, $p = .946$, $r = .02$.

✓ There was a significant interaction effect between the attractiveness of the date and the gender of the participant, $F(2, 36) = 80.43$. This effect indicates that the desirability of dates of different levels of attractiveness differed in men and women. To break down this interaction, contrasts compared each level of attractiveness to average looks, across male and female participants. These contrasts revealed significant interactions when comparing male and female scores to attractive dates compared to average-looking dates, $F(1, 18) = 43.26$, $r = .84$, and to ugly dates compared to average-looking dates, $F(1, 18) = 30.23$, $r = .79$. The interaction graph shows that although both males' and females' interest decreased as attractiveness decreased, this decrease was more pronounced for men, suggesting that when charisma is ignored, men's interest in dating a person was more influenced by their looks than women's.

✓ There was a significant interaction effect between the level of charisma of the date and the gender of the participant, $F(2, 36) = 62.45$, indicating that the desirability of dates of different levels of charisma differed in men and women. Contrasts were performed comparing each level of charisma to the middle category of 'some charisma' across male and female participants. These contrasts revealed significant interactions when comparing male and female scores to highly charismatic dates compared to dates with some charisma, $F(1, 18) = 27.20$, $r = .78$, and to dullards compared to dates with some charisma $F(1, 18) = 33.69$, $r = .81$. The interaction graph reveals that both males' and females' interest decreased as charisma decreased, but this decrease was more pronounced for females, suggesting women's interest in dating a person was more influenced by their charisma than men's.

✓ There was a significant charisma × attractiveness interaction, $F(4, 72) = 36.63$, indicating that the desirability of dates of different levels of charisma differed according to their attractiveness. Contrasts were performed comparing each level of charisma to the middle category of 'some charisma' across each level of attractiveness compared to the category of average attractiveness. The first contrast revealed a significant interaction when comparing attractive dates to average-looking dates when the date had high charisma compared to some charisma, $F(1, 18) = 21.94$, $r = .74$, and tells us that as dates became less attractive there was a greater decline in interest when charisma was low compared to when charisma was high. The second contrast, which compared attractive dates to average-looking dates when the date was a dullard compared to when they had some charisma, was not significant, $F(1, 18) = 4.09$, $p = .058$, $r = .43$. This result suggests that as dates became less attractive there was a decline in interest both when charisma was average and when there was no charisma at all. The third contrast, which compared ugly dates to average-looking dates when the date had high charisma compared to average charisma, was significant, $F(1, 18) = 6.23$, $p = .022$, $r = .51$. This contrast implies that as dates became less attractive there was a greater decline in interest when charisma was average compared to when it was high. The final contrast compared ugly dates to average-looking dates when the date was a dullard compared to when they had some charisma. This contrast was highly significant, $F(1, 18) = 88.60$, $r = .91$, and suggests that as dates became less attractive the decline in interest in dates with a bit of charisma was significantly greater than for dullards.

✓ Finally, the looks × charisma × gender interaction was significant $F(4, 72) = 24.12$. This indicates that the looks × charisma interaction described previously was different in male and female participants. Contrasts were used to break down this interaction; these contrasts compared males' and females' scores at each level of charisma relative to the middle category of some charisma across each level of attractiveness relative to the category of average attractiveness. The first contrast revealed a non-significant difference between male and female responses when comparing attractive dates to average-looking dates when the date had high charisma compared to some charisma, $F(1, 18) = 0.93$, $p = .348$, $r = .22$. This effect suggests that, for both males and females, as dates became less attractive there was a greater decline in interest when charisma was average compared to high. The second contrast investigated differences between males and females when comparing attractive dates to average-looking dates when the date was a dullard compared to when they had

LABCOAT LENI'S REAL RESEARCH 15.2

Keep the faith(ful)? ③

People can be jealous. People can be especially jealous when they think that their partner is being unfaithful. An evolutionary view of jealousy suggests that men and women have evolved distinctive types of jealousy. Specifically, a woman's sexual infidelity deprives her mate of a reproductive opportunity and could burden him with years investing in a child that is not his. Conversely, a man's sexual infidelity does not burden his mate with unrelated children, but may divert his resources from his mate's progeny. This diversion of resources is signalled by emotional attachment to another female. Consequently, men's jealousy mechanism should have evolved to prevent a mate's *sexual* infidelity, whereas in women it has evolved to prevent *emotional* infidelity. Achim Schützwohl reasoned that if this is the case, women should be on the look-out for emotional infidelity, whereas men should be watching out for sexual infidelity.

He put this hypothesis to the test in a unique study in which men and women saw sentences presented on a computer screen (Schützwohl, 2008). At each trial, participants saw a target sentence that was emotionally neutral (e.g., 'The gas station is at the other side of the

street'). However, before each of these targets, a distractor sentence was presented that could also be affectively neutral, or could indicate sexual infidelity (e.g., 'Your partner suddenly has difficulty becoming sexually aroused when he and you want to have sex') or emotional infidelity (e.g., 'Your partner doesn't say "I love you" to you anymore'). The idea was that if these distractor sentences grabbed a person's attention then (1) they would remember them, and (2) they would not remember the target sentence that came afterwards (because their attentional resources were focused on the distractor). These effects should show up only in people currently in a relationship. The outcome was the number of sentences that a participant could remember (out of 6), and the predictors were whether the person had a partner or not (**Relationship**), whether the trial used a neutral distractor, an emotional infidelity distractor or a sexual infidelity distractor, and whether the sentence was a distractor or the target following a distractor. Schützwohl analysed men and women's data seperately. The predictions are that women should remember more emotional infidelity sentences (distractors) but fewer of the targets that followed those sentences (target). For men, the same effect should be found but for sexual infidelity sentences. The data from this study are in the file **Schützwohl(2008).sav.** Labcoat Leni wants you to carry out two three-way mixed ANOVAs (one for men and the other for women) to test these hypotheses. Answers are on the companion website (or look at pages 638–642 in the original article).

Schützwohl, A. (2008). *Personality and Individual Differences, 44*, 633–644.

average charisma, $F(1, 18) = 60.67$, $r = .88$. This finding indicates that, for dates with average charisma, the reduction in interest as attractiveness went down was about the same in men and women, but for dullard dates, the decrease in interest if these dates were average-looking rather than attractive was much more dramatic in men than women. The third contrast looked for differences between males and females when comparing ugly dates to average-looking dates when the date had high charisma compared to average charisma, $F(1, 18) = 11.70$, $p = .003$, $r = .63$, and tells us that, for dates with average charisma, the reduction in interest as attractiveness went down was about the same in men and women, but for dates with high charisma, the decrease in interest if these dates were ugly rather than average-looking was much more dramatic in men than women. The final contrast looked for differences between men and women when comparing ugly dates to average-looking dates when the date was a dullard compared to when they had average charisma, $F(1, 18) = 1.33$, $p = .263$, $r = .26$. This effect suggests that for both men and women, as dates become less attractive the decline in interest in dates with average charisma was significantly greater than for dullards.

15.9. Brian's attempt to woo Jane ①

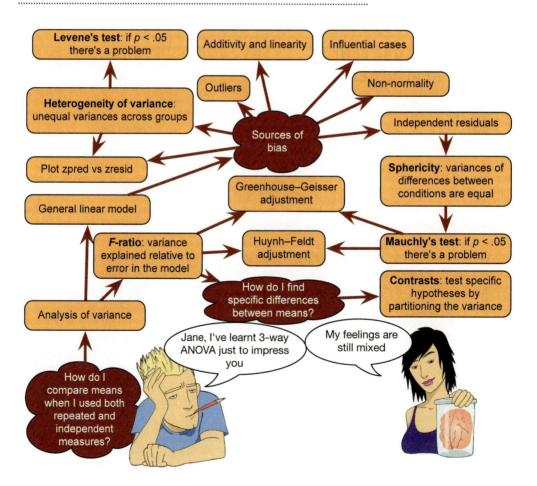

FIGURE 15.19   What Brian learnt from this chapter

15.10. What next? ②

We've discovered in this chapter that men are superficial creatures who value looks over charisma, and that women are prepared to date the hunchback of Notre Dame provided he has a sufficient amount of charisma. This is why as a 16–18-year-old my life was so complicated, because where on earth do you discover your hidden charisma? Luckily for me, some girls find alcoholics appealing. The girl I was particularly keen on at 16 was, as it turned out, keen on me too. I refused to believe this for several weeks. All of our friends were getting bored with us declaring our undying love for each other to them but then not speaking to each other; eventually they intervened. There was a party one evening and all of her friends had spent hours convincing me to ask her on a date, guaranteeing me that she would say 'yes'. I had psyched myself up, I was going to do it, I was actually going to ask a girl out on a date. My whole life had been leading up to this moment and I must not do anything to ruin it. By the time she arrived my nerves had got the better of me, and nerves made me drink alcohol, so she had to step over my paralytic corpse to get into the house. Later on, once I'd returned to semi-consciousness, my friend Paul Spreckley (see Figure 10.1) physically carried the girl in question from another room and put her next to me and then said something to the effect of 'Andy, I'm going to sit here until you ask her out'. He had a long wait but eventually, miraculously, the words came out of my mouth. What happened next is the topic for another book, not about statistics.

15.11. Key terms that I've discovered

Mixed ANOVA   Mixed design

15.12. Smart Alex's tasks

- **Task 1:** In the previous chapter we looked at an example in which participants viewed a total of nine mock adverts over three sessions. In these adverts there were three products (a brand of beer, Brain Death; a brand of wine, Dangleberry; and a brand of water, Puritan). These could be presented alongside positive, negative or neutral imagery. Over the three sessions and nine adverts, each type of product was paired with each type of imagery (read the previous chapter if you need more detail). After each advert participants rated the drinks on a scale ranging from −100 (dislike very much) through 0 (neutral) to 100 (like very much). The design had two repeated-measures independent variables: the type of drink (beer, wine or water) and the type of imagery used (positive, negative or neutral). Imagine that we also knew each participant's gender. Men and women might respond differently to the products (because, in keeping with stereotypes, men might mostly drink lager whereas women might drink wine). Reanalyse the data, taking gender (a between-group variable) into account. The data are in the file **MixedAttitude.sav**. Run a three-way mixed ANOVA on these data. ③

- **Task 2:** Text messaging and Twitter encourage communication using abbreviated forms of words (if u no wat I mean). A researcher wanted to see the effect this had on children's understanding of grammar. One group of 25 children was encouraged to send text messages on their mobile phones over a six-month period. A second group of 25 was forbidden from sending text messages for the same period (to ensure adherence, this group were given armbands that administered painful shocks in the presence of a phone signal). The outcome was a score on a grammatical test (as a percentage) that was measured both before and after the experiment. The data are in the file **TextMessages.sav**. Does using text messages affect grammar? ③

- **Task 3**: A researcher hypothesized that *Big Brother* (see Chapter 1) contestants start off with personality disorders that are exacerbated by being forced to live with people as attention-seeking as them. To test this hypothesis, she gave eight contestants a questionnaire measuring personality disorders before and after they entered the house. A second group of eight people were given the questionnaires at the same time: these people were short-listed to go into the house, but never actually went in. The data are in **BigBrother.sav**. Does the *Big Brother* house give you a personality disorder? ②

- **Task 4**: Angry Birds is a video game in which you fire birds at pigs. Some daft people think this sort of thing makes people more violent. A (fabricated) study was set up in which people played Angry Birds and a control game (Tetris) over a two-year period (one year per game). They were put in a pen of pigs for a day before the study, and after 1 month, 6 months and 12 months. Their violent acts towards the pigs were counted. The data are in the file **Angry Pigs.sav**. Does playing Angry Birds make people more violent to pigs compared to a control game? ②

- **Task 5**: A different study was conducted with the same design as in Task 4. The only difference was that the participant's violent acts in real life were monitored before the study, and after 1 month, 6 months and 12 months. Does playing Angry Birds make people more violent in general compared to a control game? (**Angry Real.sav**) ②

- **Task 6**: My wife believes that she has received less friend requests from random men on Facebook since she changed her profile picture to a photo of us both. Imagine we took 40 women who had profiles on a social networking website; 17 of them had a relationship status of 'single' and the remaining 23 had their status as 'in a relationship' (**relationship_status**). We asked these women to set their profile picture to a photo of them on their own (**alone**) and to count how many friend requests they got from men over 3 weeks, and then to switch it to a photo of them with a man (**couple**) and record their friend requests from random men over 3 weeks. The data are in the file **ProfilePicture.sav**. Run a mixed ANOVA to see if friend requests are affected by relationship status and type of profile picture. ②

- **Task 7**: Labcoat Leni's Real Research 4.2 described an important study by Johns, Hargrave, and Newton-Fisher (2012) in which they reasoned that if red was a proxy signal to indicate sexual proceptivity then men should find red female genitalia more attractive than other colours. They also recorded the men's sexual experience (**Partners**) as 'some' or 'very little'. Run a mixed ANOVA to see whether attractiveness was affected by genitalia colour (**PalePink, LightPink, DarkPink, Red**) and sexual experience (**Johns et al. (2012).sav**). Look at page 3 of Johns et al. to see how to report the results. ②

Answers can be found on the companion website.

15.13. Further reading

Field, A. P. (1998). A bluffer's guide to sphericity. *Newsletter of the Mathematical, Statistical and Computing Section of the British Psychological Society*, 6(1), 13-22. (Available in the additional material on the companion website.)

Howell, D. C. (2012). *Statistical methods for psychology* (8th ed.). Belmont, CA: Wadsworth. (Or you might prefer his *Fundamental statistics for the behavioral sciences*. Both are excellent texts.)

Multivariate analysis of variance (MANOVA)

16

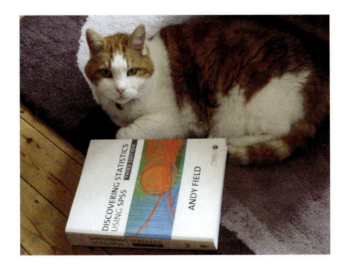

FIGURE 16.1
Fuzzy doing
some light
reading

16.1. What will this chapter tell me? ②

Having had what little confidence I had squeezed out of me by my first forays into dating and my band's unqualified failure to have an impact on the musical world, as I reached adulthood I decided that I could either kill myself or get a cat. I'd wanted to do both for years but when I was introduced to a little 4-week-old bundle of gingerness the choice was made. Fuzzy (as I named him) was born on 8 April 1996 and has been my right-hand feline ever since. He is like the Cheshire cat in Lewis Carroll's *Alice's adventures in Wonderland*[1] in that he seemingly vanishes and reappears at will: I go to find clothes in my wardrobe and notice a ginger face peering out at me, I put my pants in the laundry basket and he looks up at me from a pile of smelly socks, I go to have a bath and he's sitting in it, and I shut the

---

[1] This is one of my favourite books from my childhood. For those who haven't read it, the Cheshire cat is a big fat cat mainly remembered for vanishing and reappearing out of nowhere; on one occasion it vanished leaving only its smile behind.

bedroom door yet wake up to find him asleep next to me. His best vanishing act was a few years ago when I moved house. He'd been locked up in his travel basket (which he hates) during the move, so once we were in our new house I thought I'd let him out as soon as possible. I found a quiet room, checked the doors and windows to make sure he couldn't escape, opened the basket, gave him a cuddle and left him to get to know his new house. When I returned five minutes later, he was gone. The door had been shut, the windows closed and the walls were solid (I checked). He had literally vanished into thin air and he didn't even leave behind his smile. Before his dramatic disappearance, Fuzzy had stopped my suicidal tendencies, and there is lots of research showing that having a pet is good for your mental health. If you wanted to test this you could compare people with pets against those without to see if they had better mental health. However, the term *mental health* covers a wide range of concepts including (to name a few) anxiety, depression, general distress and psychosis. As such, we have four outcome measures and all the tests we have encountered allow us to look at only one. Fear not, when we want to compare groups on several outcome variables we can extend ANOVA to become MANOVA. That's what this chapter is all about.

16.2. When to use MANOVA ②

Over Chapters 9–15 we have seen how the general linear model can be used to detect group differences on a single outcome. However, there may be circumstances in which we are interested in several outcomes and in these cases the simple ANOVA model is inadequate. Instead, we can use **multivariate analysis of variance** (or **MANOVA**). MANOVA can be thought of as ANOVA for situations in which there are several dependent variables. The principles of ANOVA extend to MANOVA in that we can use MANOVA when there is only one independent variable or when there are several, we can look at interactions between independent variables, and we can even do contrasts to see which groups differ from each other. ANOVA can be used only in situations in which there is one dependent variable (or outcome) and so is known as a **univariate** test (meaning 'one variable'); MANOVA is designed to look at several dependent variables (outcomes) simultaneously and so is a **multivariate** test (meaning 'many variables'). There is a fairly lengthy theory section to try to explain the workings of MANOVA, but for those of you who value the little time you have on Earth, skip this section and we'll look how to do MANOVA in SPSS and interpret the output. This process will lead us to another statistical test known as **discriminant function analysis** or just **discriminant analysis**.

16.3. Introduction

16.3.1. Similarities to and differences from ANOVA ②

If we have collected data on several outcome variables then we could simply conduct a separate ANOVA for each dependent variable (read a few research papers and you'll find that it is not unusual for researchers to do this). However, we learnt in Section 2.6.1.7 that when we carry out multiple tests on the same data the Type I errors start to mount up. For this reason, we shouldn't really conduct separate ANOVAs on each outcome variable. Also, if separate ANOVAs are conducted on each outcome, then any relationship between these dependent variables is ignored and we lose this important information. MANOVA, by including all dependent variables in the same analysis, takes account of the relationship between these variables. Related to this point, ANOVA can tell us only whether groups differ along a single dimension whereas MANOVA has the power to detect whether groups differ along a combination of dimensions.

For example, we might be able to distinguish people who are married, living together or single by their happiness. 'Happiness' is a complex construct, so we might want to measure their happiness with work, socially, sexually and within themselves (self-esteem). It might not be possible to distinguish people who are married, living together or single by only one aspect of happiness (which is what an ANOVA tests) but these groups might be distinguished by *a combination* of their happiness across all four domains (which is what a MANOVA tests). In this sense MANOVA has greater potential power to detect an effect, because unlike ANOVA, it can detect whether groups differ along a combination of variables (see Jane Superbrain Box 16.1).

JANE SUPERBRAIN 16.1
The power of MANOVA ③

In theory, MANOVA has greater power than ANOVA to detect effects because it takes account of the correlations between dependent variables (Huberty & Morris, 1989). However, the issue a bit more complicated than that (isn't it always?). Tabachnick and Fidell (2007) suggest that MANOVA 'works best with highly negatively correlated DVs [dependent variables], and acceptably well with moderately correlated DVs in either direction' and that 'MANOVA also is wasteful when DVs are uncorrelated' (p. 268). The evidence is contradictory, though, with some studies showing *diminishing*

power as the correlation between dependent variables increased, while others show that power with high correlations between outcome variables is generally higher than for moderate correlations (Stevens, 1980). In fact, the power of MANOVA depends on a combination of the correlation between dependent variables and the effect size to be detected (Cole, Maxwell, Arvey & Salas, 1994). If you are expecting to find a large effect, then MANOVA will have greater power if the measures are somewhat different (even negatively correlated) and if the group differences are in the same direction for each measure. If you have two dependent variables, one of which exhibits a large group difference, and the other a small or no group difference, then power will be increased if these variables are highly correlated. Although Cole et al.'s work is limited to the case where two groups are being compared, the take-home message is that if you are interested in how powerful the MANOVA is likely to be you should consider not just the intercorrelation of dependent variables but also the size and pattern of group differences that you expect to get.

16.3.2. Choosing outcomes ②

MANOVA is probably looking like a pretty groovy test that allows you to measure hundreds of outcome variables and then sling them into an analysis. This is not the case. It is not a good idea to lump all of your dependent variables together in a MANOVA unless you have a good theoretical or empirical basis for doing so. I mentioned way back at the beginning of this book that statistical procedures are just a way of number crunching and so even if you put rubbish into an analysis you will still reach conclusions that are statistically meaningful, but are unlikely to be empirically meaningful. In circumstances where there is a good theoretical basis for including some but not all of your dependent variables, you should run separate analyses: one for the variables being tested on a heuristic basis and one for the theoretically meaningful variables. The point to take on board here is not to include lots of dependent variables in a MANOVA just because you have measured them.

16.3.3. The example for this chapter ②

Obsessive compulsive disorder (OCD) is a disorder characterized by intrusive images or thoughts that the sufferer finds abhorrent (in my case this might be the thought of someone carrying out a *t*-test on data that are not normally distributed, but in normal people it might be imagining your parents have died). These thoughts lead the sufferer to engage in activities to neutralize the unpleasantness of these thoughts (these activities can be mental, such as doing a MANOVA in my head to make me feel better about the *t*-test thought, or physical, such as touching the floor 23 times so that your parents won't die). Imagine that we were interested in the effects of cognitive behaviour therapy (CBT) on OCD. We could compare a group of OCD sufferers after CBT and after behaviour therapy (BT) with a group of OCD sufferers who are still awaiting treatment (a no treatment condition, NT).[2] Now, most psychopathologies have both behavioural and cognitive elements to them. For example, in OCD if someone had an obsession with germs and contamination, this disorder might manifest itself in obsessive hand-washing and would influence not just how many times they actually wash their hands (behaviour), but also the number of times they think about washing their hands (cognitions). If we are interested in seeing how successful a therapy is, it is not enough to look only at behavioural outcomes (such as whether obsessive behaviours are reduced); it is important to establish whether cognitions are being changed also. Hence, in this example two dependent measures were taken: the occurrence of obsession-related behaviours (**Actions**) and the occurrence of obsession-related cognitions (**Thoughts**). These dependent variables were measured on a single day and so represent the number of obsession-related behaviours/thoughts in a normal day. The data are in Table 16.1 and can be found in the file OCD.sav. Participants belonged to group 1 (CBT), group 2 (BT) or group 3 (NT), and within these groups all participants had both actions and thoughts measured.

16.4. Theory of MANOVA ③

SMART
ALEX
ONLY

The theory of MANOVA is very complex to understand without knowing matrix algebra, and frankly matrix algebra is way beyond the scope of this book (those with maths brains can consult Namboodiri, 1984; Stevens, 2002). However, I intend to give a flavour of the conceptual basis of MANOVA, using matrices, without requiring you to understand exactly how those matrices are used. Those interested in the exact underlying theory of MANOVA should read Bray and Maxwell's (1985) superb monograph.

16.4.1. Introduction to matrices ③

Despite what Hollywood would have you believe, a **matrix** does not enable you to jump acrobatically through the air, Ninja style, as time seemingly slows so that you can gracefully

---

[2] The non-psychologists out there should note that behaviour therapy works on the basis that if you stop the maladaptive behaviours the disorder will go away, whereas cognitive therapy is based on the idea that treating the maladaptive cognitions will stop the disorder.

TABLE 16.1   Data from **OCD.sav**

Group:	DV 1: Actions			DV 2: Thoughts		
	CBT (1)	BT (2)	NT (3)	CBT (1)	BT (2)	NT (3)
	5	4	4	14	14	13
	5	4	5	11	15	15
	4	1	5	16	13	14
	4	1	4	13	14	14
	5	4	6	12	15	13
	3	6	4	14	19	20
	7	5	7	12	13	13
	6	5	4	15	18	16
	6	2	6	16	14	14
	4	5	5	11	17	18
$\bar{X}$	4.90	3.70	5.00	13.40	15.20	15.00
s	1.20	1.77	1.05	1.90	2.10	2.36
s^2	1.43	3.12	1.11	3.60	4.40	5.56

$$\bar{X}_{\text{grand (Actions)}} = 4.53 \qquad \bar{X}_{\text{grand (Thoughts)}} = 14.53$$

$$s^2_{\text{grand (Actions)}} = 2.1195 \qquad s^2_{\text{grand (Thoughts)}} = 4.8780$$

contort to avoid high-velocity objects. I have worked with matrices many times, and I have never (to my knowledge) stopped time, and would certainly end up in a pool of my own innards if I ever tried to dodge a bullet. The sad reality is that a matrix is a grid of numbers arranged in columns and rows. In fact, throughout this book you have been using a matrix without even realizing it: the SPSS data editor. In the data editor we have numbers arranged in columns and rows, and this is exactly what a matrix is. A matrix can have many columns and many rows and we usually specify the dimensions of the matrix using numbers. So, a 2 × 3 matrix is a matrix with two rows and three columns, and a 5 × 4 matrix is one with five rows and four columns:

$$\begin{pmatrix} 2 & 5 & 6 \\ 3 & 5 & 8 \end{pmatrix} \qquad \begin{pmatrix} 2 & 4 & 6 & 8 \\ 3 & 4 & 6 & 7 \\ 4 & 3 & 5 & 8 \\ 2 & 5 & 7 & 9 \\ 4 & 6 & 6 & 9 \end{pmatrix}$$

2 × 3 matrix   5 × 4 matrix

You can think of these matrices in terms of each row representing the data from a single participant and each column as representing data relating to a particular variable. So, for the 5 × 4 matrix we can imagine a situation where five participants were tested on four variables: so, the first participant scored 2 on the first variable and 8 on the fourth variable.

The values within a matrix are typically referred to as *components* or *elements*. The rows and colums are called *vectors*.

A square matrix is one in which there are an equal number of columns and rows. In this type of matrix it is sometimes useful to distinguish between the diagonal components (i.e., the values that lie on the diagonal line from the top left component to the bottom right component) and the off-diagonal components (the values that do not lie on the diagonal). In the matrix below, the diagonal components are 5, 12, 2 and 6 because they lie along the diagonal line. The off-diagonal components are all of the other values. A square matrix in which the diagonal elements are equal to 1 and the off-diagonal elements are equal to 0 is known as an identity matrix:

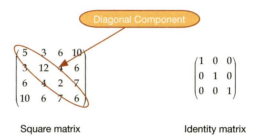

Square matrix   Identity matrix

Hopefully, the concept of a matrix should now be slightly less scary than it was previously: it is not some magical mathematical entity, merely a way of representing a data set – just like a spreadsheet. Armed with this knowledge of matrices, we can look at how they are used to conduct MANOVA.

16.4.2. Some important matrices and their functions ③

As with ANOVA, we are primarily interested in how much variance can be explained by the experimental manipulation (which in real terms means how much variance is explained by the fact that certain scores appear in certain groups). Therefore, we need to know the sum of squares due to the grouping variable (the systematic variation, SS_M), the sum of squares due to natural differences between participants (the residual variation, SS_R) and of course the total amount of variation that needs to be explained (SS_T); for more details about these sources of variation reread Chapters 8 and 11. However, I mentioned that MANOVA also takes into account several dependent variables simultaneously, and it does this by using a matrix that contains information about the variance accounted for by each dependent variable. For the univariate *F*-test (e.g., ANOVA) we calculated the ratio of systematic variance to unsystematic variance for a single dependent variable. In MANOVA, the test statistic is derived by comparing the ratio of systematic to unsystematic variance for several dependent variables. This comparison is made by using the ratio of a matrix representing the systematic variance of all dependent variables to a matrix representing the unsystematic variance of all dependent variables. To sum up, the test statistic in both ANOVA and MANOVA represents the ratio of the effect of the systematic variance to the unsystematic variance; in ANOVA these variances are single values, but in MANOVA each is a matrix containing many variances and covariances.

The matrix that represents the systematic variance (or the model sum of squares for all variables) is denoted by the letter *H* and is called the hypothesis sum of squares and cross-products matrix (or hypothesis SSCP). The matrix that represents the unsystematic variance (the residual sums of squares for all variables) is denoted by the letter *E* and is called the error sum of squares and cross-products matrix (or error SSCP). Finally, there is a matrix that represents the total amount of variance present for each dependent variable (the total sums of squares for each dependent variable) and this is denoted by T and is called the **total sum of squares and cross-products matrix** (or **total SSCP**).

Later, I will show how these matrices are used in exactly the same way as the simple sums of squares (SS_M, SS_R and SS_T) in ANOVA to derive a test statistic representing the ratio of systematic to unsystematic variance in the model. The observant among you may have noticed that the matrices I have described are all called **sum of squares and cross-products (SSCP) matrices**. It should be obvious why these matrices are referred to as sum of squares matrices, but why is there a reference to cross-products in their name?

SELF-TEST   Can you remember (from Chapter 6) what a cross-product is?

Cross-products represent a total value for the combined error between two variables (so in some sense they represent an unstandardized estimate of the total correlation between two variables). As such, whereas the sum of squares of a variable is the total squared difference between the observed values and the mean value, the cross-product is the total combined error between two variables. I mentioned earlier that MANOVA had the power to account for any correlation between dependent variables, and it does this by using these cross-products.

16.4.3. Calculating MANOVA by hand: a worked example ③

To begin with let's carry out univariate ANOVAs on each of the two dependent variables in our OCD example (see Table 16.1). A description of the ANOVA model can be found in Chapter 11, and I will draw heavily on the assumption that you have read this chapter; if you are hazy on the details then now would be a good time to (re)read it.

16.4.3.1. Univariate ANOVA for DV 1 (Actions) ②

There are three sums of squares that need to be calculated. First we need to assess how much variability there is to be explained within the data (SS_T); next we need to see how much of this variability can be explained by the model (SS_M); and finally, we have to assess how much error there is in the model (SS_R). From Chapter 11 we can calculate each of these values:

- $SS_{T(Actions)}$: The total sum of squares is obtained by calculating the difference between each of the 20 scores and the mean of those scores, then squaring these differences and adding these squared values up. Alternatively, you can get SPSS to calculate the variance for the action data (regardless of which group the score falls into) and then multiply this value by the number of scores minus 1. The degrees of freedom will be $N - 1$, in this case 29.

$$SS_T = s_{grand}^2 (N - 1)$$
$$= 2.1195(30 - 1)$$
$$= 2.1195 \times 29$$
$$= 61.47$$

- $SS_{M(Actions)}$: This value is calculated by taking the difference between each group mean and the grand mean and then squaring them. Multiply these values by the number of scores in the group and then add them together. The degrees of freedom will be $k - 1$, in this case 2.

$$SS_M = 10(4.90 - 4.53)^2 + 10(3.70 - 4.53)^2 + 10(5.00 - 4.53)^2$$

$$= 10(0.37)^2 + 10(-0.83)^2 + 10(0.47)^2$$

$$= 1.37 + 6.89 + 2.21$$

$$= 10.47$$

- $SS_{R(Actions)}$: This value is calculated by taking the difference between each score and the mean of the group from which it came. These differences are then squared and added together. Alternatively we can get SPSS to calculate the variance within each group, multiply each group variance by the number of scores minus 1 and then add them together. The degrees of freedom will be the sample size of each group minus 1 (e.g., 9) multiplied by the number of groups, $3 \times 9 = 27$.

$$SS_R = s_{CBT}^2 (n_{CBT} - 1) + s_{BT}^2 (n_{BT} - 1) + s_{NT}^2 (n_{NT} - 1)$$

$$= 1.433(10 - 1) + 3.122(10 - 1) + 1.111(10 - 1)$$

$$= (1.433 \times 9) + (3.122 \times 9) + (1.111 \times 9)$$

$$= 12.9 + 28.1 + 10$$

$$= 51$$

The next step is to calculate the average sums of squares (the mean square) for the model and for the error in the model by dividing by the degrees of freedom (see Section 11.2.6):

$$MS_M = \frac{SS_M}{df_M} = \frac{10.47}{2} = 5.235$$

$$MS_R = \frac{SS_R}{df_R} = \frac{51}{27} = 1.889$$

The final stage is to calculate F by dividing the mean squares for the model by the mean squares for the error in the model:

$$F = \frac{MS_M}{MS_R} = \frac{5.235}{1.889} = 2.771$$

16.4.3.2. Univariate ANOVA for DV 2 (Thoughts) ②

As with the data for dependent variable 1, there are three sums of squares that need to be calculated (the degrees of freedom for each are the same as above). For the total sum of squares, $SS_{T(Thoughts)}$, we have:

$$SS_T = s_{grand}^2 (n - 1)$$

$$= 4.878(30 - 1)$$

$$= 4.878 \times 29$$

$$= 141.46$$

For the model sum of squares, $SS_{M(Thoughts)}$, we have:

$$\begin{aligned} SS_M &= 10(13.40 - 14.53)^2 + 10(15.2 - 14.53)^2 + 10(15 - 14.53)^2 \\ &= 10(-1.13)^2 + 10(0.67)^2 + 10(0.47)^2 \\ &= 12.77 + 4.49 + 2.21 \\ &= 19.47 \end{aligned}$$

Finally, for the residual sum of squares, $SS_{R(Thoughts)}$, we have:

$$\begin{aligned} SS_R &= s^2_{CBT}(n_{CBT} - 1) + s^2_{BT}(n_{BT} - 1) + s^2_{NT}(n_{NT} - 1) \\ &= 3.6(10 - 1) + 4.4(10 - 1) + 5.56(10 - 1) \\ &= (3.6 \times 9) + (4.4 \times 9) + (5.56 \times 9) \\ &= 32.4 + 39.6 + 50 \\ &= 122 \end{aligned}$$

We calculate the average sums of squares (the mean square) by dividing by the degrees of freedom:

$$MS_M = \frac{SS_M}{df_M} = \frac{19.47}{2} = 9.735$$

$$MS_R = \frac{SS_R}{df_R} = \frac{122}{27} = 4.519$$

We calculate F by dividing the mean squares for the model by the residual mean squares:

$$F = \frac{MS_M}{MS_R} = \frac{9.735}{4.519} = 2.154$$

The point to take home here is that the calculations are exactly the same as if we did two separate one-way ANOVAs on each dependent variable.

16.4.3.3. The relationship between DVs: cross-products ②

We know already that MANOVA uses the same sums of squares as ANOVA, and in the next section we will see exactly how it uses these values. However, I have also mentioned that MANOVA takes account of the relationship between dependent variables by using the cross-products. There are three different cross-products that are of interest and they relate to the three sums of squares that we calculated for the univariate ANOVAs: there is a total cross-product, a cross-product due to the model and a residual cross-product. Let's look at the total cross-product (CP_T) first.

I mentioned in Chapter 6 that the cross-product was the difference between the scores and the mean in one group multiplied by the difference between the scores and the mean in the other group. In the case of the total cross-product, the mean of interest is the grand mean for each dependent variable (see Table 16.2). Hence, we can adapt the cross-product equation described in Chapter 6 using the two dependent variables. The resulting equation for the total cross-product is given by:

$$\text{CP}_\text{T} = \sum_{i=1}^{n}\left(x_{i\,(\text{Actions})} - \overline{X}_{\text{grand}\,(\text{Actions})}\right)\left(x_{i\,(\text{Thoughts})} - \overline{X}_{\text{grand}\,(\text{Thoughts})}\right) \qquad (16.1)$$

So, for each dependent variable you take each score and subtract from it the grand mean for that variable. This leaves you with two values per participant (one for each dependent variable) that should be multiplied together to get the cross-product for each participant. The total can then be found by adding the cross-products of all participants. Table 16.2 illustrates this process.

The total cross-product is a gauge of the overall relationship between the two variables. However, we are also interested in how the relationship between the dependent variables is influenced by our experimental manipulation, and this relationship is measured by the model cross-product (CP_M):

$$\text{CP}_\text{M} = \sum_{\text{grp}=1}^{k} n\left(\overline{x}_{\text{grp}\,(\text{Actions})} - \overline{X}_{\text{grand}\,(\text{Actions})}\right)\left(\overline{x}_{\text{grp}\,(\text{Thoughts})} - \overline{X}_{\text{grand}\,(\text{Thoughts})}\right) \qquad (16.2)$$

The CP_M is calculated in a similar way to the model sum of squares. First, the difference between each group mean and the grand mean is calculated for each dependent variable. The cross-product is calculated by multiplying the differences found for each group. Each product is then multiplied by the number of scores within the group (as was done with the sum of squares). Table 16.3 illustrates this principle.

Finally, we also need to know how the relationship between the two dependent variables is influenced by individual differences in participants' performances. The residual cross-product (CP_R) tells us about how the relationship between the dependent variables is affected by individual differences, or error in the model:

$$\text{CP}_\text{R} = \sum_{i=1}^{n}\left(x_{i\,(\text{Actions})} - \overline{X}_{\text{group}\,(\text{Actions})}\right)\left(x_{i\,(\text{Thoughts})} - \overline{X}_{\text{group}\,(\text{Thoughts})}\right) \qquad (16.3)$$

The CP_R is calculated in a similar way to the total cross-product, except that the group means are used rather than the grand mean. So, to calculate each of the difference scores, we take each score and subtract from it the mean of the group to which it belongs (see Table 16.4).

The observant among you may notice that the residual cross-product can also be calculated by subtracting the model cross-product from the total cross-product:

$$\begin{aligned}
\text{CP}_\text{R} &= \text{CP}_\text{T} - \text{CP}_\text{M} \\
&= 5.47 - (-7.53) \\
&= 13
\end{aligned}$$

Each of the different cross-products tells us something important about the relationship between the two dependent variables. Although I have used a simple scenario to keep the maths relatively simple, these principles can be easily extended to more complex scenarios. For example, if we had measured three dependent variables then the cross-products between pairs of dependent variables are calculated (as they were in this example) and

TABLE 16.2   Calculation of the total cross-product

Group	Actions	Thoughts	Actions − $\bar{X}_{grand\ (Actions)}$ (D_1)	Actions − $\bar{X}_{grand\ (Thoughts)}$ (D_2)	$D_1 \times D_2$
CBT	5	14	0.47	−0.53	−0.25
	5	11	0.47	−3.53	−1.66
	4	16	−0.53	1.47	−0.78
	4	13	−0.53	−1.53	0.81
	5	12	0.47	−2.53	−1.19
	3	14	−1.53	−0.53	0.81
	7	12	2.47	−2.53	−6.25
	6	15	1.47	0.47	0.69
	6	16	1.47	1.47	2.16
	4	11	−0.53	−3.53	1.87
BT	4	14	−0.53	−0.53	0.28
	4	15	−0.53	0.47	−0.25
	1	13	−3.53	−1.53	5.40
	1	14	−3.53	−0.53	1.87
	4	15	−0.53	0.47	−0.25
	6	19	1.47	4.47	6.57
	5	13	0.47	−1.53	−0.72
	5	18	0.47	3.47	1.63
	2	14	−2.53	−0.53	1.34
	5	17	0.47	2.47	1.16
NT	4	13	−0.53	−1.53	0.81
	5	15	0.47	0.47	0.22
	5	14	0.47	−0.53	−0.25
	4	14	−0.53	−0.53	0.28
	6	13	1.47	−1.53	−2.25
	4	20	−0.53	5.47	−2.90
	7	13	2.47	−1.53	−3.78
	4	16	−0.53	1.47	−0.78
	6	14	1.47	−0.53	−0.78
	5	18	0.47	3.47	1.63
$\bar{X}$ grand	4.53	14.53		$CP_T = \sum D_1 \times D_2 = 5.47$	

TABLE 16.3   Calculating the model cross-product

	$\bar{X}_{group}$ Actions	$\bar{X}_{group} - \bar{X}_{grand}$ (D_1)	$\bar{X}_{group}$ Thoughts	$\bar{X}_{group} - \bar{X}_{grand}$ (D_2)	$D_1 \times D_2$	$N(D_1 \times D_2)$
CBT	4.9	0.37	13.4	−1.13	−0.418	−4.18
BT	3.7	−0.83	15.2	0.67	−0.556	−5.56
NT	5.0	0.47	15.0	0.47	0.221	2.21
$\bar{X}_{grand}$	4.53		14.53		$CP_M = \sum N(D_1 \times D_2) = -7.53$	

entered into the appropriate SSCP matrix (see next section). As the complexity of the situation increases, so does the amount of calculation that needs to be done. At times such as these the benefit of software like SPSS becomes ever more apparent!

16.4.3.4. The total SSCP matrix (T) ③

In this example we have only two dependent variables and so all of the SSCP matrices will be 2×2 matrices. If there had been three dependent variables then the resulting matrices would all be 3×3 matrices. The total SSCP matrix, T, contains the total sums of squares for each dependent variable and the total cross-product between the two dependent variables. You can think of the first column and first row as representing one dependent variable and the second column and row as representing the second dependent variable:

	Column 1 Actions	Column 2 Thoughts
Row 1 Actions	$SS_{T(Actions)}$	CP_T
Row 1 Thoughts	CP_T	$SS_{T(Thoughts)}$

We calculated these values in the previous sections and so we can simply place the appropriate values in the appropriate cell of the matrix:

$$T = \begin{pmatrix} 61.47 & 5.47 \\ 5.47 & 141.47 \end{pmatrix}$$

From the values in the matrix (and what they represent) it should be clear that the total SSCP represents both the total amount of variation that exists within the data and the total co-dependence that exists between the dependent variables. You should also note that the off-diagonal components are the same (they are both the total cross-product) because this value is equally important for both of the dependent variables.

TABLE 16.4 Calculation of CP_R

Group	Actions	Actions − $\bar{X}_{group\ (Actions)}$ (D_1)	Thoughts	Actions − $\bar{X}_{group\ (Thoughts)}$ (D_2)	$D_1 \times D_2$
CBT	5	0.10	14	0.60	0.06
	5	0.10	11	−2.40	−0.24
	4	−0.90	16	2.60	−2.34
	4	−0.90	13	−0.40	0.36
	5	0.10	12	−1.40	−0.14
	3	−1.90	14	0.60	−1.14
	7	2.10	12	−1.40	−2.94
	6	1.10	15	1.60	1.76
	6	1.10	16	2.60	2.86
	4	−0.90	11	−2.40	2.16
$\bar{X}_{CBT}$	4.9		13.4		$\Sigma = 0.40$
BT	4	0.30	14	−1.20	−0.36
	4	0.30	15	−0.20	−0.06
	1	−2.70	13	−2.20	5.94
	1	−2.70	14	−1.20	3.24
	4	0.30	15	−0.20	−0.06
	6	2.30	19	3.80	8.74
	5	1.30	13	−2.20	−2.86
	5	1.30	18	2.80	3.64
	2	−1.70	14	−1.20	2.04
	5	1.30	17	1.80	2.34
$\bar{X}_{BT}$	3.7		15.2		$\Sigma = 22.60$
NT	4	−1.00	13	−2.00	2.00
	5	0.00	15	0	0.00
	5	0.00	14	−1.00	0.00
	4	−1.00	14	−1.00	1.00
	6	1.00	13	−2.00	−2.00
	4	−1.00	20	5.00	−5.00
	7	2.00	13	−2.00	−4.00
	4	−1.00	16	1.00	−1.00
	6	1.00	14	−1.00	−1.00
	5	0.00	18	3.00	0.00
$\bar{X}_{NT}$	5		15		$\Sigma = -10.00$

$$CP_R = \sum (D_1 \times D_2) = 13$$

16.4.3.5. The residual SSCP matrix (*E*) ③

The residual (or error) sum of squares and cross-product matrix, *E*, contains the residual sums of squares for each dependent variable and the residual cross-product between the two dependent variables. This SSCP matrix is similar to the total SSCP, except that the information relates to the error in the model:

	Column 1 Actions	Column 2 Thoughts
Row 1 Actions	$SS_{R(Actions)}$	CP_R
Row 1 Thoughts	CP_R	$SS_{R(Thoughts)}$

We calculated these values in the previous sections and so we can place the appropriate values in the appropriate cell of the matrix:

$$E = \begin{pmatrix} 51 & 13 \\ 13 & 122 \end{pmatrix}$$

The residual SSCP, therefore, represents both the unsystematic variation that exists for each dependent variable and the co-dependence between the dependent variables that is due to chance factors alone. As before, the off-diagonal elements are the same (they are both the residual cross-product).

16.4.3.6. The model SSCP matrix (*H*) ③

The model (or hypothesis) sum of squares and cross-product matrix, *H*, contains the model sums of squares for each dependent variable and the model cross-product between the two dependent variables:

	Column 1 Actions	Column 2 Thoughts
Row 1 Actions	$SS_{M(Actions)}$	CP_M
Row 1 Thoughts	CP_M	$SS_{M(Thoughts)}$

These values were calculated in the previous sections and so we can place the appropriate values in the appropriate cell of the matrix (see below). As such, the model SSCP represents both the systematic variation that exists for each dependent variable and the co-dependence between the dependent variables that is due to the model (i.e., is due to the experimental manipulation):

$$H = \begin{pmatrix} 10.47 & -7.53 \\ -7.53 & 19.47 \end{pmatrix}$$

Matrices are additive, which means that you can add (or subtract) two matrices together by adding (or subtracting) corresponding components. Now, when we calculated univariate

ANOVA we saw that the total sum of squares was the sum of the model sum of squares and the residual sum of squares (i.e., $SS_T = SS_M + SS_R$). The same is true in MANOVA except that we are adding matrices rather than single values:

$$T = H + E$$

$$= \begin{pmatrix} 10.47 & -7.53 \\ -7.53 & 19.47 \end{pmatrix} + \begin{pmatrix} 51 & 13 \\ 13 & 122 \end{pmatrix}$$

$$= \begin{pmatrix} 10.47 + 51 & -7.53 + 13 \\ -7.53 + 13 & 19.47 + 122 \end{pmatrix}$$

$$= \begin{pmatrix} 61.47 & 5.47 \\ 5.47 & 141.47 \end{pmatrix}$$

The demonstration that these matrices add up should (hopefully) help you to understand that the MANOVA calculations are conceptually the same as for univariate ANOVA – the difference is that matrices are used rather than single values.

16.4.4. Principle of the MANOVA test statistic ④

In univariate ANOVA we calculate the ratio of the systematic variance to the unsystematic variance (i.e., we divide SS_M by SS_R).[3] The conceptual equivalent would therefore be to divide the matrix H by the matrix E. There is, however, a problem in that matrices are not divisible by other matrices! However, there is a matrix equivalent to division, which is to multiply by what's known as the inverse of a matrix. So, if we want to divide H by E we have to multiply H by the inverse of E (denoted as E^{-1}). Therefore, the test statistic is based upon the matrix that results from multiplying the model SSCP with the inverse of the residual SSCP. This matrix is called **HE^{-1}**.

Calculating the inverse of a matrix is incredibly difficult and there is no need for you to understand how it is done because SPSS will do it for you. If you are interested, Stevens (2002) and Namboodiri (1984) provide accessible accounts of how to derive an inverse matrix, and having read them you could look at Oliver Twisted. Everyone else can trust me on the following:

$$E^{-1} = \begin{pmatrix} 0.0202 & -0.0021 \\ -0.0021 & 0.0084 \end{pmatrix}$$

$$HE^{-1} = \begin{pmatrix} 0.2273 & -0.0852 \\ -0.1930 & 0.1794 \end{pmatrix}$$

Remember that HE^{-1} represents the ratio of systematic variance in the model to the unsystematic variance in the model and so the resulting matrix is conceptually the same as the F-ratio in univariate ANOVA. There is another problem, though. In ANOVA, when we divide the systematic variance by the unsystematic variance we get a single figure: the F-ratio. In MANOVA, when we divide the systematic variance by the unsystematic variance we get a matrix containing several values. In this example, the matrix

[3] In reality we use the mean squares, but these values are merely the sums of squares corrected for the degrees of freedom.

contains four values, but had there been three dependent variables the matrix would have had nine values. In fact, the resulting matrix will always contain p^2 values, where p is the number of dependent variables. The problem is how to convert these matrix values into a meaningful single value. This is the point at which we have to abandon any hope of understanding the maths behind the test and talk conceptually instead.

16.4.4.1. Discriminant function variates ④

The problem of having several values with which to assess statistical significance can be simplified considerably by converting the dependent variables into underlying dimensions or factors (this process will be discussed in more detail in Chapter 17). In Chapter 8, we saw how multiple regression worked on the principle of fitting a linear model to a set of data to predict an outcome variable (the dependent variable in ANOVA terminology). This linear model was made up of a combination of predictor variables (or independent variables) each of which had a unique contribution to this linear model. We can do a similar thing here, except that we are interested in the opposite problem (i.e., predicting an independent variable from a set of dependent variables). So, it is possible to calculate underlying linear dimensions of the dependent variables. These linear combinations of the dependent variables are known as *variates* (or sometimes called *components*). In this context we wish to use these linear variates to predict which group a person belongs to (i.e., whether they were given CBT, BT or no treatment), so we are using them to discriminate groups of people. Therefore, these variates are called *discriminant functions* or discriminant function variates.

That's the theory in simplistic terms, but how do we discover these discriminant functions? Without going into too much detail, we use a mathematical procedure of maximization, such that the first discriminant function (V_1) is the linear combination of dependent variables that maximizes the differences between groups. It follows from this that the ratio of systematic to unsystematic variance (SS_M/SS_R) will be maximized for this first variate, but subsequent variates will have smaller values of this ratio. Remember that this ratio is an analogue of what the F-ratio represents in univariate ANOVA, and so in effect we obtain the maximum possible value of the F-ratio when we look at the first discriminant function. This variate can be described in terms of a linear regression equation (because it is a linear combination of the dependent variables):

$$y_i = b_0 + b_1 X_{1i} + b_2 X_{2i}$$
$$V_{1i} = b_0 + b_1 DV_{1i} + b_2 DV_{2i} \tag{16.4}$$
$$= b_0 + b_1 \text{Actions}_i + b_2 \text{Thoughts}_i$$

Equation (16.4) shows the multiple regression equation for two predictors and then extends this to show how a comparable form of this equation can describe discriminant functions. The b-values in the equation are weights (just as in regression) that tell us something about the contribution of each dependent variable to the variate in question. In regression, the values of b are obtained by the method of least squares; in discriminant function analysis the values of b are obtained from the *eigenvectors* (see Jane Superbrain Box 8.3) of the matrix HE^{-1}. We can actually ignore b_0 as well because this serves only to locate the variate in geometric space, which isn't necessary when we're using it to discriminate groups.

In a situation in which there are only two dependent variables and two groups for the independent variable, there will be only one variate. This makes the scenario very simple: by looking at the discriminant function of the dependent variables, rather than looking at the dependent variables themselves, we can obtain a single value of SS_M/SS_R for the discriminant function, and then assess this value for significance. However, in more complex cases where there are more than two dependent variables or more than three levels of the independent variable (as is the case in our example), there will be more than one variate. The number of variates obtained will be the smaller of p (the number of dependent variables) and $k - 1$ (where k is the number of levels of the independent variable). In our example, both p and $k - 1$ are 2, so we should be able to find two variates. I mentioned earlier that the b-values that describe the variates are obtained by calculating the eigenvectors of the matrix HE^{-1}, and in fact there will be two eigenvectors derived from this matrix: one with the b-values for the first variate, and one with the b-values for the second variate. Conceptually speaking, eigenvectors are the vectors associated with a given matrix that are unchanged by transformation of that matrix to a diagonal matrix (look back to Jane Superbrain Box 8.3 for a visual explanation of eigenvectors and eigenvalues). A diagonal matrix is a matrix in which the off-diagonal elements are zero, and by changing HE^{-1} to a diagonal matrix we eliminate all of the off-diagonal elements (thus reducing the number of values that we must consider for significance testing). Therefore, by calculating the eigenvectors and eigenvalues, we still end up with values that represent the ratio of systematic to unsystematic variance (because they are unchanged by the transformation), but there are considerably fewer of them.

The calculation of eigenvectors is extremely complex (insane students can consider reading Namboodiri, 1984), so you can trust me that for the matrix HE^{-1} the eigenvectors obtained are:

$$\text{eigenvector}_1 = \begin{pmatrix} 0.603 \\ -0.335 \end{pmatrix}$$

$$\text{eigenvector}_2 = \begin{pmatrix} 0.425 \\ 0.339 \end{pmatrix}$$

Replacing these values into the two equations for the variates and bearing in mind we can ignore b_0, we obtain the models described in the following equation:

$$V_{1i} = 0.603\text{Actions}_i - 0.335\text{Thoughts}_i$$
$$V_{2i} = 0.425\text{Actions}_i + 0.339\text{Thoughts}_i$$

(16.5)

It is possible to use the equations for each variate to calculate a score for each person on the variate. For example, the first participant in the CBT group carried out 5 obsessive actions, and had 14 obsessive thoughts. Therefore, this participant's score on variate 1 would be -1.675:

$$V_1 = (0.603 \times 5) - (0.335 \times 14) = -1.675$$

The score for variate 2 would be 6.87:

$$V_2 = (0.425 \times 5) + (0.339 \times 14) = 6.871$$

If we calculated these variate scores for each participant and then calculated the SSCP matrices (e.g., H, E, T and HE^{-1}) that we used previously, we would find that all of them have cross-products of zero. The reason for this is that the variates extracted from the data are orthogonal, which means that they are uncorrelated. In short, the variates extracted are independent dimensions constructed from a linear combination of the dependent variables that were measured.

This data reduction has a very useful property in that if we look at the matrix HE^{-1} calculated from the variate scores (rather than the dependent variables) we find that all of the off-diagonal elements (the cross-products) are zero. The diagonal elements of this matrix represent the ratio of the systematic variance to the unsystematic variance (i.e., SS_M/SS_R) for each of the underlying variates. So, in this example, this means that instead of having four values representing the ratio of systematic to unsystematic variance, we now have only two. This reduction may not seem a lot. However, in general if we have p dependent variables, then ordinarily we would end up with p^2 values representing the ratio of systematic to unsystematic variance; by using discriminant functions, we reduce this number to p. If there were four dependent variables we would end up with four values rather than 16 (which highlights the benefit of this process).

For the data in our example, the matrix HE^{-1} calculated from the variate scores is:

$$HE^{-1}_{\text{variate}} = \begin{pmatrix} 0.335 & 0 \\ 0 & 0.073 \end{pmatrix}$$

It is clear from this matrix that we have two values to consider when assessing the significance of the group differences. It probably seems like a complex procedure to reduce the data down in this way: however, it transpires that the values along the diagonal of the matrix for the variates (namely 0.335 and 0.073) are the *eigenvalues* of the original HE^{-1} matrix. Therefore, these values can be calculated directly from the data collected without first forming the eigenvectors. If you have lost all sense of rationality and want to see how these eigenvalues are calculated, then see Oliver Twisted. These eigenvalues are conceptually equivalent to the F-ratio in ANOVA and so the final step is to assess how large these values are compared to what we would expect if there were no effect in the population. There are four ways in which the values are assessed.

OLIVER TWISTED

Please, Sir, can I have some more … maths?

'You are a fool, Andy. I think it would be fun to check your maths so that we can see exactly how much of a village idiot you are', mocks Oliver. Luckily you can. Never one to shy from public humiliation on a mass scale, I have provided the matrix calculations for this example on the companion website. Find a mistake, go on, you know you can …

16.4.4.2. Pillai–Bartlett trace (V) ④

The **Pillai–Bartlett trace** (also known as Pillai's trace) is given by:

$$V = \sum_{i=1}^{s} \frac{\lambda_i}{1 + \lambda_i} \tag{16.6}$$

in which λ represents the eigenvalues for each of the discriminant variates and s represents the number of variates. Pillai's trace is the sum of the proportion of explained variance on the discriminant functions. As such, it is similar to the ratio of SS_M/SS_T, which is known as R^2.

For our data, Pillai's trace turns out to be 0.319, which can be transformed to a value that has an approximate F-distribution:

$$V = \frac{0.335}{1 + 0.335} + \frac{0.073}{1 + 0.073} = 0.319$$

16.4.4.3. Hotelling's T^2 ④

The **Hotelling–Lawley trace** (also known as Hotelling's T^2; Figure 16.2) is simply the sum of the eigenvalues for each variate:

$$T = \sum_{i=1}^{s} \lambda_i \tag{16.7}$$

For these data its value is 0.408 (0.335 + 0.073). This test statistic is the sum of SS_M/SS_R for each of the variates and so it compares directly to the F-ratio in ANOVA.

FIGURE 16.2
Harold Hotelling enjoying my favourite activity of drinking tea

16.4.4.4. Wilks's lambda (Λ) ④

Wilks's lambda is the product of the *unexplained* variance on each of the variates:

$$\Lambda = \prod_{i=1}^{s} \frac{1}{1 + \lambda_i} \tag{16.8}$$

(the $\prod$ symbol is similar to the summation symbol ($\sum$) that we have encountered already except that it means *multiply* rather than add up). So, Wilks's lambda represents the ratio of error variance to total variance (SS_R/SS_T) for each variate.

Large eigenvalues (which in themselves represent a large experimental effect) lead to small values of Wilks's lambda: hence statistical significance is found when Wilks's lambda is small. In this example Wilks's lambda is 0.698:

$$\Lambda = \frac{1}{1 + 0.335} \times \frac{1}{1 + 0.073} = 0.698$$

16.4.4.5. Roy's largest root ②

Roy's largest root always makes me think of some bearded statistician with a garden spade digging up an enormous parsnip (or similar root vegetable); however, it isn't a parsnip but, as the name suggests, is the eigenvalue for the first variate. So, in a sense it is the same as the Hotelling–Lawley trace but for the first variate only, that is:

$$\Theta = \lambda_{\text{largest}} \tag{16.9}$$

EVERYBODY

As such, Roy's largest root represents the proportion of explained variance to unexplained variance (SS_M/SS_R) for the first discriminant function.[4] For the data in this example, the value of Roy's largest root is 0.335 (the eigenvalue for the first variate). So, this value is conceptually the same as the *F*-ratio in univariate ANOVA. It should be apparent, from what we have learnt about the maximizing properties of these discriminant variates, that Roy's root represents the maximum possible between-groups difference given the data collected. Therefore, this statistic should in many cases be the most powerful.

16.5. Practical issues when conducting MANOVA ③

Assumptions and how to check them ③

MANOVA has similar assumptions to all of the models in this book (see Chapter 5), but extended to the multivariate case:

- **Independence**: Residuals should be statistically independent.

- **Random sampling**: Data should be randomly sampled from the population of interest and measured at an interval level.

- **Multivariate normality**: In ANOVA, we assume that our residuals are normally distributed. In the case of MANOVA, we assume that the residuals have multivariate normality.

- **Homogeneity of covariance matrices**: In ANOVA, it is assumed that the variances in each group are roughly equal (homogeneity of variance). In MANOVA we must assume that this is true for each dependent variable, but also that the correlation between any two dependent variables is the same in all groups. This assumption is examined by testing whether the population **variance–covariance matrices** of the different groups in the analysis are equal.[5]

We can correct for bias in the usual ways; however, the assumption of multivariate normality cannot be tested in SPSS and so the only practical solution is to check the assumption of univariate normality of residuals for each dependent variable in turn (see Chapter 5). This solution is practical (because it is easy to implement) and useful (because univariate normality is a necessary condition for multivariate normality), but it does not *guarantee* multivariate normality. So, I urge you to consult Stevens (2002) for some alternative options.

---

[4] This statistic is sometimes characterised as $\lambda_{\text{largest}}/1+ \lambda_{\text{largest}}$), but this is not the statistic reported by SPSS.

[5] For those of you who read about SSCP matrices, if you think about the relationship between sums of squares and variance, and cross-products and correlations, it should be clear that a variance–covariance matrix is basically a standardized form of an SSCP matrix.

The effect of violating the assumption of equality of covariance matrices is unclear, except that Hotelling's T^2 is robust in the two-group situation when sample sizes are equal (Hakstian, Roed, & Lind, 1979). The assumption can be tested using **Box's test**, which should be non-significant if the matrices are similar. Box's test is notoriously susceptible to deviations from multivariate normality and so can be non-significant not because the matrices are similar, but because the assumption of multivariate normality is not tenable. Also, as with any significance test, in large samples Box's test could be significant even when covariance matrices are relatively similar.

As a general rule, if sample sizes are equal then people tend to disregard Box's test, because (1) it is unstable, and (2) in this situation we can assume that Hotelling's and Pillai's statistics are robust (see Section 16.5.3). However, if group sizes are different, then robustness cannot be assumed. The more dependent variables you have measured, and the greater the differences in sample sizes, the more distorted the probability values become. Tabachnick and Fidell (2012) suggest that if the larger samples produce greater variances and covariances then the probability values will be conservative (and so significant findings can be trusted). However, if it is the smaller samples that produce the larger variances and covariances then the probability values will be liberal and so significant differences should be treated with caution (although non-significant effects can be trusted). Therefore, the variance–covariance matrices for samples should be inspected to assess whether the printed probabilities for the multivariate test statistics are likely to be conservative or liberal. In the event that you cannot trust the printed probabilities, there is little you can do except equalize the samples by randomly deleting cases in the larger groups (although with this loss of information comes a loss of power).

16.5.2. What to do when assumptions are violated ③

SPSS doesn't offer a non-parametric version of MANOVA; however, some ideas have been put forward based on ranked data. Although discussion of these tests is well beyond the scope of this book, there are some techniques that can be beneficial when multivariate normality or homogeneity of covariance matrices cannot be assumed (Zwick, 1985). In addition, there are robust methods for fairly straightforward designs with multiple outcome variables. For example, the Munzel–Brunner method can be implemented in the software R (Wilcox, 2012) – see Field et al. (2012) for a step-by-step guide. Although you will see a `Bootstrap...` button in the dialog box for MANOVA, it does not bootstrap the main tests and is, ultimately, disappointing.

16.5.3. Choosing a test statistic ③

Only when there is one underlying variate will the four test statistics necessarily be the same, which raises the question of which one is 'best'. As ever, when addressing this question we really need to know which has the most power, the least error and the greatest robustness to violations of test assumptions. Research investigating the power of the test statistics (Olson, 1974, 1976, 1979; Stevens, 1980) suggests that: (1) for small and moderate sample sizes the four statistics differ little in terms of power; (2) if group differences are concentrated on the first variate Roy's statistic should be the most powerful (because it takes account of only that first variate) followed by Hotelling's trace, Wilks's lambda and Pillai's trace; (3) when groups differ along more than one variate, this power order is reversed (i.e., Pillai's trace is most powerful and Roy's root is least); (4) unless sample sizes are large it's probably wise to use fewer than 10 dependent variables.

In terms of robustness, all four test statistics are relatively robust to violations of multivariate normality (although Roy's root is affected by platykurtic distributions – see Olson, 1976). Roy's root is also not robust when the homogeneity of covariance matrix assumption is untenable (Stevens, 1979). Bray and Maxwell (1985) conclude that when sample sizes are equal the Pillai–Bartlett trace is the most robust to violations of assumptions, but when sample sizes are unequal this statistic is affected by violations of the assumption of equal covariance matrices. As a rule, with unequal group sizes, check the homogeneity of covariance matrices; if they seem homogeneous and if the assumption of multivariate normality is tenable, then assume that Pillai's trace is accurate.

16.5.4. Follow-up analysis ③

The traditional approach is to follow a significant MANOVA with separate ANOVAs on each of the dependent variables. This approach might seem like a daft thing to do, given that I said earlier that multiple ANOVAs were a bad idea. I would agree, but some people argue that the ANOVAs are 'protected' by the initial MANOVA (Bock, 1975). The idea is that the overall multivariate test protects against inflated Type I error rates because if that initial test is non-significant (i.e., the null hypothesis is true) then the subsequent ANOVAs are ignored (any significance must be a Type I error because the null hypothesis is true). This notion of protection is dubious because a significant MANOVA usually reflects a significant difference for some, but not all, of the dependent variables. This argument of 'protection' applies only to the dependent variables for which group differences genuinely exist (see Bray and Maxwell, 1985, pp. 40–41) not for all dependent variables. Despite this problem, people tend to interpret ANOVAs on *all* dependent variables. Therefore, you ought to apply a Bonferroni correction to the subsequent ANOVAs (Harris, 1975).

A bigger problem is that ANOVAs don't really bear any relation to what is tested in a MANOVA. Remember that the test statistic quantifies the extent to which groups can be differentiated by a *linear combination of the outcome variables*. Subsequent ANOVAs look at the outcome variables as independent entities, not as a linear combination. An alternative is to pick apart a MANOVA with discriminant analysis, which finds the linear combination(s) of the dependent variables that best *separates* (or discriminates) the groups. The major advantage of this approach over multiple ANOVAs is that it reduces the dependent variables to a set of underlying dimensions thought to reflect substantive theoretical dimensions. As such, it is true to the ethos of MANOVA.

16.6. MANOVA using SPSS ②

16.6.1. General procedure of one-way ANOVA ②

In the remainder of this chapter we will use the OCD data to illustrate how MANOVA is done (those of you who skipped the theory section should refer to Table 16.1). Either load the data in the file **OCD.sav**, or enter the data manually. If you enter the data manually you need three columns: one column must be a coding variable for the **Group** variable (I used the codes CBT = 1, BT = 2, NT = 3), and in the remaining two columns enter the scores for each dependent variable. Figure 11.9 overviews the analysis procedure: basically, explore the data as you normally would, run the MANOVA, then follow up this analysis with a discriminant function analysis. Some of you will want to look at univariate ANOVAs, so I've included it in the diagram, but personally I wouldn't look at them.

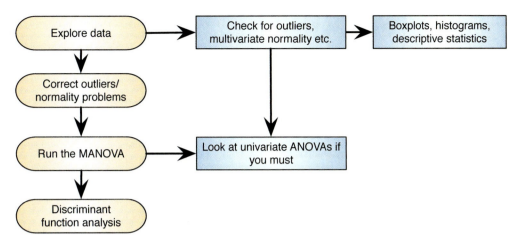

FIGURE 16.3
Overview of
the general
procedure for
MANOVA

16.6.2.   The main analysis ②

Access the main MANOVA dialog box (see Figure 16.4) by selecting Analyze General Linear Model ▸ Multivariate…. The main dialog box and options for MANOVA are very similar to those for the factorial ANOVA procedure we met in Chapter 13. The main difference is that the space labelled *Dependent Variables* has room for several variables. Select the two dependent variables from the variables list (i.e., **Actions** and **Thoughts**) and drag them to the *Dependent Variables* box (or click on ➡). Select **group** from the variables list and drag it (or click on ➡) to the *Fixed Factor(s)* box. There is also a box in which you can place covariates. For this analysis there are no covariates; however, you can apply the principles of ANCOVA to the multivariate case and conduct multivariate analysis of covariance (MANCOVA). The buttons on the right are pretty much the same as we have seen in the past few chapters.

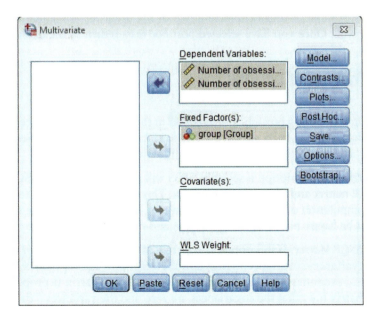

FIGURE 16.4
Main dialog
box for
MANOVA

FIGURE 16.5
Contrasts for
independent
variable(s) in
MANOVA

16.6.3. Multiple comparisons in MANOVA ②

The default way to follow up a MANOVA is to look at individual univariate ANOVAs for each dependent variable. For these tests, SPSS has the same options as in the univariate ANOVA procedure (see Chapter 11). The `Contrasts...` button opens a dialog box for specifying one of several standard contrasts for the independent variable(s) in the analysis. Table 11.6 describes what each of these tests compares, but for this example it makes sense to use a *simple* contrast that compares each of the experimental groups to the no treatment control group. The NT control group was coded as the last category (it had the highest code in the data editor), so we need to select the group variable and change the contrast to a simple contrast using the last category as the reference category (see Figure 16.5). For more details about contrasts, see Section 11.4.

Instead of running a contrast, we could carry out *post hoc* tests on the independent variable to compare each group to all other groups. To access the *post hoc* tests dialog box, click on `Post Hoc...`. The dialog box is the same as that for factorial ANOVA (see Figure 13.9) and the choice of test should be based on the same criteria as outlined in Section 11.5. For the purposes of this example, I suggest selecting two of my usual recommendations: REGWQ and Games–Howell. Once you have selected *post hoc* tests return to the main dialog box.

16.6.4. Additional options ③

To access the *Options* dialog box, click on `Options...` in the main dialog box (see Figure 16.6). The resulting dialog box is fairly similar to that for factorial ANOVA (see Section 13.4.6); however, there are a few options that are worth mentioning.

- *SSCP Matrices*: If this option is selected, SPSS will produce the model SSCP matrix, the error SSCP matrix and the total SSCP matrix. This option can be useful for understanding the computation of the MANOVA. However, if you didn't read the theory section you might be happy not to select this option and not worry about these matrices!

- *Residual SSCP Matrix*: If this option is selected, SPSS produces the error SSCP matrix, the error variance–covariance matrix and the error correlation matrix. **Bartlett's test of sphericity** examines whether the variance–covariance matrix is proportional to an identity matrix (i.e., that the covariances are zero and the variances – the values along the diagonal – are roughly equal).

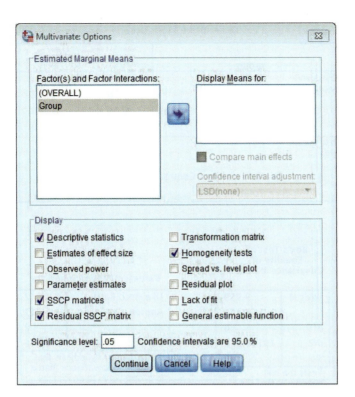

FIGURE 16.6
Additional
options in
MANOVA

ODITI'S LANTERN

MANOVA

'I, Oditi, have seen the multivariate way. To understand the hidden truth of life we must embrace complexity as though it were our attractive wife after a hard day at work. We probably shouldn't have sex with it, though. To understand complex outcomes, such as how to change people's personalities so that they worship me.. erm, I mean, worship nature, and love, and the tulips that grow where the wild wind blows, we need MANOVA. Stare into my lantern and discover all about it.'

The remaining options are the same as for factorial ANOVA and so have been described in Chapter 13).

16.7. Output from MANOVA ③

16.7.1. Preliminary analysis and testing assumptions ③

Output 16.1 shows an initial table of descriptive statistics. This table contains the overall and group means and standard deviations for each dependent variable in turn. These values correspond to those calculated by hand in Table 16.1. It is clear from the means that participants had many more obsession-related thoughts than behaviours.

Output 16.2 shows Box's test of the assumption of equality of covariance matrices (see Section 16.5.1). This statistic should be *non-significant*, which it is $p = .18$ (which is greater than .05); hence, the covariance matrices are roughly equal as assumed. Bartlett's test of

OUTPUT 16.1

Descriptive Statistics

	group	Mean	Std. Deviation	N
Number of obsession–related behaviours	CBT	4.90	1.197	10
	BT	3.70	1.767	10
	No Treatment Control	5.00	1.054	10
	Total	4.53	1.456	30
Number of obsession–related thoughts	CBT	13.40	1.897	10
	BT	15.20	2.098	10
	No Treatment Control	15.00	2.357	10
	Total	14.53	2.209	30

OUTPUT 16.2

Box's Test of Equality of Covariance Matrices[a]

Box's M	9.959
F	1.482
df1	6
df2	18168.923
Sig.	.180

Tests the null hypothesis that the observed covariance matrices of the dependent variables are equal across groups.

a. Design: Intercept + Group

Bartlett's Test of Sphericity[a]

Likelihood Ratio	.042
Approx. Chi–Square	5.511
df	2
Sig.	.064

Tests the null hypothesis that the residual covariance matrix is proportional to an identity matrix.

a. Design: Intercept + Group

sphericity tests whether the assumption of sphericity has been met and is useful only in univariate repeated-measures designs because MANOVA does not require this assumption.

16.7.2. MANOVA test statistics ③

Output 16.3 shows the main table of results. Test statistics are quoted for the intercept of the model (even MANOVA can be characterized as a linear model, although how this is done is beyond the scope of my brain) and for the group variable. For our purposes, the group effects are of interest because they tell us whether or not the therapies had an effect on the OCD clients. You'll see that SPSS lists the four multivariate test statistics, and their values correspond to those calculated in Sections 16.4.4.2–16.4.4.5. In the next column these values are transformed into an F-ratio with 2 and 26 degrees of freedom. The column of real interest, however, is the one containing the significance values of these F-ratios. For these data, Pillai's trace ($p = .049$), Wilks's lambda ($p = .050$) and Roy's largest root ($p = .020$) all reach the criterion for significance of .05. However, Hotelling's trace ($p = .051$) is non-significant by this criterion. This scenario is interesting, because the test statistic we choose determines whether or not we reject the null hypothesis that there are no between-groups differences. It again illustrates the pointlessness of having an all-or-nothing criterion for significance (see Section 2.6.2.2). However, given what we know about the robustness of Pillai's trace when sample sizes are equal, we might be well advised to trust the result of that

Multivariate Tests[a]

Effect		Value	F	Hypothesis df	Error df	Sig.
Intercept	Pillai's Trace	.983	745.230[b]	2.000	26.000	.000
	Wilks' Lambda	.017	745.230[b]	2.000	26.000	.000
	Hotelling's Trace	57.325	745.230[b]	2.000	26.000	.000
	Roy's Largest Root	57.325	745.230[b]	2.000	26.000	.000
Group	Pillai's Trace	.318	2.557	4.000	54.000	.049
	Wilks' Lambda	.699	2.555[b]	4.000	52.000	.050
	Hotelling's Trace	.407	2.546	4.000	50.000	.051
	Roy's Largest Root	.335	4.520[c]	2.000	27.000	.020

a. Design: Intercept + Group

b. Exact statistic

c. The statistic is an upper bound on F that yields a lower bound on the significance level.

test statistic, which indicates a significant difference. This example highlights the additional power associated with Roy's root (you should note how this statistic is considerably more significant than all others) when the test assumptions have been met and when the group differences are focused on one variate (which, they are in this example, as we will see later).

From this result we should probably conclude that the type of therapy employed had a significant effect on OCD. The nature of this effect is not clear from the multivariate test statistic: it tells us nothing about which groups differed from which, or about whether the effect of therapy was on the obsession-related thoughts, the obsession-related behaviours, or a combination of both. To determine the nature of the effect, a discriminant analysis would be helpful, but for some reason SPSS provides us with univariate tests instead. What a bilge rat.

16.7.3. Univariate test statistics ②

Output 16.4 initially shows a summary table of Levene's test of equality of variances for each of the dependent variables. These tests are the same as would be found if a one-way ANOVA had been conducted on each dependent variable in turn. Levene's test should be non-significant for all dependent variables if the assumption of homogeneity of variance has been met (but see Section 5.3.3.2). Output 16.4 shows that the assumption has been met, which strengthens the case for assuming that the multivariate test statistics are robust.

The next part of the output contains an ANOVA summary table for each of the dependent variables. In Sections 16.4.3.1 and 16.4.3.2, we computed various values for both actions and thoughts that are in this table: the model sum of squares (in the row labelled *Group*), the residual sum of squares (in the row labelled *Error*) and total sums of squares (in the row labelled *Corrected Total*). The F-ratios for each univariate ANOVA and their significance values are listed in the columns labelled F and Sig. These values are *identical* to those obtained if one-way ANOVA was conducted on each dependent variable independently. As such, MANOVA offers only *hypothetical* protection of inflated Type I error rates: there is no real-life adjustment made to the values obtained.

The values of p in Output 16.4 indicate that there was a non-significant difference between therapy groups in terms of both obsession-related thoughts ($p = .136$) and obsession-related behaviours ($p = .080$). We should conclude that the type of therapy had no significant effect on

Levene's Test of Equality of Error Variances[a]

	F	df1	df2	Sig.
Number of obsession–related behaviours	1.828	2	27	.180
Number of obsession–related thoughts	.076	2	27	.927

Tests the null hypothesis that the error variance of the dependent variable is equal across groups.

a. Design: Intercept + Group

Tests of Between–Subjects Effects

Source	Dependent Variable	Type III Sum of Squares	df	Mean Square	F	Sig.
Corrected Model	Number of obsession–related behaviours	10.467[a]	2	5.233	2.771	.080
	Number of obsession–related thoughts	19.467[b]	2	9.733	2.154	.136
Intercept	Number of obsession–related behaviours	616.533	1	616.533	326.400	.000
	Number of obsession–related thoughts	6336.533	1	6336.533	1402.348	.000
Group	Number of obsession–related behaviours	10.467	2	5.233	2.771	.080
	Number of obsession–related thoughts	19.467	2	9.733	2.154	.136
Error	Number of obsession–related behaviours	51.000	27	1.889		
	Number of obsession–related thoughts	122.000	27	4.519		
Total	Number of obsession–related behaviours	678.000	30			
	Number of obsession–related thoughts	6478.000	30			
Corrected Total	Number of obsession–related behaviours	61.467	29			
	Number of obsession–related thoughts	141.467	29			

a. R Squared = .170 (Adjusted R Squared = .109)

b. R Squared = .138 (Adjusted R Squared = .074)

the levels of OCD experienced by clients. Those of you who are still awake may have noticed something odd: the multivariate test statistics led us to conclude that therapy had had a significant impact on OCD, yet the univariate results indicate that therapy has not been successful.

SELF-TEST　Why might the univariate tests be non-significant when the multivariate tests were significant?

The reason for the anomaly is that the multivariate test takes account of the correlation between dependent variables and so for these data it has more power to detect group differences. With this knowledge in mind, the univariate tests are not particularly useful for interpretation, because the groups differ along a combination of the dependent variables. To see how the dependent variables interact we need to carry out a discriminant function analysis, which will be described in due course.

16.7.4. SSCP matrices ③

If you selected the two options to display SSCP matrices (Section 16.6.4), then SPSS will produce the tables in Outputs 16.5 and 16.6. The first table (Output 16.5) displays the

Between–Subjects SSCP Matrix

			Number of obsession–related behaviours	Number of obsession–related thoughts
Hypothesis	Intercept	Number of obsession–related behaviours	616.533	1976.533
		Number of obsession–related thoughts	1976.533	6336.533
	Group	Number of obsession–related behaviours	10.467	–7.533
		Number of obsession–related thoughts	–7.533	19.467
Error		Number of obsession–related behaviours	51.000	13.000
		Number of obsession–related thoughts	13.000	122.000

Based on Type III Sum of Squares

Residual SSCP Matrix

		Number of obsession–related behaviours	Number of obsession–related thoughts
Sum-of-Squares and Cross-Products	Number of obsession–related behaviours	51.000	13.000
	Number of obsession–related thoughts	13.000	122.000
Covariance	Number of obsession–related behaviours	1.889	.481
	Number of obsession–related thoughts	.481	4.519
Correlation	Number of obsession–related behaviours	1.000	.165
	Number of obsession–related thoughts	.165	1.000

Based on Type III Sum of Squares

model SSCP (*H*), which is labelled *Hypothesis Group* (I have shaded this matrix blue), and the error SSCP (*E*), which is labelled *Error* (I have shaded this matrix yellow). The values in the model and error matrices correspond to the values we calculated in Sections 16.4.3.6 and 16.4.3.5, respectively. These matrices provide insight into the pattern of the data, looking at the values of the cross-products to indicate the relationship between dependent variables. In this example, the sums of squares for the error SSCP matrix are substantially bigger than in the model (or group) SSCP matrix, whereas the absolute values of the cross-products are fairly similar. This pattern suggests that if the MANOVA is significant then it might be the relationship between dependent variables that is important rather than the individual dependent variables themselves.

Output 16.6 shows the residual SSCP matrix again, but this time it includes the variance–covariance matrix and the correlation matrix. These matrices are all related. If you look back to Chapter 6, you should remember that the covariance is the average cross-product. Likewise, the variance is the average sum of squares. Hence, the variance–covariance matrix is the average form of the SSCP matrix. Finally, we saw in Chapter 6 that the correlation was a standardized version of the covariance, so the correlation matrix represents the standardized form of the variance–covariance matrix. As with the SSCP matrix, these other matrices are useful for assessing the extent of the error in the model. The

CRAMMING SAM'S TIPS   **MANOVA**

- MANOVA is used to test the difference between groups across several dependent variables/outcomes simultaneously.
- Box's test looks at the assumption of equal covariance matrices. This test can be ignored when sample sizes are equal because when they are some MANOVA test statistics are robust to violations of this assumption. If group sizes differ this test should be inspected. If the value of *Sig.* is less than .001 then the results of the analysis should not be trusted (see Section 16.7.1).
- The table labelled *Multivariate Tests* gives us the results of the MANOVA. There are four test statistics (*Pillai's Trace, Wilks's Lambda, Hotelling's Trace* and *Roy's Largest Root*). I recommend using Pillai's trace. If the value of *Sig.* for this statistic is less than .05, then the groups differ significantly with respect to the dependent variables.
- ANOVAs can be used to follow up the MANOVA (a different ANOVA for each dependent variable). The results of these are listed in the table entitled *Tests of Between-Subjects Effects*. These ANOVAs can in turn be followed up using contrasts. Personally I don't recommend this approach and suggest conducting a *discriminant function analysis*.

variance–covariance matrix is especially useful because Bartlett's test of sphericity is based on it. Bartlett's test examines whether this matrix is proportional to an identity matrix (see earlier). Therefore, Bartlett's test tests whether the diagonal elements of the variance–covariance matrix are equal (i.e., group variances are the same), and whether the off-diagonal elements are approximately zero (i.e., the dependent variables are not correlated). In this case, the variances are quite different (1.89 compared to 4.52) and the covariances slightly different from zero (0.48), so Bartlett's test has come out as nearly significant (see Output 16.2). Although this discussion is irrelevant to the multivariate tests, I hope that by expanding upon them here you can relate these ideas back to the issues of sphericity raised in Chapter 14, and see more clearly how this assumption is tested.

16.7.5.   Contrasts ③

The univariate ANOVAs were non-significant, so we should not interpret the contrasts that we requested. However, just for practice, try the self-test.

SELF-TEST   Based on what you have learnt in previous chapters, interpret the table of contrasts in your output.

16.8.   Reporting results from MANOVA ②

Reporting a MANOVA is much like reporting an ANOVA. As you can see in Output 16.3, the multivariate tests are converted into approximate *F*s, and people often just report these

Fs just as they would for ANOVA (i.e., they give details of the F-ratio and the degrees of freedom from which it was calculated). Personally, I think the multivariate test statistic should be quoted as well. There are four different multivariate tests reported in Output 16.3; I'll report each one in turn (note that the degrees of freedom and value of F change), but in reality you would just report one of the four:

✓ Using Pillai's trace, there was a significant effect of therapy on the number of obsessive thoughts and behaviours, $V = 0.32$, $F(4, 54) = 2.56$, $p = .049$.

✓ Using Wilks's lambda, there was a significant effect of therapy on the number of obsessive thoughts and behaviours, $\Lambda = 0.70$, $F(4, 52) = 2.56$, $p = .05$.

✓ Using Hotelling's trace statistic, there was not a significant effect of therapy on the number of obsessive thoughts and behaviours, $T = 0.41$, $F(4, 50) = 2.55$, $p = .051$.

✓ Using Roy's largest root, there was a significant effect of therapy on the number of obsessive thoughts and behaviours, $\Theta = 0.35$, $F(2, 27) = 4.52$, $p = .02$.

We can also report the follow-up ANOVAs in the usual way (see Outputs 16.3 and 16.4):

✓ Using Pillai's trace, there was a significant effect of therapy on the number of obsessive thoughts and behaviours, $V = 0.32$, $F(4, 54) = 2.56$, $p = .049$. However, separate univariate ANOVAs on the outcome variables revealed non-significant treatment effects on obsessive thoughts, $F(2, 27) = 2.15$, $p = .136$, and behaviours, $F(2, 27) = 2.77$, $p = .08$.

LABCOAT LENI'S REAL RESEARCH 16.1

A lot of hot air! ④

Marzillier, S. L., & Davey, G. C. L. (2005). *Cognition and Emotion, 19*, 729–750.

Have you ever wondered what researchers do in their spare time? Well, some of them spend it tracking down the sounds of people burping and farting! Anxious people are, typically, easily disgusted. Throughout this book I have talked about how you cannot infer causality from relationships between variables. This has been a bit of a conundrum for anxiety researchers: does anxiety cause feelings of disgust or does a low threshold for being disgusted cause anxiety? Two colleagues of mine at Sussex addressed this in an unusual study in which they induced feelings of anxiety, disgust, or a neutral mood. They looked at the effect of these induced moods on feelings of anxiety, sadness, happiness, anger, disgust and contempt. To induce these moods, they used three different types of manipulation: vignettes (e.g., 'You're swimming in a dark lake and something brushes your leg' for

anxiety, and 'You go into a public toilet and find it has not been flushed. The bowl of the toilet is full of diarrhoea' for disgust), music (e.g., some scary music for anxiety, and a tape of burps, farts and vomitting for disgust), videos (e.g., a clip from *Silence of the Lambs* for anxiety and a scene from *Pink Flamingos* in which Divine eats dog faeces) and memory (remembering events from the past that had made the person anxious, disgusted or neutral).

Different people underwent anxiety, disgust and neutral mood inductions. Within these groups, the induction was done using either vignettes and music, videos, or memory recall and music for different people. The outcome variables were the change (from before to after the induction) in six moods: anxiety, sadness, happiness, anger, disgust and contempt. The data are in the file **Marzillier and Davey (2005).sav**. Draw an error bar graph of the changes in moods in the different conditions, then conduct a 3 (Mood: anxiety, disgust, neutral) × 3 (Induction: vignettes + music, videos, memory recall + music) MANOVA on these data. Whatever you do, don't imagine what their fart tape sounded like while you do the analysis. Answers are on the companion website (or look at page 738 of the original article).

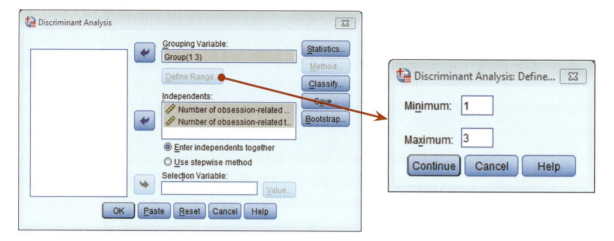

FIGURE 16.7   Main dialog box for discriminant analysis

16.9. Following up MANOVA with discriminant analysis ③

I mentioned earlier on that a significant MANOVA could be followed up using discriminant function analysis (in this section and the next we'll just call it 'discriminant analysis' because that's what SPSS calls it). In my opinion this method is the best way to follow up a significant MANOVA because a MANOVA looks at whether groups differ along *a linear combination* of outcome variables, and discriminant analysis (unlike ANOVAs) breaks down the linear combination in more detail. In discriminant analysis we look to see how we can best separate (or discriminate) a set of groups using several predictors (so it is a little like logistic regression but where there are several groups rather than two).[6] In some senses we're doing the reverse of the MANOVA: in MANOVA we predicted a set of outcome measures from a grouping variable, whereas in discriminant analysis we predict a grouping variable from a set of outcome measures. However, the basic underlying principles of these tests are the same: remember from the theory of MANOVA that it works by identifying linear variates that best differentiate the groups and these 'linear variates' are the 'functions' in discriminant function analysis.

To access the main dialog box (see Figure 16.7) select Analyze Classify ▶ ☑ Discriminant...; it lists the variables in the data editor on the left-hand side and provides two spaces on the right: one for the group variable and one for the predictors.

To run the analysis, select the variable **Group** and drag it to the box labelled *Grouping Variable* (or click on ![arrow]). Once this variable has been transferred, the Define Range... button becomes active and you should click on it to activate a dialog box in which you can specify the value of the highest and lowest coding values (1 and 3 in this case). Once you have specified the codings used for the grouping variable, you should select the variables **Actions** and **Thoughts** and drag them to the box labelled *Independents* (or click on ![arrow]). There are two options available to determine how the predictors are entered into the

---

[6] In fact, I could just as easily describe discriminant function analysis rather than logistic regression in Chapter 19 because they are different ways of achieving the same end result. However, logistic regression has far fewer restrictive assumptions and is generally more robust, which is why I have limited the coverage of discriminant analysis to this chapter.

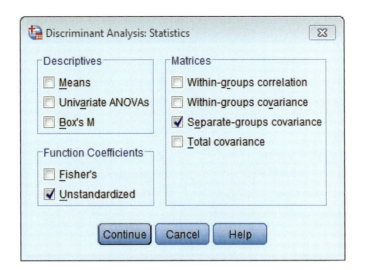

FIGURE 16.8
Statistics
options for
discriminant
analysis

model. The default is that both predictors are entered together (⊙ Enter independents together) and this is the option we require (because in MANOVA the dependent variables are analysed simultaneously).

Click on [Statistics...] to activate the dialog box in Figure 16.8. This dialog box allows us to request group means, univariate ANOVAs and Box's test of equality of covariance matrices, all of which have already been provided in the MANOVA output (so we need not ask for them again). Furthermore, we can ask for the within-group correlation and covariance matrices, which are the same as the residual correlation and covariance matrices seen in Output 16.6. There is also an option to display a *Separate-groups covariance* matrix, which can be useful for gaining insight into the relationships between dependent variables for each group (this matrix is something that the MANOVA procedure doesn't display and I recommend selecting it). Finally, we can ask for a total covariance matrix, which displays covariances and variances of the dependent variables overall. Another useful option is to select *Unstandardized* function coefficients. This option will produce the unstandardized *b*s for each variate (see equation (16.5)). When you have finished with this dialog box, click on [Continue] to return to the main dialog box.

Click on [Classify...] to access the dialog box in Figure 16.9. In this dialog box you can select how prior probabilities are determined: if your group sizes are equal then you should leave the default setting as it is; however, if you have an unbalanced design then it is beneficial to base prior probabilities on the observed group sizes. The default option for basing the analysis on the within-group covariance matrix is fine (because this is the matrix upon which the MANOVA is based). You should also request a combined-groups plot, which will plot the variate scores for each participant grouped according to the therapy they were given. The separate-groups plots show the same thing, but using different graphs for each of the groups; when the number of groups is small it is better to select a combined plot because it is easier to interpret. The remaining options are of little interest when using discriminant analysis to follow up MANOVA. The only option that is useful is the summary table, which provides an overall gauge of how well the discriminant variates classify the actual participants. When you have finished with the options click on [Continue] to return to the main dialog box.

The final options are accessed by clicking on [Save...] to access the dialog box in Figure 16.10. There are three options available, two of which relate to the predicted group memberships and probabilities of group memberships from the model. The final option is to provide the **discriminant scores**. These are the scores for each person, on each variate, obtained from equation (16.5). These scores can be useful because the variates that the

FIGURE 16.9
Discriminant
analysis
classification
options

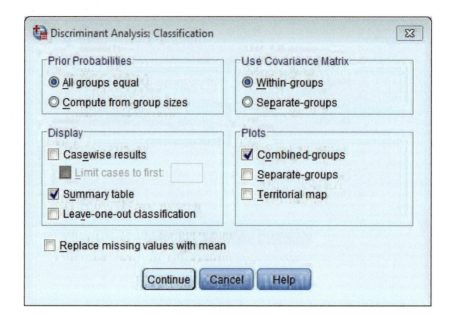

FIGURE 16.10
The save
new variables
dialog box in
discriminant
analysis

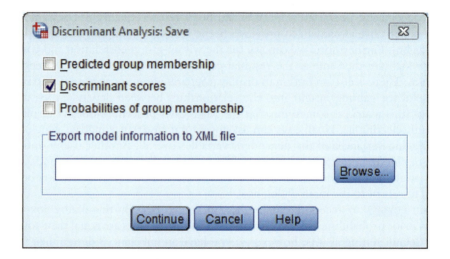

analysis identifies may represent underlying social or psychological constructs. If these constructs are identifiable, then it is useful for interpretation to know what a participant scores on each dimension.

16.10. Output from the discriminant analysis ④

Output 16.7 shows the covariance matrices for separate groups (selected in Figure 16.8). These matrices are made up of the variances of each dependent variable for each group (in fact these values are shown in Table 16.1). The covariances are obtained by taking the cross-products between the dependent variables for each group (shown in Table 16.4 as .40, 22.6 and −10) and dividing each by 9, the degrees of freedom, $N-1$ (where N is the number of observations). The values in this table are useful because they give us some idea

Covariance Matrices

group		Number of obsession–related behaviours	Number of obsession–related thoughts
CBT	Number of obsession–related behaviours	1.433	.044
	Number of obsession–related thoughts	.044	3.600
BT	Number of obsession–related behaviours	3.122	2.511
	Number of obsession–related thoughts	2.511	4.400
No Treatment Control	Number of obsession–related behaviours	1.111	-1.111
	Number of obsession–related thoughts	-1.111	5.556

of how the relationship between dependent variables changes from group to group. For example, in the CBT group behaviours and thoughts have virtually no relationship because the covariance is almost zero. In the BT group thoughts and actions are positively related, so as the number of behaviours decreases, so does the number of thoughts. In the NT condition there is a negative relationship, so if the number of thoughts increases then the number of behaviours decreases. It is important to note that these matrices don't tell us about the substantive importance of the relationships because they are unstandardized (see Chapter 6); they merely give a basic indication.

Output 16.8 shows the initial statistics from the discriminant analysis. At first we are told the eigenvalues for each variate, and you should note that the values correspond to the values of the diagonal elements of the matrix HE^{-1} (for the calculation see Oliver Twisted). These eigenvalues are converted into percentage of variance accounted for: the first variate accounts for 82.2% of variance, while the second accounts for only 17.8%. This table also shows the canonical correlation, which we can square to use as an effect size (just like R^2, which we have encountered in regression).

Eigenvalues

Function	Eigenvalue	% of Variance	Cumulative %	Canonical Correlation
1	.335[a]	82.2	82.2	.501
2	.073[a]	17.8	100.0	.260

a. First 2 canonical discriminant functions were used in the analysis.

Wilks' Lambda

Test of Function(s)	Wilks' Lambda	Chi-square	df	Sig.
1 through 2	.699	9.508	4	.050
2	.932	1.856	1	.173

The next part of the output shows the significance tests of both variates ('1 through 2' in the table), and the significance after the first variate has been removed ('2' in the table). So, effectively we test the model as a whole, and then peel away variates one at a time to see whether what's left is significant. In this case with two variates we get only two steps: the whole model, and then the model after the first variate is removed (which leaves only the second variate). When both variates are tested in combination Wilks's lambda has the

Standardized Canonical Discriminant Function Coefficients

	Function	
	1	2
Number of obsession–related behaviours	.829	.584
Number of obsession–related thoughts	-.713	.721

Structure Matrix

	Function	
	1	2
Number of obsession–related behaviours	.711*	.703
Number of obsession–related thoughts	-.576	.817*

Pooled within–groups correlations between discriminating variables and standardized canonical discriminant functions
Variables ordered by absolute size of correlation within function.

* Largest absolute correlation between each variable and any discriminant function

same value (0.699), degrees of freedom (4) and significance value (.05) as in the MANOVA (see Output 16.3). The important point to note from this table is that the two variates significantly discriminate the groups in combination ($p = .05$), but the second variate alone is non-significant, $p = .173$. Therefore, the group differences shown by the MANOVA can be explained in terms of *two* underlying dimensions in combination.

The tables in Output 16.9 are the most important for interpretation. The first table shows the standardized discriminant function coefficients for the two variates. These values are standardized versions of the values in the eigenvectors calculated in Section 16.4.4.1. Recall that if the variates can be expressed in terms of a linear regression equation (see equation (16.4)), the standardized discriminant function coefficients are equivalent to the standardized betas in regression. The structure matrix shows the same information, but in a slightly different form. The values in this matrix are the canonical variate correlation coefficients. These values indicate the substantive nature of the variates (see Chapter 17). Bargman (1970) argues that when some dependent variables have high canonical variate correlations while others have low ones, then the ones with high correlations contribute most to group separation. As such they represent the relative contribution of each dependent variable to group separation (see Bray & Maxwell, 1985, pp. 42–45). Hence, the coefficients in these tables tell us the relative contribution of each variable to the variates.

If we look at variate 1 first, thoughts and behaviours have the opposite effect (behaviour has a positive relationship with this variate whereas thoughts have a negative relationship). Given that these values (in both tables) can vary between 1 and −1, we can also see that both relationships are strong (although behaviours have slightly larger contribution to the first variate). The first variate, then, could be seen as one that differentiates thoughts and behaviours (it affects thoughts and behaviours in the opposite way). Both thoughts and behaviours have a strong positive relationship with the second variate. This tells us that this variate represents something that affects thoughts and behaviours in a similar way. Remembering that ultimately these variates are used to differentiate groups, we could say that the first variate differentiates groups by some factor that affects thoughts and behaviours differently, whereas the second variate differentiates groups on some dimension that affects thoughts and behaviours in the same way.

Output 16.10 tells us first the canonical discriminant function coefficients, which are the unstandardized versions of the standardized coefficients described above. These values are the values of b in equation (16.4) and you'll notice that they correspond to the values in the eigenvectors derived in Section 16.4.4.1 and used in equation (16.5). The values are less useful than the standardized versions, but do demonstrate from where the standardized versions come.

The centroids are the mean variate scores for each group. For interpretation we should look at the sign of the centroid (positive or negative). We can also use a combined-groups plot (selected using the dialog box in Figure 16.8). This graph plots the variate scores for each

OUTPUT 16.10

Canonical Discriminant Function Coefficients

	Function	
	1	2
Number of obsession–related behaviours	.603	.425
Number of obsession–related thoughts	–.335	.339
(Constant)	2.139	–6.857

Unstandardized coefficients

Functions at Group Centroids

group	Function	
	1	2
CBT	.601	–.229
BT	–.726	–.128
No Treatment Control	.125	.357

Unstandardized canonical discriminant functions evaluated at group means

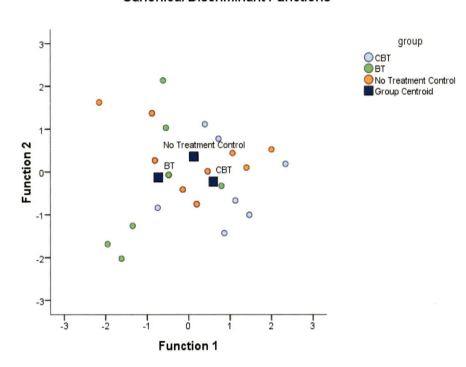

Canonical Discriminant Functions

FIGURE 16.11
Combined-groups plot

CRAMMING SAM'S TIPS   **Discriminant function analysis**

- Discriminant function analysis can be used after MANOVA to see how the dependent variables discriminate the groups.
- Discriminant function analysis identifies variates (combinations of the dependent variables), and to find out how many variates are significant look at the tables labelled *Wilks's Lambda:* if the value of *Sig.* is less than .05, then the variate is significantly discriminating the groups.
- Once the significant variates have been identified, use the table labelled *Standardized Canonical Discriminant Function Coefficients* to find out how the dependent variables contribute to the variates. High scores indicate that a dependent variable is important for a variate, and variables with positive and negative coefficients are contributing to the variate in opposite ways.
- Finally, to find out which groups are discriminated by a variate look at the table labelled *Functions at Group Centroids:* for a given variate, groups with values opposite in sign are being discriminated by that variate.

person, grouped according to the experimental condition to which that person belonged. In addition, the group centroids from Output 16.10 are shown as blue squares. The graph (Figure 16.11) and the tabulated values of the centroids (Output 16.10) tell us (look at the big squares labelled with the group initials) that variate 1 discriminates the BT group from the CBT (look at the horizontal distance between these centroids). The second variate differentiates the no treatment group from the two interventions (look at the vertical distances), but this difference is not as dramatic as for the first variate. Remember that the variates significantly discriminate the groups in combination (i.e., when both are considered).

16.11. Reporting results from discriminant analysis ②

The guiding principle in presenting data is to give the readers enough information to be able to judge for themselves what the data mean. Personally, I would suggest reporting percentage of variance explained (which gives the reader the same information as the eigenvalue but in a more palatable form) and the squared canonical correlation for each variate (this is the appropriate effect size measure for discriminant analysis). I would also report the chi-square significance tests of the variates. All of these values can be found in Output 16.8 (although remember to square the canonical correlation). It is probably also useful to quote the values in the structure matrix in Output 16.9 (which will tell the reader how the outcome variables relate to the underlying variates). Finally, although I won't reproduce it below, you could consider including a (well-edited) copy of the combined-groups centroid plot (Figure 16.11), which will help readers to determine how the variates contribute to distinguishing your groups. You could, therefore, write something like this:

✓ The MANOVA was followed up with discriminant analysis, which revealed two discriminant functions. The first explained 82.2% of the variance, canonical $R^2 = .25$, whereas the second explained only 17.8%, canonical $R^2 = .07$. In combination these discriminant functions significantly differentiated the treatment groups, $\Lambda = 0.70$, $\chi^2(4) = 9.51$, $p = .05$, but removing the first function indicated that the second function did not significantly differentiate the treatment groups, $\Lambda = 0.93$, $\chi^2(1) = 1.86$, $p = .173$. The correlations between outcomes and the discriminant functions revealed that obsessive behaviours loaded fairly evenly highly onto both functions ($r = .71$ for the first function and $r = .70$ for the second); obsessive thoughts loaded more highly on the second function ($r = .82$) than the first function ($r = -.58$). The discriminant function plot showed that the first function discriminated the BT group from the CBT group, and the second function differentiated the no treatment group from the two interventions.

16.12. The final interpretation ④

So far we have gathered an awful lot of information about our data, but how can we bring all of it together to answer our research question: can therapy improve OCD and, if so, which therapy is best? Well, the MANOVA tells us that therapy can have a significant effect on OCD symptoms, but the non-significant univariate ANOVAs suggested that this improvement is not simply in terms of either thoughts or behaviours. The discriminant analysis suggests that the group separation can be best explained in terms of one underlying dimension. In this context the dimension is likely to be OCD itself (which we can

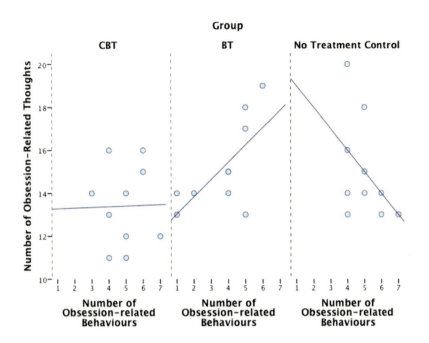

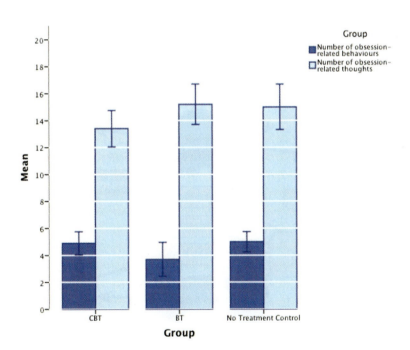

FIGURE 16.12
Graphs
showing the
relationships
(top) and
the means
and 95%
confidence
intervals
(bottom)
between the
dependent
variables in
each therapy
group

realistically presume is made up of both thoughts and behaviours). So, therapy doesn't necessarily change behaviours or thoughts *per se*, but it does influence the underlying dimension of OCD. So, the answer to the first question seems to be: yes, therapy can influence OCD, but the nature of this influence is unclear.

The next question is more complex: which therapy is best? Figure 16.12 shows graphs of the relationships between the dependent variables and the group means of the original data. The graph of the means shows that for actions, BT reduces the number of obsessive behaviours, whereas CBT and NT do not; for thoughts, CBT reduces the number of obsessive thoughts, whereas BT and NT do not (check the pattern of the bars). Looking now at the relationships between thoughts and actions, in the BT group there is a positive relationship between thoughts and actions, so the more obsessive thoughts a person has, the more obsessive behaviours they carry out. In the CBT group there is no relationship at all (thoughts and actions vary quite independently). In the no treatment group there is a negative (and non-significant, incidentally) relationship between thoughts and actions.

What we have discovered from the discriminant analysis is that BT and CBT can be differentiated from the control group based on variate 2, a variate that has a similar effect on both thoughts and behaviours. We could say then that BT and CBT are both better than a no treatment group at changing obsessive thoughts and behaviours. We also discovered that BT and CBT could be distinguished by variate 1, a variate that had the opposite effects on thoughts and behaviours. Combining this information with that in Figure 16.12, we could conclude that BT is better at changing behaviours and CBT is better at changing thoughts. So, the NT group can be distinguished from the CBT and BT graphs using a variable that affects both thoughts and behaviours. Also, the CBT and BT groups can be distinguished by a variate that has opposite effects on thoughts and behaviours. So, some therapy is better than none, but the choice of CBT or BT depends on whether you think it's more important to target thoughts (CBT) or behaviours (BT).

16.13. Brian's attempt to woo Jane ①

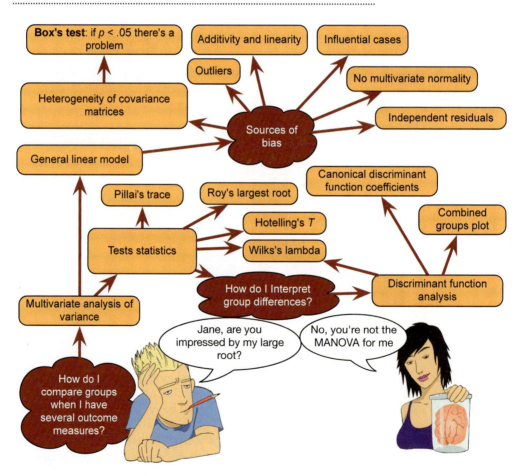

FIGURE 16.13   What Brian learnt from this chapter

16.14. What next? ②

At the beginning of this chapter we discovered that pets can be therapeutic. I left the whereabouts of Fuzzy a mystery. Now admit it, how many of you thought he was dead? He's not: he is lying next to me as I type this sentence. After frantically searching the house I went back to the room that he had vanished from to check again whether there was a hole that he could have wriggled through. As I scuttled around on my hands and knees tapping the walls, a little ginger (and sooty) face popped out from the fireplace with a look as if to say 'have you lost something?' (see **Figure 16.14**). Yep, freaked out by the whole moving experience, he had done the only sensible thing and hidden up the chimney! Cats, you gotta love 'em.

FIGURE 16.14
Fuzzy hiding up a fireplace

16.15. Key terms that I've discovered

Bartlett's test of sphericity	Hotelling–Lawley trace (T^2)	Roy's largest root
Box's test	Hypothesis SSCP (H)	Square matrix
Discriminant analysis	Identity matrix	Sum of squares and
Discriminant function variates	Matrix	cross-products matrix
Discriminant scores	Multivariate	(SSCP)
Error SSCP (E)	Multivariate analysis of variance	Total SSCP (T)
HE^{-1}	(or MANOVA)	Univariate
Homogeneity of covariance	Multivariate normality	Variance–covariance matrix
matrices	Pillai–Bartlett trace (V)	Wilks's lambda (Λ)

16.16. Smart Alex's tasks

- **Task 1**: A clinical psychologist decided to compare his patients against a normal sample. He observed 10 of his patients as they went through a normal day. He also observed 10 lecturers at the University of Sussex. He measured all participants using two dependent variables: how many chicken impersonations they did, and how good their impersonations were (as scored out of 10 by an independent farmyard noise expert). The data are in the file **Chicken.sav**. Use MANOVA and discriminant function analysis to find out whether these variables could be used to distinguish manic psychotic patients from those without the disorder. ③

- **Task 2**: A news story claimed that children who lie would become successful citizens (http://bit.ly/ammQNT). I was intrigued because although the article cited a lot of well-conducted work by Dr. Khang Lee that shows that children lie, I couldn't find anything in that research that supported the journalist's claim that children who lie become successful citizens. Imagine a Huxleyesque parallel universe in which the government was daft enough to believe the contents of this newspaper story and decided to implement a systematic programme of infant conditioning. Some infants were trained not to lie, others were brought up as normal, and a final group was trained in the art of lying. Thirty years later, they collected data on how successful these children were as adults. They measured their **salary**, and two indices of how successful they were in their **family** and **work** life, on a 0–10 scale (10 = as successful as it could possibly be, 0 = better luck in your next life). The data are in **Lying.sav**. Use MANOVA and discriminant function analysis to find out whether lying really does make you a better citizen. ③

- **Task 3**: I was interested in whether students' knowledge of different aspects of psychology improved throughout their degree (**Psychology.sav**). I took a sample of first years, second years and third years and gave them five tests (scored out of 15) representing different aspects of psychology: **Exper** (experimental psychology such as cognitive and neuropsychology); **Stats** (statistics); **Social** (social psychology); **Develop** (developmental psychology); **Person** (personality). (1) Determine whether there are overall group differences along these five measures. (2) Interpret the scale-by-scale analyses of group differences. (3) Select contrasts that test the hypothesis that second and third years will score higher than first years on all scales. (4) Select *post hoc* tests and compare these results to the contrasts. (5) Carry out a discriminant function analysis including only those scales that revealed group differences for the contrasts. Interpret the results. ④

Answers can be found on the companion website.

16.17. Further reading

Bray, J. H., & Maxwell, S. E. (1985). *Multivariate analysis of variance*. Sage University Paper Series on Quantitative Applications in the Social Sciences, 07-054. Newbury Park, CA: Sage. (This monograph on MANOVA is superb: I cannot recommend anything better.)

Huberty, C. J., & Morris, J. D. (1989). Multivariate analysis versus multiple univariate analysis. *Psychological Bulletin, 105*, 302–308.

Exploratory factor analysis

17

FIGURE 17.1
In my office
during my
Ph.D., probably
preparing some
teaching – I
had quite long
hair back then
because it hadn't
started falling out
at that point

17.1. What will this chapter tell me? ①

Having failed to become a rock star, I went to university and eventually ended up doing a Ph.D. (in Psychology) at the University of Sussex. Like many postgraduates, I taught to survive. I was allocated to second-year undergraduate statistics. I was very shy at the time, and I didn't have a clue about statistics, so standing in front of a room full of strangers and talking to them about ANOVA was about as appealing as dislocating my knees and running a marathon. I obsessively prepared for my first session so that it would go well; I created handouts, I invented examples, I rehearsed what I would say. I went in terrified but knowing that if preparation was any predictor of success then I would be OK. About half way through one of the students rose majestically from her chair. An aura of bright white light surrounded her and she appeared to me as though walking through dry ice. I guessed that she had been chosen by her peers to impart a message of gratitude for the hours of preparation I had done and the skill with which I was unclouding their brains of statistical mysteries. She stopped inches away from me. She looked into my eyes and mine raced around the floor looking for the reassurance of my shoelaces. 'No one in this room has a rabbit[1] clue what you're going on about', she spat before storming out. Scales have not been invented yet to measure how much I wished I'd run the dislocated-knees marathon that morning. To this day I have intrusive thoughts about students in my lectures walking zombie-like towards the front of the lecture theatre chanting 'No one knows what you're going on about' before devouring my brain in a rabid feeding frenzy.

The aftermath of this trauma is that I threw myself into trying to be the best teacher in the universe. I wrote detailed handouts and started using wacky examples. Based on these I was signed up by a publisher to write a book. This book. At the age of 23 I didn't realize that this was academic suicide (really, textbooks take a long time to write and they are not at all valued compared to research articles), and I also didn't realize the emotional pain I was about to inflict on myself. I soon discovered that writing a statistics book was like doing a factor analysis: in factor analysis we take a lot of information (variables) and SPSS effortlessly reduces this mass of confusion into a simple message (fewer variables). SPSS does this in a few seconds. Similarly, my younger self took a mass of information about statistics that I didn't understand and filtered it down into a simple message that I *could* understand: I became a living, breathing factor analysis … except that, unlike SPSS, it took me two years and some considerable effort.

17.2. When to use factor analysis ②

In science we often need to measure things that cannot be measured directly (so-called latent variables). For example, management researchers might be interested in measuring 'burnout', which is when someone who has been working very hard on a project (a book, for example) for a prolonged period of time suddenly finds himself devoid of motivation, inspiration, and wants to repeatedly headbutt their computer, screaming 'please, Mike, unlock the door, let me out of the basement, I need to feel the soft warmth of sunlight on my skin'. You can't measure burnout directly: it has many facets. However, you can measure different aspects of burnout: you could get some idea of motivation, stress levels, whether the person has any new ideas and so on. Having done this, it would be helpful to know whether these facets reflect a single variable. Put another way, are these different measures driven by the same underlying variable?

This chapter explores factor analysis and principal component analysis (PCA) – techniques for identifying clusters of variables. These techniques have three main uses: (1) to understand the structure of a set of variables (e.g., Spearman and Thurstone used factor analysis to try to understand the structure of the latent variable 'intelligence'); (2) to construct a questionnaire to measure an underlying variable (e.g., you might design a questionnaire to measure burnout); and (3) to reduce a data set to a more manageable size while retaining as much of the original information as possible (e.g., factor analysis can be used to solve the problem of multicollinearity that we discovered in Chapter 8 by combining variables that are collinear).

There are numerous examples of the use of factor analysis in science. Most readers will be familiar with the extroversion–introversion and neuroticism traits measured by Eysenck (1953). Most other personality questionnaires are also based on factor analysis – notably Cattell's (1966a) 16 personality factors questionnaire – and these inventories are frequently used for recruiting purposes in industry (and even by some religious groups). Economists, for example, might also use factor analysis to see whether productivity,

---

[1] She didn't say 'rabbit', but she did say a word that describes what rabbits do a lot; it begins with an 'f' and the publishers think that it will offend you.

profits and workforce can be reduced down to an underlying dimension of company growth, and Jeremy Miles told me of a biochemist who used it to analyse urine samples.

Both factor analysis and PCA aim to reduce a set of variables into a smaller set of dimensions (called 'factors' in factor analysis and 'components' in PCA). To non-statisticians, like me, the differences between a component and a factor are difficult to conceptualize (they are both linear models), and the differences are hidden away in the maths behind the techniques.[2] However, there are important differences between the techniques, which I'll discuss in due course. Most of the practical issues are the same regardless of whether you do factor analysis or PCA, so once the theory is over you can apply any advice I give to either factor analysis or PCA.

17.3. Factors and components ②

If we measure several variables, or ask someone several questions about themselves, the correlation between each pair of variables (or questions) can be arranged in a table (just like the output from a correlation analysis as seen in Chapter 7). This table is sometimes called an *R*-matrix, just to scare you. The diagonal elements of an *R*-matrix are all ones because each variable will correlate perfectly with itself. The off-diagonal elements are the correlation coefficients between pairs of variables, or questions.[3] Factor analysis attempts to achieve parsimony by explaining the maximum amount of *common variance* in a correlation matrix using the smallest number of explanatory constructs. These 'explanatory constructs' are known as **factors** (or *latent variables*) in factor analysis, and they represent clusters variables that correlate highly with each other. PCA tries to explain the maximum amount of *total variance* (not just common variance) in a correlation matrix by transforming the original variables into linear **components**.

Imagine that we wanted to measure different aspects of what might make a person popular. We could administer several measures that we believe tap different aspects of popularity. So, we might measure a person's social skills (**Social Skills**), their selfishness (**Selfish**), how interesting others find them (**Interest**), the proportion of time they spend talking about the other person during a conversation (**Talk1**), the proportion of time they spend talking about themselves (**Talk2**), and their propensity to lie to people (**Liar**). We calculate the correlation coefficients for each pair of variables and create an *R*-matrix. Figure 17.2 shows this matrix. There appear to be two clusters of interrelating variables. First, the amount that someone talks about the other person during a conversation correlates highly with both the level of social skills and how interesting the other finds that person, and social skills correlate well with how interesting others perceive a person to be. These relationships indicate that the better your social skills, the more interesting and talkative you are likely to be. Second, the amount that people talk about themselves within a conversation correlates with how selfish they are and how much they lie. Being selfish also correlates with the degree to which a person tells lies. In short, selfish people are likely to lie and talk about themselves.

---

[2] PCA is not the same as factor analysis. This doesn't stop idiots like me from discussing them as though they are. I tend to focus on the similarities between the techniques, which will reduce some statisticians (and psychologists) to tears. I'm banking on these people not needing to read this book, so I'll take my chances because I think it's easier for you if I give you a general sense of what the procedures do and not obsess too much about their differences. Once you have got the basics under your belt, feel free to obsess about their differences and complain to all of your friends about how awful the book by that imbecile Field is …

[3] This matrix is called an *R*-matrix, or *R*, because it contains correlation coefficients and *r* usually denotes Pearson's correlation (see Chapter 7) – the *r* turns into a capital letter when it denotes a matrix.

FIGURE 17.2
An *R*-matrix

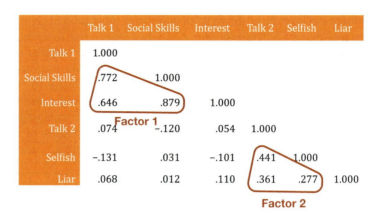

Factor analysis and PCA both aim to reduce this *R*-matrix down into a smaller set of dimensions. In factor analysis these dimensions, or factors, are estimated from the data and are believed to reflect constructs that can't be measured directly. In this example, there appear to be two clusters that fit the bill. The first 'factor' seems to relate to general sociability, whereas the second 'factor' seems to relate to the way in which a person treats others socially (we might call it *Consideration*). It might, therefore, be assumed that popularity depends not only on your ability to socialize, but also on whether you are inconsiderate towards others. PCA, in contrast, transforms the data into a set of linear components; it does not estimate unmeasured variables, it just transforms measured ones. Strictly speaking, then, we shouldn't interpret components as unmeasured variables. Despite these differences, both techniques look for variables that correlate highly with a group of other variables, but do not correlate with variables outside of that group.

17.3.1. Graphical representation ②

Factors and components can also be visualized: you can imagine factors as being the axis of a graph along which we plot variables. The coordinates of variables along each axis represent the strength of relationship between that variable and each factor. In an ideal world a variable should have a large coordinate for one of the axes, and small coordinates for any other factors. This scenario would indicate that this particular variable related to only one factor. Variables that have large coordinates on the same axis are assumed to measure different aspects of some common underlying dimension. The coordinate of a variable along a classification axis is known as a **factor loading** (or component loading). The factor loading can be thought of as the Pearson correlation between a factor and a variable (see Jane Superbrain Box 17.1). From what we know about interpreting correlation coefficients (see Section 7.4.2.2) it should be clear that if we square the factor loading we obtain a measure of the substantive importance of a particular variable to a factor.

Figure 17.3 shows such a plot for the popularity data (in which there were only two factors). The first thing to notice is that for both factors, the axis line ranges from −1 to 1, which are the outer limits of a correlation coefficient. The triangles represent the three variables that have high factor loadings (i.e., a strong relationship) with factor 1 (**Sociability**: horizontal axis) but have a low correlation with factor 2 (**Consideration**: vertical axis). Conversely, the circles represent variables that have high factor loadings with consideration but low loadings with sociability. This plot shows what we found in the

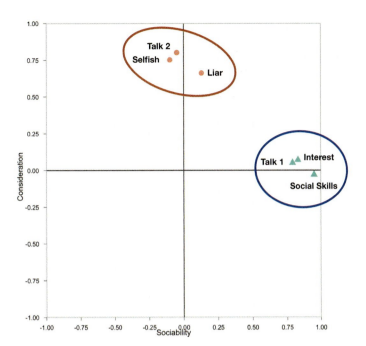

FIGURE 17.3
Example of a
factor plot

R-matrix: selfishness, the amount a person talks about themselves and their propensity to lie contribute to a factor which could be called consideration of others; and how much a person takes an interest in other people, how interesting they are and their level of social skills contribute to a second factor, sociability. Of course, if a third factor existed within these data it could be represented by a third axis (creating a 3-D graph). If more than three factors exist in a data set, then they cannot all be represented by a 2-D plot.

17.3.2. Mathematical representation ②

The axes in Figure 17.3, which represent factors, are straight lines and any straight line can be described mathematically by a familiar equation.

SELF-TEST What is the equation of a straight line/linear model?

SMART
ALEX
ONLY

Equation (17.1) reminds us of the equation describing a linear model. A component in PCA can be described in the same way. You'll notice that there is no intercept in the equation because the lines intersect at zero (hence the intercept is zero), and there is also no error term because we are simply transforming the variables. The *b*s in the equation represent the loadings.

$$Y_i = b_1 X_{1i} + b_2 X_{2i} + \cdots + b_n X_{ni}$$

$$\text{Component}_i = b_1 \text{Variable}_{1i} + b_2 \text{Variable}_{2i} + \cdots + b_n \text{Variable}_{ni}$$

(17.1)

Sticking with our example of popularity, we found that there were two components: general sociability and consideration. We can, therefore, construct an equation that describes each factor in terms of the variables that have been measured. The equations are as follows:

$$Y_i = b_1 X_{1i} + b_2 X_{2i} + \cdots + b_n X_{ni}$$

$$\text{Sociability}_i = b_1 \text{Talk1}_i + b_2 \text{Social Skills}_i + b_3 \text{Interest}_i$$
$$+ \ b_4 \text{Talk2}_i + b_5 \text{Selfish}_i + b_6 \text{Liar}_i$$

$$\text{Consideration}_i = b_1 \text{Talk1}_i + b_2 \text{Social Skills}_i + b_3 \text{Interest}_i$$
$$+ \ b_4 \text{Talk2}_i + b_5 \text{Selfish}_i + b_6 \text{Liar}_i$$

(17.2)

First, notice that the equations are identical in form: they both include all of the variables that were measured. However, the values of b in the two equations will be different (depending on the relative importance of each variable to the particular component). In fact, we can replace each value of b with the coordinate of that variable on the graph in Figure 17.3 (i.e., replace the values of b with the factor loadings). The resulting equations are as follows:

$$Y_i = b_1 X_{1i} + b_2 X_{2i} + \cdots + b_n X_{ni}$$

$$\text{Sociability}_i = 0.87 \text{Talk1}_i + 0.96 \text{Social Skills}_i + 0.92 \text{Interest}_i + 0.00 \text{Talk2}_i$$
$$- 0.10 \text{Selfish}_i + 0.09 \text{Liar}_i$$

$$\text{Consideration}_i = 0.01 \text{Talk1}_i - 0.03 \text{Social Skills}_i + 0.04 \text{Interest}_i + 0.82 \text{Talk2}_i$$
$$+ 0.75 \text{Selfish}_i + 0.70 \text{Liar}_i$$

(17.3)

Notice that, for the **Sociability** component, the values of b are high for **Talk1**, **Social Skills** and **Interest**. For the remaining variables (**Talk2**, **Selfish** and **Liar**) the values of b are very low (close to 0). This tells us that three of the variables are very important for that component (the ones with high values of b) and three are very unimportant (the ones with low values of b). We saw that this point is true because of the way that three variables clustered highly on the factor plot (Figure 17.3). The point to take on board here is that the factor plot and these equations represent the same thing: the factor loadings in the plot are simply the b-values in these equations. For the second factor, **Consideration**, the opposite pattern can be seen: **Talk2**, **Selfish** and **Liar** all have high values of b, whereas the remaining three variables have b-values close to 0. In an ideal world, variables would have very high b-values for one component and very low b-values for all other components.

The factors in factor analysis are not represented in quite the same way as components. Equation (17.4) shows how a factor is defined: the Greek letters represent matrices containing numbers. If we put the Greek letters through Andy's magical translation machine then we can stop worrying about what the matrices contain and focus on what they represent. In factor analysis, scores on the measured variables are predicted from the means of those variables plus a person's scores on the common factors (i.e., factors that explain the correlations between variables) multiplied by their factor loadings, plus scores on any unique factors within the data (factors that cannot explain the correlations between variables).

$$x = \mu + \Lambda\xi + \delta$$

$$\text{Variables} = \text{Variable Means} + (\text{Loadings} \times \text{Common Factor}) + \text{Unique Factor} \quad (17.4)$$

In a sense, the factor analysis model flips PCA on its head: in PCA we predict components from the measured variables, but in factor analysis we predict the measured variables from the underlying factors. For example, psychologists are usually interested in factors, because they're interested in how the stuff going on inside people's heads (the latent variables) affects how they answer the questions (the measured variables). The other big difference is that, unlike PCA, factor analysis contains an error term (δ is made up of both scores on unique factors and measurement error). The fact that PCA assumes that there is no measurement error upsets a lot of people who use factor analysis.

Both factor analysis and PCA are linear models in which loadings are used as weights. In both cases, these loadings can be expressed as a matrix in which the columns represent each factor and the rows represent the loadings of each variable on each factor. For the popularity data this matrix would have two columns (one for each factor) and six rows (one for each variable). This matrix, Λ, can be seen below. It is called the **factor matrix** or **component matrix** (if doing principal component analysis) – see Jane Superbrain Box 17.1 to find out about the different forms of this matrix. Try relating the elements to the loadings in equation (17.3) to give you an idea of what this matrix represents (in the case of PCA). For example, the top row represents the first variable, **Talk1**, which had a loading of .87 for the first factor (**Sociability**) and a loading of .01 for the second factor (**Consideration**).

$$\Lambda = \begin{pmatrix} 0.87 & 0.01 \\ 0.96 & -0.03 \\ 0.92 & 0.04 \\ 0.00 & 0.82 \\ -0.10 & 0.75 \\ 0.09 & 0.70 \end{pmatrix}$$

The major assumption in factor analysis (but not PCA) is that these algebraic factors represent real-world dimensions, the nature of which must be *guessed at* by inspecting which variables have high loads on the same factor. So, psychologists might believe that factors represent dimensions of the psyche, education researchers might believe they represent abilities, and sociologists might believe they represent races or social classes. However, it is an extremely contentious point: some believe that the dimensions derived from factor analysis are real only in the statistical sense – and are real-world fictions.

EVERYBODY

17.3.3. Factor scores ②

A factor can be described in terms of the variables measured and their relative importance for that factor. Therefore, having discovered which factors exist, and estimated the equation that describes them, it should be possible to estimate a person's score on a factor, based on their scores for the constituent variables; these are known as **factor scores** (or *component scores* in PCA). For example, if we wanted to derive a sociability score for a particular person after PCA, we could place their scores on the various measures into equation (17.3). This method is known as a *weighted average* and is rarely used because it is overly simplistic, but it is the easiest way to explain the principle. For example, imagine our six personality measures range from 1 to 10 and that someone scored the following: **Talk1** (4), **Social Skills** (9), **Interest** (8), **Talk2** (6), **Selfish** (8), and **Liar** (6). We could plug these values into equation (17.3) to get a score for this person's sociability and their consideration to others (see equation (17.5)). The resulting scores of 19.22 and 15.21 reflect the degree to which this person is sociable and their inconsideration towards others, respectively. This person scores higher on sociability than inconsideration. However, the scales of measurement used

JANE SUPERBRAIN 17.1

What's the difference between a pattern matrix and a structure matrix? ③

So far I've been a bit vague about factor loadings. Sometimes I've said that these loadings can be thought of as the correlation between a variable and a given factor, then at other times I've described these loadings in terms of regression coefficients (*b*). Broadly speaking, both correlation coefficients and regression coefficients represent the relationship between a variable and linear model, so my vagueness might not be the evidence of buffoonery that it initially seems. The take-home message is that factor loadings tell us about the relative contribution that a variable makes to a factor. As long as you understand that much, you'll be OK.

However, the factor loadings in a given analysis can be both correlation coefficients and regression coefficients. In a few sections' time we'll discover that the interpretation of factor analysis is helped greatly by a technique known as *rotation*. Without going into details, there are two types: orthogonal and oblique rotation (see Section 17.4.6). When orthogonal rotation is used, any underlying factors are assumed to be independent, and the factor loading *is* the correlation between the factor and the variable, but it is also the regression coefficient. Put another way, the values of the correlation coefficients are the same as the values of the regression coefficients. However, there are situations in which the underlying factors are assumed to be related or correlated to each other. In these situations, oblique rotation is used and the resulting correlations between variables and factors will differ from the corresponding regression coefficients. In this case, there are, in effect, two different sets of factor loadings: the correlation coefficients between each variable and factor (which are put in the factor structure matrix) and the regression coefficients for each variable on each factor (which are put in the factor pattern matrix). These coefficients can have quite different interpretations (see Graham, Guthrie, & Thompson, 2003).

will influence the resulting scores, and if different variables use different measurement scales, then factor scores for different factors cannot be compared. As such, this method of calculating factor scores is poor and more sophisticated methods are usually used:

$$\text{Sociability}_i = 0.87\text{Talk1}_i + 0.96\text{Social Skills}_i + 0.92\text{Interest}_i + 0.00\text{Talk2}_i$$
$$- 0.10\text{Selfish}_i + 0.09\text{Liar}_i$$
$$\text{Sociability}_i = (0.87 \times 4) + (0.96 \times 9) + (0.92 \times 8) + (0.00 \times 6)$$
$$- (0.10 \times 8) + (0.09 \times 6)$$
$$= 19.22$$

$$\text{Consideration}_i = 0.01\text{Talk1}_i - 0.03\text{Social Skills}_i + 0.04\text{Interest}_i + 0.82\text{Talk2}_i$$
$$+ 0.75\text{Selfish}_i + 0.70\text{Liar}_i$$
$$\text{Consideration}_i = (0.01 \times 4) - (0.03 \times 9) + (0.04 \times 8) + (0.82 \times 6)$$
$$+ (0.75 \times 8) + (0.70 \times 6)$$
$$= 15.21$$

$$(17.5)$$

17.3.3.1. The regression method ④

There are several sophisticated techniques for calculating factor scores that use factor score coefficients as weights rather than using the factor loadings. Factor score coefficients can be calculated in several ways. The simplest way is the regression method. In this method the factor loadings are adjusted to take account of the initial correlations between variables; in doing so, differences in units of measurement and variable variances are stabilized.

To obtain the matrix of factor score coefficients (B) we multiply the matrix of factor loadings by the inverse (R^{-1}) of the original correlation or R-matrix (this is the same process that is used to estimate the bs in ordinary regression). You might remember from the previous chapter that matrices cannot be divided (see Section 16.4.4.1). Therefore, the equivalent of dividing by a matrix is to multiply by the inverse of that matrix. Conceptually speaking, then, by multiplying the matrix of factor loadings by the inverse of the correlation matrix we are dividing the factor loadings by the correlation coefficients. The resulting factor score matrix represents the relationship between each variable and each factor, taking into account the original relationships between pairs of variables. As such, this matrix represents a purer measure of the *unique* relationship between variables and factors.

The regression technique ensures that the resulting factor scores have a mean of 0 and a variance equal to the squared multiple correlation between the estimated factor scores and the true factor values. However, the downside is that the scores can correlate not only with factors other than the one on which they are based, but also with other factor *scores* from a different orthogonal factor.

OLIVER TWISTED

Please Sir, can I have some more … matrix algebra?

'*The Matrix …*', enthuses Oliver, '… that was a good film. I want to dress in black and glide through the air as though time has stood still. Maybe the matrix of factor scores is as cool as the film.' I think you might be disappointed, Oliver, but we'll give it a shot. The matrix calculations of factor score coefficients for this example are detailed in the additional material for this chapter on the companion website. Be afraid, be very afraid …

17.3.3.2. Other methods ②

To overcome the problems associated with the regression technique, two adjustments have been proposed: the Bartlett method and the Anderson–Rubin method. The Bartlett method produces scores that are unbiased and that correlate only with their own factor. The mean and standard deviation of the scores is the same as for the regression method. However, factor scores can still correlate with each other. The Anderson-Rubin method is a modification of the Bartlett method that produces factor scores that are uncorrelated and standardized (they have a mean of 0 and a standard deviation of 1). Tabachnick and Fidell (2012) conclude that the Anderson–Rubin method is best when uncorrelated scores are required but that the regression method is preferred in other circumstances simply because it is most easily understood. Although it isn't important that you understand the maths behind any of the methods, it is important that you understand what the factor scores represent: namely, a composite score for each individual on a particular factor.

17.3.3.3. Uses of factor scores ②

There are several uses of factor scores. First, if the purpose of the factor analysis is to reduce a large set of data to a smaller subset of measurement variables, then the factor scores tell us an individual's score on this subset of measures. Therefore, any further analysis can be carried out on the factor scores rather than the original data. For example, we could carry out a *t*-test to see whether females are significantly more sociable than males using the factor scores for sociability. A second use is in overcoming collinearity problems in regression. If, following a multiple regression analysis, we have identified sources of multicollinearity then the interpretation of the analysis is compromised (see Section 8.5.3). In this situation, we can carry out a PCA on the predictor variables to reduce them to a subset of uncorrelated factors. The variables causing the multicollinearity will combine to form a component. If we then rerun the regression but using the component scores as predictor variables then the problem of multicollinearity should vanish (because the variables are now combined into a single component). There are ways in which we can ensure that the components are uncorrelated (one way is to use the Anderson–Rubin method – see above). By using uncorrelated component scores as predictors in the regression we can be confident that there will be no correlation between predictors – hence, no multicollinearity.

17.4. Discovering factors ②

By now, you should have some grasp of what a factor is and what a component is, so we will now delve into how to find or estimate these mythical beasts.

17.4.1. Choosing a method ②

There are several methods for unearthing factors in your data. The method you choose will depend on what you hope to do with the analysis. Tinsley and Tinsley (1987) give an excellent account of the different methods available. There are two things to consider: whether you want to generalize the findings from your sample to a population and whether you are exploring your data or testing a specific hypothesis. This chapter describes techniques for exploring data using factor analysis. Testing hypotheses about the structures of latent variables and their relationships to each other requires considerable complexity and can be done with computer programs such as SPSS's sister package, AMOS. Those interested in hypothesis testing techniques (known as **confirmatory factor analysis**) are advised to read Pedhazur and Schmelkin (1991: Chapter 23) for an introduction.

Assuming we want to explore our data, we then need to consider whether we want to apply our findings to the sample collected (descriptive method) or to generalize our findings to a population (inferential methods). When factor analysis was originally developed it was assumed that it would be used to explore data to generate future hypotheses. As such, it was assumed that the technique would be applied to the entire population of interest. Therefore, certain techniques assume that the sample used is the population, and so results cannot be extrapolated beyond that particular sample. Principal component analysis is an example of these techniques, as are principal factors analysis (*principal axis factoring*) and image covariance analysis (*image factoring*). Of these, principal component analysis and principal factors analysis are the preferred methods and usually result in similar solutions (see Section 17.4.3). When these methods are used, conclusions are restricted to the sample collected and generalization of the results can be achieved only if analysis using different samples reveals the same factor structure (i.e., cross-validation).

Another approach is to assume that participants are randomly selected and that the variables measured constitute the population of variables in which we're interested. By assuming this, it is possible to generalize from the sample participants to a larger population, but with the caveat that any findings hold true only for the set of variables measured (because we've assumed this set constitutes the entire population of variables). Techniques in this category include the *maximum-likelihood method* (see Harman, 1976) and Kaiser's *alpha factoring*. The choice of method depends largely on what generalizations, if any, you want to make from your data.

17.4.2. Communality ②

The idea of what variance is and how it is calculated should, by now, be an old friend with whom you enjoy tea and biscuits (if not, see Chapter 2). The total variance for a particular variable in the *R*-matrix will have two components: some of it will be shared with other variables or measures (**common variance**) and some of it will be specific to that measure (**unique variance**). We tend to use the term *unique variance* to refer to variance that can be reliably attributed to only one measure. However, there is also variance that is specific to one measure but not reliably so; this variance is called error or **random variance**. The proportion of common variance present in a variable is known as the **communality**. As such, a variable that has no unique variance (or random variance) would have a communality of 1; a variable that shares none of its variance with any other variable would have a communality of 0.

In factor analysis we are interested in finding common underlying dimensions within the data and so we are primarily interested only in the common variance. Therefore, we need to know how much of the variance present in our data is common variance. This presents us with a logical impasse: to do the factor analysis we need to know the proportion of common variance present in the data, yet the only way to find out the extent of the common variance is by carrying out a factor analysis! There are two ways to approach this problem. The first is to assume that all of the variance is common variance: we assume that the communality of every variable is 1. By making this assumption we merely transpose our original data into constituent linear components. This procedure is PCA. Remember that I said earlier that PCA assumes no measurement error? Well, by setting the communalities to 1, we are assuming that all variance is common variance (there is no random variance at all).

The second approach is to estimate the amount of common variance by estimating communality values for each variable. There are various methods of estimating communalities but the most widely used (including **alpha factoring**) is to use the squared multiple correlation (SMC) of each variable with all others. So, for the popularity data, imagine you ran a multiple regression using one measure (**Selfish**) as the outcome and the other five measures as predictors: the resulting multiple R^2 (see Section 8.2.4) would be used as an estimate of the communality for the variable **Selfish**. This second approach is used in factor analysis. These estimates allow the factor analysis to be done. Once the underlying factors have been extracted, new communalities can be calculated that represent the multiple correlation between each variable and the factors extracted. Therefore, the communality is a measure of the proportion of variance explained by the extracted factors.

17.4.3. Factor analysis or PCA? ②

I have just explained that there are two approaches to locating underlying dimensions of a data set: factor analysis and principal component analysis. These techniques differ in the communality estimates that are used. As I have hinted before, factor analysis derives a mathematical model from which factors are estimated, whereas PCA decomposes the original data into a set of linear variates (see Dunteman, 1989, Chapter 8, for more detail on the differences between the procedures). As such, only factor analysis can estimate the underlying factors, and it relies on various assumptions for these estimates to be accurate. PCA is concerned only with establishing which linear components exist within the data and how a particular variable might contribute to that component.

Should I use factor analysis or PCA?

Based on an extensive literature review, Guadagnoli and Velicer (1988) concluded that the solutions generated from PCA differ little from those derived from factor-analytic techniques. In reality, with 30 or more variables and communalities greater than 0.7 for all variables, different solutions are unlikely; however, with fewer than 20 variables and any low communalities (< 0.4) differences can occur (Stevens, 2002).

The flip side of this argument is eloquently described by Cliff (1987) who observed that proponents of factor analysis 'insist that components analysis is at best a common factor analysis with some error added and at worst an unrecognizable hodgepodge of things from which nothing can be determined' (p. 349). Indeed, feeling is strong on this issue, with some arguing that when PCA is used it should not be described as a factor analysis (oops!) and that you should not impute substantive meaning to the resulting components. Ultimately, as I hope to have made clear, they are doing slightly different things.

17.4.4.   Theory behind PCA ③

SMART
ALEX
ONLY

The theory behind factor analysis is, frankly, a bit of an arse; an arse tattooed with matrix algebra. No-one wants to look at matrix algebra when they're admiring an arse, so we'll look at the squeezable buttocks of PCA instead. Principal component analysis works in a very similar way to MANOVA and discriminant function analysis (see Chapter 16). In MANOVA, various sum of squares and cross-product matrices were calculated that contained information about the relationships between dependent variables. I mentioned before that these SSCP matrices can be converted to variance–covariance matrices, which represent the same information but in averaged form (i.e., taking account of the number of observations). I also pointed out that by dividing each element by the relevant standard deviation the variance–covariance matrices becomes standardized. The result is a correlation matrix. In PCA we usually deal with correlation matrices (although it is possible to analyse a variance–covariance matrix too), and my point is that this matrix represents the same information as an SSCP matrix in MANOVA.

In MANOVA, because we were comparing groups we ended up looking at the variates or components of the SSCP matrix that represented the ratio of the model variance to the error variance. These variates were linear dimensions that separated the groups tested, and we saw that the dependent variables mapped onto these underlying components. In short, we looked at whether the groups could be separated by some linear combination of the dependent variables. These variates were found by calculating the eigenvectors of the SSCP. The number of variates obtained was the smaller of p (the number of dependent variables) or $k - 1$ (where k is the number of groups).

In PCA we do much the same thing but using the overall correlation matrix (because we're not interested in comparing groups of scores). To simplify things a little, we take a correlation matrix and calculate the variates. There are no groups of observations, and so the number of variates calculated will always equal the number of variables measured (p). The variates are described, as for MANOVA, by the eigenvectors associated with the correlation matrix. The elements of the eigenvectors are the weights of each variable on the variate. These values are the loadings described earlier (i.e., the b-values in equation (16.5)). The largest eigenvalue associated with each of the eigenvectors provides a single indicator of the substantive importance of each component. The basic idea is that we retain components with relatively large eigenvalues and ignore those with relatively small eigenvalues.

Factor analysis works differently, but there are similarities. Rather than using the correlation matrix, factor analysis starts by estimating the communalities between variables using the SMC (as described earlier). It then replaces the diagonal of the correlation matrix (the 1s) with these estimates. Then the eigenvectors and associated eigenvalues of this matrix are computed. Again, these eigenvalues tell us about the substantive importance of the factors, and based on them a decision is made about how many factors to retain. Loadings and communalities are then estimated using only the retained factors.

EVERYBODY

17.4.5. Factor extraction: eigenvalues and the scree plot ②

In both PCA and factor analysis, not all factors are retained. The process of deciding how many factors to keep is called *extraction*. I mentioned above that eigenvalues associated with a variate indicate the substantive importance of that factor. Therefore, it is logical to retain only factors with large eigenvalues. This section looks at how we determine whether an eigenvalue is large enough to represent a meaningful factor.

How many factors should I extract?

Cattell (1966b) suggested plotting each eigenvalue (*Y*-axis) against the factor with which it is associated (*X*-axis). This graph is known as a **scree plot** (because it looks like a rock face with a pile of debris, or scree, at the bottom). I mentioned earlier that it is possible to obtain as many factors as there are variables and that each has an associated eigenvalue. By graphing the eigenvalues, the relative importance of each factor becomes apparent. Typically there will be a few factors with quite high eigenvalues, and many factors with relatively low eigenvalues, and so this graph has a very characteristic shape: there is a sharp descent in the curve followed by a tailing off (see Figure 17.4). The point of inflexion is where the slope of the line changes dramatically, and Cattell (1966b) suggested using this point as the cut-off for retaining factors. In Figure 17.4, imagine drawing two straight lines (the red dashed lines), one summarizing the vertical part of the plot and the other summarizing the horizontal part. The point of inflexion is the data point at which these two lines meet. You retain only factors to the left of the point of inflexion (and do not include the factor at the point of inflexion itself),[4] so in both examples in Figure 17.4 we would extract two factors because the point of inflexion occurs at the third data point (factor). With a sample of more than 200 participants, the scree plot provides a fairly reliable criterion for factor selection (Stevens, 2002).

Although scree plots are very useful, Kaiser (1960) recommended retaining all factors with eigenvalues greater than 1. This criterion is based on the idea that the eigenvalues represent the amount of variation explained by a factor and that an eigenvalue of 1 represents a substantial amount of variation. Jolliffe (1972, 1986) reports that **Kaiser's criterion** is too strict and suggested retaining all factors with eigenvalues more than 0.7. The difference between how many factors are retained using Kaiser's methods compared to Jolliffe's can be dramatic.

You might well wonder how the methods compare. Generally speaking, Kaiser's criterion overestimates the number of factors to retain (see Jane Superbrain Box 17.2), but there is some evidence that it is accurate when the number of variables is less than 30 and the resulting communalities (after extraction) are all greater than 0.7. Kaiser's criterion can also be accurate when the sample size exceeds 250 and the average communality is greater than or equal to 0.6. In any other circumstances you are best advised to use a scree plot, provided the sample size is greater than 200 (see Stevens, 2002, for more detail). By default, SPSS uses Kaiser's criterion to extract factors. Therefore, if you use the scree plot to determine how many factors are retained you may have to rerun the analysis specifying that SPSS extracts the number of factors you require.

As is often the case in statistics, the three criteria often provide different answers. In these situations the communalities of the factors need to be considered. Remember that communalities represent the common variance: if the values are 1 then all common variance is accounted for, and if the values are 0 then no common variance is accounted for. In both PCA and factor analysis we determine how many factors/components to extract and then re-estimate the communalities. The factors we retain will not explain all of the variance in the data (because we have discarded some information) and so the communalities

[4] In his original paper Cattell advised including the factor at the point of inflexion as well, because it represents an error factor, or 'garbage can' as he put it. However, Thurstone argued that it is better to retain too few than too many factors, and in practice the 'garbage can' factor is rarely retained.

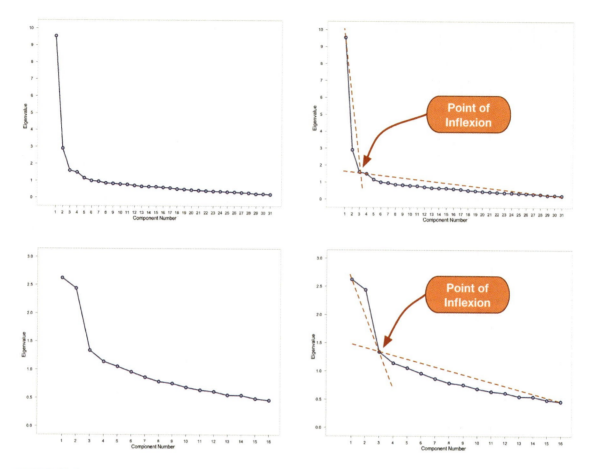

FIGURE 17.4   Examples of scree plots for data that probably have two underlying factors

after extraction will always be less than 1. The factors retained do not map perfectly onto the original variables – they merely reflect the common variance present in the data. If the communalities represent a loss of information then they are important statistics. The closer the communalities are to 1, the better our factors are at explaining the original data. It is logical that the more factors retained, the greater the communalities will be (because less information is discarded); therefore, the communalities are good indices of whether too few factors have been retained. In fact, with generalized least-squares factor analysis and maximum-likelihood factor analysis you can get a statistical measure of the goodness of fit of the factor solution (see the next chapter for more on goodness-of-fit tests). This basically measures the proportion of variance that the factor solution explains (so can be thought of as comparing communalities before and after extraction).

As a final word of advice, your decision on how many factors to extract will depend also on why you're doing the analysis; for example, if you're trying to overcome multicollinearity problems in regression, then it might be better to extract too many factors than too few.

17.4.6.   Improving interpretation: factor rotation ③

Once factors have been extracted, it is possible to calculate the degree to which variables load on these factors (i.e., calculate the loadings for each variable on each factor).

JANE SUPERBRAIN 17.2

How many factors do I retain? ③

There are fundamental problems with Kaiser's criterion (Nunnally & Bernstein, 1994). For one thing, an eigenvalue of 1 means different things in different analyses: with 100 variables it means that a factor explains 1% of the variance, but with 10 variables it means that a factor explains 10% of the variance. Clearly, these two situations are very different and a single rule that covers both is inappropriate. An eigenvalue of 1 also means only that the factor explains as much variance as a variable, which rather defeats the original intention of the analysis to reduce variables down to 'more substantive' underlying factors. Consequently, Kaiser's criterion often overestimates the number of factors. By this argument Jolliffe's criterion is even worse (a factor explains less variance than a variable).

There are more complex ways to determine how many factors to retain, but they are not easy to do in SPSS. The best is probably parallel analysis (Horn, 1965). Essentially each eigenvalue (which represents the size of the factor) is compared against an eigenvalue for the corresponding factor in many randomly generated data sets that have the same characteristics as the data being analysed. In doing so, each eigenvalue is compared to an eigenvalue from a data set that has no underlying factors. This is a bit like asking whether our observed factor is bigger than a non-existing factor. Factors that are bigger than their 'random' counterparts are retained. Of parallel analysis, the scree plot and Kaiser's criterion, Kaiser's criterion is, in general, worst and parallel analysis best (Zwick & Velicer, 1986). If you want to do parallel analysis then SPSS syntax is available (O'Connor, 2000) from https://people.ok.ubc.ca/brioconn/nfactors/nfactors.html.

Generally, you will find that most variables have high loadings on the most important factor and small loadings on all other factors. This characteristic makes interpretation difficult, and so a technique called factor **rotation** is used to discriminate between factors. If we visualize our factors as an axis along which variables can be plotted, then factor rotation effectively rotates these axes such that variables are loaded maximally to only one factor. Figure 17.5 demonstrates how this process works using an example in which there are only two factors. Imagine that a sociologist was interested in classifying university lecturers as a demographic group. She discovered that two underlying dimensions best describe this group: alcoholism and achievement (go to any academic conference and you'll see why I chose these dimensions). The first factor, alcoholism, has a cluster of variables associated with it (green circles), and these could be measures such as the number of units drunk in a week, dependency and obsessive personality. The second factor, achievement, also has a cluster of variables associated with it (red circles) and these could be measures relating to salary, job status and number of research publications. Initially, the full lines represent the factors, and by looking at the coordinates it should be clear that the red circles have high loadings for factor 2 (they are a long way up this axis) and medium loadings for factor 1 (they are not very far up this axis). Conversely, the green circles have high loadings for factor 1 and medium loadings for factor 2. By rotating the axes (dashed lines), we ensure that both clusters of variables are intersected by the factor to which they relate most. So, after rotation, the loadings of the variables are maximized on one factor (the factor that intersects the cluster) and minimized on the remaining factor(s). If an axis passes through a cluster of variables, then these variables will have a loading of approximately zero on the opposite axis. If this idea is confusing, then look at Figure 17.5 and think about

Do we have to rotate?

FIGURE 17.5
Schematic representations of factor rotation. The left graph displays orthogonal rotation, whereas the right graph displays oblique rotation (see text for more details). θ is the angle through which the axes are rotated

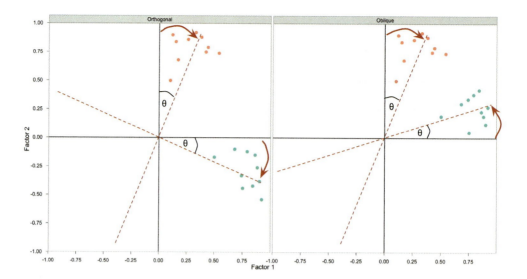

the values of the coordinates before and after rotation (this is best achieved by turning the book when you look at the rotated axes).

There are two types of rotation that can be done. The first is **orthogonal rotation**, and the left-hand side of Figure 17.5 represents this method. In Chapter 11 we saw that the term *orthogonal* means 'unrelated', and in this context it means that we rotate factors while keeping them independent, or unrelated. Before rotation, all factors are independent (i.e., they do not correlate at all) and orthogonal rotation ensures that the factors remain uncorrelated. That is why in Figure 17.5 the axes are turned while remaining perpendicular.[5] The other form of rotation is **oblique rotation**. The difference with oblique rotation is that the factors are allowed to correlate (hence, the axes of the right-hand diagram of Figure 17.5 do not remain perpendicular).

The choice of rotation depends on whether there is a good theoretical reason to suppose that the factors should be related or independent (but see my later comments on this), and also how the variables cluster on the factors before rotation. On the first point, it is probably quite rare that you would measure a set of related variables and expect their underlying dimensions to be completely independent. For example, we wouldn't expect alcoholism to be completely independent of achievement (after all, high achievement leads to high stress, which can lead to the drinks cabinet). Therefore, on theoretical grounds, we should choose oblique rotation. In fact, some argue that oblique rotation is the only sensible choice for naturally occurring data.

On the second point, Figure 17.5 demonstrates how the positioning of clusters is important in determining how successful the rotation will be (note the position of the green circles). If an orthogonal rotation was carried out on the right-hand diagram it would be considerably less successful in maximizing loadings than the oblique rotation that is displayed.

One approach is to run the analysis using both types of rotation. Pedhazur and Schmelkin (1991) suggest that if the oblique rotation demonstrates a negligible correlation between the extracted factors then it is reasonable to use the orthogonally rotated solution. If the oblique rotation reveals a correlated factor structure, then the orthogonally rotated solution should be discarded. We can check the relationships between factors using the **factor transformation matrix**, which is used to convert the unrotated factor loadings into the rotated ones. Values in this matrix represent the angle through which the axes have been rotated, or the degree to which factors have been rotated.

---

[5] This term means that the axes are at right angles to one another.

17.4.6.1. Choosing a method of factor rotation ③

SPSS has three methods of orthogonal rotation (varimax, quartimax and equamax) and two methods of oblique rotation (direct oblimin and promax). These methods differ in how they rotate the factors, so the resulting output depends on which method you select. Quartimax rotation attempts to maximize the spread of factor loadings for a variable across all factors. Therefore, interpreting variables becomes easier. However, this often results in lots of variables loading highly on a single factor. Varimax is the opposite in that it attempts to maximize the dispersion of loadings within factors. Therefore, it tries to load a smaller number of variables highly on each factor, resulting in more interpretable clusters of factors. Equamax is a hybrid of the other two approaches and is reported to behave fairly erratically (see Tabachnick and Fidell, 2012). For a first analysis, you should probably select varimax because it is a good general approach that simplifies the interpretation of factors.

The case with oblique rotations is more complex because correlation between factors is permitted. In the case of direct oblimin, the degree to which factors are allowed to correlate is determined by the value of a constant called delta. The default value in SPSS is 0, and this ensures that high correlation between factors is not allowed (this is known as direct quartimin rotation). If you choose to set delta to greater than 0 (up to 0.8), then you can expect highly correlated factors; if you set delta less than 0 (down to −0.8) you can expect less correlated factors. The default setting of zero is sensible for most analyses, and I don't recommend changing it unless you know what you are doing (see Pedhazur & Schmelkin, 1991, p. 620). Promax is a faster procedure designed for very large data sets.

In theory, the exact choice of rotation will depend largely on whether or not you think that the underlying factors should be related. If you expect the factors to be independent then you should choose one of the orthogonal rotations (I recommend varimax). If, however, there are theoretical grounds for supposing that your factors might correlate, then direct oblimin should be selected. In practice, there are strong grounds to believe that orthogonal rotations are a complete nonsense for naturalistic data, and certainly for any data involving humans (can you think of any psychological construct that is not in any way correlated with some other psychological construct?) As such, some argue that orthogonal rotations should never be used.

17.4.6.2. Substantive importance of loadings ②

Once a factor structure has been found, it is important to decide which variables make up which factors. Earlier I said that the loadings were a gauge of the substantive importance of a given variable to a given factor. Therefore, it makes sense that we use these values to place variables with factors. It is possible to assess the statistical significance of a loading (after all, it is simply a correlation coefficient or regression coefficient); however, it is not as easy as it seems (see Stevens, 2002, p. 393) because the significance of a factor loading will depend on the sample size. Stevens (2002) produced a table of critical values against which loadings can be compared. To summarize, he recommends that for a sample size of 50 a loading of .722 can be considered significant, for 100 the loading should be greater than .512, for 200 it should be greater than .364, for 300 it should be greater than .298, for 600 it should be greater than .21, and for 1000 it should be greater than .162. These values are based on an alpha level of .01 (two-tailed), which allows for the fact that several loadings will need to be tested (see Stevens, 2002, for further detail). Therefore, in very large samples, small loadings can be considered statistically meaningful.

However, the significance of a loading gives little indication of the substantive importance of a variable to a factor. We can guage importance by squaring the loading to give an estimate of the amount of variance in a factor accounted for by a variable (like R^2). In this respect Stevens (2002) recommends interpreting factor loadings with an absolute value greater than .4 (which explain around 16% of the variance in the variable). Some researchers opt for the lower criterion of .3.

17.5. Research example ②

One of the uses of factor analysis is to develop questionnaires. I have noticed that a lot of students become very stressed about SPSS. Therefore, I wanted to design a questionnaire to measure a trait that I termed 'SPSS anxiety'. I devised a questionnaire to measure various aspects of students' anxiety towards learning SPSS, the SAQ (Figure 17.6). I generated questions based on interviews with anxious and non-anxious students and came up with 23 possible questions to include. Each question was a statement followed by a 5-point Likert scale: 'strongly disagree', 'disagree', 'neither agree nor disagree', 'agree' and 'strongly agree' (SD, D, N, A, and SA, respectively). The questionnaire was designed to measure how anxious a given individual would be about learning how to use SPSS. What's more, I wanted to know whether anxiety about SPSS could be broken down into specific forms of anxiety. In other words, what latent variables contribute to anxiety about SPSS?

With a little help from a few lecturer friends I collected 2571 completed questionnaires (at this point it should become apparent that this example is fictitious!). Load the data file (**SAQ.sav**) into SPSS and have a look at the variables and their properties. The first thing to note is that each question (variable) is represented by a different column. We know that in SPSS, cases (or people's data) are stored in rows and variables are stored in columns, so this layout is consistent with past chapters. The second thing to notice is that there are 23 variables labelled **Question_01** to **Question_23** and that each has a label indicating the question. By labelling my variables I can be very clear about what each variable represents (this is the value of giving your variables full titles rather than just using restrictive column headings).

OLIVER TWISTED

Please Sir, can I have some more ... questionnaires?

'I'm going to design a questionnaire to measure one's propensity to pick a pocket or two,' says Oliver, 'but how would I go about doing it?' You'd read the useful information about the dos and don'ts of questionnaire design in the additional material for this chapter on the companion website, that's how. Rate how useful it is on a Likert scale from 1 = not useful at all, to 5 = very useful.

17.5.1. General procedure ①

Figure 17.7 shows the general procedure for conducting factor analysis or PCA. First we need to do some initial screening of the data, then once we embark on the main analysis we need to consider how many factors to retain and what rotation to use, and if we are using the analysis to look at the factor structure of a questionnaire then we would want to do a reliability analysis at the end (see Section 17.9).

The SPSS Anxiety Questionnaire (SAQ)

		SD	D	N	A	SA
1.	Statistics makes me cry	○	○	○	○	○
2.	My friends will think I'm stupid for not being able to cope with SPSS	○	○	○	○	○
3.	Standard deviations excite me	○	○	○	○	○
4.	I dream that Pearson is attacking me with correlation coefficients	○	○	○	○	○
5.	I don't understand statistics	○	○	○	○	○
6.	I have little experience of computers	○	○	○	○	○
7.	All computers hate me	○	○	○	○	○
8.	I have never been good at mathematics	○	○	○	○	○
9.	My friends are better at statistics than me	○	○	○	○	○
10.	Computers are useful only for playing games	○	○	○	○	○
11.	I did badly at mathematics at school	○	○	○	○	○
12.	People try to tell you that SPSS makes statistics easier to understand but it doesn't	○	○	○	○	○
13.	I worry that I will cause irreparable damage because of my incompetence with computers	○	○	○	○	○
14.	Computers have minds of their own and deliberately go wrong whenever I use them	○	○	○	○	○
15.	Computers are out to get me	○	○	○	○	○
16.	I weep openly at the mention of central tendency	○	○	○	○	○
17.	I slip into a coma whenever I see an equation	○	○	○	○	○
18.	SPSS always crashes when I try to use it	○	○	○	○	○
19.	Everybody looks at me when I use SPSS	○	○	○	○	○
20.	I can't sleep for thoughts of eigenvectors	○	○	○	○	○
21.	I wake up under my duvet thinking that I am trapped under a normal distribution	○	○	○	○	○
22.	My friends are better at SPSS than I am	○	○	○	○	○
23.	If I am good at statistics people will think I am a nerd	○	○	○	○	○

FIGURE 17.6   The SPSS anxiety questionnaire (SAQ)

17.5.2.   Before you begin ②

17.5.2.1.   Sample size ②

Correlation coefficients fluctuate from sample to sample, much more so in small samples than in large. Therefore, the reliability of factor analysis will depend on sample size. Many 'rules of thumb' exist for the ratio of cases to variables; a common one is to have at least 10–15 participants per variable. Although I've heard this rule bandied about on numerous occasions, its empirical basis is unclear (although Nunnally, 1978, did recommend having 10 times as many participants as variables). Based on real data, Arrindell and van der Ende (1985) concluded that the cases-to-variables ratio made little difference to the stability of factor solutions.

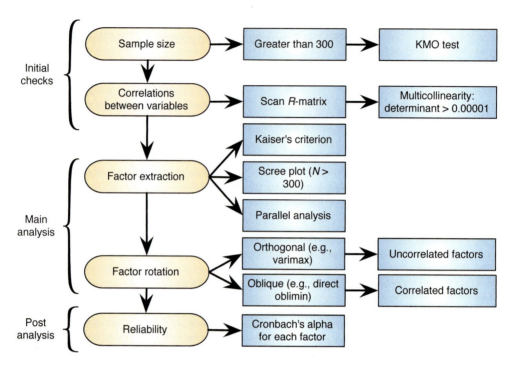

FIGURE 17.7   General procedure for factor analysis and PCA

What does matter is the overall sample size. Test parameters tend to be stable regardless of the cases-to-variables ratio (Kass & Tinsley, 1979), which is why Tabachnick and Fidell (2012) suggest that 'it is comforting to have at least 300 cases' (p. 613) and Comrey and Lee (1992) class 300 as a good sample size, 100 as poor and 1000 as excellent. However, the picture is a little more complicated than that. First, the factor loadings matter: Guadagnoli and Velicer (1988) found that if a factor has four or more loadings greater than .6 then it is reliable regardless of sample size. Furthermore, factors with 10 or more loadings greater than .40 are reliable if the sample size is greater than 150. Finally, factors with a few low loadings should not be interpreted unless the sample size is 300 or more.

Second, the communalities matter. MacCallum, Widaman, Zhang, and Hong (1999) have shown that as communalities become lower the importance of sample size increases. With all communalities above .6, relatively small samples (less than 100) may be perfectly adequate. With communalities in the .5 range, samples between 100 and 200 can be good enough provided there are relatively few factors each with only a small number of indicator variables. In the worst scenario of low communalities (well below .5) and a larger number of underlying factors they recommend samples above 500.

What's clear from this work is that a sample of 300 or more will probably provide a stable factor solution, but that a wise researcher will measure enough variables to measure adequately all of the factors that theoretically they would expect to find.

There are measures of sampling adequacy such as the **Kaiser–Meyer–Olkin measure of sampling adequacy (KMO)** (Kaiser, 1970). The KMO can be calculated for individual and multiple variables and represents the ratio of the squared correlation between variables to the squared partial correlation between variables. The KMO statistic varies between 0 and 1. A value of 0 indicates that the sum of partial correlations is large relative to the sum of correlations, indicating diffusion in the pattern of correlations (hence, factor analysis is likely to be inappropriate). A value close to 1 indicates that patterns of correlations are relatively compact and so factor analysis should yield distinct and reliable factors. Kaiser (1974) recommends accepting values greater than .5 as barely acceptable (values below this should lead you to either collect more data or rethink which variables to include). Hutcheson and Sofroniou (1999) provide appealing guidelines, especially if you like the letter M:

- Marvellous: values in the .90s

- Meritorious: values in the .80s

- Middling: values in the .70s

- Mediocre: values in the .60s

- Miserable: values in the .50s

- Merde: values below .50. (Actually they used the word 'unacceptable' but I don't like the fact that it doesn't start with the letter 'M' so I have changed it.)

17.5.2.2. Correlations between variables ③

When I was an undergraduate, my statistics lecturer always used to say 'if you put garbage in, you get garbage out'. This saying applies particularly to factor analysis because SPSS will usually find a factor solution to a set of variables. However, the solution is unlikely to have any real meaning if the variables analysed are not sensible. The first thing to do when conducting a factor analysis or PCA is to look at the correlations between variables. There are essentially two potential problems: (1) correlations that are not high enough; and (2) correlations that are too high. In both cases the remedy is to remove variables from the analysis. The correlations between variables can be checked using the *correlate* procedure (see Chapter 7) to create a correlation matrix of all variables. This matrix can also be created as part of the factor analysis. We will look at each problem in turn.

If our test questions measure the same underlying dimension (or dimensions) then we would expect them to correlate with each other (because they are measuring the same thing). Even if questions measure different aspects of the same things (e.g., we could measure overall anxiety in terms of sub-components such as worry, intrusive thoughts and physiological arousal), there should still be high correlations between the variables relating to these sub-traits. We can test for this problem first by visually scanning the correlation matrix and looking for correlations below about .3 (you could use the significance of correlations but, given the large sample sizes normally used with factor analysis, this approach isn't helpful because even very small correlations will be significant in large samples). If any variables have lots of correlations below .3 then consider excluding them. It should be immediately clear that this approach is very subjective: I've used fuzzy terms such as 'about .3' and 'lots of', but I have to because every data set is different. Analysing data really is a skill, and there's more to it than following a recipe book!

For an objective test of whether correlations (overall) are too small we can test for a very extreme scenario. If the variables in our correlation matrix did not correlate at all, then our correlation matrix would be an identity matrix (i.e., the off-diagonal components would be zero); so, if the population correlation matrix resembles an identity matrix then it means that every variable correlates very badly with all other variables (i.e., all correlation coefficients are close to zero). **Bartlett's test** tells us whether our correlation matrix is significantly different from an identity matrix. Therefore, if it is significant then it means that the correlations between variables are (overall) significantly different from zero. The trouble is that because significance depends on sample size (see Section 2.6.1.10) and in factor analysis sample sizes are very large, Bartlett's test will nearly always be significant: even when the correlations between variables are very small indeed. As such, it's not a useful test (although in the unlikely event that it is non-significant then you certainly have a big problem).

The opposite problem is when variables correlate too highly. Although mild multicollinearity is not a problem for factor analysis it is important to avoid extreme multicollinearity (i.e., variables that are very highly correlated) and **singularity** (variables that are perfectly correlated). As with regression, multicollinearity causes problems in factor analysis because it becomes impossible to determine the unique contribution to a factor of the variables that are highly correlated. Multicollinearity does not cause a problem for PCA.

Multicollinearity can be detected by looking at the determinant of the *R*-matrix, denoted $|R|$ (see Jane Superbrain Box 17.3). One simple heuristic is that the determinant of the *R*-matrix should be greater than 0.00001.

To try to avoid or to correct for multicollinearity you could look through the correlation matrix for variables that correlate very highly ($r > .8$) and consider eliminating one of the variables (or more depending on the extent of the problem) before proceeding. The problem with a heuristic such as this is that the effect of two variables correlating with $r = .9$ might be less than the effect of, say, three variables that all correlate at $r = .6$. In other words, eliminating such highly correlating variables might not be getting at the cause of the multicollinearity (Rockwell, 1975). It may take trial and error to work out which variables are creating the problem.

17.5.2.3. The distribution of data ②

As well as looking for interrelations, you might ensure that variables have roughly normal distributions and are measured at an interval level (which Likert scales are, perhaps wrongly, assumed to be). The assumption of normality is important if you wish to generalize the results of your analysis beyond the sample collected or do significance tests, but otherwise it's not. You can do factor analysis on non-continuous data; for example, if you had dichotomous variables, it's possible (using syntax) to do the factor analysis direct from the correlation matrix, but you should construct the correlation matrix from tetrachoric correlation coefficients (http://www.john-uebersax.com/stat/tetra.htm). The only hassle is computing the correlations (but see the website for software options).

17.6. Running the analysis ②

Access the main dialog box (Figure 17.9) by selecting **Analyze Dimension Reduction   ▸** **⅄ Factor…**. Simply select the variables you want to include in the analysis (remember to exclude any variables that were identified as problematic during the data screening) and transfer them to the box labelled *Variables* by clicking on ➡.

There are several options available, the first of which can be accessed by clicking on **Descriptives…** to access the dialog box in Figure 17.10. The *Univariate descriptives* option provides means and standard deviations for each variable. Most of the other options relate to the correlation matrix of variables (the *R*-matrix described earlier). The *Coefficients* option produces the *R*-matrix, and selecting the *Significance levels* option will include the significance value of each correlation in the *R*-matrix. You can also ask for the *Determinant* of this matrix, which is useful for testing for multicollinearity or singularity (see Section 17.5.2.2).

KMO and Bartlett's test of sphericity produces the Kaiser–Meyer–Olkin (see Section 17.5.2.1) measure of sampling adequacy and Bartlett's test (see Section 17.5.2.2). We have already seen the various criteria for adequacy, but with a sample of 2571 we shouldn't have cause to worry.

The *Reproduced* option produces a correlation matrix based on the model (rather than the real data). Differences between the matrix based on the model and the matrix based

JANE SUPERBRAIN 17.3

What is the determinant? ③

The determinant of a matrix is an important diagnostic tool in factor analysis, but the question of what it is is not easy to answer because it has a mathematical definition and I'm not a mathematician. However, we can bypass the maths and think about the determinant conceptually. The way that I think of the determinant is as describing the 'area' of the data. In Jane Superbrain Box 8.3 we saw the

two diagrams in Figure 17.8. At the time I used these to describe eigenvectors and eigenvalues (which describe the shape of the data). The determinant is related to eigenvalues and eigenvectors but instead of describing the height and width of the data it describes the overall area. So, in the left diagram, the determinant of those data would represent the area inside the red dashed ellipse. These variables have a low correlation so the determinant (area) is big; the biggest value it can be is 1. In the right diagram, the variables are perfectly correlated or singular, and the ellipse (red dashed line) has been squashed down to basically a straight line. In other words, the opposite sides of the ellipse have actually met each other and there is no distance between them at all. Put another way, the area, or determinant, is zero. Therefore, the determinant tells us whether the correlation matrix is singular (determinant is 0), or if all variables are completely unrelated (determinant is 1), or somewhere in between.

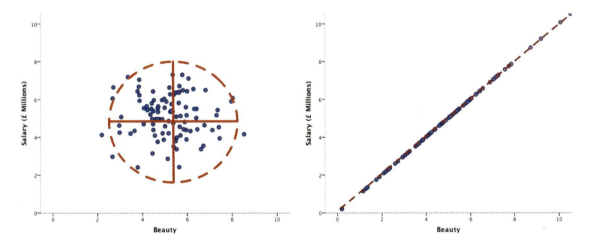

FIGURE 17.8   Data with a large (left) and small (right) determinant

on the observed data indicate the residuals of the model. SPSS produces these residuals in the lower table of the reproduced matrix, and we want relatively few of these values to be greater than .05. Luckily, to save us scanning this matrix, SPSS produces a summary of how many residuals lie above .05. The *Reproduced* option should be selected to obtain this summary. The *Anti-image* option produces an anti-image matrix of covariances and correlations. These matrices contain measures of sampling adequacy for each variable along the diagonal and the negatives of the partial correlation/covariances on the off-diagonals. The diagonal elements, like the KMO measure, should all be greater than .5 at a bare minimum if the sample is adequate for a given pair of variables. If any pair of variables has a value less than this, consider dropping one of them from the analysis. The off-diagonal elements

FIGURE 17.9
Main dialog
box for factor
analysis

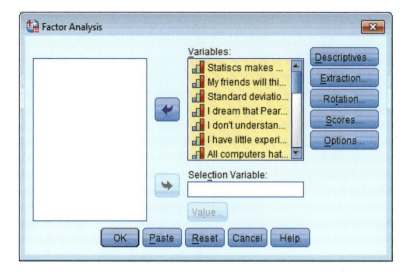

should all be very small (close to zero) in a good model. When you have finished with this
dialog box click on Continue to return to the main dialog box.

FIGURE 17.10
Descriptives in
factor analysis

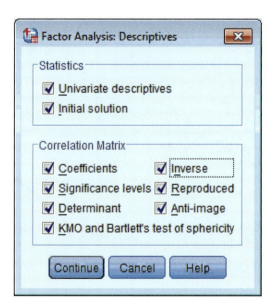

17.6.1. Factor extraction in SPSS ②

To access the *Extraction* dialog box (Figure 17.11), click on Extraction... in the main dialog
box. There are several ways of conducting a factor analysis (see Section 17.4.1). For our
purposes we will use *principal axis factoring* (Principal axis factoring ▼). In the *Analyze* box there
are two options: to analyse the *Correlation matrix* or to analyse the *Covariance matrix*
(SPSS Tip 17.1). The *Display* box has two options within it: to display the *Unrotated factor solution* and a *Scree plot*. The scree plot was described in Section 17.4.5 and is a useful
way of establishing how many factors should be retained in an analysis. The unrotated

SPSS TIP 17.1 **Correlation or covariance matrix?** ③

You should be happy with the idea that the variance–covariance matrix and correlation matrix are different versions of the same thing. However, generally the results will differ depending on which matrix you analyse. Analysing the correlation matrix is a useful default method because it takes the standardized form of the matrix; therefore, if variables have been measured using different scales this will not affect the analysis. In this example, all variables have been measured using the same measurement scale (a 5-point Likert scale), but often you will want to analyse variables that use different measurement scales. Analysing the correlation matrix ensures that differences in measurement scales are accounted for. In addition, even variables measured using the same scale can have very different variances and this creates problems for PCA. Using the correlation matrix eliminates this problem also.

Having said that, there are statistical reasons for preferring to analyse the covariance matrix: correlation coefficients are not sensitive to variations in the dispersion of data, whereas the covariance is and so it produces better-defined factor structures (Tinsley & Tinsley, 1987). However, the covariance matrix should be analysed only when your variables are commensurable.

factor solution is useful in assessing the improvement of interpretation due to rotation. If the rotated solution is little better than the unrotated solution then it is possible that an inappropriate (or less optimal) rotation method has been used.

The *Extract* box provides options pertaining to the retention of factors. You have the choice of either selecting factors with eigenvalues greater than a user-specified value or retaining a fixed number of factors. For the *Eigenvalues greater than* option the default is Kaiser's recommendation of eigenvalues over 1, but you could change this to Jolliffe's recommendation of 0.7 or any other value you want. It is probably best to run a primary analysis with the *Eigenvalues greater than* 1 option selected, select a scree plot and compare the results. If looking at the scree plot and the eigenvalues over 1 lead you to retain the same number of factors then continue with the analysis and be happy. If the two criteria give different results then examine the communalities and decide for yourself which of the two criteria to believe. If you decide to use the scree plot then you may need to redo the analysis specifying the number of factors to extract. The number of factors to be extracted can be specified by selecting *Fixed number of factors* and then typing the appropriate number in the space provided (e.g., 4).

17.6.2. Rotation ②

We have already seen that the interpretability of factors can be improved through rotation (Section 17.4.6). Click on [Rotation...] to access the dialog box in Figure 17.12. I've discussed the various rotation options in Section 17.4.6.1, but, to summarize, if there are theoretical grounds to think that the factors are independent (unrelated) then you should choose one of the orthogonal rotations (I recommend varimax) but if theory suggests that your factors might correlate then one of the oblique rotations (direct oblimin or promax) should be selected. In this example I've selected varimax.

The dialog box also has options for displaying the *Rotated solution* and a *Loading plot*. The rotated solution is displayed by default and is essential for interpreting the final rotated analysis. The loading plot will provide a graphical display of each variable plotted

FIGURE 17.11
Dialog box
for factor
extraction

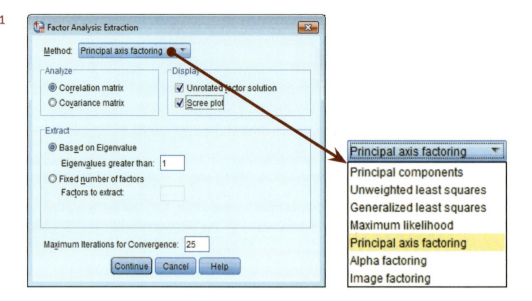

against the extracted factors up to a maximum of three factors (unfortunately SPSS cannot produce four- or five-dimensional graphs). This plot is basically similar to Figure 17.3 and it uses the factor loading of each variable for each factor. With two factors these plots are fairly interpretable, and you should hope to see one group of variables clustered close to the *X*-axis and a different group of variables clustered around the *Y*-axis. If all variables are clustered between the axes, then the rotation has been relatively unsuccessful in maximizing the loading of a variable on a single factor. With three factors these plots will strain even the most dedicated visual system, so unless you have only two factors I would probably avoid them.

A final option is to set the *Maximum Iterations for Convergence* (see SPSS Tip 19.1), which specifies the number of times that the computer will search for an optimal solution. In most circumstances the default of 25 is adequate; however, if you get an error message about convergence then increase this value.

FIGURE 17.12
Factor Analysis: Rotation dialog box

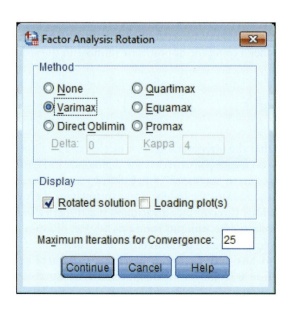

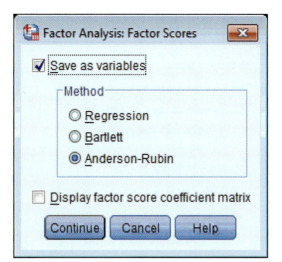

FIGURE 17.13
*Factor Analysis:
Factor* Scores
dialog box

17.6.3. Scores ②

The *Factor Scores* dialog box (Figure 17.13) can be accessed by clicking on [Scores...] in the main dialog box. This option allows you to save factor scores (see Section 17.3.3) for each case in the data editor. SPSS creates a new column for each factor extracted and then places the factor score for each case within that column. These scores can then be used for further analysis, or simply to identify groups of participants who score highly on particular factors. There are three methods of obtaining these scores, all of which were described in Section 17.3.3. If you want to ensure that factor scores are uncorrelated then select the *Anderson-Rubin* method; if correlations between factor scores are acceptable then choose the *Regression* method. As a final option, you can ask SPSS to produce the factor score coefficient matrix. This matrix is used to compute the factor scores, but realistically, we don't need to see it.

17.6.4. Options ②

The *Options* dialog box can be obtained by clicking on [Options...] in the main dialog box (Figure 17.14). Missing data are a problem for factor analysis just like most other procedures, and SPSS provides a choice of excluding cases or estimating a value for a case. Tabachnick and Fidell (2012) have an excellent chapter on data screening (see also the rather less excellent Chapter 5 of this book). Based on their advice, you should consider the distribution of missing data. If the missing data are non-normally distributed or the sample size after exclusion is too small then estimation is necessary. SPSS uses the mean as an estimate (*Replace with mean*). These procedures lower the standard deviation of variables and so can lead to significant results that would otherwise be non-significant. Therefore, if missing data are random, you might consider excluding cases. SPSS allows you to either *Exclude cases listwise*, in which case any participant with missing data for any variable is excluded, or to *Exclude cases pairwise*, in which case a participant's data are excluded only from calculations for which a datum is missing (see SPSS Tip 5.1). If you exclude cases pairwise your estimates can go all over the place, so it's probably safest to opt to exclude cases listwise unless this results in a massive loss of data.

The final two options relate to how coefficients are displayed. By default, SPSS will list variables in the order in which they are entered into the data editor. However, when

FIGURE 17.14
Factor Analysis:
options dialog
box

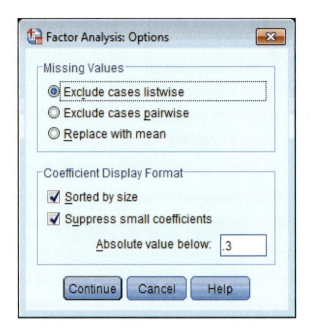

interpreting factors it is useful to list variables by size. By selecting *Sorted by size*, SPSS will order the variables by their factor loadings. In fact, it does this sorting fairly intelligently so that all of the variables that load highly on the same factor are displayed together. The second option is to *Suppress absolute values less than* a specified value (by default 0.1). This option ensures that factor loadings within ±0.1 are not displayed in the output. Again, this option is useful for interpretation. The default value is probably sensible, but on your first analysis I recommend changing it either to .3 or to a value reflecting the expected value of a significant factor loading given the sample size (see Section 17.4.6.2). This will make interpretation simpler. We know that a loading of .4 is substantial, but so we don't throw out the baby with the bath water, setting the value to 0.3 is sensible: we will see not only the substantial loadings but those close to the cut-off (e.g., a loading of .39). For this example set the value at .3.

ODITI'S LANTERN

PCA

'I, Oditi, feel that we are getting closer to finding the hidden truths behind the numbers. Factor analysis allows us to estimate variables "hidden" within the data. This technique is the very essence of the cult of undiscovered numerical truths. Once we have mastered this tool we can find out what people are really thinking, even if they don't know they're thinking it. We might find that they think that they think I'm the kind saviour of cute furry gerbils, but that underneath they know the truth … stare into my lantern to discover factor analysis.'

17.7. Interpreting output from SPSS ②

Select the same options as I have in the screen diagrams and run a factor analysis with orthogonal rotation.

SELF-TEST Having done this, select the *Direct Oblimin* option in Figure 17.12 and repeat the analysis. You should obtain two outputs identical in all respects except that one used an orthogonal rotation and the other an oblique.

To save space I set the default SPSS options such that each variable is referred to only by its label on the data editor (e.g., Question_12). On the output *you* obtain, you should find that the SPSS uses the value label (the question itself) in all of the output. When using the output refer back to Figure 17.6 to remind you of what each question was.

When you factor-analyse your own data, you might be unlucky enough to see an error message about a 'non-positive definite matrix' (see SPSS Tip 17.2). A 'non-positive definite matrix' sounds a bit like a collection of depressed numbers that lack certainty about their lives. In some ways it is.

17.7.1. Preliminary analysis ②

The first body of output concerns data screening, assumption testing and sampling adequacy. You'll find several large tables (or matrices) that tell us interesting things about our data. If you selected the *Univariate descriptives* option in Figure 17.10 then the first table

SPSS TIP 17.2   **Error messages about a 'non-positive definite matrix' ④**

Factor analysis works by looking at your correlation matrix. This matrix has to be 'positive definite' for the analysis to work. This term means lots of horrible things mathematically (e.g., the eigenvalues and determinant of the matrix have to be positive), but, in more basic terms, factors are like lines floating in space, and eigenvalues measure the length of those lines. If your eigenvalue is negative then it means that the length of your line/factor is negative too. It's a bit like me asking you how tall you are, and you responding 'I'm minus 175 cm tall'. That would be nonsense. If a factor has negative length, then that is nonsense too. When SPSS decomposes the correlation matrix to look for factors, if it comes across a negative eigenvalue it starts thinking 'oh dear, I've entered some weird parallel universe where the usual rules of maths no longer apply and things can have negative lengths, and this probably means that time runs backwards, my mum is my dad, my sister is a dog, my head is a fish, and my toe is a frog called Gerald'. It does the sensible thing and decides not to proceed. Things like the KMO test and the determinant rely on a positive definite matrix; if you don't have one they can't be computed.

The most likely reason for having a non-positive definite *R*-matrix is that you have too many variables and too few cases of data, which makes the correlation matrix a bit unstable. It could also be that you have too many highly correlated items in your matrix (singularity, for example, tends to mess things up). In any case it means that your data are bad, naughty data, and not to be trusted; if you let them loose then you have only yourself to blame for the consequences.

Other than cry, there's not that much you can do to rectify the situation. You could try to limit your items, or selectively remove items (especially highly correlated ones) to see if that helps. Collecting more data can help too. There are some mathematical fudges you can do, but they're not as tasty as vanilla fudge and they are hard to implement.

Correlation Matrix[a]

		Question_01	Question_02	Question_03	Question_04	Question_05	Question_19	Question_20	Question_21	Question_22	Question_23
Correlation	Question_01	1.000	-.099	-.337	.436	.402	-.189	.214	.329	-.104	-.004
	Question_02	-.099	1.000	.318	-.112	-.119	.203	-.202	-.205	.231	.100
	Question_03	-.337	.318	1.000	-.380	-.310	.342	-.325	-.417	.204	.150
	Question_04	.436	-.112	-.380	1.000	.401	-.186	.243	.410	-.098	-.034
	Question_05	.402	-.119	-.310	.401	1.000	-.165	.200	.335	-.133	-.042
	Question_06	.217	-.074	-.227	.278	.257	-.167	.101	.272	-.165	-.069
	Question_07	.305	-.159	-.382	.409	.339	-.269	.221	.483	-.168	-.070
	Question_08	.331	-.050	-.259	.349	.269	-.159	.175	.296	-.079	-.050
	Question_09	-.092	.315	.300	-.125	-.096	.249	-.159	-.136	.257	.171
	Question_10	.214	-.084	-.193	.216	.258	-.127	.084	.193	-.131	-.062
	Question_11	.357	-.144	-.351	.369	.298	-.200	.255	.346	-.162	-.086
	Question_12	.345	-.195	-.410	.442	.347	-.267	.298	.441	-.167	-.046
	Question_13	.355	-.143	-.318	.344	.302	-.227	.204	.374	-.195	-.053
	Question_14	.338	-.165	-.371	.351	.315	-.254	.226	.399	-.170	-.048
	Question_15	.246	-.165	-.312	.334	.261	-.210	.206	.300	-.168	-.062
	Question_16	.499	-.168	-.419	.416	.395	-.267	.265	.421	-.156	-.082
	Question_17	.371	-.087	-.327	.383	.310	-.163	.205	.363	-.126	-.092
	Question_18	.347	-.164	-.375	.382	.322	-.257	.235	.430	-.160	-.080
	Question_19	-.189	.203	.342	-.186	-.165	1.000	-.249	-.275	.234	.122
	Question_20	.214	-.202	-.325	.243	.200	-.249	1.000	.468	-.100	-.035
	Question_21	.329	-.205	-.417	.410	.335	-.275	.468	1.000	-.129	-.068
	Question_22	-.104	.231	.204	-.098	-.133	.234	-.100	-.129	1.000	.230
	Question_23	-.004	.100	.150	-.034	-.042	.122	-.035	-.068	.230	1.000
Sig. (1-tailed)	Question_01		.000	.000	.000	.000	.000	.000	.000	.000	.410
	Question_02	.000		.000	.000	.000	.000	.000	.000	.000	.000
	Question_03	.000	.000		.000	.000	.000	.000	.000	.000	.000
	Question_04	.000	.000	.000		.000	.000	.000	.000	.000	.043
	Question_05	.000	.000	.000	.000		.000	.000	.000	.000	.017
	Question_06	.000	.000	.000	.000	.000	.000	.000	.000	.000	.000
	Question_07	.000	.000	.000	.000	.000	.000	.000	.000	.000	.000
	Question_08	.000	.006	.000	.000	.000	.000	.000	.000	.000	.005
	Question_09	.000	.000	.000	.000	.000	.000	.000	.000	.000	.000
	Question_10	.000	.000	.000	.000	.000	.000	.000	.000	.000	.001
	Question_11	.000	.000	.000	.000	.000	.000	.000	.000	.000	.000
	Question_12	.000	.000	.000	.000	.000	.000	.000	.000	.000	.009
	Question_13	.000	.000	.000	.000	.000	.000	.000	.000	.000	.004
	Question_14	.000	.000	.000	.000	.000	.000	.000	.000	.000	.007
	Question_15	.000	.000	.000	.000	.000	.000	.000	.000	.000	.001
	Question_16	.000	.000	.000	.000	.000	.000	.000	.000	.000	.000
	Question_17	.000	.000	.000	.000	.000	.000	.000	.000	.000	.000
	Question_18	.000	.000	.000	.000	.000	.000	.000	.000	.000	.000
	Question_19	.000	.000	.000	.000	.000		.000	.000	.000	.000
	Question_20	.000	.000	.000	.000	.000	.000		.000	.000	.039
	Question_21	.000	.000	.000	.000	.000	.000	.000		.000	.000
	Question_22	.000	.000	.000	.000	.000	.000	.000	.000		.000
	Question_23	.410	.000	.000	.043	.017	.000	.039	.000	.000	

a. Determinant = .001

OUTPUT 17.1

will contain descriptive statistics for each variable (the mean, standard deviation and number of cases). This table is not included here, but you should have enough experience to be able to interpret it. The table also includes the number of missing cases; this summary is a useful way to determine the extent of missing data.

Output 17.1 shows the *R*-matrix (i.e., the correlation matrix)[6] produced using the *Coefficients* and *Significance levels* options in Figure 17.10. The top half of this table contains the Pearson correlation coefficient between all pairs of questions, whereas the bottom half contains the one-tailed significance of these coefficients. We can use this correlation matrix to check the pattern of relationships. First, scan the matrix for correlations greater than .3, and look for variables that only have a small number of correlations greater than this value. Then scan the correlation coefficients themselves and look for any greater than .9. If any are found then you should be aware that a problem could arise because of multicollinearity in the data.

You can also check the determinant of the correlation matrix and, if necessary, eliminate variables that you think are causing the problem. The determinant is listed at the

---

[6] To save space only columns for the first five and last five questions in the questionnaire are included.

bottom of the matrix (blink and you'll miss it). For these data its value is .001, which is greater than the necessary value of 0.00001 (see Section 17.6).[7] To sum up, all questions in the SAQ correlate reasonably well with all others and none of the correlation coefficients are excessively large; therefore, we won't eliminate any questions at this stage.

If you selected the _Inverse_ option in Figure 17.10 you'll find the inverse of the correlation matrix (R^{-1}) in your output (labelled _Inverse of Correlation Matrix_). This matrix is used in various calculations (including factor scores – see Section 17.3.3.1), but in all honesty is useful only if you want some insight into the calculations that go on in a factor analysis. Most of us have more interesting things to do, so ignore it.

If you selected the _KMO and Bartlett's test of sphericity_ and the _Anti-image_ options in Figure 17.10 then your output will contain the Kaiser–Meyer–Olkin measure of sampling adequacy and Bartlett's test of sphericity (Output 17.2) and the anti-image correlation and covariance matrices (an edited version is in Output 17.3). The anti-image correlation and covariance matrices provide similar information (remember the relationship between covariance and correlation) and so only the anti-image correlation matrix need be studied in detail because it is the most informative.

For the KMO statistic the value is .93, which is well above the minimum criterion of .5 and falls into the range of 'marvellous' (see Section 17.5.2.1), so we should be confident that the sample size is adequate for factor analysis. I mentioned before that KMO can be calculated for multiple and individual variables. The KMO values for individual variables are produced on the diagonal of the anti-image correlation matrix (I have highlighted these cells in Output 17.3). As well as checking the overall KMO statistic, we should examine the diagonal elements of the anti-image correlation matrix: the values should all be above the bare minimum of .5 (and preferably higher). For these data all values are well above .5, which is good news. If you find any variables with values below 0.5 then you should consider excluding them from the analysis (or run the analysis with and without that variable and note the difference). Removal of a variable affects the KMO statistics, so if you do remove a variable be sure to re-examine the new anti-image correlation matrix. As for the rest of the anti-image correlation matrix, the off-diagonal elements represent the partial correlations between variables. For a good factor analysis we want these correlations to be very small (the smaller, the better). So, as a final check you can look through to see that the off-diagonal elements are small (they should be for these data).

Bartlett's measure (Output 17.2) tests the null hypothesis that the original correlation matrix is an identity matrix. We want this test to be _significant_ (see Section 17.5.2.2). As I mentioned before, given the large sample sizes usually used in factor analysis this test will almost certainly be significant, and it is ($p < .001$). A non-significant test would certainly indicate a massive problem, but this significant value only really tells us that we don't have a massive problem, which is nice to know, I suppose.

KMO and Bartlett's Test   OUTPUT 17.2

Kaiser-Meyer-Olkin Measure of Sampling Adequacy.		.930
Bartlett's Test of Sphericity	Approx. Chi-Square	19334.492
	df	253
	Sig.	.000

[7] Actually the determinant of this matrix is 0.0005271; I have no idea why SPSS reports this value as .001.

Anti-image Matrices

Anti-image Correlation

	Question_01	Question_02	Question_03	Question_04	Question_05	Question_19	Question_20	Question_21	Question_22	Question_23
Question_01	.930	-.020	.053	-.167	-.156	.012	-.016	.006	.001	-.059
Question_02	-.020	.875	-.157	-.041	.010	-.029	.059	.041	-.121	-.002
Question_03	.053	-.157	.951	.084	.037	-.121	.078	.070	-.007	-.076
Question_04	-.167	-.041	.084	.955	-.134	-.034	-.004	-.086	-.033	-.017
Question_05	-.156	.010	.037	-.134	.960	-.018	-.011	-.046	.035	-.005
Question_06	.020	-.053	-.042	-.007	-.035	-.015	.051	.039	.040	.018
Question_07	.023	.016	.072	-.087	-.044	.068	.048	-.208	.013	-.008
Question_08	-.049	-.033	-.007	-.075	-.027	.047	.021	-.020	-.023	.002
Question_09	-.016	-.193	-.142	.030	-.020	-.111	.038	-.031	-.126	-.092
Question_10	-.012	-.012	-.016	.006	-.093	-.009	.043	.017	.019	.015
Question_11	-.041	.038	.064	-.022	.000	-.006	-.082	-.005	.034	.010
Question_12	-.007	.031	.087	-.154	-.058	.040	-.065	-.079	.018	-.028
Question_13	-.085	-.008	-.032	.023	.004	.009	.018	-.033	.052	-.030
Question_14	-.040	.023	.069	-.004	-.026	.044	.001	-.063	.029	-.026
Question_15	.089	.037	.008	-.062	.014	.009	-.037	.035	.025	-.024
Question_16	-.264	-.011	.081	-.036	-.096	.047	-.005	-.085	-.003	.023
Question_17	-.047	-.029	.035	-.035	-.018	-.047	.015	-.041	.010	.055
Question_18	-.023	.018	.039	-.025	.002	.030	-.003	-.072	-.024	.023
Question_19	.012	-.029	-.121	-.034	-.018	.941	.091	.031	-.115	-.038
Question_20	-.016	.059	.078	-.004	-.011	.091	.889	-.323	-.011	-.028
Question_21	.006	.041	.070	-.086	-.046	.031	-.323	.929	-.024	.013
Question_22	.001	-.121	-.007	-.033	.035	-.115	-.011	-.024	.878	-.176
Question_23	-.059	-.002	-.076	-.017	-.005	-.038	-.028	.013	-.176	.766

OUTPUT 17.3

CRAMMING SAM'S TIPS   **Preliminary analysis**

- Scan the correlation matrix; look for variables that don't correlate with any other variables, or correlate very highly ($r = .9$) with one or more other variables.
- In factor analysis, check that the determinant of this matrix is bigger than 0.00001; if it is then multicollinearity isn't a problem.
- In the table labelled *KMO and Bartlett's Test* the KMO statistic should be greater than .5 as a bare minimum; if it isn't, collect more data. You should check the KMO statistic for individual variables by looking at the diagonal of the anti-image matrices again, these values should be above .5 (this is useful for identifying problematic variables if the overall KMO is unsatisfactory).
- Bartlett's test of sphericity will usually be significant (the value of *Sig.* will be less than .05); if it's not you've got a disaster on your hands.

17.7.2.   Factor extraction ②

The first part of the factor extraction process is to determine the linear components within the data set (the eigenvectors) by calculating the eigenvalues of the *R*-matrix (see Section 17.4.4). We know that there are as many components (eigenvectors) in the *R*-matrix as there are variables, but most will be unimportant. To determine the importance of a particular vector we look at the magnitude of the associated eigenvalue. We can then apply criteria to determine which factors to retain and which to discard. By default SPSS uses Kaiser's criterion of retaining factors with eigenvalues greater than 1 (see Figure 17.11).

Output 17.4 lists the eigenvalues associated with each factor before extraction, after extraction and after rotation. Before extraction, SPSS has identified 23 factors within the

Total Variance Explained

Factor	Initial Eigenvalues			Extraction Sums of Squared Loadings			Rotation Sums of Squared Loadings		
	Total	% of Variance	Cumulative %	Total	% of Variance	Cumulative %	Total	% of Variance	Cumulative %
1	7.290	31.696	31.696	6.744	29.323	29.323	3.033	13.188	13.188
2	1.739	7.560	39.256	1.128	4.902	34.225	2.855	12.415	25.603
3	1.317	5.725	44.981	.814	3.539	37.764	1.986	8.636	34.238
4	1.227	5.336	50.317	.624	2.713	40.477	1.435	6.239	40.477
5	.988	4.295	54.612						
6	.895	3.893	58.504						
7	.806	3.502	62.007						
8	.783	3.404	65.410						
9	.751	3.265	68.676						
10	.717	3.117	71.793						
11	.684	2.972	74.765						
12	.670	2.911	77.676						
13	.612	2.661	80.337						
14	.578	2.512	82.849						
15	.549	2.388	85.236						
16	.523	2.275	87.511						
17	.508	2.210	89.721						
18	.456	1.982	91.704						
19	.424	1.843	93.546						
20	.408	1.773	95.319						
21	.379	1.650	96.969						
22	.364	1.583	98.552						
23	.333	1.448	100.000						

Extraction Method: Principal Axis Factoring.

OUTPUT 17.4

data set (we know that there should be as many eigenvectors as there are variables and so there will be as many factors as variables – see Section 17.4.4). The eigenvalues associated with each factor represent the variance explained by that particular factor; SPSS also displays the eigenvalue in terms of the percentage of variance explained (so factor 1 explains 31.696% of total variance). The first few factors explain relatively large amounts of variance (especially factor 1), whereas subsequent factors explain only small amounts of variance. SPSS then extracts all factors with eigenvalues greater than 1, which leaves us with four factors. The eigenvalues associated with these factors are again displayed (and the percentage of variance explained) in the columns labelled *Extraction Sums of Squared Loadings*. In the final part of the table (labelled *Rotation Sums of Squared Loadings*), the eigenvalues of the factors after rotation are displayed. Rotation has the effect of optimizing the factor structure, and one consequence for these data is that the relative importance of the four factors is equalized a bit. Before rotation, factor 1 accounted for considerably more variance than the remaining three (29.32% compared to 4.90%, 3.54% and 2.71%), but after rotation it accounts for only 13.19% of variance (compared to 12.42%, 8.64% and 6.24%, respectively).

Output 17.5 (left) shows the table of communalities before and after extraction. Remember that the communality is the proportion of common variance within a variable (see Section 17.4.1). Factor analysis starts by estimating the variance that is common; therefore, before extraction the communalities are a kind of best guess. Once factors have been extracted, we have a better idea of how much variance is, in reality, common. The communalities in the column labelled *Extraction* reflect this common variance. So, for example, we can say that 37.3% of the variance associated with question 1 is common, or shared, variance. Another way to look at these communalities is in terms of the proportion of variance explained by the underlying factors. Remember that after extraction we have discarded some factors

OUTPUT 17.5

Communalities

	Initial	Extraction
Question_01	.373	.373
Question_02	.188	.260
Question_03	.398	.472
Question_04	.385	.419
Question_05	.291	.299
Question_06	.427	.594
Question_07	.470	.489
Question_08	.490	.646
Question_09	.220	.339
Question_10	.197	.197
Question_11	.530	.629
Question_12	.424	.453
Question_13	.451	.474
Question_14	.393	.425
Question_15	.344	.322
Question_16	.463	.458
Question_17	.494	.575
Question_18	.492	.544
Question_19	.209	.245
Question_20	.270	.266
Question_21	.454	.468
Question_22	.167	.247
Question_23	.086	.116

Extraction Method: Principal Axis Factoring.

Factor Matrix[a]

	Factor			
	1	2	3	4
Question_18	.684			
Question_07	.663			
Question_16	.653			
Question_13	.650			
Question_11	.646	.313		
Question_12	.643			
Question_21	.633			
Question_17	.632	.359		
Question_14	.628			
Question_04	.607			
Question_03	-.605			
Question_15	.559			
Question_01	.557			
Question_06	.552		.489	
Question_08	.546	.483		
Question_05	.522			
Question_20	.407			
Question_10	.404			
Question_19	-.397			
Question_09		.460		
Question_02		.372		
Question_22				
Question_23				

Extraction Method: Principal Axis Factoring.
a. 4 factors extracted. 11 iterations required.

(in this case we've retained only four), so the communalities after extraction represent the amount of variance in each variable that can be explained by the retained factors.

Output 17.5 (right) also shows the factor matrix before rotation. This matrix contains the loadings of each variable on each factor. By default SPSS displays all loadings; however, we requested that all loadings less than .3 be suppressed in the output (see Figure 17.14) and so there are blank spaces for many of the loadings. This matrix is not particularly important for interpretation, but it is interesting to note that before rotation most variables load highly on the first factor (that is why this factor accounts for most of the variance in Output 17.4).

Factor analysis is an exploratory tool and so it should be used to guide the researcher to make various decisions: you shouldn't leave the computer to make them. One important decision is the number of factors to extract (Section 17.4.5). By Kaiser's criterion we should extract four factors (which is what SPSS has done); however, this criterion is accurate when there are fewer than 30 variables and communalities after extraction are greater than .7, or when the sample size exceeds 250 and the average communality is greater than .6. No communalities exceed .7 (Output 17.5), and the average communality can be found by adding them up and dividing by the number of communalities (9.31/23 = .405). So, both of these criteria suggest Kaiser's rule might be inappropriate for these data. We could use Jolliffe's criterion (retain factors with eigenvalues greater than .7), but there is little to recommend this criterion over Kaiser's and we'd end up with 10 factors (see Output 17.4). Finally, we could use the scree plot, which we asked SPSS to produce by using the option in Figure 17.11. This curve is difficult to interpret because there are points of inflexion at both 3 and 5 factors (Output 17.6). Therefore, we could probably justify retaining either two or four factors.

So how many factors should we extract? We need to consider that the recommendations for Kaiser's criterion are for much smaller samples than we have. Therefore, given our huge sample, and given that there is some consistency between Kaiser's criterion and the scree plot, it is reasonable to extract four factors; however, you might like to rerun the analysis specifying that SPSS extract only two factors (see Figure 17.11) and compare the results.

Output 17.7 shows an edited version of the reproduced correlation matrix that was requested using the option in Figure 17.10. The top half of this matrix (labelled *Reproduced*

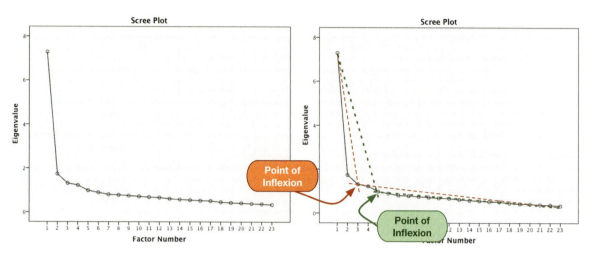

OUTPUT 17.6

Reproduced Correlations

		Question_01	Question_02	Question_03	Question_04	Question_05	Question_19	Question_20	Question_21	Question_22	Question_23
Reproduced Correlation	Question_01	.373	-.112	-.338	.393	.328	-.191	.266	.398	-.072	-.013
	Question_02	-.112	.260	.295	-.129	-.119	.237	-.192	-.201	.227	.146
	Question_03	-.338	.295	.472	-.367	-.316	.328	-.336	-.431	.242	.133
	Question_04	.393	-.129	-.367	.419	.353	-.214	.282	.429	-.092	-.021
	Question_05	.328	-.119	-.316	.353	.299	-.190	.237	.364	-.091	-.025
	Question_06	.221	-.078	-.218	.269	.249	-.167	.078	.259	-.175	-.072
	Question_07	.349	-.154	-.363	.393	.344	-.243	.230	.408	-.173	-.066
	Question_08	.345	-.044	-.258	.345	.277	-.129	.172	.283	-.086	-.055
	Question_09	-.071	.290	.295	-.092	-.092	.255	-.174	-.174	.272	.178
	Question_10	.191	-.096	-.210	.218	.194	-.149	.116	.223	-.130	-.061
	Question_11	.362	-.131	-.345	.375	.311	-.210	.213	.339	-.178	-.110
	Question_12	.374	-.189	-.407	.412	.356	-.265	.291	.447	-.158	-.057
	Question_13	.329	-.143	-.341	.371	.325	-.231	.202	.375	-.182	-.078
	Question_14	.342	-.155	-.359	.381	.333	-.238	.237	.400	-.160	-.061
	Question_15	.289	-.160	-.327	.319	.277	-.223	.204	.331	-.180	-.091
	Question_16	.401	-.193	-.426	.430	.364	-.267	.315	.457	-.152	-.063
	Question_17	.379	-.089	-.321	.393	.324	-.181	.212	.351	-.123	-.066
	Question_18	.355	-.155	-.369	.402	.354	-.249	.230	.419	-.179	-.066
	Question_19	-.191	.237	.328	-.214	-.190	.245	-.218	-.271	.211	.124
	Question_20	.266	-.192	-.336	.282	.237	-.218	.266	.329	-.122	-.059
	Question_21	.398	-.201	-.431	.429	.364	-.271	.329	.468	-.142	-.051
	Question_22	-.072	.227	.242	-.092	-.091	.211	-.122	-.142	.247	.163
	Question_23	-.013	.146	.133	-.021	-.025	.124	-.059	-.051	.163	.116
Residual[b]	Question_01		.013	.001	.042	.074	.002	-.052	-.069	-.032	.009
	Question_02	.013		.023	.017	-.001	-.034	-.010	-.004	.004	-.046
	Question_03	.001	.023		-.014	.006	.014	.011	.014	-.039	.017
	Question_04	.042	.017	-.014		.048	.028	-.039	-.018	-.006	-.013
	Question_05	.074	-.001	.006	.048		.025	-.037	-.030	-.041	-.017
	Question_06	-.004	.004	-.009	.009	.009	.000	.022	.013	.010	.003
	Question_07	-.044	-.006	-.019	.016	-.005	-.026	-.009	.075	.005	-.004
	Question_08	-.014	-.005	.000	.004	-.009	-.030	.003	.013	.006	.005
	Question_09	-.022	.024	.005	-.033	-.003	-.005	.015	.038	-.015	-.007
	Question_10	.023	.012	.017	-.003	.064	.022	-.032	-.030	-.001	-.001
	Question_11	-.005	-.013	-.006	-.007	-.013	.011	.042	.007	.016	.023
	Question_12	-.028	-.006	-.003	.030	-.009	-.001	.007	-.007	-.009	.011
	Question_13	.025	.000	.023	-.026	-.024	.004	.002	-.001	-.014	.025
	Question_14	-.004	-.009	-.012	-.030	-.017	-.016	-.011	-.001	-.009	.012
	Question_15	-.044	-.005	.015	.015	-.016	.013	.002	-.031	.012	.029
	Question_16	.098	.025	.007	-.014	.030	.000	-.050	-.036	-.003	-.019
	Question_17	-.009	.002	-.006	-.010	-.014	.018	-.007	.012	-.003	-.026
	Question_18	-.008	-.009	-.006	-.020	-.032	-.007	.005	.011	.019	-.014
	Question_19	.002	-.034	.014	.028	.025		-.031	-.004	.023	-.002
	Question_20	-.052	-.010	.011	-.039	-.037	-.031		.139	.022	.024
	Question_21	-.069	-.004	.014	-.018	-.030	-.004	.139		.013	-.017
	Question_22	-.032	.004	-.039	-.006	-.041	.023	.022	.013		.067
	Question_23	.009	-.046	.017	-.013	-.017	-.002	.024	-.017	.067	

Extraction Method: Principal Axis Factoring.

b. Residuals are computed between observed and reproduced correlations. There are 12 (4.0%) nonredundant residuals with absolute values greater than 0.05.

OUTPUT 17.7

Correlations) contains the correlation coefficients between all of the questions based on the factor model. The diagonal of this matrix contains the communalities after extraction for each variable (you can check the values against Output 17.5).

The correlations in the reproduced matrix differ from those in the *R*-matrix because they stem from the model rather than the observed data. If the model were a perfect fit of the data then we would expect the reproduced correlation coefficients to be the same as the original correlation coefficients. Therefore, to assess the fit of the model we can look at the differences between the observed correlations and the correlations based on the model. For example, if we take the correlation between questions 1 and 2, the correlation based on the observed data is $-.099$ (taken from Output 17.1). The correlation based on the model is $-.112$, which is slightly higher. We can calculate the difference as follows:

$$\text{residual} = r_{\text{observed}} - r_{\text{from model}}$$

$$\text{residual}_{Q_1 Q_2} = (-0.099) - (-0.112)$$

$$= 0.013$$

You should notice that this difference is the value quoted in the lower half of the reproduced matrix (labelled *Residual*) for questions 1 and 2 (highlighted in blue). Therefore, the lower half of the reproduced matrix contains the differences between the observed correlation coefficients and the ones predicted from the model. For a good model these values will all be small. In fact, we want most values to be less than .05. Rather than scan this huge matrix, SPSS provides a footnote summary, which states how many residuals have an absolute value greater than .05. For these data there are only 12 residuals (4%)[8] that are greater than .05. There are no hard-and-fast rules about what proportion of residuals should be below .05; however, if more than 50% are greater than .05 you probably have grounds for concern. For these data we have around 4%, which is certainly nothing to worry about.

CRAMMING SAM'S TIPS Factor extraction

- To decide how many factors to extract, look at the table labelled *Communalities* and the column labelled *Extraction*. If these values are all .7 or above and you have less than 30 variables then the SPSS default (Kaiser's criterion) for extracting factors is fine. Likewise, if your sample size exceeds 250 and the average of the communalities is .6 or greater then the default option is fine. Alternatively, with 200 or more participants the scree plot can be used.
- Check the bottom of the table labelled *Reproduced Correlations* for the percentage of 'nonredundant residuals with absolute values greater than 0.05'. This percentage should be less than 50% and the smaller it is, the better.

[8] SPSS has a weird rounding habit here. There are 253 unique correlation coefficients in the table and 12 residuals greater than .05, which is $(12/253) \times 100 = 4.74\%$. SPSS seems to round down to the nearest whole percentage value for some reason.

17.7.3. Factor rotation ②

The first analysis I asked you to run was using an orthogonal rotation. However, I also asked you to rerun the analysis using oblique rotation. In this section the results of both analyses will be reported so as to highlight the differences between the outputs. This comparison will also be a useful way to show the circumstances in which one type of rotation might be preferable to another.

17.7.3.1. Orthogonal rotation (varimax) ②

Output 17.8 shows the rotated factor matrix (called the rotated component matrix in PCA), which is a matrix of the factor loadings for each variable on each factor. This matrix contains the same information as the factor matrix in Output 17.5, except that it is calculated *after* rotation. There are several things to consider about the format of this matrix. First, factor loadings less than .3 have not been displayed because we asked for these loadings to be suppressed using the option in Figure 17.14. Second, the variables are listed in the order of size of their factor loadings because we asked for the output to be *Sorted by size* using the option in Figure 17.14. If this option was not selected the variables would be listed in the order they appear in the data editor. Finally, for all other parts of the output I suppressed the variable labels (to save space), but for this output I have used the variable labels to aid interpretation.

Compare this matrix to the unrotated solution (Output 17.5). Before rotation, most variables loaded highly on the first factor and the remaining factors didn't really get a look-in. However, the rotation of the factor structure has clarified things considerably: there are four factors and most variables load very highly on only one factor.[9] In cases where a variable loads highly on more than one factor the loading is typically higher for one factor than another. For example, 'SPSS always crashes when I try to use it' loads on both factor 1 and 2, but the loading for factor 2 (.612) is higher than for factor 1 (.366), so it makes sense to think of it as part of factor 2 more than factor 1. Remember that every variable has a loading on every factor, it just appears as though they don't in Output 17.8 because we asked that they not be printed if they were lower than .3.

The next step is to look at the content of questions that load highly on the same factor to try to identify common themes. If the mathematical factors represent some real-world construct then common themes among highly loading questions can help us identify what the construct might be. The questions that load highly on factor 1 seem to relate to different aspects of statistics; therefore, we might label this factor *fear of statistics*. The questions that load highly on factor 2 all seem to relate to using computers or SPSS. Therefore we might label this factor *fear of computers*. The three questions that load highly on factor 3 all seem to relate to mathematics; therefore, we might label this factor *fear of mathematics*. Finally, the questions that load highly on factor 4 contain some component of social evaluation from friends; therefore, we might label this factor *peer evaluation*. This analysis seems to reveal that the questionnaire is composed of four subscales: fear of statistics, fear of computers, fear of maths and fear of negative peer evaluation. There are two possibilities here. The first is that the SAQ failed to measure what it set out to (namely, SPSS anxiety) but does measure some related constructs. The second is that these four constructs are sub-components of SPSS anxiety; however, the factor analysis does not indicate which of these possibilities is true.

[9] The suppression of loadings less than .3 and ordering variables by their loading size makes this pattern really easy to see.

Rotated Factor Matrix[a]

	Factor			
	1	2	3	4
I wake up under my duvet thinking that I am trapped under a normal distribution	.594			
I weep openly at the mention of central tendency	.543			
I dream that Pearson is attacking me with correlation coefficients	.527			
People try to tell you that SPSS makes statistics easier to understand but it doesn't	.510	.398		
Standard deviations excite me	-.505			.399
Statistics makes me cry	.504			
I can't sleep for thoughts of eigenvectors	.465			
I don't understand statistics	.436			
I have little experience of computers		.753		
SPSS always crashes when I try to use it	.366	.612		
I worry that I will cause irreparable damage because of my incompetence with computers		.564		
All computers hate me	.364	.559		
Computers have minds of their own and deliberately go wrong whenever I use them	.388	.485		
Computers are useful only for playing games		.380		
Computers are out to get me		.377		
I have never been good at mathematics			.759	
I did badly at mathematics at school			.688	
I slip into a coma whenever I see an equation			.641	
My friends are better at statistics than me				.559
My friends are better at SPSS than I am				.465
My friends will think I'm stupid for not being able to cope with SPSS				.464
Everybody looks at me when I use SPSS				.375
If I'm good at statistics my friends will think I'm a nerd				.329

Extraction Method: Principal Axis Factoring.
Rotation Method: Varimax with Kaiser Normalization.[a]

a. Rotation converged in 7 iterations.

OUTPUT 17.8

17.7.3.2. Oblique rotation ②

When an oblique rotation is conducted the factor matrix is split into two matrices: the *pattern matrix* and the *structure matrix* (see Jane Superbrain Box 17.1). For orthogonal rotation these matrices are the same. The pattern matrix contains the factor loadings and is comparable to the factor matrix that we interpreted for the orthogonal rotation. The structure matrix takes into account the relationship between factors (in fact it is a product of the pattern matrix and the matrix containing the correlation coefficients between factors). Most researchers interpret the pattern matrix, because it is usually simpler; however, there are situations in which values in the pattern matrix are suppressed because of relationships between the factors. Therefore, the structure matrix is a useful double-check and Graham et al. (2003) recommend reporting both (with some useful examples of why this can be important).

For the pattern matrix for these data (Output 17.9) the same four factors seem to have emerged. Factor 1 seems to represent fear of statistics, factor 2 represents fear of peer evaluation, factor 3 represents fear of computers and factor 4 represents fear of mathematics. The structure matrix (Output 17.10) differs in that shared variance is not ignored. The picture becomes more complicated because, with the exception of factor 2, several variables load highly on more than one factor. This has occurred because of the relationship between factors 1 and 3 and between factors 3 and 4. This example should highlight why the pattern matrix is preferable for interpretative reasons: it contains information about the *unique* contribution of a variable to a factor.

The final part of the output is a correlation matrix between the factors (Output 17.11). This matrix contains the correlation coefficients between factors. As predicted from the

Pattern Matrix[a]

	Factor			
	1	2	3	4
I wake up under my duvet thinking that I am trapped under a normal distribution	.536			
I can't sleep for thoughts of eigenvectors	.470			
I weep openly at the mention of central tendency	.449			
I dream that Pearson is attacking me with correlation coefficients	.441			
Standard deviations excite me	-.435	.324		
Statistics makes me cry	.432			
People try to tell you that SPSS makes statistics easier to understand but it doesn't	.412		.358	
I don't understand statistics	.357			
My friends are better at statistics than me		.559		
My friends are better at SPSS than I am		.465		
My friends will think I'm stupid for not being able to cope with SPSS		.453		
If I'm good at statistics my friends will think I'm a nerd		.345		
Everybody looks at me when I use SPSS		.336		
I have little experience of computers			.862	
SPSS always crashes when I try to use it			.635	
All computers hate me			.562	
I worry that I will cause irreparable damage because of my incompetence with computers			.558	
Computers have minds of their own and deliberately go wrong whenever I use them			.473	
Computers are useful only for playing games			.386	
Computers are out to get me			.318	
I have never been good at mathematics				-.851
I did badly at mathematics at school				-.734
I slip into a coma whenever I see an equation				-.675

Extraction Method: Principal Axis Factoring.
Rotation Method: Oblimin with Kaiser Normalization.[a]

a. Rotation converged in 17 iterations.

OUTPUT 17.9

structure matrix, factor 2 has fairly small relationships with the other factors, but all other factors have fairly large correlations. The fact that these correlations exist tells us that the constructs measured can be interrelated. If the constructs were independent then we would expect oblique rotation to provide an identical solution to an orthogonal rotation and the factor correlation matrix should be an identity matrix (i.e., all factors have correlation coefficients of 0). Therefore, this matrix can be used to assess whether it is reasonable to assume independence between factors: for these data it appears that we cannot assume independence and so the obliquely rotated solution is probably a better representation of reality.

CRAMMING SAM'S TIPS   **Interpretation**

- If you've conduced orthogonal rotation then look at the table labelled *Rotated Component Matrix*. For each variable, note the factor/component for which the variable has the highest loading (by 'high' I mean loadings above .4 when you ignore the plus or minus sign). Try to make sense of what the factors represent by looking for common themes in the items that load on them.
- If you've conducted oblique rotation then do the same as above but for the table labelled *Pattern Matrix*. Double-check what you find by doing the same thing for the structure matrix.

Structure Matrix

	Factor			
	1	2	3	4
I wake up under my duvet thinking that I am trapped under a normal distribution	.657		.475	-.391
I weep openly at the mention of central tendency	.621		.493	-.469
Standard deviations excite me	-.596	.486	-.409	.369
People try to tell you that SPSS makes statistics easier to understand but it doesn't	.593		.564	-.366
I dream that Pearson is attacking me with correlation coefficients	.586		.472	-.458
Statistics makes me cry	.552		.407	-.449
I can't sleep for thoughts of eigenvectors	.496			
I don't understand statistics	.492		.422	-.374
My friends are better at statistics than me		.572		
My friends will think I'm stupid for not being able to cope with SPSS		.486		
My friends are better at SPSS than I am		.484		
Everybody looks at me when I use SPSS	-.360	.425		
If I'm good at statistics my friends will think I'm a nerd		.328		
I have little experience of computers			.746	-.341
SPSS always crashes when I try to use it	.486		.720	-.407
All computers hate me	.479		.676	-.415
I worry that I will cause irreparable damage because of my incompetence with computers	.414		.673	-.457
Computers have minds of their own and deliberately go wrong whenever I use them	.489		.613	-.390
Computers are out to get me	.384		.510	-.428
Computers are useful only for playing games			.437	
I have never been good at mathematics	.314		.353	-.798
I did badly at mathematics at school	.369		.478	-.783
I slip into a coma whenever I see an equation	.404		.476	-.750

Extraction Method: Principal Axis Factoring.
Rotation Method: Oblimin with Kaiser Normalization.

OUTPUT 17.10

OUTPUT 17.11

Factor Correlation Matrix

Factor	1	2	3	4
1	1.000	-.296	.483	-.429
2	-.296	1.000	-.302	.186
3	.483	-.302	1.000	-.532
4	-.429	.186	-.532	1.000

Extraction Method: Principal Axis Factoring.
Rotation Method: Oblimin with Kaiser Normalization.

On a theoretical level the dependence between our factors does not cause concern; we might expect a fairly strong relationship between fear of maths, fear of statistics and fear of computers. Generally, the less mathematically and technically minded people struggle with statistics. However, we would not necessarily expect these constructs to correlate strongly with fear of peer evaluation (because this construct is more socially based). In fact, this factor is the one that correlates the least with all others – so, on a theoretical level, things have turned out rather well.

17.7.4. Factor scores ②

Having reached a suitable solution and rotated that solution, we can look at the factor scores. SPSS will display the component score matrix *B* (see Section 17.3.3.1) from which the factor scores are calculated. I haven't reproduced this table here because I can't think of a reason why most people would want to look at it. In the original analysis we asked for scores to be calculated based on the Anderson–Rubin method. You will find these scores in the data editor. There should be four new columns of data (one for each factor) labelled *FAC1_1*, *FAC2_1*, *FAC3_1* and *FAC4_1*, respectively. If you asked for factor scores in the oblique rotation then these scores will appear in the data editor in four other columns labelled *FAC2_1* and so on.

SELF-TEST Using what you learnt in Section 8.7.6, use the *Case Summaries* command to list the factor scores for these data (given that there are over 2500 cases, you might like to restrict the output to the first 10).

Case Summaries[a]

OUTPUT 17.12

	A–R factor score 1 for analysis 1	A–R factor score 2 for analysis 1	A–R factor score 3 for analysis 1	A–R factor score 4 for analysis 1
1	-1.12974	.05090	-1.58646	-.55242
2	-.04484	-.47739	-.22126	.64055
3	.15620	-.72240	.08299	-.90901
4	.79370	.61178	-.79341	-.31779
5	-.98251	.66284	-.35819	.54788
6	-.59551	2.13562	-.53156	-.52313
7	-1.33140	-.19415	.08213	.87306
8	-.91760	-.20011	-.02149	.96984
9	1.70800	1.45700	3.03959	.65963
10	-.37637	-.77093	.06181	1.58454
Total N	10	10	10	10

a. Limited to first 10 cases.

Output 17.12 shows the factor scores for the first 10 participants. It should be pretty clear that participant 9 scored highly on factors 1 to 3 and so this person is very anxious about statistics, computing and maths, but less so about peer evaluation (factor 4). Factor scores can be used in this way to assess the relative fear of one person compared to another, or we could add the scores up to obtain a single score for each participant (which we might assume represents SPSS anxiety as a whole). We can also use factor scores in regression when groups of predictors correlate so highly that there is multicollinearity. However, people do not normally use factor scores themselves but instead sum scores on items that they have decided load on the same factor (e.g., create a score for statistics anxiety by adding up a person's scores on items 1, 3, 4, 5, 12, 16, 20 and 21).

17.7.5. Summary ②

To sum up, the analyses revealed four underlying scales in our questionnaire that may or may not relate to genuine sub-components of SPSS anxiety. It also seems as though an obliquely rotated solution was preferred due to the interrelationships between factors. The use of factor analysis is purely exploratory; it should be used only to guide future hypotheses, or to inform researchers about patterns within data sets. A great many decisions are left to the researcher using factor analysis and I urge you to make informed decisions, rather than basing decisions on the outcomes you would like to get. The next question is whether or not our scale is reliable.

17.8. How to report factor analysis ①

When reporting factor analysis we should provide our readers with enough information to form an informed opinion about what we've done. We should be clear about our criteria for extracting factors and the method of rotation used. We should also produce a table of the rotated factor loadings of all items and flag (in bold) values above a criterion level (I would personally choose .40, but see Section 17.4.6.2). We should also report the percentage of variance that each factor explains and possibly the eigenvalue too. Table 17.1 shows an example of such a table for the SAQ data (oblique rotation); note that I have also reported the sample size in the title.

In my opinion, a table of factor loadings and a description of the analysis are a bare minimum. You could consider (if it's not too large) including the table of correlations from which someone could reproduce your analysis (should they want to), and some information on sample size adequacy. For this example we might write something like this:

✓ A principal axis factor analysis was conducted on the 23 items with oblique rotation (direct oblimin). The Kaiser–Meyer–Olkin measure verified the sampling adequacy for the analysis, KMO = .93 ('marvellous' according to Hutcheson & Sofroniou, 1999), and all KMO values for individual items were greater than .77, which is well above the acceptable limit of .5 (Field, 2013). An initial analysis was run to obtain eigenvalues for each factor in the data. Four factors had eigenvalues over Kaiser's criterion of 1 and in combination explained 50.32% of the variance. The scree plot was ambiguous and showed inflexions that would justify retaining either 2 or 4 factors. We retained 4 factors because of the large sample size and the convergence of the scree plot and Kaiser's criterion on this value. Table 17.1 shows the factor loadings after rotation. The items that cluster on the same factor suggest that factor 1 represents a fear of statistics, factor 2 represents peer evaluation concerns, factor 3 a fear of computers and factor 4 a fear of maths.

17.9. Reliability analysis ②

17.9.1. Measures of reliability ③

If you're using factor analysis to validate a questionnaire, it is useful to check the reliability of your scale.

SELF-TEST   Thinking back to Chapter 1, what are reliability and test–retest reliability?

How do I tell if my questionnaire is reliable?

Reliability means that a measure (or in this case questionnaire) should consistently reflect the construct that it is measuring. One way to think of this is that, other things being equal, a person should get the same score on a questionnaire if they complete it at two different points in time (we have already discovered that this is called test–retest reliability). So, someone who is terrified of SPSS and who scores highly on our SAQ should score similarly highly if we tested them a month later (assuming they hadn't gone into some kind of

TABLE 17.1 Summary of exploratory factor analysis results for the SPSS anxiety questionnaire ($N = 2571$)

Item	Rotated Factor Loadings			
	Fear of Statistics	Peer Evaluation	Fear of Computers	Fear of Maths
I wake up under my duvet thinking that I am trapped under a normal distribution	**.54**	−.04	.17	−.06
I can't sleep for thoughts of eigenvectors	**.47**	−.14	−.08	−.05
I weep openly at the mention of central tendency	**.45**	−.05	.17	−.18
I dream that Pearson is attacking me with correlation coefficients	**.44**	.08	.18	−.19
Standard deviations excite me	**−.44**	.32	−.05	.10
Statistics makes me cry	**.43**	.10	.11	−.23
People try to tell you that SPSS makes statistics easier to understand but it doesn't	**.41**	−.04	.36	.01
I don't understand statistics	**.36**	.05	.20	−.13
My friends are better at statistics than me	−.09	**.56**	−.02	−.11
My friends are better at SPSS than I am	.07	**.47**	−.11	.04
My friends will think I'm stupid for not being able to cope with SPSS	−.18	**.45**	.04	−.05
If I'm good at statistics my friends will think I'm a nerd	.10	**.35**	.00	.07
Everybody looks at me when I use SPSS	−.22	**.34**	−.08	.01
I have little experience of computers	−.22	−.01	**.86**	.03
SPSS always crashes when I try to use it	.18	−.01	**.64**	.01
All computers hate me	.19	−.02	**.56**	−.03
I worry that I will cause irreparable damage because of my incompetence with computers	.08	−.04	**.56**	−.12
Computers have minds of their own and deliberately go wrong whenever I use them	.24	−.02	**.47**	−.03
Computers are useful only for playing games	.00	−.06	**.39**	−.06
Computers are out to get me	.11	−.13	**.32**	−.19
I have never been good at mathematics	.01	.05	−.09	**−.85**
I did badly at mathematics at school	−.01	−.11	.06	**−.73**
I slip into a coma whenever I see an equation	.08	.02	.09	**−.68**
Eigenvalues	7.29	1.74	1.32	1.23
% of variance	31.70	7.56	5.73	5.34
α	.82	.57	.82	.82

Note: Factor loadings over .40 appear in bold

SPSS-anxiety therapy in that month). Another way to look at reliability is to say that two people who are the same in terms of the construct being measured should get the same score. So, if we took two people who were equally SPSS-phobic, then they should get more or less identical scores on the SAQ. Likewise, if we took two people who loved SPSS, they should both get equally low scores. It should be apparent that the SAQ wouldn't be an accurate measure of SPSS anxiety if we took someone who loved SPSS and someone who

NICHOLS, L. A. & NICKI, R. (2004). *PSYCHOLOGY OF ADDICTIVE BEHAVIORS*, 18Â, 381–384.

LABCOAT LENI'S REAL RESEARCH 17.1

Worldwide addiction? ②

In 2007 it was estimated that around 179 million people worldwide used the Internet. From the increasing popularity (and usefulness) of the Internet has emerged a serious and recognized problem of internet addiction. To research this construct it's helpful to be able to measure it, so Laura Nichols and Richard Nicki developed the Internet Addiction Scale (Nichols & Nicki, 2004). Nichols and Nicki's 36-item questionnaire contains items such as 'I have stayed on the Internet longer than I intended to' and 'My grades/work have suffered because of my Internet use' to which responses are made on a 5-point scale (Never, Rarely, Sometimes, Frequently, Always). (Incidentally, while researching this topic I encountered

an Internet addiction recovery website that offered a whole host of resources (e.g., questionnaires, online support groups, videos, podcasts, etc.) that would keep you online for ages. It struck me that this was like having a heroin addiction recovery centre that had a huge pile of free heroin in the reception area.)

The data from 207 people in this study are in the file **Nichols & Nicki (2004).sav**. The authors dropped two items because they had low means and variances, and dropped three others because of relatively low correlations with other items. They performed a principal component analysis on the remaining 31 items. Labcoat Leni wants you to run some descriptive statistics to work out which two items were dropped for having low means/variances, then inspect a correlation matrix to find the three items that were dropped for having low correlations. Finally, he wants you to run a principal component analysis on the data. Answers are in the additional material on the companion website (or look at the original article).

was terrified of it and they got the same score! In statistical terms, the usual way to look at reliability is based on the idea that individual items (or sets of items) should produce results consistent with the overall questionnaire. So, if we take someone scared of SPSS, then their overall score on the SAQ will be high; if the SAQ is reliable then if we randomly select some items from it the person's score on those items should also be high.

The simplest way to do this in practice is to use **split-half reliability**. This method splits the scale set into two randomly selected sets of items. A score for each participant is calculated on each half of the scale. If a scale is reliable a person's score on one half of the scale should be the same (or similar) to their score on the other half. Across several participants, scores from the two halves of the questionnaire should correlate very highly. The correlation between the two halves is the statistic computed in the split-half method, with large correlations being a sign of reliability. The problem with this method is that there are several ways in which a set of data can be randomly split into two and so the results could be a product of the way in which the data were split. To overcome this problem, Cronbach (1951) came up with a measure that is loosely equivalent to creating two sets of items in every way possible and computing the correlation coefficient for each split. The average of these values is equivalent to **Cronbach's alpha, α**, which is the most common measure of scale reliability:[10]

$$\alpha = \frac{N^2 \overline{\text{cov}}}{\sum s_{\text{item}}^2 + \sum \text{cov}_{\text{item}}}$$

(17.6)

[10] Although this is the easiest way to conceptualize Cronbach's, α, whether or not it is exactly equal to the average of all possible split-half reliabilities depends on exactly how you calculate the split-half reliability (see the glossary for computational details). If you use the Spearman–Brown formula, which takes no account of item standard deviations, then Cronbach's will be equal to the average split-half reliability only when the item standard deviations are equal; otherwise α will be smaller than the average. However, if you use a formula for split-half reliability that does account for item standard deviations (such as Flanagan, 1937; Rulon, 1939) then α will always equal the average split-half reliability (see Cortina, 1993).

This equation may look complicated, but actually isn't. For each item on our scale we can calculate two things: the variance within the item, and the covariance between a particular item and any other item on the scale. Put another way, we can construct a variance–covariance matrix of all items. In this matrix the diagonal elements will be the variance within a particular item, and the off-diagonal elements will be covariances between pairs of items. The top half of the equation is simply the number of items (N) squared multiplied by the average covariance between items (the average of the off-diagonal elements in the aforementioned variance–covariance matrix). The bottom half is the sum of all the item variances and item covariances (i.e., the sum of everything in the variance–covariance matrix).

There is a standardized version of the coefficient too, which essentially uses the same equation except that correlations are used rather than covariances, and the bottom half of the equation uses the sum of the elements in the correlation matrix of items (including the 1s that appear on the diagonal of that matrix). The normal alpha is appropriate when items on a scale are summed to produce a single score for that scale (the standardized alpha is not appropriate in these cases). The standardized alpha is useful, though, when items on a scale are standardized before being summed.

17.9.2. Interpreting Cronbach's α (some cautionary tales) ②

You'll often see in books or journal articles, or be told by people, that a value of .7 to .8 is an acceptable value for Cronbach's α; values substantially lower indicate an unreliable scale. Kline (1999) notes that although the generally accepted value of .8 is appropriate for cognitive tests such as intelligence tests, for ability tests a cut-off point of .7 is more suitable. He goes on to say that when dealing with psychological constructs, values below even .7 can, realistically, be expected because of the diversity of the constructs being measured. Some even suggest that in the early stages of research, values as low as .5 will suffice (Nunnally, 1978). However, there are many reasons not to use these general guidelines, not least of which is that they distract you from thinking about what the value means within the context of the research you're doing (Pedhazur & Schmelkin, 1991).

We'll now look at some issues in interpreting alpha, which have been discussed particularly well by Cortina (1993) and Pedhazur and Schmelkin (1991). First, the value of α depends on the number of items on the scale. You'll notice that the top half of the equation for α includes the number of items squared. Therefore, as the number of items on the scale increases, α will increase. As such, it's possible to get a large value of α because you have a lot of items on the scale, and not because your scale is reliable. For example, Cortina (1993) reports data from two scales, both of which have $\alpha = .8$. The first scale has only three items, and the average correlation between items was a respectable .57; however, the second scale had 10 items with an average correlation between these items of a less respectable .28. Clearly the internal consistency of these scales differs, but according to Cronbach's α they are both equally reliable.

Second, people tend to think that alpha measures 'unidimensionality', or the extent to which the scale measures one underlying factor or construct. This is true when there is one factor underlying the data (see Cortina, 1993), but Grayson (2004) demonstrates that data sets with the same α can have very different factor structures. He showed that $\alpha = .8$ can be achieved in a scale with one underlying factor, with two moderately correlated factors and with two uncorrelated factors. Cortina (1993) has also shown that with more than 12 items, and fairly high correlations between items ($r > .5$), α can reach values around and above .7 (.65 to .84). These results show that α should not be used as a measure of 'unidimensionality'. Indeed, Cronbach (1951) suggested that if several factors exist then the formula should be applied separately to items relating to different factors. In other words, if your questionnaire has subscales, α should be applied separately to these subscales.

Eek! My alpha
is negative:
is that correct?

The final warning is about items that have a reverse phrasing. For example, in the SAQ there is one item (question 3) that was phrased the opposite way around to all other items. The item was 'standard deviations excite me'. Compare this to any other item and you'll see it requires the opposite response. For example, item 1 is 'statistics make me cry'. If you don't like statistics then you'll strongly agree with this statement and so will get a score of 5 on our scale. For item 3, if you hate statistics then standard deviations are unlikely to excite you so you'll strongly disagree and get a score of 1 on the scale. These reverse-phrased items are important for reducing response bias; participants will need to pay attention to the questions. For factor analysis, this reverse phrasing doesn't matter; all that happens is you get a negative factor loading for any reversed items (in fact, you'll see that item 3 has a negative factor loading in Output 17.9). However, these reverse-scored items will affect alpha. To see why, think about the equation for Cronbach's α. The top half incorporates the *average* covariance between items. If an item is reverse-phrased then it will have a negative relationship with other items, hence the covariances between this item and other items will be negative. The average covariance is the sum of covariances divided by the number of covariances, and by including a bunch of negative values we reduce the sum of covariances, and hence we also reduce Cronbach's α, because the top half of the equation gets smaller. In extreme cases, it is even possible to get a negative value for Cronbach's α, simply because the magnitude of negative covariances is bigger than the magnitude of positive ones. A negative Cronbach's α doesn't make much sense, but it does happen, and if it does, ask yourself whether you included any reverse-phrased items.

If you have reverse-phrased items then you also have to reverse the way in which they're scored before you conduct reliability analysis. This is quite easy. To take our SAQ data, we have one item which is currently scored as 1 = strongly disagree, 2 = disagree, 3 = neither, 4 = agree and 5 = strongly agree. This is fine for items phrased in such a way that agreement indicates statistics anxiety, but for item 3 (standard deviations excite me), disagreement indicates statistics anxiety. To reflect this numerically, we need to reverse the scale such that 1 = strongly agree, 2 = agree, 3 = neither, 4 = disagree and 5 = strongly disagree. In doing so, an anxious person still gets 5 on this item (because they'd strongly disagree with it).

To reverse the scoring find the maximum value of your response scale (in this case 5) and add 1 to it (so you get 6 in this case). Then for each person, you take this value and subtract from it the score they actually got. Therefore, someone who scored 5 originally now scores $6-5 = 1$, and someone who scored 1 originally now gets $6-1 = 5$. Someone in the middle of the scale with a score of 3 will still get $6-3 = 3$. Obviously it would take a long time to do this for each person, but we can get SPSS to do it for us.

SELF-TEST   Using what you learnt in Chapter 5, use the *compute* command to reverse-score item 3. (Clue: Remember that you are simply changing the variable to 6 minus its original value.)

17.9.3. Reliability analysis in SPSS ②

Let's test the reliability of the SAQ using the data in **SAQ.sav**. You should have reverse-scored item 3 (see above), but if you can't be bothered then load the file **SAQ (Item 3**

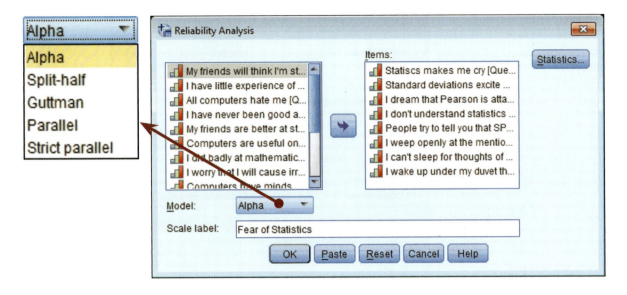

FIGURE 17.15 Main dialog box for reliability analysis.

Reversed).sav instead. Remember also that I said we should conduct reliability analysis on any subscales individually. If we use the results from our oblique rotation (Output 17.9), then we have four subscales:

1 Subscale 1 (*Fear of statistics*): items 1, 3, 4, 5, 12, 16, 20, 21

2 Subscale 2 (*Peer evaluation*): items 2, 9, 19, 22, 23

3 Subscale 3 (*Fear of computers*): items 6, 7, 10, 13, 14, 15, 18

4 Subscale 4 (*Fear of mathematics*): items 8, 11, 17

To conduct each reliability analysis on these data you need to select Analyze Scale ▶ Reliability Analysis... to display the dialog box in Figure 17.15. Select any items from the list that you want to analyse (to begin with, let's do the items from the fear of statistics subscale: items 1, 3, 4, 5, 12, 16, 20 and 21) on the left-hand side of the dialog box and drag them to the box labelled Items (or click on). Remember that you can select several items at the same time if you hold down the *Ctrl* (*Cmd* on a Mac) key while you select the variables.

There are several reliability analyses you can run, but the default option is Cronbach's α. You can change the method (e.g., to the split-half method) by clicking on Alpha ▼ to reveal a drop-down list of possibilities, but the default method is a good one to select. Also, it's a good idea to type the name of the scale (in this case 'Fear of Statistics') into the box labelled *Scale label* because this will add a header to the SPSS output with whatever you type in this box: typing a sensible name here will make your output easier to follow.

If you click on Statistics... you can access the dialog box in Figure 17.16. In the statistics dialog box you can select several things, but the one most important for questionnaire reliability is: *Scale if item deleted*. This option tells us what the value of α would be if each item were deleted. If our questionnaire is reliable then we would not expect any one item to greatly affect the overall reliability. In other words, no item should cause a substantial decrease in α. If it does then you should consider dropping that item from the questionnaire to improve reliability.

FIGURE 17.16
Statistics
for reliability
analysis

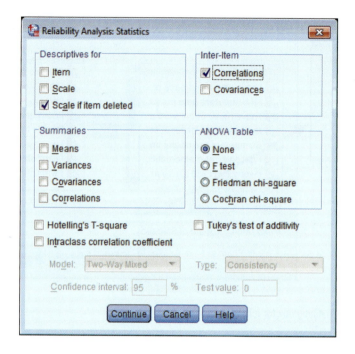

The inter-item correlations and covariances (and summaries) provide us with correlation coefficients and averages for items on our scale. We should already have these values from our factor analysis, so there is little point in selecting these options. Options like the *F test*, *Friedman chi-square* (if your data are ranked), *Cochran chi-square* (if your data are dichotomous), and *Hotelling's T-square* use these tests to compare the central tendency of different items on the questionnaire. These tests might be useful to check that items have similar distributional properties (i.e., the same average value), but given the large sample sizes you ought to be using for factor analysis, they will inevitably produce significant results even when only small differences exist between the questionnaire items.

You can also request an **intraclass correlation coefficient (ICC)**. The correlation coefficients that we encountered earlier in this book measure the relation between variables that measure different things. For example, the correlation between listening to Deathspell Omega and Satanism involves two classes of measures: the type of music a person likes and their religious beliefs. Intraclass correlations measure the relationship between two variables that measure the same thing (i.e., variables within the same class). Two common uses are in comparing paired data (such as twins) on the same measure, and assessing the consistency between judges' ratings of a set of objects (hence the reason why it is found in the reliability statistics in SPSS). If you'd like to know more, see Section 20.2.1.

Use the simple set of options in Figure 17.16 to run a basic reliability analysis. Click on Continue to return to the main dialog box and then click on OK to run the analysis.

17.9.4.   Reliability analysis output ②

Output 17.13 shows the results of this basic reliability analysis for the fear of statistics subscale. The value of Cronbach's α is presented in a small table and indicates the overall reliability of the scale. Bearing in mind what we've already noted about effects from the number of items, and how daft it is to apply general rules, we're looking for values in the region of about .7 to .8. In this case α is .821, which is certainly in the region indicated by Kline (1999), and probably indicates good reliability.

Item–Total Statistics

	Scale Mean if Item Deleted	Scale Variance if Item Deleted	Corrected Item–Total Correlation	Squared Multiple Correlation	Cronbach's Alpha if Item Deleted
Statistics makes me cry	21.76	21.442	.536	.343	.802
Standard deviations excite me	20.72	19.825	.549	.309	.800
I dream that Pearson is attacking me with correlation coefficients	21.35	20.410	.575	.355	.796
I don't understand statistics	21.41	20.942	.494	.272	.807
People try to tell you that SPSS makes statistics easier to understand but it doesn't	20.97	20.639	.572	.337	.796
I weep openly at the mention of central tendency	21.25	20.451	.597	.389	.793
I can't sleep for thoughts of eigenvectors	20.51	21.176	.419	.244	.818
I wake up under my duvet thinking that I am trapped under a normal distribution	20.96	19.939	.606	.399	.791

Reliability Statistics

Cronbach's Alpha	Cronbach's Alpha Based on Standardized Items	N of Items
.821	.823	8

OUTPUT 17.13

In the table labelled *Item-Total Statistics* the column labelled *Corrected Item-Total Correlation* has the correlations between each item and the total score from the questionnaire. In a reliable scale all items should correlate with the total. So, we're looking for items that don't correlate with the overall score from the scale: if any of these values are less than about .3 then we've got problems, because it means that a particular item does not correlate very well with the scale overall. Items with low correlations may have to be dropped. For these data, all data have item–total correlations above .3, which is encouraging.

The values in the column labelled *Cronbach's Alpha if Item Deleted* are the values of the overall α if that item isn't included in the calculation. As such, they reflect the change in Cronbach's α that would be seen if a particular item were deleted. The overall α is .821, and so all values in this column should be around that same value. We're actually looking for values of alpha greater than the overall α. If you think about it, if the deletion of an item increases Cronbach's α then this means that the deletion of that item improves reliability. Therefore, any items that have values of α in this column greater than the overall α may need to be deleted from the scale to improve its reliability. None of the items here would increase alpha if they were deleted, which is good news. It's worth noting that if items do need to be removed at this stage then you should rerun your factor analysis as well to make sure that the deletion of the item has not affected the factor structure

SELF-TEST   Run reliability analyses on the other three subscales.

Just to illustrate the importance of reverse-scoring items before running reliability analysis, Output 17.14 shows the reliability analysis for the fear of statistics subscale but done on the original data (i.e., without item 3 being reverse-scored). Note that the overall α is considerably lower (.605 rather than .821). Also, note that this item has a negative item–total correlation (which is a good way to spot if you have a potential reverse-scored item in the data that hasn't been reverse-scored). Finally, note that for item 3, the α if item deleted

Item–Total Statistics

	Scale Mean if Item Deleted	Scale Variance if Item Deleted	Corrected Item–Total Correlation	Squared Multiple Correlation	Cronbach's Alpha if Item Deleted
Statistics makes me cry	20.93	12.125	.505	.343	.521
Standard deviations excite me	20.72	19.825	-.549	.309	.800
I dream that Pearson is attacking me with correlation coefficients	20.52	11.447	.526	.355	.505
I don't understand statistics	20.58	11.714	.466	.272	.523
People try to tell you that SPSS makes statistics easier to understand but it doesn't	20.14	11.739	.501	.337	.515
I weep openly at the mention of central tendency	20.42	11.584	.529	.389	.507
I can't sleep for thoughts of eigenvectors	19.68	12.107	.353	.244	.558
I wake up under my duvet thinking that I am trapped under a normal distribution	20.13	11.189	.541	.399	.497

Reliability Statistics

Cronbach's Alpha	Cronbach's Alpha Based on Standardized Items	N of Items
.605	.641	8

OUTPUT 17.14

is .8. That is, if this item were deleted then the reliability would improve from about .6 to about .8. This, I hope, illustrates that failing to reverse-score items that have been phrased oppositely to other items on the scale will mess up your reliability analysis.

Let's now look at our subscale of peer evaluation. For our subscale of peer evaluation you should get the output in Output 17.15. The overall reliability is .57, which is nothing to bake a cake for. The overall α is quite low, and although this is in keeping with what Kline says we should expect for this kind of social science data, it is well below the statistics subscale and (as we shall see) the other two. The scale has five items, compared to seven, eight and three on the other scales, so its reliability relative to the other scales is not going to be dramatically affected by the number of items. The values in the column labelled *Corrected Item-Total Correlation* are all around .3, and smaller for item 23. These results again indicate questionable internal consistency and identify item 23 as a potential problem. The values in the column labelled *Cronbach's Alpha if Item Deleted* indicate that none of the items here would increase the reliability if they were deleted because all values in this column are less than the overall reliability of .57. The items on this subscale cover quite diverse themes of peer evaluation, and this might explain the relative lack of consistency; we probably need to rethink this subscale.

Moving on to the fear of computers subscale, Output 17.16 shows an overall α of .823, which is pretty good. The values in the column labelled *Corrected Item-Total Correlation*

OUTPUT 17.15

Item–Total Statistics

	Scale Mean if Item Deleted	Scale Variance if Item Deleted	Corrected Item–Total Correlation	Squared Multiple Correlation	Cronbach's Alpha if Item Deleted
My friends will think I'm stupid for not being able to cope with SPSS	11.46	8.119	.339	.134	.515
My friends are better at statistics than me	10.24	6.395	.391	.167	.476
Everybody looks at me when I use SPSS	10.79	7.381	.316	.106	.522
My friends are better at SPSS than I am	10.20	7.282	.378	.144	.487
If I'm good at statistics my friends will think I'm a nerd	9.65	7.988	.239	.069	.563

Reliability Statistics

Cronbach's Alpha	Cronbach's Alpha Based on Standardized Items	N of Items
.570	.572	5

OUTPUT 17.16

Item–Total Statistics

	Scale Mean if Item Deleted	Scale Variance if Item Deleted	Corrected Item–Total Correlation	Squared Multiple Correlation	Cronbach's Alpha if Item Deleted
I have little experience of computers	15.87	17.614	.619	.398	.791
All computers hate me	15.17	17.737	.619	.395	.790
Computers are useful only for playing games	15.81	20.736	.400	.167	.824
I worry that I will cause irreparable damage because of my incompetenece with computers	15.64	18.809	.607	.384	.794
Computers have minds of their own and deliberately go wrong whenever I use them	15.22	18.719	.577	.350	.798
Computers are out to get me	15.33	19.322	.491	.250	.812
SPSS always crashes when I try to use it	15.52	17.832	.647	.447	.786

Reliability Statistics

Cronbach's Alpha	Cronbach's Alpha Based on Standardized Items	N of Items
.823	.821	7

are again all above .3, which is also good. The values in the column labelled *Cronbach's Alpha if Item Deleted* show that none of the items would increase the reliability if they were deleted. This indicates that all items are positively contributing to the overall reliability.

Finally, for the fear of maths subscale, Output 17.17 shows an overall reliability of .819, which indicates good reliability. The values in the column labelled *Corrected Item-Total Correlation* are all above .3, which is good, and the values in the column labelled *Cronbach's Alpha if Item Deleted* indicate that none of the items here would increase the reliability if they were deleted because all values in this column are less than the overall reliability value.

OUTPUT 17.17

Item–Total Statistics

	Scale Mean if Item Deleted	Scale Variance if Item Deleted	Corrected Item–Total Correlation	Squared Multiple Correlation	Cronbach's Alpha if Item Deleted
I have never been good at mathematics	4.72	2.470	.684	.470	.740
I did badly at mathematics at school	4.70	2.453	.682	.467	.742
I slip into a coma whenever I see an equation	4.49	2.504	.652	.425	.772

Reliability Statistics

Cronbach's Alpha	Cronbach's Alpha Based on Standardized Items	N of Items
.819	.819	3

CRAMMING SAM'S TIPS   Reliability

- Reliability analysis is used to measure the consistency of a measure.
- Remember to reverse-score any items that were reverse-phrased on the original questionnaire before you run the analysis.
- Run separate reliability analyses for all subscales of your questionnaire.
- Cronbach's α indicates the overall reliability of a questionnaire, and values around .8 are good (or .7 for ability tests and the like).
- The *Cronbach's Alpha if Item Deleted* column tells you whether removing an item will improve the overall reliability. Values greater than the overall reliability indicate that removing that item will improve the overall reliability of the scale. Look for items that dramatically increase the value of α and remove them.
- If you remove items, rerun your factor analysis to check that the factor structure still holds.

17.10. How to report reliability analysis ②

You can report the reliabilities in the text using the symbol α and remembering that because Cronbach's α can't be larger than 1 we drop the zero before the decimal place (if we are following APA practice):

✓ The fear of computers, fear of statistics and fear of maths subscales of the SAQ all had high reliabilities, all Cronbach's $\alpha = .82$. However, the fear of negative peer evaluation subscale had relatively low reliability, Cronbach's $\alpha = .57$.

However, the most common way to report reliability analysis when it follows a factor analysis is to report the values of Cronbach's α as part of the table of factor loadings. For example, in Table 17.1 notice that in the last row of the table I quoted the value of Cronbach's α for each subscale in turn.

17.11. Brian's attempt to woo Jane ①

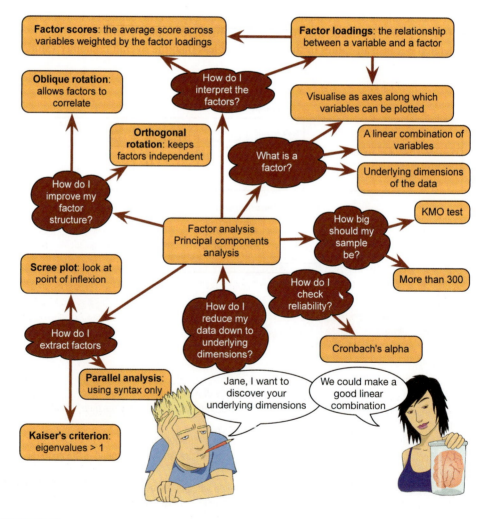

FIGURE 17.17
What Brian learnt from this chapter

17.12. What next? ②

At the age of 23 I took it upon myself to become a living homage to the digestive system. I furiously devoured articles and books on statistics (some of them I even understood), I mentally chewed over them, I broke them down with the stomach acid of my intellect, I stripped them of their goodness and nutrients, I compacted them down, and after about two years I forced the smelly brown remnants of those intellectual meals out of me in the form of a book. I was mentally exhausted at the end of it. 'It's a good job I'll never have to do that again', I thought.

17.13. Key terms that I've discovered

Alpha factoring
Anderson–Rubin method
Common factor
Common variance
Communality
Component matrix
Confirmatory factor analysis
Cronbach's α
Direct oblimin
Extraction
Equamax
Factor analysis
Factor loading

Factor matrix
Factor scores
Factor transformation matrix, Λ
Intraclass correlation coefficient (ICC)
Kaiser's criterion
Latent variable
Kaiser–Meyer–Olkin (KMO) measure of sampling adequacy
Oblique rotation
Orthogonal rotation
Pattern matrix

Principal component analysis (PCA)
Promax
Quartimax
Random variance
Rotation
Scree plot
Singularity
Split-half reliability
Structure matrix
Unique factor
Unique variance
Varimax

17.14. Smart Alex's tasks

- **Task 1**: Rerun the analysis in this chapter using principal component analysis and compare the results to those in the chapter. (Set the iterations to convergence to 30.) ②

- **Task 2**: The University of Sussex constantly seeks to employ the best people possible as lecturers. They wanted to revise the 'Teaching of Statistics for Scientific Experiments' (TOSSE) questionnaire, which is based on Bland's theory that says that good research methods lecturers should have: (1) a profound love of statistics; (2) an enthusiasm for experimental design; (3) a love of teaching; and (4) a complete absence of normal interpersonal skills. These characteristics should be related (i.e., correlated). The University revised this questionnaire to become the 'Teaching of Statistics for Scientific Experiments – Revised' (TOSSE-R). They gave this questionnaire to 239 research methods lecturers around the world to see if it supported Bland's theory. The questionnaire is in Figure 17.18, and the data are in **TOSSE-R.sav**. Conduct a factor analysis (with appropriate rotation) and interpret the factor structure. ②

- **Task 3**: Dr Sian Williams (University of Brighton) devised a questionnaire to measure organizational ability. She predicted five factors to do with organizational ability: (1) preference for organization; (2) goal achievement; (3) planning approach; (4) acceptance of delays; and (5) preference for routine. These dimensions are theoretically independent. Williams' questionnaire contains 28 items using a 7-point Likert scale (1 = strongly disagree, 4 = neither, 7 = strongly agree). She gave it to 239 people. Run a principal component analysis on the data in **Williams.sav**. ②

- **Task 4**: Zibarras, Port, and Woods (2008) looked at the relationship between personality and creativity. They used the Hogan Development Survey (HDS), which measures 11 dysfunctional dispositions of employed adults: being **volatile, mistrustful, cautious, detached, passive-aggressive, arrogant, manipulative, dramatic, eccentric, perfectionist**, and **dependent**. Zibarras et al. wanted to reduce these 11 traits and, based on parallel analysis, found that they could be reduced to three components. They ran a principal component analysis with varimax rotation. Repeat this analysis (**Zibarras et al. (2008).sav**) to see which personality dimensions clustered together (see page 210 of the original paper). ②

Answers can be found on the companion website.

FIGURE 17.18
The TOSSE-R
questionnaire

Teaching of Statistics for Scientific Experiments — Revised (TOSSE-R)

		SD	D	N	A	SA
1.	I once woke up in a vegetable patch hugging a turnip that I'd mistakenly dug up thinking it was Roy's largest root	○	○	○	○	○
2.	If I had a big gun I'd shoot all the students I have to teach	○	○	○	○	○
3.	I memorize probability values for the F-distribution	○	○	○	○	○
4.	I worship at the shrine of Pearson	○	○	○	○	○
5.	I still live with my mother and have little personal hygiene	○	○	○	○	○
6.	Teaching others makes me want to swallow a large bottle of bleach because the pain of my burning oesophagus would be light relief in comparison	○	○	○	○	○
7.	Helping others to understand sums of squares is a great feeling	○	○	○	○	○
8.	I like control conditions	○	○	○	○	○
9.	I calculate 3 ANOVAs in my head before getting out of bed	○	○	○	○	○
10.	I could spend all day explaining statistics to people	○	○	○	○	○
11.	I like it when I've helped people to understand factor rotation	○	○	○	○	○
12.	People fall asleep as soon as I open my mouth to speak	○	○	○	○	○
13.	Designing experiments is fun	○	○	○	○	○
14.	I'd rather think about appropriate dependent variables than go to the pub	○	○	○	○	○
15.	I soil my pants with excitement at the mere mention of Factor Analysis	○	○	○	○	○
16.	Thinking about whether to use repeated- or independent-measures thrills me	○	○	○	○	○
17.	I enjoy sitting in the park contemplating whether to use participant observation in my next experiment	○	○	○	○	○
18.	Standing in front of 300 people in no way makes me lose control of my bowels	○	○	○	○	○
19.	I like to help students	○	○	○	○	○
20.	Passing on knowledge is the greatest gift you can bestow on an individual	○	○	○	○	○
21.	Thinking about Bonferroni corrections gives me a tingly feeling in my groin	○	○	○	○	○
22.	I quiver with excitement when thinking about designing my next experiment	○	○	○	○	○
22.	I often spend my spare time talking to the pigeons ... and even they die of boredom	○	○	○	○	○
23.	I tried to build myself a time machine so that I could go back to the 1930s and follow Fisher around on my hands and knees licking the floor on which he'd just trodden	○	○	○	○	○
25.	I love teaching	○	○	○	○	○
26.	I spend lots of time helping students	○	○	○	○	○
27.	I love teaching because students have to pretend to like me or they'll get bad marks	○	○	○	○	○
28.	My cat is my only friend	○	○	○	○	○

17.15. Further reading

Cortina, J. M. (1993). What is coefficient alpha? An examination of theory and applications. *Journal of Applied Psychology*, 78, 98–104. (A very readable paper on Cronbach's α.)

Dunteman, G. E. (1989). *Principal components analysis*. Sage University Paper Series on Quantitative Applications in the Social Sciences, 07-069. Newbury Park, CA: Sage. (This monograph is quite high level but comprehensive.)

Pedhazur, E., & Schmelkin, L. (1991). *Measurement, design and analysis*. Hillsdale, NJ: Erlbaum. (Chapter 22 is an excellent introduction to the theory of factor analysis.)

Tabachnick, B. G., & Fidell, L. S. (2012). *Using multivariate statistics* (6th ed.). Boston: Allyn & Bacon.

18 Categorical data

FIGURE 18.1
Midway through writing the second edition of this book, things became a little strange

18.1. What will this chapter tell me? ①

We discovered in the previous chapter that I wrote a book. This book. There are a lot of good things about writing books. The main benefit is that your parents are impressed. They're not *that* impressed, because they think that a good book sells as many copies as *Harry Potter* and that people should queue outside bookshops for the latest enthralling instalment of *Discovering statistics* .... My parents are, consequently, quite baffled about how this book is seen as successful, yet I don't get invited to dinner by the Queen. Nevertheless, given that my family don't really understand what I do, books are tangible proof that I do *something*. The size of this book and the fact it has equations in it is an added bonus because it makes me look cleverer than I actually am. However, there is a price to pay, which is immeasurable mental anguish. In England we don't talk about our emotions, because we fear that if they get out into the open, civilization as we know it will collapse, so I definitely will not mention that the writing process for the second edition was so stressful that I came within one of Fuzzy's whiskers of a total meltdown. It took me two years to recover, just in time to start thinking about the third edition. Still, it was worth it because the feedback suggests that some people found the book vaguely useful. Of course, the publishers focus less on the book's helpfulness and more on sales figures and comparisons with other books. They have databases that have sales figures for this book and its competitors in different 'markets' (you are not a person, you are a 'consumer', and you don't live in a country, you live in a 'market'), and they gibber and twitch at their consoles creating pink frequency distributions (with 3-D effects) of these values. The data they get are frequency data (the number of books sold in a certain period of time). Therefore, if they wanted to compare sales of this book to its competitors, in different countries, they would need to read this chapter because it's all about analysing data for which we know only the frequency with which events occur. Of course, they won't read this chapter, but they should …

18.2. Analysing categorical data ①

So far we have looked at fitting models with categorical predictor variables, but always predicting a continuous outcome variable. Sometimes, however, we want to predict categorical outcome variables. In other words, we want to predict into which category an entity falls. For example, we might want to predict whether someone is pregnant or not, for which political party a person voted, whether a tumour is benign or malignant, whether a sports team will win, lose or draw. In all of these cases, an entity can fall into only one category, for example a woman can be pregnant or not; she can't be 'a bit pregnant'. The next two chapters deal with statistical models for categorical outcomes. We'll begin with some basic models of associations between categorical variables, then look at predicting categorical outcomes from categorical predictors, then in the next chapter we'll move on to look at predicting categorical outcomes from both categorical and continuous predictor variables.

18.3. Theory of analysing categorical data ①

We will begin by looking at the simplest situation that you could encounter; that is, quantifying the relationship between two categorical variables. With categorical variables we can't use the mean or any similar statistic because the mean of a categorical variable is completely meaningless: the numeric values you attach to different categories are arbitrary, and the mean of those numeric values will depend on how many members each category has. Therefore, when we've measured only categorical variables, we analyse the number of things that fall into each combination of categories (i.e., the frequencies). For example, a researcher was interested in whether animals could be trained to line-dance. He took 200 cats and tried to train them to line-dance by giving them either food or affection as a reward for dance-like behaviour. At the end of the week he counted how many animals could line-dance and how many could not. There are two categorical variables here: **training** (the animal was trained using either food or affection, not both) and **dance** (the animal either learnt to line-dance or it did not). By combining categories, we end up with four different categories. All we then need to do is to count how many cats fall into each category. We can tabulate these frequencies as in Table 18.1 (which shows the data for this example), and this is known as a contingency table.

18.3.1. Pearson's chi-square test ①

If we want to see whether there's a relationship between two categorical variables (i.e., does the number of cats that line-dance relate to the type of training used?) we can use Pearson's chi-square test (Fisher, 1922; Pearson, 1900). This is an extremely elegant statistic based

TABLE 18.1 Contingency table showing how many cats will line-dance after being trained with different rewards

		Training		
		Food as Reward	Affection as Reward	Total
Could They Dance?	Yes	28	48	76
	No	10	114	124
	Total	38	162	200

on the simple idea of comparing the frequencies you observe in certain categories to the frequencies you might expect to get in those categories by chance. We saw in Chapter 2 (equation (2.6)) that if we want to calculate the fit (or total error) of a model we add up the squared differences between the observed values of the outcome, and the predicted values that come from the model:

$$\text{Total error} = \sum_{i=1}^{n} \left(\text{observed}_i - \text{model}_i\right)^2 \tag{18.1}$$

This equation was the basis of our sums of squares in regression and ANOVA. When we have categorical data we use essentially the same equation. There is a slight variation in that we divide by the model scores as well, which is actually much the same process as dividing the sum of squares by the degrees of freedom in ANOVA. Basically, we're standardizing the deviation for each observation. If we add all of these standardized deviations together the resulting statistic is Pearson's chi-square (χ^2) given by:

$$\chi^2 = \sum \frac{\left(\text{observed}_{ij} - \text{model}_{ij}\right)^2}{\text{model}_{ij}} \tag{18.2}$$

in which i represents the rows in the contingency table and j represents the columns. The observed data are, obviously, the frequencies in Table 18.1, but we need to work out what the model is. When we have categorical predictors but a continuous outcome (e.g., ANOVA) the model we use is group means, but, as I've mentioned we can't work with means when we have a categorical outcome variable so we work with frequencies instead. Therefore, we use 'expected frequencies'. One way to estimate the expected frequencies would be to say 'well, we've got 200 cats in total, and four categories, so the expected value is simply 200/4 = 50'. This would be fine if, for example, we had the same number of cats that had affection as a reward as we did cats that had food as a reward, but we didn't: 38 got food and 162 got affection as a reward. Likewise there are not equal numbers that could and couldn't dance. To take account of these inequalities, when we calculate expected frequencies for each cell in the table (in this case there are four cells) we use the column and row totals for a particular cell to calculate the expected value:

$$\text{model}_{ij} = E_{ij} = \frac{\text{row total}_i \times \text{column total}_j}{n}$$

In which n is the total number of observations (in this case 200). We can calculate these expected frequencies for the four cells within our table (row total and column total are abbreviated to RT and CT, respectively):

$$\text{model}_{\text{Food, Yes}} = \frac{RT_{\text{Yes}} \times CT_{\text{Food}}}{n} = \frac{76 \times 38}{200} = 14.44$$

$$\text{model}_{\text{Food, No}} = \frac{RT_{\text{No}} \times CT_{\text{Food}}}{n} = \frac{124 \times 38}{200} = 23.56$$

$$\text{model}_{\text{Affection, Yes}} = \frac{RT_{\text{Yes}} \times CT_{\text{Affection}}}{n} = \frac{76 \times 162}{200} = 61.56$$

$$\text{model}_{\text{Affection, No}} = \frac{RT_{\text{No}} \times CT_{\text{Affection}}}{n} = \frac{124 \times 162}{200} = 100.44$$

Given that we now have these model values, all we need to do is take each value in each cell of our data table, subtract from it the corresponding model value, square the result, and then divide by the corresponding model value. Once we've done this for each cell in the table, we just add them up!

$$\chi^2 = \frac{(28-14.44)^2}{14.44} + \frac{(10-23.56)^2}{23.56} + \frac{(48-61.56)^2}{61.56} + \frac{(114-100.44)^2}{100.44}$$

$$= \frac{13.56^2}{14.44} + \frac{-13.56^2}{23.56} + \frac{-13.56^2}{61.56} + \frac{13.56^2}{100.44}$$

$$= 12.73 + 7.80 + 2.99 + 1.83$$

$$= 25.35$$

This statistic can then be checked against a distribution with known properties called the **chi-square distribution**. All we need to know is the degrees of freedom, and these are calculated as $(r-1)(c-1)$ in which r is the number of rows and c is the number of columns. Another way to think of it is as the number of levels of each variable minus one multiplied together. In this case we get $df = (2 - 1)(2 - 1) = 1$. If you were doing the test by hand, you would find a critical value for the chi-square distribution with $df = 1$ and if the observed value was bigger than this critical value you would say that there was a significant relationship between the two variables. These critical values are produced in the Appendix, and for $df = 1$ they are 3.84 ($p = .05$) and 6.63 ($p = .01$). So because the observed chi-square is bigger than these values it is significant at $p < .01$. However, SPSS will estimate the precise probability of obtaining a chi-square statistic at least as big as (in this case) 25.35 if there were no association between the variables in the population.

18.3.2. Fisher's exact test ①

There is one problem with the chi-square test, which is that the sampling distribution of the test statistic has an *approximate* chi-square distribution. The larger the sample is, the better this approximation becomes, and in large samples the approximation is good enough to not worry about the fact that it is an approximation. However, in small samples, the approximation is not good enough, making significance tests of the chi-square distribution inaccurate. This is why you often read that to use the chi-square test the expected frequencies in each cell must be greater than 5 (see Section 18.4). When the expected frequencies are greater than 5, the sampling distribution is probably close enough to a perfect chi-square distribution for us not to worry. However, when the expected frequencies are too low, it probably means that the sample size is too small and that the sampling distribution of the test statistic is too deviant from a chi-square distribution to be of any use.

Fisher came up with a method for computing the exact probability of the chi-square statistic that is accurate when sample sizes are small. This method is called **Fisher's exact test** (Fisher, 1922) even though it's not so much a test as a way of computing the exact probability of the chi-square statistic. This procedure is normally used on 2 × 2 contingency tables (i.e., two variables each with two options) and with small samples. However, it can be used on larger contingency tables and with large samples, but on larger contingency tables it becomes computationally intensive and you might find SPSS taking a long time to give you an answer. In large samples there is really no point because it was designed to overcome the problem of small samples, so you don't need to use it when samples are large.

18.3.3.   The likelihood ratio ②

An alternative to Pearson's chi-square is the likelihood ratio statistic, which is based on maximum-likelihood theory. The general idea behind this theory is that you collect some data and create a model for which the probability of obtaining the observed set of data is maximized, then you compare this model to the probability of obtaining those data under the null hypothesis. The resulting statistic is, therefore, based on comparing observed frequencies with those predicted by the model:

$$L\chi^2 = 2\sum \text{observed}_{ij} \ln\left(\frac{\text{observed}_{ij}}{\text{model}_{ij}}\right) \tag{18.3}$$

in which i and j are the rows and columns of the contingency table and ln is the natural logarithm (this is the standard mathematical function that we came across in Chapter 5, and you can find it on your calculator usually labelled as ln or $\log_e$). Using the same model and observed values as in the previous section, this would give us:

$$L\chi^2 = 2\left[28 \times \ln\left(\frac{28}{14.44}\right) + 10 \times \ln\left(\frac{10}{23.56}\right) + 48 \times \ln\left(\frac{48}{61.56}\right) + 114 \times \ln\left(\frac{114}{100.44}\right)\right]$$

$$= 2\left[28 \times 0.662 + 10 \times -0.857 + 48 \times -0.249 + 114 \times 0.127\right]$$

$$= 2\left[18.54 - 8.57 - 11.94 + 14.44\right]$$

$$= 24.94$$

As with Pearson's chi-square, this statistic has a chi-square distribution with the same degrees of freedom (in this case 1). As such, it is tested in the same way: we could look up the critical value of chi-square for the number of degrees of freedom that we have. As before, the value we have here will be significant because it is bigger than the critical values of 3.84 ($p = .05$) and 6.63 ($p = .01$). For large samples this statistic will be roughly the same as Pearson's chi-square, but is preferred when samples are small.

18.3.4.   Yates's correction ②

When you have a 2 × 2 contingency table (i.e., two categorical variables each with two categories) then Pearson's chi-square tends to produce significance values that are too small (in other words, it tends to make a Type I error). Therefore, Yates suggested a correction to the Pearson formula (usually referred to as Yates's continuity correction). The basic idea is that when you calculate the deviation from the model (the observed$_{ij}$ − model$_{ij}$ in equation (18.2)) you subtract 0.5 from the absolute value of this deviation before you square it. In plain English this means you calculate the deviation, ignore whether it is positive or negative, subtract 0.5 from the value and then square it. Pearson's equation then becomes:

$$\chi^2 = \sum \frac{\left(\left|\text{observed}_{ij} - \text{model}_{ij}\right| - 0.5\right)^2}{\text{model}_{ij}} \tag{18.4}$$

For the data in our example this just translates into:

$$\chi^2 = \frac{(13.56 - 0.5)^2}{14.44} + \frac{(13.56 - 0.5)^2}{23.56} + \frac{(13.56 - 0.5)^2}{61.56} + \frac{(13.56 - 0.5)^2}{100.44}$$

$$= 11.81 + 7.24 + 2.77 + 1.70$$

$$= 23.52$$

The key thing to note is that it lowers the value of the chi-square statistic and, therefore, makes it less significant. Although this seems like a nice solution to the problem, there is a fair bit of evidence that this overcorrects and produces chi-square values that are too small. Howell (2012) provides an excellent discussion of the problem with Yates's correction for continuity if you're interested; all I will say is that although it's worth knowing about, it's probably best ignored.

18.3.5. Other measures of association ①

There are measures of the strength of association other than the chi-square test. These measures modify the chi-square statistic to take account of sample size and degrees of freedom and try to restrict the range of the test statistic from 0 to 1 (to make them similar to the correlation coefficient described in Chapter 7). Three related measures are:

- *Phi*: This statistic is accurate for 2 × 2 contingency tables. However, for tables with more than two dimensions the value of phi may not lie between 0 and 1 because the chi-square value can exceed the sample size. Therefore, Pearson suggested the use of the contingency coefficient.

- *Contingency coefficient*: This coefficient ensures a value between 0 and 1 but, unfortunately, it seldom reaches its upper limit of 1 and for this reason Cramér devised an alternative denoted by *V*.

- *Cramér's V*: When both variables have only two categories, phi and Cramér's *V* are identical. However, when variables have more than two categories Cramér's statistic can attain its maximum of 1 – unlike the other two – and so it is the most useful.

18.3.6. Several categorical variables: loglinear analysis ③

So far we've looked at situations in which there are only two categorical variables. However, we often want to analyse more complex contingency tables in which there are three or more variables. For example, suppose we took the example we've just used but also collected data from a sample of 70 dogs. We might want to compare the behaviour in dogs to that in cats. We would now have three variables: **Animal** (dog or cat), **Training** (food as reward or affection as reward) and **Dance** (did they dance or not?). This couldn't be analysed with the Pearson chi-square and instead has to be analysed with a technique called loglinear analysis.

18.3.6.1. Chi-square as regression ④

To begin with, let's have a look at how our simple chi-square example can be expressed as a regression model. Although we already know about as much as we need to about the chi-square test, if we want to understand more complex situations life becomes considerably easier if we consider our model as a general linear model (i.e., regression). All of the general linear models we've considered in this book take the general form of:

$$\text{outcome}_i = (\text{model}) + \text{error}_i$$

For example, when we encountered multiple regression in Chapter 8 we saw that this model was written as (see equation (8.6)):

$$Y_i = (b_0 + b_1 X_{1i} + b_2 X_{2i} + \cdots + b_n X_{ni}) + \varepsilon_i$$

Also, when we came across one-way ANOVA, we adapted this regression model to conceptualize our Viagra example, as (see equation (11.1)):

$$\text{Libido}_i = b_0 + b_2 \text{High}_i + b_1 \text{Low}_i + \varepsilon_i$$

The *t*-test was conceptualized in a similar way. In all cases the same basic equation is used; it's just the complexity of the model that changes. With categorical data we can use the same model in much the same way as with regression to produce a linear model. In our current example we have two categorical variables: training (food or affection) and dance (yes they did dance or no they didn't dance). Both variables have two categories and so we can represent each one with a single dummy variable (see Section 10.5.1) in which one category is coded as 0 and the other as 1. So for training, we could code 'food' as 0 and 'affection' as 1, and we could code the dancing variable as 1 for 'yes' and 0 for 'no' (see Table 18.2).

This situation might be familiar if you think back to factorial ANOVA (Section 13.2.2) in which we also had two variables as predictors. In that situation we saw that when there are two variables the general linear model became (think back to equation (13.1)):

$$\text{Outcome}_i = (b_0 + b_1 A_i + b_2 B_i + b_3 AB_i) + \varepsilon_i$$

TABLE 18.2   Coding scheme for dancing cats

Training	Dance	Dummy (Training)	Dummy (Dance)	Interaction	Frequency
Food	No	0	0	0	10
Food	Yes	0	1	0	28
Affection	No	1	0	0	114
Affection	Yes	1	1	1	48

in which A represents the first variable, B represents the second and AB represents the interaction between the two variables. Therefore, we can construct a linear model using these dummy variables that is exactly the same as the one we used for factorial ANOVA (above). The interaction term will be the training variable multiplied by the dance variable (look at Section 10.3.2, and if it doesn't make sense look back to Section 13.2.2 because the coding is exactly the same as this example):

$$\text{outcome}_i = \left(\text{model}\right) + \text{error}_i$$

$$\text{outcome}_{ij} = \left(b_0 + b_1\text{Training}_i + b_2\text{Dance}_j + b_3\text{Interaction}_{ij}\right) + \varepsilon_{ij} \tag{18.5}$$

However, because we're using categorical data, to make this model linear we have to actually use log values and so the actual model becomes:[1]

$$\ln\left(O_i\right) = \ln\left(\text{model}\right) + \ln\left(\varepsilon_i\right)$$

$$\ln\left(O_{ij}\right) = \left(b_0 + b_1\text{Training}_i + b_2\text{Dance}_j + b_3\text{Interaction}_{ij}\right) + \ln\left(\varepsilon_{ij}\right) \tag{18.6}$$

The training and dance variables and the interaction can take the values 0 and 1, depending on which combination of categories we're looking at (Table 18.2). Therefore, to work out what the b-values represent in this model we can do the same as we did for the t-test and ANOVA and look at what happens when we replace training and dance with values of 0 and 1. To begin with, let's see what happens when we look at when training and dance are both zero. This situation represents the category of cats that got food reward and didn't line-dance. When we used this sort of model for the t-test and ANOVA the outcomes we used were taken from the observed data: we used the group means (e.g., see Sections 9.2.2 and 11.2.1). However, with a categorical outcome we use the observed frequencies (rather than observed means). In Table 18.1 we saw that there were 10 cats that had food for a reward and didn't line-dance. If we use this as the observed outcome then the model can be written as (if we ignore the error term for the time being):

$$\ln\left(O_{ij}\right) = b_0 + b_1\text{Training}_i + b_2\text{Dance}_j + b_3\text{Interaction}_{ij}$$

For cats that had food reward and didn't dance, the training and dance variables and the interaction will all be 0 and so the equation reduces to:

$$\ln\left(O_{\text{Food, No}}\right) = b_0 + \left(b_1 \times 0\right) + \left(b_2 \times 0\right) + \left(b_3 \times 0\right)$$
$$\ln\left(O_{\text{Food, No}}\right) = b_0$$
$$\ln\left(10\right) = b_0$$
$$b_0 = 2.303$$

Therefore, b_0 in the model represents the log of the observed value when all of the categories are zero. As such it's the log of the observed value of the base category (in this case cats that got food and didn't dance).

---

[1] Actually, the convention is to denote b_0 as q and the b-values as l, but I think these notational changes serve only to confuse people so I'm sticking with b because I want to emphasize the similarities to regression and ANOVA.

Now, let's see what happens when we look at cats that had affection as a reward and didn't dance. In this case, the training variable is 1 and the dance variable and the interaction are still 0. Also, our outcome now changes to be the observed value for cats that received affection and didn't dance (from Table 18.1 we can see the value is 114). Therefore, the equation becomes:

$$\ln\left(O_{\text{Affection, No}}\right) = b_0 + \left(b_1 \times 1\right) + \left(b_2 \times 0\right) + \left(b_3 \times 0\right)$$

$$\ln\left(O_{\text{Affection, No}}\right) = b_0 + b_1$$

$$b_1 = \ln\left(O_{\text{Affection, No}}\right) - b_0$$

Remembering that b_0 is the expected value for cats that had food and didn't dance, we get:

$$b_1 = \ln\left(O_{\text{Affection, No}}\right) - \ln\left(O_{\text{Food, No}}\right)$$

$$= \ln(114) - \ln(10)$$

$$= 4.736 - 2.303$$

$$= 2.433$$

The important thing is that b_1 is the difference between the log of the observed frequency for cats that received affection and didn't dance, and the log of the observed values for cats that received food and didn't dance. Put another way, within the group of cats that didn't dance it represents the difference between those trained using food and those trained using affection.

Now, let's see what happens when we look at cats that had food as a reward and danced. In this case, the training variable is 0, the dance variable is 1 and the interaction is again 0. Our outcome now changes to be the observed frequency for cats that received food and danced (from Table 18.1 we can see the value is 28). Therefore, the equation becomes:

$$\ln\left(O_{\text{Food, Yes}}\right) = b_0 + \left(b_1 \times 0\right) + \left(b_2 \times 1\right) + \left(b_3 \times 0\right)$$

$$\ln\left(O_{\text{Food, Yes}}\right) = b_0 + b_2$$

$$b_2 = \ln\left(O_{\text{Food, Yes}}\right) - b_0$$

Remembering that b_0 is the expected value for cats that had food and didn't dance, we get:

$$b_2 = \ln\left(O_{\text{Food, Yes}}\right) - \ln\left(O_{\text{Food, No}}\right)$$

$$= \ln(28) - \ln(10)$$

$$= 3.332 - 2.303$$

$$= 1.029$$

The important thing is that b_2 is the difference between the log of the observed frequency for cats that received food and danced, and the log of the observed frequency for cats that received food and didn't dance. Put another way, within the group of cats that received food as a reward it represents the difference between cats that didn't dance and those that did.

Finally, we can look at cats that had affection and danced. In this case, the training and dance variables are both 1 and the interaction (which is the value of training multiplied by the value of dance) is also 1. We can also replace b_0, b_1 and b_2 with what we now know they represent. The outcome is the log of the observed frequency for cats that received affection and danced (this expected value is 48 – see Table 18.1). Therefore, the equation becomes (I've used the shorthand of A for affection, F for food, Y for yes, and N for no):

$$\ln\left(O_{A,\,Y}\right) = b_0 + \left(b_1 \times 1\right) + \left(b_2 \times 1\right) + \left(b_3 \times 1\right)$$

$$\ln\left(O_{A,\,Y}\right) = b_0 + b_1 + b_2 + b_3$$

$$\ln\left(O_{A,\,Y}\right) = \ln\left(O_{F,\,N}\right) + \left(\ln\left(O_{A,\,N}\right) - \ln\left(O_{F,\,N}\right)\right) + \left(\ln\left(O_{F,\,Y}\right) - \ln\left(O_{F,\,N}\right)\right) + b_3$$

$$\ln\left(O_{A,\,Y}\right) = \ln\left(O_{A,\,N}\right) + \ln\left(O_{F,\,Y}\right) - \ln\left(O_{F,\,N}\right) + b_3$$

$$b_3 = \ln\left(O_{A,\,Y}\right) - \ln\left(O_{F,\,Y}\right) + \ln\left(O_{F,\,N}\right) - \ln\left(O_{A,\,N}\right)$$

$$= \ln\left(48\right) - \ln\left(28\right) + \ln\left(10\right) - \ln\left(114\right)$$

$$= -1.895$$

So, b_3 in the model really compares the difference between affection and food when the cats didn't dance to the difference between food and affection when the cats did dance. Put another way, it compares the effect of training when cats didn't dance to the effect of training when they did dance.

The final model is therefore:

$$\ln\left(O_{ij}\right) = 2.303 + 2.433\text{Training}_i + 1.029\text{Dance}_j - 1.895\text{Interaction}_{ij} + \ln\left(\varepsilon_{ij}\right)$$

The important thing to note here is that everything is exactly the same as factorial ANOVA, except that we dealt with log-transformed values (compare this section to Section 13.2.2 to see just how similar everything is). In case you still don't believe that this works as a general linear model, I've prepared a file called **Cat Regression.sav**, which contains the two variables **Dance** (0 = no, 1 = yes) and **Training** (0 = food, 1 = affection) and the interaction (**Interaction**). There is also a variable called **Observed** that contains the observed frequencies in Table 18.1 for each combination of **Dance** and **Training**. Finally, there is a variable called **LnObserved**, which is the natural logarithm of these observed frequencies (remember that throughout this section we've dealt with the log observed values).

SELF-TEST   Run a multiple regression analysis using **Cat Regression.sav** with **LnObserved** as the outcome, and **Training**, **Dance** and **Interaction** as your three predictors.

Coefficientsª

Model		Unstandardized Coefficients		Standardized Coefficients	t	Sig.
		B	Std. Error	Beta		
1	(Constant)	2.303	.000		72046662.8	.000
	Type of Training	2.434	.000	1.385	73011512.2	.000
	Did they dance?	1.030	.000	.725	27654265.1	.000
	Interaction	-1.895	.000	-1.174	-46106003	.000

a. Dependent Variable: LN (Observed Frequencies)

Output 18.1 shows the resulting coefficients table from this regression. The important thing to note is that the constant, b_0, is 2.303 as calculated above, the beta value for type of training, b_1, is 2.434 and for dance, b_2, is 1.030, both of which are within rounding error of what was calculated above. Also the coefficient for the interaction, b_3, is −1.895 as predicted. There is one interesting point, though: all of the standard errors are zero – there is *no* error at all in this model (which is also why there are no significance tests). This is because the various combinations of coding variables completely explain the observed values. This is known as a **saturated model** – I will return to this point later, so bear it in mind. For the time being, I hope this convinces you that chi-square can be conceptualized as a linear model.

OK, this is all very well, but the heading of this section did rather imply that I would show you how the chi-square test can be conceptualized as a linear model. Well, basically, the chi-square test looks at whether two variables are independent; therefore, it has no interest in the combined effect of the two variables, only their unique effect. Thus, we can conceptualize chi-square in much the same way as the saturated model, except that we don't include the interaction term. If we remove the interaction term, our model becomes:

$$\ln\left(\text{model}_{ij}\right) = b_0 + b_1 \text{Training}_i + b_2 \text{Dance}_j$$

With this new model, we cannot predict the observed values like we did for the saturated model because we've lost some information (namely, the interaction term). Therefore, the outcome from the model changes, and therefore the beta values change too. We saw earlier that the chi-square test is based on 'expected frequencies'. Therefore, if we're conceptualizing the chi-square test as a linear model, our outcomes will be these expected values. If you look back to the beginning of this chapter you'll see we already have the expected frequencies based on this model. We can recalculate the beta values based on these expected values:

$$\ln\left(E_{ij}\right) = b_0 + b_1 \text{Training}_i + b_2 \text{Dance}_j$$

For cats that had food reward and didn't dance, the training and dance variables will be 0 and so the equation reduces to:

$$\ln\left(E_{\text{Food, No}}\right) = b_0 + \left(b_1 \times 0\right) + \left(b_2 \times 0\right)$$

$$\ln\left(E_{\text{Food, No}}\right) = b_0$$

$$b_0 = \ln\left(23.56\right)$$

$$= 3.16$$

Therefore, b_0 represents the log of the expected value when all of the categories are zero.

When we look at cats that had affection as a reward and didn't dance, the training variable is 1 and the dance variable is still 0. Also, our outcome now changes to be the expected value for cats that received affection and didn't dance:

$$\ln\left(E_{\text{Affection, No}}\right) = b_0 + (b_1 \times 1) + (b_2 \times 0)$$

$$\ln\left(E_{\text{Affection, No}}\right) = b_0 + b_1$$

$$b_1 = \ln\left(E_{\text{Affection, No}}\right) - b_0$$

$$= \ln\left(E_{\text{Affection, No}}\right) - \ln\left(E_{\text{Food, No}}\right)$$

$$= \ln(100.44) - \ln(23.56)$$

$$= 1.45$$

The important thing is that b_1 is the difference between the log of the expected frequency for cats that received affection and didn't dance and the log of the expected values for cats that received food and didn't dance. In fact, the value is the same as the column marginal, that is, the difference between the total number of cats getting affection and the total number of cats getting food: $\ln(162) - \ln(38) = 1.45$. Put simply, it represents the main effect of the type of training.

When we look at cats that had food as a reward and danced, the training variable is 0 and the dance variable is 1. Our outcome now changes to be the expected frequency for cats that received food and danced:

$$\ln\left(E_{\text{Food, Yes}}\right) = b_0 + (b_1 \times 0) + (b_2 \times 1)$$

$$\ln\left(E_{\text{Food, Yes}}\right) = b_0 + b_2$$

$$b_2 = \ln\left(E_{\text{Food, Yes}}\right) - b_0$$

$$= \ln\left(E_{\text{Food, Yes}}\right) - \ln\left(E_{\text{Food, No}}\right)$$

$$= \ln(14.44) - \ln(23.56)$$

$$= -0.49$$

Therefore, b_2 is the difference between the log of the expected frequencies for cats that received food and did or didn't dance. In fact, the value is the same as the row marginal, that is the difference between the total number of cats that did and didn't dance: $\ln(76) - \ln(124) = -0.49$. In simpler terms, it is the main effect of whether or not the cat danced.

We can double-check all of this by looking at the final cell (cats that had affection and danced):

$$\ln\left(E_{\text{Affection, Yes}}\right) = b_0 + (b_1 \times 1) + (b_2 \times 1)$$

$$\ln\left(E_{\text{Affection, Yes}}\right) = b_0 + b_1 + b_2$$

$$\ln(61.56) = 3.16 + 1.45 - 0.49$$

$$4.12 = 4.12$$

The final chi-square model is therefore:

$$\ln(O_i) = \ln(\text{model}) + \ln(\varepsilon_i)$$

$$= 3.16 + 1.45\text{Training} - 0.49\text{Dance} + \ln(\varepsilon_i)$$

We can rearrange this equation to get some residuals (the error term):

$$\ln(\varepsilon_i) = \ln(O_i) - \ln(\text{model})$$

In this case, the model is merely the expected frequencies that were calculated for the chi-square test, so the residuals are the differences between the observed and expected frequencies.

SELF-TEST   To show that this all actually works, run another multiple regression analysis using **Cat Regression.sav.** This time the outcome is the log of expected frequencies **(LnExpected)** and **Training** and **Dance** are the predictors (the interaction is not included).

EVERYBODY

This section demonstrates how chi-square can work as a linear model, just like regression and ANOVA, in which the beta values tell us something about the relative differences in frequencies across categories of our two variables. If nothing else made sense I want you to leave this section aware that chi-square (and analysis of categorical data generally) can be expressed as a linear model (although we have to use log values). We can express categories of a variable using dummy variables, just as we did with regression and ANOVA, and the resulting beta values can be calculated in exactly the same way as for regression and ANOVA. In ANOVA, these beta values represented differences between the means of a particular category compared against a baseline category. With categorical data, the beta values represent the same thing, the only difference being that rather than dealing with means, we're dealing with expected values. Grasping this idea (that regression, *t*-tests, ANOVAs and categorical data analysis are basically the same) will help (me) considerably in the next section.

18.3.6.2. Loglinear analysis ③

In the previous section, after nearly reducing my brain to even more of a rotting vegetable than it already is trying to explain how categorical data analysis is just another form of regression, I ran the data through an ordinary regression using SPSS to prove that I wasn't talking complete gibberish. At the time I rather glibly said 'oh, by the way, there's no error in the model, that's odd isn't it?' and sort of passed this off by telling you that it was a 'saturated' model and not to worry too much about it because I'd explain it all later just as soon as I'd worked out what the hell was going on. That seemed like a good avoidance tactic at the time, but unfortunately I now have to explain what I was going on about.

To begin with, I hope you're now happy with the idea that categorical data can be expressed in the form of a linear model provided that we use log values (this, incidentally, is why the technique we're discussing is called *log*linear analysis). From what you hopefully already know about ANOVA and linear models generally, you should also be cosily tucked up in bed with the idea that we can extend any linear model to include any amount of predictors and any resulting interaction terms between predictors. If we can represent a simple two-variable categorical analysis in terms of a linear model, then it shouldn't amaze you to discover that if we have more than two variables this is no problem: we can extend the model by adding any new variables and the resulting interaction terms, and giving each one a parameter (b). This is all you really need to know. So, just as in multiple regression and ANOVA, if we think of things in terms of a linear model, then conceptually it becomes very easy to understand how the model expands to incorporate new variables. So, for example, if we have three predictors (A, B and C) in ANOVA we end up with three two-way interactions (AB, AC, BC) and one three-way interaction (ABC). Therefore, the resulting linear model is:

$$\text{outcome}_{ijk} = \left(b_0 + b_1 A_i + b_2 B_j + b_3 C_k + b_4 AB_{ij} + b_5 AC_{ik} + b_6 BC_{jk} + b_7 ABC_{ijk}\right) + \varepsilon_{ij}$$

In exactly the same way, if we have three variables in a categorical data analysis we get an identical model, but with an outcome in terms of logs:

$$\ln\left(O_{ijk}\right) = \left(b_0 + b_1 A_i + b_2 B_j + b_3 C_k + b_4 AB_{ij} + b_5 AC_{ik} + b_6 BC_{jk} + b_7 ABC_{ijk}\right) + \ln\left(\varepsilon_{ij}\right)$$

Obviously the calculation of beta values and expected values from the model becomes considerably more cumbersome and confusing, but that's why we invented computers – so that we don't have to worry about it. Loglinear analysis works on these principles. However, as we've seen in the two-variable case, when our data are categorical and we include all of the available terms (main effects and interactions) we get no error: our predictors can perfectly predict our outcome (the expected values). So, if we start with the most complex model possible, we will get no error. The job of loglinear analysis is to try to fit a simpler model to the data without any substantial loss of predictive power. Therefore, loglinear analysis typically works on a principle of backward elimination (yes, the same kind of backward elimination as in multiple regression – see Section 8.5.1.3). So we begin with the saturated model, and then remove a predictor from the model and using this new model we predict our data (calculate expected frequencies, just like the chi-square test) and then see how well the model fits the data (i.e., are the expected frequencies close to the observed frequencies?). If the fit of the new model is not very different from the more complex model, then we abandon the complex model in favour of the new one. Put another way, we assume the term we removed was not having a significant impact on the ability of our model to predict the observed data.

However, we don't just remove terms randomly, we do it hierarchically. So, we start with the saturated model and then remove the highest-order interaction, and assess the effect that this has. If removing the interaction term has no effect on the model then it's obviously not having much of an effect; therefore, we get rid of it and move on to remove any lower-order interactions. If removing these interactions has no effect then we carry on to any main effects until we find an effect that does affect the fit of the model if it is removed.

To put this in more concrete terms, at the beginning of the section on loglinear analysis I asked you to imagine we'd extended our training and line-dancing example to incorporate a sample of dogs. So, we now have three variables: **Animal** (dog or cat), **Training** (food or affection) and **Dance** (did they dance or not?). Just as in ANOVA this results in three main effects:

- **Animal**
- **Training**
- **Dance**

three interactions involving two variables:

- **Animal** × **Training**
- **Animal** × **Dance**
- **Training** × **Dance**

and one interaction involving all three variables:

- **Animal** × **Training** × **Dance**

When I talk about backward elimination I mean that loglinear analysis starts by including all of these effects; we then take the highest-order interaction (in this case the three-way interaction of **Animal** × **Training** × **Dance**) and remove it. We construct a new model without this interaction, and from the model calculate expected frequencies. We (well, the computer) then compare these expected frequencies (or model frequencies) to the observed frequencies using the standard equation for the likelihood ratio statistic (see Section 18.3.3). If the new model significantly changes the likelihood ratio statistic, then removing this interaction term has a significant effect on the fit of the model and we know that this effect is statistically important. If this is the case then we will stop there and say that we have a significant three-way interaction. We won't test any other effects because all lower-order effects are consumed within higher-order effects. If, however, removing the three-way interaction doesn't significantly affect the fit of the model then we move on to lower-order interactions. Therefore, we look at the **animal** × **training**, **animal** × **dance** and **training** × **dance** interactions in turn and construct models in which these terms are not present. For each model the computer again calculates expected values and compares them to the observed data using a likelihood ratio statistic.[2] Again, if any one of these models results in a significant change in the likelihood ratio then the term is retained and we won't move on to look at any main effects involved in that interaction (so if the **animal** × **training** interaction is significant the computer won't look at the main effects of animal or training). However, if the likelihood ratio is unchanged then the analysis removes the offending interaction term and moves on to look at main effects.

I mentioned that the likelihood ratio statistic (see Section 18.3.3) is used to assess each model. It should be clear how this equation can be adapted to fit any model: the observed values are the same throughout, and the model frequencies are simply the expected frequencies from the model being tested. For the saturated model, this statistic will always be 0 (because the observed and model frequencies are the same so the ratio of observed to model frequencies will be 1, and $\ln(0) = 0$), but as we've seen, in other cases it will provide a measure of how well the model fits the observed frequencies. To test whether a new model has changed the likelihood ratio, all we need do is to take the likelihood ratio for a model and subtract from it the likelihood ratio for the previous model (provided the models are hierarchically structured):

$$L\chi^2_{\text{Change}} = L\chi^2_{\text{Current Model}} - L\chi^2_{\text{Previous Model}} \tag{18.7}$$

I've tried in this section to give you a flavour of how loglinear analysis works, without getting too much into the nitty-gritty of the calculations. I've tried to show you how we can conceptualize a chi-square analysis as a linear model and then relied on what I've previously told you about ANOVA to hope that you can extrapolate these conceptual ideas to understand roughly what's going on. The curious among you might want to know exactly

---

[2] It's worth mentioning that for every model, the computation of expected values differs, and as the designs get more complex, the computation gets increasingly tedious and incomprehensible (at least to me); however, you don't need to know the calculations to get a feel for what is going on.

how everything is calculated and to these people I have two things to say: 'I don't know' and 'I know a really good place where you can buy a straitjacket'. If you're that interested then Tabachnick and Fidell (2007) has a wonderfully detailed and lucid chapter on the subject, which puts this feeble attempt to shame.

18.4. Assumptions when analysing categorical data ①

It should be obvious that the chi-square test does not rely on the assumptions discussed in Chapter 5 (for example, categorical data cannot have a normal sampling distribution because they aren't continuous). However, the chi-square test still has two important assumptions relating to (1) independence and (2) expected frequencies.

18.4.1. Independence ①

Pretty much all of the tests we have encountered in this book have made an assumption about the independence of residuals, and the chi-square test is no exception. For the chi-square test to be meaningful it is imperative that each person, item or entity contributes to only one cell of the contingency table. Therefore, you cannot use a chi-square test on a repeated-measures design (e.g., if we had trained some cats with food to see if they would dance and then trained the same cats with affection to see if they would dance we couldn't analyse the resulting data with Pearson's chi-square test).

18.4.2. Expected frequencies ①

With 2 × 2 contingency tables (two categorical variables both with two categories) no expected values should be below 5. In larger tables, and when looking at associations between three or more categorical variables (loglinear analysis, covered in Section 18.3.6), the rule is that all expected counts should be greater than 1 and no more than 20% of expected counts should be less than 5. Howell (2012) gives a nice explanation of why violating this assumption creates problems. If this assumption is broken the result is a radical reduction in test power – so dramatic, in fact, that it may not be worth bothering with the analysis at all.

In terms of remedies, if you're looking at associations between only two variables then consider using Fisher's exact test (Section 18.3.2). With three or more variables (i.e., loglinear analysis) your options are: (1) collapse the data across one of the variables (preferably the one you least expect to have an effect); (2) collapse levels of one of the variables; (3) collect more data; or (4) accept the loss of power. If you want to collapse data across one of the variables then:

1 The highest-order interaction should be non-significant.

2 At least one of the lower-order interaction terms involving the variable to be deleted should be non-significant.

Let's think about our loglinear example in which we're looking at the relationship between training (food vs. affection), whether the animal danced (yes vs. no), and the species of animal (cats vs. dogs). Say we wanted to delete the animal variable; then for this to be valid, the **animal × training × dance** variable should be non-significant, and either the **animal × training** or the **animal × dance** interaction should also be non-significant.

You can also collapse categories within a variable. So, if you had a variable of 'season' relating to spring, summer, autumn and winter, and you had very few observations in winter, you could consider reducing the variable to three categories: spring, summer, autumn/winter perhaps. However, you should combine only categories for which it makes theoretical sense.

Finally, some people overcome the problem by simply adding a constant to all cells of the table, but there really is no point in doing this because it doesn't address the issue of power.

18.4.3. More doom and gloom ①

Finally, although it's not an assumption, it seems fitting to mention in a section in which a gloomy and foreboding tone is being used that proportionately small differences in cell frequencies can result in statistically significant associations between variables if the sample is large enough (although it might need to be very large indeed). Therefore, we must look at row and column percentages to interpret any effects we get. These percentages will reflect the patterns of data far better than the frequencies themselves (because these frequencies will be dependent on the sample sizes in different categories).

18.5. Doing chi-square in SPSS ①

There are two ways in which categorical data can be entered: enter the raw scores, or enter weighted cases. We'll look at both in turn.

18.5.1. General procedure for analysing categorical outcomes ①

Figure 18.2 shows a general procedure for analysing data when you want to fit models that have both an outcome and predictor(s) that are categorical. Essentially you first look at a contingency table and check the expected frequencies. If you have one predictor then head straight to a chi-square test, but if you have more than one predictor first do a loglinear analysis (Section 18.6) and then follow up any significant effects with one or more chi-square tests. After a chi-square test it's useful to inspect the standardized residuals and compute an **odds ratio**, which is an effect size quantifying the relationship between variables.

18.5.2. Entering data ①

To begin with, let's imagine we're looking at the data from only cats. So, we want to input data about whether or not the 200 cats danced and what type of training they had.

18.5.2.1. Raw scores ①

If we input the raw scores, every row of the data editor represents each entity about which we have data (in this example, each row represents a cat). So, you would create two coding

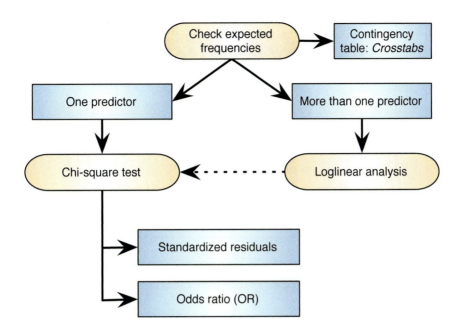

FIGURE 18.2
The general process for fitting models in which both predictors and the outcome are categorical

variables (**Training** and **Dance**) and specify appropriate numeric codes for each. The **Training** could be coded with 0 to represent a food reward and 1 to represent affection, and **Dance** could be coded with 1 to represent an animal that danced and 0 to represent one that did not. For each animal, you put the appropriate numeric code into each column. So a cat that was trained with food that did not dance would have 0 in the **Training** column and 1 in the **Dance** column. The data in the file **Cats.sav** are entered in this way and you should be able to identify the variables described. There were 200 cats in all and so there are 200 rows of data.

18.5.2.2. Weight cases ①

An alternative method of data entry is to create the same coding variables as before, but to have a third variable that represents the number of animals that fell into each combination of categories. In other words we input the frequency data (the number of cases that fall into a particular category). We could call this variable **Frequency**. Figure 18.3 shows the data editor with this third variable added. Now, instead of having 200 rows, each one representing a different animal, we have one row representing each combination of categories and a variable telling us how many animals fell into this category combination. So, the first row represents cats that had food as a reward and then danced. The variable **Frequency** tells us that there were 28 cats that had food as a reward and then danced. This information was previously represented by 28 different rows in the file **Cats.sav** and so you can see how this method of data entry saves you a lot of time. Extending this principle, we can see that when affection was used as a reward 114 cats did not dance.

To analyse data entered in this way we must tell the computer that the variable **Frequency** represents the number of cases that fell into a particular combination of categories. To do this, access the *Weight Cases* dialog box in Figure 18.4 by selecting Data ⚖ Weight Cases… . Select ⦿ Weight cases by and then drag the variable in which the number of cases is specified (in this case **Frequency**) to the box labelled *Frequency Variable* (or click on ➡). This process tells the computer that it should weight each category combination by the number in the column labelled **Frequency**. Therefore, the computer will pretend, for example, that there are 28 rows of data that have the category combination 0, 0 (representing cats trained with food and that danced). Data entered in this way are in the file **Cats Weight.sav**, and if you use this file you must remember to weight the cases as described.

FIGURE 18.3
Data entry
using weighted
cases

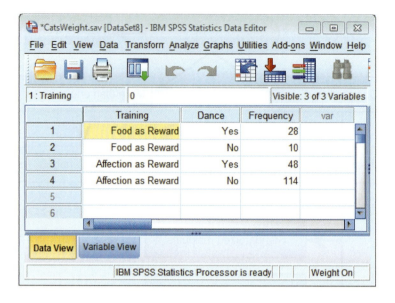

FIGURE 18.3
Data entry
using weighted
cases

18.5.3. Running the analysis ①

The first steps in Figure 18.2 are to create a contingency table using the *Crosstabs* command, check the expected frequencies and then do the chi-square test. In SPSS we can do these steps simultaneously. *Crosstabs* is accessed by selecting Analyze Descriptive Statistics ▶ Crosstabs... . Figure 18.5 shows the dialog boxes for the *Crosstabs* command (the variable **Frequency** appears because I ran the analysis on the **Cats Weight.sav** data). First, drag one of the variables of interest from the variable list to the box labelled *Row(s)* (or select it and click on ➡). For this example, I selected **Training** to be the rows of the table. Next, drag the other variable of interest (**Dance**) to the box labelled *Column(s)* (or select it and click on ➡). In addition, it is possible to select a layer variable (i.e., you can split the rows of the table into further categories). If you had a third categorical variable (as we will later in this chapter) you could split the contingency table by this variable (so layers of the table represent different categories of this third variable). If you click on Statistics... a dialog box appears in which you can specify various statistical tests. The most important options in this dialog box for categorical data are described in SPSS Tip 18.1.

Select the chi-square test, the contingency coefficient, phi and lambda and then click on Continue. If you click on Cells... a dialog box appears in which you can specify the type of data displayed in the crosstabulation table. It is important that you ask for expected counts because this is how we check the assumptions about the expected frequencies (Section 18.4). It is also useful to have a look at the row, column and total percentages because these values are usually more easily interpreted than the actual frequencies and provide some idea of the origin of any significant effects. There are two other options that are useful for breaking down a significant effect (should we get one): (1) we can select a *z*-test to compare cell counts across columns of the contingency table (☑ Compare column proportions), in which case we should use a Bonferroni correction (☑ Adjust p-values (Bonferroni method)); and (2) select standardized residuals. Once these options have been selected, click on Continue to return to the main dialog box. From here you can click on Exact... to compute Fisher's exact test (Section 18.3.2) if your sample is small or if your expected frequencies are too low (see Section 18.4). Select the *Exact* test option; we don't really need it for these data but it will be a useful way to see how it is used. Click on Continue to return to the main dialog box and then click on OK to run the analysis.

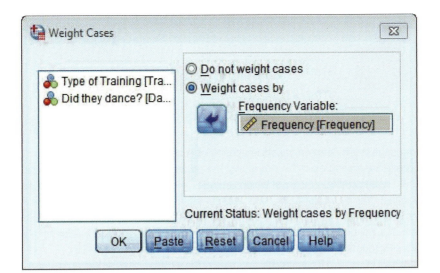

FIGURE 18.4
The dialog
box for the
weight cases
command

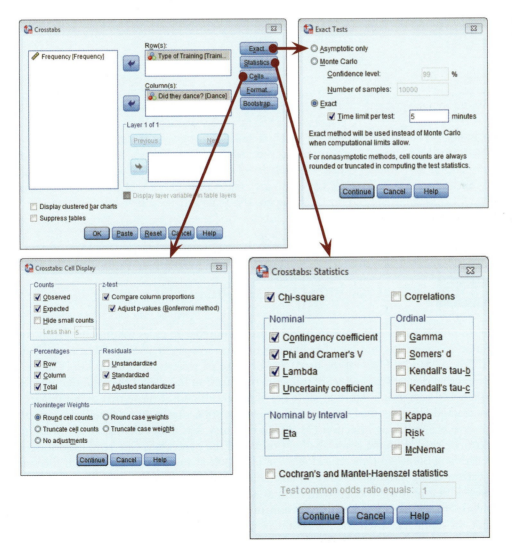

FIGURE 18.5
Dialog boxes
for the
Crosstabs
command

SPSS TIP 18.1   Statistical options for crosstabs ②

In the main dialog box there are some other tests that can be selected:

- **Chi-square**: This performs the basic Pearson chi-square test (Section 18.3.1).
- **Phi** and **Cramér's V**: These are measures of the strength of association between two categorical variables. Phi is used with 2 × 2 contingency tables (tables in which you have two categorical variables and each variable has only two categories). Phi is calculated by taking the chi-square value and dividing it by the sample size and then taking the square root of this value. If one of the two categorical variables contains more than two categories then Cramér's *V* is preferred to phi because phi fails to reach its minimum value of 0 (indicating no association) in these circumstances.
- **Goodman and Kruskal's lambda (λ)**: This statistic measures the proportional reduction in error that is achieved when membership of a category of one variable is used to predict category membership of the other variable. A value of 1 means that one variable perfectly predicts the other, and a value of 0 indicates that one variable in no way predicts the other.
- **Kendall's statistic**: This statistic is discussed in Section 7.4.4.

ODITI'S LANTERN
Dancing cats

'I, Oditi, want my followers to harness the power of dancing cats. It is a well-established fact that a dancing cat creates more energy than nuclear fusion. To solve the mysteries of statistics, we must power thousands of computers, and the only way to generate that kind of power is a stadium of dancing cats. So that you can identify a dancing cat, I have prepared a video of one … it also shows you how to do the chi-square test. Stare into my lantern and be amazed.'

18.5.4. Output for the chi-square test ①

The contingency table (Output 18.2) contains the number of cases that fall into each combination of categories and is rather like our original contingency table. We can see that in total 76 cats danced (38% of the total) and of these 28 were trained using food (36.8% of the total that danced) and 48 were trained with affection (63.2% of the total that danced). Further, 124 cats didn't dance at all (62% of the total) and of those that didn't dance, 10 were trained using food as a reward (8.1% of the total that didn't dance) and a massive 114 were trained using affection (91.9% of the total that didn't dance). The numbers of cats can be read from the rows labelled *Count* and the percentages are read from the rows labelled % *within Did they dance?* We can also look at the percentages within the training categories by looking at the rows labelled % *within Type of Training*. This tells us, for example, that of those trained with food as a reward, 73.7% danced and 26.3% did not. Similarly, for those trained with affection only 29.6% danced compared to 70.4% that didn't. In summary, when food was used as a reward most cats would dance, but when affection was used most cats refused to dance.

First, let's check that the expected frequencies assumption has been met (Section 18.4). We have a 2 × 2 table so all expected frequencies need to be greater than 5. If you look at the expected counts in the contingency table (which incidentally are the same as we calculated earlier), we see that the smallest expected count is 14.4 (for cats that were trained with food and did dance). This value exceeds 5 and so the assumption has been met. If you find an expected count lower than 5 the best remedy is to collect more data to try to boost the proportion of cases falling into each category.

The other thing to note about this table is that because we selected *Compare column proportions* in Figure 18.5 our counts have subscript letters. For example, in the row labelled *Food as Reward* the count of 10 has a subscript letter *a* and the count of 28 has a subscript letter *b*. These subscripts tell us the results of the *z*-test that we asked for: columns with different subscripts have significantly different column proportions. It's not immediately obvious what's being tested here, and to be honest with you it took me a while to fathom it out because I found I could interpret what the SPSS help files said in different ways (perhaps it's just me). However, I got there in the end, and I can confidently pass on that knowledge. We need to look within rows of the table. So, for *Food as Reward* the columns have different subscripts as I just explained, which means that proportions within the column variable (i.e., *Did they dance?*) are significantly different. The *z*-test compares the *proportion* of the total frequency of the first column that falls into the first row against the *proportion* of the total frequency of the second column that falls into the first row. So, of all the cats that danced, 36.8% had food, and of all the cats that didn't dance, 8.1% had food. The different subscripts tell us that these proportions are significantly different. Put another way, the proportion of cats that danced after food was significantly more than the proportion that didn't dance after food. To be clear, the test tells us that 36.8% is significantly different from 8.1%: it does not compare the counts themselves, so it is not the case that the count of 28 is different to the count of 10 (in this example). The self-test uses an example to illustrate this point.

If we move on to the row labelled *Affection as Reward*, the count of 114 has a subscript letter *a* and the count of 48 has a subscript letter *b*; as before, the fact they have different letters tells us that the column proportions are significantly different: in other words, 91.9% is significantly different from 63.2%. The proportion of cats that danced after affection was significantly less than the proportion that didn't dance after affection.

OUTPUT 18.2

Type of Training * Did they dance? Crosstabulation

			Did they dance?		
			No	Yes	Total
Type of Training	Food as Reward	Count	10a	28b	38
		Expected Count	23.6	14.4	38.0
		% within Type of Training	26.3%	73.7%	100.0%
		% within Did they dance?	8.1%	36.8%	19.0%
		% of Total	5.0%	14.0%	19.0%
		Std. Residual	−2.8	3.6	
	Affection as Reward	Count	114a	48b	162
		Expected Count	100.4	61.6	162.0
		% within Type of Training	70.4%	29.6%	100.0%
		% within Did they dance?	91.9%	63.2%	81.0%
		% of Total	57.0%	24.0%	81.0%
		Std. Residual	1.4	−1.7	
Total		Count	124	76	200
		Expected Count	124.0	76.0	200.0
		% within Type of Training	62.0%	38.0%	100.0%
		% within Did they dance?	100.0%	100.0%	100.0%
		% of Total	62.0%	38.0%	100.0%

Each subscript letter denotes a subset of Did they dance? categories whose column proportions do not differ significantly from each other at the .05 level.

As we saw earlier, Pearson's chi-square test examines whether there is an association between two categorical variables (in this case the type of training and whether the animal danced or not). As part of the *Crosstabs* procedure SPSS produces a table that includes the chi-square statistic and its significance value (Output 18.3). The Pearson chi-square statistic tests whether the two variables are independent. If the significance value is small enough (conventionally *Sig.* must be less than .05) then we reject the hypothesis that the variables are independent and gain confidence in the hypothesis that they are in some way related. The value of the chi-square statistic is given in the table, along with the degrees of freedom and the significance value. The value of the chi-square statistic is 25.356, which is within rounding error of what we calculated in Section 18.3.1. This value is highly significant ($p < .001$), indicating that the type of training used had a significant effect on whether an animal would dance.

A series of other statistics are also included in the table (many of which have to be requested using the options in the dialog box in Figure 18.5). *Continuity Correction* is Yates's continuity corrected chi-square (see Section 18.3.4), and its value is the same as the value we calculated earlier (23.52). This test is probably best ignored, but it does confirm the result from the main chi-square test. The *Likelihood Ratio* is the statistic we encountered in Section 18.3.3 (and is within rounding error of the value we calculated: 24.93). Again this confirms the main chi-square result, but this statistic would be preferred in smaller samples.

Underneath the chi-square table there are several footnotes relating to the assumption that expected counts should be greater than 5. If you forgot to check this assumption yourself, SPSS kindly gives a summary of the number of expected counts below 5. In this case, there were no expected frequencies less than 5 so we know that the chi-square statistic should be accurate.

The highly significant result indicates that there is an association between the type of training and whether the cat danced or not. In other words, there is a significant difference in the pattern of responses (i.e., the proportion of cats that danced to the proportion that did not) in the two training conditions. We saw from the earlier z-tests that of the cats trained with food a significantly greater proportion danced, and conversely of those trained with affection a significantly greater proportion didn't dance. Another way to look at this significant finding is that when food is used as a reward, about 74% of cats learn to dance and 26% do not, whereas when affection is used, the opposite is true (about 70% refuse to dance and 30% do dance). Therefore, we can conclude that the type of training used significantly influences the cats: they will dance for food but not for love.

How do I interpret chi-square?

OUTPUT 18.3

Chi-Square Tests

	Value	df	Asymp. Sig. (2–sided)	Exact Sig. (2–sided)	Exact Sig. (1–sided)	Point Probability
Pearson Chi-Square	25.356[a]	1	.000	.000	.000	
Continuity Correction[b]	23.520	1	.000			
Likelihood Ratio	24.932	1	.000	.000	.000	
Fisher's Exact Test				.000	.000	
Linear–by–Linear Association	25.229[c]	1	.000	.000	.000	.000
N of Valid Cases	200					

a. 0 cells (.0%) have expected count less than 5. The minimum expected count is 14.44.

b. Computed only for a 2x2 table

c. The standardized statistic is 5.023.

Having lived with a lovely cat for many years now, this supports my cynical view that they will do nothing unless there is a bowl of food waiting for them at the end of it!

If requested, SPSS produces another table (Output 18.4) containing the measures of association discussed in Section 18.3.5. For these data, Cramér's statistic is .36 out of a possible maximum value of 1. This represents a medium association between the type of training and whether the cats danced or not (if you think of it like a correlation coefficient then this represents a medium effect size). This value is highly significant ($p < .001$), indicating that a value of the test statistic that is this big is unlikely to have happened if there were no association in the population. These results confirm what the chi-square test already told us but also give us some idea of the size of the effect.

Symmetric Measures

		Value	Approx. Sig.	Exact Sig.
Nominal by Nominal	Phi	.356	.000	.000
	Cramér's V	.356	.000	.000
	Contingency Coefficient	.335	.000	.000
N of Valid Cases		200		

a. Not assuming the null hypothesis.

b. Using the asymptotic standard error assuming the null hypothesis.

18.5.5. Breaking down a significant chi-square test with standardized residuals ②

Although in a 2 × 2 contingency table, like the one we have in this example, the nature of the association can be quite clear from just the cell percentages or counts, in larger contingency tables it can be useful to do a finer-grained investigation. In a way, you can think of a significant chi-square test in much the same way as a significant interaction in ANOVA: it is an effect that needs to be broken down further. We have seen already that we can break down the effect with the z-tests that SPSS produces in the contingency table. Another easy way to break down a significant chi-square test is to use the standardized residual.

Just like regression, the residual is the error between what the model predicts (the expected frequency) and the data actually observed (the observed frequency):

$$\text{residual}_{ij} = \text{observed}_{ij} - \text{model}_{ij}$$

in which i and j represent the two variables (i.e., the rows and columns in the contingency table). This is the same as every other residual or deviation that we have encountered in this book (compare this equation to, for example, equation (2.6)). To standardize this equation, we divide by the square root of the expected frequency:

$$\text{standardized residual} = \frac{\text{observed}_{ij} - \text{model}_{ij}}{\sqrt{\text{model}_{ij}}}$$

Does this equation look familiar? Well, it's basically part of equation (18.2). The only difference is that rather than looking at squared deviations, we're looking at the pure deviation. Remember that the rationale for squaring deviations in the first place is simply to make them positive so that they don't cancel out when we add them. The chi-square statistic is based on adding together values, therefore it is important that the deviations are squared. However, if we're not planning to add up the deviations or residuals then we can inspect them in their non-squared form. There are two important things about these standardized residuals:

1   Given that the chi-square statistic is the sum of these standardized residuals (sort of), if we want to decompose what contributes to the overall association that the chi-square statistic measures, then looking at the individual standardized residuals is a good idea because they have a direct relationship with the test statistic.

2   These standardized residuals behave like any other (see Section 8.3.1.1): each one is a z-score. This is very useful because by looking at a standardized residual we can assess its significance (see Section 1.6.4). As we have learnt many times before, if the value lies outside of ± 1.96 then it is significant at $p < .05$, if it lies outside ± 2.58 then it is significant at $p < .01$ and if it lies outside ± 3.29 then it is significant at $p < .001$.

Fortunately, when we selected ☑ Standardized in Figure 18.5, SPSS produced these standardized residuals and we can see them in Output 18.2. There are four residuals: one for each combination of the type of training and whether the cats danced. When food was used as a reward the standardized residual was significant[3] for both those that danced ($z = 3.6$) and those that didn't dance ($z = -2.8$). The plus or minus sign tells us something about the direction of the effect, as do the counts and expected counts within the cells. We can interpret these standardized residuals as follows: when food was used as a reward significantly more cats than expected danced, and significantly fewer cats than expected did not dance. When affection was used as a reward the standardized residual was not significant[4] for both those that danced ($z = -1.7$) and those that didn't dance ($z = 1.4$). This tells us that when affection was used as a reward as many cats as expected danced and did not dance. In a nutshell, the cells for when food was used as a reward both significantly contribute to the overall chi-square statistic. Put another way, the association between the type of reward and dancing is mainly driven by when food is a reward.

18.5.6.   Calculating an effect size ②

Although Cramér's V is an adequate effect size (in the sense that it is constrained to fall between 0 and 1 and is, therefore, easily interpretable), a more common and probably more useful measure of effect size for categorical data is the odds ratio. Odds ratios are most interpretable in 2×2 contingency tables and are probably not useful for larger contingency tables. However, this isn't as restrictive as you might think because, as I've said more times than I care to recall in the GLM chapters, effect sizes are only ever useful when they summarize a focused comparison. A 2×2 contingency table is the categorical data equivalent of a focused comparison.

The odds ratio in its basic form is simple enough to calculate. If we look at our example, we first calculate the odds that a cat danced given that they had food as a reward. This is simply the number of cats that were given food and danced, divided by the number of cats given food that didn't dance:

$$\text{Odds}_{\text{dancing after food}} = \frac{\text{Number that had food and danced}}{\text{Number that had food but didn't dance}}$$

$$= \frac{28}{10}$$

$$= 2.8$$

---

[3] Because both values are bigger than 1.96 (when you ignore the minus sign).

[4] Because they are both smaller than 1.96 (when you ignore the minus sign)

DANIELS, E. A. (2012). *JOURNAL OF APPLIED DEVELOPMENTAL PSYCHOLOGY*, 33, 79–90.

LABCOAT LENI'S REAL RESEARCH 18.1

The impact of sexualized images on women's self-evaluations ①

Women (and increasingly men) are constantly bombarded with images of 'idealized' women in the media and there is a growing concern about how these images affect our perceptions of ourselves. Daniels (2012) conducted an interesting study in which she showed young women images of successful female athletes (e.g., Anna Kournikova) that were either images of them playing sport (performance athlete images) or images of them posing in bathing suits (sexualized images). Participants completed a short writing exercise after viewing these types of images. Each participant saw only one type of image, but several examples. Daniels then coded these written exercises and identified themes, one of which was whether women commented on their own appearance or attractiveness. Daniels hypothesized that women who viewed the sexualized images ($n = 140$) would self-objectify (i.e., this theme would be present in what they wrote) more than those who viewed the performance athlete pictures ($n = 117$, despite what the participants section of the paper implies). These are the frequencies:

	Theme Present	Theme Absent	Total
Performance athletes	20	97	117
Sexualized athletes	56	84	140

Labcoat Leni wants you to enter these data in SPSS and test Daniel's hypothesis that there is an association between the type of image viewed, and whether or not the women commented on their own appearance/attractiveness in their writing exercise **(Daniels (2012). sav)**. The answers are on the companion website, or on p. 85 of Daniels's paper.

Next we calculate the odds that a cat danced given that they had affection as a reward. This is simply the number of cats that were given affection and danced, divided by the number of cats given affection that didn't dance:

$$\text{Odds}_{\text{dancing after affection}} = \frac{\text{Number that had affection and danced}}{\text{Number that had affection but didn't dance}}$$

$$= \frac{48}{114}$$

$$= 0.421$$

The odds ratio is the odds of dancing after food divided by the odds of dancing after affection:

$$\text{Odds Ratio} = \frac{\text{Odds}_{\text{dancing after food}}}{\text{Odds}_{\text{dancing after affection}}}$$

$$= \frac{2.8}{0.421}$$

$$= 6.65$$

What this tells us is that if a cat was trained with food the odds of their dancing were 6.65 times higher than if they had been trained with affection. As you can see, this is an extremely elegant and easily understood metric for expressing the effect you've got.

18.5.7. Reporting the results of chi-square ①

When reporting Pearson's chi-square we report the value of the test statistic with its associated degrees of freedom and significance value. The test statistic, as we've seen, is denoted by χ^2. The SPSS output tells us that the value of χ^2 was 25.36, that the degrees of freedom on which this was based were 1, and that it was significant at $p < .001$ (too small to report the exact p-value). It's also useful to reproduce the contingency table and my vote would go to quoting the odds ratio too. As such, we could report:

✓ There was a significant association between the type of training and whether or not cats would dance χ^2 (1) = 25.36, $p < .001$. Based on the odds ratio, the odds of cats dancing were 6.65 times higher if they were trained with food than if trained with affection.

CRAMMING SAM'S TIPS   **Pearson chi-square test**

- If you want to test the relationship between two categorical variables you can do this with *Pearson's chi-square test* or the *likelihood ratio statistic*.
- Look at the table labelled *Chi-Square Tests*; if the *Exact Sig.* value is less than .05 for the row labelled *Pearson Chi-Square* then there is a significant relationship between your two variables.
- Check underneath this table to make sure that no expected frequencies are less than 5.
- Look at the contingency table to work out what the relationship between the variables is: look out for significant standardized residuals (values outside of ±1.96), and columns that have different letters as subscripts (this indicates a significant difference).
- Calculate the *odds ratio*.
- Report the χ^2 statistic, the degrees of freedom, the significance value and odds ratio. Also report the contingency table.

18.6.   Loglinear analysis using SPSS ②

18.6.1.   Initial considerations ②

Data are entered for loglinear analysis in the same way as for the chi-square test (see Section 18.5.2). Let's now extend the previous example to include dogs as well as cats. The data are in the file **Cats and Dogs.sav**; open this file. Notice that it has three variables (**Animal, Training** and **Dance**), and each one contains codes representing the different categories of these variables. The basic procedure is outlined in Figure 18.2, as it was for the chi-square test. First of all, we need to check the expected frequencies in the contingency table (Section 18.4.2), and we can do this with the *Crosstabs* command.

SELF-TEST   Use Section 18.5.3 to help you to create a contingency table of these data with dance as the columns, the type of training as rows and the type of animal as a layer.

BECKHAM, A. S. (1929). JOURNAL OF ABNORMAL AND SOCIAL PSYCHOLOGY, 24, 186–190.

LABCOAT LENI'S REAL RESEARCH 18.2

Is the black American happy? ①

When I was doing my psychology degree I spent a lot of time reading about the civil rights movement in the USA. Although I was supposed to be reading psychology, I became more interested in Malcolm X and Martin Luther King Jr. For this reason I find Beckham's 1929 study of black Americans such an interesting piece of research. Beckham was a black American academic who founded the psychology laboratory at Howard University, Washington, DC. His wife Ruth was the first black woman ever to be awarded a Ph.D. (also in psychology) at the University of Minnesota. To put some context on Beckham's study, it was published 36 years before the Jim Crow laws were finally overthrown by the Civil Rights Act of 1964, and at a time when black Americans were segregated, openly discriminated against and were victims of the most abominable violations of civil liberties and human rights. For a richer context I suggest reading James Baldwin's superb novel,

The fire next time. Even the language of the study and the data from it are an uncomfortable reminder of the era in which it was conducted.

Beckham sought to measure the psychological state of black Americans with three questions put to 3443 black Americans from different walks of life. He asked them whether they thought black Americans were happy, whether they personally were happy as a black American, and whether black Americans *should* be happy. They could answer only *yes* or *no* to each question. Beckham did no formal statistical analysis of his data (Fisher's article containing the popularized version of the chi-square test was published only 7 years earlier in a statistics journal that would not have been read by psychologists). I love this study, because it demonstrates that you do not need elaborate methods to answer important and far-reaching questions; with just three questions, Beckham told the world an enormous amount about very real and important psychological and sociological phenomena.

The frequency data (number of yes and no responses within each employment category) from this study are in the file **Beckham(1929).sav**. Labcoat Leni wants you to carry out three chi-square tests (one for each question that was asked). What conclusions can you draw?

The contingency table (Output 18.5) contains the number of cases that fall into each combination of categories. The top half of this table is the same as Output 18.2 because the data are the same (we've just added some dogs), and if you look back in this chapter there's a summary of what this tells us. For the dogs we can summarize the data in a similar way. In total 49 dogs danced (70% of the total) and of these 20 were trained using food (40.8% of the total that danced) and 29 were trained with affection (59.2% of the total that danced). Further, 21 dogs didn't dance at all (30% of the total) and of those that didn't dance, 14 were trained using food as a reward (66.7% of the total that didn't dance) and 7 were trained using affection (33.3% of the total that didn't dance). The numbers of dogs can be read from the rows labelled *Count* and the percentages are read from the rows labelled % *within Did they dance?* In summary, a lot more dogs danced (70%) than didn't (30%). About half of those that danced were trained with affection and about half with food as a reward. In short, dogs seem more willing to dance than cats (70% compared to 38%), and they're not too worried what training method is used.

Remember that the assumption of loglinear analysis is that there should be no expected counts less than 1, and no more than 20% less than 5 (Section 18.4.2). If you look at the expected counts in the contingency table, the smallest expected count is 10.2 (for dogs that were trained with food but didn't dance). This value still exceeds 5 and so the assumption has been met.

Type of Training * Did they dance? * Animal Crosstabulation

Animal					Did they dance? No	Did they dance? Yes	Total
Cat	Type of Training	Food as Reward	Count		10a	28b	38
			Expected Count		23.6	14.4	38.0
			% within Type of Training		26.3%	73.7%	100.0%
			% within Did they dance?		8.1%	36.8%	19.0%
			% of Total		5.0%	14.0%	19.0%
			Std. Residual		−2.8	3.6	
		Affection as Reward	Count		114a	48b	162
			Expected Count		100.4	61.6	162.0
			% within Type of Training		70.4%	29.6%	100.0%
			% within Did they dance?		91.9%	63.2%	81.0%
			% of Total		57.0%	24.0%	81.0%
			Std. Residual		1.4	−1.7	
	Total		Count		124	76	200
			Expected Count		124.0	76.0	200.0
			% within Type of Training		62.0%	38.0%	100.0%
			% within Did they dance?		100.0%	100.0%	100.0%
			% of Total		62.0%	38.0%	100.0%
Dog	Type of Training	Food as Reward	Count		14a	20b	34
			Expected Count		10.2	23.8	34.0
			% within Type of Training		41.2%	58.8%	100.0%
			% within Did they dance?		66.7%	40.8%	48.6%
			% of Total		20.0%	28.6%	48.6%
			Std. Residual		1.2	−.8	
		Affection as Reward	Count		7a	29b	36
			Expected Count		10.8	25.2	36.0
			% within Type of Training		19.4%	80.6%	100.0%
			% within Did they dance?		33.3%	59.2%	51.4%
			% of Total		10.0%	41.4%	51.4%
			Std. Residual		−1.2	.8	
	Total		Count		21	49	70
			Expected Count		21.0	49.0	70.0
			% within Type of Training		30.0%	70.0%	100.0%
			% within Did they dance?		100.0%	100.0%	100.0%
			% of Total		30.0%	70.0%	100.0%

Each subscript letter denotes a subset of Did they dance? categories whose column proportions do not differ significantly from each other at the .05 level.

18.6.2. Running loglinear analysis ②

Having established that the assumptions have been met, we can move on to the main analysis. The way to run loglinear analysis that is consistent with my section on the theory is to select Analyze Loglinear ▶ ▦ Model Selection... to access the dialog box in Figure 18.6. Select any variables that you want to include in the analysis (remember that you can select several at the same time by holding down the *Ctrl* key (*Cmd* on a Mac)) and then dragging them to the box labelled *Factor(s)* (or click on ➡). When there is a variable in this box the Define Range button becomes active. We have to tell SPSS the codes that we've used to define our categorical variables. Select a variable in the *Factor(s)* box and then click on Define Range... to activate a dialog box that allows you to specify the value of the minimum and maximum code that you've used for that variable. In fact all three variables in this example have the same codes (they all have two categories and I coded them all with 0 and 1) so we can select all three, then click on Define Range... and type 0 in the *Minimum* box and 1 in the *Maximum* box. When you've done this, click on Continue to return to the main dialog box.

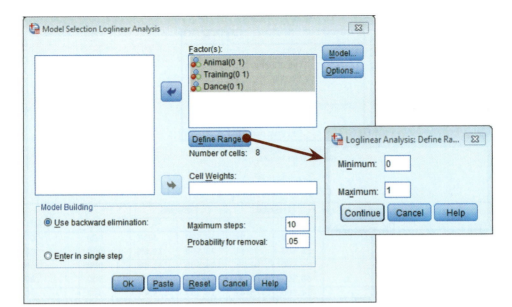

FIGURE 18.6
Main dialog box for loglinear analysis

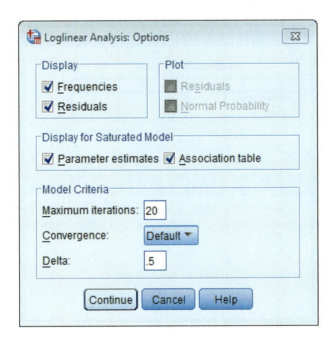

FIGURE 18.7
Options for loglinear analysis

The default options in the main box are fine; the main thing to note is that by default SPSS uses backward elimination (as I've described elsewhere). You can actually select *Enter in a single step*, which is a non-hierarchical method (in which all effects are entered and evaluated, like forced entry in multiple regression). In loglinear analysis the combined effects take precedence over lower-order effects and so there is little to recommend non-hierarchical methods.

If you click on ⬚Model… then this will open a dialog box very similar to those we saw in ANCOVA (e.g., see Figure 12.9). By default SPSS fits the saturated model; unless you have a very good reason for not fitting it, leave well alone. Clicking on ⬚Options… opens the dialog box in Figure 18.7. There are few options to play around with really (the default options are fine). You can select *Parameter estimates*, which will produce a table of parameter estimates for each effect (a z-score and associated confidence interval), and an *Association*

Data Information

		N
Cases	Valid	270
	Out of Range[a]	0
	Missing	0
	Weighted Valid	270
Categories	Animal	2
	Type of Training	2
	Did they dance?	2

a. Cases rejected because of out of range factor values.

Cell Counts and Residuals

Animal	Type of Training	Did they dance?	Observed Count[a]	Observed %	Expected Count	Expected %	Residuals	Std. Residuals
Cat	Food as Reward	No	10.500	3.9%	10.500	3.9%	.000	.000
		Yes	28.500	10.6%	28.500	10.6%	.000	.000
	Affection as Reward	No	114.500	42.4%	114.500	42.4%	.000	.000
		Yes	48.500	18.0%	48.500	18.0%	.000	.000
Dog	Food as Reward	No	14.500	5.4%	14.500	5.4%	.000	.000
		Yes	20.500	7.6%	20.500	7.6%	.000	.000
	Affection as Reward	No	7.500	2.8%	7.500	2.8%	.000	.000
		Yes	29.500	10.9%	29.500	10.9%	.000	.000

a. For saturated models, .500 has been added to all observed cells.

Goodness-of-Fit Tests

	Chi-Square	df	Sig.
Likelihood Ratio	.000	0	.
Pearson	.000	0	.

table, which will produce chi-square statistics for all of the effects in the model. This may be useful in some situations, but, as I've said before, if the higher-order interactions are significant then we shouldn't really be interested in the lower-order effects because they're confounded with the higher-order effects. When you've finished with the options, click on Continue to return to the main dialog box and then click on OK to run the analysis.

18.6.3. Output from loglinear analysis ③

Output 18.6 shows the initial output from the loglinear analysis. The first table tells us that we have 270 cases (remember that we had 200 cats and 70 dogs, and this is a useful check that no cats or dogs have been lost – they do tend to wander off). SPSS then lists all of the factors in the model and the number of levels they have (in this case all have two levels). To begin with, SPSS fits the saturated model (all terms are in the model including the highest-order interaction, in this case the **animal** × **training** × **dance** interaction). The second table gives us the observed and expected counts for each of the combinations of categories in our model. These values should be the same as the original contingency table, except that each cell has 0.5 added to it (this value is the default and is fine, but if you want to change it you can do so by changing *Delta* in Figure 18.7).

The final bit of this initial output gives us two goodness-of-fit statistics: Pearson's chi-square and the likelihood ratio statistic, both of which we came across at the beginning of this chapter. In this context we're testing the hypothesis that the frequencies predicted by the model (the expected frequencies) are significantly different from the actual frequencies in our data (the observed frequencies). Obviously, if our model is a good fit of the data then

K-Way and Higher-Order Effects

	K	df	Likelihood Ratio Chi-Square	Likelihood Ratio Sig.	Pearson Chi-Square	Pearson Sig.	Number of Iterations
K-way and Higher Order Effects[a]	1	7	200.163	.000	253.556	.000	0
	2	4	72.267	.000	67.174	.000	2
	3	1	20.305	.000	20.778	.000	4
K-way Effects[b]	1	3	127.896	.000	186.382	.000	0
	2	3	51.962	.000	46.396	.000	0
	3	1	20.305	.000	20.778	.000	0

a. Tests that k-way and higher order effects are zero.

b. Tests that k-way effects are zero.

the observed and expected frequencies should be very similar (i.e., not significantly different). Therefore, we want these statistics to be non-significant. A significant result would mean that our model was significantly different from our data (i.e., the model is a bad fit of the data). In large samples these statistics should give the same results but the likelihood ratio statistic is preferred in small samples. In this example, both statistics are 0 and yield a probability value, *p*, of '.', which is a rather confusing way of saying that the probability cannot be computed. The reason why it cannot be computed is that at this stage the model predicts the data *perfectly*. If you read the theory section this shouldn't surprise you, because I showed there that the saturated model is a perfect fit of the data and I mentioned that the resulting likelihood ratio would be zero. The interesting question is what bits of the model we can remove without significantly affecting the fit of the model.

The next part of the output (Output 18.7) tells us something about which components of the model can be removed. The first bit of the output is labelled *K-Way and Higher-Order Effects*, and there are rows showing likelihood ratio and Pearson chi-square statistics when *K* = 1, 2 and 3 (as we go down the rows of the table). The first row (*K* = 1) tells us whether removing the one-way effects (i.e., the main effects of **animal**, **training** and **dance**) and any higher-order effects will significantly affect the fit of the model. There are lots of higher-order effects here – there are the two-way interactions and a three-way interaction – and so this is basically testing whether if we remove everything from the model there will be a significant effect on the fit of the model. This effect is highly significant. If this test was non-significant (if the values of *Sig.* were above .05) then this would tell you that removing everything from your model would not affect the fit of the model (in other words, overall the combined effect of your variables and interactions is not significant). The next row of the table (*K* = 2) tells us whether removing the two-way interactions (i.e., the **animal** × **training**, **animal** × **dance** and **training** × **dance** interactions) and any higher-order effects will affect the model. In this case there is a higher-order effect (the three-way interaction) so this is testing whether removing the two-way interactions *and* the three-way interaction would affect the fit of the model. This is also highly significant, indicating that if we removed the two-way interactions and the three-way interaction then this would have a significant detrimental effect on the model. The final row (*K* = 3) is testing whether removing the three-way effect *and* higher-order effects will significantly affect the fit of the model. Now of course, the three-way interaction is the highest-order effect that we have, so this is simply testing whether removal of three-way interaction (i.e., the **animal** × **training** × **dance** interaction) will significantly affect the fit of the model. If you look at the two columns labelled *Sig.* then you can see that both chi-square and likelihood ratio tests agree that removing this interaction will significantly affect the fit of the model (because the probability value is less than .05).

The bottom of the table (*K-way Effects*) expresses the same thing but without including the higher-order effects. The first row (*K* = 1), tests whether removing the main effects (the one-way effects of **animal**, **training** and **dance**) has a significant detrimental effect on the model, and it does (because the *p*-value is less than .05). The second row (*K* = 2) tests whether removing the two-way interactions (**animal** × **training**, **animal** × **dance** and **training** × **dance**)

Partial Associations

Effect	df	Partial Chi–Square	Sig.	Number of Iterations
Animal*Training	1	13.760	.000	2
Animal*Dance	1	13.748	.000	2
Training*Dance	1	8.611	.003	2
Animal	1	65.268	.000	2
Training	1	61.145	.000	2
Dance	1	1.483	.223	2

has a significant detrimental effect on the model, and again it does ($p <.001$). This finding tells us that one or more of these two-way interactions is a significant predictor. The final row ($K = 3$) tests whether removing the three-way interaction (**animal** × **training** × **dance**) has a detrimental effect on the model. It does ($p <.001$) suggesting that this interaction is a significant predictor of the data. The results in this row are identical to the final row of the top half of the table (the *K-way and Higher Order Effects*) because it is the highest-order effect and so in the top part of the table there were no higher-order effects to include.

What this table is actually telling us is that the three-way interaction is significant: removing it from the model has a significant effect on how well the model fits the data. We also know that removing all two-way interactions has a significant effect on the model, but you have to remember that loglinear analysis should be done hierarchically and so these two-way interactions aren't of interest to us because the three-way interaction is significant (we'd look only at these effects if the three-way interaction were non-significant).

If you selected an *Association table* in Figure 18.7 then you'll get the table in Output 18.8. This table breaks down the table that we've just looked at into its component parts. So, for example, although we know from the previous output that removing all of the two-way interactions significantly affects the model, we don't know which of the two-way interactions is having the effect. This table tells us: the Pearson chi-square tests are significant for the **animal** × **dance**, **training** × **dance** and the **animal** × **training** interactions (i.e., all of them). Likewise, the previous output told us that removing the main effects of **animal**, **training** and **dance** significantly affected the fit of the model. Output 18.8 breaks this effect down to show that the main effects of **animal** and **training** are both significant ($p <.001$), but the main effect of **dance** is not ($p =.223$). However, we should ignore all of these effects because they are all confounded with the higher-order interaction of **animal** × **training** × **dance**.

If you selected the *Parameter estimates* in Figure 18.7 then you'll get the table in Output 18.9, which tells us the same thing as the previous table (i.e., it provides individual estimates for each effect) but it does so using a *z*-score rather than a chi-square test. This can be useful because we get confidence intervals, and also because the value of *z* gives us a useful comparison between effects (if you ignore the plus or minus sign, the bigger the *z*, the more significant the effect). So, if you look at the *z*-values you can see that the main effect of **animal** is the most important effect in the model ($z = 4.84$) followed by the **animal** × **training** interaction ($z = -4.82$) and then the **animal** × **training** × **dance** interaction ($z = -4.32$) and so on. However, it's worth reiterating that in this case we don't need to concern ourselves with anything other than the three-way interaction.

Output 18.10 deals with the backward elimination. SPSS will begin with the highest-order effect (in this case the **animal** × **training** × **dance** interaction); it removes it from the model, sees what effect this has, and if it doesn't have a significant effect then it moves on to the next highest effects (in this case the two-way interactions). However, we've already seen that removing the three-way interaction will have a significant effect, and this is confirmed at this stage by the table labelled *Step Summary*, which confirms that removing the three-way interaction has a significant effect on the model. Therefore, the analysis stops here: the three-way interaction is not removed and SPSS evaluates this final model using

Parameter Estimates

Effect	Parameter	Estimate	Std. Error	Z	Sig.	95% Confidence Interval	
						Lower Bound	Upper Bound
Animal*Training*Dance	1	-.360	.083	-4.320	.000	-.523	-.197
Animal*Training	1	-.402	.083	-4.823	.000	-.565	-.239
Animal*Dance	1	.197	.083	2.364	.018	.034	.360
Training*Dance	1	-.104	.083	-1.251	.211	-.268	.059
Animal	1	.404	.083	4.843	.000	.240	.567
Training	1	-.328	.083	-3.937	.000	-.492	-.165
Dance	1	-.232	.083	-2.782	.005	-.395	-.069

OUTPUT 18.9

the likelihood ratio statistic. We're looking for a non-significant test statistic, which indicates that the expected values generated by the model are not significantly different from the observed data (put another way, the model is a good fit of the data). In this case the result is very non-significant, indicating that the model is a good fit of the data.[5]

I don't need a loglinear analysis to tell me that cats are vastly superior to dogs!

The next step is to try to interpret this interaction. The first useful thing we can do is to plot the frequencies across all of the different categories. You should plot the frequencies in terms of the percentage of the total (these values can be found in the contingency table in Output 18.5 in the rows labelled *% of total*). The resulting graph is shown in Figure 18.8 and this shows what we already know about cats: they will dance (or do anything else for that matter) when there is food involved but if you train them with affection they're not interested. Dogs, on the other hand, will dance when there's affection involved (actually more dogs danced than didn't dance regardless of the type of reward, but the effect is more pronounced when affection was the training method). In fact, both animals show similar responses to food training, it's just that cats are less likely to do anything for affection compared to food. So cats are sensible creatures that do stupid stuff only when there's something in it for them (i.e., food), whereas dogs are just daft.☺

SELF-TEST Can you use the chart builder to replicate the graph in Figure 18.8?

18.6.4. Following up loglinear analysis ②

An alternative way to interpret a three-way interaction is to conduct chi-square analysis at different levels of one of your variables. For example, to interpret our **animal × training × dance** interaction, we could perform a chi-square test on training and dance but do this separately for dogs and cats (in fact the analysis for cats will be the same as the example we used for chi-square). We can then compare the results in the different animals.

[5] The fact that the analysis has stopped here is unhelpful because I can't show you how it would proceed in the event of a non-significant three-way interaction. However, it does keep things simple, and if you're interested in exploring loglinear analysis further, the task at the end of the chapter shows you what happens when the highest-order interaction is not significant.

OUTPUT 18.10

Step Summary

Step[a]		Effects	Chi-Square[c]	df	Sig.	Number of Iterations
0	Generating Class[b]	Animal*Training*Dance	.000	0	.	
	Deleted Effect 1	Animal*Training*Dance	20.305	1	.000	4
1	Generating Class[b]	Animal*Training*Dance	.000	0	.	

a. At each step, the effect with the largest significance level for the Likelihood Ratio Change is deleted, provided the significance level is larger than .050.

b. Statistics are displayed for the best model at each step after step 0.

c. For 'Deleted Effect', this is the change in the Chi-Square after the effect is deleted from the model.

Cell Counts and Residuals

Animal	Type of Training	Did they dance?	Observed Count	Observed %	Expected Count	Expected %	Residuals	Std. Residuals
Cat	Food as Reward	No	10.000	3.7%	10.000	3.7%	.000	.000
		Yes	28.000	10.4%	28.000	10.4%	.000	.000
	Affection as Reward	No	114.000	42.2%	114.000	42.2%	.000	.000
		Yes	48.000	17.8%	48.000	17.8%	.000	.000
Dog	Food as Reward	No	14.000	5.2%	14.000	5.2%	.000	.000
		Yes	20.000	7.4%	20.000	7.4%	.000	.000
	Affection as Reward	No	7.000	2.6%	7.000	2.6%	.000	.000
		Yes	29.000	10.7%	29.000	10.7%	.000	.000

Goodness-of-Fit Tests

	Chi-Square	df	Sig.
Likelihood Ratio	.000	0	.
Pearson	.000	0	.

FIGURE 18.8

Percentage of different animals who danced or not after being trained with affection or food

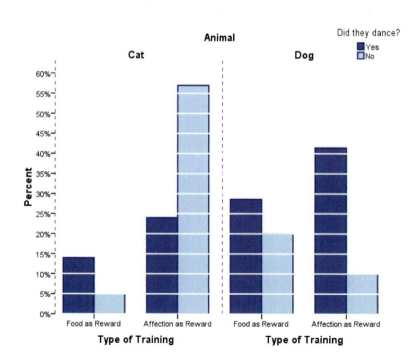

SELF-TEST   Use the split file command (see Section 5.3.2.4) to run a chi-square test on **Dance** and **Training** for dogs and cats.

Chi-Square Tests[a]

	Value	df	Asymp. Sig. (2-sided)	Exact Sig. (2-sided)	Exact Sig. (1-sided)
Pearson Chi-Square	3.932[b]	1	.047		
Continuity Correction[c]	2.966	1	.085		
Likelihood Ratio	3.984	1	.046		
Fisher's Exact Test				.068	.042
Linear-by-Linear Association	3.876	1	.049		
N of Valid Cases	70				

a. Animal = Dog

b. 0 cells (0.0%) have expected count less than 5. The minimum expected count is 10.20.

c. Computed only for a 2x2 table

The results and interpretation for cats are shown in Output 18.3 and for dogs in Output 18.11. For dogs there is still a significant relationship between the types of training and whether they danced, but it is weaker (the chi-square is 3.93 compared to 25.2 in the cats).[6] This finding seems to suggest that dogs are more likely to dance if given affection than if given food, the opposite of cats.

18.7. Effect sizes in loglinear analysis ②

As with Pearson's chi-square, one of the most elegant ways to report your effects is in terms of odds ratios. Odds ratios are easiest to understand for 2×2 contingency tables, so if you have significant higher-order interactions, or your variables have more than two categories, it is worth trying to break these effects down into logical 2×2 tables and calculating odds ratios that reflect the nature of the interaction. So, in this example we could calculate odds ratios for dogs and cats separately. We have the odds ratios for cats already (Section 18.5.6), and for dogs we would get:

$$\text{Odds}_{\text{dancing after food}} = \frac{\text{Number that had food and danced}}{\text{Number that had food but didn't dance}}$$

$$= \frac{20}{14}$$

$$= 1.43$$

$$\text{Odds}_{\text{dancing after affection}} = \frac{\text{Number that had affection and danced}}{\text{Number that had affection but didn't dance}}$$

$$= \frac{29}{7}$$

$$= 4.14$$

$$\text{Odds Ratio} = \frac{\text{Odds}_{\text{dancing after food}}}{\text{Odds}_{\text{dancing after affection}}}$$

$$= \frac{1.43}{4.14}$$

$$= 0.35$$

[6] The chi-square statistic depends on the sample size, so really you need to calculate effect sizes and compare them to make this kind of statement (unless you had equal numbers of dogs and cats).

This tells us that if a dog was trained with food the odds of their dancing were 0.35 times the odds if they were rewarded with affection (i.e., they were less likely to dance). Another way to say this is that the odds of their dancing were $1/0.35 = 2.90$ times lower if they were trained with food instead of affection. Compare this to cats where the odds of dancing were 6.65 higher if they were trained with food rather than affection. As you can see, comparing the odds ratios for dogs and cats is an extremely elegant way to present the three-way interaction term in the model.

18.8. Reporting the results of loglinear analysis ②

When reporting loglinear analysis you need to report the likelihood ratio statistic for the final model, usually denoted just by χ^2. For any terms that are significant you should report the chi-square change, or you could consider reporting the z-score for the effect and its associated confidence interval. If you break down any higher-order interactions in subsequent analyses then obviously you need to report the relevant chi-square statistics (and odds ratios). For this example we could report:

✓ The three-way loglinear analysis produced a final model that retained all effects. The likelihood ratio of this model was $\chi^2(0) = 0$, $p = 1$. This indicated that the highest-order interaction (the **animal × training × dance** interaction) was significant, $\chi^2(1) = 20.31$, $p < .001$. To break down this effect, separate chi-square tests on the **training** and **dance** variables were performed separately for dogs and cats. For cats, there was a significant association between the type of training and whether or not cats would dance, $\chi^2(1) = 25.36$, $p < .001$; this was true in dogs also, $\chi^2(1) = 3.93$, $p = .047$. Odds ratios indicated that the odds of dancing were 6.65 higher after food than affection in cats, but only 0.35 in dogs (i.e., in dogs, the odds of dancing were 2.90 times lower if trained with food compared to affection). Therefore, the analysis seems to reveal a fundamental difference between dogs and cats: cats are more likely to dance for food than affection, whereas dogs are more likely to dance for affection than food.

CRAMMING SAM'S TIPS   Loglinear analysis

- If you want to test the relationship between more than two categorical variables you can do this with *loglinear analysis*.
- Loglinear analysis is hierarchical: the initial model contains all main effects and interactions. Starting with the highest-order interaction, terms are removed to see whether their removal significantly affects the fit of the model. If it does then this term is not removed and all lower-order effects are ignored.
- Look at the table labelled *K-Way and Higher-Order Effects* to see which effects have been retained in the final model. Then look at the table labelled *Partial Associations* to see the individual significance of the retained effects (look at the column labelled *Sig.* – values less than .05 indicate significance).
- Look at the *Goodness-of-Fit Tests* for the final model: if this model is a good fit of the data then this statistic should be non-significant (*Sig.* should be bigger than .05).
- Look at the contingency table to interpret any significant effects (percentage of total for cells is the best thing to look at).

18.9. Brian's attempt to woo Jane ①

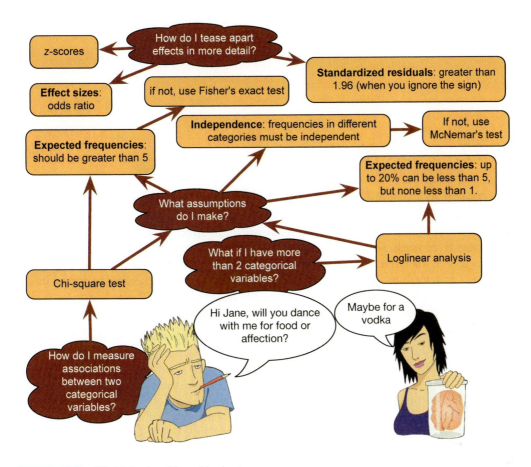

FIGURE 18.9 What Brian learnt from this chapter

18.10. What next? ①

When I wrote the first edition of this book I had always intended to do a chapter on log-linear analysis, but by the time I got to that chapter I had already written 300 pages more than I was contracted to do, and had put so much effort into the rest of it that, well, the thought of that extra chapter was making me think of large cliffs and jumping. When the second edition needed to be written, I wanted to make sure that at the very least I did a loglinear chapter. However, when I came to it, I'd already written 200 pages more than I was supposed to for this new edition, and with deadlines fading into the distance, history was repeating itself. It won't surprise you to know then that I was really happy to have written the damn thing. Fortunately the experience of this loglinear chapter taught me a valuable lesson, which is never to agree to write a chapter about something that you know very little about, and if you do then definitely don't leave it until the very end of the writing process when you're under pressure and mentally exhausted. It's lucky that we learn from our mistakes, isn't it?

18.11. Key terms that I've discovered

Chi-square distribution   Fisher's exact test   Phi
Chi-square test   Goodman and Kruskal's λ   Saturated model
Contingency table   Loglinear analysis   Yates's continuity correction
Cramér's *V*   Odds ratio

18.12. Smart Alex's tasks

- **Task 1**: Research suggests that people who can switch off from work (**Detachment**) during off-hours are more satisfied with life and have fewer symptoms of psychological strain (Sonnentag, 2012). Factors at work can affect your ability to detach when away from work. For example, a study looked at 1709 Swiss and German employees measured job stress in terms of time pressure (**Time_Pressure**) at work (no time pressure, low, medium, high and very high time pressure). Data generated to approximate Figure 1 in Sonnentag (2012) are in the file **Sonnentag (2012).sav**. Carry out a chi-square test to see if time pressure is associated with the ability to detach from work. ①

- **Task 2**: Labcoat Leni's Real Research 18.1 describes a study (Daniels, 2012) that looked at the impact of sexualized images of athletes compared to performance pictures on women's perceptions of the athlete's and of themselves. Women looked at different types of pictures (**Picture**) and then did a writing task. Daniels identified whether certain themes were present or absent in each written piece (**Theme_Present**). We have already looked at the self-evaluation theme, but Daniels also identified others including: commenting on the athlete's body/appearance (**Athletes_Body**), indicating admiration or jealousy for the athlete (**Admiration**), indicating that the athlete was a role model or motivating (**Role_Model**), and their own physical activity (**Self_Physical_Activity**). The data are in the file **Daniels (2012).sav**. Carry out a chi-square test to see whether the type of picture viewed was associated with commenting on the athlete's body/appearance. ①

- **Task 3**: Using the same data, carry out a chi-square test to see whether the type of picture viewed was associated with indicating admiration or jealousy for the athlete. ①

- **Task 4**: Using the same data, carry out a chi-square test to see whether the type of picture viewed was associated with indicating that the athlete was a role model or motivating. ①

- **Task 5**: Using the same data, carry out a chi-square test to see whether the type of picture viewed was associated with the participant commenting on their own physical activity. ①

- **Task 6**: I wrote much of the third edition of this book in the Netherlands (I have a soft spot for Holland). I noticed cultural differences to England. The Dutch travel by bike much more than the English. I noticed also that many more Dutch people cycle while steering with only one hand. I pointed this out to one of my friends, Birgit Mayer, and she said that I was being a crazy English fool and that Dutch people did not cycle one-handed. Several weeks of me pointing at one-handed cyclists and her pointing at two-handed cyclists ensued. To put it to the test I counted the number of Dutch and English cyclists who ride with one or two hands on the handlebars (**Handlebars.sav**). Can you work out which one of us is right? ①

- **Task 7**: Compute and interpret the odds ratio for Task 6. ②

- **Task 8**: Certain editors at Sage like to think they're a bit of a whiz at football (soccer if you prefer). To see whether they are better than Sussex lecturers and postgraduates we invited various employees of Sage to join in our football matches. Every player was allowed only to play in one match. Over many matches, we counted the number of players that scored goals. The data are in the file **Sage Editors Can't Play Football. sav**. Do a chi-square test to see whether more publishers or academics scored goals. We predict that Sussex people will score more than Sage people. ①

- **Task 9**: Compute and interpret the odds ratio for Task 8. ②

- **Task 10**: I was interested in whether horoscopes are just tosh. Therefore, I took 2201 people, made a note of their star sign (this variable, obviously, has 12 categories: Capricorn, Aquarius, Pisces, Aries, Taurus, Gemini, Cancer, Leo, Virgo, Libra, Scorpio and Sagittarius) and whether they believed in horoscopes (this variable has two categories: believer or unbeliever). I then sent them a horoscope in the post of what would happen over the next month. Everybody, regardless of their star sign, received the same horoscope, which read: 'August is an exciting month for you. You will make friends with a tramp in the first week of the month and cook him a cheese omelette. Curiosity is your greatest virtue, and in the second week you'll discover knowledge of a subject that you previously thought was boring, statistics perhaps. You might purchase a book around this time that guides you towards this knowledge. Your new wisdom leads to a change in career around the third week, when you ditch your current job and become an accountant. By the final week you find yourself free from the constraints of having friends, your boy/girlfriend has left you for a Russian ballet dancer with a glass eye, and you now spend your weekends doing loglinear analysis by hand with a pigeon called Hephzibah for company.' At the end of August I interviewed all of these people and I classified the horoscope as having come true, or not, based on how closely their lives had matched the fictitious horoscope. The data are in the file **Horoscope.sav**. Conduct a loglinear analysis to see whether there is a relationship between the person's star sign, whether they believe in horoscopes and whether the horoscope came true. ③

- **Task 11**: On my statistics course students have weekly SPSS classes in a computer laboratory. These classes are run by postgraduate tutors but I often pop in to help out. I've noticed in these sessions that many students are studying Facebook more than the very interesting statistics assignments that I have set them. I wanted to see the impact that this behaviour had on their exam performance. I collected data from all 260 students on my course. I checked their **Attendance** and classified them as having attended either more or less than 50% of their lab classes. Next, I classified them as being either someone who looked at **Facebook** during their lab class, or someone who never did. Lastly, after the exam, I classified them as having either passed or failed (**Exam**). The data are in **Facebook.sav**. Do a loglinear analysis on the data to see if there is an association between studying Facebook and failing your exam. ③

18.13. Further reading

Hutcheson, G., & Sofroniou, N. (1999). *The multivariate social scientist*. London: Sage.

Tabachnick, B. G., & Fidell, L. S. (2012). *Using multivariate statistics* (6th ed.). Boston: Pearson Education.

19 Logistic regression

Having a therapy
session in 2007

19.1. What will this chapter tell me? ①

Over the last couple of chapters we saw that I had gone from a child having dreams and
aspirations of being a rock star, to becoming a living (barely) statistical test. A more dramatic demonstration of my complete failure to achieve my life's ambitions I can scarcely
imagine. Having devoted far too much of my life to statistics, it was time to unlock the
latent rock star once more. The second edition of this book had left me in desperate need
of some therapy, so at the age of 29 I decided to learn to play the drums (there's a joke
in there somewhere about it being the perfect instrument for a failed musician, but really
they're much harder to play than people think). A couple of years later I had a call from
an old friend of mine, Doug, who used to be in a band that my old band Scansion used
to play with a lot: 'Remember the last time I saw you we talked about you coming and
having a jam with us?' I had absolutely no recollection whatsoever of him saying this, so
I responded 'Yes'. 'Well, how about it then?' he said. 'OK,' I said, 'you arrange it and I'll
bring my guitar.' 'No, you whelk,' he said, 'we want you to drum. Can you learn some of
the songs on the CD I gave you last year?' I'd played his band's CD and I liked it, but their
songs were ridiculously fast and there was no way on earth that I could play them. 'Sure,

no problem', I lied. I spent the next two weeks trying to become a much better drummer than I was, playing along to this CD as if my life depended on it. I'd love to report that when the rehearsal came I astounded them with my brilliance, but I didn't. I did, however, nearly have a heart attack and herniate everything in my body that it's possible to herniate. Still, we had another rehearsal, and then another and, 7 years down the line, we're still having them. The main difference now is that I play the songs at a speed that makes their old drummer sound like a sedated snail (www.myspace.com/fracture-pattern). It's curious that I started off playing guitar (which I can still play, incidentally), and then I chose drums. Within famous bands, there are always assumptions about the personalities of different musicians: the singers are egocentric, guitarists are perceived to be cool, bassists introverted and happy to blend into the background, and drummers are supposed to be crazy hedonists, autistic (enjoying counting helps) or both. I'm definitely more autistic than hedonistic. If we wanted to test what personality characteristics predict the instrument you choose to play, then we'd have a categorical outcome (type of instrument) with several categories (drums, guitar, bass, singing, keyboard, tuba, etc.) and continuous predictors (neuroticism, extroversion, etc.). We've looked at how we can quantify associations between purely categorical variables, but if we have continuous predictors too then surely there's no model on earth that can handle that kind of complexity; should we just go to the pub and have a good time instead? Actually, we can do logistic regression – bugger!

19.2. Background to logistic regression ①

In the last chapter we started to look at how we fit models of the relationships between categorical variables. We have also seen throughout the book how we can use categorical variables to predict continuous outcomes. However, we haven't looked at the reverse process: predicting categorical outcomes from continuous or categorical predictors. In a nutshell, logistic regression is multiple regression but with an outcome variable that is categorical and predictor variables that are continuous or categorical. In its simplest form, this means that we can predict which of two categories a person is likely to belong to given certain other information. A trivial example is to look at which variables predict whether a person is male or female. We might measure laziness, pig-headedness, alcohol consumption and daily flatulence. Using logistic regression, we might find that all of these variables predict the gender of the person. More important, the model we build will enable us to predict whether a new person is likely to be male or female based on these variables. So, if we picked a random person and discovered that they scored highly on laziness, pig-headedness, alcohol consumption and flatulence, then our model might tell us that, based on this information, this person is likely to be male. Logistic regression can have life-saving applications. In medical research it is used to generate models from which predictions can be made about the likelihood that a tumour is cancerous or benign (for example). A database of patients is used to establish which variables are influential in predicting the malignancy of a tumour. These variables can then be measured for a new patient and their values placed in a logistic regression model, from which a probability of malignancy could be estimated. If the probability value of the tumour being malignant is low then the doctor may decide not to carry out expensive and painful surgery that in all likelihood is unnecessary. We might not face such life-threatening decisions, but logistic regression can nevertheless be a very useful tool. When we are trying to predict membership of only two categorical outcomes the analysis is known as binary logistic regression, but when we want to predict membership of more than two categories we use multinomial (or polychotomous) logistic regression.

19.3. What are the principles behind logistic regression? ③

I don't wish to dwell on the underlying principles of logistic regression because they aren't necessary to understand the test (I am living proof of this fact). However, I do wish to draw a few parallels to ordinary regression so that you can get the gist of what's going on using a framework that will be familiar to you already. To keep things simple I will explain binary logistic regression, but most of the principles extend easily to when there are more than two outcome categories. Now would be a good time for the equation-phobes to look away. In simple linear regression, we saw that the outcome variable Y is predicted from the equation:

$$Y_i = b_0 + b_1 X_{1i} + \varepsilon_i \tag{19.1}$$

in which b_0 is the Y intercept, b_1 quantifies the relationship between the predictor and outcome, X_1 is the value of the predictor variable and ε is an error term. When there are several predictors, a similar model is used in which the outcome (Y) is predicted from a combination of each predictor variable (X) multiplied by its respective regression coefficient (b):

$$Y_i = b_0 + b_1 X_{1i} + b_2 X_{2i} + \cdots + b_n X_{ni} + \varepsilon_i \tag{19.2}$$

in which b_n is the regression coefficient of the corresponding variable X_n. However, there is a good reason why we cannot apply these linear models when the outcome variable is categorical. One of the assumptions of the linear model (i.e., regression) is that the relationship between variables is linear. In Section 8.3.2.1 we saw how important it is that the model accurately reflects the true relationship that's being modelled. Therefore, for linear regression to be a valid model, the observed data should have a linear relationship. When the outcome variable is categorical, this assumption is violated (Berry, 1993). One way around this problem is to transform the data using the logarithmic transformation (see Berry & Feldman, 1985; and Chapter 5 of this book). This transformation is a way of expressing a non-linear relationship in a linear way. Logistic regression is based on this principle: it expresses the multiple linear regression equation in logarithmic terms (called the *logit*) and thus overcomes the problem of violating the assumption of linearity. Let's now look at the logistic regression model.

Why can't I use linear regression?

In logistic regression, instead of predicting the value of a variable Y from a predictor variable X_1 or several predictor variables (Xs), we predict the *probability* of Y occurring given known values of X_1 (or Xs). The logistic regression equation bears many similarities to the regression equations just described. In its simplest form, when there is only one predictor variable X_1, the logistic regression equation from which the probability of Y is predicted is given by:

$$P(Y) = \frac{1}{1 + e^{-(b_0 + b_1 X_{1i})}} \tag{19.3}$$

in which $P(Y)$ is the probability of Y occurring, e is the base of natural logarithms, and the other coefficients form a linear combination much the same as in simple regression. In fact, you might notice that the bracketed portion of the equation is identical to the linear regression equation: there is a constant (b_0), a predictor variable (X_1) and a coefficient (or weight) attached to that predictor (b_1). Just like linear regression, it is possible to extend this equation so as to include several predictors. When there are several predictors the equation becomes:

$$P(Y) = \frac{1}{1 + e^{-(b_0 + b_1 X_{1i} + b_2 X_{2i} + \cdots + b_n X_{ni})}}$$

(19.4)

Whereas the one-predictor version of the logistic regression equation contained the simple linear regression equation, the multiple-predictor version contains the multiple regression equation.

The equation can be presented in several ways, but the version I have chosen expresses the equation in terms of the probability of Y occurring (i.e., the probability that a case belongs in a certain category). The resulting value from the equation, therefore, varies between 0 and 1. A value close to 0 means that Y is very unlikely to have occurred, and a value close to 1 means that Y is very likely to have occurred. Also, just like linear regression, each predictor variable in the logistic regression equation has its own parameter (b), which is estimated from the sample data. Whereas in linear regression these parameters are estimated using the method of least squares (Section 2.4.3), in logistic regression **maximum-likelihood estimation** is used, which selects coefficients that make the observed values most likely to have occurred. Essentially, parameters are estimated by fitting models, based on the available predictors, to the observed data. The chosen estimates of the bs will be ones that, when values of the predictor variables are placed in it, result in values of Y closest to the observed values.

19.3.1. Assessing the model: the log-likelihood statistic ③

We've seen that the logistic regression model predicts the probability of an event occurring for a given person (we denote the probability that Y occurs for the ith person as $P(Y_i)$), based on observations of whether or not the event did occur for that person (we could denote the actual outcome for the ith person as Y_i). So, for a given person, Y will be either 0 (the outcome didn't occur) or 1 (the outcome did occur), and the predicted value, $P(Y)$, will be a value between 0 (there is no chance that the outcome will occur) and 1 (the outcome will certainly occur). We saw in multiple regression that if we want to assess whether a model fits the data we can compare the observed and predicted values of the outcome (if you remember, we use R^2, which is the Pearson correlation between observed values of the outcome and the values predicted by the regression model). Likewise, in logistic regression, we use the observed and predicted values to assess the fit of the model. The measure we use is the **log-likelihood**:

$$\text{log-likelihood} = \sum_{i=1}^{N} \left[Y_i \ln\left(P(Y_i)\right) + \left(1 - Y_i\right) \ln\left(1 - P(Y_i)\right) \right]$$

(19.5)

The log-likelihood is based on summing the probabilities associated with the predicted and actual outcomes (Tabachnick & Fidell, 2012). The log-likelihood statistic is analogous to the residual sum of squares in multiple regression in the sense that it is an indicator of how much unexplained information there is after the model has been fitted. It follows, therefore, that large values of the log-likelihood statistic indicate poorly fitting statistical models, because the larger the value of the log-likelihood, the more unexplained observations there are.

19.3.2. Assessing the model: the deviance statistic ③

The **deviance** is very closely related to the log-likelihood: it's given by

$$\text{Deviance} = -2 \times \text{log-likelihood}$$

The deviance is often referred to as **−2LL** because of the way it is calculated. It's actually rather convenient to (almost) always use the deviance rather than the log-likelihood because it has a chi-square distribution (see Chapter 18 and the Appendix), which makes it easy to calculate the significance of the value.

Now, it's possible to calculate a log-likelihood or deviance for different models and to compare these models by looking at the difference between their deviances. For example, it's useful to compare a logistic regression model against some kind of baseline state. The baseline state that's usually used is the model when only the constant is included. In multiple regression, the baseline model we use is the mean of all scores (this is our best guess of the outcome when we have no other information). With a categorical outcome it doesn't make sense to use the overall mean (all we know is whether an event happened or not), so we use the frequency with which the outcome occurred instead. So, if the outcome occurs 107 times, and doesn't occur 72 times, then our best guess of the outcome will be that it occurs (because it occurs more times than it doesn't). As such, like multiple regression, our baseline model is the model that gives us the best prediction when we know nothing other than the values of the outcome: in logistic regression this will be to predict the outcome that occurs most often. This is the logistic regression model when only the constant is included. If we then add one or more predictors to the model, we can compute the improvement of the model as follows:

$$\chi^2 = \left(-2LL(\text{baseline})\right) - \left(-2LL(\text{new})\right)$$

$$= 2LL(\text{new}) - 2LL(\text{baseline})$$

$$df = k_{\text{new}} - k_{\text{baseline}}$$

(19.6)

So, we merely take the new model deviance and subtract from it the deviance for the baseline model (the model when only the constant is included). This difference is known as a likelihood ratio[1] and has a chi-square distribution with degrees of freedom equal to the number of parameters, k, in the new model minus the number of parameters in the baseline model. The number of parameters in the baseline model will always be 1 (the constant is the only parameter to be estimated); any subsequent model will have degrees of freedom equal to the number of predictors plus 1 (i.e., the number of predictors plus one parameter representing the constant).

If we build up models hierarchically (i.e., adding one predictor at a time) we can also use equation (19.6) to compare these models. For example, if you have a model (we'll call it the 'old' model) and you add a predictor (the 'new' model) to that model, you can see whether the new model has improved the fit using equation (19.6) in which the baseline model is the 'old' model. The degrees of freedom will again be the difference between the degrees of freedom of the two models.

19.3.3.   Assessing the model: R and R^2 ③

When we talked about linear regression, we saw that the multiple correlation coefficient R and its squared value R^2 were useful measures of how well the model fits the data. We've also just seen that the likelihood ratio is similar inasmuch as it is based on the level of

---

[1] You might wonder why it is called a 'ratio' when a 'ratio' usually means something is divided by something else, and we're not dividing anything here: we're subtracting. The reason is that if you subtract logs of numbers, it's the same as dividing the numbers. For example, $10/5 = 2$ and (try it on your calculator) $\log(10) - \log(5) = \log(2)$.

correspondence between predicted and actual values of the outcome. However, you can calculate a more literal version of the multiple correlation in logistic regression known as the R-statistic. This R-statistic is the partial correlation between the outcome variable and each of the predictor variables and it can vary between -1 and 1. A positive value indicates that as the predictor variable increases, so does the likelihood of the event occurring. A negative value implies that as the predictor variable increases, the likelihood of the outcome occurring decreases. If a variable has a small value of R then it contributes only a small amount to the model.

Is there a logistic regression equivalent of R^2?

The R-statistic is given by:

$$R = \sqrt{\frac{z^2 - 2df}{-2LL(\text{baseline})}} \qquad (19.7)$$

The $-2LL$ term is the deviance for the original model, the Wald statistic (z) is calculated as described in the next section, and the degrees of freedom can be read from the summary table for the variables in the equation. However, because this value of R is dependent upon the Wald statistic it is by no means an accurate measure (we'll see in the next section that the Wald statistic can be inaccurate under certain circumstances). For this reason the value of R should be treated with some caution, and it is invalid to square this value and interpret it as you would in linear regression.

There is some controversy over what would make a good analogue to the R^2 in logistic regression, but a measure described by Hosmer and Lemeshow (1989) can be easily calculated. Hosmer and Lemeshow's measure (denoted by R_L^2) is calculated as:

$$R_L^2 = \frac{-\chi^2_{\text{Model}}}{-2LL(\text{baseline})} \qquad (19.8)$$

As such, R_L^2 is calculated by dividing the model chi-square, which represents the change from the baseline (based on the log-likelihood) by the baseline chi-square (the deviance of the model before any predictors were entered). Given what the model chi-square represents (see Eq. 19.6), another way to express this is:

$$R_L^2 = \frac{\left(-2LL(\text{baseline})\right) - \left(-2LL(\text{new})\right)}{-2LL(\text{baseline})}$$

R_L^2 is the proportional reduction in the absolute value of the log-likelihood measure, and as such it is a measure of how much the badness of fit improves as a result of the inclusion of the predictor variables. It can vary between 0 (indicating that the predictors are useless at predicting the outcome variable) and 1 (indicating that the model predicts the outcome variable perfectly).

However, SPSS doesn't use this measure, it uses **Cox and Snell's** R_{CS}^2 (1989), which is based on the deviance of the model ($-2LL$(new)) and the deviance of the original model ($-2LL$(baseline)), and the sample size, n:

$$R_{CS}^2 = 1 - \exp\left(\frac{(-2LL(new)) - (-2LL(baseline))}{n}\right) \qquad (19.9)$$

However, this statistic never reaches its theoretical maximum of 1. Therefore, Nagelkerke (1991) suggested the following amendment (**Nagelkerke's** R_N^2):

$$R_N^2 = \frac{R_{CS}^2}{1 - \exp(-\frac{-2LL(baseline)}{n})} \qquad (19.10)$$

Although all of these measures differ in their computation (and the answers you get), conceptually they are somewhat the same. So, in terms of interpretation they can be seen as similar to the R^2 in linear regression in that they provide a gauge of the substantive significance of the model.

19.3.4. Assessing the contribution of predictors: the Wald statistic ②

As in linear regression, we want to know not only how well the model overall fits the data, but also the individual contribution of predictors. In linear regression, we used the estimated regression coefficients (b) and their standard errors to compute a t-statistic. In logistic regression there is an analogous statistic, the z-statistic, which follows the normal distribution. Like the t-test in linear regression, the z-statistic tells us whether the b coefficient for that predictor is significantly different from zero. If the coefficient is significantly different from zero then we can assume that the predictor is making a significant contribution to the prediction of the outcome (Y):

$$z = \frac{b}{SE_b} \qquad (19.11)$$

FIGURE 19.2   Abraham Wald writing 'I must not devise test statistics prone to having inflated standard errors' on the blackboard 100 times

Equation 19.11 shows how the z-statistic is calculated, and you can see it's basically identical to the t-statistic in linear regression (see equation (8.11)): it is the value of the regression coefficient divided by its associated standard error. The z-statistic was developed by Abraham Wald (Figure 19.2), and is known as the **Wald statistic**. SPSS actually reports the Wald statistic as z^2, which transforms it so that it has a chi-square distribution. The z-statistic is used to ascertain whether a variable is a significant predictor of the outcome; however, it should be used a little cautiously because, when the regression coefficient (b) is large, the standard error tends to become inflated, resulting in the z-statistic being underestimated (see Menard, 1995). The inflation of the standard error increases the probability of rejecting a predictor as being significant when in reality it is making a significant contribution to the model (i.e., a Type II error). In general it is probably more accurate to enter predictors hierarchically and examine the change in likelihood ratio statistics.

19.3.5. The odds ratio: exp(B) ③

More crucial to the *interpretation* of logistic regression is the value of the **odds ratio**, which is the exponential of B (i.e., e^B or exp(B)) and is an indicator of the change in odds resulting from a unit change in the predictor. As such, it is similar to the *b* coefficient in logistic regression but easier to understand (because it doesn't require a logarithmic transformation). When the predictor variable is categorical the odds ratio is easier to explain, so imagine we had a simple example in which we were trying to predict whether or not someone got pregnant from whether or not they used a condom last time they made love. The **odds** of an event occurring are defined as the probability of an event occurring divided by the probability of that event not occurring (see equation (19.12)) and should not be confused with the more colloquial usage of the word to refer to probability. So, for example, the odds of becoming pregnant are the probability of becoming pregnant divided by the probability of not becoming pregnant:

$$\text{odds} = \frac{P(\text{event})}{P(\text{no event})}$$

$$P(\text{event } Y) = \frac{1}{1 + e^{-(b_0 + b_1 X_{1i})}} \qquad (19.12)$$

$$P(\text{no event } Y) = 1 - P(\text{event } Y)$$

To calculate the change in odds that results from a unit change in the predictor, we must first calculate the odds of becoming pregnant given that a condom *wasn't* used. We then calculate the odds of becoming pregnant given that a condom *was* used. Finally, we calculate the proportionate change in these two odds.

To calculate the first set of odds, we use equation (19.3) to calculate the probability of becoming pregnant given that a condom wasn't used. If we had more than one predictor we would use equation (19.4). There are three unknown quantities in this equation: the coefficient of the constant (b_0), the coefficient for the predictor (b_1) and the value of the predictor itself (X). We'll know the value of X from how we coded the condom use variable (chances are we would've used 0 = condom wasn't used and 1 = condom was used). The values of b_1 and b_0 will be estimated for us. We can calculate the odds as in equation (19.12).

Next, we calculate the same thing after the predictor variable has changed by one unit. In this case, because the predictor variable is dichotomous, we need to calculate the odds of getting pregnant, given that a condom *was* used. So, the value of X is now 1 (rather than 0).

We now know the odds before and after a unit change in the predictor variable. It is a simple matter to calculate the proportionate change in odds by dividing the odds after a unit change in the predictor by the odds before that change:

$$\text{Odds ratio} = \frac{\text{Odds after a unit change in the predictor}}{\text{Original odds}} \qquad (19.13)$$

This proportionate change in odds is the odds ratio, and we can interpret it in terms of the change in odds: if the value is greater than 1 then it indicates that as the predictor increases, the odds of the outcome occurring increase. Conversely, a value less than 1 indicates that as the predictor increases, the odds of the outcome occurring decrease. We'll see how this works with a real example shortly.

19.3.6. Model building and parsimony ②

When you have more than one predictor, you can choose between the same methods to build your model as described for ordinary regression (Section 8.5.1). As with ordinary regression, forced entry and hierarchical methods are preferred. If you are undeterred by the criticisms of stepwise methods in the previous chapter, then as with ordinary regression you can choose between a forward or backward stepwise method. These methods work in the same way as for ordinary regression, except that different statistics are used to determine whether predictors are entered or removed from the model. For example, the forward method enters predictors based on their score statistic, then assesses removal based on the likelihood ratio statistic described in Section 18.3.3 (the *Forward: LR* method), an arithmetically less intense version of the likelihood ratio statistic called the conditional statistic (*Forward: Conditional*), or the Wald statistic (*Forward: Wald*), in which case any predictors in the model that have significance values of the Wald statistic (above the default removal criterion of .1) will be removed. Of these methods the likelihood ratio method is the best removal criterion because the Wald statistic can, at times, be unreliable (see Section 19.3.4). The opposite of the forward method is the backward method, which begins with all predictors included in the model and then removes predictors if their removal is not detrimental to the fit of the model. Whether removal is detrimental can be assessed using the same three methods as the forward approach.

Which method should I use?

As with ordinary regression, stepwise methods are best avoided for theory testing; however, they are used when no previous research exists on which to base hypotheses for testing, and in situations where causality is not of interest and you merely wish to find a model to fit your data (Agresti & Finlay, 1986; Menard, 1995). As with ordinary regression, if you do use a stepwise method then the backward method is preferable because forward methods are more likely to exclude predictors involved in suppressor effects. In terms of the test statistic used in stepwise methods, the Wald statistic, as we have seen, has a tendency to be inaccurate in certain circumstances and so the likelihood ratio method is best.

As with ordinary regression, it is best to use hierarchical methods and to build models in a systematic and theory-driven way. Although we didn't discuss this for ordinary regression (because things were getting complicated enough already), when building a model we should strive for **parsimony**. In a scientific context, parsimony refers to the idea that simpler explanations of a phenomenon are preferable to complex ones. The statistical implication of using a parsimony heuristic is that models be kept as simple as possible. In other words, do not include predictors unless they have explanatory benefit. To impliment this strategy we need to first fit the model that includes all potential predictors, and then systemmatically remove any that don't seem to contribute to the model. This is a bit like a backward stepwise method, except that the decision-making process is in the researcher's hands: they make informed decisions about what predictors should be removed. It's also worth bearing in mind that if you have interaction terms in your model then for that interaction term to be valid *you must retain the main effects involved in the interaction term as well* (even if they don't appear to contribute much).

19.4. Sources of bias and common problems ④

19.4.1. Assumptions ②

Logistic regression, like any linear model, is open to the sources of bias discussed in Chapter 5 and Section 8.3, so look back at those parts of the book. In the context of logistic regression, it's worth noting a couple of points about the assumptions of linearity and independence:

- *Linearity*: In ordinary regression we assumed that the outcome had linear relationships with the predictors. In logistic regression the outcome is categorical and so this assumption is violated, and we use the log (or *logit*) of the data. The assumption of linearity in logistic regression, therefore, assumes that there is a linear relationship between any continuous predictors and *the logit of the outcome variable*. This assumption can be tested by looking at whether the interaction term between the predictor and its log transformation is significant (Hosmer & Lemeshow, 1989). We will go through an example in Section 19.8.1.

- *Independence of errors*: In logistic regression, violating this assumption produces overdispersion, which we'll discuss in Section 19.4.4.

Logistic regression also has some unique problems. These are not sources of bias so much as things that can go wrong. SPSS solves logistic regression problems by an iterative procedure (SPSS Tip 19.1). Sometimes, instead of pouncing on the correct solution quickly, you'll notice nothing happening: SPSS begins to move infinitely slowly, or appears to have just got fed up with you asking it to do stuff and has gone on strike. If it can't find a correct solution, then sometimes it actually does give up, quietly offering you (without any apology) a result which is completely incorrect. Usually this is revealed by implausibly large standard errors. Two situations can provoke this situation, both of which are related to the ratio of cases to variables: incomplete information and complete separation.

SPSS TIP 19.1   **Error messages about 'failure to converge'** ③

Many statistical procedures use an *iterative process*, which means that SPSS attempts to estimate the parameters of the model by finding successive approximations of those parameters. Essentially, it starts by estimating the parameters with a 'best guess'. It then attempts to approximate them more accurately (known as an *iteration*). It then tries again, and then again, and so on through many iterations. It stops either when the approximations of parameters converge (i.e., at each new attempt the 'approximations' of parameters are the same or very similar to the previous attempt), or it reaches the maximum number of attempts (iterations).

Sometimes you will get an error message in the output that says something like *Maximum number of iterations were exceeded, and the log-likelihood value and/or the parameter estimates cannot converge*. What this means is that SPSS has attempted to estimate the parameters the maximum number of times (as specified in the options) but they are not converging (i.e., at each iteration SPSS is getting quite different estimates). This certainly means that you should ignore any output that SPSS has produced, and it might mean that your data are beyond help. You can try increasing the number of iterations that SPSS attempts, or make the criteria that SPSS uses to assess 'convergence' less strict.

19.4.2.   Incomplete information from the predictors ④

Imagine you're trying to predict lung cancer from smoking (a foul habit believed to increase the risk of cancer) and whether or not you eat tomatoes (which are believed to reduce the risk of cancer). You collect data from people who do and don't smoke, and from people who do and don't eat tomatoes; however, this isn't sufficient unless you collect data from all combinations of smoking and tomato eating. Suppose you ended up with the following data:

Do you smoke?	Do you eat tomatoes?	Do you have cancer?
Yes	No	Yes
Yes	Yes	Yes
No	No	Yes
No	Yes	??????

Observing only the first three possibilities does not prepare you for the outcome of the fourth. You have no way of knowing whether this last person will have cancer or not based on the other data you've collected. Therefore, SPSS will have problems unless you've collected data from all combinations of your variables. This should be checked before you run the analysis using a contingency table, and I describe how to do this in Chapter 18. While you're checking these tables, you should also look at the expected frequencies in each cell of the table to make sure that they are greater than 1 and no more than 20% are less than 5 (see Section 18.4). This is because the goodness-of-fit tests in logistic regression make this assumption.

This point applies not only to categorical variables, but also to continuous ones. Suppose that you wanted to investigate factors related to human happiness. These might include age, gender, sexual orientation, religious beliefs, levels of anxiety and even whether a person is right-handed. You interview 1000 people, record their characteristics, and whether they are happy ('yes' or 'no'). Although a sample of 1000 seems quite large, is it likely to include an 80-year-old, highly anxious, Buddhist, left-handed lesbian? If you found one such person and she was happy, should you conclude that everyone else in the same category is happy? It would, obviously, be better to have several more people in this category to confirm that this combination of characteristics is associated with happiness. One solution is to collect more data.

As a general point, whenever samples are broken down into categories and one or more combinations are empty it creates problems. These will probably be signalled by coefficients that have unreasonably large standard errors. Conscientious researchers produce and check multi-way crosstabulations of all categorical independent variables. Lazy but cautious ones don't bother with crosstabulations, but look carefully at the standard errors. Those who don't bother with either should expect trouble.

19.4.3. Complete separation ④

A second situation in which logistic regression collapses might surprise you: it's when the outcome variable can be perfectly predicted by one variable or a combination of variables. This situation is known as **complete separation**. Let's look at an example: imagine you placed a pressure pad under your door mat and connected it to your security system so that you could detect burglars when they creep in at night. However, because your teenage children (which you would have if you're old enough and rich enough to have security systems and pressure pads) and their friends are often coming home in the middle of the night, when they tread on the pad you want it to work out the probability that the person is a burglar and not one of your teenagers. Therefore, you could measure the weight of some burglars and some teenagers and use logistic regression to predict the outcome (teenager or burglar) from the weight. The graph (Figure 19.3) would show a line of triangles at zero (the data points for all of the teenagers you weighed) and a line of

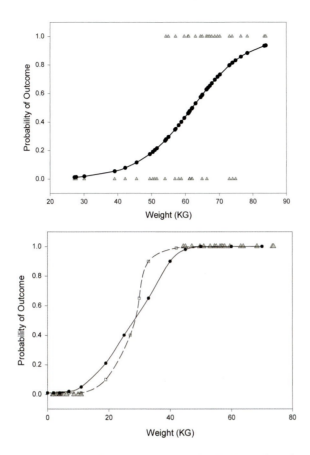

FIGURE 19.3
An example of the relationship between weight (*x*-axis) and a dichotomous outcome variable (*y*-axis, 1 = definitely a burglar, 0 = definitely not a burglar, i.e., a teenager). Note that the weights in the two groups overlap

FIGURE 19.4
An example of *complete separation*, note that the weights (*x*-axis) of the two categories in the dichotomous outcome variable (*y*-axis, 1 = definitely a burglar, 0 = definitely not a burglar, i.e., a cat) do not overlap

triangles at 1 (the data points for burglars you weighed). Note that these lines of triangles overlap (some teenagers are as heavy as burglars). We've seen that in logistic regression, SPSS tries to predict the probability of the outcome given a value of the predictor. In this case, at low weights the fitted probability follows the bottom line of the plot, and at high weights it follows the top line. At intermediate values it tries to follow the probability as it changes.

Imagine that we had the same pressure pad, but our teenage children had left home to go to university. We're now interested in distinguishing burglars from our pet cat based on weight. Again, we can weigh some cats and weigh some burglars. This time the graph (Figure 19.4) still has a row of triangles at zero (the cats we weighed) and a row at 1 (the burglars) but the rows of triangles do not overlap: there is no burglar who weighs the same as a cat – obviously there were no cat burglars in the sample (groan now at that sorry excuse for a joke). This is known as perfect separation: the outcome (cats and burglars) can be perfectly predicted from weight (anything less than 15 kg is a cat, anything more than 40 kg is a burglar). If we try to calculate the probabilities of the outcome given a certain weight then we run into trouble. When the weight is low, the probability is 0, and when the weight is high, the probability is 1, but what happens in between? We have no data in between 15 and 40 kg on which to base these probabilities. Figure 19.4 shows two possible probability curves that we could fit to these data: one much steeper than the other. Either one of these curves is valid based on the data we have available. The lack of data means that SPSS will be uncertain about how steep it should make the intermediate slope and it will try to bring the centre as close to vertical as possible, but its estimates veer unsteadily towards infinity (hence large standard errors). Complete separation often arises when too many variables are fitted to too few cases. Often the only satisfactory solution is to collect more data, but sometimes a neat answer is found by using a simpler model.

19.4.4.   Overdispersion ④

I'm a psychologist, not a statistician, and most of what I've read on **overdispersion** doesn't make an awful lot of sense to me. From what I can gather, it is when the observed variance is bigger than expected from the logistic regression model. This can happen for two reasons. The first is correlated observations (i.e., when the assumption of independence is broken) and the second is due to variability in success probabilities. For example, imagine our outcome was whether a puppy in a litter survived or died. Genetic factors mean that within a given litter the chances of success (living) depend on the litter from which the puppy came. As such success probabilities vary across litters (Halekoh & Højsgaard, 2007), this example of dead puppies is particularly good – not because I'm a cat lover, but because it shows how variability in success probabilities can create correlation between observations (the survival rates of puppies from the same litter are not independent).

Overdispersion tends to limit standard errors, which creates two problems: (1) test statistics of regression parameters are computed by dividing by the standard error (see equation (19.11)), so if the standard error is too small then the test statistic will be too big and falsely deemed significant; (2) confidence intervals are computed from standard errors, so if the standard error is too small then the confidence interval will be too narrow and make us overconfident about the likely relationship between predictors and the outcome in the population. In short, overdispersion doesn't affect the model parameters (*b*-values) themselves but biases our conclusions about their significance and population value.

SPSS produces a chi-square goodness-of-fit statistic, and overdispersion is present if the ratio of this statistic to its degrees of freedom is greater than 1 (this ratio is called the *dispersion parameter,* ϕ). Overdispersion is likely to be problematic if the dispersion parameter approaches or is greater than 2. (Incidentally, *under*dispersion is shown by values less than 1, but this problem is much less common than *over*dispersion.) There is also the *deviance* goodness-of-fit statistic, and the dispersion parameter can be based on this statistic instead (again by dividing by the degrees of freedom). When the chi-square and deviance statistics are very discrepant, then overdispersion is likely.

The effects of overdispersion can be reduced by using the dispersion parameter to rescale the standard errors and confidence intervals. For example, the standard errors are multiplied by $\sqrt{\phi}$ to make them bigger (as a function of how big the overdispersion is). You can base these corrections on the deviance statistic too, and whether you rescale using this statistic or the Pearson chi-square statistic depends on which one is bigger. The bigger statistic will have the bigger dispersion parameter (because their degrees of freedom are the same), and will make the bigger correction; therefore, correct by the bigger of the two.

CRAMMING SAM'S TIPS   Issues in logistic regression

- In logistic regression, we assume the same things as ordinary regression.
- The linearity assumption is that each predictor has a linear relationship with the log of the outcome variable.
- If we created a table that combined all possible values of all variables then we should ideally have some data in every cell of this table. If we don't then we must watch out for big standard errors.
- If the outcome variable can be predicted perfectly from one predictor variable (or a combination of predictor variables) then we have *complete separation*. This problem creates large standard errors too.
- *Overdispersion* is where the variance is larger than expected from the model. This can be caused by violating the assumption of independence. This problem makes the standard errors too small.

19.5. Binary logistic regression: an example that will make you feel eel ②

It's amazing what you find in academic journals sometimes. It's a bit of a hobby of mine trying to unearth bizarre academic papers (really, if you find any email them to me). I believe that science should be fun, and so I like finding research that makes me laugh. A research paper by Lo, Wong, Leung, Law, & Yip (2004) has (so far) made me laugh the most. Lo and colleagues report the case of a 50-year-old man who went to hospital with abdominal pain. A physical examination revealed peritonitis, so they took an X-ray of the man's abdomen. Although it somehow slipped the patient's mind to mention this to the receptionist upon arrival at the hospital, the X-ray revealed the shadow of an eel. The authors don't directly quote the man's response to this news, but I like to imagine it was something to the effect of 'Oh, that! Erm, yes, well I didn't think it was terribly relevant to my abdominal pain so I didn't mention it, but I did insert an eel into my anus. Do you think that's the problem?' Whatever he *did* say, the authors report that he admitted inserting an eel into his anus to 'relieve constipation'.

Can an eel cure constipation?

I can have a lively imagination at times, and when I read this article I couldn't help thinking about the poor eel. There it was, minding it's own business swimming about in a river (or fish tank possibly), thinking to itself 'Well, today seems like a nice day, there are no eel-eating sharks about, the sun is out, the water is nice, what could possibly go wrong?' The next thing it knows, it's being shoved up the anus of a man from Hong Kong. 'Well, I didn't see that coming', thinks the eel. Putting myself in the mind-set of an eel for a moment, he has found himself in a tight dark tunnel, there's no light, there's a distinct lack of water compared to his usual habitat, and he's probably fearing for his life. His day has gone *very* wrong. How can he escape this horrible fate? Well, doing what any self-respecting eel would do, he notices that his prison cell is fairly soft and decides 'bugger this, I'll *eat* my way out of here.'[2] Unfortunately he didn't make it, but he went out with a fight (there's a fairly unpleasant photograph in the article of the eel biting the splenic flexure). The authors conclude that: 'Insertion of a live animal into the rectum causing rectal perforation has never been reported. This may be related to a bizarre healthcare belief, inadvertent sexual behavior, or criminal assault. However, the true reason may never be known.' Quite.

OK, so this is a really grim tale.[3] It's not really very funny for the man or the eel, but it was so unbelievably bizarre that I couldn't help laughing.[4] Of course my instant reaction was that sticking an eel up your anus to 'relieve constipation' is the poorest excuse for bizarre sexual behaviour I have ever heard. But upon reflection I wondered if I was being harsh on the man – maybe an eel up the anus really can cure constipation. If we wanted to test this hypothesis, we could collect some data. Our outcome might be 'constipated' vs. 'not constipated', which is a dichotomous variable that we're trying to predict. One predictor variable

[2] Literally.

[3] As it happens, it isn't an isolated grim tale. Through this article I found myself hurtling down a road of morbid curiosity that was probably best left untravelled. Although the eel was my favourite example, I could have chosen from a very large stone (Sachdev, 1967), a test tube (Hughes, Marice, & Gathright, 1976), a baseball (McDonald & Rosenthal, 1977), an aerosol deodorant can, hose pipe, iron bar, broomstick, penknife, marijuana, bank notes, blue plastic tumbler, vibrator and primus stove (Clarke, Buccimazza, Anderson, & Thomson, 2005), or (a close second place to the eel) a toy pirate ship, with or without pirates I'm not sure (Bemelman & Hammacher, 2005). So, although I encourage you to send me bizarre research, if it involves objects in the rectum then probably don't, unless someone has managed to put Buckingham Palace up there.

[4] Possibly not as bizarre as the case study I subsequently found of a 14-year-old boy who reported to hospital because he couldn't urinate (Vezhaventhan & Jeyaraman, 2007). A small fish was discovered in his bladder that had 'swam up his penis while he was having a wee while cleaning a fish tank'. Yes, of course it did.

would be intervention (eel up the anus) vs. waiting list (no treatment). We might also want to factor in how many days the patient had been constipated before treatment. This scenario is perfect for logistic regression (but not for eels). The data are in **Eel.sav**.

I'm quite aware that many statistics lecturers do not share my unbridled joy at discussing eel-created rectal perforations with students, so I have named the variables in the file more generally:

- *Outcome* (dependent variable): **Cured** (cured or not cured).

- *Predictor* (independent variable): **Intervention** (intervention or no treatment).

- *Predictor* (independent variable): **Duration** (the number of days before treatment that the patient had the problem).

In doing so, your tutor can adapt the example to something more palatable if they wish to, but you will secretly know that it's all about having eels up your bum.

19.5.1. Building a model ①

In Section 19.3.6 we discussed the idea of building models based on the principal of parsimony. In this example, we have three potential predictors: **Intervention**, **Duration** and the **Intervention × Duration** interaction. The most complex model we can fit includes all of these variables, so the idea is that we build up to this model systematically, and then look at any terms we added that didn't improve the model and go back to a simpler model that doesn't include them. The main effect in which we're interested is whether the intervention has an effect, so the first model we might fit would be to have only **Intervention** as a predictor. As shown in Figure 19.5, we then build this model up by adding in the other main effect of **Duration** (model 2). Finally, we put in the interaction term as well (model 3). Our job is to determine which of these models best fits the data, whilst adhering to the general idea of parsimony. So, if adding the interaction term didn't improve the model then we would use model 2 as our final model. If **Duration** doesn't add anything then we'd use model 1 as the final model.

It's worth reminding you that if you want to look at an interaction *you must include any main effects involved in that interaction in the model for the interaction term to be valid*. In this example, if we want to assess the contribution of the **Duration × Intervention** interaction, we must also include **Intervention** and **Duration** into the model involving the interaction.

FIGURE 19.5
Building models based on the principal of parsimony

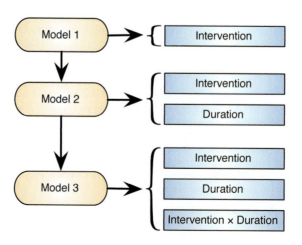

19.5.2. Logistic regression: the general procedure ①

Figure 19.6 shows the general process of conducting logistic regression analysis. First we run an initial hierarchical analysis to look at competing models. In the previous section, we identified three models that would be theoretically interesting, and we want to identify which of these three models best fits the data. Having done this, we rerun the analysis specifying this model, but also saving diagnostic statistics, which we then inspect to look for signs of bias (outliers and influential cases). We then check for linearity of the logit (in fact, it's a good idea to do this first, but it's a little complicated so I want to deal with it later in the chapter), and check for multicollinearity.

19.5.3. Data entry ①

The data should be entered as for ordinary regression: they are arranged in the data editor in three columns (one representing each variable). Looking at the data editor, you should notice that both of the categorical variables have been entered as coding variables (see Section 3.5.2.3); that is, numbers have been specified to represent categories. For ease of interpretation, the outcome variable should be coded 1 (event occurred) and 0 (event did not occur); in this case, 1 represents being cured and 0 represents not being cured. For the intervention a similar coding has been used (1 = intervention, 0 = no treatment).

19.5.4. Building the models in SPSS ②

To build the models in Figure 19.5 we need to use the main *Logistic Regression* dialog box, which can be accessed by selecting Analyze Regression ▸ Binary Logistic... . We

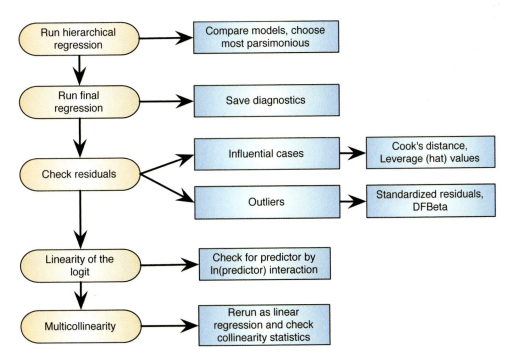

FIGURE 19.6

The process of fitting a logistic regression model

want to specify the models in a blockwise fashion so that each block maps onto each of the three models. Figure 19.7 shows the process. The main dialog box has a space to place a dependent variable (or outcome variable). In this example, the outcome was whether or not the patient was cured, so for all models, we can drag **Cured** from the variable list to the *Dependent* box (or select it and click on ). There is also a box for specifying the covariates (the predictor variables). It is possible to specify the main effect of a predictor variable (remember, this is the effect on an outcome variable of a variable *on its own*). You can also specify an interaction effect, which is the *combined* effect (on an outcome variable) of two or more variables. To specify a main effect, select one predictor (e.g., **Duration**) and then drag it to the *Covariates* box (or click on). To input an interaction, click on more than one variable on the left-hand side of the dialog box (i.e., click on several variables while holding down the *Ctrl* key, or *Cmd* on a Mac) and then click on to move them to the *Covariates* box. In this example there are only two predictors and therefore there is only one possible interaction (the **Duration × Intervention** interaction). To specify model 1 from Figure 19.5 select the **Intervention** variable and drag it to the *Covariates* box (or click on). That's model 1 sorted. To specify model 2 click on , which will clear the *Covariates* box. Model 2 in Figure 19.5 contains the main effects of **Duration** and **Intervention**, so select these variables (to select both simultaneously remember to hold down the *Ctrl* key) and drag them to the *Covariates* box (or click on). That's model 2 done. Model 3 in Figure 19.5 includes the two main effects of **Duration**, **Intervention** and the **Duration ×** **Intervention** interaction. To specify this model click on again and move these predictors to the *Covariates* box as described above, then to specify the interaction select both variables and click on . To move between models use the and buttons.

19.5.5. Method of regression ②

As with multiple regression, there are different ways of doing logistic regression. For each of the models that we specified you can select a particular method of variable entry by clicking on [Enter ▼] and then clicking on a method in the resulting drop-down menu. We are doing this analysis hierarchically, so we do want to use the [Enter ▼] method each time (i.e., we don't need to change anything) – just bear in mind that other methods exist. If you want to try out stepwise then do the self-test, which has a detailed explanation and interpretation on the companion website.

SELF-TEST   Rerun this analysis using a stepwise method *(Forward: LR)* entry method for the predictors.

19.5.6. Categorical predictors ②

SPSS needs to know which, if any, predictor variables are categorical. Click on [Categorical...] in the *Logistic Regression* dialog box to activate the dialog box in Figure 19.8. Notice that

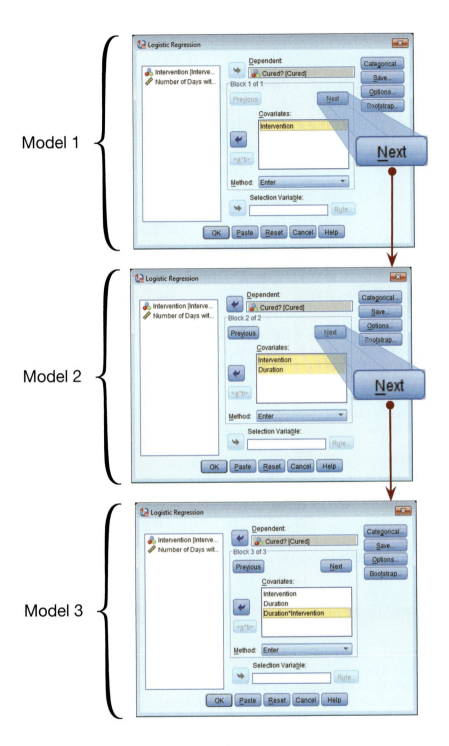

Model 1

Model 2

Model 3

FIGURE 19.7
Specifying
models using
the *Logistic
Regression*
dialog box

the covariates are listed on the left-hand side, and there is a space on the right-hand side in which categorical covariates can be placed. Select any categorical variables you have (in this example we have only one, so click on **Intervention**) and drag them to the *Categorical Covariates* box (or click on ⬆).

There are many ways in which you can treat categorical predictors, and we have looked at some of these ways when discussing dummy coding and contrasts (Sections 10.5.1 and 11.4). For logistic regression, SPSS has several 'standard' ways to code categories. By

FIGURE 19.8
Defining
categorical
variables
in logistic
regression

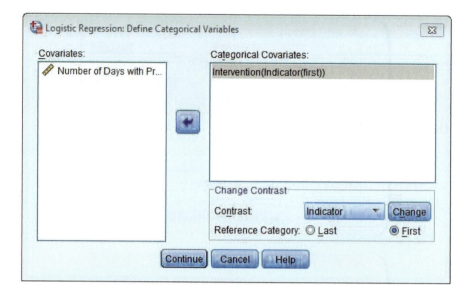

default, SPSS uses *Indicator* coding, which is standard dummy variable coding, and you can choose to have either the first or last category as your baseline. To change to a different kind of coding click on `Indicator ▾` to access a drop-down list; it is possible to select simple contrasts, difference contrasts, Helmert contrasts, repeated contrasts, polynomial contrasts and deviation contrasts, all of which were discussed in Sections 11.4.4 and 11.4.5. Let's use standard dummy coding (indicator) for this example. To reiterate, when an indicator contrast is used, levels of the categorical variable are recoded using standard dummy-variable coding (see Sections 10.5 and 11.2.1). We need only to decide whether to use the first (`◉ First`) or last (`◉ Last`) category as a baseline. In this example, it doesn't make any difference because we have only two categories, but if you had a categorical predictor with more than two categories then you should either use the highest number to code your control category in the data editor and select `◉ Last`, or use the lowest number to code your control category and specify the indicator contrast to compare against `◉ First`. In our data, I coded 'cured' as 1 and 'not cured' (our control category) as 0; therefore, select the contrast, then click on `◉ First` and then `Change` so that the completed dialog box looks like Figure 19.8.

19.5.7. Comparing the models ②

Before we look at some of the other options, we could run the analysis with the basic options we have just selected to see which model looks like the best fit. Having decided this, we could rerun the analysis and look at this model in more detail. Having selected the options that I have already described, click on `OK` in the main dialog box to run the analysis. Output 19.1 shows both how we coded our outcome variable (it reminds us that 0 = not cured, and 1 = cured)[5] and how it has coded the categorical predictors (the parameter codings for **Intervention**). We chose indicator coding and so the coding is the same as the values in the data editor (0 = no treatment, 1 = treatment). If *deviation* coding had been chosen then the coding would have been −1 (Treatment) and 1 (No

---

[5] These values are the same as the data editor, so this table might seem pointless. However, had we used codes other than 0 and 1 (e.g., 1 = not cured, 2 = cured) then SPSS would have changed these to 0 and 1, and this table informs you of which category is represented by 0 and which by 1. This is important when it comes to interpretation.

ODITI'S LANTERN

Logistic regression

'I, Oditi, believe that my loyal brethren will find it difficult to master the secrets within the data if their bowels are creaking at the seams because the curse of constipation has afflicted them. You could do the magic dance of the turtle head and hope that it brings you relief, but it is my belief that to remove an intestinal log we need log-istic regression. Stare into my lantern and feel immediate relief.'

Treatment). With a *simple* contrast, if ⊙ First was selected as the reference category the codes would have been −0.5 (**Intervention** = No Treatment) and 0.5 (**Intervention** = Treatment) and if ⊙ Last was selected as the reference category then the value of the codes would be the same but their signs would be reversed. The parameter codes are important for calculating the probability of the outcome variable ($P(Y)$), but we will come to that later.

OUTPUT 19.1

Dependent Variable Encoding

Original Value	Internal Value
Not Cured	0
Cured	1

Categorical Variables Codings

		Frequency	Parameter coding (1)
Intervention	No Treatment	56	.000
	Intervention	57	1.000

Output 19.2 shows the overall model summary statistics for each of the three models. The table labelled *Omnibus Tests of Model Coefficients* includes the chi-square statistic (which is related to −2LL) for the model overall (*Model*) and the change since the previous model (*Block*). Model 1 yields a chi-square of 9.926, which is highly significant, $p = .002$. We can compare the models using equation (19.6). For model 1, the −2LL would have been compared to that obtained from a model that included only the intercept, so we're comparing a model that includes **Intervention** against a model that has no predictors. The chi-square tells us that the model has improved significantly by adding **Intervention** as a predictor.

In model 2, we added the effect of **Duration**, and this model is a significant fit of the data because the *Model* chi-square in the table labelled *Omnibus Tests of Model Coefficients* is significant, $\chi^2(2) = 9.93$, $p = .007$. However, we're not interested in the model overall because the previous model was also a significant fit; we're interested in the improvement of model 2 over model 1 and this information is given by the chi-square for *Block*. The *Block* chi-square tells us about the change in chi-square in this block: it is the *change* in the chi-square resulting from adding **Duration** to the model. The value is obtained by taking the difference between the model chi-square for the two models (in this case 9.928 − 9.926 = 0.002). This change in the chi-square is very non-significant, $\chi^2(2) = 0.002$, $p = .964$, indicating that adding **Duration** to the model has had virtually no effect on the fit (the chi-square has hardly changed).

OUTPUT 19.2

Model 1

Omnibus Tests of Model Coefficients

		Chi-square	df	Sig.
Step 1	Step	9.926	1	.002
	Block	9.926	1	.002
	Model	9.926	1	.002

Model 2

Omnibus Tests of Model Coefficients

		Chi-square	df	Sig.
Step 1	Step	.002	1	.964
	Block	.002	1	.964
	Model	9.928	2	.007

Model 3

Omnibus Tests of Model Coefficients

		Chi-square	df	Sig.
Step 1	Step	.061	1	.805
	Block	.061	1	.805
	Model	9.989	3	.019

In model 3, we added the **Intervention** × **Duration** interaction. Again, this model is a significant fit of the data because the *Model* chi-square is significant, $\chi^2(3) = 9.99$, $p = .019$. However, as with model 2, we're interested in the *improvement* of model 3 over the previous one, and this information is given by the chi-square for *Block*. As before, the value is obtained by taking the difference between the model chi-square for the two models (in this case $9.989 - 9.928 = 0.061$). This change in the chi-square is very non-significant, $\chi^2(1) = 0.061$, $p = .805$, indicating that adding the interaction term to the model has had virtually no effect on the fit.

We could, if we wanted, look at the difference between models 1 and 3 as well, by using equation (19.6):

$$\chi^2 = \chi^2_{\text{model 3}} - \chi^2_{\text{model 1}} = 9.989 - 9.926 = 0.063$$
$$df = df_{\text{model 3}} - df_{\text{model 1}} = 3 - 1 = 2$$

We could compare this against the critical values for the chi-square distribution with 2 degrees of freedom, but we don't need to because 0.063 is so small it barely warrants turning the pages to confirm what we already know: **Duration** and the **Duration** × **Intervention** interaction add nothing to the model. Based on this comparison, we would chose model 1.

19.5.8. Rerunning the model ①

By comparing the models we have seen that **Duration** and the **Duration** × **Intervention** interaction add nothing to the model. Therefore, we should proceed with model 1. You need to rerun the analysis, but just specifying **Intervention** as a predictor (as in the top dialog box in Figure 19.7). Set the same options as before, but we'll now get some more detailed information about the model.

19.5.9. Obtaining residuals ②

As with ordinary regression, it is possible to save a set of residuals (see Section 8.3.1.1) as new variables in the data editor. These residual variables can then be examined to see how well the model fits the observed data. It makes the most sense to save these variables only once we have selected a model, which is why we didn't look at these options before. To save residuals click on [Save...] in the main *Logistic Regression* dialog box (Figure 19.7). SPSS saves each of the selected variables into the data editor but they can be listed in the output viewer by using the *Case Summaries* command (see Section 8.7.6) and selecting the residual variables of interest. The residuals box in Figure 19.9 gives us several options, and most of these are the same as those in multiple regression (refer to Section 8.6.4). The *predicted probabilities* and *predicted group memberships* are unique to logistic regression. The predicted probabilities are the probabilities of Y occurring (derived from equation (19.3)) given the values of each predictor for a given case. The predicted group membership tells us to which of the two outcome categories a participant is most likely to belong based on the model. The group memberships are based on the predicted probabilities, and I will explain these values in more detail when we consider how to interpret the residuals. As a bare minimum select the same options as in Figure 19.9. Note that these variables won't save if you activate bootstrapping (see below).

19.5.10. Further options ②

Finally, click on [Options...] in the main *Logistic Regression* dialog box to obtain the dialog box in Figure 19.10. For the most part, the default settings in this dialog box are fine. I mentioned in Section 19.5.5 that when a stepwise method is used there are default criteria for selecting and removing predictors from the model. These default settings are displayed under *Probability for Stepwise*. The probability thresholds can be changed, but there is really no need. Another

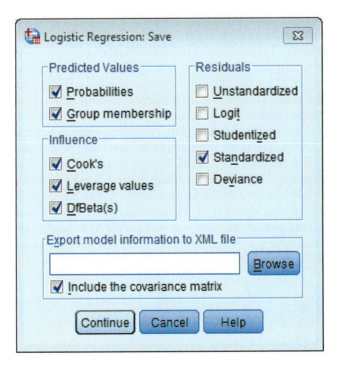

FIGURE 19.9
Dialog box for obtaining residuals for logistic regression

FIGURE 19.10
Dialog box
for logistic
regression
options

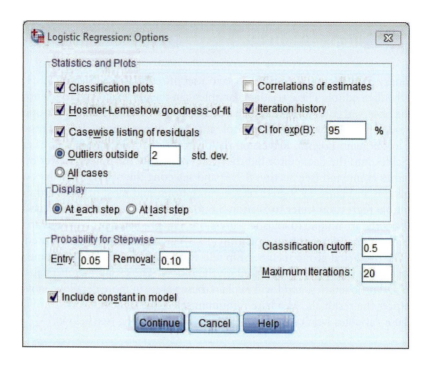

default is to arrive at a model after a maximum of 20 iterations (SPSS Tip 19.1). Unless you have a very complex model, 20 iterations will be more than adequate. We saw in Chapter 8 that regression equations contain a constant that represents the value of Y when the value of the predictors is 0. By default SPSS includes this constant in the model, but it is possible to run the analysis without this constant, and this has the effect of making the model pass through the origin (i.e., Y is 0 when X is 0). Normally we don't want to do this.

Classification plots are histograms of the actual and predicted values of the outcome variable. A classification plot is useful for assessing the fit of the model to the observed data. It is also possible to do a *Casewise listing of residuals* either for any cases for which the standardized residual is greater than 2 standard deviations (this default value is sensible, but change it if you like), or for all cases. I recommend a more thorough examination of residuals, but this option can be useful for a quick inspection. Selecting *CI for exp*(B) will produce a confidence interval (see Section 2.5.2) for the odds ratio (see Section 19.3.5); by default a 95% confidence interval is used (again, you can change it, but 95% is what is conventionally reported). You can also request the _Hosmer-Lemeshow goodness-of-fit_ statistic, which is used to assess how well the chosen model fits the data. The remaining options are fairly unimportant: you can choose to display all statistics and graphs at each stage of an analysis (the default), or only after the final model has been fitted. Finally, you can display a correlation matrix of parameter estimates for the terms in the model (*Correlation of estimates*) – the practical purpose of doing this is lost on most of us mere mortals. You can display coefficients and log-likelihood values at each iteration of the parameter estimation process (*Iteration history*), which is useful because it's the only way you can get SPSS to display the initial $-2LL$, and we need this value if we want to compute R. When you have selected all of the options that I've just described, click on $\boxed{\text{OK}}$ and watch the output spew out.

19.5.11.   Bootstrapping ②

If you use forced entry then you can also bootstrap your model by clicking on $\boxed{\text{Bootstrap...}}$ and selecting appropriate options. This function doesn't work with stepwise methods, so the button will be inactive unless you choose *Enter*. It's also worth remembering that if you activate bootstrapping then any residuals that you have asked to be saved, won't be saved. This is annoying because it means that to bootstrap the model parameters we have to run the analysis again, but deselecting the options in Figure 19.9 (I would also deselect the options in Figure 19.10 just to keep everything simple). Let's do this, select the usual bootstrapping options, and rerun the model (see Section 5.4.3) by clicking on OK.

19.6. Interpreting logistic regression ②

19.6.1. Block 0 ②

The output is split into two blocks: block 0 describes the model before **Intervention** is included, and block 1 describes the model after **Intervention** is included. As such, block 1 is the main bit in which we're interested. The bit of the block 0 output that does come in useful is in Output 19.3, and will be there only if you selected *Iteration history* in Figure 19.10. This table tells us the initial $-2LL$, which is 154.084. We'll use this value later so don't forget it.

OUTPUT 19.3

Iteration History[a,b,c]

Iteration		-2 Log likelihood	Coefficients Constant
Step 0	1	154.084	.301
	2	154.084	.303
	3	154.084	.303

a. Constant is included in the model.

b. Initial –2 Log Likelihood: 154.084

c. Estimation terminated at iteration number 3 because parameter estimates changed by less than .001.

19.6.2. Model summary ②

With **Intervention** included in the model a patient is now classified as being cured or not based on whether they had an intervention or not (waiting list). This can be explained easily if we look at the crosstabulation for the variables **Intervention** and **Cured**.[6] The model will use whether a patient had an intervention or not to predict whether they were cured or not by applying the crosstabulation shown in Table 19.1. The model predicts that all of the patients who had an intervention were cured. There were 57 patients who had an intervention, so the model predicts that these 57 patients were cured; it is correct for 41 of these patients, but misclassifies 16 people as 'cured' who were not cured (see Table 19.1). In addition, this new model predicts that all of the 56 patients who received no treatment were not cured; for these patients the model is correct 32 times but misclassifies as 'not cured' 24 people who were.

[6] The dialog box to produce this table can be obtained by selecting Analyze Descriptive Statistics ▸ Crosstabs…

TABLE 19.1   Crosstabulation of intervention with outcome status (cured or not)

		Intervention or Not	
		No Treatment	Intervention
Cured? (Cured)	Not Cured	32	16
	Cured	24	41
	Total	56	57

Output 19.4 shows summary statistics for the model,[7] but we should also look at the table that we already inspected in Output 19.2 that showed the chi-square statistic for the model (remember it was 9.926, and highly significant, $p = .002$). This chi-square statistic is derived from equation (19.6) and is the difference between the current $-2LL$ (which for this model is 144.158) and the baseline $-2LL$ (i.e., the value before **Intervention** was added, which is reported in as 154.084 in Output 19.3): $154.084 - 144.158 = 9.926$.

Output 19.4 tells us the values of Cox and Snell's and Nagelkerke's R^2, but we will discuss these a little later. There is also a classification table that indicates how well the model predicts group membership; because the model is using **Intervention** to predict the outcome variable, this classification table is the same as Table 19.1. The current model correctly classifies 32 patients who were not cured but misclassifies 16 others (it correctly classifies 66.7% of cases). The model also correctly classifies 41 patients who were cured but misclassifies 24 others (it correctly classifies 63.1% of cases). The overall accuracy of classification is, therefore, the weighted average of these two values (64.6%). So, when only the constant was included, the model correctly classified 57.5% of patients, but now, with the inclusion of **Intervention** as a predictor, this has risen to 64.6%.[8]

Output 19.5 is crucial because it tells us the estimates for the coefficients for the predictors included in the model. This section of the output gives us the coefficients and statistics for the variables that have been included in the model (namely **Intervention** and the constant). The b-values are the values that we need to replace in equation (19.3) to establish the probability that a case falls into a certain category. We saw in linear regression that the value of b represents the change in the outcome resulting from a unit change in the predictor variable. The interpretation of this coefficient in logistic regression is very similar in that it represents the change in the *logit* of the outcome variable associated with a one-unit change in the predictor variable. The logit of the outcome is the natural logarithm of the odds of Y occurring.

The output also tells us the Wald statistic (equation (19.11)).[9] This statistic tells us whether the b coefficient for that predictor is significantly different from zero. If the coefficient is significantly different from zero then we can assume that the predictor is making a significant contribution to the prediction of the outcome (Y). For these data, the Wald statistic indicates that having the intervention (or not) is a significant predictor of whether the patient is cured (note that the significance of the Wald statistic is .002, which is less than .05).

I recommended running the model once to save residuals and then again implementing bootstrapping. For the bootstrapped model you'll also see the table labelled *Bootstrap for*

---

[7] If you use bootstrapping you'll notice a load of guff below this table. Ignore it.

[8] If you go back and look at the classification tables for models 2 and 3, you'll notice they are identical to the one reported for this model, which means that adding **Duration** and the interaction term did not lead to even a single person being more accurately classified than when we include only **Intervention** as a predictor.

[9] As we have seen, the Wald statistic is b divided by its standard error ($1.229/0.40 = 3.0725$); however, SPSS quotes the Wald statistic squared, $3.0725^2 = 9.44$, as reported (within rounding error) in the table.

OUTPUT 19.4

Model Summary

Step	-2 Log likelihood	Cox & Snell R Square	Nagelkerke R Square
1	144.158[a]	.084	.113

a. Estimation terminated at iteration number 3 because parameter estimates changed by less than .001.

Classification Table[a]

			Predicted		
			Cured?		Percentage Correct
	Observed		Not Cured	Cured	
Step 1	Cured?	Not Cured	32	16	66.7
		Cured	24	41	63.1
	Overall Percentage				64.6

a. The cut value is .500

OUTPUT 19.5

Variables in the Equation

		B	S.E.	Wald	df	Sig.	Exp(B)	95% C.I.for EXP(B) Lower	Upper
Step 1[a]	Intervention(1)	1.229	.400	9.447	1	.002	3.417	1.561	7.480
	Constant	-.288	.270	1.135	1	.287	.750		

a. Variable(s) entered on step 1: Intervention.

Bootstrap for Variables in the Equation

			Bootstrap[a]					
		B	Bias	Std. Error	Sig. (2-tailed)	BCa 95% Confidence Interval Lower	Upper
Step 1	Intervention(1)	1.229	.014	.416	.004	.423	2.062
	Constant	-.288	-.002	.269	.294	-.773	.201

a. Unless otherwise noted, bootstrap results are based on 1000 bootstrap samples

Variables in the Equation in Output 19.5. This table reports the *b*-values again, but estimates the standard error based on bootstrap resampling (Section 5.4.3). The change in the standard error results in a different *p*-value for the *b* (it is .004 instead of .002), but it is still significant. More important, we get a bootstrap confidence interval for the *b*-values, which tells us that the population value of *b* falls between 0.423 and 2.062 (assuming this sample is one of the 95% for which the confidence interval contains the population value). This interval doesn't include zero so we can conclude that there is a genuine positive relationship between having the intervention (or not) and being cured (or not). The bootstrap confidence intervals will differ slightly every time you run the analysis, but they are nevertheless robust to violations of the underlying assumptions of the test.

In Section 19.3.3 we saw that we could calculate an analogue of *R* using equation (19.7). For these data, z^2 (the Wald statistic in the output) and its *df* can be read from Output 19.5 (9.447 and 1, respectively), and the baseline $-2LL$ was reported as 154.084 in Output 19.3. Therefore, *R* can be calculated as:

$$R = \sqrt{\frac{9.447 - (2 \times 1)}{154.084}}$$

$$= .22$$

In the same section we saw that Hosmer and Lemeshow's measure (R_{L}^2) can be calculated as:

$$R_{\text{L}}^2 = \frac{\left(-2LL(\text{baseline})\right) - \left(-2LL(\text{new})\right)}{-2LL(\text{baseline})}$$

$$= \frac{154.084 - 144.158}{154.084}$$

$$= .06$$

This is the same as dividing the model chi-square after **Intervention** has been entered into the model (9.93) by the baseline $-2LL$ (before any variables were entered). The resulting value of .06 is different from the one we would get by squaring R above ($R^2 = .22^2 = .05$). Two other measures of R^2, which were described in Section 19.3.3, can be found in Output 19.4: Cox and Snell's measure, which SPSS reports as .084, and Nagelkerke's adjusted value, which SPSS reports as .113. As you can see, all of these values of R^2 differ, but they can be used as effect size measures for the model.

SELF-TEST   Using equations (19.8) and (19.9), calculate the values of Cox and Snell's and Nagelkerke's R^2 reported by SPSS. (Remember the sample size, N, is 113.)

The final thing we need to look at is the odds ratio ($Exp(B)$ in the SPSS output), which was described in Section 19.3.5. SPSS reports the odds ratio as $Exp(B)$, because it is literally the exponential of the b for the predictor, in this case $e^{1.229} = 3.42$. However, most people are more familiar with the term 'odds ratio'. The odds ratio is the change in odds (see Jane Superbrain Box 8.2). If the value is greater than 1, then it indicates that as the predictor increases, the odds of the outcome occurring increase. Conversely, a value less than 1 indicates that as the predictor increases, the odds of the outcome occurring decrease. In this example, we can say that the odds of a patient who is treated being cured are 3.42 times higher than those of a patient who is not treated.

In the options (see Section 19.5.10), we requested a confidence interval for the odds ratio, and it can also be found in the output. As with any confidence interval, it is computed such that if we calculated confidence intervals for the value of the odds ratio in 100 different samples, then these intervals would include the value of the odds ratio in the population in 95 of those samples. Assuming the current sample is one of the 95 for which the confidence interval contains the true value, then we know that the population value of the odds ratio lies between 1.56 and 7.48. However, our sample could be one of the 5% that produces a confidence interval that 'misses' the population value. The important thing is that the interval doesn't contain 1 (both values are greater than 1). The value of 1 is important because it is the threshold at which the direction of the effect changes. Let me explain. Values greater than 1 mean that as the predictor variable increases, so do the odds of (in this case) being cured. However, values less than 1 mean the opposite: as the predictor variable increases, the odds of being cured *decrease*. If the confidence interval contains 1 then it means that the population value might be one that suggests that the intervention improves the probability of being cured, but equally it might be a value that suggests that the intervention decreases the probability of being cured. For our confidence interval, the fact that both limits are above 1 gives us confidence that the direction of the relationship that we have observed is true in the population (i.e., it's likely that having an intervention compared to not increases the odds of being cured). If the lower limit had been below 1 then it would

JANE SUPERBRAIN 19.1

Computing the odds ratio ③

To calculate the odds ratio, we must first calculate the odds of a patient being cured given that they *didn't* have the intervention, using equation (19.3). The parameter coding at the beginning of the output told us that patients who did not have the intervention were coded with a 0, so we use this value as X. The value of b_1 has been estimated for us as 1.229 (see *Variables in the Equation* in Output 19.5), and the coefficient for the constant can be taken from the same table and is -0.288. We can calculate the odds as:

$$P(\text{Cured}) = \frac{1}{1 + e^{-(b_0 + b_1 X_{1i})}}$$

$$= \frac{1}{1 + e^{-[-0.288 + (1.229 \times 0)]}}$$

$$= .428$$

$$P(\text{Not Cured}) = 1 - P(\text{Cured})$$

$$= 1 - .428$$

$$= .572$$

$$\text{Odds} = \frac{.428}{.572}$$

$$= .748$$

Now, we calculate the same thing after the predictor variable has changed by one unit. In this case, because the predictor variable is dichotomous, we calculate the odds of a patient being cured, given that they have had the intervention. So, the value of the intervention variable, X, is now 1 (rather than 0). The resulting calculations are as follows:

$$P(\text{Cured}) = \frac{1}{1 + e^{-(b_0 + b_1 X_{1i})}}$$

$$= \frac{1}{1 + e^{-[-0.288 + (1.229 \times 1)]}}$$

$$= .719$$

$$P(\text{Not Cured}) = 1 - P(\text{Cured})$$

$$= 1 - .719$$

$$= .281$$

$$\text{Odds} = \frac{.719}{.281}$$

$$= 2.559$$

Now that we know the odds before and after a unit change in the predictor variable, it is a simple matter to calculate the odds ratio as in equation (19.13):

$$\text{Odds ratio} = \frac{\text{Odds after a unit change in the predictor}}{\text{Original odds}}$$

$$= \frac{2.559}{0.748}$$

$$= 3.42$$

tell us that there is a chance that in the population the direction of the relationship is the opposite to what we have observed. This would mean that we could not trust that our intervention increases the odds of being cured.

Output 19.6 displays the classification plot that we requested in the *Options* dialog box. This plot is a histogram of the predicted probabilities of a patient being cured. If the model perfectly fits the data, then this histogram should show all of the cases for which the event has occurred on the right-hand side, and all the cases for which the event hasn't occurred on the left-hand side. In other words, all of the patients who were cured should appear on the right and all those who were not cured should appear on the left. In this example, the only predictor is dichotomous and so there are just two columns of cases on the plot. If the predictor is a continuous variable, the cases will be spread out across many columns. As a rule of thumb, the more the cases cluster at each end of the graph, the better; such a plot would show that when the outcome did actually occur (i.e., the patient was cured) the

Step number: 1

Observed Groups and Predicted Probabilities

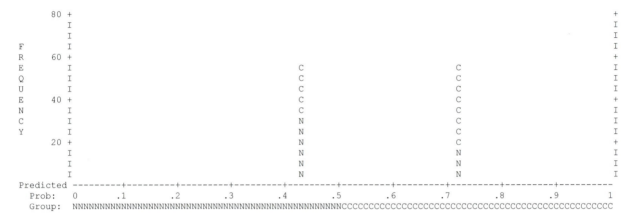

```
      80 +                                                                                          +
         I                                                                                          I
         I                                                                                          I
   F     I                                                                                          I
   R  60 +                                                                                          +
   E     I                                   C                              C                        I
   Q     I                                   C                              C                        I
   U     I                                   C                              C                        I
   E  40 +                                   C                              C                        +
   N     I                                   C                              C                        I
   C     I                                   N                              C                        I
   Y     I                                   N                              C                        I
      20 +                                   N                              C                        +
         I                                   N                              N                        I
         I                                   N                              N                        I
         I                                   N                              N                        I
Predicted ---------+---------+---------+---------+---------+---------+---------+---------+---------+---------
   Prob:  0        .1        .2        .3        .4        .5        .6        .7        .8        .9        1
   Group: NNNNNNNNNNNNNNNNNNNNNNNNNNNNNNNNNNNNNNNNNNNNNNNNNNCCCCCCCCCCCCCCCCCCCCCCCCCCCCCCCCCCCCCCCCCCCCCCCCCCC
```

Predicted Probability is of Membership for Cured
The Cut Value is .50
Symbols: N - Not Cured
         C - Cured
Each Symbol Represents 5 Cases.

OUTPUT 19.6

CRAMMING SAM'S TIPS   Model fit

- Build your model systematically and choose the most parsimonious model as the final one.
- The overall fit of the model is shown by −2*LL* and its associated chi-square statistic. If the significance of the chi-square statistic is less than .05, then the model is a significant fit of the data.
- Check the table labelled *Variables in the Equation* to see the regression parameters for any predictors you have in the model.
- For each variable in the model, look at the Wald statistic and its significance (which again should be below .05). More important, though, use the odds ratio, *Exp*(*B*), for interpretation. If the value is greater than 1 then as the predictor increases, the odds of the outcome occurring increase. Conversely, a value less than 1 indicates that as the predictor increases, the odds of the outcome occurring decrease. For the aforementioned interpretation to be reliable the confidence interval of *Exp*(*B*) should not cross 1.

predicted probability of the event occurring is also high (i.e., close to 1). Likewise, at the other end of the plot it would show that when the event didn't occur (i.e., the patient still had a problem) the predicted probability of the event occurring is also low (i.e., close to 0). This situation represents a model that correctly predicts the observed outcome data. If, however, there are a lot of points clustered in the centre of the plot then it shows that for many cases the model is predicting a probability of .5; in other words, there is little more than a 50:50 chance that these cases are predicted correctly by the model – the model could predict these cases just as accurately by tossing a coin. In Output 19.6 it's clear that cured cases are predicted relatively well by the model (the probabilities are not that close to .5), but for not cured cases the model is less good (the probability of classification is only slightly lower than .5). Also, a good model will ensure that few cases are misclassified; in this example there are a few Ns (not cured) appearing on the cured side, but more worry-ingly there are quite a few Cs (cured) appearing on the N side.

19.6.3. Listing predicted probabilities ②

It is possible to list the expected probability of the outcome variable occurring based on the final model. In Section 19.5.7 we saw that SPSS could save residuals and also predicted probabilities. SPSS saves these predicted probabilities and predicted group memberships as variables in the data editor and names them PRE_1 and PGR_1 respectively. These prob-abilities can be listed by selecting Analyze Reports ▶ 📊 Case Summaries... (see Section 8.7.6).

SELF-TEST   Use the *case summaries* function in SPSS to create a table for the first 15 cases in the file **Eel.sav** showing the values of **Cured**, **Intervention**, **Duration**, the predicted probability (**PRE_1**) and the predicted group membership (**PGR_1**) for each case.

Output 19.7 shows a selection of the predicted probabilities (because the only predictor in the model was a dichotomous variable, there will be only two different probability values). We have also listed the predictor variables to clarify from where the predicted probabilities come. The only predictor of being cured in the final model was having the intervention. This could have a value of either 1 (have the intervention) or 0 (no intervention). If these two values are placed in equation (19.3) with the respective regression coefficients, then the two probability values are derived. In fact, we calculated these values in Jane Superbrain Box 19.1; note that the calculated probabilities, P(Cured) in these equations, correspond to the values in PRE_1. These values tells us that when a patient is not treated (**Intervention** = 0, No Treatment), there is a probability of .429 that they will be cured – basically, about 43% of people get better without any treatment. However, if the patient does have the intervention (**Intervention** = 1, yes), there is a probability of .719 that they will get better – about 72% of people treated get better. When you consider that a probability of 0 indicates no chance of getting better, and a probability of 1 indicates that the patient will definitely get better, the values obtained provide strong evidence that having the intervention increases your chances of getting better (although the probability of recovery without the intervention is still not bad).

Assuming we are content that the model is accurate and that the intervention has some substantive significance, then we could conclude that our intervention (which, to remind you, was putting an eel up the anus) is the best predictor of getting better (not being con-stipated). Furthermore, including the duration of the constipation pre-intervention and its interaction with the intervention did not improve how well we could predict whether a person got better.

19.6.4. Interpreting residuals ②

Running a regression without checking how well the model fits the data is like buying a new pair of trousers without trying them on – they might look fine on the hanger but get them home and you find you're Johnny-tight-pants. The trousers do their job (they cover your legs and keep you warm) but they have no real-life value (because they cut off the blood circulation to your legs, which then have to be amputated). Likewise, regression does

OUTPUT 19.7

Case Summaries[a]

	Cured?	Intervention	Number of Days with Problem before Treatment	Predicted probability	Predicted group
1	Not Cured	No Treatment	7	.42857	Not Cured
2	Not Cured	No Treatment	7	.42857	Not Cured
3	Not Cured	No Treatment	6	.42857	Not Cured
4	Cured	No Treatment	8	.42857	Not Cured
5	Cured	Intervention	7	.71930	Cured
6	Cured	No Treatment	6	.42857	Not Cured
7	Not Cured	Intervention	7	.71930	Cured
8	Cured	Intervention	7	.71930	Cured
9	Cured	No Treatment	8	.42857	Not Cured
10	Not Cured	No Treatment	7	.42857	Not Cured
11	Cured	Intervention	7	.71930	Cured
12	Cured	No Treatment	7	.42857	Not Cured
13	Cured	No Treatment	5	.42857	Not Cured
14	Not Cured	Intervention	9	.71930	Cured
15	Not Cured	No Treatment	6	.42857	Not Cured
Total N	15	15	15	15	15

a. Limited to first 15 cases.

its job regardless of the data (it will create a model), but the real-life value of the model may be limited. So, our conclusions so far are fine in themselves, but to be sure that the model is a good one, it is important to examine the residuals. In Section 19.5.7 we saw how to get SPSS to save various residuals in the data editor. We can now interpret them.

We saw in Chapter 8 that the main purpose of examining residuals in any regression is to (1) isolate points for which the model fits poorly, and (2) isolate points that exert an undue influence on the model. To assess the former we examine the residuals, especially the Studentized residual, standardized residual and deviance statistics. To assess the latter we use influence statistics such as Cook's distance, DFBeta and leverage statistics. These statistics were explained in Section 8.3 and their interpretation in logistic regression is the same. Table 19.2 summarizes the main statistics that you should look at and what to look for, but for more detail consult Chapter 8.

If you request these residual statistics, SPSS saves them as new columns in the data editor. You can look at the values in the data editor, or produce a table by selecting Analyze Reports ▸ Case Summaries… .

The basic residual statistics for this example (Cook's distance, leverage, standardized residuals and DFBeta values) are pretty good: note that all cases have DFBetas less than 1, and leverage statistics (**LEV_1**) are very close to the calculated expected value of 0.018.

OLIVER TWISTED

Please, Sir, can I have some more … diagnostics?

'What about the trees?' protests eco-warrior Oliver. 'These SPSS outputs take up so much room, why don't you put them on the website instead?' It's a valid point, so I have produced a table of the diagnostic statistics for this example, but it's in the additional material for this chapter on the companion website.

There are also no unusually high values of Cook's distance (**COO_1**) which, all in all, means that there are no influential cases having an effect on the model. The standardized residuals all have values of less than ± 2, so there seems to be very little here to concern us.

You should note that these residuals are slightly unusual because they are based on a single predictor that is categorical. This is why there isn't a lot of variability in the values of the residuals. Also, if substantial outliers or influential cases had been isolated, you would not be justified in eliminating these cases to make the model fit better. Instead these cases should be inspected closely to try to isolate a good reason why they were unusual. It might simply be an error in inputting data, or it could be that the case was one which had a special reason for being unusual: for example, there were other medical complications that might contribute to the constipation that were noted during the patient's assessment. In such a case, you may have good reason to exclude the case and duly note the reasons why.

TABLE 19.2 Summary of residual statistics saved by SPSS

Label	Name	Comment
PRE_1	Predicted Value	
PGR_1	Predicted Group	
COO_1	Cook's Distance	Should be less than 1
LEV_1	Leverage	Lies between 0 (no influence) and 1 (complete influence). The expected leverage is $(k + 1)/N$, where k is the number of predictors and N is the sample size. In this case it would be $2/113 = .018$
SRE_1	Studentized Residual	Only 5% should lie outside ±1.96, and about 1% should lie outside ±2.58. Cases above 3 are cause for concern and cases close to 3 warrant inspection
ZRE_1	Standardized Residual	
DEV_1	Deviance	
DFB0_1	DF Beta for the Constant	Should be less than 1
DFB1_1	DF Beta for the first predictor (**Intervention**)	

CRAMMING SAM'S TIPS   Diagnostic statistics

- Look for cases that might be influencing the logistic regression model.
- Look at standardized residuals and check that no more than 5% of cases have absolute values above 2, and that no more than about 1% have absolute values above 2.5. Any case with a value above about 3 could be an outlier.
- Look in the data editor for the values of Cook's distance: any value above 1 indicates a case that might be influencing the model.
- Calculate the average leverage (the number of predictors plus 1, divided by the sample size) and then look for values greater than twice or three times this average value.
- Look for absolute values of DFBeta greater than 1.

19.6.5. Calculating the effect size ②

The best effect size to use in the context of logistic regression is the odds ratio, which we have looked at in detail and interpreted for this example in Section 19.6.2.

19.7. How to report logistic regression ②

Logistic regression is fairly rarely used in my discipline of psychology, so it's difficult to find any concrete guidelines about how to report one. My personal view is that you should report it much the same as linear regression (see Section 8.9). I'd be inclined to tabulate the results, unless it's a very simple model. As a bare minimum, report the beta values and their standard errors and significance value and some general statistics about the model (such as the R^2 and goodness-of-fit statistics). I'd also highly recommend reporting the odds ratio and its confidence interval. I'd also include the constant, so that readers of your work can construct the full regression model if they need to. You might also consider reporting the variables that were not significant predictors because this can be as valuable as knowing about which predictors were significant.

For the example in this chapter we might produce something like Table 19.3. Hopefully you can work out from where the values came by looking back through the chapter so far. I've rounded off to 2 decimal places throughout; for the R^2 there is no zero before the decimal point (because these values cannot exceed 1) but for all other values less than 1 the zero is present; I have reported the bootstrap confidence intervals for b.

TABLE 19.3 Coefficients of the model predicting whether a patient was cured [95% BCa bootstrap confidence intervals based on 1000 samples]

	b	95% CI for Odds Ratio		
		Lower	Odds	Upper
Included				
Constant	−0.29 [−0.77, 0.20]			
Intervention	1.23* [0.42, 2.06]	1.56	3.42	7.48

Note. $R^2 = .06$ (Hosmer & Lemeshow) .08 (Cox & Snell) .11 (Nagelkerke). Model $\chi^2(1) = 9.93, p < .01$. * $p < .01$.

19.8. Testing assumptions: another example ②

I am English, and a very important part of being English is believing that we can win sports events despite the crushing weight of historical evidence to the contrary. English people are genetically programmed to fail in high-pressure environments; that's a fact,[10] but as each new tournament arrives we are programmed by the media to believe that somehow

---

[10] The rugby World Cup winning side of 2003 was the exception that proves the rule. Oh, and I think we won the Ashes in 2005, but we lost them the previous 18 years in a row so that victory is hardly anything to feel smug about. Also, I don't like cricket.

England will be victorious. With every defeat, we lose a little bit of our soul. My writing of each edition of this book has coincided with a soccer-related national failure. In 1998 when I wrote the first edition, England were knocked out of the World Cup by losing a penalty shootout. In 2004 (second edition), we were knocked out of the European Championship in another penalty shootout. We didn't even manage to qualify for the 2008 European Championship (third edition); not a penalty shootout this time, just playing like cretins. Now, as I write the fourth, we have recently lost yet another penalty shootout that again sent us home from the European Championship. What is *wrong* with English footballers?

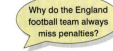

If I were the England soccer team coach, I'd take each and every one of the overpaid prima donnas and I'd kick them in the testicles. A really hard kick, just to let them know that I'm the kind of guy that'll give you a good hard kick in your testicles if you miss a penalty. Alternatively, I might use science to find out which factors predict whether or not a player will score a penalty. Then I'd kick them in the testicles. One way or another, their testicles are getting kicked.

Those of you who hate football can read this example as being factors that predict success in a free throw in basketball or netball, a penalty in hockey or a penalty kick in rugby or field goal in American football. This research question is perfect for logistic regression because our outcome variable is a dichotomy: a penalty can be either scored or missed. Imagine that past research (Eriksson, Beckham, & Vassell, 2004; Hoddle, Batty, & Ince, 1998; Hodgson, Cole, & Young, 2012) had shown that there are two factors that reliably predict whether a penalty kick will be missed or scored. The first factor is whether the player taking the kick is a worrier (this factor can be measured using a measure such as the Penn State Worry Questionnaire, PSWQ). The second factor is the player's past success rate at scoring (so whether the player has a good track record of scoring penalty kicks). It is fairly well accepted that anxiety has detrimental effects on the performance of a variety of tasks, and so it was also predicted that state anxiety might be able to account for some of the unexplained variance in penalty success.

This example is a classic case of building on a well-established model, because two predictors are already known and we want to test the effect of a new one. So, 75 football players were selected at random and before taking a penalty kick in a competition they were given a state anxiety questionnaire to complete (to assess anxiety before the kick was taken). These players were also asked to complete the PSWQ to give a measure of how much they worried about things generally, and their past success rate was obtained from a database. Finally, a note was made of whether the penalty was scored or missed. The data can be found in the file **Penalty.sav**, which contains four variables – each in a separate column:

- **Scored**: This variable is our outcome and it is coded such that 0 = penalty missed and 1 = penalty scored.

- **PSWQ**: This variable is the first predictor variable and it gives us a measure of the degree to which a player worries.

- **Previous**: This variable is the percentage of penalties scored by a particular player in their career. As such, it represents previous success at scoring penalties.

- **Anxious**: This variable is our third predictor and it is a variable that has not previously been used to predict penalty success. **Anxious** is a measure of state anxiety before taking the penalty.

SELF-TEST   Conduct a hierarchical logistic regression analysis on these data. Enter **Previous** and **PSWQ** in the first block and **Anxious** in the second (forced entry). There is a full guide on how to do the analysis and its interpretation in the additional material on the companion website.

19.8.1. Testing for linearity of the logit ③

In this example we have three continuous variables, so we have to check that each one is linearly related to the log of the outcome variable (**Scored**). I mentioned earlier in this chapter that to test this assumption we need to run the logistic regression but include predictors that are the interaction between each predictor and the log of itself (Hosmer & Lemeshow, 1989). To create these interaction terms, we need to use Transform 🔲 Compute Variable... (see Section 5.4.4). For each variable create a new variable that is the log of the original variable. For example, for **PSWQ**, create a new variable called **LnPSWQ** by entering this name into the box labelled *Target Variable* and then click on Type & Label... and give the variable a more descriptive name such as *Ln(PSWQ)*. In the list box labelled *Function group* click on *Arithmetic* and then in the box labelled *Functions and Special Variables* click on *Ln* (this is the natural log transformation) and transfer it to the command area by clicking on 🔼. When the command is transferred, it appears in the command area as 'LN(?)' and the question mark should be replaced with a variable name (which can be typed manually or transferred from the variables list). So replace the question mark with the variable **PSWQ** by either selecting the variable in the list and clicking on ➡ or just typing 'PSWQ' where the question mark is. Click on OK to create the variable.

SELF-TEST   Try creating two new variables that are the natural logs of **Anxious** and **Previous**.

To test the assumption we need to redo the analysis exactly the same way as before, except that we should force all variables in a single block (i.e., we don't need to do it hierarchically), and we also need to put in three new interaction terms of each predictor and their logs. Select Analyze Regression ▸ Binary Logistic..., then in the main dialog box click on **Scored** and drag it to the *Dependent* box (or click on ➡). Specify the main effects by clicking on **PSWQ**, **Anxious** and **Previous** while holding down the *Ctrl* key (*Cmd* on a Mac), and then drag them to the *Covariates* box (or click on ➡). To input the interactions, click on the two variables in the interaction while holding down the *Ctrl* key: for example, click on **PSWQ** then, while holding down *Ctrl*, click on **Ln(PSWQ))** and then click on >a*b> to move them to the *Covariates* box. This action specifies the **PSWQ** × **Ln(PSWQ)** interaction; specify the **Anxious** × **Ln(Anxious)** and **Previous** × **Ln(Previous)** interactions in the same way. The completed dialog box is in Figure 19.11 (note that the final **Previous** × **Ln(Previous)** interaction isn't visible, but it is there).

Output 19.8 shows the part of the output that tests the assumption. We're interested only in whether the interaction terms are significant. Any interaction that is significant indicates that the main effect has violated the assumption of linearity of the logit. All three interactions have significance values greater than .05, indicating that the assumption of linearity of the logit has been met for **PSWQ**, **Anxious** and **Previous**.

19.8.2. Testing for multicollinearity ③

In Section 8.5.3 we saw how multicollinearity can affect the parameters of a regression model. Logistic regression is just as prone to the biasing effect of collinearity, so we need

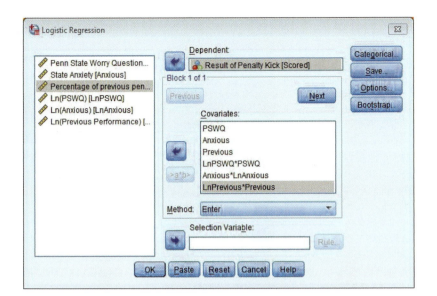

FIGURE 19.11
Dialog box
for testing the
assumption
of linearity
in logistic
regression

Variables in the Equation

OUTPUT 19.8

		B	S.E.	Wald	df	Sig.	Exp(B)
Step 1[a]	PSWQ	-.422	1.102	.147	1	.702	.656
	Anxious	-2.650	2.784	.906	1	.341	.071
	Previous	1.669	1.473	1.285	1	.257	5.309
	LnPSWQ by PSWQ	.044	.297	.022	1	.883	1.045
	Anxious by LnAnxious	.682	.650	1.102	1	.294	1.978
	LnPrevious by Previous	-.319	.315	1.025	1	.311	.727
	Constant	-3.874	14.924	.067	1	.795	.021

a. Variable(s) entered on step 1: PSWQ, Anxious, Previous, LnPSWQ * PSWQ , Anxious * LnAnxious , LnPrevious * Previous.

to test for collinearity. Unfortunately, SPSS does not have an option for producing collinearity diagnostics in logistic regression (which can create the illusion that multicollinearity doesn't matter). However, you can obtain statistics such as the tolerance and VIF by running a linear regression analysis using the same outcome and predictors.

For the penalty example in the previous section, access the *Linear Regression* dialog box by selecting Analyze Regression ▸ Linear... . The completed dialog box is shown in Figure 19.12. It is unnecessary to specify lots of options (we are using this technique only to obtain tests of collinearity) but it is essential that you click on Statistics... and then select *Collinearity diagnostics* in the dialog box. Once you have selected ☑ Collinearity diagnostics , switch off all of the default options, click on Continue to return to the *Linear Regression* dialog box, and then click on OK to run the analysis.

The results of the analysis are shown in Output 19.9. From the first table we can see that the tolerance values are 0.014 for **Previous** and **Anxious** and 0.575 for **PSWQ**. In Chapter 8 we saw various criteria for assessing collinearity. To recap, tolerance values less than 0.1 (Menard, 1995) and VIF values greater than 10 (Myers, 1990) indicate a problem. In these data the VIF values are over 70 for both **Anxious** and **Previous** indicating an issue of collinearity between the predictor variables. We can investigate this issue further by examining the table labelled *Collinearity Diagnostics*. In this table, we are given the eigenvalues of the scaled, uncentred cross-products matrix, the condition index and the variance proportions for each predictor. If any of the eigenvalues in this table are much larger than others then the uncentred cross-products matrix is said to be 'ill-conditioned', which means that the regression parameter estimates can be greatly affected by small changes in the predictors or

FIGURE 19.12
*Linear
Regression*
dialog box for
the penalty data

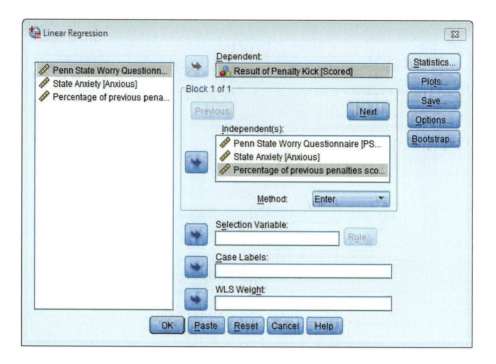

outcome. In plain English, these values give us some idea as to how accurate our regression parameters are: if the eigenvalues are fairly similar then the derived model is likely to be unchanged by small changes in the measured variables. The *condition indexes* are another way of expressing these eigenvalues and represent the square root of the ratio of the largest eigenvalue to the eigenvalue of interest (so for the dimension with the largest eigenvalue, the condition index will always be 1). For these data the final dimension has a condition index of 81.3, which is massive compared to the other dimensions. Although there are no hard-and-fast rules about how much larger a condition index needs to be to indicate collinearity problems, this case clearly shows that a problem exists.

The final step in analysing this table is to look at the variance proportions. The variance of each regression coefficient can be broken down across the eigenvalues, and the variance proportions tell us the proportion of the variance of each predictor's regression coefficient that is attributed to each eigenvalue. These proportions can be converted to percentages by multiplying them by 100. So, for example, for **PSWQ** 95% of the variance of the regression coefficient is associated with eigenvalue number 3, 4% is associated with eigenvalue number 2 and 1% is associated with eigenvalue number 1. In terms of collinearity, we are looking for predictors that have high proportions on the same *small* eigenvalue, because this would indicate that the variances of their regression coefficients are dependent. So we are interested mainly in the bottom few rows of the table (which represent small eigenvalues). In this example, 99% of the variance in the regression coefficients of both **Anxiety** and **Previous** is associated with eigenvalue number 4 (the smallest eigenvalue), which clearly indicates dependency between these variables.

The result of this analysis is pretty clear-cut: there is collinearity between state anxiety and previous experience of taking penalties, and this dependency results in the model becoming biased.

SELF-TEST   Using what you learned in Chapter 6, carry out a Pearson correlation between all of the variables in this analysis. Can you work out why we have a problem with collinearity?

Coefficients[a]

Model		Collinearity Statistics	
		Tolerance	VIF
1	Penn State Worry Questionnaire	.575	1.741
	State Anxiety	.014	71.764
	Percentage of previous penalties scored	.014	70.479

a. Dependent Variable: Result of Penalty Kick

Collinearity Diagnostics[a]

Model	Dimension	Eigenvalue	Condition Index	Variance Proportions			
				(Constant)	Penn State Worry Questionnaire	State Anxiety	Percentage of previous penalties scored
1	1	3.434	1.000	.00	.01	.00	.00
	2	.492	2.641	.00	.04	.00	.00
	3	.073	6.871	.00	.95	.01	.00
	4	.001	81.303	1.00	.00	.99	.99

a. Dependent Variable: Result of Penalty Kick

OUTPUT 19.9   Collinearity diagnostics for the penalty data

If you have identified collinearity then, unfortunately, there's not much that you can do about it. One obvious solution is to omit one of the variables (so, for example, we might stick with a model that ignores state anxiety). The problem with this should be obvious: there is no way of knowing which variable to omit. The resulting theoretical conclusions are meaningless because, statistically speaking, any of the collinear variables could be omitted. There are no statistical grounds for omitting one variable over another. Even if a predictor is removed, Bowerman and O'Connell (1990) recommend that another equally important predictor that does not have such strong multicollinearity replace it. They also suggest collecting more data to see whether the multicollinearity can be lessened. Another possibility when there are several predictors involved in the multicollinearity is to run a PCA on these predictors and to use the resulting component scores as a predictor (see Chapter 17). The safest (although unsatisfactory) remedy is to acknowledge the unreliability of the model. So, if we were to report the analysis of factors predicting penalty success, we might acknowledge that previous experience significantly predicted penalty success in the first model, but propose that this experience might affect penalty taking by increasing state anxiety. This statement would be highly speculative because the correlation between **Anxious** and **Previous** tells us nothing of the direction of causality, but it would acknowledge the inexplicable link between the two predictors.

19.9. Predicting several categories: multinomial logistic regression ③

It is possible to use logistic regression to predict membership of more than two categories; this is called *multinomial logistic regression*. Essentially, this form of logistic regression works in the same way as binary logistic regression, so there's no need for any additional equations to explain what is going on (hooray!). The analysis breaks the outcome variable

Lacourse, E., et al. (2001). *Journal of Youth and Adolescence*, 30, 321–332.

LABCOAT LENI'S REAL RESEARCH 19.1

Mandatory suicide? ②

My favourite kind of music is heavy metal. One thing that is mildly irritating about liking heavy music is that everyone assumes that you're either a moron or a miserable or aggressive bastard. When not listening (and often while listening) to heavy metal, I research clinical psychology in youths. Therefore, I was literally beside myself with excitement when I stumbled on a paper that combined these two interests: Lacourse, Claes, and Villeneuve (2001) carried out a study to see whether a love of heavy metal could predict suicide risk. Fabulous stuff!

Eric Lacourse and his colleagues used questionnaires to measure several variables: suicide risk (yes or no), marital status of parents (together or divorced/separated), the extent to which the person's mother and father were neglectful, self-estrangement/powerlessness (adolescents who have negative self-perceptions, are bored with life, etc.), social isolation (feelings of a lack of support), normlessness (beliefs that socially disapproved behaviours can be used to achieve

certain goals), meaninglessness (doubting that school is relevant to gain employment) and drug use. In addition, the authors measured liking of heavy metal; they included the sub-genres of classic (Black Sabbath, Iron Maiden), thrash metal (Slayer, Metallica), death/black metal (Obituary, Burzum) and gothic (Marilyn Manson). As well as liking, they measured behavioural manifestations of worshipping these bands (e.g., hanging posters, hanging out with other metal fans) and what the authors termed 'vicarious music listening' (whether music was used when angry or to bring out aggressive moods). They used logistic regression to predict suicide risk from these variables for males and females separately.

The data for the female sample are in the file **Lacourse et al. (2001) Females.sav**. Labcoat Leni wants you to carry out a logistic regression predicting **Suicide_Risk** from all of the predictors (forced entry). (To make your results easier to compare to the published results, enter the predictors in the same order as Table 3 in the paper: **Age, Marital_Status, Mother_Negligence, Father_Negligence, Self_Estrangement, Isolation, Normlessness, Meaninglessness, Drug_Use, Metal, Worshipping, Vicarious**). Create a table of the results. Does listening to heavy metal predict girls' suicide? If not, what does? Answers are on the companion website (or look at Table 3 in the original article).

What do I do when I have more than two outcome categories?

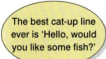

The best cat-up line ever is 'Hello, would you like some fish?'

down into a series of comparisons between two categories (which helps explain why no extra equations are really necessary). For example, if you have three outcome categories (A, B and C), then the analysis will consist of two comparisons. The form that these comparisons take depends on how you specify the analysis: you can compare everything against your first category (e.g., A vs. B and A vs. C), or your last category (e.g., A vs. C and B vs. C), or a custom category, such as B (e.g., B vs. A and B vs. C). In practice, this means that you have to select a baseline category. The important parts of the analysis and output are much the same as we have just seen for binary logistic regression.

Let's look at an example. There has been some work looking at how men and women evaluate chat-up lines (Bale, Morrison, & Caryl, 2006; Cooper, O'Donnell, Caryl, Morrison, & Bale, 2007). This research has looked at how the content (e.g., whether the chat-up line is funny, has sexual content, or reveals desirable personality characteristics) affects how favourably the chat-up line is viewed. To sum up this research, it has found that men and women like different things in chat-up lines: men prefer chat-up lines with a high sexual content, and women prefer chat-up lines that are funny and show good moral fibre.

Imagine that we wanted to assess how *successful* these chat-up lines were. We did a study in which we recorded the chat-up lines used by 348 men and 672 women in a nightclub. Our outcome was whether the chat-up line resulted in one of the following three events: the person got no response or the recipient walked away, the person obtained the recipient's phone number, or the person left the night-club with the recipient. Afterwards, the chat-up lines used in each case were rated by a panel of judges for how funny they were (0 = not funny at all, 10 = the funniest thing that I have ever heard), sexuality (0 = no sexual content at all, 10 = very sexually direct) and whether the chat-up line reflected good moral vales (0 = the chat-up line does not reflect good characteristics, 10 = the chat-up line is very indicative of good characteristics). For example, 'I may not be Fred Flintstone, but I bet I could make your bed rock' would score high on sexual content, low on good characteristics and medium on humour; 'I've been looking all over for you, the woman of my dreams' would score high on good characteristics, low on sexual content and low on humour (but high on cheese, had it been measured). We predict, based on past research, that the success of different types of chat-up line will interact with gender.

This situation is perfect for multinomial regression. The data are in the file **Chat-Up Lines.sav**. There is one outcome variable (**Success**) with three categories (no response, phone number, go home with recipient) and four predictors: funniness of the chat-up line (**Funny**), sexual content of the chat-up line (**Sex**), degree to which the chat-up line reflects good characteristics (**Good_Mate**) and the gender of the person being chatted up (**Gender**).

19.9.1. Running multinomial logistic regression in SPSS ③

To run multinomial logistic regression in SPSS, first select the main dialog box by selecting `Analyze Regression ▸ ▦ Multinomial Logistic…`. In this dialog box there are spaces to place the outcome variable (_Dependent_), any categorical predictors (_Factor(s)_) and any continuous predictors (_Covariate(s)_). In this example, the outcome variable is **Success**, so select this variable from the list and transfer it to the box labelled _Dependent_ by dragging it there or clicking on `➡`. We also have to tell SPSS whether we want to compare categories against the first category or the last, and we do this by clicking on `Reference Category…`.

SELF-TEST Think about the three categories that we have as an outcome variable. Which of these categories do you think makes most sense to use as a baseline category?

By default SPSS uses the last category, but for this example it makes most sense to use the first category (No response/walk off) because this category represents failure (the chat-up line did not have the desired effect) whereas the other two categories represent some form of success (getting a phone number or leaving the club together). To change the reference category to the first, select `◉ First Category` and then click on `Continue` to return to the main dialog box (Figure 19.13).

Next we have to specify the predictor variables. We have one categorical predictor variable, which is **Gender**, so select this variable next and transfer it to the box labelled _Factor(s)_ by dragging it there or clicking on `➡`. Finally, we have three continuous predictors or covariates (**Funny, Sex** and **Good_Mate**). You can select all of these variables simultaneously by holding down the _Ctrl_ key (_Cmd_ on a Mac) as you click on each one. Drag all three to the box labelled _Covariate(s)_ or click on `➡`. For a basic analysis in which all of these predictors are forced into the model, this is all we really need to do. However, as we saw in the regression chapter, you will often want to do a hierarchical regression, so for this analysis we'll look at how to do this in SPSS.

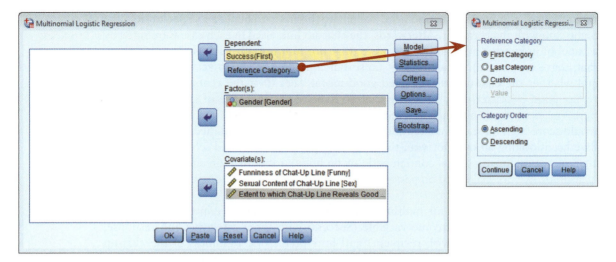

FIGURE 19.13 Main dialog box for multinomial logistic regression

19.9.1.1. Customizing the model ③

Unlike binary logistic regression, with multinomial logistic regression we can't specify interactions between predictor variables in the main dialog box. Instead we have to specify a 'custom model', and this is done by clicking on Model... to open the dialog box in Figure 19.14. You'll see that, by default, SPSS just looks at the main effects of the predictor variables. In this example, however, the main effects are not particularly interesting: based on past research, we don't necessarily expect funny chat-up lines to be successful, but we do expect them to be more successful when used on women than on men. What this prediction implies is that the *interaction* of **Gender** and **Funny** will be significant. Similarly, chat-up lines with a high sexual content might not be successful overall, but expect them to be relatively successful when used on men. Again, this means that we might not expect the **Sex** main effect to be significant, but we do expect the **Sex × Gender** interaction to be significant. As such, we need to enter some interaction terms into the model.

To customize the model we first have to select ⦿ Custom/Stepwise to activate the rest of the dialog box. There are two main ways that we can specify terms: we can force them in (by moving them to the box labelled *Forced Entry Terms*) or we can put them into the model using a stepwise procedure (by moving them into the box labelled *Stepwise Terms*). If we want to look at interaction terms, we must force the main effects into the model. If we look at interactions without the corresponding main effects being in the model then we allow the interaction term to explain variance that might otherwise be attributed to the main effect (in other words, we're not really looking at the interaction any more). So, select all of the variables in the box labelled *Factors & Covariates* by clicking on them while holding down *Ctrl* (*Cmd* on a Mac) or by selecting the first variable and then clicking on the last variable while holding down *Shift*. There is a drop-down list that determines whether you transfer these effects as main effects or interactions. We want to transfer them as main effects, so set this box to Main effects ▾ and click on ⮕.

To specify interactions we can do much the same: we can select two or more variables and then set the drop-down box to Interaction ▾ and click on ⮕. If, for example, we selected **Funny** and **Sex**, then doing this would specify the **Funny × Sex** interaction. We can also specify multiple interactions at once. For example, if we selected **Funny**, **Sex** and **Gender** and then set the drop-down box to All 2-way ▾, it would transfer *all* of the interactions involving two variables (i.e., **Funny × Sex**, **Funny × Gender** and **Sex × Gender**). You get

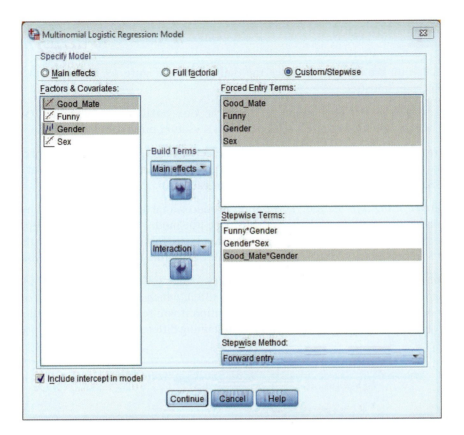

FIGURE 19.14
Specifying a
custom model

the general idea. We could also select which would automatically enter all main effects (**Funny, Sex, Good_Mate, Gender**), all interactions with two variables (**Funny × Sex, Funny × Gender, Funny × Good_Mate, Sex × Gender, Sex × Good_Mate, Gender × Good_Mate**), all interactions with three variables (**Funny × Sex × Gender, Funny × Sex × Good_Mate, Good_Mate × Sex × Gender, Funny × Good_Mate × Gender**) and the interaction of all four variables (**Funny × Sex × Gender × Good_Mate**).

In this scenario, we want to specify interactions between the ratings of the chat-up lines and gender only (we're not interested in any interactions involving three variables, or all four variables). We can either force these interaction terms into the model by putting them in the box labelled *Forced Entry Terms* or we can put them into the model using a stepwise procedure (by moving them into the box labelled *Stepwise Terms*). We'll do the latter, so interactions will be entered into the model only if they are significant predictors of the success of the chat-up line. Let's first enter the **Funny × Gender** interaction. Click on **Funny** and then **Gender** in the *Factors & Covariates* box while holding down the *Ctrl* (*Cmd* on a Mac) key. Then next to the box labelled *Stepwise Terms* change the drop-down menu to  and click on ➡. You should now see **Gender × Funny** (SPSS orders the variables in reverse alphabetical order for some reason) listed in the *Stepwise Terms* box. Specify the **Sex × Gender** and **Good_Mate × Gender** interactions in the same way. Once the three interaction terms have been specified we can decide how we want to carry out the stepwise analysis. There is a drop-down list of methods under the heading *Stepwise Method* and this list enables you to choose between forward and stepwise entry, or backward and stepwise elimination (i.e., terms are removed from the model if they do not make a significant contribution). I've described these methods elsewhere. Select forward entry for this analysis.

19.9.2. Statistics ③

If you click on <u>Statistics...</u> you will see the dialog box in Figure 19.15, in which you can specify certain statistics:

- *Pseudo R-square*: This option produces the Cox–Snell and Nagelkerke R^2 statistics. These can be used as effect sizes, so this is a useful option to select.

- *Step summary*: This option should be selected for the current analysis because we have a stepwise component to the model; this option produces a table that summarizes the predictors entered or removed at each step.

- *Model fitting information*: This option produces a table that compares the model (or models in a stepwise analysis) to the baseline (the model with only the intercept term in it and no predictor variables). This table can be useful to compare whether the model has improved (from the baseline) as a result of entering the predictors that you have.

- *Information Criteria*: This option produces Akaike's information criterion (AIC) and Schwarz's Bayesian information criterion (BIC), which are both useful for comparing models (see Section 20.4.1). Select this option if you're using stepwise methods, or if you want to compare different models containing different combinations of predictors.

FIGURE 19.15
Statistics options for multinomial logistic regression

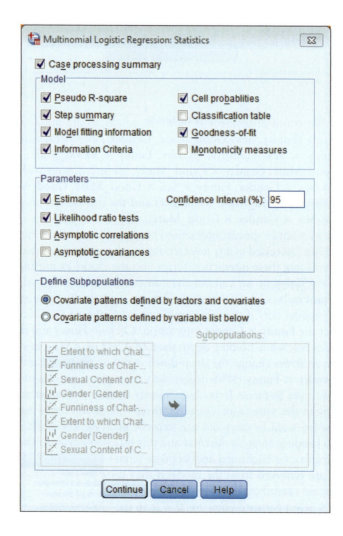

- *Cell probabilities*: This option produces a table of the observed and expected frequencies. This is basically the same as the classification table produced in binary logistic regression and is probably worth inspecting.

- *Classification table*: This option produces a contingency table of observed versus predicted responses for all combinations of predictor variables. I wouldn't select this option, unless you're running a relatively small analysis (i.e., a small number of predictors made up of a small number of possible values). In this example, we have three covariates with 11 possible values and one predictor (gender) with 2 possible values. Tabulating all combinations of these variables will create a very big table indeed.

- *Goodness-of-fit*: This option is important because it produces Pearson and likelihood ratio chi-square statistics for the model.

- *Monotonicity measures*: This option is worth selecting only if your outcome variable has two outcomes (which in our case it doesn't). It will produce measures of monotonic association such as the concordance index, which measures the probability that, using a previous example, a person who scored a penalty kick is classified by the model as having scored and can range from .5 (guessing) to 1 (perfect prediction).

- *Estimates*: This option produces the beta values, test statistics and confidence intervals for predictors in the model. This option is very important.

- *Likelihood ratio tests*: The model overall is tested using likelihood ratio statistics, but this option will compute the same test for individual effects in the model. (Basically it tells us the same as the significance values for individual predictors.)

- *Asymptotic correlations* and *Asymptotic covariances*: These produce a table of correlations (or covariances) between the betas in the model.

Set the options as in Figure 19.15 and click on `Continue` to return to the main dialog box.

19.9.3. Other options ③

If you click on `Criteria...` you'll access the dialog box in Figure 19.16 (left). Logistic regression works through an iterative process (SPSS Tip 19.1). The options available here relate to this process. For example, by default, SPSS will make 100 attempts (iterations) and the threshold for how similar parameter estimates have to be to 'converge' can be made more or less strict (the default is .0000001). You should leave these options alone unless when you run the analysis you get an error message saying something about 'failing to converge', in which case you could try increasing the *Maximum iterations* (to 150 or 200), the *Parameter convergence* (to .00001) or *Log-likelihood convergence* (to greater than 0). However, bear in mind that a failure to converge can reflect messy data and forcing the model to converge does not necessarily mean that parameters are accurate or stable across samples.

You can also click on `Options...` in the main dialog box to access the dialog box in Figure 19.16 (right). The *Scale* option here can be quite useful; I mentioned in Section 19.4.4 that overdispersion can be a problem in logistic regression because it reduces the standard errors that are used to test the significance and construct the confidence intervals of the parameter estimates for individual predictors in the model. I also mentioned that this problem could be counteracted by rescaling the standard errors. Should you be in a situation where you need to do this (i.e., you have run the analysis and found evidence of overdispersion), then you need to come to this dialog box and use the drop-down list to select to correct the standard errors by the dispersion parameter based on either the `Deviance ▼` or `Pearson ▼`

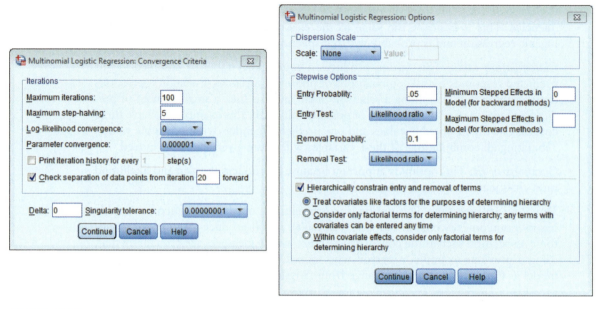

FIGURE 19.16　Criteria and options for multinomial logistic regression

FIGURE 19.17
Save options
for multinomial
logistic
regression

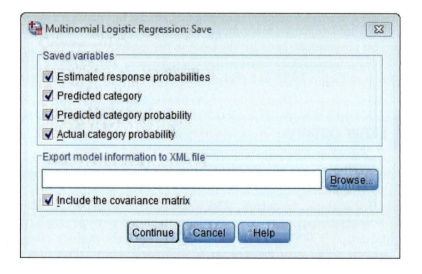

statistic. You should select whichever of these two statistics was bigger in the original analysis (because this will produce the bigger correction). Finally, if you click on [Save...] you can opt to save predicted probabilities and predicted group membership (the same as for binary logistic regression, except that they are called *Estimated response probabilities* and *Predicted category* (Figure 19.17)).

19.9.4. Interpreting the multinomial logistic regression output ③

Our SPSS output from this analysis begins with a warning (SPSS Tip 19.2). It's always nice after months of preparation, weeks entering data, years reading chapters of stupid statistics textbooks, and sleepless nights with equations chipping at your brain with little pick-axes, to see at the start of your analysis: 'Warning! Warning! Abandon ship! Flee for your life! Bad data alert! Bad data alert!' Still, such is life.

Once we have ignored the warnings, like all the best researchers do, the first part of the output tells us about our model overall (Output 19.10). Because we requested a stepwise analysis for our interaction terms, we get a table summarizing the steps in the analysis. You can see here that after the main effects were entered (model 0), the **Gender × Funny** interaction term was entered (model 1) followed by the **Sex × Gender** interaction (model 2). The chi-square statistics for each of these steps are highly significant, indicating that these interactions have a significant effect on predicting whether a chat-up line was significant (this fact is also self-evident because these terms wouldn't have been entered into the model had they not been significant). Also note that the AIC gets smaller as these terms are added to the model, indicating that the fit of the model is getting better as these terms are added (the BIC changes less, but still shows that having the interaction terms in the model results in a better fit than when just the main effects are present). Underneath the step summary, we see the statistics for the final model, which replicates the model-fitting criteria from the last line of the step summary table. This table also produces a likelihood ratio test of the overall model.

SELF-TEST   What does the log-likelihood measure?

Remember that the log-likelihood is a measure of how much unexplained variability there is in the data; therefore, the difference or change in log-likelihood indicates how much new variance has been explained by the model. The chi-square test tests the decrease in unexplained variance from the baseline model (1149.53) to the final model (871.00), which is a difference of $1149.53 - 871 = 278.53$. This change is significant, which means that our final model explains a significant amount of the original variability (in other words, it's a better fit than the original model).

The next part of the output (Output 19.11) relates to the fit of the model to the data. We know that the model is significantly better than no model, but is it a good fit to the data? The Pearson and deviance statistics test the same thing, which is whether the predicted values from the model differ significantly from the observed values. If these statistics are not significant then the model is a good fit. Here we have contrasting results: the deviance statistic says that the model is a good fit to the data ($p = .45$, which is much higher than .05), but the Pearson test indicates the opposite, namely that predicted values are significantly different from the observed values ($p < .001$). Oh dear.

SELF-TEST   Why might the Pearson and deviance statistics be different? What could this be telling us?

One answer is that differences between these statistics can be caused by overdispersion. This is a possibility that we need to look into. However, there are other reasons for this conflict: for example, the Pearson statistic can be very inflated by low expected frequencies (which could happen because we have so many empty cells, as indicated by our warning). One thing that is certain is that conflicting deviance and Pearson chi-square statistics is not

OUTPUT 19.10

Step Summary

Model	Action	Effect(s)	Model Fitting Criteria			Effect Selection Tests		
			AIC	BIC	−2 Log Likelihood	Chi-Square[a]	df	Sig.
0	Entered	Intercept, Good_Mate, Funny, Gender, Sex	937.572	986.848	917.572	.		
1	Entered	Gender * Funny	908.451	967.582	884.451	33.121	2	.000
2	Entered	Gender * Sex	899.002	967.987	871.002	13.450	2	.001

Stepwise Method: Forward Entry

a. The chi-square for entry is based on the likelihood ratio test.

Model Fitting Information

Model	Model Fitting Criteria			Likelihood Ratio Tests		
	AIC	BIC	−2 Log Likelihood	Chi-Square	df	Sig.
Intercept Only	1153.526	1163.382	1149.526			
Final	899.002	967.987	871.002	278.525	12	.000

SPSS TIP 19.2

Warning! Zero frequencies ③

Warnings

There are 504 (53.5%) cells (i.e., dependent variable levels by subpopulations) with zero frequencies.

Sometimes in logistic regression you get a warning about zero frequencies. This relates to the problem that I discussed in Section 19.4.2 of 80-year-old, highly anxious, Buddhist left-handed lesbians (well, incomplete information). Imagine we had just looked at gender as a predictor of chat-up line success. We have three outcome categories and two gender categories. There are six possible combinations of these two variables, and ideally we would like a large number of observations in each of these combinations. However, in this case, we have three variables (**Funny**, **Sex** and **Good_Mate**) with 11 possible outcomes, and **Gender** with 2 possible outcomes and an outcome variable with 3 outcomes. It should be clear that by including the three covariates, the number of combinations of these variables has escalated considerably. This error message tells us that there are some combinations of these variables for which there are no observations. So, we really have a situation where we didn't find an 80-year-old, highly anxious, Buddhist left-handed lesbian; well, we didn't find (for example) a chat-up line that was the most funny, showed the most good characteristics, had the most sexual content and was used on both a man and woman. In fact 53.5% of our possible combinations of variables had no data!

Whenever you have covariates it is inevitable that you will have empty cells, so you will get this kind of error message. To some extent, given its inevitability, we can just ignore it (in this study, for example, we have 1020 cases of data and half of our cells are empty, so we would need to at least double the sample size to stand any chance of filling those cells). However, it is worth reiterating what I said earlier that empty cells create problems, and that when you get a warning like this you should look for coefficients that have unreasonably large standard errors and if you find them be wary of them.

good news. Let's look into the possibility of overdispersion. We can compute the dispersion parameters from both statistics:

$$\phi_{\text{Pearson}} = \frac{\chi^2_{\text{Pearson}}}{df} = \frac{886.62}{614} = 1.44$$

$$\phi_{\text{Deviance}} = \frac{\chi^2_{\text{Deviance}}}{df} = \frac{617.48}{614} = 1.01$$

Goodness-of-Fit

	Chi-Square	df	Sig.
Pearson	886.616	614	.000
Deviance	617.481	614	.453

Pseudo R-Square

Cox and Snell	.239
Nagelkerke	.277
McFadden	.138

Likelihood Ratio Tests

	Model Fitting Criteria			Likelihood Ratio Tests		
Effect	AIC of Reduced Model	BIC of Reduced Model	-2 Log Likelihood of Reduced Model	Chi-Square	df	Sig.
Intercept	899.002	967.987	871.002[a]	.000	0	.
Good_Mate	901.324	960.454	877.324	6.322	2	.042
Funny	899.002	967.987	871.002[a]	.000	0	.
Gender	913.540	972.671	889.540	18.538	2	.000
Sex	899.002	967.987	871.002[a]	.000	0	.
Gender * Funny	930.810	989.941	906.810	35.808	2	.000
Gender * Sex	908.451	967.582	884.451	13.450	2	.001

The chi-square statistic is the difference in –2 log-likelihoods between the final model and a reduced model. The reduced model is formed by omitting an effect from the final model. The null hypothesis is that all parameters of that effect are 0.

a. This reduced model is equivalent to the final model because omitting the effect does not increase the degrees of freedom.

Neither of these is particularly high, and the one based on the deviance statistic is close to the ideal value of 1. The value based on Pearson is greater than 1, but not close to 2, so again does not give us an enormous cause for concern that the data are overdispersed.[11]

The output also shows us the two other measures of R^2 that were described in Section 19.3.3. The first is Cox and Snell's measure, which SPSS reports as .24, and the second is Nagelkerke's adjusted value, which SPSS reports as .28. As you can see, they are reasonably similar values and represent relatively decent-sized effects.

Output 19.12 shows the results of the likelihood ratio tests, and these can be used to ascertain the significance of predictors to the model. The first thing to note is that no significance values are produced for covariates that are involved in higher-order interactions (this is why there are blank spaces in the *Sig.* column for the effects of **Funny** and **Sex**). This table tells us, though, that gender had a significant main effect on success rates of chat-up lines, $\chi^2(2) = 18.54$, $p < .001$, as did whether the chat-up lined showed evidence of being a good partner, $\chi^2(2) = 6.32$, $p = .042$. Most interesting are the interactions which showed that the humour in the chat-up line interacted with gender to predict success at getting a date, $\chi^2(2) = 35.81$, $p < .001$; also the sexual content of the chat-up line interacted with the gender of the person being chatted up in predicting their reaction, $\chi^2(2) = 13.45$, $p = .001$. These likelihood statistics can be seen as overall statistics that tell us which predictors significantly enable us to predict the outcome category, but they don't really tell us specifically what the effect is. To see this we have to look at the individual parameter estimates.

Output 19.13 shows the individual parameter estimates. The table is split into two halves. This is because these parameters compare pairs of outcome categories. We specified the first category as our reference category; therefore, the part of the table labelled *Get*

[11] Incidentally, large dispersion parameters can occur for reasons other than overdispersion, for example omitted variables or interactions (in this example there were several interaction terms that we could have entered but chose not to), and predictors that violate the linearity of the logit assumption.

Phone Number is comparing this category against the 'No response/walked away' category. Let's look at the effects one by one; because we are just comparing two categories the interpretation is the same as for binary logistic regression (so if you don't understand my conclusions reread the start of this chapter):

- **Good_Mate**: Whether the chat-up line showed signs of good moral fibre significantly predicted whether you got a phone number or no response/walked away, $b = 0.13$, Wald $\chi^2(1) = 6.02$, $p = .014$. The odds ratio tells us that as this variable increases, so as chat-up lines show one more unit of moral fibre, the change in the odds of getting a phone number (rather than no response/walked away) is 1.14. In short, you're more likely to get a phone number than not if you use a chat-up line that demonstrates good moral fibre.

- **Funny**: Whether the chat-up line was funny did not significantly predict whether you got a phone number or no response, $b = 0.14$, Wald $\chi^2(1) = 1.60$, $p = .206$. Note that although this predictor is not significant, the odds ratio is approximately the same as for the previous predictor (which was significant). So, the effect size is comparable, but the non-significance stems from a relatively higher standard error. (Note that this effect is superseded by the interaction with gender below.)

- **Gender**: The gender of the person being chatted up significantly predicted whether they gave out their phone number or gave no response, $b = -1.65$, Wald $\chi^2(1) = 4.27$, $p = .039$. Remember that 0 = female and 1 = male, so this is the effect of females compared to males. The odds ratio tells us that as gender changes from female (0) to male (1) the change in the odds of giving out a phone number compared to not responding is 0.19. In other words, the odds of a man giving out his phone number compared to not responding are $1/0.19 = 5.26$ times more than for a woman. Men are cheap.

- **Sex**: The sexual content of the chat-up line significantly predicted whether you got a phone number or no response/walked away, $b = 0.28$, Wald $\chi^2(1) = 9.59$, $p = .002$. The odds ratio tells us that as the sexual content increased by a unit, the change in the odds of getting a phone number (rather than no response) is 1.32. In short, you're more likely to get a phone number than not if you use a chat-up line with high sexual content. (But this effect is superseded by the interaction with gender.)

- **Funny × Gender**: The success of funny chat-up lines depended on whether they were delivered to a man or a woman, because in interaction these variables predicted whether or not you got a phone number, $b = 0.49$, Wald $\chi^2(1) = 12.37$, $p < .001$. Bearing in mind how we interpreted the effect of gender above, the odds ratio tells us that as gender changes from female (0) to male (1) in combination with funniness increasing, the change in the odds of giving out a phone number compared to not responding was 1.64. In other words, as funniness increases, women become more likely to hand out their phone number than men. Funny chat-up lines are more successful when used on women than men.

- **Sex × Gender**: The success of chat-up lines with sexual content depended on whether they were delivered to a man or a woman, because in interaction these variables predicted whether or not you got a phone number, $b = -0.35$, Wald $\chi^2(1) = 10.82$, $p = .001$. Bearing in mind how we interpreted the interaction above (note that b is negative here but positive above), the odds ratio tells us that as gender changes from female (0) to male (1) in combination with the sexual content increasing, the change in the odds of giving out a phone number compared to not responding is 0.71. In other words, as sexual content increases, women become *less* likely than men to hand out their phone number. Chat-up lines with a high sexual content are more successful when used on men than women.

Parameter Estimates

Success of Chat–Up Line[a]		B	Std. Error	Wald	df	Sig.	Exp(B)	95% Confidence Interval for Exp(B) Lower Bound	Upper Bound
Get Phone Number	Intercept	−1.783	.670	7.087	1	.008			
	Good_Mate	.132	.054	6.022	1	.014	1.141	1.027	1.268
	Funny	.139	.110	1.602	1	.206	1.150	.926	1.427
	[Gender=0]	−1.646	.796	4.274	1	.039	.193	.040	.918
	[Gender=1]	0[b]	.	.	0	.	.	.	.
	Sex	.276	.089	9.589	1	.002	1.318	1.107	1.570
	[Gender=0] * Funny	.492	.140	12.374	1	.000	1.636	1.244	2.153
	[Gender=1] * Funny	0[b]	.	.	0	.	.	.	.
	[Gender=0] * Sex	−.348	.106	10.824	1	.001	.706	.574	.869
	[Gender=1] * Sex	0[b]	.	.	0	.	.	.	.
Go Home with Person	Intercept	−4.286	.941	20.731	1	.000			
	Good_Mate	.130	.084	2.423	1	.120	1.139	.967	1.341
	Funny	.318	.125	6.459	1	.011	1.375	1.076	1.758
	[Gender=0]	−5.626	1.329	17.934	1	.000	.004	.000	.049
	[Gender=1]	0[b]	.	.	0	.	.	.	.
	Sex	.417	.122	11.683	1	.001	1.518	1.195	1.928
	[Gender=0] * Funny	1.172	.199	34.627	1	.000	3.230	2.186	4.773
	[Gender=1] * Funny	0[b]	.	.	0	.	.	.	.
	[Gender=0] * Sex	−.477	.163	8.505	1	.004	.621	.451	.855
	[Gender=1] * Sex	0[b]	.	.	0	.	.	.	.

a. The reference category is: No response/Walk Off.

b. This parameter is set to zero because it is redundant.

OUTPUT 19.13

The bottom half of Output 19.13 shows the individual parameter estimates for the *Go Home with Person* category compared to the 'No response/walked away' category. We can interpret these effects as follows:

- **Good_Mate**: Whether the chat-up line showed signs of good moral fibre did not significantly predict whether you went home with the date or got a slap in the face, $b = 0.13$, Wald $\chi^2(1) = 2.42$, $p = .120$. In short, you're not significantly more likely to go home with the person if you use a chat-up line that demonstrates good moral fibre.

- **Funny**: Whether the chat-up line was funny significantly predicted whether you went home with the date or got no response, $b = 0.32$, Wald $\chi^2(1) = 6.46$, $p = .011$. The odds ratio tells us that as chat-up lines are one more unit funnier, the change in the odds of going home with the person (rather than no response) is 1.38. In short, you're more likely to go home with the person than get no response if you use a chat-up line that is funny. (This effect, though, is superseded by the interaction with gender below.)

- **Gender**: The gender of the person being chatted up significantly predicted whether they went home with the person or gave no response, $b = -5.63$, Wald $\chi^2(1) = 17.93$, $p < .001$. The odds ratio tells us that as gender changes from female (0) to male (1) the change in the odds of going home with the person compared to not responding is 0.004. In other words, the odds of a man going home with someone compared to not responding are $1/0.004 = 250$ times more likely than for a woman. Men are *really* cheap.

- **Sex**: The sexual content of the chat-up line significantly predicted whether you went home with the date or got a slap in the face, $b = 0.42$, Wald $\chi^2(1) = 11.68$, $p = .001$. The odds ratio tells us that as the sexual content increased by a unit, the change in the odds of going home with the person (rather than no response) is 1.52: you're more likely to go home with the person than not if you use a chat-up line with high sexual content.

- **Funny × Gender:** The success of funny chat-up lines depended on whether they were delivered to a man or a woman, because in interaction these variables predicted whether or not you went home with the date, $b = 1.17$, Wald $\chi^2(1) = 34.63$, $p < .001$. The odds ratio tells us that as gender changes from female (0) to male (1) in combination with funniness increasing, the change in the odds of going home with the person compared to not responding is 3.23. As funniness increases, women become more likely to go home with the person than men. Funny chat-up lines are more successful when used on women than on men.

- **Sex × Gender:** The success of chat-up lines with sexual content depended on whether they were delivered to a man or a woman, because in interaction these variables predicted whether or not you went home with the date, $b = -0.48$, Wald $\chi^2(1) = 8.51$, $p = .004$. The odds ratio tells us that as gender changes from female (0) to male (1) in combination with the sexual content increasing, the change in the odds of going home with the date compared to not responding is 0.62. As sexual content increases, women become less likely than men to go home with the person. Chat-up lines with sexual content are more successful when used on men than on women.

SELF-TEST   Use what you learnt earlier in this chapter to check the assumptions of multicollinearity and linearity of the logit.

TABLE 19.4   How to report multinomial logistic regression

	b (SE)	95% CI for Odds Ratio		
		Lower	Odds Ratio	Upper
Phone Number vs. No Response				
Intercept	−1.78 (0.67)**			
Good Mate	0.13 (0.05)*	1.03	1.14	1.27
Funny	0.14 (0.11)	0.93	1.15	1.43
Gender	−1.65 (0.80)*	0.04	0.19	0.92
Sexual Content	0.28 (0.09)**	1.11	1.32	1.57
Gender × Funny	0.49 (0.14)***	1.24	1.64	2.15
Gender × Sex	−0.35 (0.11)*	0.57	0.71	0.87
Going Home vs. No Response				
Intercept	−4.29 (0.94)***			
Good Mate	0.13 (0.08)	0.97	1.14	1.34
Funny	0.32 (0.13)*	1.08	1.38	1.76
Gender	−5.63 (1.33)***	0.00	0.00	0.05
Sexual Content	0.42 (0.12)**	1.20	1.52	1.93
Gender × Funny	1.17 (0.20)***	2.19	3.23	4.77
Gender × Sex	−0.48 (0.16)**	0.45	0.62	0.86

Note. $R^2 = .24$ (Cox & Snell), .28 (Nagelkerke). Model $\chi^2(12) = 278.53$, $p < .001$. * $p < .05$, ** $p < .01$, *** $p < .001$.

We can report the results using a table (see Table 19.4). Note that I have split the table by the outcome categories being compared, but otherwise it is the same as before. These effects are interpreted as in the previous section.

19.10. Brian's attempt to woo Jane ①

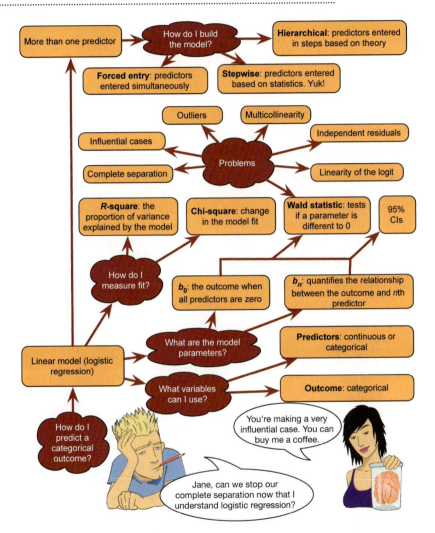

FIGURE 19.18
What Brian learnt from this chapter

19.11. What next? ①

At the age of 10 I thought I was going to be a rock star. Such was my conviction about this that even today (many years on) I'm still not entirely sure how I ended up *not* being a rock star (possible explanations are lack of talent, not being a very cool person, inability to write songs that don't make people want to throw rotting vegetables at you). Instead of the glitzy and fun life that I anticipated I am instead reduced to writing textbook chapters about things that I don't even remotely understand.

The other thing that I thought at the age of 10 was that I would marry Claire Sparks. Such was my conviction that even today I'm still not entirely sure …. Nah, I'm just kidding.

However, as a young boy I was convinced that I would get married at the age of 28. When I actually was 28 I had dedicated a lot of time to music, and far too much to trying to convince people that I was an academic. Somewhere along the line, I found myself in my mid-thirties and without a wife. I'd better get one of those, I thought to myself.[12]

19.12. Key terms that I've discovered

$-2LL$	Logistic regression	Overdispersion
Binary logistic regression	Log-likelihood	Parsimony
Complete separation	Maximum-likelihood estimation	Polychotomous logistic
Cox and Snell's R^2_{CS}	Multinomial logistic regression	regression
$Exp(B)$	Nagelkerke's R^2_N	Wald statistic
Hosmer and Lemeshow's R^2_L	Odds	

19.13. Smart Alex's tasks

- **Task 1**: A 'display rule' refers to displaying an appropriate emotion in a given situation. For example, if you receive a Christmas present that you don't like, you should smile politely and say 'Thank you, Auntie Kate, I've always wanted a rotting cabbage'. The inappropriate emotional display is to start crying and scream 'Why did you buy me a rotting cabbage, you selfish old bag?' A psychologist measured children's understanding of display rules (with a task that they could pass or fail), their age (months), and their ability to understand others' mental states ('theory of mind', measured with a false-belief task that they could pass or fail). The data are in **Display.sav**. Can display rule understanding (did the child pass the test: yes/no?) be predicted from theory of mind (did the child pass the false-belief task: yes/no?), age and their interaction? ③

- **Task 2**: Are there any influential cases or outliers in the model for Task 1? ③

- **Task 3**: Piff, Stancato, Côté, Mendoza-Dentona, and Keltner (2012) showed that people of a higher social class are more unpleasant. In the first study in their paper they observed the behaviour of drivers: they classified social class by the type of car (**Vehicle**) on a 5-point scale. They then observed whether the drivers cut in front of other cars at a busy intersection (**Vehicle_Cut**). The data are in **Piff et al. (2012) Vehicle.sav**. Do a logistic regression to see whether social class predicts whether or not a driver cut in front of other vehicles.[13] ②

- **Task 4**: In their second study, Piff et al. (2012) again observed the behaviour of drivers and classified social class by the type of car (**Vehicle**). However, they observed whether the drivers cut off a pedestrian at a crossing (**Pedestrian_Cut**). The data are in **Piff et al. (2012) Pedestrian.sav**. Do a logistic regression to see whether social class predicts whether or not a driver prevents a pedestrian from crossing. ②

- **Task 5**: Four hundred and sixty-seven lecturers completed questionnaire measures of **Burnout** (burnt out or not), **Perceived Control** (high score = low perceived control), **Coping Style** (high score = high ability to cope with stress), **Stress from Teaching** (high score = teaching creates a lot of stress for the person), **Stress from Research** (high score = research creates a lot of stress for the person) and **Stress from Providing Pastoral Care** (high score = providing pastoral care creates a lot of stress for the person). Cooper, Sloan,

---

[12] Needless to say I'm skipping over a fair few romantic events between 10 and my mid 30s – some of them more pleasant than others.

[13] I reconstructed the raw data from Figure 1 of the paper, so you will get basically the same results as reported by the authors. However, they also controlled for the age and gender of drivers, so you won't get exactly the same values (but they are pretty close).

and Williams' (1988) model of stress indicates that perceived control and coping style are important predictors of burnout. The remaining predictors were measured to see the unique contribution of different aspects of a lecturer's work to their burnout. Conduct a logistic regression to see which factors predict burnout. The data are in **Burnout.sav**. ③

- **Task 6**: An HIV researcher explored the factors that influenced condom use with a new partner (relationship less than 1 month old). The outcome measure was whether a condom was used (**Use**: condom used = 1, not used = 0). The predictor variables were mainly scales from the Condom Attitude Scale (CAS) by Sacco, Levine, Reed, and Thompson (1991): **Gender**; the degree to which the person views their relationship as 'safe' from sexually transmitted disease (**Safety**); the degree to which previous experience influences attitudes towards condom use (**Sexexp**); whether or not the couple used a condom in their previous encounter, 1 = condom used, 0 = not used, 2 = no previous encounter with this partner (**Previous**); the degree of self-control that a person has when it comes to condom use (**Selfcon**); the degree to which the person perceives a risk from unprotected sex (**Perceive**). Previous research (Sacco, Rickman, Thompson, Levine, & Reed, 1993) has shown that gender, relationship safety and perceived risk predict condom use. Carry out an analysis using **Condom.sav** to verify these previous findings, and to test whether self-control, previous usage and sexual experience predict condom use. ③

- **Task 7**: How reliable is the model for Task 6? ②

- **Task 8**: Using the final model of condom use in Task 6, what are the probabilities that participants 12, 53 and 75 will use a condom? ③

- **Task 9**: A female who used a condom in her previous encounter scores 2 on all variables except perceived risk (for which she scores 6). Use the model to estimate the probability that she will use a condom in her next encounter. ③

- **Task 10**: At the start of the chapter we looked at whether the type of instrument a person plays is connected to their personality. A musicologist got 200 singers and guitarists from bands. She noted the **Instrument** they played (Singer, Guitar), and measured two personality variables in each: **Extroversion** and **Agreeableness**. Conduct a logistic regression to see which of these variables (ignore the interaction) predicts which instrument a person plays. Data are in **Sing or Guitar.sav**. ②

- **Task 11**: Which problem associated with logistic regression might we have in the analysis for Task 10? ③

- **Task 12**: The musicologist extended her study by collecting data from 430 musicians. Again she noted the **Instrument** a person played (Singer, Guitar, Bass, Drums), and the same personality variables. However, she also measured their **Conscientiousness**. Conduct a multinomial logistic regression to see which of these three variables (ignore interactions) predicts which instrument a person plays (use drums as the reference category). The data are in **Band Personality.sav** ③

Answers can be found on the companion website.

19.14. Further reading

Baguley, T. (2012). *Serious stats: A guide to advanced statistics for the behavioural sciences*. Basingstoke: Palgrave Macmillan.

Hutcheson, G., & Sofroniou, N. (1999). *The multivariate social scientist*. London: Sage. (See Chapter 4.)

Menard, S. (1995). *Applied logistic regression analysis*. Sage University Paper Series on Quantitative Applications in the Social Sciences, 07-106. Thousand Oaks, CA: Sage. (This is a fairly advanced text, but great nevertheless.)

Mood, C. (2009). Logistic regression: Why we cannot do what we think we can do, and what we can do about it. *European Sociological Review*, 26(1), 67–82.

20 Multilevel linear models

FIGURE 20.1
On the road to
happiness

20.1. What will this chapter tell me? ①

Years at an all-boys' school carefully nurturing a morbid fear of women and a love of heavy metal had made the world of relationships a tricky place for me to inhabit. I'd always dreamt that by my mid-thirties I would have a wife and a cute little child or two to remind me of the important things in life. However, as I took my first furtive and depressing steps into middle age I found myself single, and the closest thing to a child was a ginger cat and this book. However, something remarkable had happened since my teens: rock music had become popular again, and some women liked to talk about Iron Maiden. I needed to capitalize before the ephemeral guillotine of fashion spliced this opportunity from me. I met Zoë, who was not only happy to discuss Iron Maiden, but even owned my favourite of their albums (*Piece of Mind*). She had no aversion to statistics, or soccer, and also happened to be the most beautiful woman ever placed on the face of the earth. Result. 'I'd better marry her before she realizes I'm a balding geek with slight hoarding tendencies', I thought. So that's what we did. A little later than anticipated, my dreams had come true: I started my late thirties with a wife and a cute little … book about a statistics package called R to which my wife contributed. Mental note to self: next time create a little human, not a big book.

Marriage is a leap of faith into the unknown, a shared adventure full of challenges. A bit like this chapter really, because, upon embarking on it, multilevel linear models were an 'unknown': I knew absolutely nothing about them. If you're reading this section then you probably don't know much about them either. So, we'll learn together – a shared adventure, and, oh boy, will it include some challenges …

20.2. Hierarchical data ②

In all of the analyses in this book so far we have treated data as though they are organized at a single level. However, in the real world, data are often hierarchical. This means that some variables are clustered or *nested* within other variables. For example, when I'm not writing statistics books I spend most of my time researching how anxiety develops in schoolchildren. When I run research in a school, I test children who have been assigned to different classes, and who are taught by different teachers. The classroom that a child is in could affect my results. Let's imagine I test in two different classrooms. Mr. Nervous, who is very anxious and tells children to be careful, and that things that they do are dangerous, or that they might hurt themselves, teaches the first class. Little Miss Daredevil,[1] who is carefree, tells children not to be scared of things and gives them the freedom to explore new situations, teaches the second class. One day I go into the school with a big animal carrier, which I tell the children contains an animal. I measure whether they will put their hand into the carrier to stroke the animal. Children taught by Mr. Nervous have grown up in an environment that reinforces caution, whereas children taught by Miss Daredevil have been encouraged to embrace new experiences. Therefore, we might expect Mr. Nervous's children to be more reluctant to put their hand in the box because of the classroom experiences that they have had. The classroom is a contextual variable.

What are hierarchical data?

Also, I might tell some of the children that the animal is a bloodthirsty beast, and tell others that the animal is friendly, expecting that this manipulation will affect the children's enthusiasm for stroking the animal. However, the effect of what I tell the children happens within the context of the classroom to which the child belongs. My threat information ought to have more impact on Mr. Nervous's children than on Miss Daredevil's children. Figure 20.2 illustrates this scenario: children (or cases) is the variable at the bottom of the hierarchy, known as a *level 1* variable. These children are organized by classroom (children are said to be *nested* within classes). The class to which a child belongs is a level up from the participant in the hierarchy and is said to be a *level 2* variable.

A situation with two levels is the simplest hierarchy that you can have. You can have other layers in more complex hierarchies. If we stick with our example, an obvious third level is that classrooms are nested within schools. Therefore, if I ran a study incorporating lots of different schools, as well as different classrooms within those schools, then I would have another level to the hierarchy. We can apply the same logic as before: children in the same school will be more similar to each other than to children in different schools because schools have different teaching environments and also reflect their social demographic (which can differ from school to school). Figure 20.3 shows a three-level hierarchy: the child (level 1), the class to which the child belongs (level 2) and the school within which

[1] Those of you who don't spot the Mr. Men references here, check out http://www.mrmen.com. Mr. Nervous used to be called Mr. Jelly and was a pink jelly-shaped blob, which in my opinion was better than his current incarnation.

FIGURE 20.2
An example
of a two-level
hierarchical
data structure:
children
(level 1) are
organized
within
classrooms
(level 2)

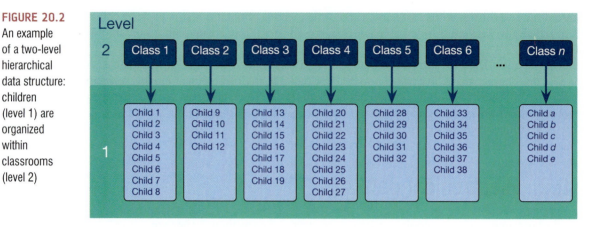

that class exists (level 3). In this situation we have two contextual variables: school and classroom.

Hierarchical data structures need not apply only to between-participants situations. We can also think of data as being nested within people. In this situation the case, or person, is not at the bottom of the hierarchy (level 1), but is further up. A good example is memory. Imagine that after giving children threat information about my caged animal I asked them a week later to recall everything they could about the animal. Let's say that I originally gave them 15 pieces of information; some children might recall all 15 pieces of information, but others might remember only 2 or 3 bits of information. The bits of information, or memories, are nested within the person and their recall depends on the person. The probability of a given memory being recalled depends on what other memories are available, and the recall of one memory may have knock-on effects for what other memories are recalled. Therefore, memories are not independent units. As such, the person acts as a context within which memories are recalled (Wright, 1998). Figure 20.4 shows this scenario: the child is our level 2 variable, and within each child there are several memories (our level 1 variable). Of course we can also have levels of the hierarchy above the child, for example, the class from which they came could be a level 3 variable. Indeed, we could even include the school again as a level 4 variable. A common situation in which cases are a contextual variable is when we take several measures over time (i.e., a repeated-measures design). In this situation measures at different points in time (level 1) are nested within cases (level 2). We look at this situation in detail in Section 20.7.

20.2.1.   The intraclass correlation ②

You might well wonder why it matters that data are hierarchical (or not). The main problem is that the contextual variables in the hierarchy introduce dependency in the data, which in plain English means that residuals will be correlated. To understand why, imagine that Charlotte and Emily are two children taught by Mr. Nervous, and Kiki and Jip are taught by Miss Daredevil. Charlotte and Emily's responses to the animal in the carrier have both been influenced by Mr. Nervous's cautious manner, so their behaviour will be similar. Likewise, Kiki and Jip's responses to the animal in the box have both been influenced by Miss Daredevil's carefree manner, so their behaviour will be similar too. Therefore, children within Mr. Nervous's class will be more similar to each other than they are to children in Miss Daredevil's class and vice versa.

This similarity is a problem because, as we saw in Chapter 5, the statistical models in this book assume that errors are independent. In other words, there is absolutely no correlation between residual scores of one child and another. When entities are sampled

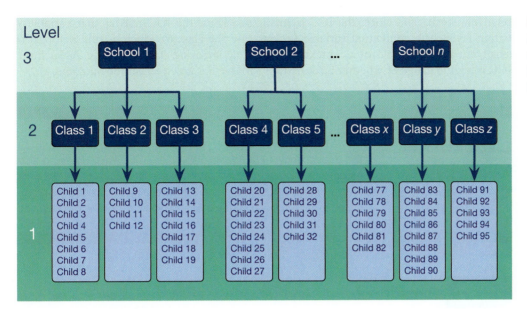

FIGURE 20.3
An example of a three-level hierarchical data structure

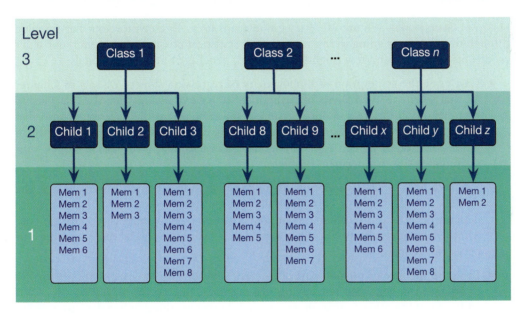

FIGURE 20.4
An example of a three-level hierarchical data structure, where the level 1 variable is a repeated measure (memories recalled)

from similar contexts, this independence is unlikely to be true (e.g., Emily and Charlotte's residuals will be correlated because their behaviour has been influenced by being taught by Mr. Nervous).

By thinking about contextual variables and factoring them into the analysis we can overcome this problem of non-independent observations. We can use the intraclass correlation (which we came across as a measure of inter-rater reliability in Section 17.9.3) to estimate the dependency between scores. We'll skip the formalities of calculating the ICC (but see Oliver Twisted if you're keen to know), and I'll try to give you a conceptual grasp of what it represents. In our two-level example of children within classes, the ICC represents the proportion of the total variability in the outcome that is attributable to the classes. It follows that if a class has had a big effect on the children within it then the variability within the class will be small (the children will behave similarly). As such, variability in the outcome within classes is minimized, and variability in the outcome between classes is maximized; therefore, the ICC is large. Conversely, if the class has little effect on the children then the outcome will vary a lot within classes, which will make differences between classes relatively small. Therefore, the ICC is small too. Thus, the ICC tells us that variability within levels of a contextual variable (in this case the class to which a child belongs) is small, but between levels of a contextual variable (comparing classes) is large. As such the ICC is a good gauge of whether a contextual variable has an effect on the outcome.

OLIVER TWISTED

Please Sir, can I have some more … ICC?

'I have a dependency on gruel', whines Oliver. 'Maybe I could measure this dependency if I knew more about the ICC.' We'll you're so high on gruel Oliver that you have rather missed the point. Still, I did write an article on the ICC once upon a time (Field, 2005a) and it's reproduced in the additional web material for your delight and amusement.

20.2.2. Benefits of multilevel models ②

Multilevel linear models (Figure 20.5) have numerous uses. To convince you that trawling through this chapter is going to reward you with statistical possibilities beyond your wildest dreams, here are just a few (slightly overstated) benefits of multilevel models:

- **Cast aside the assumption of homogeneity of regression slopes**: We saw in Chapter 12 that when we use analysis of covariance we have to assume that the relationship between our covariate and our outcome is the same across the different groups that make up our predictor variable. However, this doesn't always happen. Luckily, in multilevel models we can explicitly model this variability in regression slopes, thus overcoming this inconvenient problem.

- **Say 'bye bye' to the assumption of independence**: In Chapter 5 we saw that the models described in this book typically assume independent errors. If errors are dependent, little lizards climb out of your mattress while you're asleep and eat you. Multilevel models are specifically designed to allow you to model these relationships between residuals.

- **Laugh in the face of missing data**: I've spent a lot of this book extolling the virtues of balanced designs and not having missing data. Regression, ANOVA, ANCOVA and most of the other tests we have covered do strange things when data are missing or the design is not balanced. This can be a real pain. Missing data are a particular problem within clinical trials because it is common to attempt to collect follow-up data, often many months after treatment has ended, when patients might be difficult to track down. Of course, there are ways to correct for and impute missing data, but these techniques are often quite complicated (Yang, Li, & Shoptaw, 2008). Therefore, often when using repeated-measures designs if a single time point is missing the whole case needs to be deleted; missing data lead to more data being deleted. Multilevel models do not require complete data sets, so when data are missing for one time point they do not need to be imputed, nor does the whole case need to be deleted. Instead parameters can be estimated successfully with the available data, which offers a relatively easy solution to dealing with missing data. It is important to stress that no statistical procedure can overcome data that are missing. Good methods, designs and research execution should be used to minimize missing values, and reasons for missing values should always be explored. It is just that when using traditional statistical procedures for repeated-measures data additional procedures to account for missing data are usually necessary and can be problematic.

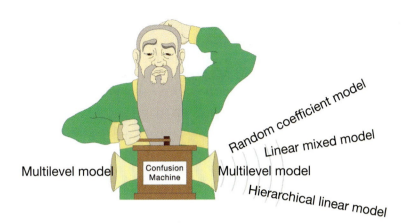

I think you'll agree that multilevel models are pretty funky. 'Is there anything they can't do?' I hear you cry. Well, no, not really.

20.3. Theory of multilevel linear models ③

The underlying theory of multilevel models is very complicated indeed – far too complicated for my little peanut of a brain to comprehend. Fortunately, the advent of computers and software like SPSS makes it possible for feeble-minded individuals such as myself to take advantage of this wonderful tool without actually needing to know the maths. Better still, this means I can get away with not explaining the maths (and really, I'm not kidding, I don't understand any of it). What I will do, though, is try to give you a flavour of what multilevel models are and what they do by describing the key concepts within the framework of linear models that has permeated this whole book.

20.3.1. An example ②

In the USA, there was a 1600% increase in cosmetic surgical and non-surgical treatments between 1992 and 2002, and 65,000 people in the UK underwent privately and publicly funded operations in 2004 (Kellett, Clarke, & McGill, 2008). With the increasing popularity of this surgery, many people are starting to question the motives of those who want to go under the knife. There are two main reasons to have cosmetic surgery: (1) to help a physical problem, such as having breast reduction surgery to relieve back ache; and (2) to change your external appearance, for example by having a face-lift. Related to this second point, one day cosmetic surgery might be performed as a psychological intervention: to improve self-esteem (Cook, Rosser, & Salmon, 2006; Kellett et al., 2008). Our first example looks at the effects of cosmetic surgery on quality of life. The variables in the data file are (**Cosmetic Surgery.sav**):

- **Post_QoL**: This variable is a measure of quality of life after the cosmetic surgery; it is our outcome variable.

- **Base_QoL**: We need to adjust our outcome for quality of life before the surgery.

- **Surgery**: This dummy variable specifies whether the person has undergone cosmetic surgery (1) or whether they are on the waiting list (0), which acts as our control group.

- **Clinic**: This variable specifies which of 10 clinics the person attended to have their surgery.

- **Age**: This variable tells us the person's age in years.

- **BDI**: People volunteering for cosmetic surgery (especially when the surgery is purely for vanity) have different personality profiles than the general public (Cook, Rosser, Toone, James, & Salmon, 2006). In particular, these people might have low self-esteem or be depressed. When looking at quality of life it is important to assess natural levels of depression, and this variable used the Beck Depression Inventory (BDI) to do just that.

- **Reason**: This dummy variable specifies whether the person had/is waiting to have surgery purely to change their appearance (0), or because of a physical reason (1).

- **Gender**: This variable specifies whether the person was a man (1) or a woman (0).

When conducting hierarchical models we work up from a very simple model to more complicated models, and we will take that approach in this chapter. In doing so I hope to illustrate multilevel modelling by attaching it to frameworks that you already understand, such as ANOVA and ANCOVA.

Figure 20.6 shows the hierarchical structure of the data. Essentially, people being treated in the same surgeries are not independent of each other because they will have had surgery from the same surgeon. Surgeons will vary in how good they are, and quality of life will to some extent depend on how well the surgery went (if they did a nice neat job then quality of life should be higher than if they left you with unpleasant scars). Therefore, people within clinics will be more similar to each other than people in different clinics. As such, the person undergoing surgery is the level 1 variable, and the clinic attended is a level 2 variable.

20.3.2. Fixed and random coefficients ③

The concepts of effects and variables should be very familiar to you by now. However, throughout the book we have viewed these concepts a bit simplistically: we have not distinguished between whether something is fixed or random. The terms 'fixed' and 'random' can be a bit confusing because they are used differently in a variety of contexts. For example, an effect in an experiment is said to be a **fixed effect** if all possible treatment conditions that a researcher is interested in are present in the experiment, but it is a **random effect** if the experiment contains only a random sample of possible treatment conditions. This distinction is important, because fixed effects can be generalized only to the situations in your experiment,

FIGURE 20.6
Diagram to show the hierarchical structure of the cosmetic surgery data set. People are clustered within clinics. Note that for each person there would be a series of variables measured: surgery, BDI, age, gender, reason and pre-surgery quality of life

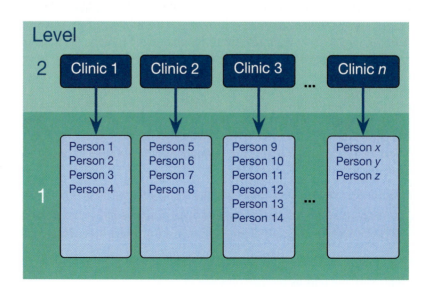

whereas random effects can be generalized beyond the treatment conditions in the experiment (provided that the treatment conditions are representative). For example, in our Viagra example from Chapter 11, the effect is fixed if we say that we are interested only in the three conditions that we had (placebo, low dose and high dose) and we can generalize our findings only to the situation of a placebo, low dose and high dose. However, if we were to say that the three doses were only a sample of possible doses (perhaps we could have tried a very high dose), then it is a random effect and we can generalize beyond just placebos, low doses and high doses. All of the effects in this book so far we have treated as fixed effects. The vast majority of academic research that you read will treat variables as fixed effects.

People also talk about **fixed variables** and **random variables**. A fixed variable is one that is not supposed to change over time (e.g., for most people their gender is a fixed variable – it never changes), whereas a random one varies over time (e.g., your weight is likely to fluctuate over time).

In the context of multilevel models we need to make a distinction between **fixed coefficients** and **random coefficients**. In the regressions, ANOVAs and ANCOVAs throughout this book we have assumed that the regression parameters are fixed. We have seen numerous times that two things characterize a linear model: the intercept, b_0, and the slope, b_1:

$$Y_i = b_0 + b_1 X_{1i} + \varepsilon_i$$

Note that the outcome (Y), the predictor (X) and the error (ε) all vary as a function of i, which normally represents a particular case of data. In other words, it represents the level 1 variable. If, for example, we wanted to predict Sam's score, we could replace the is with her name:

$$Y_{\text{Sam}} = b_0 + b_1 X_{1, \text{Sam}} + \varepsilon_{\text{Sam}}$$

This is just revision. Now, when we do a regression like this we assume that the bs are fixed and we estimate them from the data. In other words, we're assuming that the model holds true across the entire sample and that for every case of data in the sample we can predict a score using the same values of the gradient and intercept. However, we can also conceptualize these parameters as being random.[2] If we say that a parameter is random then we assume not that it is a fixed value, but that its value can vary. Up until now we have thought of regression models as having **fixed intercepts** and **fixed slopes**, but the idea that parameters can vary opens up three new possibilities for us that are shown in Figure 20.7. This figure uses our ANCOVA example from Chapter 12 and shows the relationship between a person's libido and that of their partner overall (the dashed line) and separately for the three groups in the study (a placebo group, a group that had a low dose of Viagra and a group that had a high dose).

20.3.2.1. The random intercept model ③

The simplest way to introduce random parameters into the model is to assume that the intercepts vary across contexts (or groups) – because the intercepts vary, we call them **random intercepts**. For our libido data this is like assuming that the relationship between libido and partner's libido is the same in the placebo, low- and high-dose groups (i.e., the slope is the same), but that the models for each group are in different locations (i.e., the intercepts are different). This is shown in the top panel of Figure 20.7 in which the models within the different contexts (colours) have the same shape (slope) but are located in a different geometric space (they have different intercepts).

[2] 'Random' isn't an intuitive term for us non-statisticians because it implies that values are plucked out of thin air (randomly selected). However, this is not the case – they are carefully estimated just as fixed parameters are.

FIGURE 20.7
Data sets
showing an
overall model
(dashed line)
and the models
for separate
contexts within
the data (i.e.,
groups of
cases)

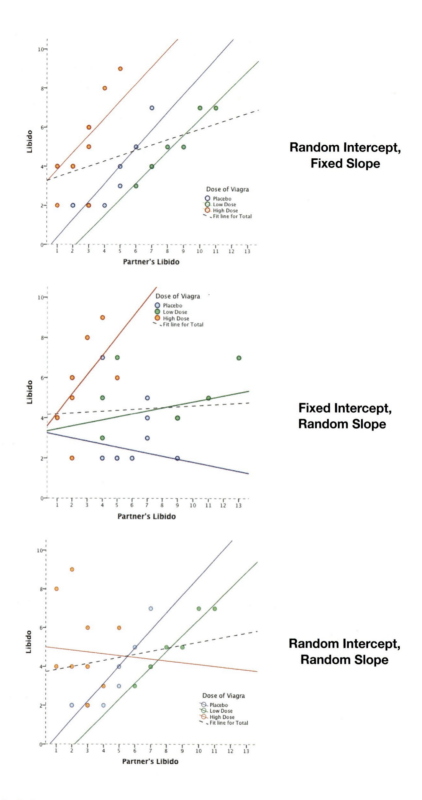

**Random Intercept,
Fixed Slope**

**Fixed Intercept,
Random Slope**

**Random Intercept,
Random Slope**

20.3.2.2. Random slope model ③

We can also assume that the slopes vary across contexts – i.e., we assume **random slopes**. For our libido data this is like assuming that the relationship between libido and partner's libido is different in the placebo, low- and high-dose groups (i.e., the slopes are different), but that the models for each group are fixed at the same geometric location (i.e., the intercepts are the same). This is what happens when we violate the assumption of homogeneity of regression slopes in ANCOVA. Homogeneity of regression slopes is the assumption that regression slopes are the same across contexts. If this assumption is not tenable then we can use a multilevel model to explicitly estimate that variability in slopes. This is shown in the middle panel of Figure 20.7 in which the models within the different contexts (colours) converge on a single intercept but have different slopes. It's worth noting that it would be unusual in reality to assume random slopes without also assuming random intercepts, because variability in the nature of the relationship (slopes) would normally create variability in the overall level of the outcome variable (intercepts). Therefore, if you assume that slopes are random you would normally also assume that intercepts are random.

20.3.2.3. The random intercept and slope model ③

The most realistic situation is to assume that both intercepts and slopes vary around the overall model. This is shown in the bottom panel of Figure 20.7 in which the models within the different contexts (colours) have different slopes but are also located in different geometric space and so have different intercepts.

20.4. The multilevel model ④

We have seen conceptually what random intercept, random slope and random intercept and slope models look like. Now let's look at how we represent the models. To keep things concrete, let's use our example and imagine that we first wanted to predict someone's quality of life (QoL) after cosmetic surgery. We can represent this as a linear model as follows:

$$\text{QoL After Surgery}_i = b_0 + b_1 \text{Surgery}_i + \varepsilon_i \tag{20.1}$$

We have seen linear models like equation (20.1) many times. In this example, we had a contextual variable, which was the clinic in which the cosmetic surgery was conducted. We might expect the effect of surgery on QoL to vary as a function of which clinic the surgery was conducted at, because surgeons will differ in their skill. This variable is a level 2 variable. As such we could allow the model that represents the effect of surgery on QoL to vary across the different contexts (clinics). We can do this by allowing the intercepts, slopes or both to vary across clinics.

To begin with, let's say we want to include a random intercept for QoL. All we do is add a component to the intercept that measures the variability in intercepts, u_{0j}. Therefore, the intercept changes from b_0 to $b_0 + u_{0j}$. This term estimates the intercept of the overall model fitted to the data, b_0, and the variability of intercepts around that overall model, u_{0j}. The overall model becomes:[3]

$$Y_{ij} = \left(b_0 + u_{0j}\right) + b_1 X_{ij} + \varepsilon_{ij} \tag{20.2}$$

The js in the equation reflect levels of the variable over which the intercept varies (in this case the clinic) – the level 2 variable. Another way that we could write this is to define

---

[3] Some people use gamma (γ), not b, to represent the parameters, but I prefer b because it makes the link to the other linear models that we have used in this book clearer.

the random intercept separately so that the model looks like an ordinary regression equation, except that the intercept has changed from a fixed, b_0, to a random one, b_{0j}, which is defined in a separate equation:

$$Y_{ij} = b_{0j} + b_1 X_{ij} + \varepsilon_{ij}$$
$$b_{0j} = b_0 + u_{0j}$$

(20.3)

Therefore, if we want to know the estimated intercept for clinic 7, we simply replace the j with 'clinic 7' in the second equation:

$$b_{0,\text{clinic 7}} = b_0 + u_{0,\text{clinic 7}}$$

If we want to include random slopes for the effect of surgery on QoL, then all we do is add a component to the slope of the overall model that measures the variability in slopes, u_{1j}. Therefore, the gradient changes from b_1 to $b_1 + u_{1j}$. This term estimates the slope of the overall model fitted to the data, b_1, and the variability of slopes in different contexts around that overall model, u_{1j}. The overall model becomes (compare to the random intercept model above):

$$Y_{ij} = b_0 + \left(b_1 + u_{1j}\right) X_{ij} + \varepsilon_{ij}$$

(20.4)

Again we can define the random slope in a separate equation to make the link to a familiar linear model even clearer. It now looks like an ordinary regression equation, except that the slope has changed from a fixed, b_1, to a random one, b_{1j}, which is defined in a separate equation:

$$Y_{ij} = b_{0i} + b_{1j} X_{ij} + \varepsilon_{ij}$$
$$b_{1j} = b_1 + u_{1j}$$

(20.5)

If we want to model a situation with random slopes *and* intercepts, then we combine the two models above. We still estimate the intercept and slope of the overall model (b_0 and b_1) but we also include the two terms that estimate the variability in intercepts, u_{0j}, and slopes, u_{1j}. The overall model becomes (compare to the two models above):

$$Y_{ij} = \left(b_0 + u_{0j}\right) + \left(b_1 + u_{1j}\right) X_{ij} + \varepsilon_{ij}$$

(20.6)

We can link this more directly to a simple linear model if we take some of these extra terms out into separate equations. We could write this model as a basic linear model, except we've replaced our fixed intercept and slope (b_0 and b_1) with their random counterparts (b_{0j} and b_{1j}):

$$Y_{ij} = b_{0j} + b_{1j} X_{ij} + \varepsilon_{ij}$$
$$b_{0j} = b_0 + u_{0j}$$
$$b_{1j} = b_1 + u_{1j}$$

(20.7)

The take-home point is that we're not doing anything terribly different from the rest of the book: it's basically just a posh linear model.

Now imagine we wanted to add in another predictor, for example quality of life before surgery. Knowing what we do about multiple regression, we shouldn't be invading the personal space of the idea that we can add this variable in with an associated beta:

$$\text{QoL After Surgery}_i = b_0 + b_1 \text{Surgery}_i + b_2 \text{QoL Before Surgery}_i + \varepsilon_i \qquad (20.8)$$

This is all revision of ideas from earlier in the book. Remember that the i represents the level 1 variable, in this case the people we tested. Therefore, we can predict a given person's quality of life after surgery by replacing the i with their name:

$$\text{QoL After}_{\text{Sam}} = b_0 + b_1 \text{Surgery}_{\text{Sam}} + b_2 \text{QoL Before}_{\text{Sam}} + \varepsilon_{\text{Sam}}$$

Now, if we want to allow the intercept of the effect of surgery on quality of life after surgery to vary across contexts then we simply replace b_0 with b_{0j}. If we want to allow the slope of the effect of surgery on quality of life after surgery to vary across contexts then we replace b_1 with b_{1j}. So, even with a random intercept and slope, our model stays much the same:

$$\text{QoL After}_{ij} = b_{0j} + b_{1j} \text{Surgery}_{ij} + b_2 \text{QoL Before}_{ij} + \varepsilon_{ij}$$
$$b_{0j} = b_0 + u_{0j} \qquad (20.9)$$
$$b_{1j} = b_1 + u_{1j}$$

Remember that the j in the equation relates to the level 2 contextual variable (clinic in this case). So, if we wanted to predict someone's score we wouldn't just do it from their name, but also from the clinic they attended. Imagine our guinea pig Sam had her surgery done at clinic 7, then we could replace the is and js as follows:

$$\text{QoL After Surgery}_{\text{Sam, clinic 7}} = b_{0, \text{ clinic 7}} + b_{1, \text{ clinic 7}} \text{Surgery}_{\text{Sam, clinic 7}}$$
$$+ b_2 \text{QoL Before Surgery}_{\text{Sam, clinic 7}} + \varepsilon_{\text{Sam, clinic 7}}$$

I want to sum up by just reiterating that all we're really doing in a multilevel model is a fancy regression in which we allow either the intercepts or slopes, or both, to vary across different contexts. All that really changes is that for every parameter that we allow to be random, we get an estimate of the variability of that parameter as well as the parameter itself. So, there isn't anything terribly complicated; we can add new predictors to the model and for each one decide whether its regression parameter is fixed or random.

20.4.1. Assessing the fit and comparing multilevel models ④

As in logistic regression (Chapter 19), the overall fit of a multilevel model is tested using a chi-square likelihood ratio test (see Section 18.3.3); SPSS reports the deviance, which is minus twice the log-likelihood, $-2LL$ (see Sections 19.3.1 and 19.3.2). Essentially, the smaller the value of the log-likelihood, the better. SPSS also produces four adjusted versions of the log-likelihood value. All of these can be interpreted in the same way as the log-likelihood, but they have been corrected for various things:

- *Akaike's information criterion (AIC)*: This statistic is a goodness-of-fit measure that is corrected for model complexity. That just means that it takes into account how many parameters have been estimated.

- *Hurvich and Tsai's criterion (AICC)*: This version of the AIC is designed for small samples.

- *Bozdogan's criterion (CAIC)*: This version of the AIC corrects not only for model complexity but also for sample size.

- *Schwarz's Bayesian criterion (BIC)*: This statistic is comparable to the AIC, but it is slightly more conservative (it corrects more harshly for the number of parameters being estimated). It should be used when sample sizes are large and the number of parameters is small.

All of these measures are similar, but the AIC and BIC are the most commonly used. None of them are intrinsically interpretable (it's not meaningful to talk about their values being large or small *per se*), but they are all useful as a way of comparing models. The value of AIC, AICC, CAIC and BIC can all be compared to their equivalent values in other models. In all cases smaller values mean better-fitting models.

Many writers recommend building up multilevel models starting with a 'basic' model in which all parameters are fixed and then adding in random coefficients as appropriate and exploring confounding variables (Raudenbush & Bryk, 2002; Twisk, 2006). One advantage of doing this is that you can compare the fit of the model as you make parameters random, or as you add in variables. To compare models we subtract the log-likelihood of the new model from the value for the old:

$$\chi^2_{\text{Change}} = \left(-2LL(\text{old})\right) - \left(-2LL(\text{new})\right)$$

$$df_{\text{Change}} = k_{\text{Old}} - k_{\text{New}}$$

(20.10)

In which k is the number of parameters in the respective model. This equation is basically the same as equation (18.7) and equation (19.6). There are two caveats to this equation: (1) it works only if full maximum-likelihood estimation is used (and not restricted maximal likelihood – see SPSS Tip 20.2); and (2) the new model contains all of the effects of the older model.

20.4.2. Types of covariance structures ④

If you have any random effects or repeated measures in your multilevel model then you can fit a *covariance structure* to each. The covariance structure specifies the form of the variance–covariance matrix (a matrix in which the diagonal elements are variances and the off-diagonal elements are covariances). There are various forms that this matrix could take, and we have to tell SPSS what form we think it *does* take. Most of the time we'll be taking an educated guess, so it is useful to run the model with different covariance structures and use the goodness-of-fit indices (the AIC, AICC, CAIC and BIC) to see whether changing the covariance structure improves the fit of the model.

The covariance structure is important because SPSS uses it as a starting point to estimate the model parameters. As such, you will get different results depending on which covariance structure you choose. If you specify a covariance structure that is too simple then you are more likely to make a Type I error (finding a parameter is significant when in reality it is not), but if you specify one that is too complex then you run the risk of a Type II error (finding parameters to be non-significant when in reality they are). SPSS has 17 different covariance structures that you can use. We will look at four of the most common. In each case I use a representation of the variance–covariance matrix to illustrate. With all of these matrices you could imagine that the rows and columns represent four different clinics in our cosmetic surgery data:

$$\begin{pmatrix} 1 & 0 & 0 & 0 \\ 0 & 1 & 0 & 0 \\ 0 & 0 & 1 & 0 \\ 0 & 0 & 0 & 1 \end{pmatrix}$$

Variance Components: This covariance structure assumes that all random effects are independent (hence, the covariances in the matrix are 0). Variances of random effects are assumed to be the same (hence, they are 1 in the matrix) and sum to the variance of the outcome variable. In SPSS this is the default covariance structure for random effects and is sometimes called the independence model.

$$\begin{pmatrix} \sigma_1^2 & 0 & 0 & 0 \\ 0 & \sigma_2^2 & 0 & 0 \\ 0 & 0 & \sigma_3^2 & 0 \\ 0 & 0 & 0 & \sigma_4^2 \end{pmatrix}$$

Diagonal: This variance structure is like variance components except that variances are assumed to be heterogeneous (this is why the diagonal of the matrix is made up of different variance terms). This structure again assumes that variances are independent and, therefore, that all of the covariances are 0. In SPSS this is the default covariance structure for repeated measures.

$$\begin{pmatrix} 1 & \rho & \rho^2 & \rho^3 \\ \rho & 1 & \rho & \rho^2 \\ \rho^2 & \rho & 1 & \rho \\ \rho^3 & \rho^2 & \rho & 1 \end{pmatrix}$$

AR(1): This stands for first-order autoregressive structure. In layman's terms, this means that the relationship between variances changes in a systematic way. If you imagine the rows and columns of the matrix to be points in time, then it assumes that the correlation between repeated measurements is highest at adjacent time points. So, in the first column, the correlation between time points 1 and 2 is ρ; let's assume that this value is .3. As we move to time point 3, the correlation between time point 1 and 3 is ρ^2, or .09. In other words, it has decreased: scores at time point 1 are more related to scores at time 2 than they are to scores at time 3. At time 4, the correlation goes down to ρ^3, or .027. So, the correlations between timepoints next to each other are assumed to be ρ, scores two intervals apart are assumed to have correlations of ρ^2, and scores three intervals apart are assumed to have correlations of ρ^3. The correlation between scores thus gets smaller over time. Variances are assumed to be homogeneous, but there is a version of this covariance structure where variance can be heterogeneous. This structure is often used for repeated-measures data (especially when measurements are taken over time such as in growth models).

$$\begin{pmatrix} \sigma_1^2 & \sigma_{21} & \sigma_{31} & \sigma_{41} \\ \sigma_{21} & \sigma_2^2 & \sigma_{32} & \sigma_{42} \\ \sigma_{31} & \sigma_{32} & \sigma_3^2 & \sigma_{43} \\ \sigma_{41} & \sigma_{42} & \sigma_{43} & \sigma_4^2 \end{pmatrix}$$

Unstructured: This covariance structure is completely general and is, therefore, the default option for random effects in SPSS. Covariances are assumed to be completely unpredictable: they do not conform to a systematic pattern.

20.5 Some practical issues ③

20.5.1. Assumptions ③

Multilevel linear models are an extension of the basic linear model, so all of the usual assumptions apply (see Chapter 5). There is a caveat, which is that a multilevel model can

CRAMMING SAM'S TIPS   Multilevel models

- Multilevel models should be used to analyse data that have a hierarchical structure. For example, you might measure depression after psychotherapy. In your sample, patients will see different therapists within different clinics. This is a three-level hierarchy with depression scores from patients (level 1) nested within therapists (level 2) who are themselves nested within clinics (level 3).
- Hierarchical models are just like regression, except that you can allow parameters to vary (this is called a random effect). In ordinary regression, parameters generally are a fixed value estimated from the sample (a fixed effect).
- If we estimate a linear model within each context (e.g., the therapist or clinic) rather than the sample as a whole, then we can assume that the intercepts of these models vary (a random intercepts model), or that the slopes of these models differ (a random slopes model) or that both vary.
- We can compare different models by looking at the difference in the value of $-2LL$. Usually we would do this when we have changed only one parameter (added one new thing to the model).
- For any model we have to assume a covariance structure. For random intercepts models the default of variance components is fine, but when slopes are random an unstructured covariance structure is often assumed. When data are measured over time an autoregressive structure (AR1) is often assumed.

sometimes solve the assumptions of independence and independent errors because we can factor in the correlations between cases caused by higher-level variables. As such, if a lack of independence is being caused by a level 2 or level 3 variable then a multilevel model should make this problem go away (although not always). As such, try to check the usual assumptions in the usual way.

There are two additional assumptions in multilevel models that relate to the random coefficients. These coefficients are assumed to be normally distributed around the overall model. So, in a random intercepts model the intercepts in the different contexts are assumed to be normally distributed around the overall model. Similarly, in a random slopes model, the slopes of the models in different contexts are assumed to be normally distributed.

Also it's worth mentioning that multicollinearity can be a particular problem in multilevel models if you have interactions that cross levels in the data hierarchy (cross-level interactions). However, centring predictors can help matters enormously (Kreft & de Leeuw, 1998), and we will see how to centre predictors in Section 20.5.4.

20.5.2. Robust multilevel models ③

Although we don't use these methods within this chapter, SPSS can produce robust confidence intervals of the model parameters found in the output tables labelled *Estimates of Fixed Effects* and *Estimates of Covariance Parameters* (e.g., see Output 20.5). You'll notice as we explore SPSS that the main dialog box for specifying a multilevel model (e.g., Figure 20.11) has a `Bootstrap...` button. Therefore, if you want robust confidence intervals for the model parameters click on `Bootstrap...` to access the bootstrap dialog box (discussed in Section 5.4.3); select ☑ Perform bootstrapping, and to get a 95% bootstrap confidence interval click ◉ Percentile or ◉ Bias corrected accelerated (BCa). Be warned that the analysis may take some time to run, and that, for complex models especially, bootstrap confidence intervals cannot always be computed.

20.5.3. Sample size and power ③

As you might well imagine, the situation with power and sample size is very complex indeed. One complexity is that we are trying to make decisions about our power to detect both fixed and random effects coefficients. Kreft and de Leeuw (1998) do a tremendous job of making sense of things for us. Essentially, the take-home message is the more data, the better. As more levels are introduced into the model, more parameters need to be estimated and the larger the sample sizes need to be. Kreft and de Leeuw conclude that if you are looking for cross-level interactions then you should aim to have more than 20 contexts (groups) in the higher-level variable, and that group sizes 'should not be too small'. They conclude by saying that there are so many factors involved in multilevel analysis that it is impossible to produce any meaningful rules of thumb.

Twisk (2006) agrees that the number of contexts relative to individuals within those contexts is important. He also points out that standard sample size and power calculations can be used but then 'corrected' for the multilevel component of the analysis (by factoring, among other things, the intraclass correlation). However, he discusses two corrections that yield very different sample sizes. He recommends using sample size calculations with caution.

20.5.4. Centring predictors ③

We encountered the concept of centring in Section 10.3.3. Essentially it is the process of transforming a variable into deviations around a fixed point. One such fixed point is the mean of the variable (grand mean centring). This form of centring is used in multilevel models too, but sometimes **group mean centring** is used instead. Group mean centring occurs when for a given variable we take each score and subtract from it the mean of the scores (for that variable) within a given group. For multilevel models, it is usually only level 1 predictors that are centred (in our cosmetic surgery example this would be predictors such as age, BDI and pre-surgery quality of life). If group mean centring is used then a level 1 variable is typically centred on means of a level 2 variable (in our cosmetic surgery data this would mean that, for example, the age of a person would be centred around the mean of age for the clinic at which the person had their surgery).

Should I centre predictors in a multilevel model?

In multilevel models centring can be a useful way to combat multicollinearity between predictor variables. It's also helpful when predictors do not have a meaningful zero point. Multilevel models with centred predictors tend to be more stable, and estimates from these models can be treated as more or less independent of each other, which might be desirable. However, as with ordinary regression (Section 10.3.3) centring has an effect on the model. There are some excellent reviews (Enders & Tofighi, 2007; Kreft & de Leeuw, 1998; Kreft, de Leeuw, & Aiken, 1995), and here I will give a very basic précis of what they say. Essentially, if you fit a multilevel model using the raw score predictors and then fit the same model but with grand mean centred predictors then the resulting models are equivalent. They will fit the data equally well, have the same predicted values, and the residuals will be the same. The parameters themselves (the *b*s) will, of course, be different but there will be a direct relationship between the parameters from the two models. Therefore, grand mean centring doesn't change the multilevel model, but it would change your interpretation of the parameters (you can't interpret them as though they are raw scores). When group mean centring is used the picture is much more complicated: the raw score model is not equivalent to the centred model in either the fixed part or the random part. One exception is when only the intercept is random (which

OLIVER TWISTED

Please Sir, can I have some more … group mean centring?

'Centring was so much fun when we did it in Chapter 10. It was like being gently tickled to sleep in a warm bath of octopuses. I want some more', gurgles Oliver as he splashes around in his bath. Fair enough, Oliver, if you want to know how to do group mean centring using SPSS, then the additional material on the companion website will tell you. Oh, and be careful with that toy pirate ship …

arguably is an unusual situation), and the group means are reintroduced into the model as level 2 variables (Kreft & de Leeuw, 1998).

If you are going to centre then you might wonder whether grand mean or group mean centring is 'better'. People learning statistics often worry about their being a 'best' way to do things, but the 'best' method usually depends on what you're trying to do. Centring is a good example. Although some people make a decision about whether to use group or grand mean centring based on some statistical criterion, there is no statistically correct choice between not centring, grand mean centring and group mean centring (Kreft et al., 1995). Enders and Tofighi (2007) make four recommendations when analysing data with a two-level hierarchy: (1) group mean centring should be used if the primary interest is in an association between variables measured at level 1 (i.e., the aforementioned relationship between surgery and quality of life after surgery); (2) grand mean centring is appropriate when the primary interest is in the level 2 variable but you want to control for the level 1 covariate (i.e., you want to look at the effect of clinic on quality of life after surgery while controlling for the type of surgery); (3) both types of centring can be used to look at the differential influence of a variable at level 1 and 2 (i.e., is the effect of surgery on quality of life post-surgery different at the clinic level than the client level?); and (4) group mean centring is preferable for examining cross-level interactions (e.g., the interactive effect of clinic and surgery on quality of life after surgery). If group mean centring is used then the group means should be reintroduced as a level 2 variable unless you want to look at the effect of your 'group' or level 2 variable uncorrected for the mean effect of the centred level 1 predictor, such as when fitting a model when time is your main explanatory variable (Kreft & de Leeuw, 1998).

20.6   Multilevel modelling using SPSS ④

SPSS is not the best program in the world for multilevel modelling. Most people who do serious multilevel modelling tend to use specialist software such as MLwiN, HLM and R. There are several excellent books that compare the various packages, and SPSS tends to fare pretty badly (Tabachnick & Fidell, 2012; Twisk, 2006). The main area where SPSS is behind its competitors is that it cannot do multilevel modelling when the outcome variable is categorical, yet this is bread and butter for the other packages mentioned. SPSS also has (and I am not the only one to say this) a completely indecipherable windows interface for doing multilevel models.

Figure 20.8 shows a very stripped down version of how we proceed with the analysis. After initial checks of the data, it is useful to build up models starting with a 'basic' model in which all parameters are fixed and then add random coefficients as appropriate before exploring confounding variables (as I mentioned in Section 20.4.1).

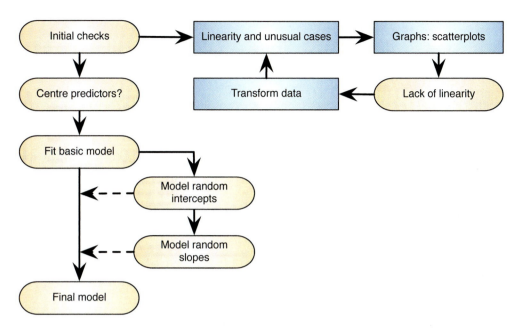

FIGURE 20.8
The basic process of fitting a multilevel model

20.6.1. Entering the data ②

Data entry depends a bit on the type of multilevel model that you wish to run: the data layout is slightly different when the same variables are measured at several points in time. However, we will look at the case of repeated-measures data in a second example. In this first example, the situation we have is very much like multiple regression in that data from each person who had surgery are not measured over multiple time points. Figure 20.9 shows the data layout. Each row represents a case of data (in this case a person who had surgery). Their scores on the various variables are simply entered in different columns. So, for example, the first person was 31 years old, had a BDI score of 12, was in the waiting list control group at clinic 1, was female and was waiting for surgery to change her appearance.

20.6.2. Ignoring the data structure: ANOVA ②

First of all, let's ground the example in something very familiar to us: ANOVA. Let's say for the time being that we were interested only in the effect that surgery has on post-operative quality of life. We could analyse this with a one-way independent ANOVA (or indeed a *t*-test), and the model is described by equation (20.1).

SELF-TEST   Using what you know about ANOVA, conduct a one-way ANOVA using **Surgery** as the predictor and **Post_QoL** as the outcome.

In reality we wouldn't do an ANOVA; I'm just using it to show you that multilevel models are not big and scary, but are simply extensions of what we have done before. Output 20.1

FIGURE 20.9
Data layout
for multilevel
modelling with
no repeated
measure

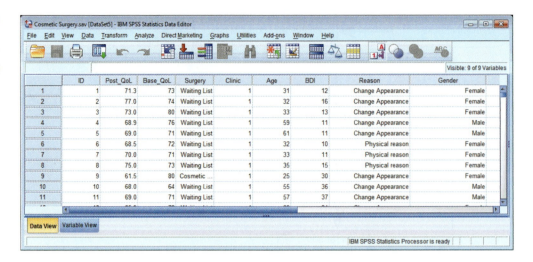

OUTPUT 20.1

ANOVA

Quality of Life After Cosmetic Surgery

	Sum of Squares	df	Mean Square	F	Sig.
Between Groups	28.620	1	28.620	.330	.566
Within Groups	23747.883	274	86.671		
Total	23776.504	275			

FIGURE 20.10
The initial
mixed models
dialog box

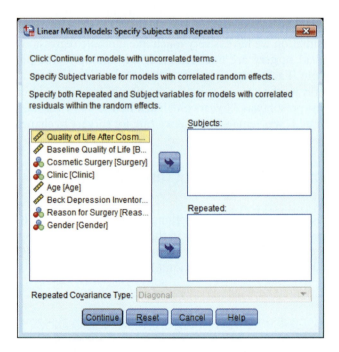

shows the results of the ANOVA that you should get if you did the self-test. We find a non-significant effect of surgery on quality of life, $F(1, 274) = 0.33$, $p = .566$.

To run a multilevel model select Analyze Mixed Models ▸ Linear…, which brings up the dialog box in Figure 20.10. This dialog box is for specifying the hierarchical structure of the data and because, for the time being, we are ignoring this hierarchical structure, we will ignore this dialog box for now.

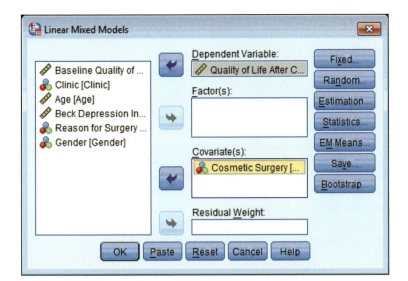

FIGURE 20.11
The main mixed models dialog box.

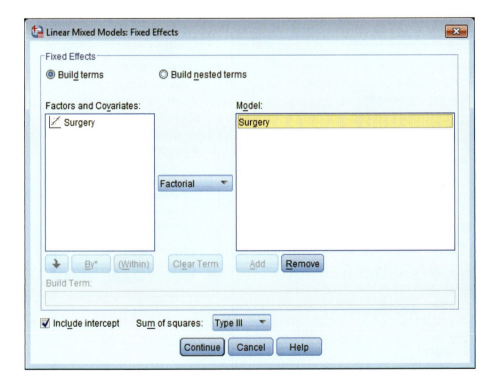

FIGURE 20.12
The dialog box for specifying fixed effects in mixed models

Click on [Continue] to move to the main dialog box (Figure 20.11), which is very similar to many other dialog boxes that we have seen before. First we specify our outcome variable, which is quality of life (QoL) after surgery, so select **Post_QoL** and drag it to the space labelled *Dependent Variable* (or click on ➡). Next, specify our predictor, which is whether or not the person has had surgery, by selecting, **Surgery** and dragging it to the space labelled *Covariate(s)*, or click on ➡ (SPSS Tip 20.1).

You'll notice several buttons at the side of the main dialog box. We use [Fixed...] to specify fixed effects in our model, and [Random...] to specify, yes, you've guessed it, random effects. To begin with we will treat our effects as fixed, so click on [Fixed...] to bring up the dialog box in Figure 20.12. We have only one variable specified as a predictor, and we want

SPSS TIP 20.1   Factor(s) or Covariate(s) ④

You might wonder why we didn't drag the **Surgery** variable to the *Factors* box, given that it is a categorical variable. If you have a categorical variable and you place it in the *Factor(s)* box then SPSS will convert it into dummy variables for you and place these dummy variables into the model. If you place it into the *Covariate(s)* box it will treat it as a linear trend. In this example, we have already coded **Surgery** as a dummy variable (i.e., 0 and 1), so it's fine to specify it as a covariate (and it makes the output a bit tidier for reasons that I won't bore you with). However, if your categorical variable had more than two categories you should certainly drag it into *Factor(s)* (and if you try out the end-of-chapter tasks you'll see that we do this). The exception is if you have ordered categories. In the second example we have a variable representing different time points. Technically, this variable is a categorical variable with four levels (each representing a point in time) but since it represents four equally spaced time points we would again want to treat it as a covariate, because by doing so we'd be looking at the linear trend of time (rather than each time point against a baseline).

FIGURE 20.13
The *Estimation* and *Statistics* options for mixed models

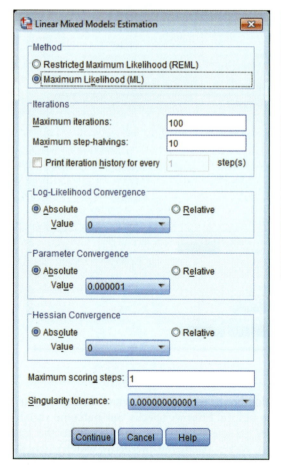

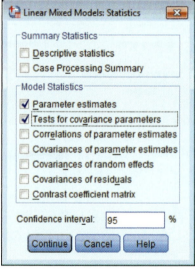

this to be treated as a fixed effect; therefore, we select it in this dialog box from the list labelled *Factors and Covariates* and then click on [Add] to transfer it to the *Model*. Click on [Continue] to return to the main dialog box.

In the main dialog box click on [Estimation...] to open the dialog box in Figure 20.13 (left). This dialog box allows you to change the parameters that SPSS will use when estimating the model. For example, if you don't get a solution then you could increase the number of iterations (SPSS Tip 19.1). The defaults can be left alone, but you do need to decide whether to use the maximum likelihood, or something called the restricted maximum-likelihood estimation method. There are pros and cons to both (see SPSS Tip 20.2), but, because we want to compare models as we build them up, we will select ⦿ Maximum Li̱kelihood (ML). Click on [Continue] to return to the main dialog box.

In the main dialog box click on [Statistics...] to open the dialog box in Figure 20.13 (right). There are two useful options in this dialog box. The first is to request *Parameter estimates*. This will give us *b*-values for each effect and their significance (so it will give us similar information to the coefficients table in multiple regression). The second useful option is *Tests for covariance parameters*, which will give us a significance test of each of the covariance estimates in the model (i.e., the values of *u* in equations (20.3), (20.5) and (20.7)). These estimates tell us about the variability of intercepts or slopes across our contextual variable and so testing them for significance can be useful (we can then say that there was significant, or not, variability in intercepts or slopes). Select these two options and then click on [Continue] to return to the main dialog box. To run the analysis, click on [OK].

SPSS TIP 20.2   Estimation ③

SPSS gives you the choice of two methods for estimating the parameters in the analysis: maximum likelihood (ML), which we have encountered before, and restricted maximum likelihood (REML). The conventional wisdom seems to be that ML produces more accurate estimates of fixed regression parameters, whereas REML produces more accurate estimates of random variances (Twisk, 2006). As such, the choice of estimation procedure depends on whether your hypotheses are focused on the fixed regression parameters or on estimating variances of the random effects. However, in many situations the choice of ML or REML will make only a small difference to the parameter estimates. Also, if you want to compare models you must use ML.

Type III Tests of Fixed Effects[a]   OUTPUT 20.2

Source	Numerator df	Denominator df	F	Sig.
Intercept	1	276	6049.727	.000
Surgery	1	276	.333	.565

a. Dependent Variable: Quality of Life After Cosmetic Surgery.

Output 20.2 shows the main table for the model. Compare this table with Output 20.1 and you'll see that there is basically no difference: we get a non-significant effect of surgery with an *F* of 0.33, and a *p* of .56. The point I want you to absorb here is that if we ignore the hierarchical structure of the data then what we are left with is something very familiar: an ANOVA/regression. The numbers are more or less exactly the same; all that has changed is that we have used different menus to get to the same endpoint.

20.6.3. Ignoring the data structure: ANCOVA ②

We have seen that there is no effect of cosmetic surgery on quality of life, but we did not take into account the quality of life before surgery. Let's, therefore, extend the example a little to look at the effect of the surgery on quality of life while taking into account the quality of life scores before surgery. Our model is now described by equation (20.8). You would normally do this analysis with an ANCOVA, through the univariate GLM menu. As in the previous section, we'll run the analysis both ways, just to illustrate that we're doing the same thing when we run a hierarchical model.

 SELF-TEST   Using what you know about ANCOVA, conduct a one-way ANCOVA using **Surgery** as the predictor, **Post_QoL** as the outcome and **Base_QoL** as the covariate.

Output 20.3 shows the results of the ANCOVA that you should get if you did the self-test. With baseline quality of life included, we find a significant effect of surgery on quality of life, $F(1, 273) = 4.04, p = .045$. Baseline quality of life also predicted quality of life after surgery, $F(1, 273) = 214.89, p < .001$.

OUTPUT 20.3

Tests of Between–Subjects Effects

Dependent Variable: Quality of Life After Cosmetic Surgery

Source	Type III Sum of Squares	df	Mean Square	F	Sig.
Corrected Model	10488.253[a]	2	5244.127	107.738	.000
Intercept	1713.257	1	1713.257	35.198	.000
Base_QoL	10459.633	1	10459.633	214.888	.000
Surgery	196.816	1	196.816	4.043	.045
Error	13288.250	273	48.675		
Total	1004494.53	276			
Corrected Total	23776.504	275			

a. R Squared = .441 (Adjusted R Squared = .437)

Select Analyze Mixed Models ▶ Linear... again, and, just like last time, ignore the first dialog box because, for now, we are ignoring the hierarchical structure of our data. We can leave the main dialog box (Figure 20.14) as it was in the last analysis except that we now need to add the baseline quality of life as another predictor. To do this, select **Base_QoL** and drag it to the space labelled *Covariate(s)* (or click on ➡).

We need to add this new variable to our model as a fixed effect, so click on Fixed to bring up the dialog box in Figure 20.15. Select **Base_QoL** in the list labelled *Factors and Covariates* and then click on Add to transfer it to the *Model*. Click on Continue to return to the main dialog box and click on OK to run the analysis.

Output 20.4 shows the main table for the model. Compare this table with Output 20.3 and you'll see that again the results are pretty similar to when we ran the analysis as ANCOVA:[4] we get a significant effect of surgery with an F of 4.08, p = .044, and a significant effect of baseline quality of life with an F of 217.25, p < .001. We can also see that the

---

[4] The values are very slightly different because here we're using maximum-likelihood methods to estimate the parameters of the model, whereas in ANCOVA we use ordinary least squares.

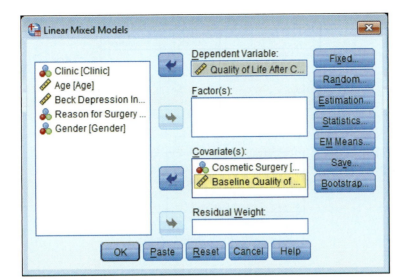

FIGURE 20.14
The main mixed models dialog box

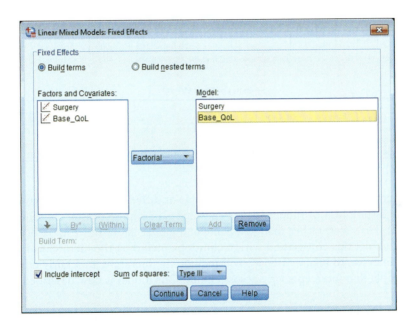

FIGURE 20.15
The dialog box for specifying fixed effects in mixed models

regression coefficient for surgery is −1.70. Hopefully this exercise has convinced you that we're just doing a regression, something you have been doing throughout this book. This technique isn't radically different, and if you think about it as just an extension of what you already know, then it's really relatively easy to understand. So, having shown you that we can do basic analyses through the mixed models command, let's now use its power to factor in the hierarchical structure of the data.

20.6.4. Factoring in the data structure: random intercepts ③

We have seen that when we factor in the pre-surgery quality of life scores, which themselves significantly predict post-surgery quality of life scores, surgery seems to positively affect quality of life. However, at this stage we have ignored the fact that our data have a hierarchical structure. Essentially we have violated the independence assumption because scores from people who had their surgery at the same clinic are likely to be related to each

OUTPUT 20.4

Model Dimension[a]

		Number of Levels	Number of Parameters
Fixed Effects	Intercept	1	1
	Surgery	1	1
	Base_QoL	1	1
Residual			1
Total		3	4

df for −2LL

a. Dependent Variable: Quality of Life After Cosmetic Surgery.

Information Criteria[a]

−2 Log Likelihood	1852.543
Akaike's Information Criterion (AIC)	1860.543
Hurvich and Tsai's Criterion (AICC)	1860.690
Bozdogan's Criterion (CAIC)	1879.024
Schwarz's Bayesian Criterion (BIC)	1875.024

−2LL

The information criteria are displayed in smaller-is-better forms.

a. Dependent Variable: Quality of Life After Cosmetic Surgery.

Type III Tests of Fixed Effects[a]

Source	Numerator df	Denominator df	F	Sig.
Intercept	1	276	39.379	.000
Surgery	1	276	4.088	.044
Base_QoL	1	276	217.249	.000

a. Dependent Variable: Quality of Life After Cosmetic Surgery.

Estimates of Fixed Effects[a]

Parameter	Estimate	Std. Error	df	t	Sig.	95% Confidence Interval Lower Bound	Upper Bound
Intercept	18.147025	2.891820	276	6.275	.000	12.454198	23.839851
Surgery	−1.697233	.839442	276	−2.022	.044	−3.349756	−.044710
Base_QoL	.665036	.045120	276	14.739	.000	.576213	.753858

a. Dependent Variable: Quality of Life After Cosmetic Surgery.

other (and certainly more related than with people at different clinics). We have seen that violating the assumption of independence can have some quite drastic consequences (see Section 11.3). However, rather than just panic and gibber about our F-ratio being inaccurate, we can model this covariation within clinics by including the hierarchical data structure in our analysis. To begin with, we will include the hierarchy in a fairly crude way by assuming simply that intercepts vary across clinics. Our model is now described by:

$$\text{QoL After Surgery}_{ij} = b_{0j} + b_1 \text{Surgery}_{ij} + b_2 \text{QoL before Surgery}_{ij} + \varepsilon_{ij}$$

$$b_{0j} = b_0 + u_{0j}$$

We again use the *Mixed Models* option by selecting Analyze Mixed Models ▶ Linear…, which will bring up the dialog box in Figure 20.10. This time, rather than ignoring this dialog box, we are going to use it to specify our level 2 variable (**Clinic**). We specify contextual variables that group participants (or subjects) in the box labelled *Subjects*. Select **Clinic** from the list of variables and drag it to the box labelled *Subjects* (or click on ⟶). The completed dialog box is shown in Figure 20.16.

Click on Continue to access the main dialog box. We don't need to change this because all we are doing in this model is changing the intercept from being fixed to random. Therefore, the main dialog box should still look like Figure 20.14. We also don't need to re-specify our fixed effects, so there is no need to click on Fixed… unless you want to check that the dialog box still looks like Figure 20.15. However, we do need to specify a random effect for the first time, so click on Random… in the main dialog box to access the dialog box in Figure 20.17. The first thing we need to do is to specify our contextual variable. We do this by selecting it from the list of contextual variables that we have told SPSS about in Figure 20.16. These

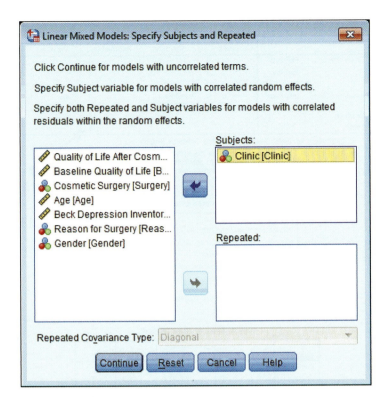

FIGURE 20.16
Specifying a
level 2 variable
in a hierarchical
linear model

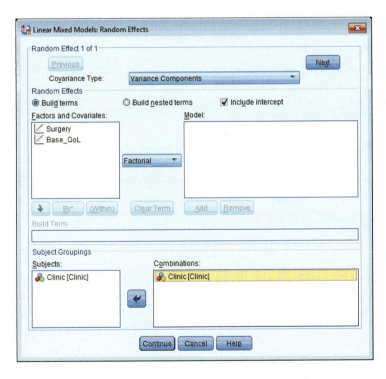

FIGURE 20.17
Dialog box
for specifying
random effects
in mixed
models

appear in the section labelled *Subjects* and because we specified only **Clinic**, this is the only variable in the list. Select this variable and drag it to the area labelled *Combinations* (or click on ➡). We want to specify only that the intercept is random, and we do this by selecting ☑ Include intercept. Notice in this dialog box that there is a drop-down list to specify the type of covariance (Variance Components ▾). For a random intercept model this default option is fine. Click on Continue to return to the main dialog box and then click on OK to run the analysis.

OUTPUT 20.5

Model Dimension[a]

		Number of Levels	Covariance Structure	Number of Parameters	Subject Variables
Fixed Effects	Intercept	1		1	
	Surgery	1		1	
	Base_QoL	1		1	
Random Effects	Intercept[b]	1	Variance Components	1	Clinic
Residual				1	
Total		4		5	

a. Dependent Variable: Quality of Life After Cosmetic Surgery.

b. As of version 11.5, the syntax rules for the RANDOM subcommand have changed. Your command syntax may yield results that differ from those produced by prior versions. If you are using version 11 syntax, please consult the current syntax reference guide for more information.

df for −2LL

Information Criteria[a]

−2 Log Likelihood	1837.490
Akaike's Information Criterion (AIC)	1847.490
Hurvich and Tsai's Criterion (AICC)	1847.712
Bozdogan's Criterion (CAIC)	1870.592
Schwarz's Bayesian Criterion (BIC)	1865.592

−2LL

The information criteria are displayed in smaller-is-better forms.

a. Dependent Variable: Quality of Life After Cosmetic Surgery.

Type III Tests of Fixed Effects[a]

Source	Numerator df	Denominator df	F	Sig.
Intercept	1	163.879	73.305	.000
Surgery	1	275.631	.139	.709
Base_QoL	1	245.020	83.159	.000

a. Dependent Variable: Quality of Life After Cosmetic Surgery.

bs

Estimates of Fixed Effects[a]

Parameter	Estimate	Std. Error	df	t	Sig.	95% Confidence Interval	
						Lower Bound	Upper Bound
Intercept	29.563601	3.452958	163.879	8.562	.000	22.745578	36.381624
Surgery	−.312999	.838551	275.631	−.373	.709	−1.963776	1.337779
Base_QoL	.478630	.052486	245.020	9.119	.000	.375248	.582012

a. Dependent Variable: Quality of Life After Cosmetic Surgery.

$Var(\varepsilon_{ij})$

Estimates of Covariance Parameters[a]

Parameter		Estimate	Std. Error	Wald Z	Sig.	95% Confidence Interval	
						Lower Bound	Upper Bound
Residual		42.497179	3.703949	11.473	.000	35.823786	50.413718
Intercept [subject = Clinic]	Variance	9.237126	5.461678	1.691	.091	2.898965	29.432742

a. Dependent Variable: Quality of Life After Cosmetic Surgery.

$Var(u_{0j})$

The output of this analysis is shown in Output 20.5. The first issue is whether allowing the intercepts to vary has made a difference to the model. We can test this using the change in −2LL (equation (20.10)). In our new model this is 1837.49 (Output 20.5), based on a total of five parameters. In the old model (Output 20.4) it was 1852.54, based on four parameters. Therefore:

$$\chi^2_{\text{Change}} = 1852.54 - 1837.49 = 15.05$$

$$df_{\text{Change}} = 5 - 4 = 1$$

The critical values for the chi-square statistic with 1 degree of freedom, given in the Appendix, are 3.84 ($p < .05$) and 6.63 ($p < .01$); therefore, this change is highly significant.

Put another way, it is important that we modelled this variability in intercepts because when we do, the fit of our model is significantly improved. We can conclude, then, that the intercepts for the relationship between surgery and quality of life (when controlling for baseline quality of life) vary significantly across the different clinics.

You will also notice that the significance of the variance estimate for the intercept (9.24) is tested using the Wald statistic, which is a standard z-score in this case ($z = 1.69$). You should be cautious in interpreting the Wald statistic because, for random parameters especially, it can be quite unpredictable (for fixed effects it should be OK). The change in $-2LL$ is much more reliable, and you should use this to assess the significance of changes to the model – just like with logistic regression (Chapter 19).

By allowing the intercept to vary we also have a new regression parameter for the effect of surgery, which is -0.31 compared to -1.70 when the intercept was fixed (Output 20.4). In other words, by allowing the intercepts to vary over clinics, the effect of surgery has decreased dramatically. In fact, it is no longer significant, $F(1, 275.63) = 0.14$, $p = .709$. This shows how, had we ignored the hierarchical structure in our data, we would have reached very different conclusions than those we have found here.

20.6.5. Factoring in the data structure: random intercepts and slopes ④

We have seen that including a random intercept is important for this model (it changes the log-likelihood significantly). We could now look at whether adding a random slope will also be beneficial by adding this term to the model. The model is now described by equation (20.9); it can be specified in SPSS with only minor modifications to the dialog boxes. All we are doing is adding another random term to the model; therefore, the only changes we need to make are in the dialog box accessed by clicking on Random... . (If you are starting from scratch then follow the instructions for setting up the dialog box in the previous section.) We need to select the predictor (**Surgery**) from the list of *Factors and Covariates* and add it to the model by clicking on Add (see Figure 20.18). Click on Continue to return to the main dialog box and then click on OK to run the analysis.

All we're interested in at this stage is estimating the effect of including the variance in slopes. Output 20.6 gives us the $-2LL$ for the new model and the value of the variance in slopes (29.63). To find the significance of the variance in slopes, we subtract this value from the $-2LL$ for the previous model. This gives us a chi-square statistic with $df = 1$ (because we have added only one new parameter to the model, the variance in slopes). In our new model the $-2LL$ is 1816 (Output 20.6) based on a total of six parameters. In the old model (Output 20.5) the $-2LL$ was 1837.49, based on five parameters. Therefore:

$$\chi^2_{\text{Change}} = 1837.49 - 1816 = 21.49$$

$$df_{\text{Change}} = 6 - 5 = 1$$

Comparing this value to the same critical values as before for the chi-square statistic with $df = 1$ (i.e., 3.84 and 6.63) shows that this change is highly significant because 21.49 is much larger than these two values. Put another way, the fit of our model significantly improved when the variance of slopes was included: there is significant variability in slopes.

Now that we know that there is significant variability in slopes, we can look to see whether the slopes and intercepts are correlated (or covary). By selecting Variance Components ▾ in the previous

FIGURE 20.18
The dialog box for specifying random effects in mixed models

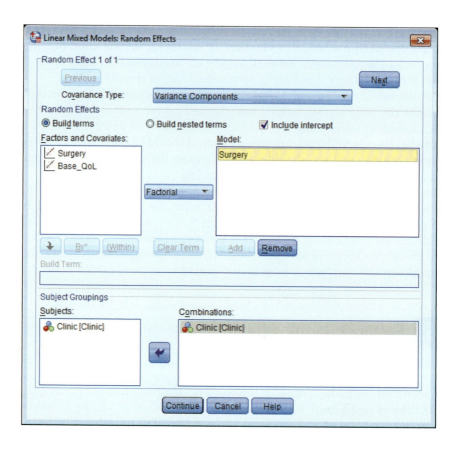

analysis, we assumed that the covariances between the intercepts and slopes were zero. Therefore, SPSS estimated only the variance of slopes. This was a useful thing to do because it allowed us to look at the effect of the variance of slopes in isolation. If we now want to include the covariance between random slopes and random intercepts we do this by clicking on Variance Components ▼ in Figure 20.18 to access the drop-down list, and selecting Unstructured ▼ instead. By changing to Unstructured ▼, we remove the assumption that the covariances between slopes and intercepts are zero, and so SPSS will estimate this covariance. As such, by changing to Unstructured ▼, we add a new term to the model that estimates the covariance between random slopes and intercepts. Redo the analysis, but change Variance Components ▼ to Unstructured ▼ in Figure 20.18.

OUTPUT 20.6

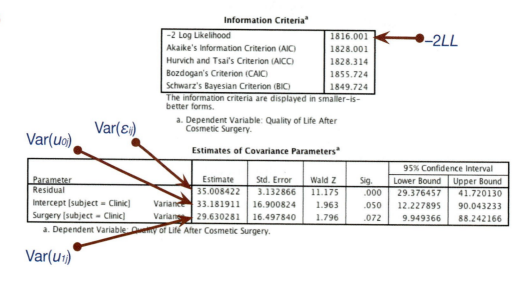

Information Criteria[a]

–2 Log Likelihood	1816.001
Akaike's Information Criterion (AIC)	1828.001
Hurvich and Tsai's Criterion (AICC)	1828.314
Bozdogan's Criterion (CAIC)	1855.724
Schwarz's Bayesian Criterion (BIC)	1849.724

The information criteria are displayed in smaller-is-better forms.

a. Dependent Variable: Quality of Life After Cosmetic Surgery.

$-2LL$

Estimates of Covariance Parameters[a]

Parameter		Estimate	Std. Error	Wald Z	Sig.	95% Confidence Interval	
						Lower Bound	Upper Bound
Residual		35.008422	3.132866	11.175	.000	29.376457	41.720130
Intercept [subject = Clinic]	Variance	33.181911	16.900824	1.963	.050	12.227895	90.043233
Surgery [subject = Clinic]	Variance	29.630281	16.497840	1.796	.072	9.949366	88.242166

a. Dependent Variable: Quality of Life After Cosmetic Surgery.

$\text{Var}(u_{0j})$ $\text{Var}(\varepsilon_{ij})$ $\text{Var}(u_{1j})$

Model Dimension[a]

		Number of Levels	Covariance Structure	Number of Parameters	Subject Variables
Fixed Effects	Intercept	1		1	
	Surgery	1		1	
	Base_QoL	1		1	
Random Effects	Intercept + Surgery[b]	2	Unstructured	3	Clinic
Residual				1	
Total		5		7	

a. Dependent Variable: Quality of Life After Cosmetic Surgery.

b. As of version 11.5, the syntax rules for the RANDOM subcommand have changed. Your command syntax may yield results that differ from those produced by prior versions. If you are using version 11 syntax, please consult the current syntax reference guide for more information.

df for −2LL

Information Criteria[a]

−2 Log Likelihood	1798.624
Akaike's Information Criterion (AIC)	1812.624
Hurvich and Tsai's Criterion (AICC)	1813.042
Bozdogan's Criterion (CAIC)	1844.967
Schwarz's Bayesian Criterion (BIC)	1837.967

−2LL

The information criteria are displayed in smaller–is–better forms.

a. Dependent Variable: Quality of Life After Cosmetic Surgery.

Type III Tests of Fixed Effects[a]

Source	Numerator df	Denominator df	F	Sig.
Intercept	1	84.954	107.284	.000
Surgery	1	9.518	.097	.762
Base_QoL	1	265.933	33.984	.000

a. Dependent Variable: Quality of Life After Cosmetic Surgery.

bs

Estimates of Fixed Effects[a]

Parameter	Estimate	Std. Error	df	t	Sig.	95% Confidence Interval	
						Lower Bound	Upper Bound
Intercept	40.102525	3.871729	84.954	10.358	.000	32.404430	47.800620
Surgery	−.654530	2.099413	9.518	−.312	.762	−5.364643	4.055583
Base_QoL	.310218	.053214	265.933	5.830	.000	.205443	.414993

a. Dependent Variable: Quality of Life After Cosmetic Surgery.

$Var(u_{0j})$ = variance of intercepts

$Var(\varepsilon_{ij})$ = variance of residuals

Estimates of Covariance Parameters[a]

Parameter		Estimate	Std. Error	Wald Z	Sig.	95% Confidence Interval	
						Lower Bound	Upper Bound
Residual		34.955705	3.116670	11.216	.000	29.351106	41.630504
Intercept + Surgery [subject = Clinic]	UN (1,1)	37.609439	18.726052	2.008	.045	14.173482	99.796926
	UN (2,1)	−36.680707	18.763953	−1.955	.051	−73.457378	.095965
	UN (2,2)	38.408857	20.209811	1.901	.057	13.694612	107.724141

a. Dependent Variable: Quality of Life After Cosmetic Surgery.

$Var(u_{1j})$ = variance of slopes

$Cov(u_{0j}, u_{1j})$ = covariance of slopes and intercepts

The output of this analysis is shown in Output 20.7. The first issue is whether adding the covariance between slopes and intercepts has made a difference to the model using the change in −2LL (equation 20.10). In our new model the −2LL is 1798.62 (Output 20.7) based on a total of seven parameters. In the old model (Output 20.6) it was 1816, based on six parameters. Therefore:

$$\chi^2_{Change} = 1816 - 1798.62 = 17.38$$

$$df_{Change} = 7 - 6 = 1$$

FIGURE 20.19

Predicted values from the model (surgery predicting quality of life after controlling for baseline quality of life) plotted against the observed values

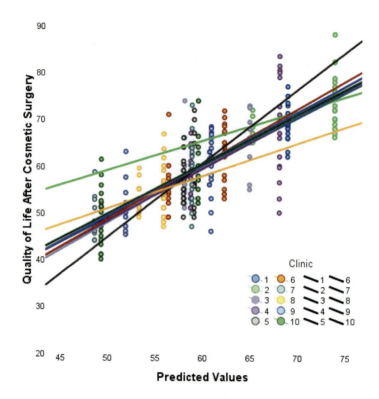

This change is highly significant at $p < .01$ because 17.38 is bigger than the critical value of 6.63 for the chi-square statistic with 1 degree of freedom (see the Appendix). Basically, the fit of our model is significantly improved when the covariance term is included in the model. The variance estimates for the intercept (37.60) and slopes (−36.68 and 38.41), and their associated significance based on the Wald test, confirm this because all three estimates are close to significance (although I reiterate my earlier point that the Wald statistic should be interpreted with caution).

Notice that the random part of the slopes now has two values (−36.68 and 38.41). The reason for this is that we changed from a covariance structure of Variance Components ▾ , which assumes that parameters are uncorrelated, to Unstructured ▾ , which makes no such assumption, and, therefore, the covariance is estimated too. The first of these values is the covariance between the random slope and random intercept, and the second is the variance of the random slopes. Covariance (Chapter 6) is an unstandardized measure of the relationship between variables. It's like a correlation. Therefore, the covariance term tells us whether there is a relationship or interaction between the random slope and the random intercept within the model. The actual size of this value is not terribly important because it is unstandardized (so we can't compare the size of covariances measured across different variables), but its direction is important. In this case the covariance is negative (−36.68), indicating a negative relationship between the intercepts and the slopes. Remember that we are looking at the effect of surgery on quality of life in 10 different clinics, so this means that, across these clinics, as the intercept for the relationship between surgery and quality of life increases, the value of the slope decreases. This is best understood using a diagram, and Figure 20.19 shows the observed values of quality of life after surgery plotted against those predicted by our model. In this diagram each line represents a different clinic. We can see that the 10 clinics differ: those with low intercepts (low values on the y-axis) have quite steep positive slopes. However, as the intercept increases (as we go from the line that crosses the y-axis at the lowest point up to the line that hits the y-axis at the highest point) the slopes of the lines get flatter (the slope decreases). The negative covariance between slope and intercept reflects this relationship. Had it been positive it would have meant the opposite: as intercepts increase, the slopes increase also.

The second term that we get with the random slope is its variance (in this case 38.41). This tells us how much the slopes vary around a single slope fitted to the entire data set (i.e., ignoring the clinic from which the data came). This confirms what our chi-square test showed us: that the slopes across clinics are significantly different.

We can conclude that the intercepts and slopes for the relationship between surgery and quality of life (when controlling for baseline quality of life) vary significantly across the different clinics. Allowing the intercept and slopes to vary results in a new regression parameter for the effect of surgery, which is -0.65 compared to -0.31 when the slopes were fixed (Output 20.5). By allowing the intercepts to vary over clinics, the effect of surgery has increased, although it is still not significant, $F(1, 9.518) = 0.10$, $p = .762$.

20.6.6. Adding an interaction to the model ④

We can build up the model by adding in another variable. One of the variables we measured was the reason for the person having cosmetic surgery: was it to resolve a physical problem or was it purely for vanity? We can add this variable to the model, and also look at whether it interacts with surgery in predicting quality of life.[5] Our model will expand to incorporate these new terms, and each term will have a regression coefficient (which we select to be fixed). Therefore, our new model can be described as in the equation below (note that all that has changed is that there are two new predictors):

$$\text{QoL After}_{ij} = b_{0j} + b_{1j}\text{Surgery}_{ij} + b_2 \text{QoL Before Surgery}_{ij}$$
$$+ b_3 \text{Reason}_{ij} + b_4 \left(\text{Reason}\times\text{Surgery}\right)_{ij} + \varepsilon_{ij}$$
$$b_{0j} = b_0 + u_{0j} \tag{20.11}$$
$$b_{1j} = b_1 + u_{1j}$$

To set up this model in SPSS is very easy and just requires some minor changes to the dialog boxes that we have already used. First, select Analyze Mixed Models ▶ Linear... ; this initial dialog box should be set up as for the previous analysis (it should look like Figure 20.16). Click on Continue to access the main dialog box. Again, assuming you're continuing the previous analysis, this dialog box will already be set up with the previous model (it should look like Figure 20.14). We have two new covariates to add to the model: the effect of the reason for the surgery (**Reason**) and the interaction of **Reason** and **Surgery**. At this stage we simply need to add **Reason** as a covariate, so select this variable and drag it to the space labelled _Covariate(s)_ (or click on ➡)[6]. The completed dialog box is in Figure 20.20.

---

[5] In reality, because we would use the change in $-2LL$ to see whether effects are significant, we would build this new model up a term at a time. Therefore, we would first include only **Reason** in the model, then in a separate analysis we would add the interaction. By doing so we can calculate the change in $-2LL$ for each effect. To save space I will put both into the model in a single step.

[6] As with **Surgery**, I've dragged **Reason** to the _Covariate(s)_ box because it is already dummy-coded (SPSS Tip 20.1).

FIGURE 20.20
The main mixed
models dialog
box

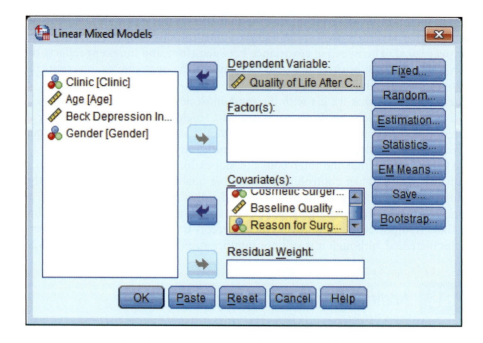

FIGURE 20.21
Specifying a
fixed effects
interaction in
mixed models

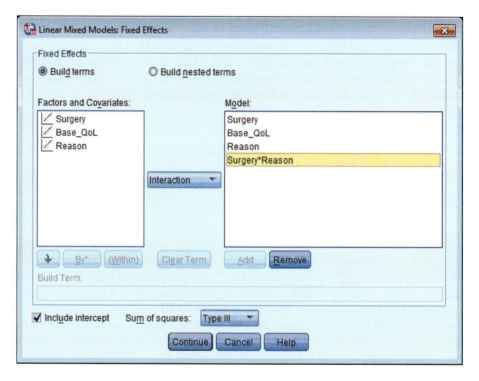

We need to add these fixed effects to our model, so click on ⬚ Fixed... ⬚ to bring up the dialog box in Figure 20.21. First, let's specify the main effect of **Reason**; to do this, select this variable in the list labelled *Factors and Covariates* and then click on ⬚ Add ⬚ to transfer it to *Model*. To specify the interaction term, first click on ⬚ Factorial ▼ ⬚ and change it to ⬚ Interaction ▼ ⬚. Next, select **Surgery** from *Factors and Covariates* and then, while holding down the *Ctrl* (*Cmd* on a Mac) key, select **Reason**. With both variables selected, click on ⬚ Add ⬚ to transfer them to *Model* as an interaction effect. The dialog box should now look like

Figure 20.21. Click on Continue to return to the main dialog box. We don't need to specify any extra random coefficients, so we can leave the dialog box accessed through Random... as it is in Figure 20.18, and we can leave the other options as they are in previous analyses. In the main dialog box click on OK to run the analysis.

OUTPUT 20.8

Model Dimension[a]

		Number of Levels	Covariance Structure	Number of Parameters	Subject Variables
Fixed Effects	Intercept	1		1	
	Surgery	1		1	
	Base_QoL	1		1	
	Reason	1		1	
	Surgery * Reason	1		1	
Random Effects	Intercept + Surgery[b]	2	Unstructured	3	Clinic
Residual				1	
Total		7		9	

a. Dependent Variable: Quality of Life After Cosmetic Surgery.

b. As of version 11.5, the syntax rules for the RANDOM subcommand have changed. Your command syntax may yield results that differ from those produced by prior versions. If you are using version 11 syntax, please consult the current syntax reference guide for more information.

df for −2LL

Information Criteria[a]

−2 Log Likelihood	1789.045
Akaike's Information Criterion (AIC)	1807.045
Hurvich and Tsai's Criterion (AICC)	1807.722
Bozdogan's Criterion (CAIC)	1848.629
Schwarz's Bayesian Criterion (BIC)	1839.629

−2LL

The information criteria are displayed in smaller-is-better forms.

a. Dependent Variable: Quality of Life After Cosmetic Surgery.

Type III Tests of Fixed Effects[a]

Source	Numerator df	Denominator df	F	Sig.
Intercept	1	108.853	122.593	.000
Surgery	1	15.863	2.167	.161
Base_QoL	1	268.920	33.647	.000
Reason	1	259.894	9.667	.002
Surgery * Reason	1	217.087	6.278	.013

a. Dependent Variable: Quality of Life After Cosmetic Surgery.

bs

Estimates of Fixed Effects[a]

Parameter	Estimate	Std. Error	df	t	Sig.	95% Confidence Interval	
						Lower Bound	Upper Bound
Intercept	42.517820	3.840055	108.853	11.072	.000	34.906839	50.128800
Surgery	−3.187677	2.165484	15.863	−1.472	.161	−7.781510	1.406157
Base_QoL	.305356	.052642	268.920	5.801	.000	.201713	.408999
Reason	−3.515148	1.130552	259.894	−3.109	.002	−5.741357	−1.288939
Surgery * Reason	4.221288	1.684798	217.087	2.506	.013	.900633	7.541944

a. Dependent Variable: Quality of Life After Cosmetic Surgery.

$Var(u_{0j})$ = variance of intercepts

$Var(\varepsilon_{ij})$ = variance of residuals

Estimates of Covariance Parameters[a]

Parameter		Estimate	Std. Error	Wald Z	Sig.	95% Confidence Interval	
						Lower Bound	Upper Bound
Residual		33.859719	3.024395	11.196	.000	28.421886	40.337948
Intercept + Surgery [subject = Clinic]	UN (1,1)	30.056340	15.444593	1.946	.052	10.978478	82.286775
	UN (2,1)	−28.083657	15.195713	−1.848	.065	−57.866706	1.699393
	UN (2,2)	29.349323	16.404492	1.789	.074	9.813593	87.774453

a. Dependent Variable: Quality of Life After Cosmetic Surgery.

$Cov(u_{0j}, u_{1j})$ = covariance of slopes and intercepts

$Var(u_{1j})$ = variance of slopes

Output 20.8 shows the resulting output, which is similar to the previous output, except that we now have two new fixed effects. The first issue is whether these new effects make a difference to the model. We can use the log-likelihood statistics again:

$$\chi^2_{\text{Change}} = 1798.62 - 1789.05 = 9.57$$

$$df_{\text{Change}} = 9 - 7 = 2$$

From the Appendix, the critical value for the chi-square statistic is 5.99 ($p < .05$, $df = 2$); therefore, this change is significant.

We can look at the effects individually in the *Type III Tests of Fixed Effects* table. This tells us that quality of life before surgery significantly predicted quality of life after surgery, $F(1, 268.92) = 33.65$, $p < .001$, surgery still did not significantly predict quality of life, $F(1, 15.86) = 2.17$, $p = .161$, but the reason for surgery, $F(1, 259.89) = 9.67$, $p = .002$, and the interaction of the reason for surgery and surgery, $F(1, 217.09) = 6.28$, $p = .013$, both did significantly predict quality of life. The *Estimates of Fixed Effects* table tells us much the same thing, except it also gives us the regression coefficients and their confidence intervals.

The values of the variance for the intercept (30.06) and the slope (29.35) are lower than in the previous model but still significant (more or less). Also the covariance between the slopes and intercepts is still negative (−28.08). As such, our conclusions about our random parameters stay much the same as in the previous model.

The interaction term is the most interesting effect, because this tells us the effect of the reason for surgery, taking account of whether or not the person had surgery. To break down this interaction we could rerun the analysis separately for the two 'reason groups'. Obviously we would remove the interaction term and the main effect of **Reason** from this analysis (because we are analysing the physical reason group separately from the group that wanted to change their appearance). As such, you need to fit the model in the previous section, but first split the file by **Reason**.

SELF-TEST   Split the file by **Reason** and then run a multilevel model predicting **Post_QoL** with a random intercept, and random slopes for **Surgery**, and including **Base_QoL** and **Surgery** as predictors.

Output 20.9 shows the parameter estimates from these analyses. For those operated on only to change their appearance, surgery almost significantly predicted quality of life after surgery, $b = -4.31$, $t(7.72) = -1.92$, $p = .09$. The negative gradient shows that in these people, quality of life was lower after surgery compared to the control group. However, for those who had surgery to solve a physical problem, surgery did not significantly predict quality of life, $b = 1.20$, $t(7.61) = 0.58$, $p = .58$. However, the slope was positive, indicating that people who had surgery scored higher on quality of life than those on the waiting list (although not significantly so). The interaction effect, therefore, reflects the difference in slopes for surgery as a predictor of quality of life in those who had surgery for physical problems (slight positive slope) and those who had surgery purely for vanity (a negative slope).

We could sum up these results by saying that quality of life after surgery, after controlling for quality of life before surgery, was lower for those who had surgery to change their appearance than those who had surgery for a physical reason. This makes sense because for those having surgery to correct a physical problem, the surgery has probably brought relief and so their quality of life will improve. However, those having surgery for vanity might well discover that having a different appearance wasn't actually at the root of their unhappiness, so their quality of life is lower.

Surgery for Cosmetic Reasons

Estimates of Fixed Effects[a,b]

Parameter	Estimate	Std. Error	df	t	Sig.	95% Confidence Interval Lower Bound	95% Confidence Interval Upper Bound
Intercept	41.786055	5.487873	77.331	7.614	.000	30.859052	52.713059
Surgery	-4.307014	2.239912	7.719	-1.923	.092	-9.505157	.891130
Base_QoL	.338492	.079035	88.619	4.283	.000	.181440	.495543

a. Reason for Surgery = Change Appearance

b. Dependent Variable: Quality of Life After Cosmetic Surgery.

Surgery for a Physical Reason

Estimates of Fixed Effects[a,b]

Parameter	Estimate	Std. Error	df	t	Sig.	95% Confidence Interval Lower Bound	95% Confidence Interval Upper Bound
Intercept	38.020790	4.666154	93.558	8.148	.000	28.755460	47.286119
Surgery	1.196550	2.081999	7.614	.575	.582	-3.647282	6.040382
Base_QoL	.317710	.068883	172.816	4.612	.000	.181749	.453670

a. Reason for Surgery = Physical reason

b. Dependent Variable: Quality of Life After Cosmetic Surgery.

CRAMMING SAM'S TIPS   **Multilevel models Output**

- The *Information Criteria* table can be used to assess the overall fit of the model. The $-2LL$ can be tested for significance with *df* = the number of parameters being estimated. It is mainly used, though, to compare models that are the same in all but one parameter by testing the difference in $-2LL$ in the two models against *df* = 1 (if only one parameter has been changed). The AIC, AICC, CAIC and BIC can also be compared across models (but not tested for significance).
- The table of *Type III Tests of Fixed Effects* tells you whether your predictors significantly predict the outcome: look in the column labelled *Sig*. If the value is less than .05 then the effect is significant.
- The table of *Estimates of Fixed Effects* gives us the regression coefficient for each effect and its confidence interval. The direction of these coefficients tells us whether the relationship between each predictor and the outcome is positive or negative.
- The table labelled *Estimates of Covariance Parameters* tells us about any random effects in the model. These values can tell us how much intercepts and slopes varied over our level 1 variable. The significance of these estimates should be treated cautiously. The exact labelling of these effects depends on which covariance structure you selected for the analysis.

20.7. Growth models ④

Growth models are extremely important in many areas of science, including psychology, medicine, physics, chemistry or economics. In a growth model the aim is to look at the rate of change of a variable over time: for example, we could look at white blood cell counts, attitudes, radioactive decay or profits. In all cases we're trying to see which model best describes the change over time.

ODITI'S LANTERN

Multilevel models

'I, Oditi, believe that you know that experimental manipulations happen within cults, erm, I mean contexts; and people within cults, erm, contexts become more similar to each other than to people outside of that cult, erm, context. To eliminate this dependency we must make everyone join our cult, erm, no, seriously, I mean we must factor the dependency by using a multilevel model. Stare into my lantern one last time and you will become worthy to call yourself one of my cult of undiscovered numerical truths.'

20.7.1. Growth curves (polynomials) ④

What is a growth curve?

Figure 20.22 shows three examples of **growth curves**: three **polynomials** representing a linear trend (the red line) otherwise known as a first-order polynomial, a quadratic trend (the green line) otherwise known as a second-order polynomial, and a cubic trend (the blue line) otherwise known as a third-order polynomial. Notice that the linear trend is a straight line, but as the polynomials increase they get more and more curved, indicating more rapid growth over time. Also, as polynomials increase, the change in the curve is quite dramatic (so dramatic that I had to adjust the scale of the y-axis on each graph to fit all three on the same diagram). This observation highlights the fact that any growth curve higher than a quadratic (or possibly cubic) trend is very unrealistic in real data. By fitting a growth model to the data we can see which trend best describes the growth of an outcome variable over time (though no one will believe that a significant fifth-order polynomial is telling us anything meaningful about the real world!).

The growth curves that we have described should seem familiar: they are the same as the trends that we described for ordered means in Section 11.4.5. What we're discussing now is really no different. There are two important things to remember when fitting growth curves: (1) you can fit polynomials up to one less than the number of time points that you have; and (2) a polynomial is defined by a simple power function. On the first point, this means that with three time points you can fit a linear and quadratic growth curve (or a first- and second-order polynomial), but you cannot fit any higher-order growth curves. Similarly, if you have six time points you can fit up to a fifth-order polynomial. This is the same basic idea as having one less contrast than the number of groups in ANOVA (see Section 11.4).

On the second point, we have to define growth curves manually in multilevel models: there is not a convenient option that we can select to do it for us. However, this is quite easy to do. If time is our predictor variable, then a linear trend is tested by including this variable alone. A quadratic or second-order polynomial is tested by including a predictor that is $time^2$, a cubic or third-order polynomial is tested by including a predictor that is $time^3$ and so on. Any polynomial is tested by including a variable that is the predictor to the power of the order of polynomial that you want to test: for a fifth-order polynomial we need a predictor of $time^5$ and for an n-order polynomial we would include $time^n$ as a predictor. Hopefully you get the general idea.

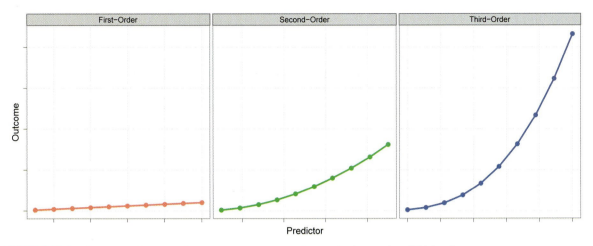

FIGURE 20.22   Illustration of a first-order (linear, red), second-order (quadratic, green) and third-order (cubic, blue) polynomial.

20.7.2.   An example: the honeymoon period ②

I once saw a brilliant talk given by Professor Daniel Kahneman, who won the 2002 Nobel Prize for Economics. In this talk Kahneman brought together an enormous amount of research on life satisfaction (he explored questions such as whether people are happier if they are richer). There was one graph in this talk that particularly grabbed my attention. It showed that, leading up to marriage, people reported greater life satisfaction, but by about two years after marriage this life satisfaction decreased back to its baseline level. This graph perfectly illustrated what people talk about as the 'honeymoon period': a new relationship/ marriage is great at first (no matter how ill suited you may be) but after six months or so the cracks start to appear and everything turns to elephant dung. Kahneman argued that people adapt to marriage; it does not make them happier in the long run (Kahneman & Krueger, 2006).[7] At the time of updating this chapter I am slap bang in the middle of this honeymoon period, so this example has particular saliency.

This talk got me thinking about whether we could apply this argument to any new relationship. Therefore, in a completely fictitious parallel world in which I concern myself with people's life satisfaction I organized a massive speed-dating event (see Chapter 15). At the start of the night I measured everyone's life satisfaction (**Satisfaction_Baseline**) on a 10-point scale (0 = completely dissatisfied, 10 = completely satisfied) and recorded their gender (**Gender**). After the speed dating I noted all of the people who had found dates. If they ended up in a relationship with the person they met on the speed-dating night then I stalked these people over the next 18 months of that relationship. At the end I had measures of their life satisfaction at 6 months (**Satisfaction_6_Months**), 12 months (**Satisfaction_12_Months**) and 18 months (**Satisfaction_18_Months**) after they entered the relationship. None of the people measured were in the same relationship (i.e., I measured life satisfaction only from one of the people in the couple).[8] Also, as is often the

---

[7] The romantics among you might be relieved to know that others have used the same data to argue the complete opposite: that married people are happier than non-married people in the long term (Easterlin, 2003).

[8] However, I could have measured both people in the couple because, using a multilevel model, I could have treated people as being nested within 'couples' to take account of the dependency in their data.

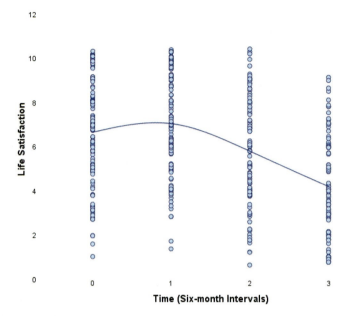

FIGURE 20.23
Life satisfaction over time

case with longitudinal data, I didn't have scores for all people at all time points because not everyone was available at the follow-up sessions. One of the benefits of a multilevel approach is that these missing data do not pose a particular problem. The data are in the file **Honeymoon Period.sav**.

Figure 20.23 shows the data. Each dot is a data point and the line shows the average life satisfaction over time. Basically, from baseline, life satisfaction rises slightly at time 1 (6 months) but then starts to decrease over the next 12 months. There are two things to note about the data. First, time 0 is before the people enter into their new relationship, yet already there is a lot of variability in their responses (reflecting the fact that people will vary in their satisfaction due to other reasons such as finances, personality and so on). This suggests that intercepts for life satisfaction differ across people. Second, there is also a lot of variability in life satisfaction after the relationship has started (time 1) and at all subsequent time points, which suggests that the slope of the relationship between time and life satisfaction might vary across people also. If we think of the time points as a level 1 variable that is nested with people (a level 2 variable) then we can easily model this variability in intercepts and slopes within people. We have a situation similar to Figure 20.4 (except with two levels instead of three).

FIGURE 20.24
The data editor for a normal repeated-measures data set

Person	Satisfaction_Base	Satisfaction_6_Months	Satisfaction_12_Months	Satisfaction_18_Months	Gender
1	6	6	5	2	Male
2	7	7	8	4	Female
3	4	6	2	2	Female
4	6	9	4	1	Male
5	6	7	6	6	Male
6	5	10	4	2	Female
7	6	6	4	2	Male
8	2	5	4		Male
9	10	9	5	6	Male

20.7.3. Restructuring the data ③

The first problem with having data measured over time is that to do a multilevel model the data need to be in a different format than we're used to. Figure 20.24 shows how we would normally set up the data editor for a repeated-measures design: each row represents a person, and the repeated-measures variable of time is represented by four different columns. If we were going to run an ordinary repeated-measures ANOVA this data layout would be fine; however, for a multilevel model we need the variable **Time** to be represented by a single column. We could enter all of the data again, but that would be a pain; luckily we don't have to do this because SPSS has a *restructure* command, which is also a pain, but not as much as retyping the data. This command enables you to take your data set and create a new data set that is organized differently (see Oliver Twisted).

OLIVER TWISTED

Please Sir, can I have some more … restructuring?

'I sat naked in the pouring rain, because SPSS had restructured my brain', sings Oliver to himself as he sits, erm, naked in the pouring rain. Horrid image. Anyway, if you would like your brain restructured then read Oliver's guide to using the restructure command in SPSS. Apparently it will restructure your data too.

SELF-TEST Use Oliver Twisted's guide to restructure the data file. Save the restructured file as **Honeymoon Period Restructured.sav**.

The restructured data are shown in Figure 20.25; it's useful to compare the restructured data with the old data file in Figure 20.24. Notice that each person is now represented by four rows (one for each time point) and that variables such as gender that are invariant over the time points have the same value within each person. However, our outcome variable (life satisfaction) does change over the four time points (the four rows for each person). You'll notice that the time points have values from 1 to 4. However, it's useful to centre this variable at 0 because our initial life satisfaction was measured before the new relationship. Therefore, an intercept of 0 is meaningful for these data: it is the value of life satisfaction when not in a relationship. By centring the scores on a baseline value of 0 we can interpret the intercept much more easily and intuitively. The easiest way to change the values is using the *compute* command to recompute **Time** to be **Time** minus 1. This will change the values from 1–4 to 0–3. If you can't be bothered with all of this use **Honeymoon Period Restructured.sav**.

SELF-TEST Use the compute command to transform **Time** into **Time** minus 1.

FIGURE 20.25
Data entry for a repeated-measures multilevel model

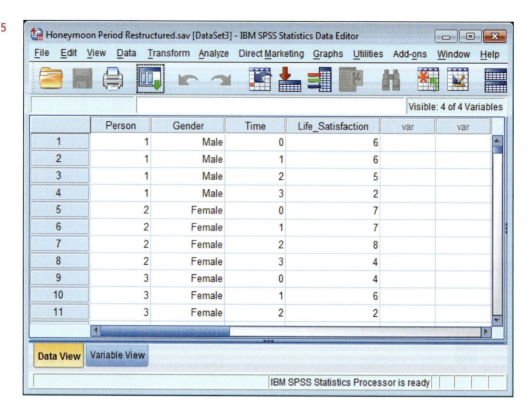

20.7.4. Running a growth model on SPSS ④

Now that we have our data set up, we can run the analysis. Essentially, we can set up this analysis in a very similar way to the previous example. First, select Analyze Mixed Models ▸ Linear… and in the initial dialog box set up the level 2 variable. In this example, life satisfaction at multiple time points is nested within people. Therefore, the level 2 variable is the person, and this variable is represented by the variable labelled **Person**. Select this variable and drag it to the box labelled *Subjects* (or click on ➡), as shown in Figure 20.26. Click on Continue to access the main dialog box.

In the main dialog box we need to set up our predictors and outcome. The outcome was life satisfaction, so select **Life_Satisfaction** and drag it to the box labelled *Dependent Variable* (or click on ➡). Our predictor, or growth variable, is **Time**, so select this variable and drag it to the box labelled *Covariate(s)*, or click on ➡, as shown in Figure 20.27.[9]

We need to add the potential growth curves that we want to test as fixed effects to our model, so click on Fixed… to bring up the *Fixed Effects* dialog box (Figure 20.28). In Section 20.7.1 we discussed different growth curves. With four time points we can fit up to a third-order polynomial. One way to do this would be to start with just the linear effect (**Time**), then run a new model with the linear and quadratic (**Time**^{2}) polynomials to see if the quadratic trend improves the model. Finally, run a third model with the linear, quadratic and cubic (**Time**^{3}) polynomial in, and see if the cubic trend adds to the model. So, basically, we add in polynomials one at a time and assess the change in $-2LL$. To specify the linear polynomial, click on **Time** and then click on Add to add it into the model. Click on Continue to return to the main dialog box.

---

[9] I have dragged **Time** to the *Covariate(s)* box because I want to treat it as a linear trend and not as a categorical variable (see SPSS Tip 20.1).

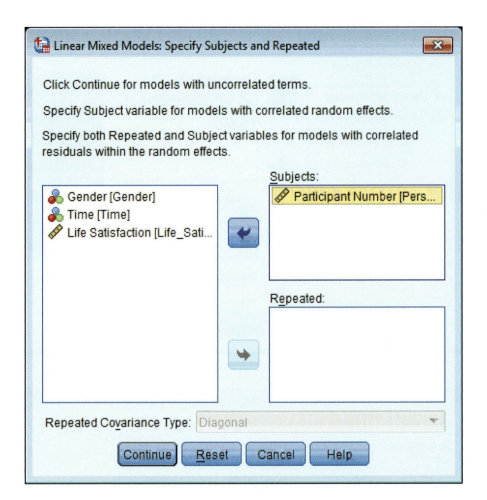

FIGURE 20.26
Setting up the
level 2 variable
in a growth
model

I mentioned earlier on that we expected the relationship between time and life satisfaction to have both a random intercept and a random slope. We need to define these parameters now by clicking on [Random...] in the main dialog box to access the dialog box in Figure 20.29. The first thing we need to do is to specify our contextual variable. We do this by selecting it from the list of contextual variables that we have told SPSS about already. These appear in the section labelled *Subjects*, and because we specified only **Person**, this variable is the only one listed. Select this variable and drag it to the area labelled *Combinations* (or click on [➡]). To specify that the intercept is random, select ☑ Include intercept, and to specify random slopes for the effect of **Time**, click on this variable in the *Factors and Covariates* list and then click on [Add] to include it in *Model*. Finally, we need to specify the covariance structure. By default, the covariance structure is set to Variance Components ▼ . However, when we have repeated measures over time it can be useful to specify a covariance structure that assumes that scores become less correlated over time (Section 20.4.2). Therefore, let's choose an autoregressive covariance structure, AR(1), and let's also assume that variances will be heterogeneous. Select AR(1): Heterogeneous ▼ from the drop-down list. Click on [Continue] to return to the main dialog box.

Click on [Estimation...] and select ◉ Maximum Likelihood (ML) and then click on [Statistics...] and select *Parameter estimates* and *Tests for covariance parameters* (see Figure 20.13). Click on [Continue] to return to the main dialog box. To run the analysis, click on [OK].

Output 20.10 shows the preliminary tables from the output. We can see that the linear trend was significant, $F(1, 106.72) = 134.26$, $p < .001$. For evaluating the improvement in the model when we add in new polynomials, we also need to note the value of $-2LL$,

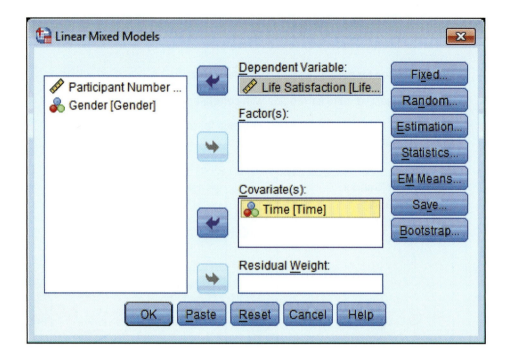

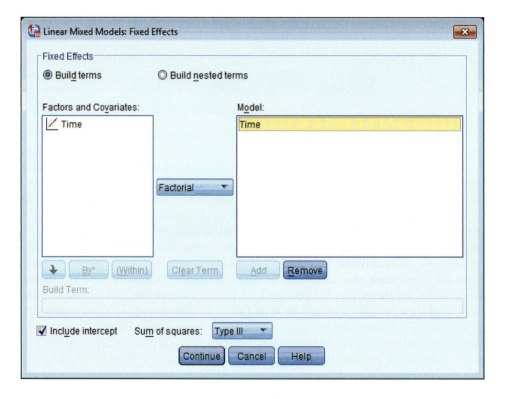

which is 1862.63, and the degrees of freedom, which are 6 (look at the row labelled *Total* in the column labelled *Number of Parameters*, in the table called *Model Dimension*).

Now, let's add the quadratic trend. To do this we return to the dialog box for fixed effects. Therefore, follow the instructions to run this analysis again until you reach the point where you click on Fixed… . The linear polynomial should already be specified from the last analysis and the dialog box will look like Figure 20.28. To add the higher-order

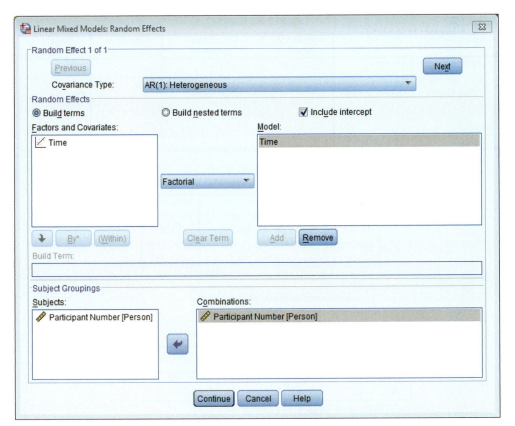

FIGURE 20.29
Defining
a random
intercept and
random slopes
in a growth
model

polynomials we need to select ⦿ Build nested terms. Select **Time** in the *Factors and Covariates* list and ⬇ will become active; click on this button and **Time** will appear in the space labelled *Model*. For the quadratic or second-order polynomial we need to define **Time**² (**Time** multiplied by itself), and we can specify this by clicking on By* to add a multiplication symbol to our term, then selecting **Time** again and clicking on ⬇. The *Build Term* bar should now read *Time*Time* (or to put it another way, **Time2**). This term is the second-order polynomial, and we click on Add to put it into the model (it will appear in the space labeled *Model*). Click on Continue to return to the main dialog box and click on OK to rerun the analysis.

The output will now include the quadratic polynomial. To see whether this quadratic trend has improved the model we need to compare the $-2LL$ for this model, to the value when only the linear polynomial was included. The value of $-2LL$ is 1802.03, as shown in Output 20.11. We have added only one term to the model so the new degrees of freedom will have risen by 1, from 6 to 7 (you can check that the new degrees of freedom are 7 in the row labelled *Total* in the column labelled *Number of Parameters*, in the table called *Model Dimension*). We can compute the change in $-2LL$ as a result of the quadratic term by subtracting the $-2LL$ for this model from the $-2LL$ for the model with only the linear trend:

$$\chi^2_{\text{Change}} = 1862.63 - 1802.03 = 60.60$$

$$df_{\text{Change}} = 7 - 6 = 1$$

From the Appendix, the critical values for the chi-square statistic for $df = 1$ are 3.84 ($p < .05$) and 6.63 ($p < .01$); therefore, this change is highly significant, because 60.60 is bigger than these values.

Model Dimension[a]

		Number of Levels	Covariance Structure	Number of Parameters	Subject Variables
Fixed Effects	Intercept	1		1	
	Time	1		1	
Random Effects	Intercept + Time	2	Heterogeneous First-Order Autoregressive	3	Person
Residual				1	
Total		4		6	

a. Dependent Variable: Life Satisfaction.

Information Criteria[a]

–2 Log Likelihood	1862.626
Akaike's Information Criterion (AIC)	1874.626
Hurvich and Tsai's Criterion (AICC)	1874.821
Bozdogan's Criterion (CAIC)	1905.119
Schwarz's Bayesian Criterion (BIC)	1899.119

The information criteria are displayed in smaller-is-better forms.

a. Dependent Variable: Life Satisfaction.

Type III Tests of Fixed Effects[a]

Source	Numerator df	Denominator df	F	Sig.
Intercept	1	113.653	1137.088	.000
Time	1	106.715	134.264	.000

a. Dependent Variable: Life Satisfaction.

Finally, let's add the cubic trend, which is defined as **Time**^{3} (or *Time*Time*Time*). Return to the dialog box for fixed effects: the linear and quadratic polynomials should already be specified and the dialog box will look like Figure 20.30. Make sure ⦿ Build nested terms is selected, then select **Time**, click on ⬇, click on By* , select **Time** again, click on ⬇, click on By* again, select **Time** for a third time, click on ⬇ and finally click on Add . This process should add the third-order polynomial (or *Time*Time*Time*) to the model,[10] as shown in Figure 20.31. Click on Continue to return to the main dialog box and click on OK to rerun the analysis.

The output will now include the cubic polynomial. To see whether this cubic trend has improved the model we again compare the $-2LL$ for this new model to the value in the previous model. The value of $-2LL$ is 1798.86, as shown in Output 20.12. We have added only one term to the model, so the new degrees of freedom will have risen by 1, from 7 to 8. We can compute the change in $-2LL$ as a result of the cubic term by subtracting the $-2LL$ for this model from the $-2LL$ for the model with the linear and quadratic trend:

$$\chi^2_{Change} = 1802.03 - 1798.86 = 3.17$$

$$df_{Change} = 8 - 7 = 1$$

[10] Should you ever want even higher-order polynomials (notwithstanding my remark about them having little real-world relevance) then you can extrapolate from what I have told you about the other polynomials; for example, for a fourth-order polynomial you go through the whole process again, but this time creating **Time**^{4} (or *Time*Time*Time*Time*).

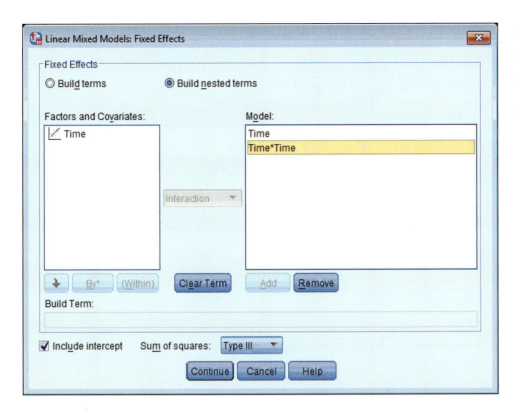

FIGURE 20.30
Specifying a linear trend (Time) and a quadratic trend (Time*Time)

OUTPUT 20.11

Information Criteria[a]

−2 Log Likelihood	1802.026
Akaike's Information Criterion (AIC)	1816.026
Hurvich and Tsai's Criterion (AICC)	1816.287
Bozdogan's Criterion (CAIC)	1851.602
Schwarz's Bayesian Criterion (BIC)	1844.602

The information criteria are displayed in smaller–is–better forms.

a. Dependent Variable: Life Satisfaction.

Using the same critical values for the chi-square statistic as before, we can conclude that this change is not significant, because 3.17 is less than the critical value of 3.84.

In the interests of parsimony, we should interpret the model that contained the quadratic term (because adding the cubic term did not improve the fit of the model). Output 20.13 shows the output for the model with the linear and quadratic trends included. The main part of the output is the table of fixed effects and the parameter estimates. These tell us that the linear, $F(1, 273.22) = 13.26, p < .001$, and quadratic, $F(1, 226.86) = 72.07, p < .001$, trends both significantly described the pattern of the data over time. These results confirm what we already know from comparing the fit of successive models. The trend in the data is best described by a second-order polynomial, or a quadratic trend. This trend reflects the initial increase in life satisfaction 6 months after finding a new partner but a subsequent reduction in life satisfaction at 12 and 18 months after the start of the relationship (Figure 20.23). The parameter estimates tell us much the same thing. It's worth remembering that this quadratic trend is only an *approximation*: if it were completely accurate then we would predict from the model that couples who had been together for 10 years would have negative life satisfaction, which is impossible, given the scale we used to measure it.

FIGURE 20.31
Specifying linear (*Time*), quadratic (*Time*Time*) and cubic (*Time*Time *Time*) trends

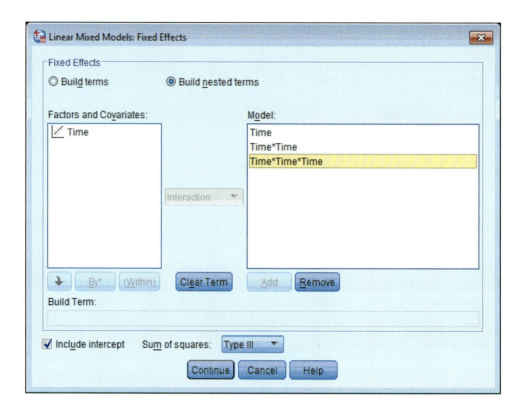

OUTPUT 20.12

Information Criteria[a]

–2 Log Likelihood	1798.857
Akaike's Information Criterion (AIC)	1814.857
Hurvich and Tsai's Criterion (AICC)	1815.193
Bozdogan's Criterion (CAIC)	1855.515
Schwarz's Bayesian Criterion (BIC)	1847.515

The information criteria are displayed in smaller–is–better forms.

a. Dependent Variable: Life Satisfaction.

The final part of the output tells us about the random parameters in the model. First of all, the variance of the random intercepts was $\text{Var}(u_{0j}) = 3.87$. This suggests that we were correct to assume that life satisfaction at baseline varied significantly across people. Also, the variance of the people's slopes varied significantly, $\text{Var}(u_{1j}) = 0.24$. This suggests also that the change in life satisfaction over time varied significantly across people too. Finally, the covariance between the slopes and intercepts (-0.37) suggests that as intercepts increased, the slope decreased. (Ideally, all of these terms should have been added in individually so that we could calculate the chi-square statistic for the change in $-2LL$ for each of them.)

20.7.5. Further analysis ④

It's worth pointing out that I've kept this growth curve analysis simple to give you the basic tools. In the example I allowed only the linear term to have a random intercept

Type III Tests of Fixed Effects[a]

Source	Numerator df	Denominator df	F	Sig.
Intercept	1	133.626	912.307	.000
Time	1	273.219	13.261	.000
Time * Time	1	226.857	72.069	.000

a. Dependent Variable: Life Satisfaction.

Estimates of Fixed Effects[a]

Parameter	Estimate	Std. Error	df	t	Sig.	95% Confidence Interval	
						Lower Bound	Upper Bound
Intercept	6.684546	.221310	133.626	30.204	.000	6.246822	7.122270
Time	.754482	.207185	273.219	3.642	.000	.346601	1.162364
Time * Time	-.562231	.066228	226.857	-8.489	.000	-.692731	-.431731

a. Dependent Variable: Life Satisfaction.

Estimates of Covariance Parameters[a]

Parameter		Estimate	Std. Error	Wald Z	Sig.	95% Confidence Interval	
						Lower Bound	Upper Bound
Residual		1.855235	.181149	10.241	.000	1.532095	2.246530
Intercept + Time [subject = Person]	Var: Intercept	3.867628	.699590	5.528	.000	2.713165	5.513318
	Var: Time	.242175	.097544	2.483	.013	.109972	.533308
	ARH1 rho	-.373673	.153978	-2.427	.015	-.631228	-.041891

a. Dependent Variable: Life Satisfaction.

LABCOAT LENI'S REAL RESEARCH 20.1

A fertile gesture ③

Most female mammals experience a phase of 'estrus' during which they are more sexually receptive, proceptive, selective and attractive. As such, the evolutionary benefit to this phase is believed to be to attract mates of superior genetic stock. However, some people have argued that this important phase became uniquely lost or hidden in human females. Geoffrey Miller and his colleagues reasoned that if the 'hidden-estrus' theory is incorrect then men should find women most attractive during the fertile phase of their menstrual cycle compared to the pre-fertile (menstrual) and post-fertile (luteal) phase.

To measure how attractive men found women in an ecologically valid way, they came up with the ingenious idea of collecting data from women working at lap-dancing clubs. These women maximize their tips from male visitors by attracting more dances. In effect the men 'try out' several dancers before choosing a dancer for a prolonged dance. For each dance the male pays a 'tip', therefore the greater the number of men choosing a

particular woman, the more her earnings will be. As such, each dancer's earnings are a good index of how attractive the male customers have found her. If the 'hidden-estrus' theory is incorrect then men will find the lap dancers more attractive during their estrus phase therefore they will earn more money. This study is a brilliant example of using a real-world phenomenon to address an important scientific question in an ecologically valid way.

The data for this study are in the file **Miller et al. (2007).sav**. The researchers collected data from several dancers (**ID**), who provided data for multiple lap-dancing shifts (so for each person there are several rows of data). They measured what phase of the menstrual cycle the women were in at a given shift (**Cyclephase**), and whether they were using hormonal contraceptives (**Contraceptive**), because this would affect their cycle. The outcome was their earnings on a given shift in dollars (**Tips**). The data are unbalanced: the women differed in the number of shifts for which they provided data (the range was 9 to 29 shifts).

Labcoat Leni wants you to carry out a multilevel model to see whether **Tips** can be predicted from **Cyclephase**, **Contraceptive** and their interaction. Is the 'estrus-hidden' hypothesis supported? Answers are on the companion website (or look at page 378 in the original article).

MILLER, G., TYBUR, J. M., & JORDAN, D. B. (2007). *EVOLUTION AND HUMAN BEHAVIOR, 28,* 375–381.

and slopes, but given that we discovered that a second-order polynomial described the change in responses, we could redo the analysis and allow random intercepts and slopes for the second-order polynomial also. To do these we would just have to specify these terms in Figure 20.29 in much the same way as we set them up as fixed effects in Figure 20.30. If we were to do this it would make sense to add the random components one at a time and test whether they have a significant impact on the model by comparing the log-likelihood values or other fit indices. Also, the polynomials I have described are not the only ones that can be used. You could test for a logarithmic trend over time, or even an exponential one.

CRAMMING SAM'S TIPS   Growth models

- Growth models are multilevel models in which changes in an outcome over time are modelled using potential growth patterns.
- These growth patterns can be linear, quadratic, cubic, logarithmic, exponential, or anything you like, really.
- The hierarchy in the data is that time points are nested within people (or other entities). As such, it's a way of analysing repeated-measures data that have a hierarchical structure.
- The *Information Criteria* table can be used to assess the overall fit of the model. The $-2LL$ can be tested for significance with $df =$ the number of parameters being estimated. It is mainly used, though, to compare models that are the same in all but one parameter by testing the difference in $-2LL$ in the two models against $df = 1$ (if only one parameter has been changed). The AIC, AICC, CAIC and BIC can also be compared across models (but not tested for significance).
- The table of *Type III Tests of Fixed Effects* tells you whether the growth functions that you have entered into the model significantly predict the outcome: look in the column labelled *Sig.* If the value is less than .05 then the effect is significant.
- The table labelled *Estimates of Covariance Parameters* tells us about any random effects in the model. These values can tell us how much intercepts and slopes varied over our level 1 variable. The significance of these estimates should be treated cautiously. The exact labelling of these effects depends on which covariance structure you selected for the analysis.
- An autoregressive covariance structure, AR(1), is often assumed in time course data such as that in growth models.

20.8.   How to report a multilevel model ③

Specific advice on reporting multilevel models is hard to come by. Also, the models themselves can take on so many forms that giving standard advice is not straightforward. If you have built up your model from one with only fixed parameters to one with a random intercept, and then random slope, it is advisable to report all stages of this process (or at the very least report the fixed-effects-only model and the final model). For any model you need to say something about the random effects. For the final model of the cosmetic surgery example you could write something like:

✓ The relationship between surgery and quality of life showed significant variance in intercepts across participants, $\text{Var}(u_{0j}) = 30.06$, $\chi^2(1) = 15.05$, $p < .01$. In addition, the slopes varied across participants, $\text{Var}(u_{1j}) = 29.35$, $\chi^2(1) = 21.49$, $p < .01$, and the slopes and intercepts negatively and significantly covaried, $\text{Cov}(u_{0j}, u_{1j}) = -28.08$, $\chi^2(1) = 17.38$, $p < .01$.

For the model itself, you have two choices. The first is to report the results rather like an ANOVA, with the *F*s and degrees of freedom for the fixed effects, and then report the parameters for the random effects in the text as well. The second is to produce a table of parameters as you would for regression. For example, you might report the cosmetic surgery example as follows:

✓ Quality of life before surgery significantly predicted quality of life after surgery, $F(1, 268.92) = 33.65$, $p < .001$, surgery did not significantly predict quality of life, $F(1, 15.86) = 2.17$, $p = .161$, but the reason for surgery, $F(1, 259.89) = 9.67$, $p = .002$, and the interaction of the reason for surgery and surgery, $F(1, 217.09) = 6.28$, $p = .013$, both significantly predicted quality of life. This interaction was broken down by conducting separate multilevel models on the 'physical reason' and 'attractiveness reason'. The models specified were the same as the main model, but excluded the main effect and interaction term involving the reason for surgery. These analyses showed that for those operated on only to change their appearance, surgery almost significantly predicted quality of life after surgery, $b = -4.31$, $t(7.72) = -1.92$, $p = .09$: quality of life was lower after surgery compared to the control group. However, for those who had surgery to solve a physical problem, surgery did not significantly predict quality of life, $b = 1.20$, $t(7.61) = 0.58$, $p = .58$. The interaction effect, therefore, reflects the difference in slopes for surgery as a predictor of quality of life in those who had surgery for physical problems (slight positive slope) and those who had surgery purely for vanity (a negative slope).

Alternatively you could present parameter information in a table:

	b	SE$_b$	95% CI
Baseline QoL	0.31	0.05	0.20, 0.41
Surgery	−3.19	2.17	−7.78, 1.41
Reason	−3.51	1.13	−5.74, −1.29
Surgery × Reason	4.22	1.68	0.90, 7.54

20.9. A message from the octopus of inescapable despair ①

When I started writing this chapter I didn't know anything about multilevel models, but by its completion I felt a tiny bit smug that I had them nailed. However, I don't, and if you now feel like you understand multilevel models too, then you're wrong. You're not wrong because you're daft, but because multilevel modelling is very complicated and this chapter barely scratches the surface of what there is to know. Multilevel models often fail to converge, with no apology or explanation, and trying to fathom out what's happening can feel like hammering nails into your head.

20.10. Brian's attempt to woo Jane ①

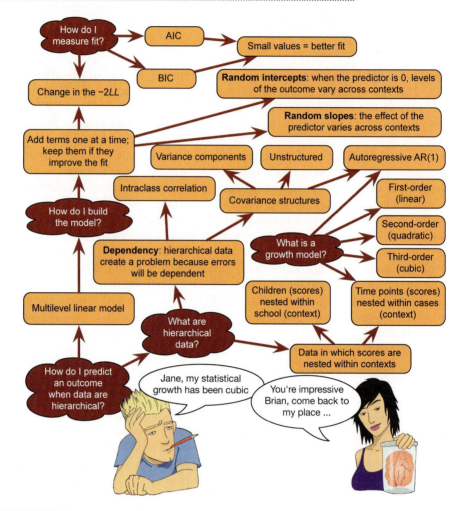

FIGURE 20.32 What Brian learnt from this chapter

20.11. What next? ②

This brings my life story up to date. Admittedly I left out some of the more colourful bits, but only because I couldn't find an extremely tenuous way to link them to statistics. We saw that over my life I managed to completely fail to achieve any of my childhood dreams. It's OK, I have other ambitions now (on a slightly smaller scale than 'rock star') and I'm looking forward to failing to achieve them too. I did at least manage to marry my lovely wife. Writing this chapter, like marriage, was a leap into the unknown. Marriage, however, has proved to be infinitely more enjoyable than writing about multilevel models. I think marriage is a useful metaphor for learning about statistics: if you think about both things logically you might never do them because they are full of uncertainty and potential scariness. However, you have to just go with your heart knowing that jumping into them will enrich you. Admittedly the kind of enrichment that marriage bestows is more obviously pleasant than knowing about autoregressive covariance structures, but statistics does give you enormous power to negotiate the scientific world (not just as practising scientists, but as normal people evaluating the often misleading media reports of scientific findings).

My wife and I think a lot about what makes a marriage work, and we think it comes down to reciprocal effort to enrich the other person's life. There is a parallel to this book: you and I have entered into a statistical relationship of sorts. For my part, I've put as much effort as I can into trying to pass on what I know about statistics, and if you have reciprocated that effort in reading the book and working through the examples, then hopefully our time together has enriched you. In return, your reactions to this book, more often than not, enrich me …

20.12. Key terms that I've discovered

AIC	Fixed effect	Polynomial
AICC	Fixed intercept	Random coefficient
AR(1)	Fixed slope	Random effect
BIC	Fixed variable	Random intercept
CAIC	Grand mean centring	Random slope
Centring	Group mean centring	Random variable
Diagonal	Growth curve	Unstructured
Fixed coefficient	Multilevel linear model	Variance components

20.13. Smart Alex's tasks

- **Task 1:** Using the cosmetic surgery example, run the analysis described in Section 20.6.5 but also including BDI, age and gender as fixed effect predictors. What differences does including these predictors make? ④

- **Task 2:** Using our growth model example in this chapter, analyse the data but include **Gender** as an additional covariate. Does this change your conclusions? ④

- **Task 3:** Hill, Abraham, and Wright (2007) examined whether providing children with a leaflet based on the 'theory of planned behaviour' increased their exercise. There were four different interventions (**Intervention**): a control group, a leaflet, a leaflet and quiz, and a leaflet and plan. A total of 503 children from 22 different classrooms were sampled (**Classroom**). The 22 classrooms were randomly assigned to the four different conditions. Children were asked 'On average over the last three weeks, I have exercised energetically for at least 30 minutes _____ times per week' after the intervention (**Post_Exercise**). Run a multilevel model analysis on these data (**Hill et al. (2007).sav**) to see whether the intervention affected the children's exercise levels (the hierarchy is children within classrooms within interventions). ④

- **Task 4:** Repeat the analysis in Task 3 but include the pre-intervention exercise scores (**Pre_Exercise**) as a covariate. What difference does this make to the results? ④

Answers can be found on the companion website.

20.14. Further reading

Baguley, T. (2012). *Serious stats: A guide to advanced statistics for the behavioural sciences.* Basingstoke: Palgrave Macmillan.

Gelman, A., & Hill, J. (2007). *Data analysis using regression and multilevel/hierarchical models.* Cambridge: Cambridge University Press.

Kreft, I., & de Leeuw, J. (1998). *Introducing multilevel modeling.* London: Sage. (This is a fantastic book that is easy to get into but has a lot of depth too.)

Twisk, J. W. R. (2006). *Applied multilevel analysis: A practical guide.* Cambridge: Cambridge University Press. (An exceptionally clearly written introduction to multilevel modelling aimed at novices. This book is the best beginners' guide that I have read.)

Epilogue: life after discovering statistics

Here's some questions that the writer sent
Can an observer be a participant?
Have I seen too much?
Does it count if it doesn't touch?
If the view is all I can ascertain,
Pure understanding is out of range.

(Fugazi, 2001)

When I wrote the first edition of this book my main ambition was to write a statistics book that I would enjoy reading. Pretty selfish, I know. I thought that if I had a reference book that had a few examples that amused me then it would make life a lot easier when I needed to look something up. I honestly didn't think anyone would buy the thing (well, apart from my mum and dad) and I anticipated a glut of feedback along the lines of 'the whole of Chapter X is completely wrong and you're an arrant fool', or 'you should be ashamed of how many trees have died in the name of this rubbish, you brainless idiot'. In fact, the publishers didn't think it would sell and made me do the typesetting to save money and cut their losses. I like to remind them of this story whenever the opportunity arises. There are several other things that I didn't expect to happen.

21.1. Nice emails

I didn't expect to receive hundreds of extremely nice emails from people who liked the book. To this day it still absolutely amazes me that anyone reads it, let alone takes the time to write me a nice email. Knowing that the book has helped people always puts a huge smile on my face. When the nice comments are followed by four pages of statistics questions, the smile fades a bit …

21.2. Everybody thinks that I'm a statistician

I should have seen this one coming, really, but since writing a statistics textbook everyone assumes that I'm a statistician. I'm not, I'm a psychologist. Consequently, I constantly disappoint people by not being able to answer their statistics questions. In fact, this book is the sum total of my knowledge about statistics; there is nothing else (statistics-wise) in my brain that isn't in this book. In fact, there is more in this book about statistics than in my brain. For example, in the logistic regression chapter there is an example on multinomial logistic regression. To write this section I read a lot about multinomial logistic regression because I'd never used it. I wrote that section about four years ago, and I've forgotten it all. Should I ever need to do a multinomial logistic regression I will read the chapter in this book and think to myself 'wow, it really sounds as though I know what I'm talking about'.

21.3. Craziness on a grand scale

The nicest thing about life after discovering statistics is the effort that people go to to demonstrate that they are even stranger than me. Figure 21.1, for example, shows how Anna Andreassen and her friends turned themselves into a human regression line after reading this book. That's right, *a human regression line*. Bonkers.

21.3.1. Catistics

Inspired by my photo of Fuzzy, people started sending me pictures of their own cat with my book (see the prelims). Checkout my *discovering catistics* Facebook page at http://ow.ly/ai6IN. There has been many a week where one of these in my inbox has turned what was going to be a steaming turd of a day into a fragrant romp through fields of tulips. How can you not get a big stupid grin on your face when you see a cat reading a statistics book?

Even more crazy, people have now started sending me pictures of dogs, parrots, lizards, and even their young children. Please, someone, send me a photo of a quokka reading my book.

FIGURE 21.1
Don't do this at home, kids … it's a human regression line

21.3.2. Cult of underlying numerical truths

Just like Oditi, I have managed to get myself a cult. It all started with two people from Exeter (UK), whom I have never met, setting up an 'Andy Field Appreciation Society' on Facebook. I didn't go there often, because it scared me a bit. But secretly I thought it was quite cool. It was almost like being the rock star that I always wanted to be, except that when people join a rock star's appreciation society they don't do it ironically. Nevertheless, beggars can't be choosers and I'm happy to overlook a technicality such as the truth if it means that I can believe that I'm popular. Anyway, I set up a Facebook page of my own (http://www.facebook.com/ProfAndyField) and a Twitter account (@ProfAndyField) and, amazingly, people follow me. I mean, not as many people as follow Justin Bieber, but more people than would follow me if I hadn't written a statistics book.

I've had a film made about the book. Admittedly it hasn't got as many special effects as *Spiderman*, but I was in equal parts crippled with laughter and utterly bemused watching the work of Julie-Renée Kabriel and her bonkers friends from Washburn University (sadly not on YouTube any more). (It was a song to the tune of 'Sweet Home Alabama' by Lynyrd Skynyrd; I once gave a talk at Aberdeen University (UK) after which I got taken to a bar and ended up, quite unexpectedly, playing drums to that song with a makeshift band of complete strangers.)

21.3.3. And then it got really weird

Possibly the icing on this bizarre cake was being invited to an autopsy by some forensic scientists in Leicester. They felt that the most appropriate reward for my book writing efforts would be to take me to see a dead body being carved up (or to spend a day visiting crime scenes). In a strange way, I can see their logic. I didn't go, because I like to live life pretending that death doesn't exist.

I was also befriended by the manager of a black metal band who, while using my book for her studies, noticed that I like black metal bands. My band was playing the next week in London and I invited them along, then they invited me back. They renamed me 'The Evil Statistic'.

All of these people have made life after *Discovering Statistics* a profoundly enjoyable experience. I never cease to be touched and amused by how enthusiastic people are about this book. When I started the first edition I never dreamed that I'd be writing a fourth edition, or that it would become such a massive part of my life. It has changed my life. I recommend writing a statistics book: you get a constant warm fuzzy feeling from strangers telling you that you've helped them, you get photos of their pets, they make films about you, they give you CDs, you get a cult, you can go to see corpses being cut up (if you like that sort of thing), join a black metal band (if their drummer's arms and legs fall off, who knows?) and have people constantly overestimate your intelligence. It's been a fantastic ride. Long may the craziness continue.

GLOSSARY

O: the amount of a clue that Sage have about how much effort I put into writing this book.

−2LL: the *log-likelihood* multiplied by minus 2. This version of the likelihood is used in *logistic regression*.

α-level: the probability of making a *Type I error* (usually this value is .05).

A Life: what you don't have when writing statistics textbooks.

Adjusted mean: in the context of *analysis of covariance* this is the value of the group mean adjusted for the effect of the *covariate*.

Adjusted predicted value: a measure of the influence of a particular case of data. It is the predicted value of a case from a model estimated without that case included in the data. The value is calculated by re-estimating the model without the case in question, then using this new model to predict the value of the excluded case. If a case does not exert a large influence over the model then its predicted value should be similar regardless of whether the model was estimated including or excluding that case. The difference between the predicted value of a case from the model when that case was included and the predicted value from the model when it was excluded is the *DFFit*.

Adjusted R^2: a measure of the loss of predictive power or *shrinkage* in regression. The adjusted R^2 tells us how much variance in the outcome would be accounted for if the model had been derived from the population from which the sample was taken.

AIC (Akaike's information criterion): a *goodness-of-fit* measure that is corrected for model complexity. That just means that it takes into account how many parameters have been estimated. It is not intrinsically interpretable, but can be compared in different models to see how changing the model affects the fit. A small value represents a better fit of the data.

AICC (Hurvich and Tsai's criterion): a *goodness-of-fit* measure that is similar to *AIC* but is designed for small samples. It is not intrinsically interpretable, but can be compared in different models to see how changing the model affects the fit. A small value represents a better fit of the data.

Alpha factoring: a method of *factor analysis*.

Alternative hypothesis: the prediction that there will be an effect (i.e., that your experimental manipulation will have some effect or that certain variables will relate to each other).

Analysis of covariance: a statistical procedure that uses the *F-ratio* to test the overall fit of a linear model, controlling for the effect that one or more *covariates* have on the *outcome variable*. In experimental research this linear model tends to be defined in terms of group means, and the resulting ANOVA is therefore an overall test of whether group means differ after the variance in the outcome variable explained by any *covariates* has been removed.

Analysis of variance: a statistical procedure that uses the *F-ratio* to test the overall fit of a linear model. In experimental research this linear model tends to be defined in terms of group means, and the resulting ANOVA is therefore an overall test of whether group means differ.

ANCOVA: acronym for *analysis of covariance*.

Anderson–Rubin method: a way of calculating *factor scores* which produces scores that are uncorrelated and *standardized* with a mean of 0 and a standard deviation of 1.

ANOVA: acronym for *analysis of variance*.

AR(1): this stands for first-order autoregressive structure. It is a covariance structure used in *multilevel linear models* in which the relationship between scores changes in a systematic way. It is assumed that the correlation between scores gets smaller over time and that variances are homogeneous. This structure is often used for repeated-measures data (especially when measurements are taken over time, such as in growth models).

Autocorrelation: when the *residuals* of two observations in a regression model are correlated.

b_i: unstandardized regression coefficient. Indicates the strength of relationship between a given predictor, i, of many and an outcome in the units of measurement of the predictor. It is the change in the outcome associated with a unit change in the predictor.

β_i: standardized regression coefficient. Indicates the strength of relationship between a given predictor, i, of many and an outcome in a *standardized* form. It is the change in the outcome (in standard deviations) associated with a one standard deviation change in the predictor.

β-level: the probability of making a *Type II error* (Cohen, 1992, suggests a maximum value of .2).

Bar chart: a graph in which a summary statistic (usually the mean) is plotted on the *y*-axis against a categorical variable on the *x*-axis (this categorical variable could represent, for example, groups of people, different times or different experimental conditions). The value of the mean for each category is shown by a bar. Different-coloured bars may be used to represent levels of a second categorical variable.

Bartlett's test of sphericity: unsurprisingly, this is a test of the assumption of *sphericity*. This test examines whether a *variance–covariance matrix* is proportional to an *identity matrix*. Therefore, it effectively tests whether the diagonal elements of the variance–covariance matrix are equal (i.e., group variances are the same), and whether the off-diagonal elements are approximately zero (i.e., the *dependent variables* are not *correlated*). Jeremy Miles, who does a lot of multivariate stuff, claims he's never ever seen a matrix that reached non-significance using this test and, come to think of it, I've never seen one either (although I do less multivariate stuff), so you've got to wonder about it's practical utility.

Beer-goggles effect: the phenomenon that people of the opposite gender (or the same, depending on your sexual orientation) appear much more attractive after a few alcoholic drinks.

Between-groups design: another name for *independent design*.

Between-subjects design: another name for *independent design*.

BIC (Schwarz's Bayesian criterion): a *goodness-of-fit* statistic comparable to the AIC, although it is slightly more conservative (it corrects more harshly for the number of parameters being estimated). It should be used when sample sizes are large and the number of parameters is small. It is not intrinsically interpretable, but can be compared in different models to see how changing the model affects the fit. A small value represents a better fit of the data.

Bimodal: a description of a distribution of observations that has two *modes*.

Binary logistic regression: *logistic regression* in which the outcome variable has exactly two categories.

Binary variable: a *categorical variable* that has only two mutually exclusive categories (e.g., being dead or alive).

Biserial correlation: a standardized measure of the strength of relationship between two variables when one of the two variables is *dichotomous.* The biserial correlation coefficient is used when one variable is a continuous dichotomy (e.g., has an underlying continuum between the categories).

Bivariate correlation: a correlation between two variables.

Blockwise regression: another name for *hierarchical regression*.

Bonferroni correction: a correction applied to the *α-level* to control the overall *Type I error rate* when multiple significance tests are carried out. Each test conducted should use a criterion of significance of the *α-level* (normally .05) divided by the number of tests conducted. This is a simple but effective correction, but tends to be too strict when lots of tests are performed.

Bootstrap: a technique from which the sampling distribution of a statistic is estimated by taking repeated samples (with replacement) from the data set (in effect, treating the data as a population from which smaller samples are taken). The statistic of interest (e.g., the *mean*, or *b* coefficient) is calculated for each sample, from which the sampling distribution of the statistic is estimated. The standard error of the statistic is estimated as the standard deviation of the sampling distribution created from the bootstrap samples. From this, confidence intervals and significance tests can be computed.

Boredom effect: refers to the possibility that performance in tasks may be influenced (the assumption is a negative influence) by boredom or lack of concentration if there are many tasks, or the task goes on for a long period of time. In short, what you are experiencing reading this glossary is a boredom effect.

Boxplot (a.k.a. box–whisker diagram)**:** a graphical representation of some important characteristics of a set of observations. At the centre of the plot is the *median*, which is surrounded by a box, the top and bottom of which are the limits within which the middle 50% of observations fall (the *interquartile range*). Sticking out of the top and bottom of the box are two whiskers which extend to the highest and lowest extreme scores, respectively.

Box's test: a test of the assumption of *homogeneity of covariance matrices*. This test should be non-significant if the matrices are roughly the same. Box's test is very susceptible to deviations from *multivariate normality*, and so may be non-significant not because the *variance–covariance matrices* are similar across groups, but because the assumption of multivariate normality is not tenable. Hence, it is vital to have some idea of whether the data meet the multivariate normality assumption (which is extremely difficult) before interpreting the result of Box's test.

Box–whisker plot: see *Boxplot*.

Brown–Forsythe *F*: a version of the *F*-ratio designed to be accurate when the assumption of *homogeneity of variance* has been violated.

CAIC (Bozdogan's criterion): a *goodness-of-fit* measure similar to the *AIC*, but correcting for model complexity and sample size. It is not intrinsically interpretable, but can be compared in different models to see how changing the model affects the fit. A small value represents a better fit of the data.

Categorical variable: The university you attend is a good example of a categorical variable: students who attend the University of Sussex are not also enrolled at Harvard or UV Amsterdam, therefore, students fall into distinct categories.

Central limit theorem: this theorem states that when samples are large (above about 30) the *sampling distribution* will take the shape of a *normal distribution* regardless of the shape of the population from which the sample was drawn. For small samples the *t*-distribution better approximates the shape of the sampling distribution. We also know from this theorem that the *standard deviation* of the sampling distribution (i.e., the *standard error* of the sample *mean*) will be equal to the standard deviation of the sample(s) divided by the square root of the sample size (N).

Central tendency: a generic term describing the centre of a *frequency distribution* of observations as measured by the *mean*, *mode* and *median*.

Centring: the process of transforming a variable into deviations around a fixed point. This fixed point can be any value that is chosen, but typically a mean is used. To centre a variable the mean is subtracted from each score. See *Grand mean centring*, *Group mean centring*.

Chartjunk: superfluous material that distracts from the data being displayed on a graph.

Chi-square distribution: a *probability distribution* of the sum of squares of several normally distributed variables. It tends to be used to test hypotheses about categorical data, and to test the fit of models to the observed data.

Chi-square test: although this term can apply to any *test statistic* having a *chi-square distribution*, it generally refers to Pearson's chi-square test of the independence of two categorical variables. Essentially it tests whether two categorical variables forming a *contingency table* are associated.

Cochran's Q: This test is an extension of *McNemar's test* and is basically a *Friedman's ANOVA* for *dichotomous* data. So imagine you asked 10 people whether they'd like to shoot Justin Timberlake, David Beckham and Simon Cowell and they could answer only 'yes' or 'no'. If we coded responses as 0 (no) and 1 (yes) we could do Cochran's test on these data.

Coefficient of determination: the proportion of variance in one variable explained by a second variable. It is *Pearson's correlation coefficient* squared.

Cohen's d: An *effect size* that expressed the difference between two means in standard deviation units. In general it can be estimated using:

$$\hat{d} = \frac{\overline{X}_1 - \overline{X}_2}{s}$$

Common factor: a *factor* that affects all measured *variables* and, therefore, explains the *correlations* between those variables.

Common variance: variance shared by two or more variables.

Communality: the proportion of a variable's variance that is *common variance*. This term is used primarily in *factor analysis*. A variable that has no *unique variance* (or *random variance*) would have a communality of 1, whereas a variable that shares none of its variance with any other variable would have a communality of 0.

Complete separation: a situation in *logistic regression* when the outcome variable can be perfectly predicted by one predictor or a combination of predictors! Suffice it to say this situation makes your computer have the equivalent of a nervous breakdown: it'll start gibbering, weeping and saying it doesn't know what to do.

Component matrix: general term for the *structure matrix* in *principal component analysis*.

Compound symmetry: a condition that holds true when both the variances across conditions are equal (this is the same as the *homogeneity of variance* assumption) and the *covariances* between pairs of conditions are also equal.

Concurrent validity: a form of *criterion validity* where there is evidence that scores from an instrument correspond to concurrently recorded external measures conceptually related to the measured construct.

Confidence interval: for a given statistic calculated for a sample of observations (e.g., the mean), the confidence interval is a range of values around that statistic that are believed to contain, with a certain probability (e.g., 95%), the true value of that statistic (i.e., the population value).

Confirmatory factor analysis (CFA): a version of *factor analysis* in which specific hypotheses about structure and relations between the *latent variables* that underlie the data are tested.

Confounding variable: a variable (that we may or may not have measured) other than the *predictor variables* in which we're interested that potentially affects an *outcome variable*.

Contaminated normal distribution: see *mixed normal distribution*.

Content validity: evidence that the content of a test corresponds to the content of the construct it was designed to cover.

Contingency table: a table representing the cross-classification of two or more *categorical variables*. The levels of each variable are arranged in a grid, and the number of observations falling into each category is noted in the cells of the table. For example, if we took the categorical variables of **glossary** (with two categories: whether an author was made to write a glossary or not), and **mental state** (with three categories: normal, sobbing uncontrollably and utterly psychotic), we could construct a table as below. This instantly tells us that 127 authors who were made to write a glossary ended up as utterly psychotic, compared to only 2 who did not write a glossary.

		Glossary		
		Author made to write glossary	No glossary	Total
Mental state	Normal	5	423	428
	Sobbing uncontrollably	23	46	69
	Utterly psychotic	127	2	129
	Total	155	471	626

Continuous variable: a variable that can be measured to any level of precision. (Time is a continuous variable, because there is in principle no limit on how finely it could be measured.)

Cook's distance: a measure of the overall influence of a case on a model. Cook and Weisberg (1982) have suggested that values greater than 1 may be cause for concern.

Correlation coefficient: a measure of the strength of association or relationship between two variables. See *Pearson's correlation coefficient*, *Spearman's correlation coefficient*, *Kendall's tau*.

Correlational research: a form of research in which you observe what naturally goes on in the world without directly interfering with it. This term implies that data will be analysed so as to look at relationships between naturally occurring variables rather than making statements about cause and effect. Compare with *cross-sectional research*, *longitudinal research* and *experimental research*.

Counterbalancing: a process of systematically varying the order in which experimental conditions are conducted. In the simplest case of there being two conditions (A and B), counterbalancing simply implies that half of the participants complete condition A followed by condition B, whereas the remainder do condition B followed by condition A. The aim is to remove systematic bias caused by *practice effects* or *boredom effects*.

Covariance: a measure of the 'average' relationship between two variables. It is the average *cross-product deviation* (i.e., the cross-product divided by one less than the number of observations).

Covariance ratio (CVR): a measure of whether a case influences the variance of the parameters in a *regression model*. When this ratio is close to 1 the case has very little influence on the variances of the model parameters. Belsey et al. (1980) recommend the following: if the CVR of a case is greater than $1 + [3(k + 1)/n]$ then deleting that case will damage the precision of some of the model's parameters, but if it is less than $1 - [3(k + 1)/n]$ then deleting the case will improve the precision of some of the model's parameters (k is the number of predictors and n is the sample size).

Covariate: a variable that has a relationship with (in terms of *covariance*), or has the potential to be related to, the *outcome variable* we've measured.

Cox and Snell's R^2_{CS}: a version of the *coefficient of determination* for logistic regression. It is based on the log-likelihood of a model (LL(new)) and the log-likelihood of the original model (LL(baseline)), and the sample size, n. However, it is notorious for not reaching its maximum value of 1 (see *Nagelkerke's R^2_N*).

Cramér's V: a measure of the strength of association between two *categorical variables* used when one of these variables has more than two categories. It is a variant of *phi* used because when one or both of the categorical variables contain more than two categories, phi fails to reach its minimum value of 0 (indicating no association).

Criterion validity: evidence that scores from an instrument correspond with (*concurrent validity*) or predict (*predictive validity*) external measures conceptually related to the measured construct.

Cronbach's α: a measure of the reliability of a scale defined by

$$\alpha = \frac{N^2 \overline{Cov}}{\sum s^2_{item} + \sum Cov_{item}}$$

in which the top half of the equation is simply the number of items (N) squared multiplied by the average covariance between items (the average of the off-diagonal elements in the *variance–covariance matrix*). The bottom half is the sum of all the elements in the *variance–covariance matrix*.

Cross-product deviations: a measure of the 'total' relationship between two variables. It is the deviation of one variable from its mean multiplied by the other variable's deviation from its mean.

Cross-sectional research: a form of research in which you observe what naturally goes on in the world without directly interfering with it, by measuring several variables at a single time point. In psychology, this term usually implies that data come from people at different age points, with different people representing each age point. See also *correlational research*, *longitudinal research*.

Cross-validation: assessing the accuracy of a model across different samples. This is an important step in *generalization*. In a *regression model* there are two main methods of cross-validation: *adjusted R^2* or data splitting, in which the data are split randomly into two halves, and a regression model is estimated for each half and then compared.

Crying: what you feel like doing after writing statistics textbooks.

Cubic trend: if you connected the means in ordered conditions with a line then a cubic trend is shown by two changes in the direction of this line. You must have at least four ordered conditions.

Currency variable: a variable containing values of money.

Date variable: a variable made up of dates. The data can take forms such as dd-mmm-yyyy (e.g., 21-Jun-1973), dd-mmm-yy (e.g., 21-Jun-73), mm/dd/yy (e.g., 06/21/73), dd.mm.yyyy (e.g., 21.06.1973).

Data View: there are two ways to view the contents of the *data editor* window. The data view shows you a spreadsheet and can be used for entering raw data. See also *variable view*.

Degrees of freedom: an impossible thing to define in a few pages, let alone a few lines. Essentially it is the number of 'entities' that are free to vary when estimating some kind of statistical parameter. In a more practical sense, it has a bearing on significance tests for many commonly used *test statistics* (such as the *F-ratio*, *t-test*, *chi-square statistic*) and determines the exact form of the *probability distribution* for these test statistics. The explanation involving soccer players in Chapter 2 is far more interesting…

Deleted residual: a measure of the influence of a particular case of data. It is the difference between the *adjusted predicted value* for a case and the original observed value for that case.

Density plot: similar to a *histogram* except that rather than having a summary bar representing the frequency of scores, it shows each individual score as a dot. They can be useful for looking at the shape of a distribution of scores.

Dependent *t*-test: see *paired-samples t-test*

Dependent variable: another name for *outcome variable*. This name is usually associated with experimental methodology (which is the only time it really makes sense) and is used because it is the variable that is not manipulated by the experimenter and so its value depends on the variables that have been manipulated. To be honest I just use the term *outcome variable* all the time – it makes more sense (to me) and is less confusing.

Deviance: the difference between the observed value of a variable and the value of that variable predicted by a statistical model.

Deviation contrast: a non-orthogonal *planned contrast* that compares the mean of each group (except for the first or last, depending on how the contrast is specified) to the overall mean.

DFBeta: a measure of the influence of a case on the values of b_i in a *regression model*. If we estimated a regression parameter b_i and then deleted a particular case and re-estimated the same regression parameter b_i, then the difference between these two estimates would be the DFBeta for the case that was deleted. By looking at the values of the DFBetas, it is possible to identify cases that have a large influence on the parameters of the regression model; however, the size of DFBeta will depend on the units of measurement of the regression parameter.

DFFit: a measure of the influence of a case. It is the difference between the *adjusted predicted value* and the original predicted value of a particular case. If a case is not influential then its DFFit should be zero – hence, we expect non-influential cases to have small DFFit values. However, we have the problem that this statistic depends on the units of measurement of the outcome and so a DFFit of 0.5 will be very small if the outcome ranges from 1 to 100, but very large if the outcome varies from 0 to 1.

Diagonal: a covariance structure used in *multilevel linear models*. In this structure variances are assumed to be heterogeneous and all of the covariances are 0.

Dichotomous: description of a variable that consists of only two categories (e.g., the variable gender is dichotomous because it consists of only two categories: male and female).

Difference contrast: a non-orthogonal *planned contrast* that compares the mean of each condition (except the first) to the overall mean of all previous conditions combined.

Direct effect: the effect of a *predictor variable* on an *outcome variable* when a *mediator* is present in the model (cf. *indirect effect*).

Direct oblimin: a method of *oblique rotation*.

Discrete variable: a variable that can only take on certain values (usually whole numbers) on the scale.

Discriminant analysis: see *discriminant function analysis*.

Discriminant function analysis: this analysis identifies and describes the *discriminant function variates* of a set of variables and is useful as a follow-up test to *MANOVA* as a means of seeing how these variates allow groups of cases to be discriminated.

Discriminant function variate: a linear combination of variables created such that the differences between group means on the transformed variable are maximized. It takes the general form

$$Variate_{1i} = b_1X_{1i} + b_2X_{2i} + \ldots + b_nX_{ni}$$

Discriminant score: a score for an individual case on a particular *discriminant function variate* obtained by substituting that case's scores on the measured variables into the equation that defines the variate in question.

Dummy variables: a way of recoding a categorical variable with more than two categories into a series of variables all of which are *dichotomous* and can take on values of only 0 or 1. There are seven basic steps to create such variables: (1) count the number of groups you want to recode and subtract 1; (2) create as many new variables as the value you calculated in step 1 (these are your dummy variables); (3) choose one of your groups as a baseline (i.e., a group against which all other groups should be compared, such as a control

group); (4) assign that baseline group values of 0 for all of your dummy variables; (5) for your first dummy variable, assign the value 1 to the first group that you want to compare against the baseline group (assign all other groups 0 for this variable); (6) for the second dummy variable assign the value 1 to the second group that you want to compare against the baseline group (assign all other groups 0 for this variable); (7) repeat this process until you run out of dummy variables.

Durbin–Watson test: a test for serial correlations between errors in *regression models*. Specifically, it tests whether adjacent residuals are correlated, which is useful in assessing the assumption of *independent errors*. The test statistic can vary between 0 and 4, with a value of 2 meaning that the residuals are uncorrelated. A value greater than 2 indicates a negative correlation between adjacent residuals, whereas a value below 2 indicates a positive correlation. The size of the Durbin–Watson statistic depends upon the number of predictors in the model and the number of observations. For accuracy, look up the exact acceptable values in Durbin and Watson's (1951) original paper. As a very conservative rule of thumb, values less than 1 or greater than 3 are definitely cause for concern; however, values closer to 2 may still be problematic depending on the sample and model.

Ecological validity: evidence that the results of a study, experiment or test can be applied, and allow inferences, to real-world conditions.

Eel: long, snakelike, scaleless fishes that lack pelvic fins. From the order Anguilliformes or Apodes, they should probably not be inserted into your anus to cure constipation (or for any other reason).

Effect size: an objective and (usually) standardized measure of the magnitude of an observed effect. Measures include Cohen's *d*, Glass's *g* and Pearson's correlations coefficient, *r*.

Equamax: a method of *orthogonal rotation* that is a hybrid of *quartimax* and *varimax*. It is reported to behave fairly erratically (see Tabachnick and Fidell, 2012) and so is probably best avoided.

Error bar chart: a graphical representation of the mean of a set

of observations that includes the 95% confidence interval of the mean. The mean is usually represented as a circle, square or rectangle at the value of the mean (or a bar extending to the value of the mean). The confidence interval is represented by a line protruding from the mean (upwards, downwards or both) to a short horizontal line representing the limits of the confidence interval. Error bars can be drawn using the standard error or standard deviation instead of the 95% confidence interval.

Error SSCP (*E*): the error sum of squares and cross-products matrix. This is a *sum of squares and cross-products matrix* for the error in a predictive *linear model* fitted to *multivariate* data. It represents the *unsystematic variance* and is the multivariate equivalent of the *residual sum of squares*.

Eta squared (η^2): an *effect size* measure that is the ratio of the *model sum of squares* to the *total sum of squares*. So, in essence, *the coefficient of determination* by another name. It doesn't have an awful lot going for it: not only is it biased, but it typically measures the overall effect of an ANOVA, and effect sizes are more easily interpreted when they reflect specific comparisons (e.g., the difference between two means).

Exp(B): the label that SPSS applies to the *odds ratio*. It is an indicator of the change in *odds* resulting from a unit change in the predictor in *logistic regression*. If the value is greater than 1 then it indicates that as the predictor increases, the odds of the outcome occurring increase. Conversely, a value less than 1 indicates that as the predictor increases, the odds of the outcome occurring decrease.

Experimental hypothesis: synonym for *alternative hypothesis*.

Experimental research: a form of research in which one or more variables are systematically manipulated to see their effect (alone or in combination) on an *outcome variable*. This term implies that data will be able to be used to make statements about cause and effect. Compare with *cross-sectional research* and *correlational research*.

Experimentwise error rate: the probability of making a *Type I error* in an experiment involving one or more statistical comparisons when the null hypothesis is true in each case.

Extraction: a term used for the process of deciding whether a *factor* in *factor analysis* is statistically important enough to 'extract' from the data and interpret. The decision is based on the magnitude of the eigenvalue associated with the factor. See *Kaiser's criterion, scree plot.*

F_{max}: see *Hartley's F_{max}.*

F-ratio: a test statistic with a known *probability distribution* (the *F*-distribution). It is the ratio of the average variability in the data that a given model can explain to the average variability unexplained by that same model. It is used to test the overall fit of the model in *simple regression* and *multiple regression*, and to test for overall differences between group means in experiments.

Factor: another name for an *independent variable* or *predictor* that's typically used when describing experimental designs. However, to add to the confusion, it is also used synonymously with *latent variable* in factor analysis.

Factor analysis: a *multivariate* technique for identifying whether the correlations between a set of observed variables stem from their relationship to one or more *latent variables* in the data, each of which takes the form of a *linear model*.

Factor loading: the *regression coefficient* of a variable for the *linear model* that describes a *latent variable* or *factor* in *factor analysis*.

Factor matrix: general term for the *structure matrix* in *factor analysis*.

Factor score: a single score from an individual entity representing their performance on some *latent variable*. The score can be crudely conceptualized as follows: take an entity's score on each of the variables that make up the factor and multiply it by the corresponding *factor loading* for the variable, then add these values up (or average them).

Factor transformation matrix, Λ: a matrix used in *factor analysis*. It can be thought of as containing the angles through which factors are rotated in factor *rotation*.

Factorial ANOVA: an analysis of variance involving two or more *independent variables* or *predictors*.

Falsification: the act of disproving a hypothesis or theory.

Familywise error rate: the probability of making a *Type I error* in any family of tests when the null hypothesis is true in each case. The 'family of tests'

can be loosely defined as a set of tests conducted on the same data set and addressing the same empirical question.

Fisher's exact test: Fisher's exact test (Fisher, 1922) is not so much a test as a way of computing the exact probability of a statistic. It was designed originally to overcome the problem that with small samples the sampling distribution of the chi-square statistic deviates substantially from a chi-square distribution. It should be used with small samples.

Fit: how sexually attractive you find a statistical test. Alternatively, it's the degree to which a statistical model is an accurate representation of some observed data. (Incidentally, it's just plain *wrong* to find statistical tests sexually attractive.)

Fixed coefficient: a coefficient or model parameter that is fixed; that is, it cannot vary over situations or contexts (cf. *Random coefficient*).

Fixed effect: An effect in an experiment is said to be a fixed effect if all possible treatment conditions that a researcher is interested in are present in the experiment. Fixed effects can be generalized only to the situations in the experiment. For example, the effect is fixed if we say that we are interested only in the conditions that we had in our experiment (e.g., placebo, low dose and high dose) and we can generalize our findings only to the situation of a placebo, low dose and high dose.

Fixed intercept: A term used in *multilevel linear modelling* to denote when the intercept in the model is fixed. That is, it is not free to vary across different groups or contexts (cf. *Random intercept*).

Fixed slope: A term used in *multilevel linear modelling* to denote when the slope of the model is fixed. That is, it is not free to vary across different groups or contexts (cf. *Random slope*).

Fixed variable: A fixed variable is one that is not supposed to change over time (e.g., for most people their gender is a fixed variable – it never changes).

Frequency distribution: a graph plotting values of observations on the horizontal axis, and the frequency with which each value occurs in the data set on the vertical axis (a.k.a. *histogram*).

Friedman's ANOVA: a non-parametric test of whether more than two related

groups differ. It is the non-parametric version of one-way *repeated-measures* ANOVA.

Generalization: the ability of a statistical model to say something beyond the set of observations that spawned it. If a model generalizes it is assumed that predictions from that model can be applied not just to the sample on which it is based, but to a wider population from which the sample came.

Glossary: a collection of grossly inaccurate definitions (written late at night when you really ought to be asleep) of things that you thought you understood until some evil book publisher forced you to try to define them.

Goodman and Kruskal's λ: measures the proportional reduction in error that is achieved when membership of a category of one variable is used to predict category membership of the other variable. A value of 1 means that one variable perfectly predicts the other, whereas a value of 0 indicates that one variable in no way predicts the other.

Goodness of fit: an index of how well a model fits the data from which it was generated. It's usually based on how well the data predicted by the model correspond to the data that were actually collected.

Grand mean: the *mean* of an entire set of observations.

Grand mean centring: grand mean *centring* means the transformation of a variable by taking each score and subtracting the mean of all scores (for that variable) from it (cf. *Group mean centring*).

Grand variance: the *variance* within an entire set of observations.

Greenhouse–Geisser estimate: an estimate of the departure from *sphericity*. The maximum value is 1 (the data completely meet the assumption of sphericity) and minimum is the *lower bound*. Values below 1 indicate departures from sphericity and are used to correct the *degrees of freedom* associated with the corresponding *F-ratios* by multiplying them by the value of the estimate. Some say the Greenhouse–Geisser correction is too conservative (strict) and recommend the *Huynh–Feldt correction* instead.

Group mean centring: group mean *centring* means the transformation of a variable by taking each score and subtracting from it the mean of the scores (for that variable) for the group to which that score belongs (cf. *Grand mean centring*).

Growth curve: a curve that summarizes the change in some outcome over time. See *Polynomial*.

Harmonic mean: a weighted version of the *mean* that takes account of the relationship between variance and sample size. It is calculated by summing the reciprocal of all observations, then dividing by the number of observations. The reciprocal of the end product is the harmonic mean:

$$H = \frac{1}{\frac{1}{n}\sum_{i=1}^{n}\frac{1}{x_i}}$$

Hartley's F_{max}: also known as the *variance ratio*, this is the ratio of the variances between the group with the biggest variance and the group with the smallest variance. This ratio is compared to critical values in a table published by Hartley as a test of *homogeneity of variance*. Some general rules are that with sample sizes (n) of 10 per group, an F_{max} less than 10 is more or less always going to be non-significant, with 15–20 per group the ratio needs to be less than about 5, and with samples of 30–60 the ratio should be below about 2 or 3.

Hat values: another name for *leverage*.

HE^{-1}: this is a matrix that is functionally equivalent to the *hypothesis SSCP* divided by the *error SSCP* in *MANOVA*. Conceptually it represents the ratio of *systematic* to *unsystematic variance*, so is a *multivariate* analogue of the *F-ratio*.

Helmert contrast: a non-orthogonal *planned contrast* that compares the mean of each condition (except the last) to the overall mean of all subsequent conditions combined.

Heterogeneity of variance: the opposite of *homogeneity of variance*. This term means that the variance of one variable varies (i.e., is different) across levels of another variable.

Heteroscedasticity: the opposite of *homoscedasticity*. This occurs when the residuals at each level of the predictor variables(s) have unequal variances. Put another way, at each point along any predictor variable, the spread of residuals is different.

Hierarchical regression: a method of *multiple regression* in which the order in which predictors are entered into the regression model is determined by the researcher based on previous research: variables already known to be predictors are entered first, new variables are entered subsequently.

Histogram: a *frequency distribution*.

Homogeneity of covariance matrices: an assumption of some *multivariate* tests such as *MANOVA*. It is an extension of the *homogeneity of variance assumption* in *univariate* analyses. However, as well as assuming that *variances* for each *dependent variable* are the same across groups, it also assumes that relationships (*covariances*) between these dependent variables are roughly equal. It is tested by comparing the population *variance–covariance matrices* of the different groups in the analysis.

Homogeneity of regression slopes: an assumption of *analysis of covariance*. This is the assumption that the relationship between the *covariate* and *outcome variable* is constant across different treatment levels. So, if we had three treatment conditions, if there's a positive relationship between the covariate and the outcome in one group, we assume that there is a similar-sized positive relationship between the covariate and outcome in the other two groups too.

Homogeneity of variance: the assumption that the variance of one variable is stable (i.e., relatively similar) at all levels of another variable.

Homoscedasticity: an assumption in regression analysis that the residuals at each level of the predictor variable(s) have similar variances. Put another way, at each point along any predictor variable, the spread of residuals should be fairly constant.

Hosmer and Lemeshow's R_L^2: a version of the *coefficient of determination* for logistic regression. It is a fairly literal translation in that it is the $-2LL$ for the model divided by the original $-2LL$, in other words, it's the ratio of what the model can explain compared to what there was to explain in the first place.

Hotelling–Lawley trace (T^2): a *test statistic* in *MANOVA*. It is the sum of the eigenvalues for each *discriminant function variate* of the data and so is conceptually the same as the *F-ratio* in *ANOVA*: it is the sum of the ratio of *systematic* and *unsystematic variance* (SS_M/SS_R) for each of the variates.

Huynh–Feldt estimate: an estimate of the departure from *sphericity*. The maximum value is 1 (the data completely meet the assumption of sphericity). Values below this indicate departures from sphericity and are used to correct the *degrees of freedom* associated with the corresponding *F-ratios* by multiplying them by the value of the estimate. It is less conservative than the *Greenhouse–Geisser estimate*, but some say it is too liberal.

Hypothesis: a prediction about the state of the world (see *experimental hypothesis* and *null hypothesis*).

Hypothesis SSCP (H): the hypothesis sum of squares and cross-products matrix. This is a *sum of squares and cross-products matrix* for a predictive *linear model* fitted to *multivariate* data. It represents the *systematic variance* and is the multivariate equivalent of the *model sum of squares*.

Identity matrix: a square matrix (i.e., having the same number of rows and columns) in which the diagonal elements are equal to 1, and the off-diagonal elements are equal to 0. The following are all examples:

$$\begin{pmatrix} 1 & 0 \\ 0 & 1 \end{pmatrix} \begin{pmatrix} 1 & 0 & 0 \\ 0 & 1 & 0 \\ 0 & 0 & 1 \end{pmatrix} \begin{pmatrix} 1 & 0 & 0 & 0 \\ 0 & 1 & 0 & 0 \\ 0 & 0 & 1 & 0 \\ 0 & 0 & 0 & 1 \end{pmatrix}$$

Independence: the assumption that one data point does not influence another. When data come from people, it basically means that the behaviour of one person does not influence the behaviour of another.

Independent ANOVA: *analysis of variance* conducted on any design in which all *independent variables* or *predictors* have been manipulated using different participants (i.e., all data come from different entities).

Independent design: an experimental design in which different treatment conditions utilize different organisms (e.g., in psychology, this would mean using different people in different treatment conditions) and so the resulting data are independent (a.k.a. between-groups or between-subjects design).

Independent errors: for any two observations in regression the *residuals* should be uncorrelated (or independent).

Independent factorial design: an experimental design incorporating two or more *predictors* (or *independent variables*) all of which have been manipulated using different participants (or whatever entities are being tested).

Independent *t*-test: a test using the *t-statistic* that establishes whether two means collected from independent samples differ significantly.

Independent variable: another name for a *predictor variable*. This name is usually associated with experimental methodology (which is the only time it makes sense) and is used because it is the variable that is manipulated by the experimenter and so its value does not depend on any other variables (just on the experimenter). I just use the term *predictor variable* all the time because the meaning of the term is not constrained to a particular methodology.

Index of mediation: a standardized measure of an *indirect effect*. In a mediation model, it is the *indirect effect* multiplied by the ratio of the standard deviation of the *predictor variable* to the standard deviation of the *outcome variable*.

Indirect effect: the effect of a *predictor variable* on an *outcome variable* through a *mediator* (cf. *direct effect*).

Interaction effect: the combined effect of two or more *predictor variables* on an *outcome variable*. It can be used to gauge *moderation*.

Interaction graph: a graph showing the means of two or more *independent variables* in which means of one variable are shown at different levels of the other variable. Unusually the means are connected with lines, or are displayed as bars. These graphs are used to help understand *interaction effects*.

Interquartile range: the limits within which the middle 50% of an ordered set of observations fall. It is the difference between the value of the *upper quartile* and *lower quartile*.

Interval variable: data measured on a scale along the whole of which intervals are equal. For example, people's ratings of this book on Amazon.com can range from 1 to 5; for these data to be interval it should be true that the increase in appreciation for this book represented by a change from 3 to 4 along the scale should be the same as the change in appreciation represented by a change from 1 to 2, or 4 to 5.

Intraclass correlation (ICC): a *correlation coefficient* that assesses the consistency between measures of the same class, that is, measures of the same thing (cf. *Pearson's correlation coefficient* which measures the relationship between variables of a different class.) Two common uses are in comparing paired data (such as twins) on the same measure, and assessing the consistency between judges' ratings of a set of objects. The calculation of these correlations depends on whether a measure of consistency (in which the order of scores from a source is considered but not the actual value around which the scores are anchored) or absolute agreement (in which both the order of scores and the relative values are considered), and whether the scores represent averages of many measures or just a single measure is required. This measure is also used in *multilevel linear models* to measure the dependency in data within the same context.

Jonckheere–Terpstra test: this statistic tests for an ordered pattern of medians across independent groups. Essentially it does the same thing as the *Kruskal–Wallis test* (i.e., test for a difference between the medians of the groups) but it incorporates information about whether the order of the groups is meaningful. As such, you should use this test when you expect the groups you're comparing to produce a meaningful order of medians.

Journal: In the context of academia a journal is a collection of articles on a broadly related theme, written by scientists, that report new data, new theoretical ideas or reviews/critiques of existing theories and data. Their main function is to induce learned helplessness in scientists through a complex process of self-esteem regulation using excessively harsh or complimentary peer feedback that has seemingly no obvious correlation with the actual quality of the work submitted.

Kaiser–Meyer–Olkin measure of sampling adequacy (KMO): the KMO can be calculated for individual and multiple variables and represents the ratio of the squared correlation between variables to the squared *partial correlation* between variables. It varies between 0 and 1: a value of 0 means that the sum of partial correlations is large relative to the sum of correlations, indicating diffusion in the pattern of correlations (hence, *factor analysis* is likely to be inappropriate); a value close to 1 indicates that patterns of correlation are relatively compact and so factor analysis should yield distinct and reliable factors. Values between .5 and .7 are mediocre, values between .7 and .8 are good, values between .8 and .9 are great and values above .9 are superb (see Hutcheson and Sofroniou, 1999).

Kaiser's criterion: a method of *extraction* in *factor analysis* based on the idea of retaining factors with associated eigenvalues greater than 1. This method appears to be accurate when the number of variables in the analysis is less than 30 and the resulting *communalities* (after *extraction*) are all greater than 0.7, or when the sample size exceeds 250 and the average communality is greater than or equal to 0.6.

Kendall's tau: a non-parametric correlation coefficient similar to *Spearman's correlation coefficient*, but should be used in preference for a small data set with a large number of tied ranks.

Kendall's *W*: this is much the same as *Friedman's ANOVA* but is used specifically for looking at the agreement between raters. So, if, for example, we asked 10 different women to rate the attractiveness of Justin Timberlake, David Beckham and Brad Pitt we could use this test to look at the extent to which they agree. Kendall's *W* ranges from 0 (no agreement between judges) to 1 (complete agreement between judges).

Kolmogorov–Smirnov test: a test of whether a distribution of scores is significantly different from a *normal distribution*. A significant value indicates a deviation from normality, but this test is notoriously affected by large samples in which small deviations from normality yield significant results.

Kolmogorov–Smirnov Z: not to be confused with the *Kolmogorov–Smirnov test* that tests whether a sample comes from a normally distributed population. This tests whether two groups have been drawn from the same population (regardless of what that population may be). It does much the same as the *Mann–Whitney test* and *Wilcoxon rank-sum test*! This test tends to have better power than the Mann–Whitney test when sample sizes are less than about 25 per group.

Kruskal–Wallis test: non-parametric test of whether more than two independent groups differ. It is the non-parametric version of one-way *independent ANOVA*.

Kurtosis: this measures the degree to which scores cluster in the tails of a frequency distribution. There are different ways to estimate kurtosis and in SPSS no kurtosis is expressed as 0 (but be careful because outside of SPSS no kurtosis is sometimes a value of 3). A distribution with positive kurtosis (*leptokurtic*, kurtosis > 0) has too many scores in the tails and is too peaked, whereas a distribution with negative kurtosis (*platykurtic*, kurtosis < 0) has too few scores in the tails and is quite flat.

Latent variable: a variable that cannot be directly measured, but is assumed to be related to several variables that can be measured.

Leptokurtic: see *Kurtosis*.

Levels of measurement: the relationship between what is being measured and the numbers obtained on a scale.

Levene's test: this tests the hypothesis that the variances in different groups are equal (i.e., the difference between the variances is zero). It basically does a one-way ANOVA on the *deviations* (i.e., the absolute value of the difference between each score and the mean of its group). A significant result indicates that the variances are significantly different – therefore, the assumption of *homogeneity of variances* has been violated. When samples sizes are large, small differences in group variances can produce a significant Levene's test.

Leverage: leverage statistics (or hat values) gauge the influence of the observed value of the outcome variable over the predicted values. The average leverage value is $(k+1)/n$ in which k is the number of predictors in the model and n is the number of participants. Leverage values can lie between 0 (the case has no influence whatsoever) and 1 (the case has complete influence over prediction). If no cases exert undue influence over the model then we would expect all of the leverage values to be close to the average value. Hoaglin and Welsch (1978) recommend investigating cases with values greater than twice the average ($2(k + 1)/n$) and Stevens (2002) recommends using three times the average ($3(k + 1)/n$) as a cut-off point for identifying cases having undue influence.

Likelihood: the probability of obtaining a set of observations given the parameters of a model fitted to those observations.

Linear model: a model that is based upon a straight line.

Line chart: a graph in which a summary statistic (usually the mean) is plotted on the *y*-axis against a categorical variable on the *x*-axis (this categorical variable could represent, for example, groups of people, different times or different experimental conditions). The value of the mean for each category is shown by a symbol, and means across categories are connected by a line. Different-coloured lines may be used to represent levels of a second categorical variable.

Logistic regression: a version of *multiple regression* in which the outcome is a *categorical variable*. If the categorical variable has exactly two categories the analysis is called *binary logistic regression*, and when the outcome has more than two categories it is called *multinomial logistic regression*.

Log-likelihood: a measure of error, or unexplained variation, in categorical models. It is based on summing the probabilities associated with the predicted and actual outcomes and is analogous to the *residual sum of squares* in multiple regression in that it is an indicator of how much unexplained information there is after the model has been fitted. Large values of the log-likelihood statistic indicate poorly fitting statistical models, because the larger the value of the log-likelihood, the more unexplained observations there are. The log-likelihood is the logarithm of the *likelihood*.

Loglinear analysis: a procedure used as an extension of the *chi-square test* to analyse situations in which we have more than two *categorical variables* and we want to test for relationships between these variables. Essentially, a *linear model* is fitted to the data that predicts expected frequencies (i.e., the number of cases expected in a given category). In this respect it is much the same as *analysis of variance* but for entirely categorical data.

Longitudinal research: a form of research in which you observe what naturally goes on in the world without directly interfering with it by measuring several variables at multiple time points. See also *correlational research*, *cross-sectional research*.

Lower-bound estimate: the name given to the lowest possible value of the *Greenhouse–Geisser estimate* of *sphericity*. Its value is $1/(k-1)$, in which k is the number of treatment conditions.

Lower quartile: the value that cuts off the lowest 25% of the data. If the data are ordered and then divided into two halves at the median, then the lower quartile is the median of the lower half of the scores.

M-estimator: a robust measure of location. One example is the median. In some cases it is a measure of location computed after outliers have been removed: unlike a *trimmed mean*, the amount of trimming used to remove outliers is determined empirically.

Mahalanobis distances: these measure the influence of a case by examining the distance of cases from the mean(s) of the predictor variable(s). One needs to look for the cases with the highest values. It is not easy to establish a cut-off point at which to worry, although Barnett and Lewis (1978) have produced a table of critical values dependent on the number of predictors and the sample size. From their work it is clear that even with large samples ($N = 500$) and five predictors, values above 25 are cause for concern. In smaller samples ($N = 100$) and with fewer predictors (namely three) values greater than 15 are problematic, and in very small samples ($N = 30$) with only two predictors values greater than 11 should be examined. However, for more specific advice, refer to Barnett and Lewis's (1978) table.

Main effect: the unique effect of a *predictor variable* (or *independent variable*) on an *outcome variable*. The term is usually used in the context of *ANOVA*.

Mann–Whitney test: a *non-parametric test* that looks for differences between two independent samples. That is, it tests whether the populations from which two samples are drawn have the same location. It is functionally the same as *Wilcoxon's rank-sum test*, and both tests are non-parametric equivalents of the *independent t-test*.

MANOVA: acronym for *multivariate analysis of variance*.

Matrix: a collection of numbers arranged in columns and rows. The values within a matrix are typically referred to as *components* or *elements*.

Mauchly's test: a test of the assumption of *sphericity*. If this test is significant then the assumption of *sphericity* has not been met and an appropriate correction must be applied to the *degrees of freedom* of the *F-ratio* in *repeated-measures ANOVA*. The test works by comparing the *variance–covariance matrix* of the data to an *identity matrix*; if the variance–covariance matrix is a scalar multiple of an *identity matrix* then sphericity is met.

Maximum-likelihood estimation: a way of estimating statistical parameters by choosing the parameters that make the data most likely to have happened. Imagine for a set of parameters that we calculated the probability (or likelihood) of getting the observed data; if this probability was high then these particular parameters yield a good fit of the data, but conversely if the probability was low, these parameters are a bad fit to our data. Maximum-likelihood estimation chooses the parameters that maximize the probability.

McNemar's test: This tests differences between two related groups (see *Wilcoxon signed-rank test* and *sign test*), when *nominal data* have been used. It's typically used when we're looking for changes in people's scores and it compares the proportion of people who changed their response in one direction (i.e., scores increased) to those who changed in the opposite direction (scores decreased). So, this test needs to be used when we've got two related dichotomous variables.

Mean: a simple statistical model of the centre of a distribution of scores. A hypothetical estimate of the 'typical' score.

Mean squares: a measure of average variability. For every *sum of squares* (which measure the total variability) it is possible to create mean squares by dividing by the number of things used to calculate the sum of squares (or some function of it).

Measurement error: the discrepancy between the numbers used to represent the thing that we're measuring and the actual value of the thing we're measuring (i.e., the value we would get if we could measure it directly).

Median: the middle score of a set of ordered observations. When there is an even number of observations the median is the average of the two scores that fall either side of what would be the middle value.

Median test: a non-parametric test of whether samples are drawn from a population with the same median. So, in effect, it does the same thing as the *Kruskal–Wallis test*. It works on the basis of producing a contingency table that is split for each group into the number of scores that fall above and below the observed median of the entire data set. If the groups are from the same population then these frequencies would be expected to be the same in all conditions (about 50% above and about 50% below).

Mediation: perfect mediation occurs when the relationship between a *predictor variable* and an *outcome variable* can be completely explained by their relationships with a third variable. For example, taking a dog to work reduces work stress. This relationship is mediated by positive mood if (1) having a dog at work increases positive mood; (2) positive mood reduces work stress; and (3) the relationship between having a dog at work and work stress is reduced to zero (or at least weakened) when positive mood is included in the model.

Mediator: a variable that reduces the size and/or direction of the relationship between a *predictor variable* and an *outcome variable* (ideally to zero) and is associated statistically with both.

Meta-analysis: this is a statistical procedure for assimilating research findings. It is based on the simple idea that we can take effect sizes from individual studies that research the same question, quantify the observed effect in a standard way (using *effect sizes*) and then combine these effects to get a more accurate idea of the true effect in the population.

Method of least squares: a method of estimating parameters (such as the *mean*, or a regression coefficient) that is based on minimizing the *sum of squared errors*. The parameter estimate will be the value, out of all of those possible, that has the smallest *sum of squared errors*.

Mixed ANOVA: *analysis of variance* used for a *mixed design*.

Mixed design: an experimental design incorporating two or more *predictors* (or *independent variables*) at least one of which has been manipulated using different participants (or whatever entities are being tested) and at least one of which has been manipulated using the same participants (or entities). Also known as a split-plot design because Fisher developed ANOVA for analysing agricultural data involving 'plots' of land containing crops.

Mixed normal distribution: a normal-looking distribution that is contaminated by a small proportion of scores from a different distribution. These distributions are not normal and have too many scores in the tails (i.e., at the extremes). The effect of these heavy tails is to inflate the estimate of the population variance. This, in turn, makes significance tests lack power.

Mode: the most frequently occurring score in a set of data.

Model sum of squares: a measure of the total amount of variability for which a model can account. It is the difference between the *total sum of squares* and the *residual sum of squares*.

Moderation: Moderation occurs when the relationship between two variables changes as a function of a third variable. For example, the relationship between watching horror films (predictor) and feeling scared at bedtime (outcome) might increase as a function of how vivid an imagination a person has (moderator).

Moderator: a variable that changes the size and/or direction of the relationship between two other variables.

Monte Carlo method: a term applied to the process of using data simulations to solve statistical problems. Its name comes from the use of Monte Carlo roulette tables to generate 'random' numbers in the pre-computer age. Karl Pearson, for example, purchased copies of *Le Monaco*, a weekly Paris periodical that published data from the Monte Carlo casinos' roulette wheels. He used these data as pseudo-random numbers in his statistical research.

Moses extreme reactions: a non-parametric test that compares the variability of scores in two groups, so it's a bit like a non-parametric *Levene's test*.

Multicollinearity: a situation in which two or more variables are very closely linearly related.

Multilevel linear model (MLM): A linear model (just like regression,

ANCOVA, ANOVA, etc.) in which the hierarchical structure of the data is explicitly considered. In this analysis regression parameters can be fixed (as in regression and ANOVA) but also random (i.e., free to vary across different contexts at a higher level of the hierarchy). This means that for each regression parameter there is a fixed component but also an estimate of how much the parameter varies across contexts (see *Fixed coefficient, Random coefficient*).

Multimodal: description of a distribution of observations that has more than two *modes*.

Multinomial logistic regression: *logistic regression* in which the outcome variable has more than two categories.

Multiple *R*: the multiple correlation coefficient. It is the correlation between the observed values of an outcome and the values of the outcome predicted by a multiple regression model.

Multiple regression: an extension of *simple regression* in which an outcome is predicted by a linear combination of two or more predictor variables. The form of the model is:

$$Y_i = \left(b_0 + b_1 X_{1i} + b_2 X_{2i} + \cdots + b_n X_{ni} \right) + \varepsilon_i$$

in which the outcome is denoted as *Y*, and each predictor is denoted as *X*. Each predictor has a regression coefficient *b* associated with it, and b_0 is the value of the outcome when all predictors are zero.

Multivariate: means 'many variables' and is usually used when referring to analyses in which there is more than one *outcome variable* (*MANOVA*, *principal component analysis*, etc.).

Multivariate analysis of variance: family of tests that extend the basic *analysis of variance* to situations in which more than one *outcome variable* has been measured.

Multivariate normality: an extension of a normal distribution to multiple variables. It is a *probability distribution* of a set of variables $v' = [v_1, v_2 \ldots v_n]$ given by:

$$f(v') = 2\pi^{-\frac{q}{2}} |\Sigma|^{-\frac{1}{2}} \exp\left\{ -\frac{1}{2}(v - \mu)' \Sigma^{-1} (v - \mu) \right\}$$

in which μ is the vector of means of the variables, and Σ is the *variance–covariance* matrix. If that made any sense to you then you're cleverer than I am.

Nagelkerke's R_N^2: a version of the *coefficient of determination* for logistic regression. It is a variation on *Cox and Snell's R_{CS}^2* which overcomes the problem that this statistic has of not being able to reach its maximum value.

Negative skew: see *Skew*.

Nominal variable: where numbers merely represent names. For example, the numbers on sports players shirts: a player with the number 1 on her back is not necessarily worse than a player with a 2 on her back. The numbers have no meaning other than denoting the type of player (full back, centre forward, etc.).

Noniles: a type of *quantile*; they are values that split the data into nine equal parts. They are commonly used in educational research.

Non-parametric tests: a family of statistical procedures that do not rely on the restrictive assumptions of parametric tests. In particular, they do not assume that the sampling distribution is normally distributed.

Normal distribution: a *probability distribution* of a random variable that is known to have certain properties. It is perfectly symmetrical (has a *skew* of 0), and has a *kurtosis* of 0.

Null hypothesis: the reverse of the *experimental hypothesis*, it says that your prediction is wrong and the predicted effect doesn't exist.

Numeric variables: variables involving numbers.

Oblique rotation: a method of *rotation* in *factor analysis* that allows the underlying factors to be correlated.

Odds: the probability of an event occurring divided by the probability of that event not occurring.

Odds ratio: the ratio of the *odds* of an event occurring in one group compared to another. So, for example, if the odds of dying after writing a glossary are 4, and the odds of dying after not writing a glossary are 0.25, then the odds ratio is 4/0.25 = 16. This means that the *odds* of dying if you write a glossary are 16 times higher than if you don't. An odds ratio of 1 would indicate that the *odds* of a particular outcome are equal in both groups.

Omega squared: an *effect size* measure associated with ANOVA that is less biased than *eta squared*. It is a (sometimes hideous) function of the *model sum of squares* and the *residual sum of squares* and isn't actually much use because it

measures the overall effect of the ANOVA and so can't be interpreted in a meaningful way. In all other respects it's great though.

One-tailed test: a test of a directional hypothesis. For example, the hypothesis 'the longer I write this glossary, the more I want to place my editor's genitals in a starved crocodile's mouth' requires a one-tailed test because I've stated the direction of the relationship (see also *two-tailed test*).

Ordinal variable: data that tell us not only that things have occurred, but also the order in which they occurred. These data tell us nothing about the differences between values. For example, gold, silver and bronze medals are ordinal: they tell us that the gold medallist was better than the silver medallist, but they don't tell us how much better (was gold a lot better than silver, or were gold and silver very closely competed?).

Ordinary least squares (OLS): a method of *regression* in which the parameters of the model are estimated using the *method of least squares*.

Orthogonal: means perpendicular (at right angles) to something. It tends to be equated to *independence* in statistics because of the connotation that perpendicular *linear models* in geometric space are completely independent (one is not influenced by the other).

Orthogonal rotation: a method of *rotation* in *factor analysis* that keeps the underlying factors independent (i.e., not correlated).

Outcome variable: a variable whose values we are trying to predict from one or more *predictor variables*.

Outlier: an observation or observations very different from most others. Outliers bias statistics (e.g., the mean) and their standard errors and confidence intervals.

Overdispersion: when the observed variance is bigger than expected from the logistic regression model. Like leprosy, you don't want it.

Paired-samples *t*-test: a test using the *t-statistic* that establishes whether two means collected from the same sample (or related observations) differ significantly.

Pairwise comparisons: comparisons of pairs of means.

Parameter: a very difficult thing to describe. When you fit a statistical model to your data, that model will consist of *variables* and parameters: variables are measured constructs that vary across entities in the sample, whereas parameters describe the relations between those variables in the population. In other words, they are constants believed to represent some fundamental truth about the measured variables. We use sample data to estimate the likely value of parameters because we don't have direct access to the population. Of course it's not quite as simple as that.

Parametric test: a test that requires data from one of the large catalogue of distributions that statisticians have described. Normally this term is used for parametric tests based on the *normal distribution*, which require four basic assumptions that must be met for the test to be accurate: a normally distributed sampling distribution (see *normal distribution*), *homogeneity of variance*, *interval* or *ratio data*, and *independence*.

Parsimony: in a scientific context, parsimony refers to the idea that simpler explanations of a phenomenon are preferable to complex ones. This idea relates to Ockham's (or Occam's if you prefer) razor, which is a phrase referring to the principle of 'shaving' away unnecessary assumptions or explanations to produce less complex theories. In statistical terms, parsimony tends to refer to a general heuristic that models be kept as simple as possible – in other words, not including variables that don't have real explanatory benefit.

Part correlation: another name for a *semi-partial correlation*.

Partial correlation: a measure of the relationship between two variables while 'controlling' the effect of one or more additional variables on both.

Partial eta squared (partial η^2): a version of *eta squared* that is the proportion of variance that a variable explains when excluding other variables in the analysis. Eta squared is the proportion of total variance explained by a variable, whereas partial eta squared is the proportion of variance that a variable explains that is not explained by other variables.

Partial out: to partial out the effect of a variable is to remove the variance that the variable shares with other variables in the analysis before looking at their relationships (see *partial correlation*).

Pattern matrix: a matrix in *factor analysis* containing the *regression* coefficients for each variable on each *factor* in the data. See also *Structure matrix*.

Pearson's correlation coefficient: Pearson's product-moment correlation coefficient, to give it its full name, is a *standardized* measure of the strength of relationship between two variables. It can take any value from −1 (as one variable changes, the other changes in the opposite direction by the same amount), through 0 (as one variable changes the other doesn't change at all), to +1 (as one variable changes, the other changes in the same direction by the same amount).

Percentiles: a type of *quantile*; they are values that split the data into 100 equal parts.

Perfect collinearity: exists when at least one predictor in a *regression model* is a perfect linear combination of the others (the simplest example being two predictors that are perfectly correlated – they have a correlation coefficient of 1).

Phi: a measure of the strength of association between two *categorical variables*. Phi is used with 2×2 *contingency tables* (tables which have two categorical variables and each variable has only two categories). Phi is a variant of the *chi square test, X^2*,

$$\phi = \sqrt{\frac{\chi^2}{N}}$$, in which n is the total

number of observations.

Pillai–Bartlett trace (V): a *test statistic* in *MANOVA*. It is the sum of the proportion of explained variance on the *discriminant function variates* of the data. As such, it is similar to the ratio of SS_M/SS_T.

Pilot fish (*Naucrates ductor*)**:** a carnivorous fish in the Carangidae family known for congregating around larger more impressive beings (e.g., sharks) and feeding parasitically from their bodies. A bit like Courtney Love.

Planned comparisons: another name for *planned contrasts*.

Planned contrasts: a set of comparisons between group means that are constructed before any data are collected. These are theory-led comparisons and are based on the idea of partitioning the variance created by the overall effect of group differences into gradually smaller portions of variance. These tests have more power than *post hoc tests*.

Platykurtic: see *Kurtosis*.

Point-biserial correlation: a standardized measure of the strength

of relationship between two variables when one of the two variables is *dichotomous*. The point-biserial correlation coefficient is used when the dichotomy is a discrete, or true, dichotomy (i.e., one for which there is no underlying continuum between the categories). An example of this is pregnancy: you can be either pregnant or not, there is no in between.

Polychotomous logistic regression: another name for *multinomial logistic regression*.

Polynomial: a posh name for a *growth curve* or trend over time. If *time* is our predictor variable, then any polynomial is tested by including a variable that is the predictor to the power of the order of polynomial that we want to test: a linear trend is tested by *time* alone, a quadratic or second-order polynomial is tested by including a predictor that is *time^2*, for a fifth-order polynomial we need a predictor of *time^5* and for an *n*th-order polynomial we would have to include *time^n* as a predictor.

Polynomial contrast: a contrast that tests for trends in the data. In its most basic form it looks for a linear trend (i.e., that the group means increase proportionately).

Population: in statistical terms this usually refers to the collection of units (be they people, plankton, plants, cities, suicidal authors, etc.) to which we want to generalize a set of findings or a statistical model.

Positive skew: see *skew*.

Post hoc tests: a set of comparisons between group means that were not thought of before data were collected. Typically these tests involve comparing the means of all combinations of pairs of groups. To compensate for the number of tests conducted, each test uses a strict criterion for significance. As such, they tend to have less power than *planned contrasts*. They are usually used for exploratory work for which no firm hypotheses were available on which to base planned contrasts.

Power: the ability of a test to detect an effect of a particular size (a value of .8 is a good level to aim for).

P-P plot: Short for a probability–probability plot. A graph plotting the cumulative probability of a variable against the cumulative probability of a particular distribution (often a normal distribution). Like a *Q-Q plot*, if values fall on the diagonal of the plot then the variable shares the same distribution as the one specified. Deviations from the diagonal show deviations from the distribution of interest.

Practice effect: refers to the possibility that participants' performance in a task may be influenced (positively or negatively) if they repeat the task because of familiarity with the experimental situation and/or the measures being used.

Predicted value: the value of an outcome variable based on specific values of the predictor variable or variables being placed into a statistical model.

Predictive validity: a form of *criterion validity* where there is evidence that scores from an instrument predict external measures (recorded at a different point in time) conceptually related to the measured construct.

Predictor variable: a variable that is used to try to predict values of another variable known as an *outcome variable*.

Principal component analysis (PCA): a *multivariate* technique for identifying the linear components of a set of variables.

Probability density function (PDF): the function that describes the probability of a random variable taking a certain value. It is the mathematical function that describes the *probability distribution*.

Probability distribution: a curve describing an idealized *frequency distribution* of a particular variable from which it is possible to ascertain the probability with which specific values of that variable will occur. For categorical variables it is simply a formula yielding the probability with which each category occurs.

Promax: a method of *oblique rotation* that is computationally faster than *direct oblimin* and so useful for large data sets.

Q-Q plot: short for a quantile–quantile plot. A graph plotting the *quantiles* of a variable against the quantiles of a particular distribution (often a normal distribution). Like a *P-P plot*, if values fall on the diagonal of the plot then the variable shares the same distribution as the one specified. Deviations from the diagonal show deviations from the distribution of interest.

Quadratic trend: if the means in ordered conditions are connected with a line

then a quadratic trend is shown by one change in the direction of this line (e.g., the line is curved in one place); the line is, therefore, U-shaped. There must be at least three ordered conditions.

Qualitative methods: extrapolating evidence for a theory from what people say or write (cf. *quantitative methods*).

Quantiles: values that split a data set into equal portions. Quartiles, for example, are a special case of quantiles that split the data into four equal parts. Similarly, *percentiles* are points that split the data into 100 equal parts and *noniles* are points that split the data into 9 equal parts (you get the general idea).

Quantitative methods: inferring evidence for a theory through measurement of variables that produce numeric outcomes (cf. *qualitative methods*).

Quartic trend: if the means in ordered conditions are connected with a line then a quartic trend is shown by three changes in the direction of this line. There must be at least five ordered conditions.

Quartiles: a generic term for the three values that cut an ordered data set into four equal parts. The three quartiles are known as the *lower quartile*, the second quartile (or *median*) and the *upper quartile*.

Quartimax: a method of *orthogonal rotation*. It attempts to maximize the spread of factor loadings for a variable across all *factors*. This often results in lots of variables loading highly onto a single *factor*.

Random coefficient: a coefficient or model parameter that is free to vary over situations or contexts (cf. *Fixed coefficient*).

Random effect: an effect is said to be random if the experiment contains only a sample of possible treatment conditions. Random effects can be generalized beyond the treatment conditions in the experiment. For example, the effect is random if we say that the conditions in our experiment (e.g., placebo, low dose and high dose) are only a sample of possible conditions (perhaps we could have tried a very high dose). We can generalize this random effect beyond just placebos, low doses and high doses.

Random intercept: A term used in *multilevel linear modelling* to denote when the intercept in the model is free to vary across different groups or contexts (cf. *Fixed intercept*).

Random slope: A term used in *multilevel linear modelling* to denote when the

slope of the model is free to vary across different groups or contexts (cf. *Fixed slope*).

Random variable: a random variable is one that varies over time (e.g., your weight is likely to fluctuate over time).

Randomization: the process of doing things in an unsystematic or random way. In the context of experimental research the word usually applies to the random assignment of participants to different treatment conditions.

Random variance: variance that is unique to a particular variable but not reliably so.

Range: the range of scores is the value of the smallest score subtracted from the highest score. It is a measure of the dispersion of a set of scores. See also *variance*, *standard deviation*, and *interquartile range*.

Ranking: the process of transforming raw scores into numbers that represent their position in an ordered list of those scores. The raw scores are ordered from lowest to highest and the lowest score is assigned a rank of 1, the next highest score is assigned a rank of 2, and so on.

Ratio variable: an *interval variable* but with the additional property that ratios are meaningful. For example, people's ratings of this book on Amazon.com can range from 1 to 5; for these data to be ratio not only must they have the properties of *interval variables*, but in addition a rating of 4 should genuinely represent someone who enjoyed this book twice as much as someone who rated it as 2. Likewise, someone who rated it as 1 should be half as impressed as someone who rated it as 2.

Regression coefficient: see b_i and β_i.

Regression line: a line on a scatterplot representing the *regression model* of the relationship between the two variables plotted.

Regression model: see *multiple regression* and *simple regression*.

Related design: another name for a *repeated-measures design*.

Related factorial design: an experimental design incorporating two or more *predictors* (or *independent variables*) all of which have been manipulated using the same participants (or whatever entities are being tested).

Reliability: the ability of a measure to produce consistent results when the same entities are measured under different conditions.

Repeated contrast: a non-orthogonal *planned contrast* that compares the mean in each condition (except the first) to the mean of the preceding condition.

Repeated-measures ANOVA: an *analysis of variance* conducted on any design in which the *independent variable* (*predictor*) or variables (*predictors*) have all been measured using the same participants in all conditions.

Repeated-measures design: an experimental design in which different treatment conditions utilize the same organisms (i.e., in psychology, this would mean the same people take part in all experimental conditions) and so the resulting data are related (a.k.a. related design or within-subject design).

Residual: The difference between the value a model predicts and the value observed in the data on which the model is based. Basically, an error. When the residual is calculated for each observation in a data set the resulting collection is referred to as the *residuals*.

Residuals: see *Residual*.

Residual sum of squares: a measure of the variability that cannot be explained by the model fitted to the data. It is the total squared *deviance* between the observations, and the value of those observations predicted by whatever model is fitted to the data.

Reverse Helmert contrast: another name for a *difference contrast*.

Roa's efficient score statistic: a statistic measuring the same thing as the *Wald statistic* but which is computationally easier to calculate.

Robust test: a term applied to a family of procedures to estimate statistics that are reliable even when the normal assumptions of the statistic are not met.

Rotation: a process in *factor analysis* for improving the interpretability of factors. In essence, an attempt is made to transform the *factors* that emerge from the analysis in such a way as to maximize *factor loadings* that are already large, and minimize factor loadings that are already small. There are two general approaches: *orthogonal rotation* and *oblique rotation*.

Roy's largest root: a *test statistic* in *MANOVA*. It is the eigenvalue for the first *discriminant function variate* of a set of observations. So, it is the same as the *Hotelling–Lawley trace* but for the first variate only. It represents the

proportion of explained variance to unexplained variance (SS_M/SS_R) for the first discriminant function.

Sample: a smaller (but hopefully representative) collection of units from a *population* used to determine truths about that population (e.g., how a given population behaves in certain conditions).

Sampling distribution: the *probability distribution* of a statistic. We can think of this as follows: if we take a *sample* from a *population* and calculate some statistic (e.g., the *mean*), the value of this statistic will depend somewhat on the sample we took. As such the statistic will vary slightly from sample to sample. If, hypothetically, we took lots and lots of samples from the population and calculated the statistic of interest we could create a frequency distribution of the values we got. The resulting distribution is what the sampling distribution represents: the distribution of possible values of a given statistic that we could expect to get from a given population.

Sampling variation: the extent to which a statistic (the mean, median, *t*, *F*, etc.) varies in samples taken from the same population.

Saturated model: a model that perfectly fits the data and, therefore, has no error. It contains all possible *main effects* and *interactions* between variables.

Scatterplot: a graph that plots values of one variable against the corresponding value of another variable (and the corresponding value of a third variable can also be included on a 3-D scatterplot).

Scree plot: a graph plotting each *factor* in a *factor analysis* (X-axis) against its associated eigenvalue (Y-axis). It shows the relative importance of each factor. This graph has a very characteristic shape (there is a sharp descent in the curve followed by a tailing off) and the point of inflexion of this curve is often used as a means of *extraction*. With a sample of more than 200 participants, this provides a fairly reliable criterion for extraction (Stevens, 2002)

Second quartile: another name for the *median*.

Semi-partial correlation: a measure of the relationship between two variables while 'controlling' the effect that one or more additional variables

has on one of those variables. If we call our variables *x* and *y*, it gives us a measure of the variance in *y* that *x* alone shares.

Shapiro–Wilk test: a test of whether a distribution of scores is significantly different from a *normal distribution*. A significant value indicates a deviation from normality, but this test is notoriously affected by large samples in which small deviations from normality yield significant results.

Shrinkage: the loss of predictive power of a regression model if the model had been derived from the population from which the sample was taken, rather than the sample itself.

Šidák correction: a slightly less conservative variant of a *Bonferroni correction*.

Sign test: tests whether two related samples are different. It does the same thing as the *Wilcoxon signed-rank test*. Differences between the conditions are calculated and the sign of this difference (positive or negative) is analysed because it indicates the direction of differences. The magnitude of change is completely ignored (unlike in Wilcoxon's test where the rank tells us something about the relative magnitude of change), and for this reason it lacks *power*. However, its computational simplicity makes it a nice party trick if ever anyone drunkenly accosts you needing some data quickly analysed without the aid of a computer … doing a sign test in your head really impresses people. Actually it doesn't, they just think you're a sad gimboid.

Simple contrast: a non-orthogonal *planned contrast* that compares the mean in each condition to the mean of either the first or last condition, depending on how the contrast is specified.

Simple effects analysis: this analysis looks at the effect of one *independent variable* (categorical *predictor variable*) at individual levels of another *independent variable*.

Simple regression: a *linear model* in which one variable or outcome is predicted from a single predictor variable. The model takes the form:
$$Y_i = (b_0 + b_1 X_i) + \varepsilon_i$$
in which Y is the outcome variable, X is the predictor, b_1 is the regression coefficient associated with the predictor and b_0 is the value of the outcome when the predictor is zero.

Simple slopes analysis: an analysis that looks at the relationship (i.e., the *simple regression*) between a *predictor variable* and an *outcome variable* at low, mean and high levels of a third (*moderator*) variable.

Singularity: a term used to describe variables that are perfectly correlated (i.e., the *correlation coefficient* is 1 or −1).

Skew: a measure of the symmetry of a *frequency distribution*. Symmetrical distributions have a skew of 0. When the frequent scores are clustered at the lower end of the distribution and the tail points towards the higher or more positive scores, the value of skew is positive. Conversely, when the frequent scores are clustered at the higher end of the distribution and the tail points towards the lower more negative scores, the value of skew is negative.

Smartreader: A free piece of software that can be downloaded from the IBM SPSS website that enables people who do not have *SPSS Statistics* installed to open and view SPSS output files.

Sobel test: A significance test of *mediation*. It tests whether the relationship between a *predictor variable* and an *outcome variable* is significantly reduced when a mediator is included in the model. It tests the *indirect effect* of the predictor on the outcome.

Spearman's correlation coefficient: a standardized measure of the strength of relationship between two variables that does not rely on the assumptions of a *parametric test*. It is *Pearson's correlation coefficient* performed on data that have been converted into ranked scores.

Sphericity: a less restrictive form of *compound symmetry* which assumes that the variances of the differences between data taken from the same participant (or other entity being tested) are equal. This assumption is most commonly found in *repeated-measures ANOVA* but applies only where there are more than two points of data from the same participant (see also *Greenhouse–Geisser correction*, *Huynh–Feldt correction*).

Split-half reliability: a measure of *reliability* obtained by splitting items on a measure into two halves (in some random fashion) and obtaining a score from each half of the scale. The correlation between the two scores, corrected to take account of the fact the correlations are based on only half of the items, is used as a measure of reliability. There are two

popular ways to do this. Spearman (1910) and Brown (1910) developed a formula that takes no account of the standard deviation of items:

$$r_{sh} = \frac{2r_{12}}{1 + r_{12}}$$

in which r_{12} is the correlation between the two halves of the scale. Flanagan (1937) and Rulon (1939), however, proposed a measure that does account for item variance:

$$r_{sh} = \frac{4r_{12} \times s_1 \times s_2}{S_T^2}$$

in which s_1 and s_2 are the standard deviations of each half of the scale, and S_T^2 is the variance of the whole test. See Cortina (1993) for more details.

Square matrix: a *matrix* that has an equal number of columns and rows.

Standard deviation: an estimate of the average variability (spread) of a set of data measured in the same units of measurement as the original data. It is the square root of the *variance*.

Standard error: the standard deviation of the *sampling distribution* of a statistic. For a given statistic (e.g., the *mean*) it tells us how much variability there is in this statistic across *samples* from the same *population*. Large values, therefore, indicate that a statistic from a given sample may not be an accurate reflection of the population from which the sample came.

Standard error of differences: if we were to take several pairs of samples from a population and calculate their means, then we could also calculate the difference between their means. If we plotted these differences between sample means as a *frequency distribution*, we would have the *sampling distribution* of differences. The standard deviation of this sampling distribution is the *standard error of differences*. As such it is a measure of the variability of differences between sample means.

Standard error of the mean (SE): the *standard error* associated with the mean. Did you really need a glossary entry to work that out?

Standardization: the process of converting a variable into a standard unit of measurement. The unit of measurement typically used is *standard deviation* units (see also *z-scores*). Standardization allows us to compare data when different units of measurement have been used (we could compare weight measured

in kilograms to height measured in inches).

Standardized: see *Standardization*.

Standardized DFBeta: a *standardized* version of *DFBeta*. These standardized values are easier to use than DFBeta because universal cut-off points can be applied. Stevens (2002) suggests looking at cases with absolute values greater than 2.

Standardized DFFit: a *standardized* version of *DFFit*.

Standardized residuals: the *residuals* of a model expressed in standard deviation units. Standardized residuals with an absolute value greater than 3.29 (actually, we usually just use 3) are cause for concern because in an average sample a value this high is unlikely to happen by chance; if more than 1% of our observations have standardized residuals with an absolute value greater than 2.58 (we usually just say 2.5) there is evidence that the level of error within our model is unacceptable (the model is a fairly poor fit of the sample data); and if more than 5% of observations have standardized residuals with an absolute value greater than 1.96 (or 2 for convenience) then there is also evidence that the model is a poor representation of the actual data.

Stepwise regression: a method of *multiple regression* in which variables are entered into the model based on a statistical criterion (the *semi-partial correlation* with the *outcome variable*). Once a new variable is entered into the model, all variables in the model are assessed to see whether they should be removed.

String variables: variables involving words (i.e., letter strings). Such variables could include responses to open-ended questions such as 'How much do you like writing glossary entries?'; the response might be 'About as much as I like placing my gonads on hot coals'.

Structure matrix: a matrix in *factor analysis* containing the *correlation coefficients* for each variable on each *factor* in the data. When *orthogonal rotations* used this is the same as the *pattern matrix*, but when oblique rotation is used these matrices are different.

Studentized deleted residual: a measure of the influence of a particular case of data. This is a standardized version of the *deleted residual*.

Studentized residuals: a variation on *standardized residuals*. A Studentized residual is an *unstandardized residual* divided by an estimate of its standard deviation that varies point by point. These residuals have the same properties as the *standardized residuals* but usually provide a more precise estimate of the error variance of a specific case.

Sum of squared errors: another name for the *sum of squares*.

Sum of squares (SS): an estimate of total variability (spread) of a set of observations around a parameter (such as the *mean*). First the *deviance* for each score is calculated, and then this value is squared. The SS is the sum of these squared deviances.

Sum of squares and cross-products matrix (SSCP matrix): a *square matrix* in which the diagonal elements represent the *sum of squares* for a particular variable, and the off-diagonal elements represent the *cross-products* between pairs of variables. The SSCP matrix is basically the same as the *variance–covariance matrix*, except that the SSCP matrix expresses variability and between-variable relationships as total values, whereas the variance–covariance matrix expresses them as average values.

Suppressor effects: situation where a predictor has a significant effect, but only when another variable is held constant.

Syntax: predefined written commands that instruct SPSS what you would like it to do (writing 'bugger off and leave me alone' doesn't seem to work …).

Systematic variation: variation due to some genuine effect (be it the effect of an experimenter doing something to all of the participants in one sample but not in other samples, or natural variation between sets of variables). We can think of this as variation that can be explained by the model that we've fitted to the data.

***t*-statistic:** Student's *t* is a *test statistic* with a known *probability distribution* (the *t*-distribution). In the context of regression it is used to test whether a regression coefficient *b* is significantly different from zero; in the context of experimental work it is used to test whether the differences between two means are significantly different from zero. See also *paired-samples t-test* and *Independent t-test*.

Tertium quid: the possibility that an apparent relationship between two variables is actually caused by the effect of a third variable on them both (often called *the third-variable problem*).

Test–retest reliability: the ability of a measure to produce consistent results when the same entities are tested at two different points in time.

Test statistic: a statistic for which we know how frequently different values occur. The observed value of such a statistic is typically used to test *hypotheses*.

Theory: although it can be defined more formally, a theory is a hypothesized general principle or set of principles that explain known findings about a topic and from which new hypotheses can be generated.

Tolerance: tolerance statistics measure *multicollinearity* and are simply the reciprocal of the *variance inflation factor* (1/VIF). Values below 0.1 indicate serious problems, although Menard (1995) suggests that values below 0.2 are worthy of concern.

Total SSCP (*T*): the total sum of squares and cross-products matrix. This is a *sum of squares and cross-products matrix* for an entire set of observations. It is the *multivariate* equivalent of the *total sum of squares*.

Total sum of squares: a measure of the total variability within a set of observations. It is the total squared *deviance* between each observation and the overall mean of all observations.

Transformation: the process of applying a mathematical function to all observations in a data set, usually to correct some distributional abnormality such as *skew* or *kurtosis*.

Trimmed mean: a statistic used in many *robust tests*. It is a mean calculated after a certain percentage of the distribution has been removed at the extremes. For example, a 20% trimmed mean is a mean calculated after the top and bottom 20% of ordered scores have been removed. Imagine we had 20 scores representing the annual income of students (in thousands, rounded to the nearest thousand: 2, 2, 2, 2, 3, 3, 3, 3, 3, 4, 4, 4, 4, 4, 4, 4, 4, 6, 35. The mean income is 5 (£5000). This value is biased by an outlier. A 10% trimmed mean will remove 10% of scores from the top and bottom of ordered scores before the mean is calculated. With 20 scores, removing 10% of scores involves removing the top and bottom 2 scores. This gives us: 2, 2, 3, 3, 3, 3, 3, 4, 4, 4, 4, 4, 4, 4, 4, the mean of which is 3.44.

The mean depends on a symmetrical distribution to be accurate, but a trimmed mean produces accurate results even when the distribution is not symmetrical. There are more complex examples of robust methods such as the *bootstrap*.

Two-tailed test: a test of a non-directional hypothesis. For example, the hypothesis 'writing this glossary has some effect on what I want to do with my editor's genitals' requires a two-tailed test because it doesn't suggest the direction of the relationship. See also *One-tailed test*.

Type I error: occurs when we believe that there is a genuine effect in our population, when in fact there isn't.

Type II error: occurs when we believe that there is no effect in the population, when in fact there is.

Unique factor: a *factor* that affects only one of many measured *variables* and, therefore, cannot explain the *correlations* between those variables.

Unique variance: variance that is specific to a particular variable (i.e., is not shared with other variables). We tend to use the term 'unique variance' to refer to variance that can be reliably attributed to only one measure, otherwise it is called *random variance*.

Univariate: means 'one variable' and is usually used to refer to situations in which only one *outcome variable* has been measured (*ANOVA*, *t-tests*, *Mann–Whitney tests*, etc.).

Unstandardized residuals: the *residuals* of a model expressed in the units in which the original outcome variable was measured.

Unstructured: a covariance structure used in *multilevel linear models*. This covariance structure is completely general. Covariances are assumed to be completely unpredictable: they do not conform to a systematic pattern.

Unsystematic variation: this is variation that isn't due to the effect in which we're interested (so could be due to natural differences between people in different samples such as differences in intelligence or motivation). We can think of this as variation that can't be explained by whatever model we've fitted to the data.

Upper quartile: the value that cuts off the highest 25% of ordered scores. If the scores are ordered and then divided into two halves at the median, then the upper quartile is the median of the top half of the scores.

Validity: evidence that a study allows correct inferences about the question it was aimed to answer or that a test measures what it set out to measure conceptually (see also *Content validity*, *Criterion validity*).

Variables: anything that can be measured and can differ across entities or across time.

Variable View: there are two ways to view the contents of the *data editor* window. The Variable View allows you to define properties of the variables for which you wish to enter data. See also *Data View*.

Variance: an estimate of average variability (spread) of a set of data. It is the sum of squares divided by the number of values on which the sum of squares is based minus 1.

Variance components: a covariance structure used in *multilevel linear models*. This covariance structure is very simple and assumes that all random effects are independent and that the variances of random effects are the same and sum to the variance of the outcome variable.

Variance–covariance matrix: a square matrix (i.e., same number of columns and rows) representing the variables measured. The diagonals represent the *variances* within each variable, whereas the off-diagonals represent the *covariances* between pairs of variables.

Variance inflation factor (VIF): a measure of *multicollinearity*. The VIF indicates whether a predictor has a strong linear relationship with the other predictor(s). Myers (1990) suggests that a value of 10 is a good value at which to worry. Bowerman and O'Connell (1990) suggest that if the average VIF is greater than 1, then multicollinearity may be biasing the regression model.

Variance ratio: see *Hartley's F_{max}*.

Variance sum law: states that the variance of a difference between two independent variables is equal to the sum of their variances.

Varimax: a method of *orthogonal rotation*. It attempts to maximize the dispersion of *factor loadings* within *factors*. Therefore, it tries to load a smaller number of variables highly onto each factor, resulting in more interpretable clusters of factors.

VIF: see *variance inflation factor*.

Wald statistic: a *test statistic* with a known *probability distribution* (a *chi-square distribution*) that is used to test whether the *b* coefficient for a predictor in a *logistic* regression model is significantly different from zero. It is analogous to the *t-statistic* in a *regression model* in that it is simply the *b* coefficient divided by its standard error. The Wald statistic is inaccurate when the regression coefficient (*b*) is large, because the standard error tends to become inflated, resulting in the Wald statistic being underestimated.

Wald–Wolfowitz runs: another variant on the *Mann–Whitney test*. Scores are rank-ordered as in the Mann–Whitney test, but rather than analysing the ranks, this test looks for 'runs' of scores from the same group within the ranked order. Now, if there's no difference between groups then obviously ranks from the two groups should be randomly interspersed. However, if the groups are different then one should see more ranks from one group at the lower end, and more ranks from the other group at the higher end. By looking for clusters of scores in this way, the test can determine if the groups differ.

Weight: a number by which something (usually a variable in statistics) is multiplied. The weight assigned to a variable determines the influence that variable has within a mathematical equation: large weights give the variable a lot of influence.

Weighted least squares: a method of *regression* in which the parameters of the model are estimated using the *method of least squares* but observations are weighted by some other variable. Often they are weighted by the inverse of their *variance* to combat *heteroscedasticity*.

Welch's *F*: a version of the *F*-ratio designed to be accurate when the assumption of *homogeneity of variance* has been violated. Not to be confused with the squelch test which is where you shake your head around

after writing statistics books to see if you still have a brain.

Wilcoxon's rank-sum test: a *non-parametric test* that looks for differences between two independent samples. That is, it tests whether the populations from which two samples are drawn have the same location. It is functionally the same as the *Mann–Whitney test*, and both tests are non-parametric equivalents of the *independent t-test*.

Wilcoxon signed-rank test: a *non-parametric test* that looks for differences between two related samples. It is the non-parametric equivalent of the *related t-test*.

Wilks's lambda (Λ): a *test statistic* in *MANOVA*. It is the product of the unexplained variance on each of the *discriminant function variates*, so it represents the ratio of error variance to total variance (SS_R/SS_T) for each variate.

Within-subject design: another name for a *repeated-measures design*.

Writer's block: something I suffered from a lot while writing this edition. It's when you can't think of any decent examples and so end up talking about sperm the whole time. Seriously, look at this book, it's all sperm this, sperm that, quail sperm, human sperm. Frankly, I'm amazed donkey sperm didn't get in there somewhere. Oh, it just did.

Yates's continuity correction: an adjustment made to the *chi-square test* when the *contingency table* is 2 rows by 2 columns (i.e., there are two categorical variables both of which consist of only two categories). In large samples the adjustment makes little difference and is slightly dubious anyway (see Howell, 2012).

z-score: the value of an observation expressed in standard deviation units. It is calculated by taking the observation, subtracting from it the mean of all observations, and dividing the result by the standard deviation of all observations. By converting a distribution of observations into z-scores a new distribution is created that has a mean of 0 and a standard deviation of 1.

APPENDIX

A.1. Table of the standard normal distribution

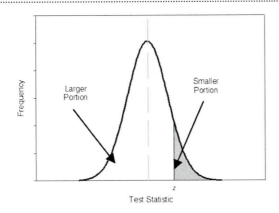

z	Larger Portion	Smaller Portion	y	z	Larger Portion	Smaller Portion	y
.00	.50000	.50000	.3989	.12	.54776	.45224	.3961
.01	.50399	.49601	.3989	.13	.55172	.44828	.3956
.02	.50798	.49202	.3989	.14	.55567	.44433	.3951
.03	.51197	.48803	.3988	.15	.55962	.44038	.3945
.04	.51595	.48405	.3986	.16	.56356	.43644	.3939
.05	.51994	.48006	.3984	.17	.56749	.43251	.3932
.06	.52392	.47608	.3982	.18	.57142	.42858	.3925
.07	.52790	.47210	.3980	.19	.57535	.42465	.3918
.08	.53188	.46812	.3977	.20	.57926	.42074	.3910
.09	.53586	.46414	.3973	.21	.58317	.41683	.3902
.10	.53983	.46017	.3970	.22	.58706	.41294	.3894
.11	.54380	.45620	.3965	.23	.59095	.40905	.3885

(Continued)

(Continued)

z	Larger Portion	Smaller Portion	y	z	Larger Portion	Smaller Portion	y
.24	.59483	.40517	.3876	.54	.70540	.29460	.3448
.25	.59871	.40129	.3867	.55	.70884	.29116	.3429
.26	.60257	.39743	.3857	.56	.71226	.28774	.3410
.27	.60642	.39358	.3847	.57	.71566	.28434	.3391
.28	.61026	.38974	.3836	.58	.71904	.28096	.3372
.29	.61409	.38591	.3825	.59	.72240	.27760	.3352
.30	.61791	.38209	.3814	.60	.72575	.27425	.3332
.31	.62172	.37828	.3802	.61	.72907	.27093	.3312
.32	.62552	.37448	.3790	.62	.73237	.26763	.3292
.33	.62930	.37070	.3778	.63	.73565	.26435	.3271
.34	.63307	.36693	.3765	.64	.73891	.26109	.3251
.35	.63683	.36317	.3752	.65	.74215	.25785	.3230
.36	.64058	.35942	.3739	.66	.74537	.25463	.3209
.37	.64431	.35569	.3725	.67	.74857	.25143	.3187
.38	.64803	.35197	.3712	.68	.75175	.24825	.3166
.39	.65173	.34827	.3697	.69	.75490	.24510	.3144
.40	.65542	.34458	.3683	.70	.75804	.24196	.3123
.41	.65910	.34090	.3668	.71	.76115	.23885	.3101
.42	.66276	.33724	.3653	.72	.76424	.23576	.3079
.43	.66640	.33360	.3637	.73	.76730	.23270	.3056
.44	.67003	.32997	.3621	.74	.77035	.22965	.3034
.45	.67364	.32636	.3605	.75	.77337	.22663	.3011
.46	.67724	.32276	.3589	.76	.77637	.22363	.2989
.47	.68082	.31918	.3572	.77	.77935	.22065	.2966
.48	.68439	.31561	.3555	.78	.78230	.21770	.2943
.49	.68793	.31207	.3538	.79	.78524	.21476	.2920
.50	.69146	.30854	.3521	.80	.78814	.21186	.2897
.51	.69497	.30503	.3503	.81	.79103	.20897	.2874
.52	.69847	.30153	.3485	.82	.79389	.20611	.2850
.53	.70194	.29806	.3467	.83	.79673	.20327	.2827

z	Larger Portion	Smaller Portion	y	z	Larger Portion	Smaller Portion	y
.84	.79955	.20045	.2803	1.14	.87286	.12714	.2083
.85	.80234	.19766	.2780	1.15	.87493	.12507	.2059
.86	.80511	.19489	.2756	1.16	.87698	.12302	.2036
.87	.80785	.19215	.2732	1.17	.87900	.12100	.2012
.88	.81057	.18943	.2709	1.18	.88100	.11900	.1989
.89	.81327	.18673	.2685	1.19	.88298	.11702	.1965
.90	.81594	.18406	.2661	1.20	.88493	.11507	.1942
.91	.81859	.18141	.2637	1.21	.88686	.11314	.1919
.92	.82121	.17879	.2613	1.22	.88877	.11123	.1895
.93	.82381	.17619	.2589	1.23	.89065	.10935	.1872
.94	.82639	.17361	.2565	1.24	.89251	.10749	.1849
.95	.82894	.17106	.2541	1.25	.89435	.10565	.1826
.96	.83147	.16853	.2516	1.26	.89617	.10383	.1804
.97	.83398	.16602	.2492	1.27	.89796	.10204	.1781
.98	.83646	.16354	.2468	1.28	.89973	.10027	.1758
.99	.83891	.16109	.2444	1.29	.90147	.09853	.1736
1.00	.84134	.15866	.2420	1.30	.90320	.09680	.1714
1.01	.84375	.15625	.2396	1.31	.90490	.09510	.1691
1.02	.84614	.15386	.2371	1.32	.90658	.09342	.1669
1.03	.84849	.15151	.2347	1.33	.90824	.09176	.1647
1.04	.85083	.14917	.2323	1.34	.90988	.09012	.1626
1.05	.85314	.14686	.2299	1.35	.91149	.08851	.1604
1.06	.85543	.14457	.2275	1.36	.91309	.08691	.1582
1.07	.85769	.14231	.2251	1.37	.91466	.08534	.1561
1.08	.85993	.14007	.2227	1.38	.91621	.08379	.1539
1.09	.86214	.13786	.2203	1.39	.91774	.08226	.1518
1.10	.86433	.13567	.2179	1.40	.91924	.08076	.1497
1.11	.86650	.13350	.2155	1.41	.92073	.07927	.1476
1.12	.86864	.13136	.2131	1.42	.92220	.07780	.1456
1.13	.87076	.12924	.2107	1.43	.92364	.07636	.1435

(Continued)

(Continued)

z	Larger Portion	Smaller Portion	y	z	Larger Portion	Smaller Portion	y
1.44	.92507	.07493	.1415	1.74	.95907	.04093	.0878
1.45	.92647	.07353	.1394	1.75	.95994	.04006	.0863
1.46	.92785	.07215	.1374	1.76	.96080	.03920	.0848
1.47	.92922	.07078	.1354	1.77	.96164	.03836	.0833
1.48	.93056	.06944	.1334	1.78	.96246	.03754	.0818
1.49	.93189	.06811	.1315	1.79	.96327	.03673	.0804
1.50	.93319	.06681	.1295	1.80	.96407	.03593	.0790
1.51	.93448	.06552	.1276	1.81	.96485	.03515	.0775
1.52	.93574	.06426	.1257	1.82	.96562	.03438	.0761
1.53	.93699	.06301	.1238	1.83	.96638	.03362	.0748
1.54	.93822	.06178	.1219	1.84	.96712	.03288	.0734
1.55	.93943	.06057	.1200	1.85	.96784	.03216	.0721
1.56	.94062	.05938	.1182	1.86	.96856	.03144	.0707
1.57	.94179	.05821	.1163	1.87	.96926	.03074	.0694
1.58	.94295	.05705	.1145	1.88	.96995	.03005	.0681
1.59	.94408	.05592	.1127	1.89	.97062	.02938	.0669
1.60	.94520	.05480	.1109	1.90	.97128	.02872	.0656
1.61	.94630	.05370	.1092	1.91	.97193	.02807	.0644
1.62	.94738	.05262	.1074	1.92	.97257	.02743	.0632
1.63	.94845	.05155	.1057	1.93	.97320	.02680	.0620
1.64	.94950	.05050	.1040	1.94	.97381	.02619	.0608
1.65	.95053	.04947	.1023	1.95	.97441	.02559	.0596
1.66	.95154	.04846	.1006	1.96	.97500	.02500	.0584
1.67	.95254	.04746	.0989	1.97	.97558	.02442	.0573
1.68	.95352	.04648	.0973	1.98	.97615	.02385	.0562
1.69	.95449	.04551	.0957	1.99	.97670	.02330	.0551
1.70	.95543	.04457	.0940	2.00	.97725	.02275	.0540
1.71	.95637	.04363	.0925	2.01	.97778	.02222	.0529
1.72	.95728	.04272	.0909	2.02	.97831	.02169	.0519
1.73	.95818	.04182	.0893	2.03	.97882	.02118	.0508

z	Larger Portion	Smaller Portion	y	z	Larger Portion	Smaller Portion	y
2.04	.97932	.02068	.0498	2.34	.99036	.00964	.0258
2.05	.97982	.02018	.0488	2.35	.99061	.00939	.0252
2.06	.98030	.01970	.0478	2.36	.99086	.00914	.0246
2.07	.98077	.01923	.0468	2.37	.99111	.00889	.0241
2.08	.98124	.01876	.0459	2.38	.99134	.00866	.0235
2.09	.98169	.01831	.0449	2.39	.99158	.00842	.0229
2.10	.98214	.01786	.0440	2.40	.99180	.00820	.0224
2.11	.98257	.01743	.0431	2.41	.99202	.00798	.0219
2.12	.98300	.01700	.0422	2.42	.99224	.00776	.0213
2.13	.98341	.01659	.0413	2.43	.99245	.00755	.0208
2.14	.98382	.01618	.0404	2.44	.99266	.00734	.0203
2.15	.98422	.01578	.0396	2.45	.99286	.00714	.0198
2.16	.98461	.01539	.0387	2.46	.99305	.00695	.0194
2.17	.98500	.01500	.0379	2.47	.99324	.00676	.0189
2.18	.98537	.01463	.0371	2.48	.99343	.00657	.0184
2.19	.98574	.01426	.0363	2.49	.99361	.00639	.0180
2.20	.98610	.01390	.0355	2.50	.99379	.00621	.0175
2.21	.98645	.01355	.0347	2.51	.99396	.00604	.0171
2.22	.98679	.01321	.0339	2.52	.99413	.00587	.0167
2.23	.98713	.01287	.0332	2.53	.99430	.00570	.0163
2.24	.98745	.01255	0325	2.54	.99446	.00554	.0158
2.25	.98778	.01222	.0317	2.55	.99461	.00539	.0154
2.26	.98809	.01191	.0310	2.56	.99477	.00523	.0151
2.27	.98840	.01160	.0303	2.57	.99492	.00508	.0147
2.28	.98870	.01130	.0297	2.58	.99506	.00494	.0143
2.29	.98899	.01101	.0290	2.59	.99520	.00480	.0139
2.30	.98928	.01072	.0283	2.60	.99534	.00466	.0136
2.31	.98956	.01044	.0277	2.61	.99547	.00453	.0132
2.32	.98983	.01017	.0270	2.62	.99560	.00440	.0129
2.33	.99010	.00990	.0264	2.63	.99573	.00427	.0126

(Continued)

(Continued)

z	Larger Portion	Smaller Portion	y	z	Larger Portion	Smaller Portion	y
2.64	.99585	.00415	.0122	2.86	.99788	.00212	.0067
2.65	.99598	.00402	.0119	2.87	.99795	.00205	.0065
2.66	.99609	.00391	.0116	2.88	.99801	.00199	.0063
2.67	.99621	.00379	.0113	2.89	.99807	.00193	.0061
2.68	.99632	.00368	.0110	2.90	.99813	.00187	.0060
2.69	.99643	.00357	.0107	2.91	.99819	.00181	.0058
2.70	.99653	.00347	.0104	2.92	.99825	.00175	.0056
2.71	.99664	.00336	.0101	2.93	.99831	.00169	.0055
2.72	.99674	.00326	.0099	2.94	.99836	.00164	.0053
2.73	.99683	.00317	.0096	2.95	.99841	.00159	.0051
2.74	.99693	.00307	.0093	2.96	.99846	.00154	.0050
2.75	.99702	.00298	.0091	2.97	.99851	.00149	.0048
2.76	.99711	.00289	.0088	2.98	.99856	.00144	.0047
2.77	.99720	.00280	.0086	2.99	.99861	.00139	.0046
2.78	.99728	.00272	.0084	3.00	.99865	.00135	.0044
2.79	.99736	.00264	.0081	⋮	⋮	⋮	⋮
2.80	.99744	.00256	.0079	3.25	.99942	.00058	.0020
2.81	.99752	.00248	.0077	⋮	⋮	⋮	⋮
2.82	.99760	.00240	.0075	3.50	.99977	.00023	.0009
2.83	.99767	.00233	.0073	⋮	⋮	⋮	⋮
2.84	.99774	.00226	.0071	4.00	.99997	.00003	.0001
2.85	.99781	.00219	.0069				

All values calculated by the author using SPSS.

A.2. Critical values of the *t*-distribution

df	Two-Tailed Test		One-Tailed Test	
	0.05	0.01	0.05	0.01
1	12.71	63.66	6.31	31.82
2	4.30	9.92	2.92	6.96
3	3.18	5.84	2.35	4.54
4	2.78	4.60	2.13	3.75
5	2.57	4.03	2.02	3.36
6	2.45	3.71	1.94	3.14
7	2.36	3.50	1.89	3.00
8	2.31	3.36	1.86	2.90
9	2.26	3.25	1.83	2.82
10	2.23	3.17	1.81	2.76
11	2.20	3.11	1.80	2.72
12	2.18	3.05	1.78	2.68
13	2.16	3.01	1.77	2.65
14	2.14	2.98	1.76	2.62
15	2.13	2.95	1.75	2.60
16	2.12	2.92	1.75	2.58
17	2.11	2.90	1.74	2.57
18	2.10	2.88	1.73	2.55
19	2.09	2.86	1.73	2.54
20	2.09	2.85	1.72	2.53
21	2.08	2.83	1.72	2.52
22	2.07	2.82	1.72	2.51
23	2.07	2.81	1.71	2.50
24	2.06	2.80	1.71	2.49
25	2.06	2.79	1.71	2.49
26	2.06	2.78	1.71	2.48
27	2.05	2.77	1.70	2.47
28	2.05	2.76	1.70	2.47
29	2.05	2.76	1.70	2.46
30	2.04	2.75	1.70	2.46
35	2.03	2.72	1.69	2.44
40	2.02	2.70	1.68	2.42
45	2.01	2.69	1.68	2.41
50	2.01	2.68	1.68	2.40
60	2.00	2.66	1.67	2.39
70	1.99	2.65	1.67	2.38
80	1.99	2.64	1.66	2.37
90	1.99	2.63	1.66	2.37
100	1.98	2.63	1.66	2.36
∞ (z)	1.96	2.58	1.64	2.33

All values computed by the author using SPSS.

A.3. Critical values of the *F*-distribution

		df (numerator)									
	p	1	2	3	4	5	6	7	8	9	10
1	.05	161.45	199.50	215.71	224.58	230.16	233.99	236.77	238.88	240.54	241.88
	.01	4052.18	4999.50	5403.35	5624.58	5763.65	5858.99	5928.36	5981.07	6022.47	6055.85
2	.05	18.51	19.00	19.16	19.25	19.30	19.33	19.35	19.37	19.38	19.40
	.01	98.50	99.00	99.17	99.25	99.30	99.33	99.36	99.37	99.39	99.40
3	.05	10.13	9.55	9.28	9.12	9.01	8.94	8.89	8.85	8.81	8.79
	.01	34.12	30.82	29.46	28.71	28.24	27.91	27.67	27.49	27.35	27.23
4	.05	7.71	6.94	6.59	6.39	6.26	6.16	6.09	6.04	6.00	5.96
	.01	21.20	18.00	16.69	15.98	15.52	15.21	14.98	14.80	14.66	14.55
5	.05	6.61	5.79	5.41	5.19	5.05	4.95	4.88	4.82	4.77	4.74
	.01	16.26	13.27	12.06	11.39	10.97	10.67	10.46	10.29	10.16	10.05
6	.05	5.99	5.14	4.76	4.53	4.39	4.28	4.21	4.15	4.10	4.06
	.01	13.75	10.92	9.78	9.15	8.75	8.47	8.26	8.10	7.98	7.87
7	.05	5.59	4.74	4.35	4.12	3.97	3.87	3.79	3.73	3.68	3.64
	.01	12.25	9.55	8.45	7.85	7.46	7.19	6.99	6.84	6.72	6.62
8	.05	5.32	4.46	4.07	3.84	3.69	3.58	3.50	3.44	3.39	3.35
	.01	11.26	8.65	7.59	7.01	6.63	6.37	6.18	6.03	5.91	5.81
9	.05	5.12	4.26	3.86	3.63	3.48	3.37	3.29	3.23	3.18	3.14
	.01	10.56	8.02	6.99	6.42	6.06	5.80	5.61	5.47	5.35	5.26
10	.05	4.96	4.10	3.71	3.48	3.33	3.22	3.14	3.07	3.02	2.98
	.01	10.04	7.56	6.55	5.99	5.64	5.39	5.20	5.06	4.94	4.85
11	.05	4.84	3.98	3.59	3.36	3.20	3.09	3.01	2.95	2.90	2.85
	.01	9.65	7.21	6.22	5.67	5.32	5.07	4.89	4.74	4.63	4.54
12	.05	4.75	3.89	3.49	3.26	3.11	3.00	2.91	2.85	2.80	2.75
	.01	9.33	6.93	5.95	5.41	5.06	4.82	4.64	4.50	4.39	4.30
13	.05	4.67	3.81	3.41	3.18	3.03	2.92	2.83	2.77	2.71	2.67
	.01	9.07	6.70	5.74	5.21	4.86	4.62	4.44	4.30	4.19	4.10
14	.05	4.60	3.74	3.34	3.11	2.96	2.85	2.76	2.70	2.65	2.60
	.01	8.86	6.51	5.56	5.04	4.69	4.46	4.28	4.14	4.03	3.94
15	.05	4.54	3.68	3.29	3.06	2.90	2.79	2.71	2.64	2.59	2.54
	.01	8.68	6.36	5.42	4.89	4.56	4.32	4.14	4.00	3.89	3.80
16	.05	4.49	3.63	3.24	3.01	2.85	2.74	2.66	2.59	2.54	2.49
	.01	8.53	6.23	5.29	4.77	4.44	4.20	4.03	3.89	3.78	3.69
17	.05	4.45	3.59	3.20	2.96	2.81	2.70	2.61	2.55	2.49	2.45
	.01	8.40	6.11	5.18	4.67	4.34	4.10	3.93	3.79	3.68	3.59
18	.05	4.41	3.55	3.16	2.93	2.77	2.66	2.58	2.51	2.46	2.41
	.01	8.29	6.01	5.09	4.58	4.25	4.01	3.84	3.71	3.60	3.51

df (denominator)

	p	df (numerator) 1	2	3	4	5	6	7	8	9	10
19	.05	4.38	3.52	3.13	2.90	2.74	2.63	2.54	2.48	2.42	2.38
	.01	8.18	5.93	5.01	4.50	4.17	3.94	3.77	3.63	3.52	3.43
20	.05	4.35	3.49	3.10	2.87	2.71	2.60	2.51	2.45	2.39	2.35
	.01	8.10	5.85	4.94	4.43	4.10	3.87	3.70	3.56	3.46	3.37
22	.05	4.30	3.44	3.05	2.82	2.66	2.55	2.46	2.40	2.34	2.30
	.01	7.95	5.72	4.82	4.31	3.99	3.76	3.59	3.45	3.35	3.26
24	.05	4.26	3.40	3.01	2.78	2.62	2.51	2.42	2.36	2.30	2.25
	.01	7.82	5.61	4.72	4.22	3.90	3.67	3.50	3.36	3.26	3.17
26	.05	4.23	3.37	2.98	2.74	2.59	2.47	2.39	2.32	2.27	2.22
	.01	7.72	5.53	4.64	4.14	3.82	3.59	3.42	3.29	3.18	3.09
28	.05	4.20	3.34	2.95	2.71	2.56	2.45	2.36	2.29	2.24	2.19
	.01	7.64	5.45	4.57	4.07	3.75	3.53	3.36	3.23	3.12	3.03
30	.05	4.17	3.32	2.92	2.69	2.53	2.42	2.33	2.27	2.21	2.16
	.01	7.56	5.39	4.51	4.02	3.70	3.47	3.30	3.17	3.07	2.98
35	.05	4.12	3.27	2.87	2.64	2.49	2.37	2.29	2.22	2.16	2.11
	.01	7.42	5.27	4.40	3.91	3.59	3.37	3.20	3.07	2.96	2.88
40	.05	4.08	3.23	2.84	2.61	2.45	2.34	2.25	2.18	2.12	2.08
	.01	7.31	5.18	4.31	3.83	3.51	3.29	3.12	2.99	2.89	2.80
45	.05	4.06	3.20	2.81	2.58	2.42	2.31	2.22	2.15	2.10	2.05
	.01	7.23	5.11	4.25	3.77	3.45	3.23	3.07	2.94	2.83	2.74
50	.05	4.03	3.18	2.79	2.56	2.40	2.29	2.20	2.13	2.07	2.03
	.01	7.17	5.06	4.20	3.72	3.41	3.19	3.02	2.89	2.78	2.70
60	.05	4.00	3.15	2.76	2.53	2.37	2.25	2.17	2.10	2.04	1.99
	.01	7.08	4.98	4.13	3.65	3.34	3.12	2.95	2.82	2.72	2.63
80	.05	3.96	3.11	2.72	2.49	2.33	2.21	2.13	2.06	2.00	1.95
	.01	6.96	4.88	4.04	3.56	3.26	3.04	2.87	2.74	2.64	2.55
100	.05	3.94	3.09	2.70	2.46	2.31	2.19	2.10	2.03	1.97	1.93
	.01	6.90	4.82	3.98	3.51	3.21	2.99	2.82	2.69	2.59	2.50
150	.05	3.90	3.06	2.66	2.43	2.27	2.16	2.07	2.00	1.94	1.89
	.01	6.81	4.75	3.91	3.45	3.14	2.92	2.76	2.63	2.53	2.44
300	.05	3.87	3.03	2.63	2.40	2.24	2.13	2.04	1.97	1.91	1.86
	.01	6.72	4.68	3.85	3.38	3.08	2.86	2.70	2.57	2.47	2.38
500	.05	3.86	3.01	2.62	2.39	2.23	2.12	2.03	1.96	1.90	1.85
	.01	6.69	4.65	3.82	3.36	3.05	2.84	2.68	2.55	2.44	2.36
1000	.05	3.85	3.00	2.61	2.38	2.22	2.11	2.02	1.95	1.89	1.84
	.01	6.66	4.63	3.80	3.34	3.04	2.82	2.66	2.53	2.43	2.34

df (denominator)

(Continued)

(Continued)

				df *(numerator)*				
	p	15	20	25	30	40	50	1000
1	.05	245.95	248.01	249.26	250.10	251.14	251.77	254.19
	.01	6157.31	6208.74	6239.83	6260.65	6286.79	6302.52	6362.70
2	.05	19.43	19.45	19.46	19.46	19.47	19.48	19.49
	.01	99.43	99.45	99.46	99.47	99.47	99.48	99.50
3	.05	8.70	8.66	8.63	8.62	8.59	8.58	8.53
	.01	26.87	26.69	26.58	26.50	26.41	26.35	26.14
4	.05	5.86	5.80	5.77	5.75	5.72	5.70	5.63
	.01	14.20	14.02	13.91	13.84	13.75	13.69	13.47
5	05	4.62	4.56	4.52	4.50	4.46	4.44	4.37
	.01	9.72	9.55	9.45	9.38	9.29	9.24	9.03
6	.05	3.94	3.87	3.83	3.81	3.77	3.75	3.67
	.01	7.56	7.40	7.30	7.23	7.14	7.09	6.89
7	.05	3.51	3.44	3.40	3.38	3.34	3.32	3.23
	.01	6.31	6.16	6.06	5.99	5.91	5.86	5.66
8	.05	3.22	3.15	3.11	3.08	3.04	3.02	2.93
	.01	5.52	5.36	5.26	5.20	5.12	5.07	4.87
9	.05	3.01	2.94	2.89	2.86	2.83	2.80	2.71
	.01	4.96	4.81	4.71	4.65	4.57	4.52	4.32
10	.05	2.85	2.77	2.73	2.70	2.66	2.64	2.54
	.01	4.56	4.41	4.31	4.25	4.17	4.12	3.92
11	.05	2.72	2.65	2.60	2.57	2.53	2.51	2.41
	.01	4.25	4.10	4.01	3.94	3.86	3.81	3.61
12	.05	2.62	2.54	2.50	2.47	2.43	2.40	2.30
	.01	4.01	3.86	3.76	3.70	3.62	3.57	3.37
13	.05	2.53	2.46	2.41	2.38	2.34	2.31	2.21
	.01	3.82	3.66	3.57	3.51	3.43	3.38	3.18
14	.05	2.46	2.39	2.34	2.31	2.27	2.24	2.14
	.01	3.66	3.51	3.41	3.35	3.27	3.22	3.02
15	.05	2.40	2.33	2.28	2.25	2.20	2.18	2.07
	.01	3.52	3.37	3.28	3.21	3.13	3.08	2.88
16	.05	2.35	2.28	2.23	2.19	2.15	2.12	2.02
	.01	3.41	3.26	3.16	3.10	3.02	2.97	2.76
17	.05	2.31	2.23	2.18	2.15	2.10	2.08	1.97
	.01	3.31	3.16	3.07	3.00	2.92	2.87	2.66
18	.05	2.27	2.19	2.14	2.11	2.06	2.04	1.92
	.01	3.23	3.08	2.98	2.92	2.84	2.78	2.58

df (denominator)

	p	15	20	25	30	40	50	1000
					df (numerator)			
19	0.05	2.23	2.16	2.11	2.07	2.03	2.00	1.88
	0.01	3.15	3.00	2.91	2.84	2.76	2.71	2.50
20	0.05	2.20	2.12	2.07	2.04	1.99	1.97	1.85
	0.01	3.09	2.94	2.84	2.78	2.69	2.64	2.43
22	0.05	2.15	2.07	2.02	1.98	1.94	1.91	1.79
	0.01	2.98	2.83	2.73	2.67	2.58	2.53	2.32
24	0.05	2.11	2.03	1.97	1.94	1.89	1.86	1.74
	0.01	2.89	2.74	2.64	2.58	2.49	2.44	2.22
26	0.05	2.07	1.99	1.94	1.90	1.85	1.82	1.70
	0.01	2.81	2.66	2.57	2.50	2.42	2.36	2.14
28	0.05	2.04	1.96	1.91	1.87	1.82	1.79	1.66
	0.01	2.75	2.60	2.51	2.44	2.35	2.30	2.08
30	0.05	2.01	1.93	1.88	1.84	1.79	1.76	1.63
	0.01	2.70	2.55	2.45	2.39	2.30	2.25	2.02
35	0.05	1.96	1.88	1.82	1.79	1.74	1.70	1.57
	0.01	2.60	2.44	2.35	2.28	2.19	2.14	1.90
40	0.05	1.92	1.84	1.78	1.74	1.69	1.66	1.52
	0.01	2.52	2.37	2.27	2.20	2.11	2.06	1.82
45	0.05	1.89	1.81	1.75	1.71	1.66	1.63	1.48
	0.01	2.46	2.31	2.21	2.14	2.05	2.00	1.75
50	0.05	1.87	1.78	1.73	1.69	1.63	1.60	1.45
	0.01	2.42	2.27	2.17	2.10	2.01	1.95	1.70
60	0.05	1.84	1.75	1.69	1.65	1.59	1.56	1.40
	0.01	2.35	2.20	2.10	2.03	1.94	1.88	1.62
80	0.05	1.79	1.70	1.64	1.60	1.54	1.51	1.34
	0.01	2.27	2.12	2.01	1.94	1.85	1.79	1.51
100	0.05	1.77	1.68	1.62	1.57	1.52	1.48	1.30
	0.01	2.22	2.07	1.97	1.89	1.80	1.74	1.45
150	0.05	1.73	1.64	1.58	1.54	1.48	1.44	1.24
	0.01	2.16	2.00	1.90	1.83	1.73	1.66	1.35
300	0.05	1.70	1.61	1.54	1.50	1.43	1.39	1.17
	.01	2.10	1.94	1.84	1.76	1.66	1.59	1.25
500	.05	1.69	1.59	1.53	1.48	1.42	1.38	1.14
	.01	2.07	1.92	1.81	1.74	1.63	1.57	1.20
1000	.05	1.68	1.58	1.52	1.47	1.41	1.36	1.11
	.01	2.06	1.90	1.79	1.72	1.61	1.54	1.16

df (denominator) (row labels, left axis)

All values computed by the author using SPSS.

A.4. Critical values of the chi-square distribution

df	p 0.05	0.01	df	p 0.05	0.01
1	3.84	6.63	25	37.65	44.31
2	5.99	9.21	26	38.89	45.64
3	7.81	11.34	27	40.11	46.96
4	9.49	13.28	28	41.34	48.28
5	11.07	15.09	29	42.56	49.59
6	12.59	16.81	30	43.77	50.89
7	14.07	18.48	35	49.80	57.34
8	15.51	20.09	40	55.76	63.69
9	16.92	21.67	45	61.66	69.96
10	18.31	23.21	50	67.50	76.15
11	19.68	24.72	60	79.08	88.38
12	21.03	26.22	70	90.53	100.43
13	22.36	27.69	80	101.88	112.33
14	23.68	29.14	90	113.15	124.12
15	25.00	30.58	100	124.34	135.81
16	26.30	32.00	200	233.99	249.45
17	27.59	33.41	300	341.40	359.91
18	28.87	34.81	400	447.63	468.72
19	30.14	36.19	500	553.13	576.49
20	31.41	37.57	600	658.09	683.52
21	32.67	38.93	700	762.66	789.97
22	33.92	40.29	800	866.91	895.98
23	35.17	41.64	900	970.90	1001.63
24	36.42	42.98	1000	1074.68	1106.97

All values computed by the author using SPSS.

REFERENCES

Agresti, A., & Finlay, B. (1986). *Statistical methods for the social sciences* (2nd ed.). San Francisco: Dellen.

Aiken, L. S., & West, S. G. (1991). *Multiple regression: Testing and interpreting interactions*. Newbury Park, CA: Sage.

Algina, J., & Olejnik, S. F. (1984). Implementing the Welch-James procedure with factorial designs. *Educational and Psychological Measurement, 44*, 39–48.

American Pyschological Association. (2010). *Publication manual of the American Psychological Association* (6th ed.). Washington DC: APA Books.

Anderson, C. A., & Bushman, B. J. (2001). Effects of violent video games on aggressive behavior, aggressive cognition, aggressive affect, physiological arousal, and pro-social behavior: A meta-analytic review of the scientific literature. *Psychological Science, 12*(5), 353–359.

Arrindell, W. A., & van der Ende, J. (1985). An empirical test of the utility of the observer-to-variables ratio in factor and components analysis. *Applied Psychological Measurement, 9*, 165–178.

Baguley, T. (2004). Understanding statistical power in the context of applied research. *Applied Ergonomics, 35*(2), 73–80.

Bale, C., Morrison, R., & Caryl, P. G. (2006). Chat-up lines as male sexual displays. *Personality and Individual Differences, 40*(4), 655–664. doi: 10.1016/j.paid.2005.07.016

Barcikowski, R. S., & Robey, R. R. (1984). Decisions in single group repeated measures analysis: statistical

tests and three computer packages. *American Statistician, 38*(2), 148–150.

Bargman, R. E. (1970). Interpretation and use of a generalized discriminant function. In R. C. Bose et al. (Eds.), *Essays in probability and statistics*. Chapel Hill: University of North Carolina Press.

Barnard, G. A. (1963). Ronald Aylmer Fisher, 1890–1962: Fisher's contributions to mathematical statistics. *Journal of the Royal Statistical Society, Series A, 126*, 162–166.

Barnett, V., & Lewis, T. (1978). *Outliers in statistical data*. New York: Wiley.

Baron, R. M., & Kenny, D. A. (1986). The moderator–mediator variable distinction in social psychological-research: Conceptual, strategic, and statistical considerations. *Journal of Personality and Social Psychology, 51*(6), 1173–1182.

Beckham, A. S. (1929). Is the Negro happy? A psychological analysis. *Journal of Abnormal and Social Psychology, 24*, 186–190.

Belia, S., Fidler, F., Williams, J., & Cumming, G. (2005). Researchers misunderstand confidence intervals and standard error bars. *Psychological Methods, 10*(4), 389–396. doi: 10.1037/1082-989x.10.4.389

Belsey, D. A., Kuh, E., & Welsch, R. (1980). *Regression diagnostics: Identifying influential data and sources of collinearity*. New York: Wiley.

Bemelman, M., & Hammacher, E. R. (2005). Rectal impalement by pirate ship: A case report. *Injury Extra, 36*, 508–510.

Berger, J. O. (2003). Could Fisher, Jeffreys and Neyman have agreed on testing? *Statistical Science, 18*(1), 1–12.

Bernard, P., Gervais, S., Allen, J., Campomizzi, S., & Klein, O. (2012). Integrating sexual objectification with object versus person recognition: The sexualized body-inversion hypothesis. *Psychological Science, 23*(5), 469–471. doi: 10.1177/0956797611434748

Berry, W. D. (1993). *Understanding regression assumptions*. Sage University Paper Series on Quantitative Applications in the Social Sciences, 07–092. Newbury Park, CA: Sage.

Berry, W. D., & Feldman, S. (1985). *Multiple regression in practice*. Sage University Paper Series on Quantitative Applications in the Social Sciences, 07–050. Beverly Hills, CA: Sage.

Board, B. J., & Fritzon, K. (2005). Disordered personalities at work. *Psychology, Crime & Law, 11*(1), 17–32.

Bock, R. D. (1975). *Multivariate statistical methods in behavioral research*. New York: McGraw-Hill.

Boik, R. J. (1981). A priori tests in repeated measures designs: Effects of nonsphericity. *Psychometrika, 46*(3), 241–255.

Bowerman, B. L., & O'Connell, R. T. (1990). *Linear statistical models: An applied approach* (2nd ed.). Belmont, CA: Duxbury.

Bray, J. H., & Maxwell, S. E. (1985). *Multivariate analysis of variance*. Sage University Paper Series on Quantitative Applications in the Social Sciences, 07-054. Newbury Park, CA: Sage.

Brown, M. B., & Forsythe, A. B. (1974). The small sample behaviour of some statistics which test the equality of several means. *Technometrics, 16*, 129–132.

Brown, W. (1910). Some experimental results in the correlation of mental abilities. *British Journal of Psychology, 3*, 296–322.

Budescu, D. V. (1982). The power of the F test in normal populations with heterogeneous variances. *Educational and Psychological Measurement, 42*, 609–616.

Budescu, D. V., & Appelbaum, M. I. (1981). Variance stabilizing transformations and the power of the F test. *Journal of Educational Statistics, 6*(1), 55–74.

Cattell, R. B. (1966a). *The scientific analysis of personality*. Chicago: Aldine.

Cattell, R. B. (1966b). The scree test for the number of factors. *Multivariate Behavioral Research, 1*, 245–276.

Çetinkaya, H., & Domjan, M. (2006). Sexual fetishism in a quail (*Coturnix japonica*) model system: Test of reproductive success. *Journal of Comparative Psychology, 120*(4), 427–432.

Chamorro-Premuzic, T., Furnham, A., Christopher, A. N., Garwood, J., & Martin, N. (2008). Birds of a feather: Students' preferences for lecturers' personalities as predicted by their own personality and learning approaches. *Personality and Individual Differences, 44*, 965–976.

Chen, P. Y., & Popovich, P. M. (2002). *Correlation: Parametric and nonparametric measures*. Thousand Oaks, CA: Sage.

Chen, X. Z., Luo, Y., Zhang, J. J., Jiang, K., Pendry, J. B., & Zhang, S. A. (2011). Macroscopic invisibility cloaking of visible light. *Nature Communications, 2*. doi: 17610.1038/ncomms1176

Clarke, D. L., Buccimazza, I., Anderson, F. A., & Thomson, S. R. (2005). Colorectal foreign bodies. *Colorectal Disease, 7*(1), 98–103.

Claxton, A., O'Rourke, N., Smith, J. Z., & DeLongis, A. (2012). Personality traits and marital satisfaction

within enduring relationships: An intra-couple discrepancy approach. *Journal of Social and Personal Relationships, 29*(3), 375-396. doi: 10.1177/0265407511431183

Cliff, N. (1987). *Analyzing multivariate data*. New York: Harcourt Brace Jovanovich.

Cohen, J. (1968). Multiple regression as a general data-analytic system. *Psychological Bulletin, 70*(6), 426–443.

Cohen, J. (1988). *Statistical power analysis for the behavioural sciences* (2nd ed.). New York: Academic Press.

Cohen, J. (1990). Things I have learned (so far). *American Psychologist, 45*(12), 1304–1312.

Cohen, J. (1992). A power primer. *Psychological Bulletin, 112*(1), 155–159.

Cohen, J. (1994). The earth is round (*p < .05*). *American Psychologist, 49*(12), 997–1003.

Coldwell, J., Pike, A., & Dunn, J. (2006) Household chaos – links with parenting and child behaviour. *Journal of Child Psychology and Psychiatry, 47*(11), 1116–1122.

Cole, D. A., Maxwell, S. E., Arvey, R., & Salas, E. (1994). How the power of MANOVA can both increase and decrease as a function of the intercorrelations among the dependent variables. *Psychological Bulletin, 115*(3), 465–474.

Collier, R. O., Baker, F. B., Mandeville, G. K., & Hayes, T. F. (1967). Estimates of test size for several test procedures based on conventional variance ratios in the repeated measures design. *Psychometrika, 32*(2), 339–352.

Comrey, A. L., & Lee, H. B. (1992). *A first course in factor analysis* (2nd ed.). Hillsdale, NJ: Erlbaum.

Cook, R. D., & Weisberg, S. (1982). *Residuals and influence in regression*. New York: Chapman & Hall.

Cook, S. A., Rosser, R., & Salmon, P. (2006). Is cosmetic surgery an effective psychotherapeutic intervention? A systematic review of the evidence. *Journal of Plastic, Reconstructive & Aesthetic Surgery, 59*, 1133–1151.

Cook, S. A., Rosser, R., Toone, H., James, M. I., & Salmon, P.

(2006). The psychological and social characteristics of patients referred for NHS cosmetic surgery: Quantifying clinical need. *Journal of Plastic, Reconstructive & Aesthetic Surgery, 59*, 54–64.

Cooper, C. L., Sloan, S. J., & Williams, S. (1988). *Occupational Stress Indicator Management Guide*. Windsor: NFER-Nelson.

Cooper, H. M. (2010). *Research synthesis and meta-analysis: A step-by-step approach* (4th ed.). Thousand Oaks, CA: Sage.

Cooper, M., O'Donnell, D., Caryl, P. G., Morrison, R., & Bale, C. (2007). Chat-up lines as male displays: Effects of content, sex, and personality. *Personality and Individual Differences, 43*(5), 1075–1085. doi: 10.1016/j.paid.2007.03.001

Cortina, J. M. (1993). What is coefficient alpha? An examination of theory and applications. *Journal of Applied Psychology, 78*, 98–104.

Cox, D. R., & Snell, D. J. (1989). *The analysis of binary data* (2nd ed.). London: Chapman & Hall.

Cronbach, L. J. (1951). Coefficient alpha and the internal structure of tests. *Psychometrika, 16*, 297–334.

Cronbach, L. J. (1957). The two disciplines of scientific psychology. *American Psychologist, 12*, 671–684.

Cumming, G. (2012). *Understanding the new statistics: Effect sizes, confidence intervals, and meta-analysis*. New York: Routledge.

Cumming, G., & Finch, S. (2005). Inference by eye: Confidence intervals and how to read pictures of data. *American Psychologist, 60*(2), 170–180. doi: 10.1037/0003-066x.60.2.170

Daniels, E. A. (2012). Sexy versus strong: What girls and women think of female athletes. *Journal of Applied Developmental Psychology, 33*, 79–90. doi: 10.1016/j.appdev.2011.12.002

Davey, G. C. L., Startup, H. M., Zara, A., MacDonald, C. B., & Field, A. P. (2003). Perseveration of checking thoughts and mood-as-input hypothesis. *Journal of Behavior Therapy & Experimental Psychiatry, 34*, 141–160.

Davidson, M. L. (1972). Univariate versus multivariate tests in repeated-measures experiments. *Psychological Bulletin, 77*, 446–452.

Davies, P., Surridge, J., Hole, L., & Munro-Davies, L. (2007). Superhero-related injuries in paediatrics: A case series. *Archives of Disease in Childhood, 92*(3), 242–243. doi: 10.1136/adc.2006.109793

DeCarlo, L. T. (1997). On the meaning and use of kurtosis. *Psychological Methods, 2*(3), 292–307.

DeCoster, J., Gallucci, M., & Iselin, A.-M. R. (2011). Best practices for using median splits, artificial categorization, and their continuous alternatives. *Journal of Experimental Psychopathology, 2*(2), 197–209. doi: 10.5127/jep.008310

DeCoster, J., Iselin, A.-M. R., & Gallucci, M. (2009). A conceptual and empirical examination of justifications for dichotomization. *Psychological Methods, 14*(4), 349–366. doi: 10.1037/a0016956

Di Falco, A., Ploschner, M., & Krauss, T. F. (2010). Flexible metamaterials at visible wavelengths. *New Journal of Physics, 12*. doi: 11300610.1088/1367-2630/12/11/113006

Domjan, M., Blesbois, E., & Williams, J. (1998). The adaptive significance of sexual conditioning: Pavlovian control of sperm release. *Psychological Science, 9*(5), 411–415.

Donaldson, T. S. (1968). Robustness of the *F*-test to errors of both kinds and the correlation between the numerator and denominator of the *F*-ratio. *Journal of the American Statistical Association, 63*, 660–676.

Dunlap, W. P., Cortina, J. M., Vaslow, J. B., & Burke, M. J. (1996). Meta-analysis of experiments with matched groups or repeated measures designs. *Psychological Methods, 1*(2), 170–177.

Dunteman, G. E. (1989). *Principal components analysis*. Sage University Paper Series on Quantitative Applications in the Social Sciences, 07-069. Newbury Park, CA: Sage.

Durbin, J., & Watson, G. S. (1951). Testing for serial correlation in least squares regression, II. *Biometrika, 30*, 159–178.

Easterlin, R. A. (2003). Explaining happiness. *Proceedings of the National Academy of Sciences, 100*(19), 11176–11183.

Efron, B., & Tibshirani, R. (1993). *An introduction to the bootstrap*. New York: Chapman & Hall.

Enders, C. K., & Tofighi, D. (2007). Centering predictor variables in cross-sectional multilevel models: A new look at an old issue. *Psychological Methods, 12*(2), 121–138.

Eriksson, S.-G., Beckham, D., & Vassell, D. (2004). Why are the English so shit at penalties? A review. *Journal of Sporting Ineptitude, 31*, 231–1072.

Erlebacher, A. (1977). Design and analysis of experiments contrasting the within- and between-subjects manipulations of the independent variable. *Psychological Bulletin, 84*, 212–219.

Eysenck, H. J. (1953). *The structure of human personality*. New York: Wiley.

Feng, J., Spence, I., & Pratt, J. (2007). Playing an action video game reduces gender differences in spatial cognition. *Psychological Science, 18*(10), 850–855. doi: 10.1111/j.1467-9280.2007.01990.x

Feng, L., Gwee, X., Kua, E. H., & Ng, T. P. (2010). Cognitive function and tea consumption in community dwelling older Chinese in Singapore. *Journal of Nutrition Health & Aging, 14*(6), 433–438.

Fesmire, F. M. (1988). Termination of intractable hiccups with digital rectal massage. *Annals of Emergency Medicine, 17*(8), 872.

Field, A. P. (1998). A bluffer's guide to sphericity. *Newsletter of the Mathematical, Statistical and Computing Section of the British Psychological Society, 6*(1), 13–22.

Field, A. P. (2000). *Discovering statistics using SPSS for Windows: Advanced techniques for the beginner*. London: Sage.

Field, A. P. (2001). Meta-analysis of correlation coefficients: A Monte Carlo comparison of fixed- and random-effects methods. *Psychological Methods, 6*(2), 161–180.

Field, A. P. (2003). Can meta-analysis be trusted? *Psychologist, 16*(12), 642–645.

Field, A. P. (2005a). Is the meta-analysis of correlation coefficients accurate when population correlations vary? *Psychological Methods, 10*(4), 444–467.

Field, A. P. (2005b). Meta-analysis. In J. Miles & P. Gilbert (Eds.), *A handbook of research methods in clinical and health psychology* (pp. 295–308). Oxford: Oxford University Press.

Field, A. P. (2005c). Sir Ronald Aylmer Fisher. In B. S. Everitt & D. C. Howell (Eds.), *Encyclopedia of Statistics in Behavioral Science* (Vol. 2, pp. 658–659). Chichester: Wiley.

Field, A. P. (2006). The behavioral inhibition system and the verbal information pathway to children's fears. *Journal of Abnormal Psychology, 115*(4), 742–752. doi: 10.1037/0021-843x.115.4.742

Field, A. P. (2012). Meta-analysis in clinical psychology research. In J. S. Comer & P. C. Kendall (Eds.), *The Oxford handbook of research strategies for clinical psychology*. Oxford: Oxford University Press.

Field, A. P. (2013). *Discovering statistics using IBM SPSS Statistics: And sex and drugs and rock 'n' roll* (4th ed.). London: Sage.

Field, A. P., & Davey, G. C. L. (1999). Reevaluating evaluative conditioning: A nonassociative explanation of conditioning effects in the visual evaluative conditioning paradigm. *Journal of Experimental Psychology – Animal Behavior Processes, 25*(2), 211–224.

Field, A. P., & Gillett, R. (2010). How to do a meta-analysis. *British Journal of Mathematical & Statistical Psychology, 63*, 665–694.

Field, A. P., & Hole, G. J. (2003). *How to design and report experiments*. London: Sage.

Field, A. P., Miles, J. N. V., & Field, Z. C. (2012). *Discovering statistics using R: And sex and drugs and rock 'n' roll*. London: Sage.

Field, A. P., & Moore, A. C. (2005). Dissociating the effects of attention and contingency awareness on evaluative conditioning effects in the visual paradigm. *Cognition and Emotion, 19*(2), 217–243.

Fienberg, S. E., Stigler, S. M., & Tanur, J. M. (2007). The William Kruskal legacy: 1919–2005. *Statistical Science, 22*(2), 255–261.

Fisher, R. A. (1921). On the probable error of a coefficient of correlation deduced from a small sample. *Metron, 1*, 3–32.

Fisher, R. A. (1922). On the interpretation of chi square from contingency tables, and the calculation of P. *Journal of the Royal Statistical Society, 85*, 87–94.

Fisher, R. A. (1925). *Statistical methods for research workers.* Edinburgh: Oliver & Boyd.

Fisher, R. A. (1925/1991). *Statistical methods, experimental design, and scientific inference.* Oxford: Oxford University Press. (Reprint.)

Fisher, R. A. (1956). *Statistical methods and scientific inference.* New York: Hafner.

Flanagan, J. C. (1937). A proposed procedure for increasing the efficiency of objective tests. *Journal of Educational Psychology, 28*, 17–21.

Friedman, M. (1937). The use of ranks to avoid the assumption of normality implicit in the analysis of variance. *Journal of the American Statistical Association, 32*, 675–701.

Gallup, G. G. J., Burch, R. L., Zappieri, M. L., Parvez, R., Stockwell, M., & Davis, J. A. (2003). The human penis as a semen displacement device. *Evolution and Human Behavior, 24*, 277–289.

Games, P. A. (1983). Curvilinear transformations of the dependent variable. *Psychological Bulletin, 93*(2), 382–387.

Games, P. A. (1984). Data transformations, power, and skew: A rebuttal to Levine and Dunlap. *Psychological Bulletin, 95*(2), 345–347.

Games, P. A., & Lucas, P. A. (1966). Power of the analysis of variance of independent groups on nonnormal and normally transformed data. *Educational and Psychological Measurement, 26*, 311–327.

Gelman, A., & Hill, J. (2007). *Data analysis using regression and multilevel/hierarchical models.* Cambridge: Cambridge University Press.

Gelman, A., & Weakliem, D. (2009). Of beauty, sex and power: Too little attention has been paid to the statistical challenges in estimating small effects. *American Scientist, 97*, 310–316.

Girden, E. R. (1992). *ANOVA: Repeated measures.* Sage University Paper Series on Quantitative Applications in the Social Sciences, 07-084. Newbury Park, CA: Sage.

Glass, G. V. (1966). Testing homogeneity of variances. *American Educational Research Journal, 3*(3), 187–190.

Glass, G. V., Peckham, P. D., & Sanders, J. R. (1972). Consequences of failure to meet assumptions underlying the fixed effects analyses of variance and covariance. *Review of Educational Research, 42*(3), 237–288.

Graham, J. M., Guthrie, A. C., & Thompson, B. (2003). Consequences of not interpreting structure coefficients in published CFA research: A reminder. *Structural Equation Modeling, 10*(1), 142–153.

Grayson, D. (2004). Some myths and legends in quantitative psychology. *Understanding Statistics, 3*(1), 101–134.

Green, C. S., & Bavelier, D. (2007). Action-video-game experience alters the spatial resolution of vision. *Psychological Science, 18*(1), 88–94. doi: 10.1111/j.1467-9280.2007.01853.x

Green, C. S., Pouget, A., & Bavelier, D. (2010). Improved probabilistic inference as a general learning mechanism with action video games. *Current Biology, 20*(17), 1573–1579. doi: 10.1016/j.cub.2010.07.040

Greenhouse, S. W., & Geisser, S. (1959). On methods in the analysis of profile data. *Psychometrika, 24*, 95–112.

Guadagnoli, E., & Velicer, W. F. (1988). Relation of sample size to the stability of component patterns. *Psychological Bulletin, 103*(2), 265–275.

Guéguen, N. (2012). Tattoos, piercings, and alcohol consumption. *Alcoholism: Clinical and Experimental Research, 36*(7), 1253–1256.

Hakstian, A. R., Roed, J. C., & Lind, J. C. (1979). Two-sample T^2 procedure and the assumption of homogeneous covariance matrices. *Psychological Bulletin, 86*, 1255–1263.

Halekoh, U., & Højsgaard, S. (2007). Overdispersion. Retrieved 18 March 2007, from http://gbi.agrsci.dk/statistics/courses/phd07/material/Day7/overdispersion-handout.pdf

Hamilton, B. L. (1977). Empirical-investigation of effects of heterogeneous regression slopes in analysis of covariance. *Educational and Psychological Measurement, 37*(3), 701–712.

Hardy, M. A. (1993). *Regression with dummy variables.* Sage University Paper Series on Quantitative Applications in the Social Sciences, 07-093. Newbury Park, CA: Sage.

Harman, B. H. (1976). *Modern factor analysis* (3rd ed., revised). Chicago: University of Chicago Press.

Harris, R. J. (1975). *A primer of multivariate statistics.* New York: Academic Press.

Hawton, K. (1989). Sexual dysfunctions. In K. Hawton, P. M. Salkovskis, J. Kirk & D. M. Clark (Eds.), *Cognitive behaviour therapy for psychiatric problems: A practical guide.* (pp. 370–405). Oxford: Oxford University Press.

Hayes, A. F. (2012). An analytical primer and computational tool for observed variable moderation, mediation, and conditional process modeling. *Manuscript submitted for publication.*

Hayes, A. F., & Cai, L. (2007). Using heteroskedasticity-consistent standard error estimators in OLS regression: An introduction and software implementation. *Behavior Research Methods, 39*(4), 709–722.

Hayes, A. F., & Matthes, J. (2009). Computational procedures for probing interactions in OLS and logistic regression: SPSS and SAS implementations. *Behavior Research Methods*, 41, 924–936.

Hedges, L. V. (1992). Meta-analysis. *Journal of Educational Statistics*, 17(4), 279–296.

Hill, C., Abraham, C., & Wright, D. B. (2007). Can theory-based messages in combination with cognitive prompts promote exercise in classroom settings? *Social Science & Medicine*, 65, 1049–1058.

Hoaglin, D., & Welsch, R. (1978). The hat matrix in regression and ANOVA. *American Statistician*, 32, 17–22.

Hoddle, G., Batty, D., & Ince, P. (1998). How not to take penalties in important soccer matches. *Journal of Cretinous Behaviour*, 1, 1–2.

Hodgson, R., Cole, A., & Young, A. (2012). The name of the game: Why can't people called Ashley score from a penalty kick? *Sporting Weakness Review*, 24(6), 574–581.

Hoffmann, F., Musolf, K., & Penn, D. J. (2012). Spectrographic analyses reveal signals of individuality and kinship in the ultrasonic courtship vocalizations of wild house mice. *Physiology & Behavior*, 105, 766–771. doi: 10.1016/j.physbeh.2011.10.011

Hollingsworth, H. H. (1980). An analytical investigation of the effects of heterogeneous regression slopes in analysis of covariance. *Educational and Psychological Measurement*, 40(3), 611–618.

Horn, J. L. (1965). A rationale and test for the number of factors in factor analysis. *Psychometrika*, 30, 179–185.

Hosmer, D. W., & Lemeshow, S. (1989). *Applied logistic regression*. New York: Wiley.

Howell, D. C. (1997). *Statistical methods for psychology* (4th ed.). Belmont, CA: Duxbury.

Howell, D. C. (2012). *Statistical methods for psychology* (8th ed.). Belmont, CA: Wadsworth.

Huberty, C. J., & Morris, J. D. (1989). Multivariate analysis versus multiple univariate analysis. *Psychological Bulletin*, 105(2), 302–308.

Hughes, J. P., Marice, H. P., & Gathright, J. B. (1976). Method of removing a hollow object from the rectum. *Diseases of the Colon & Rectum*, 19(1), 44–45.

Hume, D. (1739–40/1965). *A treatise of human nature* (L. A. Selby-Bigge, Ed.). Oxford: Clarendon Press.

Hume, D. (1748/1927). *An enquiry concerning human understanding*. Chicago: Open Court.

Hunter, J. E., & Schmidt, F. L. (2004). *Methods of meta-analysis: Correcting error and bias in research findings* (2nd ed.). Newbury Park, CA: Sage.

Hutcheson, G., & Sofroniou, N. (1999). *The multivariate social scientist*. London: Sage.

Huynh, H., & Feldt, L. S. (1976). Estimation of the Box correction for degrees of freedom from sample data in randomised block and split-plot designs. *Journal of Educational Statistics*, 1(1), 69–82.

Jackson, S., & Brashers, D. E. (1994). *Random factors in ANOVA*. Sage University Paper Series on Quantitative Applications in the Social Sciences, 07-098. Thousand Oaks, CA: Sage.

Johns, S. E., Hargrave, L. A., & Newton-Fisher N. E. (2012) Red is not a proxy signal for female genitalia in humans. *PLoS ONE*, 7(4), e34669. doi:10.1371/journal.pone.0034669

Johnson, P. O., & Neyman, J. (1936). Tests of certain linear hypotheses and their applications to some educational problems. *Statistical Research Memoirs*, 1, 57–93.

Jolliffe, I. T. (1972). Discarding variables in a principal component analysis, I: Artificial data. *Applied Statistics*, 21, 160–173.

Jolliffe, I. T. (1986). *Principal component analysis*. New York: Springer.

Jonckheere, A. R. (1954). A distribution-free k-sample test against ordered alternatives. *Biometrika*, 41, 133–145.

Judd, C. M., & Kenny, D. A. (1981). Process analysis: Estimating mediation in evaluation research. *Evaluation Research*, 5, 602–619.

Kahneman, D., & Krueger, A. B. (2006). Developments in the measurement of subjective well-being. *Journal of Economic Perspectives*, 20(1), 3–24.

Kaiser, H. F. (1960). The application of electronic computers to factor analysis. *Educational and Psychological Measurement*, 20, 141–151.

Kaiser, H. F. (1970). A second-generation little jiffy. *Psychometrika*, 35, 401–415.

Kaiser, H. F. (1974). An index of factorial simplicity. *Psychometrika*, 39, 31–36.

Kanazawa, S. (2007). Beautiful parents have more daughters: A further implication of the generalized Trivers-Willard hypothesis. *Journal of Theoretical Biology*, 244, 133–140.

Kass, R. A., & Tinsley, H. E. A. (1979). Factor analysis. *Journal of Leisure Research*, 11, 120–138.

Kellett, S., Clarke, S., & McGill, P. (2008). Outcomes from psychological assessment regarding recommendations for cosmetic surgery. *Journal of Plastic, Reconstructive & Aesthetic Surgery*, 61, 512–517.

Keselman, H. J., & Keselman, J. C. (1988). Repeated measures multiple comparison procedures: Effects of violating multisample sphericity in unbalanced designs. *Journal of Educational Statistics*, 13(3), 215–226.

Kimmel, H. D. (1957). Three criteria for the use of one-tailed tests. *Psychological Bulletin*, 54(4), 351–353. doi: 10.1037/h0046737

Kirk, R. E. (1996). Practical significance: A concept whose time has come. *Educational and Psychological Measurement*, 56(5), 746–759.

Kline, P. (1999). *The handbook of psychological testing* (2nd ed.). London: Routledge.

Klockars, A. J., & Sax, G. (1986). *Multiple comparisons*. Sage University Paper Series on Quantitative Applications in the Social Sciences, 07-061. Newbury Park, CA: Sage.

Koot, V. C. M., Peeters, P. H. M., Granath, F., Grobbee, D. E., & Nyren, O. (2003). Total and cause specific mortality among

Swedish women with cosmetic breast implants: Prospective study. *British Medical Journal, 326*(7388), 527–528.

Kreft, I. G. G., & de Leeuw, J. (1998). *Introducing multilevel modeling.* London: Sage.

Kreft, I. G. G., de Leeuw, J., & Aiken, L. S. (1995). The effect of different forms of centering in hierarchical linear models. *Multivariate Behavioral Research, 30*, 1–21.

Kruskal, W. H., & Wallis, W. A. (1952). Use of ranks in one-criterion variance analysis. *Journal of the American Statistical Association, 47*, 583–621.

Lacourse, E., Claes, M., & Villeneuve, M. (2001). Heavy metal music and adolescent suicidal risk. *Journal of Youth and Adolescence, 30*(3), 321–332.

Lambert, N. M., Negash, S., Stillman, T. F., Olmstead, S. B., & Fincham, F. D. (2012). A love that doesn't last: Pornography consumption and weakened commitment to one's romantic partner. *Journal of Social and Clinical Psychology, 31*(4), 410–438.

Lehmann, E. L. (1993). The Fisher, Neyman-Pearson theories of testing hypotheses: One theory or two? *Journal of the American Statistical Association, 88*, 1242–1249.

Lenth, R. V. (2001). Some practical guidelines for effective sample size determination. *American Statistician, 55*(3), 187–193.

Levene, H. (1960). Robust tests for equality of variances. In I. Olkin, S. G. Ghurye, W. Hoeffding, W. G. Madow & H. B. Mann (Eds.), *Contributions to probability and statistics: Essays in honor of Harold Hotelling* (pp. 278–292). Stanford, CA: Stanford University Press.

Levine, D. W., & Dunlap, W. P. (1982). Power of the F test with skewed data: Should one transform or not? *Psychological Bulletin, 92*(1), 272–280.

Levine, D. W., & Dunlap, W. P. (1983). Data transformation, power, and skew: A rejoinder to Games. *Psychological Bulletin, 93*(3), 596–599.

Lo, S. F., Wong, S. H., Leung, L. S., Law, I. C., & Yip, A. W. C. (2004). Traumatic rectal perforation by an eel. *Surgery, 135*(1), 110–111. doi: 10.1016/S0039-6060(03)00076-X

Loftus, G. R., & Masson, M. E. J. (1994). Using confidence intervals in within-subject designs. *Psychonomic Bulletin and Review, 1*(4), 476–490.

Lombardi, C. M., & Hurlbert, S. H. (2009). Misprescription and misuse of one-tailed tests. *Austral Ecology, 34*(4), 447–468. doi: 10.1111/j.1442-9993.2009.01946.x

Lord, F. M. (1967). A paradox in the interpretation of group comparisons. *Psychological Bulletin, 68*(5), 304–305.

Lord, F. M. (1969). Statistical adjustments when comparing preexisting groups. *Psychological Bulletin, 72*(5), 336–337.

Lumley, T., Diehr, P., Emerson, S., & Chen, L. (2002). The importance of the normality assumption in large public health data sets. *Annual Review of Public Health, 23*, 151–169.

Lunney, G. H. (1970). Using analysis of variance with a dichotomous dependent variable: An empirical study. *Journal of Educational Measurement, 7*(4), 263–269.

MacCallum, R. C., Widaman, K. F., Zhang, S., & Hong, S. (1999). Sample size in factor analysis. *Psychological Methods, 4*(1), 84–99.

MacCallum, R. C., Zhang, S., Preacher, K. J., & Rucker, D. D. (2002). On the practice of dichotomization of quantitative variables. *Psychological Methods, 7*(1), 19–40.

MacKinnon, D. P. (2008). *Introduction to statistical mediation analysis.* Mahwah, NJ: Erlbaum.

Mann, H. B., & Whitney, D. R. (1947). On a test of whether one of two random variables is stochastically larger than the other. *Annals of Mathematical Statistics, 18*, 50–60.

Marzillier, S. L., & Davey, G. C. L. (2005). Anxiety and disgust: Evidence for a unidirectional relationship. *Cognition and Emotion, 19*(5), 729–750.

Massar, K., Buunk, A. P., & Rempt, S. (2012). Age differences in women's tendency to gossip are mediated by their mate value. *Personality and Individual Differences, 52*, 106–109.

Mather, K. (1951). R. A. Fisher's *Statistical Methods for Research Workers*: An appreciation. *Journal of the American Statistical Association, 46*, 51–54.

Matthews, R. C., Domjan, M., Ramsey, M., & Crews, D. (2007). Learning effects on sperm competition and reproductive fitness. *Psychological Science, 18*(9), 758–762.

Maxwell, S. E. (1980). Pairwise multiple comparisons in repeated measures designs. *Journal of Educational Statistics, 5*(3), 269–287.

Maxwell, S. E., & Delaney, H. D. (1990). *Designing experiments and analyzing data.* Belmont, CA: Wadsworth.

McDonald, P. T., & Rosenthal, D. (1977). An unusual foreign body in the rectum - a baseball: Report of a case. *Diseases of the Colon & Rectum, 20*(1), 56–57.

McGrath, R. E., & Meyer, G. J. (2006). When effect sizes disagree: The case of r and d. *Psychological Methods, 11*(4), 386–401.

McNulty, J. K., Neff, L. A., & Karney, B. R. (2008). Beyond initial attraction: Physical attractiveness in newlywed marriage. *Journal of Family Psychology, 22*(1), 135–143.

Meehl, P. E. (1978). Theoretical risks and tabular asterisks: Sir Karl, Sir Ronald, and the slow progress of soft psychology. *Journal of Consulting and Clinical Psychology, 46*, 806–834.

Menard, S. (1995). *Applied logistic regression analysis.* Sage University Paper Series on Quantitative Applications in the Social Sciences, 07-106. Thousand Oaks, CA: Sage.

Mendoza, J. L., Toothaker, L. E., & Crain, B. R. (1976). Necessary and sufficient conditions for F ratios in the L * J * K factorial design with two repeated factors.

Journal of the American Statistical Association, 71, 992–993.

Mendoza, J. L., Toothaker, L. E., & Nicewander, W. A. (1974). A Monte Carlo comparison of the univariate and multivariate methods for the groups by trials repeated measures design. *Multivariate Behavioural Research, 9*, 165–177.

Meston, C. M., & Frohlich, P. F. (2003). Love at first fright: Partner salience moderates roller-coaster-induced excitation transfer. *Archives of Sexual Behavior, 32*(6), 537–544. doi: 10.1023/a:1026037527455

Miles, J. N. V., & Banyard, P. (2007). *Understanding and using statistics in psychology: A practical introduction.* London: Sage.

Miles, J. N. V., & Shevlin, M. (2001). *Applying regression and correlation: A guide for students and researchers.* London: Sage.

Mill, J. S. (1865). *A system of logic: Ratiocinative and inductive.* London: Longmans, Green.

Miller, G., Tybur, J. M., & Jordan, B. D. (2007). Ovulatory cycle effects on tip earnings by lap dancers: Economic evidence for human estrus? *Evolution and Human Behavior, 28*, 375–381.

Miller, G. A., & Chapman, J. P. (2001). Misunderstanding analysis of covariance. *Journal of Abnormal Psychology, 110*(1), 40–48. doi: 10.1037//0021-843x.110.1.40

Mishra, J., Zinni, M., Bavelier, D., & Hillyard, S. A. (2011). Neural basis of superior performance of action videogame players in an attention-demanding task. *Journal of Neuroscience, 31*(3), 992–998. doi: 10.1523/jneurosci.4834-10.2011

Morewedge, C. K., Huh, Y. E., & Vosgerau, J. (2010). Thought for food: Imagined consumption reduces actual consumption. *Science, 330*(6010), 1530–1533. doi: 10.1126/science.1195701

Muris, P., Huijding, J., Mayer, B., & Hameetman, M. (2008). A space odyssey: Experimental manipulation of threat perception and anxiety-related interpretation bias in children. *Child Psychiatry and Human Development, 39*(4), 469–480.

Myers, R. (1990). *Classical and modern regression with applications* (2nd ed.). Boston, MA: Duxbury.

Nagelkerke, N. J. D. (1991). A note on a general definition of the coefficient of determination. *Biometrika, 78*, 691–692.

Namboodiri, K. (1984). *Matrix algebra: An introduction.* Sage University Paper Series on Quantitative Applications in the Social Sciences, 07-38. Beverly Hills, CA: Sage.

Neyman, J., & Pearson, E. S. (1933). On the problem of the most efficient tests of statistical hypotheses. *Philosophical Transactions of the Royal Society of London, Series A, 231*, 289–337.

Nichols, L. A., & Nicki, R. (2004). Development of a psychometrically sound internet addiction scale: A preliminary step. *Psychology of Addictive Behaviors, 18*(4), 381–384.

Nunnally, J. C. (1978). *Psychometric theory.* New York: McGraw-Hill.

Nunnally, J. C., & Bernstein, I. H. (1994). *Psychometric theory* (3rd ed.). New York: McGraw-Hill.

O'Brien, M. G., & Kaiser, M. K. (1985). MANOVA method for analyzing repeated measures designs: An extensive primer. *Psychological Bulletin, 97*(2), 316–333.

O'Connor, B. P. (2000). SPSS and SAS programs for determining the number of components using parallel analysis and Velicer's MAP test. *Behavior Research Methods, Instrumentation, and Computers, 32*, 396–402.

Ofcom (Office of Communications) (2008). Media literacy audit: report on children's media literacy. Retrieved 25th August, 2011, from http://stakeholders.ofcom.org.uk/binaries/research/media-literacy/ml_childrens08.pdf

Olson, C. L. (1974). Comparative robustness of six tests in multivariate analysis of variance. *Journal of the American Statistical Association, 69*, 894–908.

Olson, C. L. (1976). On choosing a test statistic in multivariate analysis of variance. *Psychological Bulletin, 83*, 579–586.

Olson, C. L. (1979). Practical considerations in choosing a MANOVA test statistic: A rejoinder to Stevens. *Psychological Bulletin, 86*, 1350–1352.

Ong, E. Y. L., Ang, R. P., Ho, J. C. M., Lim, J. C. Y., Goh, D. H., Lee, C. S., et al. (2011). Narcissism, extraversion and adolescents' self-presentation on Facebook. *Personality and Individual Differences, 50*(2), 180–185. doi: 10.1016/j.paid.2010.09.022

Oxoby, R. J. (2008). On the efficiency of AC/DC: Bon Scott versus Brian Johnson. *Economic Enquiry, 47*(3), 598–602. doi: 10.1111/j.1465-7295.2008.00138.x

Pearson, E. S., & Hartley, H. O. (1954). *Biometrika tables for statisticians, Volume I.* New York: Cambridge University Press.

Pearson, K. (1894). Science and Monte Carlo. *Fortnightly Review, 55*, 183–193.

Pearson, K. (1900). On the criterion that a given system of deviations from the probable in the case of a correlated system of variables is such that it can be reasonably supposed to have arisen from random sampling. *Philosophical Magazine, 50*(5), 157–175.

Pedhazur, E., & Schmelkin, L. (1991). *Measurement, design and analysis: An integrated approach.* Hillsdale, NJ: Erlbaum.

Perham, N., & Sykora, M. (2012). Disliked music can be better for performance than liked music. *Applied Cognitive Psychology, 26*(4), 550–555.

Piff, P. K., Stancato, D. M., Côté, S., Mendoza-Dentona, R., & Keltner, D. (2012). Higher social class predicts increased unethical behavior. *Proceedings of the National Academy of Sciences, 109*(11), 4086–4091.

Plackett, R. L. (1983). Karl Pearson and the chi-squared test. *International Statistical Review, 51*(1), 59–72.

Preacher, K. J., & Hayes, A. F. (2004). SPSS and SAS procedures for estimating indirect effects in simple mediation models. *Behavior Research Methods Instruments & Computers, 36*(4), 717–731.

Preacher, K. J., & Hayes, A. F. (2008a). Asymptotic and resampling strategies for assessing and comparing indirect effects in multiple mediator models. *Behavior Research Methods, 40*(3), 879–891.

Preacher, K. J., & Hayes, A. F. (2008b). Contemporary approaches to assessing mediation in communication research. In A. F. Hayes, M. D. Slater & L. B. Snyder (Eds.), *The Sage sourcebook of advanced data analysis methods for communication research* (pp. 13–54). Thousand Oaks, CA: Sage.

Preacher, K. J., & Kelley, K. (2011). Effect size measures for mediation models: Quantitative strategies for communicating indirect effects. *Psychological Methods, 16*(2), 93–115. doi: 10.1037/a0022658

Ratcliff, R. (1993). Methods for dealing with reaction-time outliers. *Psychological Bulletin, 114*(3), 510–532.

Raudenbush, S. W., & Bryk, A. S. (2002). *Hierarchical linear models* (2nd ed.). Thousand Oaks, CA: Sage.

Rockwell, R. C. (1975). Assessment of multicollinearity: The Haitovsky test of the determinant. *Sociological Methods and Research, 3*(4), 308–320.

Rogosa, D. (1981). On the relationship between the Johnson-Neyman region of significance and statistical tests of parallel within group regressions. *Educational and Psychological Measurement, 41*(73–84).

Rosenthal, R. (1991). *Meta-analytic procedures for social research* (2nd ed.). Newbury Park, CA: Sage.

Rosenthal, R., Rosnow, R. L., & Rubin, D. B. (2000). *Contrasts and effect sizes in behavioural research: A correlational approach.* Cambridge: Cambridge University Press.

Rosnow, R. L., & Rosenthal, R. (2005). *Beginning behavioral research: A conceptual primer* (5th ed.). Upper Saddle River, NJ: Pearson/Prentice Hall.

Rosnow, R. L., Rosenthal, R., & Rubin, D. B. (2000). Contrasts and correlations in effect-size estimation. *Psychological Science, 11*, 446–453.

Rouanet, H., & Lépine, D. (1970). Comparison between treatments in a repeated-measurement design: ANOVA and multivariate methods. *British Journal of Mathematical and Statistical Psychology, 23*, 147–163.

Rowe, R., Costello, E. J., Angold, A., Copeland, W. E., & Maughan, B. (2010). Developmental pathways in oppositional defiant disorder and conduct disorder. *Journal of Abnormal Psychology, 119*(4), 726–738. doi: 10.1037/a0020798

Rulon, P. J. (1939). A simplified procedure for determining the reliability of a test by split-halves. *Harvard Educational Review, 9*, 99–103.

Ruxton, G. D., & Neuhauser, M. (2010). When should we use one-tailed hypothesis testing? *Methods in Ecology and Evolution, 1*(2), 114–117. doi: 10.1111/j.2041-210X.2010.00014.x

Sacco, W. P., Levine, B., Reed, D., & Thompson, K. (1991). Attitudes about condom use as an AIDS-relevant behavior: Their factor structure and relation to condom use. *Psychological Assessment: A Journal of Consulting and Clinical Psychology, 3*(2), 265–272.

Sacco, W. P., Rickman, R. L., Thompson, K., Levine, B., & Reed, D. L. (1993). Gender differences in aids-relevant condom attitudes and condom use. *AIDS Education and Prevention, 5*(4), 311–326.

Sachdev, Y. V. (1967). An unusual foreign body in the rectum. *Diseases of the Colon & Rectum, 10*(3), 220–221.

Salsburg, D. (2002). *The lady tasting tea: How statistics revolutionized science in the twentieth century.* New York: Owl Books.

Savage, L. J. (1976). On re-reading R. A. Fisher. *Annals of Statistics, 4*, 441–500.

Scanlon, T. J., Luben, R. N., Scanlon, F. L., & Singleton, N. (1993). Is Friday the 13th bad for your health? *British Medical Journal, 307*, 1584–1586.

Scariano, S. M., & Davenport, J. M. (1987). The effects of violations of independence in the one-way ANOVA. *American Statistician, 41*(2), 123–129.

Schützwohl, A. (2008). The disengagement of attentive resources from task-irrelevant cues to sexual and emotional infidelity. *Personality and Individual Differences, 44*, 633–644.

Senn, S. (2006). Change from baseline and analysis of covariance revisited. *Statistics in Medicine, 25*, 4334–4344. doi: 10.1002/sim.2682

Shackelford, T. K., LeBlanc, G. J., & Drass, E. (2000). Emotional reactions to infidelity. *Cognition & Emotion, 14*(5), 643–659.

Shee, J. C. (1964). Pargyline and the cheese reaction. *British Medical Journal, 1*(539), 1441.

Sobel, M. E. (1982). Asymptotic intervals for indirect effects in structural equations models. In S. Leinhart (Ed.), *Sociological methodology 1982* (pp. 290–312). San Francisco: Jossey-Bass.

Sonnentag, S. (2012). Psychological detachment from work during leisure time: The benefits of mentally disengaging from work. *Current Directions in Psychological Science, 21*(2), 114–118. doi: 10.1177/0963721411434979

Spearman, C. (1910). Correlation calculated with faulty data. *British Journal of Psychology, 3*, 271–295.

Stevens, J. P. (1979). Comment on Olson: Choosing a test statistic in multivariate analysis of variance. *Psychological Bulletin, 86*, 355–360.

Stevens, J. P. (1980). Power of the multivariate analysis of variance tests. *Psychological Bulletin, 88*, 728–737.

Stevens, J. P. (2002). *Applied multivariate statistics for the social sciences* (4th ed.). Hillsdale, NJ: Erlbaum.

Strahan, R. F. (1982). Assessing magnitude of effect from rank-order correlation coeffients. *Educational and Psychological Measurement, 42*, 763–765.

Stuart, E. W., Shimp, T. A., & Engle, R. W. (1987). Classical-conditioning of consumer attitudes – Four experiments in an advertising context. *Journal of Consumer Research, 14*(3), 334–349.

Studenmund, A. H., & Cassidy, H. J. (1987). *Using econometrics: A practical guide*. Boston: Little, Brown.

Tabachnick, B. G., & Fidell, L. S. (2007). *Using multivariate statistics* (5th ed.). Boston: Pearson/Allyn & Bacon.

Tabachnick, B. G., & Fidell, L. S. (2012). *Using multivariate statistics* (6th ed.). Boston: Pearson Education.

Terpstra, T. J. (1952). The asymptotic normality and consistency of Kendall's test against trend, when ties are present in one ranking. *Indagationes Mathematicae, 14,* 327–333.

Tinsley, H. E. A., & Tinsley, D. J. (1987). Uses of factor analysis in counseling psychology research. *Journal of Counseling Psychology, 34,* 414–424.

Tomarken, A. J., & Serlin, R. C. (1986). Comparison of ANOVA alternatives under variance heterogeneity and specific noncentrality structures. *Psychological Bulletin, 99,* 90–99.

Toothaker, L. E. (1993). *Multiple comparison procedures*. Sage University Paper Series on Quantitative Applications in the Social Sciences, 07-089. Newbury Park, CA: Sage.

Tufte, E. R. (2001). *The visual display of quantitative information* (2nd ed.). Cheshire, CT: Graphics Press.

Tuk, M. A., Trampe, D., & Warlop, L. (2011). Inhibitory spill-over: Increased urinating urgency facilitates impulse control in unrelated domains. *Psychological Science, 22,* 627–633.

Tukey, J. W. (1960). A survey of sampling from contaminated normal distributions. In I. Olkin, S. G. Ghurye, W. Hoeffding, W. G. Madow, & H. B. Mann (Eds.), *Contributions to Probability and statistics: Essays in honor of Harold Hotelling, Issue 2* (pp. 448–485). Stanford, CA: Stanford University Press.

Twenge, J. M. (2000). The age of anxiety? Birth cohort change in anxiety and neuroticism, 1952–1993. *Journal of Personality and Social Psychology, 79*(6), 1007–1021.

Twisk, J. W. R. (2006). *Applied multilevel analysis: A practical guide*. Cambridge: Cambridge University Press.

Umpierre, S. A., Hill, J. A., & Anderson, D. J. (1985). Effect of Coke on sperm motility. *New England Journal of Medicine, 313*(21), 1351.

Vezhaventhan, G., & Jeyaraman, R. (2007). Unusual foreign body in urinary bladder: A case report. *Internet Journal of Urology, 4*(2).

Wainer, H. (1972). A practical note on one-tailed tests. *American Psychologist, 27*(8), 775–776. doi: 10.1037/h0020482

Wainer, H. (1984). How to display data badly. *American Statistician, 38*(2), 137–147.

Welch, B. L. (1951). On the comparison of several mean values: An alternative approach. *Biometrika, 38,* 330–336.

Wilcox, R. R. (2010). *Fundamentals of modern statistical methods: Substantially improving power and accuracy*. New York: Springer.

Wilcox, R. R. (2012). *Introduction to robust estimation and hypothesis testing* (3rd ed.). Burlington, MA: Elsevier.

Wilcoxon, F. (1945). Individual comparisons by ranking methods. *Biometrics, 1,* 80–83.

Wildt, A. R., & Ahtola, O. (1978). *Analysis of covariance*. Sage University Paper Series on Quantitative Applications in the Social Sciences, 07-012. Newbury Park, CA: Sage.

Wilkinson, L. (1999). Statistical methods in psychology journals: Guidelines and explanations. *American Psychologist, 54*(8), 594–604.

Williams, J. M. G. (2001). *Suicide and attempted suicide*. London: Penguin.

Wright, D. B. (1998). Modeling clustered data in autobiographical memory research: The multilevel approach. *Applied Cognitive Psychology, 12,* 339–357.

Wright, D. B. (2003). Making friends with your data: Improving how statistics are conducted and reported. *British Journal of Educational Psychology, 73,* 123–136.

Wright, D. B., London, K., & Field, A. P. (2011). Using bootstrap estimation and the plug-in principle for clinical psychology data. *Journal of Experimental Psychopathology, 2*(2), 252–270. doi: 10.5127/jep.013611

Wu, Y. W. B. (1984). The effects of heterogeneous regression slopes on the robustness of 2 test statistics in the analysis of covariance. *Educational and Psychological Measurement, 44*(3), 647–663.

Yang, X. W., Li, J. H., & Shoptaw, S. (2008). Imputation-based strategies for clinical trial longitudinal data with nonignorable missing values. *Statistics in Medicine, 27*(15), 2826–2849.

Yates, F. (1951). The influence of *Statistical Methods for Research Workers* on the development of the science of statistics. *Journal of the American Statistical Association, 46,* 19–34.

Zabell, S. L. (1992). R. A. Fisher and fiducial argument. *Statistical Science, 7*(3), 369–387.

Zibarras, L. D., Port, R. L., & Woods, S. A. (2008). Innovation and the 'dark side' of personality: Dysfunctional traits and their relation to self-reported innovative characteristics. *Journal of Creative Behavior, 42*(3), 201–215.

Ziliak, S. T., & McCloskey, D. N. (2008). *The cult of statistical significance: how the standard error costs us jobs, justice and lives*. Michigan: University of Michigan.

Zimmerman, D. W. (2004). A note on preliminary tests of equality of variances. *British Journal of Mathematical & Statistical Psychology, 57,* 173–181.

Zwick, R. (1985). Nonparametric one-way multivariate analysis of variance: A computational approach based on the Pillai–Bartlett trace. *Psychological Bulletin, 97*(1), 148–152.

Zwick, W. R., & Velicer, W. F. (1986). Comparison of five rules for determining the number of components to retain. *Psychological Bulletin, 99*(3), 432–442.

INDEX

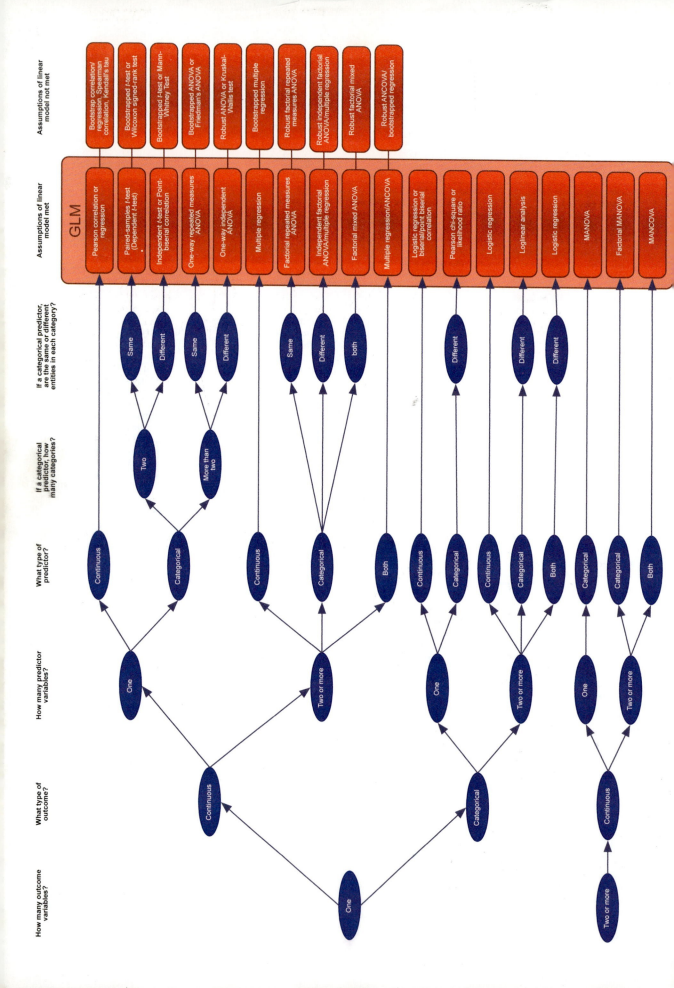